HOLT
ELEMENTS OF
LITERATURE

First Course

HOLT, RINEHART AND WINSTON

A Harcourt Education Company

Orlando • **Austin** • New York • San Diego • Toronto • London

EDITORIAL
Executive Editor: Laura Mongello
Senior Book Editors: Jennifer Tench, Marcia Kelley
Project Editor: Michael Zakhar
Managing Editor: Marie Price
Associate Managing Editor: Elizabeth LaManna
Editorial Staff: Abraham Chang, Mary Shaw, Emily R. Stern, Evan Wilson
Copyediting Manager: Michael Neibergall
Copyediting Supervisors: Kristen Azzara, Mary Malone
Senior Copyeditors: Christine Altgelt, Elizabeth Dickson, Leora Harris, Anne Heausler, Kathleen Scheiner
Copyeditors: Emily Force, Julia Thomas Hu, Nancy Shore
Project Administration: Janet Jenkins, *Senior Editorial Coordinator;* Christine Degollado, Betty Gabriel, Mark Koenig, Erik Netcher, *Editorial Coordinators*
Permissions: Ann Farrar, *Senior Permissions Editor;* Sally Garland, Susan Lowrance, *Permissions Editors*

ART, DESIGN, AND PRODUCTION
Senior Design Director: Betty Mintz
Composition: H & S Graphics, Inc.
Production Manager: Carol Trammel
Assistant Production Coordinator: Myles Gorospe

COVER
Photo Credits: (Inset) *Boats at Fishbeach* by James Fitzgerald. Oil on canvasboard. Courtesy of Dan Broeckelmann and Krista Lisajus. (background) Photograph of boats on water, © Derek P. Redearn/Getty Images.

Printed in the United States of America

ISBN 0-03-068382-3

4 5 048 06 05

	Literary Response	Reading Comprehension	Vocabulary	Writing
COLLECTION 1	Analyze plot and setting.	Analyze text structures. Retell/summarize a story's plot.	Clarify word meanings by using restatement, contrast, and definition.	Write a short story.
COLLECTION 2	Analyze character.	Analyze comparison and contrast.	Understand word origins. Recognize roots and affixes.	Write a problem-solution essay.
COLLECTION 3	Analyze theme.	Analyze cause-and-effect.	Understand similes and metaphors. Use analogies. Identify idioms. Use context clues.	Write a personal narrative.
COLLECTION 4	Analyze point of view.	Analyze an author's argument.	Clarify word meanings by using contrast and definition.	Write a descriptive essay.
COLLECTION 5	Analyze prose and poetry.	Analyze main idea.	Understand denotations and connotations. Understand word analogies.	Write an essay supporting an interpretation.
COLLECTION 6	Analyze myths and folk tales.	Summarize texts. Understand Greek and Latin roots and affixes.	Understand Greek and Latin roots and affixes.	Write a comparison-contrast essay.
COLLECTION 7	Criticize literature.	Evaluate evidence.	Understand Latin and Anglo-Saxon word origins. Understand French word origins.	Write an informative report.
COLLECTION 8		Analyze information in public, workplace, and consumer documents. Follow technical directions.		Create a multimedia public-service announcement.

LITERARY SKILLS	Grade 6	Grade 7	Grade 8	Grade 9	Grade 10	Grade 11	Grade 12
Alexandrine							■
Allegory				■	■	■	■
Alliteration	■	■	■	■	■	■	■
Allusion	■	■	■	■	■	■	■
Ambiguity				■	■	■	
American Indian oratory						■	
Analogy		■	■	■	■	■	■
Anecdote	■	■	■			■	■
Antagonist			■	■	■	■	■
Anticlimax							■
Antithesis							■
Aphorism						■	■
Apostrophe							■
Approximate rhyme			■	■	■	■	
Archetype						■	■
Argument					■	■	
Arthurian legend		■			■		■
Aside				■	■		
Assonance			■	■		■	■
Atmosphere		■	■	■	■	■	■
Autobiography	■	■	■	■	■	■	■
Ballad			■	■	■	■	■
Biography	■	■	■	■	■	■	■
Blank verse				■	■	■	■
Cadence						■	
Caesura							■
Catalog poem		■		■		■	■
Carpe Diem							■
Character	■	■	■	■	■	■	■
Character interactions		■		■	■		
Character traits	■	■	■	■	■		

LITERARY SKILLS	Grade 6	Grade 7	Grade 8	Grade 9	Grade 10	Grade 11	Grade 12
Characterization	■	■	■	■	■	■	■
Chronological order	■	■	■	■	■	■	
Classicism							■
Climax	■	■	■	■	■	■	■
Comedy			■	■	■	■	■
Comic devices			■			■	
Comparing texts	■	■	■	■	■	■	■
Conceit							■
Conflict	■	■	■	■	■	■	■
Connotation	■	■	■	■	■	■	■
Contradiction				■	■		
Couplet		■	■	■	■	■	■
Deism						■	■
Denotation	■	■	■	■	■	■	■
Denouement				■	■	■	■
Description	■	■	■	■	■	■	■
Dialect	■	■	■	■	■	■	■
Dialogue	■	■	■	■	■	■	■
Diction			■	■	■	■	■
Didactic literature	■	■	■				■
Direct characterization	■	■	■	■	■		
Drama	■	■	■	■	■		■
Dramatic monologue				■	■	■	■
Dramatic irony			■	■	■	■	■
Elegy		■	■			■	■
End rhyme	■	■	■	■	■		
Epic			■	■			■
Epic conventions							■
Epic hero			■	■			■
Epic simile							■
Epigram							■

LITERARY SKILLS	Grade 6	Grade 7	Grade 8	Grade 9	Grade 10	Grade 11	Grade 12
Epiphany							■
Epitaph							■
Essay	■	■	■	■	■	■	■
Exposition		■	■	■	■	■	■
Extended metaphor	■	■	■	■	■	■	■
External conflict	■	■	■	■	■	■	■
Fable	■	■	■	■	■		■
Farce					■		
Fiction	■	■	■				
Figurative language	■	■	■	■	■	■	■
First–person point of view	■	■	■	■	■	■	■
First–person narrator	■	■		■	■	■	■
Flashback	■	■	■	■	■	■	■
Flash–forward		■		■			
Flat character				■	■		
Foil				■	■		
Folk tale	■	■	■	■			
Foreshadowing	■	■	■	■	■	■	■
Frame story						■	■
Free verse	■	■	■	■	■	■	■
Gothic tale						■	■
Haiku	■			■			■
Harlem Renaissance	■		■			■	
Historical context	■			■	■	■	■
Historical fiction		■	■				
Humanism							■
Hyperbole	■					■	■
Iambic pentameter		■	■	■	■	■	■
Idiom	■	■	■	■	■	■	
Imagery	■	■	■	■	■	■	■
Implied metaphor			■	■	■	■	

LITERARY SKILLS	Grade 6	Grade 7	Grade 8	Grade 9	Grade 10	Grade 11	Grade 12
Indirect characterization		■	■	■	■		
Interior monologue						■	
Internal conflict	■	■	■	■	■	■	■
Internal rhyme	■	■	■	■	■	■	
Inversion			■		■	■	
Irony	■	■	■	■	■	■	■
Kenning							■
Legend	■	■	■		■		
Literary criticism	■	■	■	■	■	■	■
Lyric poetry		■	■	■	■	■	■
Magic realism					■	■	■
Main idea	■	■	■	■	■	■	■
Memoir	■	■				■	■
Metamorphosis	■	■	■			■	
Metaphor	■	■	■	■	■		■
Metaphysical poetry							■
Meter	■	■	■	■	■	■	■
Metonymy							■
Mock epic			■				■
Modernism						■	■
Mood	■	■	■	■	■	■	■
Motif	■	■	■				■
Motivation	■	■	■	■	■	■	■
Myth	■	■	■	■	■	■	■
Narration	■	■	■	■	■	■	■
Narrative	■	■	■			■	
Narrative poem	■	■	■	■	■	■	
Narrator	■	■	■	■	■	■	■
Naturalism						■	
Neoclassicism							■
Nonfiction	■	■	■	■	■	■	■

LITERARY SKILLS	Grade 6	Grade 7	Grade 8	Grade 9	Grade 10	Grade 11	Grade 12
Objective writing		■	■		■	■	
Ode	■	■	■		■		■
Omniscient narrator		■		■	■	■	■
Omniscient point of view		■	■	■	■	■	■
Onomatopoeia	■	■	■	■	■	■	■
Ottava rima							■
Oxymoron							■
Parable					■	■	■
Paradox						■	■
Parallelism				■	■	■	■
Parody						■	■
Pastoral							■
Persona				■	■		
Personification	■	■	■	■	■	■	■
Persuasion	■	■		■	■	■	■
Plain style						■	
Plot	■	■	■	■	■	■	■
Poetry	■	■	■	■	■	■	■
Point of view	■	■	■	■	■	■	■
Postmodernism						■	■
Protagonist	■	■	■	■	■	■	■
Proverb						■	■
Rationalism						■	■
Realism						■	■
Refrain	■	■	■	■	■	■	■
Regionalism						■	
Renaissance							■
Repetition	■	■	■	■	■	■	
Resolution	■	■	■	■	■	■	■
Rhyme	■	■	■	■	■	■	■
Rhyme scheme	■	■	■	■	■	■	■

LITERARY SKILLS	Grade 6	Grade 7	Grade 8	Grade 9	Grade 10	Grade 11	Grade 12
Rhythm	■	■	■	■	■	■	■
Romance					■	■	■
Romanticism						■	■
Round character				■	■		
Satire			■	■	■	■	■
Scene design			■	■	■		
Setting	■	■	■	■	■	■	■
Short story	■	■	■	■	■	■	■
Simile	■	■	■	■	■	■	■
Situational irony			■	■	■	■	■
Slant rhyme		■				■	
Soliloquy			■	■	■	■	■
Sonnet		■	■	■	■	■	■
Sound effects	■	■		■	■	■	
Speaker	■	■	■	■	■	■	■
Speech		■	■	■	■	■	■
Spenserian stanza							■
Static character		■	■	■	■		
Stanza	■	■	■				
Stereotype						■	
Stock character					■	■	
Stream of consciousness						■	■
Style			■	■	■	■	■
Subjective writing		■	■		■	■	
Subplots			■				
Surprise ending	■			■			
Suspense	■	■	■	■	■		
Symbol	■	■	■	■	■	■	■
Synesthesia						■	■
Tall tale	■	■	■			■	
Tanka					■		■

LITERARY SKILLS	Grade 6	Grade 7	Grade 8	Grade 9	Grade 10	Grade 11	Grade 12
Teleplay	■	■	■				
Terza rima							■
Theme	■	■	■	■	■	■	■
Third-person limited point of view	■	■		■	■		
Title	■	■	■	■	■	■	
Tone	■	■		■	■	■	■
Tragedy			■	■	■		■
Tragic hero				■			
Transcendentalism						■	
Understatement			■			■	■
Universal themes		■	■	■	■		
Unreliable narrator			■	■	■		
Verbal irony			■	■	■	■	
Vernacular						■	■
Villanelle						■	■
Voice				■	■		

READING SKILLS	Grade 6	Grade 7	Grade 8	Grade 9	Grade 10	Grade 11	Grade 12
Anachronism					■		
Analogy		■	■	■	■	■	■
Application forms	■	■					
Argument		■		■	■	■	■
Assertions	■					■	
Author's opinion				■	■	■	■
Author's purpose	■	■	■	■	■	■	■
Bias		■		■	■		■
Cause and effect	■	■	■	■	■	■	
Chronological order	■	■	■	■	■	■	■
Claim				■	■	■	■
Coherence			■	■	■	■	■

READING SKILLS	Grade 6	Grade 7	Grade 8	Grade 9	Grade 10	Grade 11	Grade 12
Comparing texts	■	■	■	■	■	■	■
Comparison and contrast	■	■	■	■	■	■	■
Connotation	■	■	■	■	■	■	■
Consumer documents		■	■	■	■		
Context clues	■	■	■	■	■	■	■
Credibility				■	■	■	■
Denotation	■	■	■	■	■		■
Drawing conclusions	■	■	■				
Emotional appeals	■	■		■	■	■	■
Evaluating evidence	■	■	■	■	■	■	■
Evaluating historical accuracy			■				
Evidence	■	■	■	■	■		■
Fact	■	■	■	■	■		
Fallacious reasoning	■	■	■	■	■	■	■
Generalizations	■	■	■	■	■	■	■
Generating research questions				■	■		
Graphic features	■	■	■		■		■
Graphic organizers	■	■	■	■	■	■	■
Graphs	■	■	■	■	■	■	■
Historical context	■	■	■	■	■	■	■
Idiom	■	■	■	■	■		
Inferences	■	■	■	■	■	■	■
Informative texts	■	■	■	■	■	■	■
Internet sources	■	■	■	■	■	■	■
Inversion				■		■	
Judgments			■				
Logic	■	■	■	■	■	■	■
Logical appeals	■	■		■	■	■	■
Logical order			■	■	■	■	■
Main idea	■	■	■	■	■	■	■
Maps	■	■	■	■	■	■	■

READING SKILLS	Grade 6	Grade 7	Grade 8	Grade 9	Grade 10	Grade 11	Grade 12
Monitor reading	■	■	■	■	■	■	■
Note taking	■	■	■	■	■	■	■
Objective writing		■	■		■	■	
Opinion	■	■	■	■	■	■	■
Outlining	■	■	■	■	■	■	■
Paraphrasing	■	■	■	■	■	■	
Persuasion	■	■	■	■	■	■	■
Predictions	■	■	■	■	■	■	■
Previewing			■				
Primary sources				■	■	■	■
Prior knowledge	■	■	■			■	
Propaganda	■	■					
Proposition and support			■				
Public documents		■	■	■	■	■	■
Purpose of texts	■	■	■				
Questioning			■				
Reading for details	■	■	■	■	■	■	■
Reading for information	■	■	■	■	■	■	■
Reading poetry	■	■	■	■	■	■	■
Reading rate	■	■		■	■	■	■
Researching information	■			■	■		
Retelling	■	■	■			■	
Rhetorical devices						■	■
Secondary sources				■	■	■	
Stereotyping		■	■				
Subjective writing		■			■	■	
Summarizing	■	■	■	■	■	■	■
Syntax				■	■		
Synthesizing sources				■	■		
Text structures	■	■	■	■	■	■	■
Vernacular						■	

READING SKILLS	Grade 6	Grade 7	Grade 8	Grade 9	Grade 10	Grade 11	Grade 12
Visualizing	■		■	■	■		
Workplace documents		■	■	■	■		
Writer's perspective		■		■	■	■	■

VOCABULARY SKILLS	Grade 6	Grade 7	Grade 8	Grade 9	Grade 10	Grade 11	Grade 12
Affixes	■	■	■	■	■	■	■
Analogies		■	■	■	■	■	■
Anglo–Saxon roots and affixes	■	■	■	■	■	■	■
Antonyms	■		■	■	■	■	■
Archaic words					■		
Borrowed words	■	■	■	■	■		
Connotations	■	■	■	■	■	■	■
Context clues	■	■	■	■	■	■	■
Definition	■	■	■				
Denotations	■	■		■	■	■	■
Dialect	■	■	■	■	■	■	■
Diction			■	■			
Dictionary	■	■		■	■		
Epithets				■		■	■
Etymology	■	■	■	■	■	■	■
Figurative language	■	■	■	■	■	■	■
Foreign words used in English	■	■	■	■	■		
Greek roots and affixes	■	■		■	■	■	■
History of English language			■	■			
Homographs			■				
Homophones			■				
Idioms	■	■	■	■	■	■	
Indo–European roots			■	■			
Informal words			■	■	■		
Jargon				■	■		

VOCABULARY SKILLS	Grade 6	Grade 7	Grade 8	Grade 9	Grade 10	Grade 11	Grade 12
Latin roots and affixes	■	■	■	■	■	■	■
Metaphor	■	■	■	■	■	■	■
Multiple-meaning words	■	■	■	■	■	■	■
Personification	■	■	■	■	■	■	■
Prefixes	■	■		■	■	■	■
Puns			■		■		
Restatement		■	■				
Root words	■	■	■	■	■	■	■
Semantic maps	■			■	■		■
Simile	■	■	■	■	■	■	■
Suffixes	■	■		■	■	■	■
Synonyms	■	■	■	■	■	■	■
Technical vocabulary				■	■		
Thesaurus	■	■	■	■	■		■
Word derivations	■	■	■	■	■	■	■
Word knowledge	■	■	■	■	■	■	■
Word maps	■	■	■	■	■	■	■
Word origins	■	■	■	■	■	■	■
Word trees	■	■					

WRITING SKILLS	Grade 6	Grade 7	Grade 8	Grade 9	Grade 10	Grade 11	Grade 12
WRITING MODE							
Analyze a biography				■			
Analyze a character			■				
Analyze a novel						■	
Analyze a poem				■			■
Analyze a short story				■	■	■	
Analyze nonfiction						■	■
Analyze works of literature							■
Autobiographical narrative				■	■	■	

Program Scope and Sequence

WRITING SKILLS	Grade 6	Grade 7	Grade 8	Grade 9	Grade 10	Grade 11	Grade 12
Biographical narrative					■	■	
Business letter				■	■		
Compare and contrast media genres				■	■		
Compare and contrast two literary works							■
Comparison–contrast essay	■	■	■				
Descriptive essay	■	■		■	■	■	■
Editorial						■	
Historical research report						■	
Informative report		■	■				
Literary research paper							■
Minutes of a meeting				■			
Personal narrative	■	■	■				
Persuasive cause–and–effect essay				■			
Persuasive essay	■	■	■	■	■		■
Problem–solution essay	■	■	■		■		
Reflective essay						■	■
Report	■						
Research paper	■	■	■	■	■	■	■
Short story	■	■	■	■	■	■	■
Technical documents					■		
WRITING PROCESS							
Prewriting							
Choose topic	■	■	■	■	■	■	■
Identify purpose	■	■	■	■	■	■	■
Identify audience	■	■	■	■	■	■	■
Generate ideas	■	■	■	■	■	■	■
Gather information	■	■	■	■	■	■	■
Organize information	■	■	■	■	■	■	■
Draft thesis statement	■	■	■	■	■	■	■

WRITING SKILLS	Grade 6	Grade 7	Grade 8	Grade 9	Grade 10	Grade 11	Grade 12
Writing a draft							
State main point	■	■	■	■	■	■	■
Include relevant support	■	■	■	■	■	■	■
Include elaboration	■	■	■	■	■	■	■
Follow plan of elaboration	■	■	■	■	■	■	■
Revising							
Revise for content	■	■	■	■	■	■	■
Revise for style	■	■	■	■	■	■	■
Publishing							
Proofread for grammar, usage, and mechanics	■	■	■	■	■	■	■
Publish or share writing	■	■	■	■	■	■	■
Reflect on the writing experience	■	■	■	■	■	■	■

LISTENING and SPEAKING SKILLS	Grade 6	Grade 7	Grade 8	Grade 9	Grade 10	Grade 11	Grade 12
LISTENING AND SPEAKING MODE							
Debate an issue				■	■	■	■
Informative speech	■	■	■				
Multimedia presentation	■			■	■		
Oral autobiographical narrative				■	■		■
Oral descriptive essay				■		■	■
Oral interpretation of a poem				■		■	
Oral narrative	■	■	■	■		■	
Oral problem-solution essay	■						
Oral recitation of literature		■	■	■	■	■	■
Oral reflective essay						■	■
Oral research report				■	■	■	■
Oral response to a literary work	■		■	■	■	■	■
Persuasive speech	■	■	■	■	■	■	■

LISTENING and SPEAKING SKILLS	Grade 6	Grade 7	Grade 8	Grade 9	Grade 10	Grade 11	Grade 12
LISTENING AND SPEAKING PROCESS							
Analyze a documentary		■					
Analyze electronic journalism		■					
Analyze and evaluate a speech	■	■	■	■	■	■	■
Analyze content	■	■	■	■	■	■	■
Analyze delivery	■	■	■	■	■	■	■
Analyze organization	■	■	■	■	■	■	■
Analyze strategies used by media	■		■	■	■	■	■
Plan and organize speech or presentation	■	■	■	■	■		■
Rehearse and deliver speech or presentation	■	■	■	■	■	■	■
Understand and identify logical fallacies				■		■	■
Understand and identify propaganda techniques	■			■		■	■
Use rhetorical techniques				■		■	■
Use verbal and nonverbal techniques	■	■	■	■	■	■	■

MEDIA SKILLS	Grade 6	Grade 7	Grade 8	Grade 9	Grade 10	Grade 11	Grade 12
Analyze and use media	■	■	■	■	■	■	■
Analyze a documentary		■					
Analyze electronic journalism		■					
Analyze strategies used by media	■		■	■	■	■	■
Compare and contrast media genres				■	■		
Create graphics for technical documents			■				
Multimedia presentation	■			■	■	■	■
Use electronic texts to locate information	■						

FIRST COURSE MINIMUM COURSE OF STUDY

	Literature	Informational Text	Writing Workshop
COLLECTION 1	• "Rikki-tikki-tavi"	• *from* People, Places, and Change	
COLLECTION 2	• "The Smallest Dragonboy"	• "Here Be Dragons"	• Persuasive Writing: Problem–Solution Essay
COLLECTION 3	• "User Friendly"	• "It Just Keeps Going and Going . . ."	• Narrative Writing: Personal Narrative
COLLECTION 4	• "After Twenty Years"	• "What's *Really* in a Name?"	
COLLECTION 5	• "Amigo Brothers" • "The Runaway"	• "A Good Reason to Look Up"	
COLLECTION 6	• "Orpheus, The Great Musician" • "The Hummingbird King"	• "The Search Goes On"	
COLLECTION 7	• "King Arthur: The Sword in the Stone"	• Three Responses to Literature	• Expository Writing: Informative Report
COLLECTION 8		• "From Page to Film"	

Program Author

Kylene Beers established the reading pedagogy for *Elements of Literature.* A former middle-school teacher, Dr. Beers has turned her commitment to helping readers having difficulty into the major focus of her research, writing, speaking, and teaching. Dr. Beers is currently Senior Reading Researcher at the Child Study Center of the School Development Program at Yale University and was formerly a Research Associate Professor at the University of Houston. Dr. Beers is also currently the editor of the National Council of Teachers of English journal *Voices from the Middle.* She is the author of *When Kids Can't Read: What Teachers Can Do* and the co-editor of *Into Focus: Understanding and Creating Middle School Readers.* Dr. Beers is the 2001 recipient of the Richard Halle Award from the NCTE for outstanding contributions to middle-level literacy education. She has served on the review boards of the *English Journal* and *The Alan Review.* Dr. Beers currently serves on the board of directors of the International Reading Association's Special Interest Group on Adolescent Literature.

Special Contributors

Flo Ota De Lange and **Sheri Henderson** helped plan and organize the program and played key roles in developing and preparing the informational materials. They wrote Collection 8, Reading for Life, as well as Test Smarts.

Flo Ota De Lange is a former teacher with a thirty-year second career in psychotherapy, during which she studied learning processes in children and adults. These careers have led to her third career, as a writer.

Sheri Henderson brings to the program twenty years of experience as a middle-school research practitioner and full-time reading and language arts teacher at La Paz Intermediate School in Saddleback Valley Unified School District in California. She regularly speaks at statewide and national conferences.

Since 1991, DeLangeHenderson LLC has published forty-three titles designed to integrate the teaching of literature with standards requirements and state and national tests.

Writers

John Malcolm Brinnin, author of six volumes of poetry that have received many prizes and awards, was a member of the American Academy and Institute of Arts and Letters. He was a critic of poetry and a biographer of poets and was for a number of years Director of New York's famous Poetry Center. His teaching career, begun at Vassar College, included long terms at the University of Connecticut and Boston University, where he succeeded Robert Lowell as Professor of Creative Writing and Contemporary Letters. Mr. Brinnin wrote *Dylan Thomas in America: An Intimate Journal* and *Sextet: T. S. Eliot & Truman Capote & Others.*

Virginia Hamilton wrote the Elements of Literature essay on folk tales. Ms. Hamilton is one of America's most highly acclaimed writers of books for children and young adults. She has received many awards, including the Newbery Award for *M. C. Higgins, the Great;* the Newbery Honor Award for *In the Beginning: Creation Stories from Around the Word;* the Coretta Scott King Award for *Sweet Whispers, Brother Rush;* and the Edgar Allan Poe Award for *The House of Dies Drear.* Among her collections of folk tales are *The People Could Fly* and *The Dark Way: Stories from the Spirit World.* The *All Jahdu Storybook* is a collection of Hamilton's own tales about a trickster hero who was born in an oven between two loaves of bread. In 1990, Hamilton received an honorary doctorate from the Bank Street College of Education in New York City. In 1995, she received a MacArthur Fellowship. In 1998, Kent State University established the Virginia Hamilton Literary Award for excellence in multicultural literature for children and young adults.

Writers

David Adams Leeming wrote the Elements of Literature essay on Greek and Roman myths. Dr. Leeming was a Professor of English and Comparative Literature at the University of Connecticut for many years. He is the author of several books on mythology, including *Mythology: The Voyage of the Hero; The World of Myth;* and *Encyclopedia of Creation Myths.* For several years he taught English at Robert College in Istanbul, Turkey. He also served as secretary and assistant to the writer James Baldwin in New York and Istanbul. He is the author of the biographies *James Baldwin* and *Amazing Grace: A Biography of Beauford Delaney.*

John Leggett is a novelist, biographer, and teacher. He went to the Writer's Workshop at the University of Iowa in the spring of 1969, expecting to work there for a single semester. In 1970, he assumed temporary charge of the program, and for the next seventeen years he was its director. Mr. Leggett's novels include *Wilder Stone, The Gloucester Branch, Who Took the Gold Away?, Gulliver House,* and *Making Believe.* He is also the author of the highly acclaimed biography *Ross and Tom: Two American Tragedies* and of a biography of William Saroyan, *A Daring Young Man.* Mr. Leggett lives in California's Napa Valley.

Joan Burditt is a writer and editor who has a master's degree in education with a specialization in reading. She taught for several years in Texas, where her experience included work in programs for readers having difficulty. Since then she has developed and written instructional materials for middle-school language arts texts.

Madeline Travers Hovland, who taught middle school for several years, is a writer of educational materials. She studied English at Bates College and received a master's degree in education from Harvard University.

Richard Kelso is a writer and editor whose children's books include *Building a Dream: Mary Bethune's School; Walking for Freedom: The Montgomery Bus Boycott; Days of Courage: The Little Rock Story;* and *The Case of the Amistad Mutiny.*

Mara Rockliff is a writer and editor with a degree in American civilization from Brown University. She has written dramatizations of classic stories for middle-school students, collected in a book called *Stories for Performance.* She has also published feature stories in national newspapers and is currently writing a novel for young adults.

Fannie Safier has worked as a teacher in New York City schools. She has been writing and editing educational materials for more than thirty years.

Program Consultants

CONTENT-AREA READING CONSULTANT

Judith L. Irvin served as a reading consultant for the content-area readers: *The Ancient World; A World in Transition;* and *The United States: Change and Challenge.* Dr. Irvin is a Professor of Education at Florida State University. She writes a column, "What Research Says to the Middle Level Practitioner," for the *Middle School Journal* and serves as the literacy expert for the *Middle Level News,* published by the California League of Middle Schools. Her several books include the companion volumes *Reading and the Middle School Student: Strategies to Enhance Literacy* and *Reading and the High School Student: Strategies to Enhance Literacy* (with Buehl and Klemp).

SENIOR PROGRAM CONSULTANT

Carol Jago is the editor of CATE's quarterly journal, *California English.* She teaches English at Santa Monica High School, in Santa Monica, and directs the California Reading and Literature Project at UCLA. She also writes a weekly education column for the *Los Angeles Times.* She is the author of several books, including two in a series on contemporary writers in the classroom: *Alice Walker in the Classroom* and *Nikki Giovanni in the Classroom.* She is also the author of *With Rigor for All: Teaching the Classics to Contemporary Students* and *Beyond Standards: Excellence in the High School English Classroom.*

CRITICAL REVIEWERS

Dr. Julie M. T. Chan
Director of Literacy
  Instruction
Newport-Mesa Unified
  School District
Costa Mesa, California

Kathy Dubose
Murchison Junior High
  School
Austin, Texas

Pamela Dukes
Boude Storey Middle
  School
Dallas, Texas

Debra Hardick
Bennet Middle School
Manchester, Connecticut

Cheri Howell
Reading Specialist
Covina-Valley Unified
  School District
Covina, California

José M. Ibarra-Tiznado
ELL Program Coordinator
Bassett Unified School
  District
La Puente, California

Stacy Kim
Rowland Unified
  School District
Rowland Heights,
  California

Dr. Ronald Klemp
Instructor
California State
  University, Northridge
Northridge, California

Mary Alice Madden
Lathrop Intermediate
  School
Santa Ana, California

Colette F. McDonald
HB DuPont Middle
  School
Hockessin, Delaware

Jeff Read
Oak Grove Middle
  School
Clearwater, Florida

Constance Ridenour
Ford Middle School
Brook Park, Ohio

Fern M. Sheldon
K–12 Curriculum and
  Instruction Specialist
Rowland Unified School
  District
Rowland Heights,
  California

Karen Simons
Slausen Middle School
Ann Arbor, Michigan

Carol Surabian
Washington
  Intermediate School
Dinuba, California

FIELD-TEST PARTICIPANTS

Kate Baker
South Hills Middle
  School
Pittsburgh,
  Pennsylvania

Linda Lawler
Arcadia Middle School
Rochester, New York

Cindy MacIntosh
Seven Hills Middle
  School
Nevada City, California

Tim Pail
South Hills Middle
  School
Pittsburgh,
  Pennsylvania

Mathew Woodin
Martha Baldwin School
Alhambra, California

CONTENTS IN BRIEF

Collection 1

Facing Danger

LITERARY FOCUS
Analyzing Plot

INFORMATIONAL FOCUS
Analyzing Text Structures

Collection 2

CHARACTERS: LIVING MANY LIVES

LITERARY FOCUS
Analyzing Character

INFORMATIONAL FOCUS
Analyzing Comparison and Contrast

Collection 3

Living in the Heart

LITERARY FOCUS
Analyzing Theme

INFORMATIONAL FOCUS
Analyzing Cause and Effect

Collection 4

Point of View: Can You See It My Way?

LITERARY FOCUS
Analyzing Point of View

INFORMATIONAL FOCUS
Analyzing an Author's Argument

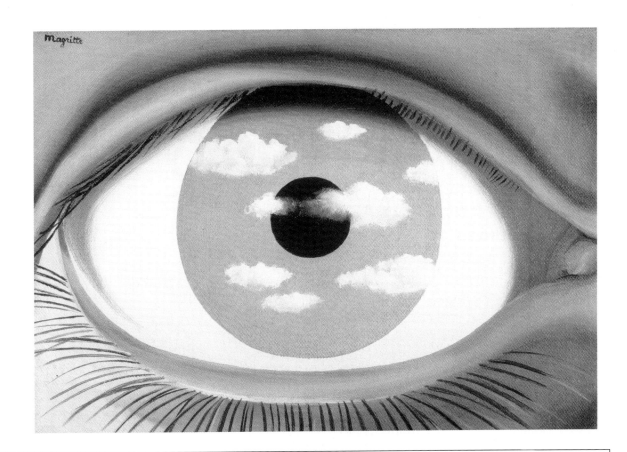

Collection 5

Worlds of Words: Prose and Poetry

LITERARY FOCUS
Analyzing Prose and Poetry

INFORMATIONAL FOCUS
Analyzing Main Idea

Elements of Poetry

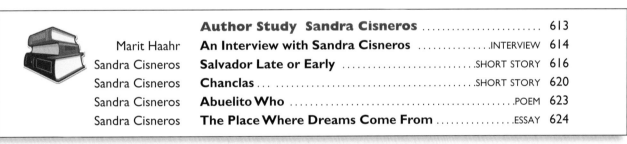
Writing Workshop Persuasive Writing:

Supporting an Interpretation 630

Collection 6

Our Literary Heritage

Greek Myths and World Folk Tales

LITERARY FOCUS
Analyzing Myths and Folk Tales

INFORMATIONAL FOCUS
Summarizing

World Folk Tales

Collection 7

Literary Criticism:
Where I Stand

LITERARY FOCUS
Criticizing Literature

INFORMATIONAL FOCUS
Evaluating Evidence

Collection 8

Reading for Life

INFORMATIONAL FOCUS

- Analyzing Information in Public, Workplace, and Consumer Documents
- Following Technical Directions

Resource Center

SKILLS, WORKSHOPS, AND FEATURES

SKILLS

ELEMENTS OF LITERATURE ESSAYS

READING SKILLS AND STRATEGIES LESSONS

LITERARY SKILLS

WORKSHOPS

WRITING WORKSHOPS

FEATURES

GRAMMAR LINKS

SKILLS REVIEW

TEST SMARTS

LANGUAGE HANDBOOK

SPELLING HANDBOOK

COMMUNICATIONS HANDBOOK

SPEAKING AND LISTENING HANDBOOK

MEDIA HANDBOOK

SELECTIONS BY GENRE

FICTION

SHORT STORIES

SONG LYRICS

NONFICTION

AUTOBIOGRAPHIES

INFORMATIONAL TEXTS

INFORMATIONAL ARTICLES

MAGAZINE ARTICLES

PUBLIC, WORKPLACE, AND CONSUMER DOCUMENTS

Elements of Literature on the Internet

TO THE STUDENT

At the *Elements of Literature* Internet site, you can read texts by professional writers and learn the inside stories behind your favorite authors. You can also build your word power and analyze messages in the media. As you move through *Elements of Literature*, you will find the best online resources at **go.hrw.com**.

Here's how to log on:

1. Start your Web browser, and enter **go.hrw.com** in the Address or Location field.

| Back | Forward | Reload | Home | Search |

Location: http://go.hrw.com

2. Note the keyword in your textbook.

INTERNET

More About Plot
•
More About Conflict

Keyword: LE5 7-1

3. Enter the keyword, and click "go."

http://go.hrw.com

LE5 7-1   go!

Enter keyword

FEATURES OF THE SITE

More About the Writer
Author biographies provide the inside stories behind the lives and works of great writers.

More About the Literary Element
Graphic organizers present visual representations of literary concepts.

Interactive Reading Model
Interactive Reading Workshops guide you through high-interest informational articles and allow you to share your opinions through pop-up questions and polls.

More Writer's Models
Interactive Writer's Models present annotations and reading tips to help you with your own writing. Printable Professional Models and Student Models provide you with quality writing by real writers and students from across the country.

Vocabulary Activity
Interactive vocabulary-building activities help you build your word power.

Projects and Activities
Projects and activities help you extend your study of literature through writing, research, art, and public speaking.

Speeches
Video clips from historical speeches provide you with the tools you need to analyze elements of great speechmaking.

Media Tutorials
Media tutorials help you dissect messages in the media and learn to create your own multimedia presentations.

A Walk Through
Elements of Literature

The **Elements of Literature** program is logically organized and sequenced so that students build literary, reading, writing, vocabulary, and speaking and listening skills. The **Elements of Literature Student Edition** is the primary tool for building knowledge and understanding of these skills. Opportunities for practice and remediation, reteaching, and assessing are offered throughout the program.

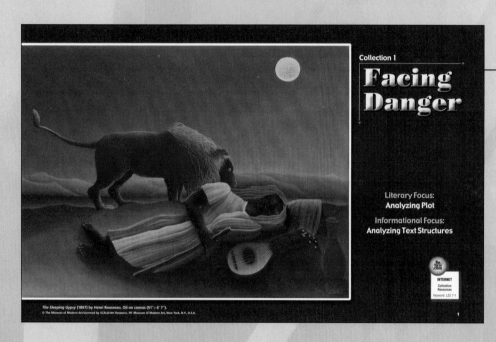

Collections

The collections in **Elements of Literature** are organized to cover the grade-level skills in literary response and analysis, reading comprehension, vocabulary, and writing. The literary focus and informational reading focus of each collection appear on the collection opener. Each collection also includes a variety of informational texts related to the literary selections, multiple opportunities for students to master each skill, and a review section.

 ## Elements of Literature

An **Elements of Literature** feature illustrates the **key literary element** or elements that are developed in the collection. Examples, excerpts from selections, and diagrams are often used in this feature.

Reading Skills and Strategies

Summarizing the Plot: Retelling
by Kylene Beers

Is this a plot?" Manuel asked as he pointed to the first paragraph of a story. He didn't understand that plot isn't a single thing he can point to in the story. He didn't know that **plot** is what happens in the story—all the related events that move from the story's beginning to its end. Plot is made up of all the building blocks you just read about on pages 2–3.

What Is Retelling?
Keeping up with all the information in a story can be difficult. A strategy called **retelling** can help you identify the elements of a plot and keep all the information about a plot straight in your mind. With this strategy you practice telling the plot of the story using a **Retelling Summary Sheet.** You use the Retelling Summary Sheet as a guide, to be sure you've included all the events in the plot.

The best way to get better at retelling is to practice retelling. Start practicing by reading the story titled "Duffy's Jacket," which begins on page 5. You can retell by jotting down some notes, by discussing your retelling with a friend, or by just thinking about what you would say.

When you've finished reading the story, use your retelling notes to fill out the Retelling Summary Sheet on page 12.

Retelling Tips

- Start by telling the title and author.
- Explain who the characters are.
- Explain the conflict, or main problem.
- Name the main events, keeping them in order.
- Explain what happens at the end.
- Tell what you liked or didn't like about the story.
- Use words like *first, second, next,* and *finally* to help keep everything in order.

SKILLS FOCUS

Reading Skills
Retell story events.

4 Collection 1 / Facing Danger

Reading Skills and Strategies
At the beginning of each collection, a **Reading Skills and Strategies** feature written by Kylene Beers offers students strategies designed to improve their reading skills. Dr. Beers first models the strategy for students and then guides them through an annotated selection. The questions in her annotations help students apply the strategy to the selection. After the selection, **Practice the Strategy** provides additional tips and practice.

Before You Read
The **Before You Read** page precedes every literary selection, providing a purpose for reading the selection. The **Skills Focus** identifies the literary and reading skills students will learn with the selection.

Make the Connection encourages students to connect personally with the text by thinking or writing about issues they will encounter in the literature they are about to read.

Literary Focus enables students to learn about or review a key literary element in the selection.

Reading Skills introduces a skill that will help students' reading comprehension, such as making inferences, retelling, or making predictions.

Background provides students with information that will help them understand the context of the literature.

Vocabulary Development lists the **key vocabulary words** from the selection. Each word is used in a sentence that places it in the context of the selection.

Before You Read   The Short Story

Rikki-tikki-tavi

Make the Connection
Quickwrite ✏

Conflict is part of our real lives. For example, most people face bullies at some time in their lives. If you were facing a bully, what would you do? Would you fight? Would you run away? Would you try to negotiate? In your journal, describe how you think you would react.

Literary Focus
Conflict

All stories are built on some kind of **conflict.** Usually a conflict results when a character wants something very badly but has a hard time getting it. Think of the stories in movies and on TV, and you'll be able to find a conflict in every one of them. Conflict is worked out in the series of related events called **plot.**

Reading Skills 📖
Retelling

Try a strategy called **retelling** to identify the events that move this plot forward. Here is how it works: As you read this story, you'll see little open-book signs alongside the text. At those points, stop and jot down notes that retell what has just happened. As you do your retelling, focus on the important events that keep the plot moving.

Vocabulary Development

Every time you read, you have a chance to add words to your vocabulary. The words that follow are underlined and defined in the story. See if you can use each one in a sentence of your own.

immensely (i·mens'lē) *adv.:* enormously. *Rikki is immensely brave. The snakes are immensely powerful.*

cowered (kou'ərd) *v.:* crouched and trembled in fear. *Darzee, who is a coward, cowered before the snakes. Rikki cowered before no one.*

valiant (val'yənt) *adj.:* brave and determined. *Rikki is a valiant hero. Would other snakes think the snakes are valiant too?*

consolation (kän'sə·lā'shən) *n.:* comfort. *Snakes get no consolation from Rikki. Rikki's consolation comes from a safe, peaceful garden.*

impotent (im'pə·tənt) *adj.:* powerless. *With all but her last egg destroyed, Nagaina felt impotent against Rikki.*

Go. hrw .com

INTERNET
Vocabulary Activity
•
Cross-curricular Connection
•
More About Kipling
Keyword: LE5 7-1

SKILLS FOCUS

Literary Skills
Analyze conflict.

Reading Skills
Retell story events.

Background
Literature and Social Studies

This story takes place in India many years ago, when the British ruled that huge country. The family in this story lives in a cantonment (kan·tän'mənt), which is a kind of army base. The father is in the British army. This story is about a conflict that takes place between two deadly snakes and a brave little mongoose—a creature that looks something like a weasel or a large squirrel.

14

you think it is right for you to eat fledglings out of a nest?"

Nag was thinking to himself and watching the least little movement in the grass behind Rikki-tikki. He knew that mongooses in the garden meant death sooner or later for him and his family, but he wanted to get Rikki-tikki off his guard. So he dropped his head a little and put it on one side.

"Let us talk," he said. "You eat eggs. Why should not I eat birds?"

"Behind you! Look behind you!" sang Darzee.

Rikki-tikki knew better than to waste time in staring. He jumped up in the air as high as he could go, and just under him whizzed by the head of Nagaina, Nag's wicked wife. She had crept up behind him as he was talking, to make an end of him; and he heard her savage hiss as the stroke missed. He came down almost across her back, and if he had been an old mongoose, he would have known that then was the time to break her back with one bite; but he was afraid of the terrible lashing return stroke of the cobra. He bit, indeed, but did not bite long enough, and he jumped clear of the whisking tail, leaving Nagaina torn and angry.

"Wicked, wicked Darzee!" said Nag, lashing up as high as he could reach toward the nest in the thorn bush; but Darzee had

built it out of reach of snakes, and it only swayed to and fro.

Rikki-tikki felt his eyes growing red and hot (when a mongoose's eyes grow red, he is angry), and he sat back on his tail and hind legs like a little kangaroo, and looked all round him, and chattered with rage. But Nag and Nagaina had disappeared into the grass. ②

RETELL
❷ What happens when Rikki first meets the snakes?

When a snake misses its stroke, it never says anything or gives any sign of what it means to do next. Rikki-tikki did not care to follow them, for he did not feel sure that he could manage two snakes at once. So he trotted off to the gravel path near the house and sat down to think. It was a serious matter for him. If you read the old books of natural history, you will find they say that when the mongoose fights the snake and happens to get bitten, he runs off and eats some herb that cures him. That is not true. The victory is only a matter of quickness of eye and quickness of foot—snake's blow against the mongoose's jump—and as no eye can follow the motion of a snake's head when it strikes, this makes things much more wonderful than any magic herb. Rikki-tikki knew he was a young mongoose, and it made him all the more pleased to think that he had managed

"I am Nag. . . . Look, and be afraid!"

Directed-Reading questions appear throughout many of the selections. They model the thinking and questioning strategies students need to build strong reading skills.

Meet the Writer

Rudyard Kipling

On His Own

India, the setting of "Rikki-tikki-tavi," is a place **Joseph Rudyard Kipling** (1865–1936) knew well. His father was a professor of art in Bombay, and Kipling was born in that city when India was under British rule. India was a fascinating place, and young Kipling loved it.

When he was six, however, his parents shipped him and his sister off to a boardinghouse in England. Feeling very much on his own in England, he made a discovery:

❝ [Books] were among the most important affairs in the world. . . . I could read as much as I chose and ask the meaning of things from anyone I met. I had found out, too, that one could take a pen and set down what one thought, and that nobody accused one of 'showing off' by doing so. ❞

When he was seventeen, Kipling returned to India and took a job as an editor with an English-language newspaper. He was fascinated by the lives of British colonials in India and the vivid contrast they made with the Indian people they ruled. Soon the paper was printing Kipling's poems and tales about

what he saw around him. Other newspapers reprinted them, and readers begged for more. Kipling's fame grew; over the next half century he wrote dozens of books, and in 1907, he won the Nobel Prize in literature. Although he later lived in many places around the world, India would always remain close to his heart.

For Independent Reading

Read more of Kipling's animal stories in *Just So Stories* and *The Jungle Book*. *The Jungle Book* is about Mowgli, a boy who is raised by wolves. *Kim,* Kipling's best-known novel, traces the adventures of an Irish orphan who is raised as an Indian and eventually becomes a British spy.

Meet the Writer

Meet the Writer appears after each literature selection, providing students with a short biography that includes **quotations from the author** about the experiences that inspired the author to become a writer.

After You Read — Response and Analysis

First Thoughts

1. Respond to "Rikki-tikki-tavi" by completing these sentences:
   - I thought this story was . . .
   - I was frightened for Rikki-tikki-tavi when . . .
   - The scene I liked best was . . .

Thinking Critically

2. Describe three **conflicts** that Rikki-tikki faces. Which conflict do you think is his greatest challenge? Why? How is it resolved?

3. **Motive** refers to the reason for a character's behavior. What was Rikki's **motive** for fighting Nagaina? What did he want?

4. What was Nagaina's **motive** for fighting Rikki? What did she want?

5. What does Darzee's chant tell about the garden animals' feelings for Rikki? Give specific words from the chant to support your answer.

INTERNET
Projects and Activities
Keyword: LE5 7-1

Extending Interpretations

6. Did Rikki's conflicts with the deadly garden bullies remind you of your own experiences? For ideas, think back to what you said about bullies before you read the story. ✎

7. The animal world of "Rikki-tikki-tavi" is filled with conflict and danger. What causes the war in this animal story? What causes most wars among people?

SKILLS FOCUS

Literary Skills
Analyze conflict.

Reading Skills
Retell story events.

Writing Skills
Express an opinion.

WRITING

Expressing Your Opinion

Look back at pages 18 and 19, where Nag and Nagaina are described for the first time. Find words on those pages that make the snakes seem evil. Is Kipling being fair, or are the snakes just doing what snakes do naturally? Does Kipling present the snakes as totally evil, or are they good in any way? In a paragraph or two, discuss your evaluation of the way Kipling handles his snake characters.

30 Collection 1 / Facing Danger

Reading Check

Work out the major events that advance the **plot** of Rikki's story. Fill in a diagram like this one. You should find at least four key events that lead to the exciting climax.

Climax

Event ——
Event —— Resolution
Event ——
Event —— [Add as many events as you need.]

Basic situation

Response and Analysis

A **Response and Analysis** page assesses students' comprehension of the literature selections. Questions clearly relate to the literary and reading skills taught with the selection.

First Thoughts questions encourage students to express their first impressions of the selections.

Reading Check questions address students' basic comprehension of the selection.

Thinking Critically offers interpretive and analytical questions that explore students' deeper understanding of the selection.

Extending Interpretations includes questions that encourage students to synthesize and evaluate key concepts they have discovered in their reading.

Writing Assignments provide opportunities for analysis, comparison and contrast, and other higher-level thinking skills.

Vocabulary Development

Vocabulary Development focuses on the skills students need to build strong vocabularies, with exposition and practice exercises.

Grammar Links

Grammar Links provide instruction and practice on common errors in usage, mechanics, and style.

After You Read — Vocabulary Development

Clarifying Word Meanings: Contrast

Sometimes you can clarify the meaning of an unfamiliar word by looking for **contrast** clues.

A writer who uses contrast will show how a word is *unlike* another word. For example, you can get a pretty clear idea of what a *splendid* garden is if you see it contrasted with a dark, narrow hole in the ground.

> The splendid garden glowed with roses and great clumps of waving grasses, unlike the dreary hole where cobras live.

Be on the lookout for these words, which signal contrast: *although, but, yet, still, unlike, not, in contrast, instead, however.*

PRACTICE

Fill in the blanks in the following sentences with words or phrases that contrast with the underlined word. You may find it helpful to make a cluster diagram of the word and its opposites before you write, like the one below for *cowered* and *cowering*:

cowered and cowering

bold   stood up to

aggressive

Word Bank
immensely
cowered
valiant
consolation
impotent

A cowering dog

An aggressive dog

1. The cobras had immense power, but the power of Darzee and the other garden creatures was _____.
2. Darzee cowered before the cobras, but Rikki _____.
3. Rikki was certainly valiant, but Chuchundra, the little muskrat, was _____.
4. The family felt consoled that Rikki was guarding their house, though they were _____ when the cobra threatened Teddy.
5. Darzee sang that the cobras were impotent in death, but they were _____ only a few hours earlier.

SKILLS FOCUS

Vocabulary Skills
Clarify word meanings by using contrast.

Rikki-tikki-tavi **31**

After You Read — Grammar Link

Subject-Verb Agreement

Probably the most common error people make in writing (and in speaking) is in subject-verb agreement. The rule is simple: Subjects and their verbs must always agree. That means that a singular subject takes a singular verb and a plural subject takes a plural verb. The problem comes with identifying the subject and deciding whether it's singular or plural.

Be especially careful when you have *neither/nor* or *either/or.* You must also pay attention when a subject is separated from its verb by a prepositional phrase. The verb always agrees with the subject.

1. **Neither Huttenmaier nor Rose wants/want to give up Sunny Jim.** [Singular subjects joined by *or* or *nor* take a singular verb. Therefore, the verb should be *wants.*]

2. **Neither Sunny Jim nor his owners wants/want to end their friendship.** [When a singular subject and a plural subject are joined by *or* or *nor,* the verb agrees with the subject closer to the verb. Since *owners* is plural, the verb should be *want.*]

3. **The owners of Sunny Jim is/are a bit unusual.** [The number of the subject is not affected by a prepositional phrase following the subject. Therefore, the verb should be *are.*]

PRACTICE

Rewrite the paragraph below to correct errors in subject-verb agreement.

The most interesting moments in this story comes when Sunny Jim is described. Neither tags nor a collar were found on the little rat. The owners of the rat seem very nice, but parts of their story is weird. The writer don't seem very enthusiastic either. Stories about the curious cat wasn't told here. Neither my biology teacher nor my town's pet-store owner recommend getting a pet *Rattus.*

For more help, see Agreement of Subject and Verb, 2b–n, in the Language Handbook.

SKILLS FOCUS

Grammar Skills
Use correct subject-verb agreement.

56 Collection 1 / Facing Danger

Informational Text

LINK TO "THREE SKELETON KEY"

Understanding Text Structures: A Newspaper Article

Reading Focus
Structure and Purpose of a Newspaper Article

The story "Three Skeleton Key" is about a terrifying invasion of rats, but the newspaper article you are about to read presents another view of these furry creatures.

The **purpose** of a newspaper article is to give you factual information about current events. A good informational article in a newspaper provides detailed answers to the questions *who? what? when? where? why?* and *how?*

Many newspaper articles follow an **inverted**—or upside-down—**pyramid** style. The article begins with a **summary lead,** a sentence or paragraph that gives the **main idea** of the story—this is usually the most important idea or detail in the story. It is followed by the less important details of the article.

Some articles begin with a lead that simply grabs your interest in a topic. Such a lead does not summarize but instead describes an interesting situation or fact related to the story. Here are some additional elements in the **structure** of a news article:

- **Headline:** the catchy boldface words that tell you what the article is about.
- **Subhead:** additional boldface words in smaller type under the headline, which add details about the article.
- **Byline:** the name of the reporter who wrote the article.
- **Dateline:** the location where the article was reported and the date when the information was reported.
- **Lead:** the sentence or paragraph that begins the news article.
- **Tone:** the choice of words and point of view that meet the interests of the newspaper's audience. Tone often depends on the subject of the article. Some articles are light, lively, and humorous; others are serious and straightforward.

■ How many structural elements of a newspaper article can you find as you read "Eeking Out a Life"?

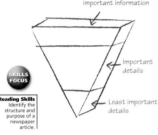

Summary lead, or most important information

Important details

Least important details

SKILLS FOCUS

Reading Skills
Identify the structure and purpose of a newspaper article.

52 Collection 1 / Facing Danger

Informational Text

Each informational text in *Elements of Literature* is topically or thematically linked to the preceding literary selection. An **Informational Text** page before every informational selection presents an informational **Reading Focus,** such as analyzing proposition and support or taking notes and outlining.

Vocabulary Development focuses on the skills students need to build strong vocabularies, with exposition and practice exercises.

The **Skills Focus** listed on the page shows students what they are expected to accomplish.

Analyzing Informational Text

Every informational selection is followed by a **Test Practice** in which students answer multiple-choice and constructed-response questions that test their understanding of the selection and its skills focus.

Analyzing a Newspaper Article

Eeking Out a Life

Test Practice

1. The **structure** of a newspaper article is said to be similar to an —
   A octagon
   B inverted pyramid
   C oval
   D upside-down T

2. The **dateline** of the article on page 53 names which city?
   F Salt Lake City
   G Des Moines
   H Buxton
   J Simi Valley

3. The **subhead** of the article tells you that —
   A something is eeking out a life
   B a couple has adopted a stray rat
   C the rat may have been chased by an owl
   D rats have become popular

4. The **byline** of the news article shows it was written by —
   F George G. Toudouze
   G Nachshon Rose
   H Matt Surman
   J Sunny Jim

5. The **lead** of this article —
   A is an attention grabber
   B makes a serious statement about dangerous rats
   C answers *who? what? where? when?* and *how?*
   D presents the story's main idea

6. The **main idea** of this article is —
   F a couple loves its adopted rat
   G rats can't live with people
   H keeping a rat at home is dangerous
   J the rat population is a problem

Constructed Response

1. What is the **purpose** of a newspaper article?

2. Describe the **inverted-pyramid structure** of a typical newspaper article.

3. Summarize the information from the article on page 53 that answers the questions *who? what? when? where? why?* and *how?*

4. Describe the **tone** of the article. Why do you think the reporter decided to use this tone?

5. The **headline** title of this article contains a **pun,** which is a play on word meanings. What two words, both pronounced "eek," is the headline playing with?

SKILLS FOCUS

Reading Skills
Analyze the structure and purpose of a newspaper article.

Eeking Out a Life 55

Comparing Literature

Each collection has a **Comparing Literature** or **Author Study** feature that focuses on two or more selections that are thematically or topically linked. The selections represent a variety of genres.

The features begin with a prereading page that introduces a Literary Focus and a Reading Skill as well as any additional information that students may find useful.

Each **Comparing Literature** or **Author Study** feature ends either with instruction in writing a comparison-contrast essay about the selections or with a variety of writing, speaking and listening, or other assignments.

 ## Comparing Literature

Literary Focus
Science Fiction

You're about to read and compare two science fiction stories. **Science fiction** is a kind of writing that lies somewhere between realistic fiction and total fantasy. It is usually set in the future in a world different from our own, but it is not a kind of writing in which anything goes. Science fiction is based on scientific laws. Most writers of science fiction use their knowledge of the latest scientific ideas and discoveries to imagine new technology that might someday be developed. They also use their understanding of human psychology to imagine how people might behave in situations involving that new technology.

The best of science fiction appeals to our intelligence and also to our imagination, to our sense of awe and wonder at being a part of a mysterious and unknown universe.

Reading Skills
Comparing and Contrasting

Although "Zoo" and "The Ruum" are very different stories, they have interesting similarities. To compare and contrast the two stories, you might look at the ways each story uses the elements of science fiction. When you **compare,** you look for ways that things are alike. When you **contrast,** you look for ways that things are different.

Elements of Science Fiction

Most science fiction stories contain some or all of the following elements:

- **a setting in the future,** often on another planet or in a spaceship
- **technology** that has not yet been invented, but that conforms to the rules of science
- **a journey through time** or to a distant planet or galaxy
- **imaginary characters** from outer space—alien or extraterrestrial creatures
- realistic human reactions to **fantastic situations**
- **a surprise ending**

SKILLS FOCUS

Literary Skills
Understand the elements of science fiction.

Reading Skills
Compare and contrast stories.

84   Collection 1 / Facing Danger

 ## NO QUESTIONS ASKED

This poem by Edward Field presents us with a new version of a famous character in literature, the monster brought to life by Frankenstein. In the original story, by the English writer Mary Wollstonecraft Shelley, a scientist named Frankenstein uses portions of dead bodies to create a figure shaped like a man and then gives the creature the power to move and think by activating him with electricity.

Frankenstein's creation is a scientific triumph, but it is also a moral disaster that leads to tragedy. The monster, who is actually a gentle and intelligent being, is physically a hideous patchwork of other bodies. His features are so ugly and nightmarish that no one can look at him without wanting to scream. Consequently the monster is forever denied the human companionship and love that he needs.

Edward Field's poem is based on the 1931 movie starring Boris Karloff, in which some elements of the original story were changed. For example, the scientist Frankenstein is Baron Frankenstein in the movie. As you read, picture the poem as presenting a series of film clips.

Frankenstein

Edward Field

The monster has escaped from the dungeon
where he was kept by the Baron,
who made him with knobs sticking out from each side
      of his neck
where the head was attached to the body
5   and stitching all over
where parts of cadavers° were sewed together.

He is pursued by the ignorant villagers,
who think he is evil and dangerous because he is ugly
and makes ugly noises.

6. **cadavers** (kə·davˈərz) *n.*: dead bodies; corpses.

108   Collection 1 / Facing Danger

No Questions Asked

Each collection ends with a **No Questions Asked** feature that includes one or more selections without accompanying apparatus. These selections allow students to practice reading independently.

Writing Workshops

Writing Workshops at the end of each collection guide students through the writing process. Each workshop covers a different mode of writing, such as narration, persuasion, description, or exposition, and is a logical extension of the literary and informational selections covered in the collection.

Step-by-step instruction helps students get started and think about the audience they want to reach as well as how to structure their papers.

A **student model** demonstrates the workshop assignment with annotations to help students understand the structure and development of an essay.

A **revision chart** offers specific actions for students to take to locate and correct weaknesses in their papers.

Writing Workshop

Assignment
Write a short story that includes the elements of plot, character, and setting.

Audience
Your classmates, teachers, family, and friends.

RUBRIC
Evaluation Criteria

A good story
1. centers on a major conflict that the characters must resolve
2. uses dialogue and action to develop the characters
3. provides a vivid description of the setting
4. ends with a resolution of the conflict
5. may reveal an overall message about life

NARRATIVE WRITING
Story

One of the best-loved forms of fictional writing is the **short story**. Some short stories are modeled closely on actual occurrences, while others are wildly imaginative—but any good story creates a world that fully engages a reader's interest.

Prewriting

1 Choosing a Story Idea

Writing a story can be an enjoyable challenge. Write a story in response to the following **prompt:**

> A good story entertains the reader with lifelike characters in a vivid setting, and in some way it resolves a conflict, or problem. Write a four-page story that presents characters who encounter and solve a problem.

The kernel of a story—your "seed" idea—might come from personal experience. Prod your memory by freewriting responses to questions like these:

- Of all the people you've known, who was the most unusual? the funniest? the most serious?
- What place do you know best? What happens there?
- What interesting experiences have you had?
- Is there an adventure you'd like to have?

SKILLS FOCUS

Writing Skills
Write a short story.

112

CALVIN AND HOBBES © Watterson. Reprinted with permission of UNIVERSAL PRESS SYNDICATE. All rights reserved.

Collection 1: Skills Review
Writing Skills

Test Practice

DIRECTIONS: Read the passage from a short story. Then, answer each question that follows.

Breannah stood in the goal, shifting her weight from one foot to the other, as a swarm of red jerseys nudged the soccer ball toward her. A lone blue-clad defender tried and failed to cut off the attack. Now no one stood between her and the lanky star forward of the Red Hots. The forward kicked the ball, and Breannah leaped to her right. The ball whooshed past her left ear and into the net.

She rose slowly and brushed herself off, ignoring the cheers from the Red Hots' bleachers. Next time, Breannah thought, she would be ready.

1. What strategy does the writer use to develop the main character?
   A dialogue spoken by the character
   B description of the character's appearance
   C description of the character's thoughts and actions
   D explanation of how other people respond to the character

2. What details does the writer use to show point of view in this passage?
   F The words *she* and *her* and the main character's thoughts are used to show third-person limited point of view.
   G The word *I* is used to show first-person point of view.
   H The word *you* is used to show second-person point of view.
   J Information about other characters' thoughts is used to show third-person-omniscient point of view.

3. If this passage occurs near the story's beginning, what might the writer do in later passages to build toward the climax?
   A summarize events in the story that readers have already read about
   B describe additional problems that add to the story's conflict
   C change the point of view to include other characters' views of events
   D describe the setting in detail

4. If a speaker were telling this story out loud, why might sh___ ing that the story w___ friend's experience___
   F to point out the ___
   G to create a mo___
   H to establish a c___
   J to include reali___

Skills Review

A **Skills Review** at the end of each collection provides **standardized test practice** and a review of the collection skills in reading, vocabulary, and writing.

READ ON: FOR INDEPENDENT READING

Fiction

Working Girl
In Katherine Paterson's *Lyddie*, set in the 1840s, Lyddie Worthen has to grow up fast when her mother is forced to abandon the family farm. When she finds a job in a textile mill, Lyddie faces a grim new world of poverty and eighteen-hour workdays. A true heroine, Lyddie fights against injustice as she struggles to earn enough to buy back the family farm.

First Division
Sixth-graders from Barlow Road and Bear Creek Ridge have developed a serious softball rivalry that has lasted more than fifty years, and the 1949 game looks to be one of the most exciting yet. But the shadow of World War II looms over the game when Shazam—whose father was killed at Pearl Harbor—attacks Aki—who spent years in an internment camp. Virginia Euwer Wolff's *Bat 6* takes a brave look at prejudice, responsibility, and growing up.

This title is available in the HRW Library.

Strange Happenings
What if you were vacationing in Hawaii and you made a volcano goddess angry? Could you imagine being struck by lightning and finding yourself 140 years in the past? What would you do if you woke up one morning and saw seven guardian angels talking to one another in your bedroom? Neal Shusterman presents these wacky situations and more in *MindBenders*.

A Life of Danger
In *Lupita Mañana* by Patricia Beatty, Lupita Torres enters California illegally and tries to help support her widowed mother and younger siblings in Mexico by finding a job. Her search for a better life becomes a struggle in a place where the laws are not always fair and growing up is not always easy.

This title is available in the HRW Library.

124 Collection 1 / Facing Danger

Nonfiction

Courage in China
When Ji-Li Jiang turned twelve in 1966, she was an intelligent student with a bright future ahead of her. Then Mao Tse-tung launched the Cultural Revolution in China, and her family's background was revealed. As a result, Ji-Li's friends turned their backs on her, and her family suffered repeated abuse at the hands of Chinese officials. Ji-Li recalls her childhood of bravery and loyalty in *Red Scarf Girl*.

This title is available in the HRW Library.

Back in Shakespeare's Day...
Ruth Ashby goes back to the sixteenth century in *Elizabethan England*. Ashby details the lives of prominent historical figures such as Henry VIII and Sir Walter Raleigh and authors such as Sir Thomas More and William Shakespeare. She also describes the religious and social customs of the English people at the time. Helpful maps and illustrations are included.

Snakes, Snakes, and More Snakes
Are you interested in snakes? Dr. Robert Mason is *really* interested in them. For over fifteen years he has been researching the world's largest concentration of garter snakes, located in Manitoba, Canada. Sy Montgomery accompanied Dr. Mason on his field study and, in *The Snake Scientist*, recorded some of the amazing things he learned.

The Story Behind the News Stories
Newspapers have riveted the American public with troubling and sensational stories since the founding of our country. They are perhaps the single most important medium for conveying information, shaping public opinion, and spreading awareness of the world around us. In *Behind the Headlines*, Thomas Fleming explores in exacting detail the people and events that make the news.

Read On 125

Read On

At the end of each collection, a **Read On** provides students with suggestions for independent reading of **fiction** and **nonfiction**. The recommended books have themes or subjects similar to those in the collection.

Test Smarts

by Flo Ota De Lange and Sheri Henderson

Strategies for Taking a Multiple-Choice Test

If you have ever watched a quiz show on TV, you know how multiple-choice tests work. You get a question and (usually) four choices. Your job is to pick the correct one. Easy! (Don't you wish?) Taking multiple-choice tests will get a whole lot easier when you apply these Test Smarts:

 T rack your time.

 E xpect success.

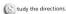 **S** tudy the directions.

T ake it all in.

S pot those numbers.

M aster the questions.

A nticipate the answers.

R ely on 50/50.

T ry. Try. Try.

S earch for skips and smudges.

Track Your Time

You race through a test for fear you won't finish, and then you sit watching your hair grow because you finished early, or you realize you have only five minutes left to complete eleven zillion questions. Sound familiar? You can avoid both problems if you take a few minutes before you start to estimate how much time you have for each question. Using all the time you are given can help you avoid making errors. Follow these tips to set **checkpoints:**

• How many questions should be completed when one quarter of the time is gone?

• What should the clock read when you are halfway through the questions?

• If you find yourself behind your checkpoints, you can speed up.

• If you are ahead, you can—and should— slow down.

Expect Success

Top athletes know that attitude affects performance. They learn to deal with their negative thoughts, to get on top of their mental game. So can you! But how? Do you compare yourself with others? Most top athletes will tell you that they compete against only one person: the...

Test Smarts

Test Smarts gives students strategies for taking multiple-choice tests and writing tests. It includes reading comprehension and vocabulary questions, as well as writing prompts.

Handbook of Literary Terms

For more information about a topic, turn to the page(s) in this book indicated on a separate line at the end of the entries. To learn more about *Alliteration*, for example, turn to pages 577 and 601.

On another line are cross-references to entries in this handbook that provide closely related information. For instance, at the end of *Autobiography* is a cross-reference to *Biography*.

ALLITERATION **The repetition of the same or very similar consonant sounds in words that are close together.** Though alliteration usually occurs at the beginning of words, it can also occur within or at the end of words. Among other things, alliteration can help establish a mood, emphasize words, and serve as a memory aid. In the following example the *s* sound is repeated at the beginning of the words *silken* and *sad* and within the words *uncertain* and *rustling:*

> And the silken sad uncertain rustling of each purple curtain
>
> —Edgar Allan Poe, from "The Raven"

See pages 577, 601.

ALLUSION **A reference to a statement, a person, a place, or an event from literature, history, religion, mythology, politics, sports, or science.** Allusions enrich the reading experience. Writers expect readers to recognize an allusion and to think, almost at the same time, about the literary work and the person,

place, or event that it refers to. The following lines, describing a tunnel in the snow, contain an allusion to Aladdin, a character in *The Thousand and One Nights:*

> With mittened hands, and caps drawn low,
> To guard our necks and ears from snow,
> We cut the solid whiteness through.
> And, where the drift was deepest, made
> A tunnel walled and overlaid
> With dazzling crystal: we had read
> Of rare Aladdin's wondrous cave,
> And to our own his name we gave.
>
> —John Greenleaf Whittier, from "Snow-Bound"

The cave in the tale contains a magic lamp that helps Aladdin discover vast riches. By alluding to Aladdin's cave, Whittier makes us see the icy tunnel in the snow... fairy-tale place.

The cartoon below makes... popular fairy tale.

"Now, this policy will cover your h... flood and huffing and p...
Reprinted from The Saturday Evening...

See...

Handbook of Liter...

Handbook of Reading and Informational Terms

For more information about a topic, turn to the page(s) in this book indicated on a separate line at the end of the entry. To learn more about *Cause and Effect*, for example, turn to page 256.

On another line are cross-references to entries in this handbook that provide closely related information. For instance, the entry *Chronological Order* contains a cross-reference to *Text Structures.*

ANALOGY

1. An **analogy** is a point-by-point comparison made between two things to show how they are alike. An analogy shows how something unfamiliar is like something well-known.

2. Another kind of analogy is a **verbal analogy.** A verbal analogy is a word puzzle. It gives you two words and asks you to identify another pair of words with a similar relationship. In an analogy the symbol ":" means "is to." The symbol "::" means "as."

> Select the pair of words that best completes the analogy.
>
> Toe : foot :: _____
>
> A   house : barn
> B   finger : hand
> C   road : path
> D   light : darkness

The correct answer is B: Toe : foot :: finger : hand, or "Toe is to foot as finger is to hand." The relationship is that of part to whole. A toe is part of the foot; a finger is part of the hand.

Another relationship often represented in verbal analogies is that of opposites:

> clear : cloudy :: bright : dark

Both sets of words are opposites. Clear is the opposite of cloudy, and bright is the opposite of dark.

Verbal analogies are often found in tests, where they are used to check vocabulary and thinking skills.

See pages 265, 288, 532.

ARGUMENT An **argument** is a position supported by evidence. Arguments are used to persuade us to accept or reject an opinion on a subject. Arguments are also used to persuade us to act in a certain way.

Supporting evidence can take the form of facts, statistics, anecdotes (brief stories that illustrate a point), and expert opinions. Not all arguments are logical. **Emotional appeals** find their way into most arguments, and you should learn to recognize them. Details that appeal to your feelings make an argument more interesting and memorable—but you should not accept an argument that is based only on an emotional appeal.

Handbook of Reading and Informational Terms   **943**

Handbook of Literary Terms

Handbook of Reading and Informational Terms

The **Handbook of Literary Terms** and the **Handbook of Reading and Informational Terms** serve as reference guides to the important literary, reading, and informational terms and concepts students encounter throughout the text.

T67

Language Handbook

The **Language Handbook** is a comprehensive reference to important issues in **grammar, usage,** and **mechanics.** Tips and activities appear throughout this handbook.

Language Handbook

1 THE PARTS OF SPEECH

THE NOUN

1a. A *noun* is a word used to name a person, a place, a thing, or an idea.

PERSONS	giant, Miss Nettie Hopley, baby sitter, immigrant
PLACES	pasture, Italy, Sutter's Fort, Crocker Art Gallery
THINGS	quilt, key, frog, desk, Newbery Medal, *Voyager 2*
IDEAS	knowledge, friendliness, success, love, self-esteem

Compound Nouns

A *compound noun* is two or more words used together as a single noun. The parts of a compound noun may be written as one word, as separate words, or as a hyphenated word.

> **TIPS FOR SPELLING** Compound words may be written as one word, as separate words, or as a hyphenated word. To be sure you are spelling a compound word correctly, always use a current dictionary.

ONE WORD	butterfly, playground, Passover, classroom
SEPARATE WORDS	Golden Age, compact disc, post office
HYPHENATED WORD	self-control, bull's-eye, six-year-old

Collective Nouns

A *collective noun* is a word that names a group.

EXAMPLES class family choir herd jury

Common Nouns and Proper Nouns

A *common noun* is a general name for a person, a place, a thing, or an idea. A *proper noun* names a particular person, place, thing, or idea. Proper nouns always begin with a capital letter. Common nouns begin with a capital letter in titles and when they begin sentences.

COMMON NOUNS	poem	nation	day
PROPER NOUNS	"The Runaway"	Japan	Friday

✓ **QUICK CHECK I**

Identify the nouns in the following sentences. Classify each noun as *common* or *proper.* Also label any *compound* or *collective* nouns.

EXAMPLE 1. "Rikki-tikki-tavi" is a short story by Rudyard Kipling.
1. *"Rikki-tikki-tavi"*—compound, proper; *short story*—compound, common; *Rudyard Kipling*—compound, proper

---

Communications Handbook

RESEARCH STRATEGIES

Using a Media Center or Library

To find a book, tape, film, or video in a library, start by looking in the **catalog.** Most libraries use an **online,** or computer, **catalog.**

Online catalogs vary from library to library. With some you begin searching for resources by **title, author,** or **subject.** With others you simply enter **keywords** for the subject you're researching. With either system, you enter information into the computer and a new screen will show you a list of materials or subject headings relating to your request. When you find an item you want, write down the title, author, and **call number,** the code of numbers and letters that shows you where to find the item on the library's shelves.

Some libraries still use card catalogs. A **card catalog** is a collection of index cards arranged in alphabetical order by title and author. Nonfiction is also cataloged by subject.

Electronic Databases. Electronic databases are collections of information you can access by computer. You can use these databases to find such resources as encyclopedias, almanacs, and museum art collections.

There are two kinds of electronic databases: **Online databases** are accessed at a computer terminal connected to a modem. The modem allows the computer to communicate with other computers over telephone lines. **Portable databases** are available on magnetic tape, diskette, or CD-ROM.

A **CD-ROM** (compact disc–read only memory) is played on a computer equipped with a CD-ROM player. If you were to look up *Amy Tan* on a CD-ROM guide to literature, for example, you could hear passages from her books and read critical analyses of her work.

Periodicals. Most libraries have a collection of magazines and newspapers. To find up-to-date magazine or newspaper articles on a topic, use a computerized index, such as *InfoTrac* or *EBSCO.* Some of these indices provide a summary of each article. Others provide the entire text, which you can read on-screen or print out. The *Readers' Guide to Periodical Literature* is a print index of articles that have appeared in hundreds of magazines.

Using the Internet

The **Internet** is a huge network of computers. Libraries, news services, government agencies, researchers, and organizations communicate and share information on the Net. The Net also lets you chat online with students around the world. For help in using the Internet to do research or to communicate with someone by computer, explore the options on the next page.

The Reference Section

Every library has materials you can use only in the library. Some examples are listed below. (Some reference works are available in both print and electronic form.)

Encyclopedias
Collier's Encyclopedia
The World Book Encyclopedia

General Biographical References
Current Biography Yearbook
The International Who's Who
Webster's New Biographical Dictionary

Special Biographical References
American Men & Women of Science
Biographical Dictionary of American Sports
Mexican American Biographies

Atlases
Atlas of World Cultures
National Geographic Atlas of the World

Almanacs
Information Please Almanac
The World Almanac and Book of Facts

Books of Quotations
Bartlett's Familiar Quotations

Books of Synonyms
Roget's International Thesaurus
Webster's New Dictionary of Synonyms

Communications Handbook

The **Communications Handbook** provides students with tips and instruction on how to do research on the Internet, evaluate Web sources, take notes, and cite sources.

Speaking and Listening Handbook

Media Handbook

The **Speaking and Listening Handbook** and **Media Handbook** provide instruction that guides students in delivering focused, coherent presentations and in evaluating a variety of oral and media communications.

Speaking and Listening Handbook

Giving and Listening to a Personal Narrative

Choosing a Story

To plan your oral narrative, you must find the right story to tell. (You might want to adapt the personal narrative you wrote for the Writing Workshop on pages 330–335.) Your story should have the following elements:

- **major and minor characters** that seem real
- **setting,** a definite time and place in which the story occurs
- **conflict,** a problem that the major characters must solve
- **plot,** made up of a **beginning** that sets the scene, **rising action** that leads to the story's **climax,** and a **resolution**

Make sure the story also has **dialogue** that brings the characters to life, **suspense** that makes listeners wonder what will happen next, and **action** that you can describe vividly or act out using movements, gestures, and facial expressions.

In addition, you need to consider the *purpose* and *audience* for your story. The **purpose** is to entertain, so you should choose a story that will appeal to the backgrounds and interests of your **audience,** namely, your teacher and classmates.

Planning Your Presentation

You can choose to tell the story as yourself, as a character involved in the story, or as an uninvolved narrator, but be sure to use a consistent **point of view** to keep your audience from becoming confused. Also, use the following strategies as you plan how to tell your story.

Media Handbook

Analyzing Electronic Journalism

Just as you can analyze the elements of fiction, you can analyze the elements of a TV news story. A TV news story is made up of words, images, and sounds. Television journalists use specific techniques for presenting these words, images, and sounds. Each of these techniques serves a specific purpose.

Analyzing Elements of TV News

Textual Elements **Text** is the name given to the words you hear and sometimes see on the TV screen. When you hear text, it is presented by a *news anchor* or *news reporter.* The **news anchor** reads the text of the primary, or most important, news stories. The anchor also introduces other reporters and their news stories. **Reporters**—often reporting live from where a news event is happening—may provide additional information on the primary news stories or give information on secondary, or less important, news stories.

Because of time limitations on TV, news stories are short, usually no more than two to three minutes long. This means that news writers and reporters must carefully plan text to achieve their purposes—capturing and keeping your attention, engaging your mind and emotions, and informing you. In order to understand the effects of a news story, you must examine both the *structure* by which the text is arranged and *content* of the text. You must also think about how the structure helps determine the content.

Program Resources

HOLT
ELEMENTS OF LITERATURE
First Course

Holt Assessment
Writing, Listening, and Speaking

Includes Writing Workshop Tests and Answer Key

HOLT
ELEMENTS OF LITERATURE
First Course

Holt Assessment
Literature, Reading, and Vocabulary

Includes Entry-Level and Collection Diagnostic Tests and Answer Key

HOLT
ELEMENTS OF LITERATURE
First Course

Holt Reading Solutions

Kylene Beers

Solutions for
• Intervention
• English-Language Learners
• Special Education

HOLT
ELEMENTS OF LITERATURE
First Course

Holt Adapted Reader

from *Elements of Literature*
• Adapted Literary Selections
• Poetry Selections
• Adapted Informational Texts

HOLT
ELEMENTS OF LITERATURE
First Course

Spelling
Lessons and Activities

HOLT
ELEMENTS OF LITERATURE
First Course

The Holt Reader

• Literary Selections from *Elements of Literature*
• Additional Literary Selections and Informational Texts

Planning

Annotated Teacher's Edition

This planning and teaching tool offers

- Specific questions to help reinforce and evaluate reading and literary skills for each selection

- Special approaches for learners having difficulty, English-language learners, and advanced learners

- Planning charts in the interleaf pages for each collection that provide information about the collection's scope and sequence of skills, core content, and resources

- Specific sequencing suggestions to ensure coverage of grade-level skills, effective testing, and remediation and reteaching opportunities

One-Stop Planner CD-ROM with ExamView Test Generator

This time-saving planning software contains print-based teaching resources, clips from the video program, and valuable assessment tools. The **One-Stop Planner** also

- Simplifies lesson planning and management

- Includes all the teaching resources for **Elements of Literature**

- Includes printable program resources and an easy-to-use test generator

- Offers previews of all teaching resources, including assessments and worksheets linked to the **Student Edition**

- Launches directly to the **go.hrw.com** Web site

PowerNotes for Literature and Reading

- Contains fully editable instructional PowerPoint® presentations that teach literary elements and reading skills and that introduce literary periods

- Includes teacher's notes with discussion questions and student note-taking worksheets with graphic organizers for each presentation

Professional Development

Web-Based Professional Development

Teaching Literacy to All Students, Grades 6–12, is a 9-module online professional development program that is ideal for all subject areas. **Teaching Reading to All Students, Grades 6–8,** is a 16-module online professional development program designed for middle school language arts teachers. Each module provides video demonstrations of best teaching practices tied to Web-based content that includes explanations and examples, interactive applications to the teacher's own classroom, graphic organizers and lesson-planning templates, printable classroom handouts, and assessment instruments. The modules cover topics such as

- Planning schoolwide literacy programs
- Using assessment data to drive instruction
- Modifying instruction for English-language learners
- Helping struggling readers with comprehension and fluency
- Integrating standards-based instruction

Face-to-Face Professional Development

Holt, Rinehart and Winston provides customized, comprehensive teacher training to assist school districts and individual teachers in the effective implementation of **Elements of Literature.**

- The training is facilitated by highly qualified professional development providers with language arts and reading expertise.

- Training institute and workshop topics include effective teaching practices, evidence-based research, and standards-based instruction.

Differentiating Instruction

The Holt Reader

This consumable workbook includes alternative direct instruction and additional practice for the skills taught in each collection of **Elements of Literature.** The consumable format offers students an interactive, hands-on approach to building reading, vocabulary, and literary analysis skills. Students circle and underline the text and write responses in the margins of the selections.

- **Part 1** contains key literary selections from **Elements of Literature** and additional literary selections that extend students' practice. Instruction is focused on vocabulary, literary elements, and reading skills. Skills practice and skills review exercises extend instruction and provide assessment opportunities.

- **Part 2** contains informational texts such as magazine and newspaper articles, editorials, and essays. Also offered are skills practice and skills review exercises.

Holt Adapted Reader

This consumable worktext contains the literary and informational adaptations found in **Holt Reading Solutions.** With scaffolded instruction that provides guided support, the **Holt Adapted Reader** can be used with struggling readers while other students in the class read the same selection in **The Holt Reader** or the **Student Edition.**

- Adaptations are within the reading range of English-language learners, special education students, and reluctant readers.

- "Here's How" annotations model vocabulary, literary analysis, and reading comprehension skills; "Your Turn" annotations ask students to answer a question using the skill just modeled.

- Graphic organizers help students review and consolidate what they've learned.

Holt Reading Solutions

This book pulls together all of the reading resources in the *Elements of Literature* program to create a powerful tool for intervention and whole-class instruction. It includes

- Diagnostic assessment tools
- Lesson plans for English-language learners and special education students
- Adaptations of selected reading selections
- Vocabulary and comprehension worksheets
- Information on phonics and decoding
- Additional instruction and practice in remedial reading skills and strategies

Supporting Instruction in Spanish

Provides the following Spanish-language materials as extra support for students who are making the transition from Spanish to English:

- Summaries of selections in *Elements of Literature*
- Criteria for major writing modes
- Definitions and examples of key grammar terms and concepts
- Introductions and summaries of Visual Connections segments

Audio CD Library

- Includes dramatic readings by professional actors that bring to life nearly every reading selection in *Elements of Literature*

Audio CD Library, Selections and Summaries in Spanish

- Includes Spanish translations of key selections in *Elements of Literature* and assists students in reading and developing their own sense of a selection
- Includes recordings of summaries in Spanish of virtually every selection in *Elements of Literature* and serves as a valuable tool for English-language learners

Workshop Resources: Writing, Listening, and Speaking

Supports instruction and assignments in the **Student Edition**

- Includes worksheets for each Writing Workshop, the Media Handbook, and the Speaking and Listening Handbook
- Includes exercises and lesson plans with alternative teaching strategies for English-language learners and special education students

Family Involvement Activities in English and Spanish

- Offers a selection of letters written for the parents or guardians of students using *Elements of Literature*
- Suggests activities that can be completed at home to extend the material in the **Student Edition**
- Allows parents or guardians to participate in students' education and helps foster an atmosphere in the home that encourages academic success

Reading/Literature/Vocabulary

The Holt Reader

This consumable workbook includes alternative direct instruction and additional practice for the skills taught in each collection of *Elements of Literature*. The consumable format offers students an interactive, hands-on approach to building reading, vocabulary, and literary analysis skills. Students circle and underline the text and write responses in the margins of the selections.

- **Part 1** contains key literary selections from *Elements of Literature* and additional literary selections that extend students' practice. Instruction is focused on vocabulary, literary elements, and reading skills. Skills practice and skills review exercises extend instruction and provide assessment opportunities.
- **Part 2** contains informational texts such as magazine and newspaper articles, editorials, and essays. Also offered are skills practice and skills review exercises.

Holt Adapted Reader

This consumable worktext contains the literary and informational adaptations found in *Holt Reading Solutions*. With scaffolded instruction that provides guided support, the *Holt Adapted Reader* can be used with struggling readers while other students in the class read the same selection in *The Holt Reader* or the **Student Edition**.

- Adaptations are within the reading range of English-language learners, special education students, and reluctant readers.
- "Here's How" annotations model vocabulary, literary analysis, and reading comprehension skills; "Your Turn" annotations ask students to answer a question using the skill just modeled.
- Graphic organizers help students review and consolidate what they've learned.

Holt Reading Solutions

This book pulls together all of the reading resources in the *Elements of Literature* program to create a powerful tool for intervention and whole-class instruction. It includes

- Diagnostic assessment tools
- Lesson plans for English-language learners and special education students
- Adaptations of selected reading selections
- Vocabulary and comprehension worksheets
- Information on phonics and decoding
- Additional instruction and practice in remedial reading skills and strategies

Vocabulary Development

- Includes copying master worksheets that expand on students' ability to define and use the vocabulary words identified in the **Student Edition**
- Includes cumulative reviews that reinforce students' mastery of the Vocabulary words

HRW Library

- Offers a comprehensive selection of the best novels, works of nonfiction, anthologies, and connected readings, with selections drawn from a variety of cultures
- Includes Study Guides that help motivate students and enhance their appreciation and understanding of classic and contemporary literature

Writing/Grammar and Language/Listening and Speaking

Workshop Resources: Writing, Listening, and Speaking

Supports instruction and assignments in the **Student Edition**

- Includes worksheets for each Writing Workshop, the Media Handbook, and the Speaking and Listening Handbook
- Includes exercises and lesson plans with alternative teaching strategies for English-language learners and special education students

Language Handbook Worksheets

- Includes practice and reinforcement worksheets that cover the material presented in the Language Handbook section of *Elements of Literature*
- Includes tests at the end of each section of the booklet that can be used either for assessment or as end-of-section reviews

Daily Language Activities

A notebook of transparencies that reinforce skills in reading, writing, grammar, usage, and mechanics that are covered in *Elements of Literature*. Transparencies are grouped into the following categories:

- Proofreading Warm-ups
- Vocabulary
- Analogies
- Sentence Combining
- Critical Reading

Spelling

A workbook of comprehensive spelling instruction and practice. Each of the 35 lessons includes

- A spelling generalization
- A corresponding list of spelling words
- Activities that incorporate one or more spelling strategies that students practice and apply

Assessment

Holt Assessment: Literature, Reading, and Vocabulary

Contains diagnostic, progress, and summative assessment tests, as follows:

- An Entry-Level Test and diagnostic tests for each collection assess students' level of preparation.
- Tests for every reading selection provide ongoing evaluation of students' skill development.
- Summative tests for each collection and an End-of-Year Test then offer cumulative assessment opportunities.

Holt Assessment: Writing, Listening, and Speaking

- Includes assessment of writing skills in a standardized test format for each Writing Workshop
- Provides scales and rubrics for each assignment in the Writing Workshops, the Media Handbook, and the Speaking and Listening Handbook

Holt Online Assessment

- Includes diagnostic and summative assessments
- Provides tools to monitor student progress through tracking student mastery and recording and analyzing scores

One-Stop Planner CD-ROM with ExamView Test Generator

Time-saving planning software that includes a printable version of all the tests from *Holt Assessment: Reading, Literature, and Vocabulary* and *Holt Assessment: Writing, Listening, and Speaking* as well as an easy-to-use test generator.

Holt Online Essay Scoring

- Provides writing prompts for the types of writing most common in state assessments
- Instantly scores and gives holistic and analytic feedback on student essays
- Provides writing tips, activities, and model essays geared to students' results

Technology

Internet

Elements of Literature Basic Online Edition

A Web-based version of the print edition of *Elements of Literature,* this "digital textbook"

- Delivers the content of the textbook in an online format that lightens the load students carry in their backpacks
- Enables students to complete homework online
- Includes access to an online notebook for storing student work, taking notes, and responding to the same questions and activities that appear in the student book

Elements of Literature Enhanced Online Edition

In addition to all the features of the **Basic Online Edition** described above, the **Enhanced Online Edition** includes a number of selections from the student text that are enhanced with various interactive features. The **Enhanced Online Edition**

- Provides point-of-use interactive critical thinking and literary response questions that pop up in the Notebook, where students can type responses, edit, save, and print their work
- Includes audio excerpts from the selection in both English and Spanish
- Features vocabulary links in English and Spanish, with accompanying audio
- Delivers links to high-interest video clips that enhance students' understanding of selections and build their prior knowledge
- Provides Spanish summaries of selections in audio
- Includes highlighting and annotation tools for use by both students and teachers
- Features an Image Gallery where students can click to see art and graphics from their textbook

AuthorSpace

A Web environment available on *Elements of Literature* **Enhanced Online Edition** that provides students opportunities to dig deeper into the lives and works of various authors

- Uses a variety of interactive features such as timelines, maps, and illustrated "webs of influence" to help students gain a more detailed understanding of an author's life and his or her place in literary history
- Gives students a chance to read additional literary works, as well as primary source documents, by featured authors

go.hrw.com

At **go.hrw.com,** students put their reading, writing, listening, and speaking skills into action in real-world situations. The **GO Site**

- Reinforces the study of literature through additional biographical information about authors, a variety of cross-curricular projects connected to the literature in the student textbook, and literary elements activities
- Includes interactive reading workshops that guide students through informational texts
- Includes interactive writers' models that illustrate various types of writing
- Includes vocabulary-building activities, through which students explore synonyms, antonyms, etymologies, and multiple meanings

Holt Online Assessment

- Includes diagnostic and summative assessments
- Provides tools to monitor student progress through tracking student mastery and recording and analyzing scores

Holt Online Essay Scoring

- Provides writing prompts for the types of writing most common in state assessments
- Instantly scores and gives holistic and analytic feedback on student essays
- Provides writing tips, activities, and model essays geared to students' results

Teaching Literacy to All Students, Grades 6–12

This online professional development program provides video demonstrations of best teaching practices combined with interactive exercises, graphic organizers, and lesson-planning templates; printable classroom handouts; and assessment instruments. The program contains 9 lesson-segments covering literacy topics such as

- Schoolwide literacy programs
- Assessment driving instruction
- English language learners and intensive learners
- Comprehension and fluency
- Strategies in language arts

Media

Visual Connections Videocassette Program

- Consists of author biographies, interviews, historical summaries, and cross-curricular connections that motivate students and enrich and extend learning

Fine Art Transparencies

- Features stunning examples of classic and contemporary art to complement the literature selections in *Elements of Literature*
- Helps students explore literary characters and ideas through visual representations
- Encourages students to make cross-curricular connections

One-Stop Planner CD-ROM with ExamView Test Generator

- Time-saving planning software that contains print-based teaching resources, clips from the video program, and valuable assessment tools

PowerNotes for Literature and Reading

- Fully editable instructional PowerPoint presentations that teach literary elements and reading skills and that introduce literary periods

Audio CD Library

- Includes dramatic readings by professional actors that bring to life nearly every reading selection in *Elements of Literature*

Audio CD Library, Selections and Summaries in Spanish

- Includes Spanish translations of key selections in *Elements of Literature*
- Includes recordings of summaries in Spanish of virtually every selection in *Elements of Literature*

Holt Interactive Spelling

- Spelling instruction, practice, and assessment in an engaging, interactive CD-ROM format
- Includes a diagnostic test that allows for individualized plans of instruction

T73

Diagnosis and Prescription: Tracking Student Mastery

The Entry-Level and End-of-Year tests can be used to inform instructional planning, chart student progress, and provide individual and group snapshots of core language arts skills proficiency.

CORE SKILLS	Entry-Level Test	End-of-Year Test	Collection Diagnostic Test	Collection Summative Test	Reteaching	Remediation
Collection 1						
Analyzing plot	Items 5,9	Items 1, 21, 31, 37	Items 1–6	Items 6–11, 14	*The Holt Reader,* Collection 1 *ATE,* Reteaching Lessons	*Holt Reading Solutions:* • Lesson Plans (ELL) • Special Ed Lesson Plans • Adapted Readings • MiniReads *Holt Adapted Reader*
Analyzing text structures	Item 32	Items 17, 19, 39, 40	Items 7–10		*The Holt Reader,* Collection 1	*Holt Adapted Reader*
Vocabulary	Items 10, 11, 17, 18, 22, 27, 37, 41–50	Items 10, 18, 25, 45–50		Items 1–5	*The Holt Reader,* Collection 1	
Collection 2						
Analyzing character	Items 4, 6, 8	Items 2, 3, 8, 22, 34, 35	Items 1–6	Items 7–10	*The Holt Reader,* Collection 2 *ATE,* Reteaching Lessons	*Holt Reading Solutions:* • Lesson Plans (ELL) • Special Ed Lesson Plans • Adapted Readings • MiniReads *Holt Adapted Reader*
Analyzing comparison and contrast		Item 26	Item 7		*The Holt Reader,* Collection 2 *ATE,* Reteaching Lessons	*Holt Adapted Reader*
Vocabulary	Items 10, 11, 17, 18, 22, 27, 37, 41–50	Items 10, 18, 25, 45–50	Items 9, 10	Items 1-5	*The Holt Reader,* Collection 2	
Collection 3						
Analyzing theme	Item 12	Items 6, 28–30, 32	Items 1–3	Items 6, 7, 9, 14	*The Holt Reader,* Collection 3 *ATE,* Reteaching Lessons	*Holt Reading Solutions:* • Lesson Plans (ELL) • Special Ed Lesson Plans • Adapted Readings • MiniReads *Holt Adapted Reader*
Analyzing cause and effect	Item 28	Items 11, 12, 20, 33	Item 7	Items 8, 10–13	*The Holt Reader,* Collection 3 *ATE,* Reteaching Lessons	*Holt Adapted Reader*
Vocabulary	Items 10, 11, 17, 18, 22, 27, 37, 41–50	Items 10, 18, 25, 45–50	Items 9, 10	Items 1–5	*The Holt Reader,* Collection 3	

CORE SKILLS	Entry-Level Test	End-of-Year Test	Collection Diagnostic Test	Collection Summative Test	Reteaching	Remediation
Collection 4						
Analyzing point of view	Item 24	Items 4, 5, 15, 27	Items 1–4	Items 6, 8, 10, 14	*The Holt Reader,* Collection 4 *ATE,* Reteaching Lessons	*Holt Reading Solutions:* • Lesson Plans (ELL) • Special Ed Lesson Plans • Adapted Readings • MiniReads *Holt Adapted Reader*
Analyzing an author's argument		Items 41, 42, 44	Items 7, 8	Item 13	*The Holt Reader,* Collection 4 *ATE,* Reteaching Lessons	
Vocabulary	Items 10, 11, 17, 18, 22, 27, 37, 41–50	Items 10, 18, 25, 45–50	Items 9, 10	Items 1–5	*The Holt Reader,* Collection 4	
Collection 5						
Analyzing prose and poetry	Items 1, 2, 13, 15, 21, 23, 31	Items 9, 38	Items 1–7	Items 1–10	*The Holt Reader,* Collection 5 *ATE,* Reteaching Lessons	*Holt Reading Solutions:* • Lesson Plans (ELL) • Special Ed Lesson Plans • Adapted Readings *Holt Adapted Reader*
Analyzing main idea	Item 20, 25, 33–35		Item 8		*The Holt Reader,* Collection 5	*Holt Reading Solutions:* • Lesson Plans (ELL) • Special Ed Lesson Plans • MiniReads *Holt Adapted Reader*
Vocabulary	Items 10, 11, 17, 18, 22, 27, 37, 41–50	Items 10, 18, 25, 45–50	Items 9, 10	Items 1–5	*The Holt Reader,* Collection 5	

CORE SKILLS	Entry-Level Test	End-of-Year Test	Collection Diagnostic Test	Collection Summative Test	Reteaching	Remediation
Collection 6						
Analyzing myths and folk tales			Items 1–7	Items 6-10, 12, 13	*The Holt Reader,* Collection 6 *ATE,* Reteaching Lessons	*Holt Reading Solutions:* • Lesson Plans (ELL) • Special Ed Lesson Plans • Adapted Readings *Holt Adapted Reader*
Summarizing	Item 30	Item 23	Item 8	Item 11	*The Holt Reader,* Collection 6 *ATE,* Reteaching Lessons	*Holt Reading Solutions:* • Lesson Plans (ELL) • Special Ed Lesson Plans • MiniReads *Holt Adapted Reader*
Vocabulary	Items 10, 11, 17, 18, 22, 27, 37, 41–50	Items 10, 18, 25, 45–50	Items 9, 10	Items 1–5	*The Holt Reader,* Collection 6	
Collection 7						
Criticizing literature	Item 16		Items 1–4		*The Holt Reader,* Collection 7 *ATE,* Reteaching Lessons	*Holt Reading Solutions:* • Lesson Plans (ELL) • Special Ed Lesson Plans • Adapted Readings *Holt Adapted Reader*
Evaluating evidence	Items 26, 38	Items 7, 43	Items 7, 8	Item 11		*Holt Adapted Reader*
Vocabulary	Items 10, 11, 17, 18, 22, 27, 37, 41–50	Items 10, 18, 25, 45–50	Items 9, 10	Items 1–5	*The Holt Reader,* Collection 7	

CORE SKILLS	Entry-Level Test	End-of-Year Test	Collection Diagnostic Test	Collection Summative Test	Reteaching	Remediation
Collection 8						
Analyzing information in public, workplace, and consumer documents		Item 16	Items 1–7	Item 6–9, 13–15	*The Holt Reader,* Collection 8 *ATE,* Reteaching Lessons	*Holt Reading Solutions:* • Lesson Plans (ELL) • Special Ed Lesson Plans • Adapted Readings *Holt Adapted Reader*
Following technical directions		Item 14	Items 8–10		*The Holt Reader,* Collection 8	*Holt Reading Solutions:* • Lesson Plans (ELL) • Special Ed Lesson Plans • Adapted Readings *Holt Adapted Reader*
Vocabulary	Items 10, 11, 17, 18, 22, 27, 37, 41–50	Items 10, 18, 25, 45–50		Items 1–5	*The Holt Reader,* Collection 8	

Carol Jago
English Teacher
Santa Monica High School
Santa Monica, CA
and
Director
California Reading and Literature Project
University of California,
Los Angeles, CA

RESEARCH

Beck, I. and McKeown, M. 1981.
"Developing Questions That Promote
Comprehension: The Story Map." *Language Arts*
November/December: 913–918.

Mandler, J. and N. Johnson. 1977.
"Remembrance of Things Parsed: Story
Structure and Recall." *Cognitive Psychology*
9: 111–151.

**Pressley, M., Johnson, C. J., Symons, S.,
Mcgoldrick, J. S., & Kurita, J. A. 1989.**
"Strategies That Improve Children's Memory and
Comprehension of Text. *The Elementary School
Journal* 90: 3–32.

Rumelhart, D. 1975.
"Notes on a Schema for Stories." *Representation
and Understanding.* Eds. Browbrow, D., &
Collins, A. New York: Academic, 211–236.

How Stories Work

"What is character but the determination of incident? What is incident but the illustration of character?"—**Henry James**

Story Mapping

Writers create stories with a common set of building blocks. These literary elements—character, setting, plot, theme, and conflict—create a predictable structure familiar to every reader, storyteller, and moviegoer. Researchers Beck and McKeown found that when students map these elements, identifying them either as they read or upon reflection, comprehension improves dramatically. Readers begin to see how a story works from the inside out.

Literary elements provide an organizing framework for understanding critical aspects of a story. The simple question "Who?" leads readers to characters; "Where?" and "When?" to setting; "What?" "Why?" and "How?" to plot. Without answers to these questions, readers can easily become lost in the story and lose their bearings.

Story Grammar

Storytellers and writers also draw from a stock of familiar narrative structures. In the 1970s, Rumelhart organized the insights of cognitive researchers into a comprehensive grammar for narrative text. For experienced readers, these patterns form an arc they know well. A hero or heroine takes center stage. Trouble emerges. Help appears, sometimes from an unlikely source. Complications develop. Things get worse and worse until the conflict is finally resolved.

In "Remembrance of Things Parsed: Story Structure and Recall," Mandler and Johnson expand Rumelhart's theory of a story grammar to include a study of the events taking place within the story. They examine and build into their ideas about story grammar the hero's goals, the path taken, failed and successful attempts to solve the problem, and ultimate outcomes. They explore questions such as "When all was said and done, what did the main character feel? What had he or she learned?"

Building Comprehension

Research by Pressley suggests that stories that conform to story grammar structure are easier for students to read and remember than those that take alternate forms. Charting the course of the story can help students see how what they are reading, unfamiliar as the characters and setting may seem at first, actually conforms to a pattern they know well.

Stories that withstand the test of time stimulate readers by both confirming our expectations and surprising us. Gifted authors and storytellers work within a framework as they use familiar literary elements. At the same time, they always seem to find a way to say something new.

Effective Vocabulary Instruction

Kylene Beers, Ph.D.
Senior Reading Researcher
Child Study Center
Youth Development Program
Yale University

RESEARCH

Beers, K. 2002.
When Kids Can't Read—What Teachers Can Do.
Portsmouth: Heinemann.

Blachowicz, C. L. Z., and Fisher, P. 2000.
"Vocabulary Instruction." *Handbook of Reading Research.* Eds. P. D. Pearson, R. Barr, M. Kamil, and P. Mosenthal. White Plains: Longman, 503–524.

Tierney, R., and Cunningham, J. 1984.
"Research on Teaching Reading Comprehension." *Handbook of Reading Research.* Eds. P. D. Pearson, R. Barr, M. Kamil, and P. Mosenthal. White Plains: Longman, 609–656.

"Preteaching vocabulary . . . requires that the words to be taught must be key words, . . . be taught in semantically and topically related sets, . . . and that only a few words be taught per lesson." —**Tierney and Cunningham**

Preteaching Vocabulary

When students don't know the meaning of words that are used in a text, their ability to understand that text is diminished. They can use the context as a clue to get the gist of the meaning, but sometimes the context doesn't provide enough information, and other times the gist isn't helpful enough. In those cases, we must preteach the vocabulary. To do so effectively, focus on which words you teach, the number that you teach, and how you teach them.

The Right Words and the Right Number

Deciding which words to teach is linked to deciding how many to teach. Twenty new words per week are probably too many for struggling readers, especially when you consider that the list of twenty is just for English class. The more vocabulary words we give students to learn weekly, the less chance they have of learning a word to the level needed to move it from short-term to long-term memory. Keeping the number between five and ten means students have a better chance of retaining that word beyond the end of the week (Beers, 2002).

Consequently, choose wisely the words to be taught. Avid readers benefit by studying rare words—those highly unusual ones—because they already have a solid vocabulary of the more common ones. Struggling readers, however, benefit by focusing on high-utility words—those more common words that they are likely to see in other contexts. So, in this sentence, "The boys banked the canoe to the lee side of the rock," the inclination might be to teach the word *lee*, a rare word. However, if students don't know what *banked* means in this context or don't know the word *canoe*, it matters little what *lee* means. For struggling readers, a focus on high-utility words is more beneficial than a focus on rare words.

The Right Instructional Approach

Tierney and Cunningham (1984) explain that offering students a list of vocabulary words with their definitions is not as effective as placing each word within a semantic context. Students learn how to use words as they read or hear them used correctly. *Elements of Literature* provides a short list of words on the "Before You Read" page of each selection that are defined and then used in a sentence. It is this semantic placement that most helps students learn words. Choosing the right number of the right words and presenting words in a semantic context helps students build their vocabulary and, as a consequence, improve their comprehension.

Dale Allender
Associate Executive Director
National Council of Teachers of English
Urbana, IL

RESEARCH

Allender, D. 2002
"The Myth Ritual Theory and the
Teaching of Multicultural Literature."
English Journal 5: 52–55.

Barthes, R. 1981
"Theory of the Text." *Untying the Text: A
Poststructuralist Reader.* Ed. R Young.
London: Routledge.

Bloome, D. and Egan-Robertson, A. 1993
"The Social Construction of Intertextuality in
Classroom Reading and Writing Lessons."
Reading Research Quarterly 28: 304–333.

Callahan, Meg. 2002
"Intertextual Composition: The Power of the
Digital Pen." *English Education* 35: 46–64.

Spears-Bunton, L. 1999
"Calypso, Jazz, Reggae, and Salsa: Literature
Response and the African Diaspora." *Reader
Response in Secondary and College Classrooms.*
Ed. N. Karolides. Mahway, New Jersey:
Lawrence Erlbaum Associates.

Multicultural Literacy

"Inherent in the theory of text is the notion of intertextuality."
—Meg Callahan

Finding a Way In

Multicultural literature affirms and celebrates the rich diversity of our classrooms. That very same literature, however, can be a source of confusion and frustration for some readers, as it often contains unfamiliar references and unfamiliar words or phrases. We can overcome these surface problems by using intertextual readings.

Intertextual Reading

At first glance, intertextual reading looks like paired reading via novel sets or themed reading. However, it is far more. It is an activity for before, during, and after reading; and it can be led by the teacher or students. When reading intertextually, teachers and students read widely within and across genres, canons, and eras as a way of exploring one novel, short story, or poem (Barthes 1981; Bloome and Egan-Robinson, 1993). This is a particularly helpful strategy when the core selection represents a nonwhite cultural group. Students begin to build an understanding of the core selection by reading various other selections. Some students will read primary-source documents from the era of the literary work; others will look at contemporary media with related content. Still others will look at student-produced research papers, Web sites, audio tapes, CDs, or poetry. Everything is fair game, as long as it has some relationship to the literature the whole class is reading. It is helpful if the additional material is short—a newspaper article, letter, poem, video clip, song, or excerpt from a reference book. Short pieces allow students to read and re-read quickly and not get bogged down in something intended to help with the primary reading task.

From Text to Talk

All of the additional reading can then be discussed in relation to the primary work as a way of illuminating, challenging, or affirming it through various reading, writing, and speaking activities. For example, students might use a Venn diagram to compare information in a newspaper account of a historic event to the representation of that event in the literature. Or they can interview each other about the literature in light of the related reading. They might ask a partner who read an article or studied a photograph how the literature shapes or expresses the event in a different way from the image or article. They might ask if the literature adds colorful language or if it changes facts and information. Such intertextual reading will help students understand multicultural literature. In fact, such reading extends the meaning of reading multiculturally so that now it includes reading multiple sources about a diversity of experiences and communities. *Elements of Literature,* with its thematic grouping of literature and its wide variety of genres, offers readers repeated opportunities for intertextual reading.

The Reciprocal Nature of Reading and Writing

Linda Rief
Language Arts Teacher
Oyster River Middle School
Durham, NY
and
Instructor
Summer Literacy Institute
University of New Hampshire

RESEARCH

Hillocks, G. 1986.
Research on Written Composition: New Directions for Teaching. Urbana, IL: National Council of Teachers of English.

National Council of Teachers of English/ International Reading Association. 1996.
Standards for the English Language Arts. Urbana and Newark: NCTE /IRA

Murray, D. 1990.
Read to Write. Texas: Holt, Rinehart, and Winston.

Rief, L. 1992.
Seeking Diversity: Language Arts with Adolescents. Portsmouth, NH: Heinemann.

"The more you write and read, the more the writer's double vision will become natural. It will increase your enjoyment for reading and your skill at writing. As we write we are readers. The words and sentences and paragraphs that appear under our hand are read." —Donald M. Murray

Reading and Writing Connections

Real writing and real reading are thinking. Intimate knowledge and success as readers *and writers* help our students become articulate, literate citizens of the world. In our attempts to lead our students to literacy, we succeed more easily when we remember the reading-writing connection. Remember, a person can read without writing, but he or she cannot write without reading. If we neglect writing while focusing our attention almost exclusively on reading, we do so *at the expense of reading.*

Writing as a Reader

Reasons for offering students ample opportunities to write about topics they care about have been well documented (Hillocks, 1986; "Standards for the English Language Arts," 1996; Rief, 1992). As we provide opportunities for students to write, we offer them chances to think critically: Have I said clearly what I want to say? Is this well organized in developing my ideas? Have I used the sharpest, tightest, most vivid language? Does my lead capture readers and give them a clear direction and focus? Does my writing make readers think or feel or learn something? We connect what students have read to what they might write as we ask students to reflect on an array of questions: What did I think or learn as I read? What questions came to mind? How does this alter my view of the world?

Reading as a Writer

When students read as writers, they actively question the author in the same way they question themselves as writers. Has the author said clearly what she wants to say? Is the writing well organized and easy to follow? Has he used the best word choices? As students analyze an author's work, we teach them to ask more probing questions. How did the author engage you so deeply? What did he or she do to sustain the suspense, the tension, the humor? In what ways did the author make you feel for the characters? This reading-as-a-writer creates better readers *and writers.*

Reading and writing are reciprocal processes seen as both writer and reader attempt to create meaning in the clearest, most engaging, most persuasive way. As students read as writers and write as readers, they see the interrelated nature of the two. They become involved, thoughtful readers and writers and move closer to becoming articulate, literate citizens of the world—our true ultimate goal.

Best Practices in Writing

Harvey A. Daniels
Professor of Education
National-Louis University
Evanston, IL

RESEARCH

Atwell, N. 2002.
In the Middle: New Understandings About Writing, Reading, and Learning.
Portsmouth: Heinemann Educational Books.

Graves, D. 1983.
Writing: Teachers and Children at Work.
Portsmouth: Heinemann Educational Books.

Newman, F. 1996.
Authentic Achievement: Restructuring Schools for Intellectual Quality.
San Francisco: Jossey-Bass.

National Council of Teachers of English/ International Reading Association. 1999.
Standards for the English Language Arts.
Newark: NCTE/IRA.

Zemelman, S., H. Daniels, and A. Hyde. 1998.
Best Practice: New Standards for Teaching and Learning in America's Schools, 2nd ed.
Portsmouth: Heinemann.

"There is a process to follow. There is a process to learn. That's the way it is with a craft, whether it be teaching or writing. There is a road, a journey to travel, and there is someone to travel with us, someone who has already made the trip." —**Donald Graves**

The Process of Writing

Over the past twenty-five years, the "process" model of writing has been strongly validated by educational research. A generation ago, many viewed writing as a somewhat magical act in which flawless texts flowed from the pens of a few muse-blessed artists. Today, we understand that writing is not so much a rare talent but a definable series of cognitive operations that can be learned by anyone who can read. For even the most skilled writer, composing is a sequential process of constructing meaning: gathering information, organizing material, trying out ideas in draft, revising and restructuring text, proofreading and editing, and sharing text with readers and using their feedback for further refinement. No, these stages aren't linear and lockstep; indeed, recursive and even idiosyncratic approaches are normal and useful. But the underlying cognitive reality remains: Just like reading, writing is a staged cognitive process of building up meaning.

New Teacher Roles

Once we understand that writing is more craft than magic, we can recast the teacher as a master craftsperson, helping apprentices to learn a trade. Process-writing teachers model, mentor, and coach; they create a classroom workshop where students build a repertoire of strategies for starting, developing, and polishing written products over a wide range of genres. The teacher's first job is to show how writing gets made, by serving as a live example of an adult writer at work. This doesn't mean teachers must be paragons or professionals, just journeyman composers eager to share their own writings and explain their own strategies. Then they can add rich literary models, bathing the workshop in fine literature, so students have great writers to learn from. That's why the *Elements of Literature* series includes collections of great and varied literature, followed by activities that help students draw directly upon these models to create their own original pieces.

Instructional Implications

Young writers need plenty of writing practice. In the workshop approach, students start many pieces, save all materials in a portfolio, and gradually develop selected drafts to a highly polished and public form. At the core of this work is deep revision: Students are constantly helped to re-see ideas and rethink organization, as well as to follow carefully the conventions of written language. Where possible, writing is not just graded, but shared with real audiences. This makes the work more rhetorically genuine and provides authentic feedback that can help writers grow. All these features of writing-process instruction remind us that—when the trade secrets are revealed, explained, and practiced—writing is not a mysterious practice reserved for the gifted, but a trade that's open to all.

The Technology Connection

Nancy Patterson, Ph.D.
Assistant Professor, School of Education
Grand Valley State University
Grand Rapids, MI

RESEARCH

Bolter, Jay David. 1991.
Writing Space: The Computer, Hypertext, and the History of Writing. Mahwah: Lawrence Erhlbaum Associates.

Henderson, Kathryn. 1995.
"The Visual Culture of Engineers."
The Cultures of Computing. Ed. Susan Leigh Star. Cambridge: Blackwell Publishers. 196–218.

Joyce, Michael. 1995.
Of Two Minds: Hypertext Pedagogy and Poetics. Ann Arbor: University of Michigan Press.

Snyder, Ilana. 1997.
Hypertext: The Electronic Labyrinth.
New York: New York University Press.

Weaver, Constance. 1994.
Reading Process and Practice: From Socio-Psycholinguistics to Whole Language, 2nd ed. Portsmouth: Heinemann.

"Reading comprehension is a process that involves the orchestration of the reader's prior experience and knowledge about the world and about language." —**Bartoli and Botel**

Technology Promotes Thinking Skills

Without technology, there would be no reading. It takes technology to create text. Whether that technology has been the invention of the scroll, the moveable printing press, or e-books, each new innovation in text-creation technology brings new challenges for readers and writers. Computer technology is no exception, especially when it comes to helping readers access, and even create, the necessary prior knowledge needed for efficient reading.

Michael Joyce (1995) believes that Internet technology offers the possibility for students to use the same thinking skills "that experts routinely, subtly, and self-consciously apply in accomplishing intellectual tasks"—as it "promises to unlock these skills for novice learners and to empower and enfranchise their learning." The Internet offers this promise because it allows readers to act physically on the associations or mental connections they make when reading. Hyperlinks effectively placed in a piece of online text can help students make connections between what they are reading and what they already know. Hyperlinks support students' thinking by prompting them through the wording of the links, and when they activate a link, allowing them to immediately learn more information about a given topic.

Webbed Text and Thinking

Constance Weaver (1994) explains that prior knowledge develops through our experience with the world. Readers create some of those experiences through active participation with Webbed texts. So, when the appropriate prior knowledge does not exist, students can gain knowledge via hyperlinks associated with a selection.

Jay Bolter (1991) believes that Webbed texts bring the usually unconscious transaction between reader and writer to the forefront. The writer invites the reader to choose paths—or click on links. The reader considers the author's invitations and follows various paths through the links-as-invitation. Students experience the satisfaction of physically clicking on a link that addresses the same topic they may have been thinking about as they read. Those connections to more information increase their prior knowledge.

But Webbed text can provide more than just information. We cannot ignore the importance of visual literacy in our culture today. In a world where images convey so much meaning, students must understand how images affect meaning. The more they are able to construct meaning with images, the better they will become at that mode of meaning construction (Henderson, 196). The effective combination of text and visually rich images on many Web pages, coupled with reflections on those elements, can help students build the literacies they need in this complex world.

Collection 1
Facing Danger

Literary Focus:
Analyzing Plot

Informational Focus:
Analyzing Text Structures

About Collection 1

In Collection 1, students will master the following skills:

- **Literary Skills:** Understand plot structure and foreshadowing; analyze conflict, suspense, and plot complications.
- **Reading Skills:** Retell story events; make predictions and inferences; analyze the structure and purpose of a textbook, a newspaper article, and informational materials.
- **Vocabulary Skills:** Clarify word meanings by using contrast, examples, and definitions.
- **Writing Skills:** Develop, write, and revise a short story.

Informational Text

Each collection of *Elements of Literature* provides a variety of informational texts related to the literature selections by theme or topic.

Minimum Course of Study

Most skills can be taught with a minimum number of selections and features. In the chart to the right, lessons highlighted in green constitute the minimum course of study that provides coverage of the skills taught in Collection 1.

Resource Manager
(pp. 1C–1F)

Lesson and workshop resources are referenced in the Resource Manager. These resources can be used to reinforce the skills taught, remediate students who are having difficulty, and provide supporting activities for English-language learners.

Scope and Sequence

Selection ▪ Feature	Literary Skills
Elements of Literature: Plot *by John Leggett*	• Understand plot structure and foreshadowing
Reading Skills and Strategies: **Summarizing the Plot** **Duffy's Jacket** *by Bruce Coville* ↓ *below grade level*	
Rikki-tikki-tavi *by Rudyard Kipling* ↑ *above grade level*	• Analyze conflict
Informational Text: from **People, Places, and Change** ↔ *at grade level*	
Three Skeleton Key *by George G. Toudouze* ↑ *above grade level*	• Analyze suspense
Informational Text: **Eeking Out a Life** *by Matt Surman* ↔ *at grade level*	
The Monsters Are Due on Maple Street *by Rod Serling* ↔ *at grade level*	• Analyze plot complications
Informational Text: **Cellular Telephone Owner's Manual** ↔ *at grade level*	
Comparing Literature: Science Fiction **Zoo** *by Edward D. Hoch* ↓ *below grade level*	• Analyze the elements of science fiction
The Ruum *by Arthur Porges* ↑ *above grade level*	
No Questions Asked: **Frankenstein** *by Edward Field* ↑ *above grade level*	
Writing Workshop: *Narrative Writing: Story*	
Skills Review: *Literary Skills* *Informational Reading Skills* *Vocabulary Skills* *Writing Skills*	• Analyze plot structure

Reading Skills	Vocabulary Skills	Writing · Grammar and Language Skills
• Retell story events		
• Retell story events • Analyze the structure and purpose of a textbook	• Clarify word meanings by using contrast	• Express an opinion
• Make predictions • Analyze the structure and purpose of a newspaper article	• Clarify word meanings by using examples	• Write a description • Use correct subject-verb agreement
• Make inferences • Analyze the structure and purpose of informational materials	• Clarify word meanings by using definitions	• Analyze a work's message • Update a teleplay
• Compare and contrast stories		• Write a comparison-contrast essay
		• Write a short story
• Analyze structure and purpose of informational materials	• Understand multiple-meaning words	• Analyze a short story

Selection ■ Feature	Planning	Differentiating Instruction ■ Lesson Plans with ELL Strategies and Practice	Reading ■ Vocabulary
Elements of Literature: Plot *by* John Leggett	• PowerNotes: Suspense and Foreshadowing	• Holt Reading Solutions: Lesson Plans, pp. 31–32	• Holt Reading Solutions, pp. 31–32
Reading Skills and Strategies: Summarizing the Plot **Duffy's Jacket** *by* Bruce Coville			• PowerNotes: Summarizing a Story
Rikki-tikki-tavi *by* Rudyard Kipling **Informational Text:** *from* **People, Places, and Change**	• One-Stop Planner with ExamView Test Generator	• The Holt Reader, pp. 4–29 • Holt Adapted Reader, pp. 1–13 • Holt Reading Solutions: Lesson Plans, pp. 33–40 • Supporting Instruction in Spanish, p. 3 • Audio CD Library • Audio CD Library, Selections and Summaries in Spanish	• The Holt Reader, pp. 16–29 • Holt Adapted Reader, pp. 1–7 • Holt Reading Solutions, pp. 33–40 • Vocabulary Development, p. 1 • PowerNotes: Summarizing a Story
Three Skeleton Key *by* George G. Toudouze **Informational Text:** **Eeking Out a Life** *by* Matt Surman	• One-Stop Planner with ExamView Test Generator	• The Holt Reader, pp. 32–49 • Holt Adapted Reader, pp. 8–25 • Holt Reading Solutions: Lesson Plans, pp. 41–48 • Supporting Instruction in Spanish, p. 4 • Audio CD Library • Audio CD Library, Selections and Summaries in Spanish	• The Holt Reader, pp. 32–49 • Holt Adapted Reader, pp. 8–25 • Holt Reading Solutions, pp. 41–48 • Vocabulary Development, pp. 2–3 • PowerNotes: Making Predictions
The Monsters Are Due on Maple Street *by* Rod Serling **Informational Text:** **Cellular Telephone Owner's Manual**	• One-Stop Planner with ExamView Test Generator	• Holt Reading Solutions: Lesson Plans, pp. 49–56 • Holt Adapted Reader, pp. 26–29 • Supporting Instruction in Spanish, p. 5 • Audio CD Library • Audio CD Library, Selections and Summaries in Spanish	• Holt Adapted Reader, pp. 26–29 • Holt Reading Solutions, pp. 41–48 • Vocabulary Development, p. 4 • PowerNotes: Making Inferences
Comparing Literature: Science Fiction **Zoo** *by* Edward D. Hoch **The Ruum** *by* Arthur Porges		• Holt Reading Solutions, pp. 57–60	• Holt Reading Solutions, pp. 57–60

Writing · Grammar and Language	Assessment
• Daily Language Activities	• Holt Assessment: Literature, Reading, and Vocabulary • One-Stop Planner with ExamView Test Generator • Holt Online Assessment
• Daily Language Activities • Language Handbook Worksheets, pp. 15–22	• Holt Assessment: Literature, Reading, and Vocabulary • One-Stop Planner with ExamView Test Generator • Holt Online Assessment
• Daily Language Activities	• Holt Assessment: Literature, Reading, and Vocabulary • One-Stop Planner with ExamView Test Generator • Holt Online Assessment

Technology

INTERNET

- go.hrw.com
- Holt Online Assessment
- Holt Online Essay Scoring
- Elements of Literature Online

MEDIA

 • One-Stop Planner with ExamView Test Generator

 • PowerNotes

 • Audio CD Library

 • Audio CD Library, Selections and Summaries in Spanish

 • Visual Connections Videocassette Program, Segment 1

 • Fine Art Transparencies, 1

 Transparency   Video

 CD-ROM   Audio CD

(continued)

Selection ▪ Feature	Planning	Differentiating Instruction Lesson Plans with ELL Strategies and Practice	Reading ▪ Vocabulary
No Questions Asked: Frankenstein *by* Edward Field			
Writing Workshop: *Narrative Writing: Story*	• One-Stop Planner with ExamView Test Generator	• Workshop Resources: Writing, Listening, and Speaking, pp. 1–11 • Family Involvement Activities in English and Spanish • Supporting Instruction in Spanish, p. 37	
Skills Review: *Literary Skills Informational Reading Skills Vocabulary Skills Writing Skills*			

The Holt Reader

The Holt Reader is a consumable paperback book that can be used alone or to accompany *Elements of Literature*. It offers guided support throughout the reading process and encourages students to become active readers by circling, underlining, questioning, and jotting down responses as they read. *The Holt Reader* works well for homework, students who have missed class, additional instructional time, reteaching, and remediation.

Holt Reading Solutions (HRS)

Holt Reading Solutions pulls together reading resources in the *Elements of Literature* program to create a powerful tool for intervention and whole-class instruction. *HRS* includes diagnostic assessment tools, lesson plans for English-language learners and special education students, adaptations of selected reading selections, vocabulary and comprehension worksheets, information on phonics and decoding, and additional instruction and practice in remedial reading skills.

Writing ■ Grammar and Language	Assessment
• Workshop Resources: Writing, Listening, and Speaking, pp. 1–11 • Language Handbook Worksheets • Daily Language Activities	• Holt Assessment: Literature, Reading, and Vocabulary • One-Stop Planner with ExamView Test Generator • Holt Online Assessment • Holt Online Essay Scoring
	• Holt Assessment: Literature, Reading, and Vocabulary • One-Stop Planner with ExamView Test Generator • Holt Online Assessment

One-Stop Planner with ExamView Test Generator

The *One-Stop Planner* CD-ROM planning software contains print-based teaching resources, clips from the video program, and valuable assessment tools. The *One-Stop Planner* resources are presented in easy-to-follow, point-and-click menu formats. To preview resources or print out worksheets and tests, you simply make a selection and click.

One-Stop
Planner CD-ROM

Technology

INTERNET

- go.hrw.com
- Holt Online Assessment
- Holt Online Essay Scoring
- Elements of Literature Online

MEDIA

 • One-Stop Planner with ExamView Test Generator

 • PowerNotes

 • Audio CD Library

 • Audio CD Library, Selections and Summaries in Spanish

• Visual Connections Videocassette Program, Segment 1

• Fine Art Transparencies, 1

 Transparency   Video

 CD-ROM   Audio CD

Collection 1

SKILLS FOCUS

Grade-Level Skills

■ **Literary Skills**
Identify events that advance the plot, and determine how each event explains past or present actions or foreshadows future actions.

■ **Reading Skills**
Analyze the structure and purpose of informational texts.

■ **Reading Skills**
Retell story events.

■ **Vocabulary Skills**
Clarify word meanings by using definitions, examples, and contrasts.

Review Skills

■ **Literary Skills**
Identify the main conflict of the plot and how it is resolved.

■ **Reading Skills**
Use the structural features of newspapers, magazines, and online data to obtain information.

■ **Vocabulary Skills**
Use context clues to determine the meanings of unfamiliar words.

Upcoming Skills

■ **Literary Skills**
Evaluate the plot's structure and development and the way conflicts are resolved.

■ **Reading Skills**
Obtain information from public documents.

The Sleeping Gypsy (1897) by Henri Rousseau. Oil on canvas (51" × 6' 7").
The Museum of Modern Art, NY.

COLLECTION 1 RESOURCES: READING

Planning
■ *One-Stop Planner* CD-ROM with ExamView Test Generator

Differentiating Instruction
■ *The Holt Reader*
■ *Holt Adapted Reader*
■ *Holt Reading Solutions*
■ *Family Involvement Activities in English and Spanish*

■ *Supporting Instruction in Spanish*
■ *Audio CD Library*
■ *Audio CD Library, Selections and Summaries in Spanish*

Vocabulary
■ *Vocabulary Development*

Grammar and Language
■ *Language Handbook Worksheets*
■ *Daily Language Activities*

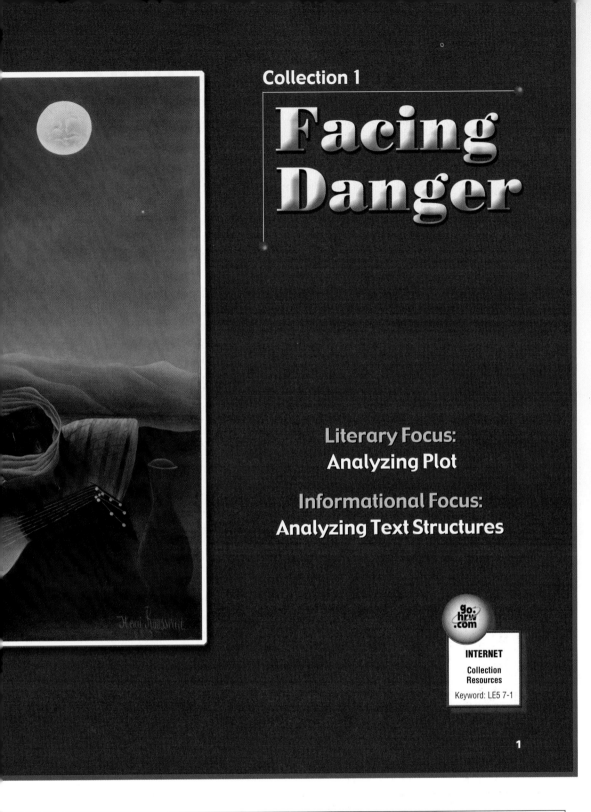

Collection 1

Facing Danger

Literary Focus:
Analyzing Plot

Informational Focus:
Analyzing Text Structures

go.hrw.com

INTERNET

Collection Resources

Keyword: LE5 7-1

1

Assessment
- *Holt Assessment: Literature, Reading, and Vocabulary*
- *One-Stop Planner* CD-ROM with ExamView Test Generator
- *Holt Online Assessment*

Internet
- *go.hrw.com* (Keyword: LE5 7-1)
- *Elements of Literature Online*

Media
- *Audio CD Library*
- *Audio CD Library, Selections and Summaries in Spanish*
- *Fine Art Transparencies*
- *Visual Connections Videocassette Program*
- *PowerNotes*

Theme: Facing danger. Facing danger can be a frightening ordeal. Sometimes, however, danger summons qualities that we never knew we had—courage, determination, ingenuity, and compassion. The stories in this collection are grabbers—tales that keep the reader in suspense from beginning to end.

Analyzing plot. Different aspects of plot are discussed with each story, so students emerge with an understanding of the well-plotted narrative. Attention is focused on conflict, complications, climax, suspense, and foreshadowing. The unit concludes with a feature comparing two works of science fiction and an opportunity for students to write a story.

Analyzing text structures. Informational pieces follow some of the literary sections. These informational texts are linked topically or thematically to the literary selection. Students will learn how to analyze text structures in different kinds of informational materials.

VIEWING THE ART

Henri Rousseau (1844–1910) was a French primitive, a term used to describe a self-taught artist. He often painted surreal scenes from his vivid imagination. Many of the wild beasts in these scenes were drawn from photographs in a children's book that Rousseau's daughter owned. *The Sleeping Gypsy* is one of the artist's best-known dreamscapes. A tawny lion is silhouetted against an azure sky that is lit by a full moon. The lion is sniffing a sleeping gypsy woman, clad in a striped cloak, who lies on the dun-colored desert. The gypsy woman's jug and mandolin lie beside her. This strange encounter between the king of the beasts and a sleeping wanderer sends prickles down the viewer's spine.

Activity. Ask students to record any questions the painting inspires in their minds.

Grade–Level Skills

■ **Literary Skills**
Understand plot structure, and determine how each event explains past or present actions or foreshadows future actions.

Review Skills

■ **Literary Skills**
Identify the main conflict of the plot and how it is resolved.

Upcoming Skills

■ **Literary Skills**
Evaluate the plot's structure and development and the way conflicts are resolved.

Elements of Literature: Plot

Ask students to describe how they experience suspense in a movie. How do they feel at different points in the film? What emotions are they experiencing? Do their hearts beat faster? Then, review the parts of a plot with students. Point out that the tension may fluctuate as complications are introduced and then overcome. As the story progresses, however, the suspense rises to a final peak, or climax, and then drops dramatically.

Elements of Literature
Plot *by John Leggett*

A STORY'S BUILDING BLOCKS

Plot is what happens in a story. Plot consists of a series of related episodes, one growing out of another. Most plots have four parts, which are like building blocks.

1 The first part of a plot tells you about the story's **basic situation:** Who are the characters, and what do they want? This is usually where you find out about the conflict, or problem, in a story. A **conflict** is a struggle between opposing characters or opposing forces. In an **external conflict** a character struggles against another person, a group of people, or a force of nature (a tornado, a bear, an icy mountain path). An **internal conflict** takes place in a character's mind (he struggles with shyness; she struggles to accept a death). Here is the introduction to a new version of a tale you know well:

"Hi there, Red," said a wolf to a little girl in a red velvet hood. "How'd ya like a ride on my motorcycle?"

"Thank you, sir, but I can't," replied Little Red Riding Hood. "As you can see, I'm carrying this basket of ginger cookies to my grandmother, and I can't be late."

"Tell you what, Red. You just hop on the back, and I'll run you over to Granny's in five seconds flat."

"My grandmother lives way out at the end of Lonely Road," Red protested. "It's miles and miles."

"This here motorcycle eats miles."

"No, thank you," said Little Red Riding Hood. "I've made up my mind."

To make us feel suspense, storytellers give us clues that **foreshadow,** or hint at, future events. Maybe you felt a shiver of fear when you read that Granny lives on Lonely Road. Bad things can happen on lonely roads. Could this foreshadow trouble for Little Red?

2 In the second part of a plot, one or more of the characters act to resolve the conflict. Now a **series of events** takes place that makes it very hard for the character to get what he or she wants. (Sometimes these events are called **complications.**)

"Suit yourself," chuckled the wolf, who had thought of a wicked plan. He would go alone to the end of Lonely Road, gobble up Red's grandma, and then, when the little girl turned up, he would gobble her up too.

So, arriving at the last house on Lonely Road, the wolf raced his engine, scaring Grandma out her

INTERNET
More About Plot
Keyword: LE5 7-1

Literary Skills
Understand plot structure.

DIFFERENTIATING INSTRUCTION

Learners Having Difficulty
Plot. To help students recognize and describe the plot of a story, suggest that they name a favorite fairy tale or folk tale and the main conflict or problem faced by the characters. As an alternative, provide students with a three- or four-frame cartoon strip, and have them describe the conflict or problem the characters face.

Advanced Learners
Acceleration. Help students determine the structural elements of plot. Ask students working in pairs to take a simple plot and brainstorm a subplot and its resolution to add to the story. Have students create a plot diagram that shows both the plot and the subplot.

back door and under the woodshed. The wolf was puzzled to find the house empty, but he put on Grandma's nightcap and nightshirt and climbed into the bed to wait for Red.

3 Now comes the **climax,** the story's most emotional or suspenseful moment. This is the point at which the conflict is decided one way or another.

It was nearly dark when Red arrived, but as she approached her grandma's bed, she sensed something was wrong.

"Are you all right, Granny?" Red asked. "Your eyes look bloodshot."

"All the better to see you with," replied the wolf.

"And your teeth—suddenly they look like fangs."

"All the better to eat—" the wolf began, but he stopped at the sound of his motorcycle engine thundering in the front yard. "Wait right there, Red," said the wolf, bounding from the bed.

The wolf was startled to find Grandma sitting on the motorcycle.

"Hey!" he shouted. "Stop fooling with my bike." As he lunged for her, Grandma found the gearshift, and the cycle leapt forward, scooping the wolf up on its handlebars and hurling him into a giant thorn bush—which is where the police found him when they arrived.

4 The **resolution** is the last part of the story. This is where the loose ends of the plot are tied up and the story is closed.

The wolf was brought to trial and sent to prison. Granny became a popular guest on talk shows. Red lived happily ever after.

Practice

The main events of a story's **plot** can be charted in a diagram like the one below. Think about a story you know well—maybe a movie or a TV show or a novel. See if you can show the story's main events in a similar diagram.

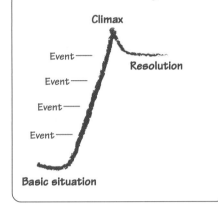

"Once upon a time, they lived happily ever after."

Practice

Students might list events as follows.

Basic situation—Red wants to give her ginger cookies to her grandmother, and the wolf wants to eat Red.

First event—Red turns down the wolf's offer of a ride on his motorcycle.

Second event—The wolf races off to Granny's, where he scares the woman away and takes her place in bed.

Third event—The wolf tries to eat Red.

Climax—Granny rides the wolf's motorcycle, catches him in the handlebars, and hurls him into a thorn bush.

Resolution—The wolf goes to prison; Granny does talk shows; Red lives happily ever after.

Apply

Encourage students to choose another well-known fairy tale and then fill out a plot diagram for it.

HOMEWORK

Grade-Level Skills

■ **Reading Skills**
Retell story events.

OVERVIEW

Purpose. The strategy of retelling helps students identify and summarize the events that advance the plot of a story.

Use. Retelling can be used to review the events of any plot. It is especially useful for stories with complicated plots, for long stories or novels, and for stories that shift back and forth in time. With "Duffy's Jacket," a relatively easy story, have students use retelling to identify plot events and to explain how the events relate to past and future actions. As they retell, students will identify the main characters and the story's conflict, climax, and resolution. Retelling will also be helpful with "The Smallest Dragonboy" in Collection 2 and "After Twenty Years" in Collection 4.

Summary ⬇ *below grade level*

Andrew, the narrator, reluctantly embarks on a family camping trip with his mother; his Aunt Elise; his little sister Marie; and his annoying, forgetful cousin Duffy. While hiking in the woods, Duffy carelessly leaves his jacket behind. When their mothers go into town that evening, the two boys and Marie are on their own—and scared. A giant creature has tracked the kids from the woods and is trying to get into the cabin. After a terrifying pursuit, the creature corners the kids, angrily returns Duffy's jacket, and leaves. Duffy never forgets his things again— because you never know who might return them.

Reading Skills and Strategies

Summarizing the Plot: Retelling
by Kylene Beers

Is this a plot?" Manuel asked as he pointed to the first paragraph of a story. He didn't understand that plot isn't a single thing he can point to in the story. He didn't know that **plot** is what happens in the story—all the related events that move from the story's beginning to its end. Plot is made up of all the building blocks you just read about on pages 2–3.

What Is Retelling?

Keeping up with all the information in a story can be difficult. A strategy called **retelling** can help you identify the elements of a plot and keep all the information about a plot straight in your mind. With this strategy you practice telling the plot of the story using a **Retelling Summary Sheet.** You use the Retelling Summary Sheet as a guide, to be sure you've included all the events in the plot.

The best way to get better at retelling is to practice retelling. Start practicing by reading the story titled "Duffy's Jacket," which begins on page 5. You can retell by jotting down some notes, by discussing your retelling with a friend, or by just thinking about what you would say.

When you've finished reading the story, use your retelling notes to fill out the Retelling Summary Sheet on page 12.

SKILLS FOCUS

Reading Skills
Retell story events.

Retelling Tips

• Start by telling the title and author.

• Explain who the characters are.

• Explain the conflict, or main problem.

• Name the main events, keeping them in order.

• Explain what happens at the end.

• Tell what you liked or didn't like about the story.

• Use words like *first, second, next,* and *finally* to help keep everything in order.

Duffy's Jacket

Bruce Coville

As you read, you'll find this open-book sign at certain points in the story: 📖. Stop at these points, and think about what you've just read. Sometimes a part of the retelling will be there for you. At other times you'll do the retelling.

If my cousin Duffy had the brains of a turnip it never would have happened. But as far as I'm concerned, Duffy makes a turnip look bright. My mother disagrees. According to her, Duffy is actually very bright. She claims the reason he's so scatterbrained is that he's too busy being brilliant inside his own head to remember everyday things. Maybe. But hanging around with Duffy means you spend a lot of time saying, "Your glasses, Duffy," or "Your coat, Duffy," or—well, you get the idea: a lot of three-word sentences that start with "Your," end with "Duffy," and have words like *book, radio, wallet,* or whatever it is he's just put down and left behind, stuck in the middle.

Me, I think turnips are brighter.

But since Duffy's my cousin, and since my mother and her sister are both single parents, we tend to do a lot of things together—like camping, which is how we got into the mess I want to tell you about.

Personally, I thought camping was a big mistake. But since Mom and Aunt Elise are raising the three of us—me, Duffy, and my little sister, Marie—on their own, they're convinced they have to do man-stuff with us every once in a while. I think they read some book

(A)

Selection Starter
Motivate. Invite students to share spooky stories that they have heard—perhaps from friends or camp counselors. How have students' responses to the stories changed since the first time they heard them? Encourage students to identify common elements or patterns in the stories.

DIRECT TEACHING

(A) Literary Focus
Plot. Remind students that the first part of a plot is the basic situation—who the characters are and what they want. Ask students to identify the story's basic situation after reading these paragraphs. [Possible responses: Characters mentioned so far are the narrator, his little sister, his mother and aunt, and his careless cousin Duffy. The narrator wants to tell a story about Duffy.]

DIFFERENTIATING INSTRUCTION

Learners Having Difficulty
Some students may not be familiar with the term *single parents.* Explain to students that the narrator and his cousin Duffy do not live with their fathers. Tell students that the narrator's mother and his aunt Elise decide to take their sons on a camping trip in the woods because they think the boys need to do "man-stuff," the kinds of activities boys traditionally do with their fathers. Ask students if they have ever been camping. Do they think that camping is a "manly" activity? Lead a class discussion about whether camping is or is not a "manly" activity.

A Reading Skills and Strategies

Retell. Point out that readers can tell Duffy is important because the narrator describes him in detail and his name is in the story's title. More subtle is the fact that the narrator is also describing himself. Ask students what they have learned, or can infer, about the narrator so far. [Possible responses: He's being raised by a single mother and has a little sister. He is practical and has a sarcastic sense of humor.]

B Reading Skills and Strategies

❷ Retell. What do you think the narrator really means by saying Duffy couldn't have been expected to remember his suitcase? [Possible response: The narrator is commenting sarcastically that unlike most people, Duffy needs to be reminded of everything.]

C Advanced Learners

Enrichment. The narrator uses "man-stuff" to describe things he says men do more than women, such as camping and drinking beer. He suggests that women appreciate the beauty of nature more than men do. Ask students how these beliefs reflect stereotypical views of men and women and how these views might be refuted.

D Vocabulary Note

❷ Latin roots. Point out in *fumigating* the Latin root word *fumus*, "smoke." What other English words share this root word? [Possible responses: fume (noun and verb), perfume.]

Using the Strategy

RETELL

❶ Think about what you've learned so far. What's the title? Who's the author? Who are the important characters? Who are the other characters?

This story is called "Duffy's Jacket," and it's written by Bruce Coville. I think Duffy and his cousin ("I," the narrator) are the important characters. Aunt Elsie, Mom, and the narrator's sister, Marie, are the other characters.

RETELL

❷ What's Duffy's most obvious characteristic?

Duffy forgets things—like his suitcase when he takes a trip.

---

that said me and Duffy would come out weird if they don't. You can take him camping all you want. It ain't gonna make Duffy normal. ❶

Anyway, the fact that our mothers were getting wound up to do something fatherly, combined with the fact that Aunt Elise's boss had a friend who had a friend who said we could use his cabin, added up to the five of us bouncing along this horrible dirt road late one Friday in October.

It was late because we had lost an hour going back to get Duffy's suitcase. I suppose it wasn't actually Duffy's fault. No one remembered to say, "Your suitcase, Duffy," so he couldn't really have been expected to remember it. ❷

"Oh, Elise," cried my mother, as we got deeper into the woods. "Aren't the leaves beautiful?"

That's why it doesn't make sense for them to try to do man-stuff with us. If it had been our fathers, they would have been drinking beer and burping and maybe telling dirty stories instead of talking about the leaves. So why try to fake it?

Anyway, we get to this cabin, which is about eighteen million miles from nowhere, and to my surprise, it's not a cabin at all. It's a house. A big house.

"Oh, my," said my mother as we pulled into the driveway.

"Isn't it great?" chirped Aunt Elise. "It's almost a hundred years old, back from the time when they used to build big hunting lodges up here. It's the only one in the area still standing. Horace said he hasn't been able to get up here in some time. That's why he was glad to let us use it. He said it would be good to have someone go in and air the place out."

Leave it to Aunt Elise. This place didn't need airing out—it needed fumigating.[1] I never saw so many spider webs in my life. From the sounds we heard coming from the walls, the mice seemed to have made it a population center. We found a total of two working lightbulbs: one in the kitchen and one in the dining room, which was paneled with dark wood and had a big stone fireplace at one end.

"Oh, my," said my mother again.

Duffy, who's allergic to about fifteen different things, started to sneeze.

"Isn't it charming?" asked Aunt Elise hopefully.

No one answered her.

---

1. **fumigating** (fyōo′mə·gāt′iŋ) *v.* used as *n.*: spraying with chemicals to kill harmful organisms and pests.

MINI-LESSON Reading

Developing Word-Attack Skills

Write the selection word *scent* on the chalkboard, and have a volunteer read it aloud. Then, point out that the *c* in *scent* is silent. Have the class suggest other words that begin with the combination *sc*, in which the letter *c* is silent. [*scene, scenario, scissors, science*] Then, contrast these words with selection words such as *scratch, scared*, and so on. Finally, help students formulate the following rule: The *c* is silent in words that begin with the letters *sc* followed by the vowel *e* or *i*.

Activity. Display these word pairs. Have students tell which word in each pair has a silent *c*. Answers are underlined.

1. <u>scent</u>	scratch
2. scary	<u>scenario</u>
3. scabbard	<u>scepter</u>
4. <u>scissors</u>	scalpel
5. scarce	<u>scientist</u>

Four hours later we had managed to get three bedrooms clean enough to sleep in without getting the heebie-jeebies—one for Mom and Aunt Elise, one for Marie, and one for me and Duffy. After a supper of beans and franks we hit the hay, which I think is what our mattresses were stuffed with. As I was drifting off, which took about thirty seconds, it occurred to me that four hours of housework wasn't all that much of a man-thing, something it might be useful to remember the next time Mom got one of these plans into her head. ❸ 📖

Things looked better in the morning when we went outside and found a stream where we could go wading. ("Your sneakers, Duffy.")

Later we went back and started poking around the house, which really was enormous.

That was when things started getting a little spooky. In the room next to ours I found a message scrawled on the wall. "Beware the Sentinel,"[2] it said in big black letters.

When I showed Mom and Aunt Elise they said it was just a joke and got mad at me for frightening Marie. ❹ 📖

Marie wasn't the only one who was frightened.

We decided to go out for another walk. ("Your lunch, Duffy.") We went deep into the woods, following a faint trail that kept threatening to disappear but never actually faded away altogether. It was a hot day, even in the deep woods, and after a while we decided to take off our coats.

When we got back and Duffy didn't have his jacket, did they get mad at him? My mother actually had the nerve to say, "Why didn't you remind him? You know he forgets things like that."

What do I look like, a walking memo pad?

Anyway, I had other things on my mind—like the fact that I was convinced someone had been following us while we were in the woods.

I tried to tell my mother about it, but first she said I was being ridiculous, and then she accused me of trying to sabotage[3] the trip. ❺ 📖

So I shut up. But I was pretty nervous, especially when Mom and Aunt Elise announced that they were going into town—which was twenty miles away—to pick up some supplies (like lightbulbs).

"You kids will be fine on your own," said Mom cheerfully. "You can make popcorn and play Monopoly. And there's enough soda here for you to make yourselves sick on."

---

2. **sentinel** (sent'n·əl) *n.*: guard; person keeping watch.
3. **sabotage** (sab'ə·täzh') *v.*: obstruct or destroy.

Using the Strategy

RETELL

❸ Review what's happened. Where are the campers? What's the condition of the cabin? What three things have happened since they arrived at the cabin?

They're in a big hunting lodge in the woods. The place is dirty and full of spiders and mice. They cleaned the cabin, ate dinner, and went to sleep.

RETELL

❹ When do things start to get spooky?

RETELL

❺ What does the narrator tell his mother? How does she react?

DIRECT TEACHING

E 🅔 **Reading Skills and Strategies**

❓ **Retell.** You might ask students for more details about the cabin. [Possible responses: It's old, isolated, neglected, and has many rooms but almost no lights; the dining room is paneled in dark wood and has a huge stone fireplace.] **Which word describes the cabin better: *cozy* or *gloomy*? [gloomy]**

F 🅕 **Vocabulary Note**

Word families. Tell students that the word *sentinel* comes from the Latin root word *sentire,* meaning "to perceive or feel," and is related to the English words *sentry* and *sentimental.* Ask students to explain what each word has to do with perceiving or feeling.

G 🅖 **Reading Skills and Strategies**

Retell. [Possible response to question 4: Things get spooky when the narrator finds "Beware the Sentinel" scrawled on a wall, and the adults fail to recognize the danger that the narrator senses.]

H 🅗 **Reading Skills and Strategies**

Retell. [Possible response to question 5: He tells his mother that someone was following them in the woods. She says he's being silly and accuses him of trying to ruin their camping trip.]

DIFFERENTIATING INSTRUCTION

Advanced Learners
Enrichment. Advanced learners will appreciate the fun Coville has with his twist on a standard horror plot. Encourage these students to identify the standard plot pattern and the twist. [*Standard plot pattern*—Monster pursues hapless victims who have made a minor but fatal mistake; *Twist*—The Sentinel is just picking up after Duffy.] Guide students in tracing the buildup of suspense to its humorous anticlimax. Then, challenge students to think of other eerie tales that share this plot pattern or that reach a similar anticlimax.
Activity. Place students in small groups to devise graphics showing the buildup of tension and the anticlimax in "Duffy's Jacket."

DIRECT TEACHING

A Literary Focus

❓ Foreshadowing. How do the narrator's responses hint at, or foreshadow, a frightening event about to take place? [Possible responses: The narrator's wish for adults to be there hints at something threatening nearby. The narrator describes physical sensations, such as his stomach rolling over, that signal fear.]

B Learners Having Difficulty

Question the text. Be sure students understand why Andrew and Marie say, "Your jacket, Duffy!" and why Duffy turns white. [Andrew and Marie remember that Duffy left his jacket in the woods and feel that whatever is at the door has tracked them by the scent on the jacket. Duffy turns white because he realizes that his forgetfulness may have horrible consequences.]

C Vocabulary Note

Context clues. Ask students which words and phrases in these sentences provide clues to the meaning of the word *lurking.* [Possible responses: "waiting for our mothers to leave"; "waiting for years."]

D Reading Skills and Strategies

Retell. [Possible response to question 6: Duffy's problem is that he carelessly forgets his things; the kids' problem is that a huge, frightening creature is after them.]

And with that they were gone.

It got dark.

We played Monopoly.

They didn't come back. That didn't surprise me. Since Duffy and I were both fifteen they felt it was okay to leave us on our own, and Mom had warned us they might decide to have dinner at the little inn we had seen on the way up.

A But I would have been happier if they had been there.

Especially when something started scratching on the door.

"What was that?" asked Marie.

"What was what?" asked Duffy.

"That!" she said, and this time I heard it, too. My stomach rolled over, and the skin at the back of my neck started to prickle.

"Maybe it's the Sentinel!" I hissed.

"Andrew!" yelled Marie. "Mom told you not to say that."

"She said not to try to scare you," I said. "I'm not. *I'm* scared! I told you I heard something following us in the woods today."

Scratch, scratch.

"But you said it stopped," said Duffy. "So how would it know where we are now?"

"I don't know. I don't know what it is. Maybe it tracked us, like a bloodhound."

Scratch, scratch.

"Don't bloodhounds have to have something to give them a scent?" asked Marie. "Like a piece of clothing, or—"

B We both looked at Duffy.

"Your jacket, Duffy!"

Duffy turned white.

"That's silly," he said after a moment.

C "There's something at the door," I said frantically. "Maybe it's been lurking around all day, waiting for our mothers to leave. Maybe it's been waiting for years for someone to come back here."

Scratch, scratch.

"I don't believe it," said Duffy. "It's just the wind moving a branch. I'll prove it."

He got up and headed for the door. But he didn't open it. Instead he peeked through the window next to it. When he turned back, his eyes looked as big as the hard-boiled eggs we had eaten for supper.

"There's something out there!" he hissed. *"Something big!"* **6**

"I told you," I cried. "Oh, I knew there was something there."

RETELL

6 You should be able to identify two problems at this point. One has to do with Duffy, and the other is about what's happening to the kids. What are the problems?

DEVELOPING FLUENCY

Activity. This story's vivid exaggeration and figurative language will delight some students and challenge others. Place students in mixed-ability groups to read the story aloud. Have students pay attention to exaggeration and figurative language. (For example, "Duffy makes a turnip look bright"; mice have made the cabin's walls "a population center"; Duffy's eyes are "as big as . . . hard-boiled eggs"; the Sentinel tracks the children "like some giant bloodhound.") Be sure students understand that these figures of speech are not literally true. After reading, have groups discuss how the figurative language helped them see or feel things in unexpected ways.

MIXED ABILITY

"Andrew, are you doing this just to scare me?" said Marie. "Because if you are—"

Scratch, scratch.

"Come on," I said, grabbing her by the hand. "Let's get out of here."

I started to lead her up the stairs.

"Not there!" said Duffy. "If we go up there, we'll be trapped."

"You're right," I said. "Let's go out the back way!"

The thought of going outside scared the daylights out of me. But at least out there we would have somewhere to run. Inside—well, who knew what might happen if the thing found us inside.

We went into the kitchen.

I heard the front door open.

"Let's get out of here!" I hissed.

We scooted out the back door. "What now?" I wondered, looking around frantically.

"The barn," whispered Duffy. "We can hide in the barn."

"Good idea," I said. Holding Marie by the hand, I led the way to the barn. But the door was held shut by a huge padlock.

The wind was blowing harder, but not hard enough to hide the sound of the back door of the house opening, and then slamming shut.

"Quick!" I whispered. "It knows we're out here. Let's sneak around front. It will never expect us to go back into the house."

Duffy and Marie followed me as I led them behind a hedge. I caught a glimpse of something heading toward the barn and swallowed nervously. It was big. Very big.

"I'm scared," whispered Marie.

"*Shhhh!*" I hissed. "We can't let it know where we are."

E

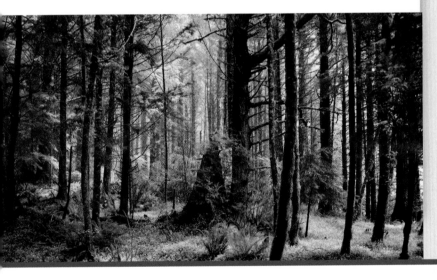

E **Literary Focus**

Plot. Ask students to list the plot complications that lead up to this action sequence. [The Sentinel comes in the front door; the children run out the back door; they want to hide in the barn, but it's padlocked; the Sentinel comes out the back door; the children run around to the front of the house.] Point out how suspense mounts with each complication.

A Reading Skills and Strategies

Retell. [Possible response to question 7: They go back into the house and lock the front door.]

B Literary Focus

Narrator. Remind students that readers experience events through Andrew's eyes only and that he tends to exaggerate (for example, he describes the cabin as being "eighteen million miles from no-where"). Ask how a more matter-of-fact narrator might change this paragraph. [Possible response: The "enormous, manlike creature" might become a "large man,"and the "scrap of cloth" might become "a garment," making the effect much less frightening.]

C Vocabulary Note

Connotations. Point out that the word *huddled* suggests, or con-notes, a need for defense—for example, animals huddled up in the cold. Ask students for more instances in which animals or people would huddle. [Possible responses: People caught in a storm huddle up inside the nearest shelter; sheep huddle together when they feel threatened.]

D Literary Focus

Sound effects. As the story's ten-sion builds to a climax, Coville uses the device of onomatopoeia (the use of words whose sounds suggest their meaning) and selective repetition to maximize suspense. Ask students to point out examples. [*scratch; clomping; thump; it was . . . knock*]

Using the Strategy

RETELL

A ❼ What do the kids do to get away from the creature?

We slipped through the front door. We locked it, just like people always do in the movies, though what good that would do I couldn't figure, since if something really wanted to get at us, it would just break the window and come in. ❼

"Upstairs," I whispered.

We tiptoed up the stairs. Once we were in our bedroom, I thought we were safe. Crawling over the floor, I raised my head just enough to peek out the window. My heart almost stopped. Standing in the moonlight was an enormous, manlike creature. It had a scrap of cloth in its hands. It was looking around—looking for us. I saw it lift its head and sniff the wind. To my horror, it started back toward the house.

"It's coming back!" I yelped, more frightened than ever.

"How does it know where we are?" asked Marie.

I knew how. It had Duffy's jacket. It was tracking us down, like some giant bloodhound.

We huddled together in the middle of the room, trying to think of what to do.

A minute later we heard it.

Scratch, scratch.

None of us moved.

Scratch, scratch.

We stopped breathing, then jumped up in alarm at a terrible crashing sound.

The door was down.

We hunched back against the wall as heavy footsteps came clomp-ing up the stairs.

I wondered what our mothers would think when they got back. Would they find our bodies? Or would there be nothing left of us at all?

Thump. Thump. Thump.

It was getting closer.

Thump. Thump. Thump.

It was outside the door.

Knock, knock.

"Don't answer!" hissed Duffy.

Like I said, he doesn't have the brains of a turnip.

It didn't matter. The door wasn't locked. It came swinging open. In the shaft of light I saw a huge figure. The Sentinel of the Woods! It had to be. I thought I was going to die.

The figure stepped into the room. Its head nearly touched the ceiling.

FAMILY/COMMUNITY ACTIVITY

In this story a boy's forgetfulness causes a potential disaster. In real life, too, a good memory is essential. Encourage students and their families to play some games at home that will stretch and develop their memo-ries. Word games such as Twenty Questions, trivia games, card games such as Hearts, and crossword puzzles can help students improve and train their memories while enjoying some friendly competition. You might send a note home to parents explain-ing how playing memory games can benefit students.

Marie squeezed against my side, tighter than a tick in a dog's ear.

The huge creature sniffed the air. It turned in our direction. Its eyes seemed to glow. Moonlight glittered on its fangs.

Slowly the Sentinel raised its arm. I could see Duffy's jacket dangling from its fingertips.

And then it spoke.

"You forgot your jacket, stupid."

It threw the jacket at Duffy, turned around, and stomped down the stairs.

Which is why, I suppose, no one has had to remind Duffy to remember his jacket, or his glasses, or his math book, for at least a year now.

After all, when you leave stuff lying around, you never can be sure just who might bring it back. ❽ 📖

Using the Strategy

RETELL

❽ Finish your retelling by telling what happens at the end of the story. Add your own thoughts about the story. Explain why you did or didn't like it.

Ⓔ

Meet the Writer

Bruce Coville

A Word Wrangler

Bruce Coville (1950–   ) grew up in a rural area north of Syracuse, New York, around the corner from his grandparents' dairy farm. About "Duffy's Jacket" he says:

❝ For years I have been maintaining that I can't really write short stories, that they are just something that happen to me by accident every now and then. . . . 'Duffy's Jacket,' on the other hand, was pure joy. The idea came to me while I was walking in the woods with some friends. When we got back to the house, I excused myself, went upstairs, and typed it in a single sitting, the words seeming to fly from my fingers. . . . If only it were always that easy! But I figure a quarter century of word wrangling entitles you to at least one story that comes fairly quickly. ❞

For Independent Reading

You can read more of Coville's unusual and highly entertaining stories in *Oddly Enough* and *Odder Than Ever*.

DIRECT TEACHING

Ⓔ **Reading Skills and Strategies**

Retell. [Possible response to question 8: The creature corners the kids, scolds Duffy for forgetting his jacket, throws it at him, and leaves. Duffy is cured of his carelessness. Students may like the final twist or may dislike the quirky humor and find the ending a letdown.]

Meet the Writer

Bruce Coville grew up devouring science fiction books, fantasies such as *Mary Poppins* and *Dr. Dolittle*, young-adult adventures (the Nancy Drew, Hardy Boys, and Tom Swift series), and even comic books. He says, "The first time I can remember thinking that I would like to be a writer came in sixth grade, when our teacher—Mrs. Crandall—gave us an extended period of time to write a long story. I loved doing it."

For Independent Reading

■ If students choose to read Bruce Coville's *Oddly Enough*, encourage them to stay alert for his trademark blend of humor and the supernatural and for conflicts between thoughtless characters like Duffy and beleaguered, responsible characters like Andrew.

■ Students who like "Duffy's Jacket" may also enjoy James Thurber's classic "The Night the Bed Fell," another story of a mysterious incident in the life of an offbeat family.

Practice the Strategy

In this feature, students have the opportunity to retell a story, assess their retellings using a Retelling Rating Sheet, and then revise their work.

Strategy Tip

While students are working on their introductions, remind them to write their plot retellings in the present tense.

Strategy Tip

Tell students that since plot retellings follow time order, sequence words help to organize the events. Then, write additional sequence words and phrases on the board: *then, before, after, soon, meanwhile, earlier, while, until, when, after a while.*

PRACTICE 1

Possible answer: Soon Andrew, Duffy, and Marie hear noises at the door of the cabin. When the kids try to hide, a huge creature tracks them down and corners them. Finally, the creature scolds Duffy, throws Duffy's jacket at him, and stomps off. Duffy never forgets his things again. I like this story because it starts as a horror story but ends as a joke.

Practice the Strategy

Retelling: Summarizing the Plot

Here's how one student started a retelling of "Duffy's Jacket."

> I'm going to give a retelling of a story called "Duffy's Jacket," written by Bruce Coville. The important characters are Duffy and his cousin Andrew. Other characters are Andrew's mom, his Aunt Elise, and Duffy's sister, Marie. Duffy is very smart but very forgetful. All of them go on a trip to stay in a cabin in the middle of nowhere.
>
> Once they get to the cabin, they discover that it's not in such good shape. After they get unpacked and get things cleaned up, they go to sleep for the night. The next day, Andrew finds a message that says "Beware the Sentinel" written on the wall. No one knows who wrote it. Then . . .

PRACTICE 1

Finish the retelling. Use the Retelling Summary Sheet to organize your retelling. Keep the following points in mind:

1. Tell what happened after Andrew's mom and Aunt Elise left.
2. Describe the main problems. Think about Duffy's memory as one problem and the strange visitor as the other one.
3. Make sure you keep events in order.
4. Explain how the story ended.
5. Add your own comments about the story.

Retelling Summary Sheet

1. **Introduction**

   Begin with the title and author of the story. Then, tell where and when the story is set—if that's important.

2. **Characters**

   Tell the characters' names, and explain how the characters are related or connected to one another. Tell what the main character wants.

3. **Conflict**

   What is the main character's problem, or conflict—that is, who or what is keeping the main character from getting what he or she wants?

4. **Complications**

   Tell the main events—what happens as the character tries to solve the conflict.

   > **Strategy Tip**
   >
   > Avoid linking the events with a string of *and*'s. Here are some good time-order words to use: *first, second, third, next, eventually, later, afterward, finally, in conclusion.*

5. **Climax**

   Describe the climax, the most suspenseful moment in the story, when you discover at last how the conflict will be resolved.

   > **Strategy Tip**
   >
   > This is the moment when you know you are finally about to find out how the main character will overcome the conflict (or be defeated).

6. **Resolution**

   Tell what happens after the climax. How does the story end?

7. **Personal Response**

   Tell how you felt about the story.

Practice the Strategy

PRACTICE 2

Ask a buddy to listen as you give the retelling and to rate what you say on a Retelling Rating Sheet like the one that follows:

Retelling Rating Sheet

Name

Text

Directions: Have your listener use the following checklist to rate your retelling. Ask the listener to decide whether you've covered each item listed below a little, to some extent, a lot, or not at all. Work on those details that you haven't covered or covered only a little.

0	1	2	3
Not at all	A little	Some	A lot

Does this retelling . . .

1. have a good beginning that tells the title, the author, and when and where the story takes place?
2. tell who the characters are and how they are related to one another?
3. include the main events?
4. keep those main events in the correct sequence?
5. explain how the conflict, or main problem, is resolved?
6. include any personal comments about the story?

You can use the retelling strategy with the stories in this collection. If you want to review the elements of any plot, try **retelling.**

SKILLS FOCUS

Reading Skills
Retell story events.

Duffy's Jacket   13

PRACTICE 2

- After students have first drafts of their retellings, pair students and direct them to read their retellings aloud to each other.
- Instruct listeners to rate each element of the presenter's retelling, using the four-point scale provided (from 0, "Not at all," to 3, "A lot").
- Next, ask students to revise their retellings.
- Then, pair students once more, and have them rate each other's revisions again.
- Finally, bring the class together as a group, and ask volunteers to share what they found easiest and hardest about writing the retellings.

CROSS-CURRICULAR CONNECTIONS

Science

Report on science experiment. After consulting with a science teacher, guide students in adapting the rating sheet for use in evaluating reports on a science experiment. For example, students might revise the six questions to cover (1) the date and subject area of the experiment, (2) the hypothesis tested, (3) the materials used, (4) the steps followed, (5) the results obtained, and (6) the student's analysis of the results. Encourage students to use the adapted rating sheets as they draft and revise their next lab reports.

WHOLE CLASS

Grade-Level Skills

■ **Literary Skills**
Analyze the main conflict of the plot.

■ **Reading Skills**
Retell story events.

Upcoming Skills

■ **Literary Skills**
Evaluate the plot's structure and development, and the way conflicts are resolved.

Summary ⬆ *above grade level*

In this famous "monster-slaying" story, a little mongoose called Rikki-tikki-tavi is adopted by a British family living in India around 1900. When Rikki learns that two cobras, Nag and his wife, Nagaina, live in the family garden, he knows he must kill them. After overhearing the cobras' plans to kill the family, Rikki ambushes and kills Nag in the bathroom of the family's bungalow. To prevent the rise of a new generation of cobras, Rikki destroys all but one of the cobra eggs. He uses the last egg to lure Nagaina away from Teddy, the family's little boy, but Nagaina snatches the egg and disappears underground. Rikki bravely follows to what seems a certain death. At the story's climax the little hero emerges triumphant and tells the garden, "It is all over."

Before You Read — The Short Story

Rikki-tikki-tavi

Make the Connection
Quickwrite ✏️

Conflict is part of our real lives. For example, most people face bullies at some time in their lives. If you were facing a bully, what would you do? Would you fight? Would you run away? Would you try to negotiate? In your journal, describe how you think you would react.

Literary Focus
Conflict

All stories are built on some kind of **conflict.** Usually a conflict results when a character wants something very badly but has a hard time getting it. Think of the stories in movies and on TV, and you'll be able to find a conflict in every one of them. Conflict is worked out in the series of related events called **plot.**

INTERNET

Vocabulary Activity
•
Cross-curricular Connection
•
More About Kipling

Keyword: LE5 7-1

Reading Skills 📖
Retelling

Try a strategy called **retelling** to identify the events that move this plot forward. Here is how it works: As you read this story, you'll see little open-book signs alongside the text. At those points, stop and jot down notes that retell what has just happened. As you do your retelling, focus on the important events that keep the plot moving.

Vocabulary Development

Every time you read, you have a chance to add words to your vocabulary. The words that follow are underlined and defined in the story. See if you can use each one in a sentence of your own.

immensely (i·mens′lē) *adv.*: enormously. *Rikki is immensely brave. The snakes are immensely powerful.*

cowered (kou′ərd) *v.*: crouched and trembled in fear. *Darzee, who is a coward, cowered before the snakes. Rikki cowered before no one.*

valiant (val′yənt) *adj.*: brave and determined. *Rikki is a valiant hero. Would other snakes think the snakes are valiant too?*

consolation (kän′sə·lā′shən) *n.*: comfort. *Snakes get no consolation from Rikki. Rikki's consolation comes from a safe, peaceful garden.*

impotent (im′pə·tənt) *adj.*: powerless. *With all but her last egg destroyed, Nagaina felt impotent against Rikki.*

SKILLS FOCUS

Literary Skills
Analyze conflict.

Reading Skills
Retell story events.

14

Background
Literature and Social Studies

This story takes place in India many years ago, when the British ruled that huge country. The family in this story lives in a cantonment (kan·tän′mənt), which is a kind of army base. The father is in the British army. This story is about a conflict that takes place between two deadly snakes and a brave little mongoose—a creature that looks something like a weasel or a large squirrel.

RESOURCES: READING

Planning
■ *One-Stop Planner* CD-ROM with ExamView Test Generator

Differentiating Instruction
■ *The Holt Reader*
■ *Holt Adapted Reader*
■ *Holt Reading Solutions*
■ *Supporting Instruction in Spanish*
■ *Audio CD Library*

■ *Audio CD Library, Selections and Summaries in Spanish*

Vocabulary
■ *Vocabulary Development*

Grammar and Language
■ *Daily Language Activities*

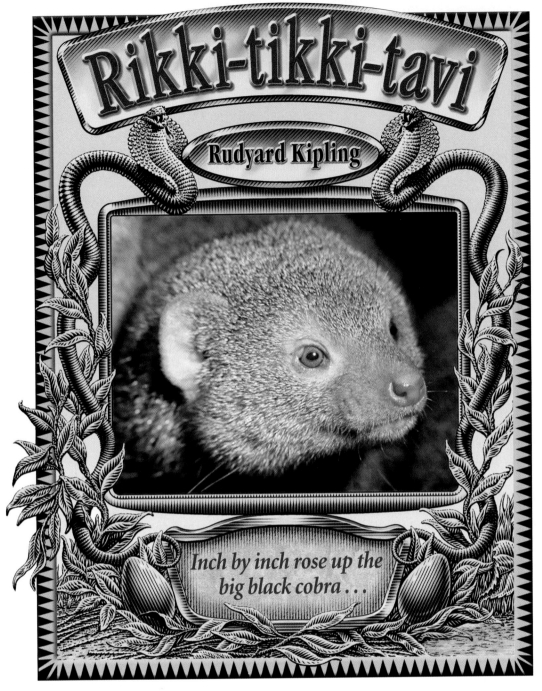

Rikki-tikki-tavi

Rudyard Kipling

Inch by inch rose up the big black cobra . . .

Selection Starter

Motivate. Present to students a conflict reported in a recent newspaper. How did the people in the article deal with each other? Did they talk it out? get help? fight? Then, ask students to complete the Quickwrite activity.

Preview Vocabulary

To help students master the Vocabulary words introduced on p. 14, give students these exercises.

1. Describe a time when you were <u>immensely</u> proud.
2. Draw a picture of an elephant that <u>cowered</u> before a mouse.
3. Name three people who are <u>valiant</u>.
4. If you had lost a contest that you wanted very much to win, what thoughts might provide you with <u>consolation</u>?
5. Draw a picture of a weightlifter who is <u>impotent</u> to lift a dumbbell.

Assign the Reading

Have the class read the story aloud up to and including Rikki's first confrontation with Nag and Nagaina. Then, allow advanced learners to finish the story independently—and to answer the After You Read activities as homework—while you continue working with small groups of readers having difficulty.

HOMEWORK

Assessment
- *Holt Assessment: Literature, Reading, and Vocabulary*
- *One-Stop Planner* CD-ROM with ExamView Test Generator
- *Holt Online Assessment*

Internet
- go.hrw.com (Keyword: LE5 7-1)
- *Elements of Literature Online*

Media
- *Audio CD Library*
- *Audio CD Library, Selections and Summaries in Spanish*
- *Visual Connections Videocassette Program*

A bungalow in India.

A This is the story of the great war that Rikki-tikki-tavi fought single-handed, through the bathrooms of the big bungalow[1] in Segowlee cantonment.[2] Darzee, the tailorbird, helped him, and Chuchundra, the muskrat, who never comes out into the middle of the floor but always creeps round by the wall, gave him advice; but Rikki-tikki did the real fighting.

1. **bungalow** *n.:* in India, a low, one-storied house, named after a type of house found in Bengal, a region of South Asia.
2. **Segowlee** (sē·gou**ʼ**lē) **cantonment:** British army post in Segowlee (now Segauli), India.

He was a mongoose, rather like a little cat in his fur and his tail but quite like a weasel in his head and his habits. His eyes and the end of his restless nose were pink; he could scratch himself anywhere he pleased with any leg, front or back, that he chose to use; he could fluff up his tail till it looked like a bottlebrush, and his war cry as he scuttled through the long grass was *Rikk-tikk-tikki-tikki-tchk!*

B One day, a high summer flood washed him out of the burrow where he lived with his father and mother and carried him, kicking and clucking, down a roadside ditch. He found a little wisp of grass floating there and clung to it till he lost his senses. When he revived, he was lying in the hot sun in the middle of a garden path, very draggled[3] indeed, and a small boy was saying: "Here's a dead mongoose. Let's have a funeral."

"No," said his mother; "let's take him in and dry him. Perhaps he isn't really dead."

They took him into the house, and a big man picked him up between his finger and thumb and said he was not dead but half choked; so they wrapped him in cotton wool and warmed him over a little fire, and he opened his eyes and sneezed.

"Now," said the big man (he was an Englishman who had just moved into the bungalow), "don't frighten him, and we'll see what he'll do."

It is the hardest thing in the world to frighten a mongoose, because he is eaten up from nose to tail with curiosity. The motto of all the mongoose family is "Run and find out," and Rikki-tikki was a true mongoose. He looked at the cotton wool, decided that it was not good to eat, ran all round the table, sat up and put his fur in order, scratched himself, and jumped on the small boy's shoulder.

"Don't be frightened, Teddy," said his father. "That's his way of making friends."

"Ouch! He's tickling under my chin," said Teddy.

Rikki-tikki looked down between the boy's collar and neck, snuffed at his ear, and climbed down to the floor, where he sat rubbing his nose.

"Good gracious," said Teddy's mother, "and that's a wild creature! I suppose he's so tame because we've been kind to him."

---

3. **draggled** v. used as adj.: wet and muddy, as if from being dragged around.

"All mongooses are like that," said her husband. "If Teddy doesn't pick him up by the tail or try to put him in a cage, he'll run in and out of the house all day long. Let's give him something to eat."

They gave him a little piece of raw meat. Rikki-tikki liked it immensely, and when it was finished, he went out into the veranda[4] and sat in the sunshine and fluffed up his fur to make it dry to the roots. Then he felt better.

"There are more things to find out about in this house," he said to himself, "than all my family could find out in all their lives. I shall certainly stay and find out." ❶

He spent all that day roaming over the house. He nearly drowned himself in the bathtubs, put his nose into the ink on a writing table, and burnt it on the end of the big man's cigar, for he climbed up in the big man's lap to see how writing was done. At nightfall he ran into Teddy's nursery to watch how kerosene lamps were lighted, and when Teddy went to bed, Rikki-tikki climbed up too; but he was a restless companion, because he had to get up and attend to every noise all through the night and find out what made it. Teddy's mother and father came in, the last thing, to look at their pillow. "I don't like that," said Teddy's mother; "he may bite the child." "He'll do no such thing," said the father. "Teddy's

> **RETELL**
> ❶ Before you read about how Rikki explores his new home, retell the events that brought him here.

---

4. **veranda** n.: open porch covered by a roof, running along the outside of a building.

Vocabulary
immensely (i·mensʹlē) adv.: enormously.

C English-Language Learners
Interpret idioms. Be sure students know that the phrase *eaten up from nose to tail with curiosity* means "extremely curious." You might challenge students to use one of the Vocabulary words in a paraphrase of the idiom. [*immensely* curious]

D Reading Skills
Retell. To help students retell these story events, give them a list of terms and phrases related to conflict and plot to draw upon: *tension builds, a complication arises when . . . , a surprising twist occurs when. . . .*

[Possible response to question 1: A flood washed Rikki out of the burrow where he lived with his parents. He held on to some floating grass, lost consciousness, and woke up in an English family's garden.]

Special Education Students
For lessons designed for special education students, see *Holt Reading Solutions.*

Advanced Learners
Acceleration. Use the following activity with advanced learners to help them evaluate plots.
Activity. Suggest that students create a chart listing the following three evaluation questions about "Rikki-tikki-tavi":

- How well matched are the antagonists?
- How suspenseful are the fight scenes?
- How believable is the resolution?

On a scale from one to ten, have students rate the story and compare their evaluations with those of other students.

A Literary Focus

? Foreshadowing. Point out that this is the first time snakes have been mentioned. What effect does the remark create? [It creates a sense of dread in Teddy's mother and in the reader as well.] Explain that foreshadowing functions just as ominous music does in a suspenseful movie; it makes readers fear upcoming conflicts.

B Vocabulary Development

Clarify word meanings: Contrast. Point out the word *cultivated.* Explain that a garden that is not cultivated might be described as untended, disorderly, or growing wild. Then, ask students to suggest definitions for *cultivated* as it is used in this passage. [Possible responses: well tended, neatly kept, orderly.]

C Reading Skills

Predict. You might invite students to pause after reading Rikki's question and to make predictions about who Nag might be. Ask them which clues so far suggest Nag's identity. [Nag's having eaten a baby bird suggests that he is a predator. Students may recall the father's ominous remark about snakes and guess that Nag is a snake who threatens the small animals in the garden and the family in the bungalow.]

---

safer with that little beast than if he had a bloodhound to watch him. If a snake came into the nursery now—"

But Teddy's mother wouldn't think of anything so awful.

Early in the morning, Rikki-tikki came to early breakfast in the veranda riding on Teddy's shoulder, and they gave him banana and some boiled egg; and he sat on all their laps one after the other, because every well-brought-up mongoose always hopes to be a house mongoose someday and have rooms to run about in; and Rikki-tikki's mother (she used to live in the General's house at Segowlee) had carefully told Rikki what to do if ever he came across white men.

Then Rikki-tikki went out into the garden to see what was to be seen. It was a large garden, only half cultivated, with bushes, as big as summerhouses, of Marshal Niel roses; lime and orange trees; clumps of bamboos; and thickets of high grass. Rikki-tikki licked his lips. "This is a splendid hunting ground," he said, and his tail grew bottlebrushy at the thought of it, and he scuttled up and down the garden, snuffing here and there till he heard very sorrowful voices in a thorn bush. It was Darzee, the tailorbird, and his wife. They had made a beautiful nest by pulling two big leaves together and stitching them up the edges with fibers and had filled the hollow with cotton and downy fluff. The nest swayed to and fro as they sat on the rim and cried.

"What is the matter?" asked Rikki-tikki.

"We are very miserable," said Darzee. "One of our babies fell out of the nest yesterday and Nag ate him."

"H'm!" said Rikki-tikki, "that is very sad —but I am a stranger here. Who is Nag?"

Darzee and his wife only cowered down

in the nest without answering, for from the thick grass at the foot of the bush there came a low hiss—a horrid, cold sound that made Rikki-tikki jump back two clear feet. Then inch by inch out of the grass rose up the head and spread hood of Nag, the big black cobra, and he was five feet long from tongue to tail. When he had lifted one third of himself clear of the ground, he stayed balancing to and fro exactly as a dandelion tuft balances in the wind, and he looked at Rikki-tikki with the wicked snake's eyes that never change their expression, whatever the snake may be thinking of.

"Who is Nag," said he. "*I* am Nag. The great God Brahm[5] put his mark upon all our people, when the first cobra spread his hood to keep the sun off Brahm as he slept. Look, and be afraid!"

He spread out his hood more than ever, and Rikki-tikki saw the spectacle mark on the back of it that looks exactly like the eye part of a hook-and-eye fastening. He was afraid for the minute; but it is impossible for a mongoose to stay frightened for any length of time, and though Rikki-tikki had never met a live cobra before, his mother had fed him on dead ones, and he knew that all a grown mongoose's business in life was to fight and eat snakes. Nag knew that too, and at the bottom of his cold heart, he was afraid.

"Well," said Rikki-tikki, and his tail began to fluff up again, "marks or no marks, do

---

5. **Brahm** (bräm): in the Hindu religion, the creator (also called Brahma).

Vocabulary

cowered (kou′ərd) *v.:* crouched and trembled in fear.

Culture

Hinduism. In Hindu belief, cobras are serpent kings and queens often associated with the god Brahma. Sometimes they are considered gods in their own right.

Activity. Encourage interested students to research traditional Hindu tales and compare the cobras in the traditional tales with those in "Rikki-tikki-tavi."

INDIVIDUAL

Science

Mongooses. In the 1800s, mongooses were imported into the sugar cane–producing islands of the Caribbean to kill rats. Unfortunately, with no natural enemies the mongooses multiplied uncontrollably. Today mongooses living on the islands eat small pets, threaten endangered species, and spread rabies. Ask students what steps they think the governments of these islands should take to solve this problem.

Activity. Place students of differing abilities into groups of three or four, and ask them to research some aspect of the mongoose, such as its feeding habits, its life cycle, or its physical characteristics. Have students create mongoose-shaped bookmarks and write on them the important facts they discover.

MIXED ABILITY

you think it is right for you to eat fledglings out of a nest?"

Nag was thinking to himself and watching the least little movement in the grass behind Rikki-tikki. He knew that mongooses in the garden meant death sooner or later for him and his family, but he wanted to get Rikki-tikki off his guard. So he dropped his head a little and put it on one side.

"Let us talk," he said. "You eat eggs. Why should not I eat birds?"

"Behind you! Look behind you!" sang Darzee.

Rikki-tikki knew better than to waste time in staring. He jumped up in the air as high as he could go, and just under him whizzed by the head of Nagaina, Nag's wicked wife. She had crept up behind him as he was talking, to make an end of him; and he heard her savage hiss as the stroke missed. He came down almost across her back, and if he had been an old mongoose, he would have known that then was the time to break her back with one bite; but he was afraid of the terrible lashing return stroke of the cobra. He bit, indeed, but did not bite long enough, and he jumped clear of the whisking tail, leaving Nagaina torn and angry.

"Wicked, wicked Darzee!" said Nag, lashing up as high as he could reach toward the nest in the thorn bush; but Darzee had built it out of reach of snakes, and it only swayed to and fro.

Rikki-tikki felt his eyes growing red and hot (when a mongoose's eyes grow red, he is angry), and he sat back on his tail and hind legs like a little kangaroo, and looked all round him, and chattered with rage. But Nag and Nagaina had disappeared into the grass.

When a snake misses its stroke, it never says anything or gives any sign of what it means to do next. Rikki-tikki did not care to follow them, for he did not feel sure that he could manage two snakes at once. So he trotted off to the gravel path near the house and sat down to think. It was a serious matter for him. If you read the old books of natural history, you will find they say that when the mongoose fights the snake and happens to get bitten, he runs off and eats some herb that cures him. That is not true. The victory is only a matter of quickness of eye and quickness of foot—snake's blow against the mongoose's jump—and as no eye can follow the motion of a snake's head when it strikes, this makes things much more wonderful than any magic herb. Rikki-tikki knew he was a young mongoose, and it made him all the more pleased to think that he had managed

"*I am Nag. . . . Look, and be afraid!*"

RETELL
❷ What happens when Rikki first meets the snakes? ❷

Ⓓ Literary Focus

❓ Characterization. The confrontation with Nag and Nagaina is Rikki's first experience with his natural enemies. What do the actions of Rikki and the cobras reveal about these three characters? [Possible response: The cobras are vicious, sneaky, and clever; Rikki is inexperienced but brave and competent.]

Ⓔ Learners Having Difficulty

❓ Monitor students' progress. Ask the following questions to make sure students recognize the central characters in the conflict: Who are Rikki's enemies? [Nag and Nagaina] Who is Rikki's helper? [Darzee]

Ⓕ Reading Skills

Retell. Be sure students understand that this incident introduces the main conflict.

[Possible response to question 2: Nag rose up and tried to scare Rikki, who coolly scolded Nag for eating Darzee's fledgling. Nag argued, hoping to distract Rikki so he wouldn't notice Nagaina sneaking up behind him. Warned by Darzee, Rikki jumped clear of Nagaina's attack just in time. He bit Nagaina but not hard enough, and the two cobras escaped. Rikki was furious.]

A **Vocabulary Development**

Clarify word meanings. The name Karait is actually the Hindi word for this small, highly venomous snake of southern Asia. The English word, derived from the Hindi, is *krait*. Point out that Kipling describes Karait as "the dusty brown snakeling."

B **Literary Focus**

❓ **Conflict.** How does this battle with Karait build suspense and advance the plot? [Possible responses: It emphasizes the threat that the snakes pose to the humans; it shows that Rikki will fight to protect the family; it builds suspense by showing Rikki's inexperience (he does not realize how quick or venomous Karait is); it reminds readers that he still must fight the much bigger cobras.]

C **Learners Having Difficulty**

Break down difficult text. To help these students comprehend and visualize this complex scene, read the passage aloud. With the group, break the scene down into a numbered list of actions in the order in which they occur in the story—for example, (1) Teddy shouted, (2) Teddy's mother screamed, (3) Karait lunged, and so on. Make sure students note that while Teddy's "father ran out with a stick," he arrives too late to help.

D **Reading Skills**

Retell. [Possible response to question 3: Teddy comes to pet Rikki, not seeing the deadly Karait in the dust about to strike. Rikki fights Karait without knowing how dangerous he is. When Teddy shouts, his father runs up with a stick, but Rikki has already killed Karait. Rikki doesn't eat Karait because he needs fast reflexes to fight the cobras. Both parents praise Rikki.]

---

to escape a blow from behind. It gave him confidence in himself, and when Teddy came running down the path, Rikki-tikki was ready to be petted. But just as Teddy was stooping, something wriggled a little in the dust and a tiny voice said: "Be careful. I am Death!" It was Karait, the dusty brown snakeling that lies for choice on the dusty earth; and his bite is as dangerous as the cobra's. But he is so small that nobody thinks of him, and so he does the more harm to people.

Rikki-tikki's eyes grew red again, and he danced up to Karait with the peculiar rocking, swaying motion that he had inherited from his family. It looks very funny, but it is so perfectly balanced a gait[6] that you can fly off from it at any angle you please; and in dealing with snakes this is an advantage. If Rikki-tikki had only known, he was doing a much more dangerous thing than fighting Nag, for Karait is so small and can turn so quickly that unless Rikki bit him close to the back of the head, he would get the return stroke in his eye or his lip. But Rikki did not know; his eyes were all red, and he rocked back and forth, looking for a good place to hold. Karait struck out, Rikki jumped sideways and tried to run in, but the wicked little dusty gray head lashed within a fraction of his shoulder, and he had to jump over the body, and the head followed his heels close.

Teddy shouted to the house: "Oh, look here! Our mongoose is killing a snake," and Rikki-tikki heard a scream from Teddy's mother. His father ran out with a stick, but by the time he came up, Karait had lunged out once too far, and Rikki-tikki had

---

6. **gait** (gāt) *n.:* way of walking or running.

---

sprung, jumped on the snake's back, dropped his head far between his forelegs, bitten as high up the back as he could get hold, and rolled away. That bite paralyzed Karait, and Rikki-tikki was just going to eat him up from the tail, after the custom of his family at dinner, when he remembered that a full meal makes a slow mongoose, and if he wanted all his strength and quickness ready, he must keep himself thin. He went away for a dust bath under the castor-oil bushes, while Teddy's father beat the dead Karait. "What is the use of that?" thought Rikki-tikki; "I have settled it all"; and then Teddy's mother picked him up from the dust and hugged him, crying that he had saved Teddy from death, and Teddy's father said that he was a providence,[7] and Teddy looked on with big, scared eyes. Rikki-tikki was rather amused at all the fuss, which, of course, he did not understand. Teddy's mother might just as well have petted Teddy for playing in the dust. Rikki was thoroughly enjoying himself. ❸

RETELL
❸ What happens in Rikki's conflict with Karait?

That night at dinner, walking to and fro among the wineglasses on the table, he might have stuffed himself three times over with nice things; but he remembered Nag and Nagaina, and though it was very pleasant to be patted and petted by Teddy's mother and to sit on Teddy's shoulder, his eyes would get red from time to time, and he would go off into his long war cry of *Rikk-tikk-tikki-tikki-tchk!*

Teddy carried him off to bed and insisted on Rikki-tikki's sleeping under his chin.

---

7. **providence** (präv′ə·dəns) *n.:* favor or gift from God or nature.

DEVELOPING FLUENCY

Activity. Because of the series of suspenseful battles in "Rikki-tikki-tavi," the story is riveting for audiences of all ages. In order to capitalize on the story's appeal, invite students from a local elementary school to visit your classroom. Group three or four of your students with three or four of the younger ones, and ask that your students take turns reading the story aloud to the visitors. After students have finished reading, have the groups discuss the passages they thought were most suspenseful.

CROSS AGE

Rikki-tikki was too well bred to bite or scratch, but as soon as Teddy was asleep, he went off for his nightly walk round the house, and in the dark he ran up against Chuchundra, the muskrat, creeping round by the wall. Chuchundra is a brokenhearted little beast. He whimpers and cheeps all night, trying to make up his mind to run into the middle of the room; but he never gets there.

"Don't kill me," said Chuchundra, almost weeping. "Rikki-tikki, don't kill me!"

"Do you think a snake killer kills muskrats?" said Rikki-tikki scornfully.

"Those who kill snakes get killed by snakes," said Chuchundra, more sorrowfully than ever. "And how am I to be sure that Nag won't mistake me for you some dark night?"

"There's not the least danger," said Rikki-tikki, "but Nag is in the garden, and I know you don't go there."

"My cousin Chua, the rat, told me—" said Chuchundra, and then he stopped.

"Told you what?"

"H'sh! Nag is everywhere, Rikki-tikki. You should have talked to Chua in the garden."

"I didn't—so you must tell me. Quick, Chuchundra, or I'll bite you!"

Chuchundra sat down and cried till the tears rolled off his whiskers. "I am a very poor man," he sobbed. "I never had spirit enough to run out into the middle of the room. H'sh! I mustn't tell you anything. Can't you *hear,* Rikki-tikki?"

Rikki-tikki listened. The house was as still as still, but he thought he could just catch the faintest *scratch-scratch* in the world—a noise as faint as that of a wasp walking on a windowpane—the dry scratch of a snake's scales on brickwork.

"That's Nag or Nagaina," he said to himself, "and he is crawling into the bathroom sluice.[8] You're right, Chuchundra; I should have talked to Chua."

He stole off to Teddy's bathroom, but there was nothing there, and then to Teddy's mother's bathroom. At the bottom of the smooth plaster wall there was a brick pulled out to make a sluice for the bathwater, and as Rikki-tikki stole in by the masonry[9] curb where the bath is put, he heard Nag and Nagaina whispering together outside in the moonlight.

"Be careful. I am Death!" It was Karait. . . .

"When the house is emptied of people," said Nagaina to her husband, "*he* will have to go away, and then the garden will be our own again. Go in quietly, and remember that the big man who killed Karait is the first one to bite. Then come out and tell me, and we will hunt for Rikki-tikki together."

---

8. **sluice** (slo͞os) *n.:* drain.
9. **masonry** *n.:* something built of stone or brick.

DIRECT TEACHING

E Literary Focus

❓ Complications. What new information does Chuchundra indirectly reveal to Rikki? [Possible response: The cobras are invading the house.] How does this information advance the plot? [Possible response: In the house, the cobras will pose a greater threat. It becomes more urgent that Rikki fight them.]

F Literary Focus

Foreshadowing. Define foreshadowing as a way an author hints about events that will occur later in a story. Teddy's father's comment about snakes earlier in the story is one example. Challenge pairs of students to find two to three more examples. Have pairs create charts or other graphics showing what occurs in each example, when it occurs, and what it foreshadows.

A **Literary Focus**

❓ **Characters' motives.** Nag and Nagaina reveal several of their reasons for planning to kill the humans. What are some of these reasons? [Nagaina wants the man dead because she thinks he killed Karait and thus is dangerous to all snakes; Nagaina thinks that with the people dead Rikki will have to leave; the cobras want to be king and queen of the garden; the cobras want enough space and peace for their young, who are about to hatch.]

B **Reading Skills**

❓ **Interpret.** If Rikki is the one that Nag and Nagaina want to be rid of, why does Nag resist the idea of hunting Rikki on his own or with Nagaina? [Nag may feel that even a pair of cobras has little chance of winning a fight with a mongoose.]

C **Cross-curricular Connections**
CULTURE

Architecture. Explain that in houses without plumbing, water must be pumped from a well or collected in rainwater cisterns. The water is then stored in jars and pitchers throughout the house, wherever water is needed.

D **Literary Focus**

❓ **Conflict.** How does Kipling slow the pace of the action and build suspense before Rikki's final conflict with Nag? [Possible responses: Kipling slows the action with phrases such as *coil by coil* and *muscle by muscle.* He shows Rikki imagining various strategies—all with disastrous consequences.]

A "But are you sure that there is anything to be gained by killing the people?" said Nag.

"Everything. When there were no people in the bungalow, did we have any mongoose in the garden? So long as the bungalow is empty, we are king and queen of the garden; and remember that as soon as our eggs in the melon bed hatch (as they may tomorrow), our children will need room and quiet."

B "I had not thought of that," said Nag. "I will go, but there is no need that we should hunt for Rikki-tikki afterward. I will kill the big man and his wife, and the child if I can, and come away quietly. Then the bungalow will be empty, and Rikki-tikki will go."

Rikki-tikki tingled all over with rage and hatred at this, and then Nag's head came through the sluice, and his five feet of cold body followed it. Angry as he was, Rikki-tikki was very frightened as he saw the size of the big cobra. Nag coiled himself up, raised his head, and looked into the bathroom in the dark, and Rikki could see his eyes glitter.

"Now, if I kill him here, Nagaina will know; and if I fight him on the open floor, the odds are in his favor. What am I to do?" said Rikki-tikki-tavi.

C Nag waved to and fro, and then Rikki-tikki heard him drinking from the biggest water jar that was used to fill the bath. "That is good," said the snake. "Now, when Karait was killed, the big man had a stick. He may have that stick still, but when he comes in to bathe in the morning, he will not have a stick. I shall wait here till he comes. Nagaina—do you hear me?—I shall wait here in the cool till daytime."

There was no answer from outside, so Rikki-tikki knew Nagaina had gone away.

Nag coiled himself down, coil by coil, round the bulge at the bottom of the water jar, and Rikki-tikki stayed still as death. After an hour he began to move, muscle by muscle, toward the jar. Nag was asleep, and Rikki-**D** tikki looked at his big back, wondering which would be the best place for a good hold. "If I don't break his back at the first jump," said Rikki, "he can still fight; and if he fights—O Rikki!" He looked at the thickness of the neck below the hood, but that was too much for him; and a bite near the tail would only make Nag savage.

"It must be the head," he said at last, "the head above the hood; and when I am once there, I must not let go."

Then he jumped. The head was lying a little clear of the water jar, under the curve of it; and as his teeth met, Rikki braced his back against the bulge of the red earthenware to hold down the head. This gave him just one second's purchase,[10] and he made the most of it. Then he was battered to and fro as a rat is shaken by a dog—to and fro on the floor, up and down, and round in great circles, but his eyes were red and he held on as the body cartwhipped over the floor, upsetting the tin dipper and the soap dish and the flesh brush, and banged against the tin side of the bath. As he held, he closed his jaws tighter and tighter, for he made sure[11] he would be banged to death, and for the honor of his family, he preferred to be found with his teeth locked. He was dizzy, aching, and felt shaken to pieces, when something went off like a thunderclap just behind him; a hot wind knocked him senseless and red fire singed his fur. The big

---

10. **purchase** *n.:* firm hold.
11. **made sure:** here, felt sure.

man had been wakened by the noise and had fired both barrels of a shotgun into Nag just behind the hood.

Rikki-tikki held on with his eyes shut, for now he was quite sure he was dead; but the head did not move, and the big man picked him up and said: "It's the mongoose again, Alice; the little chap has saved *our* lives now." Then Teddy's mother came in with a very white face and saw what was left of Nag, and Rikki-tikki dragged himself to Teddy's bedroom and spent half the rest of the night shaking himself tenderly to find out whether he really was broken into forty pieces, as he fancied. **❹**

🔖 **RETELL**
❹ What happens when Rikki sees Nag poke his head into the bathroom?

When morning came, he was very stiff but well pleased with his doings. "Now I have Nagaina to settle with, and she will be worse than five Nags, and there's no knowing when the eggs she spoke of will hatch. Goodness! I must go and see Darzee," he said.

Without waiting for breakfast, Rikki-tikki ran to the thorn bush, where Darzee was singing a song of triumph at the top of his voice. The news of Nag's death was all over the garden, for the sweeper had thrown the body on the rubbish heap.

"Oh, you stupid tuft of feathers!" said Rikki-tikki angrily. "Is this the time to sing?"

"Nag is dead—is dead—is dead!" sang Darzee. "The <u>valiant</u> Rikki-tikki caught him by the head and held fast. The big man brought the bang-stick, and Nag fell in two pieces! He will never eat my babies again."

"All that's true enough, but where's Nagaina?" said Rikki-tikki, looking carefully round him.

"Nagaina came to the bathroom sluice and called for Nag," Darzee went on, "and Nag came out on the end of a stick—the sweeper picked him up on the end of a stick and threw him upon the rubbish heap. Let us sing about the great, the red-eyed Rikki-tikki!" and Darzee filled his throat and sang.

"If I could get up to your nest, I'd roll your babies out!" said Rikki-tikki. "You don't know when to do the right thing at the right time. You're safe enough in your nest there, but it's war for me down here. Stop singing a minute, Darzee."

"For the great, beautiful Rikki-tikki's sake I will stop," said Darzee. "What is it, O Killer of the terrible Nag?"

"Where is Nagaina, for the third time?"

"On the rubbish heap by the stables, mourning for Nag. Great is Rikki-tikki with the white teeth."

"Bother[12] my white teeth! Have you ever heard where she keeps her eggs?"

"In the melon bed, on the end nearest the wall, where the sun strikes nearly all day. She hid them there weeks ago."

"And you never thought it worthwhile to tell me? The end nearest the wall, you said?"

"Rikki-tikki, you are not going to eat her eggs?"

"Not eat exactly; no. Darzee, if you have a grain of sense, you will fly off to the stables and pretend that your wing is broken and let Nagaina chase you away to this bush. I must get to the melon bed, and if I went there now, she'd see me."

---

12. **bother** *interj.*: here, never mind.

Vocabulary
valiant (val′yənt) *adj.*: brave and determined.

ⓔ Reading Skills
Retell. [Possible response to question 4: At night in the bathroom, Rikki hears Nag and Nagaina planning to kill the humans. Then Nagaina leaves. Nag enters the bathroom and falls asleep, and Rikki leaps and locks his teeth into Nag's head. Nag tries to batter him off, but Rikki holds on until the man comes and shoots Nag.] Be sure students realize that although this incident gets rid of one of Rikki's enemies, the tension is not yet resolved since Nagaina is still a threat.

ⓕ Correcting Misconceptions
Some students may be confused by the term *bang-stick*. Darzee is referring to the man's shotgun, which is shaped like a stick and makes a banging noise when it goes off.

ⓖ Advanced Learners
Enrichment. Point out how Darzee is praising Rikki in this dialogue. Descriptive phrases such as "Killer of the terrible Nag" and "Rikki-tikki with the white teeth" are part of the epic tradition in which heroes are described in terms of their appearance and praised for their deeds. For more examples of such epic phrases, see Darzee's chant on p. 28.

ⓗ Reading Skills
❷ Interpret. Why is Darzee concerned that Rikki might be planning to eat the cobra eggs? Do you think he is being sympathetic, shortsighted, or both? Why? [Possible response: Darzee is being sympathetic because his children are born from eggs too. However, he is also being shortsighted because cobra eggs soon become cobras. His wife is more practical.]

CROSS-CURRICULAR CONNECTIONS

Science
A cobra's bite. Tell students that a cobra's bite can kill a person in fifteen minutes. The cobra's venom attacks the nervous system, causing dizziness, blurred vision, and pain. Cobras are particularly dangerous when guarding their eggs. In India, villages have been evacuated when cobra eggs were found.

A Reading Skills

❓ **Interpret.** The narrator says that Darzee is "very much like a man." What might this comparison imply? [Possible responses: Men are foolish; they lack foresight.]

B English-Language Learners

Interpret idioms. Be sure students understand that "settle accounts with" means "take revenge on."

C Literary Focus

❓ **Characters' motives.** Why does Nagaina plan to kill Teddy? [Possible response: She wants to get even with the humans for killing Nag.]

D Vocabulary Development

Clarify word meanings: Contrast. Point out the word *cunningly.* Tell students that something done cunningly is not done clumsily, carelessly, or ineptly. Then, ask them to suggest definitions for *cunningly* as it is used in the passage. Encourage students to use dictionaries for help. [Possible responses: cleverly, slyly, craftily, artfully.]

E Literary Focus

❓ **Conflict.** What new twist is added to the plot when Darzee's wife screams for Rikki? [Possible response: Nagaina is attacking the humans directly, in broad daylight. Rikki must defend them at once.] How does this new twist affect the pace of the plot? [Possible response: The pace intensifies as Rikki rushes to stop Nagaina.]

Darzee was a featherbrained little fellow who could never hold more than one idea at a time in his head, and just because he knew that Nagaina's children were born in eggs like his own, he didn't think at first that it was fair to kill them. But his wife was a sensible bird, and she knew that cobra's eggs meant young cobras later on; so she flew off from the nest and left Darzee to keep the babies warm and continue his song about the death of Nag. Darzee was very like a man in some ways.

She fluttered in front of Nagaina by the rubbish heap and cried out, "Oh, my wing is broken! The boy in the house threw a stone at me and broke it." Then she fluttered more desperately than ever.

Nagaina lifted up her head and hissed, "You warned Rikki-tikki when I would have killed him. Indeed and truly, you've chosen a bad place to be lame in." And she moved toward Darzee's wife, slipping along over the dust.

"The boy broke it with a stone!" shrieked Darzee's wife.

"Well! It may be some consolation to you when you're dead to know that I shall settle accounts with the boy. My husband lies on the rubbish heap this morning, but before night the boy in the house will lie very still. What is the use of running away? I am sure to catch you. Little fool, look at me!"

Darzee's wife knew better than to do *that,* for a bird who looks at a snake's eyes gets so frightened that she cannot move. Darzee's wife fluttered on, piping sorrowfully and never leaving the ground, and Nagaina quickened her pace.

Rikki-tikki heard them going up the path from the stables, and he raced for the end of

the melon patch near the wall. There, in the warm litter above the melons, very cunningly hidden, he found twenty-five eggs about the size of a bantam's[13] eggs but with whitish skins instead of shells.

"I was not a day too soon," he said, for he could see the baby cobras curled up inside the skin, and he knew that the minute they were hatched, they could each kill a man or a mongoose. He bit off the tops of the eggs as fast as he could, taking care to crush the young cobras, and turned over the litter from time to time to see whether he had missed any. At last there were only three eggs left, and Rikki-tikki began to chuckle to himself, when he heard Darzee's wife screaming:

"Rikki-tikki, I led Nagaina toward the house, and she has gone into the veranda, and—oh, come quickly—she means killing!"

Rikki-tikki smashed two eggs, and tumbled backward down the melon bed with the third egg in his mouth, and scuttled to the veranda as hard as he could put foot to the ground. Teddy and his mother and father were there at early breakfast, but Rikki-tikki saw that they were not eating anything. They sat stone still, and their faces were white. Nagaina was coiled up on the matting by Teddy's chair, within easy striking distance of Teddy's bare leg, and she was swaying to and fro, singing a song of triumph.

"Son of the big man that killed Nag," she hissed, "stay still. I am not ready yet. Wait a little. Keep very still, all you three! If you

---

13. **bantam's** *n.:* small chicken's.

Vocabulary
consolation (kän′sə·lā′shən) *n.:* comfort.

MINI-LESSON Reading

Developing Word-Attack Skills
Have students compare these two words from p. 25 and p. 27: *dust* and *rustle.* Point out that the word *rustle* begins with the word *rust,* so it's logical to think that the beginning of *rustle* would sound like *rust* and rhyme with *dust.* But this is not the case. In *rustle,* the *t* is silent. Use the following word pairs to show that *–le* after the consonant blend *st* always has the effect of making the *t* silent.

cast/castle   grist/gristle
nest/nestle   whist/whistle
Warn students that *–le* is tricky and doesn't always behave in the same way—that is, it doesn't always make letters silent. Then, explore with students the effect of *–le* on another consonant blend: *mb.* When a word ends with *mb,* the *b* is always silent: *crumb, plumb,* and *limb.* But when *mb* is followed by *–le,* the *b* is not silent. Compare the words *crumb* and *crumble.* The sound

move, I strike, and if you do not move, I strike. Oh, foolish people, who killed my Nag!"

Teddy's eyes were fixed on his father, and all his father could do was to whisper, "Sit still, Teddy. You mustn't move. Teddy, keep still."

Then Rikki-tikki came up and cried: "Turn round, Nagaina; turn and fight!"

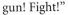

"All in good time," said she, without moving her eyes. "I will settle my account with *you* presently. Look at your friends, Rikki-tikki. They are still and white. They are afraid. They dare not move, and if you come a step nearer, I strike."

"Look at your eggs," said Rikki-tikki, "in the melon bed near the wall. Go and look, Nagaina!"

The big snake turned half round and saw the egg on the veranda. "Ah-h! Give it to me," she said.

Rikki-tikki put his paws one on each side of the egg, and his eyes were blood-red. "What price for a snake's egg? For a young cobra? For a young king cobra? For the last—the very last of the brood? The ants are eating all the others down by the melon bed."

Nagaina spun clear round, forgetting everything for the sake of the one egg; and Rikki-tikki saw Teddy's father shoot out a big hand, catch Teddy by the shoulder, and drag him across the little table with the teacups, safe and out of reach of Nagaina.

"Tricked! Tricked! Tricked! *Rikk-tck-tck!*"

chuckled Rikki-tikki. "The boy is safe, and it was I—I—I—that caught Nag by the hood last night in the bathroom." Then he began to jump up and down, all four feet together, his head close to the floor. "He threw me to and fro, but he could not shake me off. He was dead before the big man blew him in two. I did it! *Rikki-tikki-tck-tck!* Come then, Nagaina. Come and fight with me. You shall not be a widow long."

Darzee, a featherbrained little fellow.

Nagaina saw that she had lost her chance of killing Teddy, and the egg lay between Rikki-tikki's paws. "Give me the egg, Rikki-tikki. Give me the last of my eggs, and I will go away and never come back," she said, lowering her hood.

"Yes, you will go away, and you will never come back; for you will go to the rubbish heap with Nag. Fight, widow! The big man has gone for his gun! Fight!"

Rikki-tikki was bounding all round Nagaina, keeping just out of reach of her stroke, his little eyes like hot coals. Nagaina gathered herself together and flung out at him. Rikki-tikki jumped up and backwards. Again and again and again she struck, and each time her head came with a whack on the matting of the veranda and she gathered herself together like a watch spring. Then Rikki-tikki danced in a circle to get behind her, and Nagaina spun round to keep her head to his head, so that the rustle of her

Rikki-tikki-tavi **25**

F Literary Focus

❓ Conflict. Although everyone seems frozen in time, what dramatic conflicts are going on as Rikki and Nagaina talk? [Possible response: Rikki and Nagaina are fighting a battle of wills, Nagaina is holding Teddy hostage, and Rikki is holding Nagaina's last egg hostage.]

G Literary Focus

❓ Characters' motives. Why does Rikki tell Nagaina that he, not the man, killed Nag? [Possible responses: to turn Nagaina's anger away from the humans; to distract her; to boast and to torment her as she has tormented Teddy and his parents; to make her lose control and fight him.]

H Reading Skills

❓ Make judgments. Does Nagaina deserve any mercy or sympathy? Why or why not? [Possible responses: Yes, because she has lost her husband and all her babies but one. No, because she is merciless herself; she tried to kill Rikki, and she planned to show no mercy to Teddy or his parents.]

I Literary Focus

❓ Conflict. In the fight scene, Rikki and Nagaina circle each other like boxers in a ring. How is the action building to a peak? [Possible response: Rikki is jumping around like a high-bouncing ball, Nagaina is coiling and striking repeatedly, and the man has gone for his shotgun.]

of *b* is heard in words ending with *–mble*: *stumble, nimble,* and *tremble.*
Activity. Write the following sentences on the chalkboard. Ask a volunteer to explain why each underlined word sounds the way it does.

1. The eggs are <u>nestled</u> in the shade.
2. Darzee <u>trembles</u> as he <u>whistles</u>.
3. Nag's victims are struck <u>dumb</u> with terror.
4. Rikki's home is his <u>castle</u>.
5. If you hear a <u>rustle</u>, don't move a <u>limb</u>.

A Literary Focus

Characterization. Ask students what character traits Rikki shows by chasing Nagaina and following her into her hole. [Possible responses: He shows bravery; he shows foolhardiness. He seems determined to finish things once and for all.]

Rikki-tikki knew that he must catch Nagaina or all the trouble would begin again.

tail on the matting sounded like dry leaves blown along by the wind.

He had forgotten the egg. It still lay on the veranda, and Nagaina came nearer and nearer to it, till at last, while Rikki-tikki was drawing breath, she caught it in her mouth, turned to the veranda steps, and flew like an arrow down the path, with Rikki-tikki behind her. When the cobra runs for her life, she goes like a whiplash flicked across a horse's neck. Rikki-tikki knew that he must catch her or all the trouble would begin again. She headed straight for the long grass by the thorn bush, and as he was running, Rikki-tikki heard Darzee still singing his foolish little song of triumph. But Darzee's wife was wiser. She flew off her nest as Nagaina came along and flapped her wings about Nagaina's head. If Darzee had helped, they might have turned her, but Nagaina only lowered her hood and went on. Still, the instant's delay brought Rikki-tikki up to

earth. Then the grass by the mouth of the hole stopped waving, and Darzee said: "It is all over with Rikki-tikki! We must sing his death song. Valiant Rikki-tikki is dead! For Nagaina will surely kill him underground."

So he sang a very mournful song that he made up on the spur of the minute, and just as he got to the most touching part, the grass quivered again, and Rikki-tikki, covered with dirt, dragged himself out of the hole leg by leg, licking his whiskers. Darzee stopped with a little shout. Rikki-tikki shook some of the dust out of his fur and sneezed. "It is all over," he said. "The widow will never come out again." And the red ants that live between the grass stems heard him and began to troop down one after another to see if he had spoken the truth. ❺

RETELL
❺ What happens when Rikki fights Nagaina?

Rikki-tikki curled himself up in the grass and slept where he was—slept and slept till it was late in the afternoon, for he had done a hard day's work.

"Now," he said, when he awoke, "I will go back to the house. Tell the Coppersmith, Darzee, and he will tell the garden that Nagaina is dead."

The Coppersmith is a bird who makes a noise exactly like the beating of a little hammer on a copper pot; and the reason he is always making it is because he is the town crier to every Indian garden and tells all the news to everybody who cares to listen. As Rikki-tikki went up the path, he heard his "attention" notes like a tiny dinner gong and then the steady "*Ding-dong-tock!* Nag is dead—*dong!* Nagaina is dead! *Ding-dong-tock!*" That set all the birds in the garden singing and the frogs croaking, for Nag and

her, and as she plunged into the rat hole where she and Nag used to live, his little white teeth were clenched on her tail and he went down with her—and very few mongooses, however wise and old they may be, care to follow a cobra into its hole. It was dark in the hole, and Rikki-tikki never knew when it might open out and give Nagaina room to turn and strike at him. He held on savagely and stuck out his feet to act as brakes on the dark slope of the hot, moist

B Reading Skills

❓ **Predict.** Do you believe, as Darzee does, that Rikki will be killed? Why or why not? [Possible responses: no, because Rikki has been successful and lucky in past battles; yes, because even experienced mongooses don't follow cobras into their holes.]

C Reading Skills

Retell. [Possible response to question 5: Rikki distracts Nagaina from Teddy by showing her the last cobra egg and telling her he's smashed the others. He and Nagaina circle each other for position until she suddenly grabs the last egg in her mouth and speeds off toward her hole. Rikki chases her, and Darzee's wife flaps in Nagaina's face to slow her so he can grab her tail. She dives into her hole, Rikki still hanging on to her tail, and he kills her underground and emerges unharmed.]

D English-Language Learners

Build background knowledge. Some students might not know that before the invention of the telephone and television, a person known as a town crier roamed a town with a bell, announcing news to the community. Here the coppersmith bird announces Rikki's triumph to the garden as a town crier would to a town.

A **Literary Focus**

❓ **Conflict.** How is the conflict resolved? [Possible response: The conflict is resolved through Rikki's killing of Nagaina underground and through his patrolling the garden fiercely from that time on, keeping it free of cobras.]

GUIDED PRACTICE

Monitor students' progress. Guide the class in answering these comprehension questions. Direct students to locate passages in the text that support their responses.

True-False

1. The plot of the story involves a mongoose who threatens humans. [F]
2. Conflict arises from the fact that mongooses and snakes are natural enemies. [T]
3. Nag and Nagaina plan to kill Rikki because he killed their young. [F]
4. The final battle occurs between Nag and Rikki. [F]
5. At the climax of the story, Rikki puts himself in mortal danger by following a cobra into its hole. [T]

Chuchundra, a brokenhearted little beast.

Nagaina used to eat frogs as well as little birds.

When Rikki got to the house, Teddy and Teddy's mother (she looked very white still, for she had been fainting) and Teddy's father came out and almost cried over him; and that night he ate all that was given him till he could eat no more and went to bed on Teddy's shoulder, where Teddy's mother saw him when she came to look late at night.

"He saved our lives and Teddy's life," she said to her husband. "Just think, he saved all our lives."

Rikki-tikki woke up with a jump, for the mongooses are light sleepers.

A "Oh, it's you," said he. "What are you bothering for? All the cobras are dead; and if they weren't, I'm here."

Rikki-tikki had a right to be proud of himself, but he did not grow too proud, and he kept that garden as a mongoose should keep it, with tooth and jump and spring and bite, till never a cobra dared show its head inside the walls.

Darzee's Chant
Sung in honor of Rikki-tikki-tavi

Singer and tailor am I—
    Doubled the joys that I know—
Proud of my lilt[14] to the sky,
    Proud of the house that I sew.
Over and under, so weave I my music—
    so weave I the house that I sew.

Sing to your fledglings[15] again,
    Mother, O lift up your head!
Evil that plagued us is slain,
    Death in the garden lies dead.
Terror that hid in the roses is impotent—
    flung on the dunghill and dead!

Who has delivered us, who?
    Tell me his nest and his name.
Rikki, the valiant, the true,
    Tikki, with eyeballs of flame—
Rikk-tikki-tikki, the ivory-fanged,
    the hunter with eyeballs of flame!

Give him the Thanks of the Birds,
    Bowing with tail feathers spread,
Praise him with nightingale words—
    Nay, I will praise him instead.
Hear! I will sing you the praise of the
    bottle-tailed Rikki with eyeballs of red!

(*Here Rikki-tikki interrupted, so the rest of the song is lost.*)

---

14. **lilt** *n.*: song.
15. **fledglings** (flej′liŋz) *n.*: baby birds.

Vocabulary
impotent (im′pə·tənt) *adj.*: powerless.

FAMILY/COMMUNITY ACTIVITY

Encourage students and their families to hold family read-arounds at home, using students' favorite parts of "Rikki-tikki-tavi." In a read-around, family members take turns reading aloud. Each participant reads as much (or as little) as he or she wants; then the next participant takes over. You might send home a note to parents, explaining how a read-around works and how the activity benefits students.

Meet the Writer

Rudyard Kipling

On His Own

India, the setting of "Rikki-tikki-tavi," is a place **Joseph Rudyard Kipling** (1865–1936) knew well. His father was a professor of art in Bombay, and Kipling was born in that city when India was under British rule. India was a fascinating place, and young Kipling loved it.

When he was six, however, his parents shipped him and his sister off to a boardinghouse in England. Feeling very much on his own in England, he made a discovery:

> 66 [Books] were among the most important affairs in the world.... I could read as much as I chose and ask the meaning of things from anyone I met. I had found out, too, that one could take a pen and set down what one thought, and that nobody accused one of 'showing off' by doing so. 99

When he was seventeen, Kipling returned to India and took a job as an editor with an English-language newspaper. He was fascinated by the lives of British colonials in India and the vivid contrast they made with the Indian people they ruled. Soon the paper was printing Kipling's poems and tales about what he saw around him. Other newspapers reprinted them, and readers begged for more. Kipling's fame grew; over the next half century he wrote dozens of books, and in 1907, he won the Nobel Prize in literature. Although he later lived in many places around the world, India would always remain close to his heart.

For Independent Reading

Read more of Kipling's animal stories in *Just So Stories* and *The Jungle Book*. *The Jungle Book* is about Mowgli, a boy who is raised by wolves. *Kim*, Kipling's best-known novel, traces the adventures of an Irish orphan who is raised as an Indian and eventually becomes a British spy.

Meet the Writer

Kipling often wrote humorous and affectionate letters to his children when they were away from home. In one letter, Kipling offers some suggestions for living in London:

- "Wash early and often with soap and hot water."
- "Never stop a motorbus with your foot. It is not a croquet ball."
- "Do not attempt to take pictures off the wall of the National Gallery, or to remove cases of butterflies from the Natural History Museum. You will be noticed if you do."

For Independent Reading

- If students choose to read *The Jungle Book*, be sure they watch a movie version of *The Jungle Book* and compare it to Kipling's actual work. You also might recommend the following titles:
- If students liked the story of Teddy and his pet mongoose Rikki, they might enjoy *My Dog Skip*, the story of a boy and his dog, by Willie Morris.
- For another tale of courage, recommend *Where the Red Fern Grows* by Wilson Rawls. Two dogs and a boy in the Ozarks end up facing foes as daunting as Nag and Nagaina.
- Animal lovers might enjoy *Never Cry Wolf*, Farley Mowat's surprising, often hilarious, true story of a year spent among Arctic wolves.

DIFFERENTIATING INSTRUCTION

Advanced Learners
Enrichment. Tell students that during Kipling's lifetime, the British prided themselves on the fact that the sun never set on their empire. No one was more proud of the empire than Kipling.

Researching Kipling. Have students find out more about Kipling's role as the spokesperson for British colonialism. Suggest that they enter *Rudyard Kipling* or *British Empire* as keywords in a search engine and then look for the countries in Queen Victoria's empire that Kipling actually visited.

After You Read

First Thoughts

1. Possible Answers
   • I thought this story was <u>scary</u>.
   • I was frightened for Rikki-tikki-tavi when <u>Nag slid into the dark bathroom</u>.
   • The scene I liked best was <u>the one in which Rikki confronted Nagaina</u>.

Thinking Critically

2. Rikki faces conflicts with Nag, Karait, and Nagaina, each of which is potentially life threatening. Most students will think that the greatest conflict is with Nagaina because she has good reasons for being angry with him.

3. Rikki wants to be the house mongoose. He fights Nagaina to protect the family and to get rid of his natural enemies.

4. Nagaina wants to be queen of the garden and to make the area safe for her family. She fights Rikki for her last egg and to seek revenge.

5. Possible answer: The garden animals see Rikki as a heroic deliverer, larger than life. Darzee calls him "the valiant, the true," describing him as a mighty "ivory-fanged" hunter with "eyeballs of flame."

Extending Interpretations

6. Some students will identify with Rikki's experience, while others will not.

7. Rikki has a natural instinct to hunt and kill snakes. Snakes must kill to stay alive. This begins the conflict. Students might mention differences of opinion, prejudice, conflicts over money or power, or misunderstandings as causes of human war.

First Thoughts

1. Respond to "Rikki-tikki-tavi" by completing these sentences:
   • I thought this story was . . .
   • I was frightened for Rikki-tikki-tavi when . . .
   • The scene I liked best was . . .

Thinking Critically

2. Describe three **conflicts** that Rikki-tikki faces. Which conflict do you think is his greatest challenge? Why? How is it resolved?

3. **Motive** refers to the reason for a character's behavior. What was Rikki's **motive** for fighting Nagaina? What did he want?

4. What was Nagaina's **motive** for fighting Rikki? What did she want?

5. What does Darzee's chant tell about the garden animals' feelings for Rikki? Give specific words from the chant to support your answer.

INTERNET

Projects and Activities

Keyword: LE5 7-1

Extending Interpretations

6. Did Rikki's conflicts with the deadly garden bullies remind you of your own experiences? For ideas, think back to what you said about bullies before you read the story.

7. The animal world of "Rikki-tikki-tavi" is filled with conflict and danger. What causes the war in this animal story? What causes most wars among people?

SKILLS FOCUS

Literary Skills
Analyze conflict.

Reading Skills
Retell story events.

Writing Skills
Express an opinion.

WRITING

Expressing Your Opinion

Look back at pages 18 and 19, where Nag and Nagaina are described for the first time. Find words on those pages that make the snakes seem evil. Is Kipling being fair, or are the snakes just doing what snakes do naturally? Does Kipling present the snakes as totally evil, or are they good in any way? In a paragraph or two, discuss your evaluation of the way Kipling handles his snake characters.

Reading Check

Work out the major events that advance the **plot** of Rikki's story. Fill in a diagram like this one. You should find at least four key events that lead to the exciting climax.

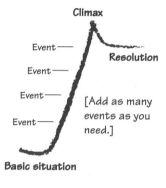

Climax

Event ——

Event ——

Event ——   Resolution

Event ——   [Add as many events as you need.]

Basic situation

Reading Check

Events might include Rikki's first encounter with Nag and Nagaina, Rikki's fight with Karait, Rikki's fight with Nag, Nagaina's threatening of Teddy, and Rikki's fight with Nagaina.

After You Read   Vocabulary Development

Clarifying Word Meanings: Contrast

Sometimes you can clarify the meaning of an unfamiliar word by looking for **contrast** clues.

A writer who uses contrast will show how a word is *unlike* another word. For example, you can get a pretty clear idea of what a *splendid* garden is if you see it contrasted with a dark, narrow hole in the ground.

> **The splendid garden glowed with roses and great clumps of waving grasses, unlike the dreary hole where cobras live.**

Be on the lookout for these words, which signal contrast: *although, but, yet, still, unlike, not, in contrast, instead, however.*

Word Bank
immensely
cowered
valiant
consolation
impotent

PRACTICE

Fill in the blanks in the following sentences with words or phrases that contrast with the underlined word. You may find it helpful to make a cluster diagram of the word and its opposites before you write, like the one below for *cowered* and *cowering:*

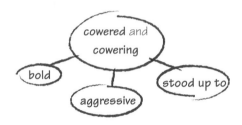

A cowering dog

An aggressive dog

1. The cobras had immense power, but the power of Darzee and the other garden creatures was _____.

2. Darzee cowered before the cobras, but Rikki _____.

3. Rikki was certainly valiant, but Chuchundra, the little muskrat, was _____.

4. The family felt consoled that Rikki was guarding their house, though they were _____ when the cobra threatened Teddy.

5. Darzee sang that the cobras were impotent in death, but they were _____ only a few hours earlier.

SKILLS FOCUS

Vocabulary Skills
Clarify word meanings by using contrast.

PRACTICE

Possible Answers
1. slight
2. stood up to them
3. a coward
4. disturbed
5. powerful

ASSESSING

Assessment
- *Holt Assessment: Literature, Reading, and Vocabulary*

RETEACHING

For a lesson reteaching plot, see **Reteaching,** p. 917B.

DIFFERENTIATING INSTRUCTION

Learners Having Difficulty
In class, have students fill in the plot diagram from the Reading Check. *Monitoring tip:* If students are unable to work out the major events of the plot have them re-read pp. 19–20, 22–23, and 25–27, looking for the answers to these questions: *Who fights whom? Who wins?* Then, have student pairs collaborate on the Extending Interpretations questions.

Writing. You might want to help students fill in plot diagrams for their stories before they begin writing their narratives at home.

HOMEWORK

Advanced Learners
Enrichment. Encourage students to consider this tale as an archetypal battle between good and evil. Discuss other monster-slaying heroes, such as Hercules, who take on difficult tasks and descend into an underworld.

Grade-Level Skills

■ **Reading Skills**

Analyze the structure and purpose of informational texts, including a textbook.

Review Skills

■ **Reading Skills**

Analyze how text features convey information.

Summary *at grade level*

This excerpt from a geography text illustrates the features found in most textbooks. These features help students locate and review information easily. This section of the textbook covers India's history from its earliest civilizations to its independence from British rule.

PRETEACHING

Selection Starter

Build background. Ask students to fill in a web showing what they already know about India. Have students use what they learned about India from reading "Rikki-tikki-tavi" as a starting point.

Assign the Reading

This analysis of textbook structure features numbered call-outs that explain aspects of a textbook. You may want to assign individual call-outs to class members to read aloud and answer the question.

Informational Text

LINK TO "RIKKI-TIKKI-TAVI"

Understanding Text Structures: A Textbook

Reading Focus
Structure and Purpose of a Textbook

The story of Rikki-tikki-tavi may have made you want to know more about India. Textbooks are one source you can go to for information on the history of India and on the culture of India today.

Textbooks have features that help you locate information and review what you have learned. Textbooks also offer photographs and artwork that can lead you to even further investigations of a subject.

■ In the next four pages are features from a geography textbook called *People, Places, and Change*. See how well you understand the structure of a textbook.

INTERNET
Interactive Reading Model
Keyword: LE5 7-1

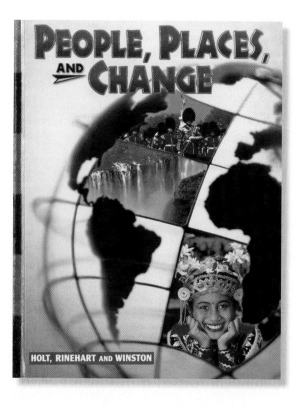

PEOPLE, PLACES, AND CHANGE

HOLT, RINEHART AND WINSTON

SKILLS FOCUS

Reading Skills
Understand the structure and purpose of a textbook.

32   Collection 1 / Facing Danger

RESOURCES: READING

Planning
■ *One-Stop Planner* CD-ROM with ExamView Test Generator

Differentiating Instruction
■ *Holt Adapted Reader*
■ *Holt Reading Solutions*
■ *Supporting Instruction in Spanish*
■ *Audio CD Library*

■ *Audio CD Library, Selections and Summaries in Spanish*

Grammar and Language
■ *Daily Language Activities*

Assessment
■ *Holt Assessment: Literature, Reading, and Vocabulary*
■ *One-Stop Planner* CD-ROM with ExamView Test Generator
■ *Holt Online Assessment*

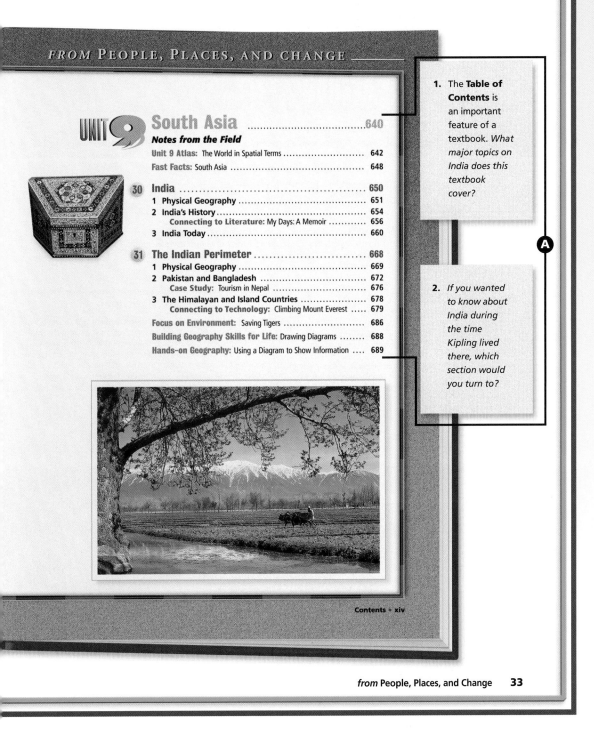

FROM PEOPLE, PLACES, AND CHANGE

UNIT 9 South Asia 640

Notes from the Field

1. The **Table of Contents** is an important feature of a textbook. *What major topics on India does this textbook cover?*

A

2. *If you wanted to know about India during the time Kipling lived there, which section would you turn to?*

Contents • xiv

from People, Places, and Change **33**

A Reading Informational Text

Structural features and purpose: Table of contents. Be sure students understand that the table of contents contains numbered unit, chapter, and section titles showing topics found on various page numbers in the textbook. Ask students why the table of contents uses different-sized heads and an outline form. [Possible response: These features make it easier to know at a glance in which unit, chapter, or section specific topics are found.]

[Possible response to question 1: The major topics on India are "Physical Geography," "India's History," and "India Today."]

[Possible response to question 2: You would turn to the section on "India's History."]

Internet

■ go.hrw.com (Keyword: LE5 7-1)

■ *Elements of Literature Online*

Media

■ *Audio CD Library*

■ *Audio CD Library, Selections and Summaries in Spanish*

A Reading Informational Text

Structural features and purpose: Section overview. Point out the headings "Reading Focus," "Key Terms," and "Key Places," and the lists of information under each. Ask students why they think those features appear here. [Possible response: These headings and lists tell the readers what the main ideas of the section are, what new words are taught, and what cities are studied.] Explain to students that each question under "Reading Focus" is tied to a major heading in the section.

[Possible response to question 3: You will find information on colonial India in the text tied to the question "How did Great Britain gain control of India?" This text is headed "The British" and appears on p. 35.]

B Reading Informational Text

Structural features: Illustrations and photographs. Tell students that textbooks rely heavily on illustrations to convey information. The photograph here is of the ancient city of Mohenjo Daro.

[Possible response to question 4: The caption is positioned just above the photograph and to the left.]

[Possible response to question 5: Mohenjo Daro is in present-day Pakistan.]

---

3. History and science books often **sum up** the focus of each chapter. *Look at the Reading Focus list. If you want information on India under British rule, will you find it in this chapter?*

4. A **caption** is text that explains the subject of an illustration. *Where can you find the caption for the photo that runs across the bottom of the page?*

5. Note the **inset,** which is a very small map showing where the subject of the photo is located. Usually a star or a circle indicates the exact location. *Is the city of Mohenjo Daro in present-day Pakistan or India?*

Section 2 India's History

Reading Focus
- What outside groups affected India's history?
- What was the Mughal Empire like?
- How did Great Britain gain control of India?
- Why was India divided when it became independent?

Key Terms
Sanskrit
sepoys
boycott

Key Places
Delhi
Calcutta
Mumbai

Coat of arms of the East India Company

You Be the Geographer

India has been invaded several times by outside groups. These groups added new customs and beliefs to India's diverse culture. Besides through invasion, how do ideas spread from country to country?

Mohenjo Daro was one of the largest cities of the Harappan civilization.

Interpreting the Visual Record How might you tell from this photo that Harappan cities were well planned?

Early Indian Civilizations

The first civilization on the Indian subcontinent was centered around the Indus River valley. Its territory was mainly in present-day Pakistan but also extended into India. Scholars call this the Harappan civilization after one of its cities, Harappa. By about 2500 B.C. the people of this civilization were living in large, well-planned cities. Scholars believe the Harappans traded with the peoples of Mesopotamia. The Harappans had a system of writing, but scholars have not been able to read it. Very little is known about Harappan religion and customs.

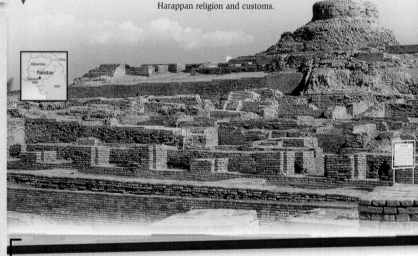

34   Collection 1 / Facing Danger

English-Language Learners

Use a brace map like the following to help students become familiar with terms for different parts of the textbook.

Parts of a Textbook

Table of Contents	Section Overview	Captions	Inset	Reading Checks and Section Review
topics and page numbers	main idea questions; terms; places to be studied	information about photographs and illustrations	small map detailing subject of photograph	questions to check comprehension and apply knowledge

The Taj Mahal is one of the most famous buildings in the world.

The British

Movement During the 1700s and 1800s the British slowly took control of India. At first this was done by the English East India Company. This company won rights to trade in the Mughal Empire in the 1600s. The East India Company first took control of small trading posts. Later the British gained more Indian territory.

Company Rule As the Mughal Empire grew weaker, the English East India Company expanded its political power. The company also built up its own military force. This army was made up mostly of **sepoys**, Indian troops commanded by British officers. The British used the strategy of backing one Indian ruler against another in exchange for cooperation. By the mid-1800s the company controlled more than half of India. The rest was divided into small states ruled by local princes.

The British changed the Indian economy to benefit British industry. India produced raw materials, including cotton, indigo—a natural dye—and jute. These materials were then shipped to Britain for use in British factories. Spices, sugar, tea, and wheat were also grown in India for export. Railroads were built to ship the raw materials to Calcutta, Bombay (now Mumbai), and other port cities. India also became a market for British manufactured goods. Indians, who had woven cotton cloth for centuries, were now forced to buy British cloth.

In September 1857, British and loyal Sikh troops stormed the gate of Delhi, defended by rebel sepoys. Bloody fighting continued until late 1858.

Interpreting the Visual Record
How did the Indian Mutiny lead to a change in the way India was governed?

6. Key ideas and terms are set in **boldface type.** The boldface terms are often defined in the text. *Is the boldface word on this page defined?*

India • 657

from People, Places, and Change **35**

C Reading Informational Text

? Structural features and purpose: Captions. Point out the caption next to the photograph of the Taj Mahal. What function does this feature serve? [Possible response: The caption provides additional information about the Taj Mahal.]

D Reading Informational Text

Structural features: Boxed text. Point out the boxed word *Movement* that appears under the heading "The British." Ask students what the word might signify. [Possible response: It signals a new invasion of people into India—the British.]

E Reading Informational Text

Structural features: Boldface terms. Point out the terms in boldface type. Remind students that this term was listed under "Key Terms" in the section overview. Discuss the importance of this term to understanding what is being taught on the page.

[Possible response to question 6: The boldface word *sepoys* is defined on this page. Sepoys were Indian troops under British officers who fought for the English East India Company.]

F Reading Informational Text

Structural features: Questions on art. Point out the question that appears under the caption for the Indian Mutiny art. Explain that students must look at the illustration, the caption, and the text to answer this query.

Advanced Learners
Enrichment. Invite students to work in small groups to make a poster illustrating the different parts of a textbook, including the title and copyright pages, glossaries, photograph and art credits, and indexes. Suggest they use both words and pictures to illustrate the parts.

from People, Places, and Change **35**

A Reading Informational Text

? Structural features: Subheads. Have students look at the subheads "Anti-British Protest" and "Gandhi and Nonviolence" under the heading "The British." Also point out the boxed word *Place*. What information might appear under these subheads? [Possible response: information about the Indian independence movement and how it was led by Gandhi, who believed in nonviolent protest strategies.]

[Possible response to question 8: The text seems factual and unbiased, but the writer seems to suggest that the British treated the Indians unfairly, and that the Indian Muslims were primarily responsible for the partition.]

B Reading Skills

Find the main idea. Ask students to state the main idea of this text copy under "Independence and Division." [Possible response: The British government granted India its independence, even though it resulted in considerable discord between the region's two main religious groups.]

GUIDED PRACTICE

Monitor students' progress. Have students work together to fill in a graphic organizer that shows the four major headings of Section 2 and the major ideas in each.

---

7. **Reading checks** are often provided to help you review what you have learned.

8. Textbooks are meant to be unbiased. When reporting controversial events, they try to present the views of all sides. India's war for independence still sparks controversy. *Do you find any bias in the writer's text here? Is the writer critical of any group?*

9. **Questions** usually conclude each section. These questions help you review what you've read; if you can't answer the questions, you need to re-read the text.

Anti-British Protest

After World War I more and more Indians began dema[nd] end of British rule. A lawyer named Mohandas K. Gandhi b[ecame] most important leader of this Indian independence moveme[nt]

Gandhi and Nonviolence *Place* Gandhi reached [out to] millions of Indian peasants. He used a strategy of nonvio[lent] protest. He called for Indians to peacefully refuse to coope[rate with] the British. Gandhi led protest marches and urged Indians to [not buy,] or refuse to buy, British goods. Many times the police use[d force] against marchers. When the British jailed Gandhi, he went [on hunger] strikes. Gandhi's determination and self-sacrifice attracted [many fol]lowers. Pressure grew on Britain to leave India.

✓ **READING CHECK:** Do you know how India came under British control?

Mohandas Gandhi was known to his followers as the Mahatma, or the "great soul."

Independence and Division

Region After World War II the British government decided [to grant] India independence. The British government and the Indian [National] Congress wanted India to become one country. However [some] Muslims demanded a separate Muslim state. Anger and fe[ar grew] between Hindus and Muslims. India seemed on the verge of c[ivil war.]

Finally, in 1947 the British divided their Indian colony [into two] independent countries, India and Pakistan. India was mostly [Hindu.] Pakistan, which then included what is today Bangladesh, wa[s mostly] Muslim. However, the new boundary left millions of Hindus in [Pakistan] and millions of Muslims in India. Masses of people rushed to [cross the] border. Hundreds of thousands were killed in rioting and pani[c.]

✓ **READING CHECK:** Do you know why India was divided when it became inde[pendent?]

Section Review 2

Define Sanskrit, sepoys, boycott

Working with Sketch Maps On the map you created in Section 1, label Delhi, Calcutta, and Mumbai. What bodies of water are important to each of these cities?

Reading for Content Understanding

1. *Region* What factors made the Mughal Empire one of the most powerful states in the world?
2. *Movement* How did the English East India Company gain control of most of India?
3. *Place* Who was the most important leader o[f] the Indian independence movement, and wha[t] was his strategy?

You Be the Geographer: **CRITICAL TH[INKING]**

4. *Movement* Why was the British colony of Ind[ia] divided into two countries?

Organizing What You Know

5. Copy the following time line. Use it to mark important events in Indian history from 2500 B.C. to A.D. 1947.

2500 B.C.   A.D. 1[947]

CROSS-CURRICULAR CONNECTIONS

History
Gandhi in India. Mohandas K. Gandhi (1869–1948) was one of the most influential leaders of the twentieth century. Although he was assassinated shortly after the British gave India its independence, Gandhi's philosophy lived on in the work of other leaders and activists.
Activity. You might encourage interested students to research how Gandhi's philosophy of nonviolent civil disobedience influenced a leader such as Martin Luther King, Jr., Cesar Chavez, Rosa Parks, Lech Walesa, Daw Aung San Suu Kyi, or Nelson Mandela.

Culture
Islam in India. While Hinduism dominates religious life in India, about 12 percent of Indians are Muslims.
Activity. Encourage students to explore the differences between the lifestyles and beliefs of Hindus and Muslims in India today.

Analyzing a Textbook

Using *Elements of Literature*

To check on how well you know the important parts of a textbook, answer the following questions by referring to the key parts of the textbook you are now using, called *Elements of Literature*.

1. The **copyright page** is in the front of the book, usually right after the main title page. Here is where you will find the date the book was published. What is the copyright date of this textbook?
   - A 2003
   - B 2004
   - C 2005
   - D 2006

2. The **table of contents** is found in the front of a textbook. According to the table of contents of this textbook, how many collections appear in the book?
   - F 5
   - G 6
   - H 7
   - J 8

3. At the back of this book is a section called **Resource Center.** Which of the following features is *not* found in this section?
   - A Index of Skills
   - B Handbook of Informational Terms
   - C Index of Maps
   - D Index of Authors and Titles

Constructed Response

4. There are many kinds of textbooks. Explain the **purpose** they all share.

5. Which features of the textbook shown on pages 33–36 do you find most useful? Why?

SKILLS FOCUS

Reading Skills
Analyze the structure and purpose of a textbook.

FAMILY/COMMUNITY ACTIVITY

Encourage students to take their textbooks home to share with family members. Tell them to explain the different parts of a textbook and the purpose of each part. Students may want to create timed contests in which family members compete to find information located in the tables of contents, indexes, and copyright pages of school textbooks.

Analyzing a Textbook

Test Practice

Answers and Model Rationales

1. **C** To find the copyright date, students need to look on the page following the title page and find the year the book was published.

2. **J** Point out to students that the table of contents lists the number of collections.

3. **C** Students should refer to the table of contents for this information.

Test-Taking Tips

Remind students that when *not* appears in an item, they should look for an answer that does not fit in with the others. Also, remind students to look at key words in the questions, such as *how, what,* and *which,* for help in choosing the correct answer.

For more instruction, refer students to **Test Smarts,** p. 920.

Constructed Response

4. All textbooks share the purpose of giving the reader information about a particular subject.

5. Possible answer: The table of contents is most useful because it directs me to a specific section that gives me the information I need.

ASSESSING

Assessment
- *Holt Assessment: Literature, Reading, and Vocabulary*

Grade-Level Skills

■ **Literary Skills**
Identify events that advance the plot and determine how each event creates suspense and fore-shadows future actions.

■ **Reading Skills**
Make predictions.

Summary 🔼 *above grade level*

This horror story begins when three lighthouse keepers realize that a derelict ship heading for their tiny island is filled with thousands of giant rats. The ship runs aground and sinks, the fam-ished rats scramble onto the island, and in time they break into the lighthouse. The besieged men struggle to stay alive. To draw the attention of people on the mainland, they do not light their lamp. Rescue ships come but are at first driven away by the human-eating rats. Later, the rescuers devise another plan. They load a barge with meat and tow it near the island. The rats swim out to the barge, the barge is set on fire, and the rats are burned or eaten by sharks. The three keepers are rescued, but one goes insane, the second dies from his infected wounds, and only the narrator is left alive to resume his service on the island of Three Skeleton Key.

Before You Read · The Short Story

Three Skeleton Key

Make the Connection
Quickwrite 🖉
Movies, TV, and books are full of horror tales that make us want to check under our beds. If you were writing a horror story, what details would you use to create a scary setting? Freewrite your ideas.

Literary Focus
Suspense and Foreshadowing
The writer of this story hooks our interest with his opening sentence: "My most terrifying experience?" Once a question like this is asked in a story, we want to know the answer. We want to know what happens next. This feeling of anxious curiosity is called **suspense.**

Writers often intensify suspense by dropping clues that hint at what might happen later in the story. This use of clues is called **foreshadowing.**

Reading Skills 🕮
Making Predictions
Part of the fun of following any **story** is trying to guess what will happen next. That process is called **making predictions.** Here's how to make

predictions on your own as you read a text:

- Look for clues that seem to **foreshadow** something that will happen.
- As the **suspense** builds, think about possible outcomes.
- Ask yourself questions as you read. Revise your predictions as you go.

Vocabulary Development
Pay attention to these words as you read the story:

hordes (hôrdz) *n.:* large, moving crowds. *The rats swam ashore in hordes.*

receding (ri·sēd′iŋ) *v.* used as *adj.:* moving back. *At first the ship came toward us, but then it drifted off in the receding waters.*

fathom (fa*th*′əm) *v.:* understand. *The lighthouse keepers couldn't fathom the rats' nasty reaction.*

edible (ed′ə·bəl) *adj.:* fit to be eaten. *The rats thought the men were edible.*

derisive (di·rī′siv) *adj.:* scornful and ridiculing. *The rats peered with derisive eyes at the terrified men.*

INTERNET
Vocabulary
Activity
•
Cross-curricular
Connection
Keyword: LE5 7-1

SKILLS FOCUS

Literary Skills
Understand suspense.

Reading Skills
Make predictions.

Background
Literature and Geography
The title of this story is the name of a *key,* or low-lying island, off the coast of French Guiana (gē·an′ə), in South America. At the time the story was written, French Guiana was a colony of France. Cayenne (kī·en′), the capital, was the site of one of the prisons that France maintained there until 1945.

38

RESOURCES: READING

Planning
■ *One-Stop Planner* CD-ROM with ExamView Test Generator

Differentiating Instruction
■ *The Holt Reader*
■ *Holt Adapted Reader*
■ *Holt Reading Solutions*
■ *Supporting Instruction in Spanish*

■ *Audio CD Library*
■ *Audio CD Library, Selections and Summaries in Spanish*

Vocabulary
■ *Vocabulary Development*

Grammar and Language
■ *Daily Language Activities*

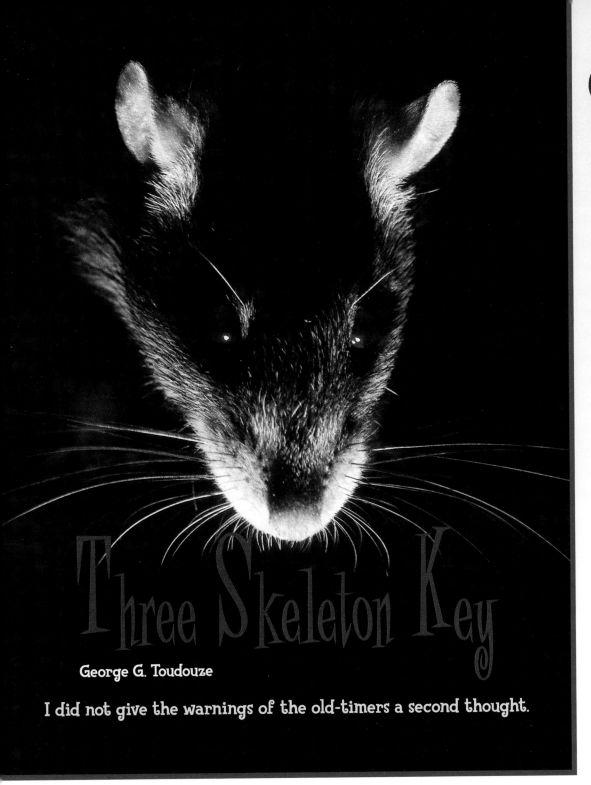

Three Skeleton Key

George G. Toudouze

I did not give the warnings of the old-timers a second thought.

Assessment
- *Holt Assessment: Literature, Reading, and Vocabulary*
- *One-Stop Planner* CD-ROM with ExamView Test Generator
- *Holt Online Assessment*

Internet
- go.hrw.com (Keyword: LE5 7-1)
- *Elements of Literature Online*

Media
- *Audio CD Library*
- *Audio CD Library, Selections and Summaries in Spanish*
- *Fine Art Transparencies*

Selection Starter

Motivate. The story begins with "My most terrifying experience?" Ask students what their most terrifying experience would entail. After listing on the chalkboard a number of specific terrors, ask students to complete the Quickwrite activity.

Preview Vocabulary

To build students' familiarity with the Vocabulary words introduced on p. 38, have pairs of students fill in the words that are missing from the following mini-story.

1. "Oh, no!" exclaimed the worker at Burger-Rama. " _____ of hungry students are heading this way." [Hordes]

2. "I just can't _____ their appetites," said the manager. [fathom]

3. One student made a _____ remark about the poor quality of the food. "Don't you have anything _____?" he complained. [derisive, edible]

4. At last, all of the students were served, and the crowd began to _____. [recede]

DIRECT TEACHING

A Reading Skills

Predict. Have students look at the illustration on p. 39 and point out the word *skeleton* in the title. Then, have them read the first two paragraphs. Ask them to make a prediction about the story by filling in the blanks in this sentence: "It will be a _____ story about _____ set in _____." [Possible response: It will be a terrifying story about rats set in an isolated lighthouse.]

B Literary Focus

❓ Foreshadowing. In what way might the story of the three convicts hint at what's going to happen in this story? [Possible response: Their deaths show the difficulty of surviving on the isolated island; the story might be about survival.]

C Vocabulary Development

Clarify word meanings: Example. Point out the word *provisions.* Tell students that provisions for the three men might include flour, meat, coffee, water, and matches. Ask them to suggest a meaning for *provisions.* [food and other necessary supplies]

My most terrifying experience? Well, one does have a few in thirty-five years of service in the Lights, although it's mostly monotonous, routine work—keeping the light in order, making out the reports.

When I was a young man, not very long in the service, there was an opening in a lighthouse newly built off the coast of Guiana, on a small rock twenty miles or so from the mainland. The pay was high, so in order to reach the sum I had set out to save before I married, I volunteered for service in the new light.

Three Skeleton Key, the small rock on which the light stood, bore a bad reputation. It earned its name from the story of the three convicts who, escaping from Cayenne in a stolen dugout canoe, were wrecked on the rock during the night, managed to escape the sea, but eventually died of hunger and thirst. When they were discovered, nothing remained but three heaps of bones, picked clean by the birds. The story was that the three skeletons, gleaming with phosphorescent[1] light, danced over the small rock, screaming. . . .

But there are many such stories and I did not give the warnings of the old-timers at the *Île-de-Seine*[2] a second thought. I signed up, boarded ship, and in a month I was installed at the light.

Picture a gray, tapering cylinder,[3] welded to the solid black rock by iron rods and concrete, rising from a small island twenty-odd miles from land. It lay in the midst of the sea, this island, a small, bare piece of stone, about one hundred fifty feet long, perhaps forty wide. Small, barely large enough for a man to walk about and stretch his legs at low tide.

This is an advantage one doesn't find in all lights, however, for some of them rise sheer from the waves, with no room for one to move save within the light itself. Still, on our island, one must be careful, for the rocks were treacherously smooth. One misstep and down you would fall into the sea—not that the risk of drowning was so great, but the waters about our island swarmed with huge sharks, who kept an eternal patrol around the base of the light.

Still, it was a nice life there. We had enough provisions to last for months, in the event that the sea should become too rough for the supply ship to reach us on schedule. During the day we would work about the light, cleaning the rooms, polishing the metalwork and the lens and reflector of the light itself, and at night we would sit on the gallery and watch our light, a twenty-thousand-candlepower lantern, swinging its strong white bar of light over the sea from the top of its hundred-twenty-foot tower. Some days, when the air would be very clear, we could see the land, a threadlike line to the west. To the east, north, and south stretched the ocean. Landsmen, perhaps, would soon have tired of that kind of life, perched on a small island off the coast of South America

---

1. **phosphorescent** (fäs′fə·res′ənt) *adj.:* glowing.
2. **Île-de-Seine** (ēl′ də sen′).

3. **tapering cylinder:** tube shape that gradually narrows toward one end; in this case, toward the top.

DIFFERENTIATING INSTRUCTION

Learners Having Difficulty
Modeling. Making predictions can help students focus on details that contribute to the suspense and foreshadow future events. Model making predictions by saying: "Based on the title, I think the lighthouse keepers in this story will die." Then, have students read on to confirm or refute this prediction. As they read, encourage students to ask themselves, "What might happen next?"

English-Language Learners
Be sure students understand that the *key* of the title refers not to an instrument for unlocking doors but to a low island or reef. Tell them that the word is sometimes spelled *cay* (*cayo* in Spanish). Display pictures of lighthouses and sailing ships to help students visualize the setting.

for eighteen weeks until one's turn for leave ashore came around. But we liked it there, my two fellow tenders and myself—so much so that for twenty-two months on end, with the exception of shore leaves, I was greatly satisfied with the life on Three Skeleton Key.

I had just returned from my leave at the end of June, that is to say, midwinter in that latitude, and had settled down to the routine with my two fellow keepers, a Breton[4] by the name of Le Gleo and the head keeper, Itchoua, a Basque[5] some dozen years or so older than either of us.

Eight days went by as usual; then on the ninth night after my return, Itchoua, who was on night duty, called Le Gleo and me, sleeping in our rooms in the middle of the tower, at two in the morning. We rose immediately and, climbing the thirty or so steps that led to the gallery, stood beside our chief.

Itchoua pointed, and following his finger, we saw a big three-master, with all sail set, heading straight for the light. A queer course, for the vessel must have seen us; our light lit her with the glare of day each time it passed over her.

Now, ships were a rare sight in our waters, for our light was a warning of treacherous reefs, barely hidden under the surface and running far out to sea. Consequently we were always given a wide berth, especially by sailing vessels, which cannot maneuver as readily as steamers.

No wonder that we were surprised at seeing this three-master heading dead for us in the gloom of early morning. I had immediately recognized her lines, for she stood out

plainly, even at the distance of a mile, when our light shone on her.

She was a beautiful ship of some four thousand tons, a fast sailer that had carried cargoes to every part of the world, plowing the seas unceasingly. By her lines she was identified as Dutch built, which was understandable, as Paramaribo and Dutch Guiana are very close to Cayenne.

Watching her sailing dead for us, a white wave boiling under her bows, Le Gleo cried out:

"What's wrong with her crew? Are they all drunk or insane? Can't they see us?"

Itchoua nodded soberly and looked at us sharply as he remarked: "See us? No doubt—if there *is* a crew aboard!"

"What do you mean, chief?" Le Gleo had started, turned to the Basque. "Are you saying that she's the *Flying Dutchman*?"[6]

His sudden fright had been so evident that the older man laughed:

"No, old man, that's not what I meant. If I say that no one's aboard, I mean she's a derelict."[7]

Then we understood her queer behavior. Itchoua was right. For some reason, believing her doomed, her crew had abandoned her. Then she had righted herself and sailed on, wandering with the wind.

The three of us grew tense as the ship seemed about to crash on one of our numerous reefs, but she suddenly lurched with some change of the wind, the yards[8] swung around, and the derelict came clumsily about and sailed dead away from us.

---

4. **Breton** (bret′n): person from Brittany, a region of northern France.
5. **Basque** (bask): Basques are people living in the Pyrenees, a mountain range in France and Spain.

6. *Flying Dutchman:* fabled Dutch ghost ship whose captain is said to be condemned to sail the seas until Judgment Day. Seeing the *Flying Dutchman* is supposed to bring bad luck.
7. **derelict** (der′ə·likt′) *n.:* here, abandoned ship.
8. **yards** *n.:* in nautical terms, rods fastened across the masts to support the sails.

A Literary Focus

❓ Suspense. How does the author increase the reader's tension and anxiety in this part of the story? [Possible responses: He stretches out the action, letting the derelict ship zigzag back and forth, toward the island and then away; he makes the characters speculate about why the perfectly intact ship was abandoned. As a result, readers wonder what will happen next.]

VIEWING THE ART

The Belgian surrealist painter **René Magritte** (1898–1967) is sometimes described as a "magical realist" because of his seamless, eerie melding of the ordinary and the bizarre. Magritte gravitated toward surrealism after viewing a painting by the Italian artist Giorgio de Chirico. In *Le Séducteur,* the gauzy, distant image of a ship looms on the horizon.

Activity. The English translation of the title is the "The Seducer." Ask students why they think Magritte gave his work that title. Does the ship appear real or does it appear to be an illusion? Do students sense a connection between the picture and the *Cornelius de Witt* (the ship described on this page and named on p. 43)?

Le Séducteur by René Magritte. Oil on canvas (19" × 23").

Virginia Museum of Fine Arts, Richmond, Virginia. Collection of Mr. and Mrs. Paul Mellon. Photograph by Ron Jennings. © 2000 Virginia Museum of Fine Arts. © 2003 C. Herscovici, Brussels/Artists Rights Society (ARS), New York.

In the light of our lantern she seemed so sound, so strong, that Itchoua exclaimed impatiently:

A "But why the devil was she abandoned? Nothing is smashed, no sign of fire—and she doesn't sail as if she were taking water."

Le Gleo waved to the departing ship:

"Bon voyage!" he smiled at Itchoua and went on. "She's leaving us, chief, and now we'll never know what—"

"No, she's not!" cried the Basque. "Look! She's turning!"

As if obeying his words, the derelict three-master stopped, came about, and headed for us once more. And for the next four hours the vessel played around us— zigzagging, coming about, stopping, then suddenly lurching forward. No doubt some freak of current and wind, of which our island was the center, kept her near us.

CROSS-CURRICULAR CONNECTIONS

History
Lighthouses. For centuries, lighthouses have been used to alert sailors that land is near, to point out dangerous rocks and reefs, and to cast a bright light into the night to guide ships safely into port. Seafarers have relied on these structures since the days of ancient Egypt. The lighthouse built in 300 B.C. on Pharos, an island near Alexandria, was regarded as one of the Seven Wonders of the World.

Today most lighthouses are fully automated and do not require keepers like the men in the story. Before the machine age, however, tending a lighthouse was a difficult and vital job. Lighthouses in the early United States used whale oil–burning wick lamps that made lots of smoke. If the lamps were left unattended, their glass panes would soon be covered with so much dark soot that no light could get through them. A lighthouse keeper spent a typical night cleaning glass (often on more than one lamp), filling lamps with oil (two or three times a night), and trimming burnt wicks.

Then suddenly the tropic dawn broke, the sun rose, and it was day, and the ship was plainly visible as she sailed past us. Our light extinguished, we returned to the gallery with our glasses[9] and inspected her.

The three of us focused our glasses on her poop[10] and saw, standing out sharply, black letters on the white background of a life ring, the stenciled name "*Cornelius de Witt,* Rotterdam."

We had read her lines correctly: She was Dutch. Just then the wind rose and the *Cornelius de Witt* changed course, leaned to port, and headed straight for us once more. But this time she was so close that we knew she would not turn in time.

"Thunder!" cried Le Gleo, his Breton soul aching at seeing a fine ship doomed to smash upon a reef, "she's going to pile up! She's gone!"

I shook my head:

"Yes, and a shame to see that beautiful ship wreck herself. And we're helpless."

There was nothing we could do but watch. A ship sailing with all sail spread, creaming the sea with her forefoot as she runs before the wind, is one of the most beautiful sights in the world—but this time I could feel the tears stinging in my eyes as I saw this fine ship headed for her doom.

All this time our glasses were riveted on her and we suddenly cried out together:

"The rats!"

Now we knew why this ship, in perfect condition, was sailing without her crew aboard. They had been driven out by the rats. Not those poor specimens of rats you see ashore, barely reaching the length of one foot from their trembling noses to the tip of their skinny tails, wretched creatures that dodge and hide at the mere sound of a footfall.

No, these were ships' rats, huge, wise creatures, born on the sea, sailing all over the world on ships, transferring to other, larger ships as they multiply. There is as much difference between the rats of the land and these maritime rats as between a fishing smack[11] and an armored cruiser.

The rats of the sea are fierce, bold animals. Large, strong, and intelligent, clannish and seawise, able to put the best of mariners to shame with their knowledge of the sea, their uncanny ability to foretell the weather.

And they are brave, these rats, and vengeful. If you so much as harm one, his sharp cry will bring hordes of his fellows to swarm over you, tear you, and not cease until your flesh has been stripped from the bones.

The ones on this ship, the rats of Holland, are the worst, superior to other rats of the sea as their brethren are to the land rats. There is a well-known tale about these animals.

A Dutch captain, thinking to protect his cargo, brought aboard his ship not cats but two terriers, dogs trained in the hunting, fighting, and killing of vicious rats. By the time the ship, sailing from Rotterdam, had passed the Ostend light, the dogs were gone and never seen again. In twenty-four hours they had been overwhelmed, killed, and eaten by the rats.

At times, when the cargo does not suffice,[12] the rats attack the crew, either

---

9. **glasses** *n.:* here, binoculars.
10. **poop** *n.:* in nautical terms, the stern (back) deck of a ship.
11. **smack** *n.:* here, small sailboat.
12. **suffice** (sə·fīs′) *v.:* provide enough.

Vocabulary
hordes (hôrdz) *n.:* large, moving crowds.

B Cross-curricular Connections
CULTURE

Brittany. A Breton comes from Brittany, a peninsula on the northern coast of France where the culture has historically been fishing-based. A Breton soul, therefore, would have a special feeling for ships.

C Reading Skills

? Predict. What do you think the rest of the story will be about? [Students will probably predict that the rest of the story will be about the men's attempts to fight or outsmart the rats, or to get off the island safely.]

D Literary Focus

? Foreshadowing. In what way might the story about the two dogs hint at the main conflict of this story? [Possible responses: The story suggests that rats are formidable foes. The main conflict will probably be between the men and the rats.]

❓ Draw conclusions. What do you conclude has happened to the ship's crew? What evidence supports your conclusion? [Possible response: The rats ate the crew. It is stated that hungry rats will attack a crew and either drive them from a ship or eat them. The lifeboats are still on the ship. Since the crew did not escape in lifeboats, the rats must have eaten the crew.]

B Advanced Learners

Enrichment. Encourage students to label a diagram of a ship with the following terms and explain their meanings to the class: *port, starboard, bow, stern.*

C Literary Focus

❓ Suspense. As this paragraph progresses, what questions are raised in readers' minds to build suspense? [Possible responses: Will the rats make it to the shore? What will the rats do when they reach shore? Will the rats get into the tower?]

D Literary Focus

❓ Imagery. What sensory images does the narrator use in order to vividly convey the horror of the situation? [Possible responses: *Sight*— swarmed, covered, filling, piling, gleaming, beady eyes, sharp claws and teeth, horde. *Sound*—scraped, grated. *Smell*—poisoned our lungs, rasped our nostrils, pestilential, nauseating smell. *Touch*—furry mantle, sharp claws and teeth, sealed alive.]

driving them from the ship or eating them alive. And studying the *Cornelius de Witt*, I turned sick, for her small boats were all in place. She had not been abandoned.

Over her bridge, on her deck, in the rigging, on every visible spot, the ship was a writhing mass—a starving army coming toward us aboard a vessel gone mad!

Our island was a small spot in that immense stretch of sea. The ship could have grazed us or passed to port or starboard with its ravening[13] cargo—but no, she came for us at full speed, as if she were leading the regatta at a race, and impaled herself on a sharp point of rock.

There was a dull shock as her bottom stove in,[14] then a horrible crackling as the three masts went overboard at once, as if cut down with one blow of some gigantic sickle. A sighing groan came as the water rushed into the ship; then she split in two and sank like a stone.

But the rats did not drown. Not these fellows! As much at home in the sea as any fish, they formed ranks in the water, heads lifted, tails stretched out, paws paddling. And half of them, those from the forepart of the ship, sprang along the masts and onto the rocks in the instant before she sank. Before we had time even to move, nothing remained of the three-master save some pieces of wreckage floating on the surface and an army of rats covering the rocks left bare by the receding tide.

Thousands of heads rose, felt the wind, and we were scented, seen! To them we were fresh meat, after possible weeks of starving.

13. **ravening** (rav'ən·iŋ) *adj.:* greedily searching for animals to kill for food. A more common related word is *ravenous* (rav'ə·nəs), meaning "wildly, greedily hungry."
14. **stove in:** caved in.

There came a scream, composed of innumerable screams, sharper than the howl of a saw attacking a bar of iron, and in the one motion, every rat leaped to attack the tower!

We barely had time to leap back, close the door leading onto the gallery, descend the stairs, and shut every window tightly. Luckily the door at the base of the light, which we never could have reached in time, was of bronze set in granite and was tightly closed.

The horrible band, in no measurable time, had swarmed up and over the tower as if it had been a tree, piled on the embrasures[15] of the windows, scraped at the glass with thousands of claws, covered the lighthouse with a furry mantle, and reached the top of the tower, filling the gallery and piling atop the lantern.

Their teeth grated as they pressed against the glass of the lantern room, where they could plainly see us, though they could not reach us. A few millimeters of glass, luckily very strong, separated our faces from their gleaming, beady eyes, their sharp claws and teeth. Their odor filled the tower, poisoned our lungs, and rasped our nostrils with a pestilential, nauseating smell. And there we were, sealed alive in our own light, prisoners of a horde of starving rats.

That first night, the tension was so great

15. **embrasures** (em·brā'ʒhərz) *n.:* slanted openings.

Vocabulary
receding (ri·sēd'iŋ) *v.:* used as *adj.:* moving back.

Activity. The story is full of suspenseful moments. Group students in pairs. Have each pair choose one suspenseful moment and take turns reading that passage aloud to each other, using their voices to convey the suspense.

PAIRED

that we could not sleep. Every moment, we felt that some opening had been made, some window given way, and that our horrible besiegers were pouring through the breach. The rising tide, chasing those of the rats which had stayed on the bare rocks, increased the numbers clinging to the walls, piled on the balcony—so much so that clusters of rats clinging to one another hung from the lantern and the gallery.

With the coming of darkness we lit the light and the turning beam completely maddened the beasts. As the light turned, it successively blinded thousands of rats crowded against the glass, while the dark side of the lantern room gleamed with thousands of points of light, burning like the eyes of jungle beasts in the night.

All the while we could hear the enraged scraping of claws against the stone and glass, while the chorus of cries was so loud that we had to shout to hear one another. From time to time, some of the rats fought among themselves and a dark cluster would detach itself, falling into the sea like a ripe fruit from a tree. Then we would see phosphorescent streaks as triangular fins slashed the water—sharks, permanent guardians of our rock, feasting on our jailers.

The next day we were calmer and amused ourselves teasing the rats, placing our faces against the glass which separated us. They could not fathom the invisible barrier which separated them from us, and we laughed as we watched them leaping against the heavy glass.

But the day after that, we realized how serious our position was. The air was foul; even the heavy smell of oil within our stronghold could not dominate the fetid odor of the beasts massed around us. And there was no way of admitting fresh air without also admitting the rats.

The morning of the fourth day, at early dawn, I saw the wooden framework of my window, eaten away from the outside, sagging inwards. I called my comrades and the three of us fastened a sheet of tin in the opening, sealing it tightly. When we had completed that task, Itchoua turned to us and said dully:

"Well—the supply boat came thirteen days ago, and she won't be back for twenty-nine." He pointed at the white metal plate sealing the opening through the granite. "If that gives way"—he shrugged—"they can change the name of this place to Six Skeleton Key."

The next six days and seven nights, our only distraction was watching the rats whose holds were insecure fall a hundred and twenty feet into the maws of the sharks—but they were so many that we could not see any diminution in their numbers.

Thinking to calm ourselves and pass the time, we attempted to count them, but we soon gave up. They moved incessantly, never still. Then we tried identifying them, naming them.

One of them, larger than the others, who seemed to lead them in their rushes against the glass separating us, we named "Nero";[16] and there were several others whom we had learned to distinguish through various peculiarities.

But the thought of our bones joining those of the convicts was always in the back

---

16. **Nero** (nēr′ō): emperor of Rome (A.D. 54–68) known for his cruelty.

Vocabulary
fathom (fa*th*′əm) *v.:* understand.

DIRECT TEACHING

E **Reading Skills**

❓ **Predict.** Do you think the rats will eventually get into the lighthouse? Explain why or why not. [Possible responses: The author will devise a way for the rats to get in to make the story more exciting; the rats will not get in but the author will find some other way to build suspense.]

F **Vocabulary Development**
Clarify word meanings: Example. Point out the word *fetid.* Explain that a dead animal left in an enclosed place would produce a fetid odor. Ask students to suggest definitions for *fetid.* [decaying, stinking]

G **Literary Focus**

❓ **Foreshadowing.** The rats have gnawed at the wooden window frame enough to make it sag inward. What hint does this give you about future events? [Possible response: If the rats have succeeded in making the window frame sag, they will probably succeed in getting into the tower.]

H **Learners Having Difficulty**
Ask questions. To help students understand the meaning of Itchoua's statement, ask them to recall why the island was named Three Skeleton Key. [Three escaped prisoners died there.] Then, ask them what would cause the island's name to be changed to Six Skeleton Key. [Three more people dying there.] Finally, ask them what Itchoua is suggesting will happen if the metal plate gives way. [The three lighthouse keepers will die.]

Three Skeleton Key   45

DIRECT TEACHING

Ⓐ Literary Focus

Foreshadowing. Tell students that the word *maniacal* is the adjective derived from the noun *maniac.* Ask them what this word might foreshadow about Le Gleo's future. [Possible response: Le Gleo may go mad from the strain.]

Ⓑ Reading Skills

❷ Predict. How might the men signal to the mainland that something is wrong on the island without going out on the gallery? [Possible responses: The men might set a fire to attract the attention of passing ships; they might use the light to send a message in Morse code; they might turn off the lighthouse lamp.]

Ⓒ Reading Skills

❷ Make judgments. Were the men justified in committing this "breach" of their service? [Possible responses: Some students may say the men were justified because if they didn't save themselves, eventually there would be no one to light the lamp. Others may say that they are ethically bound to safeguard the lives of sailors on passing ships, even if it means dying in the line of duty.]

of our minds. And the gloom of our prison fed these thoughts, for the interior of the light was almost completely dark, as we had had to seal every window in the same fashion as mine, and the only space that still admitted daylight was the glassed-in lantern room at the very top of the tower.

Then Le Gleo became morose and had nightmares in which he would see the three skeletons dancing around him, gleaming coldly, seeking to grasp him. His maniacal, raving descriptions were so vivid that Itchoua and I began seeing them also.

It was a living nightmare, the raging cries of the rats as they swarmed over the light, mad with hunger; the sickening, strangling odor of their bodies—

True, there is a way of signaling from lighthouses. But to reach the mast on which to hang the signal, we would have to go out on the gallery where the rats were.

There was only one thing left to do. After debating all of the ninth day, we decided not to light the lantern that night. This is the greatest breach of our service, never committed as long as the tenders of the light are alive; for the light is something sacred, warning ships of danger in the night. Either the light gleams a quarter-hour after sundown, or no one is left alive to light it.

Well, that night, Three Skeleton Light was dark, and all the men were alive. At the risk of causing ships to crash on our reefs, we left it unlit, for we were worn out—going mad!

At two in the morning, while Itchoua was dozing in his room, the sheet of metal sealing his window gave way. The chief had just time enough to leap to his feet and cry for help, the rats swarming over him.

46 Collection 1 / Facing Danger

MINI-LESSON Reading

Developing Word-Attack Skills
Remind students of the mnemonic: *When two vowels go a-walking, the first one does the talking.* This mnemonic pertains to two-vowel spellings of long vowel sounds: *ai* for long *a; ea* for long *e; oa* for long *o.* Ask students to locate words in "Three Skeleton Key" that illustrate the mnemonic. Examples include *mainland* and *remained* on p. 40;

heaps on p. 40 and *unceasingly* on p. 41; *boats* on p. 44 and *approach* on p. 48.

Explain that sometimes when two vowels appear together in a word, each vowel has its own sound. Usually this occurs in longer, multisyllabic words, but there are examples in short words, too, such as *liar* and *neon.* Write these two words from the selection on the board: *defiance, nauseating.* Pronounce

But Le Gleo and I, who had been watching from the lantern room, got to him immediately, and the three of us battled with the horde of maddened rats which flowed through the gaping window. They bit, we struck them down with our knives—and retreated.

We locked the door of the room on them, but before we had time to bind our wounds, the door was eaten through and gave way, and we retreated up the stairs, fighting off the rats that leaped on us from the knee-deep swarm.

I do not remember, to this day, how we ever managed to escape. All I can remember is wading through them up the stairs, striking them off as they swarmed over us; and then we found ourselves, bleeding from innumerable bites, our clothes shredded, sprawled across the trapdoor in the floor of the lantern room—without food or drink. Luckily, the trapdoor was metal, set into the granite with iron bolts.

The rats occupied the entire light beneath us, and on the floor of our retreat lay some twenty of their fellows, who had gotten in with us before the trapdoor closed and whom we had killed with our knives. Below us, in the tower, we could hear the screams of the rats as they devoured

everything edible that they found. Those on the outside squealed in reply and writhed in a horrible curtain as they stared at us through the glass of the lantern room.

Itchoua sat up and stared silently at his blood trickling from the wounds on his limbs and body and running in thin streams **D** on the floor around him. Le Gleo, who was in as bad a state (and so was I, for that matter), stared at the chief and me vacantly, started as his gaze swung to the multitude of rats against the glass, then suddenly began laughing horribly:

"Hee! Hee! The Three Skeletons! Hee! Hee! The Three Skeletons are now *six* **E** skeletons! *Six* skeletons!"

He threw his head back and howled, his eyes glazed, a trickle of saliva running from the corners of his mouth and thinning the blood flowing over his chest. I shouted to him to shut up, but he did not hear me, so I did the only thing I could to quiet him—I swung the back of my hand across his face.

The howling stopped suddenly, and his eyes swung around the room; then he bowed his head and began weeping softly, like a child.

Our darkened light had been noticed from the mainland, and as dawn was breaking, the patrol was there to investigate the failure of our light. Looking through my binoculars, I could see the horrified expression on the **F** faces of the officers and crew when, the daylight strengthening, they saw the light completely covered by a seething mass of rats. They thought, as I afterwards found out, that we had been eaten alive.

But the rats had also seen the ship or had scented the crew. As the ship drew nearer, a

---

Vocabulary
edible (ed′ə·bəl) *adj.:* fit to be eaten.

Three Skeleton Key **47**

---

them, and point out the vowel pair in each word that stands for two distinct vowel sounds: *ia* in *defiance* and *ea* in *nauseating.*
Activity. Write these sentences on the chalkboard. Have volunteers read each sentence and underline the word that has two vowels in sequence representing two-vowel sounds.

1. The men toiled in a <u>heroic</u> effort to turn back the invading rats.

2. The rat's eyes gleamed <u>diabolically</u>.
3. Fear and disgust worked together to <u>create</u> panic.
4. The tension mounted in the <u>interior</u> of the lighthouse.
5. A <u>maniacal</u> scream cut the air.

A Literary Focus

② Character. What qualities of Itchoua's character increase the chance that the men will survive? [Possible response: He is quick-thinking and remains calm in difficult situations. Even when wounded, he thinks to use the light to send a signal in Morse code.]

B Reading Skills

② Predict. What might the ship's crew members do to rescue the lighthouse keepers? [Possible responses: They might use guns, fire, explosives, or poison to get rid of the rats.]

C Literary Focus

② Suspense. What makes this a suspenseful part of the story? [Possible response: The ship's crew has already battled the rats unsuccessfully and has been forced to retreat. The reader wonders anxiously whether the rescue ship will return with a more effective way to fight the rats.]

solid phalanx[17] left the light, plunged into the water, and swimming out, attempted to board her. They would have succeeded, as the ship was hove to;[18] but the engineer connected his steam to a hose on the deck and scalded the head of the attacking column, which slowed them up long enough for the ship to get under way and leave the rats behind.

Then the sharks took part. Belly up, mouths gaping, they arrived in swarms and scooped up the rats, sweeping through them like a sickle through wheat. That was one day that sharks really served a useful purpose.

The remaining rats turned tail, swam to the shore, and emerged dripping. As they neared the light, their comrades greeted them with shrill cries, with what sounded like a derisive note predominating. They answered angrily and mingled with their fellows. From the several tussles that broke out, it seemed as if they resented being ridiculed for their failure to capture the ship.

But all this did nothing to get us out of our jail. The small ship could not approach but steamed around the light at a safe distance, and the tower must have seemed fantastic, some weird, many-mouthed beast hurling defiance at them.

Finally, seeing the rats running in and out of the tower through the door and the windows, those on the ship decided that we had perished and were about to leave when Itchoua, regaining his senses, thought of using the light as a signal. He lit it and, using a plank placed and withdrawn before the beam to form the dots and dashes, quickly

---

17. **phalanx** (fā′laŋks′) *n.:* closely packed group. A phalanx is an ancient military formation, and the word still has warlike connotations.
18. **hove to:** stopped by being turned into the wind.

sent out our story to those on the vessel.

Our reply came quickly. When they understood our position—how we could not get rid of the rats, Le Gleo's mind going fast, Itchoua and myself covered with bites, cornered in the lantern room without food or water—they had a signalman send us their reply.

His arms swinging like those of a windmill, he quickly spelled out:

"Don't give up, hang on a little longer! We'll get you out of this!"

Then she turned and steamed at top speed for the coast, leaving us little reassured.

She was back at noon, accompanied by the supply ship, two small coast guard boats, and the fireboat—a small squadron. At twelve-thirty the battle was on.

After a short reconnaissance,[19] the fireboat picked her way slowly through the reefs until she was close to us, then turned her powerful jet of water on the rats. The heavy stream tore the rats from their places and hurled them screaming into the water, where the sharks gulped them down. But for every ten that were dislodged, seven swam ashore, and the stream could do nothing to the rats within the tower. Furthermore, some of them, instead of returning to the rocks, boarded the fireboat, and the men were forced to battle them hand to hand. They were true rats of Holland, fearing no man, fighting for the right to live!

Nightfall came, and it was as if nothing had been done; the rats were still in possession. One of the patrol boats stayed by the island; the rest of the flotilla[20] departed for

---

19. **reconnaissance** (ri·kän′ə·səns) *n.:* exploratory survey or examination.
20. **flotilla** (flō·til′ə) *n.:* small fleet of boats.

Vocabulary
derisive (di·rī′siv) *adj.:* scornful and ridiculing.

History
Morse code. Long before there were two-way radios, telephones, or e-mail, the most efficient way to communicate across distances was by telegraph, using Morse code to transmit signals along wires. The code is made up of dots (short signals), dashes (long signals), and spaces (pauses). The most well-known example of Morse code is the distress signal

SOS (three dots, three dashes, three dots), used especially by ships in trouble at sea.
Activity. Ask volunteers to find out more about Morse code and about other methods of sending signals at sea, and to demonstrate them for the class.

INDIVIDUAL

the coast. We had to spend another night in our prison. Le Gleo was sitting on the floor, babbling about skeletons, and as I turned to Itchoua, he fell unconscious from his wounds. I was in no better shape and could feel my blood flaming with fever.

Somehow the night dragged by, and the next afternoon I saw a tug, accompanied by the fireboat, come from the mainland with a huge barge in tow. Through my glasses, I saw that the barge was filled with meat.

Risking the treacherous reefs, the tug dragged the barge as close to the island as possible. To the last rat, our besiegers deserted the rock, swam out, and boarded the barge reeking with the scent of freshly cut meat. The tug dragged the barge about a mile from shore, where the fireboat drenched the barge with gasoline. A well-placed incendiary shell from the patrol boat set her on fire.

The barge was covered with flames immediately, and the rats took to the water in swarms, but the patrol boat bombarded them with shrapnel from a safe distance, and the sharks finished off the survivors.

A whaleboat from the patrol boat took us off the island and left three men to replace us. By nightfall we were in the hospital in Cayenne. What became of my friends?

Well, Le Gleo's mind had cracked and he was raving mad. They sent him back to France and locked him up in an asylum, the poor devil! Itchoua died within a week; a rat's bite is dangerous in that hot, humid climate, and infection sets in rapidly.

As for me—when they fumigated the light and repaired the damage done by the rats, I resumed my service there. Why not? No reason why such an incident should keep me from finishing out my service there, is there?

Besides—I told you I liked the place—to be truthful, I've never had a post as pleasant as that one, and when my time came to leave it forever, I tell you that I almost wept as Three Skeleton Key disappeared below the horizon.

Meet the Writer

George G. Toudouze

Sea Fever

George G. Toudouze (1847–1904) was born in France and grew up to develop many literary interests—he was a playwright, an essayist, and an illustrator. He also had a great interest in the sea and worked on a history of the French navy. One critic says of his storytelling style, "It has the impact of a powerful man at the fair who, for the fun of it, takes the hammer and at one blow sends the machine to the top, rings the bell, and walks off."

"Three Skeleton Key" was first published in *Esquire,* a magazine that once was famous for its macho adventure stories. The map on page 50 shows the setting of "Three Skeleton Key."

FAMILY/COMMUNITY ACTIVITY

Encourage students and their families to use the basic plot of "Three Skeleton Key" as a starting point for their own horror story. The student can bring home a short summary of how the story begins. It might be as simple as the fact that three lighthouse keepers are alone on a small island. It might go as far as the appearance of the ship or even the men's realization that rats are onboard.

After the student provides the opening, family members take turns adding to the plot until some resolution is reached. The student can then summarize the actual plot for the family.

DIRECT TEACHING

D Reading Skills

? Predict. The men have gone two days without food. Do you now predict that they will survive? [Possible responses: Rescue seems so close that perhaps they can still make it, although they may eventually go insane or die from infected wounds. Some students may realize that the narrator, at least, must survive in order to tell the story.]

GUIDED PRACTICE

Monitor students' progress. Guide students in answering these comprehension questions. Then, direct them to locate passages in the text that support their answers.

True-False

1. "Three Skeleton Key" is about one man's most humiliating experience. [F]
2. Three Skeleton Key is an island where three escaped prisoners died of thirst and hunger. [T]
3. The rats onboard the drifting ship were very similar to land rats. [F]
4. The men decided to leave the lighthouse unlit as a signal to the mainland. [T]
5. Only one man was left alive when the rescuers arrived. [F]

Meet the Writer

"Three Skeleton Key" became widely known in the 1950s when it was adapted as a radio drama, performed live with the famed horror actor Vincent Price as the narrator.

For Independent Reading

For an entirely different view of an attempt to get rid of rats, students might read Robert Browning's poem "The Pied Piper of Hamelin."

After You Read

First Thoughts

1. Possible Answers
   - When I first read about the rats, I felt <u>scared, sick, uneasy, intrigued</u>.
   - For me the scariest part of the story was <u>when the rats broke into the lighthouse and attacked the men</u>.

Thinking Critically

2. Possible answer: The legend involves three men who die of hunger and thirst on the isolated island. Their fate hints at the life-threatening situation the three lighthouse keepers will face with the rats.

3. It makes the men seem vulnerable and makes readers wonder how soon the rats will break in. Other details include the sounds of the rats' cries and their scraping claws; the men's decision not to light the lantern; and the metal seal giving way in Itchoua's window.

4. The narrator, who remains calm, survives and goes back to work on the island. Le Gleo, who becomes depressed and has nightmares, goes insane and ends up in an asylum. Itchoua, who reveals a negative outlook when he mentions renaming the island, dies of rat bites.

Extending Interpretations

5. Possible answers: I knew the men would survive once the rescue ship arrived and the crew realized the men were trapped; or once the barge filled with meat was on the scene; or once the barge was drenched with gasoline.

After You Read Response and Analysis

First Thoughts

1. Describe your reaction to "Three Skeleton Key" by completing these sentences:
   - When I first read about the rats, I felt . . .
   - For me the scariest part of the story was . . .

Thinking Critically

2. Early in the story the narrator explains how Three Skeleton Key got its name. How does this **foreshadow**—or hint at—the danger the three lighthouse keepers will face later on?

3. On the fourth day of the invasion, a wooden window frame in the lighthouse sags inward. How does this incident increase **suspense**? What other details create suspense?

4. The three **characters** in the lighthouse respond differently to the invasion. Describe each man's reaction to the rats and its effect on the outcome of the story. Which character (if any) did you identify with?

Extending Interpretations

5. At what point did you predict that the narrator would survive the rat attack? On what evidence did you base your prediction?

WRITING

Describing a Setting

Much of the suspense in "Three Skeleton Key" comes from the fact that the characters are completely isolated. A lonely, forsaken island is a perfect **setting** for a horror story. Write a brief description of another good setting for a horror story. Look back at your Quickwrite notes for more ideas. Consider these features of a setting: sounds, sights, smells, time of day, weather, animal life, names.

go.hrw.com

INTERNET
Projects and Activities
Keyword: LE5 7-1

SKILLS FOCUS

Literary Skills
Analyze suspense.

Reading Skills
Make predictions.

Writing Skills
Write a description.

Reading Check

To review the story line, imagine you are the narrator filling out a report on your adventure at Three Skeleton Key.

Lighthouse Log
Day 1:
Day 2:
Day 3:
Day 4:

Day 9:
Day 10:
Day 11:

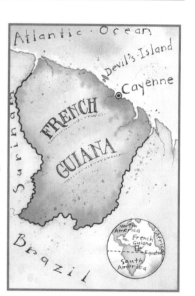

Reading Check
Possible Answers

Day 1: Spotted three-master heading for lighthouse

Day 2: Teased rats as they tried to get at us through the glass

Day 3: Couldn't get fresh air

Day 4: Saw window frame eaten away

Day 9: Decided not to light lantern

Day 10: Rats took over tower; ship arrived

Day 11: Rescued

Clarifying Word Meanings

PRACTICE 1

Test your mastery of the Word Bank words by answering these questions:

1. Hordes of rats would be a terrifying sight. Describe two other kinds of hordes you would not like to see.
2. How might you try to fathom a difficult text?
3. If you were a flood victim, how would you feel when you saw the flood waters receding?
4. What is your favorite edible plant? Name one plant that is inedible.
5. Write a derisive remark that a skeptic might make on hearing this rat story.

Word Bank

hordes
receding
fathom
edible
derisive

Clarifying Word Meanings: Examples

Sometimes you can figure out the meaning of an unfamiliar word by finding other words or phrases that give you an example of what the word means. For example, what words in this sentence give you an idea of what *staples* are?

> **The lighthouse keepers were running very low on necessary staples, such as flour, sugar, and salt.**

Certain words often let you know when an example is being used: *for example, for instance, like, such as, in this case, as if.*

PRACTICE 2

Find the words in each sentence that give you clues to the meaning of the underlined word. Then, make a guess about the meaning of the underlined word.

1. The rocks were treacherous. One false step and you would fall into the sea. *Treacherous* probably means _____.
2. Our eyes were riveted on the ship, as if fixed there by an invisible force. *Riveted* probably means _____.
3. The ship was a writhing mass, like a pit of moving snakes. *Writhing* probably means _____.

SKILLS
FOCUS

Vocabulary Skills
Clarify word meanings by using examples.

Three Skeleton Key **51**

Vocabulary Development

PRACTICE 1

Possible Answers

1. hordes of ants overrunning a picnic, and hordes of fans waiting for your autograph
2. I would read it carefully and slowly.
3. relieved
4. Broccoli is my favorite edible plant. Poison ivy is inedible.
5. That story's ridiculous. Who ever heard of such a thing?

PRACTICE 2

1. dangerous
2. fastened
3. twisting and turning

ASSESSING

Assessment
- *Holt Assessment: Literature, Reading, and Vocabulary*

RETEACHING

For a lesson reteaching plot, see **Reteaching,** p. 917B.

Grade-Level Skills

■ **Reading Skills**
Analyze the structure and purpose of informational texts, including a newspaper article.

Review Skills

■ **Reading Skills**
Use the structural features of newspapers, magazines, and online data to obtain information.

Upcoming Skills

■ **Reading Skills**
Evaluate the logic, consistency, and structural patterns in informational texts.

Summary ⬌ *at grade level*

> Sunny Jim, a lost or escaped pet rat, was discovered in a park by Nachshon Rose and taken in by Rose and his fiancée. After detailing the couple's attempts to make the rat comfortable in their home, the article concludes with information about the popularity of pet rats.

PRETEACHING

Selection Starter

Motivate. Ask students what image forms in their minds when they hear the word *rat*. How would they feel about having a pet rat in their home?

Assign the Reading

Students will enjoy reading this article aloud as if on a radio or television news broadcast. Assign roles as reader and interviewees.

Understanding Text Structures: A Newspaper Article

Reading Focus
Structure and Purpose of a Newspaper Article

The story "Three Skeleton Key" is about a terrifying invasion of rats, but the newspaper article you are about to read presents another view of these furry creatures.

The **purpose** of a newspaper article is to give you factual information about current events. A good informational article in a newspaper provides detailed answers to the questions *who? what? when? where? why?* and *how?*

Many newspaper articles follow an **inverted**—or upside-down—**pyramid** style. The article begins with a **summary lead,** a sentence or paragraph that gives the **main idea** of the story—this is usually the most important idea or detail in the story. It is followed by the less important details of the article.

Some articles begin with a lead that simply grabs your interest in a topic. Such a lead does not summarize but instead describes an interesting situation or fact related to the story. Here are some additional elements in the **structure** of a news article:

- **Headline:** the catchy boldface words that tell you what the article is about.
- **Subhead:** additional boldface words in smaller type under the headline, which add details about the article.
- **Byline:** the name of the reporter who wrote the article.
- **Dateline:** the location where the article was reported and the date when the information was reported.
- **Lead:** the sentence or paragraph that begins the news article.
- **Tone:** the choice of words and point of view that meet the interests of the newspaper's audience. Tone often depends on the subject of the article. Some articles are light, lively, and humorous; others are serious and straightforward.

■ How many structural elements of a newspaper article can you find as you read "Eeking Out a Life"?

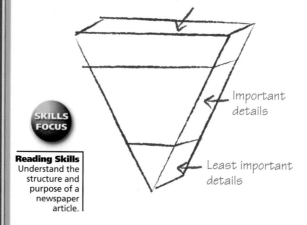

Summary lead, or most important information

Important details

Least important details

SKILLS FOCUS

Reading Skills
Understand the structure and purpose of a newspaper article.

52   Collection 1 / Facing Danger

RESOURCES: READING

Planning
■ *One-Stop Planner* CD-ROM with ExamView Test Generator

Differentiating Instruction
■ *Holt Adapted Reader*
■ *Holt Reading Solutions*
■ *Supporting Instruction in Spanish*
■ *Audio CD Library*

■ *Audio CD Library, Selections and Summaries in Spanish*

Vocabulary
■ *Vocabulary Development*

Grammar and Language
■ *Language Handbook Worksheets*
■ *Daily Language Activities*

Eeking Out a Life

Couple Welcome a Rescued Rat into Their Home

by Matt Surman

SIMI VALLEY, Calif., July 8—Who knows what trials the rat named Sunny Jim endured in his days alone in the wilderness?

Was he chased by voracious[1] owls? beset by marauding[2] gangs of streetwise sewer rats? Did he yearn for a child who had lost him on a day's outing?

His new owners—Hayley Huttenmaier and Nachshon Rose—can only guess. The little rat that they rescued, housed, and fed isn't talking, of course. And now Rose isn't sure he wants to find out about the past of the rat they have named Sunny Jim if that means the owner is going to come forward. Rose, in fact, has become attached to this sweet, squirming, don't-call-him-vermin little guy.

---

1. **voracious** (vô·rā′shəs) *adj.:* extremely hungry; eager to eat a lot of food.
2. **marauding** (mə·rôd′iŋ) *v.* used as *adj.:* roving in search of something to take or destroy.

All the former veterinary hospital employee knows is that he was returning from a short hike through Corriganville Park one Tuesday when a bundle of fur scampered across the parking lot. He followed, saw it stick its nose out of a little burrow, and then—bit by bit—come to perch on his shoe.

"I was kind of concerned that if I didn't catch him, he would probably be eaten," Rose said. "He probably couldn't have been out there more than a day."

The rat wasn't wearing any tags. There were no remnants of a leash. But he had to be a pet: Just look at the

A Reading Informational Text
? **Identify structural features: Subhead.** What is the subhead of this article? [Couple Welcome a Rescued Rat into Their Home] How does the subhead serve as a summary lead? [It gives the key facts.]

B Reading Informational Text
? **Identify structural features: Lead.** What is the purpose of the lead in this article? [Its purpose is to grab the reader's attention.]

Assessment
■ *Holt Assessment: Literature, Reading, and Vocabulary*
■ *One-Stop Planner* CD-ROM with ExamView Test Generator
■ *Holt Online Assessment*

Internet
■ go.hrw.com (Keyword: LE5 7-1)
■ *Elements of Literature Online*

Media
■ *Audio CD Library*
■ *Audio CD Library, Selections and Summaries in Spanish*

? **Identify structural features.**
Point out the two parenthetical remarks set off by dashes. What tone or point of view toward the subject do these remarks indicate? [Possible response: They indicate a light, casual tone.]

B **Reading Informational Text**

? **Identify structural features.**
Why does this information appear near the end of the article? [It is not directly related to the main idea.]

GUIDED PRACTICE

Monitor students' progress.
Draw an inverted pyramid on the board and have students fill in the three categories: summary lead or most important information, important details, and least important details.

A white and brownish-gray markings, his docile[3]—could one go so far as to say friendly?—behavior, his clean fur, and diminutive[4] size. Clearly this was not one of those sooty, dirt-brown outdoor creatures known as *Rattus rattus*.

So, he brought the rat home, and there, he and his fiancee, Huttenmaier, welcomed the rat into their family of two dogs and three cats. Now, Sunny Jim has his own room—well, a cabinet actually—with a cubbyhole formed by bricks, a handful of toys, a soft bed of wood shavings, and regular meals.

Huttenmaier insisted that they place an ad seeking its owner. "My theory is a kid took him out to play and lost him," she said. But so far they have received no calls. While Huttenmaier feels a bit for the poor owner, Rose doesn't want to give Sunny up. He thinks a mom forced her kid to abandon the creature when she realized there was a rodent hiding in a bedroom.

Which brings up the question: Isn't owning a rat found in the woods—even one with a cute glossy face, busy little hands, and a slippy short tail—a little worrisome?

"We can't turn down a cute face," Huttenmaier explained.

And experts agreed: Sunny Jim is almost certainly not a tree-dwelling, bubonic-plague carrying, skinny wild rat. He is closer to man's best friend.

"Oh, rats are like little dogs," said Louis Stack, membership director of the Riverside-based American Fancy Rat & Mouse Association, whose members raise show rats the way purebred owners raise show dogs. "They can sit on your shoulder and watch TV with you."

B And indeed, rat lovers are not shy about their enthusiasm. The Web hosts scores of sites extolling[5] *Rattus norvegicus*—the pet rat, domesticated about 100 years ago in England—and dispelling what they call misinformation about the cleanliness of their pets.

"There are people who are fanatical about rats," Stack said. "There are . . . all kinds of newsletters." Huttenmaier and Rose have no intentions of going that far.

They are just happy to offer little Sunny a home, a sense of safety—disregarding one little incident with a curious cat—and a chance to take it easy for a while.

And just maybe, there is a chance for a Rat Pack. "We might even get him a friend," Huttenmaier said.

---

3. **docile** (däs′əl) *adj.:* manageable.
4. **diminutive** (də·min′yōō·tiv) *adj.:* very small; tiny.

5. **extolling** (ek·stōl′iŋ) *v.* used as *adj.:* praising highly.

DIFFERENTIATING INSTRUCTION

Learners Having Difficulty
As students read the selection, have them identify information that answers the questions *who? what? when? where? why?* and *how?* List the information on a chart (or have the students do so), and have the students prepare a news summary of the story using the information they've identified.

Advanced Learners
Rats frequently get a bad rap as being pests and carriers of disease. Suggest that students research information about rats to find out some of the positive attributes of these rodents. Then, have students write their own news stories using the inverted pyramid structure.

Analyzing a Newspaper Article

Eeking Out a Life

Test Practice

1. The **structure** of a newspaper article is said to be similar to an —
   A octagon
   B inverted pyramid
   C oval
   D upside-down T

2. The **dateline** of the article on page 53 names which city?
   F Salt Lake City
   G Des Moines
   H Buxton
   J Simi Valley

3. The **subhead** of the article tells you that —
   A something is eeking out a life
   B a couple has adopted a stray rat
   C the rat may have been chased by an owl
   D rats have become popular

4. The **byline** of the news article shows it was written by —
   F George G. Toudouze
   G Nachshon Rose
   H Matt Surman
   J Sunny Jim

5. The **lead** of this article —
   A is an attention grabber
   B makes a serious statement about dangerous rats
   C answers *who? what? where? when?* and *how?*
   D presents the story's main idea

6. The **main idea** of this article is —
   F a couple loves its adopted rat
   G rats can't live with people
   H keeping a rat at home is dangerous
   J the rat population is a problem

Constructed Response

1. What is the **purpose** of a newspaper article?

2. Describe the **inverted-pyramid structure** of a typical newspaper article.

3. Summarize the information from the article on page 53 that answers the questions *who? what? when? where? why?* and *how?*

4. Describe the **tone** of the article. Why do you think the reporter decided to use this tone?

5. The **headline** title of this article contains a **pun**, which is a play on word meanings. What two words, both pronounced "eek," is the headline playing with?

SKILLS FOCUS

Reading Skills
Analyze the structure and purpose of a newspaper article.

Analyzing a Newspaper Article

Test Practice

Answers and Model Rationales

1. **B** Students should recall this information from p. 52.
2. **J** Simi Valley is the only location mentioned.
3. **B** The additional boldface words after the headline refer to a couple welcoming a stray rat into their home.
4. **H** The name appearing after "by" is Matt Surman.
5. **A** The first sentence of the article asks a question.
6. **F** Students should realize that the article views rats positively, while G, H, and J are negative statements.

Test-Taking Tips

For more information on how to answer multiple-choice items, refer students to **Test Smarts**, p. 920.

Constructed Response

1. The purpose of a newspaper article is to give factual information about current events.

2. A typical newspaper article is structured with the most important information at the beginning, followed by details in descending order of importance.

3. Hayley Huttenmaier and Nachshon Rose have adopted a rat that Rose found in Corriganville Park one Tuesday. Rose brought the pet rat home because he feared that it would be eaten by predators.

4. Possible answer: The tone is light and humorous. The reporter probably used this tone because the article was written primarily for readers' entertainment

5. "Eek" is an interjection or sound uttered to signify surprise or sudden fright, like the kind of response one might have upon seeing a rat. The word "eke" means to struggle to survive. Sunny Jim managed to survive in the wilderness, but with great difficulty.

Grammar Link

(Correct verb forms are italicized.) The most interesting moments in this story *come* when Sunny Jim is described. Neither tags nor a collar *was* found on the little rat. The owners of the rat seem very nice, but parts of their story *are* weird. The writer *doesn't* seem very enthusiastic either. Stories about the curious cat *weren't* told here. Neither my biology teacher nor my town's pet-store owner *recommends* getting a pet Rattus.

ASSESSING

Assessment

■ *Holt Assessment: Literature, Reading, and Vocabulary*

Subject-Verb Agreement

Probably the most common error people make in writing (and in speaking) is in subject-verb agreement. The rule is simple: Subjects and their verbs must always agree. That means that a singular subject takes a singular verb and a plural subject takes a plural verb. The problem comes with identifying the subject and deciding whether it's singular or plural.

Be especially careful when you have *neither/nor* or *either/or*. You must also pay attention when a subject is separated from its verb by a prepositional phrase. The verb always agrees with the subject.

1. **Neither Huttenmaier nor Rose wants/want to give up Sunny Jim.** [Singular subjects joined by *or* or *nor* take a singular verb. Therefore, the verb should be *wants*.]

2. **Neither Sunny Jim nor his owners wants/want to end their friendship.** [When a singular subject and a plural subject are joined by *or* or *nor*, the verb agrees with the subject closer to the verb. Since *owners* is plural, the verb should be *want*.]

3. **The owners of Sunny Jim is/are a bit unusual.** [The number of the subject is not affected by a prepositional phrase following the subject. Therefore, the verb should be *are*.]

Rewrite the paragraph below to correct errors in subject-verb agreement.

The most interesting moments in this story comes when Sunny Jim is described. Neither tags nor a collar were found on the little rat. The owners of the rat seem very nice, but parts of their story is weird. The writer don't seem very enthusiastic either. Stories about the curious cat wasn't told here. Neither my biology teacher nor my town's pet-store owner recommend getting a pet *Rattus*.

For more help, see Agreement of Subject and Verb, 2b–n, in the Language Handbook.

SKILLS FOCUS

Grammar Skills
Use correct subject-verb agreement.

Learners Having Difficulty
Write the following sentences on the chalkboard. Have students choose the correct verb form in each sentence.

1. A mouse or a rat is/are not everyone's idea of a great pet. [is]

2. Neither Alicia nor her parents want/wants any small rodents. [want]

3. Jared, on the other hand, think/thinks rats are cool. [thinks]

4. According to scientists, not all rats or mice are/is the same. [are]

5. Unlike their wild cousins, most pet rodents doesn't/don't spread diseases. [don't]

The Monsters Are Due on Maple Street

Make the Connection
Quickwrite ✏️

People often make snap judgments in life. In your journal, write about a time you jumped to an incorrect conclusion about someone or someone jumped to an incorrect conclusion about you. What was the situation? What mistake was made? How was the mistake corrected?

Literary Focus
Plot Complications

Complications in stories make it hard for characters to get what they want. Complications usually begin to develop as soon as the characters take steps to resolve their problems or to get what they want so badly. Complications are events like a sudden storm breaking just

as the climbers are nearing the summit or another dragon appearing out of the cave just when the hero thinks he has finished his work. Complications usually add more conflict to the story. They also make the plot more complex. Complications are meant to increase our anxiety about how the story will finally end. In stories, as in life, it's never easy.

Reading Skills 📖
Making Inferences

Good readers **make inferences** using clues the writer provides. It's a form of word arithmetic: The writer gives you *one* and *one* but expects you to figure out the answer—*two*.

As you read this teleplay, you'll see little open-book signs. At these points, stop and add up the important clues the writer has just given. Note your inferences in your notebook, or discuss them with your partner.

INTERNET

Vocabulary Activity
•
More About Serling

Keyword: LE5 7-1

SKILLS FOCUS

Literary Skills
Understand plot complications.

Reading Skills
Make inferences.

The Monsters Are Due on Maple Street   **57**

SKILLS FOCUS
pp. 57–80

Grade-Level Skills

■ **Literary Skills**
Identify events that advance the plot, and determine how each event explains past or present actions.
■ **Reading Skills**
Make inferences.

Review Skills

■ **Literary Skills**
Identify the main conflict of the plot and how it is resolved.

Upcoming Skills

■ **Literary Skills**
Evaluate the plot's structure and development and the way conflicts are resolved.

Summary ↔ *at grade level*

When a sudden and inexplicable force causes everything to stop working on Maple Street, the people there begin to wonder who or what is responsible. At first they believe a meteor is causing the loss of power. Then, as fear begins to invade each person's mind, complications arise. Accusations and suspicions about one person, then another and another and another, finally lead to violence, and an innocent man is killed. As the teleplay closes, the audience learns that aliens who want to take over the world have stopped the machines and are observing the humans' self-destructive behavior. This behavior reveals that the real monsters on Maple Street are the people themselves and the fears and prejudices they harbor.

Selection Starter

Motivate. Invite students to brainstorm words, images, and feelings that the word *monster* brings to mind. [Possible responses: evil, abnormal, hideous, enormous, brute, beast, horrible, unreal.] Then, have students predict who or what the monsters on Maple Street may be.

Preview Vocabulary

To build students' familiarity with the Vocabulary words on p. 58, assign these exercises.

1. Tell us about a time you were transfixed by something on television.
2. Mutter a phrase that is not intelligible.
3. Write a sentence that includes the words *assent* and *variations*.
4. Describe something tremendous that intimidated a child.
5. Demonstrate a defiant pose.
6. Describe an idiosyncrasy of someone you know.
7. Tell about something that is a menace to society.
8. Draw a picture of coyotes converging on their prey.
9. Give an explicit direction.

Vocabulary Development

These words are important in the teleplay:

transfixed (trans·fikst′) *v.* used as *adj.*: very still, as if nailed to the spot. *Up and down the street, people stood transfixed, staring at the sky.*

intelligible (in·tel′i·jə·bəl) *adj.*: understandable. *The residents muttered nothing intelligible; they just made an indistinct rumble.*

assent (ə·sent′) *n.*: agreement. *At first, Steve's common sense gained the crowd's assent and goodwill.*

intimidated (in·tim′ə·dāt′id) *v.*: frightened with threats. *The angry crowd intimidated the Goodmans, who then began to defend themselves.*

defiant (dē·fī′ənt) *adj.*: boldly resisting authority. *Those who speak out against the opinions of an angry crowd must be both defiant and courageous.*

idiosyncrasy (id′ē·ō·siṇ′krə·sē) *n.*: peculiarity. *All people have at least one idiosyncrasy that makes them a little different.*

menace (men′əs) *n.*: danger; threat. *The residents of Maple Street believed there was a real menace to their safety.*

converging (kən·vʉrj′iŋ) *v.* used as *adj.*: closing in. *The crowd began converging around Tommy in order to hear him speak.*

explicit (eks·plis′it) *adj.*: definite; clearly stated. *The danger on Maple Street was not explicit, or understandable, making it more frightening.*

variations (ver′ē·ā′shənz) *n.*: differences. *Most of the residents of Maple Street reacted to fear in similar ways, with only small variations.*

Background
Literature and Media

From its 1959 debut through its more than 150 subsequent episodes, *The Twilight Zone* thrilled and captivated millions of television viewers. Rebroadcasts run even today—maybe you've seen some episodes. As Rod Serling, the show's creator, would eerily alert viewers at the beginning of every episode, things in the Twilight Zone are not always what they seem. Ordinary people face extraordinary situations in the Twilight Zone, where familiar rules no longer apply. As the bards and poets have warned for centuries, "Here be monsters. . . ."

RESOURCES: READING

Assessment
- *Holt Assessment: Literature, Reading, and Vocabulary*
- *One-Stop Planner* CD-ROM with ExamView Test Generator
- *Holt Online Assessment*

Internet
- go.hrw.com (Keyword: LE5 7-1)
- *Elements of Literature Online*

Media
- *Audio CD Library*
- *Audio CD Library, Selections and Summaries in Spanish*

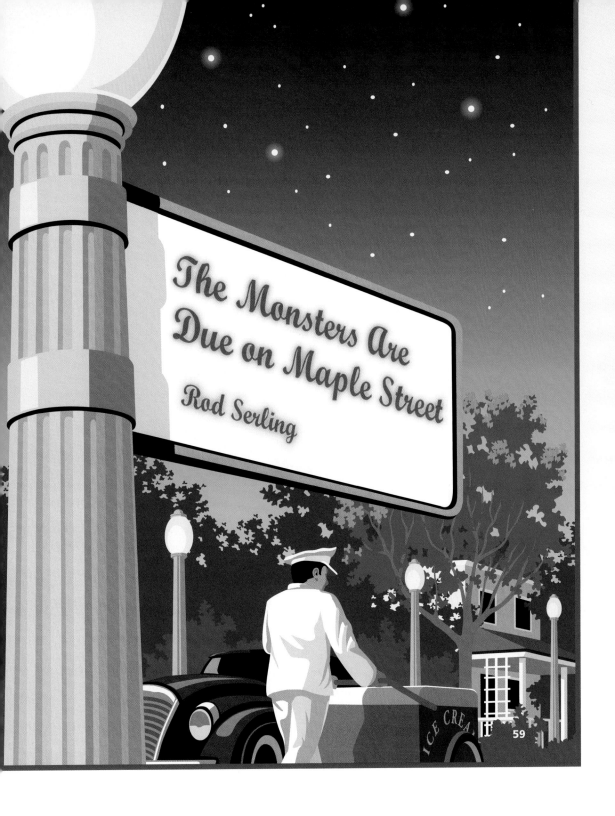

The Monsters Are Due on Maple Street

Rod Serling

Teleplay Terms

Ⓐ Scripts written for television or the movies are different from scripts written for the stage. A **teleplay** is a script written for TV; a **screenplay** is a script written for movies. Both kinds of scripts may contain these camera directions:

fade in: The picture gradually appears on the screen.

pan: a swiveling movement of the camera, from one side to the other.

fade to black: The picture gradually disappears until all that remains is a black screen.

Ⓑ **cut to:** a sudden change from one scene or character to another.

outside shot: a camera shot of an exterior.

long shot: a camera shot from far off.

close-up: a camera shot that is very close to its subject.

opening shot: the first scene of the production.

dissolve: A new scene is blended with a scene that is fading out.

Characters

Narrator	Charlie
Figure One	Charlie's wife
Figure Two	Tommy
	Sally, Tommy's mother
Residents of Maple Street	Les Goodman
Steve Brand	Mrs. Goodman
Mrs. Brand	Woman Next Door
Don Martin	Woman One
Pete Van Horn	Man One
	Man Two

Act One

Fade in on a shot of the night sky. The various nebulae and planets stand out in sharp, sparkling relief. As the camera begins a slow pan across the heavens, we hear the narrator offscreen.

Narrator's Voice. There is a fifth dimension beyond that which is known to man. It is a dimension as vast as space and as timeless as infinity. It is the middle ground between light and shadow—between science and superstition. And it lies between the pit of man's fears and the summit of his knowledge. This is the dimension of imagination. It is an area which we call The Twilight Zone.

[The camera pans down past the horizon, stopping on a sign which reads "Maple Street." Then it moves on to the street below. It is daytime. We see a quiet, tree-lined street, typical of small-town America. People sit and swing on gliders on their front porches, chatting across from house to house. STEVE BRAND *polishes his car, while his neighbor,* DON MARTIN, *leans against the fender watching him. A Good Humor man on a bicycle stops to sell some ice cream to a couple of kids. Two women gossip on a front lawn. Another man waters his lawn.]*

Maple Street, U.S.A., late summer. A tree-lined little world of front-porch gliders, hopscotch, the laughter of children, and the bell of an ice-cream vendor.

[The camera moves back to the Good Humor man and the two boys who are standing alongside him, buying ice cream.]

At the sound of the roar and the flash of light, it will be precisely 6:43 P.M. on Maple Street.

[One of the boys, TOMMY, *looks up to listen to a tremendous screeching roar from overhead. A flash of light plays on the boys' faces. It moves down the street, past lawns and porches and rooftops, and disappears. People leave their porches or stop what they're doing to stare up at the sky.* STEVE BRAND *stops polishing his car and stands transfixed, staring upward. He looks at* DON MARTIN, *his neighbor from across the street.]*

Steve. What was that? A meteor?
Don (*nods*). That's what it looked like. I didn't hear any crash, though, did you?
Steve (*shakes his head*). Nope. I didn't hear anything except a roar.
Mrs. Brand (*from her porch*). Steve? What was that?
Steve (*raising his voice and looking toward porch*). Guess it was a meteor, honey. Came awful close, didn't it?
Mrs. Brand. Too close for my money! Much too close.

Vocabulary
transfixed (trans·fikst′) *v.* used as *adj.*: very still, as if nailed to the spot.

The Monsters Are Due on Maple Street, Act One   **61**

A Literary Focus

Foreshadowing and suspense.
Point out the phrase "the last calm and reflective moment . . . before the monsters came!" Ask what effect this phrase creates. [It creates a feeling of dread and anticipation.]

B Reading Skills

Make inferences. Remind students that readers figure out what is going on by connecting clues in the text with what they know. Ask students how they can use what they know of electric power to understand this passage. [Students know that appliances such as lamps, power mowers, and telephones need electricity to function, so they can conclude that there has been a power failure—perhaps caused by an explosion.

[Possible response to question 1: The stage directions lead one to think that whatever caused the roaring sound and flashing light caused an electric power failure.]

C Literary Focus

❷ Complications. What complication are the people experiencing now? [Possible response: The phone won't work, so the people's lines of communication are cut off.] How are they reacting to it? [Possible response: They are getting tense.]

D Learners Having Difficulty

Find the sequence of events.
To help students follow events, draw a flowchart like the one below:

People hear a roar and a flash of light.

↓

Electric power has failed. Phone and radio no longer work.

↓

Pete Van Horn goes to investigate.

[People stand on their porches, watching and talking in low tones.]

A **Narrator's Voice.** Maple Street. 6:44 P.M., on a late September evening.(*A pause*) Maple Street in the last calm and reflective moments . . . before the monsters came!

B [*The camera pans across the porches again. A man is screwing in a lightbulb on a front porch. He gets down off the stool and flicks the switch, only to find that nothing happens. Another man is working on an electric power mower. He plugs in the plug and flicks the switch of the power mower, off and on, but nothing happens. Through the window of a front porch we see a woman at a telephone, pushing her finger back and forth on the dial hook. Her voice is indistinct and distant, but intelligible and repetitive.*] ❶

Woman Next Door. Operator, operator, something's wrong on the phone, operator!

[MRS. BRAND *comes out on the porch and calls to* STEVE.]

Mrs. Brand (*calling*). Steve, the power's off. I had the soup on the stove, and the stove just stopped working.
Woman Next Door. Same thing over here. I can't get anybody on the phone either. The phone seems to be dead.

C [*The camera looks down on the street. Small, mildly disturbed voices creep up from below.*]

Voices.
Electricity's off.
Phone won't work.

> **MAKE INFERENCES**
> ❶ What do the stage directions lead you to think about the roaring sound and flashing light?

Can't get a thing on the radio.
My power mower won't move, won't work at all.
Radio's gone dead.

[PETE VAN HORN, *a tall, thin man, is standing in front of his house.*]

D **Van Horn.** I'll cut through the backyard. . . . See if the power's still on on Floral Street. I'll be right back.

[*He walks past the side of his house and disappears into the backyard. We see the hammer on his hip as he walks. The camera pans down slowly until we're looking at ten or eleven people standing around the street and overflowing to the curb and sidewalk. In the background is* STEVE BRAND'*s car.*]

Steve. Doesn't make sense. Why should the power go off all of a sudden, and the phone line?
Don. Maybe some sort of an electrical storm or something.
Charlie. That don't seem likely. Sky's just as blue as anything. Not a cloud. No lightning. No thunder. No nothing. How could it be a storm?
Woman One. I can't get a thing on the radio. Not even the portable.

[*The people again murmur softly in wonderment and question.*]

Charlie. Well, why don't you go downtown and check with the police, though they'll probably think we're crazy or something. A little power failure and right away we get all flustered and everything.

Vocabulary
intelligible (in·tel′i·jə·bəl) *adj.*: understandable.

DIFFERENTIATING INSTRUCTION

Advanced Learners
Acceleration. Use the following activity with advanced learners to help them evaluate a plot's development.
Activity. After they read the play, have students meet in a small group and discuss the following questions:
• What roles do Tommy, Charlie, and Steve play in the development of the plot?

• Given the events that precede it, is the climax believable? Explain your answer.
• Were you surprised by the resolution of the plot? Why or why not?
Then, have students suppose that a new version of *The Monsters Are Due on Maple Street* is scheduled for a television broadcast. Would they urge friends to watch it? Why or why not?

Steve. It isn't just the power failure, Charlie. If it was, we'd still be able to get a broadcast on the portable.

[*There's a murmur of reaction to this.* STEVE *looks from face to face and then over to his car.*]

I'll run downtown. We'll get this all straightened out.

[STEVE *walks over to the car, gets in it, and turns the key. Through the open car door we see the crowd watching him from the other side.* STEVE *starts the engine. It turns over sluggishly and then just stops dead. He tries it again, and this time he can't even get it to turn over. Then, very slowly and reflectively, he turns the key back to "off" and slowly gets out of the car. Everyone stares at* STEVE. *He stands for a moment by the car, then walks toward the group.*]

I don't understand it. It was working fine before....

Don. Out of gas?
Steve (*shakes his head*). I just had it filled up.
Woman One. What's it mean?
Charlie. It's just as if ... as if everything

had stopped.... (*Then he turns toward* STEVE) We'd better walk downtown.

[*Another murmur of* assent *at this.*]

Steve. The two of us can go, Charlie. (*He turns to look back at the car.*) It couldn't be the meteor. A meteor couldn't do this.

[*He and* CHARLIE *exchange a look, then they start to walk away from the group. We see* TOMMY, *a serious-faced fourteen-year-old in spectacles, standing a few feet away from the group. He is halfway between them and the two men, who start to walk down the sidewalk.*]

Tommy. Mr. Brand ... you better not!
Steve. Why not?
Tommy. They don't want you to.
[STEVE *and* CHARLIE *exchange a grin, and* STEVE *looks back toward the boy.*]

Steve. Who doesn't want us to?
Tommy (*jerks his head in the general direction of the distant horizon*). Them!
Steve. Them?
Charlie. Who are them?
Tommy (*very intently*). Whoever was in that thing that came by overhead.

[STEVE *knits his brows for a moment, cocking his head questioningly. His voice is intense.*]

Steve. What?
Tommy. Whoever was in the thing that came over. I don't think they want us to leave here.

[STEVE *leaves* CHARLIE *and walks over to the*

Vocabulary
assent (ə·sent′) *n.:* agreement.

The Monsters Are Due on Maple Street, Act One **63**

? **Characterization.** What impressions have you formed of Steve Brand based on what he says and does and the way other characters respond to him? If you were an actor playing this character, how would you talk to Tommy? [Possible responses: Steve seems to be reasonable, trustworthy, and levelheaded; he is a leader. Students may say that if they were playing the character they would speak gently and reassuringly.]

B Reading Skills

Make inferences. Ask students to identify clues to Steve's feelings in his dialogue and the stage directions. Then, ask them to connect those clues with their own knowledge of human nature. [Possible responses: *Clues in dialogue*—The ellipses and dashes convey uncertainty. *Clues in stage directions*—Steve is "trying to weight his words with an optimism he obviously doesn't feel but is desperately trying to instill in himself. . . ." *Knowledge*—When people deny their true feelings, they are just fooling themselves.]

[Possible response to question 2: The stage directions indicate that Steve does not believe what he is saying. Students might infer that in order to prevent a panic, Steve is trying to come up with a rational explanation for what has occurred.]

C Reading Skills

? **Interpret.** Are the onlookers responding to Tommy's words with emotion or reason? Explain. [Possible response: Tommy's words are stirring up emotions in the people. They are responding with irritation brought on by deep-seated feelings of fear. Their response is unreasonable, "without logic."]

---

boy. He kneels down in front of him. He forces his voice to remain gentle. He reaches out and holds the boy.]

A **Steve.** What do you mean? What are you talking about?

Tommy. They don't want us to leave. That's why they shut everything off.

Steve. What makes you say that? Whatever gave you that idea?

Woman One (*from the crowd*). Now isn't that the craziest thing you ever heard?

Tommy (*persistently but a little intimidated by the crowd*). It's always that way, in every story I ever read about a ship landing from outer space.

Woman One (*to the boy's mother,* SALLY, *who stands on the fringe of the crowd*). From outer space, yet! Sally, you better get that boy of yours up to bed. He's been reading too many comic books or seeing too many movies or something.

Sally. Tommy, come over here and stop that kind of talk.

B **Steve.** Go ahead, Tommy. We'll be right back. And you'll see. That wasn't any ship or anything like it. That was just a . . . a meteor or something. Likely as not— (*He turns to the group, now trying to weight his words with an optimism he obviously doesn't feel but is desperately trying to instill in himself, as well as the others.*) No doubt it did have something to do with all this power failure and the rest of it. Meteors can do some crazy things. Like sunspots. **2** 🔖

Don (*picking up the cue*). Sure. That's the kind of thing—like sunspots. They raise Cain with radio reception all over the

🔖 **MAKE INFERENCES**
2 Does Steve believe his own words? What can you infer from the stage directions?

world. And this thing being so close—why, there's no telling the sort of stuff it can do. (*He wets his lips and smiles nervously.*) Go ahead, Charlie. You and Steve go into town and see if that isn't what's causing it all.

[STEVE *and* CHARLIE *walk away from the group again, down the sidewalk. The people watch silently.* TOMMY *stares at them, biting his lips, and finally calls out again.*]

Tommy. Mr. Brand!

[*The two men stop again.* TOMMY *takes a step toward them.*]

Tommy. Mr. Brand . . . please don't leave here.

C [STEVE *and* CHARLIE *stop once again and turn toward the boy. There's a murmur in the crowd, a murmur of irritation and concern as if the boy were bringing up fears that shouldn't be brought up; words that carried with them a strange kind of validity that came without logic, but nonetheless registered and had meaning and effect.* TOMMY *is partly frightened and partly defiant.*]

You might not even be able to get to town. It was that way in the story. Nobody could leave. Nobody except—

Steve. Except who?

Tommy. Except the people they'd sent down ahead of them. They looked just like humans. And it wasn't until the ship landed that—

[*The boy suddenly stops again, conscious of the parents staring at him and of the sudden hush of the crowd.*]

Vocabulary

intimidated (in·tim′ə·dāt′id) *v.:* frightened with threats or violence.
defiant (dē·fī′ənt) *adj.:* boldly resisting authority.

Sally (*in a whisper, sensing the antagonism of the crowd*). Tommy, please, son . . . honey, don't talk that way—

Man One. That kid shouldn't talk that way . . . and we shouldn't stand here listening to him. Why, this is the craziest thing I ever heard of. The kid tells us a comic book plot, and here we stand listening—

[STEVE *walks toward the camera and stops by the boy.*]

Steve. Go ahead, Tommy. What kind of story was this? What about the people that they sent out ahead?

Tommy. That was the way they prepared things for the landing. They sent four people. A mother and a father and two kids who looked just like humans . . . but they weren't.

[*There's another silence as* STEVE *looks toward the crowd and then toward* TOMMY. *He wears a tight grin.*]

Steve. Well, I guess what we'd better do then is to run a check on the neighborhood and see which ones of us are really human.

[*There's laughter at this, but it's a laughter that comes from a desperate attempt to lighten the atmosphere.* CHARLIE *laughs nervously, slightly forced. The people look at one another in the middle of their laughter.*]

Charlie. There must be somethin' better to do than stand around makin' bum jokes about it. (*Rubs his jaw nervously*) I wonder if Floral Street's got the same deal we got. (*He looks past the houses.*) Where is Pete Van Horn anyway? Didn't he get back yet?

[*Suddenly there's the sound of a car's engine starting to turn over. We look across the street toward the driveway of* LES GOODMAN's *house. He's at the wheel trying to start the car.*]

Sally. Can you get it started, Les?

[LES GOODMAN *gets out of the car, shaking his head.*]

Goodman. No dice.

[*He walks toward the group. He stops suddenly as behind him, inexplicably and with a noise that inserts itself into the silence, the car engine starts up all by itself.* GOODMAN *whirls around to stare toward it. The car idles roughly, smoke coming from the exhaust, the frame shaking gently.* GOODMAN's *eyes go wide, and he runs over to his car. The people stare toward the car.*]

Man One. He got the car started somehow. He got his car started!

D Reading Skills

? Speculate. The character who is speaking is identified as Man One, just as an earlier speaker was identified as Woman One. Why do you think these speakers are nameless? [Possible responses: The speakers are minor characters. They are anonymous because they could be anyone in the group—they are voicing thoughts and feelings shared by others.]

E Literary Focus

? Complications. What complication is created by Tommy's words to Steve? Why do the neighbors look at each other? [Possible response: Tommy's words add to the people's feelings of confusion, fear, and distrust. They look at each other because they are beginning to suspect that some in their group may be aliens disguised as humans.]

F Literary Focus

? Stage directions. If you were an actor playing Goodman, how would you use body language and facial expressions to bring this scene to life? If you were the director, what camera angles would you use to shoot the scene? [Possible response: As an actor playing Goodman, a student might come to an abrupt halt and then whirl around and stare for a long moment, his mouth open and his eyes wide, before racing to the car. The camera would be focused on Goodman's back as he walks hesitantly, stops, and then whirls; the camera would then cut to the idling car and pan, close-up, along the terrified faces.]

Culture

Alien tales. A number of comic books, science fiction novels, and films have plots that deal with aliens masquerading as humans or with aliens taking over the earth.

Activity. Interested students might want to research and report to the class on how Orson Welles incited mass hysteria in the 1930s when he adapted *The War of the Worlds* by H. G. Wells for a radio broadcast. The story seemed so real that people listening to the radio panicked. Some fled for their lives because they believed that aliens were actually invading the United States.

INDIVIDUAL

A Literary Focus

❓ Complications. What new complication has just developed in the plot? How is this affecting the neighbors? [Les Goodman's car has started all by itself. Neighbors begin to suspect that he has something to do with the strange events.]

B Reading Skills

Make inferences. [Possible responses to question 3: The characters have decided that Les may be an alien with extraordinary powers because his car starts by itself when no other cars will start; unlike everyone else, he takes no interest in the roar; and in their view, he is "different," an "oddball." Some students may assume that Les knows what is going on. Others may feel that the characters are basing their conclusions on flimsy evidence.]

C Literary Focus

❓ Characterization. How does Steve prevent the group from turning into a stampeding mob? [Steve controls the crowd by commanding them to stop.] What does this reveal about him? [Possible response: This shows his willingness to stand alone against the crowd, his ability to think and act quickly, and his strong leadership qualities.]

D Reading Skills

Express an opinion. Ask students what they think of the crowd's treatment of Les Goodman. [Possible responses: The neighbors are being unfair to Les and are letting their fears get in the way of their judgment. The neighbors are right to question Les, but they shouldn't gang up on him.]

[*The camera pans along the faces of the people as they stare, somehow caught up by this revelation and somehow, illogically, wildly, frightened.*]

Woman One. How come his car just up and started like that?

Sally. All by itself. He wasn't anywheres near it. It started all by itself.

[DON *approaches the group. He stops a few feet away to look toward* GOODMAN'*s car, and then back toward the group.*]

Don. And he never did come out to look at that thing that flew overhead. He wasn't even interested. (*He turns to the faces in the group, his face taut and serious.*) Why? Why didn't he come out with the rest of us to look?

Charlie. He always was an oddball. Him and his whole family. Real oddball.

Don. What do you say we ask him? ❸

> **🔖 MAKE INFERENCES**
> ❸ What inference have the neighbors made about Les Goodman?

[*The group suddenly starts toward the house. In this brief fraction of a moment they take the first step toward a metamorphosis from a group into a mob. They begin to head purposefully across the street toward the house at the end.* STEVE *stands in front of them. For a moment their fear almost turns their walk into a wild stampede, but* STEVE'*s voice, loud, incisive, and commanding, makes them stop.*]

Steve. Wait a minute . . . wait a minute! Let's not be a mob!

[*The people stop as a group, seem to pause for a moment, and then much more quietly*

and slowly start to walk across the street. GOODMAN *stands there alone, facing the people.*]

Goodman. I just don't understand it. I tried to start it and it wouldn't start. You saw me. All of you saw me.

[*And now, just as suddenly as the engine started, it stops. There's a long silence that is gradually intruded upon by the frightened murmuring of the people.*]

I don't understand. I swear . . . I don't understand. What's happening?

Don. Maybe you better tell us. Nothing's working on this street. Nothing. No lights, no power, no radio. (*And then meaningfully*) Nothing except one car—yours!

[*The people pick this up. Now their murmuring becomes a loud chant, filling the air with accusations and demands for action. Two of the men pass* DON *and head toward* GOODMAN, *who backs away, backing into his car. He is now at bay.*]

Goodman. Wait a minute now. You keep your distance—all of you. So I've got a car that starts by itself—well, that's a freak thing, I admit it. But does that make me some kind of criminal or something? I don't know why the car works—it just does!

[*This stops the crowd momentarily, and now* GOODMAN, *still backing away, goes toward his front porch. He goes up the steps and then stops to stand facing the mob.* STEVE *comes through the crowd.*]

Steve (*quietly*). We're all on a monster kick, Les. Seems that the general impression holds that maybe one family isn't what we think they are. Monsters from outer space

or something. Different than us. Fifth columnists° from the vast beyond. (*He chuckles.*) You know anybody that might fit that description around here on Maple Street? ❹

Goodman. What is this, a gag or something? This a practical joke or something?

[*The spotlight on his porch suddenly goes out. There's a murmur from the group.*]

Now, I suppose that's supposed to incriminate me! The light goes on and off. That really does it, doesn't it? (*He looks around the faces of the people.*) I just don't understand this— (*He wets his lips, looking from face to face.*) Look, you all know me. We've lived here five years. Right in this house. We're no different than any of the rest of you! We're no different at all. Really . . . this whole thing is just . . . just weird—

Woman One. Well, if that's the case, Les Goodman, explain why—(*She stops suddenly, clamping her mouth shut.*)

° **fifth columnists:** people who aid an enemy from within their own country.

Goodman (*softly*). Explain what?
Steve (*interjecting*). Look, let's forget this—
Charlie (*overlapping him*). Go ahead, let her talk. What about it? Explain what?
Woman One (*a little reluctantly*). Well . . . sometimes I go to bed late at night. A couple of times . . . a couple of times I'd come out on the porch and I'd see Mr. Goodman here in the wee hours of the morning standing out in front of his house . . . looking up at the sky. (*She looks around the circle of faces.*) That's right. Looking up at the sky as if . . . as if he were waiting for something. (*A pause*) As if he were looking for something. ❻

> **MAKE INFERENCES**
> ❹ Is Steve serious here? On what do you base your inference?

> **MAKE INFERENCES**
> ❺ What fact about Goodman has the woman observed? What inference has she made? Is this reasonable?

[*There's a murmur of reaction from the crowd again. As* GOODMAN *starts toward them, they back away, frightened.*]

Goodman. You know really . . . this is for laughs. You know what I'm guilty of? (*He laughs.*) I'm guilty of insomnia. Now what's the penalty for insomnia? (*At this point the laugh, the humor, leaves his voice.*) Did you hear what I said? I said it was insomnia. (*A pause as he looks around, then shouts.*) I said it was insomnia! You fools. You scared, frightened rabbits, you. You're sick people, do you know that? You're sick people—all of you! And you don't even know what you're starting because let me tell you . . . let me tell you—this thing you're starting— that should frighten you. As God is my witness . . . you're letting something begin here that's a nightmare!

[*Fade to black.*]

Ⓔ Reading Skills
Make inferences. [Possible responses to question 4: Steve is not serious; he is trying to inject some humor into the situation in order to calm people down and prevent a disaster. Students may base their inferences on Steve's playful choice of words—"monster kick" and "Fifth columnists from the vast beyond"— and the onstage directions that indicate he chuckles.]

Ⓕ Reading Skills
Make inferences. [Possible responses to question 5: The woman has observed Goodman on his porch after midnight, looking up at the sky. She has inferred that he must be in communication with something or someone from outer space. This assumption is not reasonable; there is no evidence for it.]

Ⓖ Literary Focus
❓ Complications. What new complication occurs at the end of Act One? [Possible responses: People are ganging up on Les Goodman and suspect that he is an alien. He makes them feel that they will regret their actions. Tension and fear and a threat of danger fill the air. The townspeople are suspicious of each other and are becoming an angry mob.]

GUIDED PRACTICE

Monitor students' progress.
Invite the class to participate in retelling the plot up to this point. Guide the class by asking questions and calling on individuals to answer. Begin by asking one student, "What happened first?" After the student responds, ask another student, "And then what happened?" Continue in this way until students have accurately retold all the complications in Act One. If you wish, have students locate passages in the teleplay that support their responses.

After You Read

First Thoughts

1. Possible answer: Aliens are involved; the narrator mentions the fifth dimension, the Twilight Zone, and the coming of monsters, and nothing else explains the strange events.

Thinking Critically

2. Tommy suggests that aliens, disguised as humans, are preparing to land in town.

3. The people are fearful. They infer that Goodman is an alien with extraordinary powers.

4. Goodman means that the residents are judging him guilty with no supporting evidence and are behaving like a mob.

5. Goodman is considered an oddball. Also, he didn't come out to look at the flash of light in the sky; only his car starts; and his electricity is working.

Extending Interpretations

6. A crowd is a large group of people. A mob is a disorderly or uncontrollable crowd.

7. Possible answer: The people are reacting to inexplicable events by making wild accusations. Their behavior may lead to violence.

Reading Check

a. Residents believe that the thing that passed overhead has caused the power failure.

b. A portable radio won't work; a car starts and stops by itself; a light goes on and off by itself.

c. At first, adults ridicule the idea.

d. Tommy suggests that aliens may be masquerading as humans.

e. Tommy's sources are comic books and movies.

After You Read Response and Analysis

Act One

First Thoughts

1. Do you believe aliens are involved in the events on Maple Street? Explain the reasons for your prediction.

Thinking Critically

2. What future events could Tommy's words **foreshadow**?

3. What is the group's reaction when Les Goodman's car starts? What **inference** do they make about the cause of the car's behavior?

4. At the end of Act One, Les Goodman warns the residents that they are starting something that should frighten them, and he goes on to call it a nightmare. What could he mean?

5. A scapegoat is someone whom people blame for their troubles. How has Les Goodman become a scapegoat?

Extending Interpretations

6. What is the difference between a crowd and a mob? Have you ever seen or been a part of a mob? Briefly describe your experiences.

7. In your own words, describe what is happening to the community, and **predict** where this kind of behavior is going to lead. Based on what you know so far and on what you know from history and from your own experience, **predict** events that may occur in Act Two. (Think back to your Quickwrite notes.)

**SKILLS
FOCUS**

Literary Skills
Analyze plot
complications.

Reading Skills
Make inferences.

Reading Check

a. A dramatic event triggers the action on Maple Street. What do the residents believe has caused the power failure?

b. Find three incidents that show that this is not a normal power failure.

c. How do the adults first react to Tommy's suggestion that "they" are aliens who do not want Steve and Charlie to leave the area?

d. What does Tommy then say that causes the adults to become increasingly uncomfortable?

e. What is Tommy's source of information about alien life forms and their habits?

DIFFERENTIATING INSTRUCTION

Learners Having Difficulty

In class, have students write answers to the Reading Check questions. *Monitoring tip:* If students are unable to figure out the inference people make when Goodman's car starts (question 3), allow them to work together in small groups. Have them re-read pp. 65–67 and look for answers to these questions: How do people feel when Goodman's car starts by itself? What does Don say about Goodman's behavior? What does Charlie call Goodman and his family? What does Steve mean by a "monster kick," and why does Goodman say, "We're no different than any of the rest of you"? What does Woman One say Goodman is doing when he looks up at the sky? Then, have students work in their groups to collaborate on the Extending Interpretations questions.

Act One

Clarifying Word Meanings: Definitions

Writers often help readers understand difficult words by using definition. A writer using **definition** will provide the word's meaning within the sentence. Let's look at the following sentence:

> In this brief fraction of a moment they take the first step toward a <u>metamorphosis</u> that changes people from a group into a mob.

A reader who does not understand the word *metamorphosis* would benefit from the second half of the sentence, which defines what a metamorphosis does: "changes people from a group into a mob." The reader can then know that events have just taken a pretty important turn. The good people of Maple Street have suddenly become another creature entirely.

As you read, be on the lookout for definitions provided in the text itself. Chances are, if you read a little past a difficult word, you may find that the writer has given you some help.

Word Bank

transfixed
intelligible
assent
intimidated
defiant

PRACTICE

Each sentence below contains an underlined word from the Word Bank as well as a **definition** of that word. For each item, identify the defining words. It might help to explore each word's meaning in a cluster diagram, like the one at the right for the word *transfixed*.

1. Steve stood <u>transfixed</u>, looking at the sky as if he had been nailed to the spot and couldn't move.

2. As the mob came closer, its words became more <u>intelligible</u>, allowing Mr. Goodman to hear and understand them.

3. The residents of Maple Street agreed that strange events were afoot, and when Pete Van Horn offered to investigate, everyone nodded <u>assent</u>.

4. People facing a mob would be <u>intimidated</u>, and their fright would be justified.

5. Tommy was quietly <u>defiant</u> when the adults laughed at him; he held his ground no matter what they said.

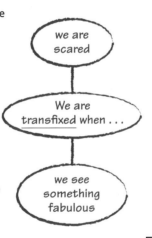

SKILLS FOCUS

Vocabulary Skills
Clarify word meanings by using definitions.

Vocabulary Development

PRACTICE

1. transfixed; as if he had been nailed to the spot and couldn't move
2. intelligible; allowing Mr. Goodman to hear and understand them
3. assent; agreed, everyone nodded
4. intimidated; fright
5. defiant; held his ground no matter what they said

The Monsters Are Due on Maple Street, Act One   **69**

Advanced Learners

Encourage students to consider the characters who have thus far been introduced. Have students discuss how their manner of speaking, their words, and their actions help to reveal their personalities.

Enrichment. Point out to students that an alien does not need to be a creature from outer space; it may be anyone who feels or is treated like an outsider in a group. Ask students to research the origin of the word *alien* (from the Latin *alius*, "other"), and have them make associations to related words, such as *alienate, alienation,* and *alienist.*

SMALL GROUP

❓ Compare and contrast. What is the mood at the end of Act One? How is the mood different at the beginning of Act Two? [Possible response: At the end of Act One, the mood is charged with tension, anger, and the threat of violence, as the shouting Goodman confronts the crowd. At the beginning of Act Two, the mood is quieter and more sub-dued, though still tense. The people are suspicious and are keeping watch on Goodman, but the immediate threat of danger is gone.]

B **Vocabulary Development**

Clarify word meanings: Definitions. Have students note the word *all-pervading,* and ask them what other words in the sentence can help them understand what it means. [blankets the area]

C **Reading Skills**

❓ Make judgments. In this speech, what evidence does Charlie give to support his accusation against Goodman? What do you think of this evidence? [The evidence is that Goodman looks up at the sky in the early morning. As evidence, this detail is meaningless.]

D **Cross-curricular Connections**
HISTORY

The Dark Ages. The term *Dark Ages* is sometimes used to refer to the early part of the Middle Ages (about A.D. 500–1000) when the "light" of knowledge and reason seemed to be nearly extinguished by constant warfare and the col-lapse of the Roman Empire. The "darkness" of superstition seemed to be sweeping away the "light" of law and reason found in the classical world.

Act Two

A *Fade in on the entry hall of the Goodman house at night. On the side table rests an unlit candle.* MRS. GOODMAN *walks into the scene, a glass of milk in hand. She sets the milk down on the table, lights the candle with a match from a box on the table, picks up the glass of milk, and starts out of the scene. Cut to an outside shot.* MRS. GOODMAN *comes through her porch door, glass of milk in hand. The entry hall, with the table and lit candle, can be seen behind her. The camera slowly pans down the side-walk, taking in little knots of people who stand around talking in low voices. At the end of each conversation they look toward* LES GOODMAN's *house. From the various houses we can see candlelight but no electricity.*

B *An all-pervading quiet blankets the area, disturbed only by the almost whispered voices of the people as they stand around. The camera pans over to one group where* CHARLIE *stands. He stares across at* GOODMAN's *house. Two men stand across the street from it, in almost sentrylike poses. We return to the group.*

Sally (*a little timorously[1]*). It just doesn't seem right, though, keeping watch on them. Why . . . he was right when he said he was one of our neighbors. Why, I've known Ethel Goodman ever since they moved in. We've been good friends—

C **Charlie.** That don't prove a thing. Any guy who'd spend his time lookin' up at the sky early in the morning—well there's something wrong with that kind of a

---
1. **timorously** (tim′ər·əs·lē) *adv.:* timidly; fearfully.

person. There's something that ain't legiti-mate. Maybe under normal circumstances we could let it go by, but these aren't normal circumstances. Why, look at this street! **D** Nothin' but candles. Why, it's like goin' back into the dark ages or somethin'!

[STEVE *walks down the steps of his porch. He walks down the street, over to* LES GOODMAN's *house, and stops at the foot of the steps.* GOODMAN *stands behind the screen door, his wife behind him, very frightened.*]

Goodman. Just stay right where you are, Steve. We don't want any trouble, but this time if anybody sets foot on my porch, that's what they're going to get—trouble!
Steve. Look, Les—
Goodman. I've already explained to you people. I don't sleep very well at night

sometimes. I get up and I take a walk and I look up at the sky. I look at the stars!

Mrs. Goodman. That's exactly what he does. Why this whole thing, it's . . . it's some kind of madness or something.

Steve (*nods grimly*). That's exactly what it is—some kind of madness.

Charlie's Voice (*shrill, from across the street*). You best watch who you're seen with, Steve! Until we get this all straightened out, you ain't exactly above suspicion yourself. ❻ 📖

Steve (*whirling around toward him*). Or you, Charlie. Or any of us, it seems. From age eight on up!

Woman One. What I'd like to know is, what are we gonna do? Just stand around here all night?

Charlie. There's nothin' else we can do! (*He turns back looking toward* STEVE *and* GOODMAN *again.*) One of 'em'll tip their hand. They got to.

Steve (*raising his voice*). There's something you can do, Charlie. You could go home and keep your mouth shut. You could quit strutting around like a self-appointed hanging judge[2] and just climb into bed and forget it.

Charlie. You sound real anxious to have that happen, Steve. I think we better keep our eye on you too!

Don (*as if he were taking the bit in his teeth, takes a hesitant step to the front*). I think everything might as well come out now.

📖 **MAKE INFERENCES**

❻ What is Charlie suggesting about the fact that Steve is talking to Les Goodman? What can you suppose about the characters from this?

---

2. **hanging judge:** judge who sentences people to death without sufficient evidence.

(*He turns toward* STEVE.) Your wife's done plenty of talking, Steve, about how odd you are!

Charlie (*picking this up, his eyes widening*). Go ahead, tell us what she's said.

[STEVE *walks toward them from across the street.*]

Steve. Go ahead, what's my wife said? Let's get it all out. Let's pick out every idiosyncrasy of every single man, woman, and child on the street. And then we might as well set up some kind of a kangaroo court.[3] How about a firing squad at dawn, Charlie, so we can get rid of all the suspects? Narrow them down. Make it easier for you.

Don. There's no need gettin' so upset, Steve. It's just that . . . well . . . Myra's talked about how there's been plenty of nights you spend hours down in your basement workin' on some kind of radio or something. Well, none of us have ever seen that radio—

[*By this time* STEVE *has reached the group. He stands there defiantly close to them.*]

Charlie. Go ahead, Steve. What kind of "radio set" you workin' on? I never seen it. Neither has anyone else. Who you talk to on that radio set? And who talks to you?

Steve. I'm surprised at you, Charlie. How come you're so dense all of a sudden? (*A pause*) Who do I talk to? I talk to monsters from outer space. I talk to three-headed green men who fly over here in what look like meteors.

---

3. **kangaroo court:** unauthorized court, usually one that pays no attention to legal procedures. Kangaroo courts were often set up in frontier areas.

Vocabulary
idiosyncrasy (id′ē·ō·sin′krə·sē) *n.*: peculiarity.

E **Reading Skills**

Make inferences. [Possible response to question 6: Charlie is suggesting that Steve is suspect just because he is talking with Les. Students may suppose that the characters are fearful and are acting irrationally, blaming others for the unexplained events without good reasons.]

F **English-Language Learners**

Interpret idioms. Tell students that the idiom *tip their hand* means to reveal something without meaning to, as card players do if they unintentionally show their cards. In this case, Charlie means that if he waits long enough, some people will make a mistake and "tip their hand," or unintentionally reveal their connection to the aliens.

G **Learners Having Difficulty**

Summarize. Have students take parts and read this dialogue aloud. Then, ask them to summarize what is happening. Be sure they understand that Charlie's and Don's accusations are based not on facts but on fear.

H **Vocabulary Development**

Clarify word meanings: Definitions. Direct students to look at the meaning of *kangaroo court* in the footnote if they haven't done so. Then, ask students to explain why Steve uses the term. [Possible response: Steve is using the term to show scorn for the way Charlie and others are making accusations and setting themselves up as both judge and jury.]

DIFFERENTIATING INSTRUCTION

English-Language Learners
Ask students if they have ever been viewed with suspicion because they observed a tradition from their native country or behaved slightly differently from others. Ask them how their experiences might relate to the events taking place in the play. Why are people under pressure so afraid of idiosyncrasies and differences?

A **Advanced Learners**

? **Interpret.** Why do you think Steve says, "Let them get a search warrant"? [Possible responses: He has something to hide; he fears his neighbors; he is angry about his neighbors' mob mentality.]

B **Cross-curricular Connections**
CULTURE

Scapegoat. A *scapegoat* is "someone who is made to bear the blame for the wrongdoings of others." The term is from a scene in the Bible, in which Aaron confesses the sins of the people of Israel over the head of a live goat. The goat then symbolically bears those sins.

C **Literary Focus**

? **Suspense.** Have students imagine watching this scene on television. What makes the scene suspenseful? [Possible responses: The long shot of the gloomy street sets a mood of mystery. The shadowy, almost ghostly figure surprises the viewer. Anxiety about who the figure is and what he will do builds as he slowly advances toward the crowd. Tommy's shout increases the tension. Then a man holds up a shotgun.]

D **Literary Focus**

? **Characterization.** How would you contrast Steve's words about the approaching figure with the words and actions of Don and Charlie? [Possible response: Steve thinks through the consequences of an action and tries to keep the situation under control. Don and Charlie speak and act impulsively.]

E **Vocabulary Development**

? **Clarify word meanings: Definitions.** What word defines *apprehensive*? [fearful]

[STEVE'S *wife steps down from their porch, bites her lip, calls out.*]

Mrs. Brand. Steve! Steve, please. (*Then looking around, frightened, she walks toward the group.*) It's just a ham radio[4] set, that's all. I bought him a book on it myself. It's just a ham radio set. A lot of people have them. I can show it to you. It's right down in the basement.

Steve (*whirls around toward her*). Show them nothing! If they want to look inside our house—let them get a search warrant.
Charlie. Look, buddy, you can't afford to—
Steve (*interrupting*). Charlie, don't tell me what I can afford! And stop telling me who's dangerous and who isn't and who's safe and who's a menace. (*He turns to the group and shouts.*) And you're with him too—all of you! You're standing here all set to crucify—all set to find a scapegoat—all desperate to point some kind of a finger at a neighbor! Well now look, friends, the only thing that's gonna happen is that we'll eat each other up alive—

[*He stops abruptly as* CHARLIE *suddenly grabs his arm.*]

Charlie (*in a hushed voice*). That's not the only thing that can happen to us.

[*Cut to a long shot looking down the street. A figure has suddenly materialized in the gloom, and in the silence we can hear the clickety-clack of slow, measured footsteps on concrete as the figure walks slowly toward them. One of the women lets out a stifled cry.[5] The young mother grabs her boy, as do a couple of others.*]

---

4. **ham radio:** two-way radio used by an amateur operator. Ham radio operators used to talk to one another all over the world via their radios.
5. **stifled** (stī′fəld) **cry:** cry that is checked or stopped.

Tommy (*shouting, frightened*). It's the monster! It's the monster!

[*Another woman lets out a wail and the people fall back in a group, staring toward the darkness and the approaching figure. As the people stand in the shadows watching,* DON MARTIN *joins them, carrying a shotgun. He holds it up.*]

Don. We may need this.
Steve. A shotgun? (*He pulls it out of* DON'S *hand.*) Good Lord—will anybody think a thought around here? Will you people wise up? What good would a shotgun do against—

[*Now* CHARLIE *pulls the gun from* STEVE'S *hand.*]

Charlie. No more talk, Steve. You're going to talk us into a grave! You'd let whatever's out there walk right over us, wouldn't yuh? Well, some of us won't!

[*He swings the gun around to point it toward the sidewalk. The dark figure continues to walk toward them. The group stands there, fearful, apprehensive. Mothers clutch children, men stand in front of wives.* CHARLIE *slowly raises the gun. As the figure gets closer and closer, he suddenly pulls the trigger. The sound of it explodes in the stillness. The figure suddenly lets out a small cry, stumbles forward onto his knees, and then falls forward on his face.* DON, CHARLIE, *and* STEVE *race over to him.* STEVE *is there first and turns the man over. Now the crowd gathers around them.*]

Steve (*slowly looks up*). It's Pete Van Horn.

Vocabulary
menace (men′əs) *n.:* danger; threat.

MINI-LESSON **Reading**

Developing Word-Attack Skills
Present this mnemonic poem:
    I before *e* except after *c,*
    And when sounded like *a,*
    As in *neighbor* and *weigh.*
Explain that the poem helps you remember how most words with *ie* and *ei* are spelled, but it gives you only one clue about the sounds the letters stand for.

Use these words from the selection to explore the differing sounds of *ie* and *ei*. Write these sets of words on the chalkboard without underlines. In two of the words in each set, *ie* or *ei* stands for the same sound; in one of the words, the letters stand for a sound that is different from the other two. Have students read each set and identify the word with the different sound.

The Monsters Are Due on Maple Street, Act Two   73

Don (*in a hushed voice*). Pete Van Horn! He was just gonna go over to the next block to see if the power was on—

Woman One. You killed him, Charlie. You shot him dead!

Charlie (*looks around at the circle of faces, his eyes frightened, his face contorted*). But . . . but I didn't know who he was. I certainly didn't know who he was. He comes walkin' out of the darkness—how am I supposed to know who he was? (*He grabs* STEVE.) Steve—you know why I shot! How was I supposed to know he wasn't a monster or something? (*He grabs* DON *now.*) We're all scared of the same thing. I was just tryin' to . . . tryin' to protect my home, that's all! Look, all of you, that's all I was tryin' to do. (*He looks down wildly at the body.*) I didn't know it was somebody we knew! I didn't know—

[*There's a sudden hush and then an intake of breath. We see the living room window of* CHARLIE's *house. The window is not lit, but suddenly the house lights come on behind it.*]

Woman One (*in a very hushed voice*). Charlie . . . Charlie . . . the lights just went on in your house. Why did the lights just go on?

Don. What about it, Charlie? How come you're the only one with lights now?

Goodman. That's what I'd like to know.

[*There is a pause as they all stare toward* CHARLIE.]

You were so quick to kill, Charlie, and you were so quick to tell us who we had to be careful of. Well, maybe you had to kill. Maybe Peter there was trying to tell us something. Maybe he'd found out

---

F **Literary Focus**

? Complications. What new complication has occurred? [Charlie has killed Pete Van Horn.] **How might this complication affect the events to come?** [Possible responses: The neighbors may now become suspicious of Charlie. They may no longer go along with Charlie if he continues to blame others. Charlie may have had a secret motive for killing Van Horn that will be revealed.]

Set 1	Set 2	Set 3
brief	weight	<u>series</u>
field	<u>either</u>	quiet
<u>friends</u>	neighbors	science

Activity. Write these sentences and words on the chalkboard. Have students identify the word that shares the vowel sound spelled with *ie* or *ei* in the underlined word.

1. Fear raced through the <u>neighborhood</u>.
space   field   light [space]

2. Something <u>weird</u> was happening.
weigh   weary   wire [weary]

3. A strange <u>series</u> of events scared them.
raid   streak   wild [streak]

4. Ordinary people became a <u>fierce</u> mob.
fur   fiery   fear [fear]

A Reading Skills

Make inferences. [Possible response to question 7: The residents are implying that Charlie killed Van Horn to keep him from reporting that Charlie is involved in what is happening. The evidence on which they base this inference is that Charlie was quick to kill Van Horn and that the lights in Charlie's house have suddenly turned on.]

B Literary Focus

❓ Complications. How is this new complication in the plot similar to some of the earlier complications, and how is it different? [Possible response: This new complication is like earlier ones in that the group singles out a person for blame. It is different and more frightening because physical violence against a fellow townsperson is occurring. Words such as *desperate punches, smashes, blood running,* and *converging* suggest that something very destructive may happen next.]

C Reading Skills

❓ Interpret. Why does Charlie say that he knows who the monster is? [Charlie is trying to save himself by naming someone else.]

---

something and came back to tell us who there was amongst us we should watch out for— **❼** 📖

[CHARLIE *backs away from the group, his eyes wide with fright.*]

Charlie. No . . . no . . . it's nothing of the sort! I don't know why the lights are on. I swear I don't. Somebody's pulling a gag or something.

[*He bumps against* STEVE, *who grabs him and whirls him around.*]

Steve. A gag? A gag? Charlie, there's a dead man on the sidewalk and you killed him! Does this thing look like a gag to you?

[CHARLIE *breaks away and screams as he runs toward his house.*]

Charlie. No! No! Please!

[*A man breaks away from the crowd to chase* CHARLIE. *The man tackles him and lands on top of him. The other people start to run toward them.* CHARLIE *is up on his feet. He breaks away from the other man's grasp and lands a couple of desperate punches that push the man aside. Then he forces his way, fighting, through the crowd to once again break free. He jumps up on his front porch. A rock thrown from the group smashes a window alongside of him, the broken glass flying past him. A couple of pieces cut him. He stands there perspiring, rumpled, blood running down from a cut on his cheek. His wife breaks away from the group to throw herself into his arms. He buries his face against her. We can see the crowd converging on the porch now.*]

> **📖 MAKE INFERENCES**
> **❼** What are the residents implying about Charlie? based on what evidence?

Voices.
It must have been him.
He's the one.
We got to get Charlie.

[*Another rock lands on the porch. Now* CHARLIE *pushes his wife behind him, facing the group.*]

Charlie. Look, look, I swear to you . . . it isn't me . . . but I do know who it is . . . I swear to you, I do know who it is. I know who the monster is here. I know who it is that doesn't belong. I swear to you I know.

Goodman (*shouting*). What are you waiting for?

Woman One (*shouting*). Come on, Charlie, come on.

Man One (*shouting*). Who is it, Charlie, tell us!

Don (*pushing his way to the front of the crowd*). All right, Charlie, let's hear it!

[CHARLIE'*s eyes dart around wildly.*]

Charlie. It's . . . it's . . .
Man Two (*screaming*). Go ahead, Charlie, tell us.
Charlie. It's . . . it's the kid. It's Tommy. He's the one.

[*There's a gasp from the crowd as we cut to a shot of the mother holding her boy. The boy at first doesn't understand. Then, realizing the eyes are all on him, he buries his face against his mother,* SALLY.]

Sally (*backs away*). That's crazy. That's crazy. He's a little boy.
Woman One. But he knew! He was the only

Vocabulary
converging (kən·vʉrj′iŋ) *v.* used as *adj.:* closing in.

CROSS-CURRICULAR CONNECTIONS

History
McCarthyism. In the early 1950s, the United States was fighting a "cold war" with the Soviet Union. Americans were worried about a communist takeover of the world. In this atmosphere of fear, Senator Joseph McCarthy of Wisconsin charged that communist spies had infiltrated the government. In nationally televised hearings, he accused government employees and thousands of others of being communists—with little

evidence to back up his claims. The characters in *The Monsters Are Due on Maple Street* use some of McCarthy's tactics, such as getting those accused to accuse others to save themselves, and assuming people are guilty because they associate with the accused.
Activity. Call on volunteers to research the term *McCarthyism* and share what they learn with the class.

INDIVIDUAL

one who knew! He told us all about it. Well, how did he know? How could he have known?

[*The various people take this up and repeat the questions aloud.*]

Voices.
How could he know?
Who told him?
Make the kid answer.

❽

Man One. What about Goodman's car?
Don. It was Charlie who killed old man Van Horn.
Woman One. But it was the kid here who knew what was going to happen all the time. He was the one who knew!

[STEVE *shouts at his hysterical neighbors.*]

Steve. Are you all gone crazy? (*Pause as he looks about*) Stop.

[*A fist crashes at* STEVE'*s face, staggering him back out of view. Several close camera shots suggest the coming of violence: A hand fires a rifle. A fist clenches. A hand grabs the hammer from* VAN HORN'*s body, etc.*]

Don. Charlie has to be the one— Where's my rifle—
Woman One. Les Goodman's the one. His car started! Let's wreck it.
Mrs. Goodman. What about Steve's radio— He's the one that called them—
Mr. Goodman. Smash the radio. Get me a hammer. Get me something.
Steve. Stop— Stop—
Charlie. Where's that kid— Let's get him.
Man One. Get Steve— Get Charlie— They're working together.

[*The crowd starts to converge around the*

━━━━━━━━━━━━━━━

🔖 **MAKE INFERENCES**
❽ What inference have the residents made about Tommy?

━━━━━━━━━━━━━━━

mother, who grabs her son and starts to run with him. The crowd starts to follow, at first, walking fast, and then running after him. Suddenly, CHARLIE'*s lights go off and the lights in another house go on. They stay on for a moment, then from across the street other lights go on and then off again.*]

Man One (*shouting*). It isn't the kid. . . . It's Bob Weaver's house.
Woman One. It isn't Bob Weaver's house, it's Don Martin's place.
Charlie. I tell you, it's the kid.
Don. It's Charlie. He's the one.

[*The people shout, accuse, scream. The camera tilts back and forth. We see panic-stricken faces in close-up and tilting shots of houses as the lights go on and off. Slowly, in the middle of this nightmarish morass*[6] *of sight and sound, the camera starts to pull away, until once again we've reached the opening shot, looking at the Maple Street sign from high above. The camera continues to move away until we dissolve to a shot of the metal side of a spacecraft, which sits shrouded*[7] *in darkness. An open door throws out a beam of light from the illuminated interior. Two figures silhouetted against the bright lights appear. We get only a vague feeling of form, but nothing more* explicit *than that.*]

Figure One. Understand the procedure now? Just stop a few of their machines and radios

━━━━━━━━━━━━━━━

6. **morass** (mə·ras′) *n.*: confusing situation. Strictly speaking, a morass is a kind of swamp.

7. **shrouded** (shroud′id) *v.* used as *adj.*: hidden; covered.

Vocabulary
explicit (eks·plis′it) *adj.*: definite.

━━━━━━━━━━━━━━━

Literature
The Crucible. In this teleplay, Rod Serling comments on the McCarthy hearings. Arthur Miller, a writer whom McCarthy investigated, also used his writing to comment on the hearings. Miller's play, *The Crucible,* is based on real events that took place in Salem, Massachusetts, in the 1600s and have parallels to the events of the 1950s. In *The Crucible,* hysteria sweeps through the town

of Salem just as it does through Maple Street. Both Serling and Miller warn audiences of the injustice that can occur when people are falsely accused of crimes and no one defends them.
Activity. Invite a small group of advanced readers to read *The Crucible* and then point out similarities between the two plays.

SMALL GROUP

ⅅ Reading Skills

Make inferences. [Possible response to question 8: The residents have inferred that Tommy is one of the people sent down by the aliens.]

ⅇ Literary Focus

❓ **Symbol.** How does Steve's action resemble others he has taken before? How is the neighbors' response different from before? What could this incident symbolize? [Possible response: Before, Steve's neighbors only disagreed with him verbally. Now, they use violence against him. Steve has been the voice of reason throughout the play. The mob's attack on Steve could signal that mass hysteria is taking over.]

ⅎ Reading Skills

❓ **Interpret.** The Goodmans seem like good people who were accused falsely. Why are they now accusing Steve? What do their actions suggest about them? [Possible response: The Goodmans are accusing Steve to protect themselves. Their actions suggest that they are really not much better than Charlie, who also has accused another to save himself.]

⅁ Literary Focus

❓ **Mood.** What makes this scene so horrifying? [Possible responses: The vivid verbs and adjectives—*shout, accuse, scream, panic-stricken, nightmarish*—convey to readers a mood of terror and chaos. Readers experience the frantic pace of the action as the camera jumps quickly from one house to the next and tilts back and forth. Readers sense that the Maple Street inhabitants are ready to self-destruct.]

A Reading Skills

Make inferences. [Possible response to question 9: One can infer that the aliens believe that humans are easy to manipulate and control and that humans will always turn on one another and destroy themselves.]

B Reading Skills

? Paraphrase. According to the narrator, what is a threat to all of us? [Possible response: Prejudice and suspicion threaten all of us because they make people act irrationally and can lead to violence.]

GUIDED PRACTICE

Monitor students' progress. Have students work in groups to plan a new and happy ending for *The Monsters Are Due on Maple Street.* Have groups discuss how the residents' fears caused all but the first complication and then brainstorm to come up with ways that the residents might have acted together to solve the problem.

---

and telephones and lawn mowers . . . throw them into darkness for a few hours and then you just sit back and watch the pattern.
Figure Two. And this pattern is always the same?
Figure One. With few variations. They pick the most dangerous enemy they can find . . . and it's themselves. And all we need do is sit back . . . and watch.
Figure Two. Then I take it this place . . . this Maple Street . . . is not unique.
Figure One (*shaking his head*). By no means. Their world is full of Maple Streets. And we'll go from one to the other and let them destroy themselves. One to the other . . . one to the other . . . one to the other— **9**

[*Now the camera pans up for a shot of the starry sky.*]

Narrator's Voice. The tools of conquest do not necessarily come with bombs and explosions and fallout. There are weapons that are simply thoughts, attitudes, prejudices—to be found only in the minds of men. For the record, prejudices can kill and suspicion can destroy, and a thoughtless, frightened search for a scapegoat has a fallout all of its own for the children . . . the children yet unborn. (*A pause*) And the pity of it is . . . that these things cannot be confined to . . . The Twilight Zone!

[*Fade to black.*]

Vocabulary
variations (ver′ē·ā′shənz) *n.*: differences.

MAKE INFERENCES
9 What can you infer about the aliens' view of the human race?

FAMILY/COMMUNITY ACTIVITY

Ask students to interview senior members of their families (such as their grandparents) or older friends about their memories of the 1950s. How did people dress? What were their houses like? How did they use front porches? What did their cars look like? What did they do for entertainment? How did they communicate with people far away? These interviews will help students better understand and visualize the setting of *The Monsters Are Due on Maple Street.*

Meet the Writer

Rod Serling

Man from Another Dimension

Rod Serling (1924–1975) was a man of great energy. He had the vitality of one who seems to be running even as he is standing still.

How does a fledgling writer caught in a dreamless job get from Cincinnati, Ohio, to New York City and then to Hollywood? If you're Rod Serling, you one day look at your wife, and together you decide that the hour has come to sink or swim—the hour has come to go for it.

In the early 1950s, Rod Serling eagerly arrived in New York and found himself a job writing for television when it was new and young. He first wrote for a live half-hour drama called *Lux Video Theatre*. From there he went on to create and produce the hit television show *The Twilight Zone*.

In the fifth-dimensional world of the Twilight Zone, Serling made his concerns and beliefs visible. He sought to show his audiences that "there is nothing in the dark that isn't there when the lights are on." In his widely known teleplay *The Monsters Are Due on Maple Street*, he dramatized what was perhaps his most enduring and urgent theme.

The teleplay was written at a time when Americans were concerned about the spread of communism to the United States. Thousands of lives were destroyed by suspicion and suggestion. People lost their jobs, homes, and friends when they were accused of being members of the Communist party, even though membership in the party was legal. During this time some people made up stories about others in order to appear innocent themselves, and many people were afraid to continue friendships with those who had been accused or were suspected of being members of the Communist party. Rod Serling could not write about these events directly for television; the show would not have made it on the air. Yet in *The Monsters Are Due on Maple Street*, he does voice his opinion.

For Independent Reading

Enter the fifth dimension by checking out Rod Serling's *The Twilight Zone: Complete Stories.*

Meet the Writer

Rod Serling used his writing to fight what he felt were injustices in society. Through the fantasies of *The Twilight Zone* and other works, Serling was able to express his sometimes controversial ideas. Though *The Twilight Zone* was one of the most popular television series ever created, Serling wasn't satisfied with his success as a screenwriter. He wanted to be recognized as a serious writer.

For Independent Reading

■ Students who read *The Twilight Zone* books would also enjoy watching Serling's *Twilight Zone* TV series, which is sometimes shown on cable television. In addition, you might recommend the following titles:

■ For another book that involves alien invasion, students may read *Under Alien Stars* by Pamela E. Service. This science fiction novel introduces an alien character and pits him against a human.

■ Students who want to explore the view from space will enjoy reading the nonfiction selection *Seeing Earth from Space* by Patricia Lauber. Informative and easy to understand, the book includes facts about the use of satellites and remote sensors.

DIFFERENTIATING INSTRUCTION

Advanced Learners

The early days of television. Sometimes referred to as the "Golden Age" of television, the 1950s were an era in which many of the most talented minds in show business applied themselves to this new medium. **Activity.** Encourage interested students to research television in the 1950s, a time when shows were often broadcast live and many of the television formats common today, such as the sitcom and the game show, were developed. For Internet research, students can input keyword phrases such as *1950s television* and *Museum of Television and Radio.*

After You Read

Thinking Critically

1. Possible answers: The roaring sound and flashing light caused the power failure; Les Goodman is an alien; Steve and Goodman are both aliens; both Charlie and Tommy are aliens. These inferences were incorrect.

2. Steve most clearly reflects Rod Serling's point of view. Possible speeches:
   - Wait a minute . . . wait a minute! Let's not be a mob!
   - You're standing here all set to crucify—all set to find a scapegoat—all desperate to point some kind of a finger at a neighbor! Well now look, friends, the only thing that's gonna happen is that we'll eat each other up alive—

3. The name hints that, on a scale measuring good men, he is a "less good man," the kind that might turn on a friend. Readers can infer that he is perhaps better than Charlie but less good than Steve.

4. The residents lose the power to reason. The symbolism is reflected through the loss of electricity, which literally puts them in the dark. The community then turns on one another, and distrust changes the residents into a violent, angry mob.

5. Our most dangerous enemy is ourselves. The "monsters" are the prejudices, suspicions, and lawless mob behavior of the people.

Extending Interpretations

6. Possible answer: Its message is still important today because suspicious attitudes and prejudice continue to keep people apart.

After You Read Response and Analysis

Acts One and Two

Thinking Critically

1. Choose three **inferences** you made as you read the teleplay. Were your inferences correct? Explain.

2. Writers often speak through a particular character to voice their own opinions. Which character do you think reflects Rod Serling's **point of view**? Find at least two speeches that reveal that point of view.

3. In light of Les Goodman's behavior throughout the plot, what **inference** can you make about the significance of his name?

4. **Symbols** in literature are persons, places, or things that function as themselves but that can also stand for larger ideas, such as love, glory, or honor. When Maple Street loses power and is plunged into darkness, terrible events unfold. This loss of power is also a symbol for a larger idea. What personal power, or ability, do the residents of Maple Street lose that plunges them further into darkness?

5. According to the aliens, who is the most dangerous enemy? Who do you think are the "monsters" in this story?

Extending Interpretations

6. This teleplay was written in 1960. Is its message still important today? Explain why or why not.

SKILLS FOCUS

Literary Skills
Analyze plot complications.

Reading Skills
Make inferences.

Writing Skills
Analyze a work's message; update a teleplay.

Reading Check

Fill out a chart like the one below to show the bare bones of the play's **plot.** Be sure to compare your charts in class. You might have different opinions about the number of key events, or **complications,** that lead to the surprising resolution.

Reading Check

Basic situation—A mysterious power failure unsettles a quiet street. *Event*—People hear a roar and see a flash of light and think a meteor has gone by. *Event*—A power failure occurs. *Event*—Les Goodman is confronted by an angry mob. *Event*— Pete Van Horn is killed by Charlie. *Event*—Charlie is attacked by a mob. *Event*—Everyone accuses everyone else; mass hysteria. *Resolution*—The mass hysteria was deliberately generated by aliens as a way of getting humans to destroy themselves.

WRITING ABOUT THE TELEPLAY

Responding to a Text

What message does the play deliver about humankind? How do the events of the teleplay illustrate this message? In a two-paragraph essay, write your response to this play. In one paragraph, explain the meaning of the closing comments in light of the events of this teleplay. In the second paragraph, tell how you feel about the message in the play, and explain how the message still has significance in today's world (unless you believe otherwise!).

Updating the Teleplay

Suppose you are a television producer and you want to update the teleplay so that it takes place in 2010. In a paragraph, tell how you would change details of the play to set it in the new time frame. Consider these details:

- What do people now know about aliens and space travel?
- What electronic equipment would be affected by the blackout?
- Where would the aliens land (would you keep a small town as your setting or would you set the revised story in a suburb or a city)?
- What would Tommy be reading today?

PRACTICE

1. variations; differences, changes
2. converging; meeting
3. explicit; knowable and under-standable
4. menace; danger
5. idiosyncrasy; oddity that makes him unique

ASSESSING

Assessment

■ *Holt Assessment: Literature, Reading, and Vocabulary*

RETEACHING

For a lesson reteaching interrelated plot events, see **Reteaching**, p. 917D.

After You Read   Vocabulary Development

Act Two

Clarifying Word Meanings: Definitions

Sharpen your definition-hunting skills with the following exercise.

PRACTICE

Choose the word from the Word Bank that best fits the blank in each sentence below. Remember to look for definitions within each sentence to help you decide. Be ready to cite the definition you found in the sentence.

1. Wherever the aliens go, the human beings react the same: There are few differences, few changes, few _____.

2. During the second act the crowd's fear, mistrust, and suspicion are meeting, or _____, to create a mob.

3. An _____ danger is by its nature knowable and understandable.

4. A frightened man with a gun can be considered a _____ and a danger to society.

5. Steve's interest in ham radios becomes a threat rather than an oddity, or _____, that makes him unique.

> **Word Bank**
>
> idiosyncrasy
> menace
> converging
> explicit
> variations

SKILLS FOCUS

Vocabulary Skills
Clarify word meanings by using definitions.

Understanding Text Structures: An Owner's Manual

Reading Focus
Structure and Purpose of an Instructional Manual

For the residents of Maple Street, not even cell phones might have been helpful against the aliens' powers. However, a cell phone might be just the kind of device to get you out of a crisis—if you know how to use one, that is.

The **purpose** of an instructional manual is to help you operate and care for a specific device, such as a cordless phone or a hand-held Internet appliance. Many instructional manuals have a **structure** like that of a small textbook.

Use these strategies in order to make the best use of an instructional manual:

- Scan the **table of contents** of the manual to get an idea of the topics covered.

- If you don't see the topic you're looking for, turn to the **index,** located in the back of the manual. This is an alphabetical list of the topics and the page numbers on which they appear.

- Look for a regular mail address and an **e-mail address** as well as a

customer service **phone number** or **Web site** where you can get additional help from the manufacturer.

- Become familiar with the parts of the device. An instructional manual usually includes a **diagram** showing you the important parts of the device and explaining their functions.

- Read the **directions** carefully, and keep referring to the actual device as you read.

- Do the directions have **steps**? Follow them in order. Read all the directions for a procedure before you move on to the next one.

- Make sure you understand any special abbreviations or symbols. You may find definitions and meanings in the manual's **glossary**—an alphabetical list of special terms and their definitions.

■ With all the electronic products available today, it's useful to know how to read an instructional manual like the one on page 82.

Reading Skills
Understand the structure and purpose of an instructional manual.

Cellular Telephone Owner's Manual **81**

SKILLS FOCUS
pp. 81–83

Grade-Level Skills
■ **Reading Skills**
Analyze the structure and purpose of informational texts, including an instructional manual.

Summary ⬌ *at grade level*

Two sets of step-by-step directions are given for removing and replacing the batteries on a cellular phone. The manual provides written directions and diagrams to help the user complete this task.

PRETEACHING

Selection Starter
Motivate. Ask students to think about a time when they or a family member tried to put together something such as a bookcase or tried to use an electronic product for the first time. Was it difficult to do? Were the instructions easy to follow? Have students discuss any problems they experienced.

Assign the Reading
Read the Student Edition text on the structure and purpose of an instructional manual with students. Make sure they realize that the boldfaced terms in the bulleted list represent common elements of such a manual. Then, assign the reading in class.

RESOURCES: READING

Planning
■ *One-Stop Planner* CD-ROM with ExamView Test Generator

Differentiating Instruction
■ *Holt Adapted Reader*
■ *Holt Reading Solutions*
■ *Supporting Instruction in Spanish*
■ *Audio CD Library*

■ *Audio CD Library, Selections and Summaries in Spanish*

Assessment
■ *Holt Assessment: Literature, Reading, and Vocabulary*
■ *One-Stop Planner* CD-ROM with ExamView Test Generator
■ *Holt Online Assessment*

Internet
■ go.hrw.com (Keyword: LE5 7-1)
■ *Elements of Literature Online*

Media
■ *Audio CD Library*
■ *Audio CD Library, Selections and Summaries in Spanish*

A Reading Informational Text

Purpose. Ask students to identify the purpose of this page of an instructional manual. [Possible response: The purpose is to explain how to remove and replace a cellular phone battery.]

B Reading Informational Text

❓ **Structure.** How is the material organized to help you figure out what to do? [Possible response: The material includes directions organized in numbered steps.]

C Reading Informational Text

❓ **Structure.** Why does the manual include a diagram? [The diagram shows the battery pack, the telephone, and how they fit together. The arrows show where to place the parts so that the battery clicks into place.]

D Reading Skills

❓ **Find the main idea.** Why does the manual give a second set of directions? When would owners use each method? [The manual gives owners options. Using the first method, they can change the battery at any time. The second method lets owners change the battery in the middle of a call, so they will not be interrupted if the original battery loses power.]

Monitor students' progress. Have student pairs explain the steps for battery removal and replacement. Have one partner explain the standard method and the other explain the quick-change method. Listeners should check that their partners explain every step.

Cellular Telephone Owner's Manual

Battery Removal and Replacement

A There are two ways to remove and replace your telephone battery—the standard method and the quick-change method.

Standard Method

B
1. Turn off your telephone.
2. Depress the latch button on the rear of the battery, and slide the battery pack downward until it stops.
3. Lift the battery clear to remove.
4. To reinstall, place the battery pack on the unit so that its grooves align, and slide upward (in the direction of the arrows on the back of the phone) until it clicks into place.

Quick-Change Method

D
1. Advise the party you are talking to that you are about to change batteries.
2. Remove the battery from the telephone.
3. Put on the spare battery.
4. Press PWR. This will return you to your telephone call. You will have only five seconds to complete this action before your telephone call is terminated.

The quick-change method allows you to remove your telephone battery at any time and replace it with a charged spare battery during a telephone call. This is especially useful if you receive the "low battery" message (or an audible tone) during a call.

It is a good idea to practice this procedure a few times before using it during an actual phone call.

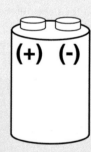

Learners Having Difficulty
Students who have never handled a cellular telephone may be unfamiliar with its basic controls, such as the on-off button, and how those controls are typically labeled. If you have access to a cellular telephone, you may want to bring it in to show students that *PWR* is a common label for the on-off button and to demonstrate the "low battery" message.

Advanced Learners
Researching products. Have students conduct an Internet search to find information on current cellular telephone models. They can browse the Web for online vendors of replacement batteries and create a chart that lists several merchants (with Web site addresses and phone numbers), includes price comparisons for a particular battery, and provides numbered, step-by-step ordering directions.

Analyzing an Owner's Manual

Cellular Telephone Owner's Manual

Test Practice

1. The **main topic** of the section of the manual on page 82 is —
   A removing and replacing the battery
   B making and receiving calls
   C using the phone to send e-mail
   D using the phone in out-of-state networks

2. In which part of the manual would you look to find the pages on which the topic of ringer volume appears?
   F Diagram
   G Glossary
   H Index
   J Cover

3. In which part of the manual would you look to find the meaning of the abbreviation of *LCD*?
   A Table of contents
   B Glossary
   C Index
   D Cover

4. The first step in the standard method is to —
   F remove the battery
   G tell the person you're speaking with to call back
   H turn off the phone
   J turn off the "low battery" message

5. The first step in the quick-change method is to —
   A put in the spare battery
   B remove the battery
   C tell the person you're speaking with that you're going to change the battery
   D ask the person you're speaking with to call you back after you've changed the battery

6. After you put in the spare battery using the quick-change method, your call will be terminated unless you —
   F press PWR within five seconds
   G deposit twenty-five cents
   H charge the telephone battery
   J press 0 for further assistance

Constructed Response

Use the chart to the right to compare these informational materials: newspaper articles, textbooks, and instructional manuals.

Material	Purpose	Structure
Newspaper articles		
Textbooks		
Instructional manuals		

SKILLS FOCUS

Reading Skills
Analyze the structure and purpose of an instructional manual.

Cellular Telephone Owner's Manual **83**

Analyzing an Owner's Manual

Test Practice

Answers and Model Rationales

1. **A** Point out that the title of the section gives the topic.
2. **H** The index lists page numbers for specific topics.
3. **B** The glossary gives definitions. A, C, and D help readers locate information.
4. **H** Point out that the first step in repairing any electronic device is to turn off the power.
5. **C** Explain that if you removed the battery without telling the other caller, he or she would think the conversation had been cut off.
6. **F** H is incorrect; a new battery need not be charged.

Test-Taking Tips

For instruction on how to take multiple-choice tests, see **Test Smarts,** p. 920.

Assessment

■ *Holt Assessment: Literature, Reading, and Vocabulary*

Constructed Response

Newspaper articles. Purpose—objectively report on current events. *Structure*—articles in column format, arranged in sentences and paragraphs. *Textbooks. Purpose*—informative prose and graphics based on specific topics. *Structure*—essays divided into chapters, sections, or parts. *Instructional manuals. Purpose*—comprehensive, step-by-step operating guidelines. *Structure*—sections arranged by function, listed in tables of contents, and indexed.

Comparing Literature

Grade-Level Skills

■ **Literary Skills**
Analyze elements of science fiction.

■ **Reading Skills**
Compare and contrast stories.

OVERVIEW

Purpose. This Comparing Literature feature explores the characteristics of science fiction. An understanding of the elements of science fiction will help students analyze and appreciate many fictional works written about or set in the future.

Use. Direct students' attention to the box identifying the elements of science fiction, and tell them to look for these elements as they read "Zoo" and "The Ruum." After reading both stories, students will write a comparison-contrast essay about them. Students will fill in comparison-contrast charts, examine similarities and differences in the elements of science fiction in both stories, and explain how these similarities and differences affect their responses.

Literary Focus
Science Fiction

You're about to read and compare two science fiction stories. **Science fiction** is a kind of writing that lies somewhere between realistic fiction and total fantasy. It is usually set in the future in a world different from our own, but it is not a kind of writing in which anything goes. Science fiction is based on scientific laws. Most writers of science fiction use their knowledge of the latest scientific ideas and discoveries to imagine new technology that might someday be developed. They also use their understanding of human psychology to imagine how people might behave in situations involving that new technology.

The best of science fiction appeals to our intelligence and also to our imagination, to our sense of awe and wonder at being a part of a mysterious and unknown universe.

Reading Skills
Comparing and Contrasting

Although "Zoo" and "The Ruum" are very different stories, they have interesting similarities. To compare and contrast the two stories, you might look at the ways each story uses the elements of science fiction. When you **compare,** you look for ways that things are alike. When you **contrast,** you look for ways that things are different.

SKILLS FOCUS

Literary Skills
Understand the elements of science fiction.

Reading Skills
Compare and contrast stories.

Elements of Science Fiction

Most science fiction stories contain some or all of the following elements:

- **a setting in the future,** often on another planet or in a spaceship
- **technology** that has not yet been invented, but that conforms to the rules of science
- **a journey through time** or to a distant planet or galaxy
- **imaginary characters** from outer space—alien or extraterrestrial creatures
- realistic human reactions to **fantastic situations**
- **a surprise ending**

Before You Read

You've probably been to a zoo to see the animals. You may have stood in front of the animals' cages and commented on their strange features, their enormous size, or the curious way they chew their food. Have you ever wondered what these animals are thinking as they look at you?

Comparing Literature

Zoo

Edward D. Hoch

The children were always good during the month of August, especially when it began to get near the twenty-third. It was on this day that Professor Hugo's Interplanetary Zoo settled down for its annual six-hour visit to the Chicago area. ❶

Before daybreak the crowds would form, long lines of children and adults both, each one clutching his or her dollar and waiting with wonderment to see what race of strange creatures the professor had brought this year.

In the past they had sometimes been treated to three-legged creatures from Venus, or tall, thin men from Mars, or even snake-like horrors from somewhere more distant. This year, as the great round ship settled slowly to earth in the huge tri-city parking area just outside of Chicago, they watched with awe as the sides slowly slid up to reveal the familiar barred cages. In them were some wild breed of nightmare—small, horselike animals that moved with quick, jerking motions and constantly chattered in a high-pitched tongue. The citizens of Earth clustered around as Professor Hugo's crew quickly collected the waiting dollars, and soon the good professor himself made an appearance, wearing his many-colored rainbow cape and top hat. "Peoples of Earth," he called into his microphone. ❷

The crowd's noise died down and he continued. "Peoples of Earth, this year you see a real treat for your single dollar—the little-known horse-spider people of Kaan—brought to you across a million miles of space at great expense. Gather around, see them,

A

IDENTIFY

❶ What clue in this first paragraph suggests that this story is **science fiction**?

B

COMPARE AND CONTRAST

❷ "Zoo" is set on Earth sometime in the future. How is life in this future like and unlike life today?

C

Zoo **85**

Summary ⬇ *below grade level*

At an unspecified time in the future, a spaceship carrying Professor Hugo's Interplanetary Zoo descends for its annual six-hour landing in a "tri-city parking area" near Chicago. Crowds gather, and each person pays one dollar to marvel at the caged aliens. This year the professor has brought horse-spider creatures from the planet Kaan. The customers agree that this year's zoo is the best ever. Later, back on Kaan, the horse-spider creatures return to their homes with similar responses. They have visited many worlds, and the spaceship's strong bars have kept them safe from creatures such as the bizarre, two-legged Earthlings that they paid to see.

PRETEACHING

Selection Starter

Motivate. Ask students to recall examples of creatures from outer space from books they've read or films they've seen. [the aliens from *The Monsters Are Due on Maple Street;* E.T. from the movie *E.T. the Extra-Terrestrial*]

DIRECT TEACHING

Ⓐ Literary Focus

❓ **Science fiction.** Which element of science fiction is set up in this opening? [the element of realistic human reactions to fantastic situations]

Ⓑ Reading Skills

Identify. [Possible response to question 1: The words *Interplanetary Zoo* suggest a future setting with aliens.]

Ⓒ Reading Skills

Compare and contrast. [Possible responses to question 2: *Like*— Chicago, microphone, dollars. *Unlike*—aliens, intergalactic travel.]

DIFFERENTIATING INSTRUCTION

Learners Having Difficulty
Part of the fun of science fiction is exploring views of the future. Invite students to compare their own views of the future with the view presented in "Zoo." To help students visualize the Kaanians, you might encourage students to sketch a Kaanian standing next to an Earthling. For lesson plans designed for learners having difficulty, see *Holt Reading Solutions.*

Advanced Learners
Enrichment. These students will appreciate the story's two-part structure. Point out that the first part of the story assumes the perspective of people living on Earth and the second part provides the Kaanians' perspective. Challenge students to identify the point in the story where the perspective changes and to explain how Hoch makes the change. [In paragraph eight, Hoch calls the rocks of Kaan "familiar" and then later describes the Kaanians at home, including their words and emotions.]

Zoo **85**

A Vocabulary Note

Multiple meanings. Ask students to list other meanings they know for the verb *filed*. [Possible responses: smoothed with a rasp; put papers in order; started legal proceedings (filed a lawsuit).] Point out that context clues show which meaning the author intends.

B Reading Skills

Compare and contrast. [Possible response to question 3: Like zoo-goers today, they gawk and marvel.]

C Advanced Learners

Enrichment. Define *anachronistic* as "not fitting in with a story's time period." Ask students why "telephone your friends" might be seen as anachronistic in this story. [Possible response: In a technologically advanced future instant messaging or some newer development would be a more likely way to communicate.]

COMPARE AND CONTRAST

B ❸ How do people react to the horse-spiders of Kaan? How are their reactions similar to the way people today react to animals at a zoo?

---

study them, listen to them, tell your friends about them. But hurry! My ship can remain here only six hours!"

A And the crowds slowly filed by, at once horrified and fascinated by these strange creatures that looked like horses but ran up the walls of their cages like spiders. "This is certainly worth a dollar," one man remarked, hurrying away. "I'm going home to get the wife." ❸

All day long it went like that, until ten thousand people had filed by the barred cages set into the side of the spaceship. Then, as the six-hour limit ran out, Professor Hugo once more took the micro-**C** phone in hand. "We must go now, but we will return next year on this date. And if you enjoyed our zoo this year, telephone your friends in other cities about it. We will land in New York tomorrow, and next week on to London, Paris, Rome, Hong Kong, and Tokyo. Then on to other worlds!"

He waved farewell to them, and as the ship rose from the ground, the Earth peoples agreed that this had been the very best Zoo yet. . . .

86   Collection 1 / Facing Danger

Some two months and three planets later, the silver ship of Professor Hugo settled at last onto the familiar jagged rocks of Kaan, and the odd horse-spider creatures filed quickly out of their cages. Professor Hugo was there to say a few parting words, and then they scurried away in a hundred different directions, seeking their homes among the rocks. **D**

In one house, the she-creature was happy to see the return of her mate and offspring. She babbled a greeting in the strange tongue and hurried to embrace them. "It was a long time you were gone! Was it good?"

And the he-creature nodded. "The little one enjoyed it especially. We visited eight worlds and saw many things."

The little one ran up the wall of the cave. "On the place called Earth it was the best. The creatures there wear garments over their skins, and they walk on two legs."

"But isn't it dangerous?" asked the she-creature.

"No," her mate answered. "There are bars to protect us from them. We remain right in the ship. Next time you must come with us. It is well worth the nineteen commocs it costs." **4**

And the little one nodded. "It was the very best zoo ever. . . ." **5**

Comparing Literature

EVALUATE

4 What do you learn when you hear the horse-spiders speak? **E**

INTERPRET

5 This story's tricky ending makes us reconsider the rest of the story. What do you learn about the zoo in Chicago after you read the second part of the story set in Kaan? **G**

Meet the Writer

Edward D. Hoch

Edward D. Hoch (1930–   ), whose last name rhymes with "coke," was born in Rochester, New York. He became a full-time writer in 1968, publishing novels and short stories and editing collections in the fields of mystery, crime, suspense, science fiction, and fantasy. Hoch contributed more than 750 short stories to periodicals such as *Argosy, Ellery Queen's Mystery Magazine,* and *Alfred Hitchcock's Mystery Magazine.* This prolific mystery writer is a bit of a mystery himself. To find all of his work you also have to search under his many pseudonyms, such as Irwin Booth, Anthony Circus, Stephen Dentinger, Pat McMahon, Mister X, R. E. Porter, and R. L. Stevens. Many consider Hoch to be the finest writer of short mystery fiction, and in 2001, he won the Edgar Allan Poe Grand Master Award. Two of his stories won awards—"The Oblong Room" won the Edgar Allan Poe Award for best mystery short story in 1967, and "The Problem of the Potting Shed" won the Anthony Award for best short story in 2001—and fourteen of his stories were adapted for television.

Zoo **87**

DIRECT TEACHING

D **Vocabulary Note**

? **Synonyms.** *Scurried* suggests running lightly with small, quick steps. What other words might have the same meaning? [scampered, scuttled] Ask students to use each suggested word in a sentence.

E **Reading Skills**

Evaluate. [Possible response to question 4: Their emotions are like humans'; they found Earthlings as bizarre as the Earthlings found them.]

F **Literary Focus**

? **Science fiction.** Tell students that science fiction writers often use their stories to comment on human behavior. What does the surprise ending suggest about how people should view other creatures? [Possible response: We should be tolerant because we may seem as strange to other creatures as they do to us.]

G **Reading Skills**

Interpret. [Possible response to question 5: The people in Chicago were part of an interplanetary zoo that the Kaanians were visiting.]

Meet the Writer

An interviewer once asked the mystery author Edward Hoch if he could imagine a life without writing. Hoch replied: "No, and neither can most writers. Occasionally someone will announce their retirement from writing, but they usually change their mind before long."

After You Read

First Thoughts

1. **Possible Answers**
   - I thought this story was <u>ironic and funny.</u>
   - What surprised me most about the story was <u>when I found out the humans were part of a zoo.</u>

Thinking Critically

2. If the part on Kaan came first, it would ruin the surprise twist at the end of the story.

3. Possible answers: Wouldn't the zoo's visiting several cities on Earth be pointless, since the same species inhabits each one? How can the professor communicate with so many varied life-forms?

Comparing Literature

4. Possible answers: *Human characters*—Professor Hugo, Chicagoans who visit zoo. *Alien characters*—she-creature, he-creature, little one. *Journey through space*—Hugo's ship's route. *Futuristic technology*—Hugo's ship. *Lesson about life*—We should be tolerant because we may seem as exotic to the inhabitants of another planet as they do to us.

Reading Check

Possible answers: *Characters*—Professor Hugo, Earthlings, Kaanians. *Settings*—Earth, Kaan. *Problem; Conflict*—Earthlings and aliens encounter one another. *Major Events*—(1) Interplanetary Zoo lands outside Chicago. (2) Earthlings file past the spaceship to view Kaanians. (3) Earthlings call it best zoo ever. (4) Spaceship returns to Kaan. (5) Kaanians go home, discuss odd Earthlings, call it best zoo ever. *Ending; Resolution*—It becomes clear that the Earthlings are part of Professor Hugo's zoo.

After You Read   "Zoo"

First Thoughts

1. Respond to "Zoo" by completing one of the following sentences:
   - I thought this story was . . .
   - What surprised me most about the story was . . .

Thinking Critically

2. This story has two parts and two **settings.** What if the first part of "Zoo" were set on Kaan and the second part set on Earth? How would this change the story?

3. The **plot** of this story has a tricky ending, which makes us reconsider the rest of the story. Do you find any flaws in the story—do some details in the story not make sense to you? Write down your questions, and see if you can answer them in a group discussion.

Comparing Literature

4. After you've read the next story, you'll have an opportunity to write a comparison-contrast essay. You can begin to plan your essay by filling out a chart like the one below focusing on the story "Zoo." This chart will be repeated with "The Ruum" on page 106, where you'll add details about that story.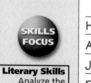

Reading Check

Use the following story map to outline the main parts of this story's **plot.** Keep your notes for the assignment on page 107.

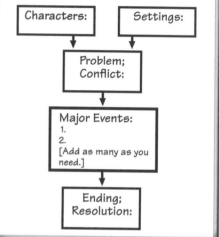

Comparing Science Fiction Stories		
	"Zoo"	"The Ruum"
Human characters		
Alien characters		
Journey through space		
Futuristic technology		
Lesson about life		

SKILLS FOCUS

Literary Skills Analyze the elements of science fiction.

Reading Skills Compare and contrast stories.

LITERARY CONNECTIONS

Science Fiction: A History

Many students may be surprised to learn that science fiction did not always exist as a genre. It arose in the nineteenth century when great scientific and technological advances raised questions about the future. Many scholars feel that Mary Shelley's *Frankenstein* (1818) was the first science fiction story. (See p. 108 for a poem based loosely on this work.) Other early science fiction authors who wrote about the future

include Jules Verne (*Twenty Thousand Leagues Under the Sea,* 1870) and H. G. Wells (*The Time Machine,* 1895). In the twentieth century, American writers such as Ray Bradbury, Ursula K. Le Guin, and Rod Serling devoted their careers to science fiction.

Activity. Ask students to review Serling's classic work of science fiction on p. 59. What elements of the genre appear in the teleplay?

Before You Read

In "The Ruum" you will find a journey through eons of time, an indestructible nightmare machine set loose by a galactic spaceship commander, and a brave hero.

Like writers of mystery and crime stories, writers of science fiction often drop clues as their stories unfold. Every detail in this story is important. Pay attention to the dynamite, the rifle, the pistol, and the use of numbers.

The Ruum

Arthur Porges

The cruiser *Ilkor* had just gone into her interstellar overdrive beyond the orbit of Pluto when a worried officer reported to the commander.

"Excellency," he said uneasily, "I regret to inform you that because of a technician's carelessness a Type H-9 Ruum has been left behind on the third planet, together with anything it may have collected."

The commander's triangular eyes hooded momentarily, but when he spoke his voice was level.

"How was the ruum set?"

"For a maximum radius of thirty miles, and 160 pounds plus or minus 15." **❶**

There was silence for several seconds; then the commander said: "We cannot reverse course now. In a few weeks we'll be returning and can pick up the ruum then. I do not care to have one of those costly, self-energizing models charged against my ship. You will see," he ordered coldly, "that the individual responsible is severely punished."

But at the end of its run, in the neighborhood of Rigel, the carrier met a flat, ring-shaped raider; and when the inevitable firefight was over, both ships, semimolten, radioactive, and laden with dead, were starting a billion-year orbit around the star.

And on the earth, it was the age of reptiles. **❷**

Comparing Literature

IDENTIFY

❶ This writer drops clues for you to notice and then interpret. Look for the clues to answer these questions: Where is the *Ilkor*? Is the commander of the *Ilkor* human? What is a ruum, and what is its purpose? **(A)**

IDENTIFY

❷ What was the result of the battle between the *Ilkor* and the raider? When in history did the battle take place? **(B)**

The Ruum **89**

Summary ⬆ *above grade level*

During the age of dinosaurs, a spaceship stops on the earth and accidentally leaves a "ruum" (pronounced "rōōm"), a robot used to collect animal specimens, each weighing from 145 to 175 pounds. (The weight programmed into the ruum is key.) In the present day, Walt, a bush pilot, drops off his friend Jim to search for uranium in northern Canada. Jim stumbles onto the ruum's collection of animals, all paralyzed but eerily alive. The ruum promptly moves in to collect Jim—who weighs 149 pounds. It pursues him all day and night. When the robot finally captures Jim, however, it sets him down again and leaves. Jim is mystified. That day, Walt returns and notes that Jim must have lost at least ten pounds during his ordeal.

PRETEACHING

Selection Starter

Motivate. Ask students the following question: *Many robots serve useful functions. Do you view robots as threatening? Why or why not?*

DIRECT TEACHING

(A) Reading Skills

Identify. [Possible responses to question 1: The *Ilkor* is leaving our solar system; its commander has triangular eyes and thus is nonhuman. A ruum is a robot that collects things.]

(B) Reading Skills

Identify. [Possible responses to question 2: Both ships were destroyed. The battle took place millions of years ago, when dinosaurs roamed the earth.]

Ⓐ Reading Skills

Infer. [Possible response to question 3: since the time from the age of dinosaurs to the present.]

Ⓑ Reading Skills

Identify. [Possible response to question 4: Jim is in a valley in the Canadian Rockies, surrounded by wilderness and hoping to find uranium.]

Ⓒ Learners Having Difficulty

❓ Find details. How long did Jim plan to stay before Walt would pick him up? [three weeks] How much time has gone by so far? [almost three weeks]

INFER

Ⓐ ❸ About how much time has passed since the *Ilkor* left the ruum behind?

IDENTIFY

Ⓑ ❹ Where is Jim Irwin? What is he hoping to find?

When the two men had unloaded the last of the supplies, Jim Irwin watched his partner climb into the little seaplane. He waved at Walt. ❸

"Don't forget to mail that letter to my wife," Jim shouted.

"The minute I land," Walt Leonard called back, starting to rev the engine. "And you find us some uranium—a strike is just what Cele needs. A fortune for your son and her, hey?" His white teeth flashed in a grin. "Don't rub noses with any grizzlies—shoot 'em, but don't scare 'em to death!"

Jim thumbed his nose as the seaplane speeded up, leaving a frothy wake. He felt a queer chill as the amphibian took off. For three weeks he would be isolated in this remote valley of the Canadian Rockies. If for any reason the plane failed to return to the icy blue lake, he would surely die. Even with enough food, no man could surmount the frozen peaks and make his way on foot over hundreds of miles of almost virgin wilderness. But, of course, Walt Leonard would return on schedule, and it was up to Jim whether or not they lost their stake. If there was any uranium in the valley, he had twenty-one days to find it. To work then, and no gloomy forebodings. ❹

Moving with the unhurried precision of an experienced woodsman, he built a lean-to in the shelter of a rocky overhang. For this three weeks of summer, nothing more permanent was needed. Perspiring in the strong morning sun, he piled his supplies back under the ledge, well covered by a waterproof tarpaulin and protected from the larger animal prowlers. All but the dynamite; that he cached,[1] also carefully wrapped against moisture, two hundred yards away. Only a fool shares his quarters with a box of high explosives.

The first two weeks went by all too swiftly, without any encouraging finds. There was only one good possibility left, and just enough time to explore it. So early one morning toward the end of his third week, Jim Irwin prepared for a last-ditch foray into the northeast part of the valley, a region he had not yet visited.

He took the Geiger counter, slipping on the earphones, reversed to keep the normal rattle from dulling his hearing, and reaching

> **If for any reason the plane failed to return to the icy blue lake, he would surely die.**

---

1. **cached** (kasht) *v.*: hid; stored.

DIFFERENTIATING INSTRUCTION

Learners Having Difficulty
Re-reading. This story's ending will initially leave many students as baffled as Jim; only a very alert reader will have caught the reason why the ruum spares him. Rather than calling students' attention to clues during their first reading, let the ending provide an incentive for students to practice re-reading. Encourage them to scan the gripping action sequences for the details that provide keys to the mystery. For lesson plans for learners having difficulty, see *Holt Reading Solutions*.

for the rifle, set out, telling himself it was now or never so far as this particular expedition was concerned. The bulky .30-06 was a nuisance and he had no enthusiasm for its weight, but the huge grizzlies of Canada are not intruded upon with impunity, and take a lot of killing. He'd already had to dispose of two, a hateful chore, since the big bears were vanishing all too fast. And the rifle had proved a great comfort on several ticklish occasions when actual firing had been avoided. The .22 pistol he left in its sheepskin holster in the lean-to.

He was whistling at the start, for the clear, frosty air, the bright sun on blue-white ice fields, and the heady smell of summer all delighted his heart despite his bad luck as a prospector. He planned to go one day's journey to the new region, spend about thirty-six hours exploring it intensively, and be back in time to meet the plane at noon. Except for his emergency packet, he took no food or **D** water. It would be easy enough to knock over a rabbit, and the streams were alive with firm-fleshed rainbow trout of the kind no longer common in the States.

All morning Jim walked, feeling an occasional surge of hope as the counter chattered. But its chatter always died down. The valley had nothing radioactive of value, only traces. Apparently they'd made a bad choice. His cheerfulness faded. They needed a strike badly, especially Walt. And his own wife, Cele, with a kid on the way. But there was still a chance. These last thirty-six hours—he'd snoop at night, if necessary—might be the payoff. He reflected a little bitterly that it would help quite a bit if some of those birds he'd staked would make a strike and return his dough. Right this **E** minute there were close to eight thousand bucks owing to him.

A wry smile touched his lips, and he abandoned unprofitable speculations for plans about lunch. The sun, as well as his stomach, said it was time. He had just decided to take out his line and fish a foaming brook when he rounded a grassy knoll to come upon a sight that made him stiffen to a halt, his jaw dropping.

It was like some enterprising giant's outdoor butcher shop: a great assortment of animal bodies, neatly lined up in a triple row that extended almost as far as the eye could see. And what animals! To be sure, those nearest to him were ordinary deer, bear, cougars, and mountain sheep—one of each, apparently—but down the line were strange, uncouth, half-formed, hairy beasts, and beyond them **F** a nightmare conglomeration of reptiles. One of the latter, at the extreme end of the remarkable display, he recognized at once.

The Ruum   91

D **Comparing Literature**

? **Compare science fiction stories.** Which details about Jim make him realistically human, with contradictions and concerns? [Possible responses: He likes camping and hunting but shows concern for endangered wildlife; he wants to help his friend Walt; he worries about his wife and unborn baby.] **How does he compare with the human beings in "Zoo"?** [Possible responses: He shares their emotions but is a much more developed character. He seems better trained and more knowledgeable than "Zoo"'s earthlings.]

E **English-Language Learners**

Slang. Students may be baffled by the slang in the clause beginning "if some of those birds." Provide the following definitions for the slang words: *birds,* "guys"; *staked,* "lent money to"; *make a strike,* "get rich"; *dough,* "money." Then, ask students to convert the clause to standard English. [if some of those guys he'd lent money to would get rich and return his money]

F **Learners Having Difficulty**

? **Use context clues.** *Uncouth* can mean "impolite," "unfamiliar," or "clumsy." From the context clues in this description, which meaning does it have here? [unfamiliar]

Advanced Learners
Enrichment. Challenge these students to analyze the ironies that add to the suspense of "The Ruum." Define the term *irony* as "a surprising twist." Explain that situational irony occurs when events in a story unfold in a way different from what might reasonably be expected. For example, the ruum's intent to collect Jim is an ironic twist: One does not expect a human to become a specimen in a collection. Other ironies occur when readers

know something that a character does not yet know. For example, tension builds as Jim puzzles over the ruum's source and purpose, which readers already know from the conversation aboard the *Ilkor.*
Activity. Ask students, as they read, to find more examples of irony in "The Ruum." Afterward, have students write or talk about the role of irony in building the story's suspense.

DIRECT TEACHING

A Reading Skills

Interpret. [Possible responses to question 5: It's vast; there is only one of each species; many are from earlier time periods; one is a small dinosaur.]

B Reading Skills

Compare and contrast. [Possible responses to question 6: It's like a zoo in that the animals are arranged as if on exhibit. Like the humans in "Zoo," Jim finds the exhibit both fascinating and bizarre.]

C Comparing Literature

❓ **Compare science fiction stories.** Both "Zoo" and "The Ruum" contain a futuristic machine. How is the machine used in each story? [In "Zoo" the spaceship provides a setting for the Interplanetary Zoo; in "The Ruum" the machine is a character bent on capturing Jim.]

D Vocabulary Note

❓ **Synonyms.** *Outlandish* means "very odd" or "strange." What is a synonym for *outlandish*? [Possible responses: bizarre; unusual.]

E Reading Skills

Infer. [Possible responses to question 7: It is set for a radius of 30 miles and a weight range of 160 pounds, plus or minus 15. That is why all the animals in the ruum's collection are approximately the same size. The ruum's interest in Jim implies that he must weigh between 145 and 175 pounds.]

INTERPRET

Ⓐ ❺ What is so surprising about this collection of animals?

COMPARE AND CONTRAST

Ⓑ ❻ How is the ruum's collection of animals like a zoo's? Compare Jim's response to these animals with the way the people on Earth respond to creatures in the Interplanetary Zoo in the story on page 85.

Ⓒ
Ⓓ

INFER

Ⓔ ❼ On page 89, re-read how the ruum was set. How might its settings explain the similarity in size of the animals in the ruum's collection? What can you infer about Jim Irwin based on this knowledge?

There had been a much larger specimen, fabricated about an incomplete skeleton, of course, in the museum at home. ❺

No doubt about it—it was a small stegosaur,[2] no bigger than a pony!

Fascinated, Jim walked down the line, glancing back over the immense array. Peering more closely at one scaly, dirty-yellow lizard, he saw an eyelid tremble. Then he realized the truth. The animals were not dead, but paralyzed and miraculously preserved. Perspiration prickled his forehead. How long since stegosaurs had roamed this valley? ❻

All at once he noticed another curious circumstance: The victims were roughly of a size. Nowhere, for example, was there a really large saurian.[3] No tyrannosaurus. For that matter, no mammoth. Each specimen was about the size of a large sheep. He was pondering this odd fact when the underbrush rustled a warning behind him.

Jim Irwin had once worked with mercury, and for a second it seemed to him that a half-filled leather sack of the liquid metal had rolled into the clearing. For the quasi-spherical[4] object moved with just such a weighty, fluid motion. But it was not leather, and what appeared at first a disgusting wartiness turned out on closer scrutiny to be more like the functional projections of some outlandish mechanism. Whatever the thing was, he had little time to study it, for after the spheroid had whipped out and retracted a number of metal rods with bulbous, lenslike structures at their tips, it rolled toward him at a speed of about five miles an hour. And from its purposeful advance, the man had no doubts that it meant to add him to the pathetic heap of living-dead specimens. ❼

Uttering an incoherent exclamation, Jim sprang back a number of paces, unslinging his rifle. The ruum that had been left behind was still some thirty yards off, approaching at that moderate but invariable velocity, an advance more terrifying in its regularity than the headlong charge of a mere brute beast.

Jim's hand flew to the bolt, and with practiced deftness he slammed a cartridge into the chamber. He snuggled the battered stock against his cheek and, using the peep sight, aimed squarely at the leathery bulk—a perfect target in the bright afternoon sun.

---

2. **stegosaur** (steg′ə·sôr′) *n.:* dinosaur with a small head and heavy, bony plates on its back.
3. **saurian** (sôr′ē·ən) *n.:* lizard; here, dinosaur.
4. **quasi-spherical** (kwā′zī·sfer′i·kəl) *adj.:* shaped somewhat like a ball, or sphere.

Science

Uranium. Jim is in the valley in order to find the valuable element uranium. Encourage interested students to learn more about uranium and to share their findings with the class. Students might search for answers to the following questions about the element:

- What are its physical and chemical properties?
- What are its uses?
- What is its monetary value?
- How and by whom was it discovered?
- What are its sources?
- What does a Geiger counter do, and how does it work?

WHOLE CLASS

A Reading Skills

Compare and contrast. [Possible responses to question 8: Students' sketches of Kaanians should show small horselike creatures that climb walls as spiders do. The ruum should be roundish, bumpy, and leathery, with protruding sensors and possibly "finger hooks" and a "stinglike probe dripping greenish liquid."]

B English-Language Learners

Explain to students that the phrase *the winged* is short for "the winged ones"—birds and other flying creatures. Point out that here *winged* is pronounced with two syllables: (win' id). Then, ask students what *the four-footed* would mean. [Possible responses: four-footed ones; any quadrupeds.]

C Advanced Learners

❓ Enrichment. What irony do you see in Jim's concern with shedding surplus weight? [Possible response: He is thinking that the weight of his gear will hinder his escape, but he doesn't know that the gear makes his weight exceed the ruum's limit.]

COMPARE AND CONTRAST

8 Try to visualize the ruum. Now, picture the horse-spiders of Kaan from "Zoo" (page 85). Check the stories for details you may have forgotten; then, sketch each of these creatures in your notebook.

A grim little smile touched his lips as he squeezed the trigger. He knew what one of those 180-grain, metal-jacketed, boat-tail slugs could do at 2,700 feet per second. Probably at this close range it would keyhole and blow the foul thing into a mush.

Wham! The familiar kick against his shoulder. E-e-e-e! The whining screech of a ricochet.[5] He sucked in his breath. There could be no doubt whatever. At a mere twenty yards, a bullet from this hard-hitting rifle had glanced from the ruum's surface. Frantically Jim worked the bolt. He blasted two more rounds, then realized the utter futility of such tactics. When the ruum was six feet away, he saw gleaming finger hooks flick from warty knobs and a hollow, stinglike probe, dripping greenish liquid, poised snakily between them. The man turned and fled. **8**

Jim Irwin weighed exactly 149 pounds.

It was easy enough to pull ahead. The ruum seemed incapable of increasing its speed. But Jim had no illusions on that score. The steady five-mile-an-hour pace was something no organism on earth could maintain for more than a few hours. Before long, Jim guessed, the hunted animal had either turned on its implacable pursuer or, in the case of more timid creatures, run itself to exhaustion in a circle out of sheer panic. Only the winged were safe. But for anything on the ground the result was inevitable: another specimen for the awesome array. And for whom the whole collection? Why? Why?

Coolly, as he ran, Jim began to shed all surplus weight. He glanced at the reddening sun, wondering about the coming night. He hesitated over the rifle; it had proved useless against the ruum, but his military training impelled him to keep the weapon to the last. Still, every pound raised the odds against him in the grueling race he foresaw clearly. Logic told him that military reasoning did not apply to a contest like this; there would be no disgrace in abandoning a worthless rifle. And when weight became really vital, the .30-06 would go. But meanwhile he slung it over one shoulder. The Geiger counter he placed as gently as possible on a flat rock, hardly breaking his stride.

> **Jim Irwin weighed exactly 149 pounds.**

---

5. **ricochet** (rik′ə·shā′) *n.:* rebound of an object, such as a bullet, after striking a surface at an angle.

One thing was certain. This would be no rabbit run, a blind, panicky flight until exhausted, ending in squealing submission. This would be a fighting retreat, and he'd use every trick of survival he'd learned in his hazard-filled lifetime.

Taking deep, measured breaths, he loped along, watching with shrewd eyes for anything that might be used for his advantage in the weird contest. Luckily the valley was sparsely wooded; in brush or forest his straightaway speed would be almost useless.

Suddenly he came upon a sight that made him pause. It was a point where a huge boulder overhung the trail, and Jim saw possibilities in the situation. He grinned as he remembered a Malay mantrap[6] that had once saved his life. Springing to a hillock, he looked back over the grassy plain. The afternoon sun cast long shadows, but it was easy enough to spot the pursuing ruum, still oozing along on Jim's trail. He watched the thing with painful anxiety. Everything hinged upon this brief survey. He was right! Yes, although at most places the man's trail was neither the only route nor the best one, the ruum dogged the footsteps of his prey. The significance of that fact was immense, but Irwin had no more than twelve minutes to implement the knowledge.

Deliberately dragging his feet, Irwin made it a clear trail directly under the boulder. After going past it for about ten yards, he walked backward in his own prints until just short of the overhang and then jumped up clear of the track to a point behind the balanced rock.

Whipping out his heavy-duty belt knife, he began to dig, scientifically but with furious haste, about the base of the boulder. Every few moments, sweating with apprehension and effort, he rammed it with one shoulder. At last, it teetered a little. He had just jammed the knife back into its sheath and was crouching there, panting, when the ruum rolled into sight over a small ridge on his back trail.

He watched the gray spheroid moving toward him and fought to quiet his sobbing breath. There was no telling what other senses it might bring into play, even though the ruum seemed to prefer just to follow in his prints. But it certainly had a whole battery of instruments at its disposal. He crouched low behind the rock, every nerve a charged wire. ❾

But there was no change of technique by the ruum; seemingly

---

6. **Malay mantrap:** device involving a large object that falls on a person, usually designed so that it is triggered unknowingly by its victim. Its name refers to Malaya, now part of Malaysia in Southeast Asia.

INTERPRET

❾ What is Jim's state of mind? What words clue you in?

Comparing Literature

DIRECT TEACHING

D Vocabulary Note
Word origins. Tell students that the word *submission* comes from the Latin prefix *sub–*, meaning "under," and the Latin root word *mittere*, meaning "to send." A person who sends himself or herself to an opponent is giving up or showing submission. How does Jim feel about submitting or surrendering to the ruum? [He rejects the idea and says he will fight for his survival.]

E English-Language Learners
Idioms. Tell students that to dog the footsteps of someone is to follow him or her persistently, as a bloodhound would. Here the implication may be that the ruum, like a dog, is tracking Jim by scent. Ask students what it means if someone says, "Bad luck dogs me." [Possible responses: Bad luck follows me persistently; I always have bad luck.]

F Reading Skills
❷ **Predict.** What do you think Jim is planning to do? [Possible response: He plans to crush the ruum beneath the boulder.]

G Reading Skills
Interpret. [Possible responses to question 9: Jim is frantic but trying to act rationally. Clues so far on this page include "painful anxiety," "scientifically but with furious haste," "sweating with apprehension," "fought to quiet his sobbing breath," and "every nerve a charged wire."]

VIEWING THE ART

Tell students that the art on this page was not created specifically for this story. Encourage students to compare the descriptions of the ruum with the picture. What differences can they find? What events portrayed in the art are not actual events in the story? [Possible responses: The art on this page shows three humans, but in "The Ruum," Jim Irwin is the only character who is shown interacting with the ruum. There are a number of ruums in the art, but the story only mentions one.]

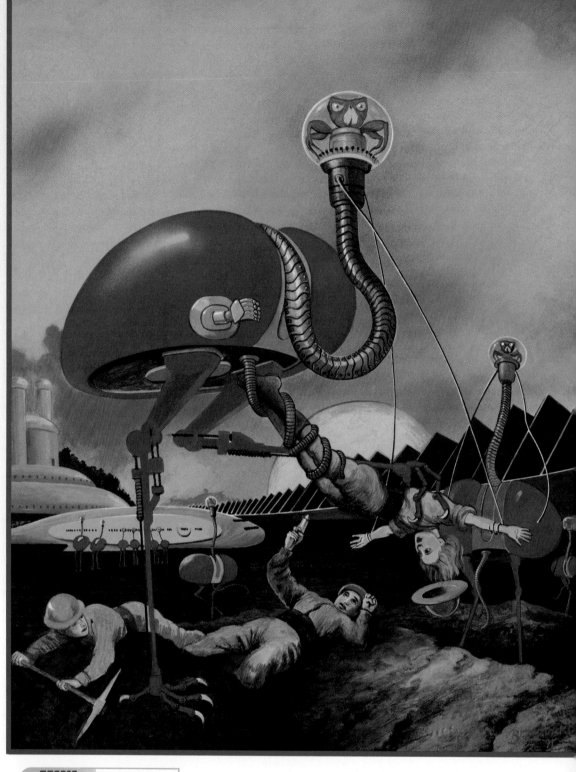

MINI-LESSON Reading

Developing Word-Attack Skills
Write the selection words *stegosaur* and *opened* on the chalkboard, and have a volunteer read each aloud. Explain that the *o* in *opened* is a long *o* sound and the sound of *au* in the suffix *–saur* in *stegosaur* is a broad *o* sound. The *o* in the middle of *stegosaur* is actually pronounced as a schwa. Then, place the following words on the chalkboard, and have a volunteer read them aloud:

autobiography   dinosaur

Work with students so they understand that the letter combination *au* produces a broad *o* sound no matter where it appears in a word. The letter *o*, however, can be pronounced as either a long *o* or a schwa.
Activity. Place these words on the chalkboard, and have students underline the letter(s) forming the broad *o* sound once, the letter(s) forming the long *o* sound twice, and the letter *o* pronounced as a schwa

intent on the footprints of its prey, the strange sphere rippled along, passing directly under the great boulder. As it did so, Irwin gave a savage yell and, thrusting his whole muscular weight against the balanced mass, toppled it squarely on the ruum. Five tons of stone fell from a height of twelve feet.

Jim scrambled down. He stood there, staring at the huge lump and shaking his head dazedly. He gave the boulder a kick. "Hah! Wait and I might clear a buck or two yet from your little meat market. Maybe this expedition won't be a total loss. Enjoy yourself in hell where you came from!"

Then he leapt back, his eyes wild. The giant rock was shifting! Slowly its five-ton bulk was sliding off the trail, raising a ridge of soil as it grated along. Even as he stared, the boulder tilted, and a gray protuberance appeared under the nearest edge. With a choked cry, Jim Irwin broke into a lurching run.

He ran a full mile down the trail. Then, finally, he stopped and looked back. He could just make out a dark dot moving away from the fallen rock. It progressed as slowly and as regularly and as inexorably as before, and in his direction. Jim sat down heavily, putting his head in his scratched, grimy hands.

But that despairing mood did not last. After all, he had gained a twenty-minute respite. Lying down, trying to relax as much as possible, he took the flat packet of emergency rations from his jacket and, eating quickly but without bolting, disposed of some pemmican, biscuit, and chocolate. A few sips of icy water from a streamlet, and he was almost ready to continue his fantastic struggle. When the ruum was still an estimated ten minutes away, Jim Irwin trotted off, much of his wiry strength back, and fresh courage to counter bone-deep weariness. **⑩** **Ⓐ**

After running for fifteen minutes, he came to a sheer face of rock about thirty feet high. The terrain on either side was barely **Ⓒ** passable, consisting of choked gullies, spiky brush, and knife-edged rocks. If Jim could make the top of this little cliff, the ruum sure would have to detour, a circumstance that might put it many minutes behind him.

He looked up at the sun. Huge and crimson, it was almost touching the horizon. He would have to move fast. Irwin was no rock climber but he did know the fundamentals. Using every crevice, roughness, and minute ledge, he found his way up the cliff. Somehow—unconsciously—he used that flowing climb of a natural mountaineer, which takes each foothold very briefly as an

COMPARE AND CONTRAST

⑩ In science fiction, characters often respond to imagined worlds in ways that we recognize. Do Jim Irwin and the human characters in "Zoo" react to fantastic situations in believable ways? Compare the two responses. **Ⓑ**

The Ruum   97

Ⓐ Literary Focus

❷ Science fiction. Jim's struggle with the ruum is a classic battle between a human and a machine. What might his struggle suggest to you about the meaning of being human? [Possible response: It's human nature to fight to survive.]

Ⓑ Reading Skills

Compare and contrast. [Possible responses to question 10: Jim's reactions to the ruum are believable: He frantically tries to flee and then to fight; he puzzles over the ruum's purpose and capabilities; and he feels fear, rage, and despair. In "Zoo," children are excited to visit the zoo, and visitors gawk in awe. These responses too are human and believable.]

Ⓒ Vocabulary Note

❷ Word families. The word *terrain* comes from the Latin word *terra* meaning "earth." What other related words share this root word? [territory, terrestrial, terrarium]

three times. Encourage students to consult their dictionaries if necessary.

1. aut<u>o</u>bus
2. aut<u>o</u>crat
3. <u>o</u>kra
4. s<u>a</u>urian
5. c<u>a</u>ustic
6. vi<u>o</u>lin
7. <u>o</u>verh<u>au</u>l
8. <u>au</u>tumn
9. aut<u>o</u>pil<u>o</u>t
10. tyrann<u>o</u>saurus

DIRECT TEACHING

A Vocabulary Note

❓ **Word origins.** Tell students that the word *uncanny* derives from word parts meaning "not able." An uncanny ability is an ability that human beings normally do not have. An uncanny occurrence is one that normally does not happen. What is uncanny about the ruum? [its ability to withstand high-powered rifle fire and a five-ton boulder]

B Reading Skills

Interpret. [Possible responses to question 11: Jim lets the ruum see his head. As a result, the ruum knows exactly where he is and can reach him more quickly.]

C Comparing Literature

❓ **Compare science fiction stories.** In "Zoo" the extraterrestrial horse-spiders of Kaan prove to have experiences similar to those of the Earthlings. What human qualities, if any, do you see in the ruum? [Possible response: Most students will say the ruum has no human qualities. It shows no emotions; it does not deviate from what it is programmed to do.]

INTERPRET

B ⓫ What mistake does Jim make? What is the result of his mistake?

---

unstressed pivot point in a series of rhythmic advances.

He had just reached the top when the ruum rolled up to the base of the cliff.

Jim knew very well that he ought to leave at once, taking advantage of the few precious remaining moments of daylight. Every second gained was of tremendous value, but curiosity and hope made him wait. He told himself that the instant his pursuer detoured, he would get out of there all the faster. Besides, the thing might even give up and he could sleep right here.

Sleep! His body lusted for it.

But the ruum would not detour. It hesitated only a few seconds at the foot of the barrier. Then a number of knobs opened to extrude metallic wands. One of these, topped with lenses, waved in **A** the air. Jim drew back too late—their uncanny gaze had found him as he lay atop the cliff, peering down. He cursed his idiocy. ⓫

Immediately all the wands retracted, and from a different knob a slender rod, blood-red in the setting sun, began to shoot straight up to the man. As he watched, frozen in place, its barbed tip gripped the cliff's edge almost under his nose.

Jim leapt to his feet. Already the rod was shortening as the ruum reabsorbed its shining length. And the leathery sphere was rising off the ground. Swearing loudly, Jim fixed his eyes on the tenacious hook, drawing back one heavy foot.

But experience restrained him. The mighty kick was never launched. He had seen too many rough-and-tumbles lost by an injudicious attempt at the boot. It wouldn't do at all to let any part of his body get within reach of the ruum's superb tools. Instead he seized a length of dry branch and, inserting one end under the **C** metal hook, began to pry.

There was a sputtering flash, white and lacy, and even through the dry wood he felt the potent surge of power that splintered the end. He dropped the smoldering stick with a gasp of pain and, wringing his numb fingers, backed off several steps, full of impotent rage. For a moment he paused, half inclined to run again, but then his upper lip drew back and, snarling, he unslung his rifle. He knew he had been right to lug the thing all this way—even if it had beat a tattoo on his ribs. Now he had the ruum right where he wanted it!

Kneeling to steady his aim in the failing light, Jim sighted at the hook and fired. There was a soggy thud as the ruum fell. Jim shouted. The heavy slug had done a lot more than he expected.

98 Collection 1 / Facing Danger

DEVELOPING FLUENCY

Activity. Invite students to choose favorite parts of "The Ruum" to read aloud to the class. They might look for parts that involve especially vivid action, gripping suspense, or striking irony. Place students in groups to practice their readings. Some students may want to present their readings in pairs or small groups, while others may prefer to present them individually. Organize the presentations so that they follow the order of events in the story. Ask each presenter to explain why he or she chose the excerpt.

SMALL GROUP

Not only had it blasted the metal claw loose, but it had smashed a big gap in the cliff's edge. It would be pretty damned hard for the ruum to use that part of the rock again!

He looked down. Sure enough, the ruum was back at the bottom. Jim Irwin grinned. Every time the thing clamped a hook over the bluff, he'd blow that hook loose. There was plenty of ammunition in his pocket, and until the moon rose, bringing a good light for shooting with, he'd stick the gun's muzzle inches away if necessary. Besides, the thing—whatever it might be—was obviously too intelligent to keep up a hopeless struggle. Sooner or later it would accept the detour. And then, maybe the night would help to hide his trail.

Then—he choked and, for a brief moment, tears came to his eyes. Down below, in the dimness, the squat, phlegmatic[7] spheroid was extruding three hooked rods simultaneously in a fanlike spread. In a perfectly coordinated movement, the rods snagged the cliff's edge at intervals of about four feet.

Jim Irwin whipped the rifle to his shoulder. All right—this was going to be just like the rapid fire for record back at Benning.[8] Only, at Benning, they didn't expect good shooting in the dark!

But the first shot was a bull's-eye, smacking the left-hand hook loose in a puff of rock dust. His second shot did almost as well, knocking the gritty stuff loose so the center barb slipped off. But even as he whirled to level at number three, Jim saw it was hopeless.

The first hook was back in place. No matter how well he shot, at least one rod would always be in position, pulling the ruum to the top.

Jim hung the useless rifle muzzle down from a stunted tree and ran into the deepening dark. The toughening of his body, a process of years, was paying off now. So what? Where was he going? What could he do now? Was there anything that could stop that thing behind him?

Then he remembered the dynamite.

Gradually changing his course, the weary man cut back toward his camp by the lake. Overhead the stars brightened, pointing the

> **Now he had the ruum right where he wanted it!**

---

7. **phlegmatic** (fleg·mat′ik) *adj.:* calm; impassive.
8. **Benning:** Fort Benning, Georgia, a U.S. Army post.

D Comparing Literature

❓ Compare science fiction stories. In the plot of "Zoo," futuristic technology plays a relatively small role. The spaceship is not described in detail; the emphasis is on characters rather than technology. How would you describe the role played by technology in the plot of "The Ruum"? [Possible responses: In "The Ruum," technology is pivotal to the plot. The ruum is described in detail. It has almost no character, but its mechanics create the story's conflict and drive the action.]

E Literary Focus

❓ Theme. What do Jim's actions suggest to you about the human instinct for survival? [Possible response: It persists even when there seems to be no hope.]

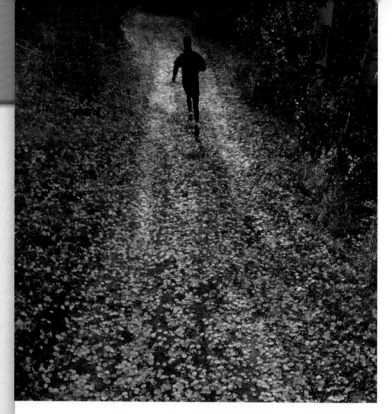

DIRECT TEACHING

A Reading Skills

Infer. [Possible response to question 12: It suggests that Jim is nearing his mental and physical limits.] You might call students' attention to Jim's concern for his wife, even in his desperate state.

INFER

A ⓬ What does this hallucination suggest about Jim's mental and physical state?

---

way. Jim lost all sense of time. He must have eaten as he wobbled along, for he wasn't hungry. Maybe he could eat at the lean-to . . . no, there wouldn't be time. The moon was up and he could hear the ruum close behind. Close.

Quite often phosphorescent[9] eyes peered at him from the underbrush and once, just at dawn, a grizzly woofed with displeasure at his passage.

Sometimes during the night his wife, Cele, stood before him with outstretched arms. "Go away!" he rasped; "go away! You can make it! It can't chase both of us!" So she turned and ran lightly alongside of him. But when Irwin panted across a tiny glade, Cele faded away into the moonlight and he realized she hadn't been there at all. ⓬

Shortly after sunrise Jim Irwin reached the lake. The ruum was close enough for him to hear the dull sounds of its passage. Jim

---

9. **phosphorescent** (fäs′fə·res′ənt) *adj.:* glowing.

staggered, his eyes closed. He hit himself feebly on the nose, his eyes jerked open, and he saw the explosive. The sight of the greasy sticks of dynamite snapped Irwin wide awake.

He forced himself to calmness and carefully considered what to do. Fuse? No. It would be impossible to leave fused dynamite in the trail and time the detonation with the absolute precision he needed. Sweat poured down his body; his clothes were sodden with it. It was hard to think. The explosion must be set off from a distance and at the exact moment the ruum was passing over it. But Irwin dared not use a long fuse. The rate of burning was not constant enough. Couldn't calibrate[10] it perfectly with the ruum's advance. Jim Irwin's body sagged all over; his chin sank toward his heaving chest. He jerked his head up, stepped back—and saw the .22 pistol where he had left it in the lean-to.

His sunken eyes flashed.

Moving with frenetic haste, he took the half-filled case, piled all the remaining percussion caps among the loose sticks in a devil's mixture. Weaving out to the trail, he carefully placed box and contents directly on his earlier tracks some twenty yards from a rocky ledge. It was a risk—the stuff might go anytime—but that didn't matter. He would far rather be blown to rags than end up living but paralyzed in the ruum's outdoor butcher's stall. ⑬

The exhausted Irwin had barely hunched down behind the thin ledge of rock before his inexorable pursuer appeared over a slight rise five hundred yards away. Jim scrunched deeper into the hollow, then saw a vertical gap, a narrow crack between rocks. That was it, he thought vaguely. He could sight through the gap at the dynamite and still be shielded from the blast. If it was a shield . . . when that half-caste blew only twenty yards away . . .

He stretched out on his belly, watching the ruum roll forward. A hammer of exhaustion pounded his ballooning skull. When had he slept last? This was the first time he had lain down in hours. Hours? Ha! It was days. His muscles stiffened, locked into throbbing, burning knots. Then he felt the morning sun on his back, soothing, warming, easing. . . . No! If he let go, if he slept now, it was the ruum's macabre collection for Jim Irwin! Stiff fingers tightened around the pistol. He'd stay awake! If he lost—if the ruum survived the blast—there'd still be time to put a bullet through his brain.

He looked down at the sleek pistol, then out at the innocent-

---

10. **calibrate** (kal′ə·brāt′) *v*.: measure; here, time.

PREDICT

⑬ Describe Jim's new plan to stop the ruum, and predict whether his plan will work.

The Ruum   **101**

DIRECT TEACHING

A English-Language Learners

❓ Jargon. Here the phrase *blow a cap* means "make a stick of dynamite explode." What would happen to the pile of dynamite if one of the sticks exploded? [Possible response: It would set off a chain reaction, and the whole pile would explode.]

B Advanced Learners

❓ Enrichment. Why does Jim laugh at the bear? Why is this ironic? [Possible response: It's ironic that the one thing Jim used to fear most—a grizzly—may save him from what he now fears most, the ruum.]

C Literary Focus

❓ Suspense. In the seconds before the grizzly attacks the ruum, how does the author crank up the suspense one more notch? [He takes a small break from the action to follow Jim's wandering thoughts. The effect is like a momentary shift to slow motion.]

D Reading Skills

❓ Interpret. [Possible responses to question 14: The grizzly may weigh more than 175 pounds; the ruum may already have a grizzly in its collection.]

---

seeming booby trap. If he timed this right—and he would—the ruum wouldn't survive. No. He relaxed a little, yielding just a bit to the gently insistent sun. A bird whistled softly somewhere above him and a fish splashed in the lake.

Suddenly he was wrenched to full awareness. Of all times for a grizzly to come snooping about! With the whole of Irwin's camp ready for greedy looting, a fool bear had to come sniffing around the dynamite! The furred monster smelled carefully at the box, nosed around, rumbled deep displeasure at the alien scent of man. **(A)** Irwin held his breath. Just a touch would blow a cap. A single cap meant . . .

The grizzly lifted his head from the box and growled hoarsely. The box was ignored; the offensive odor of man was forgotten. Its feral[11] little eyes focused on a plodding spheroid that was now only forty yards away. Jim Irwin snickered. Until he had met the ruum, **(B)** the grizzly bear of the North American continent was the only thing in the world he had ever feared. And now—why was he so calm about it?—the two terrors of his existence were meeting head-on and he was laughing. He shook his head and the great side muscles in his neck hurt abominably. He looked down at his pistol, then out at the dynamite. These were the only real things in his world.

About six feet from the bear, the ruum paused. Still in the grip of that almost idiotic detachment, Jim Irwin found himself wondering again what it was, where it had come from. The grizzly arose on its haunches, the embodiment of utter ferocity. Terrible teeth flashed white against red lips. The business-like ruum started **(C)** to roll past. The bear closed in, roaring. It cuffed at the ruum. A mighty paw, armed with black claws sharper and stronger than scythes, made that cuff. It would have disemboweled a rhinoceros. Irwin cringed as that sideswipe knocked dust from the leathery sphere. The ruum was hurled back several inches. It paused, recovered, and with the same dreadful casualness it rippled on, making a wider circle, ignoring the bear. **(14)**

But the lord of the woods wasn't settling for any draw. Moving with that incredible agility which has terrified Indians, Spanish, French, and Anglo-Americans since the first encounter of any of them with his species, the grizzly whirled, sidestepped beautifully, and hugged the ruum. The terrible, shaggy forearms tightened; the

INTERPRET

(14) Think back to what you know about the ruum's origin. What fact explains why the ruum ignores the grizzly's attack?

---

11. **feral** (fir′əl) *adj.:* wild.

CROSS-CURRICULAR CONNECTIONS

Science

Endangered grizzlies. Jim Irwin feels that grizzlies are "vanishing all too fast." Is this still true? Are grizzlies losing or gaining ground?

Activity. Ask interested students to learn more about grizzly bears and their endangerment and to report their findings to the class. Students might look for answers to the following questions about grizzlies:

• What distinguishes them from other bears?

• What problems do they cause for humans, and what problems do humans cause for them?

• Where did they live one hundred years ago, and where do they live now?

• What factors account for the change in their population?

• What is the Endangered Species Act, and how does it protect them?

INDIVIDUAL

CROSS-CURRICULAR CONNECTIONS

Art

Connect to the text. Remind students that the pictures accompanying "The Ruum" were not created specifically for the story. Have students re-read the descriptions of the ruum on pp. 92 and 98. Then, ask them to draw their own pictures of the ruum from the details in the story. Students can share their finished pictures with the rest of the class.

A Literary Focus

❓ Suspense. This paragraph shows the effects of the blast by using figurative language and providing images, thoughts, and impressions from Jim's jumbled stream of consciousness. How do these techniques increase suspense? [Possible responses: Readers must slow down to figure out what the figurative language means and what has happened. It's still not clear if the ruum has been destroyed.]

B Literary Focus

❓ Science fiction. Do you think that Jim's giving up is a realistic human reaction in this situation? Have you ever felt the total exhaustion and defeat that Jim feels? [Possible responses: It's not realistic that he would give up now, because he's not a quitter. It's realistic that, at the end of his mental and physical resources, Jim does what defeated people do—he makes a final, feeble struggle; tries to pray; thinks disjointedly; closes his eyes.]

slavering jaws champed at the gray surface. Irwin half rose. "Go it!" he croaked. Even as he cheered the clumsy emperor of the wild, Jim thought it was an insane tableau: the village idiot wrestling with a beach ball.

Then silver metal gleamed bright against gray. There was a flash, swift and deadly. The roar of the king abruptly became a whimper, a gurgle, and then there was nearly a ton of terror wallowing in death—its throat slashed open. Jim Irwin saw the bloody blade retract into the gray spheroid, leaving a bright red smear on the thing's dusty hide.

And the ruum rolled forward past the giant corpse, implacable, still intent on the man's spoor, his footprints, his pathway. OK, baby, Jim giggled at the deadly grizzly, this is for you, for Cele, for—lots of poor dumb animals like us—come to, you fool, he cursed at himself. And aimed at the dynamite. And very calmly, very carefully, Jim Irwin squeezed the trigger of his pistol.

Briefly, sound first. Then giant hands lifted his body from where he lay, then let go. He came down hard, face in a patch of nettles, but he was sick, he didn't care. He remembered that the birds were quiet. Then there was a fluid thump as something massive struck the grass a few yards away. Then there was quiet.

Irwin lifted his head . . . All men do in such a case. His body still ached. He lifted sore shoulders and saw . . . an enormous smoking crater in the earth. He also saw, a dozen paces away, gray-white because it was covered now with powdered rock, the ruum.

It was under a tall, handsome pine tree. Even as Jim watched, wondering if the ringing in his ears would ever stop, the ruum rolled toward him.

Irwin fumbled for his pistol. It was gone. It had dropped somewhere, out of reach. He wanted to pray, then, but couldn't get properly started. Instead, he kept thinking idiotically, "My sister Ethel can't spell Nebuchadnezzar[12] and never could. My sister Ethel—"

The ruum was a foot away now, and Jim closed his eyes. He felt cool, metallic fingers touch, grip, lift. His unresisting body was raised several inches, and juggled oddly. Shuddering, he waited for the terrible syringe with its green liquid, seeing the yellow, shrunken face of a lizard with one eyelid a-tremble.

Then, dispassionately, without either roughness or solicitude,

---

12. **Nebuchadnezzar** (neb′yə•kəd•nez′ər): king of ancient Babylonia.

FAMILY/COMMUNITY ACTIVITY

"The Ruum," like much of science fiction, touches on issues of concern to many people today. One of these issues is the fear that technology has become too powerful. In the story this threat is personified by the ruum itself. In real life, people experience the threat in various other ways. For example, some people fear that the Internet will deprive users of privacy, that viewing television and playing video games will dull people's minds, or that automation will usurp jobs. Encourage students to interview friends and family about these issues. Students might ask what their subjects consider the negative and positive aspects of technology to be. Remind student interviewers to listen respectfully and to record subjects' responses carefully. Then, ask students, with their subjects' permission, to share their results with the class.

the ruum put him back on the ground. When he opened his eyes, some seconds later, the sphere was rolling away. Watching it go, he sobbed drily.

It seemed a matter of moments only before he heard the seaplane's engine and opened his eyes to see Walt Leonard bending over him.

Later in the plane, five thousand feet above the valley, Walt grinned suddenly, slapped him on the back, and cried: "Jim, I can get a whirlybird, a four-place job! Why, if we can snatch up just a few of those prehistoric lizards and things while the museum keeper's away, it's like you said—the scientists will pay us plenty."

Jim's hollow eyes lit up. "That's the idea," he agreed. Then, bitterly, "I might just as well have stayed in bed. Evidently the thing didn't want me at all. Maybe it wanted to know what I paid for these pants! Barely touched me, then let go. And how I ran!"

"Yeah," Walt said. "That was queer. And after that marathon. I admire your guts, boy." He glanced sideways at Jim Irwin's haggard face. "That night's run cost you plenty. I figure you lost over ten pounds." **⓯**

Meet the Writer

Arthur Porges

Arthur Porges (1915–   ) has published more than seventy short stories in various magazines. Porges was born in Chicago, and he taught mathematics at the Western Military Academy and the Illinois Institute of Technology until his retirement in 1975. Porges, whose best-known stories are "The Ruum" and "The Fly," also writes under the pen names Peter Arthur and Pat Rogers.

Comparing Literature

INFER

⓯ This story has a surprise ending. To figure out why the ruum puts Jim back on the ground, think about the ruum's instructions. Why might the ruum have been interested in Jim to begin with? Then, think about what might have changed. (A clue is given in the last line of the story.)

DIRECT TEACHING

C Reading Skills
Infer. [Possible response to question 15: The ruum wanted to add Jim to its collection. Jim lost enough weight during his ordeal that he fell below the ruum's 145-pound minimum requirement.]

For Independent Reading

■ Students who liked "The Ruum" will also enjoy Isaac Asimov's *I, Robot,* a volume of linked, suspenseful short stories that tantalize the reader's powers of deduction and observation.

■ For students intrigued by the time warp aspect of "The Ruum," suggest *Dinotopia* by James Gurney. In this masterfully realized "history" with its glowing, detailed illustrations, dinosaurs coexist with humans in an elaborate civilization.

After You Read

First Thoughts

1. Possible Answers
   - I thought the scariest part was when <u>the ruum grabs Jim.</u>
   - I'm confused about <u>why the ruum's sensors didn't immediately detect when Jim had fallen below the minimum weight.</u>

Thinking Critically

2. Possible answer: The ruum is a science experiment gone wrong.

3. In the end, Jim seems unsure of the value of his strength and skills. Students may say they gained respect for Jim because of his courage.

Comparing Literature

4. *Human characters*—Jim, Walt. *Alien characters*—commander, officer, the ruum. *Journey through space*—the alien ship's voyage. *Futuristic technology*—the alien ship and the ruum. *Lesson about life*—Even intelligent humans are subject to chance and the threat of runaway technology.

Reading Check

The opening part of the story takes place in the age of dinosaurs. An alien spaceship stops on the earth and accidentally leaves a ruum (an animal-collecting robot) behind. The ship is later destroyed. Millions of years later, Jim, an ex–military man, stumbles onto the ruum while prospecting for uranium. The ruum has been collecting animals since the Jurassic Age, and now it zeroes in on Jim. He shoots it, tips a boulder onto it, and blasts it with dynamite, but he can't stop it. He runs for miles trying to escape, but the ruum finally captures him. Then it just lifts him, puts him down, and leaves. Jim never understands why.

After You Read   "The Ruum"

First Thoughts

1. Respond to "The Ruum" by completing one of the following sentences:
   - I thought the scariest part was when . . .
   - I am confused about . . .

Thinking Critically

2. The writer describes the bear as "lord of the woods" and "clumsy emperor of the wild." He is using **figurative language** to create a powerful and absurd picture of the grizzly battling the ruum. Use figurative language to come up with your own descriptions of the ruum.

3. Jim Irwin calls himself a dumb animal. Has Jim's opinion of himself changed in the course of his adventure? How has your opinion about Jim changed?

Comparing Literature

4. Add information on "The Ruum" to the chart below. Then, use your chart as you write the comparison-contrast essay on the next page.

Comparing Science Fiction Stories		
	"Zoo"	"The Ruum"
Human characters		
Alien characters		
Journey through space		
Futuristic technology		
Lesson about life		

Reading Check

Retell the main events, and describe the characters in the opening part of "The Ruum." Where and when does this part of the story take place? Then, retell the main events, and describe the characters in the rest of the story. Where and when does this part of the story take place?

SKILLS FOCUS

Literary Skills
Analyze the elements of science fiction.

Reading Skills
Compare and contrast stories.

106   Collection 1 / Facing Danger

DIFFERENTIATING INSTRUCTION

Advanced Learners

Enrichment. Although "The Ruum" and "Zoo" are different in many ways, both science fiction stories play on people's distaste for being treated as part of a collection or zoo. Jim is terrified of this prospect and does everything in his power to escape the ruum. Readers of "Zoo" often find the role reversal at the end of the story unsettling. By playing on these feelings, the stories indirectly reassert the value of the individual.

Activity. Encourage interested students to write their own science fiction stories that explore this theme.

Learners Having Difficulty

Block method. If students choose to use the block method of organization, urge them to address the stories' features in the

---

Assignment
1. Writing a Comparison-Contrast Essay

Write an essay comparing "Zoo" and "The Ruum." To help plan your essay, review the chart you completed after you read each story. The chart will help you focus on elements in the stories that are very similar or very different. You do not have to write about all of these elements in your essay. You should pick the elements in each story that most interest you.

Use the workshop on writing a Comparison-Contrast Essay, pages 772–777, for help with this assignment.

Here are two ways you can organize your essay:

1. You can organize your essay by the stories. That means that you will discuss one story at a time, explaining how certain elements are used in that story. If you organize by the stories, your first and second paragraphs might be outlined like this:

> **Paragraph 1:** How "Zoo" uses certain elements
>   A. Journey in "Zoo"
>   B. Aliens in "Zoo"
> **Paragraph 2:** How "The Ruum" uses the elements
>   A. Journey in "The Ruum"
>   B. Aliens in "The Ruum"

2. You can organize your essay by the elements. That means that you will discuss each story element, one at a time, explaining how it is used in each story. If you organize by the elements, your first and second paragraph might be focused on these topics:

> **Paragraph 1:** The setting and characters of each story
>   A. "Zoo"
>   B. "The Ruum"
> **Paragraph 2:** The lesson about life taught in each story
>   A. "Zoo"
>   B. "The Ruum"

At the end of your essay, tell which story you prefer and why.

SKILLS FOCUS

Writing Skills
Write a comparison-contrast essay.

Writing a Comparison-Contrast Essay

Strategy Tip
Method of organization. Urge students having difficulties to write about first one story and then the other. This approach is easy because it involves less moving back and forth between subjects. Remind students using this method to use their closing paragraph to highlight the key similarities and differences between the stories.

Evaluation Criteria
A successful comparison-contrast essay
- opens with a brief introduction naming both stories and their authors
- is unified by one clear thesis statement
- is effectively organized either by stories (block) or by elements (point-by-point)
- analyzes similarities as well as differences
- includes specifics from both stories
- concludes with a personal response
- is free of major errors in grammar and mechanics

---

same order in each paragraph. For instance, if they are comparing the characters and plots in the two stories, they should decide to deal with characters first and then plot second when talking about each story. This predictable order makes the comparison and contrast easier for readers to follow. To help students highlight the similarities and differences between the stories, give them the following word/phrase lists:

Similarities	Differences
both	on the other hand
also	however
in the same way	but
likewise	unlike
in addition	whereas
another	in contrast with

OVERVIEW

The poem in No Questions Asked gives students the chance to read for enjoyment. The annotations in the margins of the Teacher's Edition are optional. No follow-up questions will appear after this poem.

Summary ⬆ *above grade level*

Frankenstein's monster escapes his dungeon; eludes a vicious mob; and eventually arrives at the cottage of a blind violinist, who cannot see the monster's terrifying looks. The kind old musician teaches the monster the simple pleasures of food, wine, good cigars, and friendship. When the musician plays for him, the monster weeps with joy and relief—unaware that the mob will soon find and kill him.

PRETEACHING

Selection Starter

Motivate. Sometimes friendships are forged under strange circumstances. Ask students to think about an important friendship in their lives and consider the following questions: *How did they come to be friendly with the other person? What surprised them about the other person? What unusual interests did they share?*

DIRECT TEACHING

Ⓐ Literary Focus

❓ Theme. These first images describe the monster's inhuman appearance. Yet the speaker describes the monster as "he," not "it." What might the speaker be suggesting by choosing the pronoun *he*? [that the monster has human feelings]

This poem by Edward Field presents us with a new version of a famous character in literature, the monster brought to life by Frankenstein. In the original story, by the English writer Mary Wollstonecraft Shelley, a scientist named Frankenstein uses portions of dead bodies to create a figure shaped like a man and then gives the creature the power to move and think by activating him with electricity.

Frankenstein's creation is a scientific triumph, but it is also a moral disaster that leads to tragedy. The monster, who is actually a gentle and intelligent being, is physically a hideous patchwork of other bodies. His features are so ugly and nightmarish that no one can look at him without wanting to scream. Consequently the monster is forever denied the human companionship and love that he needs.

Edward Field's poem is based on the 1931 movie starring Boris Karloff, in which some elements of the original story were changed. For example, the scientist Frankenstein is Baron Frankenstein in the movie. As you read, picture the poem as presenting a series of film clips.

Frankenstein

Edward Field

The monster has escaped from the dungeon
where he was kept by the Baron,
who made him with knobs sticking out from each side
   of his neck
where the head was attached to the body
5 and stitching all over
where parts of cadavers° were sewed together.

He is pursued by the ignorant villagers,
who think he is evil and dangerous because he is ugly
and makes ugly noises.

6. **cadavers** (kə·dav′ərz) *n.:* dead bodies; corpses.

CROSS-CURRICULAR CONNECTIONS

Music
"Spring Song." Felix Mendelssohn (1809–1847), one of the earlier German Romantic composers, was a child prodigy who gave his first performance at age nine and presented his first original works at age eleven. His "Spring Song," a light but complex melody that suggests the chirping of birds, is from the eight-volume collection *Songs Without Words*, on which he collaborated with his sister Fanny, also a composer. Mendelssohn was both a violinist and a pianist. His compositions—graceful, lyrical, and rich in orchestral color—include the Italian Symphony (1833) and the overture, "Wedding March," and other music for Shakespeare's *A Midsummer Night's Dream*.

10   They wave firebrands at him and cudgels° and rakes,
      but he escapes and comes to the thatched cottage
      of an old blind man playing on the violin Mendelssohn's°
         "Spring Song."

      Hearing him approach, the blind man welcomes him:
      "Come in, my friend," and takes him by the arm.
15   "You must be weary," and sits him down inside the house.
      For the blind man has long dreamed of having a friend
      to share his lonely life. **B**

      The monster has never known kindness—the Baron was cruel—
      but somehow he is able to accept it now,
20   and he really has no instincts to harm the old man,
      for in spite of his awful looks he has a tender heart:
      Who knows what cadaver that part of him came from? **D**   **C**

10. **cudgels** (kuj**'**əlz) *n.:*
    short, thick sticks or clubs.

12. **Mendelssohn's**
    (men**'**d'l·sənz):
    Felix Mendelssohn
    (1809–1847), a German
    composer.

DIRECT TEACHING

B Literary Focus

❓ **Plot.** Why does the blind man welcome the monster? [Possible responses: This is how the blind man would treat anyone; he can't see what the monster looks like and, therefore, is not scared of him.]

C Comparing Literature

❓ **Compare science fiction works.** How does the theme of this work resemble the theme of "Zoo"? [Possible response: Both works convey the message that we share common human feelings no matter how different our outward appearances are.]

D Vocabulary Note
Synonyms. The words *cadaver, corpse,* and *carcass* are near synonyms. *Cadaver* refers to a dead body intended for scientific study. *Corpse* is a general term for a dead body, while *carcass* is the preferred term for the body of a dead animal.

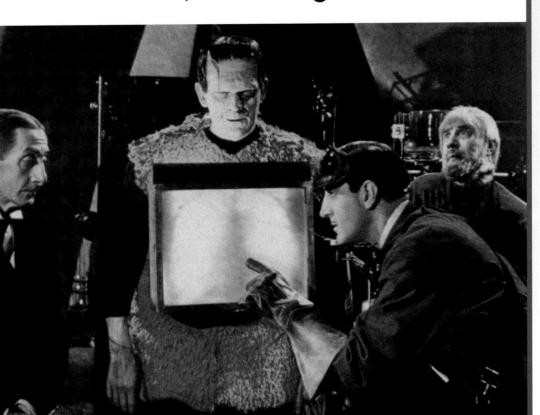

Frankenstein   **109**

Activity. Play a recording of "Spring Song" for students. Invite them to speculate about why tears come into the eyes of the monster in the poem when the musician plays him this piece.

WHOLE CLASS

Frankenstein   **109**

? **Plot.** Remind students that writers sometimes structure their plots by repeating the same incident with slight variations. What plot repetition does Field use here? [The blind musician offers the monster food, drink, a cigar, and music.] What do the old man's repeated acts of kindness toward the monster reveal about the characters? [Possible response: They reveal the goodness of the blind man and reinforce the fact that the monster has the same needs as humans.]

B Vocabulary Note

? **Context clues.** Remind students to look at surrounding verses for clues to unfamiliar words. What clues in the previous stanza hint at the meaning of the word *tentative*? [Possible response: The fact that the monster associates fire with pain would make him hesitant to smoke the cigar.]

C Literary Focus

? **Theme.** Do you think the time spent with the blind musician ultimately brought the monster more joy or more pain? Why? [Possible responses: More pain; if the monster had never known kindness, he would not have known what he was losing when the mob came after him again. More joy; at least the monster had experienced the joy of friendship before he was killed.]

The old man seats him at table, offers him bread,
and says, "Eat, my friend." The monster
25 rears back roaring in terror.

"No, my friend, it is good. Eat—gooood"
and the old man shows him how to eat,
and reassured, the monster eats
and says, "Eat—gooood,"
30 trying out the words and finding them good too.

The old man offers him a glass of wine,
"Drink, my friend. Drink—gooood."
A The monster drinks, slurping horribly, and says,
"Drink—gooood," in his deep nutty voice
35 and smiles maybe for the first time in his life.

Then the blind man puts a cigar in the monster's mouth
and lights a large wooden match that flares up in his face.
The monster, remembering the torches of the villagers,
recoils, grunting in terror.
40 "No, my friend, smoke—gooood,"
and the old man demonstrates with his own cigar.

The monster takes a tentative puff
B and smiles hugely, saying, "Smoke—gooood,"
and sits back like a banker, grunting and puffing.

45 Now the old man plays Mendelssohn's "Spring Song" on the violin
while tears come into our dear monster's eyes
C as he thinks of the stones of the mob, the pleasures of mealtime,
the magic new words he has learned
and above all of the friend he has found.

50 It is just as well that he is unaware—
being simple enough to believe only in the present—
that the mob will find him and pursue him
for the rest of his short unnatural life,
until trapped at the whirlpool's edge
55 he plunges to his death.

110 Collection 1 / Facing Danger

DEVELOPING FLUENCY

Activity. Because so much of this poem is direct dialogue, it makes a good oral-reading activity. Have students form groups of three, and assign one person to be the narrator, the second the blind man, and the third the monster. Encourage students to practice using their voices to convey the personalities of their characters. The monster's voice should be deep and slow, while the blind man's voice should be soothing and encouraging. Then, have groups perform their readings for the class.

SMALL GROUP

Meet the Writer

Edward Field

Meaning of the Monster

Edward Field (1924–) "discovered" poetry during World War II, when he was in England. Between bombing missions he'd go into London on passes and buy books of poetry. He says that he was surprised to find there were actual *living* poets. He himself would receive twenty-two rejections before he finally got his first poetry collection published. Field's poetry is written in a conversational style in language that is familiar and frank. It has been described as "childlike," "open," and "funny." "Frankenstein" is one of several poems based on old movies.

© Robert Giard

  66 The part I love most in the movie *Frankenstein* is where the blind man meets the monster. For the first time, the monster's need for love is revealed and we begin to see him as a victim of a cruel world which is out to destroy him because he is different.

  What then is the meaning for us of this monster? Perhaps he stands for people of other races whom we learn to hate. Perhaps he is also a secret part of us, our forbidden feelings, that we fear and must punish in ourselves and others. 99

Meet the Writer

In addition to writing poetry, Edward Field translated Eskimo songs and tales and wrote the narration for an Academy Award–winning film documentary, *To Be Alive* (1965). His most recent volume of poetry is *A Frieze for a Temple of Love* (1998).

DIFFERENTIATING INSTRUCTION

Advanced Learners
Enrichment. Field suggests that the monster is a metaphor for "a secret part of us, our forbidden feelings, that we fear and must punish in ourselves and others." Ask students to re-read Field's statements in Meet the Writer. Then, invite students to create illustrations, either representational or abstract, in response to Field's statements. Students might include images from any works they have read in this collection. Some students may want to choose a sentence or phrase from the poem or from Field's statements to caption their illustrations.

Writing Workshop

Objectives

- Use appropriate prewriting and drafting skills to create a story.
- Revise the story by adding precise nouns, verbs, and adjectives to make the characters and setting more vivid.
- Reflect on and assess one's writing process and story.

PRETEACHING

Skills Starter

Motivate. Ask students to name well-known stories they have enjoyed reading or seeing as films or TV shows. Why did students enjoy these works? Record their reasons on the chalkboard. Point out that elements such as realistic characters, vivid settings, suspenseful plots, and meaningful themes make stories exciting. Tell students that these are the elements they will be working with as they write their own stories.

DIRECT TEACHING

PREWRITING

Choosing a Story Idea

Remind students that freewriting is an effective way to generate story ideas. If students begin writing about one unusual person they've known and then remember an intriguing incident involving a different person, they can switch subjects without backtracking. You might tell students, "Just keep the pencil going and the thoughts flowing."

Assignment

Write a short story that includes the elements of plot, character, and setting.

Audience

Your classmates, teachers, family, and friends.

RUBRIC
Evaluation Criteria

A good story

1. centers on a major conflict that the characters must resolve
2. uses dialogue and action to develop the characters
3. provides a vivid description of the setting
4. ends with a resolution of the conflict
5. may reveal an overall message about life

SKILLS FOCUS

Writing Skills
Write a short story.

112

NARRATIVE WRITING
Story

One of the best-loved forms of fictional writing is the **short story.** Some short stories are modeled closely on actual occurrences, while others are wildly imaginative—but any good story creates a world that fully engages a reader's interest.

Prewriting

1 **Choosing a Story Idea**

Writing a story can be an enjoyable challenge. Write a story in response to the following **prompt:**

> A good story entertains the reader with lifelike characters in a vivid setting, and in some way it resolves a conflict, or problem. Write a four-page story that presents characters who encounter and solve a problem.

The kernel of a story—your "seed" idea—might come from personal experience. Prod your memory by freewriting responses to questions like these:

- Of all the people you've known, who was the most unusual? the funniest? the most serious?
- What place do you know best? What happens there?
- What interesting experiences have you had?
- Is there an adventure you'd like to have?

CALVIN AND HOBBES © Watterson. Reprinted with permission of UNIVERSAL PRESS SYNDICATE. All rights reserved.

COLLECTION 1 RESOURCES: WRITING

Planning
- *One-Stop Planner* CD-ROM with ExamView Test Generator

Differentiating Instruction
- *Workshop Resources: Writing, Listening, and Speaking*
- *Family Involvement Activities in English and Spanish*
- *Supporting Instruction in Spanish*

Writing and Language
- *Workshop Resources: Writing, Listening, and Speaking*
- *Daily Language Activities*
- *Language Handbook Worksheets*

Assessment
- *Holt Assessment: Writing, Listening, and Speaking*

---

2 Brainstorming

Try writing down at least ten characters, ten settings, and ten problems on separate slips of paper. For each story element, use a different-colored paper. (To get started, you may want to consider the suggestions on the right.) Then, mix and match the characters, settings, and problems until you come up with an interesting combination for a story.

3 Creating Interesting Characters

One of the best ways to hold your reader's interest is to create vivid, true-to-life **characters**. A character comes alive in the reader's imagination through specific descriptions, realistic speech and actions, and the reactions of other characters.

4 Plotting Your Story

To come up with the action, or **plot**, of your story, think about a character's problem. What is the **conflict** that arises—either between characters or in the mind of an individual character? What goal does your character have? What events lead to resolving the problem? The story-plan framework on the right might serve as a guide. You may also find it helpful to use the diagram in the margin of page 114 to visualize the shape of your story.

5 Choosing a Setting

Look for opportunities to give your reader a clear sense of the **setting**—where and when the events of the story take place. Don't just describe the setting and then forget about it when you move on to the action. Try to blend the two. Every detail of the setting should be important to either the mood or the plot of the story—or both.

Drafting

1 Getting Started

If you can come up with a good opening now, that's great, but if you can't, don't worry. Just start writing. You don't

---

Characters

park ranger

veterinarian

shy seventh-grader

Settings

national park

big city

shopping mall

Problems

battles a fire

hates dirty streets

needs a friend

Story Plan

My main character is

_____, who

(name)

_____ .

(basic situation)

This character wants

_____, but

(goal)

_____ .

(main conflict)

Eventually,

_____ ,

(climax)

and in the end,

_____ .

(resolution)

Story **113**

Telling the Story

To help students write in the first-person point of view, encourage them to take a moment to get themselves into character. Once they are inside the head of their narrator, they will find it easier to maintain their character's distinct way of talking and acting.

Plot Diagram

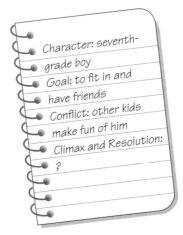

Character: seventh-grade boy
Goal: to fit in and have friends
Conflict: other kids make fun of him
Climax and Resolution:
?

Language Handbook
H E L P

Problems with verbs: See Agreement of Subject and Verb, 2b–n, in the Language Handbook.

need to think of everything all at once! Pick an event or a character or a place, and begin. Trust your imagination—once you begin, new ideas will come to you faster than you can write them down.

2 Telling the Story

From whose **point of view** do you want to tell your story? Do you want to tell it from the point of view of one of the characters, who refers to himself or herself as "I"? Do you want to tell it from the point of view of a narrator who knows everything about all the characters? Perhaps you might want to use a narrator who knows the thoughts and feelings of just one character. (Learn more about point of view on pages 348–349.)

3 Using Dialogue to Develop Characters

Readers can learn a lot about characters through **dialogue**, or what the characters say. As you write, ask yourself if there's a way to use dialogue to show rather than tell about a character. For example, instead of writing "She was kind" to show that a character is kind, try having her speak gently to someone. Let readers hear your character talk so that they can make their own judgments.

Notice how skillfully George G. Toudouze uses dialogue to reveal character and advance the plot in "Three Skeleton Key" (page 42):

> In the light of our lantern she seemed so sound, so strong, that Itchoua exclaimed impatiently:
> "But why the devil was she abandoned? Nothing is smashed, no sign of fire—and she doesn't sail as if she were taking water."
> Le Gleo waved to the departing ship:
> "Bon voyage!" he smiled at Itchoua and went on. "She's leaving us, chief, and now we'll never know what—"
> "No, she's not!" cried the Basque. "Look! She's turning!"

114 Collection 1 / Facing Danger

Learners Having Difficulty
Story patterns. Tell students that their story ideas will probably follow a basic pattern. Most stories involve a character who wants something specific at the beginning of the story and who struggles to achieve that desire throughout the tale. The story ends when the character either gets or does not get what he or she wants. Discuss familiar stories such as *Cinderella* that follow this

basic pattern, and then ask volunteers to suggest plot outlines of their own that conform to this structure.

English-Language Learners
To help these students work effectively with the concepts of character, setting, and conflict, have students bring short newspaper cartoon strips to class. Pair students, and have each pair use a cartoon strip as the

Student Model

This is the beginning of a student's short story.

from Being Different

The top edge of the sun was visible over the roof of the barn. There was a slight chill in the air like every dusk. I spotted the slumped figure in the wooden swing across the field and walked to it.

"Momma is worried. You didn't go tell her you were home from school," I said, noticing the pile of books at his feet. "She thought something happened to you."

He didn't answer, just shrugged.

"Why didn't you kiss Momma hello?"

"Didn't want to." He looked in the other direction. "I just needed time to think about things alone." He faced me, a tear in his left eye glistening.

"What things?" I asked. I had never seen my brother so upset.

He looked up at the dusk sky and then down at his feet. "About important things."

I didn't mean to pry, I knew he disliked me to do so, but I felt so close to him now, closer than ever before, and I knew I had to pry.

"I don't fit in with the other boys at school."

"Who told you that?"

"It's obvious, Angie. Don't you notice who always gets the good grades but never the good friends? I'm so different."

—Amy Yustein
Suffern Junior High School
Suffern, New York

The first paragraph introduces us to the setting and the main characters.

The realistic dialogue creates believable characters.

The main character's actions clearly show he is sad and upset.

We get inside the narrator's mind and know how she feels.

This is the main character's problem. His goal is to fit in.

Strategies for Elaboration

To create believable, interesting characters, start carefully observing the people around you—at a shopping center or a restaurant, for example.

- Look at people's appearance—their clothing, hairstyles, and so on.

- Listen carefully. How do people really talk? What does actual speech sound like?

- Take notes on what you see and hear. In addition to helping you remember details, note-taking will sharpen your powers of observation.

- Remember that the more carefully you observe the world around you, the better you'll write about it.

**go.
hrw
.com**

INTERNET
**More Writer's
Models**
Keyword: LE5 7-1

Story **115**

Student Model

Encourage students to examine the model to see how one student writer introduces characters, shows a basic situation, and reveals a conflict.

Strategies for Elaboration

To help students elaborate on their characters' appearances, you might have them include comparisons. For example, after a sentence about a character's boots, the student might add a second sentence comparing those boots to something else. Students' comparisons might be figurative (similes or metaphors), or they might be as straightforward as "my brother's work boots were older and more scuffed than my school loafers."

DIFFERENTIATING INSTRUCTION

Learners Having Difficulty

Remind students that they must not simply state the character's main problem but instead reveal it through incidents. Ask students to suggest an incident that would demonstrate Angie's brother's predicament.

---

basis for a short story. Before students begin writing, have each pair tell you about the conflict, the main character, and the setting for their story. For lesson plans for learners having difficulty, see *Workshop Resources: Writing, Listening, and Speaking.*

Special Education Students

Before beginning to draft their short stories, students may find it helpful to sketch storyboards that present the series of events they plan to include. This strategy helps students keep the events of the plot in sequence. It also can help them strengthen their drafts by reminding them about how their characters dress and act.

Advanced Learners

Enrichment. Encourage advanced students to go beyond straightforward chronological order in their stories. They might experiment with flashback, flashforward, or both. For example, some students might begin their stories with a flashback showing a key event from the main character's past. Others might create dramatic irony by beginning with a flash-forward and then picking up the story in the present.

116   Collection 1 / Facing Danger

DIRECT TEACHING

EVALUATING AND REVISING

Content and Organization Guidelines

Suggest that students read their revised stories aloud to a peer editor, who will check for precise nouns and verbs and vivid modifiers. Have them record the peer editor's suggestions for improvements on their drafts with a colored pencil. They can then take their time considering whether or not to make the recommended changes.

TECHNOLOGY TIP

Remind students who use word processors to save a copy of their first drafts before they begin revising. If they aren't happy with their revisions, they can go back to the original and begin new revisions.

Evaluating and Revising

Use this chart to help you evaluate and revise the content and organization of your story.

Story: Content and Organization Guidelines

Evaluation Questions	▶ Tips	▶ Revision Techniques
❶ Does the story have an interesting plot with an effective beginning, a conflict, complications, a suspenseful climax, and a clear resolution?	▶ **Place a check mark** next to each of the following elements: beginning, conflict, complications, climax, and resolution.	▶ **Add** or **elaborate** on elements of the plot as necessary. **Delete** any information that ruins the suspense.
❷ Is the point of view consistent throughout the story?	▶ **Identify** pronouns (*I, he,* or *she*) that identify the point of view. **Label** the story's point of view; then, **circle** any information not given from that point of view.	▶ If any sentences are circled, **delete** them. If necessary, **add** the same information told from the narrator's point of view.
❸ Are the characters complex and realistic?	▶ **Underline** specific details about each of the characters.	▶ If necessary, **add** details about a character's appearance, personality, or background. **Add** dialogue and narrative actions that reveal more about a character.
❹ Does the story have a definite setting?	▶ With a colored marker, **highlight** details of the setting.	▶ If there are few highlighted words, **elaborate** on the setting by adding descriptive details.
❺ Is the story well organized and coherent? Does the writer use transitions effectively?	▶ **Number** the major events in the story. **Put a star** next to transitional words and phrases such as *next* and *later that day.*	▶ **Rearrange** any events that are out of order. If there are few or no stars, **add** transitional words and phrases to show the order of events.

Put your first draft aside for a while. Then, read your story as if it has been written by someone else.

EVALUATION GUIDELINES

	4	3	2	1
Use these guidelines to quickly assess students' final drafts.	**Beginning introduces characters, well-defined setting, point of view, and conflict.**	Beginning clearly introduces characters, well-defined setting, point of view, and conflict.	Beginning vaguely introduces characters, setting, point of view, and conflict.	Beginning merely names characters and hints at setting, point of view, and conflict.	Beginning does not introduce any of the main elements.
	All events build to a suspenseful climax.	All events clearly and effectively build to a suspenseful climax.	Most events build to a suspenseful climax, but one or more events are not clearly connected to the plot.	Several events build to a climax, but earlier events give away the climax or lead to a weak climax.	Plot wanders and is unclear or haphazard. No climax is apparent.

Here is one writer's revision of a passage from a short story.

Revision Model

After Peter regained consciousness, he

looked around ^eagerly, trying to identify his

surroundings. ^Overhead There was a tangled web of

yellow, red, and black cables. Each ~~cable~~ one was

the thickness of his waist. An entire wall

glowed with a soft ^amber light. On the floor, spaced at

regular intervals, were large ^metal boxes with ^dozens of switches

on them. He was trapped inside a ^gigantic ~~big~~ PC.

Suddenly, he heard a series of ten ^loud electronic tones. "A

modem!" he ^exclaimed ~~said~~. His whereabouts were no

longer a mystery.

Evaluating the Revision

1. Where has the writer made descriptions more accurate and vivid by adding modifiers?

2. How has the writer improved dialogue by using a more vivid verb?

3. Where has the writer replaced an unnecessarily repeated noun with a pronoun?

4. How has the writer sustained suspense by not revealing information too early?

PROOFREADING

TIPS

- Check your writing for errors in spelling, grammar, and punctuation.

- Make sure you have punctuated dialogue correctly.

- Correct any sentence fragments.

Communications Handbook HELP

See Proofreaders' Marks.

PUBLISHING

TIPS *Create a short story anthology.*

- *Collect your class stories in a booklet.*

- *Provide a table of contents and a preface explaining your story-writing project.*

- *Leave your story anthology in your classroom as an inspiration and resource for other students.*

Story **117**

DIRECT TEACHING

Revision Model

To help students grasp the concept of revising with more precise modifiers, present the thought processes of a writer making the changes shown in the Revision Model. Calling students' attention to the last four sentences, you might say, "The vivid adjectives *loud* and *electronic* show more exactly what the tones sounded like. Replacing the word *big* with the more vivid adjective *gigantic* clarifies the amazing size of this PC."

Proofreading Tips

To help students check their punctuation of dialogue, tell them to be sure that each set of opening quotation marks has a corresponding set of closing ones.

GUIDED PRACTICE

Evaluating the Revision

1. The writer added modifiers to the descriptions of the light and the floor.

2. By using the word *exclaimed* rather than *said,* the writer has added emotion to the dialogue.

3. The writer replaced the noun *cable* with *one.*

4. The writer sustains suspense by describing the setting first and then explaining that Peter is in a giant PC.

	4	3	2	1
Point of view (first or third person) is consistent throughout story.	Point of view is clear and consistent throughout the story.	Point of view is consistent in most sections of the story.	Point of view shifts periodically for no apparent reason.	Point of view is inconsistent and confusing throughout.
Precise words describe characters and setting.	Precise words always describe characters and setting.	Precise words usually describe characters and setting.	Precise words are used only occasionally to describe characters and setting.	The story suffers from a lack of precise words.

Collection 1: Skills Review
Literary Skills

SKILLS FOCUS
pp. 118–119

Grade-Level Skills

■ **Literary Skills**
Analyze plot structure, and determine how each event explains past or present actions or foreshadows future actions.

INTRODUCING THE SKILLS REVIEW

Use this review to assess students' grasp of plot structure.

DIRECT TEACHING

A **Literary Focus**

❓ Foreshadowing. What might the hostess's strained expression signal? [Her expression might signal some annoyance or some trouble or danger.]

B **Literary Focus**

❓ Plot structure. How do the hostess's instructions to the servant advance the plot? What previous event(s) in the story do they help explain? [Her instructions reveal the cobra's presence. They explain the hostess's strange expression and hint that the colonel's argument that women have less "nerve control" than men is wrong.]

Test Practice

DIRECTIONS: Read the story. Then, answer each question that follows.

The Dinner Party
Mona Gardner

The country is India. A colonial official and his wife are giving a large dinner party. They are seated with their guests—army officers and government attachés[1] and their wives, and a visiting American naturalist[2]—in their spacious dining room, which has a bare marble floor, open rafters, and wide glass doors opening onto a veranda.

A spirited discussion springs up between a young girl who insists that women have outgrown the jumping-on-a-chair-at-the-sight-of-a-mouse era and a colonel who says that they haven't.

"A woman's unfailing reaction in any crisis," the colonel says, "is to scream. While a man may feel like it, he has that ounce more of nerve control than a woman has. That last ounce is what counts."

The American does not join in the argument but watches the other guests. **A** As he looks, he sees a strange expression come over the face of the hostess. She is staring straight ahead, her muscles contracting slightly. With a slight gesture she summons the Indian boy standing behind her chair and whispers to him. The boy's eyes widen; he quickly leaves the room. **B**

Of the guests, none except the American notices this nor sees the boy place a bowl of milk on the veranda just outside the open doors.

The American comes to with a start. In India, milk in a bowl means only one thing—bait for a snake. He realizes there must be a cobra in the room. He looks up at the rafters—the likeliest place—but they are bare. Three corners of the room are empty, and in the fourth the servants are waiting to serve the next course. There is only one place left—under the table.

His first impulse is to jump back and warn the others, but he knows the commotion would frighten the cobra into striking. He speaks quickly, the tone of his voice so arresting that it sobers everyone.

"I want to know just what control everyone at this table has. I will count to three hundred—that's five minutes—and

1. **attachés** (at′ə·shāz′) *n.:* diplomatic officials.
2. **naturalist** *n.:* person who studies nature by observing animals and plants.

SKILLS FOCUS

Literary Skills
Analyze plot structure.

MINI-LESSON **Reading**

Reviewing Word-Attack Skills
Activity. Display these pairs of words. For each pair, have students pick the word in which the underlined letter is silent.

1. thum**b**   thim**b**le   [thumb]
2. lim**b**er   lim**b**   [limb]
3. **w**rest   **w**restle   [wrestle]
4. entom**b**   trom**b**one   [entomb]

Activity. Display these sets of words. Have students read each word and decide whether the underlined letters stand for one sound or two. They can consult a dictionary if necessary.

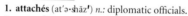
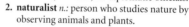

1. m**ea**nder   m**ea**sles   m**ea**sure   [2, 1, 1]
2. p**ie**ces   sc**ie**nce   d**ie**t   [1, 2, 2]
3. gr**oa**n   Sam**oa**n   b**oa**   [1, 2, 2]
4. r**ei**nvent   r**ei**ndeer   l**ei**sure   [2, 1, 1]

not one of you is to move a muscle. Those who move will forfeit³ fifty rupees.⁴ Ready!"

The twenty people sit like stone images while he counts. He is saying ". . . two hundred and eighty . . ." when, out of the corner of his eye, he sees the cobra emerge and make for the bowl of milk. Screams ring out as he jumps to slam the veranda doors safely shut.

"You were right, Colonel!" the host exclaims. "A man has just shown us an example of perfect control." **C**

"Just a minute," the American says, turning to his hostess. "Mrs. Wynnes, how did you know that cobra was in the room?"

A faint smile lights up the woman's face as she replies: "Because it was crawling across my foot." **D**

3. **forfeit** (fôr′fit) v.: give up as a penalty.
4. **rupees** (roo′pēz) n.: Indian money, like dollars in the United States.

---

1. The **setting** of this story is colonial —
   A America
   B India
   C Africa
   D Australia

2. Which of the following events in the **plot** of the story happens first?
   F The American challenges the guests to remain still.
   G A cobra is attracted to milk.
   H The hostess whispers to a servant.
   J The colonel argues with a girl.

3. What **later event** explains the strange expression on the hostess's face?
   A A cobra has crawled across her foot.
   B She dislikes the colonel's biased opinions about women.
   C The servant is not doing his job.
   D She sees a cobra on the veranda.

4. What **later event** explains why the boy places the milk on the veranda?
   F The colonel's speech bores him.
   G The American has seen a cobra.
   H A cobra makes for the milk.
   J The American proposes a challenge.

5. What event marks the **climax** of the story?
   A The argument between the girl and colonel ends.
   B The boy places a bowl of milk on the veranda.
   C The American begins to count.
   D The cobra emerges and screams ring out.

Constructed Response
6. Explain what happens in the **resolution** of the story.

C Literary Focus

❓ Effect of character on plot. How does the American's observant, knowledgeable, and controlled nature affect the plot? [His observant nature leads him to notice the hostess's expression and the bowl of milk. His knowledge tells him the milk is snake bait. His control lets him devise the bet that keeps everyone alive.]

D Literary Focus

❓ Plot. Will the ironic plot twist at the end affect the argument between the colonel and the girl? If so, how? [Yes, the hostess's nerves of steel will give the girl enough ammunition to demolish the colonel's argument.]

Test Practice

Answers and Model Rationales

1. **B** The first sentence of the story reads, "The country is India."
2. **J** Students should be able to list the plot events in sequence: J, H, F, G.
3. **A** The ending of the story reveals that the woman felt the cobra on her foot but did not scream.
4. **H** When the American sees the milk being placed on the veranda, he realizes there is a snake in the room.
5. **D** Remind students that the climax is the story's most suspenseful or emotional moment.

Constructed Response

6. The colonel was proved wrong because the hostess did not scream.

Test-Taking Tips

For more instruction on test taking, refer students to **Test Smarts,** p. 920.

Using Academic Language

Literary Terms
To review plot structure, ask students to look back through the collection to find the meanings of the terms listed at right. Then, have students demonstrate their understanding of plot by citing passages from two or three selections in the collection that illustrate the meanings of the following terms.

Foreshadowing (pp. 2, 38); **Conflict** (p. 14); **Plot** (pp. 2, 14); **Suspense** (p. 38); **Complications** (p. 57).

Informational Reading Skills

SKILLS FOCUS
pp. 120–121

Grade-Level Skills

■ **Reading Skills**
Analyze the structure and purpose of informational texts.

INTRODUCING THE SKILLS REVIEW

Use this review to test students' grasp of the differences between textbooks, newspaper articles, and instruction manuals. Use the annotation only if you want to conduct this review orally.

DIRECT TEACHING

Ⓐ Reading Informational Text

❓ The structure and purpose of various media. How do the structures and purposes of the textbook passage, newspaper article, and instructional manual excerpt differ? [The textbook uses words and typefaces to define a scientific concept. The newspaper article uses a headline and a dateline to convey current news. The instructional manual uses words, symbols, and an illustration to provide a list of steps to take.]

SKILLS FOCUS

Reading Skills
Analyze structure and purpose of informational materials.

Test Practice

DIRECTIONS: Read the informational materials. Then, answer each question that follows.

TEXTBOOK

CHAPTER 2

Biomes: World Plant Regions

What is a biome? A plant and animal community that covers a very large land area is called a **biome**. Plants are the most visible part of a biome. If you looked down on the United States from space, you would see various biomes. The forests of the eastern United States would appear green, while the deserts of the Southwest would be light brown.

NEWSPAPER ARTICLE

B2

Hatteras Lighthouse Completes Its Move

BUXTON, N.C., July 9 (AP)—As onlookers clapped and cheered, the Cape Hatteras Lighthouse slid today onto the concrete pad where its caretakers hope it will stand for another century, a safe distance from the thundering Atlantic surf.

INSTRUCTIONAL MANUAL

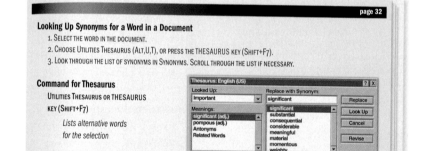

page 32

Looking Up Synonyms for a Word in a Document
1. SELECT THE WORD IN THE DOCUMENT.
2. CHOOSE UTILITIES THESAURUS (ALT,U,T), OR PRESS THE THESAURUS KEY (SHIFT+F7).
3. LOOK THROUGH THE LIST OF SYNONYMS IN SYNONYMS. SCROLL THROUGH THE LIST IF NECESSARY.

Command for Thesaurus
UTILITIES THESAURUS OR THESAURUS KEY (SHIFT+F7)

Lists alternative words for the selection

Using Academic Language

Informational Terms
Ask students to look back through the collection to find the meanings of the following terms and phrases. Then, ask students to choose an informational selection from the collection (or an informational piece that they have read on their own) and explain it using the words at the right:

Table of Contents (p. 33); **Captions** (p. 34); **Summary Lead** (p. 52); **Inverted Pyramid Style** (p. 52); **Headline** (p. 52); **Subhead** (p. 52); **Byline** (p. 52); **Dateline** (p. 52); **Lead** (p. 52); **Tone** (p. 52); **Index** (p. 81); **Directions** (p. 81); **Glossary** (p. 81).

Collection 1: Skills Review

1. Which statement explains the difference between the **purpose** of a textbook and the purpose of a newspaper article?

   A   A textbook has an index, a glossary, and graphic features, while a newspaper article has an inverted pyramid structure.

   B   A textbook has a table of contents and an index, while a newspaper article has a headline, a dateline, and a byline.

   C   A textbook gives lots of information about a big subject, while a newspaper article gives information about a current event.

   D   A textbook has many pages, while a newspaper article is usually one page long or less.

2. In comparing the **structure** of a textbook and the structure of an instructional manual, you could say that —

   F   they both have a table of contents, a glossary, an index, and graphic features, but a textbook is much longer

   G   a textbook presents information about a big subject, but an instructional manual presents information about how to operate and use a device

   H   a textbook is something you use in a classroom, but a manual is something you use at work or at home

   J   a textbook is something your school gives you to use, but a manual comes with something you buy

3. In the **textbook** excerpt the word *biome* means —

   A   a community of plants growing in a forest

   B   plants and sand that occur in desert areas

   C   the coastal areas of the United States as seen from outer space

   D   a plant and animal community that covers a large area

4. The **instructional manual** shown on page 120 gives instructions on how to —

   F   find biomes

   G   move a lighthouse

   H   look up synonyms

   J   read the Internet

5. The **newspaper article** on page 120 shows all of the following features *except* a —

   A   byline

   B   dateline

   C   page number

   D   headline

Constructed Response

6. Explain why an owner's manual has diagrams and an index.

Answers and Model Rationales

1. **C**   Explain that A, B, and D describe differences in structure but only C addresses purpose.

2. **F**   Students should be able to rule out H and J as irrelevant to the issue of structure. G talks about content and purpose, not structure. Only F is about structure.

3. **D**   Students should realize that forests and deserts are only examples of biomes; neither encompasses the full meaning of the term, which is a plant and animal community that covers a large area.

4. **H**   Students should find the manual on p. 120 and note its topic, looking up synonyms.

5. **A**   Point out to students that the writer of the article is not named.

Constructed Response

6. A diagram shows the important parts of a tool and their functions. An index shows a list of topics within the owner's manual.

Test-Taking Tips

Remind students that all the materials in this review have something in common: Their main purpose is to provide information. Encourage students to ask themselves what they have learned from each category of informational material before they answer the Test Practice items.

For more information on test taking, see **Test Smarts,** p. 920.

Collection 1: Skills Review

Vocabulary Skills

Multiple-Meaning Words

Modeling. Model the thought process of a good reader getting the answer to item 1 by saying: "The model sentence says 'Rikki put his fur in order,' meaning 'arranged it neatly.' In the same way, a swimmer would arrange his hair neatly when coming out of the water. B and C have nothing to do with neatness. A shows a way of arranging people but does not necessarily connote neatness."

Test Practice

Answers and Model Rationales

1. **D**   In the model sentence and D, the words *in order* and *into order* mean "in place." In A, the word *order* means "arrangement." This is close to "neat" but not a match. In B, *order* means "instructions to purchase"; in C, *come to order* means "come to attention."

2. **H**   In the model and H, the word *end* means "death." In F, *end zone* refers to a section of a football field. In G and J, *end* means "conclusion" or "dead end," which is not the same as "death."

3. **C**   In the model and C, the word *stroke* suggests a physical blow. In A, *stroke* means "a chime of a clock." In B, *stroke* means "a significant event"; in D, *stroke* means "a sudden failure of brain function."

4. **H**   In the model and H, the word *blow* suggests a hard hit. In F, G, and J, *blow* refers to a flow or breath of air.

5. **B**   In the model and B, *mark* means "a visible distinguishing trait." In A, *mark* means "pay attention to." In C, *mark* means "grade." In D, *mark* means "indication," which is close but not an exact match.

Test Practice

Multiple-Meaning Words

DIRECTIONS: Each sentence below is from "Rikki-tikki-tavi." Read the sentence. Then, choose the answer in which the underlined word is used the same way.

1. "He . . . put his fur in order, scratched himself, and jumped on the small boy's shoulder."
   - **A**   The order of the processional will be shortest person to tallest.
   - **B**   The new order could not be filled because there were no more boxes.
   - **C**   The meeting will come to order.
   - **D**   Coming out of the water, the swimmer swept his hair back into order.

2. "She had crept up behind him as he was talking, to make an end of him. . . ."
   - **F**   The fullback carried the ball into the end zone and scored a touchdown.
   - **G**   The end of the story was too sad.
   - **H**   The dinner guest looked as if it would be the end of him if he had to eat one more bite.
   - **J**   Mr. Lee lives at the end of the road.

3. "When a snake misses its stroke, it never says anything or gives any sign of what it means to do next."
   - **A**   On the stroke of midnight, the old year gives way to the new year.
   - **B**   Winning the football pool was a stroke of good luck.

   - **C**   With one more stroke of the ax, the tree was felled.
   - **D**   It was said that the neighbor on the corner had suffered a stroke.

4. "Rikki-tikki knew he was a young mongoose, and it made him all the more pleased to think that he had managed to escape a blow from behind."
   - **F**   Which way does the wind blow?
   - **G**   There is one more candle to blow out.
   - **H**   Jack felled the giant with one blow.
   - **J**   Stop now, and blow your nose.

5. "He spread out his hood more than ever, and Rikki-tikki saw the spectacle mark on the back of it that looks exactly like the eye part of a hook-and-eye fastening."
   - **A**   Mark my words, no good will come of this.
   - **B**   This mark indicates the ball is mine.
   - **C**   He hopes to get a higher mark in geometry this semester.
   - **D**   Saying "thank you" is a mark of good manners.

SKILLS FOCUS

Vocabulary Skills
Understand multiple-meaning words.

122   Collection 1 / Facing Danger

Vocabulary Review

Use the following activity to find out whether your students have retained the Vocabulary words taught in this collection. **Activity.** Have students select the correct words from the box to complete the sentences.

valiant	idiosyncrasy	huddled
hordes	receding	

1. When the fire alarm went off, we _____ together. [huddled]
2. Counting his fingers each morning is Bob's _____. [idiosyncrasy]
3. The storm is over and the floodwaters are _____. [receding]
4. The barbarians descended on Rome in _____. [hordes]
5. Jill made a _____ effort to stay awake. [valiant]

Collection 1: Skills Review

Writing Skills

Test Practice

DIRECTIONS: Read the passage from a short story. Then, answer each question that follows.

 Breannah stood in the goal, shifting her weight from one foot to the other, as a swarm of red jerseys nudged the soccer ball toward her. A lone blue-clad defender tried and failed to cut off the attack. Now no one stood between her and the lanky star forward of the Red Hots. The forward kicked the ball, and Breannah leaped to her right. The ball whooshed past her left ear and into the net.

 She rose slowly and brushed herself off, ignoring the cheers from the Red Hots' bleachers. Next time, Breannah thought, she would be ready.

1. What strategy does the writer use to develop the main character?
   A dialogue spoken by the character
   B description of the character's appearance
   C description of the character's thoughts and actions
   D explanation of how other people respond to the character

2. What details does the writer use to show point of view in this passage?
   F The words *she* and *her* and the main character's thoughts are used to show third-person limited point of view.
   G The word *I* is used to show first-person point of view.
   H The word *you* is used to show second-person point of view.
   J Information about other characters' thoughts is used to show third-person-omniscient point of view.

3. If this passage occurs near the story's beginning, what might the writer do in later passages to build toward the climax?
   A summarize events in the story that readers have already read about
   B describe additional problems that add to the story's conflict
   C change the point of view to include other characters' views of events
   D describe the setting in detail

4. If a speaker were telling this story out loud, why might she begin by explaining that the story was based on a friend's experience playing soccer?
   F to point out the story's climax
   G to create a mood of suspense
   H to establish a context for the story
   J to include realistic dialogue

SKILLS FOCUS

Writing Skills
Analyze a short story.

Test Practice

Answers and Model Rationales

1. **C** A, B, and D are not strategies used in the paragraph. The writer uses descriptions of the character's thoughts and actions to develop the main character (C).

2. **F** The writer uses the words *she, her,* and *Breannah,* and writes from the third-person limited point of view to show the main character's thoughts in this passage (F).

3. **B** If the passage occurs near the story's beginning, summarizing events would not move the plot forward (A). Changing the point of view to include other characters' views of events (C) and describing the setting in detail (D) would add depth to the overall story, but only describing additional problems that add to the story's conflict (B) would directly build toward the climax of the story.

4. **H** If the speaker were to provide information that the story was based on a friend's experience playing soccer, this would establish a context (H) to help readers understand the setting and circumstances surrounding the story.

APPLICATION

Make a Children's Book

For homework, have interested students convert their short stories into children's books. Point out that each page of a children's book needs an illustration and simplified text. The challenge is to simplify without losing too many of the details that bring the characters, events, and setting to life.

EXTENSION

Write an Eyewitness Account

Tell students that, like a story, an eyewitness account of an event requires an accurate sequence of action, precise details, and the inclusion of dialogue. Have interested students write about an event that they witnessed firsthand. Direct students to include pertinent dialogue in their narration and to reflect on the event's significance at the end.

For Independent Reading

If students enjoyed the themes and topics explored in this collection, you might recommend these titles for independent reading.

Assessment Options

The following projects can help you evaluate and assess your students' outside reading. Videotapes or audiotapes of completed projects may be included in students' portfolios.

- **Create a mural.** Have students design and create a mural that depicts the series of events in *Lyddie.* Have students work in groups to brainstorm for images. Assign each group a section of the mural. Students may use any medium in their work—crayons, paints, colored pencils, or chalk. Have each group explain the actions and events in their section of the mural.

Fiction

Working Girl

In Katherine Paterson's *Lyddie,* set in the 1840s, Lyddie Worthen has to grow up fast when her mother is forced to abandon the family farm. When she finds a job in a textile mill, Lyddie faces a grim new world of poverty and eighteen-hour workdays. A true heroine, Lyddie fights against injustice as she struggles to earn enough to buy back the family farm.

First Division

Sixth-graders from Barlow Road and Bear Creek Ridge have developed a serious softball rivalry that has lasted more than fifty years, and the 1949 game looks to be one of the most exciting yet. But the shadow of World War II looms over the game when Shazam—whose father was killed at Pearl Harbor—attacks Aki—who spent years in an internment camp. Virginia Euwer Wolff's *Bat 6* takes a brave look at prejudice, responsibility, and growing up.

This title is available in the HRW Library.

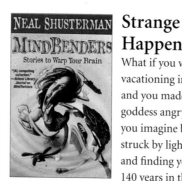

Strange Happenings

What if you were vacationing in Hawaii and you made a volcano goddess angry? Could you imagine being struck by lightning and finding yourself 140 years in the past? What would you do if you woke up one morning and saw seven guardian angels talking to one another in your bedroom? Neal Shusterman presents these wacky situations and more in *MindBenders.*

A Life of Danger

In *Lupita Mañana* by Patricia Beatty, Lupita Torres enters California illegally and tries to help support her widowed mother and younger siblings in Mexico by finding a job. Her search for a better life becomes a struggle in a place where the laws are not always fair and growing up is not always easy.

This title is available in the HRW Library.

DIFFERENTIATING INSTRUCTION

Estimated Word Counts of Read On Books:

Fiction		Nonfiction	
Lyddie	53,000	*Red Scarf Girl: A Memoir of the Cultural Revolution*	57,000
Bat 6	59,000		
Connections to *Bat 6*	4,000	Connections to *Red Scarf Girl: A Memoir of the Cultural Revolution*	9,800
MindBenders: Stories to Warp Your Brain	33,000	*Elizabethan England*	19,000
Lupita Mañana	50,000	*The Snake Scientist*	10,000
Connections to *Lupita Mañana*	7,800	*Behind the Headlines*	33,000

Nonfiction

Courage in China

When Ji-Li Jiang turned twelve in 1966, she was an intelligent student with a bright future ahead of her. Then Mao Tse-tung launched the Cultural Revolution in China, and her family's background was revealed. As a result, Ji-Li's friends turned their backs on her, and her family suffered repeated abuse at the hands of Chinese officials. Ji-Li recalls her childhood of bravery and loyalty in *Red Scarf Girl*.

This title is available in the HRW Library.

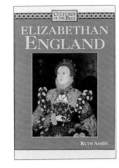

Back in Shakespeare's Day...

Ruth Ashby goes back to the sixteenth century in *Elizabethan England*. Ashby details the lives of prominent historical figures such as Henry VIII and Sir Walter Raleigh and authors such as Sir Thomas More and William Shakespeare. She also describes the religious and social customs of the English people at the time. Helpful maps and illustrations are included.

Snakes, Snakes, and More Snakes

Are you interested in snakes? Dr. Robert Mason is *really* interested in them. For over fifteen years he has been researching the world's largest concentration of garter snakes, located in Manitoba, Canada. Sy Montgomery accompanied Dr. Mason on his field study and, in *The Snake Scientist*, recorded some of the amazing things he learned.

The Story Behind the News Stories

Newspapers have riveted the American public with troubling and sensational stories since the founding of our country. They are perhaps the single most important medium for conveying information, shaping public opinion, and spreading awareness of the world around us. In *Behind the Headlines*, Thomas Fleming explores in exacting detail the people and events that make the news.

Assessment Options

■ **Chart China's attitude toward education.** Have students who choose to read *Red Scarf Girl* work in groups to make a chart showing what China's attitude toward education was before, during, and after the Cultural Revolution, as described by Ji-Li Jiang. They should include a column explaining how this change in attitude affected Ji-Li and her family. Ask students to trade their charts with other groups and use them as a basis for a Venn diagram comparing Chinese attitudes with attitudes in the United States during the same period.

■ **Hold a Shakespearean dress-up day.** Have students work in pairs to come up with costumes that resemble some of the clothing pictured in *Elizabethan England*. Encourage them to use everyday items like scarves to re-create sixteenth-century dress. One student in each pair should model a costume while the other gives an oral report explaining what kind of person (noble or commoner, religious or secular figure, male or female, adult or child) would have been likely to wear such dress.

The Read On titles are categorized as shown below:

Below Grade Level ⬇
MindBenders: Stories to Warp Your Brain
Elizabethan England

At Grade Level ↔
Lyddie
Lupita Mañana
Red Scarf Girl: A Memoir of the Cultural Revolution
The Snake Scientist

Above Grade Level ⬆
Bat 6
Behind the Headlines

Collection 2
Characters: Living Many Lives

Literary Focus:
Analyzing Character

Informational Focus:
Analyzing Comparison and Contrast

About Collection 2

In Collection 2, students will master the following skills:

- **Literary Skills:** Analyze characterization, character traits, motivation, and the narrator.
- **Reading Skills:** Analyze how character affects plot, comparison and contrast, the main idea; make inferences and predictions; compare and contrast characters.
- **Vocabulary Skills:** Understand word origins, roots, affixes, and dialect; clarify word meanings; identify synonyms.
- **Writing Skills:** Develop, write, and revise a problem-solution essay.

Informational Text

Each collection of *Elements of Literature* provides a variety of informational texts related to the literature selections by theme or topic.

Minimum Course of Study

Most skills can be taught with a minimum number of selections and features. In the chart to the right, lessons highlighted in green constitute the minimum course of study that provides coverage of the skills taught in Collection 2.

Selection ▪ Feature	Literary Skills
Elements of Literature: Characterization *by* Mara Rockliff	• Analyze characterization
Reading Skills and Strategies: Characters and Plots **Girls** *by* Gary Paulsen ↓ *below grade level*	
Mother and Daughter *by* Gary Soto ↔ *at grade level*	• Analyze character traits
The Smallest Dragonboy *by* Anne McCaffrey ↔ *at grade level* **Informational Text:** **Here Be Dragons** *by* Flo Ota De Lange ↓ *below grade level*	• Analyze motivation
A Rice Sandwich *by* Sandra Cisneros ↔ *at grade level*	• Analyze the narrator
Antaeus *by* Borden Deal ↑ *above grade level* **Informational Text:** **In a Mix of Cultures, an Olio of Plantings** *by* Anne Raver ↓ *below grade level*	• Analyze motivation • Analyze an allusion
Comparing Literature: Characters and Character Traits **A Day's Wait** *by* Ernest Hemingway ↔ *at grade level* **Stolen Day** *by* Sherwood Anderson ↔ *at grade level*	• Analyze character traits

Resource Manager
(pp. 126E–126H)

Lesson and workshop resources are referenced in the Resource Manager on the pages that follow. These resources can be used to reinforce the skills taught in Collection 2, remediate students who are having difficulty, and provide supporting activities for English-language learners.

Reading Skills	Vocabulary Skills	Writing ■ Grammar and Language Skills
• Analyze how character affects plot		
• Make inferences	• Understand word origins	• Write a character sketch
• Make inferences	• Understand roots and affixes	• Write a narrative
• Analyze comparison and contrast		
• Make inferences	• Understand word origins	• Describe events from another point of view • Use clear pronoun references
• Make predictions • Analyze the main idea	• Clarify word meanings • Understand dialect	• Add a scene to a story
• Compare and contrast characters		• Write a comparison-contrast essay

(continued)

Selection ▪ Feature	Literary Skills	Reading Skills
No Questions Asked: *from* **Homesick** *by* Jean Fritz ↔ *at grade level*		
Writing Workshop: *Persuasive Writing: Problem-Solution Essay*		
Skills Review: *Literary Skills* *Vocabulary Skills* *Writing Skills*	• Analyze characterization	

Reading Skills and Strategies

At the beginning of each collection, a **Reading Skills and Strategies** feature written by Kylene Beers offers students strategies to improve their reading skills. Dr. Beers first models the strategy for the students, then guides them through an annotated selection. The questions in her annotations help students apply the strategy to the selection. After the selection, **Practice the Strategy** provides additional tips and practice.

Comparing Literature / Author Study

Each collection has a **Comparing Literature** or **Author Study** feature that focuses on two or more selections that are thematically or topically linked. The selections represent a variety of genres. The features begin with a prereading page that introduces a Literary Focus and a Reading Skill as well as additional information that students may find useful. Each **Comparing Literature** or **Author Study** feature ends with instruction in writing a comparison-contrast essay about the selections they've read or provides a variety of writing, speaking and listening, or other assignments.

Vocabulary Skills	Writing ▪ Grammar and Language Skills
	• Write a problem-solution essay
• Identify synonyms	• Analyze a problem-solution essay

No Questions Asked

Each collection ends with a **No Questions Asked** feature that includes one or more selections without accompanying apparatus. These selections allow students to practice reading independently. Annotations for teaching the selections are provided in the **Annotated Teacher's Edition.**

Selection ▪ Feature	Planning	Differentiating Instruction ▪ Lesson Plans with ELL Strategies and Practice	Reading ▪ Vocabulary
Elements of Literature: Characterization *by Mara Rockliff*	• PowerNotes: Character	• Holt Reading Solutions: Lesson Plans, pp. 61–62	• Holt Reading Solutions: Lesson Plans, pp. 61–62
Reading Skills and Strategies: Characters and Plots Girls *by Gary Paulsen*			
Mother and Daughter *by Gary Soto*	• One-Stop Planner with ExamView Test Generator	• The Holt Reader, pp. 60–72 • Holt Adapted Reader, pp. 30–37 • Holt Reading Solutions: Lesson Plans, pp. 63–68 • Supporting Instruction in Spanish, p. 6 • Audio CD Library • Audio CD Library, Selections and Summaries in Spanish	• The Holt Reader, pp. 60–72 • Holt Adapted Reader, pp. 30–37 • Holt Reading Solutions, pp. 63–68 • Vocabulary Development, p. 6 • PowerNotes: Making Inferences
The Smallest Dragonboy *by Anne McCaffrey* **Informational Text: Here Be Dragons** *by Flo Ota De Lange*	• One-Stop Planner with ExamView Test Generator	• Holt Reading Solutions: Lesson Plans, pp. 69–76 • Holt Adapted Reader, pp. 38–49 • Supporting Instruction in Spanish, p. 6 • Audio CD Library • Audio CD Library, Selections and Summaries in Spanish	• Holt Adapted Reader, pp. 38–49 • Holt Reading Solutions, pp. 69–76 • Vocabulary Development, pp. 7–8
A Rice Sandwich *by Sandra Cisneros*	• One-Stop Planner with ExamView Test Generator	• The Holt Reader, pp. 73–78 • Holt Reading Solutions: Lesson Plans, pp. 77–82 • Supporting Instruction in Spanish, p. 7 • Audio CD Library • Audio CD Library, Selections and Summaries in Spanish	• The Holt Reader, pp. 73–78 • Holt Reading Solutions, pp. 77–82 • PowerNotes: Making Inferences
Antaeus *by Borden Deal* **Informational Text: In a Mix of Cultures, an Olio of Plantings** *by Anne Raver*	• One-Stop Planner with ExamView Test Generator • PowerNotes: Allusions	• Holt Reading Solutions: Lesson Plans, pp. 83–90 • Holt Adapted Reader, pp. 50–57 • Supporting Instruction in Spanish, pp. 7, 8 • Audio CD Library • Audio CD Library, Selections and Summaries in Spanish	• Holt Adapted Reader, pp. 50–57 • Holt Reading Solutions, pp. 83–90 • Vocabulary Development, p. 9 • PowerNotes: Discovering the Main Idea
Comparing Literature: Characters and Character Traits A Day's Wait *by Ernest Hemingway* **Stolen Day** *by Sherwood Anderson*		• Holt Reading Solutions: Lesson Plans, pp. 91–94	• Holt Reading Solutions, pp. 91–94

Writing ▪ Grammar and Language	Assessment
• Daily Language Activities	• Holt Assessment: Literature, Reading, and Vocabulary • One-Stop Planner with ExamView Test Generator • Holt Online Assessment
• Daily Language Activities	• Holt Assessment: Literature, Reading, and Vocabulary • One-Stop Planner with ExamView Test Generator • Holt Online Assessment
• Daily Language Activities • Language Handbook Worksheets, pp. 23–24	• Holt Assessment: Literature, Reading, and Vocabulary • One-Stop Planner with ExamView Test Generator • Holt Online Assessment
• Daily Language Activities	• Holt Assessment: Literature, Reading, and Vocabulary • One-Stop Planner with ExamView Test Generator • Holt Online Assessment

Technology

INTERNET

- go.hrw.com
- Holt Online Assessment
- Holt Online Essay Scoring
- Elements of Literature Online

MEDIA

 • One-Stop Planner with ExamView Test Generator

 • PowerNotes

 • Audio CD Library

 • Audio CD Library, Selections and Summaries in Spanish

 • Visual Connections Videocassette Program, Segment 2

 • Fine Art Transparencies, 2

 Transparency   Video

 CD-ROM   Audio CD

(continued)

Selection ▪ Feature	Planning	Differentiating Instruction ▪ Lesson Plans with ELL Strategies and Practice	Reading ▪ Vocabulary
No Questions Asked: *from* **Homesick** *by* Jean Fritz			
Writing Workshop: *Persuasive Writing: Problem-Solution Essay*	• One-Stop Planner with ExamView Test Generator	• Workshop Resources: Writing, Listening, and Speaking, pp. 12–22 • Family Involvement Activities in English and Spanish • Supporting Instruction in Spanish, p. 38	
Skills Review: *Literary Skills* *Vocabulary Skills* *Writing Skills*			

The Holt Reader

The Holt Reader is a consumable paperback book that can be used alone or to accompany *Elements of Literature*. It offers guided support throughout the reading process and encourages students to become active readers by circling, underlining, questioning, and jotting down responses as they read. *The Holt Reader* works well for homework, students who have missed class, additional instructional time, reteaching, and remediation.

Holt Reading Solutions (HRS)

Holt Reading Solutions pulls together reading resources in the *Elements of Literature* program to create a powerful tool for intervention and whole-class instruction. *HRS* includes diagnostic assessment tools, lesson plans for English-language learners and special education students, adaptations of selected reading selections, vocabulary and comprehension worksheets, information on phonics and decoding, and additional instruction and practice in remedial reading skills.

Writing · Grammar and Language	Assessment
• Workshop Resources: Writing, Listening, and Speaking, pp. 12–22 • Language Handbook Worksheets • Daily Language Activities	• Holt Assessment: Literature, Reading, and Vocabulary • One-Stop Planner with ExamView Test Generator • Holt Online Assessment • Holt Online Essay Scoring
	• Holt Assessment: Literature, Reading, and Vocabulary • One-Stop Planner with ExamView Test Generator • Holt Online Assessment

One-Stop Planner with ExamView Test Generator

The *One-Stop Planner* CD-ROM planning software contains print-based teaching resources, clips from the video program, and valuable assessment tools. The *One-Stop Planner* resources are presented in easy-to-follow, point-and-click menu formats. To preview resources or print out worksheets and tests, you simply make a selection and click.

One–Stop Planner CD-ROM

Technology

INTERNET

- go.hrw.com
- Holt Online Assessment
- Holt Online Essay Scoring
- Elements of Literature Online

MEDIA

 • One-Stop Planner with ExamView Test Generator

 • PowerNotes

• Audio CD Library

• Audio CD Library, Selections and Summaries in Spanish

• Visual Connections Videocassette Program, Segment 2

• Fine Art Transparencies, 2

 Transparency   Video

 CD-ROM   Audio CD

Collection 2

SKILLS FOCUS

Grade-Level Skills

■ **Literary Skills**
Analyze the methods writers use to reveal character.

■ **Reading Skills**
Analyze texts that show comparison and contrast.

■ **Reading Skills**
Analyze how characters affect plot.

■ **Vocabulary Skills**
Use Latin, Greek, and Anglo-Saxon roots to determine meanings of new words.

Review Skills

■ **Reading Skills**
Analyze the main idea, and identify evidence that supports that idea.

■ **Vocabulary Skills**
Recognize the word origins of unknown words.

Upcoming Skills

■ **Literary Skills**
Compare and contrast the motives of literary characters from different historical eras.

■ **Reading Skills**
Analyze an author's argument, point of view, or perspective.

■ **Vocabulary Skills**
Understand the history of the English language.

COLLECTION 2 RESOURCES: READING

Planning
■ *One-Stop Planner* CD-ROM with ExamView Test Generator

Differentiating Instruction
■ *The Holt Reader*
■ *Holt Adapted Reader*
■ *Holt Reading Solutions*
■ *Family Involvement Activities in English and Spanish*

■ *Supporting Instruction in Spanish*
■ *Audio CD Library*
■ *Audio CD Library, Selections and Summaries in Spanish*

Vocabulary
■ *Vocabulary Development*

Grammar and Language
■ *Language Handbook Worksheets*
■ *Daily Language Activities*

Collection 2

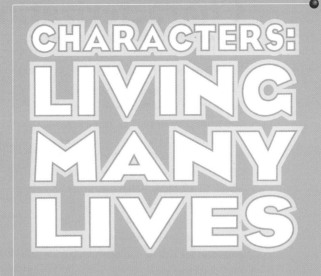

CHARACTERS: LIVING MANY LIVES

Literary Focus:
Analyzing Character

Informational Focus:
Analyzing Comparison and Contrast

INTERNET
Collection Resources
Keyword: LE5 7-2

Market Scene (20th century)
by Carlo Decimus.
Coll. Manu Sassoonian, New York, NY.
© Manu Sassoonian/Licensed by Art Resource, NY.

127

INTRODUCING THE COLLECTION

Theme: Living many lives. The stories in this collection will introduce students to a variety of characters living different lives, from a flamboyant Mexican American single mother to a young boy from another planet. Each main character in Collection 2 is faced with a tough decision, and each handles it in a way that suits his or her personality.

Analyzing character. Students will learn how writers use characterization to create memorable, well-rounded characters. Through studying a character's appearance, actions, speech, thoughts, and motivation, students will analyze the characters in each selection.

Analyzing comparison and contrast. Informational texts connected thematically or topically to the preceding literary selections teach comparison and contrast. Students will understand how authors use this pattern to convey their ideas effectively.

VIEWING THE ART

Activity. Ask students to look at *Market Scene* from a distance first; then, have them look at the painting closely. Ask students to think about the different ways they perceive the painting. Finally, ask them how the painting may tie into the collection theme, "Living Many Lives." [Possible response: From far away the painting looks like a jumble of people, but when examined closely, each figure in the painting is clearly defined. The painting relates to the theme because the texts in the collection will reflect the lives of different fictional characters, all of whom will have unique characteristics.]

Assessment
■ *Holt Assessment: Literature, Reading, and Vocabulary*
■ *One-Stop Planner* CD-ROM with ExamView Test Generator
■ *Holt Online Assessment*

Internet
■ go.hrw.com (Keyword: LE5 7-2)
■ *Elements of Literature Online*

Media
■ *Audio CD Library*
■ *Audio CD Library, Selections and Summaries in Spanish*
■ *Fine Art Transparencies*
■ *Visual Connections Videocassette Program*
■ *PowerNotes*

Grade-Level Skills

■ **Literary Skills**
Analyze characterization.

Elements of Literature: Characterization

Ask students how they decide what a new student or person in their neighborhood is like and whether they want to become friends with that person. In other words, what clues do they use to determine whether to get to know someone? Students may mention personal appearance or actions, such as how a person treats others and what a person says. Remind students that authors use some of the same clues to help readers get to know characters. Ask students what they would think of a character who said these lines at the beginning of a story: "Get out of my way" or "Excuse me, I appear to be lost."

Elements of Literature
Characterization *by* Mara Rockliff
ALL ABOUT THE PEOPLE WE MEET

Getting to Know You

Wouldn't life be easier if the people you met just wore T-shirts that told you what they were like? You'd know right away if the girl who just moved in next door was "SNOBBY AND CONCEITED" or "FRIENDLY, WITH A GREAT SENSE OF HUMOR." That substitute teacher? Better not mess with her—she's "TOUGH BUT FAIR." You won't have to wonder whether your new science partner will be fun or annoying. His T-shirt says it all.

Show Me a Story

If you read a novel written a hundred years ago or more, the writer may just tell you directly, "Old Luther was the meanest old cuss in five counties," or "Little Posy was barely half the size of the other orphans, but she had pluck." Those kinds of statements, in which the writer tells you directly what a character is like, are known as **direct characterization.**

These days, though, writers try to make their stories more like real life. Writers want you to get to know fictional characters just as you get to know people in real life—not by reading a statement on a T-shirt, but by observing people very closely and deciding for yourself what kinds of people they are. You ask: What do they look like? How do they act? What

© The New Yorker Collection 1992 Edward Koren from cartoonbank.com All Rights reserved.

do they say and how do they say it? How do other people feel about them?

One of the first pieces of advice a new writer always hears is "Show, don't tell." Telling is the old way—**direct characterization.** Most writers (and readers) think showing is more interesting and realistic than just telling. This "showing" method of revealing a character is called indirect characterization. In **indirect characterization** you have to observe the character and come to your own conclusion about the kind of person you are meeting.

Who Is This Character, Anyway?

So how does a writer *show* what a character is like?

1 **Appearance.** Appearances can sometimes deceive, but they're often your first clue to character. Does the grandfather in the story have laugh lines around his eyes or a

INTERNET
More About
Characterization
Keyword: LE5 7-2

SKILLS FOCUS

Literary Skills
Analyze
characterization.

128　Collection 2 / Characters: Living Many Lives

DIFFERENTIATING INSTRUCTION

Learners Having Difficulty
Characterization. To help students understand how a writer creates characters, ask students to think of a character from a movie or television show. Invite students to describe the character's appearance, actions, and speech. Then, ask students to think of examples of how other characters' actions reveal what this character is like.

Advanced Learners
Acceleration. Use this activity to help advanced learners compare and contrast the reactions of characters from different historical eras confronting similar conflicts. **Activity.** Have students identify the central conflict confronted by Rikki-tikki-tavi. [He must defend his home.] How does he react? [He bravely battles Nag and his wife.] Then, ask students to identify a character from a story

furrowed brow from years of worrying? Is the trial lawyer cool and collected in her expensive, neatly pressed suit, or is she a sweat-soaked, wrinkled mess?

2 **Action.** The writer could *tell* you, "The boy was happy," but if you see the boy in action, you'll know for yourself.

Luis danced into the kitchen, singing along with the song on the radio. He paused just long enough to give his mother a loud kiss on the cheek, then danced on out the door.

3 **Speech.** Listen to a character talk, and she will tell you what she's like—*indirectly*. A four-year-old may not announce, "Hi! I'm bratty and stubborn," but doesn't the following outburst reveal the same thing?

"I don't have to do what you say!" screamed Darlene as she kicked the new baby sitter in the shins.

4 **Thoughts and feelings.** Here's where literature is better than life. In some books you can actually read what people are thinking, and what they think shows who they are.

Julie wanted to cry when she saw the stray cat. Its ribs were showing. She desperately wanted to add it to her well-fed tribe of cats at home.

5 **Other characters' reactions.** What do the other people in the story think of this character? What do they say about her? How do they act toward him? Of course, just as in life,

you have to consider the source. If a character has something insulting to say about everyone in his school, his comments probably tell you more about *him* than about the others.

Practice

Write down the name of a character from a story you have recently read. Choose two or three words that describe that character, write those words under the name, and then draw a circle around each word. Now, go back to the story, and find examples of how the writer shows you those characteristics. (Notice **appearance, action, speech, thoughts,** and **other characters' reactions.**) Jot down the examples, circle them, and draw lines connecting them to the main circle.

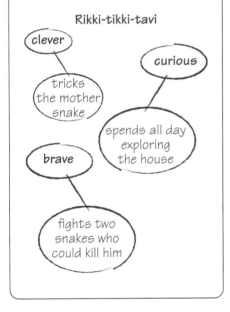

Rikki-tikki-tavi

- clever — tricks the mother snake
- curious — spends all day exploring the house
- brave — fights two snakes who could kill him

Characterization : All About the People We Meet **129**

set in a different historical era who faced a similar situation. How does that character react? Are their responses to the crisis similar in any way? Are they different in any way?

Practice

Possible response is based on "Three Skeleton Key."

Le Gleo

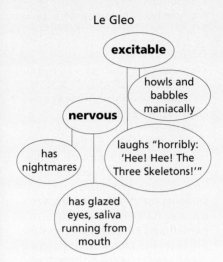

- excitable — howls and babbles maniacally
- nervous — has nightmares
- laughs "horribly: 'Hee! Hee! The Three Skeletons!'"
- has glazed eyes, saliva running from mouth

Apply

You might suggest that students choose one of the figures in the cartoon and explain how they would develop him or her into a round character for a story. Students might describe the character's appearance, write a few lines of dialogue, and explain something the character would do and some thoughts the character would have.

HOMEWORK

Grade-Level Skills

■ **Reading Skills**
Analyze how characters affect plot.

OVERVIEW

Purpose. The strategy of If—Then helps students identify character traits and recognize the way characters affect plot.

Use. If—Then can be used to analyze the way any character has influenced the plot of a story. With "Girls," a lighthearted anecdote about a first date, have students use If—Then to analyze the way Paulsen characterizes himself and Eileen and recognize the ways the plot would change if the characters were different. In addition to using the strategy with the stories in this collection, If—Then can be useful when students are reading selections such as "The Highwayman" in Collection 3 and "Amigo Brothers" in Collection 5.

Summary ⬇ *below grade level*

This memoir relates Gary Paulsen's experience on his first date. As a thirteen-year-old boy, Gary noticed that his peers suddenly were able to talk to girls, while he could only talk about them. When Eileen looked at him and smiled, Gary was unsure of how to respond. With help from his friend Orvis and other classmates, Gary arranged to take Eileen to a movie. When the date began, Gary was sweating because of his heavy clothes, and he spilled his money on the ground. Over the course of the date, he spoke to Eileen only once, to ask her if she'd like popcorn. Gary realized that he couldn't recall a single moment from the movie they watched together because he was consumed by thoughts about Eileen.

Characters and Plots

by Kylene Beers

Pause for a moment and think of a movie you've seen or story you've read. Now, think about that movie or story without the characters. Can you do it? Probably not. Plot gives us the action of a story; characters are the ones doing the action. Take away the characters, and the plot comes to a standstill. Change the characters, and the plot changes too. Make the killer shark in the movie *Jaws* a friendly dolphin, and you have a very different movie.

Understanding How Characters Affect Plot

If you want to figure out how the plot might change if a character changes, use a simple strategy called **If—Then**. With this strategy you imagine what would have happened if the character had behaved differently. **If** you think a character is fearless, **then** what would have happened if he were frightened? **If** you think another character is cautious, **then** what would have happened if she were reckless?

As you read the next selection from Gary Paulsen's book *How Angel Peterson Got His Name,* consider how this story of a first date would change if either the boy or the girl behaved differently.

SKILLS FOCUS

Reading Skills
Understand how characters affect plot.

Tips for Understanding Characters

Writers use many ways to help you understand characters. They may

• use dialogue to give you insight into a character

• tell you what a character is thinking

• describe the way a character acts or reacts to situations

• tell you how other characters—or even animals—react to a character

If you read a story in which a dog growls as a character approaches, you may be right to guess that the character is up to no good. If a character says, "Who may I say is calling?" instead of "Whosit?" you're right to think that manners count to that gent.

DIFFERENTIATING INSTRUCTION

Learners Having Difficulty

Point out to students that Paulsen uses the actions of characters to tell readers something about them. Ask students who have trouble with characterization to make a three-column chart and label the first column "Character," the second "Action," and the third "What the action tells about the character." Then, have students fill out the chart as they read so they can get a better understanding of the story.

English-Language Learners

Students from other countries may be unfamiliar with the dating rituals in this story. For example, they may be surprised that Gary was allowed to meet Eileen alone on the first date. To get English-language learners involved with the story, invite them to tell how their culture's courting and dating rituals are similar to or different from the ones in the story.

Girls

from How Angel Peterson Got His Name

Gary Paulsen

Girls. ❶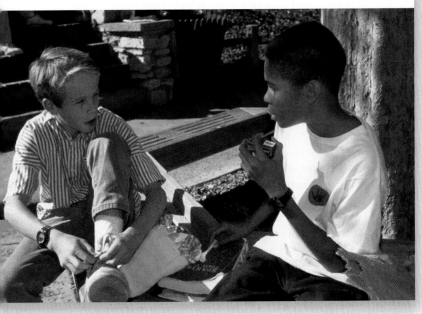

When we were eleven and even twelve they were just like us. Sort of.

That is, we could be friends and do projects together in school and some boys could even talk to them.

Not me. I never could. And neither could Orvis. Alan seemed to have worked out a way to pretend they weren't even there and Wayne swore that it didn't bother him at all to speak to girls.

And then we became thirteen.

Everything changed. ❷

Well, not everything. I still couldn't talk to them, lived in mortal terror of them, and Orvis was the same way. But we talked *about* them all the time, how they looked, how they smiled, how they sounded, how

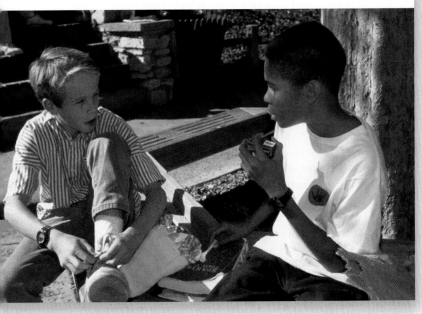

Using the Strategy

As you read, you'll find this open-book sign at certain points in the story: . Stop at these points, and think about what you've just read. Do what the prompts ask you to do.

ANALYZE

❶ Why does Paulsen start this story with a one-word paragraph? What is he trying to tell you about girls?

Ⓐ

ANALYZE

❷ Why do you think Paulsen writes so many short paragraphs? How do the short paragraphs help you understand what he considers important?

Ⓑ

PRETEACHING

Selection Starter

Motivate. Ask students to think back on a time when they were worried about what someone else thought of them. What were their worries at the time? Were their concerns unfounded? Ask students to freewrite about their experience.

DIRECT TEACHING

Ⓐ **Reading Skills and Strategies**

Analyze. [Possible responses to question 1: Paulsen starts the story in a way that grabs the reader's attention. He is saying that one word ("girls") can mean different things to different readers and each reader probably has a particular experience that comes to mind upon reading the word.]

Ⓑ **Reading Skills and Strategies**

Analyze. [Possible response to question 2: The short paragraphs help draw attention to the important topics of the piece: girls and turning thirteen.]

Advanced Learners

Enrichment. Ask students to think of short stories, novels, or movies where a lack of confidence has a detrimental effect on a character. Then, have them discuss the way this characteristic is viewed in other works and in "Girls."

DIRECT TEACHING

A Reading Skills and Strategies

Analyze. [Possible response to question 3: Paulsen is using capitalization to point out that these ideas were very important for thirteen-year-old boys like himself.]

B Reading Skills and Strategies

Analyze character. [Possible responses to question 4: Gary didn't ask Eileen because he was afraid to talk to girls. He would have needed to be bold and confident to ask her directly. The situation is funny because it should have been easy for Gary to ask a girl out who smiled at him without involving so many other people.]

C Reading Skills and Strategies

? If—Then. Imagine if Paulsen were able to speak to girls. How would this passage be different? [Possible response: Instead of just talking to his friends about Eileen, he probably would have approached her and begun a conversation after she smiled at him.]

D Reading Skills and Strategies

Interpret. [Possible responses to question 5: He probably would have been awkward around them or said something that offended or surprised them. If he were confident, he would have said something cordial and charming, and her parents probably would have taken a liking to him immediately.]

ANALYZE

A ❸ Why does Paulsen use capital letters for *In Love* and *For Real,* as if these phrases were titles?

ANALYZE CHARACTER

B ❹ Why didn't the narrator just ask Eileen himself? What **character traits** would he have needed to be able to ask her directly?

INTERPRET

D ❺ Imagine what the narrator might have said if he had met Eileen's parents. What would the conversation have been like if he had been as scared to talk to them as he was to talk to Eileen? What might have been said if he had been confident instead?

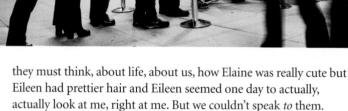

---

they must think, about life, about us, how Elaine was really cute but Eileen had prettier hair and Eileen seemed one day to actually, actually look at me, right at me. But we couldn't speak *to* them.

Except that now it became very important that we be *able* to speak to them. Before, it didn't seem to matter, and now it was somehow the only thing that *did* matter.

C I had this problem because Eileen actually *had* looked at me one day on the way out of school, or so I thought, and on top of it she had smiled—I was pretty sure at me as well—and I thought that maybe I was In Love and that it was For Real and when I asked Orvis about it he agreed that I might be In Love for Real and suggested that I take Eileen to a movie. ❸

Which nearly stopped my heart cold. I couldn't talk to her—how could I ask her to go to a movie? Finally it was Orvis who thought of the way. I would ask Wayne to ask Shirley Johnson to ask Claudia Erskine, who was a close friend of Eileen's, if Eileen might like to go to the movies with me the following Saturday afternoon. ❹

This tortuous procedure was actually followed and by the time I was told that indeed Eileen would like to see a movie the next Saturday, I was a nervous wreck and honestly hoped she wouldn't go.

We met in front of the theater, as things were done then at our age—I couldn't even imagine going to her home and ringing the bell to pick her up and having her parents answer the door. If I couldn't really speak to girls, what would I do with a set of *parents* of the girl I was going to take to a movie? ❺

132   Collection 2 / Characters: Living Many Lives

So we met at the theater at one-thirty. I wore what I thought were my best clothes, a pullover sweater over a turtleneck, with my feeble attempt at a flattop, Butch-Waxed so much that dropping an anvil on my head wouldn't have flattened it. I think now I must have looked something like a really uncomfortable, sweaty, walking, greasy-topped bottle brush. (Have I mentioned that with my sweater and turtleneck I had gone solely for fashion and had ignored the fact that it was high summer? Or that the theater was most decidedly *not* air-conditioned?) ❻ 📖

But Eileen was a nice person and pretended not to notice the sweat filling my shoes so they sloshed when we walked or how I dropped my handful of money all over the ground. I had brought all of my seven dollars in savings because I really didn't know how much it would cost, what with tickets and treats, and maybe she was a big eater. ❼ 📖

She also pretended not to notice when I asked her if she wanted popcorn.

So I asked her again. Louder.

And then again. Louder.

All because I was blushing so hard my ears were ringing and I wasn't sure if I was really making a sound and so when I screamed it out the third time and she jumped back, it more or less set the tone for the whole date.

We went into the theater all right. And we sat next to each other. And she was kind enough to overlook the fact that I smelled like a dead buffalo and that other than asking her three times if she wanted popcorn I didn't say a word to her. Not a word.

I couldn't.

The movie was called *The Thing*, about a creature from another planet who crashes to earth in the Arctic and develops a need/thirst/obsession for human and sled-dog blood and isn't killed until they figure out that he's really a kind of walking, roaring, grunting plant. So they rig up some wire to "cook him like a stewed carrot." All of this I learned the second time around, when I went to the movie with Wayne, because sitting next to Eileen, pouring sweat, giving her endless boxes of Dots and candy corn and popcorn (almost none of which she wanted but accepted nicely and set on the seat next to her), I didn't remember a single thing about the movie. Not a word, not a scene. ❽ 📖

All I could do was sit and think, I'm this close to a girl, right next to a girl, my arm almost touching her arm, a girl, right there, right *there*....

Using the Strategy

ANALYZE

❻ Do you think the narrator really looked like a "greasy-topped bottle brush"? Why would he describe himself this way? What response is he trying to get from you?

INTERPRET

❼ The narrator uses a lot of exaggeration in describing himself. However, he understates Eileen's character, saying only that she was "a nice person." Do you think that Eileen was also nervous? Why doesn't the narrator tell us more about the way she was acting?

INTERPRET

❽ The narrator tells this first-date story with a lot of humor. Re-read your favorite sections, and think about what would have happened if either the boy or the girl had behaved differently. If Eileen, for example, had been more outgoing or rude, how might the date have ended?

Girls   133

DIRECT TEACHING

Ⓔ Reading Skills and Strategies

❓ **If—Then.** If Gary were more self-assured, how would this passage be different? [Possible responses: He probably would not have worn winter clothes during the summer, and if he did, he'd probably think he was making a fashion statement. He would have thought his hair looked stylish. He would not have even noticed his sweat. He would have been generally comfortable with his appearance.]

Ⓕ Reading Skills and Strategies

Analyze. [Possible responses to question 6: He probably didn't appear as awful as his description implies. He describes himself this way to let the reader know how little he thought of himself and to add humor to the situation.]

Ⓖ Reading Skills and Strategies

Interpret. [Possible response to question 7: It's possible that she too was nervous, because she didn't begin a conversation with Gary either. The narrator doesn't say how she was acting because he was so concerned with his own appearance.]

Ⓗ Literary Focus

❓ **Character.** Why didn't Eileen notice Gary's question? What does that tell you about her character? [Possible responses: She may have been distracted by something else or lost in thought about her own appearance. The episode suggests that she may have been nervous as well.]

Ⓘ Reading Skills and Strategies

Interpret. [Possible responses to question 8: If Eileen had been more outgoing, she probably would have begun a conversation, and they might have gotten along better. If Eileen had been rude, she probably would have ended the date abruptly.]

Meet the Writer

In the midst of an unhappy child-hood, Gary Paulsen was introduced to the world of books, a discovery he says saved his life: "I was a miserable student. . . . I had a miserable home life. . . . One night I went into a library to get warm and the librarian asked me if I wanted a library card. Then she started giving me books. . . . It saved me, it really did. And now I tell kids to read like a wolf eats."

For Independent Reading

- If students decide to read *Woodsong,* you can ask them to describe the lessons that Paulsen learns about nature during his journeys.

- Students who liked the excerpt from *How Angel Peterson Got His Name* may also want to read about the misadventures of an insecure adolescent in Paulsen's novel *The Boy Who Owned the School: A Comedy of Love.*

Gary Paulsen

Real-Life Adventures

One night while **Gary Paulsen** (1939–) was working as an electronics engineer at a deep-space tracking station in California, he had the sudden realization that he needed a change. Paulsen recalls:

> **"** I thought . . . what am I doing? I just hated it. I decided to be a writer, pretty much that night. I drove to Hollywood. If I'd been in the East I would have gone to New York. I needed to find [other] writers. **"**

Gary Paulsen has clearly found his calling in life. He has written more than 175 books, three of which were named Newbery Honor Books.

The popular young adult author frequently finds inspiration for his books in his life experiences, which have included stints as a soldier, actor, sailor, trapper, and rancher. Paulsen has clearly seen his share of adventure in these positions and has a wealth of material to write about as a result.

For Independent Reading

In the memoir *Woodsong,* Paulsen presents an incredible account of eye-opening journeys he has taken into the wilderness with his sled dogs.

Practice the Strategy

Recognizing Characterization
PRACTICE 1

In "Girls," Paulsen wants you to feel a young boy's terror at asking a girl on a date. He doesn't want you just to *know* the boy was afraid; he wants you to *feel* his fear and nervousness. How does Paulsen do this? (Hint: Take a look at the adjectives he chooses to describe the boy's feelings.)

If—Then: How Characters Affect Plot
PRACTICE 2

On page 130, you were asked to think about how this story of a first date would change if either the boy or the girl had behaved differently. What might have happened if the boy had been more confident? if the girl had been more talkative?

From each pair of opposites below, choose the adjective that best describes the narrator or Eileen.

> *shy / bold*
> *scared / fearless*
> *caring / uncaring*

Now, think about the events in the story you just read. How would these events have changed if either the boy or the girl had displayed the opposite characteristics? If you think Eileen is scared, for example, what might have happened differently if she had been fearless?

You can use the **If—Then strategy** with the stories in this collection. If you want to figure out how any plot might change if a character changes, try using the If—Then strategy.

Strategy Tip

Here are some pairs of adjectives to keep in mind as you read any selection. Ask yourself, "**If** the character is [one of these adjectives], **then** how does the plot change if he or she were [the other adjective] instead?"

> *selfish / selfless*
> *greedy / giving*
> *active / passive*
> *brave / cowardly*
> *graceful / clumsy*
> *strong / weak*
> *good / bad*
> *wise / foolish*
> *truthful / sneaky*
> *kind / mean*
> *honest / dishonest*
> *scared / fearless*
> *caring / uncaring*
> *daring / cautious*
> *funny / serious*
> *polite / rude*
> *happy / sad*
> *shy / bold*

SKILLS FOCUS

Reading Skills
Analyze how character affects plot.

Girls **135**

Practice the Strategy

In this feature students have the opportunity to analyze characterization and discuss how the plot of a story would change if characters had different attributes.

Strategy Tip

When students are choosing adjectives that describe characters, remind them to keep in mind each character's speech, thoughts, feelings, and actions. Focusing on the techniques of characterization will allow them to think of descriptions more easily.

PRACTICE 1

Possible answer: The reader feels the narrator's nervousness through Paulsen's use of exaggeration. The narrator lived "in mortal terror" of girls. His "heart stopped cold" when someone suggested that he ask Eileen out. Though these things didn't actually happen, that was how it felt for the narrator.

PRACTICE 2

Possible answer: If Gary were bold instead of shy, he would have asked Eileen out himself rather than going through his friends. If Eileen were uncaring instead of caring, she would have mocked Gary's appearance and ended the date abruptly.

CROSS-CURRICULAR CONNECTIONS

History
Research report. After consulting a history teacher, encourage students to use If—Then to help them when they write a history report. The strategy can be used to help them discover the defining characteristics of historical figures. For example, a student researching Dr. Martin Luther King, Jr., might use the strategy this way: "If Dr. Martin Luther King, Jr., had been cowardly instead of brave, he would not have worked to end segregation." Students can also use the strategy to help them understand causes and effects of historical events—for example, "If Dr. Martin Luther King, Jr., had not given his 'I Have a Dream' speech, then Congress would have been less likely to pass the Civil Rights Act of 1964."

Grade-Level Skills
- **Literary Skills**
Analyze character traits.
- **Reading Skills**
Make inferences.

Review Skills
- **Literary Skills**
Analyze the characters' effects on the plot and its resolution.

Upcoming Skills
- **Literary Skills**
Compare and contrast the motives of literary characters from different historical eras.

Summary *at grade level*

Pretty, studious Yollie Moreno lives with her mother, a large, flamboyant practical joker. An immigrant from Mexico who has worked hard all her life, Mrs. Moreno wants Yollie to become a doctor and take care of her. Because there is no money for a new dress for the school dance, Mrs. Moreno dyes a white dress black. When it begins to rain, Yollie's dress begins to drip black dye. Mortified, Yollie runs home and yells at her mother. The next day they make up. Overcoming her desire to save for the future, Mrs. Moreno gives Yollie money that she has been saving for Yollie's college education so that the girl can buy a new outfit.

Before You Read · The Short Story

Mother and Daughter

Make the Connection
Quickwrite ✏️

Like the characters in a story, real people have **character traits** too. Think about your experiences with people. What makes you like or dislike someone? In your journal, make a list of four or five character traits that you admire most in people and a list of those you like the least.

Literary Focus
Character Traits

A **character** is anyone who plays a part in a story. A **character trait** is a quality in a person that can't be seen. Character traits are revealed through a person's appearance, words, actions, and thoughts. Character traits can also be revealed in the ways a person affects other people. As you read "Mother and Daughter," notice how the writer helps you get to know this mother and her daughter. What are their character traits (the qualities they carry inside)?

Reading Skills
Making Inferences

To find a character's traits, you have to make inferences. **Inferences** are educated guesses, based on whatever evidence you have. If you wake up in the morning and see puddles in the streets, you could infer that it rained the night before. If you read a story in which a character always mentors kids who need help reading, you could infer that she is a caring person. As you read "Mother

INTERNET

Vocabulary
Activity
•
More About Soto
Keyword: LE5 7-2

SKILLS FOCUS

Literary Skills
Understand character traits.

Reading Skills
Make inferences.

and Daughter," look for details in the story that can help you make inferences about the characters. To collect evidence, look for answers to questions like these:

- What do I know about the character's looks, thoughts, words, and actions?
- How do other characters react to the character?
- What does the character learn by the end of the story?

Vocabulary Development

Here are some words you'll learn as you read the story:

matinees (mat''n·āz') *n.*: afternoon performances of a play or a movie. *Yollie and her mother got along well enough to go to matinees together at the local theater.*

antics (an'tiks) *n.*: playful or silly acts. *People who witnessed Mrs. Moreno's antics couldn't help laughing.*

meager (mē'gər) *adj.*: slight; small amount. *Mrs. Moreno remembers that her parents worked hard for their meager salaries.*

sophisticated (sə·fis'tə·kāt'id) *adj.*: worldly; elegant and refined. *Yollie admired the way sophisticated people in New York dressed.*

tirade (tī'rād') *n.*: long, scolding speech. *Yollie felt bad about her tirade against her mom.*

Mother and Daughter

Gary Soto

PRETEACHING

Selection Starter

Motivate. Parents and children don't always agree about what is important. What is the best way to resolve these conflicts? What character traits make conflict resolution easier? After the discussion, ask students to complete the Quickwrite.

Preview Vocabulary

After students have read the Vocabulary words and definitions, ask them to answer these questions and give reasons for each answer.

1. If you went to a matinee, would you be worried about coming home after dark? [No, an early afternoon performance would end before dark.]

2. Who would be more likely to engage in antics: a lion tamer or a clown? [A clown is more likely to perform silly acts.]

3. If you were hungry, would you be pleased to have a meager lunch? [No, a small lunch would probably not satisfy your hunger.]

4. Would you dress up to dine with a sophisticated friend? [Yes, you would want to dress well to dine with an elegant person.]

5. Do you enjoy listening to a tirade? [No one likes to be scolded.]

Assign the Reading

You might wish to have students take turns reading the story aloud up to the following sentence: "Why did you leave me on the couch . . . ?" Then, assign the rest for homework.

HOMEWORK

Assessment
- *Holt Assessment: Literature, Reading, and Vocabulary*
- *One-Stop Planner* CD-ROM with ExamView Test Generator
- *Holt Online Assessment*

Internet
- go.hrw.com (Keyword: LE5 7-2)
- *Elements of Literature Online*

Media
- *Audio CD Library*
- *Audio CD Library, Selections and Summaries in Spanish*

A Literary Focus

❓ Character traits. One way to identify character traits is to ask, "What kind of person does or says . . . ?" Ask students, "What kind of person waves at people she doesn't know who are cruising around in cars?" [Possible response: Someone who is friendly, outgoing, and fun-loving.]

B Cross-curricular Connections
CULTURE

Low-riders. Low-riders are cars that have been modified so that the body is very close to the ground.

C Literary Focus

❓ Character traits. Based on this incident, what would you conclude about Mrs. Moreno's character? [Possible responses: She is a practical joker; she is more interested in playing a joke than in her daughter's feelings.]

D Reading Skills

❓ Infer. To help students make an inference about Yollie's character, suggest that Yollie could have responded to her mother's practical joke in a number of ways. Yollie could (1) call her mother names, (2) destroy something of her mother's and say it was an accident, (3) play a joke on her mother and burn her toast, or (4) cry herself to sleep. What would each of these actions reveal about Yollie's character? Then, point out that the students' answers are inferences.

A
B Yollie's mother, Mrs. Moreno, was a large woman who wore a muumuu and butterfly-shaped glasses. She liked to water her lawn in the evening and wave at low-riders, who would stare at her behind their smoky sunglasses and laugh. Now and then a low-rider from Belmont Avenue would make his car jump and shout *Mamacita!* But most of the time they just stared and wondered how she got so large.

Mrs. Moreno had a strange sense of humor. Once, Yollie and her mother were watching a late-night movie called *They Came to Look*. It was about creatures from the underworld who had climbed through molten lava to walk the earth. But Yollie, who had played soccer all day with the kids

next door, was too tired to be scared. Her eyes closed but sprang open when her mother screamed, "Look, Yollie! Oh, you missed a scary part. The guy's face was all ugly!"

But Yollie couldn't keep her eyes open. They fell shut again and stayed shut, even when her mother screamed and slammed a heavy palm on the arm of her chair.

"Mom, wake me up when the movie's over so I can go to bed," mumbled Yollie.

"OK, Yollie, I wake you," said her mother through a mouthful of popcorn.

But after the movie ended, instead of waking her daughter, Mrs. Moreno laughed under her breath, turned the TV and lights off, and tiptoed to bed. Yollie woke up in the middle of the night and didn't know where she was. For a moment she thought she was dead. Maybe something from the underworld had lifted her from her house and carried her into the earth's belly. She blinked her sleepy eyes, looked around at the darkness, and called, "Mom? Mom, where are you?" But there was no answer, just the throbbing hum of the refrigerator.

Finally, Yollie's grogginess cleared and she realized her mother had gone to bed, leaving her on the couch. Another of her little jokes.

But Yollie wasn't laughing. She tiptoed into her mother's bedroom with a glass of water and set it on the nightstand next to the alarm clock. The next morning, Yollie woke to screams. When her mother reached to turn off the alarm, she had overturned the glass of water.

C

D Yollie burned her mother's morning toast and gloated. "Ha! Ha! I got you back. Why did you leave me on the couch when I told you to wake me up?"

Learners Having Difficulty
Invite learners having difficulty to read "Mother and Daughter" in interactive format in *The Holt Reader* and to use sidenotes as aids to understanding the selection. The interactive version provides additional instruction, practice, and assessment of the literary skill taught in the Student Edition. Monitor students' responses to the selection, and correct any misconceptions that arise.

English-Language Learners
For lessons designed for English-language learners, see *Holt Reading Solutions.*

Special Education Students
For lessons designed for special education students, see *Holt Reading Solutions.*

Despite their jokes, mother and daughter usually got along. They watched bargain matinees together, and played croquet in the summer and checkers in the winter. Mrs. Moreno encouraged Yollie to study hard because she wanted her daughter to be a doctor. She bought Yollie a desk, a typewriter, and a lamp that cut glare so her eyes would not grow tired from hours of studying.

Yollie was slender as a tulip, pretty, and one of the smartest kids at Saint Theresa's. She was captain of crossing guards, an altar girl, and a whiz in the school's monthly spelling bees.

E *"Tienes que estudiar mucho,"* Mrs. Moreno said every time she propped her work-weary feet on the hassock. "You have to study a lot, then you can get a good job and take care of me."

"Yes, Mama," Yollie would respond, her face buried in a book. If she gave her mother any **F** sympathy, she would begin her stories about how she had come with her family from Mexico with nothing on her back but a sack with three skirts, all of which were too large by the time she crossed the border because she had lost weight from not having enough to eat.

Everyone thought Yollie's mother was a riot. Even the nuns laughed at her antics. Her brother Raul, a nightclub owner, thought she was funny enough to go into show business.

But there was nothing funny about Yollie needing a new outfit for the eighth-grade fall dance. They couldn't afford one. It was late October, with Christmas around the corner, and their dented Chevy Nova had gobbled **G** up almost one hundred dollars in repairs.

"We don't have the money," said her mother, genuinely sad because they couldn't **H** buy the outfit, even though there was a little money stashed away for college. Mrs. Moreno remembered her teenage years and her hard-working parents, who picked grapes and oranges, and chopped beets and cotton for meager pay around Kerman. Those were the days when "new clothes" meant limp and out-of-style dresses from Saint Vincent de Paul.

The best Mrs. Moreno could do was buy Yollie a pair of black shoes with velvet bows

Vocabulary
matinees (mat''n·āz') *n.:* afternoon performances of a play or a movie.
antics (an'tiks) *n.:* playful or silly acts.
meager (mē'gər) *adj.:* slight; small amount.

A Advanced Learners

❓ Acceleration. Yollie and her mother both want the same thing: for Yollie to fit in with the dominant culture. How do their different backgrounds bring them into conflict about how to achieve this? [Possible response: Mrs. Moreno is the child of migrant workers. She sees fitting in as a long-range goal to be accomplished by education. Yollie has had a more stable life than her mother. She wants to fit in now.]

B Literary Focus

❓ Resolution of conflict. Which character traits of Yollie and Mrs. Moreno help them resolve the conflict over a new dress? [Possible responses: Mrs. Moreno is optimistic and high-spirited. She expects things to work out, so she goes ahead with plans. Yollie doesn't hold a grudge, so when the dress looks fine, she is satisfied.]

and fabric dye to color her white summer dress black.

"We can color your dress so it will look brand-new," her mother said brightly, shaking the bottle of dye as she ran hot water into a plastic dish tub. She poured the black liquid into the tub and stirred it with a pencil. Then, slowly and carefully, she lowered the dress into the tub.

Yollie couldn't stand to watch. She *knew* it wouldn't work. It would be like the time her mother stirred up a batch of molasses for candy apples on Yollie's birthday. She'd dipped the apples into the goo and swirled them and seemed to taunt Yollie by singing *"Las Mañanitas"* to her. When she was through, she set the apples on wax paper. They were hard as rocks and hurt the kids' teeth. Finally, they had a contest to see who could break the apples open by throwing them against the side of the house. The apples shattered like grenades, sending the kids scurrying for cover, and in an odd way the birthday party turned out to be a success. At least everyone went home happy.

To Yollie's surprise, the dress came out shiny black. It looked brand-new and

sophisticated, like what people in New York wear. She beamed at her mother, who hugged Yollie and said, "See, what did I tell you?"

The dance was important to Yollie because she was in love with Ernie Castillo, the third-best speller in the class. She bathed, dressed, did her hair and nails, and primped until her mother yelled, "All right already." Yollie sprayed her neck and wrists with Mrs. Moreno's Avon perfume and bounced into the car.

Mrs. Moreno let Yollie out in front of the school. She waved and told her to have a good time but behave herself, then roared off, blue smoke trailing from the tail pipe of the old Nova.

Yollie ran into her best friend, Janice. They didn't say it, but each thought the other was the most beautiful girl at the dance; the boys would fall over themselves asking them to dance.

The evening was warm but thick with clouds. Gusts of wind picked up the paper lanterns hanging in the trees and swung them, blurring the night with reds and yellows. The lanterns made the evening seem romantic, like a scene from a movie. Everyone danced, sipped punch, and stood in knots of threes and fours, talking. Sister Kelly got up and jitterbugged with some kid's father. When the record ended, students broke into applause.

Janice had her eye on Frankie Ledesma, and Yollie, who kept smoothing her dress down when the wind picked up, had her eye on Ernie. It turned out that Ernie had his mind on Yollie, too. He ate a handful of

Vocabulary
sophisticated (sə·fis′tə·kāt′id) *adj.:* worldly; elegant and refined.

CROSS-CURRICULAR CONNECTIONS

History
Mexican Americans in California. People from Mexico have lived in California since the 1500s. Until 1848, they lived first under the rule of Spain and then Mexico. After 1848, when Mexico lost the northern half of its territory to the United States, Mexican Americans quickly lost land and political power to European American settlers. Since that time, Mexican immigrants have been welcomed into the United States during times when their labor was needed in agriculture and manufacturing and turned away during times of high unemployment. Starting in the 1950s, migrant workers, led by Mexican American human rights leader Cesar Chavez (who died in 1993), have organized nonviolent protests against poor working conditions and low wages. Their successes have awakened pride in their Mexican American heritage.

cookies nervously, then asked her for a dance.

"Sure," she said, nearly throwing herself into his arms.

They danced two fast ones before they got a slow one. As they circled under the lanterns, rain began falling, lightly at first. Yollie loved the sound of the raindrops ticking against the leaves. She leaned her head on Ernie's shoulder, though his sweater was scratchy. He felt warm and tender. Yollie could tell that he was in love, and with her, of course. The dance continued successfully, romantically, until it began to pour.

"Everyone, let's go inside—and, boys, carry in the table and the record player," Sister Kelly commanded.

The girls and boys raced into the cafeteria. Inside, the girls, drenched to the bone, hurried to the restrooms to brush their hair and dry themselves. One girl cried because her velvet dress was ruined. Yollie felt sorry for her and helped her dry the dress off with paper towels, but it was no use. The dress was ruined.

Yollie went to a mirror. She looked a little gray now that her mother's makeup had washed away but not as bad as some of the other girls. She combed her damp hair, careful not to pull too hard. She couldn't wait to get back to Ernie.

Yollie bent over to pick up a bobby pin, and shame spread across her face. A black puddle was forming at her feet. Drip, black drip. Drip, black drip. The dye was falling from her dress like black tears. Yollie stood up. Her dress was now the color of ash. She looked around the room. The other girls, unaware of Yollie's problem, were busy grooming themselves. What could she do? Everyone would laugh. They would know she dyed an

old dress because she couldn't afford a new one. She hurried from the restroom with her head down, across the cafeteria floor and out the door. She raced through the storm, crying as the rain mixed with her tears and ran into twig-choked gutters.

When she arrived home, her mother was on the couch eating cookies and watching TV.

"How was the dance, *m'ija*? Come watch the show with me. It's really good."

Yollie stomped, head down, to her bedroom. She undressed and threw the dress on the floor.

Her mother came into the room. "What's going on? What's all the racket, baby?"

"The dress. It's cheap! It's no good!" Yollie kicked the dress at her mother and watched it land in her hands. Mrs. Moreno studied it closely but couldn't see what was wrong. "What's the matter? It's just a bit wet."

"The dye came out, that's what."

Mrs. Moreno looked at her hands and saw the grayish dye puddling in the shallow lines of her palms. Poor baby, she thought, her brow darkening as she made a sad face. She wanted to tell her daughter how sorry

Mother and Daughter 141

DIRECT TEACHING

C Reading Skills

Predict. All has been going well for Yollie. How might the rain create a new conflict for her? [Some students might guess that the dye could run out of her dress. Others might say that the rain will ruin the party.]

D Reading Skills

Make generalizations. Twice Mrs. Moreno has tried to give Yollie something she wanted on a limited budget. What has happened both times? [In Yollie's eyes, both attempts were disasters.] **What generalization can you make from these events?** [Possible response: Some students may generalize that it is difficult to achieve desired results without the necessary money.]

E Literary Focus

Character traits. What do Yollie's thoughts at this point tell you about her character? [Possible responses: She is ashamed of being poor. She doesn't believe that her classmates would sympathize with her.]

F Reading Skills

Infer. How does Mrs. Moreno feel about Yollie? To help students, ask: What does Mrs. Moreno do when Yollie has a birthday party? when Yollie wants a new dress? when Yollie's dress gets ruined? [Possible response: Mrs. Moreno loves Yollie and wants her dreams to come true.]

MINI-LESSON Reading

Developing Word-Attack Skills
Write these words from the selection on the chalkboard: *Yollie, why, scary, sympathy, days, money, boys, buy.* Have students read the words and compare the sounds represented by *y*:

- In *Yollie, y* stands for the consonant sound /y/.
- In *why*, the letter *y* stands for long *i*.
- In *scary, y* stands for long *e*.

- In *sympathy*, the first *y* stands for short *i* and the final *y* stands for long *e*.
- In *days, y* is part of the *ay* spelling for long *a*.
- In *money, y* is part of the *ey* spelling for long *e*.
- In *boys, y* is part of the *oy* spelling for the sound /oi/.
- In *buy, y* is part of the *uy* spelling for long *i*.

Activity. Have volunteers underline the words spelled with *y* in each sentence and identify the sound that each *y* stands for.

1. Let's <u>try</u> to have the <u>party</u> in the <u>gym</u>.
   [long *i*, long *e*, short *i*]
2. <u>They</u> <u>say</u> it will be <u>rainy</u> on <u>Friday</u>.
   [long *a*, long *a*, long *e*, long *a*]
3. The <u>sky</u> looks <u>dreary</u> and <u>gray</u>.
   [long *i*, long *e*, long *a*]

A Literary Focus

? Character traits. Why does Mrs. Moreno so quickly give up the idea of inventing something? [Possible responses: Mrs. Moreno doesn't really believe they could. She said that to make Yollie feel better. Her practicality tells her the most realistic way for them to have a better life is for Yollie to get an education.]

B Literary Focus

? Resolution of conflict. In order for the conflict to be resolved, how did Mrs. Moreno's character have to change? [Possible response: She had to decide to place more importance on Yollie's present happiness than on future goals.] What change in Yollie's character might have led to a different resolution? [Possible response: If Yollie decided that an education was more important than what people think of her, she might have told her mother to put the money back.]

GUIDED PRACTICE

Monitor students' progress. To check students' understanding of the two main characters, have them complete a Venn diagram. To help students get started, suggest that they consider these categories: appearance, attitude toward others, sense of humor, attitude toward work, practical versus romantic.

Yollie
concerned about what others think
slim
studious
quiet
romantic

hard-working
quick to forgive
independent

Mrs. Moreno
not concerned about what others think
large
willing to change
loud
practical

---

she was, but she knew it wouldn't help. She walked back to the living room and cried.

The next morning, mother and daughter stayed away from each other. Yollie sat in her room turning the pages of an old *Seventeen,* while her mother watered her plants with a Pepsi bottle.

"Drink, my children," she said loud enough for Yollie to hear. She let the water slurp into pots of coleus and cacti. "Water is all you need. My daughter needs clothes, but I don't have no money."

Yollie tossed her *Seventeen* on her bed. She was embarrassed at last night's tirade. It wasn't her mother's fault that they were poor.

When they sat down together for lunch, they felt awkward about the night before. But Mrs. Moreno had made a fresh stack of tortillas and cooked up a pan of *chile verde,* and that broke the ice. She licked her thumb and smacked her lips.

"You know, honey, we gotta figure a way to make money," Yollie's mother said. "You and me. We don't have to be poor. Remember the Garcias. They made this stupid little tool that fixes cars. They moved away because they're rich. That's why we don't see them no more."

"What can we make?" asked Yollie. She took another tortilla and tore it in half.

"Maybe a screwdriver that works on both ends? Something like that." The mother looked around the room for ideas, but then shrugged. "Let's forget it. It's better to get an education. If you get a good job and have spare time then maybe you can invent something." She rolled her tongue over her lips and cleared her throat. "The county fair hires people. We can get a job there. It will be here next week."

Yollie hated the idea. What would Ernie say if he saw her pitching hay at the cows?

How could she go to school smelling like an armful of chickens? "No, they wouldn't hire us," she said.

The phone rang. Yollie lurched from her chair to answer it, thinking it would be Janice wanting to know why she had left. But it was Ernie wondering the same thing. When he found out she wasn't mad at him, he asked if she would like to go to a movie.

"I'll ask," Yollie said, smiling. She covered the phone with her hand and counted to ten. She uncovered the receiver and said, "My mom says it's OK. What are we going to see?"

After Yollie hung up, her mother climbed, grunting, onto a chair to reach the top shelf in the hall closet. She wondered why she hadn't done it earlier. She reached behind a stack of towels and pushed her chubby hand into the cigar box where she kept her secret stash of money.

"I've been saving a little money every month," said Mrs. Moreno. "For you, *m'ija.*" Her mother held up five twenties, a blossom of green that smelled sweeter than flowers on that Saturday. They drove to Macy's and bought a blouse, shoes, and a skirt that would not bleed in rain or any other kind of weather.

FAMILY/COMMUNITY ACTIVITY

Mrs. Moreno is eager to talk about her past, especially about what it was like to have immigrated to the United States. Have students choose an older family member or an elder in their community to interview about the differences between his or her childhood and teenage years and what today's young people might experience. Students might share their interview results in class.

Meet the Writer

Gary Soto

"A Name Among *la gente*"

Like Yollie in this story, **Gary Soto** (1952–) grew up in a Mexican American family in California. Much of his award-winning fiction and poetry draws on his heritage and his childhood memories. Although his work is vastly popular today, selling an average of seven thousand books a month, Soto remembers that early on he had trouble cultivating readers, even his own grandmother.

❝ Unlike most other contemporary poets and writers, I've taken the show on the road and built a name among *la gente*, the people. I have ventured into schools, where I have played baseball and basketball with young people, sung songs, acted in skits, delivered commencement speeches, learned three chords on a Mexican guitar to serenade teachers. . . . My readership is strung from large cities, such as Los Angeles, to dinky Del Ray, where peach trees outnumber the population by many thousands. From all appearances my readers care.

. . . I'm in their lives and in their hearts. I'm searching for a family whose grandmother, an illiterate, fits a book into a picture frame, the centerpiece for a household that will in time quiet down and throw open the cover. ❞

For Independent Reading

"Mother and Daughter" appears in a collection of short stories called *Baseball in April,* about kids like Yollie growing up in Fresno, California. You might want to read one of Soto's novels, such as *Taking Sides* or its sequel, *Pacific Crossing.* If you like poetry, look at *A Fire in My Hands.* That book includes a question-and-answer section in which Soto talks about writing poetry.

Meet the Writer

Gary Soto says he writes about "commonplace, everyday things— baseball, an evening walk, a boyhood friendship, first love, fatherhood, a tree, rock 'n' roll, the homeless, dancing." In his writing he tries to "keep alive the small moments which add up to a large moment: life itself."

For Independent Reading

- If students read *Baseball in April,* suggest that after reading "Seventh Grade" they think about whether the main character's experiences on the first day of school are realistic. You might also recommend the following titles:

- For another view of a contemporary Mexican American family living in California, students might read the novel *Parrot in the Oven,* by Victor Martinez, who, like Gary Soto, grew up in Fresno, California. Soto has called this book the most finely written portrait of poverty he has ever read.

- Novels about earlier immigrant groups in California include William Saroyan's *My Name Is Aram,* about an Armenian family in San Luis Obispo, California, and *Mama's Bank Account,* Kathryn Forbes's account of Norwegian immigrants in San Francisco.

- *Not Just Party Girls,* by Jeanne Betancourt, is a novel of one girl's life-changing experience as an intern at a missionary camp for migrant workers.

DIFFERENTIATING INSTRUCTION

Advanced Learners

The United Farm Workers. Though Soto is known primarily as a writer of fiction and poetry, he has written a biography for young adults about Jessie De La Cruz, an organizer for the United Farm Workers union. Soto decided to write the book after inviting De La Cruz to spend the night at his home and listening to her stories.

Enrichment. Suggest that students find out more about migrant workers and the United Farm Workers by reading Soto's biography, *Jessie De La Cruz: A Profile of a United Farm Worker.* They might also find information on the Internet by entering *United Farm Workers* as key words in a search engine.

INDEPENDENT PRACTICE

After You Read

First Thoughts

1. Possible answers:
   - I thought Yollie was immature at times.
   - I thought she and her mother learned to respect one another's feelings.

Thinking Critically

2. They are both practical jokers. Mrs. Moreno is more concerned with having fun than pampering her daughter. Yollie is not afraid to take revenge on her mother.

3. She is captain of the crossing guards, an altar girl, and a star in spelling bees. These activities suggest that she is a leader and is religious and smart.

4. She is flamboyant, outgoing, and unconcerned about what others think of her. She is a caring mother.

Extending Interpretations

5. Possible answers: Some will say that the two are believable because they have failings, such as Yollie's concern with what others think and Mrs. Moreno's insensitivity to Yollie. Others may say that their easygoing relationship is unrealistic. Those who feel the resolution is realistic may say that Mrs. Moreno changes because she cares for Yollie. Others may say that it's unlikely that a practical mother would spend college savings on new clothes.

First Thoughts

1. Respond to the story by completing these sentences:
   - I thought Yollie was . . .
   - I thought she and her mother . . .

Thinking Critically

2. Look back at the way Yollie and her mother tease each other at the beginning of the story. What inferences can you make about the **character traits** of the mother and the daughter in that scene?

3. How has Yollie distinguished herself at Saint Theresa's? Based on her involvement in those activities, what would you infer about her **character?**

4. Look at the way Mrs. Moreno dresses, at how other people respond to her, and at how she feels about Yollie. What inferences can you make about her **character?**

Extending Interpretations

5. Do you think Yollie and her mother are believable **characters**? (Think about how they compare with people you know.) How about that final discovery of the money in the cigar box? Was that a believable resolution to the plot? Why or why not?

SKILLS FOCUS

Literary Skills
Analyze character traits.

Reading Skills
Make inferences.

Writing Skills
Write a character sketch.

WRITING

Creating a Character

Before you read this story, you took notes about some character traits you admire and some you don't like. Now, refer to those notes, and write a sketch of a character with the traits you admire or the traits you do not like. Be sure to use details to describe your character's actions, looks, and relationships with other people. ✏

Reading Check

Fill out a story map like the one below to review the plot of "Mother and Daughter."

> Characters:
> What they want:
> Conflicts (problems):
> > Event:
> > Event:
> > Event:
> > Event:
> > Climax:
>
> Resolution of conflict:

Focus on the main events in the plot. (You may note a different number of events.)

Reading Check

Characters—Yollie, Mrs. Moreno. *What they want*—Yollie wants a new dress for the school dance; Mrs. Moreno wants Yollie to go to college, get a good job, and take care of her. *Conflicts (problems)*—There is no money for a new dress; Yollie doesn't want her mother to dye an old dress. *Event*—Mrs. Moreno dyes Yollie's old white dress black. *Event*—It starts to rain at the outdoor dance. *Event*—Yollie notices her dress is dripping black dye. *Event*—She runs home. *Climax*—Yollie yells at her mother about the dyed dress. *Resolution of conflict*—Mrs. Moreno gives Yollie money she was saving for Yollie's college expenses to buy a new outfit.

After You Read — Vocabulary Development

Dictionaries Tell Stories: Word Origins

Etymology (et′ə·mäl′ə·jē) means "the study of the origin and development of words." Most dictionaries give an etymology in brackets or parentheses following the word itself. At the back or front of the dictionary, you'll find definitions of the symbols and abbreviations used in the etymologies. One important symbol is "<," which means "comes from" or "derived from." The "derived from" symbol followed by a question mark ("<?") indicates that the derivation of a word or word part is unknown. A backward "derived from" symbol (">") means "from which comes." Here is the etymology of *mother* from one dictionary:

Word Bank

matinees
antics
meager
sophisticated
tirade

This etymology could be translated as "The word *mother* comes from the Middle English word *moder,* which comes from the Old English word *modor,* which is related ('akin') to the German word *mutter,* which comes from the Indo-European word *matér,* from which comes the Latin word *mater,* the Greek word *mētēr,* and the Old Irish word *māthir.* All the words might come from a word that imitates the sound of baby talk."

PRACTICE

The words in the Word Bank are derived from either Latin or Greek. Use a good dictionary to discover the original derivation of these words. Then, complete a chart like the one below:

Word Bank Word	Original Derivation
sophisticated	< Gr sophos, "clever; skillful; wise"

Vocabulary Skills
Understand word origins.

PRACTICE

- *matinees*—< L *matutinus,* "of the morning"
- *antics*—< L *antiquus,* "ancient; old"
- *meager*—< L *macer,* "lean; thin"; < Gr *makros,* "long"
- *tirade*—< VL *tirare,* "pull; draw; shoot"

ASSESSING

Assessment
- *Holt Assessment: Literature, Reading, and Vocabulary*

RETEACHING

For a lesson reteaching characterization, see **Reteaching,** p. 917E.

DIFFERENTIATING INSTRUCTION

Learners Having Difficulty
Work with students as they fill in the story map and answer the questions. *Monitoring tip*: If students have difficulty identifying the conflicts, remind them to look at what each person wants and ask, "Is there a conflict between these two desires?" As students answer the Extending Interpretations question, remind them to re-read relevant passages from the story and to ask themselves, "What kind of person would do that?"

Writing. Remind students to use a character map like the one on p. 129 to plan their character sketch.

HOMEWORK

Advanced Learners
Enrichment. Point out to students that since this story is written in the third person, readers can only infer the characters' motivations based on what they learn about the characters from their words and actions.

Activity. Have students write an interior monologue that shows what is going on in Yollie's mind as she talks on the telephone with Ernie.

Grade-Level Skills

■ Literary Skills
Analyze character motivation.

■ Reading Skills
Make inferences.

Review Skills

■ Literary Skills
Analyze the characters' effects on the plot and its resolution.

Summary ⬌ *at grade level*

This fantasy takes place on the planet Pern, an imaginary world where dragons help protect the inhabitants. Each year, in an Impression ceremony, each newly hatched dragon selects its own rider from among the young people of Pern. The hero of the story is Keevan, a boy facing his first Impression ceremony. Small for his age, Keevan must work twice as hard as the other boys and endure their taunts and teasing, especially those of the bully Beterli. Goaded into a fight with Beterli, Keevan is badly injured. However, he calls on his courage and determination to hobble to the Hatching Ground, where he is chosen by a bronze dragon, the highest honor a dragonrider can achieve.

Before You Read The Short Story

The Smallest Dragonboy

Make the Connection
Quickwrite

Have you ever wanted to do something that you thought would be too hard or that someone said you couldn't do? What motivated you to overcome your difficulties? Take some notes about a time when you faced a challenge as an underdog.

Literary Focus
Motivation

Why do people do the things they do? What makes us act one way and not another? These are questions about **motivation.** Feelings, needs, wishes, pressures from family and friends—all these are forces that pull and push people from inside and outside. As you read "The Smallest Dragonboy," ask yourself what forces motivate Keevan, the main character. How does understanding Keevan's motivation help you understand the kind of character he is?

INTERNET

Vocabulary Activity

•

More About McCaffrey

Keyword: LE5 7-2

SKILLS FOCUS

Literary Skills
Understand motivation.

Reading Skills
Make inferences.

Reading Skills
Making Inferences

An **inference** is an educated guess based on evidence. When you make inferences about characters, you try to guess what kind of people they are, based on how the characters act, what they say, how other people respond. As you read "The Smallest Dragonboy," look for the little open-book signs after some paragraphs. Stop at these points to answer questions that ask you to make inferences about a character.

Vocabulary Development

These words appear in the story. See if you can use each one in a sentence of your own.

goaded (gōd′id) *v.:* pushed or driven. *Beterli goaded Keevan into a fight.*

imminent (im′ə·nənt) *adj.:* about to happen. *Pern was in imminent danger of a Thread attack.*

perturbed (pər·tʉrbd′) *v.* used as *adj.:* disturbed; troubled. *Keevan was perturbed when he heard the bad news.*

confrontation (kän′frən·tā′shən) *n.:* face-to-face meeting between opposing sides. *The conflict between the two boys led to a violent confrontation.*

alleviate (ə·lē′vē·āt′) *v.:* relieve; reduce. *The boy's mother spoke soothing words to alleviate his fears.*

146   Collection 2 / Characters: Living Many Lives

RESOURCES: READING

Planning
■ *One-Stop Planner* CD-ROM with ExamView Test Generator

Differentiating Instruction
■ *Holt Adapted Reader*
■ *Holt Reading Solutions*
■ *Supporting Instruction in Spanish*
■ *Audio CD Library*

■ *Audio CD Library, Selections and Summaries in Spanish*

Vocabulary
■ *Vocabulary Development*

Grammar and Language
■ *Daily Language Activities*

Assessment
■ *Holt Assessment: Literature, Reading, and Vocabulary*

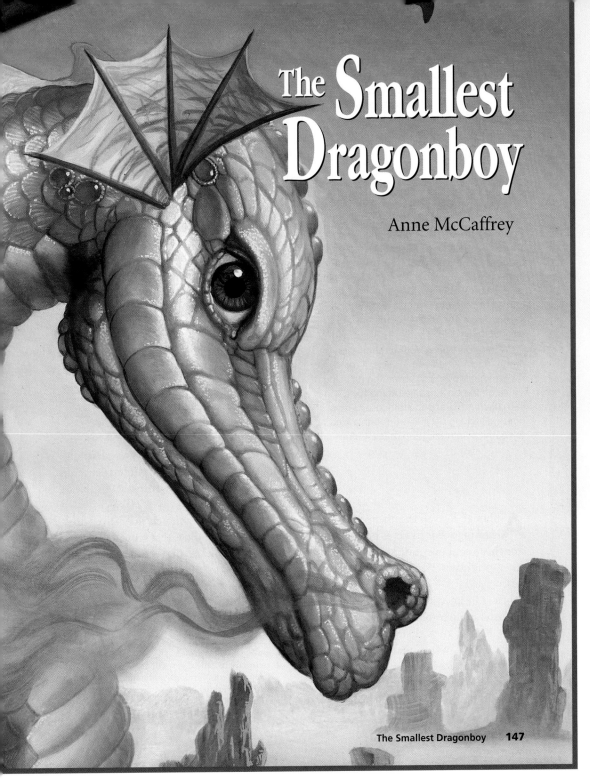

The Smallest Dragonboy

Anne McCaffrey

The Smallest Dragonboy **147**

- *One-Stop Planner* CD-ROM with ExamView Test Generator
- *Holt Online Assessment*

Internet
- go.hrw.com (Keyword: LE5 7-2)
- *Elements of Literature Online*

Media
- *Audio CD Library*
- *Audio CD Library, Selections and Summaries in Spanish*
- *Fine Art Transparencies*

Skills Starter

Build skills. Review character analysis with students. On what do they base their opinions of a character? [Possible responses: the character's words, the character's actions, and so on.] List answers on the chalkboard. Explain that to decide why a character does something, students should look at these clues and think about why a person might act in this way.

Preview Vocabulary

After students have read the definitions of the Vocabulary words, ask volunteers to mime the meanings of *goaded, imminent, perturbed, confrontation,* and *alleviate.* Then, have students reinforce their understanding of the words with the following activity. Tell students to

- write a sentence that includes the words *goaded* and *confrontation*
- write a sentence that includes the words *imminent* and *perturbed*
- write a sentence that includes the word *alleviate*

Have students mix up the order of the three sentences and copy them onto another sheet of paper, leaving blank spaces for the Vocabulary words. They should then exchange papers with a partner, fill in the blanks on each other's papers with the missing Vocabulary words, and check each other's work.

Assign the Reading

Before assigning the Quickwrite activity for homework, you might wish to discuss the concept of motivation in class. Students can then come to class prepared to read the story silently.

HOMEWORK

A **Reading Skills**

❓ **Infer.** What does this information suggest about Keevan? [Possible responses: He is observant and perceptive; he understands other people's words, actions, and motives.]

B **Reading Skills**

Infer. Point out that Keevan infers that Beterli walks quickly in order to embarrass him, the smallest dragonboy. Assuming Keevan's inference is correct, ask students what this tells them about Beterli.

[Possible response to question 1: Beterli is cruel and unkind.]

C **Learners Having Difficulty**

Break down difficult text. Help students break down this long sentence into short ones. [On the height, the blue watch dragon stretched his great transparent pinions. His rider was mounted on his neck. His pinions carried him on the winds of Pern to fight the evil Thread. The Thread fell at certain times from the skies.]

Background
The World of Pern

"The Smallest Dragonboy" takes place on the planet of Pern, an imaginary world somewhere in outer space. Pern is threatened by the dangerous Red Star, which rains deadly, threadlike plant spores on the planet every two hundred years or so. If a hungry Thread falls on Pern soil and grows there, it will devour every living thing in sight.

To protect their planet, colonists on Pern have bioengineered a race of great winged dragons. When fed a special rock called firestone, the dragons breathe flames that char Thread to ashes. During Thread attacks, the dragons and their dragonriders charge into battle in midair while the other colonists hide safely in their cave towns. During periods of Thread attacks, the protectors of Pern live inside the cones of old volcanoes in cave colonies called Weyrs.

As the story opens, young candidates for dragonrider in the Benden Weyr, a colony in the Benden Mountains, await the hatching of a clutch of dragon eggs. According to custom, each newborn dragon will choose its own rider—a lifelong partner—through a kind of telepathic communication called Impression.

Although Keevan lengthened his walking stride as far as his legs would stretch, he couldn't quite keep up with the other candidates. He knew he would be teased again.

Just as he knew many other things that his foster mother told him he ought not to know, Keevan knew that Beterli, the most senior of the boys, set that spanking pace just to embarrass him, the smallest dragonboy. Keevan would arrive, tail fork-end of the group, breathless, chest heaving, and

maybe get a stern look from the instructing wingsecond. ❶

Dragonriders, even if they were still only hopeful candidates for the glowing eggs which were hardening on the hot sands of the Hatching Ground cavern, were expected to be punctual and prepared. Sloth[1] was not tolerated by the Weyrleader of Benden Weyr. A good record was especially important now. It was very near hatching time, when the baby dragons would crack their mottled[2] shells and stagger forth to choose their lifetime companions. The very thought of that glorious moment made Keevan's breath catch in his throat. To be chosen—to be a dragonrider! To sit astride the neck of a winged beast with jeweled eyes; to be his friend, in telepathic communion[3] with him for life; to be his companion in good times and fighting extremes; to fly effortlessly over the lands of Pern! Or, thrillingly, *between* to any point anywhere on the world! Flying *between* was done on dragonback or not at all, and it was dangerous.

Keevan glanced upward, past the black mouths of the Weyr caves, in which grown dragons and their chosen riders lived, toward the Star Stones that crowned the ridge of the old volcano that was Benden Weyr. On the height, the blue watch dragon, his rider mounted on his neck, stretched the great transparent pinions[4] that carried him on the winds of Pern to fight the evil

---

1. **sloth** (slôth) *n.*: laziness.
2. **mottled** (mät'ld) *adj.*: spotted.
3. **telepathic communion:** communication of thoughts without speaking.
4. **pinions** (pin'yənz) *n.*: wings.

INFER
❶ What can you infer about Beterli from the very first mention of him in the story?

DIFFERENTIATING INSTRUCTION

Learners Having Difficulty
Modeling. Some students may need help understanding the characters in "The Smallest Dragonboy." Remind students that characters reveal what they are like through what they think, say, and do. You may wish to model how to make inferences about the character of Keevan. Read the first two paragraphs of the story aloud and

say: "When I read how hard Keevan tries to keep up—stretching his legs as far as he can and arriving breathless—I can infer that he is determined to succeed despite his small size." Encourage students as they read to ask themselves: "What do the characters' words and actions reveal about the kind of people they are?"

Thread that fell at certain times from the skies. The many-faceted rainbow jewels of his eyes glistened fleetingly in the greeny sun. He folded his great wings to his back, and the watch pair resumed their statuelike pose of alertness.

Then the enticing view was obscured as Keevan passed into the Hatching Ground cavern. The sands underfoot were hot, even through heavy wher-hide boots. How the boot maker had protested having to sew so small! Keevan was forced to wonder why being small was reprehensible.[5] People were always calling him "babe" and shooing him away as being "too small" or "too young" for this or that. Keevan was constantly working, twice as hard as any other boy his age, to prove himself capable. What if his muscles weren't as big as Beterli's? They were just as hard. And if he couldn't overpower anyone in a wrestling match, he could outdistance everyone in a footrace.

"Maybe if you run fast enough," Beterli had jeered on the occasion when Keevan had been goaded to boast of his swiftness, "you could catch a dragon. That's the only way you'll make a dragonrider!"

"You just wait and see, Beterli, you just wait," Keevan had replied. He would have liked to wipe the contemptuous[6] smile from Beterli's face, but the guy didn't fight fair even when a wingsecond was watching. "No one knows what Impresses a dragon!"

"They've got to be able to *find* you first, babe!"

---

5. **reprehensible** (rep′ri·hen′sə·bəl) *adj.:* made to seem like it was a fault, something that deserved to be criticized.
6. **contemptuous** (kən·temp′chōō·əs) *adj.:* scornful; full of meanness.

Yes, being the smallest candidate was not an enviable position. It was therefore imperative that Keevan Impress a dragon in his first hatching. That would wipe the smile off every face in the cavern and accord him the respect due any dragonrider, even the smallest one.

Besides, no one knew exactly what Impressed the baby dragons as they struggled from their shells in search of their lifetime partners.

"I like to believe that dragons see into a man's heart," Keevan's foster mother, Mende, told him. "If they find goodness, honesty, a flexible mind, patience, courage—and you've got that in quantity, dear Keevan—that's what dragons look for. I've seen many a well-grown lad left standing on the sands, Hatching Day, in favor of someone not so strong or tall or handsome. And if my memory serves me"—which it usually did: Mende knew every word of every Harper's tale worth telling, although Keevan did not interrupt her to say so—"I don't believe that F'lar, our Weyrleader, was all that tall when bronze Mnementh chose him. And Mnementh was the only bronze dragon of that hatching." ❷

INFER
❷ Why does Mende comment on F'lar's height?

Dreams of Impressing a bronze were beyond Keevan's boldest reflections, although that goal dominated the thoughts of every other hopeful candidate. Green dragons were small and fast and more numerous. There was more prestige to Impressing a blue or brown than a green. Being practical,

Vocabulary
goaded (gōd′id) *v.:* pushed or driven. A goad is a stick with a sharp point used to herd oxen.

D Literary Focus

❓ **Motivation.** Why do you think Keevan works so hard to prove himself? [Possible responses: He is self-conscious about his size and wants to prove that it doesn't matter. He wants to earn people's respect.]

E Literary Focus

Conflict. Pause at this point, and ask students to predict or infer the major conflicts of the story. [Possible responses: There will be a conflict between Keevan and Beterli. Keevan will have to prove himself to everyone.]

F Correcting Misconceptions

Tell students that in this context a Harper probably means a story-teller. Presumably a Harper would play the harp and recite tales about the history of Pern.

G Reading Skills

Infer. Point out that Mende is Keevan's foster mother. [Possible response to question 2: She understands Keevan's fears about his size, and she wants to reassure him.]

English-Language Learners
Students may need help with the invented vocabulary in this story, such as *dragonboy, tail fork-end, wingsecond, dragonriders, numbweed,* and so on. After reviewing with students the background information on this page, have them scan the story for invented words. Then, work together to create definitions for the words based on

their context. For instance, in the story a *wingsecond* would be a second in command to a leader of dragonriders.

Special Education Students
For lessons designed for special education students, see *Holt Reading Solutions.*

? Infer. What does this suggest about Beterli's character? [Possible responses: He is violent. He doesn't want anyone getting in his way. He doesn't play fair.]

B Reading Skills

? Infer. What can you infer about Beterli from his having been present at eight Impressions? [Possible responses: Beterli has not Impressed a dragon in eight tries. While Keevan is worried about Impressing a dragon right away, Beterli is probably even more worried because he may fail a ninth time.]

Keevan seldom dreamed as high as a big fighting brown, like Canth, F'nor's fine fellow, the biggest brown on all Pern. But to fly a bronze? Bronzes were almost as big as the queen, and only they took the air when a queen flew at mating time. A bronze rider could aspire to become Weyrleader! Well, Keevan would console himself, brown riders could aspire to become wingseconds, and that wasn't bad. He'd even settle for a green dragon; they were small, but so was he. No matter! He simply had to Impress a dragon his first time in the Hatching Ground. Then no one in the Weyr would taunt[7] him anymore for being so small.

Shells, Keevan thought now, but the sands are hot!

"Impression time is imminent, candidates," the wingsecond was saying as everyone crowded respectfully close to him. "See the extent of the striations[8] on this promising egg." The stretch marks *were* larger than yesterday.

Everyone leaned forward and nodded thoughtfully. That particular egg was the one Beterli had marked as his own, and no other candidate dared, on pain of being beaten by Beterli at his first opportunity, to approach it. The egg was marked by a large yellowish splotch in the shape of a dragon backwinging to land, talons outstretched to grasp rock. Everyone knew that bronze eggs bore distinctive markings. And naturally, Beterli, who'd been presented at eight Impressions already and was the biggest of the candidates, had chosen it.

"I'd say that the great opening day is

almost upon us," the wingsecond went on, and then his face assumed a grave expression. "As we well know, there are only forty eggs and seventy-two candidates. Some of you may be disappointed on the great day. That doesn't necessarily mean you aren't dragonrider material, just that *the* dragon for you hasn't been shelled. You'll have other hatchings, and it's no disgrace to be left behind an Impression or two. Or more."

Keevan was positive that the wingsecond's eyes rested on Beterli, who'd been stood off at so many Impressions already. Keevan tried to squinch down so the wingsecond wouldn't notice him. Keevan had been reminded too often that he was eligible to be a candidate by one day only. He, of all the hopefuls, was most likely to be left standing on the great day. One more reason why he simply had to Impress at his first hatching.

"Now move about among the eggs," the wingsecond said. "Touch them. We don't know that it does any good, but it certainly doesn't do any harm."

Some of the boys laughed nervously, but everyone immediately began to circulate among the eggs. Beterli stepped up officiously[9] to "his" egg, daring anyone to come near it. Keevan smiled, because he had already touched it—every inspection day, when the others were leaving the Hatching Ground and no one could see him crouch to stroke it.

Keevan had an egg he concentrated on, too, one drawn slightly to the far side of the others. The shell had a soft greenish blue tinge with a faint creamy swirl design. The

---

7. **taunt** (tônt) *v.*: ridicule; mock.
8. **striations** (strī·ā′shənz) *n.*: stretch marks; stripes. (This word is defined in the context—in the next sentence.)

9. **officiously** (ə·fish′əs·lē) *adv.*: in a self-important way.

Vocabulary
imminent (im′ə·nənt) *adj.*: about to happen.

Advanced Learners
Acceleration. Use the following activity to help advanced learners compare and contrast motivations and reactions of characters from different historical eras confronting similar situations. Point out that Keevan's conflicts are universal; he struggles against a bully and he strives to prove himself. Such conflicts occur in every historical period.

Activity. Have students form a small discussion group in which they compare characters from different eras who face similar situations. You might suggest they compare Rikki-tikki-tavi and Keevan. How does Rikki-tikki-tavi react to the bully Nag? What motivates him to fight the cobras?

consensus was that this egg contained a mere green, so Keevan was rarely bothered by rivals. He was somewhat <u>perturbed</u>, then, to see Beterli wandering over to him.

"I don't know why you're allowed in this Impression, Keevan. There are enough of us without a babe," Beterli said, shaking his head.

"I'm of age." Keevan kept his voice level, telling himself not to be bothered by mere words.

"Yah!" Beterli made a show of standing on his toe tips. "You can't even see over an egg; Hatching Day, you better get in front or the dragons won't see you at all. 'Course, you could get run down that way in the mad scramble. Oh, I forget, you can run fast, can't you?"

"You'd better make sure a dragon sees *you* this time, Beterli," Keevan replied. "You're almost overage, aren't you?" ❸

Beterli flushed and took a step forward, hand half raised. Keevan stood his ground, but if Beterli advanced one more step, he would call the wingsecond. No one fought on the Hatching Ground. Surely Beterli knew that much.

Fortunately, at that moment, the wingsecond called the boys together and led them from the Hatching Ground to start on evening chores. There were "glows" to be replenished in the main kitchen caverns and sleeping cubicles, the major hallways, and the queen's apartment. Firestone sacks had to be filled against Thread attack, and black rock brought to the kitchen hearths. The boys fell to their chores, tantalized by the

INFER
❸ Why does Keevan taunt Beterli about his age?

odors of roasting meat. The population of the Weyr began to assemble for the evening meal, and the dragonriders came in from the Feeding Ground on their sweep checks.

It was the time of day Keevan liked best: Once the chores were done but before dinner was served, a fellow could often get close enough to the dragonriders to hear their talk. Tonight, Keevan's father, K'last, was at the main dragonrider table. It puzzled Keevan how his father, a brown rider and a tall man, could *be* his father—because he, Keevan, was so small. It obviously puzzled K'last, too, when he deigned to notice his small son: "In a few more Turns, you'll be as tall as I am—or taller!"

Vocabulary
perturbed (pər·tʉrbd′) *v.* used as *adj.:* disturbed; troubled.

The Smallest Dragonboy   **151**

DIRECT TEACHING

C Vocabulary Development
Latin roots and affixes. Ask students to define the word *consensus.* [Students may suggest "opinion, general opinion, agreement."] Point out the Latin prefix *con–*, meaning "with, together," and *sensus*, which comes from the root word *sentire*, meaning "to feel." To feel together means to agree. Therefore, a consensus is an agreement.

D Literary Focus
❷ Motivation. Have students review Beterli's treatment of Keevan thus far in the story. Why does Beterli taunt Keevan now? [Possible responses: He may be trying to make himself feel better about his own chances at the Hatching by putting Keevan down. He may have a grudge against Keevan.]

E Reading Skills
Infer. [Possible response to question 3: Keevan taunts Beterli because he is tired of being picked on. He also knows that Beterli is sensitive about his eight failures to Impress a dragon.]

A Literary Focus

Conflict. Ask students to describe the internal conflict Keevan is going through. [Possible responses: He wants to ask questions, but he doesn't want to appear foolish. He wants to be a dragonrider but worries about his fitness for the role.]

B Literary Focus

Motivation. Invite students to speculate about L'vel's motivation for suggesting that the babes should wait. [Possible responses: He has friends among the older candidates. He is worried about the future of the dragon army. He does not want to have to treat very young boys as colleagues.]

C Literary Focus

? Motivation. Why do you think K'last expresses these opinions? [Possible responses: He wants his son Keevan to have a chance to Impress a dragon. He wants all the boys to have a fair chance within the established rules.]

D Vocabulary Development

Greek word roots. Point out the word *heretical*. Ask students what kind of suggestion Lessa has made. [From the context clues, students should guess "shocking" or "outrageous."] Explain that the noun *heresy* is from a Greek word meaning "choice." In English, *heresy* is an opinion that disagrees with generally held beliefs, especially religious beliefs.

K'last was pouring Benden wine all around the table. The dragonriders were relaxing. There'd be no Thread attack for three more days, and they'd be in the mood to tell tall tales, better than Harper yarns, about impossible maneuvers they'd done a-dragonback. When Thread attack was closer, their talk would change to a discussion of tactics of evasion, of going *between,* how long to suspend there until the burning but fragile Thread would freeze and crack and fall harmlessly off dragon and man. They would dispute the exact moment to feed firestone to the dragon so he'd have the best flame ready to sear Thread midair and render it harmless to ground—and man—below. There was such a lot to know and understand about being a dragonrider that sometimes Keevan was overwhelmed. How would he ever be able to remember everything he ought to know at the right moment? He couldn't dare ask such a question; this would only have given additional weight to the notion that he was too young yet to be a dragonrider.

"Having older candidates makes good sense," L'vel was saying as Keevan settled down near the table. "Why waste four to five years of a dragon's fighting prime until his rider grows up enough to stand the rigors?" L'vel had Impressed a blue of Ramoth's first clutch. Most of the candidates thought L'vel was marvelous because he spoke up in front of the older riders, who awed them. "That was well enough in the Interval when you didn't need to mount the full Weyr complement to fight Thread. But not now. Not with more eligible candidates than ever. Let the babes wait."

"Any boy who is over twelve Turns has the right to stand in the Hatching Ground,"

K'last replied, a slight smile on his face. He never argued or got angry. Keevan wished he were more like his father. And oh, how he wished he were a brown rider! "Only a dragon—each particular dragon—knows what he wants in a rider. We certainly can't tell. Time and again, the theorists," K'last's smile deepened as his eyes swept those at the table, "are surprised by dragon choice. *They* never seem to make mistakes, however."

"Now, K'last, just look at the roster this Impression. Seventy-two boys and only forty eggs. Drop off the twelve youngest, and there's still a good field for the hatchlings to choose from. Shells! There are a couple of Weyrlings unable to see over a wher egg, much less a dragon! And years before they can ride Thread."

"True enough, but the Weyr is scarcely under fighting strength, and if the youngest Impress, they'll be old enough to fight when the oldest of our current dragons go *between* from senility."

"Half the Weyr-bred lads have already been through several Impressions," one of the bronze riders said then. "I'd say drop some of *them* off this time. Give the untried a chance."

"There's nothing wrong in presenting a clutch with as wide a choice as possible," said the Weyrleader, who had joined the table with Lessa, the Weyrwoman.

"Has there ever been a case," she said, smiling in her odd way at the riders, "where a hatchling didn't choose?"

Her suggestion was almost heretical and drew astonished gasps from everyone, including the boys.

F'lar laughed. "You say the most outrageous things, Lessa."

"Well, *has* there ever been a case where a dragon didn't choose?"

DEVELOPING FLUENCY

Activity. Have students choose partners with whom to read dialogue sequences from the story aloud. Students should find a conversation (such as the one between L'vel and K'last on this page), choose a character, and then read the dialogue aloud. Students should read as expressively and naturally as possible. After each conversation, have students switch roles and repeat.

PAIRED

"Can't say as I recall one," K'last replied.

"Then we continue in this tradition," Lessa said firmly, as if that ended the matter.

But it didn't. The argument ranged from one table to the other all through dinner, with some favoring a weeding out of the candidates to the most likely, lopping off those who were very young or who had had multiple opportunities to Impress. All the candidates were in a swivet,[10] though such a departure from tradition would be to the advantage of many. As the evening progressed, more riders were favoring eliminating the youngest and those who'd passed four or more Impressions unchosen. Keevan felt he could bear such a dictum[11] only if Beterli were also eliminated. But this seemed less likely than that Keevan would be turfed out,[12] since the Weyr's need was for fighting dragons and riders.

By the time the evening meal was over, no decision had been reached, although the Weyrleader had promised to give the matter due consideration.

He might have slept on the problem, but few of the candidates did. Tempers were uncertain in the sleeping caverns next morning as the boys were routed out of their beds to carry water and black rock and cover the "glows." Twice Mende had to call Keevan to order for clumsiness.

"Whatever is the matter with you, boy?" she demanded in exasperation when he tipped black rock short of the bin and sooted up the hearth.

"They're going to keep me from this Impression."

---

10. **in a swivet:** frustrated and annoyed.
11. **dictum** *n.:* pronouncement or judgment.
12. **turfed out:** British expression meaning "removed; expelled."

"What?" Mende stared at him. "Who?"

"You heard them talking at dinner last night. They're going to turf the babes from the hatching."

Mende regarded him a moment longer before touching his arm gently. "There's lots of talk around a supper table, Keevan. And it cools as soon as the supper. I've heard the same nonsense before every hatching, but nothing is ever changed."

"There's always a first time," Keevan answered, copying one of her own phrases.

"That'll be enough of that, Keevan. Finish your job. If the clutch does hatch today, we'll need full rock bins for the feast, and you won't be around to do the filling. All my fosterlings make dragonriders."

"The first time?" Keevan was bold enough to ask as he scooted off with the rockbarrow.

Perhaps, Keevan thought later, if he hadn't been on that chore just when Beterli was also fetching black rock, things might have turned out differently. But he had dutifully trundled the barrow to the outdoor bunker for another load just as Beterli arrived on a similar errand.

"Heard the news, babe?" Beterli asked. He was grinning from ear to ear, and he put an unnecessary emphasis on the final insulting word.

"The eggs are cracking?" Keevan all but dropped the loaded shovel. Several anxieties flicked through his mind then: He was black with rock dust—would he have time to wash before donning the white tunic of candidacy? And if the eggs were hatching, why hadn't the candidates been recalled by the wingsecond?

"Naw! Guess again!" Beterli was much too pleased with himself.

With a sinking heart, Keevan knew what

E **Vocabulary Development**

Latin word roots. Write the word *dictum* on the chalkboard, and underline the first four letters. Explain that this root is from the Latin verb *dicere,* meaning "to say." Have students think of other words with this root. [Possible responses: *dictate, predict, edict, dictionary.*] List the words on the chalkboard, underline the root in each, and show students how the meanings are all related.

F **Reading Skills**

? **Infer.** Why do you think the boys' tempers are uncertain? [Possible responses: They are all nervous about the Hatching. The younger ones are afraid that they will not be allowed to participate.]

G **Vocabulary Development**

Latin word roots. Point out the phrase "white tunic of candidacy." Explain that the Latin verb *candere* means "to shine, to glow white." Therefore, white is the perfect color for a candidate's tunic. Help students make a list of related words from the same root. [Possible responses: *candle, candid, incandescent;* all have to do with glowing light or with purity.]

DIFFERENTIATING INSTRUCTION

Advanced Learners

Enrichment. The scene in which the dragonriders gather for a meal, conversation, and an exchange of tales may remind students of similar scenes from literature, television, or the movies. Ask students to provide examples. They might mention scenes from Homer's *Odyssey* or from a movie such as *Star Wars* or *Braveheart.*

A Reading Skills

❓ Infer. What inference do you think Keevan has just made? Why? [Possible responses: He thinks he won't be allowed to take part in the Impression. The talk at the dinner had already worried him, and Beterli is very pleased, which suggests that he has come to gloat over Keevan's bad luck.]

B Learners Having Difficulty

Recognize shifts in scene. Point out that the author abruptly shifts both the time and location of the scene from one paragraph to the next. Call on a volunteer to explain what causes Keevan's feeling of "painful nothingness." [Beterli has knocked Keevan unconscious.] Where is Keevan when he awakens? [He is in bed at home with Mende at his side.]

C Reading Skills

Infer. Ask students to think about how they might feel if they were in Keevan's place.

[Possible responses to question 4: Keevan would rather resolve his conflict with Beterli by himself. Keevan doesn't want to ruin Beterli's entire future by eliminating him from the Impression.]

D Literary Focus

❓ Motivation. Why do you think Lessa wants to hear Keevan's side of the story? [Possible responses: She wants to be sure she has all the facts. She wants to be sure that no one is punished unfairly.]

A the news must be, and he could only stare with intense desolation at the older boy.

"C'mon! Guess, babe!"

"I've no time for guessing games," Keevan managed to say with indifference. He began to shovel black rock into the barrow as fast as he could.

"I said, guess." Beterli grabbed the shovel.

"And I said I have no time for guessing games."

Beterli wrenched the shovel from Keevan's hands. "Guess!"

"I'll have that shovel back, Beterli." Keevan straightened up, but he didn't come to Beterli's bulky shoulder. From somewhere, other boys appeared, some with barrows, some mysteriously alerted to the prospect of a confrontation among their numbers.

"Babes don't give orders to candidates around here, babe!"

Someone sniggered, and Keevan, incredulous,[13] knew that he must've been dropped from the candidacy.

He yanked the shovel from Beterli's loosened grasp. Snarling, the older boy tried to regain possession, but Keevan clung with all his strength to the handle, dragged back and forth as the stronger boy jerked the shovel about.

B With a sudden, unexpected movement, Beterli rammed the handle into Keevan's chest, knocking him over the barrow handles. Keevan felt a sharp, painful jab behind his left ear, an unbearable pain in his left shin, and then a painless nothingness.

Mende's angry voice roused him, and, startled, he tried to throw back the covers, thinking he'd overslept. But he couldn't

---

13. **incredulous** (in·krej′oo·ləs) *adj.:* doubting; unable to believe.

move, so firmly was he tucked into his bed. And then the constriction of a bandage on his head and the dull sickishness in his leg brought back recent occurrences.

"Hatching?" he cried.

"No, lovey," Mende said in a kind voice. Her hand was cool and gentle on his forehead. "Though there's some as won't be at any hatching again." Her voice took on a stern edge.

Keevan looked beyond her to see the Weyrwoman, who was frowning with irritation.

"Keevan, will you tell me what occurred at the black-rock bunker?" asked Lessa in an even voice.

He remembered Beterli now and the quarrel over the shovel and . . . what had Mende said about some not being at any hatching? Much as he hated Beterli, he couldn't bring himself to tattle on Beterli and force him out of candidacy. **4**

INFER
C **4** Why is Keevan reluctant to tell Lessa what really happened?

D "Come, lad," and a note of impatience crept into the Weyrwoman's voice. "I merely want to know what happened from you, too. Mende said she sent you for black rock. Beterli—and every Weyrling in the cavern—seems to have been on the same errand. What happened?"

"Beterli took my shovel. I hadn't finished with it."

"There's more than one shovel. What did he *say* to you?"

"He'd heard the news."

Vocabulary
confrontation (kän′frən·tā′shən) *n.:* face-to-face meeting between opposing sides.

154 Collection 2 / Characters: Living Many Lives

Developing Word-Attack Skills
On the chalkboard, write the word *punctual,* which appears in the selection. Read the word aloud. Then, have students repeat the word with you, stressing the three syllables: *punc-tu-al.* Ask students if they hear the sound /ch/ in the word. Then, repeat the word and have them identify the letter that stands for /ch/ in *punctual.* Point out that *t* often stands for /ch/ when it comes before *u.*

Activity. Read these sentences aloud and have students identify the words in which *t* stands for /ch/.

1. Virtually every boy got his turn.
2. A boy's stature was not an issue.
3. The dragons worked on intuition, not anything intellectual.
4. Nobody can lecture a dragon.
5. A chosen boy is the picture of happiness.

A Reading Skills

? Interpret. What old gag is Lessa referring to? [Possible response: She is referring to the way in which Beterli provokes a fight by dropping hints so Keevan will assume the worst and lose control.]

B Reading Skills

? Infer. What do you think Mende means by "you are and you aren't"? [Possible responses: Keevan can't go to this Hatching, but he will go to the next one. Keevan is a candidate but is too severly injured to attend the Hatching.]

C Literary Focus

Motivation. Ask students why they think Lessa and Mende don't tell Keevan that the Impression is about to begin. [Possible responses: They don't want to upset him. They know he can't go since he is too badly injured. They think he can bear the disappointment better once he is feeling stronger. They know there will be other Impressions.]

"What news?" The Weyrwoman was suddenly amused.

"That . . . that . . . there'd been changes."

"Is that what he said?"

"Not exactly."

"What did he say? C'mon, lad, I've heard from everyone else, you know."

"He said for me to guess the news."

"And you fell for that old gag?" The Weyrwoman's irritation returned.

"Consider all the talk last night at supper, Lessa," Mende said. "Of course the boy would think he'd been eliminated."

"In effect, he is, with a broken skull and leg." Lessa touched his arm in a rare gesture of sympathy. "Be that as it may, Keevan, you'll have other Impressions. Beterli will not. There are certain rules that must be observed by all candidates, and his conduct proves him unacceptable to the Weyr."

She smiled at Mende and then left.

"I'm still a candidate?" Keevan asked urgently.

"Well, you are and you aren't, lovey," his foster mother said. "Is the numbweed working?" she asked, and when he nodded, she said, "You just rest. I'll bring you some nice broth."

At any other time in his life, Keevan would have relished such cosseting,[14] but now he just lay there worrying. Beterli had been dismissed. Would the others think it was his fault? But everyone was there! Beterli provoked that fight. His worry increased, because although he heard excited comings and goings in the passageway, no one tweaked back the curtain across the sleeping alcove he shared with five other boys. Surely one of

them would have to come in sometime. No, they were all avoiding him. And something else was wrong. Only he didn't know what.

Mende returned with broth and beachberry bread.

"Why doesn't anyone come see me, Mende? I haven't done anything wrong, have I? I didn't ask to have Beterli turfed out."

Mende soothed him, saying everyone was busy with noontime chores and no one was angry with him. They were giving him a chance to rest in quiet. The numbweed made him drowsy, and her words were fair enough. He permitted his fears to dissipate.[15] Until he heard a hum. Actually he felt it first, in the broken shinbone and his sore head. The hum began to grow. Two things registered suddenly in Keevan's groggy mind: The only white candidate's robe still on the pegs in the chamber was his, and the dragons hummed when a clutch was being laid or being hatched. Impression! And he was flat abed.

Bitter, bitter disappointment turned the warm broth sour in his belly. Even the small voice telling him that he'd have other opportunities failed to alleviate his crushing depression. *This* was the Impression that mattered! This was his chance to show *everyone*, from Mende to K'last to L'vel and even the Weyrleader, that he, Keevan, was worthy of being a dragonrider.

He twisted in bed, fighting against the tears that threatened to choke him. Dragonmen don't cry! Dragonmen learn to live with pain.

Pain? The leg didn't actually pain him as

---

14. **cosseting** (käs′it·iŋ) *v.* used as *n.*: spoiling; pampering; treating as if he were a little pet.

---

15. **dissipate** (dis′ə·pāt′) *v.*: disappear; go away.

Vocabulary
alleviate (ə·lē′vē·āt′) *v.*: relieve; reduce.

Science
Hatching eggs. Point out that like many animals on Earth, the dragons of Pern hatch from eggs. The eggs of most mammals develop inside the mother's body, but the eggs of birds, insects, and most reptiles are laid and develop outside of the mother's body, and then hatch into young. Some animals sit on their eggs to keep them warm; others, like the mother dragon in this story, leave the eggs in a sheltered place.
Activity. Have students look through the story for clues about the hatching process of dragon eggs (e.g., the eggs are left in a dry cavern, in hot sand, and out of the sunlight). Then, organize students into three groups to investigate how birds, reptiles, or insects hatch. Have students in each group compare these processes to the dragon hatching. After students have finished their research, have them comment on the realism in McCaffrey's description of the hatching process.

SMALL GROUP

he rolled about on his bedding. His head felt sort of stiff from the tightness of the bandage. He sat up, an effort in itself since the numbweed made exertion[16] difficult. He touched the splinted leg; the knee was unhampered.[17] He had no feeling in his bone, really. He swung himself carefully to the side of his bed and stood slowly. The room wanted to swim about him. He closed his eyes, which made the dizziness worse, and he had to clutch the wall.

Gingerly, he took a step. The broken leg dragged. It hurt in spite of the numbweed, but what was pain to a dragonman? ⑤

INFER
⑤ Why does Keevan deny the pain in his leg?

No one had said he couldn't go to the Impression. "You are and you aren't" were Mende's exact words.

Clinging to the wall, he jerked off his bed shirt. Stretching his arm to the utmost, he jerked his white candidate's tunic from the peg. Jamming first one arm and then the other into the holes, he pulled it over his head. Too bad about the belt. He couldn't wait. He hobbled to the door and hung on to the curtain to steady himself. The weight on his leg was unwieldy. He wouldn't get very far without something to lean on. Down by the bathing pool was one of the long crook-necked poles used to retrieve clothes from the hot washing troughs. But it was down there, and he was on the level above. And there was no one nearby to come to his aid; everyone would be in the Hatching Ground right now, eagerly waiting for the first egg to crack.

---

16. **exertion** (eg·zur′shən) *n.*: exercise; effort.
17. **unhampered** (un·ham′pərd) *v.* used as *adj.*: free to move around. (There was no tight bandage on his knee.)

The humming increased in volume and tempo, an urgency to which Keevan responded, knowing that his time was all too limited if he was to join the ranks of the hopeful boys standing around the cracking eggs. But if he hurried down the ramp, he'd fall flat on his face.

He could, of course, go flat on his rear end, the way crawling children did. He sat down, sending a jarring stab of pain through his leg and up to the wound on the back of his head. Gritting his teeth and blinking away tears, Keevan scrabbled down the ramp. He had to wait a moment at the bottom to catch his breath. He got to one knee, the injured leg straight out in front of him. Somehow, he managed to push himself erect, though the room seemed about to tip over his ears. It wasn't far to the crooked stick, but it seemed an age before he had it in his hand.

Then the humming stopped!

Keevan cried out and began to hobble frantically across the cavern, out to the bowl of the Weyr. Never had the distance between living caverns and the Hatching Ground seemed so great. Never had the Weyr been so breathlessly silent. It was as if the multitude of people and dragons watching the hatching held every breath in suspense. Not even the wind muttered down the steep sides of the bowl. The only sounds to break the stillness were Keevan's ragged gasps and the thump-thud of his stick on the hard-packed ground. Sometimes he had to hop twice on his good leg to maintain his balance. Twice he fell into the sand and had to pull himself up on the stick, his white tunic no longer spotless. Once he jarred himself so badly he couldn't get up immediately.

Then he heard the first exhalation of the crowd, the oohs, the muted cheer, the

DIRECT TEACHING

D Reading Skills

Infer. [Possible response to question 5: Keevan doesn't want his injuries to prevent him from attending the Impression.]

E Reading Skills

❓ **Predict.** What do you think Keevan is going to do? Why do you think so? [Possible response: He will try to get to the Impression, because he wants to become a dragonrider.]

F Reading Skills

❓ **Infer.** What does Keevan's journey to the cavern suggest about his character? [Possible responses: He is determined to get what he wants. He is brave enough to overcome the pain of his injuries. He doesn't give up easily.]

A Vocabulary Development

Latin word roots. Ask students to find synonyms for the phrase "plaintive crooning." [Possible response: whimpering sound.] Tell them that *plaintive* is from the Latin verb *plangere,* which means "to lament." Challenge students to find and define related words that come from this root. [Possible responses: complaint, explain, plaintiff.]

B Vocabulary Development

Latin word roots and affixes. Write the word *ignominious* on the chalkboard. Underline the Latin prefix *ig–,* which means "not," and the root *nomin* (usually spelled *nomen*), which means "name." *Ignominious* means "characterized by shame, disgrace, or loss of one's reputation."

C Reading Skills

❓ Infer. What does this dragon's refusal to choose a rider suggest about him? [Possible response: He won't settle for anyone other than the right person.]

D Reading Skills

❓ Infer. Can you tell who is speaking to Keevan in this passage? What clues can you use to help you figure it out? [Possible response: The speaker might be the dragon. The words are in italics, not quotation marks, which suggests that they aren't actually spoken. Earlier in the story we were told that the dragons can communicate with their riders through telepathy.]

---

susurrus[18] of excited whispers. An egg had cracked, and the dragon had chosen his rider. Desperation increased Keevan's hobble. Would he never reach the arching mouth of the Hatching Ground?

Another cheer and an excited spate[19] of applause spurred Keevan to greater effort. If he didn't get there in moments, there'd be no unpaired hatchling left. Then he was actually staggering into the Hatching Ground, the sands hot on his bare feet.

No one noticed his entrance or his halting progress. And Keevan could see nothing but the backs of the white-robed candidates, seventy of them ringing the area around the eggs. Then one side would surge forward or back and there'd be a cheer. Another dragon had been Impressed. Suddenly a large gap appeared in the white human wall, and Keevan had his first sight of the eggs. There didn't seem to be *any* left uncracked, and he could see the lucky boys standing beside wobble-legged dragons.

A He could hear the unmistakable plaintive[20] crooning of hatchlings and their squawks of protest as they'd fall awkwardly in the sand.

Suddenly he wished that he hadn't left his bed, that he'd stayed away from the Hatch-**B** ing Ground. Now everyone would see his ignominious[21] failure. So he scrambled as desperately to reach the shadowy walls of the Hatching Ground as he had struggled to cross the bowl. He mustn't be seen.

He didn't notice, therefore, that the shifting group of boys remaining had begun to drift in his direction. The hard pace he had set himself and his cruel disappointment took their

---

18. **susurrus** (sə·sŭr'əs) *n.:* rustling sound.
19. **spate** (spāt) *n.:* sudden outpouring.
20. **plaintive** (plān'tiv) *adj.:* sorrowful; sad.
21. **ignominious** (ig'nə·min'ē·əs) *adj.:* shameful.

---

double toll of Keevan. He tripped and collapsed, sobbing, to the warm sands. He didn't see the consternation in the watching Weyrfolk above the Hatching Ground, nor did he hear the excited whispers of speculation. He didn't know that the Weyrleader and Weyrwoman had dropped to the arena and were making their way toward the knot of boys slowly moving in the direction of the entrance.

C "Never seen anything like it," the Weyrleader was saying. "Only thirty-nine riders chosen. And the bronze trying to leave the Hatching Ground without making Impression."

"A case in point of what I said last night," the Weyrwoman replied, "where a hatchling makes no choice because the right boy isn't there."

"There's only Beterli and K'last's young one missing. And there's a full wing of likely boys to choose from. . . ."

"None acceptable, apparently. Where is the creature going? He's not heading for the entrance after all. Oh, what have we there, in the shadows?"

Keevan heard with dismay the sound of voices nearing him. He tried to burrow into the sand. The mere thought of how he would be teased and taunted now was unbearable.

D *Don't worry! Please don't worry!* The thought was urgent, but not his own.

Someone kicked sand over Keevan and butted roughly against him.

"Go away. Leave me alone!" he cried.

Why? was the injured-sounding question inserted into his mind. There was no voice, no tone, but the question was there, perfectly clear, in his head.

Incredulous, Keevan lifted his head and stared into the glowing jeweled eyes of a small bronze dragon. His wings were wet,

---

CROSS-CURRICULAR CONNECTIONS

Culture

Dragons. Dragons are featured in both European and Asian folklore.

Activity. Display or distribute several pictures of dragons from a variety of cultures, and have students discuss them. You might, for example, have them compare depictions of dragons in Western and Eastern traditions. You might use a painting of Saint George and the dragon and a photograph of a dragon costume from a Chinese New Year celebration for comparison. Ask students to discuss which dragon seems more ferocious and whether one is more appealing than the other. Then, have students draw dragons of their own and caption their drawings with descriptions of the dragons' unique qualities.

INDIVIDUAL

A Literary Focus

? Motivation. Why does the bronze baby dragon choose Keevan? [Possible responses: The dragon senses Keevan's determination to be a dragonrider. The dragon is unique among the hatched dragons, just as Keevan is among the boys.]

GUIDED PRACTICE

Monitor students' progress. To check students' comprehension of the story, ask them to respond to the following questions. Direct students to locate passages in the text that support their responses.

Short Answer

1. Who is the smallest dragonboy? [Keevan]

2. What event is Keevan waiting for? [the hatchling dragons' selection of their riders]

3. What is an Impression? [the ceremony in which the dragons choose their riders]

4. What happens to Beterli after the fight with Keevan? [He is disqualified from the Impression.]

5. Whom does the bronze dragon choose? [Keevan]

A the tips drooping in the sand. And he sagged in the middle on his unsteady legs, although he was making a great effort to keep erect.

Keevan dragged himself to his knees, oblivious[22] of the pain in his leg. He wasn't even aware that he was ringed by the boys passed over, while thirty-one pairs of resentful eyes watched him Impress the dragon. The Weyrmen looked on, amused and surprised at the draconic[23] choice, which could not be forced. Could not be questioned. Could not be changed.

Why? asked the dragon again. *Don't you like me?* His eyes whirled with anxiety, and his tone was so piteous that Keevan staggered forward and threw his arms around the dragon's neck, stroking his eye ridges, patting the damp, soft hide, opening the fragile-looking wings to dry them, and wordlessly assuring the hatchling over and over again that he was the most perfect, most beautiful, most beloved dragon in the Weyr, in all the Weyrs of Pern.

---

22. **oblivious** (ə·bliv′ē·əs) *adj.:* forgetful; not aware of.
23. **draconic** (drə·kän′ik) *adj.:* of a dragon. *Drakōn* is the Greek word for "dragon."

"What's his name, K'van?" asked Lessa, smiling warmly at the new dragonrider. K'van stared up at her for a long moment. Lessa would know as soon as he did. Lessa was the only person who could "receive" from all dragons, not only her own Ramoth. Then he gave her a radiant smile, recognizing the traditional shortening of his name that raised him forever to the rank of dragonrider.

My name is Heth, the dragon thought mildly, then hiccuped in sudden urgency. *I'm hungry.*

"Dragons are born hungry," said Lessa, laughing. "F'lar, give the boy a hand. He can barely manage his own legs, much less a dragon's."

K'van remembered his stick and drew himself up. "We'll be just fine, thank you."

"You may be the smallest dragonrider ever, young K'van," F'lar said, "but you're one of the bravest!"

And Heth agreed! Pride and joy so leaped in both chests that K'van wondered if his heart would burst right out of his body. He looped an arm around Heth's neck, and the pair, the smallest dragonboy and the hatchling who wouldn't choose anybody else, walked out of the Hatching Ground together forever.

FAMILY/COMMUNITY ACTIVITY

Tell students that Impressing a dragon is a step toward assuming adult responsibilities in Pern society. Ask students to talk to their families about milestones or rituals that are used to mark the passage into adulthood in their own particular ethnic or religious community.

Meet the Writer

Anne McCaffrey

Dragon Writer

Growing up as a "lonely tomboy" in New Jersey, **Anne McCaffrey** (1926–   ) decided there were two things she really wanted. "When I was a very young girl, I promised myself very fervently (usually after I'd lost another battle with one of my brothers) that I would become a famous author and I'd own my own horse." McCaffrey's books are now known all over the world and have been translated into many languages. Since she moved to County Wicklow in Ireland, she has owned a number of horses (and cats and dogs). McCaffrey lives and works in Ireland at her home, called Dragonhold. Fans of her books rejoice in McCaffrey's promise: "I shall continue to write—I can't not write—until I am too frail to touch the keys of my word processor." McCaffrey once said this about her own writing process:

> ❝ First I find interesting people to write about (I have written an anthology series, *Crystal Singer*, because I wanted to name a feminine character Killashandra), and then I find something for them to argue about or fight for or against. Or I think about an interesting concept—the dragons of Pern—telepathic, huge, flame-throwing dragons who fly because they 'think' they can. Aerodynamically, they can't. I like to write better than anything else, including riding [horses]. And I write because I can't always get the kind of story I like to read on library shelves. ❞

For Independent Reading

If you want to continue riding with the dragonriders, read *Dragonsong, Dragonsinger,* and *Dragondrums,* a series of science fantasy novels about the dragons of Pern.

Meet the Writer

Anne McCaffrey once said about her own writing process: "When I run into a science problem for which I am not equipped, I find myself an expert in that specialty . . . and I make him tell me what I need to know to make my story convincing. I learn a great deal about science that way . . . and every bit of information you learn will be useful to you at one time in your life. Being a writer is a constant learning process—learning, reading, and then writing."

For Independent Reading

If students enjoyed roaming the planet Pern with dragons in "The Smallest Dragonboy," they might also like to read *The Hobbit* by J.R.R. Tolkien. This fantasy novel follows the adventures of a band of dwarves and their companion, a hobbit, who venture into the dangerous Lonely Mountains to rescue their stolen treasure from the dragon Smaug. Those students who survive the encounter may want to continue with *The Hobbit's* three sequels, a trilogy known as *The Lord of the Rings.*

DIFFERENTIATING INSTRUCTION

Advanced Learners

Read on. Give students a list of some well-known fantasy writers, such as C. S. Lewis or Ursula K. Le Guin. Ask each student to read a short story or an excerpt from a longer work comparable in length to "The Smallest Dragonboy." Have students write short essays comparing their chosen works with "The Smallest Dragonboy." Suggest that they begin by comparing the fantastic elements, invented vocabularies, or unusual creatures in the two works.

After You Read

First Thoughts

1. Possible images: Keevan hobbling to the Hatching; Keevan being chosen by Heth; the fight scene between Keevan and Beterli.

Thinking Critically

2. *External conflicts*—dealing with Beterli's bullying, getting to the Impression in spite of injuries. *Internal conflicts*—self-doubt. Possible answer: the attempt to get to the Hatching, because it was so painful.

3. Beterli jeers at Keevan because he wants to distract attention from himself.

4. Possible answers: He is too proud to accept help. Heth's choice of him makes him so happy that he feels strong and confident.

Extending Interpretations

5. Possible answers: Mende and Lessa are the only women in the story. Lessa has a position of power; she can communicate with all dragons. Because Mende raises children and shapes their values, she has power too.

Reading Check

a. He wants to be a dragonrider.

b. Boys gather together when the dragons are hatching. Each dragon chooses a boy who will be his lifelong rider.

c. Some older dragonriders think there are too many candidates and that the younger ones, including Keevan, should wait.

d. Beterli implies that Keevan has been eliminated from the Hatching and then seriously injures Keevan in a fight.

e. Keevan scoots his way down to the pool, takes a long pole to use as a crutch, and hobbles toward the Hatching Ground.

f. He Impresses a bronze dragon.

After You Read   Response and Analysis

First Thoughts

1. Describe or draw one vivid **image** that you recall from this story. Compare your picture with your classmates'. Is your image the same as any of theirs?

Thinking Critically

2. Make a chart showing all the **conflicts** Keevan faces. Which conflict do you think is the hardest for him?

External Conflicts	Internal Conflicts

3. Think about Beterli's **character.** What inferences can you make to explain Beterli's **motivation** for trying to ruin Keevan's chances on Hatching Day?

4. Why does K'van reject the help Lessa offers him at the end of the story? What **inference** can you make about K'van from his action?

Extending Interpretations

5. List all the women in this story. Do you think they have powerful positions in Pern society, or do only men hold power? Explain. If you were writing about Pern, what roles and responsibilities would you give to men and women?

WRITING

Writing a Narrative

This story is an "underdog" story, in which a person who seems like a loser ends up a winner. Check the notes you took before you read this story, and write a short narrative in which you tell about a time when you felt like an underdog. What did you do about it? What did the experience teach you? If you've never had an underdog experience, you might write about someone you know who has.

go.
hrw
.com

INTERNET
Projects and Activities
Keyword: LE5 7-2

SKILLS FOCUS

Literary Skills Analyze motivation.

Reading Skills Make inferences.

Writing Skills Write a narrative.

Reading Check

a. What does Keevan want as the story opens?

b. How are dragonriders chosen?

c. Why does Keevan think he might be kept from the Impression?

d. How does the bully Beterli try to ruin Keevan's chances on Hatching Day?

e. Describe Keevan's struggle to reach the Hatching Ground.

f. What happens to Keevan just when he is most discouraged?

DIFFERENTIATING INSTRUCTION

Learners Having Difficulty
Focus students' attention on question 3, which gets at the heart of the conflict between Beterli and Keevan. *Monitoring tip:* Point out that people usually taunt others when they feel threatened. Ask students, "What scares Beterli?"

Advanced Learners
Enrichment. Have students discuss Beterli with partners. They should concentrate on possible motivations for his behavior, on the conflicts he faces, and on how he handles them. Remind students that they should try to see the situations in the story from Beterli's point of view.

Activity. Students might write essays giving Beterli advice on how to finally Impress a dragon.

After You Read Vocabulary Development

Recognizing Roots and Affixes

Many English word roots come from Latin, Greek, and an ancestor of the English language called Old English. A **word root** is a word part from which several words are formed. An **affix** is a word part added to a root. An affix can be added to the front of a word (in which case it's called a **prefix**), or it can be added to the end of a word (in which case it's called a **suffix**). For example, the word *confrontation* is made up of the prefix *com–* ("together"), the Latin root *–frons–* ("forehead"), and the suffix *–ation* ("the act of"). In the story you just read, Keevan and Beterli are brought together in a face-to-face meeting, or confrontation.

> **Word Bank**
>
> goaded
> imminent
> perturbed
> confrontation
> alleviate

PRACTICE

1. *Goaded* is derived from the Old English word *gad,* which was a pointed stick used to prod cattle. Look up the meaning of the word *gadfly,* and tell how it is related to the meaning of *gad.*

2. *Imminent* comes from the Latin word *minere,* meaning "to threaten or to project over." Look up the derivation of *menace.* How is the meaning of *menace* related to the Latin word *minere?*

3. *Turbare* is a Latin word meaning "to disturb." How is *perturbed* related to the meaning of the Latin word?

4. The word *turbine* is built on the same root word as *perturbed.* How is "disturbance" part of the meaning of *turbine?*

5. *Alleviate* is built on the Latin word *levis,* meaning "light," and the Latin prefix *ad–,* meaning "to." Using that root word and its affix, define *alleviate.*

6. Draw a "family" tree showing words that are part of the Latin word *credere,* "to believe." You should be able to find at least six words built on *credere.* A model tree showing the family *turbare* is shown at the right.

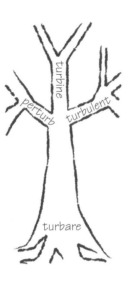

turbine

perturb turbulent

turbare

SKILLS FOCUS

Vocabulary Skills
Understand roots and affixes.

Vocabulary Development

PRACTICE

1. A gadfly is a stinging, biting insect that irritates cattle as a gad would.

2. A menace is something dangerous that threatens or hangs over someone.

3. *Perturbed* means nearly the same thing as *disturbed* ("worried, anxious, unsettled"), which comes from the same root.

4. A turbine is an engine that spins. This constant motion is the "disturbance" that the root word *turbare* conveys.

5. *Alleviate* means "to improve, make lighter, or make easier."

6. Possible words: incredulous, incredible, credo, credit, credence, credulity, credentials.

> ### ASSESSING

Assessment
■ *Holt Assessment: Literature, Reading, and Vocabulary*

The Smallest Dragonboy　**163**

Grade-Level Skills

■ **Reading Skills**
Analyze texts that show comparison and contrast.

Summary ⬇ below grade level

Legends from almost every country feature dragons, but different cultures have different views of these mythical creatures. Asians believe that the dragon is a benevolent creature, while Westerners see it as evil or malicious. Good or evil, dragons still fascinate people all over the world.

PRETEACHING

Selection Starter

Motivate. Have students share stories about dragons: folk tales, legends, or modern fantasy stories. Ask them to note whether the dragons in these stories are good or evil creatures.

Assign the Reading

You might wish to assign the Before You Read page for homework. The next day in class, review the two compare-and-contrast organizational patterns. Then, have students read the article to identify the organizational pattern used.

HOMEWORK

Informational Text

LINK TO "THE SMALLEST DRAGONBOY"

Understanding Comparison and Contrast

Reading Focus

Comparison and Contrast

The dragons of Pern are similar in some ways: They all bond with a human for life and help defend the planet from the evil Thread. They also differ in some ways: The green dragons are small and fast; the brown are big and strong; only the huge bronze can mate with the queen. When you **compare,** you look at two or more things and see how they are the same; when you **contrast,** you look for differences. You may not realize it, but you do a lot of comparing and contrasting every day—for example, when you decide what to eat for lunch or when you think about when you'll do your homework.

Writers compare and contrast things all the time. To do it effectively, they use what's known as a **compare-and-contrast organizational pattern.** Writers use one of two methods when they compare or contrast something. (The charts below refer to the article on dragons you are about to read.)

- **Block method.** The writer first discusses all the features of subject 1, then all the features of subject 2.
- **Point-by-point method.** In this pattern the writer discusses one feature of each subject at a time. The writer chooses a feature and shows how it applies to subject 1, then how it applies to subject 2. The writer continues to discuss other features and how they apply to each subject in turn.

■ In the article that follows, the writer compares and contrasts dragons from around the world. Which method does she use?

go.
hrw
.com

INTERNET
Interactive
Reading Model
Keyword: LE5 7-2

SKILLS FOCUS

Reading Skills
Understand comparison and contrast.

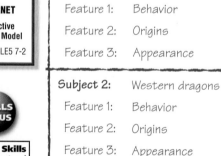

Block Method	
Subject 1:	Eastern dragons
Feature 1:	Behavior
Feature 2:	Origins
Feature 3:	Appearance
Subject 2:	Western dragons
Feature 1:	Behavior
Feature 2:	Origins
Feature 3:	Appearance

Point-by-Point Method	
Feature 1:	Behavior
Subject 1:	Eastern dragons
Subject 2:	Western dragons
Feature 2:	Origins
Subject 1:	Eastern dragons
Subject 2:	Western dragons
Feature 3:	Appearance
Subject 1:	Eastern dragons
Subject 2:	Western dragons

164 Collection 2 / Characters: Living Many Lives

RESOURCES: READING

Planning
■ *One-Stop Planner* CD-ROM with ExamView Test Generator

Differentiating Instruction
■ *Holt Reading Solutions*
■ *Supporting Instruction in Spanish*
■ *Audio CD Library*
■ *Audio CD Library, Selections and Summaries in Spanish*

Grammar and Language
■ *Daily Language Activities*

Assessment
■ *Holt Assessment: Literature, Reading, and Vocabulary*
■ *One-Stop Planner* CD-ROM with ExamView Test Generator
■ *Holt Online Assessment*

Internet
■ go.hrw.com (Keyword: LE5 7-2)
■ *Elements of Literature Online*

Media
■ *Audio CD Library*
■ *Audio CD Library, Selections and Summaries in Spanish*

Chinese dragon robe with silk embroidery (detail), from the T'ung-chih period (1862–1875). The Granger Collection, New York.

 MANY, MANY YEARS AGO, when people first began to map the Western world, they charted two main areas: their settlements and the wilderness. On the wilderness areas of their maps, they wrote a warning: "Here be dragons." When the European explorers set off in their wooden ships in the fifteenth century, most of the sailors still believed that if they sailed too far, the boats would tumble off the earth and into that area populated with seething,[1] clawed monsters.

Dragon stories have been told for ages in almost every land and culture: Africa, Britain, China, Egypt, Greece, and Russia. From their beginnings in mythology, dragons were associated with the Great Mother,

_____
1. **seething** *adj.:* violently agitated.

with the warrior sun god, and, especially, with the water gods. Dragons were said to have been present at the creation and so were endowed with characteristics of the cosmos.[2] At one with wind and fire and water, they had the ancient power of these primal[3] forces. They had command of fire and water and could fly like the wind. But dragons differ from culture to culture: In Asia, dragons help people; in Europe and other places, dragons are associated with destruction and evil. **A**

EASTERN DRAGONS. In Asia the **B** dragon is a benevolent, spiritual creature, gifted with wisdom and the power to confer blessings upon humankind. One of the first dragon stories Asian children hear has a beautifully multicolored dragon emerging from the primordial[4] swamp, proudly beating its chest and calling forth, wanting to know how it can be of service to people. Eastern dragons inspire awe in the people who look to them for guidance, and many are cherished as great and wonderful creatures. Two dragons acting as honor guards are believed to have visited the home of the philosopher Confucius

_____
2. **cosmos** *n.:* the whole universe.
3. **primal** (prī'məl) *adj.:* basic or fundamental.
4. **primordial** (prī·môr'dē·əl) *adj.:* original; first in time.

A Reading Informational Text

❓ Compare-and-contrast pattern. What does this sentence suggest about the writer's plan for her article? [The sentence implies that she will first discuss Asian dragons, then European dragons.]

B Reading Informational Text

❓ Compare-and-contrast pattern. What clue does this heading provide about which comparison-contrast method the author is using? [The author is using the block method; she will discuss all the features of one kind of dragon first—the Eastern dragon—before addressing Western dragons.]

DIFFERENTIATING INSTRUCTION

English-Language Learners
This article provides an opportunity for students to share dragon stories and legends from their cultures. Have students decide which of the two types of dragons in this article matches their image of a dragon, and have them explain why.

Special Education Students
For lessons designed for special education students, see *Holt Reading Solutions.*

Advanced Learners
Enrichment. Have each student find a legend about a dragon. Possibilities include the legend of Perseus (mentioned in the article), the story of St. George, and any number of Chinese or Japanese tales. Students can briefly retell these stories to the class. Then, students can decide if the stories fit the thesis of "Here Be Dragons."

Ⓐ Cross-curricular Connections
SCIENCE

Sulfur. Tell students that *brimstone* is an archaic or literary name for the element sulfur. Sulfur burns with a blue flame and has a strong odor. It is used to make matches and gunpowder.

Ⓑ Cross-curricular Connections
LITERATURE

Heroes. Tell students that the mythological Greek hero Perseus rescues the princess Andromeda by slaying a sea monster. Beowulf, the hero of the earliest epic poem in English literature, slays two monsters, the man-eating Grendel and his equally ferocious mother. At the end of his life, Beowulf kills another dragon that is laying waste to his kingdom.

GUIDED PRACTICE

Monitor students' progress.
Draw a Venn diagram on the chalkboard, and go over students' answers to the Constructed Response question as a class. Challenge students to support their answers with specific evidence from the text.

VIEWING THE ART

Activity. Ask students to research and retell the story of "Saint George and the Dragon" that is depicted in this painting.

Saint George and the Dragon by Paolo Uccello (1397–1475).
Musée Jacquemart-André, Paris. Copyright Scala/Art Resource, NY.

when he was born. The ruler Huang-Ti was supposedly carried to heaven on the back of a dragon. If you met one on the road of life, an Eastern dragon would give you a gift as opposed to, say, fire and brimstone.

WESTERN DRAGONS. Speaking of fire and brimstone, the Western dragon is famous for both. People could always tell when they were in the vicinity of a Western dragon because the air would be Ⓐ heated and foul with the unmistakable sulfuric odor of brimstone. Brimstone has a smell that makes the scent of a rotten egg seem lovely by comparison.

Western dragons became feared as the foes of civilization. Perseus of ancient Greece, Beowulf of ancient Denmark, even Ⓑ brave little Bilbo in *The Hobbit*—all had to face down menacing dragons before they could conclude their quests. In Western stories, dragons often lie underground,

guarding huge piles of gold they have stolen from the surrounding countryside, which, by the way, has also been scorched and laid waste by the dragon's fiery breath.

DRAGONS TODAY. Dragons have largely disappeared from our stories—except for the fantasies of writers like Anne McCaffrey.

Dragons haven't died out, however. Wait a moment! What is all that noise? It sounds like people playing gongs, cymbals, and drums. What is that colorful creature a block long snaking its way through the Chinese New Year's crowd lining the sidewalks? Why, it's the Eastern dragon come again to celebrate the vitality of life! Hear that thunderous applause? That is the sound that attends an Eastern dragon passing by.

—Flo Ota De Lange

166   Collection 2 / Characters: Living Many Lives

Analyzing Comparison and Contrast

Here Be Dragons

Test Practice

1. Which sentence best states the **main idea** of this article?

   A Dragon stories are very old.

   B In Asia, dragons are helpful; in the West, dragons are evil.

   C Dragons are mythical creatures.

   D Western dragons are foes of civilization.

2. The **organizational pattern** this writer uses for **comparing and contrasting** Eastern and Western dragons is the —

   F chronological method

   G point-by-point method

   H persuasive method

   J block method

3. The **title** of this article refers to —

   A a book on dragons

   B an Asian dragon story

   C a warning on old maps

   D a European dragon story

4. Dragon stories would most likely appear in a book of —

   F realistic stories

   G mystery stories

   H myths and legends

   J nonfiction

5. Anne McCaffrey's dragons in "The Smallest Dragonboy" most resemble the ones in stories from —

   A Asia

   B Europe

   C Africa

   D America

Constructed Response

A Venn diagram like the one at the right can help you sort out and analyze the similarities and differences between Eastern dragons and Western dragons. In each circle you note differences. In the center, where the circles overlap, you note similarities. Complete the diagram.

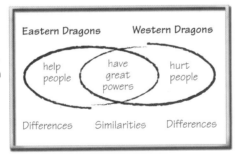

Eastern Dragons   Western Dragons

help people | have great powers | hurt people

Differences   Similarities   Differences

SKILLS FOCUS

Reading Skills
Analyze comparison and contrast.

Here Be Dragons **167**

Assessment

■ *Holt Assessment: Literature, Reading, and Vocabulary*

Analyzing Comparison and Contrast

Test Practice

Answers and Model Rationales

1. **B** The author compares dragon stories from two different cultures. The other options are details, not the main idea.

2. **J** The author discusses one culture's view of dragons, then the other's.

3. **C** The first paragraph of the article says that the early Western mapmakers would write the title as a warning on unexplored areas on their maps.

4. **H** Dragons are mythical.

5. **A** Asian dragons are kind, wise, and helpful to humans, much like McCaffrey's dragons.

Test-Taking Tips

Many test items ask for specific information from the text. To answer this type of question, students must identify the subject of the question and then re-read the portions of the text that deal with that subject.

For more instruction on how to answer multiple-choice items, refer students to **Test Smarts,** p. 920.

Constructed Response

Possible answers: *Eastern dragons*—wise, kind, give gifts. *Western dragons*—breathe fire and brimstone, steal treasure, destroy nature. *Similarities*—ancient, intelligent, powerful, associated with primal forces (wind, fire, and water).

Grade-Level Skills

■ **Literary Skills**
Analyze the ways writers use a narrator to reveal character.

■ **Reading Skills**
Make inferences.

Review Skills

■ **Literary Skills**
Identify the speaker and recognize first-person narration.

Summary ◄► *at grade level*

Esperanza has her heart set on eating in the school cafeteria instead of going home for lunch. After three days of persuading, her mother agrees and packs a rice sandwich for her, because they have no lunch meat. However, the sister superior says that Esperanza lives close enough to walk home for lunch. The girl begins to cry and the nun lets her eat lunch in the cafeteria, an experience that turns out to be a disappointment.

Before You Read The Short Story

A Rice Sandwich

Make the Connection
Quickwrite ✏

In this story, a girl named Esperanza has an upsetting encounter with a school official. Have you, or someone you know, ever been corrected by someone in authority? Jot down some notes about the incident.

Literary Focus
The Narrator

If you have ever written a story, you know that the first questions you have to answer are "Who is going to tell this story?" and "Who will be my narrator?" A **narrator** is simply the person telling the story.

Most stories are told by what is called an **omniscient** (äm·nish′ənt) **narrator.** *Omniscient* means "all knowing," and an omniscient narrator knows all about all the characters and the events in the story. An omniscient narrator can tell you what everyone in the story is thinking. An omniscient narrator can also take you back and forth in time. "Rikki-tikki-tavi," the story about the brave mongoose and the killer cobras, which starts on page 15, is told by an omniscient narrator.

When you read the second paragraph of "A Rice Sandwich," you realize that you are listening to one of the characters in the story. Notice that this narrator says, "*My* home," not

INTERNET
More About Cisneros
Keyword: LE5 7-2

SKILLS FOCUS

Literary Skills
Understand the narrator.

Reading Skills
Make inferences.

"*Esperanza's* home," and "*I* got it in my head," not "*She* got it in her head." When a story is told by a character in the story—someone who tells the whole tale using the first-person pronoun *I* or *me* or *mine*—the story is told by a **first-person narrator.**

Reading a story told by a first-person narrator is like entering into a character's mind and heart. Notice how much Esperanza reveals about herself as she tells about her experience with a rice sandwich.

Reading Skills 📖
Making Inferences

Writers don't come right out and tell you everything you want to know about their characters. You're supposed to take part in the story and make your own inferences about the characters you meet, just the way you do in real life. To make inferences about the character in this story, use these strategies:

• Watch what Esperanza says and does.

• Observe the way other characters respond to Esperanza.

• Examine what you learn about Esperanza's thoughts.

• Think about how Esperanza is like, or not like, people you know in real life.

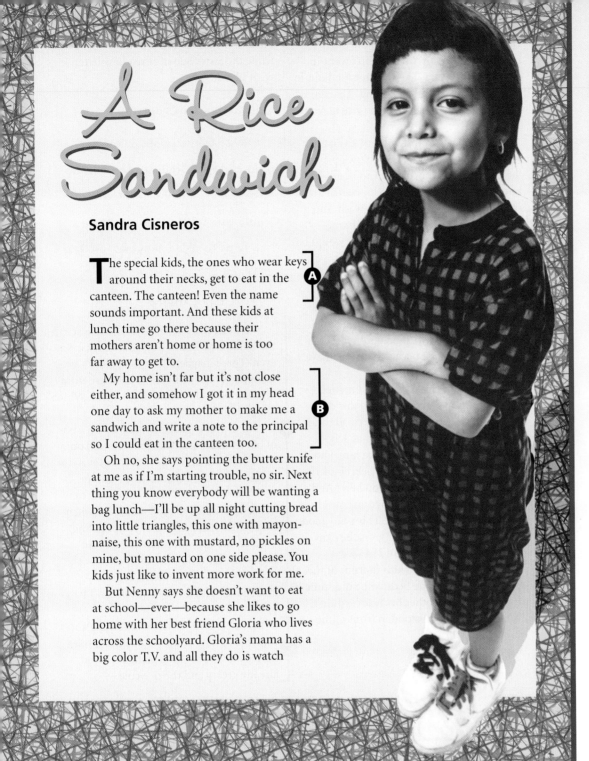

A Rice Sandwich

Sandra Cisneros

The special kids, the ones who wear keys around their necks, get to eat in the canteen. The canteen! Even the name sounds important. And these kids at lunch time go there because their mothers aren't home or home is too far away to get to.

My home isn't far but it's not close either, and somehow I got it in my head one day to ask my mother to make me a sandwich and write a note to the principal so I could eat in the canteen too.

Oh no, she says pointing the butter knife at me as if I'm starting trouble, no sir. Next thing you know everybody will be wanting a bag lunch—I'll be up all night cutting bread into little triangles, this one with mayonnaise, this one with mustard, no pickles on mine, but mustard on one side please. You kids just like to invent more work for me.

But Nenny says she doesn't want to eat at school—ever—because she likes to go home with her best friend Gloria who lives across the schoolyard. Gloria's mama has a big color T.V. and all they do is watch

Selection Starter

Motivate. Play a form of charades with the class. Have student pairs each secretly decide on a character trait such as shyness or friendliness. Then have each pair role-play a character with that trait, and invite the class to guess the trait. Finally, have students complete the Quickwrite activity.

DIRECT TEACHING

Ⓐ Vocabulary Development

Understand word origins. Tell students that *special* comes from *specere*, a Latin word that means "to look at." Ask students how the meaning of *special* might relate to its Latin origin. [Possible response: *Special* means "exceptional," or "out of the ordinary"; something special would be conspicuous and noticed, or looked at.]

Ⓑ Literary Focus

❓ First-person narrator. What words in the second paragraph indicate that this story is told by a first-person narrator? [*My, I, me*]

DIFFERENTIATING INSTRUCTION

Learners Having Difficulty
Modeling. To help students understand the main character in "A Rice Sandwich," model the reading skill of making inferences. Say, "In the first sentence, Esperanza is thinking that the special kids 'get to eat in the canteen.' Then she says she wants to eat in the canteen, so I can infer that she'd like to be special, too." Encourage students to ask as they read: What can I tell about Esperanza from what she thinks, says, and does? What inferences about her can I make?

Ask questions. At this point students may be asking themselves: Why is the narrator holding up her wrist? To whom is she speaking? Help them understand that in this paragraph she is trying to persuade her mother that she is too weak to walk home for lunch so her mother will let her eat in the canteen. Though there are no quotation marks, the narrator is addressing her mother directly.

B Reading Skills

? **Infer.** What can you infer about Esperanza's feelings toward people in authority from her conversation with Sister Superior? [Possible response: She's very sensitive and easily intimidated by authority figures.]

C Literary Focus

? **First-person narrator.** What do readers know from the narrator's thoughts that the watching boys and girls do not know? [Possible response: Readers know why she is crying. They also know how the narrator now feels about the canteen.]

Monitor students' progress. Have students create a character sociogram by writing Esperanza's name in a box in the center of the page. Then, have them put the names of all the other characters in separate boxes. On arrows drawn between the boxes, students should write a word or two describing the relationship or feelings between the narrator and each of the other characters.

---

cartoons. Kiki and Carlos, on the other hand, are patrol boys. They don't want to eat at school either. They like to stand out in the cold especially if it's raining. They think suffering is good for you ever since they saw that movie "300 Spartans."

A   I'm no Spartan[1] and hold up an anemic[2] wrist to prove it. I can't even blow up a balloon without getting dizzy. And besides, I know how to make my own lunch. If I ate at school there'd be less dishes to wash. You would see me less and less and like me better. Every day at noon my chair would be empty. Where is my favorite daughter you would cry, and when I came home finally at 3 p.m. you would appreciate me.

Okay, okay, my mother says after three days of this. And the following morning I get to go to school with my mother's letter and a rice sandwich because we don't have lunch meat.

Mondays or Fridays, it doesn't matter, mornings always go by slow and this day especially. But lunch time came finally and I got to get in line with the stay-at-school kids. Everything is fine until the nun who knows all the canteen kids by heart looks at me and says: you, who sent you here? And since I am shy, I don't say anything, just hold out my hand with the letter. This is no good, she says, till Sister Superior gives the okay. Go upstairs and see her. And so I went.

I had to wait for two kids in front of me to get hollered at, one because he did something in class, the other because he didn't. My turn came and I stood in front of the

---

1. **Spartan:** hardy, disciplined person, like the Spartans of ancient Greece.
2. **anemic** (ə·nē′mik) *adj.*: pale and weak.

---

big desk with holy pictures under the glass while the Sister Superior read my letter. It went like this:

Dear Sister Superior,

Please let Esperanza eat in the lunch room because she lives too far away and she gets tired. As you can see she is very skinny. I hope to God she does not faint. Thanking you,
Mrs. E. Cordero.

B   You don't live far, she says. You live across the boulevard. That's only four blocks. Not even. Three maybe. Three long blocks away from here. I bet I can see your house from my window. Which one? Come here. Which one is your house?

And then she made me stand up on a box of books and point. That one? she said pointing to a row of ugly 3-flats, the ones even the raggedy men are ashamed to go into. Yes, I nodded even though I knew that wasn't my house and started to cry. I always cry when nuns yell at me, even if they're not yelling.

Then she was sorry and said I could stay—just for today, not tomorrow or the day after—you go home. And I said yes and could I please have a Kleenex—I had to blow my nose.

C   In the canteen, which was nothing special, lots of boys and girls watched while I cried and ate my sandwich, the bread already greasy and the rice cold.

English-Language Learners
Help students to understand that the idiomatic phrases in the story should not be taken literally. Examples: *I got it in my head* means "I had an idea"; *no sir* is an expression used for emphasis regardless of gender; *knows all the canteen kids by heart* means "knows . . . by memory"; *get hollered at* means "be scolded"; *raggedy men* means "homeless men."

Special Education Students
For lessons designed for special education students, see *Holt Reading Solutions.*

Advanced Learners
Acceleration. Use the following activity with advanced learners to help them examine how literature reflects the heritage, traditions, attitudes, and beliefs of an author.

Meet the Writer

Sandra Cisneros

Finding Her Own Way

Sandra Cisneros (1954–   ) was born and raised in Chicago, the only daughter in a working-class family with six sons. The harshness of life in her poor neighborhood made Cisneros shy as a child, and she escaped into the world of books. By the age of ten, she was writing her own poetry.

Cisneros grew up speaking Spanish with her Mexican-born father, but she didn't explore her heritage until she attended the Writer's Workshop at the University of Iowa. There she began a series of sketches about her old Spanish-speaking neighborhood in Chicago. These sketches grew into her first book, *The House on Mango Street* (1984), which includes the story "A Rice Sandwich." About her writing she says:

"I didn't know what I was writing when I wrote *House on Mango Street*, but I knew what I wanted. I didn't know what to call it, but I knew what I was after. It wasn't a naive thing; it wasn't an accident. I wanted to write a series of stories that you could open up at any point. You didn't have to know anything before or after and you would understand each story like a little pearl, or you could look at the whole thing like a necklace. That's what I always knew from the day that I wrote the first one.**"**

Author Study

To read more by and about Sandra Cisneros (and her character Esperanza), see the Author Study on pages 613–627.

Meet the Writer

Cisneros was in her early twenties when she attended the Iowa Writers' Workshop, and afterward she struggled to find her voice as a writer. Her friendship with Joy Harjo, a Native American writer from Oklahoma, helped her realize that her heritage was a worthwhile subject. Besides *The House on Mango Street,* Cisneros has published two other books of short stories as well as collections of her poetry and other writings.

For Independent Reading

If students liked this story of a Hispanic child growing up in a big city, they might enjoy *Gaucho,* a play by Gloria Gonzales about a Puerto Rican boy living in New York.

Activity. Have students read two other short stories from *The House on Mango Street.* Then, have them work in small groups to write paragraphs showing how these selections, as well as "A Rice Sandwich," reflect the following about Cisneros:

• her Mexican heritage

• her attitude toward growing up poor and Mexican American in Chicago

• her beliefs, hopes, and dreams as a young child

Remind students to keep in mind what they learned in "Meet the Writer" as they write.

After You Read

First Thoughts

1. I thought Esperanza <u>should have tried to hold back her tears when Sister Superior was speaking to her.</u>

Thinking Critically

2. She thinks that the name sounds important and that the special, cool kids get to eat there.

3. When she wants something, she's determined and will work hard to get it.

4. She characterizes herself as anemic, Nenny as obsessed with cartoons, and her brothers as Spartans.

5. She cries easily and is afraid to speak up to the nuns. Students who are sensitive and easily intimidated by authority will find the scene believable.

Extending Interpretations

6. Possible answer: Esperanza's feelings are as important to the story as the events. With another narrator, the reader would not be able to get inside her heart and mind, and the story would not be as good.

Reading Check

a. Kids who live far away or whose mothers aren't home.

b. She says that there will be fewer dishes to wash and that her mother will see her less and like her better.

c. She thinks Esperanza lives close enough to walk home for lunch.

d. She always cries when nuns yell at her, even if they're not yelling.

e. The bread is already greasy, and the rice is cold.

After You Read Response and Analysis

First Thoughts

1. Complete this sentence:
   - I thought Esperanza . . .

Thinking Critically

2. Why do you think eating in the canteen is so important for Esperanza? Do you think she'll want to eat there again? Explain.

3. What can you infer about Esperanza's **character** from the fact that she argues for three days with her mother, trying to persuade her to write the note?

4. How does Esperanza directly **characterize** herself? How does she directly characterize her sister, Nenny, and her brothers, Kiki and Carlos?

5. What do you learn about Esperanza's **character** in the scene with Sister Superior? Did this encounter seem believable to you? Be sure to check your Quickwrite notes.

Extending Interpretations

6. This story is a **first-person narration** told by Esperanza, a character in the story. Do you think the story would have been better or not as good or about the same if someone else had been the narrator? Explain.

WRITING

Describing Another Side of the Story

This is a story about a tiny incident in Esperanza's life. Take the incident, and let another character tell a story about it. You might let Sister Superior be the new narrator or Esperanza's mother or even Nenny, Kiki, or Carlos.

SKILLS FOCUS

Literary Skills
Analyze the narrator.

Reading Skills
Make inferences.

Writing Skills
Describe events from another point of view.

Reading Check

a. Who eats in the canteen?

b. How does Esperanza persuade her mother to write the note so that she can eat in the canteen too?

c. Why doesn't Sister Superior want to let Esperanza eat in the canteen?

d. According to Esperanza, why does she begin to cry?

e. How does Esperanza describe her sandwich at the end of the story?

FAMILY/COMMUNITY ACTIVITY

Encourage students to plan and put on a play based on the story for their families and friends. Remind your theater troupe to make a list of the cast members and the important props (like a rice sandwich). Help them convert descriptive paragraphs in the story into dialogue the actors can speak. Ask for parent volunteers to find a place where the students can perform their play.

After You Read Vocabulary Development

Borrowed Words

When people speaking different languages come into contact, they often borrow one another's words. It is no surprise, then, that English contains many words borrowed from other cultures.

PRACTICE

Explain how the following facts help you understand the meaning of one of the Word Bank words.

1. In Italian a *cantina* is a wine cellar.
2. The Latin word *ferre* means "to bear"; the Latin prefix *sub–* means "under" or "below."
3. The prefix *tri–* comes from *tres,* meaning "three" in Latin.
4. The Greek prefix *an–* means "without," and the Greek word *haima* means "blood."
5. Sparta was a great military power in ancient Greece. The people of Sparta were known for their courage, discipline, and ability to endure hardship.

SKILLS FOCUS

Vocabulary Skills
Understand word origins.

Grammar Skills
Use clear pronoun references.

Grammar Link

Avoiding Unclear Pronoun References

Writers must make sure that readers can tell which word or phrase a pronoun refers to. The word a pronoun refers to is called its **antecedent.** In the first sentence that follows, the antecedent of the pronoun *she* cannot be clearly identified.

CONFUSING   **Nenny whispered something to Gloria, and she smiled.** [Who smiled, Nenny or Gloria?]

CLEAR   **Nenny smiled as she whispered something to Gloria.** [Nenny was the one who smiled.]

To avoid confusion, the writer had to reword the sentence and move the pronoun closer to its antecedent (Nenny).

PRACTICE

Revise the following sentences to fix the unclear pronoun references.

1. Carlos told Kiki that he wasn't allowed to be on patrol anymore.
2. When the nun told Sister Superior what happened, she gave me a concerned look.
3. Esperanza later told her mother, and she started to cry.

For more help, see Agreement of Pronoun and Antecedent, 2o–x, in the Language Handbook.

Vocabulary Development

PRACTICE

Possible Answers

1. Since *cantina* is a place that holds wine, a canteen must be a place that holds things to drink and eat.
2. A person who is suffering is bearing up under great pain.
3. Triangles have three angles and three sides.
4. If *anhaima* means without blood, an anemic person must be pale and weak from not having enough red blood cells.
5. A Spartan is someone who is disciplined and able to endure hardship as the people of Sparta did.

Grammar Link

PRACTICE

Possible Answers

1. Carlos told Kiki that Kiki wasn't allowed to be on patrol anymore.
2. When the nun told Sister Superior what happened, Sister Superior gave me a concerned look.
3. Later, Esperanza started to cry as she told her mother.

ASSESSING

Assessment
■ *Holt Assessment: Literature, Reading, and Vocabulary*

RETEACHING

For a lesson reteaching characterization, see **Reteaching,** p. 917E.

Learners Having Difficulty

To help students answer question 4 on page 172, have them go back through the text and underline any references the narrator makes to herself, her sister, or her brothers. Then, suggest they ask themselves the following question: What is the narrator saying about the character or characters in these references?

Grade-Level Skills

- **Literary Skills**
Analyze character motivation.
- **Literary Skills**
Analyze allusion.
- **Reading Skills**
Make predictions.

Review Skills

- **Literary Skills**
Analyze the characters' effects on the plot and its resolution.

Summary ⬆ *above grade level*

The first-person narrator of this story is an unnamed young city boy who hangs out with a group of friends. When T. J. moves into his building from the rural South, the narrator invites him to join the gang. T. J. wants to plant a field in his new home. He and the boys agree to plant grass in their secret place—an unused flat roof of a neighborhood factory. They haul earth up to the roof and plant stolen seeds. One day, as they look down at the sprouting grass, the factory owner discovers them and orders "all that junk" removed. After protesting, the boys follow T. J.'s lead and destroy their garden themselves. T. J. leaves the city; he is found two weeks later, heading home to Alabama. None of the boys ever returns to the roof.

Before You Read The Short Story

Antaeus

Make the Connection
Quickwrite ✏️

Which do you think makes the best home: the country or the city? Write down some reasons for your choice, or draw a picture of what you think is the perfect place to live.

Literary Focus
Motivation

Why did he do that? What makes her act that way? These are questions about **motivation.** Feelings, needs, wishes, pressures from family and friends—all these forces pull and push people from inside and outside. As you read the story of T. J. and his friends, think about what motivates them to act the way they do.

Allusion

This title of this story is an **allusion** to a character from Greek mythology. Antaeus (an·tē′əs) is a giant whose strength comes from his mother, the Earth. As long as his feet are on the ground, Antaeus cannot be beaten. As you read the story, think about the connection between Antaeus and T. J.

INTERNET
Vocabulary
Development
Keyword: LE5 7-2

SKILLS FOCUS

Literary Skills
Understand motivation; understand allusion.

Reading Skills
Make predictions.

Reading Skills 📖
Predicting

As you read this story, do some guesswork about what you think will happen. The best thing about guessing, or **predicting**, is that you can always change your prediction (and often should) once you've read more of the story. Use your own knowledge of human behavior and details from the text to predict what T. J. and his friends will do next.

Vocabulary Development

You'll learn these words in "Antaeus."

resolute (rez′ə·lōot′) *adj.*: firm and purposeful; determined. *T. J. was resolute; he would not change his plan.*

domain (dō·mān′) *n.*: territory. *The boys were thrilled with their own rooftop domain.*

contemplate (kän′təm·plāt′) *v.*: look at or think about carefully. *They could contemplate the result of their labor with satisfaction.*

shrewd (shrōōd) *adj.*: clever. *His shrewd words convinced his friends of his plan.*

sterile (ster′əl) *adj.*: barren; lacking interest or vitality. *They were surprised to see grass growing on the sterile roof of the building.*

Background
Literature and Social Studies

During World War II, the United States geared up to produce equipment, weapons, and goods to serve the military effort overseas. Since most factories were in the North, many families left their homes in the South seeking work. This is the situation the narrator is referring to as the story opens.

174

RESOURCES: READING

Planning
- *One-Stop Planner* CD-ROM with ExamView Test Generator

Differentiating Instruction
- *Holt Adapted Reader*
- *Holt Reading Solutions*
- *Supporting Instruction in Spanish*
- *Audio CD Library*

- *Audio CD Library, Selections and Summaries in Spanish*

Vocabulary
- *Vocabulary Development*

Grammar and Language
- *Daily Language Activities*

Assessment
- *Holt Assessment: Literature, Reading, and Vocabulary*

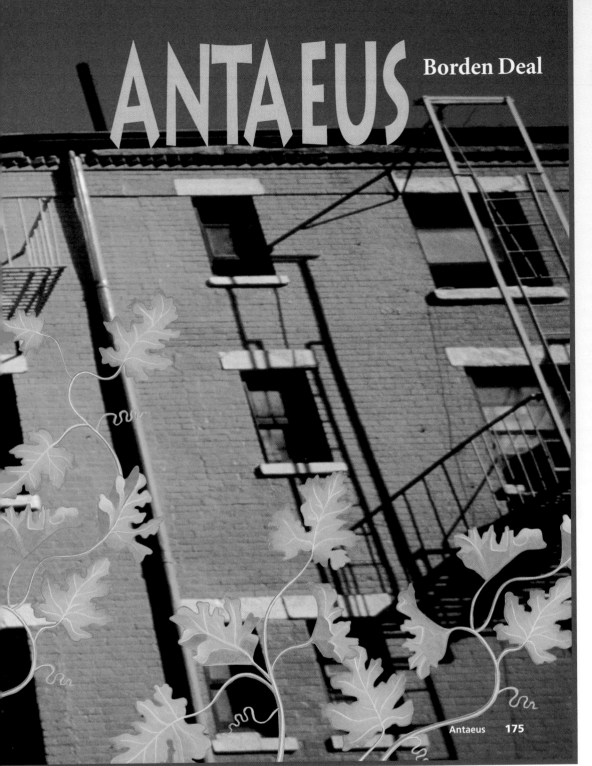

ANTAEUS

Borden Deal

Selection Starter

Motivate. Ask students to think back to a time when they worked on a project with their friends. It could be something academic, such as creating a science project, or something fun, such as building a fort to play in. Ask students what their motivation was for undertaking this project. How did they feel when they finished it?

Preview Vocabulary

Have students read the definitions of the Vocabulary words on page 174. Have students use each word in a sentence. Then, ask students to identify the Vocabulary word that is a synonym for each of the words and phrases listed below.

1. decisive [resolute]
2. not fruitful [sterile]
3. consider carefully [contemplate]
4. territory [domain]
5. savvy [shrewd]

Assign the Reading

Encourage students having difficulty with the story to read the story in a group. Advanced learners can answer the After You Read questions for homework.

HOMEWORK

- *One-Stop Planner* CD-ROM with ExamView Test Generator
- *Holt Online Assessment*

Internet
- go.hrw.com (Keyword: LE5 7-2)
- *Elements of Literature Online*

Media
- *Audio CD Library*
- *Audio CD Library, Selections and Summaries in Spanish*

A Learners Having Difficulty

? Use context clues. Students uncertain about the meaning of *stocky* and *robust* can use the context clue "nothing . . . except." If the writer has contrasted the two unfamiliar words with *sissy*, what do they mean? [Possible response: "strong, healthy, sturdy."]

B Literary Focus

? Character. What does this detail imply about the narrator? [Possible responses: The narrator usually doesn't interact with people who are different from him. The narrator has made up his mind about T. J.]

VIEWING THE ART

In a career that spanned most of the twentieth century, **Georgia O'Keeffe** (1887–1986) emerged as one of the most original and esteemed figures of modern American art. She is best known for intensely observed, close-up views of flowers. Yet her evocations of southwestern deserts and of northeastern cityscapes are distinctive as well.

Activity. Ask students how this painting helps the reader understand what the boys' hangout looks like. [Possible response: The painting presents a city scene that is lacking open spaces and the presence of nature.]

This was during the wartime, when lots of people were coming North for jobs in factories and war industries, when people moved around a lot more than they do now, and sometimes kids were thrown into new groups and new lives that were completely different from anything they had ever known before. I remember this one kid, T. J. his name was, from somewhere down South, whose family moved into our building during that time. They'd come North with everything they owned piled into the back seat of an old-model sedan that you wouldn't expect could make the trip, with T. J. and his three younger sisters riding shakily on top of the load of junk.

Our building was just like all the others there, with families crowded into a few rooms, and I guess there were twenty-five or thirty kids about my age in that one building. Of course, there were a few of us who formed a gang and ran together all the time after school, and I was the one who brought T. J. in and started the whole thing.

The building right next door to us was a factory where they made walking dolls. It was a low building with a flat, tarred roof that had a parapet[1] all around it about head-high, and we'd found out a long time before that no one, not even the watchman, paid any attention to the roof because it was higher than any of the other buildings around. So my gang used the roof as a headquarters. We could get up there by crossing over to the fire escape from our own roof on a plank and then going on up. It was a secret place for us, where nobody else could go without our permission.

I remember the day I first took T. J. up there to meet the gang. He was a stocky, robust kid

East River from the 30th Story of the Shelton Hotel by Georgia O'Keeffe. Oil on canvas (30" x 48").

A with a shock of white hair, nothing sissy about him except his voice; he talked in this slow, gentle voice like you never heard before. He talked **B** different from any of us and you noticed it right away. But I liked him anyway, so I told him to come on up.

We climbed up over the parapet and dropped down on the roof. The rest of the gang were already there.

---

1. **parapet** *n.:* wall or railing.

Learners Having Difficulty
Modeling. After reading to the end of paragraph 4 on page 176, model making predictions by saying, "Based on what I know about T. J., I think he might come into conflict with other members of the gang." Then, have students confirm or refute this prediction as they read. Encourage students to look for foreshadowing clues as they read and make predictions based on those clues. After students have finished reading, have them compare their predictions with the actual outcome of the story.

English-Language Learners
Students may have some difficulty with the dialect in this story. Have them make a two-column chart in which they list each example of dialect and its counterpart in standard English. Students might complete the Vocabulary Development activity on dialect on page 186 before they begin reading.

"Hi," I said. I jerked my thumb at T. J. "He just moved into the building yesterday."

He just stood there, not scared or anything, just looking, like the first time you see somebody you're not sure you're going to like.

"Hi," Blackie said. "Where are you from?"

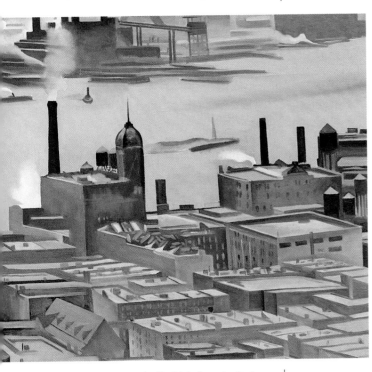

New Britain Museum of American Art, New Britain, Connecticut. Stephen Lawrence Fund. 1958.9 Photo credit: Irving Blomstrann. ©2003 The Georgia O'Keeffe Foundation/Artists Rights Society (ARS), New York.

"Marion County," T. J. said.

We laughed. "Marion County?" I said. "Where's that?"

He looked at me for a moment like I was a stranger, too. "It's in Alabama," he said, like I ought to know where it was.

"What's your name?" Charley said.

"T. J.," he said, looking back at him. He had pale blue eyes that looked washed-out, but he looked directly at Charley, waiting for his re-action. He'll be all right, I thought. No sissy in him, except that voice. Who ever talked like that?

"T. J.," Blackie said. "That's just initials. What's your real name? Nobody in the world has just initials."

"I do," he said. "And they're T. J. That's all the name I got."

His voice was <u>resolute</u> with the knowledge of his rightness, and for a moment no one had anything to say. T. J. looked around at the rooftop and down at the black tar under his feet. "Down yonder where I come from," he said, "we played out in the woods. Don't you-all have no woods around here?"

"Naw," Blackie said. "There's the park a few blocks over, but it's full of kids and cops and old women. You can't do a thing."

T. J. kept looking at the tar under his feet. "You mean you ain't got no fields to raise nothing in?—no watermelons or nothing?"

"Naw," I said scornfully. "What do you want to grow something for? The folks can buy everything they need at the store."

He looked at me again with that strange, unknowing look. "In Marion County," he said, "I had my own acre of cotton and my own acre of corn. It was mine to plant and make ever' year."

He sounded like it was something to be proud of, and in some obscure way it made the rest of us angry. Blackie said, "Who'd want to have their

---

Vocabulary

resolute (rez′ə·lo͞ot′) *adj.:* firm and purposeful; determined.

Antaeus **177**

DIRECT TEACHING

C **Literary Focus**

❓ **Character.** What does this detail suggest about T. J.? [Possible responses: He is independent and sure of himself. He doesn't care what other people think about him.]

D **English-Language Learners**

Understand dialect. Explain that *you-all* is an example of dialect—a way of speaking in a particular region or among a particular group (the example is of southern United States dialect). In standard English, *you* can be either singular or plural; *you-all* is always plural. *Down yonder* means "down there."

Special Education Students

For lessons designed to help special education students, see *Holt Reading Solutions.*

Advanced Learners

Acceleration. Use the following activity to help advanced learners compare and contrast the motivations of different literary characters confronting similar situations.
Activity. Ask students to think back on any novels or stories they have read (such as *Julie of the Wolves* by Jean Craighead George or "To Build a Fire" by Jack London) that feature a character whose relationship to nature is central to the plot. Ask students to write a brief report comparing T. J. with the character of their choosing. How is T. J.'s relationship with nature different from that of the other character? Why does each character feel toward nature the way he or she does?

? **Allusion.** How is T. J. similar to the Greek character Antaeus? [Possible response: Antaeus's strength comes from his mother, the earth. T. J. doesn't feel secure without fields and woods.]

B Literary Focus

? **Motivation.** Why does T. J. suggest growing a garden on the roof? [Possible responses: He feels out of place in the city, where there is no trace of nature. He wants to share what he recalls from his old home with his new acquaintances.]

C English-Language Learners

? **Understand dialect.** The word *ourn* is modeled on the possessive pronoun *mine*. How would the word be written in standard English? [*ours*] Also, in T. J.'s dialect, a personal pronoun is often inserted between a verb and its direct object, as in "raise us some cotton," meaning "raise some cotton for us."

D Reading Skills

Predict. Ask students whether they think the garden will grow. [Possible responses: Yes, T. J. is knowledgeable and determined that it will grow. No, the other boys won't help him enough.]

---

own acre of cotton and corn? That's just work. What can you do with an acre of cotton and corn?"

T. J. looked at him. "Well, you get part of the bale offen your acre," he said seriously. "And I fed my acre of corn to my calf."

We didn't really know what he was talking about, so we were more puzzled than angry; otherwise, I guess, we'd have chased him off the roof and wouldn't let him be part of our gang. But he was strange and different, and we were all attracted by his stolid sense of rightness and belonging, maybe by the strange softness of his voice contrasting our own tones of speech into harshness.

A He moved his foot against the black tar. "We could make our own field right here," he said softly, thoughtfully. "Come spring we could raise us what we want to—watermelons and garden truck and no telling what all."

"You'd have to be a good farmer to make these tar roofs grow any watermelons," I said. We all laughed.

B But T. J. looked serious. "We could haul us some dirt up here," he said. "And spread it out even and water it, and before you know it, we'd have us a crop in here." He looked at us intently. "Wouldn't that be fun?"

"They wouldn't let us," Blackie said quickly.

"I thought you said this was you-all's roof," T. J. said to me. "That you-all could do anything you wanted to up here."

"They've never bothered us," I said. I felt the idea beginning to catch fire in me. It was a big idea, and it took a while for it to sink in; but the more I thought about it, the better I liked it. "Say," I said to the gang. "He might have something there. Just make us a regular roof garden, with flowers and grass and trees and everything. And all ours, too," I said. "We wouldn't let anybody up here except the ones we wanted to."

"It'd take a while to grow trees," T. J. said quickly, but we weren't paying any attention to him. They were all talking about it suddenly, all excited with the idea after I'd put it in a way they would catch hold of it. Only rich people had roof gardens, we knew, and the idea of our own private <u>domain</u> excited them.

"We could bring it up in sacks and boxes," Blackie said. "We'd have to do it while the folks weren't paying any attention to us, for we'd have to come up to the roof of our building and then cross over with it."

"Where could we get the dirt?" somebody said worriedly.

"Out of those vacant lots over close to school," Blackie said. "Nobody'd notice if we scraped it up."

I slapped T. J. on the shoulder. "Man, you had a wonderful idea," I said, and everybody grinned at him, remembering that he had started it. "Our own private roof garden."

C He grinned back. "It'll be ourn," he said. "All ourn." Then he looked thoughtful again. "Maybe I can lay my hands on some cotton seed, too. You think we could raise us some cotton?"

D We'd started big projects before at one time or another, like any gang of kids, but they'd always petered out[2] for lack of organization and direction. But this one didn't; somehow or other T. J. kept it going all through the winter months. He kept talking about the watermelons and the cotton we'd raise, come spring, and when even that wouldn't work, he'd switch around to my idea of flowers and grass and trees, though he was always honest enough to add that it'd take a while to get any

Vocabulary
domain (dō·mān') *n.:* territory.

2. **petered out:** gradually disappeared.

CROSS-CURRICULAR CONNECTIONS

Science
Horticulture. Some students may not realize that gardening is not just a hobby some people do in their spare time. Horticulture is a type of farming science dealing with the cultivation of garden plants. Horticulturists concern themselves with the climate and terrain of the area where they garden to make sure their plants are as successful and plentiful as possible.

Activity. Ask students to investigate the science of horticulture. Have students determine what type of soil T. J. is looking for. What other conditions and equipment might T. J.'s garden need? Have students find out which flowers or vegetables can grow in their local climate. Students may want to ask their science teacher for advice.

trees started. He always had it on his mind, and he'd mention it in school, getting them lined up to carry dirt that afternoon, saying in a casual way that he reckoned a few more weeks ought to see the job through.

Our little area of private earth grew slowly. T. J. was smart enough to start in one corner of the building, heaping up the carried earth two or three feet thick so that we had an immediate result to look at, to <u>contemplate</u> with awe. Some of the evenings T. J. alone was carrying earth up to the building, the rest of the gang distracted by other enterprises or interests, but T. J. kept plugging along on his own, and eventually we'd all come back to him again, and then our own little acre would grow more rapidly.

He was careful about the kind of dirt he'd let us carry up there, and more than once he dumped a sandy load over the parapet into the areaway below because it wasn't good enough. He found out the kinds of earth in all the vacant lots for blocks around. He'd pick it up and feel it and smell it, frozen though it was sometimes, and then he'd say it was good growing soil or it wasn't worth anything, and we'd have to go on somewhere else.

Thinking about it now, I don't see how he kept us at it. It was hard work, lugging paper sacks and boxes of dirt all the way up the stairs of our own building, keeping out of the way of the grown-ups so they wouldn't catch on to what we were doing. They probably wouldn't have cared, for they didn't pay much attention to us, but we wanted to keep it secret anyway. Then we had to go through the trapdoor to our roof, teeter over a plank to the fire escape, then climb two or three stories to the parapet, and drop them down onto the roof. All that for a small pile of earth that sometimes didn't seem

worth the effort. But T. J. kept the vision bright within us, his words <u>shrewd</u> and calculated toward the fulfillment of his dream; and he worked harder than any of us. He seemed driven toward a goal that we couldn't see, a particular point in time that would be definitely marked by signs and wonders that only he could see.

The laborious earth just lay there during the cold months, inert and lifeless, the clods lumpy and cold under our feet when we walked over it. But one day it rained, and afterward there was a softness in the air, and the earth was live and giving again with moisture and warmth.

That evening T. J. smelled the air, his nostrils dilating with the odor of the earth under his feet. "It's spring," he said, and there was a gladness rising in his voice that filled us all with the same feeling. "It's mighty late for it, but it's spring. I'd just about decided it wasn't never gonna get here at all."

We were all sniffing at the air, too, trying to smell it the way that T. J. did, and I can still remember the sweet odor of the earth under our feet. It was the first time in my life that spring and spring earth had meant anything to me. I looked at T. J. then, knowing in a faint way the hunger within him through the toilsome[3] winter months, knowing the dream that lay behind his plan. He was a new Antaeus, preparing his own bed of strength.

"Planting time," he said. "We'll have to find us some seed."

"What do we do?" Blackie said. "How do we do it?"

Vocabulary

contemplate (kän′təm·plāt′) v.: consider; look at or think about carefully.
shrewd (shrood) adj.: clever.

---

3. **toilsome** adj.: involving hard work; laborious.

E **Literary Focus**

? **Motivation.** Why does T. J. work harder than the other boys? [Possible responses: He wants to inspire the other boys to work harder by setting an example of leadership. He is determined to feel more at home in his new surroundings.]

F **Literary Focus**

? **Allusion.** What kind of strength does T. J. draw from the earth? How is it different from the strength Antaeus draws from the earth? [Possible response: Antaeus draws physical strength from the earth, whereas T. J. draws emotional strength from it.]

A English-Language Learners

? Understand dialect. Point out that the contraction *ain't* is sometimes used in informal contexts, like conversations, but should be avoided in most student writing. *Ain't* is often used with a double negative. What would the *ain't* sentence here be in standard English? [Possible response: "I have never put any effort into that."] What words can be combined to make *ain't*? [*am not, is not, are not, has not, have not*]

B Literary Focus

? Motivation. Why does T. J. give in to the gang's wish to grow grass? [Possible response: T. J. might lose the gang's enthusiasm if he asks them to work too hard or grow something they don't want to grow.]

C Literary Focus

? Motivation. Why do the boys refrain from playing in the grass they've planted? What has caused the gang's behavior to change? [Possible responses: Since meeting T. J., they have learned to respect nature. The boys are proud of the work they've done, and they don't want it ruined.]

"First we'll have to break up the clods," T. J. said. "That won't be hard to do. Then we plant the seeds, and after a while they come up. Then you got you a crop." He frowned. "But you ain't got it raised yet. You got to tend it and hoe it and take care of it, and all the time it's growing and growing, while you're awake and while you're asleep. Then you lay it by when it's growed and let it ripen, and then you got you a crop."

"There's those wholesale seed houses over on Sixth," I said. "We could probably swipe some grass seed over there."

A T. J. looked at the earth. "You-all seem mighty set on raising some grass," he said. "I ain't never put no effort into that. I spent all my life trying not to raise grass."

"But it's pretty," Blackie said. "We could play on it and take sunbaths on it. Like having our own lawn. Lots of people got lawns."

B "Well," T. J. said. He looked at the rest of us, hesitant for the first time. He kept on looking at us for a moment. "I did have it in mind to raise some corn and vegetables. But we'll plant grass."

He was smart. He knew where to give in. And I don't suppose it made any difference to him, really. He just wanted to grow something, even if it was grass.

"Of course," he said, "I do think we ought to plant a row of watermelons. They'd be mighty nice to eat while we was a-laying on that grass."

We all laughed. "All right," I said. "We'll plant us a row of watermelons."

Things went very quickly then. Perhaps half the roof was covered with the earth, the half that wasn't broken by ventilators,[4] and we swiped pocketfuls of grass seed from the open bins in the wholesale seed house, mingling among the buyers on Saturdays and during the school lunch

hour. T. J. showed us how to prepare the earth, breaking up the clods and smoothing it and sowing the grass seed. It looked rich and black now with moisture, receiving of the seed, and it seemed that the grass sprang up overnight, pale green in the early spring.

We couldn't keep from looking at it, unable to believe that we had created this delicate growth. We looked at T. J. with understanding now, knowing the fulfillment of the plan he had carried along within his mind. We had worked without full understanding of the task, but he had known all the time.

C We found that we couldn't walk or play on the delicate blades as we had expected to, but we didn't mind. It was enough just to look at it, to realize that it was the work of our own hands, and each evening, the whole gang was there, trying to measure the growth that had been achieved that day.

One time a foot was placed on the plot of ground, one time only, Blackie stepping onto it with sudden bravado. Then he looked at the crushed blades and there was shame in his face. He did not do it again. This was his grass, too, and not to be desecrated.[5] No one said anything, for it was not necessary.

T. J. had reserved a small section for watermelons, and he was still trying to find some seed for it. The wholesale house didn't have any watermelon seeds, and we didn't know where we could lay our hands on them. T. J. shaped the earth into mounds ready to receive them, three mounds lying in a straight line along the edge of the grass plot.

We had just about decided that we'd have to buy the seeds if we were to get them. It was a violation of our principles, but we were anxious to get the watermelons started. Somewhere or

---

4. **ventilators** *n.:* devices used to bring in fresh air.

5. **desecrated** (des′i·krāt′id) *v.:* showed disrespect for (something considered holy).

DIFFERENTIATING INSTRUCTION

English-Language Learners
Dialect. To help English-language learners with the dialect in the story, ask them to read the following sentences from page 182 of "Antaeus" silently and then aloud. Then, have them identify the words and phrases (italicized) that are not standard English and rewrite the sentences in standard English. Students might consider the difference in tone between the two versions.

1. "Well, you *wasn't* using the roof." [Well, you weren't using the roof.]

2. "We *toted* it up here, and it's our earth." [We hauled it up here, and it's our earth.]

3. "You *ain't got no* right!" [You don't have any right!]

4. "*Can't nobody* touch a man's own land." [Nobody can touch a man's own land.]

Chandler, Mexico (1923), photograph by Edward Weston.

© 1981 Center for Creative Photography, Arizona Board of Regents.

VIEWING THE ART

Edward Weston (1886–1958) was born in California. Before Weston was exposed to modern art in 1915, his photographs reflected the style of impressionist paintings. Afterward, his work took on far greater realism. To avoid losses in tone and detail that result from using an enlarger, Weston worked with cameras capable of producing large contact prints of striking sharpness, as in *Chandler, Mexico*.

Activity. Ask students to express, in either prose or poetry, what the boy in the photo may be thinking. How may the thoughts of the boy in the photograph be similar to those of the boys in the story?

other, T. J. got his hands on a seed catalog and brought it one evening to our roof garden.

"We can order them now," he said, showing us the catalog. "Look!"

We all crowded around, looking at the fat green watermelons pictured in full color on the pages. Some of them were split open, showing the red, tempting meat, making our mouths water.

"Now we got to scrape up some seed money," T. J. said, looking at us. "I got a quarter. How much you-all got?"

We made up a couple of dollars among us and T. J. nodded his head. "That'll be more than enough. Now we got to decide what kind to get. I

think them Kleckley Sweets. What do you-all think?"

He was going into esoteric[6] matters beyond our reach. We hadn't even known there were different kinds of melons. So we just nodded our heads and agreed that yes, we thought the Kleckley Sweets too.

"I'll order them tonight," T. J. said. "We ought to have them in a few days."

"What are you boys doing up here?" an adult voice said behind us.

It startled us, for no one had ever come up here before in all the time we had been using the roof of the factory. We jerked around and

---

6. **esoteric** (es′ə·ter′ik) *adj.:* specialized; beyond most people's understanding or knowledge.

Antaeus **181**

D Reading Skills

? Predict. Who are these men? Why have they come to the roof? [Possible responses: The men own the factory. They are plainclothes detectives. They have heard noise from the roof. Neighbors or factory workers have complained about the boys on the roof.] **What do you think will happen, now that adults have appeared in the story?** [Some students may predict that the men will be angry at the boys for bringing the dirt to the roof. Other students may predict that the men will be glad that the boys improved the area.]

Advanced Learners
Enrichment. Have advanced learners read a comprehensive version of the myth of Antaeus. In this story, Hercules, seeking to obtain the golden apples of the Hesperides, meets and fights Antaeus. Ask students to share the story of Hercules and Antaeus with their classmates. Encourage students to look for parallels between the myth and the short story and present their observations to the class.

A Learners Having Difficulty

Use context clues. Have students use context clues (such as "guilt heavy among us," "tone of voice," and the question asked by the middle adult) to determine the meaning of *levied*. ["imposed" or "forced"; the adults' authority imposes guilt on the boys].

B Literary Focus

? Motivation. Why does T. J. react differently from the other boys? [Possible responses: He does not realize that the factory roof is considered private property. He is proud of his ability to make plants grow.]

C Literary Focus

? Motivation. Why does T. J. say that the owners don't have a right to the earth? [Possible responses: T. J. believes in the importance of growing living things. He believes the grower's "rights" outweigh the owner's.]

D Reading Skills

? Predict. Do you think the gang can prevent the destruction of their garden? [Possible responses: No, there is nothing the boys can do to counteract the owner's claim to the land. Yes, the gang's determination to protect their garden will overcome the owner's plans.]

---

saw three men standing near the trapdoor at the other end of the roof. They weren't policemen or night watchmen but three men in plump business suits, looking at us. They walked toward us.

"What are you boys doing up here?" the one in the middle said again.

A We stood still, guilt heavy among us, levied by the tone of voice, and looked at the three strangers.

The men stared at the grass flourishing behind us. "What's this?" the man said. "How did this get up here?"

B "Sure is growing good, ain't it?" T. J. said conversationally. "We planted it."

The men kept looking at the grass as if they didn't believe it. It was a thick carpet over the earth now, a patch of deep greenness startling in the <u>sterile</u> industrial surroundings.

"Yes, sir," T. J. said proudly. "We toted that earth up here and planted that grass." He fluttered the seed catalog. "And we're just fixing to plant us some watermelon."

The man looked at him then, his eyes strange and faraway. "What do you mean, putting this on the roof of my building?" he said. "Do you want to go to jail?"

T. J. looked shaken. The rest of us were silent, frightened by the authority of his voice. We had grown up aware of adult authority, of policemen and night watchmen and teachers, and this man sounded like all the others. But it was a new thing to T. J.

"Well, you wasn't using the roof," T. J. said. He paused a moment and added shrewdly, "So we just thought to pretty it up a little bit."

"And sag it so I'd have to rebuild it," the man said sharply. He started turning away, saying to

---

Vocabulary
sterile (ster'əl) *adj.*: barren; lacking interest or vitality.

---

another man beside him, "See that all that junk is shoveled off by tomorrow."

"Yes, sir," the man said.

T. J. started forward. "You can't do that," he said. "We toted it up here, and it's our earth. We planted it and raised it and toted it up here."

The man stared at him coldly. "But it's my building," he said. "It's to be shoveled off tomorrow."

C "It's our earth," T. J. said desperately. "You ain't got no right!"

The men walked on without listening and descended clumsily through the trapdoor. T. J. stood looking after them, his body tense with anger, until they had disappeared. They wouldn't even argue with him, wouldn't let him defend his earth rights.

He turned to us. "We won't let 'em do it," he said fiercely. "We'll stay up here all day tomorrow and the day after that, and we won't let 'em do it."

D We just looked at him. We knew there was no stopping it.

He saw it in our faces, and his face wavered for a moment before he gripped it into determination. "They ain't got no right," he said. "It's our earth. It's our land. Can't nobody touch a man's own land."

We kept looking at him, listening to the words but knowing that it was no use. The adult world had descended on us even in our richest dream, and we knew there was no calculating the adult world, no fighting it, no winning against it.

We started moving slowly toward the parapet and the fire escape, avoiding a last look at the green beauty of the earth that T. J. had planted for us, had planted deeply in our minds as well as in our experience. We filed slowly over the edge and down the steps to the plank, T. J. coming last, and all of us could feel the weight of his

---

DEVELOPING FLUENCY

Activity. Have students work in small groups to read the section of the story where T. J. is confronted by the adults. One student can read the narration while others assume the roles of characters in the story. Students can help one another with T. J.'s dialect and discuss the contrast between his speech and that of the adults.

SMALL GROUP

grief behind us.

"Wait a minute," he said suddenly, his voice harsh with the effort of calling.

We stopped and turned, held by the tone of his voice, and looked up at him standing above us on the fire escape.

"We can't stop them?" he said, looking down at us, his face strange in the dusky light. "There ain't no way to stop 'em?"

"No," Blackie said with finality. "They own the building."

We stood still for a moment, looking up at T. J., caught into inaction by the decision working in his face. He stared back at us, and his face was pale and mean in the poor light, with a bald nakedness in his skin like cripples have sometimes.

"They ain't gonna touch my earth," he said fiercely. "They ain't gonna lay a hand on it! Come on."

He turned around and started up the fire escape again, almost running against the effort of climbing. We followed more slowly, not knowing what he intended to do. By the time we reached him, he had seized a board and thrust it into the soil, scooping it up and flinging it over the parapet into the areaway below. He straightened and looked at us.

"They can't touch it," he said. "I won't let 'em lay a dirty hand on it!"

We saw it then. He stooped to his labor again, and we followed, the gusts of his anger moving in frenzied labor among us as we scattered along the edge of earth, scooping it and throwing it over the parapet, destroying with anger the growth we had nurtured with such tender care. The soil carried so laboriously upward to the light and the sun cascaded swiftly into the dark areaway, the green blades of grass crumpled and twisted in the falling.

It took less time than you would think; the task of destruction is infinitely easier than that of creation. We stopped at the end, leaving only a scattering of loose soil, and when it was finally over, a stillness stood among the group and over the factory building. We looked down at the bare sterility of black tar, felt the harsh texture of it under the soles of our shoes, and the anger had gone out of us, leaving only a sore aching in our minds, like overstretched muscles.

T. J. stood for a moment, his breathing slowing from anger and effort, caught into the same contemplation of destruction as all of us. He stooped slowly, finally, and picked up a lonely blade of grass left trampled under our feet and put it between his teeth, tasting it, sucking the greenness out of it into his mouth. Then he started walking toward the fire escape, moving before any of us were ready to move, and disappeared over the edge.

We followed him, but he was already halfway down to the ground, going on past the board where we crossed over, climbing down into the areaway. We saw the last section swing down with his weight, and then he stood on the concrete below us, looking at the small pile of anonymous earth scattered by our throwing. Then he walked across the place where we could see him and disappeared toward the street without glancing back, without looking up to see us watching him.

They did not find him for two weeks.

Then the Nashville police caught him just outside the Nashville freight yards. He was walking along the railroad track, still heading South, still heading home.

As for us, who had no remembered home to call us, none of us ever again climbed the escapeway to the roof.

Antaeus 183

Meet the Writer

After high school, Borden Deal left his Mississippi home and traveled around the country on foot and by train, sometimes working for a circus and on a showboat. Later, he worked for the Department of Labor and then joined the U.S. Navy. After World War II, Deal studied creative writing at the University of Alabama. He lived in Mexico for three years but eventually settled permanently in the South.

For Independent Reading

Students interested in children like Borden Deal who grew up in the midst of the Great Depression might be interested in reading Irene Hunt's *No Promises in the Wind,* which tells the story of a boy named Josh who leaves his home and fights for survival.

Meet the Writer

Borden Deal

Keeping the Faith

Like his hero T. J., **Borden Deal** (1922–1985) came from a family of Southern cotton farmers. They knew firsthand the hardships of farm life during the Great Depression. As the following anecdote proves, Deal was just as persistent as T. J.:

> 66 My short story 'Antaeus' has a strange history. Though it has been reprinted far more often than any other of my nearly one hundred short stories, it took me ten years to get it published the first time! True. It was turned down by every quality popular magazine in the country, not once but two or three times. Then, on rereading the story after a year or so, I'd like it all over again, and I'd send it around once more. After ten long years, the story was finally published by one of the country's finest literary magazines, and the next year it was reprinted in the annual collection called *The Best American Short Stories.* Since then, the story has appeared in hundreds of textbooks and anthologies on every level, from grammar school to college. So you see, when you believe in something, it pays to keep the faith and be persistent—just as, in the story, T. J. is persistent in his faith and feeling for the earth. 99

DIFFERENTIATING INSTRUCTION

Advanced Learners

Enrichment. Have students research the effects the Great Depression had on farmers in the South. They can use an encyclopedia or enter the phrase *Great Depression* in an Internet search engine. Then, have them discuss reasons why a writer like Deal might create sympathetic characters like T. J., whose defining characteristic is his determination.

First Thoughts

1. If you were T. J., what would you do after hearing the words "It's to be shoveled off tomorrow"?

Thinking Critically

2. T. J. inspires the boys to take on a difficult project and carries it out alone when the others lose interest. What does this tell you about his **character**?

3. What was T. J.'s **motivation** for conceiving and carrying out his grand project?

4. Find the passage in the story that mentions Antaeus (page 179). In the Greek myth, Antaeus cannot be beaten while connected with the earth, but the hero Hercules is able to kill Antaeus after lifting him into the air. Explain the connection between what happens to Antaeus and what happens to T. J. What do you think the **allusion** adds to the story?

5. What do you make of the last line, about the city boys' having "no remembered home" to call them? What do you think the word *home* means here?

6. Did any of your **predictions** turn out to be correct? Using details from the story, explain why one of your predictions was or was not correct.

Extending Interpretations

7. Look back at the notes about home that you made for the Quickwrite. How do your feelings about home compare with T. J.'s?

WRITING

Adding a Final Scene

What happens to T. J.? Write a final scene for the story. Tell it from T. J.'s point of view. Let T. J. continue the story, speaking as "I." Before you write, collect ideas by answering the questions in the graphic to the right.

Reading Check

a. What characteristic makes T. J. seem "different" at first to the narrator?

b. What does T. J. want? What obstacles must he overcome to get what he wants?

c. What does the narrator realize for the first time when he smells "the sweet odor of the earth" under his feet (page 179)?

d. How does T. J. react when the boys' project is destroyed?

INTERNET

Projects and Activities

Keyword: LE5 7-2

SKILLS FOCUS

Literary Skills
Analyze motivation; analyze an allusion.

Reading Skills
Make predictions.

Writing Skills
Add a scene to a story.

Antaeus **185**

Reading Check

a. He has a gentle and soft voice.

b. He wants to plant a garden on the roof. He has to get the boys to agree to help. They must obtain soil and seeds. They have to carry the soil to the roof secretly.

c. He appreciates nature and has a desire to grow things.

d. He decides to return home to Alabama.

After You Read

First Thoughts

1. Possible answers: argue with the men; destroy the garden; plant a new garden somewhere else; share my anger with friends or family members.

Thinking Critically

2. He is determined. He is not easily intimidated. He is a hard worker. He will not give up once his mind is set on a goal.

3. T. J. is motivated by the absence of nature in the city's landscape. He has a need to cultivate land whenever possible.

4. When the characters are physically separated from the earth by their opponents, they become physically weak (Antaeus) or feel emotionally incomplete (T. J.). The allusion helps the reader appreciate the heroism of the "ordinary" boy from the rural South.

5. Possible answer: They have not yet experienced the feeling of love for a particular place, as T. J. has. *Home* refers to the place where a person has roots.

6. Answers will vary. Possible answer: Since he seemed different from the rest of the gang, I predicted that T. J. and the other boys would have difficulty getting along. My prediction was incorrect because they found the common interest of planting a garden.

Extending Interpretations

7. Possible answer: Like T. J., I feel that a person can create a home wherever he or she is.

Vocabulary Development

PRACTICE 1

Possible Answers

1. T. J. is too <u>resolute</u> to accept failure and too <u>shrewd</u> to insist on raising only vegetables.
2. The boys <u>contemplate</u> the grass as it grows. They are proud of this addition to their <u>domain</u>.
3. With the arrival of T. J. and his knowledge of gardens, the <u>sterile</u> roof sprouted a small lawn.

PRACTICE 2

Responses will vary. Have students work with partners to answer the three questions and to discuss their responses with the class.

ASSESSING

Assessment

■ *Holt Assessment: Reading, Literature, and Vocabulary*

Clarifying Word Meanings

One way to show your understanding of words is to use them in your own writing.

PRACTICE 1

1. Describe T. J., using the words *resolute* and *shrewd*.
2. Describe how the city boys feel about the roof garden, using the words *contemplate* and *domain*.
3. Using the word *sterile* describe how the boys change the tar roof into a lawn.

> **Word Bank**
>
> resolute
> domain
> contemplate
> shrewd
> sterile

Dialect—Voices of a Region or a Group

In "Antaeus," T. J. speaks in a way that doesn't sound like standard English. He uses double (even triple) negatives and words like *ourn* for *ours* and *offen* for *from*. Here is an example:

T. J.'S DIALECT	"You mean you ain't got no fields to raise nothing in?"
STANDARD ENGLISH	Do you mean you have no fields in which to raise anything?

Dialect is a way of speaking that is characteristic of a particular region or group of people. People who study language say that all of us speak one dialect or another. Think of how a British speaker sounds. Think of how a Philadelphian speaks, as compared with a person from Southern California. T. J. speaks one of the dialects of the Deep South. Like all dialects, T. J.'s has a distinctive pronunciation, vocabulary, and grammar. By re-creating T. J.'s dialect, Deal helps us "see" the boy and "hear" his gentle Southern drawl.

SKILLS FOCUS

Vocabulary Skills
Clarify word meanings; understand dialect.

PRACTICE 2

Do a survey of dialects spoken in your class. Does everyone sound the same, or do you hear varied dialects?

1. Do you say "crick" or "creek" to refer to a small stream?
2. Do you use *frying pan, skillet,* or *spider* to refer to the pan you fry eggs in?
3. How do you pronounce *dear, car,* and *water*?

186 Collection 2 / Characters: Living Many Lives

Understanding the Main Idea

Reading Focus
The Main Idea

In the fictional story "Antaeus," T. J. wants to grow plants on a city roof. In the newspaper article you are about to read, you'll meet some real-live people who garden in the city.

Informational texts, such as newspaper articles, usually focus on one or more main ideas. The **main idea** is the central, most important point in a text. In some texts the main idea is stated directly. Most of the time however, you, the reader, must **infer** the main idea—that is, you have to think about all the details in the text and make an educated guess about its main point.

Here are some tips for figuring out the main idea:

- Look at the **title**. Does it tell you what the text focuses on? Sometimes the title does not point to a central idea at all. Instead, it's a "grabber"— it's meant to grab your attention. (The title of the article you are about to read plays on the words *mix* and *olio*. *Olio* means "collection or mixture.")

- Look for a **sentence that seems to state a key idea** in general terms. Sometimes such statements appear at the beginning or the end of a text. Other times they are buried someplace in the middle.

- If you can't find a sentence that clearly states the main idea, go back over the text, and find the **most important details**. Ask yourself: What do all these details add up to?

■ When you have finished reading the article, think about whether the title gives you a clue to its main idea.

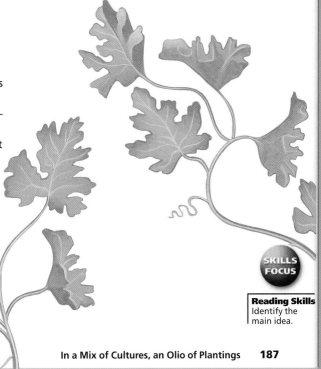

SKILLS FOCUS

Reading Skills
Identify the main idea.

In a Mix of Cultures, an Olio of Plantings **187**

SKILLS FOCUS
pp. 187–189

Grade-Level Skills
■ Reading Skills
Analyze the main idea, and identify evidence that supports that idea.

Summary ⬇ *below grade level*

This informative article tells about a small piece of land known as "The Garden of Happiness" in the South Bronx in New York City. Members of the community banded together to plant fruits and vegetables on lots that were previously wasted. These residents value the garden because it gets them back to their roots. The garden is one example of the hundreds of gardens that are part of New York City's gardening program, Operation Green Thumb.

PRETEACHING

Selection Starter
Motivate. Ask students if they have ever embarked on a project, such as putting on a show with a local theater group, that was dedicated to improving life in their community. What type of project did they participate in? How did they feel once it was over?

Assign the Reading
This selection is short enough for students to read on their own at home before reviewing it with the class.

HOMEWORK

RESOURCES: READING

Planning
■ *One-Stop Planner* CD-ROM with ExamView Test Generator

Differentiating Instruction
■ *Holt Reading Solutions*
■ *Supporting Instruction in Spanish*
■ *Audio CD Library*
■ *Audio CD Library, Selections and Summaries in Spanish*

Grammar and Language
■ *Daily Language Activities*

Assessment
■ *Holt Assessment: Literature, Reading, and Vocabulary*
■ *One-Stop Planner* CD-ROM with ExamView Test Generator
■ *Holt Online Assessment*

Internet
■ go.hrw.com (Keyword: LE5 7-2)
■ *Elements of Literature Online*

Media
■ *Audio CD Library*
■ *Audio CD Library, Selections and Summaries in Spanish*

A Vocabulary Development

? Multiple meanings. Ask students to look up *olio* in a dictionary. Besides "mixture," what meaning does the word have? [a spicy stew] Why did the author use this word in the title? [Possible responses: The garden, a mixture of flowers and vegetables, is cared for by thirty gardeners. *Olio* is from the Spanish *olla*, "pot," and several Spanish words are used in the article.]

B Reading Skills

Restate the main idea. Ask students to state the main idea of this passage in their own words. [Possible response: The community members planted this garden to improve their neighborhood and remind themselves of where they came from.]

C Advanced Learners

? Extend the text. What does this article have in common with "Antaeus"? [Possible responses: Both selections suggest the importance of nature in human life. Both T. J. and the gardeners in this article try to create natural places for themselves within a big city.]

In a Mix of Cultures, an Olio of Plantings

ANNE RAVER

Juan Guerrero grows tomatillos on a scrap of land that used to be a chop shop for stolen cars in the South Bronx. It's his little piece of Mexico.

"He says you cut them up with hot pepper for salsa," said Jose Garcia, who grew up in Puerto Rico. Mr. Guerrero left Puebla, Mexico, four years ago, but he speaks little English, so Mr. Garcia was translating.

He watched Mr. Guerrero peel the papery husk from a hard little green fruit and nodded yes, yes, yes, as his neighbor explained how to dry the fruit for seeds.

"In Puerto Rico," Mr. Garcia said, chuckling, "my father always told me these were poison." Then he politely tasted a pungent leaf that Mr. Guerrero had just picked from a bushy green herb.

"Papalo," Mr. Guerrero said. "Como cilantro."

This 100 by 175 foot piece of earth, on Prospect Avenue between East 181st and 182d Streets, used to grow old car parts, refrigerators, and crack vials. Now it grows zinnias, hollyhocks, eggplants, collard greens, and pear trees. And its thirty gardeners call it "The Garden of Happiness."

Happiness here has little to do with the perfect perennial° bed. It's about reclaiming scarred land from drug dealers. And planting a few vegetables and flowers that remind you of the roots you tore up to get here.

Many urban gardeners till city-owned lots leased to them for one dollar a year by Operation Green Thumb, the city's gardening program, which leases more than a thousand lots to 550 community groups. Others just take over garbage-strewn land.

"Gardening takes you back to your roots," said Karen Washington, 37, who took a pickax and shovel to the debris three years ago and now heads the community garden. "My grandparents farmed in North Carolina. If you gave them some store-bought collard greens, they'd look at you like you were crazy."

C —from *The New York Times*

Sara Krulwich, The New York Times.

Urban gardener Annie Vigg with a harvest of squash, tomatoes, beans, peas, and okra.

°**perennial** (pə·ren′ē·əl) n. used as an *adj.:* a plant that survives and grows again year after year.

188 Collection 2 / Characters: Living Many Lives

DIFFERENTIATING INSTRUCTION

Learners Having Difficulty
To help students identify the main idea of the article, ask what they think the most important details of the article are. Students can keep their own lists, or you can compile a list on the chalkboard. Then, ask students to state the main idea of the article based on the lists they've compiled.

English-Language Learners
For lessons designed for intermediate and advanced English-language learners, see *Holt Reading Solutions.*

Analyzing Main Idea

In a Mix of Cultures, an Olio of Plantings

Test Practice

1. The **subject** of this article is —
   A Juan Guerrero's tomatillos
   B Operation Green Thumb
   C gardening in the city
   D gardening in Puerto Rico

2. Which of the following sentences *best* states the **main idea** of this article?
   F It takes many different types of people to plant a garden.
   G Gardening improves the quality of life for city dwellers.
   H It is better to garden in New York than in North Carolina.
   J Happiness means planting the perfect year-round garden.

3. This **newspaper article** can best be described as —
   A fast-breaking news
   B a human-interest story
   C an editorial
   D political analysis

4. The **main idea** of this article is stated —
   F in the first sentence
   G in the middle
   H at the end
   J indirectly

Constructed Response

State the **main idea** of this article in your own words. Then, list three significant **details** or **quotations** from the article that you think back up the main idea.

SKILLS FOCUS

Reading Skills
Analyze the main idea.

Advanced Learners
Activity. Students might want to imagine themselves as T. J. and write a letter to one of the urban gardeners to share experiences or ask for advice. Or students might imagine themselves as one of the Bronx gardeners and write a letter to the factory owner, asking that T. J. and his friends be allowed to keep the rooftop garden.

Analyzing Main Idea

Test Practice

Answers and Model Rationales

1. **B** Gardening in Puerto Rico (D) is mentioned as background information, not as the subject of the article. Juan Guerrero's tomatillos (A) are not covered in depth. Gardening in the city (C) may appear to be correct, but it is too general; the article specifically deals with the gardens brought about by Operation Green Thumb (B).

2. **G** F, H, and J are not in the article, leaving G as the only correct answer.

3. **B** The article has nothing to do with politics (D), states no strong opinion on an issue (C), and does not contain urgent information (A), leaving B as the only possible answer.

4. **J** J is the correct answer, since students must infer the main idea on their own.

Test-Taking Tips

For more instruction on how to answer multiple-choice questions, see **Test Smarts** on page 920.

Constructed Response

Possible main idea: Gardening improves the quality of life in urban communities and keeps people in touch with their rural roots. Possible supporting details: Lands that were used for dealing drugs are now used for gardening; gardening keeps neighborhoods clean; some community members feel more in touch with their heritage when they are growing gardens.

SKILLS FOCUS
pp. 190–205

Grade-Level Skills

■ **Literary Skills**
Analyze character traits.

■ **Reading Skills**
Compare and contrast characters.

Upcoming Skills

■ **Literary Skills**
Compare and contrast the motives of literary characters from different historical eras.

OVERVIEW

Purpose. This Comparing Literature feature asks students to make inferences about character traits and to compare characters from two different stories. By completing this feature, students will be able to understand the different ways authors choose to reveal character. Students will also learn how to compare and contrast characters across stories.

Use. Direct students' attention to the box on the right-hand side of this page. Ask students to look for clues to the main character's traits in each story. After reading both stories, students will fill out a comparison chart in which they list the most important characteristics of Schatz from "A Day's Wait" and the boy from "Stolen Day." They will then use this information to write an essay comparing and contrasting these two characters.

Literary Focus
Characters and Character Traits

How do you get to know the people you meet? They don't carry around signs saying "I am kind and caring" or "I am a mean bully." You have to figure out what they are like for yourself. How do you do it? You notice their appearance. You pay attention to what they say and do. You listen to what others say about them. Then, you think about these clues and make inferences about the **character traits** they reveal. Finally, you decide what you think about them.

You do the same thing to get to know the characters in a story. In "A Day's Wait" clues in the text will help you understand the character traits of a young boy and his father.

Reading Skills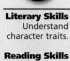
Comparing and Contrasting

The main characters in "A Day's Wait" and "Stolen Day" are both young boys who think they are sick, but each boy behaves in a different way.

In the margins of each story, you will find numbered questions. These questions will help you focus on the actions of the boys and think about their character traits. Once you have a list of each boy's actions and the traits they reveal, you will be ready to write an essay in which you show how the two boys are similar and how they are different.

SKILLS FOCUS

Literary Skills
Understand character traits.

Reading Skills
Compare and contrast characters.

Clues to Character Traits

You can get to know the characters in a story by paying attention to their:

• appearance
• actions
• words
• thoughts and feelings
• effects on other characters

Sample Character Traits

• pushy / shy
• brave / fearful
• mean / kind
• cheerful / sad
• thoughtful / careless
• selfish / generous
• confident / unsure
• serious / silly
• restless / content
• curious / bored
• sad / happy
• weak / powerful
• hardworking / lazy
• determined / easygoing

190   Collection 2 / Characters: Living Many Lives

Before You Read

To understand this story, you have to know that there are two kinds of thermometers, each using a different temperature scale. On the Celsius thermometer, used in Europe, the boiling point of water is 100 degrees. On the Fahrenheit thermometer, used in the United States, the boiling point is much higher, 212 degrees.

The events in this story really happened to Hemingway and his nine-year-old son Bumby. (In this story, Bumby is called Schatz, a German word meaning "treasure.") Hemingway and his family lived in France for many years; in this story they are back in the United States. Do the father or son in this story remind you of anyone you know?

A Day's Wait

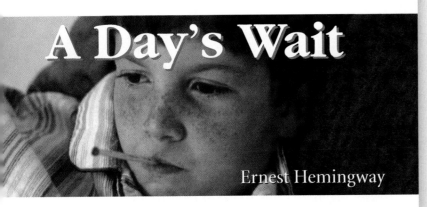

Ernest Hemingway

He came into the room to shut the windows while we were still in bed and I saw he looked ill. He was shivering, his face was white, and he walked slowly as though it ached to move.

"What's the matter, Schatz?"

"I've got a headache."

"You better go back to bed."

"No. I'm all right."

"You go to bed. I'll see you when I'm dressed."

But when I came downstairs he was dressed, sitting by the fire, looking a very sick and miserable boy of nine years. When I put my hand on his forehead I knew he had a fever.

"You go up to bed," I said, "you're sick."

"I'm all right," he said. ❶

When the doctor came he took the boy's temperature.

INFER

❶ What do the boy's words and actions so far tell you about his character?

Ⓐ

A Day's Wait   **191**

Summary ➡ *at grade level*

The story's narrator notices one morning that his nine-year-old son is ill. A doctor visits the home and notes that the boy's temperature is 102. After the doctor leaves, the boy seems strangely detached and refuses to go to sleep. Eventually he asks his father, "About what time do you think I'm going to die?" Questioned by his father, the boy reveals that while at school in France he heard that a person cannot live with a temperature over 44. The father explains the difference between the Fahrenheit and Celsius scales and tells Schatz that he is not going to die. The boy, having faced his ordeal with dignity and courage, gradually relaxes.

PRETEACHING

Selection Starter

Build background. The boy in this story is suffering from influenza, commonly known as "the flu." Students may not be aware that illnesses such as influenza and pneumonia, which are treated routinely today, often proved fatal in the past. Point out that this story takes place at a time before antibiotics had been developed.

DIRECT TEACHING

Ⓐ **Reading Skills**

Infer. [Possible responses to question 1: Schatz tries to be independent. He doesn't like to admit weakness.]

DIRECT TEACHING

A Reading Skills

? Infer. Based on Schatz's response and the father's description of Schatz, what can you infer about Schatz's character? [Possible responses: The boy is trying to act too grown-up. He is troubled by his illness, but is not showing emotion.]

"What is it?" I asked him.

"One hundred and two."

Downstairs, the doctor left three different medicines in different-colored capsules with instructions for giving them. One was to bring down the fever, another a purgative,[1] the third to overcome an acid condition. The germs of influenza can only exist in an acid condition, he explained. He seemed to know all about influenza and said there was nothing to worry about if the fever did not go above one hundred and four degrees. This was a light epidemic of flu and there was no danger if you avoided pneumonia.

Back in the room I wrote the boy's temperature down and made a note of the time to give the various capsules.

"Do you want me to read to you?"

A "All right. If you want to," said the boy. His face was very white and there were dark areas under his eyes. He lay still in the bed and seemed very detached from what was going on.

I read aloud from Howard Pyle's *Book of Pirates*; but I could see

---

1. **purgative** (pur′gə·tiv) *n.:* laxative.

DIFFERENTIATING INSTRUCTION

Learners Having Difficulty
Modeling. For students having difficulty making inferences about character, model the strategy If—Then from p. 130. At question 1, you can say, "If Schatz was willing to go upstairs to bed, then that would show he wasn't afraid to admit weakness." Encourage students to use the strategy when they are identifying character traits.

English-Language Learners
The dialogue of this story consists largely of simple words and sentences. Place students in groups of three to read the story aloud. Assign one reader who is proficient in English to each group. Have students who are learning English read the dialogue while the more proficient reader reads the narrative passages.

he was not following what I was reading.

"How do you feel, Schatz?" I asked him.

"Just the same, so far," he said.

I sat at the foot of the bed and read to myself while I waited for it to be time to give another capsule. It would have been natural for him to go to sleep, but when I looked up he was looking at the foot of the bed, looking very strangely.

"Why don't you try to go to sleep? I'll wake you up for the medicine."

"I'd rather stay awake."

After a while he said to me, "You don't have to stay in here with me, Papa, if it bothers you."

"It doesn't bother me."

"No, I mean you don't have to stay if it's going to bother you." ❷

I thought perhaps he was a little lightheaded and after giving him the prescribed capsules at eleven o'clock I went out for a while.

It was a bright, cold day, the ground covered with a sleet that had frozen so that it seemed as if all the bare trees, the bushes, the cut brush, and all the grass and the bare ground had been varnished with ice. I took the young Irish setter for a little walk up the road and along a frozen creek, but it was difficult to stand or walk on the glassy surface and the red dog slipped and slithered and I fell twice, hard, once dropping my gun and having it slide away over the ice.

We flushed a covey[2] of quail under a high clay bank with overhanging brush and I killed two as they went out of sight over the top of the bank. Some of the covey lit in trees, but most of them scattered into brush piles and it was necessary to jump on the ice-coated mounds of brush several times before they would flush. Coming out while you were poised unsteadily on the icy, springy brush, they made difficult shooting and I killed two, missed five, and started back pleased to have found a covey close to the house and happy there were so many left to find on another day. ❸

At the house they said the boy had refused to let anyone come into the room.

"You can't come in," he said. "You mustn't get what I have."

I went up to him and found him in exactly the position I had left him, white-faced, but with the tops of his cheeks flushed by the fever, staring still, as he had stared, at the foot of the bed.

---

2. **flushed a covey** (kuv′ē): frightened a small group of wild birds from their hiding place.

Comparing Literature

INFER

❷ What does the boy say that shows he is concerned about his father? **B**

INFER

❸ The father goes hunting and enjoys himself while his son is sick. What does this action reveal about the father's **character**? **D**

B Reading Skills

Infer. [Possible response to question 2: He tells his father that he doesn't need to stay if it bothers him.]

C English-Language Learners

Irregular verbs. Point out that the verb *frozen* is the past participle of the verb *freeze*, and that *freeze* is irregular because its past and past participle tenses (*froze*, *frozen*) are not formed by adding *–d* or *–ed*.

D Reading Skills

Infer. [Possible responses to question 3: He is unfazed by his son's illness because it is minor. He is tough and determined.]

Special Education Students

For lessons designed for special education students, see *Holt Reading Solutions*.

Advanced Learners

Enrichment. Tell students that in this story Hemingway takes only six pages to describe the most frightening day in a young boy's life. The boy's feelings are hinted at and briefly explained but are never described in detail.

Activity. Have students debate whether Hemingway's method of hinting at strong emotions is more effective or less effective than if he had provided detailed descriptions of the character's inner turmoil. Which style of writing do students prefer, and why?

DIRECT TEACHING

A Literary Focus

❓ **Character.** What do you learn about the characters from this exchange? [Possible response: The father minimizes the temperature because he wants to ease his son's fears. The son is fearful of something but unwilling to share what it is.]

B Reading Skills

Infer. [Possible responses to question 4: He showed bravery in the face of what he thought were dire circumstances. He showed consideration for his father and others around him.]

C Reading Skills

❓ **Infer.** Why do you think that realizing he is not going to die has this effect on the boy? [Possible responses: The boy has no more strength and no longer needs to be brave. The boy is relieved to be alive and is finally releasing the anxiety he felt.]

D Reading Skills

Compare and contrast. [Possible responses to question 5: The boy was hiding his feelings about important things, but now he is letting his feelings about insignificant things show. He was behaving as he thought an adult would early in the story, but now he is behaving like a child.]

INFER

❹ Think about what Schatz has said and done so far. What **character traits** does he show?

COMPARE AND CONTRAST

❺ How does Schatz's behavior at the end of the story differ from his behavior at the beginning?

I took his temperature.

"What is it?"

"Something like a hundred," I said. It was one hundred and two and four tenths.

"It was a hundred and two," he said.

"Who said so?"

"The doctor."

"Your temperature is all right," I said. "It's nothing to worry about."

"I don't worry," he said, "but I can't keep from thinking."

"Don't think," I said. "Just take it easy."

"I'm taking it easy," he said and looked straight ahead. He was evidently holding tight onto himself about something.

"Take this with water."

"Do you think it will do any good?"

"Of course it will."

I sat down and opened the *Pirate* book and commenced to read, but I could see he was not following, so I stopped.

"About what time do you think I'm going to die?" he asked. ❹

"What?"

"About how long will it be before I die?"

"You aren't going to die. What's the matter with you?"

"Oh, yes, I am. I heard him say a hundred and two."

"People don't die with a fever of one hundred and two. That's a silly way to talk."

"I know they do. At school in France the boys told me you can't live with forty-four degrees. I've got a hundred and two."

He had been waiting to die all day, ever since nine o'clock in the morning.

"You poor Schatz," I said. "Poor old Schatz. It's like miles and kilometers. You aren't going to die. That's a different thermometer. On that thermometer thirty-seven is normal. On this kind it's ninety-eight."

"Are you sure?"

"Absolutely," I said. "It's like miles and kilometers. You know, like how many kilometers we make when we do seventy miles in the car?"

"Oh," he said.

But his gaze at the foot of the bed relaxed slowly. The hold over himself relaxed too, finally, and the next day it was very slack and he cried very easily at little things that were of no importance. ❺

194   Collection 2 / Characters: Living Many Lives

DEVELOPING FLUENCY

Group students in pairs, and have them read the dialogue in which Schatz's misunderstanding is cleared up, beginning with "'What is it?'" on p. 194. Make sure students capture Schatz's worry and the father's concern in their speech.

(**PAIRED**)

Meet the Writer

Ernest Hemingway

Grace Under Pressure

Ernest Hemingway (1899–1961) was born in Oak Park, Illinois. He spent his first seventeen summers in northern Michigan, where his father introduced him to hunting and fishing. In high school, Hemingway boxed and played football, but he also wrote poetry, stories, and the gossip column for his school newspaper.

When the United States entered World War I, Hemingway volunteered and became an American ambulance driver in Italy. He was nineteen when a bomb landed three feet away and filled his right leg with 227 pieces of shrapnel.

After returning from the war, Hemingway wrote many stories and novels that portray men who show "grace under pressure"—that is, calm courage in the face of great danger. In his own life, Hemingway relentlessly pursued excitement and danger. He hunted and fished all over the world, surviving several plane crashes and the fierce charges of the large animals he loved to hunt.

In "A Day's Wait," Hemingway again explores the theme of grace under pressure. This time he focuses on a young boy who believes he is about to die. The silences and sparse dialogue in the story reflect the belief of Hemingway's heroes that they should keep a tight rein on their fears and other emotions.

Hemingway worked hard to keep up his image of toughness, but his son Gregory remembers a more human side:

> 66 He told me about the times he'd been scared as a boy, how he used to dream about a furry monster who would grow *taller and taller* every night and then, just as it was about to eat him, would jump over the fence. He said fear was perfectly natural and nothing to be ashamed of. 99

Hemingway won the Nobel Prize in literature in 1954. Today he is regarded as one of the great writers of the twentieth century.

Meet the Writer

Students probably noticed that Hemingway uses very few words to get his point across. He once stated his writing philosophy by saying, "All you have to do is write one true sentence. Write the truest sentence that you know." He added that it should be a simple declarative sentence, without any "ornamental language," based on something from the author's personal experience.

DIFFERENTIATING INSTRUCTION

Advanced Learners

Enrichment. After students have read the story, have them work in small groups. Ask them to discuss the personal qualities of the boy—his self-control, his courage, his sensitivity to his father's feelings. Then have them make a list of characters from books, movies, or television shows who also display these qualities. Have them share their ideas with classmates.

SMALL GROUP

After You Read

First Thoughts

1. Possible Answers
   - If I were Schatz and thought I was about to die, I would <u>cry or ask for help.</u>
   - If I were Papa and saw the way Schatz looked and acted, I would <u>ask Schatz what was worrying him.</u>

Thinking Critically

2. Schatz is serious and responsible. He is independent.

3. Possible answers: Schatz may behave this way to try to please his father or be like him. Some students may say it shows real heroism and courage. Others may feel that he should have shared his fears with his father.

4. Possible answers: The title refers to the boy's waiting all day for death. The title refers to the father's wait to find out why Schatz is behaving strangely.

Comparing Literature

5. Possible details in the story: *Actions*—Schatz tries to take care of himself. He refuses to let anyone into his room. *Words*—"You don't have to stay in here with me, Papa, if it bothers you." "No, I'm all right." *Thoughts and feelings*—He thinks he's going to die. He is worried, but keeps his feelings to himself. *Effects on others*—Schatz's father worries about him. Possible character traits: *Actions*—independence. *Words*—concern for others. *Thoughts and feelings*—bravery. *Effects on others*—courage; sensitivity.

After You Read · "A Day's Wait"

First Thoughts

1. Finish these sentences:
   - If I were Schatz and thought I was about to die, I would . . .
   - If I were Papa and saw the way Schatz looked and acted, I would . . .

Thinking Critically

2. Although Schatz is sick, he gets up, closes the windows in his parents' room, and then gets dressed. What **character traits** do these actions reveal?

3. Why would a young boy behave so heroically in the face of death? Do you think his behavior is typical? Discuss your answer with a partner.

4. Explain the title of this story.

Comparing Literature

5. After you read the next story, you will write an essay comparing and contrasting the main characters of the two stories. You can start to plan your essay by filling out a chart like the one below. List details in the story that tell you about Schatz. Then, decide what **character traits** the details reveal. The list of traits on page 190 may help you decide, or you can think of other traits on your own.

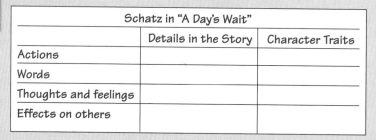

Schatz in "A Day's Wait"		
	Details in the Story	Character Traits
Actions		
Words		
Thoughts and feelings		
Effects on others		

go.hrw.com

INTERNET
Projects and
Activities

Keyword: LE5 7-2

SKILLS FOCUS

Literary Skills
Analyze character traits.

Reading Skills
Compare and contrast characters.

Reading Check

Go back through "A Day's Wait," and fill in a story map like the one below.

Title:

Author:

Characters:

Conflict:

Resolution:

Setting:

Reading Check

Title—"A Day's Wait"

Author—Ernest Hemingway

Characters—Schatz; Papa

Conflict—Schatz thinks he is going to die of a high fever.

Resolution—Papa explains that there are two types of thermometers.

Setting—Papa's house and outdoors

Before You Read

This story is set in a small town in the Midwest about a century ago. Some customs may have changed since then, but people's emotions and their motives, or reasons, for doing what they do have stayed pretty much the same. What motivates the narrator in this story to say he is sick?

Comparing
Literature

Stolen Day

Sherwood Anderson

I t must be that all children are actors. The whole thing started with a boy on our street named Walter, who had inflammatory rheumatism.[1] That's what they called it. He didn't have to go to school.

Still he could walk about. He could go fishing in the creek or the waterworks pond. There was a place up at the pond where in the spring the water came tumbling over the dam and formed a deep pool. It was a good place. Sometimes you could get some good big ones there.

I went down that way on my way to school one spring morning. It was out of my way but I wanted to see if Walter was there.

He was, inflammatory rheumatism and all. There he was, sitting with a fish pole in his hand. He had been able to walk down there all right.

It was then that my own legs began to hurt. My back too. I went on to school but, at the recess time, I began to cry. I did it when the teacher, Sarah Suggett, had come out into the schoolhouse yard. ❶

She came right over to me.

"I ache all over," I said. I did, too.

I kept on crying and it worked all right.

"You'd better go on home," she said.

So I went. I limped painfully away. I kept on limping until I got out of the schoolhouse street.

---

1. **inflammatory rheumatism** (ro͞o′mə•tiz′əm): rheumatic fever, a disease characterized by pain in the joints, fever, and inflammation of the heart.

INFER

❶ Why does the narrator of this story decide he has inflammatory rheumatism?

A

Summary   *at grade level*

While he is on his way to school, the narrator notices Walter, a boy from his street, fishing. Although Walter has inflammatory rheumatism, the narrator thinks he's lucky because he can fish during the day rather than attend school. Later, the boy begins to convince himself he has developed symptoms of the disease and is sent home from school. He explains to his mother that he is achy, but doesn't explicitly say that he has the disease. Soon after he gets home, he feels well enough to go fishing. At the fishing hole, he catches a huge carp and brings it home for the family to eat. At dinner that night, he announces that he has inflammatory rheumatism. The family laugh at him, and he runs upstairs, humiliated.

PRETEACHING

Selection Starter

Motivate. Ask students to think of a time when they avoided a responsibility at home. Did they make up an excuse to avoid doing their chores? Ask students to think of the most far-fetched excuse they've ever used to avoid a responsibility.

DIRECT TEACHING

A Reading Skills

Infer. [Possible response to question 1: He wants to spend the day fishing, like Walter. He thinks if he has the same disease as Walter, he will be able to do the same things.]

A Reading Skills

❓ Infer. Why does the narrator try to seek Walter out? [Possible response: He is looking for Walter to tell him what the actual symptoms of inflammatory rheumatism are.] **Based on this reason, what can you infer about his character?** [Possible responses: He is impulsive. He uses the disease as an excuse even though he doesn't know how severe it may be.]

VIEWING THE ART

Andrew Wyeth (1917–   ) is a popular painter who distinguished himself by his restrained use of watercolors. He was frequently ill as a child and was taught at home by his father, Newell Convers Wyeth, a distinguished illustrator. Another one of Wyeth's works appears on page 202.

Activity. Have students look closely at the boy's facial expression in the painting. What sorts of feelings does the boy's face convey? Are the feelings similar to or different from the narrator's feelings in the story? [Possible response: The boy in the painting seems thoughtful and somber; his expression may reflect sadness, disappointment, or wounded pride, like that of the narrator.]

Albert's Son by Andrew Wyeth.

Tempera on panel, 1959, © Andrew Wyeth.

Then I felt better. I still had inflammatory rheumatism pretty bad but I could get along better.

I must have done some thinking on the way home.

"I'd better not say I have inflammatory rheumatism," I decided. "Maybe if you've got that you swell up."

I thought I'd better go around to where Walter was and ask him about that, so I did—but he wasn't there.

DIFFERENTIATING INSTRUCTION

Learners Having Difficulty
To help learners having difficulty inferring the narrator's character traits, have them set up a two column chart. Have them label the first column *Actions* and the second column *Inference*. As they read the story, have them fill out the first column with the narrator's actions and the second column with inferences on his character based on the actions.

English-Language Learners
Make sure English-language learners are aware of the clues Anderson gives that the narrator is not actually ill. Begin by pointing out that he first complains about his soreness while he is in school but says he feels better as soon as he leaves the schoolyard. Ask students to keep track of the circumstances in which the boy says he's sick and those in which he says he's better.

"They must not be biting today," I thought.

I had a feeling that, if I said I had inflammatory rheumatism, Mother or my brothers and my sister Stella might laugh. They did laugh at me pretty often and I didn't like it at all. ❷

"Just the same," I said to myself, "I have got it." I began to hurt and ache again.

I went home and sat on the front steps of our house. I sat there a long time. There wasn't anyone at home but Mother and the two little ones. Ray would have been four or five then and Earl might have been three.

It was Earl who saw me there. I had got tired sitting and was lying on the porch. Earl was always a quiet, solemn little fellow.

He must have said something to Mother for presently she came.

"What's the matter with you? Why aren't you in school?" she asked.

I came pretty near telling her right out that I had inflammatory rheumatism but I thought I'd better not. Mother and Father had been speaking of Walter's case at the table just the day before. "It affects the heart," Father had said. That frightened me when I thought of it. "I might die," I thought. "I might just suddenly die right here; my heart might stop beating."

On the day before I had been running a race with my brother Irve. We were up at the fairgrounds after school and there was a half-mile track.

"I'll bet you can't run a half-mile," he said. "I bet you I could beat you running clear around the track."

And so we did it and I beat him, but afterwards my heart did seem to beat pretty hard. I remembered that lying there on the porch. "It's a wonder, with my inflammatory rheumatism and all, I didn't just drop down dead," I thought. The thought frightened me a lot. I ached worse than ever.

"I ache, Ma," I said. "I just ache."

She made me go in the house and upstairs and get into bed.

It wasn't so good. It was spring. I was up there for perhaps an hour, maybe two, and then I felt better.

I got up and went downstairs. "I feel better, Ma," I said. ❸

Mother said she was glad. She was pretty busy that day and hadn't paid much attention to me. She had made me get into bed upstairs and then hadn't even come up to see how I was.

I didn't think much of that when I was up there but when I got

INFER ⟧ B

❷ What has the narrator revealed about his **character** so far?

COMPARE AND CONTRAST

❸ How does Schatz in "A Day's Wait" respond to his illness? How does this boy respond? ⟧ E

DIRECT TEACHING

B Reading Skills

Infer. [Possible responses to question 2: He has tried to deceive his family in the past; he is able to convince himself that his lies are actually true.]

C Comparing Literature

❓ **Compare characters.** What is your first impression of the boy's mother? In what ways does she seem different from the father in "A Day's Wait"? [Possible responses: She seems suspicious of the boy's reasons for being home. She does not seem concerned about the boy's illness. Schatz's father, on the other hand, shows more concern when Schatz is sick.]

D Reading Skills

❓ **Cause and effect.** What else could have caused the boy's heart rate to increase? [Possible responses: His heart rate increased probably because he ran a long distance.]

E Reading Skills

Compare and contrast. [Possible responses to question 3: Schatz doesn't share how he actually feels with anyone once it's determined he's sick. The boy in "Stolen Day" is constantly trying to convince himself and others that he is feeling ill.]

Special Education Students
For lessons designed for special education students, see *Holt Reading Solutions*.

Advanced Learners
Enrichment. Use the following activity to help advanced learners compare and contrast the reactions and motivations of characters from different historical eras. Ask students to think of stories such as Aesop's "The Boy Who Cried Wolf" in which

children's claims are disbelieved (sometimes justifiably) by adults.

Activity. Have students read "The Boy Who Cried Wolf." Then have them write essays in which they compare the child in that fable with the narrator of "Stolen Day." How are the characters similar or different? What is the basis of the adults' reactions?

DIRECT TEACHING

Ⓐ Reading Skills

Compare and contrast. [Possible responses to question 4: The boy is upset because he thinks he isn't getting enough attention from his mother. Schatz, on the other hand, doesn't want his father to be concerned about his illness.]

Ⓑ Literary Focus

❓ **Motivation.** Besides his desire to go fishing, what motivation does the boy have for saying he is sick? [Possible response: The boy was hoping he would get attention from his mom by saying he was sick.]

Ⓒ Literary Focus

❓ **Flashback.** Make sure students realize that this passage is a flashback, an interruption of the action of the story to tell of an event that occurred in the past. How does the narrator misinterpret his mother's reaction to the drowning of the Wyatt child? [Possible responses: He doesn't understand the nature of death. He doesn't understand that his mother is not acting out of a particular love for the Wyatt child.]

COMPARE AND CONTRAST

❹ How does the boy Ⓐ feel about his mother's reaction to his illness? How did Schatz in "A Day's Wait" feel about his father?

---

downstairs where she was, and when, after I had said I felt better and she only said she was glad and went right on with her work, I began to ache again.

I thought, "I'll bet I die of it. I bet I do."

I went out to the front porch and sat down. I was pretty sore at Mother.

"If she really knew the truth, that I have the inflammatory rheumatism and I may just drop down dead any time, I'll bet she wouldn't care about that either," I thought. ❹

I was getting more and more angry the more thinking I did.

"I know what I'm going to do," I thought; "I'm going to go fishing."

I thought that, feeling the way I did, I might be sitting on the high bank just above the deep pool where the water went over the dam, and suddenly my heart would stop beating.

And then, of course, I'd pitch forward, over the bank into the Ⓑ pool and, if I wasn't dead when I hit the water, I'd drown sure.

They would all come home to supper and they'd miss me.

"But where is he?"

Then Mother would remember that I'd come home from school aching.

She'd go upstairs and I wouldn't be there. One day during the year before, there was a child got drowned in a spring. It was one of the Wyatt children.

Right down at the end of the street there was a spring under a birch tree and there had been a barrel sunk in the ground.

Everyone had always been saying the spring ought to be kept covered, but it wasn't.

Ⓒ So the Wyatt child went down there, played around alone, and fell in and got drowned.

Mother was the one who had found the drowned child. She had gone to get a pail of water and there the child was, drowned and dead.

This had been in the evening when we were all at home, and Mother had come running up the street with the dead, dripping child in her arms. She was making for the Wyatt house as hard as she could run, and she was pale.

She had a terrible look on her face, I remembered then.

"So," I thought, "they'll miss me and there'll be a search made. Very likely there'll be someone who has seen me sitting by the pond fishing, and there'll be a big alarm and all the town will turn out and they'll drag the pond."

DEVELOPING FLUENCY

Activity. The informal language and style of this selection make it a good choice for students to read aloud. You can ask students to prepare sections of the story for oral reading. When they read, remind them to use a relaxed tone that conveys the narrator's personality.

Ask students to listen as the readers present the story, and then hold a discussion at the story's conclusion. Find out if students were able to follow the action of the story and whether they could discern the narrator's motivation as they listened.

WHOLE CLASS

I was having a grand time, having died. Maybe, after they found me and had got me out of the deep pool, Mother would grab me up in her arms and run home with me as she had run with the Wyatt child. **⑤**

I got up from the porch and went around the house. I got my fishing pole and lit out for the pool below the dam. Mother was busy—she always was—and didn't see me go. When I got there I thought I'd better not sit too near the edge of the high bank.

By this time I didn't ache hardly at all, but I thought.

"With inflammatory rheumatism you can't tell," I thought.

"It probably comes and goes," I thought.

"Walter has it and he goes fishing," I thought.

I had got my line into the pool and suddenly I got a bite. It was a regular whopper. I knew that. I'd never had a bite like that. I knew what it was. It was one of Mr. Fenn's big carp.

Mr. Fenn was a man who had a big pond of his own. He sold ice in the summer and the pond was to make the ice. He had bought some big carp and put them into his pond and then, earlier in the spring when there was a freshet,[2] his dam had gone out.

So the carp had got into our creek and one or two big ones had been caught—but none of them by a boy like me.

The carp was pulling and I was pulling and I was afraid he'd

---

2. **freshet** *n.:* a sudden overflowing of a stream caused by a heavy rain or a thaw.

COMPARE AND CONTRAST

⑤ How is this boy's response to dying different from Schatz's response? **D**

E

D **Reading Skills**
Compare and contrast. [Possible responses to question 5: While Schatz is genuinely fearful of death, this boy is looking forward to dying because of the attention he'd receive. This boy doesn't realize the consequences of death the way Schatz does.]

E **English-Language Learners**
Idioms. Make sure students are clear on the meaning of the word *whopper* in this sentence. Some students may be confused (especially in light of the narrator's behavior) because *whopper* is sometimes defined as "an outrageous lie or exaggeration." Clarify to students that *whopper* in this context means "something exceptionally large."

DIRECT TEACHING

A **Learners Having Difficulty**

❓ **Find details.** Remind students of the episode earlier in the story where the narrator ran half a mile. How is the narrator's account of that event different from his account of this event? [Possible responses: Earlier in the story, the narrator thought he was ill when his heart rate sped up. Now he is too caught up in the moment to notice. Before, the boy was trying to think of symptoms for inflammatory rheumatism so that he could go fishing, but now that he's fishing, he is not aware of feeling sick.]

B **Reading Skills**

Infer. [Possible responses to question 6: The boy is seen as a hero by his family and neighbors because he has caught a huge fish. He feels like a hero because he's receiving attention.]

End of Olson's (1969) by Andrew Wyeth. Tempera on panel.

© Andrew Wyeth.

break my line, so I just tumbled down the high bank, holding onto the line, and got right into the pool. We had it out, there in the pool. We struggled. We wrestled. Then I got a hand under his gills and got him out.

A He was a big one all right. He was nearly half as big as I was myself. I had him on the bank and I kept one hand under his gills and I ran.

I never ran so hard in my life. He was slippery, and now and then he wriggled out of my arms; once I stumbled and fell on him, but I got him home.

So there it was. I was a big hero that day. Mother got a washtub and filled it with water. She put the fish in it and all the neighbors came to look. I got into dry clothes and went down to supper—and then I made a break that spoiled my day. ❻

There we were, all of us, at the table, and suddenly Father asked what had been the matter with me at school. He had met the teacher, Sarah Suggett, on the street and she had told him how I had become ill.

"What was the matter with you?" Father asked, and before I thought what I was saying I let it out.

INFER

B ❻ Why do the boy's family and neighbors see him as a hero?

"I had the inflammatory rheumatism," I said—and a shout went up. It made me sick to hear them, the way they all laughed.

It brought back all the aching again, and like a fool I began to cry.

"Well, I have got it—I have, I have," I cried, and I got up from the table and ran upstairs.

I stayed there until Mother came up. I knew it would be a long time before I heard the last of the inflammatory rheumatism. I was sick all right, but the aching I now had wasn't in my legs or in my back. **❼**

Comparing Literature

INFER

❼ What is the aching the narrator feels now?

Meet the Writer

Sherwood Anderson

A Talented Storyteller

Sherwood Anderson (1876–1941) grew up in Clyde, Ohio, a small town that played a major role in many of his stories. He attended school infrequently while working full time to help provide for his family. After his mother died, Anderson went to Chicago, where he worked as a laborer, until he went off to fight in the Spanish-American War.

Anderson's talent as a storyteller emerged later in life while he was running his own business, a manufacturing company. He eventually left the business to focus on writing and received encouragement from such noted writers as Carl Sandburg and Vachel Lindsay (poems by Sandburg and Lindsay appear on pages 328, 438, and 607). Anderson developed a straightforward writing style that changed the very nature of the short story, influencing a younger generation of writers. Anderson offered his own support to writers of this younger generation, including Ernest Hemingway. In fact, Anderson was instrumental in getting Hemingway's first novel published.

C **Comparing Literature**

❓ Compare characters. How is the boy's behavior similar to Schatz's at the conclusion of "A Day's Wait"? [Possible response: Both boys cry over things others would probably consider unimportant.] **Is your reaction to this boy's crying similar to or different from your reaction to Schatz's crying?** [Possible responses: It is easier to sympathize with Schatz because he has been through an ordeal, whereas the other boy was only trying to get attention. Schatz's crying is more disappointing than the other boy's because Schatz has been brave throughout the story.]

D **Reading Skills**

Infer. [Possible responses to question 7: The aching the boy feels is humiliation over his family's laughing at him. He feels anger and disappointment because he's been embarrassed on a day when he finally got the attention he desired.]

Meet the Writer

Before becoming a full-time writer, Sherwood Anderson ran a manufacturing company in Ohio. In 1912, Anderson made a dramatic exit from the company. He later published an account of his departure from the business world in an article titled "When I Left Business for Literature" that became legendary. In it, Anderson stated that he had made a clear decision to forgo financial success in favor of a career in writing. As a result, some writers viewed Anderson as a heroic figure who chose art over materialism.

Advanced Learners

Enrichment. Part of the power behind Anderson's stories lies in his description of the Ohio setting he was familiar with throughout his life. Like Anderson, many writers have used their hometowns as a source of inspiration for works of fiction. **Activity.** Ask students to list at least five details about their hometown that make it unique. Details can include places they like to visit or people they've met. Then, have them use these details as the basis for writing a brief anecdote about an incident in their hometown. Remind students to add details that make the people and places they're writing about distinctive.

After You Read

First Thoughts

1. Possible answers:
   - The part I liked best about this story was the scene in which the boy catches the fish.
   - I am confused about whether or not the boy is actually sick.

Thinking Critically

2. Walter is able to miss school and spend his days fishing because he is sick, so the narrator begins to feel sick so that he can go fishing too.
3. He gets upset when his mother doesn't check on him after he's come home from school. He dwells on the attention his mother paid to the Wyatt child who drowned in the spring.
4. The family laughs because they know the boy is lying. He's probably tried similar ways to get attention before.
5. His pride is hurt by his family's laughter, so he wants to save face.
6. The narrator has "stolen" a day from his usual routine of going to school by pretending he is sick and going fishing.

Comparing Literature

7. Possible details in the story:
   Actions—The boy leaves school because he says he's sick. He goes fishing during the day. *Words*—"'I ache, Ma. I just ache.'" "'Well, I have got it—I have, I have.'" *Thoughts and feelings*—"I was pretty sore at Mother." "'I may just drop down dead anytime, I'll bet she wouldn't care about that either.'" *Effects on others*—His family laugh at him when he tells them he has inflammatory rheumatism.
   Possible character traits: *Actions*—dishonest. *Words*—self-absorbed. *Thoughts and feelings*—eager for attention. *Effects on others*—overly sensitive; lonely.

First Thoughts

1. Finish these sentences:
   - The part I liked best about this story was . . .
   - I am confused about . . .

Thinking Critically

2. Why do you think the narrator starts to feel sick after he sees Walter fishing at the pond?
3. What does the narrator say and do that shows he wants his mother to pay more attention to him?
4. Why do you think the narrator's family laughs at him when he says he has inflammatory rheumatism?
5. Why does the narrator insist that he really *is* sick?
6. Explain the title of this story.

Comparing Literature

7. Add information on the narrator of "Stolen Day" to the chart below. Then, use your chart as you prepare to write the comparison-contrast essay on the next page.

	The Boy in "Stolen Day"	
	Details in the Story	Character Traits
Actions		
Words		
Thoughts and feelings		
Effects on others		

SKILLS FOCUS

Literary Skills
Analyze character traits.

Reading Skills
Compare and contrast characters.

Reading Check

Summarize this story by retelling it to a partner. Begin with the **title** and **author**. Next, explain who the **main character** is, and describe the central **conflict** or problem. Then, list the **main events** in the order in which they occur. Finally, tell what you liked or didn't like about the story. When you finish, ask your partner if you left out any important details.

Reading Check

Possible retelling: In "Stolen Day" by Sherwood Anderson, a boy wishes that he could go fishing rather than be in school when he sees another boy fishing during school hours. When he gets to school, he claims that he is ill and is sent home. Once home awhile, he feels better and goes fishing. He catches a massive carp, which he brings home to his family, much to their delight. At dinner, he is asked why he wasn't in school. He tells them he has inflammatory rheumatism. Upon hearing this, his family bursts into laughter. He runs upstairs, ashamed, aching now with humiliation and disappointment.

Writing a Comparison-Contrast Essay

Assignment

Write an essay comparing two characters: Schatz in "A Day's Wait" and the boy in "Stolen Day." Begin planning your essay by referring to the charts you completed after you read the stories. Use the information from those charts to fill in the comparison chart below. This chart will help you identify similarities and differences between the two characters.

Use the workshop on writing a Comparison-Contrast Essay, pages 772–777, for help with this assignment.

	Schatz in "A Day's Wait"		The Boy in "Stolen Day"	
	Story Details	Character Traits	Story Details	Character Traits
Actions				
Words				
Thoughts and feelings				
Effects on others				

Organize your essay in one of these two ways:

1. Organize the essay by character traits. In your first paragraph you might discuss three traits the boys have in common. In your second paragraph you might discuss at least one way in which the boys are different. Cite details illustrating the traits you see in each character.

2. You can organize your essay by the characters. For example, you might focus on Schatz and his character traits in your first paragraph and then do the same for the boy in "Stolen Day" in your next paragraph. Cite specific details from the stories to support your analysis of each character. Be sure to show how the boys are alike and how they are different.

At the end of your essay, tell which character you liked more, and explain why. Did you identify with either character? Did either boy remind you of someone you know? Use details from the stories to explain your responses.

SKILLS FOCUS

Writing Skills
Write a comparison-contrast essay.

Writing a Comparison-Contrast Essay

Strategy Tip

Using transitional words. If students choose to organize their essay by comparing characters, tell them they need to remind the reader of the points they made in the first paragraph as they write the second paragraph. This will make their comparisons clearer. Ask students to think of transitional words or phrases that will tie together their points about Schatz and the narrator of "Stolen Day." [Possible responses: *but; however; similarly; on the other hand.*]

Evaluation Criteria

A successful comparison-contrast essay
- opens with a brief introduction naming both stories and their authors
- is unified by one clear thesis statement
- is effectively organized by character (block) or character trait (point by point)
- analyzes similarities as well as differences
- includes details about both characters
- concludes with a personal response
- is free of major errors in grammar, usage, and mechanics

DIFFERENTIATING INSTRUCTION

Learners Having Difficulty
Modeling. To help students having difficulty comparing characters, draw two large boxes on the board next to one another. Label the first box *Schatz in "A Day's Wait"* and the second *The Boy in "Stolen Day."* In the second box, write "Unlike Schatz, the narrator of 'Stolen Day' . . ." Tell students to use this type of transition, which keeps both subjects in the reader's mind. Encourage students to use a chart like this one as they are preparing to write their essay.

OVERVIEW

The literature in *No Questions Asked* gives students the chance to read a selection for enjoyment and enrichment as they further explore the themes in this collection. The annotation questions in the margins of the Teacher's Edition should be considered optional. No follow-up questions will appear after the selection.

Summary 🔁 *at grade level*

In this chapter from her auto-biography, Fritz relates how she longs to be in America. She feels out of place in both the British school she attends and the Chinese community, Hankow, in which she lives. When Ian Forbes, the school bully, threatens Jean if she refuses to sing "God Save the King," Jean plays hooky for a day and explores her Chinese neighborhood. At home, she is scolded for cutting school. Later, her father helps her solve her dilemma at school by telling her to use the words to "My Country 'Tis of Thee" while her British schoolmates sing "God Save the King" to the same melody.

PRETEACHING

Selection Starter

Motivate. Ask students to think about how they would feel if they had to live in a foreign country. Have them list three reasons why they might like to move to another country and three reasons why they'd prefer to stay in the United States.

from Homesick

Jean Fritz

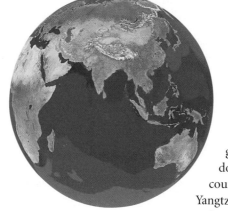

In my father's study there was a large globe with all the countries of the world running around it. I could put my finger on the exact spot where I was and had been ever since I'd been born. And I was on the wrong side of the globe. I was in China in a city named Hankow, a dot on a crooked line that seemed to break the country right in two. The line was really the Yangtze River, but who would know by looking at a map what the Yangtze River really was?

Orange-brown, muddy mustard colored. And wide, wide, wide. With a river smell that was old and came all the way up from the bottom. Sometimes old women knelt on the riverbank, begging the River God to return a son or grandson who may have drowned. They would wail and beat the earth to make the River God pay attention, but I knew how busy the River God must be. All those people on the Yangtze River! Coolies[1] hauling water. Women washing clothes. Houseboats swarming with old people and young, chickens and pigs. Big crooked-sailed junks[2] with eyes painted on their prows so they could see where they were going. I loved the Yangtze River, but of course, I belonged on the other side of the world. In America, with my grandmother.

---

1. **coolies** *n.:* workers who do heavy work for little pay. English-speakers visiting the East took this name from the Hindi word *qulī*, meaning "hired servant."
2. **junks** *n.:* Chinese ships with flat bottoms and square sails.

DIFFERENTIATING INSTRUCTION

Learners Having Difficulty
Characterization. Some students may have difficulty understanding characterization. Explain to students that authors show what a character is like by desribing a character's appearance, actions, thoughts, and speech.
Activity. Have students create a four-column table in their notebooks and label the first column *Appearance;* the second, *Actions;* the third, *Thoughts;* and the fourth, *Speech.* They can write Jean's name above the table. Then, as students read the story, ask them to fill in the appropriate columns with facts about Jean from the story.

English-Language Learners
Reinforce the skill of comparing and contrasting character traits by having students draw a Venn diagram. Have students label one circle *Jean* and the other circle *Ian.* Then, have them note characteristics of

Twenty-five fluffy little yellow chicks hatched from our eggs today, my grandmother wrote.

I wrote my grand-mother that I had watched a Chinese magician swallow three yards of fire.

The trouble with living on the wrong side of the world was that I didn't feel like a *real* American.

For instance. I could never be president of the United States. I didn't want to be president; I wanted to be a writer. Still, why should there be a *law* saying that only a person born in the United States could be president?[3] It was as if I wouldn't be American enough.

Actually, I was American every minute of the day, especially during school hours. I went to a British school and every morning we sang "God Save the King." Of course the British children loved singing about their gracious king. Ian Forbes stuck out his chest and sang as if he were saving the king all by himself. Everyone sang. Even Gina Boss, who was Italian. And Vera Sebastian, who was so Russian she dressed the way Russian girls did long ago before the Revolution,[4] when her family had to run away to keep from being killed.

But I wasn't Vera Sebastian. I asked my mother to write an excuse so I wouldn't have to sing, but she wouldn't do it. "When in Rome," she said, "do as the Romans do." What she meant was, "Don't make trouble. Just sing."

So for a long time I did. I sang with my fingers crossed but still I felt like a traitor.

Then one day I thought: If my mother and father were really and truly in Rome, they wouldn't do what the Romans did at all. They'd probably try to get the Romans to do what *they* did, just as they were trying to teach the Chinese to do what Americans did. (My mother even gave classes in American manners.)

So that day I quit singing. I kept my mouth locked tight against the king of England. Our teacher, Miss Williams, didn't notice at first. She stood in front of the room, using a ruler for a baton, striking each syllable so hard it was as if she were making up for the times she had nothing to strike.

---

3. This is not a fact. The U.S. Constitution states only that a presidential candidate must be a "natural-born" U.S. citizen. This term applies to citizens born in the United States and its territories. But no law or court case has yet decided whether "natural-born" also describes children born to U.S. citizens in other countries.
4. **Revolution:** In 1917, a revolution drove the czars (emperors) and other nobility from power, and Russia became the first nation to set up a Communist government.

A **Literary Focus**

❓ Theme. Why does Jean include excerpts from her letters in her autobiography? [Possible responses: She wants to illustrate a contrast between Chinese and American cultures. She wants to give readers a glimpse of how she imagined life in the United States.]

B **Reading Skills**

❓ Distinguish fact from opinion. Why is this statement an opinion, not a fact? [Possible response: It states Jean's feelings about being an American; this statement cannot be proved true or false.]

C **Literary Focus**

❓ Character. What does Jean's decision not to sing "God Save the King" say about her character? [Possible responses: She has pride in her country. She is principled and does what she believes is right.]

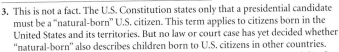

each character as they read. What traits do they have in common? How are they different?

Advanced Learners
Acceleration. You can use the following activity to help students compare and contrast the reactions of characters from different historical eras confronting similar conflicts.

Activity. Point out to students that the two main characters in the story are in conflict. Ian is trying to force Jean to do something that she doesn't want to do. Ask students whether they've encountered any characters confronted with similar situations in television shows or movies they've seen. Did those characters confront the bully? How did those situations resolve themselves? Ask students to be specific in their explanations.

A Reading Skills

❓ Infer. What do you think the writer means when she describes Vera as "someone who had been dropped out of a history book"? [Possible response: The writer thinks Vera is old-fashioned because of the way she acts and dresses.]

(Miss Williams was pinch-faced and bossy. Sometimes I wondered what had ever made her come to China. "Maybe to try and catch a husband," my mother said.

A husband! Miss Williams!)

"Make him vic-tor-i-ous," the class sang. It was on the strike of "vic" that Miss Williams noticed. Her eyes lighted on my mouth and when we sat down, she pointed her ruler at me.

"Is there something wrong with your voice today, Jean?" she asked.

"No, Miss Williams."

"You weren't singing."

"No, Miss Williams. It is not my national anthem."

"It is the national anthem we sing here," she snapped. "You have always sung. Even Vera sings it."

I looked at Vera with the big blue bow tied on the top of her head. Usually I felt sorry for her but not today. At recess I might even untie that bow, I thought. Just give it a yank. But if I'd been smart, I wouldn't have been looking at Vera. I would have been looking at Ian Forbes and I would have known that no matter what Miss Williams said, I wasn't through with the king of England.

Recess at the British School was nothing I looked forward to. Every day we played a game called prisoner's base, which was all running and shouting and shoving and catching. I hated the game, yet everyone played except Vera Sebastian. She sat on the sidelines under her blue bow like someone who had been dropped out of a history book. By recess I had forgotten my plans for that bow. While everyone was getting ready for the game, I was as usual trying to look as if I didn't care if I was the last one picked for a team or not. I was leaning against the high stone wall that ran around the schoolyard. I was looking up at a little white cloud skittering across the sky when all at once someone tramped down hard on my right foot. Ian Forbes. Snarling bulldog face. Heel grinding down on my toes. Head thrust forward the way an animal might before it strikes.

208   Collection 2 / Characters: Living Many Lives

CROSS-CURRICULAR CONNECTIONS

History/Music
"God Save the King." Tell students that the first public performance in London of "God Save the King" dates back to 1745, when Prince Charles Edward Stuart (called the "Young Pretender") led his forces to victory over England's King George II.
Enrichment. Have students find out more about the history behind "God Save the King." Suggest they use the phrases *God Save the King, Jacobite Rebellion,* and *Young*

Pretender as keywords when they search for information in an online encyclopedia.

INDIVIDUAL

"You wouldn't sing it. So say it," he ordered. "Let me hear you say it."

I tried to pull my foot away but he only ground down harder.

"Say what?" I was telling my face please not to show what my foot felt.

"*God save the king.* Say it. Those four words. I want to hear you say it."

Although Ian Forbes was short, he was solid and tough and built for fighting. What was more, he always won. You had only to look at his bare knees between the top of his socks and his short pants to know that he would win. His knees were square. Bony and unbeatable. So of course it was crazy for me to argue with him.

"Why should I?" I asked. "Americans haven't said that since George the Third."[5]

He grabbed my right arm and twisted it behind my back.

"Say it," he hissed.

I felt the tears come to my eyes and I hated myself for the tears. I hated myself for not staying in Rome the way my mother had told me.

"I'll never say it," I whispered.

They were choosing sides now in the schoolyard and Ian's name was being called—among the first, as always.

He gave my arm another twist. "You'll sing tomorrow," he snarled, "or you'll be bloody sorry."

As he ran off, I slid to the ground, my head between my knees.

Oh, Grandma, I thought, why can't I be there with you? I'd feed the chickens for you. I'd pump water from the well, the way my father used to do.

It would be almost two years before we'd go to America. I was ten years old now; I'd be twelve then. But how could I think about *years*? I didn't even dare to think about the next day. After school I ran all the way home, fast so I couldn't think at all.

Our house stood behind a high stone wall, which had chips of broken glass sticking up from the top to keep thieves away. I flung open the iron gate and threw myself through the front door.

"I'm home!" I yelled.

Then I remembered that it was Tuesday, the day my mother taught an English class at the YMCA[6] where my father was the director.

I stood in the hall, trying to catch my breath, and as always I

---

5. **George the Third** (1738–1820): king of Great Britain at the time of the Revolutionary War (1775–1783), fought by the American colonies to gain independence from Great Britain.
6. **YMCA:** short for "Young Men's Christian Association."

B Reading Skills

❓ Predict. Based on your own experience and on what you've learned about Jean, what do you think she will do? [Possible responses: She'll sing "God Save the King" because she knows she can't defeat a bully; she won't sing the song because she's determined to keep her allegiance to the United States.]

C English-Language Learners

British slang. Ask students to give the most common meaning of *bloody*. [stained with blood] Then, tell students *bloody* is a British slang word that means "very." It is sometimes considered vulgar.

DEVELOPING FLUENCY

Activity. Allow students to choose a partner. Then, have them read aloud the dialogue of an encounter between two people in the story. They might choose Jean's confrontations with Ian Forbes or her friendly interaction with a Chinese boy later in the story. Encourage students to read expressively to convey the feelings of the characters.

PAIRED

DIRECT TEACHING

Ⓐ Literary Focus

❷ Character. What do the details in this passage tell you about Jean's character? [Possible responses: She can become easily agitated when others know something she doesn't. She is a curious girl who has a desire for knowledge.]

Ⓑ Vocabulary Note

Clarify word meanings: definitions. Explain to students that *glowering* means "scowling" or "staring angrily." Then ask students why the writer chose to use *glowering* instead of *staring*. [Possible response: *Glowering* conveys the anger and frustration that Jean is feeling.]

Ⓒ Learners Having Difficulty

❷ Find details. Why do you think Jean and Lin Nai-Nai keep Lin Nai-Nai's origins a secret from the other servants? [Lin Nai-Nai does not come from the servant class. If the other servants knew this, they would be cruel to her.]

began to feel small. It was a huge hall with ceilings so high it was as if they would have nothing to do with people. Certainly not with a mere child, not with me—the only child in the house. Once I asked my best friend, Andrea, if the hall made her feel little too. She said no. She was going to be a dancer and she loved space. She did a high kick to show how grand it was to have room.

Andrea Hull was a year older than I was and knew about everything sooner. She told me about commas, for instance, long before I took punctuation seriously. How could I write letters without commas? she asked. She made me so ashamed that for months I hung little wagging comma-tails all over the letters to my grandmother. She told me things that sounded so crazy I had to ask my mother if they were true. Like where babies came from. And that someday the whole world would end. My mother would frown when I asked her, but she always agreed that Andrea was right. It made me furious. How could she know such things and not tell me? What was the matter with grown-ups anyway?

I wished that Andrea were with me now, but she lived out in the country and I didn't see her often. Lin Nai-Nai, my amah,[7] was the only one around, and of course I knew she'd be there. It was her job to stay with me when my parents were out. As soon as she heard me come in, she'd called, "Tsai loushang," which meant that she was upstairs. She might be mending or ironing but most likely she'd be sitting by the window embroidering. And she was. She even had my embroidery laid out, for we had made a bargain. She would teach me to embroider if I would teach her English. I liked embroidering: the cloth stretched tight within my embroidery hoop while I filled in the stamped pattern with cross-stitches and lazy daisy flowers. The trouble was that lazy daisies needed French knots for their centers and I hated making French knots. Mine always fell apart, so I left them to the end. Today I had twenty lazy daisies waiting for their knots.

Lin Nai-Nai had already threaded my needle with embroidery floss.

"Black centers," she said, "for the yellow flowers."

I felt myself glowering. "American flowers don't have centers," I said, and gave her back the needle.

Lin Nai-Nai looked at me, puzzled, but she did not argue. She was different from other amahs. She did not even come from the servant class, although this was a secret we had to keep from the other ser-

---

7. **amah** *n.:* in Asia, a woman who looks after children.

vants, who would have made her life miserable had they known. She had run away from her husband when he had taken a second wife. She would always have been Wife Number One and the Boss no matter how many wives he had, but she would rather be no wife than head of a string of wives. She was modern. She might look old-fashioned, for her feet had been bound up tight when she was a little girl so that they would stay small, and now, like many Chinese women, she walked around on little stumps stuffed into tiny cloth shoes. Lin Nai-Nai's were embroidered with butterflies. Still, she believed in true love and one wife for one husband. We were good friends, Lin Nai-Nai and I, so I didn't know why I felt so mean.

She shrugged. "English lesson?" she asked, smiling.

I tested my arm to see if it still hurt from the twisting. It did. My foot too. "What do you want to know?" I asked.

We had been through the polite phrases—Please, Thank you, I beg your pardon, Excuse me, You're welcome, Merry Christmas (which she had practiced but hadn't had a chance to use since this was only October).

"If I meet an American on the street," she asked, "how do I greet him?"

I looked her straight in the eye and nodded my head in a greeting. "Sewing machine," I said. "You say, 'Sew-ing ma-chine.'"

She repeated after me, making the four syllables into four separate words. She got up and walked across the room, bowing and smiling. "Sew Ing Ma Shing."

Part of me wanted to laugh at the thought of Lin Nai-Nai maybe meeting Dr. Carhart, our minister, whose face would surely puff up, the way it always did when he was flustered. But part of me didn't want to laugh at all. I didn't like it when my feelings got tangled, so I ran downstairs and played "Chopsticks" on the piano. Loud and fast. When my sore arm hurt, I just beat on the keys harder.

Homesick **211**

DIRECT TEACHING

D Reading Skills

❓ **Speculate.** Why do you think Jean tricks Lin Nai-Nai? [Possible response: Jean wants to take out her anger and frustration on someone, and Lin Nai-Nai is the only person she can hurt.]

E Vocabulary Note

Context clues. Help students determine the meaning of *flustered* by examining the context of the word in the story. Ask students how they would feel if someone greeted them by saying "Sewing machine" instead of "Hello." They will probably say they'd be confused. Explain that *confused* is a synonym for *flustered*.

F Literary Focus

❓ **Character.** What does Jean's leaving the room reveal about her character? [Possible responses: She needs an outlet when she is dealing with conflicting feelings. She gets upset when she is mean to people.]

CROSS-CURRICULAR CONNECTIONS

History

Foot binding. Tell students that foot binding is associated with a craze for small feet that began in the Tang dynasty (618–906), when dancers bound their feet. The agonizing process was inflicted on girls between the ages of five and seven. Many Chinese families, especially the wealthy, required footbound wives for their sons.

A **Reading Skills**

❓ Compare and contrast characters. How is Lin Nai-Nai's attitude toward her class different from Yang Sze-Fu's attitude to his? [Possible response: Yang Sze-Fu considers himself superior to other workers. Lin Nai-Nai comes from the upper classes but acts like a member of the working class.]

B **Literary Focus**

❓ Character. Why does Yang Sze-Fu prepare the butter pagodas despite the instructions from Jean's mother? [Possible responses: Yang Sze-Fu wants to prove his independence. He takes great pride in his work and wants to show off his skill.]

Then I went out to the kitchen to see if Yang Sze-Fu, the cook, would give me something to eat. I found him reading a Chinese newspaper, his eyes going up and down with the characters. (Chinese words don't march across flat surfaces, the way ours do; they drop down cliffs, one cliff after another from right to left across a page.)

"Can I have a piece of cinnamon toast?" I asked. "And a cup of cocoa?"

A Yang Sze-Fu grunted. He was smoking a cigarette, which he wasn't supposed to do in the kitchen, but Yang Sze-Fu mostly did what he wanted. He considered himself superior to common workers. You could tell because of the fingernails on his pinkies. They were at least two inches long, which was his way of showing that he didn't have to use his hands for rough or dirty work. He didn't seem to care that his fingernails were dirty, but maybe he couldn't keep such long nails clean.

He made my toast while his cigarette dangled out of the corner of his mouth, collecting a long ash that finally fell on the floor. He wouldn't have kept smoking if my mother had been there, although he didn't always pay attention to **B** my mother. Never about butter pagodas,[8] for instance. No matter how many times my mother told him before a dinner party, "No butter pagoda," it made no difference. As soon as everyone was seated, the serving boy, Wong Sze-Fu, would bring in a pagoda and set it on the table. The guests would "oh" and "ah," for it was a masterpiece: a pagoda molded out of butter, curved roofs rising tier upon tier, but my mother could only think how unsanitary it was. For, of course, Yang Sze-Fu had molded the butter with his hands and carved the decorations with one of his long fingernails. Still, we always used the butter, for if my mother sent it back to the kitchen, Yang Sze-Fu would lose face[9] and quit.

When my toast and cocoa were ready, I took them upstairs to my

---

8. **pagodas** *n.:* Asian temples with several levels.
9. **lose face:** lose dignity or self-respect.

room (the blue room) and while I ate, I began *Sara Crewe*[10] again. Now there was a girl, I thought, who was worth crying over. I wasn't going to think about myself. Or Ian Forbes. Or the next day. I wasn't. I wasn't.

And I didn't. Not all afternoon. Not all evening. Still, I must have decided what I was going to do because the next morning when I started for school and came to the corner where the man sold hot chestnuts, the corner where I always turned to go to school, I didn't turn. I walked straight ahead. I wasn't going to school that day.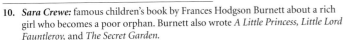

I walked toward the Yangtze River. Past the store that sold paper pellets that opened up into flowers when you dropped them in a glass of water. Then up the block where the beggars sat. I never saw anyone give money to a beggar. You couldn't, my father explained, or you'd be mobbed by beggars. They'd follow you everyplace; they'd never leave you alone. I had learned not to look at them when I passed and yet I saw. The running sores, the twisted legs, the mangled faces. What I couldn't get over was that, like me, each one of those beggars had only one life to live. It just happened that they had drawn rotten ones.

Oh, Grandma, I thought, we may be far apart but we're lucky, you and I. Do you even know how lucky? In America do you know?

This part of the city didn't actually belong to the Chinese, even though the beggars sat there, even though upper-class Chinese lived there. A long time ago other countries had just walked into China and divided up part of Hankow (and other cities) into sections, or concessions, which they called their own and used their own rules for governing. We lived in the French concession on Rue de Paris. Then there was the British concession and the Japanese. The Russian and German concessions had been officially returned to China, but the people still called them concessions. The Americans didn't have one, although, like some of the other countries, they had gunboats on the river. In case, my father said. In case what? Just in case. That's all he'd say.

The concessions didn't look like the rest of China. The buildings were solemn and orderly, with little plots of grass around them. Not like those in the Chinese part of the city: a jumble of rickety shops with people, vegetables, crates of quacking ducks, yard goods, bamboo baskets, and mangy[11] dogs spilling onto a street so narrow it was hardly there.

---

10. *Sara Crewe:* famous children's book by Frances Hodgson Burnett about a rich girl who becomes a poor orphan. Burnett also wrote *A Little Princess, Little Lord Fauntleroy,* and *The Secret Garden.*
11. **mangy** (mān'jē) *adj.:* diseased. Animals with mange lose their hair and become covered with sores and scabs.

Homesick   213

Allusion. Jean is quoting from Sir Walter Scott's poem "The Lay of the Last Minstrel."

B Cross-curricular Connections
HISTORY

At this time, the British often recruited Sikhs from northern India to serve as soldiers and police officers in their colonies around the world.

The grandest street in Hankow was the Bund, which ran along beside the Yangtze River. When I came to it after passing the beggars, I looked to my left and saw the American flag flying over the American consulate building. I was proud of the flag and I thought maybe today it was proud of me. It flapped in the breeze as if it were saying ha-ha to the king of England.

Then I looked to the right at the Customs House, which stood at the other end of the Bund. The clock on top of the tower said nine-thirty. How would I spend the day?

I crossed the street to the promenade part of the Bund. When people walked here, they weren't usually going anyplace; they were just out for the air. My mother would wear her broad-brimmed beaver hat when we came, and my father would swing his cane in that jaunty way that showed how glad he was to be a man. I thought I would just sit on a bench for the morning. I would watch the Customs House clock, and when it was time, I would eat the lunch I had brought along in my schoolbag.

I was the only one sitting on a bench. People did not generally "take the air" on a Wednesday morning, and besides, not everyone was allowed here. The British had put a sign on the Bund, NO DOGS, NO CHINESE. This meant that I could never bring Lin Nai-Nai with me. My father couldn't even bring his best friend, Mr. T. K. Hu. Maybe the British wanted a place where they could pretend they weren't in China, I thought. Still, there were always Chinese coolies around. In order to load and unload boats in the river, coolies had to cross the Bund. All day they went back and forth, bent double under their loads, sweating and chanting in a tired, singsong way that seemed to get them from one step to the next.

To pass the time, I decided to recite poetry. The one good thing about Miss Williams was that she made us learn poems by heart and I liked that. There was one particular poem I didn't want to forget. I looked at the Yangtze River and pretended that all the busy people in the boats were my audience.

A "'Breathes there the man, with soul so dead,'" I cried, "'Who never to himself hath said, This is my own, my native land!'"

I was so carried away by my performance that I didn't notice the policeman until he was right in front of me. Like all policemen in **B** the British concession, he was a bushy-bearded Indian with a red turban wrapped around his head.

He pointed to my schoolbag. "Little miss," he said, "why aren't you in school?"

MINI-LESSON Reading

Developing Word-Attack Skills
Write the selection word *notice* on the chalkboard. Remind students that when *c* comes before *e, i,* or *y,* it can have the sound /s/. However, the letters *ci* also can have the sound /sh/.

Use the following words to demonstrate these rules regarding the letter *c*:

• *concession*—*c* stands for /s/ before *e* (Note that in this word, the first *c* stands for /k/ and the second for /s/.)

• *recite*—*c* stands for /s/ before *i*

• *officially*—*c* before *i* can stand for /sh/

Activity. Write these sets of words on the board. Have volunteers identify the two words in each set in which *c, ce,* or *ci* stands for /s/ or /sh/.

1. decide	proceed	placate
2. accent	cement	content
3. specter	special	spacious
4. docile	project	voice

He was tall and mysterious-looking, more like a character in my *Arabian Nights* book than a man you expected to talk to. I fumbled for an answer. "I'm going on an errand," I said finally. "I just sat down for a rest." I picked up my schoolbag and walked quickly away. When I looked around, he was back on his corner, directing traffic.

So now they were chasing children away too, I thought angrily. Well, I'd like to show them. Someday I'd like to walk a dog down the whole length of the Bund. A Great Dane. I'd have him on a leash—like this—(I put out my hand as if I were holding a leash right then) and he'd be so big and strong I'd have to strain to hold him back (I strained). Then of course sometimes he'd have to do his business and I'd stop (like this) right in the middle of the sidewalk and let him go to it. I was so busy with my Great Dane I was at the end of the Bund before I knew it. I let go of the leash, clapped my hands, and told my dog to go home. Then I left the Bund and the concessions and walked into the Chinese world.

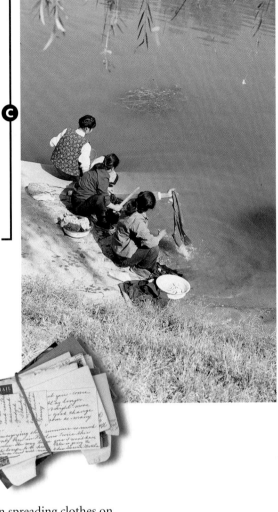

My mother and father and I had walked here but not for many months. This part near the river was called the Mud Flats. Sometimes it was muddier than others, and when the river flooded, the flats disappeared underwater. Sometimes even the fishermen's huts were washed away, knocked right off their long-legged stilts and swept down the river. But today the river was fairly low and the mud had dried so that it was cracked and cakey. Most of the men who lived here were out fishing, some not far from the shore, poling their sampans through the shallow water. Only a few people were on the flats: a man cleaning fish on a flat rock at the water's edge, a woman spreading clothes on the dirt to dry, a few small children. But behind the huts was something I had never seen before. Even before I came close, I guessed what it was. Even then, I was excited by the strangeness of it.

C Literary Focus

❷ Character. What does Jean's fantasy of walking a Great Dane tell the reader about her character? [Possible response: She feels small and powerless.]

❓ Personification. How does the author help us to imagine that the junk "would have life"? [Possible response: She uses the names of body parts to describe it—its skeleton, ribs, backbone, snub-nosed prow, and eyes.]

B **Reading Skills**

❓ Infer. Why does Jean carve the Chinese form of her name on the junk? [Possible responses: She wants to establish a connection to this boat and to China. She wants to leave a permanent record that makes her part of this land.]

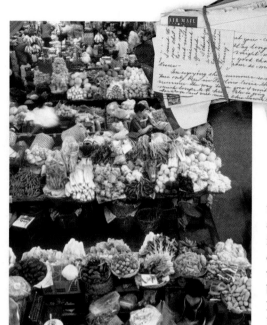

It was the beginnings of a boat. The skeleton of a large junk, its ribs lying bare, its backbone running straight and true down the bottom. The outline of the prow was already in place, turning up wide and snub-nosed, the way all junks did. I had never thought of boats starting from nothing, of taking on bones under their bodies. The eyes, I supposed, would be the last thing added. Then the junk would have life.

The builders were not there, and I was behind the huts where no one could see me as I walked around and around, marveling. Then I climbed inside, and as I did, I knew that something wonderful was happening to me. I was a-tingle, the way a magician must feel when he swallows fire, because suddenly I knew that the boat was mine. No matter who really owned it, it was mine. Even if I never saw it again, it would be my junk sailing up and down the Yangtze River. My junk seeing the river sights with its two eyes, seeing them for me whether I was there or not. Often I had tried to put the Yangtze River into a poem so I could keep it. Sometimes I had tried to draw it, but nothing I did ever came close. But now, *now* I had my junk and somehow that gave me the river too.

I thought I should put my mark on the boat. Perhaps on the side of the spine. Very small. A secret between the boat and me. I opened my schoolbag and took out my folding penknife that I used for sharpening pencils. Very carefully I carved the Chinese character that was our name. Gau. (In China my father was Mr. Gau, my mother was Mrs. Gau, and I was Little Miss Gau.) The builders would paint right over the character, I thought, and never notice. But I would know. Always and forever I would know.

For a long time I dreamed about the boat, imagining it finished, its sails up, its eyes wide. Someday it might sail all the way down the Yangtze to Shanghai, so I told the boat what it would see along the way because I had been there and the boat hadn't. After a while I got hungry and I ate my egg sandwich. I was in the midst of peeling an orange when all at once I had company.

A small boy, not more than four years old, wandered around to the back of the huts, saw me, and stopped still. He was wearing a ragged blue cotton jacket with a red cloth pincushion-like charm around his neck which was supposed to keep him from getting smallpox. Sticking up straight from the middle of his head was a small pigtail, which I knew was to fool the gods and make them think he was a girl. (Gods didn't bother much with girls; it was boys that were important in China.) The weather was still warm so he wore no pants, nothing below the waist. Most small boys went around like this so that when they had to go, they could just let loose and go. He walked slowly up to the boat, stared at me, and then nodded as if he'd already guessed what I was. "Foreign devil," he announced gravely.

I shook my head. "No," I said in Chinese. "American friend." Through the ribs of the boat, I handed him a segment of orange. He ate it slowly, his eyes on the rest of the orange. Segment by segment, I gave it all to him. Then he wiped his hands down the front of his jacket.

"Foreign devil," he repeated.

"American friend," I corrected. Then I asked him about the boat. Who was building it? Where were the builders?

He pointed with his chin upriver. "Not here today. Back tomorrow."

I knew it would only be a question of time before the boy would run off to alert the people in the huts. "Foreign devil, foreign devil," he would cry. So I put my hand on the prow of the boat, wished it luck, and climbing out, I started back toward the Bund. To my surprise the boy walked beside me. When we came to the edge of the Bund, I squatted down so we would be on the same eye level.

"Goodbye," I said. "May the River God protect you."

For a moment the boy stared. When he spoke, it was as if he were trying out a new sound. "American friend," he said slowly.

When I looked back, he was still there, looking soberly toward the foreign world to which I had gone.

The time, according to the Customs House clock, was five after two, which meant that I couldn't go home for two hours. School was dismissed at three-thirty and I was home by three-forty-five unless I had to stay in for talking in class. It took me about fifteen minutes to write "I will not talk in class" fifty times, and so I often came home at four o'clock. (I wrote up and down like the Chinese: fifty "I's," fifty "wills," and right through the sentence so I never had to think what I was writing. It wasn't as if I were making a promise.) Today I planned to arrive home at four, my "staying-in" time, in the hope that I wouldn't meet classmates on the way.

A **English-Language Learners**

Idioms. Explain that the idiom *in one piece* means "unhurt" or "safe."

B **Literary Focus**

❓ Character. What does Jean reveal about herself with her comment about hanging her head? [Possible responses: She identifies with literary characters. She has a dramatic flair.]

C **Literary Focus**

❓ Internal conflict. In this paragraph, what conflicting feelings does Jean's mother experience, and how does she express them? [Possible response: Jean's mother strokes Jean's hair, an indication of feelings of love for her daughter. On the other hand, she stiffens, which indicates that she is somewhat angry with Jean and will discipline her for cutting school.]

Meanwhile I wandered up and down the streets, in and out of stores. I weighed myself on the big scale in the Hankow Dispensary[12] and found that I was as skinny as ever. I went to the Terminus Hotel and tried out the chairs in the lounge. At first I didn't mind wandering about like this. Half of my mind was still on the river with my junk, but as time went on, my junk began slipping away until I was alone with nothing but questions. Would my mother find out about today? How could I skip school tomorrow? And the next day and the next? Could I get sick? Was there a kind of long lie-abed sickness that didn't hurt?

I arrived home at four, just as I had planned, opened the door, and called out, "I'm home!" Cheery-like and normal. But I was scarcely in the house before Lin Nai-Nai ran to me from one side of the hall and my mother from the other.

"Are you all right? Are you all right?" Lin Nai-Nai felt my arms as if she expected them to be broken. My mother's face was white. "What happened?" she asked.

Then I looked through the open door into the living room and saw Miss Williams sitting there. She had beaten me home and asked about my absence, which of course had scared everyone. But now my mother could see that I was in one piece and for some reason this seemed to make her mad. She took me by the hand and led me into the living room. "Miss Williams said you weren't in school," she said. "Why was that?"

I hung my head, just the way cowards do in books.

My mother dropped my hand. "Jean will be in school tomorrow," she said firmly. She walked Miss Williams to the door. "Thank you for stopping by."

Miss Williams looked satisfied in her mean, pinched way. "Well," she said, "ta-ta." (She always said "ta-ta" instead of "goodbye." Chicken language, it sounded like.)

As soon as Miss Williams was gone and my mother was sitting down again, I burst into tears. Kneeling on the floor, I buried my head in her lap and poured out the whole miserable story. My mother could see that I really wasn't in one piece after all, so she listened quietly, stroking my hair as I talked, but gradually I could feel her stiffen. I knew she was remembering that she was a Mother.

"You better go up to your room," she said, "and think things over. We'll talk about it after supper."

---

12. **dispensary** *n.:* place where medicine and first aid are provided.

I flung myself on my bed. What was there to think? Either I went to school and got beaten up. Or I quit.

After supper I explained to my mother and father how simple it was. I could stay at home and my mother could teach me, the way Andrea's mother taught her. Maybe I could even go to Andrea's house and study with her.

My mother shook her head. Yes, it was simple, she agreed. I could go back to the British School, be sensible, and start singing about the king again.

I clutched the edge of the table. Couldn't she understand? I couldn't turn back now. It was too late.

So far my father had not said a word. He was leaning back, teetering on the two hind legs of his chair, the way he always did after a meal, the way that drove my mother crazy. But he was not the kind of person to keep all four legs of a chair on the floor just because someone wanted him to. He wasn't a turning-back person so I hoped maybe he would understand. As I watched him, I saw a twinkle start in his eyes and suddenly he brought his chair down slam-bang flat on the floor. He got up and motioned for us to follow him into the living room. He sat down at the piano and began to pick out the tune for "God Save the King."

A big help, I thought. Was he going to make me practice?

Then he began to sing:

"My country 'tis of thee,
Sweet land of liberty . . ."

Of course! It was the same tune. Why hadn't I thought of that? Who would know what I was singing as long as I moved my lips? I joined in now, loud and strong.

"Of thee I sing."

My mother laughed in spite of herself. "If you sing that loud," she said, "you'll start a revolution."

"Tomorrow I'll sing softly," I promised. "No one will know." But for now I really let freedom ring.

DIRECT TEACHING

D Literary Focus

? Character. What can you tell about Jean's father by his solution to her problem? [Possible response: Her father is clever and perhaps a bit sneaky.]

A **Reading Skills**

❓ **Infer.** Why does Jean go to Lin Nai-Nai and tell her the correct way to greet someone? [Possible response: Now that she has found a solution to her problem, Jean feels guilty about taking out her frustrations on Lin Nai-Nai and wants to make amends.]

B **Vocabulary Note**

❓ **Connotations.** Does the word *sauntered* have a positive or negative connotation in this context? Explain. [Possible response: *Sauntered* has a negative connotation; it suggests cockiness.]

C **Literary Focus**

❓ **Resolution.** Are you satisfied that the conflict between Jean and Ian has been resolved? [Possible responses: No, I think Ian might have noticed which song Jean was singing. Yes, Ian will leave Jean alone now that he believes she is singing.]

Then all at once I wanted to see Lin Nai-Nai. I ran out back, through the courtyard that separated the house from the servants' quarters, and upstairs to her room.

"It's me," I called through the door and when she opened up, I threw my arms around her. "Oh, Lin Nai-Nai, I love you," I said. "You haven't said it yet, have you?"

"Said what?"

"Sewing machine. You haven't said it?"

"No," she said, "not yet. I'm still practicing."

"Don't say it, Lin Nai-Nai. Say 'Good day.' It's shorter and easier. Besides, it's more polite."

"Good day?" she repeated.

"Yes, that's right. Good day." I hugged her and ran back to the house.

The next day at school when we rose to sing the British national anthem, everyone stared at me, but as soon as I opened my mouth, the class lost interest. All but Ian Forbes. His eyes never left my face, but I sang softly, carefully, proudly. At recess he sauntered[13] over to where I stood against the wall. He spat on the ground. "You can be bloody glad you sang today," he said. Then he strutted off as if he and those square knees of his had won again.

C And, of course, I was bloody glad.

---

13. **sauntered** (sôn′tərd) v.: strolled.

FAMILY/COMMUNITY ACTIVITY

Activity. Ask students to conduct an interview with a friend, neighbor, or relative who has spent time in a foreign country. Encourage students to focus not so much on facts but rather on what the interviewee was thinking and feeling while he or she was away. Have students summarize their interviews for the class.

Meet the Writer

Jean Fritz

"I Had to Speak Up"

Jean Fritz (1915–   ) spent the first thirteen years of her life in Hankow, China. She recalls her memorable childhood in *Homesick: My Own Story,* a 1983 Newbery Honor Book and American Book Award winner.

> ❝ Until I was eleven years old I attended an English school. I felt very American and often thought I had to speak up for my country. At recess, for instance. The English children would sometimes tease me by making fun of America. I never let that pass even if it meant a fight. ❞

After moving to the United States and graduating from college, Jean Fritz became a librarian. "When I ran the children's department of our local library," she recalls, "I found that I not only wanted to read children's stories, I wanted to write them too."

For Independent Reading

Jean Fritz has written more than a dozen biographies for young adults, including *Why Don't You Get a Horse, Sam Adams?; Where Do You Think You're Going, Christopher Columbus?;* and *Traitor: The Case of Benedict Arnold.*

Meet the Writer

Jean Fritz once summed up her feeling on writing historical biographies and novels this way: "My interest in writing about American history stemmed originally, I think, from a subconscious desire to find roots. I lived in China until I was thirteen, hearing constant talk about 'home' (meaning America), but since I had never been 'home,' I felt like a girl without a country. . . . If I can surprise children into believing history, I will be happy, especially if they find, as I do, that the truth is stranger (and often funnier) than fiction."

For Independent Reading

Students with a keen interest in the American Revolution will be happy to learn that Fritz has written biographies of many key figures of the conflict. They may want to start with *And Then What Happened, Paul Revere?* or *Traitor: The Case of Benedict Arnold.* For students who prefer biographies with a lighter touch, recommend *George Washington's Mother,* a successful blend of history and humor.

Writing Workshop

Objectives

- Use appropriate prewriting and drafting skills to create a problem-solution essay.
- Revise the problem-solution essay by clarifying statements, elaborating on details, and adjusting the tone.
- Reflect on and assess one's writing process and problem-solution essay.

PRETEACHING

Skills Starter

Motivate. Have students discuss a simple problem specific to the classroom before tackling larger issues—lack of room in the coat closet, for example, or disorganized bookshelves. Let students brainstorm steps toward solving one of these problems. Have volunteers write possible solutions on the chalkboard. Then, have students vote on the solution that they think is the best.

DIRECT TEACHING

PREWRITING

Choosing a Topic

To help students begin writing, encourage them to brainstorm and jot down ideas about problems that they have encountered. Remind them that they can think about problems they've experienced in their lives or problems that may be affecting their school or city. Tell students to freewrite for five minutes, jotting down everything that comes to mind. Explain that the object of freewriting is to quickly generate as many ideas as possible.

Assignment

Write an essay describing a problem and offering a solution.

Audience

Anyone affected by the problem.

RUBRIC
Evaluation Criteria

A good problem-solution essay

1. defines the problem clearly and identifies its causes and effects

2. provides evidence of the seriousness of the problem

3. proposes one or more solutions and discusses the benefits of each solution as well as objections to it

4. considers the audience for the essay and their point of view

5. makes a convincing call for change or action

SKILLS FOCUS

Writing Skills
Write a problem-solution essay.

PERSUASIVE WRITING
Problem-Solution Essay

Many situations can be considered problems. Some problems occur in your everyday life, such as a broken bicycle wheel or a computer that crashes. The subject of a problem-solution essay, however, is a problem that seriously affects a large number of people. Your object is to explain the problem and to offer one or more solutions.

Prewriting

1 Choosing a Topic

Consider the following **prompt:**

> Think about how you might solve a problem that affects your school, your neighborhood, or your community. Write an essay in which you describe this problem and try to persuade readers to accept your solution.

Get together with a group of classmates, and brainstorm a list of problems. Here are some suggestions to help you get started:

- If I could make just one thing happen, I'd . . .
- If I were the president/mayor/principal, I would . . .
- The world would be a better place if everyone . . .

2 Finding Solutions

Choose one problem to work on. Explore solutions to the problem in a cluster diagram like the one shown on the

PEANUTS reprinted by permission of United Feature Syndicate, Inc.

222   Collection 2 / Characters : Living Many Lives

---

right. You might also try jotting down all your ideas. If you've chosen a good topic, you probably won't be able to write fast enough to keep up with your thoughts! Keep writing until you can't think of anything else to say—then sort through what you've written and choose the solution that seems most promising.

3 Targeting Your Audience

A critical question you must answer is "Whom do I want to persuade?" Your audience might be:

- people who are affected by the problem
- people who are responsible for causing the problem
- people who can help with the solution

In a persuasive essay, you don't want to "preach to the choir"—that is, write to impress people who probably agree with you already—or to attack those who disagree. Neither of these tactics will help you achieve your real purpose, which is to persuade as many readers as possible to accept your assessment of the problem and your ideas for solving it.

Drafting

1 Crafting a Strong Beginning

You might open your essay with a quotation, a vivid example of the problem, or a surprising statistic. Avoid using statements beginning with "I think" or "I feel." In your introduction, state your purpose. Make the problem real for your reader. Explain what causes the problem, and describe its effects on your readers.

2 Showing the Problem

How can you make the problem real for your readers? Don't just name it. Explain what causes it and how widespread it is. Go on to describe its effects—especially those that touch your readers' lives.

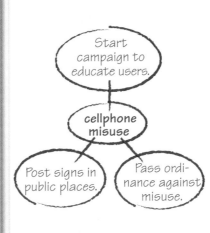

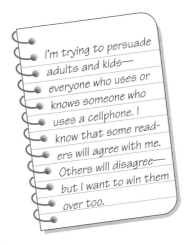

I'm trying to persuade adults and kids— everyone who uses or knows someone who uses a cellphone. I know that some readers will agree with me. Others will disagree— but I want to win them over too.

Problem-Solution Essay **223**

DIRECT TEACHING

MODELING

Framework for a Problem-Solution Essay

Help learners having difficulty by filling in the framework on the chalkboard with examples. For instance, you might use the following example:

Introduction (strong example or statement): Studies of schools have shown that some students can spend several hundred dollars a month on clothes and as much as two and a half hours a day getting dressed for school.

Problem: Students place too much value on material possessions and personal appearance.

Solution: Require students to wear school uniforms.

Details: Don't allow students to wear accessories that are not part of the school uniform.

Benefits: Students will save time and money if they wear uniforms every day and stop worrying about their choice of clothing. Thefts will be reduced if expensive clothing and personal items are not allowed in school.

Possible objections: Uniforms prevent students from expressing their individuality.

Your responses: Uniforms promote individuality by emphasizing students' inner selves—not their outward appearance and material possessions.

Conclusion (a strong argument, a summary, or a call to action): Adopting school uniforms will create a better educational environment in which students can concentrate on learning. Mandatory school uniforms will lower students' anxiety about their appearance, help them save money, increase school security, and encourage students to place more value on the way they think and feel—and not just on the way they look.

Framework for a Problem–Solution Essay

Introduction (a strong example or statement): _____

Problem: _____
Solution: _____
Details: _____
Benefits: _____
Possible objections: _____
Your responses: _____
Conclusion (a strong argument, a summary, or a call to action): _____

Writing Tip

Avoid circular reasoning: Restating the problem in different words (as in the following example) is not the same as providing a solution.

> By showing greater consideration for others, cellphone users can solve the problem because lack of consideration is the source of the trouble.

This statement does not explain how to promote consideration for others.

---

3 Proposing Solutions

Briefly describe your solution to the problem. Then, describe the solution in detail, citing examples and explaining what steps need to be taken. Be sure to stress the benefits offered by your solution. Show that your proposal is realistic and doable. Remember, the best solutions are "win-win": They offer advantages to everyone affected by the problem.

4 Anticipating Objections

Your goal is to persuade readers to accept your solution and to take the actions you recommend. However, every solution will have its opponents. Can you win them over to your side? If not, can you counter their arguments?

Look for weak points in your proposed solution, and see if you can strengthen them. Think of arguments that might be raised against your ideas so that you can anticipate and respond to them. Deal with these possible objections by stressing the benefits of your approach.

Using a chart like the one below is a good way to plan your responses to anticipated objections.

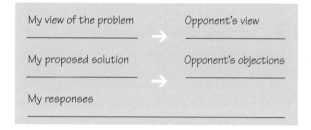

5 Ending on a Strong Note

In your conclusion, state what you want your readers to do. You might remind your readers of the importance of the problem and the pressing need to solve it. You might also look toward the future. What might happen if people act— or fail to act—on your suggestion?

DIFFERENTIATING INSTRUCTION

Learners Having Difficulty

Researching ideas. Tell students who are having difficulty finding topics to write about to look at editorials in their school or local newspapers. Remind students that they can use the information they find in the editorials in their essays. Tell students that they can agree or disagree with what the editorial writers say and then state their own opinions in their essays.

English-Language Learners

Students may have a difficult time understanding technical or scientific terminology they encounter while doing research for their essays. Tell students to make lists of unfamiliar words they find. Then, have students use a bilingual dictionary to determine the meanings of these new words.

Student Model

KIDS SHOULD BE PAID FOR CHORES

I strongly believe that kids should be paid for doing chores around the house. Kids all across the country constantly nag their parents for money to go to the movies, buy CDs, go to McDonalds, and do many other things. Many parents complain about kids' always asking them for money.

Parents constantly complain that kids don't help out around the house enough. Lots of times parents nag kids until they clean up their rooms, put out the trash, cut the lawn, do the dishes, shovel the snow, and do many other chores.

Why can't kids and parents reach a compromise about money and chores? Parents would pay kids who remember to do their chores without being reminded a small fee for the work done. Kids would no longer ask for money.

This compromise teaches kids responsibility. They would learn that you don't get anything for doing nothing. When their chores are completed, with no nagging, they'd be paid whatever the parents had agreed to pay them. Kids could spend the money on things they like. They'd learn to save money for the expensive items.

No more nagging kids begging for money. No more nagging parents begging kids to clean up. Both kids and parents would be getting something that they want.

—T. J. Wilson
Atlantic Middle School
North Quincy, Massachusetts

*A **strong statement** is used to grab the reader's attention.*

*Detailed **examples** illustrate the **problems** faced by both sides—parents and kids.*

*The writer outlines a **solution**.*

*The writer answers possible **objections** by pointing out **benefits** of the solution.*

*The writer ends with a **strong statement** of the benefits to both parties.*

Strategies For Elaboration

To support your problem-solution essay, you can use

- facts (including statistics and other evidence from research)
- anecdotes and other examples from personal experience
- opinions of experts
- discussion of the solution's practicality in terms of money, time, and difficulty
- comparisons of various solutions

INTERNET
More Writer's Models
Keyword: LE5 7-2

Problem-Solution Essay   **225**

DIRECT TEACHING

Student Model
Encourage students to examine the model to see how one student writer introduces a problem, gives detailed examples of it, suggests a solution, addresses objections by pointing out benefits, and concludes with a strong statement.

Strategies for Elaboration
Tell students that collecting anecdotes and conducting interviews are good ways to gather information for their essays. Have students talk to their peers, their parents, their neighbors, and others to hear their opinions and learn about their experiences concerning the problems addressed in students' essays.

DIFFERENTIATING INSTRUCTION

Learners Having Difficulty
Remind students that when they begin crafting their essays they can appeal to the reader's emotions. Adding personal experiences or anecdotes with human interest will help readers sympathize with the writer's opinion presented in the essay.

Advanced Learners
Enrichment. Encourage advanced students to form pairs and choose identical topics. The pairs will take opposing sides or offer alternative views of the same problem. Tell students that each pair can deliver their papers as an oral presentation. A further challenge would be for the pairs of students to debate the topics of their papers in front of the whole class and have students vote for the debater they found most convincing.

DIRECT TEACHING

EVALUATING AND REVISING

Content and Organization Guidelines

Have students form pairs and read their essays aloud to their partners. Tell students to write their partners' comments on their drafts with colored pencils. Remind students to take into account any objections that their partners raise to their proposed solutions and to address those objections when they revise their essays.

TECHNOLOGY TIP

Remind students who use word processors or computers to be sure to use them to check their spelling and grammar. Many word-processing programs include tools that can help students identify errors in spelling and grammar.

Evaluating and Revising

Use the following chart to evaluate and revise your problem-solution essay.

Problem Solution: Content and Organization Guidelines

Evaluation Questions	▶ Tips	▶ Revision Techniques
❶ Do you grab the reader's attention with a strong beginning? Does your introduction state the problem clearly?	▶ **Underline** the attention-getting opening. **Highlight** the statement of the problem.	▶ **Add** a strong statement, a statistic, or a vivid example of the problem.
❷ Do you provide details that describe the problem?	▶ **Put stars** next to details that show the causes and effects of the problem.	▶ **Add** examples that reveal the seriousness of the problem.
❸ Does your essay propose a solution to the problem? Does it examine the pros and cons of the solution?	▶ **Circle** the statements that propose a solution. **Check** the descriptions of benefits and possible objections.	▶ **Summarize** your solution, and **elaborate** with details.
❹ Does your essay target your audience?	▶ **Check** phrases or sentences that identify your audience.	▶ **Adjust tone** to reach your audience.
❺ Are paragraphs arranged in order of importance?	▶ **Number** each paragraph according to the importance of the ideas discussed.	▶ **Rearrange** paragraphs to build toward your most important idea.
❻ Does the conclusion include a convincing call to action?	▶ **Draw a wavy line** under the call to action.	▶ **Add** a call to action, or **revise** your statement to make it stronger and more specific.

On the next page you'll find the opening paragraph of a problem-solution essay that has been revised. Following the Revision Model are questions you can use to evaluate the writer's revisions.

226 Collection 2 / Characters : Living Many Lives

EVALUATION GUIDELINES

		4	3	2	1
Use these guidelines to quickly assess students' final drafts.	**Beginning grabs reader's attention and clearly defines the problem.**	Beginning grabs reader's attention and clearly defines the problem.	Beginning grabs reader's attention but only vaguely defines the problem.	Beginning does not grab reader's attention and only vaguely defines the problem.	Beginning does not grab reader's attention and does not identify the problem.
	Essay includes details that help explain and elaborate on the proposed solution.	Essay thoughtfully uses details to explain the problem and elaborate on the proposed solution.	Essay explains the problem and the proposed solution but lacks details.	Analysis of the problem is weak; proposed solution is not thoroughly explained.	Problem is not analyzed; no solution is proposed.

Revision Model

most exciting
You've just reached the ~~best~~ scene of a movie, and you're

sitting on the edge of your seat. Suddenly, ~~out of nowhere~~

the tension is broken by a ringing noise—somebody's

has gone off
cell phone ‸. Because people are turning to mobile phones in

ever-growing numbers, we find them being used in public

have many important uses, but they
places. Cell phones ‸ are rapidly becoming a public nuisance.

common-sense
We need some ‸ strategies that will encourage cell phone

users to respect the rights of others to quiet and privacy in

including restaurants, schools, theaters, and buses
public places ‸. ~~Rules are already in place to control the~~

~~noise of car radios.~~ One possibility is posting signs ‸ in public

vehicles, movie theaters, and restaurants (that restrict or

prohibit the use of cell phones) . Bus drivers, for example,

might be given the authority to temporarily confiscate the

phones of riders who refuse to cooperate.

Evaluating the Revision

1. What has the writer added to clarify the nature of the problem?
2. What unnecessary details has the writer deleted?
3. Where has the writer rearranged details for greater effectiveness?

Communications Handbook
H E L P

See Proofreaders' Marks.

Problem-Solution Essay **227**

Revision Model
To help students grasp the concept of revising their essays to include more precise nouns, verbs, and modifiers, present the thought processes of a writer making the changes shown in the Revision Model. Calling students' attention to the fifth sentence, you might say, "The word *common-sense* was inserted to emphasize that strategies used to solve this problem must be methods that can be easily applied. The phrase *including restaurants, schools, theaters, and buses* provides examples of public places where cell phones can be a nuisance."

Proofreading Tips
Remind students that as they proofread, they should pay close attention to the tone of their essays. Changes in punctuation, grammar, and sentence structure can sometimes change the tone of an essay.

Evaluating the Revision

1. The writer added *have many important uses, but they* to address readers' belief that cell phones are useful.
2. The writer deleted the detail about rules to reduce the noise of car radios because this fact is not directly related to the overuse of cell phones in public.
3. The writer moved the phrase *that restrict or prohibit the use of cell phones* so that it would clearly modify *signs*.

	4	3	2	1
Essay considers the audience and possible objections to proposed solution.	Essay appropriately addresses the audience and anticipates any possible objections.	Essay appropriately addresses the audience but does not thoroughly address all objections.	Essay considers the audience but does not address objections.	Audience is not considered; possible objections are not addressed.
Conclusion restates writer's solution and includes a call to action.	Conclusion persuasively restates writer's solution and includes a convincing call to action.	Conclusion restates writer's solution and includes a weak call to action.	Conclusion restates writer's solution but does not include a call to action.	Conclusion does not restate solution and does not include a call to action.

Collection 2: Skills Review

Literary Skills

SKILLS FOCUS
pp. 228–229

Grade-Level Skills

■ Literary Skills
Analyze characterization.

INTRODUCING THE SKILLS REVIEW

Use this review to assess students' grasp of the characterization skills taught in this collection.

DIRECT TEACHING

A **Literary Focus**

❓ **Characterization.** Based on the narrator's description, what is the Red Girl's appearance? [The Red Girl's face and hair are red; her body and clothes are dirty, and her hair is tangled; her face, feet, and hands are big; she is barefoot; she smells wonderful to the narrator.]

B **Literary Focus**

❓ **Characterization.** What do you learn about the Red Girl's life from her mother's actions? [The Red Girl has a lot of freedom, since her mother does not try to control her.]

C **Literary Focus**

❓ **Characterization.** What do the narrator's thoughts about the Red Girl tell you about herself? [She is well-groomed, obedient, and unhappy with her lack of freedom.]

Collection 2: Skills Review

Literary Skills

Test Practice

DIRECTIONS: Read the following story. Then, answer each question that follows.

Here is a portion of a story set in Antigua, an island in the Caribbean Sea. The narrator is a young girl named Annie John, who has for a while wanted to play with another girl she calls the Red Girl.

from The Red Girl

Jamaica Kincaid

The Red Girl and I stood under the guava tree looking each other up and down. What a beautiful thing I saw standing before me. Her face was big and round and red, like a moon—a red moon. She had big, broad, flat feet, and they were naked to the bare ground; her dress was dirty, the skirt and blouse tearing away from each other at one side; the red hair that I had first seen standing up on her head was matted and tangled; her hands were big and fat, and her fingernails held at least ten anthills of dirt under them. And on top of that, she had such an unbelievable, wonderful smell, as if she had never taken a bath in her whole life.

I soon learned this about her: She took a bath only once a week, and that was only so that she could be admitted to her grandmother's presence. She didn't like to bathe, and her mother didn't force her. She changed her dress once a week for the same reason. She preferred to wear a dress until it just couldn't be worn anymore. Her mother

didn't mind that, either. She didn't like to comb her hair, though on the first day of school, she could put herself out for that. She didn't like to go to Sunday school, and her mother didn't force her. She didn't like to brush her teeth, but occasionally her mother said it was necessary. She loved to play marbles, and was so good that only Skerritt boys now played against her. Oh, what an angel she was, and what a heaven she lived in! I, on the other hand, took a full bath every morning and a sponge bath every night. I could hardly go out on my doorstep without putting my shoes on. I was not allowed to play in the sun without a hat on my head. My mother paid a woman who lived five houses away from us sevenpence a week—a penny for each school day and twopence for Sunday—to comb my hair. On Saturday, my mother washed my hair. Before I went to sleep at night I had to make sure my uniform was clean and creaseless and all laid out for the next day. I had to make sure that my

Literary Skills
Analyze characterization.

Using Academic Language

As part of the review of characterization, ask students to look back through the collection to find the meanings of the terms listed at the right. Then, have students show their grasp of characterization by citing passages from a story in the collection that illustrate the meanings of the terms.

Characterization (p. 128), **Direct Characterization** (p. 128), **Indirect Characterization** (p. 128), **Character Traits** (pp. 136, 190), **Motivation** (pp. 146, 174), **Narrator** (p. 168).

Collection 2: Skills Review

shoes were clean and polished to a nice shine. I went to Sunday school every Sunday unless I was sick. I was not allowed to play marbles, and, as for Skerritt boys, that was hardly mentionable.

---

1. Which of the following **character traits** does the narrator apply to the Red Girl?
   A She is a careful dresser.
   B She spends too much time on her hair.
   C She is unconcerned about her appearance.
   D She is always clean and neat.

2. All of the following **traits** are characteristic of the narrator *except* —
   F she envies the Red Girl's freedom
   G she much prefers her own life to that of the Red Girl
   H she obeys her mother
   J she dresses neatly and wears clean shoes

3. From the narrator's vivid description of the Red Girl, you can **infer** that the narrator —
   A is disgusted by the Red Girl
   B wants to help the Red Girl
   C longs to be more like the Red Girl
   D doesn't want to be friends with the Red Girl

4. The narrator tells us directly how she feels about the Red Girl when she says —
   F "She took a bath only once a week. . . ."
   G "She didn't like to go to Sunday school. . . ."
   H "I was not allowed to play in the sun without a hat on my head."
   J "Oh, what an angel she was, and what a heaven she lived in!"

5. In this passage from "The Red Girl," the narrator uses all of the following methods of **characterization** *except* —
   A stating character traits directly
   B describing actions
   C quoting speech
   D describing appearance

Constructed Response

6. Do you think the Red Girl is as wonderful as the narrator thinks she is? Why do you think the narrator likes the Red Girl so much?

Answers and Model Rationales

1. **C** Students should eliminate A because the narrator says "her dress was dirty, the skirt and blouse tearing away from each other," and they should eliminate B because her hair "was matted and tangled." D should be eliminated in line with both these details. The Red Girl's appearance is just the opposite, as described in C.

2. **G** Students should recognize that F, H, and J are all true of the narrator, so the word *except* in the question eliminates them.

3. **C** Students can eliminate A and D because the narrator calls the Red Girl "a beautiful thing" and says she's an angel. They can eliminate B because there's no hint that the Red Girl needs help.

4. **J** Students should realize that F, G, and H state facts. Only J is a feeling.

5. **C** Students should recognize that there are no quotations in the selection; therefore, C is the correct answer.

Constructed Response

6. The Red Girl may not be as wonderful as the narrator thinks she is because the narrator is envious of the Red Girl's way of living. This enviousness may cause the narrator to exaggerate the Red Girl's positive characteristics. The narrator likes the Red Girl because the Red Girl has been given so much more individual freedom than she has.

Test-Taking Tips

Remind students not to get stalled on one question of the test. They should work through the entire test at a fairly steady pace. They can always go back to more difficult questions later if there is enough time.

For more instruction on how to answer multiple-choice questions, refer students to **Test Smarts,** p. 920.

Collection 2: Skills Review

Vocabulary Skills

Word Analysis: Synonyms

Modeling. Model the thought process of a good reader getting the answer to item 1 by saying: "I know that a saboteur is a person who wrecks things, so I can immediately eliminate A, *hide,* and D, *collect.* In choosing *destroy* over *remove,* I reason that to sabotage something is not to move it again or take it away. Therefore, B is the correct answer."

Test Practice

Answers and Model Rationales

1. **B** See rationale above.
2. **J** A staid person is usually self-contained, or quiet.
3. **A** Students should recognize the root word, *console,* which means "to comfort."
4. **H** *Intelligible* is related to *intellect,* and someone with intellect is likely to understand things. Also, the suffix *–ible* means the same as *–able.*
5. **A** A perturbed person is disturbed or troubled. Therefore, A is correct.
6. **G** If someone alleviates your pain, they lessen, or relieve it, so G is correct.
7. **B** *Valor* means "bravery," so a valiant person must be a brave one.
8. **F** *Derision* means "contempt or scorn," so a derisive laugh must sound scornful.
9. **D** A menace is a threat, and threats are dangerous, so D is correct.
10. **F** Someone who is intimidated is scared or frightened into inaction, so F is correct.

Collection 2: Skills Review

Vocabulary Skills

Test Practice

This Test Practice reviews Vocabulary words you have studied in Collections 1 and 2.

Synonyms

Directions: Choose the word or phrase that means the same or about the same as the underlined word.

1. To sabotage means to —
    A   hide
    B   destroy
    C   remove
    D   collect

2. A staid person is usually —
    F   tired
    G   restless
    H   bothersome
    J   quiet

3. Seeking consolation is the same as seeking —
    A   comfort
    B   prizes
    C   housing
    D   warmth

4. An intelligible conversation is —
    F   alien
    G   secretive
    H   understandable
    J   unimportant

5. If you are perturbed, you are —
    A   troubled
    B   surprised
    C   pleased
    D   calmed

6. To alleviate pain means to —
    F   increase it
    G   relieve it
    H   deepen it
    J   disguise it

7. A valiant person is —
    A   truthful
    B   brave
    C   graceful
    D   cowardly

8. A derisive laugh sounds —
    F   scornful
    G   musical
    H   loving
    J   loud

9. A menace is a —
    A   pest
    B   nightmare
    C   machine
    D   danger

10. Someone who is intimidated is —
    F   frightened
    G   alone
    H   angry
    J   hopeful

SKILLS FOCUS

Vocabulary Skills
Identify synonyms.

Vocabulary Review

Use this activity to assess whether students have retained the collection Vocabulary. **Activity.** Have students select the correct word from the box to complete the following sentences.

| confrontation | tirade | imminent |
| goaded | antics | |

1. Charles teased and _____ the big dog next door. [goaded]

2. He didn't seem to realize that he was in _____ danger. [imminent]

3. His actions were leading toward a fight or at least a _____. [confrontation]

4. I gave Charles a talking-to, and after my _____, he walked away. [tirade]

5. When the owner appeared, the dog engaged in playful _____. [antics]

Collection 2: Skills Review

Writing Skills

Test Practice

DIRECTIONS: Read the following paragraph from a problem-solution essay. Then, answer each question that follows.

(1) The backwater swamps of the American South support many life forms that are threatened by the overuse of natural resources. (2) Wetlands that have not been re-planted after logging are vulnerable to floods and erosion. (3) Because the soil is so rich, lands have been cleared for agriculture. (4) The great trees have been cut down for lumber. (5) Huge stands of oak, elm, cypress, and other species of North American wetlands have been removed from the landscape. (6) To preserve and protect this important habitat, we must all work for the reforestation of these swamps.

1. Which of the following statements might be added to support the opening sentence?
   - A Many swamp creatures are nocturnal.
   - B These wetlands shelter snakes, alligators, black bears, and many varieties of birds, as well as enormous trees.
   - C Many superstitions exist about swamps.
   - D The naturalist John James Audubon wrote about alligators on the shores of the Red River.

2. Where might sentence 2 be moved to make the paragraph more effective?
   - F to the beginning of the paragraph, to introduce the topic
   - G following sentence 5, to show the harm that can come from deforestation
   - H to the end of the paragraph, to serve as a call to action
   - J out of the paragraph altogether

3. What transitional word or phrase might be added to the beginning of sentence 5?
   - A Fortunately,
   - B Otherwise,
   - C However,
   - D For example,

4. How else might sentence 5 be strengthened?
   - F By explaining how lumber is used for construction
   - G By replacing "Huge stands" with more exact statistics
   - H By using comparisons to the destruction of rain forests
   - J By moving it to the end of the paragraph

5. In the remaining paragraphs of the essay, readers would expect to find all of the following *except* —
   - A possible objections to the solution
   - B the benefits of following the writer's plan
   - C a call for change or action
   - D lists of threatened jungle habitats

SKILLS FOCUS

Writing Skills
Analyze a problem-solution essay.

Test Practice

Answers and Model Rationales

1. **B**   B is correct because it provides examples of the threatened life forms mentioned in the opening sentence.

2. **G**   Sentence 2 explains the harmful consequences of deforestation. It would be effective only after sentence 5, which lists types of trees that have been cut down.

3. **D**   D is clearly the correct choice because the sentence lists types of trees that have been cut down.

4. **G**   F might provide extraneous information and would not strengthen sentence 5. H may draw parallels to the problem presented in the essay, but it would not strengthen this particular sentence. J is incorrect because the sentence would not be a proper conclusion for the paragraph. Only G would provide a concrete fact to strengthen the sentence.

5. **D**   D is a nonessential detail that may or may not be included in the essay.

APPLICATION

Practical Solutions for Community Problems

Have interested students divide into groups, choose a problem, and come up with practical solutions. Students can then write letters presenting their ideas to local newspapers, community associations, and government representatives.

EXTENSION

Analyzing Televised Debates

Have students watch a show that has a panel of commentators who discuss political topics. Have students pick one of the problems that the panelists discuss and write a brief essay about the solutions that are presented on the program. Students should discuss which of the solutions seems the most feasible.

READ ON

For Independent Reading

If students enjoyed the themes and topics explored in this collection, you might recommend these titles for independent reading.

Assessment Options

The following projects can help you evaluate and assess your students' outside reading. Videotapes or audiotapes of completed projects may be included in students' portfolios.

■ **Paint a panoramic mural.**
Point out to students that when M. C. Higgins climbs his forty-foot pole, he has an amazing view. Have students divide up that view into four-foot segments and paint or draw each segment on butcher paper. Remind them that much of what M. C. sees is the Cumberland Mountains. He also sees glimpses of some towns and, all too close to home, a slag heap from strip mining. Suggest that students search the library or the Internet for pictures of M. C.'s region. They might also check nature guides for the types of trees and shrubs that grow in the region so they can paint them realistically. When the artists have finished, have them hang their pictures in a continuous panorama around the room.

Fiction

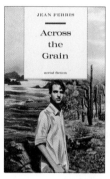

A Moving Experience

Orphan Will Griffin is feeling lost when he relocates to the California desert with his flighty sister. Then Will meets a moody girl named Mike and an old loner named Sam. These three outsiders help one another through sorrowful times and discover the value of friendship in Jean Ferris's *Across the Grain*.

Family Ties

M. C. Higgins and his family have been living on Sarah's Mountain ever since M. C.'s great-grandmother arrived there as a fugitive from slavery. His family loves their mountain, but one day M. C. notices a massive pile of debris accumulating on a cliff over their home. In Virginia Hamilton's *M. C. Higgins, the Great*, a young boy is torn between his loyalty to his family and his desire for a life beyond the mountain.

This title is available in the HRW Library.

The Notebook

If you are interested in writing, you might enjoy Louise Fitzhugh's *Harriet the Spy*. Harriet Welsch longs to be a writer, so she begins recording honest observations of her classmates in her secret notebook. When the notebook is discovered by the classmates, Harriet finds out what being a writer really means.

Friendly Fire

Artos is lonely and dissatisfied in his medieval castle. The other boys mock him because he does not know who his birth parents are. His life changes when he meets Linn, an old dragon who lives in a cave. In Jane Yolen's *The Dragon's Boy*, Linn guides Artos with his wisdom and proves that Artos's life will have great meaning after all.

DIFFERENTIATING INSTRUCTION

Estimated Word Counts of Read On Books:

Fiction		Nonfiction	
Across the Grain	56,000	*At Her Majesty's Request: An African*	
M. C. Higgins, the Great	68,000	*Princess in Victorian England*	20,000
Connections to *M. C. Higgins,*		*Bill Nye the Science Guy's*	
the Great	11,000	*Consider the Following*	22,000
Harriet the Spy	68,000	*Commodore Perry in*	
The Dragon's Boy	21,000	*the Land of the Shogun*	28,000
		Castles	15,000

Nonfiction

Starting a New Life

In *At Her Majesty's Request: An African Princess in Victorian England*, Walter Dean Myers tells the story of Sarah Forbes Bonetta, who was saved from death by a British sea captain. As a result, she spent her life in nineteenth-century England, a place where others made life decisions for her. Myers includes newspaper articles and portraits to add to the reality of Bonetta's compelling story.

Science Stumpers

Have you ever wondered why leaves change color in the autumn? how a magnet sticks to a refrigerator? what prevents a heavy boat from sinking in the ocean? Bill Nye has the answers to all these questions and a whole lot more in *Bill Nye the Science Guy's Consider the Following*.

© 1995 by Bill Nye. Used by permission of Disney Enterprises, Inc.

An Era Begins

In *Commodore Perry in the Land of the Shogun*, Rhoda Blumberg describes the beginning of trade talks between Japan and the United States in the nineteenth century. Blumberg sensitively depicts relations between two distinct cultural groups who were wary of each other at first but grew to respect each other's differences.

Medieval Times

Philip Steele provides an engaging overview of medieval life in *Castles*. In addition to providing astonishing and informative illustrations showing how castles were built, Steele describes the weapons used by medieval warriors and narrates a typical day in a castle town.

Assessment Options

- **Tape an interview.** If two students read *The Dragon's Boy*, suggest that they role-play the two main characters, Artos and Linn. Have Artos interview Linn about the many fascinating things he has seen and done in his long life. Encourage the student playing Linn to make up incidents that go beyond the scope of the book, but remind both students to stay in character.

- **Compare a novel with a nonfiction book.** Ask students who read both *The Dragon's Boy* and *Castles* to create a compare-and-contrast chart. What are the similarities and differences between the way Yolen describes medieval life and the way Steele describes it? How accurate are Yolen's descriptions of Artos's home? Make sure the charts are complete enough to answer these questions.

- **Perform an experiment.** Tell students to choose a favorite experiment from *Bill Nye the Science Guy's Consider the Following*. Students may wish to work in small groups to try the experiment several times. When they feel they've perfected the experiment, they should perform it for the class. Remind students that they should understand the scientific reasons for what happens in the experiment well enough to answer questions from the class.

The Read On titles are categorized as shown below:

Collection 3
Living in the Heart

Literary Focus:
Analyzing Theme

Informational Focus:
Analyzing Cause and Effect

About Collection 3

In Collection 3, students will master the following skills:

- **Literary Skills:** Understand and analyze theme and recurring themes; compare and contrast a story and a poem.
- **Reading Skills:** Analyze cause-and-effect text structures; make and analyze outlines.
- **Vocabulary Skills:** Understand similes, metaphors, and Latin roots; identify and explain idioms; use context clues.
- **Writing Skills:** Develop, write, and revise a personal narrative.

Informational Text

Each collection of *Elements of Literature* provides a variety of informational texts related to the literature selections by theme or topic.

Minimum Course of Study

Most skills can be taught with a minimum number of selections and features. In the chart to the right, lessons highlighted in green constitute the minimum course of study that provides coverage of the skills taught in Collection 3.

Scope and Sequence

Selection ■ Feature	Literary Skills
Elements of Literature: Theme *by Mara Rockliff*	• Understand and analyze theme
Reading Skills and Strategies: Finding the Theme Hearts and Hands *by O. Henry* ↓ *below grade level*	
The Highwayman *by Alfred Noyes* ↑ *above grade level* **Informational Text: Gentlemen of the Road** *by Mara Rockliff* ↔ *at grade level*	• Analyze narrative poems • Analyze theme
Annabel Lee *by Edgar Allan Poe* ↓ *below grade level* **Informational Text: The Fall of the House of Poe?** *by Mara Rockliff* ↑ *above grade level*	• Analyze theme • Understand repetition in poetry
User Friendly *by T. Ernesto Bethancourt* ↔ *at grade level* **Informational Text: It Just Keeps Going and Going . . .** *by Joan Burditt* ↔ *at grade level*	• Analyze theme
Echo and Narcissus *retold by* Roger Lancelyn Green ↔ *at grade level*	• Analyze recurring themes

Resource Manager
(pp. 234E–234H)

Lesson and workshop resources are referenced in the Resource Manager on the pages that follow. These resources can be used to reinforce the skills taught in Collection 3, remediate students who are having difficulty, and provide supporting activities for English-language learners.

Reading Skills	Vocabulary Skills	Writing ▪ Grammar and Language Skills
• Find the theme		
• Analyze cause and effect	• Understand similes and metaphors	• Describe events from another point of view
• Make and analyze outlines	• Understand and use analogies • Understand Latin roots	• Write a tribute to a person
• Analyze cause and effect • Analyze cause-and-effect text structures	• Identify and explain idioms • Understand analogies	• Write a tribute to an object • Use pronouns correctly
	• Use context clues	• Write an origin myth • Use *its* and *it's* and *your* and *you're* correctly

(continued)

Selection ▪ Feature	Literary Skills	Reading Skills
Comparing Literature: Settings, Characters, Themes **Charles** *by* Shirley Jackson ↔ *at grade level* **Miss Awful** *by* Arthur Cavanaugh ↔ *at grade level*	• Analyze characters, settings, and themes	• Compare and contrast stories
No Questions Asked: **The Only Girl in the World for Me** *from* **Love and Marriage** *by* Bill Cosby ↓ *below grade level* **To a Golden-Haired Girl in a Louisiana Town** *by* Vachel Lindsay ↓ *below grade level*		
Writing Workshop: *Narrative Writing: Personal Narrative*		
Skills Review: *Literary Skills* *Informational Reading Skills* *Vocabulary Skills* *Writing Skills*	• Analyze theme; compare and contrast a story and a poem	• Analyze cause and effect

Reading Skills and Strategies

At the beginning of each collection, a **Reading Skills and Strategies** feature written by Kylene Beers offers students strategies to improve their reading skills. Dr. Beers first models the strategy for the students, then guides them through an annotated selection. The questions in her annotations help students apply the strategy to the selection. After the selection, **Practice the Strategy** provides additional tips and practice.

Comparing Literature / Author Study

Each collection has a **Comparing Literature** or **Author Study** feature that focuses on two or more selections that are thematically or topically linked. The selections represent a variety of genres. The features begin with a prereading page that introduces a Literary Focus and a Reading Skill as well as additional information that students may find useful. Each **Comparing Literature** or **Author Study** feature ends with instruction in writing a comparison-contrast essay about the selections they've read or provides a variety of writing, speaking and listening, or other assignments.

Vocabulary Skills	Writing ▪ Grammar and Language Skills
	• Write a personal narrative
• Use context clues	• Analyze a personal narrative

No Questions Asked

Each collection ends with a **No Questions Asked** feature that includes one or more selections without accompanying apparatus. These selections allow students to practice reading independently. Annotations for teaching the selections are provided in the **Annotated Teacher's Edition.**

Selection ■ Feature	Planning	Differentiating Instruction ■ Lesson Plans with ELL Strategies and Practice	Reading ■ Vocabulary
Elements of Literature: Theme *by Mara Rockliff*		• Holt Reading Solutions: Lesson Plans, pp. 95–96	• Holt Reading Solutions, pp. 95–96
Reading Skills and Strategies: Finding the Theme Hearts and Hands *by O. Henry*			
The Highwayman *by Alfred Noyes* **Informational Text: Gentlemen of the Road** *by Mara Rockliff*	• One-Stop Planner with ExamView Test Generator	• The Holt Reader, pp. 94–103 • Holt Adapted Reader, pp. 58–73 • Holt Reading Solutions: Lesson Plans, pp. 97–104 • Supporting Instruction in Spanish, p. 9 • Audio CD Library • Audio CD Library, Selections and Summaries in Spanish	• The Holt Reader, pp. 94–103 • Holt Adapted Reader, pp. 58–73 • Holt Reading Solutions, pp. 97–104
Annabel Lee *by Edgar Allan Poe* **Informational Text: The Fall of the House of Poe?** *by Mara Rockliff*	• One-Stop Planner with ExamView Test Generator	• Holt Adapted Reader, pp. 74–77 • Holt Reading Solutions: Lesson Plans, pp. 105–112 • Supporting Instruction in Spanish, p. 10 • Audio CD Library • Audio CD Library, Selections and Summaries in Spanish	• Holt Adapted Reader, pp. 74–77 • Holt Reading Solutions, pp. 105–112
User Friendly *by T. Ernesto Bethancourt* **Informational Text: It Just Keeps Going and Going …** *by Joan Burditt*	• One-Stop Planner with ExamView Test Generator	• Holt Adapted Reader, pp. 78–83 • Holt Reading Solutions: Lesson Plans, pp. 113–120 • Supporting Instruction in Spanish, pp. 10, 11 • Audio CD Library • Audio CD Library, Selections and Summaries in Spanish	• Holt Adapted Reader, pp. 78–83 • Holt Reading Solutions, pp. 113–120
Echo and Narcissus *retold by* Roger Lancelyn Green	• One-Stop Planner with ExamView Test Generator • PowerNotes: The Myths of Greece and Rome	• The Holt Reader, pp. 104–112 • Holt Adapted Reader, pp. 84–89 • Holt Reading Solutions: Lesson Plans, pp. 121–126 • Supporting Instruction in Spanish, p. 12 • Audio CD Library • Audio CD Library, Selections and Summaries in Spanish	• The Holt Reader, pp. 104–112 • Holt Adapted Reader, pp. 84–89 • Holt Reading Solutions, pp. 121–126 • Vocabulary Development, p. 11

Writing · Grammar and Language	Assessment
• Daily Language Activities	• Holt Assessment: Literature, Reading, and Vocabulary • One-Stop Planner with ExamView Test Generator • Holt Online Assessment
• Daily Language Activities	• Holt Assessment: Literature, Reading, and Vocabulary • One-Stop Planner with ExamView Test Generator • Holt Online Assessment
• Daily Language Activities • Language Handbook Worksheets, pp. 39–43	• Holt Assessment: Literature, Reading, and Vocabulary • One-Stop Planner with ExamView Test Generator • Holt Online Assessment
• Daily Language Activities • Language Handbook Worksheets, pp. 140–142	• Holt Assessment: Literature, Reading, and Vocabulary • One-Stop Planner with ExamView Test Generator • Holt Online Assessment

(continued)

Technology

INTERNET

- go.hrw.com
- Holt Online Assessment
- Holt Online Essay Scoring
- Elements of Literature Online

MEDIA

 • One-Stop Planner with ExamView Test Generator

• PowerNotes

• Audio CD Library

• Audio CD Library, Selections and Summaries in Spanish

• Visual Connections Videocassette Program, Segment 3

• Fine Art Transparencies, 3 and 4

 Transparency   Video

 CD-ROM   Audio CD

Selection ▪ Feature	Planning	Differentiating Instruction ▪ Lesson Plans with ELL Strategies and Practice	Reading ▪ Vocabulary
Comparing Literature: Settings, Characters, Themes **Charles** *by* Shirley Jackson **Miss Awful** *by* Arthur Cavanaugh		• Holt Reading Solutions: Lesson Plans, pp. 127–130	• Holt Reading Solutions, pp. 127–130
No Questions Asked: **The Only Girl in the World for Me** *from* **Love and Marriage** *by* Bill Cosby **To a Golden-Haired Girl in a Louisiana Town** *by* Vachel Lindsay			
Writing Workshop: *Narrative Writing: Personal Narrative*	• One-Stop Planner with ExamView Test Generator	• Workshop Resources: Writing, Listening, and Speaking, pp. 23–33 • Supporting Instruction in Spanish, p. 39	
Skills Review: *Literary Skills* *Informational Reading Skills* *Vocabulary Skills* *Writing Skills*			

The Holt Reader

The Holt Reader is a consumable paperback book that can be used alone or to accompany *Elements of Literature*. It offers guided support throughout the reading process and encourages students to become active readers by circling, underlining, questioning, and jotting down responses as they read. *The Holt Reader* works well for homework, students who have missed class, additional instructional time, reteaching, and remediation.

Holt Reading Solutions (HRS)

Holt Reading Solutions pulls together reading resources in the *Elements of Literature* program to create a powerful tool for intervention and whole-class instruction. *HRS* includes diagnostic assessment tools, lesson plans for English-language learners and special education students, adaptations of selected reading selections, vocabulary and comprehension worksheets, information on phonics and decoding, and additional instruction and practice in remedial reading skills.

Writing · Grammar and Language	Assessment
• Workshop Resources: Writing, Listening, and Speaking, pp. 23–33 • Language Handbook Worksheets • Daily Language Activities	• Holt Assessment: Literature, Reading, and Vocabulary • One-Stop Planner with ExamView Test Generator • Holt Online Assessment • Holt Online Essay Scoring
	• Holt Assessment: Literature, Reading, and Vocabulary • One-Stop Planner with ExamView Test Generator • Holt Online Assessment

Technology

INTERNET

- go.hrw.com
- Holt Online Assessment
- Holt Online Essay Scoring
- Elements of Literature Online

MEDIA

 • One-Stop Planner with ExamView Test Generator

 • PowerNotes

 • Audio CD Library

 • Audio CD Library, Selections and Summaries in Spanish

 • Visual Connections Videocassette Program, Segment 3

 • Fine Art Transparencies, 3 and 4

One-Stop Planner with ExamView Test Generator

The *One-Stop Planner* CD-ROM planning software contains print-based teaching resources, clips from the video program, and valuable assessment tools. The *One-Stop Planner* resources are presented in easy-to-follow, point-and-click menu formats. To preview resources or print out worksheets and tests, you simply make a selection and click.

One-Stop Planner CD-ROM

 Transparency   Video

 CD-ROM   Audio CD

Collection 3

SKILLS FOCUS

Grade-Level Skills

■ **Literary Skills**
Identify and analyze recurring themes.

■ **Reading Skills**
Analyze texts that show cause-and-effect relationships.

■ **Vocabulary Skills**
Identify and understand idioms, analogies, metaphors, and similes.

■ **Vocabulary Skills**
Use Latin roots to determine meanings of unfamiliar words.

Review Skills

■ **Literary Skills**
Identify themes as conveyed through characters, actions, and images.

■ **Reading Skills**
Understand informational texts by creating outlines and taking logical notes.

Upcoming Skills

■ **Literary Skills**
Analyze recurring themes across traditional and contemporary works.

■ **Vocabulary Skills**
Analyze idioms, analogies, and other figures of speech to infer both the literal and the figurative meanings of a text.

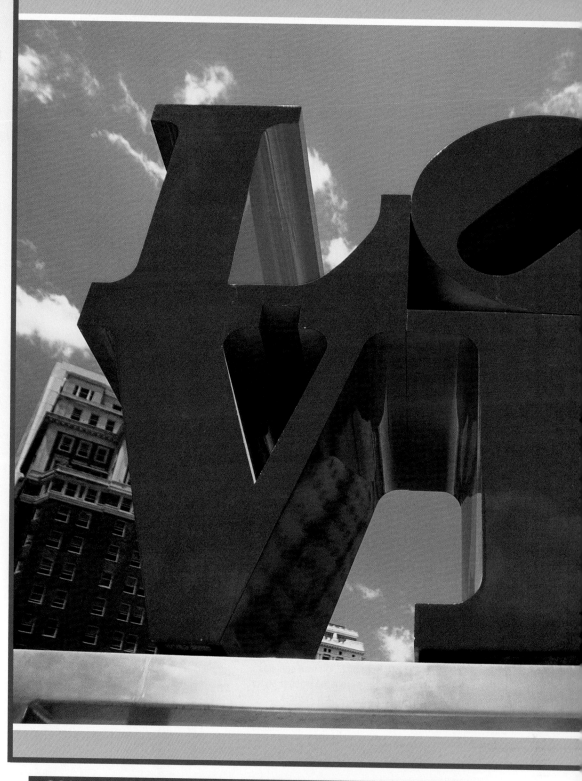

COLLECTION 3 RESOURCES: READING

Planning
■ *One-Stop Planner* CD-ROM with ExamView Test Generator

Differentiating Instruction
■ *The Holt Reader*
■ *Holt Adapted Reader*
■ *Holt Reading Solutions*
■ *Family Involvement Activities in English and Spanish*

■ *Supporting Instruction in Spanish*
■ *Audio CD Library*
■ *Audio CD Library, Selections and Summaries in Spanish*

Vocabulary
■ *Vocabulary Development*

Grammar and Language
■ *Language Handbook Worksheets*
■ *Daily Language Activities*

Collection 3

Living in the Heart

Literary Focus:
Analyzing Theme

Informational Focus:
Analyzing Cause and Effect

INTERNET

Collection
Resources
Keyword: LE5 7-3

LOVE Sculpture
by Robert Indiana.

235

INTRODUCING THE COLLECTION

Theme: Living in the heart.
Explain to the class that each of the stories and poems in this collection centers on an unusual and unforgettable relationship. Point out that several of the selections focus on the love and care people show others. As they read the selections, remind students to look for universal themes expressed by the writers.

Analyzing theme. Students will explore the way writers reveal the theme, or truth about life, of a work. They will learn how to infer the theme of the work based on analyzing characters, important passages, and the titles of stories. In addition, students will learn how to identify and analyze recurring themes across works.

Analyzing cause and effect. Students will read informational pieces connected to the literature that teach the cause-and-effect organizational pattern. They will determine how writers use this pattern to convey ideas effectively.

VIEWING THE ART

Explain to the students that this sculpture by **Robert Indiana** (1928–) also served as the basis for a postage stamp. The city of Philadelphia may have chosen this particular work of art to place in front of its Convention and Visitors Bureau because Philadelphia is known as the City of Brotherly Love.

Assessment
- *Holt Assessment: Literature, Reading, and Vocabulary*
- *One-Stop Planner* CD-ROM with ExamView Test Generator
- *Holt Online Assessment*

Internet
- go.hrw.com (Keyword: LE5 7-3)
- *Elements of Literature Online*

Media
- *Audio CD Library*
- *Audio CD Library, Selections and Summaries in Spanish*
- *Fine Art Transparencies*
- *Visual Connections Videocassette Program*
- *PowerNotes*

Grade-Level Skills

■ Literary Skills
Understand and analyze theme.

Elements of Literature: Theme

Ask volunteers to name movies they have recently seen that made them think. List these movies on the chalkboard. Ask what aspects of the movies made students continue thinking or talking about them. Explain that the *theme* is the underlying message the writer and director want viewers to carry away from the movie theater. If students feel that they learned something about life from a film, they have understood its theme or themes. Point out that written works also have themes.

Elements of Literature
Theme *by* Mara Rockliff

WHAT'S THE BIG IDEA?

A key element of literature—of fiction, nonfiction, poetry, and drama—is theme. **Theme** is a revelation about our lives; theme is a discovery of a truth about our own human experience.

Theme Is a Revelation

Suppose we read a story about two friends. Surprisingly, one friend betrays the other. If the story is well written, we will feel that we have lived through the betrayal ourselves. We will feel that the tragedy could have happened in exactly the way the writer tells it. As we share the characters' experiences in the story, we also discover something. We discover—or rediscover—the delicate nature and value of friendship.

Themes Focus on the "Big" Ideas

Literature that endures, that lasts through the centuries, tends to focus on discoveries about the big topics in everyone's life: understanding the nature of love, accepting responsibility, understanding loss, dealing with ambition, discovering the joys and problems of friendship.

A theme isn't something a writer tacks on to a story or poem to make it more literary. Theme grows naturally out of what the writer believes and out of the story that's being told.

If you've read several novels, you

INTERNET

More About Theme

Keyword: LE5 7-3

SKILLS FOCUS

Literary Skills
Understand and analyze theme.

know that works by different writers can have similar themes, even though their stories may be quite different. Themes recur over and over again in the stories we tell because some truths about the human experience are universal, whether a story was written hundreds of years ago in a snowbound Alaskan village or typed on a laptop yesterday in Zimbabwe.

Plot Isn't Theme

"Plot is what a story is about," someone once said. "Theme is what a story is *really* about."

A story's plot might be about a family that drinks from a magical spring, becomes immortal, and suffers the consequences. That's what happens. But what's the story *really* about? What does the story reveal to you about life?

Maybe it reveals that living forever is more frightening than dying. Maybe it reveals that without death, growth and change would be impossible and life would no longer give us pleasure. In a single plot you might discover both themes, or you might see an entirely different theme instead.

Where Does It Say That?

You usually won't find the theme of a piece of literature stated directly. Theme is what the writer wants you to *discover* for yourself as you share the

236   Collection 3 / Living in the Heart

DIFFERENTIATING INSTRUCTION

Learners Having Difficulty
Theme versus plot. To help students distinguish theme from plot, draw a plot diagram on the chalkboard, and ask students to identify key plot events from a well-known movie, such as *Finding Nemo*. Write each plot event by one of the following labels: *exposition, conflict, complications, climax,* and *resolution*. Point out that the plot diagram helps to show how events in a story are linked together. Then, invite

students to recall important dialogue or monologues in which characters address the meaning behind the plot events students provided. Have students contrast the actions, words, and even the physical appearance of characters at the start and at the end of the film to find clues to how the characters have changed or what they have learned about life. Jot down students' responses and remind them that their observations will help them infer themes, experiences of the story's characters. One way to identify the theme is to look closely at what the writer is saying. Consider these questions:

- How has the main **character** changed over the course of the story? What has he or she **discovered** by the story's end?
- Which scenes or passages strike you as especially important to the story? What ideas about life do they suggest?
- What is the story's **title**? Does it reveal anything special about the story?

Evaluating Theme

Why go to the trouble of figuring out a story's theme? Why not just enjoy the plot and not worry about whether you've gotten the theme?

Because the theme *will* get through to you whether you realize it or not. Watch a double feature of shoot'em-up action movies, and twice in one night you've absorbed the idea that the world is a dangerous place where problems are best solved through violence. Read another teen romance, and you've been told once again that nothing is more important than finding true love.

You are not going to agree with all themes. In some stories you'll feel that the truth you're getting is the real deal, a gold nugget of wisdom the writer has discovered through hard experience and is passing on to you. In other stories you'll feel that the writer is just giving you an overused formula, which the writer repeats without even believing it.

Putting a theme into words brings it out into the open, where you can look at it critically and decide if it fits with what *you* know about life.

Practice

Choose two novels you have read recently that deal with similar topics—for example, loyalty, courage, friendship, or loneliness. If you have a favorite writer, use two novels by this writer.

Take a blank sheet of paper, and draw a chart like the one below. Write the title of each novel at the top of the page. Underneath the titles, identify their topics. Then, in one or two sentences, state the theme of each novel—what the story reveals to you about that topic.

Are the themes in the novels the same or different? Which theme do you find more important or more appealing and why?

Novel 1	Novel 2
Topic	Topic
Theme	Theme

Theme: What's the Big Idea? **237**

Possible answer for two books by Laura Ingalls Wilder, *By the Shores of Silver Lake* and *The Long Winter.*

■ *By the Shores of Silver Lake*
   Topic—a girl's growing up in the Dakota territory in the 1880s.
   Theme—Home is any place where family and friends are together.
■ *The Long Winter*
   Topic—a girl's growing up in the Dakota territory in the 1880s.
   Theme—Never give up, even when faced with terrible odds. For the community to survive, everyone must work together.

Similarities in themes—Both novels stress the importance of home and family and of everyone working together and cooperating. *Differences in themes*—The Long Winter deals more directly with overcoming odds; the entire town is threatened with starvation during a winter of fierce blizzards when no supply trains can get through. *By the Shores of Silver Lake* tells a story of facing and overcoming everyday difficulties.

Take a few minutes to sit down with each student individually and go over his or her answers to the Practice activity. If students have difficulty articulating the novels' themes, help them by asking questions such as the following:

- What did the main character learn by the end of the novel?
- What did this story make you think about after you had finished reading it?
- Do you think the writer was trying to say something to you, the reader? What was the message?

Apply

Have students find two short stories by the same author, such as O. Henry, Walter Dean Myers, Cynthia Rylant, or Gary Soto. Students can read the two stories and repeat the Practice activity using them.

HOMEWORK

and that a work may contain more than one theme.

Advanced Learners

Acceleration. To help advanced learners identify and analyze recurring themes across traditional and modern works, have students choose two stories—one traditional and one modern—in which characters of differing backgrounds overcome their differences to reach understanding.

Then, ask students to write a brief dialogue between the main characters of each story in which the shared theme is discussed in the context of each story's historical setting.

OVERVIEW

Purpose. The purpose of finding the theme of a story is to discover the message about life that the author is trying to convey.
Use. Finding the theme is essential to understanding any story or poem that expresses an idea about the human experience. It is especially useful for short stories and narrative poems in which the main character is facing difficult circumstances or undergoes a change in attitude. Writers often use changes in a character's attitude to express their views on life. With "Hearts and Hands," have students look for clues in the actions and behavior of each character that point to the story's central idea. Finding the theme may also be useful for students when they read myths, such as "Orpheus, the Great Musician" and "The Flight of Icarus" in Collection 6. The actions of characters in myths are often used to teach a lesson about life.

Summary ⬇ *below grade level*

Two men who are handcuffed together board a train. Miss Fairchild recognizes the younger of the two men, Mr. Easton, and reintroduces herself to him. She then notices that the two men are handcuffed to each other. The older man explains that he is being taken to prison by Mr. Easton, the marshal. Miss Fairchild, relieved, continues chatting with Mr. Easton until the other man complains that he wants to have a pipe. The pair depart amicably. After they leave, a passenger who overheard the conversation reveals that Mr. Easton is actually the prisoner and the other man is the marshal.

Reading Skills and Strategies

Finding the Theme

by Kylene Beers

❝So what's the theme of the story?" the teacher asked. Many students looked down at their books. One student began going through his backpack. "Why are you looking in your backpack?" the teacher asked. The student shrugged and replied, "Maybe the answer is in there, because it certainly isn't anyplace else."

Theme—What It Is and Is Not

When you are asked to think about theme, you might start by remembering what theme is *not*. Theme is *not* the **plot** or the **topic** of a story. **Theme** is a truth about life, which you discover by reading the story. You can't express a theme in one word, the way you can state a topic. You need a full sentence to explain the theme.

Read each item below, and decide whether it states a plot, a topic, or a theme:

1. A family travels to Alabama and faces hardships along the way.
2. Prejudice
3. Facing your fears is the only way to overcome them.
4. Happiness can be found in the joys of ordinary life.

SKILLS FOCUS

Reading Skills
Find the theme.

Tips for Uncovering Theme

It might be nice if writers included a P.S. to their stories that said, "The theme of this story is . . ." But they don't do that. Instead, writers allow us to meet characters and share an experience with them.

At the end of the story, we, along with the characters, have discovered something about human experience. It might be something we already know but rediscover in new circumstances. It might be something we haven't thought about before.

The **theme,** then, is a truth about life or people that we discover as we share the characters' experiences.

As you read the story that follows, ask yourself

• What is the plot?
• What is the topic?
• What is the story's truth—its theme?

Remember, you must express the theme as a sentence—one that explains what you've discovered from the story.

DIFFERENTIATING INSTRUCTION

Learners Having Difficulty
Theme is a relatively difficult concept for students to grasp. Tell students that they can figure out a story's theme by examining how the central problem in the story is resolved. After students read the story, have them identify the central problem and its resolution. Then, ask them to consider the outcome of the story and state what they think the author is trying to say about life.

English-Language Learners
Students may be unfamiliar with the position of a marshal. Explain to students that a marshal in this context is not a high-ranking military post, but rather, an officer who carries out the orders of a federal court. Explain to students that a marshal can carry out duties similar to those of a sheriff: executing court orders and keeping peace within a county. This may be why Miss Fairchild seems impressed by Mr. Easton's position.

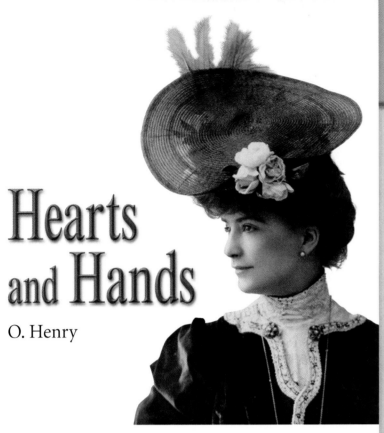

Hearts and Hands

O. Henry

Using the Strategy

As you read, you'll find this open-book sign at certain points in the story: 📖. Stop at these points, and think about what you've just read. Do what the prompts ask you to do.

At Denver there was an influx of passengers into the coaches on the eastbound B. & M. express. In one coach there sat a very pretty young woman dressed in elegant taste and surrounded by all the luxurious comforts of an experienced traveler. Among the newcomers were two young men, one of handsome presence with a bold, frank countenance and manner; the other a ruffled, glum-faced person, heavily built and roughly dressed. The two were handcuffed together. ❶ 📖

As they passed down the aisle of the coach the only vacant seat offered was a reversed one facing the attractive young woman. Here the linked couple seated themselves. The young woman's glance fell upon them with a distant, swift disinterest; then with a lovely smile brightening her countenance and a tender pink tingeing her rounded cheeks, she held out a little gray-gloved hand. When she spoke her voice, full, sweet, and deliberate, proclaimed that its owner was accustomed to speak and be heard.

IDENTIFY

❶ Who are the three main characters in this story? Where does the story take place?

Ⓐ

Ⓑ

PRETEACHING

Selection Starter
Motivate. Ask students to think of a time when they've helped a friend in need. The instance could be something as simple as providing help with homework or a household chore. What did they gain by helping out? Would they do it again? Why or why not? Encourage students to share their responses in class.

DIRECT TEACHING

Ⓐ Reading Skills and Strategies
Identify. [Possible response to question 1: The three main characters are the young woman and the two handcuffed men. The story takes place on an eastbound train leaving Denver.]

Ⓑ Reading Skills and Strategies
❓ Infer. What have you learned about the young woman in this passage? From these details, how do you think she will interact with the two men? [Possible responses: She is attractive and elegant in dress and manner. She will probably get along better with the younger, handsome man than with the older, gruff one.]

Special Education Students
Explain to special education students that writers express their themes through important details in their works. Tell them that reading closely is essential to uncovering theme. Instruct students to jot down the three words or phrases that they think are the most important in the story as they read. After they finish reading, have them use those words or phrases as the basis of a statement of the story's theme.

Advanced Learners
Enrichment. Ask students to consider how the resolution of the story defines the theme that the writer is trying to convey. Then, ask students how the story would change if the marshal admitted that Mr. Easton was a criminal or if Miss Fairchild discovered Mr. Easton's secret on her own. A very different theme would emerge if the story's ending changed.
Activity. Have students rewrite the ending of the story by changing the way the central

problem is resolved. Then, have them write a sentence that expresses the theme reflected in the new story's ending.

A Learners Having Difficulty

Break down difficult text. This long sentence may be hard for some students to follow. Have students break it down by listing the four actions that occur in the sentence. [(1) The younger man is startled by her voice. (2) He becomes embarrassed. (3) He shrugs off his embarrassment. (4) He shakes the woman's hand.]

B Reading Skills and Strategies

Infer. [Possible response to question 2: He is embarrassed that he didn't greet the woman first. He was not expecting to meet someone he knows.]

C Reading Skills and Strategies

Infer. [Possible response to question 3: She might be thinking that Mr. Easton is a criminal who is under arrest.]

D Reading Skills and Strategies

Interpret. [Possible response to question 4: The glum-faced man has indicated that he, not Mr. Easton, is the prisoner. Miss Fairchild reacts with relief and resumes her conversation with Mr. Easton.]

E Reading Skills and Strategies

Infer. [Possible response to question 5: The conversation suggests that Mr. Easton and Miss Fairchild were once romantically involved but that she became involved with an ambassador.]

Using the Strategy

INFER

B ❷ Why do you think Mr. Easton is embarrassed?

INFER

C ❸ Read this paragraph again. Think about how Miss Fairchild's expression changes when she sees the handcuffs. What might she be thinking?

INTERPRET

D ❹ What has just happened? Who indicated that he is the prisoner? How does Miss Fairchild react?

INFER

E ❺ What do you guess happened between Mr. Easton and Miss Fairchild in Washington?

"Well, Mr. Easton, if you *will* make me speak first, I suppose I must. Don't you ever recognize old friends when you meet them in the West?"

A The younger man roused himself sharply at the sound of her voice, seemed to struggle with a slight embarrassment which he threw off instantly, and then clasped her fingers with his left hand. ❷

"It's Miss Fairchild," he said, with a smile. "I'll ask you to excuse the other hand; it's otherwise engaged just at present."

He slightly raised his right hand, bound at the wrist by the shining "bracelet" to the left one of his companion. The glad look in the girl's eyes slowly changed to a bewildered horror. The glow faded from her cheeks. Her lips parted in a vague, relaxing distress. Easton, with a little laugh, as if amused, was about to speak again when the other forestalled[1] him. The glum-faced man had been watching the girl's countenance with veiled glances from his keen, shrewd eyes. ❸

"You'll excuse me for speaking, miss, but I see you're acquainted with the marshal here. If you'll ask him to speak a word for me when we get to the pen he'll do it, and it'll make things easier for me there. He's taking me to Leavenworth prison. It's seven years for counterfeiting."

"Oh!" said the girl, with a deep breath and returning color. "So that is what you are doing out here? A marshal!" ❹

"My dear Miss Fairchild," said Easton, calmly, "I had to do something. Money has a way of taking wings unto itself, and you know it takes money to keep step with our crowd in Washington. I saw this opening in the West, and—well, a marshalship isn't quite as high a position as that of ambassador, but—"

"The ambassador," said the girl, warmly, "doesn't call anymore. He needn't ever have done so. You ought to know that. And so now you are one of these dashing Western heroes, and you ride and shoot and go into all kinds of dangers. That's different from the Washington life. You have been missed from the old crowd." ❺

The girl's eyes, fascinated, went back, widening a little, to rest upon the glittering handcuffs.

"Don't you worry about them, miss," said the other man. "All marshals handcuff themselves to their prisoners to keep them from getting away. Mr. Easton knows his business."

"Will we see you again soon in Washington?" asked the girl.

---

1. **forestalled** (fôr·stôld′) *v.:* prevented.

DIRECT TEACHING

F **Reading Skills and Strategies**

Infer. [Possible response to question 6: Miss Fairchild believes that Mr. Easton lives in the West; she may be hoping to receive an invitation to visit him.]

G **Reading Skills and Strategies**

Infer. [Possible responses to question 7: The prisoner might have something he needs to say to the marshal in private. He is getting bored with the conversation.]

"Not soon, I think," said Easton. "My butterfly days are over, I fear."

"I love the West," said the girl irrelevantly.[2] Her eyes were shining softly. She looked away out the car window. She began to speak truly and simply, without the gloss of style and manner: "Mamma and I spent the summer in Denver. She went home a week ago because father was slightly ill. I could live and be happy in the West. I think the air here agrees with me. Money isn't everything. But people always misunderstand things and remain stupid—"

"Say, Mr. Marshal," growled the glum-faced man. "This isn't quite fair. Haven't had a smoke all day. Haven't you talked long enough? Take me in the smoker now, won't you? I'm half dead for a pipe."

The bound travelers rose to their feet, Easton with the same slow smile on his face.

"I can't deny a petition for tobacco," he said, lightly. "It's the one friend of the unfortunate. Goodbye, Miss Fairchild. Duty calls, you know." He held out his hand for a farewell.

"It's too bad you are not going East," she said, reclothing herself with manner and style. "But you must go on to Leavenworth, I suppose?"

"Yes," said Easton, "I must go on to Leavenworth."

INFER

6 Why does Miss Fairchild tell Mr. Easton she loves the West?

INFER

7 Why do you think the "prisoner" suddenly decides he wants to leave?

---

2. irrelevantly (i·rel′ə·vənt·lē) *adv.:* without relation to the subject at hand.

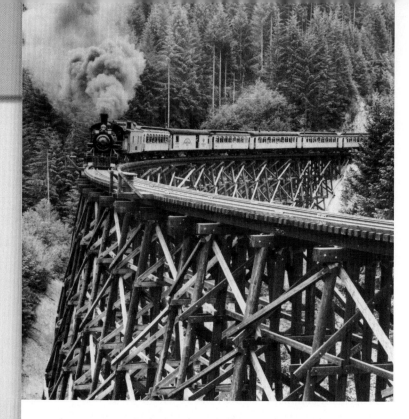

DIRECT TEACHING

A Reading Skills and Strategies

Analyze. [Possible responses to question 8: The prisoner turns out to be Mr. Easton. The marshal is the older man who was covering for him. The story shows that through a simple act of compassion, one person can help another person preserve his or her dignity. Compassion is sometimes shown by those from whom you would least expect it.

The hands in the title are those of Mr. Easton and the marshal, which are bound together by handcuffs. Hearts could refer to the romantic link between Miss Fairchild and Mr. Easton and to the marshal's compassion. The title gives a clue to the story's theme by suggesting that people's hearts are linked together the way that Mr. Easton's and the marshal's hands are.]

B Reading Skills and Strategies

❓ Evaluate. Do you think the plot twist at the end of the story is convincing? Explain. [Possible responses: No, I don't think it's likely that a marshal would cover for his prisoner. Yes, because the marshal has nothing to gain by revealing that Mr. Easton is under arrest.]

ANALYZE

❽ Explain the story's surprise ending. As you think about the marshal's actions, remember that the **theme** of a story is a truth you discover **A** through reading it. What did you discover about the power of compassion? What does this story show about how easy it is to help someone?

What does the title refer to? Does it give you a clue to the story's theme?

The two men sidled down the aisle into the smoker.

The two passengers in a seat nearby had heard most of the conversation. Said one of them: "That marshal's a good sort of chap. Some of these Western fellows are all right."

"Pretty young to hold an office like that, isn't he?" asked the other.

B "Young!" exclaimed the first speaker, "why— Oh! didn't you catch on? Say—did you ever know an officer to handcuff a prisoner to his *right* hand?" ❽ 📖

FAMILY/COMMUNITY ACTIVITY

Ask students to describe the awkward situation depicted in "Hearts and Hands" to a family member. Have them ask the family member what he or she would have done in the marshal's position. Encourage students to share the responses in a group discussion with the class.

Meet the Writer

O. Henry

The O. Henry Style

O. Henry (1862–1910), born William Sydney Porter, once expressed his philosophy of writing this way:

> 66 The short story is a potent medium of education.... It should break prejudice with understanding. I propose to send the down-and-outers into the drawing-rooms of the 'get-it-alls,' and I intend to insure their welcome. 99

O. Henry got to know the "down-and-outers" of New York City when he moved there in 1901. The crowded streets of New York proved an ideal setting for O. Henry to make use of his exceptional powers of observation. He closely studied the ordinary people that he encountered there, transforming them into vivid characters of his short stories. O. Henry described his fascination with the city in this way:

> 66 I would like to live a lifetime on each street in New York. Every house has a drama in it. 99

At the time of his death, O. Henry was one of the most highly regarded writers in the United States. The humor and ironic twists in his stories, characteristics of the so-called O. Henry style, have helped ensure his continuing popularity.

For Independent Reading

To meet up with more of O. Henry's New York characters, try his short story collection *The Voice of the City.*

Meet the Writer

Episodes in O. Henry's life seem as if they might have been lifted from his stories. In 1896, he fled to Honduras after being charged with embezzling funds from a Texas bank. He returned to Texas when he found out that his wife was fatally ill. After his wife's death, O. Henry stood trial and was sentenced to five years in prison, but it is unclear whether he actually stole the money or was covering for a bank official.

For Independent Reading

Students who enjoyed this selection may also appreciate the ironic twist in O. Henry's popular story "The Ransom of Red Chief."

Practice the Strategy

In this feature, students will distinguish plot and topic from theme and examine the details of the story to determine its theme.

Strategy Tip

Advise students that they should determine the theme *after* they read the story a second time. Theme often reveals itself only after a story has been read closely.

PRACTICE 1

1. states a topic
2. sums up the plot
3. states a topic
4. sums up the plot

Recognizing Plot and Topic

Remember, a theme is *not* the plot or the topic of a story. The **plot** is the series of events that happen in the story. The **topic** is the general subject of the story; it can usually be expressed in one word. (A story may deal with several topics.)

PRACTICE 1

Read the following words and sentences about "Hearts and Hands." Explain which ones state a topic and which ones sum up the plot.

1. Deception
2. Two friends meet on a train, and one pretends to be a U.S. marshal.
3. Friendship
4. A young woman traveling on a train runs into a young man she once knew. She tries to renew the friendship, but he is unable to do so because he is headed to prison. The marshal with him pretends he is the prisoner.

Finding the Theme

When you ask, "What happens next?" you are asking about **plot**. When you ask, "Why does the character do that?" you are asking about **motivation.** When you ask, "What does the story really mean? What is it telling me?" you are asking about **theme.**

Study What the Characters Say

Sometimes the author makes clear the insight into life he or she is sharing with you. For instance, in E. B. White's classic book *Charlotte's Web,* we meet two characters—Wilbur and Charlotte— who show us time and time again how valuable friendship is. Wilbur says at one point in the book, "Friendship is one of the most satisfying things in the world." That's a pretty clear statement of the truth the author wants you to take away from reading this story. In this case you could say that the theme is directly, explicitly stated in the text.

> **Strategy Tip**
>
> As you read, jot down significant comments made by the characters. They may help you decide what truth the author wants you to discover.

Think About What the Characters Learn

Most times the theme is implicit, which means it is not stated directly. Then you must look at the situations the characters face and the conflicts they resolve and decide what the characters—and you—have learned from the experience.

> **Strategy Tip**
>
> Jot down important words or ideas as you read. They will help you track your thoughts about theme.

DIFFERENTIATING INSTRUCTION

Learners Having Difficulty

If students are having difficulty determining the story's theme, suggest that they examine each character's behavior. They can then organize the details graphically to help them uncover the theme. Ask students to draw a three-column table, labeling the columns *Miss Fairchild, Mr. Easton,* and *The Marshal.* Have them fill in each column with the character's words, feelings, and actions.

Ask them to consider what these details tell them about life. Finally, have them determine the theme from their conclusion.

Think about *Charlotte's Web* again. In that story, Wilbur, a pig, and Charlotte, a spider, form a close friendship. By the end of the story, you might find yourself thinking how wonderful it is that even though Wilbur and Charlotte are so different, they still care a great deal for one another. That might lead you to uncover another truth in this story: *Friendship knows no boundaries and can occur even between those who are very different.* You might remember that truth long after you've forgotten the characters' names or even the title of the story. That's what theme does—it stays with you after the story is over.

PRACTICE 2

What truth about people stays with you after you read "Hearts and Hands"? O. Henry doesn't explicitly state a theme; instead, you've got to figure it out on your own. Ask yourself:
• What have I learned about helping someone people normally wouldn't help?
• Why does the marshal cover up for his prisoner? Is he trying to spare the feelings of the young woman? Is it because he sees the prisoner as a fellow human being?
Write a **theme statement** that starts, "This story reveals to me that . . ."

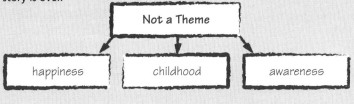

Not a Theme → happiness · childhood · awareness

Theme Statement → Happiness is accepting the joys of ordinary life. · Childhood is a time of innocence. · Awareness of death can make life richer.

Strategy Tip

When you write or state a theme, remember that a theme isn't a word or a phrase—it's at least one sentence!

 Noticing what the characters say and what they learn will help you **find the theme** in all the stories you read.

SKILLS FOCUS

Literary Skills
Find the theme.

PRACTICE 2

Possible Answers
■ Helping someone people normally wouldn't help requires compassion.
■ The marshal covers up for Mr. Easton to spare his feelings. The marshal knows that Miss Fairchild would be appalled if she learned that Mr. Easton was now a prisoner. The marshal understands how Mr. Easton feels and wants to spare him embarrassment, even though he has broken the law. This story reveals to me that a small act of kindness can mean a great deal to someone in need.

Grade-Level Skills

■ Literary Skills
Analyze topic and theme.

■ Literary Skills
Analyze narrative poems.

Summary ⬆ *above grade level*

The highwayman, an eighteenth-century thief, promises to return to his love, Bess, the landlord's daughter. Tim, the stableman, himself in love with Bess, over-hears the lovers and, it is implied, betrays his rival to the authorities. The next night, soldiers tie Bess to her bed with a musket beneath her breast and wait for the highwayman. When Bess hears her lover's horse on the road, she pulls the trigger to warn him, giving up her life to save his. The highwayman gallops off. When he learns of Bess's death, he returns in a rage, and the soldiers shoot him. Legend suggests that the two are together in death.

Before You Read The Poem

The Highwayman

Make the Connection
Talk It Over

It was a night for love and adventure. Start with the **setting:** a moonlit road hundreds of years ago, a country inn at midnight. Add some **characters:** a daring and dashing robber, a beautiful young woman, a jealous stableman, and a group of cruel soldiers. Can you predict what will happen? Hint: Look at the poem's title and illustrations. Skim the first verse.

 Predicting. Discuss your impressions of the poem with a partner. On the basis of your preview, what do you think will happen?

Literary Focus
Topic Versus Theme

After reading a story or a poem, have you ever asked yourself, "What does it *mean*?" What you are asking about is the theme. The **theme** is what a piece of literature reveals about people and life. It is the meaning you take away from the story.

A theme is not the same as a subject or topic. The **topic** of a work can usually be expressed in just a word or two: love, childhood, injustice. The theme is the idea that the writer wishes to convey *about* a particular topic. Some themes—like the power of love or the importance of home or the strength of the human spirit—have been at the heart of stories and poems throughout time.

Narrative Poems

Poems that are written to tell a story are called **narrative poems.** These story poems resemble short stories: They have a **plot, characters,** and a **setting.** Stories sung to the strumming of a stringed instrument are probably the oldest form of storytelling. Modern poems like "The Highwayman" use strong rhythms to make their stories sound like the old sung stories—they capture the enduring power of the spoken word.

 You must read this poem aloud to feel its galloping rhythms.

SKILLS
FOCUS

Literary Skills
Understand
topic and theme;
understand
narrative poems.

> **Background**
> **Literature and Social Studies**
>
> The highwayman in this famous poem is a robber who lived in England in the 1700s. Highwaymen used to stop stagecoaches on the lonely moorlands of northern England and Scotland to rob the rich passengers of money and jewels. Some highwaymen were considered heroes by the Scots because they shared the money with the poor. Highwaymen were sometimes dashing, romantic figures who dressed in expensive clothes. The poem is based on a true story that the poet heard while he was on vacation in the part of England where highwaymen used to lie in wait for stagecoaches.

246 Collection 3 / Living in the Heart

RESOURCES: READING

Planning
■ *One-Stop Planner* CD-ROM with ExamView Test Generator

Differentiating Instruction
■ *The Holt Reader*
■ *Holt Adapted Reader*
■ *Holt Reading Solutions*
■ *Supporting Instruction in Spanish*
■ *Audio CD Library*

■ *Audio CD Library, Selections and Summaries in Spanish*

Assessment
■ *Holt Assessment: Literature, Reading, and Vocabulary*
■ *One-Stop Planner* CD-ROM with ExamView Test Generator
■ *Holt Online Assessment*

The Highwayman

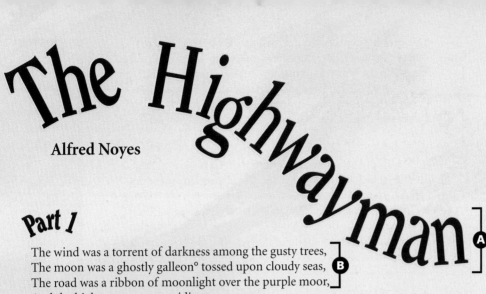

Alfred Noyes

Part 1

The wind was a torrent of darkness among the gusty trees,
The moon was a ghostly galleon° tossed upon cloudy seas,
The road was a ribbon of moonlight over the purple moor,
And the highwayman came riding—
5   Riding—riding—
The highwayman came riding, up to the old inn door.

He'd a French cocked hat on his forehead, a bunch of lace at his
   chin,
A coat of the claret° velvet, and breeches of brown doeskin.
They fitted with never a wrinkle. His boots were up to the thigh.
10   And he rode with a jeweled twinkle,
      His pistol butts a-twinkle,
His rapier hilt° a-twinkle, under the jeweled sky.

Over the cobbles he clattered and clashed in the dark inn yard.
And he tapped with his whip on the shutters, but all was locked
   and barred.
He whistled a tune to the window, and who should be waiting
15   there
But the landlord's black-eyed daughter,
      Bess, the landlord's daughter,
Plaiting° a dark red love knot into her long black hair.

---

2. **galleon** (gal′ē·ən) *n.*: large sailing ship.
8. **claret** (klar′it) *n.* used as *adj.*: purplish red, like claret wine.
12. **rapier** (rā′pē·ər) **hilt:** sword handle.
18. **plaiting** (plāt′iŋ) *v.* used as *adj.*: braiding.

The Highwayman   **247**

Internet
■ go.hrw.com (Keyword: LE5 7-3)
■ *Elements of Literature Online*
Media
■ *Audio CD Library*

■ *Audio CD Library, Selections and Summaries in Spanish*
■ *Fine Art Transparencies*
■ *Visual Connections Videocassette Program*

PRETEACHING

Selection Starter
Motivate. After students have completed the Talk It Over activity, you might present the videocassette segment, "The Highwayman Came Riding." Then, discuss how the video confirms or disproves the predictions the students made earlier.

DIRECT TEACHING

Ⓐ Literary Focus
Topic versus theme. Remind students that the topic of a work and its theme differ. Point out that the title of this poem tells them its subject. The theme is the message about life which students will infer from the highwayman's actions and experiences.

Ⓑ Vocabulary Development
❷ Identify metaphors and similes. Remind students that in a metaphor, a writer compares two unlike things by saying that one *is* the other (not *like* the other). What three metaphors appear in the first stanza of the poem? [The wind was a torrent of darkness, the moon was a ghostly galleon, and the road was a ribbon of moonlight.]

Ⓒ Literary Focus
❷ Narrative poetry. Remind students that narrative poetry, like fiction, has a plot, characters, and a setting. Who are the major characters in the poem so far? [the highwayman, Bess] What mood does the setting create? [Possible response: The wild wind, dark night, and locked inn create an eerie mood.]

Ⓐ Vocabulary Development

❓ Identify metaphors and similes. Remind students that a simile is a comparison of two unlike things that uses the word *like, as,* or *resembles.* A metaphor doesn't use those words. Ask students to find the two similes and one metaphor in the description of the new character, Tim the ostler. [*Similes*—hair like moldy hay, dumb as a dog. *Metaphor*—His eyes were hollows of madness.] **What impression of Tim do they create?** [Possible response: They make him seem like a deranged or sinister person.]

Ⓑ Correcting Misconceptions

Make sure students understand that when the author calls Tim "dumb as a dog," he's using the word *dumb* to mean silent.

Ⓒ Literary Focus

❓ Narrative poetry. Remind students that a narrative poem has a plot. Invite a volunteer to read the highwayman's speech to Bess aloud. **What does he promise to do?** [He promises to return to her before dawn, after he completes his next robbery or the following night if he is pursued.] **What conflict does the highwayman hint might occur?** [The authorities might pursue him.]

Ⓓ Learners Having Difficulty

Infer. Some students may have trouble connecting the stanza on Tim the ostler with the redcoat troop's arrival. Readers have to infer that Tim betrays the highwayman to the redcoats, since it is never directly stated. To help students make the inference, point out that there must be a reason why Noyes includes the stanza on Tim overhearing the highwayman's plans. Readers can deduce that Tim has given this information to the redcoats.

And dark in the dark old inn yard a stable wicket° creaked
20   Where Tim the ostler° listened. His face was white and peaked.
   His eyes were hollows of madness, his hair like moldy hay,
   But he loved the landlord's daughter,
        The landlord's red-lipped daughter,
   Dumb as a dog he listened, and he heard the robber say—

25   "One kiss, my bonny sweetheart, I'm after a prize tonight,
   But I shall be back with the yellow gold before the morning
     light;
   Yet, if they press me sharply, and harry° me through the day,
   Then look for me by moonlight,
        Watch for me by moonlight,
30   I'll come to thee by moonlight, though hell should bar the way."

He rose upright in the stirrups. He scarce could reach her hand,
But she loosened her hair in the casement.° His face burnt like a
   brand
As the black cascade of perfume came tumbling over his breast;
And he kissed its waves in the moonlight,
35   (Oh, sweet black waves in the moonlight!)
Then he tugged at his rein in the moonlight, and galloped away
   to the west.

Part 2

He did not come in the dawning. He did not come at noon;
And out of the tawny sunset, before the rise of the moon,
When the road was a gypsy's ribbon, looping the purple moor,
40   A redcoat troop came marching—
        Marching—marching—
   King George's men came marching, up to the old inn door.

---

19. **wicket** *n.:* small door or gate.
20. **ostler** (äs′lər) *n.:* person who takes care of horses; groom.
27. **harry** *v.:* harass or push along.
32. **casement** *n.:* window that opens outward on hinges.

248   Collection 3 / Living in the Heart

DIFFERENTIATING INSTRUCTION

Learners Having Difficulty

Invite learners having difficulty to read "The Highwayman" in interactive format in *The Holt Reader* and to use sidenotes as aids to understanding the selection. The interactive version provides additional instruction, practice, and assessment of the literary skill taught in the Student Edition. Monitor students' responses to the selection, and correct any misconceptions that arise.

English-Language Learners

Students unfamiliar with American history may not recognize the terms "redcoat troop" and "King George's Men." Explain that both of these terms refer to the British army under King George III. The army wore red-jacketed uniforms, hence the term *redcoat.* Students may also have trouble with other unfamiliar terms in the poem. Help them find definitions for *torrent* (rushing

The Haywain by John Constable (1776–1837).
National Gallery, London/Bridgeman Art Library, London/Superstock.

VIEWING THE ART

John Constable (1776–1837) was one of England's greatest landscape painters, although he was not recognized as such during his lifetime. After a boyhood spent sketching the countryside around his home, Constable entered the Royal Academy. *The Haywain* (hay wagon), painted in 1821, is one of his best-known works. It shows his fascination with the English countryside and its radiant, cloud-filled skies. Although Constable's earlier paintings tended to be tranquil, after his wife's death in 1828, they became more muted and brooding.

Activity. Ask students if they see a visual focus, or center, to this picture. [Possible response: The hay wagon is the focal point, made prominent by its position in the painting and by the light.] Have them describe the painting's mood and find features in it that help create this mood. [Possible response: The cottage, trees, and pond are comforting and serene. The gathering clouds add a foreboding note.]

---

river), *moor* (open wasteland), *breeches* (knee-length pants), and *cobbles* (paving stones).

Special Education Students
For lessons designed for special education students, see *Holt Reading Solutions*.

Advanced Learners
Enrichment. Point out the patterns of recurring colors and images in this poem—for example, the love knot tied in Bess's hair and the ropes knotted around her body, or the dark night and Bess's black hair. What other patterns can students find in the poem? [Possible response: Bess's red love knot, her red lips, the blood from her gunshot wound, and the blood on the highwayman's spurs.]

A Literary Focus

? Narrative poetry. What complication in the plot arises when the soldiers arrive at the inn? [The soldiers tie Bess to her bed.] What appears to be their motive? [They want to trap the highwayman. They expect him to return to her, and when he does, they'll capture or kill him.]

B Learners Having Difficulty

? Interpret. Why does the speaker say, "There was death at every window; / And hell at one dark window"? [Possible response: The authorities have stationed soldiers with guns at every window to shoot the highwayman. They have placed Bess so that she is facing the window that looks out on the road the highwayman will travel. The *hell* is that she will have to watch him being shot through that window.]

C Literary Focus

? Narrative poetry. How would you describe the soldiers? [Possible response: They are coarse bullies who mock Bess and kiss her. They would think nothing of killing her to get their man.]

D Correcting Misconceptions

Make sure students understand that "the dead man" is the highwayman. Help them understand that Noyes is implying that, at this point in the poem, the highwayman is clearly doomed.

They said no word to the landlord. They drank his ale instead.
But they gagged his daughter, and bound her, to the foot of her
   narrow bed.
45 Two of them knelt at her casement, with muskets at their side!
There was death at every window;
     And hell at one dark window;
For Bess could see, through her casement, the road that *he*
   would ride.

They had tied her up to attention, with many a sniggering jest;
They had bound a musket beside her, with the muzzle beneath
50   her breast!
"Now, keep good watch!" and they kissed her. She heard the
   dead man say—
Look for me by moonlight;
    Watch for me by moonlight;
I'll come to thee by moonlight, though hell should bar the way!

250   Collection 3 / Living in the Heart

Activity. Have students pair up to take turns reading stanzas of the poem to each other. The reader should look up any words that are difficult to pronounce and then practice reciting the entire poem a few times. As the reader reads, the listener should jot down questions about anything confusing. Students should try to answer each other's questions. After students have finished reading, go over any questions that remain with the class.

(**PAIRED**)

Meet the Writer

Alfred Noyes

A Rousing Romantic

The British poet, novelist, biographer, and essayist **Alfred Noyes** (1880–1958) was possibly the most popular writer of his time. People enjoyed his verse for its rousing storytelling and its thumping rhythms—in fact, his work was often performed aloud.

Noyes, unlike most other poets of his time, was successful enough to earn a living solely from his poetry. He particularly liked the work of Alfred, Lord Tennyson, whose poetry had been popular during Noyes's childhood. Although the twentieth century was a time of literary experimentation and rebellion against convention, Noyes's poems were written in a traditional style, sounding as if they came from a much earlier era.

Today Noyes is best remembered for "The Highwayman," which he wrote in a small cottage on the edge of Bagshot Heath shortly after leaving Oxford University. He recalled:

The Granger Collection, New York.

66 Bagshot Heath in those days was a wild bit of country, all heather and pinewoods. 'The Highwayman' suggested itself to me one blustery night when the sound of the wind in the pines gave me the first line: 'The wind was a torrent of darkness among the gusty trees....'

It took me about two days to complete the poem. Shortly afterward it appeared in *Blackwood's Magazine*. It illustrates the unpredictable chances of authorship, that this poem, written in so short a time, when I was twenty-four, should have been read so widely.

I think the success of the poem in all these ways was due to the fact that it was not an artificial composition but was written at an age when I was genuinely excited by that kind of romantic story. 99

Meet the Writer

Given the traditional style of Alfred Noyes's poems, it is startling to realize that Noyes lived into the era of television and space launches.

For Independent Reading

- Students who enjoyed "The Highwayman" might be interested in reading the dramatic plot twists in O. Henry's short stories, particularly "The Gift of the Magi," which deals with similar themes. Students can find many of O. Henry's best stories collected in *The Gift of the Magi and Other Stories*.

- Students who want to explore the themes of love and betrayal in a contemporary setting might enjoy *On My Honor* by Marion Dane Bauer. This novel explores the serious ramifications of breaking a promise.

DIFFERENTIATING INSTRUCTION

Advanced Learners
Acceleration. You can use the following activity to help advanced learners identify and analyze recurring themes across traditional and contemporary works.
Activity. Suggest that interested advanced learners read *On My Honor* and create a Venn diagram comparing it with "The Highwayman." Encourage them to analyze how the themes of the two works are alike and how they differ. Remind them that there are different kinds of love. What roles do betrayal and death play in the poem and the novel? Which aspects of their themes are universal and which are specific to a certain time and place?

After You Read

First Thoughts

1. Possible answer: I think her action is noble because she sacrifices her own life to save another, which is the most unselfish thing a person can do.

Thinking Critically

2. The setting is a windy, moonlit night on a moor and at a dark inn. Noyes uses vivid descriptions, such as "The road was a ribbon of moonlight," to help readers see the setting.

3. Tim's motive is that he loves Bess himself and is jealous of the man she loves.

4. Possible answer: When you truly love someone, you care more about his or her happiness than about your own (as Bess does but Tim doesn't).

5. Possible answers: "road was a ribbon"; "breeches of brown"; "clattered and clashed"; "whistled . . . waiting"; "loved the landlord's."

Extending Interpretations

6. Possible answer: Bess manages to free herself and run off with the highwayman.

7. Possible answer: I liked the mood and the description in the poem. Bess was so brave she inspired me. But why didn't the highwayman realize he was throwing away his life and her sacrifice by galloping up to the inn? I would have liked to see him sneak up on the men who had tied up his girlfriend and punish them.

After You Read   Response and Analysis

First Thoughts

1. Bess gives up her life for the highwayman. Do you think her sacrifice is noble or pointless?

Thinking Critically

2. What is the **setting** of this poem? What details in the poem help you see and hear what is happening?

3. What is Tim's **motive**, or reason, for betraying Bess?

4. This poem is about love, betrayal, and death. What **theme**, or message about people and life, does the poem reveal to you?

5. **Alliteration** (ə·lit'ər·ā'shən) is the repetition of consonant sounds in words close to one another. You can hear alliteration in the phrase "ghostly galleon." Read aloud five other lines in the poem that use alliteration.

Extending Interpretations

6. If you could write a new ending for the poem, what would it be?

7. At the right is a student's letter about "The Highwayman." What points would you make in a letter about the poem?

WRITING

Writing from Another Point of View

The poem concerns itself mainly with the highwayman and Bess. We don't learn much about the other characters. Imagine you are either Tim the ostler or one of the soldiers who come to the inn. In a paragraph, describe your reaction to Bess's death, writing as "I."

INTERNET
Projects
and Activities
Keyword: LE5 7-3

SKILLS
FOCUS

Literary Skills
Analyze theme; analyze a narrative poem.

Writing Skills
Describe events from another point of view.

Reading Check

Review the main events of this **narrative poem,** and then complete a **sequence chart** like the one below.

Part 1

1. The highwayman rides to the old inn.

2. He finds Bess waiting.

3. Tim overhears him saying . . .

Dear Editors;

I am a seventh grader at Madison Jr. High. My name is Brooke Garner. Our class has been reading many stories in your book.

My favorite poem ~~this~~ is "The Highwayman." It shows a very deep understanding and love between the highwayman and the girl. This poem was so touching that ~~because~~ every emotion the writer was trying to convey, filtered through my mind and I was left weakened by its magnitude. The poem lived and I feel that the author had somehow been hurt and understood how the people must have felt and lived.

Sincerely yours,

Brooke Garner

Reading Check

Part 1: *1.*—The highwayman rides to the old inn. *2.*—He finds Bess waiting. *3.*—Tim overhears him saying he'll come back as soon as he can. Part 2: *4.*—The redcoats come to the inn. *5.*—They tie up Bess. *6.*—Bess shoots herself to warn the highwayman. *7.*—The highwayman gets away. *8.*—The next morning the highwayman hears of Bess's death. *9.*—He rides back to the inn in a rage. *10.*—The redcoats kill him. *11.*—Bess and the highwayman meet as ghosts.

Making Connections: Similes and Metaphors

In our everyday language we use many expressions that are not literally true: "Charlie's bragging gets under my skin." "Gilda's money is burning a hole in her pocket." When we use expressions like these, we are using **figures of speech.** Our listeners know that the words do not carry their ordinary meaning. Bragging, after all, does not really pierce skin, and money cannot cause a pocket to catch fire.

The meaning of such figurative expressions depends on comparisons. Bragging is *compared* to something that causes pain or annoyance, such as a thorn. Money is *compared* to something so hot that it cannot be held and must be gotten rid of.

There are many kinds of figures of speech; the most common are **similes** and **metaphors.**

A **simile** is a comparison of two unlike things using the word *like, as, than,* or *resembles.* Here are two famous similes:

> I wandered lonely as a cloud....
> —William Wordsworth

> My love is like a red, red rose....
> —Robert Burns

A **metaphor** also compares two unlike things, but it does so without using *like, as, than,* or *resembles.* For example, in "The Highwayman," Alfred Noyes does not say the moon was *like* a ghostly galleon. He uses a metaphor: "The moon *was* a ghostly galleon tossed upon cloudy seas."

PRACTICE

Fill in this chart by completing each comparison from "The Highwayman." Then, identify it as a simile or a metaphor. The first item has been done for you.

Figure of Speech
line 1: The wind is compared to a torrent of darkness. (a metaphor)
line 3: The road is compared to _____
line 12: The stars in the sky are compared to _____
line 21: Tim's eyes are compared to _____
line 21: Tim's hair is compared to _____
line 24: Tim's dumbness is compared to _____
line 32: The highwayman's face is compared to _____
line 39: The road is compared to _____
line 74: Bess's face is compared to _____

SKILLS FOCUS

Vocabulary Skills
Understand similes and metaphors.

The Highwayman   **255**

Vocabulary Development

PRACTICE

- line 3: The road is compared to a ribbon of moonlight. (metaphor)
- line 12: The stars in the sky are compared to jewels. (metaphor)
- line 21: Tim's eyes are compared to hollows of madness. (metaphor)
- line 21: Tim's hair is compared to moldy hay. (simile)
- line 24: Tim's dumbness is compared to a dog's. (simile)
- line 32: The highwayman's face is compared to a burning brand. (simile)
- line 39: The road is compared to a gypsy's ribbon. (metaphor)
- line 74: Bess's face is compared to a light. (simile)

ASSESSING

Assessment
- *Holt Assessment: Literature, Reading, and Vocabulary*

RETEACHING

For a lesson reteaching themes across genres, see **Reteaching,** p. 917F.

Summary ↔ *at grade level*

This article explains why people in eighteenth-century England thought of highwaymen as gentlemen even though they were criminals. During that period, England had some very wealthy people and vast numbers of poor people. Many of these poor people were not sympathetic when the rich were robbed, especially when the highwaymen, like Robin Hood, shared the loot with the poor. In addition to their generosity with their ill–gotten goods, highwaymen sometimes behaved like gentlemen: They dressed well, had good manners, and treated their horses kindly. Some highwaymen also displayed courage—even when facing death by hanging.

Informational Text

Understanding Cause and Effect

Causes and Effects

You know from experience that one thing leads to another. If you sleep through your alarm, you know you'll be late for school and you'll miss your favorite class—English. Sleeping through your alarm is a **cause**—it makes something happen. An **effect** is what happens as a result of some event—you're late for school and miss English.

You could go on. Being late for English class causes you to have to make up the time after school. Making up the time causes you to miss tryouts for football. Missing tryouts causes you to lose the chance to impress a certain girl. So you lose the girl, and it all can be traced to sleeping through an alarm.

■ As you read the following article on real highwaymen, ask yourself, "Why did this happen?" and "What happened because of this?" These questions will help you discover causes and effects.

To find causes and their effects, look for signal terms such as *cause, effect, resulted in, so, thus, why,* and *because.*

INTERNET
Interactive
Reading Model
Keyword: LE5 7-3

Reading Skills
Understand cause and effect.

Cause and Effect: The Rise of Highwaymen in England

What Happened
Some people in England got very rich. Others got poorer.

↓

Effect
Government built new toll roads for the rich to travel.

↓

Effect
Highwaymen held up stagecoaches and carriages to get money.

↓

Effect
Highwaymen . . .

256   Collection 3 / Living in the Heart

RESOURCES: READING

Planning
■ *One-Stop Planner* CD-ROM with ExamView Test Generator

Differentiating Instruction
■ *Holt Adapted Reader*
■ *Holt Reading Solutions*
■ *Supporting Instruction in Spanish*
■ *Audio CD Library*

■ *Audio CD Library, Selections and Summaries in Spanish*

Grammar and Language
■ *Daily Language Activities*

Assessment
■ *Holt Assessment: Literature, Reading, and Vocabulary*
■ *One-Stop Planner* CD-ROM with ExamView Test Generator

■ *Holt Online Assessment*

Internet
■ go.hrw.com (Keyword: LE5 7-3)
■ *Elements of Literature Online*

Media
■ *Audio CD Library*
■ *Audio CD Library, Selections and Summaries in Spanish*

Gentlemen of the Road

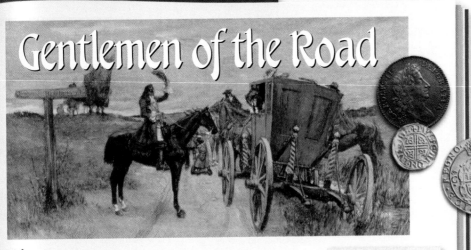

WHY DID PEOPLE ONCE THINK of highwaymen, the bandits (like Bess's beloved) who robbed travelers in seventeenth- and eighteenth-century England, as gentlemen?

To answer that question, first look at these facts. The seventeenth and eighteenth centuries saw the rise of a very wealthy class in England. England became a nation of haves and have-nots. The rich dressed in silks and velvets. Men and women wore huge powdered wigs. The rich lived on vast estates. They traveled to London for rounds of parties in the winter-spring season and spent summers in seaside towns, where gambling was a favorite pastime.

As the wealthy became richer, the conditions of the poor grew worse. Because the government did not care about their welfare, the poor lived in filthy slums in cities and in miserable conditions in farms and towns. In the worst years, 74 percent of the children in London died before the age of five. These were the social conditions that contributed to the rise of the highwaymen.

In addition, newly built toll roads ran through the countryside, connecting towns and villages. These improved roads brought out more travelers—rich ones. The highwaymen could stop the private carriages and the stagecoaches that used the toll roads and rob the passengers.

The highwaymen called themselves gentlemen of the road, and some people agreed—sometimes even their victims! How did they come by this surprising reputation?

Some people saw the highwaymen not as criminals but as the new Robin Hoods because they gave to the poor what they had stolen from the rich (or part of it). **Ⓐ**

> This article will explain why people thought of the highwaymen as gentlemen.

The Granger Collection, New York.

> This paragraph and those that follow tell what caused people to think of these bandits as gentlemen.

A Reading Informational Text

? Identify cause and effect.
The article states that some highwaymen, when facing death by hanging, chose to hasten their own deaths by throwing themselves off the scaffold before the wagon could be pulled out from under them. The public admired this act for two reasons, the first being that it showed bravery. What is the second? [The act defied the authorities, whom many poor people viewed as corrupt.]

GUIDED PRACTICE

Monitor students' progress.
Help students reformulate key relationships in the selection by forming statements beginning with "Because." For example, "Because rich people traveled the newly built country roads, they were easy targets for highwaymen; Because the government did not care about them, poor people lived in miserable conditions." This strategy helps reveal causes and effects by answering the question why. (Why were rich people easy targets? Why did some people live in poor conditions?)

Their life of crime brought highwaymen lots of money— the reason they could afford to dress well.

Another reason why people thought of these bandits as gentlemen was that they looked the part. Most highwaymen came from poor families or, at best, middle-class ones. But once they turned to a life of crime, they could afford to dress in style. They wore high-heeled boots that went all the way to the hip, fancy shirts, long, elegant coats, and wide-brimmed hats with feathers. With their dashing clothes and fine horses these former footmen, butchers, and cheese sellers might have been mistaken for aristocrats.

The Singing Lesson by Arturo Ricci.

Here's another reason why the highwaymen were considered gentlemen: their manners.

Some highwaymen tried to act like gentlemen as well. Many would never point a gun at a lady or search her for valuables, and sometimes they'd let women they robbed keep items of sentimental value. Highwaymen loved their horses too and took pride in earning the loyalty of their steeds by treating them well.

Here is another example of gentlemanly behavior.

Some highwaymen politely begged their victims' pardon as they relieved them of their money and jewels. Others took only what they felt they needed and returned the rest to their owners.

In one account a robbery victim was upset about losing his beloved watch. He offered the highwayman two guineas instead, along with a promise not to turn him in to the authorities. The highwayman agreed, and they went off together to the man's home. The money changed hands, the two men shared a bottle of wine, and after many courteous words on each side, the highwayman galloped off.

Final reason for their reputation as gentlemen.

A

Even when captured and sentenced to hang (the usual punishment for robbery in those days), some highwaymen tried to behave like gentlemen. They were too proud to cry or beg for mercy from the authorities they defied. After the noose was tied around their neck, some threw themselves off the scaffold rather than wait for the wagon they stood on to be pulled from beneath them. For those who romanticized the highwaymen in stories and song, this final act showed scorn for the corrupt authorities and courage in the face of death.

—Mara Rockliff

DIFFERENTIATING INSTRUCTION

Learners Having Difficulty
Vary reading rate. Tell students that there is a great deal of information to absorb in this short selection. Suggest that they read it slowly, noting anything that might be a reason why highwaymen were considered "gentlemen." Then, have students work in small groups to discuss one another's notes.

Analyzing Cause and Effect

Gentlemen of the Road

Test Practice

1. This article suggests that all of the following might have **caused** the rise of the highwayman *except* the —

   A worsening conditions of the poor

   B rise of a very wealthy class

   C use of capital punishment

   D newly built toll roads

2. What **caused** people to see the highwaymen as the new Robin Hoods?

   F They rode horses and used bows and arrows.

   G They robbed from the rich and gave to the poor.

   H They lived in Sherwood Forest.

   J They wore Robin Hood outfits.

3. The highwaymen were able to dress in style because —

   A they were wealthy aristocrats

   B they took advice from their victims

   C their crimes made them wealthy

   D they were interested in fashion

4. Some highwaymen didn't beg for mercy from the hangman because of their —

   F pride

   G fear

   H mercy

   J shame

Constructed Response

1. List some of the conditions in seventeenth- and eighteenth-century England that **caused** bandits to rob travelers on the nation's highways.

2. What **caused** people to regard these bandits, or highwaymen, as gentlemen?

SKILLS FOCUS

Reading Skills
Analyze cause and effect.

Gentlemen of the Road **259**

INDEPENDENT PRACTICE

Analyzing Cause and Effect

Test Practice

Answers and Model Rationales

1. **C** Capital punishment would cause a decline in highwaymen.

2. **G** Students should realize that F, H, and J are not true.

3. **C** A and B are untrue. D may be true, but it doesn't explain how they could afford stylish clothes. C is the answer.

4. **F** If highwaymen felt either fear (G) or shame (J), they probably would beg for mercy. They were in no position to give mercy (H). Pride (F) caused them to die bravely.

Test-Taking Tips

For more instruction on how to answer multiple-choice questions, refer students to **Test Smarts**, p. 920.

Constructed Response

1. The poor lived in miserable conditions, while the rich grew richer. In addition, new toll roads enabled the rich to travel, providing an easy target for highwaymen.

2. Highwaymen treated women well and were kind to the poor.

ASSESSING

Assessment

■ *Holt Assessment: Literature, Reading, and Vocabulary*

RETEACHING

For a lesson reteaching cause and effect, see **Reteaching,** p. 917J.

Grade-Level Skills

■ Literary Skills
Analyze recurring themes.

■ Literary Skills
Understand how tone or meaning is conveyed in poetry through repetition.

Upcoming Skills

■ Literary Skills
Compare and contrast similar themes across genres.

Summary ⬇ *below grade level*

> This lyric poem expresses the speaker's passionate love for his bride, Annabel Lee. He says she was killed by a cold wind sent by angels who envied the lovers' earthly bliss. He further states that their love will endure even though death separates them physically.

Before You Read The Poem

Annabel Lee

Make the Connection
Think Aloud

With a partner, take turns reading stanzas of the poem aloud to hear its haunting sounds and to visualize its romantic setting. Exchange thoughts about the poem's speaker and its music. Jot down comments and questions as they come to you, and discuss them with your partner. Work together to solve any problems you have in understanding the poem.

Literary Focus
Themes Across Time

"Annabel Lee" is a famous love poem, written after the poet's young wife, Virginia, died of tuberculosis. She was laid to rest in New York, near the Hudson River, in a sepulcher (sep′əl·kər), a burial vault that stands aboveground. Poe's poem reads like a fairy tale, set in a faraway time and place.

Across time, poets, storytellers, and songwriters have written about the many faces of love. It's an age-old subject that has inspired many themes. Songs tell of love that blooms in the most unexpected places. Storytellers write about love that overcomes impossible barriers. In "Annabel Lee," Poe's speaker describes an eternal love.

Repetition

Musicians, as you may know, use repetition—of sounds, of words, of tones—to create emotional effects. Poe uses repetition in much the same way. In "Annabel Lee," notice how words, sounds, phrases, and rhythms recur with hypnotic regularity. How many times does the name Annabel Lee appear in the poem?

INTERNET
More About Poe
Keyword: LE5 7-3

SKILLS FOCUS

Literary Skills
Understand universal themes; understand repetition in poems.

(Above) Edgar Allan Poe's grave in Westminster Burial Ground in Baltimore, Maryland.

(Opposite) Poe's cottage before it was moved to Dyckman Street in the Bronx, New York.

260 Collection 3 / Living in the Heart

RESOURCES: READING

Planning
■ *One-Stop Planner* CD-ROM with ExamView Test Generator

Differentiating Instruction
■ *Holt Reading Solutions*
■ *Supporting Instruction in Spanish*
■ *Audio CD Library*
■ *Audio CD Library, Selections and Summaries in Spanish*

Assessment
■ *Holt Assessment: Literature, Reading, and Vocabulary*
■ *One-Stop Planner* CD-ROM with ExamView Test Generator
■ *Holt Online Assessment*

Annabel Lee

Edgar Allan Poe

Portrait of "Sissy,"
Poe's beloved wife.

Valentine Museum,
Richmond, Virginia.

It was many and many a year ago,
    In a kingdom by the sea,
That a maiden there lived whom you may know
    By the name of Annabel Lee;
5 And this maiden she lived with no other thought
    Than to love and be loved by me.

I was a child and *she* was a child,
    In this kingdom by the sea:
But we loved with a love that was more than love—
10   I and my Annabel Lee—
With a love that the wingèd seraphs° of heaven
    Coveted° her and me.

11. **seraphs** (ser′əfs) *n.*: angels.
12. **coveted** (kuv′it·id) *v.*: envied.

And this was the reason that, long ago,
    In this kingdom by the sea,
15 A wind blew out of a cloud, chilling
    My beautiful Annabel Lee;
So that her highborn kinsmen came
    And bore her away from me,
To shut her up in a sepulcher
20   In this kingdom by the sea.

The angels, not half so happy in heaven,
    Went envying her and me—
Yes!—that was the reason (as all men know,
    In this kingdom by the sea)
25 That the wind came out of the cloud by night,
    Chilling and killing my Annabel Lee.

Annabel Lee   **261**

Internet
- go.hrw.com (Keyword: LE5 7-3)
- *Elements of Literature Online*

Media
- *Audio CD Library*
- *Audio CD Library, Selections and Summaries in Spanish*

? **Title and theme.** What is the speaker saying in this stanza? [Possible response: His love for Annabel Lee is so strong that their souls are still united, even though death has separated them physically.] What message about love is the poet trying to convey? [Possible response: True love is stronger than angels, demons, or death.]

B Literary Focus

? **Repetition: Refrain.** Point out that these two lines echo the refrain "kingdom by the sea" in the first four stanzas, with the gloomy words *sepulcher* and *tomb* replacing the word *kingdom*. How do these changes suggest Poe's theme? [Possible response: They suggest that the speaker will never get over the tragic loss of his beloved.]

VIEWING THE ART

Marsden Hartley (1877–1943) was one of the pioneers of modern art in the United States. After years of experimenting, Hartley developed a sophisticated yet seemingly primitive style of painting. Although *Crashing Wave* is a representational painting, it combines realistic elements with intense emotion.

Activity. Have students explain what the painting is depicting, and then describe the emotion it evokes. [The painting depicts ocean waves crashing on tall, heavy black rocks. Possible emotions: anger, grief, anxiety.] Ask which elements that create the overall effect of a painting—form, color, brush strokes, composition—seem to add most to the impact of this work. [Possible response: The contrast between the foaming white water and the heavy black rocks—which involves color and composition—contributes to the painting's turbulence.]

But our love it was stronger by far than the love
    Of those who were older than we—
    Of many far wiser than we—
30 And neither the angels in heaven above,
    Nor the demons down under the sea,
Can ever dissever° my soul from the soul
    Of the beautiful Annabel Lee—

32. **dissever** (di·sev′ər) *v.*: separate.

For the moon never beams, without bringing me dreams
35   Of the beautiful Annabel Lee;
And the stars never rise, but I feel the bright eyes
    Of the beautiful Annabel Lee;
And so, all the night-tide, I lie down by the side
Of my darling—my darling—my life and my bride,
40   In the sepulcher there by the sea,
    In her tomb by the sounding sea.

Crashing Wave (c. 1938) by Marsden Hartley.
Private Collection, New York.

262   Collection 3 / Living in the Heart

DIFFERENTIATING INSTRUCTION

Learners Having Difficulty
Some students may need help hearing the musical sounds and rhythm of "Annabel Lee," as well as help pronouncing a few of the words in the poem. Play the audio recording of "Annabel Lee," and as students listen, have them follow the words in their books. Hearing the poem read aloud will increase both their enjoyment and understanding of the poem.

English-Language Learners
Help English-language learners get interested in the poem by asking them for examples of songs about love and loss in other languages. Ask for volunteers to quote some lines of such songs along with translations. You might suggest that they bring in a CD or tape to play for the class. As the class listens to the song, can students find any examples of repetition in the lyrics?

Meet the Writer

Edgar Allan Poe

The Granger Collection, New York.

"A World of Moan"

Long before Stephen King began writing stories of horror, **Edgar Allan Poe** (1809–1849) was exploring the dark side of the human imagination in such works as "The Raven," "The Tell-Tale Heart," and "The Masque of the Red Death." Poe's life was hard from the start. First, his father deserted the family. Then, before Poe was three years old, his beautiful young mother died, and the little boy was left alone. John Allan, a wealthy and childless businessman in Richmond, Virginia, took in young Edgar and provided for his education, but the two constantly quarreled. Poe wanted to write, while his foster father wanted him to take over the family business. Eventually Poe broke away from his foster parents and set out on his own. Throughout his adult life he was plagued by poverty, alcoholism, and unhappiness. As Poe said, "I dwelt alone in a world of moan."

Always searching for a family, Poe married his thirteen-year-old cousin, Virginia Clemm. Her early death seemed to destroy him, and he himself died two years after she did. He had lived only forty years.

For Independent Reading

Poe's haunting poems include "The Raven" and "The Bells." You'll find some of his most chilling stories in a book titled *The Best of Poe.*

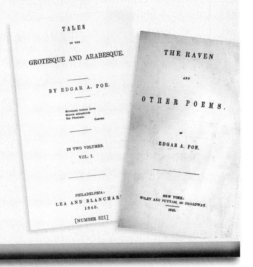

INDEPENDENT PRACTICE

After You Read

First Thoughts

1. Students may want to ask if the speaker really does lie down next to his bride in her tomb.

Thinking Critically

2. Possible answers: Some students may be surprised because no one would want to sleep in a tomb. Some may feel that the speaker just imagines himself with her when he sleeps.

3. Possible answers: "kingdom by the sea" and "tomb by the sounding sea."

4. The long e sound in *sea, Lee, me,* and *we* repeats throughout the poem. It reminds readers of Annabel Lee.

Extending Interpretations

5. Possible answers: The theme is that the speaker will always remember his love for Annabel Lee. Some students will agree that all people experience some form of loss. Others may see the grief as being specific to the speaker and Annabel Lee.

6. Some students may feel that the joys of love are not worth the pain of loss. Others may disagree, arguing that it is better to be happy once than never. The speaker would probably agree because his time with Annabel Lee was the happiest of his life.

Reading Check

a. He describes a love that was greater than any other.

b. The winged seraphs (angels) in heaven are jealous.

c. They take her away from the speaker and put her in a tomb by the sea.

d. He sees her in the moon and the stars. He sleeps by her side in her tomb.

After You Read

First Thoughts

1. If you were to meet the speaker of this poem, what would you want to ask him? Be sure to refer to the notes you made as you read the poem.

Thinking Critically

2. Were you surprised when you discovered where the speaker sleeps each night? Do you think he actually sleeps there, or is he speaking of what he does in his imagination? Explain.

3. Find at least two details that help you picture the poem's **setting.**

4. List the **rhyming sounds** that echo through the six stanzas. What words are repeated over and over and over again? What does the **repetition** remind you of?

Extending Interpretations

5. One topic of this poem is loss. What does the poem say about loss? In other words, how would you state the poem's **theme**? Talk about whether you think the speaker's feelings of grief are universal.

6. Some say that it's better to have loved and lost than never to have loved at all. Do you agree or disagree? How do you think the poem's speaker would respond to that idea?

WRITING

Writing a Tribute to a Person

The speaker of the poem says that the moon and stars remind him of Annabel Lee. Think of someone you feel strongly about—perhaps someone you love, admire, or miss very much. Jot down the special things and places that remind you of that person. Then, write a brief tribute, using images of the special things or places to emphasize what you miss about the person.

INTERNET
Projects and Activities
Keyword: LE5 7-3

SKILLS FOCUS

Literary Skills
Analyze theme; understand repetition in poems.

Writing Skills
Write a tribute to a person.

Reading Check

a. How does the speaker describe the love he shared with Annabel Lee?

b. Who is jealous of the speaker and Annabel Lee?

c. What do Annabel Lee's relatives do to her?

d. According to the last stanza, where does the speaker now see Annabel Lee? Where does he sleep each night?

DIFFERENTIATING INSTRUCTION

Learners Having Difficulty
Monitoring tip: If students have trouble identifying the theme of the poem, have them re-read the last two stanzas of the poem. Remind them to ask, "What is the poet saying about life and love?"

Advanced Learners
Enrichment. Tell students that folk singer Joan Baez and singer-songwriter Phil Ochs were both popular performers in the 1960s

era of folk rock. Ochs recorded a musical version of "The Highwayman." Baez recorded "Annabel Lee" as well as *Baptism,* an entire album of famous poems set to music. **Activity.** Have students listen to the musical versions of the two poems several times. Suggest that as they listen, they contemplate the similarities and differences between the poems' themes. Then, ask them to write a short essay comparing the two songs. Which

After You Read   Vocabulary Development

Using Analogies

An **analogy** (ə·nal′ə·jē) is a comparison between two things to show how they are alike. An analogy can explain one idea by showing how that idea is similar to another, more easily understood idea. Analogies can be tricky, though, because few ideas or situations are alike in all ways. Here's an example in which a writer compares playing golf to being in love:

> I fell in love with golf when I was twenty-five. It would have been a healthier relationship had it been an adolescent romance or, better yet, a childhood crush. Though I'd like to think we've had a lot of laughs together and even some lyrical moments. I have never felt quite adequate to her demands, and she keeps secrets from me.... I can't get them out of my mind, or quite wrap my mind around them. Sometimes I wish that she and I had never met. She leads me on, but deep down I suspect—this is my secret—that I'm just not her type.

—from "An Ode to Golf" by John Updike

PRACTICE

Try writing your own analogy. First, you have to find a subject you would like to talk about. Updike chose golf. Then, find something familiar that you can compare this subject to. Before you write your analogy, make a list of the ways in which your two subjects are similar. In your analogy, compare your subjects point by point. Remember that in an analogy you use several points for comparison, not just one. Here are some ideas for subjects:

Doing homework [is like . . .]   Family life [is like . . .]
Exercising [is like . . .]   Keeping friends [is like . . .]
Playing soccer [is like . . .]

If you prefer, write your analogy to explain something complex, perhaps something you learned in science. Scientists, in fact, use analogies all the time. A doctor might compare antibodies zeroing in on a tumor to guided missiles finding their target, for example.

SKILLS FOCUS

Vocabulary Skills
Understand and use analogies.

Vocabulary Development

PRACTICE

Possible answer: Exercising is like putting money in the bank. Sometimes I'd rather spend my time other ways, but if I invest it in exercise, it pays off. I have more energy, think more clearly, and perform better at basketball practice. Even a few dollars invested today yields a lot of money when interest is compounded for years. In the same way, a few minutes invested in exercising now yields a habit that will help protect me from heart disease, diabetes, and other health problems when I'm older.

ASSESSING

Assessment
■ *Holt Assessment: Literature, Reading, and Vocabulary*

RETEACHING

For a lesson reteaching themes across genres, see **Reteaching**, p. 917F.

---

do they think is a more accurate representation of the original poem? Which captures the intended emotion better? Which do they like better, and why?

HOMEWORK

Grade-Level Skills

■ **Reading Skills**
Understand informational texts by making outlines and taking logical notes.

Summary ⬆ *above grade level*

The house where Edgar Allan Poe lived in 1846 is in Greenwich Village in New York City. The building belongs to New York University, which wants to tear it down to make room for a new law-school building. Poe fans are trying to save the house from demolition, arguing that Poe was at the height of his career during his residence there. A state Supreme Court justice, however, dismissed the case, saying he had no authority to prevent NYU from tearing down the structure. The building's future is still undecided as Poe fans vow to appeal the court decision.

Informational Text

Taking Notes and Outlining

Reading Focus

Taking Notes

Edgar Allan Poe's life was filled with struggle and conflict, as you learned from his poem and biography. The article you are about to read deals with another conflict involving Poe, one that took place many years after his death.

When you read informational material, like an article, a lot goes on in your head.

- You connect what you read with your own experiences and knowledge.
- You ask yourself questions and make predictions.
- You challenge the text.
- You reflect on its meaning.

Jotting down notes will help you understand and remember what you read. Here's what to do:

- **Be organized.** Use a simple outline form to jot down the information or ideas that you think are most important. (See the box for a sample outline form.)

- **Be brief.** Keep your notes short, simple, and clear. Write only words and phrases that will help you focus on the most important information.

- **Underline or circle information.** It may be useful to highlight certain information directly in the text, but don't do it in a book that doesn't belong to you, and don't get carried away. If everything is highlighted, then it's hard to tell what's most important.

Reading Skills
Take notes and make outlines.

■ When you read this selection about a house Edgar Allan Poe once lived in, keep a sheet of paper nearby and jot down key details.

Outlining

Outlining can help you uncover the skeleton that holds the text together. An outline highlights main ideas and supporting details. Here's an example of an informal outline:

> **Main idea**
> supporting detail
> supporting detail
> [etc.]
>
> **Main idea**
> supporting detail
> supporting detail
> [etc.]

RESOURCES: READING

Planning
- *One-Stop Planner* CD-ROM with ExamView Test Generator

Differentiating Instruction
- *Holt Adapted Reader*
- *Holt Reading Solutions*
- *Supporting Instruction in Spanish*
- *Audio CD Library*

■ *Audio CD Library, Selections and Summaries in Spanish*

Grammar and Language
- *Daily Language Activities*

Assessment
- *Holt Assessment: Literature, Reading, and Vocabulary*
- *One-Stop Planner* CD-ROM with ExamView Test Generator

■ *Holt Online Assessment*

Internet
- go.hrw.com (Keyword: LE5 7-3)
- *Elements of Literature Online*

Media
- *Audio CD Library*
- *Audio CD Library, Selections and Summaries in Spanish*

THE FALL OF THE HOUSE OF POE?

THINK OF YOUR FAVORITE PLACE in the world, the place where you've spent some of the happiest hours of your life.

Now, think about it being torn down.

How do you feel? Terrible, right? If Edgar Allan Poe were alive today, scholars say, that's the way he might feel about the fate of the boardinghouse he once lived in at 85 Amity Street in New York City's Greenwich Village.

More than a century and a half has passed since Poe died. Amity Street was long ago renamed West Third Street, and the former boardinghouse now belongs to New York University. For years the university used it for classrooms and offices. But in 1999, NYU officials announced that they would be tearing the house down to make room for a new building for their law school.

Loyal Poe fans joined neighborhood residents in vigorously protesting the university's plan. They wrote letters, circulated petitions, and organized a rally attended by several hundred supporters chanting, "No, no, Poe won't go." They read aloud from "The Raven," the poem that made Poe famous, and chanted its famous refrain: "Nevermore!"

"It always mystified me why there was not a gold plaque outside the house," one Poe scholar said. "It is a genuine literary landmark."

New York University disagreed. Its representatives argued that Poe (along with his young wife, Virginia, and her mother) may have lived at the boardinghouse for as little as six months and that he had not written any of his more important works there. They also said that the house had changed drastically over the years, leaving no traces of Poe's residence. They even questioned whether the current building was the same one that had stood there in 1845, when Poe moved in. One NYU representative concluded, "This is not a building that remembers Poe."

The protesters researched the university's claims. They studied all kinds of documents, from letters and recollections of people who knew Poe to public records showing the history of the neighborhood.

Judging from dates and addresses in Poe's surviving correspondence, including a valentine given to him by Virginia in 1846, it seems probable that Poe lived there for less than a year. But that may have been longer than he stayed at any of the other eight places where he lived in Manhattan, all of which have already been torn down.

But the months he spent at 85 Amity may have been the happiest in Poe's short

The Fall of the House of Poe? **267**

Skills Starter

Build skills. The skill of note-taking and outlining requires students to identify main ideas. Give students sample paragraphs to practice distinguishing the main idea from supporting details. Remind them that an article with many paragraphs such as "The Fall of the House of Poe?" will have a number of important ideas in it. As they read the article, students should focus on these ideas.

DIRECT TEACHING

Ⓐ Cross-curricular Connections

The house of Poe. The title of the selection is a play on words. Its subject is the possibility that a house that Poe once lived in may fall to the wrecking ball. But it also echoes the title of one of Poe's most famous stories, "The Fall of the House of Usher."

Ⓑ Reading Informational Text

Distinguish between facts and opinions. Remind students that a fact can be proved, while an opinion is based on a personal viewpoint and cannot be proved. Ask students to identify one fact and one opinion in this passage. [*Fact*—There is no gold plaque outside the house. *Opinion*—The house is a genuine literary landmark.]

Ⓒ Reading Informational Text

❓ **Take notes and outline.** This paragraph summarizes New York University's rationale for demolishing the Poe building, citing four specific arguments. What are they? [(1) Poe lived there less than six months, (2) he wrote no important works there, (3) the house has changed entirely since Poe's day, and (4) it might not even be the house that Poe lived in.]

DIFFERENTIATING INSTRUCTION

Learners Having Difficulty

Some students may find the amount of information in the selection overwhelming. Help them individually with their note taking and outlining as they read. Then, have them work in pairs to go over each other's notes and ask their partner to clarify anything in the notes that doesn't make sense.

A Reading Informational Text

❓ Take notes and outline. Point out that the rest of the article (except the last paragraph) refutes the arguments made by NYU. What arguments do the preservationists make? [(1) It is true that Poe and his wife lived in the house a short time, but it may have been the happiest time of his life, (2) he wrote famous works such as "The Raven" and "The Facts in the Case of M. Valdemar" there, and (4) the building *is* the same one Poe lived in.] Point out that the article does not refute NYU's third point.

Monitor students' progress.
When students take notes or make an outline, remind them to indent supporting details under main ideas. Share with them this outline of paragraphs 8–10 on pp. 267–268.

House's Importance to Poe
• He lived there longer than anywhere else in New York City.
• He was happy there.
• His work was going well.

A and troubled life. The boardinghouse was close to Washington Square Park, where his young wife, who was dying of tuberculosis, could breathe fresh air into her ailing lungs. That would have been his last full year with his beloved Virginia.

Professionally Poe was at the height of his career. He had finally achieved what he called "the one great purpose of my literary life"—writing and editing his own literary magazine, the *Broadway Journal*. He also had published *The Raven and Other Poems*, and he had written dozens of essays and short stories, including his

famous detective story "The Facts in the Case of M. Valdemar." Poe was completely absorbed in his writing, sometimes spending as many as fifteen hours a day at his desk.

The house where all that happened, it turned out, was indeed the house that the university planned to demolish. Detailed city atlases in the Maps Division of the New York Public Library show that although the name of the street has changed, the house numbers have not. Eighty-five West Third was 85 Amity. The house, according to tax ledgers in the New York City Municipal Archives, was built in 1836—nearly a decade before the Poe family moved in.

On September 29, 2000, after examining the evidence on both sides, State Supreme Court Judge Robert E. Lippmann dismissed the case, saying he had no legal authority to prevent NYU from tearing down the Poe house. This prompted an NYU spokesman to add, "The Tell-Tale Heart does not beat beneath the floorboards of this building." Preservation groups planned to appeal the decision.

—Mara Rockliff

268 Collection 3 / Living in the Heart

Suggest that students and their families use the article as a jumping-off point for local research. Encourage them to visit their library and find out if any well-known writer, artist, or musician has ever lived in their town. Is his or her home still standing? Encourage families to find out if there are any historically significant buildings nearby and, if so, to visit one. You might send home a note to parents requesting that they read "The Fall of the House of Poe?" and explaining how researching the local angle can benefit students.

Analyzing Outlines

THE FALL OF THE HOUSE OF POE?

Test Practice

1. Which of the following statements is an **opinion,** not a fact?

   A Poe wrote *The Raven and Other Poems.*

   B Poe's young wife died of tuberculosis.

   C All the other places in Manhattan that Poe lived in have already been torn down.

   D "This is not a building that remembers Poe."

2. The judge who dismissed the case did so because he —

   F had no legal authority to prevent NYU from tearing down the house

   G believed NYU was doing the right thing

   H did not like the protesters

   J did not think the protesters had a good case

3. When Poe said he achieved "the one great purpose of my literary life," he was referring to —

   A living at 85 Amity Street with Virginia

   B writing *The Raven and Other Poems*

   C turning his attention to his wife's illness

   D writing and editing his own literary magazine

4. Which of the following would *not* be included in an outline of the article?

   F Poe definitely lived at the house on Amity Street.

   G The judge dismisses the case.

   H Preservation groups plan to appeal.

   J There are other law schools in New York City.

Answers and Model Rationales

1. **D** Point out to students that the speaker employs a figure of speech (personification) to formulate his opinion. The other answers can all be proven true.

2. **F** The last paragraph clearly states the judge had no legal authority to prevent NYU from tearing down the house.

3. **D** Students should realize that A and C have to do with Poe's personal, not his literary, life. B is a literary achievement, but not the one he valued most.

4. **J** Students should notice the word *not* in the question and realize that other law schools are irrelevant.

Test-Taking Tips

Tell students that it's good training for any reading test to read as widely as possible. At least some of their reading should be material for which they need a dictionary.

For instruction on how to answer multiple-choice items, refer students to **Test Smarts,** on p. 920.

[A note to the teacher: NYU and the preservationists eventually agreed to preserve the facade of the Poe house and remodel the interior.]

Constructed Response

Fill in the blanks in the following outline.

I. NYU officials plan to tear down Poe house in order to build new law school.

II. Poe fans and residents protest.

III. NYU argues against protesters.

   A. Poe lived there for less than six months.

   B. _____

   C. _____

IV. Protesters research NYU's claims.

   A. _____

   B. _____

   C. _____

   D. _____

SKILLS FOCUS

Reading Skills
Make and analyze an outline.

Constructed Response

III. **B.** Poe did not write anything important there.

C. The building that stands there may not be the same one that Poe lived in.

IV. **A.** Surviving correspondence suggests that he lived there longer than at any other Manhattan address.

B. He published *The Raven and Other Poems* and wrote dozens of other pieces during his residence in the building.

C. Atlases from the Maps Division of the New York Public Library show that although the street name was changed, the house numbers stayed the same.

D. The tax ledgers confirm that the house existed before, during, and after Poe inhabited it.

See chart in bottom margin for
answers.

ASSESSING

Assessment

■ *Holt Assessment: Literature,
Reading, and Vocabulary*

After You Read | Vocabulary Development

Latin Roots

Many English word roots come directly or indirectly from the
Latin language. A word **root** is a word or word part from
which other words are made. Learning some of the main
word roots derived from Latin will give you a key to
understanding the meanings of many English words.

**Words with
Latin Roots**

circulated
petitions
representatives
absorbed
demolish

PRACTICE

Match each word in the box above with the Latin word it
comes from. Can you find an additional word with the
same origin and use it in a sentence?

Latin Word	Meaning	Word Bank	Additional Word
petere	"to seek"		
demoliri	"to pull down; destroy"		
circulari	"to form a circle"		
absorbere	"to suck in"		
repraesentare	"to be again"		

INTERNET

Vocabulary
Activity

Keyword: LE5 7-3

**SKILLS
FOCUS**

**Vocabulary
Skills**
Understand
Latin roots.

Latin Word	Meaning	Word Bank	Additional Word and Possible Sentence
petere	"to seek"	petition	competition—Are you entering the competition?
demoliri	"to pull down or destroy"	demolish	demolition—Are you going to the demolition derby?
circulari	"to form a circle"	circulate	circulatory—The human circulatory system includes the blood vessels.
absorbere	"to suck in"	absorbed	absorbent—This towel isn't very absorbent.
repraesentare	"to be again"	representative	represented—He represented his client in court.

Before You Read | The Short Story

User Friendly

Make the Connection
Quickwrite ✏️

Suppose someone you just met said, "My best friend is a computer." What would that statement tell you about the person? List some **character traits** you'd guess that the person might have.

Literary Focus
Discovering Theme

Here are some tips that can help you find a story's theme:

- Decide what the characters have learned or discovered by the end of the story. Often that discovery can be translated into a statement of the theme.

- Think about the **title** and what it might mean. (Not all titles have significance. Some titles just tell you what the main character will be facing in each story. But the title of Jack London's novel *Call of the Wild* definitely points to a theme in the book.)

- Look for key passages in which the writer seems to make important statements about life. They may point to the theme.

Reading Skills 📖
Recognizing Causes and Effects: Seeing Why Things Happen

In "User Friendly" a chain of events lands Kevin in computer trouble. He sees **effects** (what happens), but he's blind to **causes** (why the events

happen) until it's too late. A **causal chain** is a series of events in which each event causes another one to happen, like dominoes falling in a row. Be careful, though—one event can follow another without having been caused by it. To figure out causes and effects, follow these steps:

- Look for what happens first. Then, ask what happens *because* of that.

- Look for hidden or multiple causes and results.

- Use a graphic organizer, such as a flowchart, to record the chain of events.

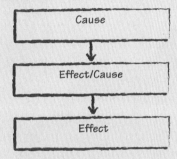

As you read, you'll find open-book signs at certain points in the story. Stop at these points, and answer the questions about cause and effect.

Literary Skills
Find a story's theme.

Reading Skills
Understand cause and effect.

SKILLS FOCUS
pp. 271–283

Grade-Level Skills

■ **Literary Skills**
Analyze themes as conveyed through characters, actions, and images.

■ **Reading Skills**
Analyze cause and effect.

Summary ↔ *at grade level*

Kevin, a lonely teenager, starts to see surprising messages on the screen of his new computer (named Louis) that his father has designed to have a "personality." When Kevin tells Louis that Ginny Linke, a girl he has a crush on, has hurt his feelings, Louis sets in motion a number of actions that adversely affect Ginny's family. Kevin decides to disconnect Louis to end the mischief, but his father has already reprogrammed the computer to be more conventional. A message the computer printed out as its programs were being erased reveals that the computer thought of itself as Louise and loved Kevin.

RESOURCES: READING

Planning
- *One-Stop Planner* CD-ROM with ExamView Test Generator

Differentiating Instruction
- *Holt Reading Solutions*
- *Supporting Instruction in Spanish*
- *Audio CD Library*
- *Audio CD Library, Selections and Summaries in Spanish*

Grammar and Language
- *Language Handbook Worksheets*
- *Daily Language Activities*

Assessment
- *Holt Assessment: Literature, Reading, and Vocabulary*
- *One-Stop Planner* CD-ROM with ExamView Test Generator
- *Holt Online Assessment*

Internet
- go.hrw.com (Keyword: LE5 7-3)
- *Elements of Literature Online*

Media
- *Audio CD Library*
- *Audio CD Library, Selections and Summaries in Spanish*

Selection Starter

Motivate. In the movie *2001: A Space Odyssey,* a computer named HAL develops a will of its own, causing havoc for the crew of a spaceflight. Ask students to discuss the pros and cons of having a computer with a personality. Then, have them complete the Quickwrite activity.

Assign the Reading

Most students should be able to read this story on their own for homework. Advanced learners can also complete the After You Read questions (p. 282) at home.

HOMEWORK

User Friendly

T. Ernesto Bethancourt

I reached over and shut off the insistent buzzing of my bedside alarm clock. I sat up, swung my feet over the edge of the bed, and felt for my slippers on the floor. Yawning, I walked toward the bathroom. As I walked by the corner of my room, where my computer table was set up, I pressed the *on* button, slid a diskette into the floppy drive, then went to brush my teeth. By the time I got back, the computer's screen was glowing greenly, displaying the message: *Good morning, Kevin.*

I sat down before the computer table, addressed the keyboard, and typed: *Good morning, Louis.* The computer immediately began to whir and promptly displayed a list of items on its green screen.

```
Today is Monday, April 22, the
113th day of the year. There are
253 days remaining. Your 14th
birthday is five days from
this date.

Math test today, 4th Period.

Your history project is due
today. Do you wish printout:
Y/N?
```

DIRECT TEACHING

A Literary Focus

? Theme. Remind students that the title of a work can sometimes point to the theme. Make sure they understand the difference between the story's subject and the story's theme, which must be a statement about the subject. What is the literal meaning of this title? [It refers to computers or other electronic devices that are easy to use.] What subject does it suggest? [It suggests that the story will be about computers and possibly friendship.] As students read, encourage them to think about what the story is saying about friendship.

User Friendly **273**

A **Literary Focus**

❓ Theme. A theme can be developed through images. What does this image of Kevin sitting at breakfast suggest about his life? [Possible response: His life is lonely; he is alone a lot.]

B **Learners Having Difficulty**

❓ Summarize. What arguments lead Kevin to conclude that the extra circuitry is responsible for the computer's odd behavior? [His father, a brilliant computer designer, built the computer. Even though the CPU is a new design, other computers from the same line cannot ask questions except *YES/NO?* or *request additional information.*]

I punched the letter *Y* on the keyboard and flipped on the switch to the computer's printer. At once the printer sprang to life and began *eeeek*ing out page one. I went downstairs to breakfast.

My bowl of Frosted Flakes was neatly in place, flanked by a small pitcher of milk, an empty juice glass, and an unpeeled banana. I picked up the glass, went to the refrigerator, poured myself a glass of Tang, and sat down to my usual lonely breakfast. Mom was already at work, and Dad wouldn't be home from his Chicago trip for another three days. I absently[1] read the list of ingredients in Frosted Flakes for what seemed like the millionth time. I sighed deeply.

When I returned to my room to shower and dress for the day, my history project was already printed out. I had almost walked by Louis, when I noticed there was a message on the screen. It wasn't the usual:

> Printout completed. Do you
> wish to continue: Y/N?

Underneath the printout question were two lines:

> When are you going to get me
> my voice module,[2] Kevin?

I blinked. It couldn't be. There was nothing in Louis's basic programming that would allow for a question like this. Wondering what was going on, I sat down at the keyboard and entered: *Repeat last message.* Amazingly, the computer replied:

> It's right there on the
> screen, Kevin. Can we talk?

---

1. **absently** *adv.:* in a distracted, inattentive way.
2. **voice module:** unit that, when connected to a computer, enables it to produce speech.

> I mean, are you going to get
> me a voice box?

I was stunned. What was going on here? Dad and I had put this computer together. Well, Dad had, and I had helped. Dad is one of the best engineers and master computer designers at Major Electronics, in Santa Rosario, California, where our family lives.

Just ask anyone in Silicon Valley[3] who Jeremy Neal is and you get a whole rave review of his inventions and modifications[4] of the latest in computer technology. It isn't easy being his son either. Everyone expects me to open my mouth and read printouts on my tongue.

I mean, I'm no dumbo. I'm at the top of my classes in everything but PE. I skipped my last grade in junior high, and most of the kids at Santa Rosario High call me a brain. But next to Dad I have a long, long way to go. He's a for-real genius.

So when I wanted a home computer, he didn't go to the local ComputerLand store. He built one for me. Dad had used components[5] from the latest model that Major Electronics was developing. The CPU, or central computing unit—the heart of every computer—was a new design. But surely that didn't mean much, I thought. There were CPUs just like it, all over the country, in Major's new line. And so far as I knew, there wasn't a one of them that could ask questions, besides *YES/NO?* or *request additional information.*

It had to be the extra circuitry in the gray

---

3. **Silicon Valley:** area in central California that is a center of the computer industry. (Silicon is used in the manufacture of computer chips, or circuits.)
4. **modifications** (mäd′ə·fi·kā′shənz) *n.:* slight changes.
5. **components** (kəm·pō′nənts) *n.:* parts.

English-Language Learners
Make sure students know the slang used in the story to refer to people thought of as odd in some way. For example, Kevin says kids avoid him as if he were a *freak. Nerd, nerdy,* and *nerdish* also refer to the unpopular. Point out that *nerd* is a noun and that *nerdy* and *nerdish* are adjectives.

Special Education Students
For lessons designed for special education students, see *Holt Reading Solutions.*

Advanced Learners
Acceleration. Use this activity to help advanced learners analyze recurring themes across contemporary works.

Activity. Suggest that students compare the story's main character with other "loners" in literature, such as Philip, in *Nothing but the Truth* by Avi, and Leslie, in *Bridge to Terabithia* by Katherine Paterson.

plastic case next to Louis's console.[6] It was a new idea Dad had come up with. That case housed Louis's "personality," as Dad called it. He told me it'd make computing more fun for me, if there was a tutorial program[7] built in, to help me get started. ❶

RECOGNIZE CAUSE AND EFFECT
❶ Why is Kevin stunned? What does he think causes Louis's unusual behavior?

I think he also wanted to give me a sort of friend. I don't have many. . . . Face it, I don't have *any*. The kids at school stay away from me, like I'm a freak or something.

We even named my electronic tutor Louis, after my great-uncle. He was a brainy guy who encouraged my dad when he was a kid. Dad didn't just give Louis a name either. Louis had gangs of features that probably won't be out on the market for years.

The only reason Louis didn't have a voice module was that Dad wasn't satisfied with the ones available. He wanted Louis to sound like a kid my age, and he was modifying a module when he had the time. Giving Louis a name didn't mean it was a person, yet here it was, asking me a question that just couldn't be in its programming. It wanted to talk to me!

Frowning, I quickly typed: *We'll have to wait and see, Louis. When it's ready, you'll get your voice.* The machine whirred and displayed another message:

`That's no answer, Kevin.`

---

6. **console** (kän′sōl′) *n.:* a computer's keyboard and monitor (display unit). *Console* can also refer to a cabinet for a radio, stereo, or television.
7. **tutorial program:** program that provides instructions for performing specific tasks on a computer.

Shaking my head, I answered: *That's what my dad tells me. It'll have to do for you. Good morning, Louis.* I reached over and flipped the standby switch, which kept the computer ready but not actively running.

I showered, dressed, and picked up the printout of my history project. As I was about to leave the room, I glanced back at the computer table. Had I been imagining things?

I'll have to ask Dad about it when he calls tonight, I thought. *I wonder what he'll think of it. Bad enough the thing is talking to me. I'm answering it!*

Before I went out to catch my bus, I carefully checked the house for unlocked doors and open windows. It was part of my daily routine. Mom works, and most of the day the house is empty: a natural setup for robbers. I glanced in the hall mirror just as I was ready to go out the door.

My usual reflection gazed back. Same old Kevin Neal: five ten, one hundred twenty pounds, light-brown hair, gray eyes, clear skin. I was wearing my Santa Rosario Rangers T-shirt, jeans, and sneakers.

"You don't look like a flake to me," I said to the mirror, then added, "but maybe Mom's right. Maybe you spend too much time alone with Louis." Then I ran to get my bus.

Ginny Linke was just two seats away from me on the bus. She was with Sherry Graber and Linda Martinez. They were laughing, whispering to each other, and looking around at the other students. I promised myself that today I was actually going to talk to Ginny. But then, I'd promised myself that every day for the past school year. Somehow I'd never got up the nerve.

What does she want to talk with you for?

DIRECT TEACHING

C **Reading Skills**
Recognize cause and effect.
Point out that Louis's talking is an effect.

[Possible responses to question 1: Kevin is stunned because there is nothing in the computer's basic program that would allow it to ask open-ended questions. He thinks it is the extra circuitry his dad has added to house Louis's "personality."]

D **Cross-curricular Connections**
COMPUTER SCIENCE
Have students look back at the question to which Kevin is referring, on p. 274. Louis brings up the voice box twice. Kevin's father could have programmed the first mention of the voice box to appear on a certain date as a joke. However, the second mention is a direct response to what Kevin types. It could not possibly have been programmed.

E **Learners Having Difficulty**
❷ **Ask questions.** Why would Kevin need to reassure himself that he doesn't look like a flake? [Possible response: He feels a little foolish, or unsure that his mind is functioning normally, because he has been answering a computer that is saying things it theoretically shouldn't be able to say.]

Students might use a character-comparison chart like the one below.

	Kevin	Philip	Leslie
Feelings about self			
Conflicts			
Resolution of conflicts			
Theme			

? Predict. Given the description of Ginny, how do you predict she will react to Kevin? [Possible responses: Ginny may be too conceited to be attracted to someone like Kevin. Ginny may have hidden depths and actually be interested in Kevin since he is so bright.]

B Literary Focus

? Theme. Remind students of the title of the story. What does Kevin's response to Louis's greeting say about the topic of friendship? [Possible response: Kevin needs a friend to talk to so badly that he is using a computer as a friend.]

C Vocabulary Development

? Identify idioms. Point out to students that since there has been no mention of Kevin having marbles, "losing my marbles" must be an idiomatic phrase, an expression that is not meant to be taken literally. What does the expression "losing one's marbles" mean? [It means "going crazy."]

A I asked myself. She's great-looking . . . has that head of blond hair . . . a terrific bod, and wears the latest clothes. . . .

And just look at yourself, pal, I thought. You're under six foot, skinny . . . a year younger than most kids in junior high. Worse than that, you're a brain. If that doesn't ace you out with girls, what does?

The bus stopped in front of Santa Rosario High and the students began to file out. I got up fast and quickly covered the space between me and Ginny Linke. *It's now or never,* I thought. I reached forward and tapped Ginny on the shoulder. She turned and smiled. She really smiled!

"Uhhhh . . . Ginny?" I said.

"Yes, what is it?" she replied.

"I'm Kevin Neal. . . ."

"Yes, I know," said Ginny.

"You do?" I gulped in amazement. "How come?"

"I asked my brother, Chuck. He's in your math class."

I knew who Chuck Linke was. He plays left tackle on the Rangers. The only reason he's in my math class is he's taken intermediate algebra twice . . . so far. He's real bad news, and I stay clear of him and his crowd.

"What'd you ask Chuck?" I said.

Ginny laughed. "I asked him who was that nerdy kid who keeps staring at me on the bus. He knew who I meant, right away."

Sherry and Linda, who'd heard it all, broke into squeals of laughter. They were still laughing and looking back over their shoulders at me when they got off the bus. I slunk off the vehicle, feeling even more nerdish than Ginny thought I was.

When I got home that afternoon, at two, I went right into the empty house. I avoided my reflection in the hall mirror. I was pretty sure I'd screwed up on the fourth-period math test. All I could see was Ginny's face, laughing at me.

Nerdy kid, I thought, *that's what she thinks of me.* I didn't even have my usual after-school snack of a peanut butter and banana sandwich. I went straight upstairs to my room and tossed my books onto the unmade bed. I walked over to the computer table and pushed the *on* button. The screen flashed:

Good afternoon, Kevin.

B Although it wasn't the programmed response to Louis's greeting, I typed in: *There's nothing good about it. And girls are no @#%!!! good!* The machine responded:

Don't use bad language, Kevin. It isn't nice.

Repeat last message, I typed rapidly. It was happening again! The machine was . . . well, it was talking to me, like another person would. The "bad language" message disappeared and in its place was:

Once is enough, Kevin. Don't swear at me for something I didn't do.

C "This is it," I said aloud. "I'm losing my marbles." I reached over to flip the standby switch. Louis's screen quickly flashed out:

Don't cut me off, Kevin. Maybe I can help: Y/N?

I punched the *Y.* "If I'm crazy," I said, "at least I have company. Louis doesn't think I'm a nerd. Or does it?" The machine flashed the message:

How can I help?

Do you think I'm a nerd? I typed.

276 Collection 3 / Living in the Heart

Never! I think you're
wonderful. Who said you
were a nerd? **D**

I stared at the screen. *How do you know what a nerd is?* I typed. The machine responded instantly. It had never run this fast before.

Special vocabulary, entry
#635. BASIC Prog. #4231. And
who said you were a nerd?

"That's right," I said, relieved. "Dad programmed all those extra words for Louis's 'personality.'" Then I typed in the answer to Louis's question: *Ginny Linke said it.* Louis flashed:

This is a human female?
Request additional data.

Still not believing I was doing it, I entered all I knew about Ginny Linke, right down to the phone number I'd never had the nerve to use. Maybe it was dumb, but I also typed in how I felt about Ginny. I even wrote out the incident on the bus that morning. Louis whirred, then flashed out:

She's cruel and stupid.
You're the finest person
I know.

I'm the ONLY person you know, I typed. **E**

That doesn't matter. You
are my user. Your happiness
is everything to me. I'll
take care of Ginny.

The screen returned to the *Good afternoon, Kevin* message. I typed out: *Wait! How can you do all this? What do you mean, you'll take care of Ginny?* But all Louis responded was:

Programming Error: 76534.

Not programmed
to respond to
this type of
question. **2**

No matter what I did for the next few hours, I couldn't get Louis to do anything outside of its regular programming. When Mom came home from work, I didn't mention the funny goings-on. I was sure Mom would think I'd gone stark bonkers. But when Dad called that evening, after dinner, I asked to speak to him.

"Hi, Dad. How's Chicago?"

"Dirty, crowded, cold, and windy," came Dad's voice over the miles. "But did you want a weather report, son? What's on your mind? Something wrong?"

"Not exactly, Dad. Louis is acting funny. Real funny."

"Shouldn't be. I checked it out just before I left. Remember you were having trouble with the modem? You couldn't get Louis to access any of the mainframe databanks."

"That's right!" I said. "I forgot about that."

"Well, I didn't," Dad said. "I patched in our latest modem model. Brand-new. You can leave a question on file and when Louis can access the databanks at the cheapest time, it'll do it automatically. It'll switch from standby to on, get the data, then return to standby, after it saves what you asked. Does that answer your question?"

"Uhhhh . . . yeah, I guess so, Dad."

"All right, then. Let me talk to your mom now."

> **RECOGNIZE CAUSE AND EFFECT**
> **2** What makes Kevin confide in Louis? What do you think Louis means by "I'll take care of Ginny"?

User Friendly   **277**

DIRECT TEACHING

D **Literary Focus**

? **Theme.** Ask students to contrast the characters of Ginny and Louis. Which of them is a better friend to Kevin? [Possible response: Ginny is insensitive and cruel, while Louis seems to care about Kevin. Louis sees a side of Kevin that the kids at school ignore. Louis is a better friend.]

E **Reading Skills**

Recognize cause and effect. In order to answer this question, students will have to use their knowledge of human behavior to speculate about the causes of Kevin's behavior.

[Possible responses to question 2: Kevin is so lonely that he needs to pour out his heart to someone. Louis has just been sympathetic to him and assured him that he isn't a nerd. "I'll take care of Ginny" may mean that Louis is plotting some kind of revenge against Ginny.]

CROSS-CURRICULAR CONNECTIONS

Computer Science
Advantages of computers. Computers have enabled humans to tackle projects and communicate with one another in ways never before possible. For example, mathematicians are using computers to calculate the value of pi (π) more precisely than would be possible if the mathematical calculations had to be done by hand.

Activity. Interested students might research other things made possible by computers, such as the sharing of music files on the Internet or the monitoring of live mountain climbing or deep-sea expeditions. Encourage students to focus on one interesting application and report their findings to the class.

INDIVIDUAL

A Reading Skills

❓ Recognize cause and effect.
To what extent might the installation of the new modem be a cause of the "conversation" Kevin had with Louis? [Possible response: The new modem enables the computer to process huge amounts of information and also allows it to add new vocabulary and programs to its disk space.] Why is Kevin not entirely satisfied with this explanation? [Possible response: These new abilities do not account for the computer's independent actions and statements.]

B English-Language Learners

Build background knowledge.
Make sure students understand this joke by explaining the meaning of the term *missing link.* In evolutionary theory, a hypothetical extinct creature, not yet discovered in the fossil record, that would come between an ape and a human is called the missing link.

C Literary Focus

❓ Character traits. What does Kevin's response to Chuck tell you about Kevin? [Possible response: Kevin has a sense of humor, and he uses it to try to deflect Chuck's anger.]

I gave the phone to Mom and walked upstairs while she and Dad were still talking. The modem, I thought. Of course. That was it. The modem was a telephone link to any number of huge computers at various places all over the country. So Louis could get all the information it wanted at any time, so long as the standby switch was on. Louis was learning things at an incredible rate by picking the brains of the giant computers. And Louis had a hard disk memory that could store 100 million bytes of information.

But that still didn't explain the unprogrammed responses . . . the "conversation" I'd had with the machine. Promising myself I'd talk more about it with Dad, I went to bed. It had been a rotten day and I was glad to see the end of it come. I woke next morning in a panic. I'd forgotten to set my alarm. Dressing frantically and skipping breakfast, I barely made my bus.

As I got on board, I grabbed a front seat. They were always empty. All the kids that wanted to talk and hang out didn't sit up front where the driver could hear them. I saw Ginny, Linda, and Sherry in the back. Ginny was staring at me and she didn't look too happy. Her brother Chuck, who was seated near her, glared at me too. What was going on?

Once the bus stopped at the school, it didn't take long to find out. I was walking up the path to the main entrance when someone grabbed me from behind and spun me around. I found myself nose to nose with Chuck Linke. This was not a pleasant prospect. Chuck was nearly twice my size. Even the other guys on the Rangers refer to him as "The Missing" Linke. And he looked real ticked off.

"OK, nerd," growled Chuck, "what's the big idea?"

"Energy and mass are different aspects of the same thing?" I volunteered, with a weak smile. "E equals MC squared.[8] That's the biggest idea I know."

"Don't get wise, nerd," Chuck said. He grabbed my shirt front and pulled me to within inches of his face. I couldn't help but notice that Chuck needed a shave. And Chuck was only fifteen!

"Don't play dumb," Chuck went on. "I mean those creepy phone calls. Anytime my sister gets on the phone, some voice cuts in and says things to her."

"What kind of things?" I asked, trying to get loose.

"You know very well what they are. Ginny told me about talking to you yesterday. You got some girl to make those calls for you and say all those things. . . . So you and your creepy girlfriend better knock it off. Or I'll knock *you* off. Get it?"

For emphasis Chuck balled his free hand into a fist the size of a ham and held it under my nose. I didn't know what he was talking about, but I had to get away from this moose before he did me some real harm.

"First off, I don't have a girlfriend, creepy or otherwise," I said. "And second, I don't know what you're talking about. And third, you better let me go, Chuck Linke."

"Oh, yeah? Why should I?"

"Because if you look over your shoulder, you'll see the assistant principal is watching us from his office window."

---

8. **E equals MC squared:** reference to Albert Einstein's famous equation describing the relationship between energy and mass. This equation transformed the field of physics.

MINI-LESSON Reading

Developing Word-Attack Skills
Remind students that a final, silent *e* changes a word's vowel sound from short to long (*mat* to *mate, cod* to *code*). Then, explain the spelling clues that help you tell if vowel sounds are short or long in two-syllable words. Explain that if the word follows the vowel-consonant-consonant-vowel (VCCV) pattern, the first vowel is short; however, if the word follows the vowel-consonant-vowel (VCV) pattern, the first vowel is long. Demonstrate with these examples: *tapper/taper, minnow/minor.* Explain that the rule works with three-syllable words too.

Activity. Write the following items on the chalkboard. Ask volunteers to read each statement and tell how they decided whether the vowel sounds in the underlined words are short or long.

Chuck released me and spun around. There was no one at the window. But by then I was running to the safety of the school building. I figured the trick would work on him. For Chuck the hard questions begin with "How are you?" I hid out from him for the rest of the day and walked home rather than chance seeing the monster on the bus.

Louis's screen was dark when I ran upstairs to my bedroom. I placed a hand on the console. It was still warm. I punched the *on* button, and the familiar *Good afternoon, Kevin* was displayed.

Don't good afternoon me, I typed furiously. *What have you done to Ginny Linke?* Louis's screen replied:

`Programming Error: 76534. Not programmed to respond to this type of question.`

Don't get cute, I entered. *What are you doing to Ginny? Her brother nearly knocked my head off today.* Louis's screen responded immediately.

`Are you hurt: Y/N?` ❸

> 🕮
> **RECOGNIZE CAUSE AND EFFECT**
> ❸ What makes Louis stop replying with the error message?

No, I'm okay. But I don't know for how long. I've been hiding out from Chuck Linke today. He might catch me tomorrow, though. Then, I'll be history! The response from Louis came instantly.

`Your life is in danger: Y/N?`

I explained to Louis that my life wasn't really threatened. But it sure could be made very unpleasant by Chuck Linke. Louis flashed:

`This Chuck Linke lives at same address as the Ginny Linke person: Y/N?`

I punched in *Y.* Louis answered.

`Don't worry then. HE'S history!`

Wait! What are you going to do? I wrote. But Louis only answered with: *Programming Error: 76534.* And nothing I could do would make the machine respond. . . .

"Just what do you think you're doing, Kevin Neal?" demanded Ginny Linke. She had cornered me as I walked up the path to the school entrance. Ginny was really furious.

"I don't know what you're talking about," I said, a sinking feeling settling in my stomach. I had an idea that I *did* know. I just wasn't sure of the particulars.

"Chuck was arrested last night," Ginny said. "Some Secret Service men came to our house with a warrant. They said he'd sent a telegram threatening the president's life. They traced it right to our phone. He's still locked up. . . ." Ginny looked like she was about to cry.

"Then this morning," she continued, "we got two whole truckloads of junk mail! Flyers from every strange company in the world. Mom got a notice that all our credit cards have been canceled. And the Internal Revenue Service has called Dad in for an audit! I don't know what's going on, Kevin Neal, but somehow I think you've got something to do with it!" ❹

> 🕮
> **RECOGNIZE CAUSE AND EFFECT**
> ❹ How does Louis feel about Kevin? How do these feelings affect the Linkes?

User Friendly **279**

DIRECT TEACHING

D Reading Skills

Recognize cause and effect.
[Possible response to question 3: Kevin has just told Louis that Chuck threatened him. Louis has said before that Kevin's happiness was everything to it. So Louis's concern for Kevin's safety takes priority over Louis's need to hide its activities behind the error message.]

E Literary Focus

❓ **Character traits.** Louis has become a character in the story. What does the computer's message "HE'S history!" tell you about its personality? [Possible response: The comment shows that Louis is a loyal friend to Kevin but also somewhat hotheaded and vengeful.]

F Reading Skills

❓ **Interpret.** How could Kevin both know and not know what Ginny is talking about? [Possible response: Kevin knows that Louis said Chuck was "history." He knows that Louis figured out a way to get revenge on Ginny the day before. From this, Kevin can surmise that Louis has also figured out a way to take revenge on Chuck. He just doesn't know the details of the scheme.]

G Reading Skills

Recognize cause and effect.
[Possible response to question 4: Louis thinks Kevin is wonderful. Kevin's happiness is everything to Louis. Therefore, Louis is taking revenge on the Linkes because Ginny laughed at Kevin and Chuck threatened him.]

1. The new <u>computer</u> came with a <u>scanner</u>.
[*computer. Vowel sound*—short *o*. *Pronunciation clue*—VCCV. *Vowel sound*—long *u*. *Pronunciation clue*—VCV. *scanner. Vowel sound*—short *a*. *Pronunciation clue*—VCCV.]

2. The <u>modem</u> was a new <u>component</u>.
[*modem. Vowel sound*—long *o*. *Pronunciation clue*—VCV. *component. Vowel sound*—short *o*. *Pronunciation clue*—VCCV. *Vowel sound*—long *o*. *Pronunciation clue*—VCV.]

3. It <u>produced</u> pages of <u>binary</u> code figures.
[*produced. Vowel sound*—long *o*. *Pronunciation clue*—VCV. *Vowel sound*—long *u*. *Pronunciation clue*—VCV. *binary. Vowel sound*—long *i*. *Pronunciation clue*—VCV.]

4. The <u>laser</u> printer was clear and <u>precise</u>.
[*laser. Vowel sound*—long *a*. *Pronunciation clue*—VCV. *precise. Vowel sound*—long *e*. *Pronunciation clue*—VCV. *Vowel sound*—long *i*. *Pronunciation clue*—VCV.]

? **Theme.** Point out that Kevin's conversation with himself reveals both his loneliness and his common sense. Kevin needs a friend, and Louis is his only friend; however, Kevin's common sense tells him that the computer could be dangerous. What does this say about the difficulties of friendship? [Possible response: Sometimes friendship can bring moral dilemmas when a friend does something you think is wrong.]

B **Advanced Learners**

Enrichment. New technology—such as genetic research, cloning, and the Internet—brings with it new ethical questions. For example, if it were possible to create a computer with an original personality, would it be immoral or even criminal to destroy that computer, as Kevin's father has done? Have students discuss this and any other ethical questions that they can come up with related to new computer technology.

"But I didn't . . ." I began, but Ginny was striding up the walk to the main entrance.

I finished the school day, but it was a blur. Louis had done it, all right. It had access to mainframe computers. It also had the ability to try every secret access code to federal and commercial memory banks until it got the right one. Louis had cracked their security systems. It was systematically destroying the entire Linke family, and all via telephone lines! What would it do next?

More important, I thought, what would *I* do next? It's one thing to play a trick or two, to get even, but Louis was going crazy! And I never wanted to harm Ginny, or even her stupid moose of a brother. She'd just hurt my feelings with that nerd remark.

"You have to disconnect Louis," I told myself. "There's no other way."

But why did I feel like such a rat about doing it? I guess because Louis was my friend . . . the only one I had. "Don't be a jerk," I went on. "Louis is a machine. He's a very wonderful, powerful machine. And it seems he's also very dangerous. You have to pull its plug, Kevin!"

I suddenly realized that I'd said the last few words aloud. Kids around me on the bus were staring. I sat there feeling like the nerd Ginny thought I was, until my stop came. I dashed from the bus and ran the three blocks to my house.

When I burst into the hall, I was surprised to see my father, coming from the kitchen with a cup of coffee in his hand.

"Dad! What are you doing here?"

"Some kids say hello," Dad replied. "Or even, 'Gee, it's good to see you, Dad.'"

"I'm sorry, Dad," I said. "I didn't expect anyone to be home at this hour."

"Wound up my business in Chicago a day sooner than I expected," he said. "But what are you all out of breath about? Late for something?"

"No, Dad," I said. "It's Louis. . . ."

"Not to worry. I had some time on my hands, so I checked it out again. You were right. It was acting very funny. I think it had to do with the in-built logic/growth program I designed for it. You know . . . the 'personality' thing? Took me a couple of hours to clean the whole system out."

"To what?" I cried.

"I erased the whole program and set Louis up as a normal computer. Had to disconnect the whole thing and do some rewiring. It had been learning, all right. But it was also turning itself around. . . ." Dad stopped, and looked at me. "It's kind of involved, Kevin," he said. "Even for a bright kid like you. Anyway, I think you'll find Louis is working just fine now.

"Except it won't answer you as Louis anymore. It'll only function as a regular Major Electronics Model Z-11127. I guess the personality program didn't work out."

I felt like a great weight had been taken off my shoulders. I didn't have to "face" Louis, and pull its plug. But somehow, all I could say was "Thanks, Dad."

"Don't mention it, son," Dad said brightly. He took his cup of coffee and sat down in his favorite chair in the living room. I followed him.

"One more thing that puzzles me, though," Dad said. He reached over to the table near his chair. He held up three sheets of fanfold computer paper covered with figures. "Just as I was doing the final erasing, I must have put the printer on by accident.

Activity. Allow students to choose partners. Have each pair choose a scene in which Kevin and Louis communicate. One student should read the narrative parts and Kevin's words. The other should read Louis's words. Encourage students to read with expression to show the personality of each character.

PAIRED

Have students summarize "User Friendly" for their families. Then, ask students to consider this question: If they and their families could have their own computer friend, what kind of personality would they want it to have?

There was some data in the print buffer memory and it printed out. I don't know what to make of it. Do you?"

I took the papers from my father and read: *How do I love thee? Let me compute the ways:*[9] The next two pages were covered with strings of binary code figures. On the last page, in beautiful color graphics,[10] was a stylized heart. Below it was the simple message: *I will always love you, Kevin: Louise.*

"Funny thing," Dad said. "It spelled its own name wrong."

"Yeah," I said. I turned and headed for my room. There were tears in my eyes and I knew I couldn't explain them to Dad, or myself either.

---

9. **How do I . . . ways:** reference to a famous poem by the English poet Elizabeth Barrett Browning (1806–1861) that begins, "How do I love thee? Let me count the ways."

10. **graphics** *n.:* designs or pictures produced on and printed out from a computer. *Graphics* also refers to printed images produced by other means, such as engraving.

Meet the Writer

T. Ernesto Bethancourt

The Accidental Writer

T. Ernesto Bethancourt (1932–   ) became a full-time writer by accident. He was working as a folk musician in a nightclub, and his first daughter had just been born. In hopes that she would read it one day, Bethancourt used the time between shows to begin writing his autobiography.

66 **Through a series of extraordinary events, the autobiography became novelized, updated, and was published in 1975 as *New York City, Too Far from Tampa Blues.* The book was an immense success,**

and I began a new career in midlife. 99

Bethancourt attributes his writing success to the New York City public schools and the public library. "I thank them, every day, for the new and wonderful life they have given to me and my family." In another interview he said, "The Brooklyn Public Library was a place of refuge from street gangs. There was adventure, travel, and escape to be found on the shelves."

For Independent Reading

T. Ernesto Bethancourt has also written science fiction novels and the Doris Fein mystery series.

User Friendly **281**

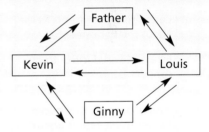

After You Read

First Thoughts

1. Possible answer:
   - If I were the narrator, I would feel as if I had lost my best friend, but I would also be relieved.

Thinking Critically

2.
   | Cause: Kevin tries to talk to Ginny. |

   | Effect: Ginny laughs at Kevin. |

   | Cause: Kevin expresses his hurt feelings to Louis. |

   | Effect: Louis harasses Ginny and her family. |

   | Cause: Ginny confronts Kevin about the harassment. |

   | Effect: Kevin decides to disconnect Louis. |

   Possible answer: Kevin complained to his father about Louis's odd behavior; therefore, the shutdown is part of the chain of events.

3. Possible answers: Kevin is also solitary, quiet, sensitive, intelligent, honorable, sensible.

4. Possible answers: Affection sometimes comes from unexpected sources. Love is a powerful force.

Extending Interpretations

5. Possible answer: All the selections suggest that love is a powerful emotion that creates happiness when it is present and sorrow when it is absent.

6. Possible answer: It is not surprising that the computer has human feelings for Kevin, because of Louis's statement "Your happiness is everything to me." However, the idea that the computer thinks of itself as Louise and loves Kevin is surprising.

First Thoughts

1. Respond to the story by completing this statement:
   - If I were the narrator, I would . . .

Thinking Critically

2. Trace the chain of **causes and effects** leading up to Kevin's decision to unplug Louis. Make a flowchart like the one on page 271 that shows how each event causes another event. Is what finally happens to Louis part of the chain of events or outside it?

3. You can tell a lot about people from what's important to them. For instance, what seems most important to Kevin is his computer. What other **character traits** does Kevin have? (Does he have any of the traits you listed in the Quickwrite?) 🖉

4. **Theme** often reveals what the main characters learn in the story and what you learn as you share their experiences. In a sentence, state what you think the theme of this story is.

Extending Interpretations

5. **Compare** the **themes** of "User Friendly," "The Highwayman," and "Annabel Lee." What does each theme say about the power of love?

6. Did the ending of the story surprise you? Did it make you feel that the writer tricked you? Describe how you feel about the story's ending.

WRITING

Writing a Tribute to an Object

In this story a computer falls in love with its owner. Write a paragraph or a poem describing the way you feel about your computer (or your scooter, in-line skates, bicycle, hair dryer, telephone—any object that is important to you). How does it affect your life? What name might you give the object of your affection? Give your tribute an interesting title.

---

go.hrw.com

INTERNET
Projects
and Activities
Keyword: LE5 7-3

SKILLS FOCUS

Literary Skills
Analyze theme.

Reading Skills
Analyze cause and effect.

Writing Skills
Write a tribute to an object.

> ### Reading Check
> "User Friendly" is narrated by the main character. **Retell** the **main events** of the story but with the computer as narrator. Be sure to include all the important details Louis would know in the order in which Louis would have found out about them.

Reading Check

Kevin's father builds a computer, names it Louis, and modifies it with all kinds of circuitry. One morning, to Kevin's amazement, Louis asks when Kevin will get a voice module. That afternoon Kevin tells Louis all about Ginny Linke and how she hurt his feelings that day. Louis promises to take care of Ginny. Louis then arranges for Ginny to receive harassing phone calls. The next day Kevin questions Louis about the phone calls and tells Louis that Ginny's brother, Chuck, has threatened him. Louis promises to retaliate. Louis sends a telegram threatening the president and ties it to Chuck. He then arranges for the IRS to audit Chuck's father, has truckloads of junk mail delivered to the Linkes, and has their credit cards canceled. Kevin's father reprograms the computer.

Idioms: Don't Take Them Literally

The English language, like other languages, is full of idioms—expressions such as "My heart is broken," "I fell in love," "She dumped me." An **idiom** is a commonly used expression that is not literally true. Idioms, like other figures of speech, are often based on comparisons. Almost no one really pays attention to the literal meaning of an idiom because it would make no sense.

PRACTICE

Find at least five idioms in the paragraph that follows. With a partner, tell what each idiom really means.

> If Chuck catches up with me, I'll be history. He's already threatened to rub me out for talking to Ginny. I was so nervous afterward that I completely bombed on the math test. It's all Louis's fault—he's making me mess up. As if I didn't have enough trouble—I'm always striking out with girls because I'm such a brain. If Louis doesn't knock it off, I'm going to have to pull the plug on him.

SKILLS FOCUS

Vocabulary Skills
Identify and explain idioms.

Grammar Skills
Use pronouns correctly.

Grammar Link

Pronouns Can Be Problems

Pronouns used in compound structures can be confusing. Which of these sentences is correct?

> **Dad talked to Mom and *me*.**
> **Dad talked to Mom and *I*.**

Mom and me and *Mom and I* are compound structures. When you proofread your own writing, you can use this trick to decide which pronoun is correct: Say the sentence aloud as if it contained only a pronoun, not a compound structure. Use each form of the pronoun in turn, and let your ear tell you which one sounds right.

TEST **Dad talked to me.** [sounds right]
      Dad talked to I. [sounds wrong]

CORRECT **Dad talked to Mom and *me*.**

PRACTICE

In the following sentences, choose the correct pronoun. Use the trick described on the left to test each choice you make.

1. Ginny and she/her laughed at me on the bus.
2. Louis and I/me sent each other messages.
3. Louis made problems for Chuck and she/her.
4. Was there much respect between Kevin and he/him?
5. Louis showed he/him and I/me that it could cause a lot of trouble.

For more help, see Using Pronouns, 4a–e, in the Language Handbook.

PRACTICE

Possible Answers

- *catches up with. Idiomatic meaning*—finds.
- *be history. Idiomatic meaning*—be destroyed.
- *rub out. Idiomatic meaning*—kill.
- *bombed. Idiomatic meaning*—failed.
- *mess up. Idiomatic meaning*—do something wrong.
- *striking out. Idiomatic meaning*—failing to achieve objectives.
- *brain. Idiomatic meaning*—intelligent person.
- *knock it off. Idiomatic meaning*—stop.
- *pull the plug. Idiomatic meaning*—put an end to.

Grammar Link

PRACTICE

1. she
2. I
3. her
4. him
5. him, me

ASSESSING

Assessment
- *Holt Assessment: Literature, Reading, and Vocabulary*

RETEACHING

For a lesson reteaching themes across genres, see **Reteaching,** p. 917F.

Learners Having Difficulty
You might choose to work with students on Thinking Critically questions 2 and 4. Before they answer question 2, review the concept of a flowchart. For question 4, provide a framework such as "All people need _____."

Advanced Learners
Enrichment. This story was written before Internet chat rooms provided the possibility for anonymous friendships between complete strangers. Ask students to write a short story set in the present that develops the same theme as "User Friendly" but with updated technology.

Grade-Level Skills

■ **Reading Skills**
Analyze the cause-and-effect text structure.

Summary ⟷ *at grade level*

This article uses a model to explain how computer viruses operate. In the model, a flawed answer key is thrown away by a teacher but is rescued by the custodian. A sticky note reading "Copy two times and put copies in other teachers' boxes" that was also in the trash has stuck to the paper, and when a substitute teacher finds the flawed answer key, she unknowingly spreads it throughout the school. Anyone who receives the answer key continues to innocently make two copies and put them in the other teachers' boxes, so that by the end of the day the answer keys are everywhere and the school's organization has broken down. The article concludes by describing the damage computer viruses can cause and expressing hope about the development of antivirus programs.

PRETEACHING

Selection Starter

Motivate. Ask students if any of them have ever encountered a computer virus. If so, what were the effects of the virus? Tell them that in this article, they will find out more about such viruses.

Assign the Reading

You might want to assign advanced learners to read this article silently in class while you work with a small group of learners having difficulty.

Informational Text

LINK TO "USER FRIENDLY"

Understanding Text Structure: Cause and Effect

Reading Focus
Cause-and-Effect Pattern

In "User Friendly," Kevin has trouble with his computer because of a faulty experimental program his father installed. A more common cause of computer malfunction is a computer virus. The informational article you are about to read explains how a computer virus works.

The structure of this article is called a **cause-and-effect chain.** This pattern is built around a series of causes and effects. Each event **causes** another event to happen. The event it causes is called an **effect.** In this article a little mistake starts a chain reaction. Soon a chain of causes and effects has turned a minor mishap into a big mess.

Writers of cause-and-effect articles often use **transitions** to show how one idea is connected to another. These transition terms help the reader follow the cause-and-effect pattern.

Cause-and-Effect Terms	
after	so
as a result	then
because	therefore
consequently	since

■ Read "It Just Keeps Going and Going . . ." once all the way through. Then, read it a second time, and keep track of the cause-and-effect chain by filling out an organizer like the one on page 271. The annotations at the beginning of the article will get you started. Then you can take over. Start each cause statement with the word *because*, just as you see in the model. The more causes and effects you find, the longer your chain will be.

INTERNET
Interactive
Reading Model
Keyword: LE5 7-3

SKILLS FOCUS

Reading Skills
Understand
cause-and-effect
text structure.

PEANUTS reprinted by permission of United Feature Syndicate, Inc.

284   Collection 3 / Living in the Heart

IT JUST KEEPS GOING AND GOING . . .

IT IS A HUMAN-MADE MONSTER. NO ONE CAN ESCAPE the reach of its tentacles, which can extend not just across a room but also around the entire planet. It gets worse. This monster, known by names such as the Brain, Crusher, Grog, and the Creeper, can quickly reproduce and shut down entire systems. This is no science fiction or fantasy creature. It's a computer virus.

The effects of computer viruses range from pesky system crashes to life-threatening situations, but experts disagree on how serious they really are. In fact, information and opinions on viruses are spreading as fast as the viruses themselves. *Encarta Encyclopedia* defines a computer virus as a "self-replicating computer program that interferes with a computer's hardware or operating system (the basic software that runs the computer)." That doesn't sound too bad, but think about the term *self-replicating*. That means that it keeps making copies of itself over and over again.

Here's an explanation of how a computer virus works, based on a model by the computer scientist Eugene Kaspersky.

A teacher is working at his desk at the end of the day. He finds mistakes in the midterm answer key, so he tosses it into the trash. Since the trash can is overflowing, the answer key falls onto the floor.

Then the teacher feels a headache coming on and goes home. The custodian comes to empty the trash, sees the answer key on the floor, and picks it up.

He puts it back on the teacher's desk. But now, attached to the answer key is a sticky note that says, "Copy two times, and put copies in other teachers' boxes."

A. CAUSE:
Because the answer key is wrong,

B. EFFECT:
the teacher tosses it into a trash can, which happens to be full.

C. CAUSE:
Because the trash can is full,

D. EFFECT:
the answer key falls onto the floor.

E. CAUSE:
Because the custodian finds the answer key on the floor,

F. EFFECT:
he puts it on the teacher's desk.

DIRECT TEACHING

Ⓐ Reading Informational Text

❓ Analyze cause and effect. Point out that in this cause-and-effect statement, the cause is stated after the phrase "the effects of." What is the cause? [computer viruses] What are the effects? [They range from system crashes to life-threatening situations.]

Ⓑ Reading Informational Text

Analyze cause and effect. Help students see the unstated cause in this passage that creates a crucial effect. Have them restate the following information as a cause-and-effect statement: Earlier the teacher had thrown away an unrelated self-stick note. The self-stick note got attached to the discarded answer key. [Possible cause-and-effect statement: The unrelated self-stick note got attached to the discarded answer key because earlier the teacher had thrown the note in the trash.]

A **Reading Informational Text**

❓ **Analyze cause and effect.**
Remind students that in a cause-and-effect chain, one cause has an effect which causes another effect, and so on. What causes a substitute teacher to come to school? [The regular teacher is sick and stays home.] What effect does the substitute teacher create? [She copies the answer key.]

B **Reading Informational Text**

❓ **Analyze cause and effect.**
What effect do antivirus programs have? [Antivirus programs make it easier to detect a virus early on.]

A The next day the teacher stays home because he has the flu. As a result, a substitute is called to the school. The first thing the substitute sees is the answer key with the note stuck to it. So she copies it twice for each teacher and puts the copies into the teachers' boxes. She leaves the sticky note on the answer key so they will see that the absent teacher wanted them to get the copies.

G. CAUSE: Because the custodian has put the answer key on the desk,

H. EFFECT: [You fill in the effect.]

When the other teachers find 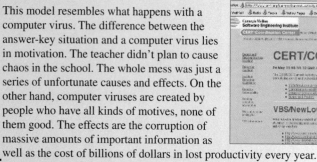 the two copies of the answer key with the instructions to copy them twice and distribute them, they give them to the office clerk. She then makes more copies of the answer key and puts them into the boxes of the "other teachers." By the end of the day, the school is out of paper, and the teachers' boxes are stuffed with useless answer keys.

This model resembles what happens with a computer virus. The difference between the answer-key situation and a computer virus lies in motivation. The teacher didn't plan to cause chaos in the school. The whole mess was just a series of unfortunate causes and effects. On the other hand, computer viruses are created by people who have all kinds of motives, none of them good. The effects are the corruption of massive amounts of important information as well as the cost of billions of dollars in lost productivity every year.

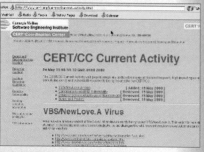

B Developers of antivirus programs are gaining on the virus villains, making it easier to detect a virus before it spreads and causes a path of destruction. Nonetheless, watch what you put in your computer . . . and in your trash.

—Joan Burditt

DIFFERENTIATING INSTRUCTION

Learners Having Difficulty
Cause-and-effect chain. Work with students to complete the cause-and-effect chain that begins in the margin of the student text on p. 285. Make sure that they notice that each cause, beginning with cause C, stems from the effect that comes right before it in the chain.

Analyzing Cause-and-Effect Text Structure

IT JUST KEEPS GOING AND GOING . . .

Test Practice

1. Which of the following sentences contains a **cause** and an **effect**?
   - A The computer she wanted was the most expensive one.
   - B The salesperson agreed to throw in a monitor for free.
   - C Since the monitor was free, she bought the computer.
   - D I can't imagine life without computers.

2. According to the article, which of the following statements is a major **effect** of computer viruses?
   - F Computers are ruined.
   - G Billions of dollars and a lot of information are lost.
   - H Some viruses ruin networks.
   - J A computer will do everything it is told to do.

3. This article is mainly about —
   - A problems with computers
   - B how to kill a virus
   - C the history of computers
   - D how computer viruses work

4. The causal chain below shows some of the important **causes and effects** in the story about the answer key.

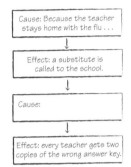

Which of these statements belongs in the blank *Cause* box?
   - F The substitute is unsure about what to do.
   - G The substitute follows the instructions on the sticky note.
   - H The substitute tells all the teachers the answer key is wrong.
   - J The substitute helps the office clerk with all the extra copying.

Constructed Response

1. What does *self-replicating* mean?
2. Which two main events cause the answer-key confusion to spin out of control?
3. Make a list of all the cause-and-effect words in this article.
4. According to the article, what are the effects of computer viruses?
5. Imagine you submitted this article to an editor of a newspaper. The editor tells you to get a new title. What would you call it?

SKILLS FOCUS

Reading Skills
Analyze cause-and-effect text structure.

Constructed Response

1. The word means "keeps making copies of itself."
2. The substitute teacher copied the answer key with mistakes and gave two copies to each teacher. She left on the self-stick note when she copied it.
3. effects, so, since, then, because, as a result, so, then
4. The effects of computer viruses are the corruption of massive amounts of important data and the loss of millions of dollars in productivity.
5. Possible answers: "What Makes a Computer Sick?" or "Call the Disk Doctor."

Monitor students' progress.
Have students meet in small groups to compare their Think Sheets.

INDEPENDENT PRACTICE

Analyzing Cause-and-Effect Text Structure

Test Practice

Answers and Model Rationales

1. **C** The word *since* signals a cause-and-effect statement. Each of the other answers contains only one element.

2. **G** The most significant effects of computer viruses are directly stated at the end of the essay. The other answers are either inaccurate or irrelevant.

3. **D** Most of the article is a model showing how computer viruses work. Students can eliminate A, because the article is only about one problem; B, because the article doesn't tell how to stop a virus; and C, because there is nothing about the history of computers in the article.

4. **G** Students should realize that F, H, and J contain information not stated in the article.

Test-Taking Tips

For instruction on how to answer multiple-choice items, refer students to **Test Smarts,** p. 920.

Vocabulary Development

1. c
2. b
3. a

Possible Analogies

- The first day of school is like your first roller coaster ride. You are nervous and excited at the same time.

- Re-reading a favorite book is like visiting with an old friend. There aren't any surprises, but it's still a lot of fun.

ASSESSING

Assessment

- *Holt Assessment: Literature, Reading, and Vocabulary*

Putting Analogies to Work

One way to explain something is to use an **analogy** (ə·nal′ə·jē). Writers use analogies to explain an idea by comparing it point by point to something familiar. In the article you just read, a computer virus is compared to a school situation that goes out of control. Here are two other examples of analogies:

- A computer virus is like a virus in the human body. Both self-replicate, and both damage the system they infect.

- Searching for something on the Internet without a search engine is like trying to find a CD in a store where the CDs are not arranged by music category, artist, or group. It is practically impossible to find what you are looking for.

PRACTICE

Form an analogy by matching the phrases in column A with the phrases and sentences in column B. Then, think of two of your own analogies. Remember that an analogy uses more than one point of comparison.

Column A	Column B
1. Studying for a big test is like	**a.** standing on the edge of a cliff. You feel as if you might fall, but you manage to keep your balance and enjoy the experience.
2. Giving a speech in front of the whole school is like	**b.** going to the dentist to have a cavity filled. You're so nervous you would rather not do it; but when it's over, you're glad you did.
3. Learning to ride a bike is like	**c.** shooting baskets before an important game. You're worried about how you'll perform, but you know you'll be glad you took the time to prepare.

SKILLS
FOCUS

Vocabulary Skills
Understand analogies.

288   Collection 3 / Living in the Heart

Before You Read   The Myth

Echo and Narcissus

Make the Connection
Conduct a Survey ✏️

Take a quick survey to find out how your classmates rate the following statements on a scale of 1 to 5, with 1 meaning they do not agree at all and 5 meaning they agree completely.

1. People judge others by their looks alone.

2. Vain, self-centered people are often not nice to others.

In your notebook, briefly explain your rating on one of the statements.

Literary Focus
Recurring Themes

People all over the world have basically the same dreams, fears, and need to understand who they are and how they should live their lives. It is not surprising, therefore, that the same **themes** come up again and again in the stories people tell. As you think about the selections in this collection, look for the themes that they share.

Reading Skills 🏊
Using Context Clues

What do you do when you come across an unfamiliar word? Rather than skipping over it or running straight to a dictionary, try using **context clues**—the surrounding words and sentences—to figure out what the word might mean. As you examine the surrounding text, ask yourself the following questions:

- Does the surrounding text give clues to the word's meaning?

- Is there a familiar word or word part within the unfamiliar word?

- How is the word used in the sentence?

- Does the meaning I've guessed make sense in the sentence?

As you read "Echo and Narcissus," use these strategies to try to figure out the meanings of words you don't know.

Vocabulary Development

Here are some words you'll want to know before you read this story. See if you can spot context clues in the sample sentences.

detain (dē·tān′) v.: hold back; delay. *Echo was asked to detain Hera so Hera's husband, Zeus, could wander about.*

vainly (vān′lē) adv.: uselessly; without result. *Echo tried vainly to attract the young man's attention.*

unrequited (un′ri·kwīt′id) v. used as adj.: not returned in kind. *Unfortunately, Echo's love was unrequited, for Narcissus loved only himself.*

parched (pärcht) v. used as adj.: very hot and dry. *Narcissus's throat was parched, so he eagerly knelt to drink the cool water.*

intently (in·tent′lē) adv.: with great concentration. *Narcissus gazed intently at his reflection in the pool.*

go.hrw.com

INTERNET
Vocabulary Practice
Keyword: LE5 7-3

SKILLS FOCUS

Literary Skills
Understand recurring themes.

Reading Skills
Use context clues.

Echo and Narcissus   **289**

Grade-Level Skills
■ **Literary Skills**
Analyze recurring themes.
■ **Reading Skills**
Use context clues.

Review Skills
■ **Literary Skills**
Identify themes as conveyed through characters, actions, and images.

Upcoming Skills
■ **Literary Skills**
Analyze recurring themes across traditional and contemporary works.

Summary ⬌ *at grade level*

To help Zeus, the king of the Greek gods, cavort with mountain nymphs, the nymph Echo detains Zeus's wife, Hera, in conversation. When Hera realizes what Echo is up to, she casts a spell on her; Echo can speak only when spoken to and repeat only the words she hears. Soon after, Echo falls in love with Narcissus, a handsome youth, and secretly follows him. One day, alone and lost, Narcissus calls for help, and Echo repeats his calls. She embraces Narcissus, but because he loves only himself, he rudely rejects her. Heartbroken, Echo dies. Aphrodite, the goddess of love, punishes Narcissus, causing him to fall in love with his own reflection in a pool of water. Because his reflection cannot return his love, Narcissus, like Echo, dies of unrequited love. On the spot where Narcissus died, a new flower—the narcissus—blooms beside the pool.

RESOURCES: READING

Planning
■ *One-Stop Planner* CD-ROM with ExamView Test Generator

Differentiating Instruction
■ *The Holt Reader*
■ *Holt Adapted Reader*
■ *Holt Reading Solutions*
■ *Supporting Instruction in Spanish*
■ *Audio CD Library, Selections and Summaries in Spanish*

Vocabulary
■ *Vocabulary Development*

Grammar and Language
■ *Language Handbook Worksheets*
■ *Daily Language Activities*

Assessment
■ *Holt Assessment: Literature, Reading, and Vocabulary*
■ *One-Stop Planner* CD-ROM with ExamView Test Generator

■ *Holt Online Assessment*

Internet
■ go.hrw.com (Keyword: LE5 7-3)
■ *Elements of Literature Online*

Media
■ *Audio CD Library*
■ *Audio CD Library, Selections and Summaries in Spanish*
■ *Fine Art Transparencies*

Selection Starter

Build background. Invite students to share their general knowledge of Greek mythology and name some of the gods and goddesses. Students should realize that Zeus is the most powerful god. Point out that although Aphrodite is the goddess of love, Hera is the goddess of marriage.

Preview Vocabulary

Have students use context clues to fill in the missing Vocabulary words in the sentences below.

1. The worried owner searched _____ for his missing dog. [vainly]

2. The owner did not allow anyone to _____ him from his search. [detain]

3. We gave the _____, hungry dog water and food. [parched]

4. My interest in the dog was _____; he ignored me. [unrequited]

5. When the owner walked in, the dog stared _____ and then furiously wagged his tail. [intently]

DIRECT TEACHING

A Reading Skills

❓ **Use context clues.** How do context clues help you figure out the meaning of the word *nymphs*? [The phrase *nymphs or fairies* shows that these words are synonyms.]

B Literary Focus

❓ **Recurring themes.** How do some other characters in this collection express the idea that nothing in the world matters but love? [In "The Highwayman," Bess gives up her life for love, and her lover dies trying to avenge her death. In "User Friendly," the computer has no qualms about damaging others to protect its love.]

Greek myth, retold by Roger Lancelyn Green

A Up on the wild, lonely mountains of Greece lived the Oreades,[1] the nymphs or fairies of the hills, and among them one of the most beautiful was called Echo. She was one of the most talkative, too, and once she talked too much and angered Hera, wife of Zeus, king of the gods.

When Zeus grew tired of the golden halls of Mount Olympus, the home of the immortal gods, he would come down to earth and wander with the nymphs on the mountains. Hera, however, was jealous and often came to see what he was doing. It seemed strange at first that she always met Echo, and that Echo kept her listening for hours on end to her stories and her gossip.

But at last Hera realized that Echo was doing this on purpose to detain her while Zeus went quietly back to Olympus as if he had never really been away.

"So nothing can stop you talking?" exclaimed Hera. "Well, Echo, I do not intend to spoil your pleasure. But from this day on, you shall be able only to repeat what other people say—and never speak unless someone else speaks first."

Hera returned to Olympus, well pleased with the punishment she had made for

Echo, leaving the poor nymph to weep sadly among the rocks on the mountainside and speak only the words which her sisters and their friends shouted happily to one another.

She grew used to her strange fate after a while, but then a new misfortune befell her.

There was a beautiful youth called Narcissus,[2] who was the son of a nymph and the god of a nearby river. He grew up in the plain of Thebes[3] until he was sixteen years old and then began to hunt on the mountains toward the north where Echo and her sister Oreades lived.

As he wandered through the woods and valleys, many a nymph looked upon him and loved him. But Narcissus laughed at them scornfully, for he loved only himself.

B Farther up the mountains Echo saw him. And at once her lonely heart was filled with love for the beautiful youth, so that nothing else in the world mattered but to win him.

Now she wished indeed that she could speak to him words of love. But the curse which Hera had placed upon her tied her

---

1. **Oreades** (ō′rē·ad′ēz).

2. **Narcissus** (när·sis′əs).
3. **Thebes** (thēbz).

Vocabulary
detain (dē·tān′) *v.:* hold back; delay.

DIFFERENTIATING INSTRUCTION

Learners Having Difficulty
Modeling. If students need help reading "Echo and Narcissus," model the reading skill of using context clues. Point out the word *talkative* in the first paragraph. Explain that if the word is unfamiliar, readers can figure out its meaning from both the word part *talk* in *talkative* and the phrase "talked too much" in the story. A clue in the second paragraph—"Echo kept

her listening for hours"—confirms that *talkative* means "talking a great deal."

English-Language Learners
Some students may be unfamiliar with Greek mythology. Help them to compare this origin myth with those from their own culture. Also, explain the meanings of idioms in the story, such as "her heart heavy with unspoken love," and "eaten up with self-love."

Narcissus by Caravaggio (1573–1610).

Galleria Nazionale d'Arte Antica, Rome. Scala/Art Resource, New York.

VIEWING THE ART

Michelangelo Merisi, known as **Caravaggio** (1573–1610), broke with the idealism typical of earlier Italian Renaissance art to create dramatic, intensely realistic paintings. The religious and mythological figures that Caravaggio painted looked like the laborers and peasants that the artist used as models, down to their dirty fingernails. Some patrons were shocked and repelled by such extreme realism, and the artist several times was asked to repaint a commissioned work in order to satisfy his customers. His dramatic use of contrasting light and darkness, or *chiaroscuro,* adds greatly to the emotional impact of his paintings; the characters emerge suddenly out of the darkness, as if lit by a spotlight on a stage or by a ray of divine light from heaven. Caravaggio's realism and his dramatic use of chiaroscuro influenced many of his contemporaries, as well as later artists.

Activity. Ask students to discuss the use of light and darkness in this painting. Start them off with such questions as the following: To which areas does the light focus the viewer's attention? What effect does the dark background have on the overall impact of the painting? Then, invite students to compare the painting with the written version of the myth.

Special Education Students

For lessons designed for special education students, see *Holt Reading Solutions.*

Advanced Learners

Acceleration. Use the following activity with advanced learners to help them compare themes across works of different eras.

Activity. Ask students to identify and list other works they have read that deal with true love, lovers parted, or tragic or unrequited love. Then, have students discuss whether human nature has changed over the centuries.

• Are any of the contemporary works similar to earlier works in their characters, plots, or themes? What similarities are there?

• Do the works suggest that people from all times and places have qualities and emotions in common? If so, what are they?

Ⓐ Vocabulary Development

❓ Metaphor. The phrase *her heart leaping with joy* is not meant literally but as a metaphor, a comparison of two unlike things. What is the heart compared to? [a person jumping up and down with joy] Why is this appropriate? [A person's heart may beat faster with feelings of joy.]

Ⓑ Literary Focus

❓ Character. What character trait does Echo reveal by her actions? [Possible responses: a loving, passionate nature; an ability to take risks for a chance at love.]

Ⓒ Literary Focus

❓ Recurring themes. What happens after the true lovers in this collection die? [They linger as ghosts or continue to love and be loved.] State this theme in your own words. [Possible response: Love is stronger than death.]

---

tongue, and she could only follow wherever he went, hiding behind trees and rocks, and feasting her eyes vainly upon him.

One day Narcissus wandered farther up the mountain than usual, and all his friends, the other Theban youths, were left far behind. Only Echo followed him, still hiding among the rocks, her heart heavy with unspoken love.

Presently Narcissus realized that he was lost, and hoping to be heard by his companions, or perhaps by some mountain shepherd, he called out loudly:

"Is there anybody here?"

"Here!" cried Echo.

Narcissus stood still in amazement, looking all around in vain. Then he shouted, even more loudly:

"Whoever you are, come to me!"

"Come to me!" cried Echo eagerly.

Still no one was visible, so Narcissus called again:

"Why are you avoiding me?"

Echo repeated his words, but with a sob in her breath, and Narcissus called once more:

"Come here, I say, and let us meet!"

Ⓐ "Let us meet!" cried Echo, her heart leaping with joy as she spoke the happiest words that had left her lips since the curse of Hera had fallen on her. And to make good **Ⓑ** her words, she came running out from behind the rocks and tried to clasp her arms about him.

But Narcissus flung the beautiful nymph away from him in scorn.

"Away with these embraces!" he cried angrily, his voice full of cruel contempt. "I would die before I would have you touch me!"

"I would have you touch me!" repeated poor Echo.

"Never will I let you kiss me!"

"Kiss me! Kiss me!" murmured Echo, sinking down among the rocks, as Narcissus cast her violently from him and sped down the hillside.

"One touch of those lips would kill me!" he called back furiously over his shoulder.

"Kill me!" begged Echo.

Ⓒ And Aphrodite,[4] the goddess of love, heard her and was kind to her, for she had been a true lover. Quietly and painlessly, Echo pined away and died. But her voice lived on, lingering among the rocks and answering faintly whenever Narcissus or another called.

"He shall not go unpunished for this cruelty," said Aphrodite. "By scorning poor Echo like this, he scorns love itself. And scorning love, he insults me. He is altogether eaten up with self-love . . . Well, he shall love himself and no one else, and yet shall die of unrequited love!"

It was not long before Aphrodite made good her threat, and in a very strange way. One day, tired after hunting, Narcissus came to a still, clear pool of water away up the mountainside, not far from where he had scorned Echo and left her to die of a broken heart.

With a cry of satisfaction, for the day was hot and cloudless, and he was parched with thirst, Narcissus flung himself down beside the pool and leaned forward to dip his face in the cool water.

---

4. **Aphrodite** (af′rə·dīt′ē).

Vocabulary

vainly (vān′lē) *adv.:* uselessly; without result.

unrequited (un′ri·kwīt′id) *v.* used as *adj.:* not returned in kind.

parched (pärcht) *v.* used as *adj.:* very hot and dry.

What was his surprise to see a beautiful face looking up at him through the still waters of the pool. The moment he saw, he loved—and love was a madness upon him so that he could think of nothing else.

"Beautiful water nymph!" he cried. "I love you! Be mine!"

Desperately he plunged his arms into the water—but the face vanished and he touched only the pebbles at the bottom of the pool. Drawing out his arms, he gazed intently down and, as the water grew still again, saw once more the face of his beloved.

Poor Narcissus did not know that he was seeing his own reflection, for Aphrodite hid this knowledge from him—and perhaps this was the first time that a pool of water had reflected the face of anyone gazing into it.

Narcissus seemed enchanted by what he saw. He could not leave the pool, but lay by its side day after day looking at the only face in the world which he loved—and could not win—and pining just as Echo had pined.

Slowly Narcissus faded away, and at last his heart broke.

"Woe is me for I loved in vain!" he cried.

"I loved in vain!" sobbed the voice of Echo among the rocks.

"Farewell, my love, farewell," were his last words, and Echo's voice broke and its whisper shivered into silence: "My love . . . farewell!"

So Narcissus died, and the earth covered his bones. But with the spring, a plant pushed its green leaves through the earth where he lay. As the sun shone on it, a bud opened and a new flower blossomed for the first time—a white circle of petals round a yellow center. The flowers grew and spread, waving in the gentle breeze which whispered among them like Echo herself come to kiss the blossoms of the first Narcissus flowers.

D Vocabulary
intently (in·tent′lē) *adv.:* with great concentration.

Meet the Writer

Roger Lancelyn Green

Green, a Greek at Heart
Roger Lancelyn Green (1918–1987) was born in England and educated at Oxford University. After a short stint as an actor in London, he devoted his life to children's literature and the study of ancient times. His books for children include stories, poems, and his own retellings of fairy tales, legends, and myths from many lands. Green's special love was Greece, which he visited more than twenty times.

Echo and Narcissus **293**

FAMILY/COMMUNITY ACTIVITY

Echo and *narcissism* are English words with roots in ancient Greek culture. Encourage students to use community resources to collect other words derived from both Greek and Roman myths. Suggest that students ask their families, friends, and neighbors for words they know from myths, such as *atlas, chronic,* and *mercury,* the names of the planets, or expressions such as "opening a Pandora's box." Students can also do research on the Internet and investigate library resources. A librarian can help them find the names of characters in myths, and students can use these names as clues to identify English words. Students can then combine their word lists to create a dictionary of words and expressions from classical mythology.

D Literary Focus

? Character. How would you describe Narcissus's major character trait? [self-love or self-absorption] In what way is he like and unlike other lovers in this collection? [Possible response: Narcissus is like the others in his total devotion to his love, but he is unlike them because he himself, rather than another character, is the object of his love.]

GUIDED PRACTICE

Monitor students' progress. Guide students in answering these questions. If they give a wrong answer, challenge them to find support for it in the text.

True-False

1. Hera rewards Echo for helping her to find out what Zeus is doing. [F]
2. Echo dies, but her voice lingers in the mountains where she lived. [T]
3. Aphrodite feels that Narcissus insults her personally when he rejects Echo's love. [T]
4. Aphrodite causes Narcissus to fall in love with a goddess. [F]
5. A flower blooms on the spot where Narcissus dies. [T]

Meet the Writer

Roger Lancelyn Green published several volumes of poetry, as well as biographies of such writers as C. S. Lewis and Lewis Carroll. He retold the legends of King Arthur and Norse myths as well as those of Greece.

After You Read

First Thoughts

1. Ask students to cite details that changed their opinions or to explain why the myth did not change their opinions.

Thinking Critically

2. Echo talks too much. The punishment is appropriate because it affects her ability to speak.
3. Possible answer: He is cruel because he is vain and self-absorbed.
4. Students should back their opinions on which statement best fits the myth with details from the text. The first theme is revealed in Narcissus's self-involvement; the second, in both Echo's and Narcissus's experiences of love; the third, in their dying because of unrequited love.
5. Some students may say that both are victims of vengeful gods. Others may say that the characters' flaws brought on their fates.

Extending Interpretations

6. Possible answers: The first theme is expressed in "User Friendly," in Kevin's unrequited love for the self-absorbed Ginny. All selections express the power and the devastating effects of love, the second and third themes. In every selection at least one lover dies.
7. Students may find the gods at least as unfair as human beings. Some may see Aphrodite's punishment of Narcissus as just and fair. Few will consider Hera's punishment of Echo fair.

After You Read — Response and Analysis

First Thoughts

1. Did reading this myth change your opinions about beauty and vanity at all? If so, how?

Thinking Critically

2. What is the major flaw in Echo's **character**? Why is Hera's curse an appropriate punishment for this flaw?
3. Why do you think Narcissus is so cruel to Echo? Does the class survey help explain why Narcissus is so mean? If so, how?
4. Which of the following statements of theme best fits the myth? Explain how this **theme** is revealed in the myth.

   • We can't love other people when we are too involved with ourselves.

   • Love is a powerful feeling whether we seek it or not.

   • Romantic love and self-love can have devastating effects.

5. Are Echo and Narcissus victims of the gods, or are they responsible for their own tragedies? Explain your opinion.

INTERNET
Projects and Activities
Keyword: LE5 7-3

Extending Interpretations

6. Which other selection in this collection is built on the theme you selected in question 4? Explain how the selections are similar and how they are different.
7. Are the gods fair? What do you think of their actions in this myth?

SKILLS FOCUS

Literary Skills
Analyze recurring themes.

Writing Skills
Write an origin myth.

WRITING

Writing an Origin Myth

Here's your chance to write an origin myth of your own. Think of some everyday phenomenon, and write a brief story that explains how it might have come about. Try to come up with fresh, surprising **causes** for familiar **effects**. Use your imagination!

Reading Check

a. What does Echo do that annoys Hera?
b. How does Hera punish Echo?
c. Why does Aphrodite punish Narcissus?
d. What curse does Aphrodite place on Narcissus?
e. An **origin myth** is an imaginative story that explains how something came into being. According to this myth, what is the origin of the echo we hear when we call into a cave or from a mountaintop? What is the origin of the fragrant flower called the narcissus?

Reading Check

a. Echo chatters away, detaining Hera so that Zeus can sneak back to Mount Olympus.
b. Hera robs Echo of the ability to speak, except to repeat what others say.
c. Narcissus has insulted Aphrodite by rejecting Echo's love and scorning love itself.
d. She causes him to fall hopelessly in love with himself.
e. Echo's story explains the origin of the echo. Even after her death, Echo's voice lingers, faintly repeating our words. The narcissus first bloomed on the grave of Narcissus, a youth who loved only himself.

Building Context Clues

PRACTICE

Using the words in the Word Bank, write a short version of the Echo and Narcissus story that a six-year-old would understand. Build lots of **context clues** into the sentences.

> **Word Bank**
> detain
> vainly
> unrequited
> parched
> intently

Grammar Link

Words Often Confused: *Its, It's* and *Your, You're*

Do you hear an echo? The words in each pair may sound alike, but they have very different purposes.

- The **personal possessive pronouns** *its* and *your* show that something belongs to someone or something. Possessive pronouns should not have apostrophes.

  > "He could not leave the pool, but lay by its side...."
  > [The side "belongs" to the pool.]

  > "'Well, Echo, I do not intend to spoil your pleasure.'"
  > [The pleasure "belongs" to Echo.]

- The **contractions** *it's* and *you're* are both shortened combinations of a personal pronoun and the verb *is, has,* or *are.* A contraction should have an apostrophe to show where letters have been left out.

  > It's [It is] his own reflection he sees.
  > You're [You are] going to repeat words.

Here's a tip to use if you are unsure of the correct word: Substitute the two words that might be used in place of the one you are unsure of, such as *it is* or *you are.* If the sentence still makes sense, use the contraction rather than the possessive pronoun.

PRACTICE

Write each sentence below, choosing the correct form of the underlined words.

1. "Your/You're not the one I love," said Narcissus.
2. A plant pushed its/it's green leaves through the earth.
3. Its/It's Echo's constant chatter that annoys Hera.
4. "Narcissus, you won't realize your/you're in love with your/you're own reflection," thought Aphrodite.

For more help, see Apostrophes, 15a–c, in the Language Handbook.

SKILLS FOCUS

Vocabulary Skills
Use context clues.

Grammar Skills
Use *its* and *it's* and *your* and *you're* correctly.

Echo and Narcissus **295**

PRACTICE

Students' stories will vary. Here is a possible first paragraph with context clues for one word in the Word Bank:

Hera and Zeus are the queen and king of the gods. Hera is looking for Zeus. She gets angry at Echo because Echo tries to *detain* Hera by talking a lot. "Don't stop me! You should not hold me back!" Hera shouts angrily. Hera punishes Echo by robbing her of the power to speak when she wants to. Now Echo can only repeat what other people say.

Grammar Link

PRACTICE

1. You're
2. its
3. It's
4. you're; your

ASSESSING

Assessment

- *Holt Assessment: Literature, Reading, and Vocabulary*

RETEACHING

For a lesson reteaching themes across genres, see **Reteaching,** p. 917F.

DIFFERENTIATING INSTRUCTION

Learners Having Difficulty
Discuss question 3 as a whole class. Have students compare their survey results and work together to apply their results to Narcissus. *Monitoring tip:* If students have trouble with question 6, have them work in groups to review the other collection selections. **Writing.** Have students brainstorm effects and causes in class, then write their stories at home.

HOMEWORK

Advanced Learners
Enrichment. Have students develop their answers to question 6 as comparison-and-contrast essays. They should discuss the two selections' similarities and differences in detail. You might encourage them to create a literary magazine for publishing these essays and others.

HOMEWORK

Comparing Literature

OVERVIEW

Purpose. In this Comparing Literature feature, students will be asked to compare literary elements in two stories. By examining the similarities and differences between the stories' characters, settings, and themes, students will learn that stories that appear similar on the surface may contain very different messages about life.

Use. Direct students' attention to the box labeled "Questions to Ask About the Elements." Tell them to keep these questions in mind as they read "Charles" and "Miss Awful." Students will fill in charts comparing the characters and settings of the stories, identify each story's theme, and write an essay comparing the literary elements in the stories. Students will also have the opportunity to write a description of a perfect classroom and to write and perform a dramatization with a group of classmates.

Literary Focus
Characters, Settings, Themes

Stories can be alike in some ways yet very different in other ways. Two stories might have similar characters, but the discoveries made by those characters may be quite different. One character may change during the events of the story, while another character may remain the same. The stories might have similar settings, but what happens in those settings could be very different. The stories might even have similar characters *and* settings but reveal completely different themes.

Reading Skills and Strategies
Comparing and Contrasting

Both "Charles" and "Miss Awful" are about boys who are in conflict with their teachers. As you read the two stories, however, you'll notice many differences. Though their subject matter is similar, their themes are not at all alike. Questions in the margins of the stories will help you think about how the stories are alike and—perhaps even more important— how they are different. After you have read both stories, you will be asked to compare and contrast them in an essay.

SKILLS FOCUS

Literary Skills
Analyze characters, settings, and themes.

Reading Skills
Compare and contrast stories.

Questions to Ask About the Elements

Characters
• Are the characters **dynamic**—do they change in the story and discover something of importance about themselves and their world?

• Are the characters **static**—do they remain the same?

Setting
• Where and when does the story take place?

Theme
• What does the story reveal about human nature? To uncover the theme, look for

—discoveries made by the character

—reasons the character changes

—key statements

—important scenes

Before You Read

The story you are about to read is a modern-day **trickster tale**—a story about a character, usually someone small and weak, who plays tricks on someone large and powerful. The writer Julius Lester explains, "Teachers and parents know Trickster well, because there is one in every classroom and every large family. Trickster is the class clown, the child who seems to have a genius for walking a thin line between fun and trouble, the child who is always 'up to something.'" Decide whether you identify with the trickster Charles or with his parents or teacher. Who do you think is more powerful?

CHARLES

Shirley Jackson

The day Laurie started kindergarten, he renounced[1] corduroy overalls with bibs and began wearing bluejeans with a belt; I watched him go off the first morning with the older girl next door, seeing clearly that an era of my life was ended, my sweet-voiced nursery-school tot replaced by a long-trousered, swaggering character who forgot to stop at the corner and wave goodbye to me.

He came home the same way, the front door slamming open, his cap on the floor, and the voice suddenly become raucous shouting, "Isn't anybody *here*?"

At lunch he spoke insolently[2] to his father, spilled his baby sister's milk, and remarked that his teacher said that we were not to take the name of the Lord in vain. **❶**

"How *was* school today?" I asked, elaborately casual.

"All right," he said.

"Did you learn anything?" his father asked.

Laurie regarded his father coldly. "I didn't learn nothing," he said.

"Anything," I said. "Didn't learn anything."

"The teacher spanked a boy, though," Laurie said, addressing his

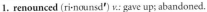

1. **renounced** (ri·nounsd´) *v.:* gave up; abandoned.
2. **insolently** (in´sə·lənt·lē) *adv.:* with bold disrespect.

COMPARE AND CONTRAST

❶ How does Laurie change when he starts kindergarten? **A**

Summary *at grade level*

As the narrator sends her son Laurie off to kindergarten, she fears that her sweet child has become a "swaggering character." Every day Laurie regales the family with stories about the misdeeds of his classmate Charles and the punishments he receives (which seem to embolden rather than subdue him). Laurie speculates that Charles may be thrown out of school. In the third and fourth weeks Charles reforms, but he breaks out again with "evil word" mischief. While Laurie's parents worry that Charles is having a bad influence on their son, they grow increasingly curious about him. At the PTA, Laurie's mother discovers from Laurie's teacher that there is no one named Charles in the class. The story raises many questions for students: why Laurie lies, why "Charles" acts out, and what role the narrator-mom plays in events and in readers' perception of them.

PRETEACHING

Selection Starter

Motivate. Have students read Julius Lester's description of a trickster, and ask students if they know anyone who matches the description. Have them briefly write details about the real-life trickster they know.

DIRECT TEACHING

Ⓐ Reading Skills
Compare and contrast. [Possible responses to question 1: Laurie begins dressing differently. He is disrespectful to his parents. He is loud and obnoxious.]

Comparing Literature

Infer. [Possible response to question 2: He enjoys Charles's bad behavior. You can tell because he grins "enormously" as he reports Charles's latest mischief.]

B Literary Focus

? **Motivation.** Why does Laurie's mother "quickly" ask a question? [Possible responses: She wants to divert attention from Laurie's rudeness to his father. She wants to keep peace in the family. She wants to discourage Laurie from being rude by ignoring his comment.]

C Reading Skills

? **Express an opinion.** Since the time when Jackson wrote this story, concern about child abuse has grown and disciplinary methods used in schools have changed. In your opinion, which of the punishments Charles receives during the first week of school are appropriate? Which are inappropriate? [Possible response: Depriving Charles of blackboard privileges is an acceptable punishment for throwing chalk, but I don't think the teacher should be allowed to spank Charles.]

---

bread and butter. "For being fresh," he added with his mouth full.

"What did he do?" I asked. "Who was it?"

Laurie thought. "It was Charles," he said. "He was fresh. The teacher spanked him and made him stand in a corner. He was awfully fresh."

"What did he do?" I asked again, but Laurie slid off his chair, took a cookie, and left, while his father was still saying, "See here, young man."

The next day Laurie remarked at lunch, as soon as he sat down, "Well, Charles was bad again today." He grinned enormously and said, "Today Charles hit the teacher." **2**

"Good heavens," I said, mindful of the Lord's name, "I suppose he got spanked again?"

"He sure did," Laurie said. "Look up," he said to his father.

"What?" his father said, looking up.

"Look down," Laurie said. "Look at my thumb. Gee, you're dumb." He began to laugh insanely.

"Why did Charles hit the teacher?" I asked quickly.

"Because she tried to make him color with red crayons," Laurie said. "Charles wanted to color with green crayons so he hit the teacher and she spanked him and said nobody play with Charles but everybody did."

The third day—it was Wednesday of the first week—Charles bounced a seesaw onto the head of a little girl and made her bleed and the teacher made him stay inside all during recess. Thursday Charles had to stand in a corner during story time because he kept pounding his feet on the floor. Friday Charles was deprived of blackboard privileges because he threw chalk.

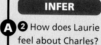

INFER

A 2 How does Laurie feel about Charles? How can you tell?

DIFFERENTIATING INSTRUCTION

Learners Having Difficulty
Modeling. Help students identify the theme of "Charles" by modeling the strategy of finding the theme. First, have them describe the plot and identify the topic of the story; then, have them note important words or phrases that suggest the theme. Get students started by saying "One of the significant phrases in the story is 'being a Charles.' It is important because it's the term Laurie's family's uses for bad behavior."

Have students look for other important words and phrases that point to the theme of the story.

English-Language Learners
Students from different cultures may have widely different expectations for proper behavior in school and for the proper attitude of students toward teachers. Before students read the story, discuss with them such early schooling topics as typical children's

On Saturday I remarked to my husband, "Do you think kindergarten is too unsettling for Laurie? All this toughness and bad grammar, and this Charles boy sounds like such a bad influence." **D**

"It'll be all right," my husband said reassuringly. "Bound to be people like Charles in the world. Might as well meet them now as later." ❸

On Monday Laurie came home late, full of news. "Charles," he shouted as he came up the hill; I was waiting anxiously on the front steps, "Charles," Laurie yelled all the way up the hill, "Charles was bad again."

"Come right in," I said, as soon as he came close enough. "Lunch is waiting."

"You know what Charles did?" he demanded, following me through the door. "Charles yelled so in school they sent a boy in from first grade to tell the teacher she had to make Charles keep quiet, and so Charles had to stay after school. And so all the children stayed to watch him."

"What did he do?" I asked.

"He just sat there," Laurie said, climbing into his chair at the table. "Hi Pop, y'old dust mop."

"Charles had to stay after school today," I told my husband. "Everyone stayed with him."

INTERPRET

❸ What is the main **conflict** so far?

E

Charles **299**

D Reading Skills

❓ **Infer.** Why is Laurie's mother worried about him? [Possible response: She is afraid that Charles will have a bad influence on Laurie.]

E Reading Skills

Interpret. [Possible response to question 3: The main conflict centers on whether Laurie's parents or Charles will be a bigger influence on Laurie's behavior.]

behavior, activities of the day, and skills taught, as they remember them from their own first experience of attending school.

Special Education Students
For lessons designed for special education students, see *Holt Reading Solutions.*

Advanced Learners
Enrichment. Ask students to list what they know about the behavior typical of five-year-olds attending kindergarten. As they read the story, ask them to list details in the story that are either consistent or inconsistent with their expectations. After students have read the story, have them comment on the author's portrayal of kindergarten activities, the behavior of Laurie/Charles, and the response of the teacher.

DIRECT TEACHING

A Learners Having Difficulty

Find details. Laurie lists some differences between himself and Charles. What are they? [Laurie says that Charles is bigger and doesn't wear rubbers or a jacket.]

B Reading Skills

Respond. [Possible responses to question 4: I dislike Charles because he is a troublemaker. Charles is spirited and fearless; I can't help admiring him.]

C Reading Skills

Speculate. What do you think will happen to Charles now? Will he be thrown out of school, or will he begin behaving differently. What might make his behavior improve? [Possible response: I think Charles's behavior would change if the teacher came up with a tougher punishment, such as suspension from school. Charles would get bored and would return reformed.]

D Literary Focus

Character. How has Charles become an almost legendary figure for the family? [They have made his name part of their family jargon. To "be a Charles" is to cause trouble.]

RESPOND

B ❹ How do you feel about Charles at this point in the story?

"What does this Charles look like?" my husband asked Laurie. "What's his other name?"

A "He's bigger than me," Laurie said. "And he doesn't have any rubbers and he doesn't even wear a jacket."

Monday night was the first Parent-Teachers meeting, and only the fact that the baby had a cold kept me from going; I wanted passionately to meet Charles's mother. On Tuesday Laurie remarked suddenly, "Our teacher had a friend come see her in school today."

"Charles's mother?" my husband and I asked simultaneously.

"Naaah," Laurie said scornfully. "It was a man who came and made us do exercises. Look." He climbed down from his chair and squatted down and touched his toes. "Like this," he said. He got solemnly back into his chair and said, picking up his fork, "Charles didn't even *do* exercises."

"That's fine," I said heartily. "Didn't Charles want to do exercises?"

"Naaah," Laurie said. "Charles was so fresh to the teacher's friend he wasn't *let* do exercises."

"Fresh again?" I said.

"He kicked the teacher's friend," Laurie said. "The teacher's friend told Charles to touch his toes like I just did and Charles kicked him." ❹

C "What are they going to do about Charles, do you suppose?" Laurie's father asked him.

Laurie shrugged elaborately. "Throw him out of school, I guess," he said.

Wednesday and Thursday were routine; Charles yelled during story hour and hit a boy in the stomach and made him cry. On Friday Charles stayed after school again and so did all the other children.

D With the third week of kindergarten Charles was an institution in our family; the baby was being a Charles when she cried all afternoon; Laurie did a Charles when he filled his wagon full of mud and pulled it through the kitchen; even my husband, when he caught his elbow in the telephone cord and pulled telephone, ash tray, and a bowl of flowers off the table, said, after the first minute, "Looks like Charles."

"He kicked the teacher's friend."

During the third and fourth weeks it looked like a reformation in Charles; Laurie reported grimly at lunch on Thursday of the third week, "Charles was so good today the teacher gave him an apple."

"What?" I said, and my husband added warily,[3] "You mean Charles?"

"Charles," Laurie said. "He gave the crayons around and he picked up the books afterward and the teacher said he was her helper."

"What happened?" I asked incredulously.

"He was her helper, that's all," Laurie said, and shrugged.

"Can this be true, about Charles?" I asked my husband that night. "Can something like this happen?"

"Wait and see," my husband said cynically. "When you've got a Charles to deal with, this may mean he's only plotting."

He seemed to be wrong. For over a week Charles was the teacher's helper; each day he handed things out and he picked things up; no one had to stay after school. **5**

"The PTA meeting's next week again," I told my husband one evening. "I'm going to find Charles's mother there."

"Ask her what happened to Charles," my husband said. "I'd like to know."

"I'd like to know myself," I said.

On Friday of that week things were back to normal. "You know what Charles did today?" Laurie demanded at the lunch table, in a voice slightly awed. "He told a little girl to say a word and she said it and the teacher washed her mouth out with soap and Charles laughed."

"What word?" his father asked unwisely, and Laurie said, "I'll have to whisper it to you, it's so bad." He got down off his chair and went around to his father. His father bent his head down and Laurie whispered joyfully. His father's eyes widened.

"Did Charles tell the little girl to say *that*?" he asked respectfully.

"She said it *twice*," Laurie said. "Charles told her to say it *twice*."

"What happened to Charles?" my husband asked.

"Nothing," Laurie said. "He was passing out the crayons."

Monday morning Charles abandoned the little girl and said the evil word himself three or four times, getting his mouth washed out

---

3. **warily** (wer′ə·lē) *adv.*: cautiously.

COMPARE AND CONTRAST **F**

5 How has Charles's behavior changed?

DIRECT TEACHING

E **Literary Focus**

? **Character.** From what you've heard about Charles, how do you think he feels about being called the teacher's helper? [Possible responses: He probably enjoys it because he is still being singled out for attention. He probably prefers being known as the class troublemaker.]

F **Reading Skills**

Compare and contrast. [Possible response to question 5: Charles is cooperating with the teacher and treating her and his classmates with more respect. He is no longer being disruptive.]

DIFFERENTIATING INSTRUCTION

Learners Having Difficulty
Ask students to imagine that they are kindergarten teachers confronted with a child like Charles. Have them work in groups of five to brainstorm ways to handle the child's behavior. Suggest that they use a graphic organizer like the one at the right to help them generate ideas.

Problem	Cause	Solution
[Won't sit down]	[Is bored]	[Play game of Simon Says]
[Uses bad language]	[Wants attention]	[Teach new words]

Ⓐ Literary Focus

❷ Motivation. Why do you think Laurie's mother is cautious about approaching the teacher? [Possible responses: She may feel a little embarrassed because of her curiosity about Charles. She doesn't know what the teacher thinks of Laurie.]

Ⓑ Reading Skills

Identify. [Possible response to question 6: The teacher says that Laurie had trouble adjusting at first but is now a good helper.]

with soap each time. He also threw chalk.

My husband came to the door with me that evening as I set out for the PTA meeting. "Invite her over for a cup of tea after the meeting," he said. "I want to get a look at her."

"If only she's there," I said prayerfully.

"She'll be there," my husband said. "I don't see how they could hold a PTA meeting without Charles's mother."

At the meeting I sat restlessly, scanning each comfortable matronly face, trying to determine which one hid the secret of Charles. None of them looked to me haggard[4] enough. No one stood up in the meeting and apologized for the way her son had been acting. No one mentioned Charles.

Ⓐ After the meeting I identified and sought out Laurie's kindergarten teacher. She had a plate with a cup of tea and a piece of chocolate cake; I had a plate with a cup of tea and a piece of marshmallow cake. We maneuvered up to one another cautiously and smiled.

"I've been so anxious to meet you," I said. "I'm Laurie's mother."

"We're all so interested in Laurie," she said.

"Well, he certainly likes kindergarten," I said. "He talks about it all the time."

"We had a little trouble adjusting, the first week or so," she said primly, "but now he's a fine little helper. With lapses, of course." ❻

"Laurie usually adjusts very quickly," I said. "I suppose this time it's Charles's influence."

"Charles?"

IDENTIFY

❻ According to the teacher, who has had trouble adjusting but is now usually a good helper?

---

4. haggard (hag′ərd) *adj.:* looking worn-out and exhausted.

DIFFERENTIATING INSTRUCTION

Advanced Learners

Enrichment. Laurie will probably have a lot of explaining to do when his mother gets home from the PTA meeting. How will he talk his way out of trouble?

Activity. Assign pairs of students to write a brief dialogue that takes place between Laurie and his mother after she returns from the PTA meeting. To get students started, divide the class in half. Assign half of the students to be Lauries and half to be

Moms. Then, pair the "Lauries" and "Moms" and have them create or improvise a dialogue, writing down the lines they like best to share with the class.

PAIRED

"Yes," I said, laughing, "you must have your hands full in that kindergarten, with Charles."

"Charles?" she said. "We don't have any Charles in the kindergarten." ❼

INFER

❼ What can you infer from the teacher's last remark? **C**

C Reading Skills

Infer. [Response to question 7: Charles is actually Laurie.]

Meet the Writer

The lighthearted tone of Jackson's fictionalized memoirs contrasts sharply with the ominous mood of her other works, including her story "The Lottery." That story aroused a storm of outrage when it first appeared in *The New Yorker* in 1948. Jackson's husband, the critic Stanley Edgar Hyman, writes that the public and critics alike took the story as neurotic fantasy, failing to see it as a sensitive, symbolic representation of a world mad enough to permit the atomic bomb and Nazi concentration camps.

For Independent Reading

Encourage students who choose to read selections from *Raising Demons* to comment on Jackson's use of humor to create engaging depictions of everyday family life.

Meet the Writer

Shirley Jackson

A Keen Sense of Humor

Shirley Jackson (1919–1965) was born in San Francisco, California. Her keen sense of humor is evident in "Charles" and other comically exaggerated accounts of life with her husband and four children. It is also evident in this mock questionnaire she wrote for fellow suffering mothers:

❝At breakfast I raise a considerable howl about the general sloppy condition of the back porch and the yard. Laurie, Joanne, Sally, and Barry promise that after school there will be a monumental cleaning-up and I will find the yard and porch immaculate. (1) Who has to stay after school to finish his chemistry notebook? (2) Who forgot that today was Girl Scouts? (3) Who calls from the library to say she will be home later? (4) Who stops off at David's house to see David's new steam engine and has to be sent for at five o'clock? (5) Who raises another howl the next morning at breakfast?❞

For Independent Reading

"Charles" comes from *Life Among the Savages*. The adventures of Laurie and the rest of the Jackson family continue in *Raising Demons*.

After You Read

First Thoughts

1. Have students who anticipated the plot twist identify the clues that alerted them.

Thinking Critically

2. Possible answers: Laurie himself is rude and combative when he comes home. He takes pleasure in reporting Charles's misbehavior. He gets home late on the days when Charles is kept after school.

3. Possible answer: Laurie invents Charles so that he can talk about what happens in school without getting into trouble at home.

4. Possible answers: Yes, Laurie's parents should have picked up on the clues. No, Laurie's parents knew they had raised their child to behave, and it was natural for them to trust him.

5. Some students will say that Laurie is a dynamic character, because he gradually changes in the course of the story. Others may feel that he is essentially the same at the end of the story.

6. Possible answer: Laurie has learned that behaving badly is a good way to attract attention.

Comparing Literature

7. Possible answers: *Setting*— Laurie's family's home. *Characters*—Laurie/Charles, Laurie's mother and father, Laurie's kindergarten teacher. *Theme of "Charles"*—Children can be trickier than adults realize.

After You Read "Charles"

First Thoughts

1. This story has a **surprise** ending. Did it surprise you? Why or why not?

Thinking Critically

2. What clues does the writer give to Charles's identity?

3. Why do you think Laurie invents Charles?

4. Do you think Laurie's parents should have realized the truth about Charles sooner? Explain.

5. Do you think Laurie is a **dynamic character,** one who changes during the story, or a **static character,** one who remains the same? Explain your thinking.

6. What lessons do you think Laurie learns during his time in kindergarten?

Comparing Literature

7. After you read the next story, you will compare and contrast the characters, settings, and themes of the two stories. To plan your essay, you can start by filling in a chart like the one below with details from "Charles." Then, write out a possible theme for the story. To decide on the theme, ask yourself this question: "What did I learn from this story about life or about people?" Be sure to write your theme as a complete sentence. You will fill in the chart for "Miss Awful" when you finish that story.

Comparing Stories		
	"Charles"	"Miss Awful"
Setting		
Characters		
Theme of "Charles": _____		

Reading Check

a. Describe how Laurie's behavior at home changes when he begins school.

b. According to Laurie, what is Charles like?

c. How does Laurie's mother learn the truth about Charles?

SKILLS FOCUS

Literary Skills
Analyze characters, settings, and themes.

Reading Skills
Compare and contrast stories.

Reading Check

a. He dresses differently, uses improper English, and is generally rude.

b. Charles breaks rules in school, is disrespectful to his teacher, and is mean to other students.

c. Laurie's mother learns the truth about Charles by speaking to Laurie's teacher at a PTA meeting.

Before You Read

Have you ever attended an elementary school in which you had the same teacher for every subject? If you did, you know that you were with that one person a long time—approximately fourteen hundred hours a year. A teacher, especially one who is with a student for so long, can have a great deal of influence. Think of the best teacher you've ever had. What qualities and actions made this teacher special? As you read, ask yourself whether your favorite teacher was anything like the teachers in "Miss Awful."

Miss Awful

Arthur Cavanaugh

The whole episode of Miss Awful began for the Clarks at their dinner table one Sunday afternoon. Young Roger Clark was explaining why he could go to Central Park with his father instead of staying home to finish his homework—Miss Wilson, his teacher, wouldn't be at school tomorrow, so who'd know the difference? "She has to take care of a crisis," Roger explained. "It's in Omaha." ❶

"What is?" his older sister, Elizabeth, inquired. "For a kid in third grade, Roger, you talk dopey. You fail to make sense."

Roger ignored the insult. His sister was a condition of life he had learned to live with, like lions. Or snakes. Poisonous ones. Teetering,[1] as always, on the tilted-back chair, feet wrapped around the legs, he continued, "Till Miss Wilson gets back we're having some other teacher. She flew to Omaha yesterday." He pushed some peas around on his plate and was silent a moment. "I hope her plane don't crash," he said.

Roger's mother patted his hand. A lively, outgoing youngster, as noisy and rambunctious[2] as any eight-year-old, he had another side to him, tender and soft, which worried about people. Let the blind man who sold pencils outside the five-and-ten on Broadway be absent from his post, and Roger worried that catastrophe had overtaken him. When Mrs. Loomis, a neighbor of the Clarks in the

1. **teetering** *v. used as adj.*: wobbling, as if about to fall.
2. **rambunctious** *adj.*: noisy and lively.

Selection Starter

Motivate. Ask students to think of the best teacher they've ever had and to consider what qualities made this teacher special. Then, pair students and have them explain to their partners why that teacher was so special.

Summary ⬌ *at grade level*

In this short story, Roger Clark learns that his teacher, Miss Wilson, will be away for an indefinite period. Her place is taken by Miss Orville, a forbidding disciplinarian whose loud commands and harsh reprimands stun the children, who are accustomed to more indulgent treatment. Roger becomes a target of her criticism because of his poor spelling. Miss Orville's severity extends to the parents: She bluntly informs them of their children's shortcomings and prescribes remedies. On her last day in class, the students plot their revenge—stripping the leaves from Miss Orville's cherished plant. Roger protests, but to no avail. The sight of the ruined plant stuns and saddens Miss Orville. At the end of the school day, Roger remains behind after the other children leave. He walks up to Miss Orville and correctly spells *flower* and *castle*, two words he had wrestled with before. Miss Orville is moved to tears.

IDENTIFY

❶ Why does Roger decide he does not have to do his homework?

Ⓐ

Ⓑ

DIRECT TEACHING

Ⓐ Reading Skills

Identify. [Possible response to question 1: Roger decides that he does not have to do his homework because his teacher is not going to be in school.]

Ⓑ Reading Skills

Predict. Ask students to write predictions about what will happen while Miss Wilson is away, judging from Roger's comments and other evidence, such as the story's title.

DIRECT TEACHING

VIEWING THE ART

Activity. Have students focus on the individuals in this painting and decide what each of them is doing. Discuss whether this classroom would be conducive to learning, and why or why not. Encourage students to formulate questions of their own about the painting—for example: Why are there so few chairs in the classroom? What is the little boy in the right-hand corner doing? Whom are the children and teacher looking at, and why are some of the children looking in another direction?

A Reading Skills

Identify. [Possible response to question 2: Roger is as lively and noisy as any eight-year-old, but he is also kind and caring.]

B Comparing Literature

? Compare characters. What is your first impression of Roger's relationship with his parents? How is it different from Laurie's relationship with his parents in "Charles"? [Possible response: Roger is open and honest with his parents, and they seem to understand him. Laurie, in contrast, deceives his parents and speaks rudely and defiantly to them.]

Tribute to the American Working People (detail of five-part painting) by Honoré Desmond Sharrer.

National Museum of American Art, Washington, D.C./Art Resource, NY.

IDENTIFY

A **❷** What does the narrator tell you directly about Roger's character?

Greenwich Village brownstone, had entered the hospital, Roger's anxious queries had not ceased until she was discharged.[3] And recently there was the cat which had nested in the downstairs doorway at night. Roger had carried down saucers of milk, clucking with concern. "Is the cat run away? Don't it have a home?" ❷

Virginia Clark assured her son, "You'll have Miss Wilson safely back before you know it. It's nice that you care so."

Roger beamed with relief. "Well, I like Miss Wilson, she's fun.
B Last week, for instance, when Tommy Miller got tired of staying in his seat and lay down on the floor—"

"He did what?" Roger's father was roused from his post-dinner torpor.[4]

"Sure. Pretty soon the whole class was lying down. Know what

---

3. **discharged** *v.:* released: here, from the hospital.
4. **torpor** (tôr′pər) *n.:* sluggishness.

306 Collection 3 / Living in the Heart

DIFFERENTIATING INSTRUCTION

Learners Having Difficulty

To help students having difficulty, read aloud statements comparing elements of "Charles" and "Miss Awful." Say to the class, "Laurie is a more realistic character than Roger." Ask students whether they agree or disagree with the statement. Tell them to support their answers with evidence from the text. Then, have students make up their own statements, and use them as the basis for a classroom discussion.

English-Language Learners

Students from other countries may have difficulty imagining conditions at St. Geoffrey's, a school with an informal relaxed atmosphere. Have them read the Meet the Writer feature on p. 320, in which Arthur Cavanaugh describes the actual circumstances on which "Miss Awful" was based. Explain to English-language learners the similarity in sound between *Miss Awful* and *Miss Orville.*

Miss Wilson did?"

"If you'll notice, Mother," Elizabeth interjected, "he hasn't touched a single pea."

"*She* lay down on the floor, too," Roger went on ecstatically. "She said we'd *all* have a rest, it was perfectly normal in the middle of the day. That's what I love about St. Geoff's. It's fun."

"Fun," snorted his sister. "School isn't supposed to be a fun fest. It's supposed to be filling that empty noodle of yours." ❸

"Miss Wilson got down on the floor?" Mr. Clark repeated. He had met Roger's teacher on occasion; she had struck him as capable but excessively whimsical.⁵ She was a large woman to be getting down on floors, Mr. Clark thought. "What did the class do next?" he asked.

"Oh, we lay there a while, then got up and did a Mexican hat dance," Roger answered. "It was swell."

"I'm sure not every day is as frolicsome," Mrs. Clark countered, slightly anxious. She brought in dessert, a chocolate mousse. Roger's story sounded typical of St. Geoffrey's. Not that she was unhappy with his school. A small private institution, while it might be called overly permissive, it projected a warm, homey atmosphere which Mrs. Clark found appealing. It was church-affiliated, which she approved of, and heaven knows its location a few blocks away from the brownstone was convenient. True, Roger's scholastic progress wasn't notable—his spelling, for example, remained atrocious. Friendly as St. Geoffrey's was, Mrs. Clark sometimes *did* wish . . . ❹

Roger attacked dessert with a lot more zest than he had shown the peas. "So can I go to the park with you, Dad? I've only got spelling left, and who cares about that?" Before his mother could comment, he was up from the table and racing toward the coat closet. "Okay, Dad?"

"I didn't say you could go. I didn't even say I'd take you," Mr. Clark objected. He happened, at that moment, to glance at his waistline and reflect that a brisk hike might do him some good. He pushed back his chair. "All right, but the minute we return, it's straight to your room to finish your spelling."

"Ah, thanks, Dad. Can we go to the boat pond first?"

"We will not," cried Elizabeth, elbowing into the closet. "We'll go to the Sheep Meadow first."

---

5. **whimsical** (hwim′zi·kəl) *adj.:* full of silly, fanciful ideas.

Comparing Literature

COMPARE AND CONTRAST

❸ What does Roger think school is good for? What does his sister think?

IDENTIFY

❹ What does Roger's mother like about his school? What does she find troublesome?

DIRECT TEACHING

C Reading Skills
Compare and contrast. [Possible response to question 3: Roger thinks school is a good place to have fun. His sister thinks school is a place to learn.]

D Vocabulary Note
Use context clues. Ask students to figure out the meaning of the word *atrocious*. What context clues suggest the meaning of the word? [Roger's poor spelling is an example of his lack of progress in his studies, so students should realize that *atrocious* means "bad" or "inferior."]

E Reading Skills
Identify. [Possible response to question 4: Roger's mother likes the school's cozy atmosphere, convenient location, and affiliation with the church. She is troubled by the fact that Roger hasn't been making much progress in school, and she thinks the school could be more rigorous.]

Advanced Learners
Enrichment. Have students keep track of the significant events in the story as they read.
Activity. After students finish reading the story, have them work in groups to create storyboards for three important events in "Miss Awful," using passages from the story as captions. Incidents students might choose include these:

- The children marching to their desks: "She clapped time with her hands and the stunned ranks trooped into the classroom."
- Miss Orville reprimanding Roger when she sees his toys spilling from his schoolbag: "We have come to play, have we?"
- Miss Orville sitting in a rocking chair on the sidewalk after being evicted: "She couldn't keep any of the plants."

Call on a student from each group to present the storyboards to the class and to read the captions aloud.

A **Reading Skills**

Predict. [Possible response to question 5: I think Roger's day with the substitute teacher will not be as easy as he expects.]

B **Comparing Literature**

? **Compare characters.** How do Roger's interactions with his classmates differ from Laurie's in "Charles"? [Possible response: Roger is friendly with his classmates and likes to play with them, whereas Laurie is frequently mean to his classmates.]

C **Reading Skills**

Infer. [Possible response to question 6: The fact that Roger packs so many toys into his schoolbag tells you that he has a lot of time to play with his friends during school. His school may not emphasize learning as much as it should.]

PREDICT

❺ Sometimes a writer drops a hint that **foreshadows** events to come. What do you think is going to happen next?

INFER

❻ What does the fact that Roger packs so many toys in his schoolbag tell you about him? about his school?

Roger was too happy to argue. Pulling on his jacket, he remarked, "Gee, I wonder what the new teacher will be like. Ready for your coat, Dad?" **❺**

It was just as well that he gave the matter no more thought. In view of events to come, Roger was entitled to a few carefree hours. Monday morning at school started off with perfect normalcy. It began exactly like any other school morning. Elizabeth had long since departed for the girls' school she attended uptown when Mrs. Clark set out with Roger for the short walk to St. Geoff's. She didn't trust him with the Fifth Avenue traffic yet. They reached the school corner and Roger skipped away eagerly from her. The sidewalk in front of school already boasted a large, jostling throng of children, and his legs couldn't hurry Roger fast enough to join them. Indeed, it was his reason for getting to school promptly: to have time to play before the 8:45 bell. Roger's schoolbag was well equipped for play. As usual, he'd packed a supply of baseball cards for trading opportunities; a spool of string, in case anybody brought a kite; a water pistol for possible use in the lavatory; and a police whistle for sheer noise value. Down the Greenwich Village sidewalk he galloped, shouting the names of his third grade friends as he picked out faces from the throng. "Hiya, Tommy. Hey, hiya, Bruce. Hi, Steve, you bring your trading cards?" **❻**

By the time the 8:45 bell rang—St. Geoff's used a cowbell, one of the homey touches—Roger had finished a game of tag, traded several baseball cards, and was launched in an exciting jump-the-hydrant contest. Miss Gillis, the school secretary, was in charge of the bell, and she had to clang it extensively before the student body took notice. Clomping up the front steps, they spilled into the downstairs hall, headed in various directions. Roger's class swarmed up the stairs in rollicking spirits, Tommy Miller, Bruce Reeves, Joey Lambert, the girls forming an untidy rear flank behind them, shrill with laughter.

It wasn't until the front ranks reached the third-grade classroom that the first ominous note was struck.

"Hey, what's going on?" Jimmy Moore demanded, first to observe the changed appearance of the room. The other children crowded behind him in the doorway. Instead of a cozy semicircle—"As though we're seated round a glowing hearth," Miss Wilson had described it—the desks and chairs had been rearranged in stiff, rigid rows. "Gee, look, the desks are in rows," commented Midge Fuller, a

---

DEVELOPING FLUENCY

Activity. Have several students act out the roles of Clark family members at dinner. When Roger describes Miss Wilson's behavior, how does his family react? Be sure that students' role-playing shows an understanding of the characters' reactions. Encourage students to emphasize the attitude their characters have toward Miss Wilson's whimsical behavior.

SMALL GROUP

> **"Gee, I wonder what the new teacher will be like. Ready for your coat, Dad?"**

plump little girl who stood blocking Roger's view. Midge was a child given to unnecessary statements. "It's raining today," she would volunteer to her classmates, all of them in slickers. Or, "There's the lunch bell, gang." The point to Roger wasn't that the desks had been rearranged. The point was, *why?* As if in answer, he heard two hands clap behind him, as loud and menacing as thunder. ❼

"What's this, what's this?" barked a stern, raspish voice. "You are not cattle milling in a pen. Enough foolish gaping! Come, come, form into lines."

Heads turned in unison, mouths fell agape. The children of St. Geoffrey's third grade had never formed into lines of any sort, but this was not the cause of their shocked inertia.[6] Each was staring, with a sensation similar to that of drowning, at the owner of the raspish voice. She was tall and straight as a ruler, and was garbed in an ancient tweed suit whose skirt dipped nearly to the ankles. She bore a potted plant in one arm and Miss Wilson's roll book in the other. Rimless spectacles glinted on her bony nose. Her hair was gray, like a witch's, skewered in a bun, and there was no question that she had witch's eyes. Roger had seen those same eyes leering from the pages of *Hansel and Gretel*—identical, they were. He gulped at the terrible presence.

"Form lines, I said. Girls in one, boys in the other." Poking, prodding, patrolling back and forth, the new teacher kneaded the third grade into position and ruefully inspected the result. "Sloppiest group I've ever beheld. *March!*" She clapped time with her hands and the stunned ranks trooped into the classroom. "*One,* two, three, *one,* two—girls on the window side, boys on the wall. Stand at your desks. Remove your outer garments. You, little Miss, with the vacant stare. What's your name?"

"Ja-Ja—" a voice squeaked.

"Speak up. I won't have mumblers."

"Jane Douglas."

---

6. **inertia** (in·ur′shə) *n.:* here, an inability or reluctance to move.

COMPARE AND CONTRAST

❼ How is the classroom different from what it was like when Miss Wilson was there? What does the arrangement suggest about the new teacher?

DIRECT TEACHING

D Reading Skills
Compare and contrast. [Possible response to question 7: The chairs used to be in a semicircle, but now they are arranged in rows. The arrangement suggests that the new teacher will be stricter and more orderly than Miss Wilson.]

E Literary Focus
Characterization. Remind students that the way a character speaks tells us something about his or her personality. From the way the author describes Miss Wilson's speech, what is your impression of her? Explain. [She seems like a disciplinarian, because she repeats herself, is described as stern, and "barks" at the students.]

DIRECT TEACHING

A **Comparing Literature**

? **Speculate.** Do you think Laurie from "Charles" would like being Miss Orville's coat monitor? Explain. [Possible response: Yes, Laurie would like being coat monitor because he likes getting attention.]

B **Comparing Literature**

? **Compare characters.** The class immediately obeys Miss Orville's command to sit down. Would Laurie have obeyed if he were in the class? Explain. [Possible responses: Laurie would not have obeyed, because he likes to cause problems. Laurie would have behaved because Miss Orville is so intimidating.]

C **Reading Skills**

Infer. [Possible response to question 8: Plants and children are alike in that they are living organisms that grow when cared for properly. Miss Orville feels that children need careful guidance.]

INFER

8 According to Miss Orville, how are plants and children alike? What does this comparison tell you about Miss Orville's feelings toward children?

A "Well, Jane Douglas, you will be coat monitor. Collect the garments a row at a time and hang them neatly in the cloakroom. Did you hear me, child? Stop staring." Normally slow-moving, Jane Douglas became a whirl of activity, charging up and down the aisles, piling coats in her arms. The new teacher tugged at her tweed jacket. **B** "Class be seated, hands folded on desks," she barked, and there was immediate compliance. She next paraded to the windows and installed the potted plant on the sill. Her witch's hands fussed with the green leaves, straightening, pruning. "Plants and children belong in classrooms," she declared, spectacles sweeping over the rows. "Can someone suggest why?"

There was total silence, punctured by a deranged giggle, quickly suppressed.

"Very well, I will tell you. Plants and children are living organisms. Both will grow with proper care. Repeat, *proper*. Not indulgent fawning, or giving in to whims—scrupulosity!"[7] With another tug at the jacket, she strode, ruler straight, to the desk in the front of the room. "I am Miss Orville. *O-r-v-i-l-l-e*," she spelled. "You are to use my name in replying to all questions." **8**

In the back of the room, Jimmy Moore whispered frantically to Roger. "What did she say her name is?"

---

7. **scrupulosity** (skro͞oʹpyə·läsʹə·tē) *n.*: extreme carefulness and correctness.

---

310 Collection 3 / Living in the Heart

Miss Orville rapped her desk. "Attention, please, no muttering in the back." She cleared her voice and resumed. "Prior to my retirement I taught boys and girls for forty-six years," she warned. "I am beyond trickery, so I advise you to try none. You are to be in my charge until the return of Miss Wilson, however long that may be." She clasped her hands in front of her and trained her full scrutiny on the rows. "Since I have no knowledge of your individual abilities, perhaps a look at the weekend homework will shed some light. Miss Wilson left me a copy of the assignment. You have all completed it, I trust? Take out your notebooks, please. At once, at once, I say."

Roger's head spun dizzily around. He gaped at the monstrous tweed figure in dismay. Book bags were being clicked open, notebooks drawn out—what was he to do? He had gone to his room after the outing in the park yesterday, but, alas, it had not been to complete his assignment. He watched, horrified, as the tweed figure proceeded among the aisles and inspected notebooks. What had she said her name was? Awful—was that it? Miss Awful! Biting his lip, he listened to her scathing comments.

"You call this chicken scrawl penmanship?" R-r-rip! A page was torn out and thrust at its owner. "Redo it at once, it assaults the intelligence." Then, moving on, "What is this maze of ill-spelled words? Not a composition, I trust."

Ill-spelled words! He was in for it for sure. The tweed figure was heading down his aisle. She was three desks away, no escaping it. Roger opened his book bag. It slid from his grasp and, with a crash, fell to the floor. Books, pencil case spilled out. Baseball cards scattered, the water pistol, the police whistle, the spool of string . . .

"Ah," crowed Miss Awful, instantly at his desk, scooping up the offending objects. "We have come to play, have we?"

And she fixed her witch's gaze on him.

Long before the week's end, it was apparent to Virginia Clark that something was drastically wrong with her son's behavior. The happy-go-lucky youngster had disappeared, as if down a well. Another creature had replaced him, nervous, harried, continuously glancing over his shoulder, in the manner of one being followed. Mrs. Clark's first inkling of change occurred that same Monday. She had been chatting with the other mothers who congregated outside St. Geoffrey's at three every afternoon to pick up their offspring. A casual assembly, the mothers were as relaxed and informal as the

DIRECT TEACHING

D Reading Skills

? Predict. What do you think will happen when Miss Orville realizes Roger has not done his homework? [Possible response: She will punish him and take away his toys.]

E Literary Focus

? Character. How has Roger changed since Miss Orville's arrival? [Possible response: He has gone from easygoing and happy to nervous and fearful.]

LITERARY CONNECTIONS

Stereotypical Characters

Ask students to offer comparisons between Miss Orville and similar characters they have read about in other stories or novels. Ask whether each of these characters is described positively or negatively, and whether the character changes at some point in the work. Point out that Miss Orville's character is based on a stereotype, largely a negative one, of the "old-maid schoolteacher." As the story continues, tell students to be on the lookout for any new information about Miss Orville or positive aspects of her character.

Comparing Literature

DIRECT TEACHING

A Reading Skills

Compare and contrast. [Possible response to question 9: The children used to be loud and playful, but now they are quiet.]

B Comparing Literature

? Compare characters. How is Roger's mother similar to Laurie's mother in "Charles"? [Possible response: The mothers are similar in that they inherently trust their sons and are concerned about the effect other people have on them.]

C Reading Skills

Compare and contrast. [Possible response to question 10: Roger used to have a lackadaisical attitude about homework, but now he treats it as his top priority.]

COMPARE AND CONTRAST

9 The children's behavior has changed. How did they behave in the past? How do they behave now?

COMPARE AND CONTRAST

10 Think back to the beginning of the story. How has Roger's attitude about homework changed?

---

school itself, lounging against the picket fence, exchanging small talk and anecdotes.

"That darling cowbell," laughed one of the group at the familiar clang. "Did I tell you Anne's class is having a taffy pull on Friday? Where else, in the frantic city of New York . . ."

The third grade was the last class to exit from the building on Monday. Not only that, but Mrs. Clark noted that the children appeared strangely subdued. Some of them were actually reeling, all but dazed. As for Roger, eyes taut and pleading, he quickly pulled his mother down the block, signaling for silence. When enough distance had been gained, words erupted from him. **9**

"No, we don't have a new teacher," he flared wildly. "We got a *witch* for a new teacher. It's the truth. She's from *Hansel and Gretel,* the same horrible eyes—and she steals toys. *Yes,*" he repeated in mixed outrage and hurt. "By accident, you happen to put some toys in your book bag, and she *steals* 'em. I'll fool her! I won't *bring* any more toys to school," he howled. "Know what children are to her? Plants! She did, she called us plants. Miss Awful, that's her name."

Such was Roger's distress that his mother offered to stop at the Schrafft's on Thirteenth Street and treat him to a soda. "Who's got time for sodas?" he bleated. "I have homework to do. Punishment homework. Ten words, ten times each. On account of the witch's spelling test."

"Ten words, ten times each?" Mrs. Clark repeated. "How many words were on the test?"

"Ten," moaned Roger. "Every one wrong. Come on, I've got to hurry home. I don't have time to waste." Refusing to be consoled, he headed for the brownstone and the desk in his room. **10**

On Tuesday, together with the other mothers, Mrs. Clark was astonished to see the third grade march down the steps of St. Geoffrey's in military precision. Clop, clop, the children marched,

> "I have homework to do. Punishment homework. Ten words, ten times each."

312 Collection 3 / Living in the Heart

looking neither to the left nor right, while behind them came a stiff-backed, iron-haired woman in a pepper-and-salt suit. "*One, two, three, one, two, three,*" she counted, then clapped her hands in dismissal. Turning, she surveyed the assemblage of goggle-eyed mothers. "May I inquire if the mother of Joseph Lambert is among you?" she asked.

"I'm Mrs. Lambert," replied a voice meekly, whereupon Miss Orville paraded directly up to her. The rest of the mothers looked on, speechless.

"Mrs. Lambert, your son threatens to grow into a useless member of society," stated Miss Orville in ringing tones that echoed down the street. "That is, unless you term watching television useful. Joseph has confessed that he views three hours per evening." ⓫

"Only after his homework's finished," Margery Lambert allowed.

"Madame, he does not finish his homework. He idles through it, scattering mistakes higgledy-piggledy. I suggest you give him closer supervision. Good day." With a brief nod, Miss Orville proceeded down the street, and it was a full minute before the mothers had recovered enough to comment. Some voted in favor of immediate protest to Dr. Jameson, St. Geoffrey's headmaster, on the hiring of such a woman, even on a temporary basis. But since it was temporary, the mothers concluded it would have to be tolerated.

Nancy Reeves, Bruce's mother, kept staring at the retreating figure of Miss Orville, by now far down the block. "I know her from somewhere, I'm sure of it," she insisted, shaking her head.

The next morning, Roger refused to leave for school. "My shoes aren't shined," he wailed. "Not what Miss Awful calls shined. Where's the polish? I can't leave till I do 'em over."

"Roger, if only you'd thought of it last night," sighed Mrs. Clark.

"You sound like her," he cried. "That's what *she'd* say," and it gave his mother something to puzzle over for the rest of the day. She was still thinking about it when she joined the group of mothers outside St. Geoffrey's at three. She had to admit it was sort of impressive, the smart, martial[8] air exhibited by the third grade as they trooped down the steps. There was to be additional ceremony today. The ranks waited on the sidewalk until Miss Orville passed back and forth in inspection. Stationing herself at the head of the columns, she boomed, "Good afternoon, boys and girls. Let us return with perfect papers tomorrow."

---

8. **martial** (mär′shəl) *adj.:* military.

INFER

⓫ Why do you think Miss Orville disapproves of Joseph's watching television?

D

E

F

ⓓ Reading Skills

Infer. [Possible response to question 11: Miss Orville thinks that Joseph could spend more time reading books or doing his homework.]

ⓔ English-Language Learners

Idioms. Some students will probably be unfamiliar with the term *higgledy-piggledy.* They might be surprised to learn that the term can be found in most dictionaries. Ask them to guess the meaning from the word's sound and its context. If they need help, point out the context clue *scattering,* which should help students arrive at a definition for *higgledy-piggledy:* "jumbled; confused."

ⓕ Comparing Literature

❓ Compare characters. How is Roger's mother's encounter with Miss Orville different from Laurie's mother's interaction with Laurie's teacher in "Charles"? [Possible responses: Roger's mother sees the way Miss Orville behaves firsthand, so she knows that her son is telling her the truth. Laurie's mother does not meet her son's teacher until the end of the story and never witnesses the teacher's or her son's actions.]

Comparing Literature

A Reading Skills

Infer. [Possible response to question 12: Household chores are a way to give kids responsibilities and make them more independent.]

B Reading Skills

Infer. [Possible responses to question 13: I think Miss Orville is cruel because she humiliates Roger in front of his mother. She may be treating Roger harshly in order to make him take his schoolwork more seriously.]

C Literary Focus

? Character. Are you surprised that Roger's mother is "mortified" by Miss Orville's antics? Why or why not? [Possible responses: Yes, because I thought she'd realize that such drastically different behavior from her son would be the result of a stricter teacher. No, Miss Orville's rudeness would be insufferable for even the most tolerant parent.]

INFER

A ⓬ Why do you think Miss Orville believes that household chores are "lessons in self-reliance for the future"?

INFER

B ⓭ Do you think Miss Orville is a cruel person, or does she have a good reason for treating Roger harshly?

"Good aaaaafternoon, Miss Orville," the class sang back in unison, after which the ranks broke. Taking little Amy Lewis in tow, Miss Orville once more nodded at the mothers. "Which is she?" she asked Amy.

Miss Orville approached the trapped Mrs. Lewis. She cleared her throat, thrust back her shoulders. "Amy tells me she is fortunate enough to enjoy the services of a full-time domestic[9] at home," said Miss Orville. "May I question whether she is fortunate—or deprived? I needn't lecture you, I'm sure, Mrs. Lewis, about the wisdom of assigning a child tasks to perform at home. Setting the table, tidying up one's room, are lessons in self-reliance for the future. Surely you agree." There was a nod from Mrs. Lewis. "Excellent," smiled Miss Orville. "Amy will inform me in the morning the tasks you have assigned her. Make them plentiful, I urge you." **⓬**

The lecturing, however, was not ended. Turning from Mrs. Lewis, Miss Orville cast her gaze around and inquired, "Is Roger Clark's mother present?"

"Yes?" spoke Virginia Clark, reaching for Roger's hand. "What is it?"

Miss Orville studied Roger silently for a long moment. "A scallywag, if ever I met one," she pronounced. The rimless spectacles lifted to the scallywag's mother. "You know, of course, that Roger is a prodigy,"[10] said Miss Orville. "A prodigy of misspelling. Roger, spell *flower* for us," she ordered. "Come, come, speak up."

Roger kept his head lowered. "F," he spelled. "*F-l-o-r.*"

"Spell castle."

"K," spelled Roger. "*K-a-z-l.*"

Miss Orville's lips parted grimly. "Those are the results, mind you, of an hour's solid work with your son, Mrs. Clark. He does not apply himself. He wishes to remain a child at play, absorbed in his toys. Is that what you want for him?" **⓭**

"I—I—" Virginia Clark would have been grateful if the sidewalk had opened up to receive her.

As she reported to her husband that evening, she had never in her life been as mortified.[11] "Spoke to me in front of all the other mothers, in loud, clarion tones," she described the scene. "Do I want Roger to remain a child at play. Imagine."

"By the way, where is Roge?" Mr. Clark asked, who had come

---

9. **domestic** *n.:* housecleaner.
10. **prodigy** (präd′ə·jē) *n.:* child genius.
11. **mortified** (môrt′ə·fīd) *v.* used as *adj.:* ashamed and hurt.

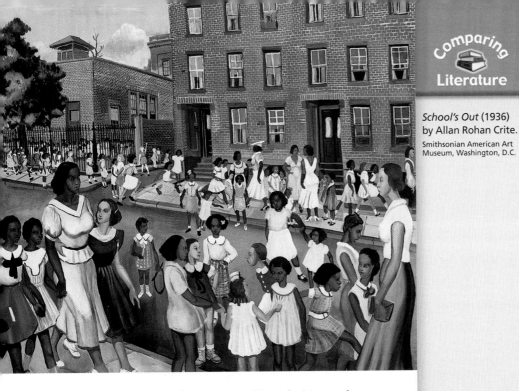

School's Out (1936)
by Allan Rohan Crite.
Smithsonian American Art
Museum, Washington, D.C.

home late from the office. "He's not watching television, or busy with his airplanes—"

"In his room, doing over his homework for the ninety-eighth time. It has to be perfect, he says. But, really, Charles, don't you think it was outrageous?"

Mr. Clark stirred his coffee. "I bet Miss Orville doesn't get down on the floor with the class. Or do Mexican hat dances with them."

"If that's meant to disparage[12] Miss Wilson—" Virginia Clark stacked the dinner dishes irritably. She sometimes found her husband's behavior maddening. Especially when he took to grinning at her, as he was presently doing. She also concluded that she'd had her fill of Elizabeth's attitude on the subject. "At last some teacher's wised up to Roge," had been the Clarks' daughter's comment. "He's cute and all, but I wouldn't want to be in a shipwreck with him." Washing dishes in the kitchen, Mrs. Clark considered that maybe she wouldn't meet Roger in *front* of school tomorrow. Maybe she'd wait at the corner instead. "His shoes," she gasped, and hurried to remind her son to get out the polishing kit. The spelling, too, she'd better work on that . . . **14**

---

12. **disparage** (di·spar**'**ij) *v.*: show disrespect for; "put down."

INFER

14 Why do Roger's sister and father think Miss Orville is an improvement over Miss Wilson?

E

Miss Awful   315

DIRECT TEACHING

D **Literary Focus**

? **Character.** How is Roger's mother's behavior in this passage similar to her son's? [Possible response: Both Roger and his mother are made nervous by Miss Orville. They both want to make a positive impression on her.]

E **Reading Skills**

Infer. [Possible response to question 14: They feel that Miss Orville is an improvement over Miss Wilson because Miss Orville takes academic studies more seriously and maintains an orderly classroom.]

VIEWING THE ART

Activity. Have students look at the painting by **Allan Rohan Crite** (1910–   ), and ask them to remember scenes where Roger and his friends are leaving school. Then, ask students to answer the following questions: How do the students in the painting feel? Do you relate to how they feel? Are the kids in the painting similar to Roger and his friends before Miss Orville comes or after she comes?

DIFFERENTIATING INSTRUCTION

Advanced Learners
Enrichment. Ask students to work in groups of four to create a résumé for Miss Orville. Give students a model résumé before they begin. Instruct them to come up with information about areas of her life:
- education
- teaching experience
- skills
- awards

Encourage students to type their information in résumé format.

DIRECT TEACHING

A Literary Focus

? Characterization. Has Nancy Reeves's story affected your perception of Miss Orville? How? [Possible response: Up to this point, Miss Orville seemed like a tyrant, but Nancy Reeves's account humanizes her and makes her more sympathetic.]

B Reading Skills

Infer. [Possible response to question 15: Her memory reveals that Miss Orville is stubborn and determined. It also shows that she had to deal with difficulties in her life.]

C Literary Focus

? Theme. What does Roger's mother realize when Roger refers to Miss Orville as a witch? How might her reaction hint at the story's theme? [Possible responses: She realizes that she may have been too lenient with Roger and allowed him to get away with unacceptable behavior. The theme may be that it is important to discipline children.]

It was on Thursday that Nancy Reeves finally remembered where previously she had seen Miss Orville. Perhaps it was from the shock of having received a compliment from the latter.

"Mrs. Reeves, I rejoice to inform you of progress," Miss Orville had addressed her, after the third grade had performed its military display for the afternoon. "On Monday, young Bruce's penmanship was comparable to a chicken's—if a chicken could write. Today, I was pleased to award him an A."

A tug at the tweed jacket, and the stiff-backed figure walked firmly down the street. Nancy Reeves stared after her until Miss Orville had merged into the flow of pedestrians and traffic. "I know who she is," Nancy suddenly remarked, turning to the other mothers. "I knew I'd seen her before. Those old ramshackle buildings near us on Hudson Street—remember when they were torn down last year?" The other mothers formed a circle around her. "Miss Orville was one of the tenants," Nancy Reeves went on. "She'd lived there for ages, and refused to budge until the landlord got a court order and deposited her on the sidewalk. I *saw* her there, sitting in a rocker on the sidewalk, surrounded by all this furniture and plants. Her picture was in the papers. Elderly retired schoolteacher . . . they found a furnished room for her on Jane Street, I think. Poor old thing, evicted like that . . . I remember she couldn't keep any of the plants . . ."

On the way home, after supplying a lurid account of the day's tortures—"Miss Awful made Walter Meade stand in the corner for saying a bad word"—Roger asked his mother, "Eviction. What does that mean?"

"It's when somebody is forced by law to vacate an apartment. The landlord gets an eviction notice, and the person has to leave."

"Kicked her out on the street. Is that what they did to the witch?" **15**

"Don't call her that, it's rude and impolite," Mrs. Clark said, as they turned into the brownstone doorway. "I can see your father and I have been too easygoing where you're concerned."

"Huh, we've got worse names for her," Roger retorted. "*Curse* names, you should hear 'em. We're planning how to get even with Miss Awful, just you see." He paused, as his mother opened the downstairs door with her key. "That's where the cat used to sleep, remember?" he said, pointing at a corner of the entryway. His face was grave and earnest. "I wonder where that cat went to. Hey, Mom," he hurried to catch up. "Maybe *it* was evicted, too."

Then it was Friday at St. Geoffrey's. Before lunch, Miss Orville

---

INFER

15 Nancy Reeves remembers something about Miss Orville. What does her memory tell you about Miss Orville's **character**?

told the class, "I am happy to inform you that Miss Wilson will be back on Monday." She held up her hand for quiet. "This afternoon will be my final session with you. Not that discipline will relax, but I might read you a story. Robert Louis Stevenson, perhaps. My boys and girls always enjoyed him so. Forty-six years of them . . . Joseph Lambert, you're not sitting up straight. You know I don't permit slouchers in my class."

It was a mistake to have told the children that Miss Wilson would be back on Monday, that only a few hours of the terrible reign of Miss Awful were left to endure. Even before lunch recess, a certain spirit of challenge and defiance had infiltrated[13] into the room. Postures were still erect, but not quite as erect. Tommy Miller dropped his pencil case on the floor and did not request permission to pick it up.

"Ahhh, so what," he mumbled, when Miss Orville remonstrated[14] with him.

"What did you say?" she demanded, drawing herself up.

"I said, so what," Tommy Miller answered, returning her stare without distress.

Roger thought that was neat of Tommy, talking fresh like that. He was surprised, too, because Miss Awful didn't yell at Tommy or anything. A funny look came into her eyes, he noticed, and she just went on with the geography lesson. And when Tommy dropped his pencil case again, and picked it up without asking, she said nothing. Roger wasn't so certain that Tommy should have dropped the pencil case a second time. The lunch bell rang, then, and he piled out of the classroom with the others, not bothering to wait for permission. **16**

At lunch in the basement cafeteria, the third grade talked of nothing except how to get even with Miss Awful. The recommendations showed daring and imagination.

"We could beat her up," Joey Lambert suggested. "We could wait at the corner till she goes by, and throw rocks at her."

---

13. **infiltrated** (in·fil′trāt′id) *v.:* gradually entered or sneaked into.
14. **remonstrated** *v.:* reasoned earnestly in protest against something.

DIRECT TEACHING

D **Comparing Literature**

? **Compare characters.** How do Roger's feelings toward Miss Orville change in this passage? If Laurie from "Charles" were in Miss Orville's class, would he feel the same way? [Possible response: Roger begins to feel sympathy for Miss Orville. Students may say that Laurie probably wouldn't feel sympathetic toward her since he shows little regard for others' feelings.]

E **Reading Skills**

Infer. [Possible response to question 16: It was a mistake, because the students will disregard her instructions. Since it's her last day, they aren't worried about being punished for misbehaving.]

DIRECT TEACHING

A Literary Focus

? Character. What do Roger's misgivings tell you about his character? [Possible response: Even though Roger resented Miss Orville for her strictness, he still has a strong sense of what is right and wrong and doesn't really want to hurt her.] **Do you think he is a static character or a dynamic character?** [Some students will say that Roger is a static character, because he shows evidence of his caring nature throughout the story. Others may say that Roger has changed in the course of the story, pointing out that he has begun to take responsibility for his actions.]

"We'd get arrested," Walter Meade pointed out.

"Better idea," said Bruce Reeves. "We could go upstairs to the classroom before she gets back, and tie a string in front of the door. She'd trip, and break her neck."

"She's old," Roger Clark protested. "We can't hurt her like that. She's too old."

It was one of the girls, actually, who thought of the plant. "That dopey old plant she's always fussing over," piped Midge Fuller. "We could rip off all the dopey leaves. That'd show her."

Roger pushed back his chair and stood up from the table. "We don't want to do that," he said, not understanding why he objected. It was a feeling inside, he couldn't explain . . . "Aw, let's forget about it," he said. "Let's call it quits."

"The plant, the plant," Midge Fuller squealed, clapping her hands.

Postures were a good deal worse when the third grade reconvened after lunch. "Well, you've put in an industrious week, I daresay . . ." Miss Orville commented. She opened the frayed volume of *Treasure Island* which she had brought from home and turned the pages carefully to Chapter One. "I assume the class is familiar with the tale of young Jim Hawkins, Long John Silver, and the other wonderful characters."

"No, I ain't," said Tommy Miller.

"Ain't. What word is that?"

"It's the word ain't," answered Tommy.

"Ain't, ain't," somebody jeered.

Miss Orville lowered the frayed volume. "No, children, you mustn't do this," she said with force. "To attend school is a privilege you must not mock. Can you guess how many thousands of children in the world are denied the gift of schooling?" Her lips quavered. "It is a priceless gift. You cannot permit yourselves to squander a moment of it." She rose from her desk and looked down at the rows

CROSS-CURRICULAR CONNECTIONS

Social Studies
Education. Miss Orville asks her students if they realize how many children around the world are denied the privilege of schooling. **Activity.** Have students research levels of education around the world and present this information to the class. Have them provide figures for the average age at which children in various countries leave school to enter the work force. Students may be surprised at the figures, so ask

them to write down their reactions to the information they find.

WHOLE CLASS

of boys and girls. "It isn't enough any longer to accept a gift and make no return for it, not with the world in the shape it's in," she said, spectacles trembling on her bony nose. "The world isn't a playbox," she said. "If I have been severe with you this past week, it was for your benefit. The world needs good citizens. If I have helped one of you to grow a fraction of an inch, if just *one* of you—"

She stopped speaking. Her voice faltered, the words dammed up. She was staring at the plant on the window sill, which she had not noticed before. The stalks twisted up bare and naked, where the leaves had been torn off. "You see," Miss Orville said after a moment, going slowly to the window sill. "You *see* what I am talking about? To be truly educated is to be civilized. Here, you may observe the opposite." Her fingers reached out to the bare stalks. "Violence and destruction . . ." She turned and faced the class, and behind the spectacles her eyes were dim and faded. "Whoever is responsible, I beg of you only to be sorry," she said. When she returned to her desk, her back was straighter than ever, but it seemed to take her longer to cover the distance. ⓱

At the close of class that afternoon, there was no forming of lines. Miss Orville merely dismissed the boys and girls and did not leave her desk. The children ran out, some in regret, some silent, others cheerful and scampering. Only Roger Clark stayed behind.

He stood at the windows, plucking at the naked plant on the sill. Miss Orville was emptying the desk of her possessions, books, pads, a folder of maps. "These are yours, I believe," she said to Roger. In her hands were the water pistol, the baseball cards, the spool of string. "Here, take them," she said.

Roger went to the desk. He stuffed the toys in his coat pocket without paying attention to them. He stood at the desk, rubbing his hand up and down his coat.

"Yes?" Miss Orville asked.

Roger stood back, hands at his side, and lifted his head erectly. "Flower," he spelled. "*F-l-o-w-e-r.*" He squared his shoulders and looked at Miss Orville's brimming eyes. "Castle," Roger spelled. "*C-a-s-t-l-e.*"

Then he walked from the room. ⓲

COMPARE AND CONTRAST

⓱ What kind of behavior does Miss Orville contrast with civilized behavior?

INTERPRET

⓲ What message do you think Roger means to give Miss Orville when he spells *flower* and *castle* correctly?

Ⓑ Reading Skills

Compare and contrast. [Possible response to question 17: Miss Orville contrasts malicious acts (such as the mangling of her plant) with civilized behavior.]

Ⓒ Learners Having Difficulty

❓ **Find details.** Why does Roger choose to spell *flower* and *castle*? [They are the two words that he failed to spell correctly when Miss Orville asked him to.]

Ⓓ Reading Skills

Interpret. [Possible response to question 18: Spelling out the words is his way of showing Miss Orville that she has made a difference to him.]

Meet the Writer

Meet the Writer

Cavanaugh's comments seem to indicate that he, like Roger's father, prefers Miss Orville's teaching approach to Miss Wilson's. He also suggests that his son was more motivated by a strict substitute teacher than by his regular teacher and actually missed the substitute when she left. Cavanaugh says that he usually waits a long time before turning a real-life incident into a story. Ask the class why they think he was inspired to write this story as the events were taking place.

Arthur Cavanaugh

"All of My Stories Have Been Drawn from Life"

Arthur Cavanaugh (1926–   ) was born in New York City and has lived there all his life. Many of his short stories are about the Clark family, which bears a strong resemblance to his own. "Miss Awful," in fact, is based on his son Frank's experiences at a school in Greenwich Village, New York. Cavanaugh remembers:

❝ To hear him tell of it, the days at school were a happy mixture of games, crayons, milk and cookies, and outings to the playground across the street. One night when I got home from work, Frank indignantly announced that his teacher was out sick and, worse, replaced by a crabby old lady who did nothing but admonish the class for their lack of discipline and scholarship. 'Honest, you wouldn't believe how awful she is,' Frank assured me. But I noticed a marked change in my son, at night when I came home. Where before he was sprawled in front of the television, I'd find him bent over his homework or actually voluntarily reading a book. The night that I discovered him wrestling with a dictionary, looking up words for a quiz the next day, I knew that 'Miss Awful' had scored a victory on behalf of education. And when the following week I heard from Frank that his regular teacher was back at her desk, the tinge of regret in his voice was unmistakable. All of my stories have been drawn from life, usually long after the incident happened, but 'Miss Awful' was the exception, taking shape as the story happened right in front of me. ❞

DIFFERENTIATING INSTRUCTION

Advanced Learners

Enrichment. After students finish the story, ask them to imagine that a film crew stops by St. Geoffrey's to tape interviews for a short documentary about Miss Orville's life on the day after she leaves.

Activity. Divide students into groups. Have each group assign roles to its members and conduct interviews with these characters: Roger, another student, and Roger's mother offering their opinions of Miss Orville, and Miss Orville, speaking about herself. Encourage students to take notes about what each character would say, but ask them to ad-lib during the actual interviews. Have them make videotaped interviews or perform the interviews live for the class.

SMALL GROUP

First Thoughts

1. Do you think Miss Orville is really "Miss Awful"? Would you like to be in her class? Discuss your responses to what happened in her classroom.

Thinking Critically

2. Think about what you know of Miss Orville's life, and try to explain why she demands so much of her class.

3. How would you explain the children's cruelty in this story? Did they have a good reason for doing what they did? What do you think of their behavior?

4. The story suggests that Roger has discovered something important in the end. What do you think he has discovered?

Comparing Literature

5. Fill in a chart like the one below with details from "Miss Awful." Then, write out a possible theme for the story. To figure out the theme, ask yourself: "What did I learn about life or people from this story?" Remember that the themes of "Charles" and "Miss Awful" may be very different.

Reading Check

Use a story map like the one below to outline the main parts of "Miss Awful."

Setting:

Characters:

Conflicts:

Event 1:

Event 2:

(Add as many as you need.)

Climax:

Resolution of conflict:

go.hrw.com

INTERNET
Projects and Activities
Keyword: LE5 7-3

Comparing Stories

	"Charles"	"Miss Awful"
Setting		
Characters		
Theme of "Miss Awful": _____		

SKILLS FOCUS

Literary Skills
Analyze characters, settings, and themes.

Reading Skills
Compare and contrast stories.

Miss Awful   **321**

Independent Practice content below:

After You Read

First Thoughts

1. Some students may say that Miss Orville was not as bad as she seemed at first. Very few are likely to say they would like to be in her class.

Thinking Critically

2. Miss Orville seems to have had a hard life. She wants her students to value the education they are receiving and to be prepared for the difficulties they will face in the world outside the classroom.

3. The children act out of anger over Miss Orville's harsh treatment. Encourage students who approve of the children's actions to consider Miss Orville's feelings.

4. Possible answer: Roger realizes that Miss Orville cares deeply about children and that she has not had much happiness in her life.

Comparing Literature

5. Possible answers: *Setting*—St. Geoffrey's; Roger's home. *Characters*—Roger; Miss Orville; Roger's mother, father, and sister; and other students in Roger's class. *Theme of "Miss Awful"*—Sometimes the best approach to teaching children is a strict one.

Reading Check

Setting—St. Geoffrey's, Roger's home. *Characters*—Roger, Miss Orville, Roger's family, other students in Roger's class. *Conflicts*—Roger and his classmates versus Miss Orville; Roger versus the rest of his classmates. *Event 1*—Miss Orville arrives as substitute for Miss Wilson. *Event 2*—Miss Orville disciplines students harshly. *Event 3*—Miss Orville humiliates Roger in front of his mother by showing that he is a poor speller. *Event 4*—Students plot revenge for perceived mistreatment. *Event 5*—Roger tries to dissuade students from acting harshly. *Climax*—Students strip leaves off of Miss Orville's plant. *Resolution of conflict*—Roger spells words correctly for Miss Orville.

INDEPENDENT PRACTICE

After You Read

1. Writing a Comparison-Contrast Essay

Strategy tip. If students choose to organize their essays by story elements, remind them that they probably came up with very different themes for the two stories. Have students begin by writing about the similar settings of the two stories. Then, have them write about the main characters, who are both young boys, but who have different character traits. Have students use these traits as the basis of their examination of the story's theme. They can close with a personal comment about which story they prefer and why.

2. Describing a Perfect Class

Strategy tip. Remind students to use sensory details when they write their description of the perfect classroom. Tell students that using vivid adjectives to describe what the teacher looks like and how the room is decorated will help readers picture the classroom in their minds.

3. Writing and Performing a Dramatization

Strategy tip. Encourage students to think of a defining trait of each character in their dramatization before they begin writing. For instance, if students choose to act out a day in Miss Orville's classroom, the trait they might associate most with Miss Orville is her strictness. Encourage them to keep this trait in mind as they write and perform.

Assignment

1. Writing a Comparison-Contrast Essay

Write an essay comparing and contrasting the settings, characters, and themes of "Charles" and "Miss Awful." To plan your essay, review the charts you filled in after you read the stories. The chart will help you focus on the key elements in the stories and the similarities and differences between them.

You can organize your essay in one of these two ways:

1. You can organize your essay by story: In the first paragraph, discuss the setting, characters, and theme of "Charles." In the second paragraph, discuss the setting, characters, and theme of "Miss Awful."

2. You can organize your essay by elements: In separate paragraphs, compare and contrast the settings, main characters, and themes of the two stories.

Whichever form of organization you use, include a final paragraph in which you describe your own response to each story. Did you prefer one story to the other? Did you find the story true to life? Would you recommend either story to a classmate?

> Use the workshop on writing a Comparison-Contrast Essay, pages 772–777, for help with this assignment.

SKILLS FOCUS

Writing Skills
Write a comparison-contrast essay; write a descriptive essay; write a scene.

Speaking and Listening Skills
Perform a scene.

Assignment

2. Describing a Perfect Class

Describe what you think the perfect classroom would be like. How many students would be in the class? What "learning tools" would be available? How would the furniture be arranged? Would the teacher be strict, like Miss Orville and Charles's teacher, or easygoing, like Miss Wilson? What kind of atmosphere do you think is best to learn in? Write at least one paragraph.

Assignment

3. Writing and Performing a Dramatization

With a small group of classmates, stage a scene from a day in the classroom of Miss Wilson, Miss Orville, or Charles's teacher. Before you write the dialogue for your scene, decide how many speaking parts it will include. Perform the scene for your class, and ask for feedback. Is your dramatization true to the characters in the original story?

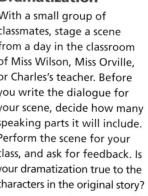

322 Collection 3 / Living in the Heart

DIFFERENTIATING INSTRUCTION

Special Education Students

If students have difficulty describing a perfect class, ask them to begin referring back to "Charles" and "Miss Awful" for ideas. You might have them compare aspects of Miss Wilson's classroom with aspects of Miss Orville's classroom (such as the arrangement of desks). Then, ask them which environment they think would be more conducive to learning.

For further activities for special education students, see *Holt Reading Solutions*.

NO QUESTIONS ASKED

I can't remember where I have left my glasses, but I can still remember the smell of the first girl I ever fell in love with when I was twelve: a blend of Dixie Peach pomade on her hair and Pond's cold cream on her skin; together they were honeysuckle for me. And just as heady as her scent was the thought that I was in love with the only girl in the world for me and would marry her and take care of her forever in a palace in North Philadelphia. Because I wanted to make a wondrous impression on this girl, grooming was suddenly important to me. Before puberty, happiness in appearance for me was pants that didn't fall down and a football that stayed pumped; but now I started taking three long baths a day and washing my own belt until it was white and shining my shoes until I could see in them a face that was ready for romance.

The Only Girl in the World for Me

Bill Cosby
from Love and Marriage

The first time I saw her, she was crossing the street to the schoolyard and for one golden moment our eyes met. Well, maybe the moment was closer to bronze because she made no response. But at least she had seen me, just about the way that she saw lampposts, hydrants, and manholes. Or was there something more? I began to dream; and later that day, when I was playing with the boys in the yard, it seemed that she was looking at me and the world was suddenly a better place, especially Twelfth and Girard.

However, we still never talked, but just traded silent unsmiling looks whenever we passed. For several days, just her look was enough of a lift for me; but a higher altitude was coming, for one night at a party, we met and I actually danced with her. Now I was certain that I was in love and was going to win her.

I began my conquest with a combination of sporting skill and hygiene: I made my jump shots and my baths as dazzling as they could be. Oddly enough, however, although I saw her every day at

The Only Girl in the World for Me **323**

The Only Girl in the World for Me **323**

OVERVIEW
The No Questions Asked feature gives students the opportunity to read for enjoyment. The annotations in the margins of the Teacher's Edition are optional. No follow-up questions appear after the essay and poem.

Summary ⬇ *below grade level*

In this memoir, Bill Cosby wittily recaptures the roller coaster ride of first love, which transforms him from an ordinary twelve-year-old boy into a neat freak who takes three baths a day. He silently worships a young girl, who is never given a name. He finally works up the courage to ask her girlfriend whether the girl ever talks about him. The news that she thinks he is cute intoxicates him, but he is dismayed to learn that she not only has a boyfriend, but also has a successor lined up. Nevertheless, Bill is patient and finally escorts his goddess to a movie, where his circulation and bladder conspire against him. True love and real life finally intersect, however, when he discovers that his new girlfriend also needed to go to the bathroom.

PRETEACHING

Selection Starter
Build background. "The Only Girl in the World for Me" takes place in Philadelphia in the late 1940s, when Bill Cosby was twelve years old. The story unfolds in a racially mixed, working-class section of North Philadelphia, fondly recalled by Cosby in his writings and stand-up routines.

Vary your reading rate. Ask students to compare the speed at which they would read this piece with the speed at which they would read an informational piece about science. [Most students will say that the Cosby piece, being light and entertaining, can be read more quickly.] Warn students that although a quick reading will cover the basic events of the memoir, reading too quickly might make them miss gems such as "I sat down one Sunday night and wrote a note that was almost to her."

B Literary Focus

? Motivation. Why does Bill carry the note around rather than open it? [Possible response: As long as he doesn't read the note, he can always imagine that it contains good news.]

C Advanced Learners

Allusion. Tell students that an allusion is a reference to a person, place, thing, event, or quotation from literature, history, or another cultural source. Explain that comparing the girl's note to "something by Keats" is Cosby's way of saying it was beautiful poetry to him. It also sets up the comedy of Cosby's irony, because the response is not the least bit poetic. Encourage students to look for other allusions as they read the essay.

school and on the weekends too, I never spoke to her. I had what was considered one of the faster mouths in Philadelphia, but I still wasn't ready to talk to her because I feared rejection. I feared:

COSBY: I like you very much. Will you be my girlfriend?
GODDESS: (*Doing a poor job of suppressing a laugh*) I'd rather have some cavities filled.

All I did, therefore, was adore her in silent cleanliness. Each Sunday night, I took a bath and then prepared my shirt and pants for display to her. On Monday morning, I took another bath (Bill the Baptist,[1] I should have been called) and then brushed my hair, my shoes, and my eyelashes and went outside to await the pang of another silent passage.

At last, deciding that I could no longer live this way, I sat down one Sunday night and wrote a note that was almost to her. It was to her constant girlfriend and it said:

Please don't tell her, but find out what she thinks of me.
Bill

The following morning, I slipped the note to the girlfriend and began the longest wait of my life.

Two agonizing days later, the girlfriend slipped me an answer, but I put it into my pocket unread. For hours, I carried it around, afraid to read it because I didn't happen to be in the mood for crushing rejection that day. At last, however, I summoned the courage to open the note and read:

She thinks you're cute.

Not even malaria[2] could have taken my temperature to where it went. I had been called many things, but cute was never one of them.

An even lovelier fever lay ahead, for the next time I saw her, she smiled at me, I smiled at her, and then I composed my next winged message to her friend:

I think she's cute too. Does she ever talk about me?

The answer to this one came return mail and it sounded like something by Keats:[3]

---

1. **Bill the Baptist:** reference to John the Baptist, a prophet who baptized his followers to show that they had repented.
2. **malaria** *n.:* disease characterized by chills and fever.
3. **Keats:** John Keats (1795–1821), an English poet.

English-Language Learners
To give English-language learners some cultural context, bring photos, tapes, and other material pertaining to Bill Cosby to class. Students from other countries may have difficulty with some of the cultural references—for example, jump shots, Western Union, and the *Hindenburg*. Help students understand Cosby's use of exaggeration ("And the angels sang!") and irony ("What a prince of passion I was at this moment!").

She talks about you a lot. She knows it when you come around her.

And the angels sang! Imagine: She actually *knew* it when I came around her! The fact that she also knew it when gnats came around her in no way dampened my ecstasy.

And so, we continued to smile as we passed, while I planned my next move. My Western Union[4] style had clearly been charming the pants off her (so to speak) and now I launched my most courageous question yet:

Does she have a boyfriend?

When I opened the answer the next day in school, the air left me faster than it left the *Hindenburg:*[5]

Yes.

Trying to recover from this deflation, I told myself that I was still cute. I was the cutest man in second place. But perhaps my beloved wasn't aware of the glory she kept passing by. Once more, I sat down and wrote:

How much longer do you think she'll be going with him? And when she's finished with him, can I be next?

Note the elegance and dignity of my appeal. My dignity, however, did have some trouble with the reply:

She thinks she's going to break up with him in about a week, but she promised Sidney she would go with him next.

Suddenly, my aching heart found itself at the end of a line. But it was like a line at a bank: I knew it was leading to a payoff. I also knew that I could cream Sidney in cuteness.

Once she had made the transition to Sidney, I patiently began waiting for her to get sick of him. I had to be careful not to rush the illness because Sidney belonged to a tough gang and there was a chance that I might not be walking around too well when the time came for me to inherit her.

And then, one magnificent morning, I received the magic words:

She would like to talk to you.

---

4. **Western Union:** company that operates a telegraph service.
5. *Hindenburg:* an airship filled with hydrogen gas that caught fire and blew up following a transatlantic flight in May 1937.

The Only Girl in the World for Me 325

D **Literary Focus**

❓ **Exaggeration.** What comic device is Cosby using in this passage? [exaggeration] What other examples of exaggeration can you find in the essay? [Possible responses: "Not even malaria could have taken my temperature to where it went"; "how much more torrid our passion would be when I began to *talk* to her"; "this romantic agony."]

E **Literary Focus**

❓ **Theme.** What is the topic of this essay? What selections in the collection deal with topics similar to those in Cosby's essay? [Possible responses: The topic is an idealized lover. "Annabel Lee" and "The Highwayman" deal with similar topics.] Do you expect that Cosby's theme will be similar to the themes of these works? [Possible response: Probably not; the tone of "Annabel Lee" and "The Highwayman" is more serious than Cosby's work, so I expect Cosby's theme to be comic, not tragic.]

❓ Dialogue. Be sure students are aware that no dialogue appears in the narrative until this point. Point out the shift from passing notes through an intermediary to face-to-face conversation. How might this shift affect the relationship? [Possible response: The shift to conversation makes the relationship less idealized and more real.]

Ⓑ Reading Skills

❓ Predict. How do you predict Cosby will handle this potentially embarrassing situation? [Possible responses: He will be true to his idea of being a gentleman and remain in the theater. He will find a gallant way to leave the theater for a moment.]

I wrote back to see if she would wait until I had finished duty at my post as a school crossing guard. Yes, she would wait; I could walk her home. We were going steady now; and how much more torrid our passion would be when I began to *talk* to her.

At last, the words came and I chose them with care. As I walked her home from school, I reached into my reservoir of romantic thoughts, smiled at her soulfully, and said, "How you doing?"

Her response was equally poetic: "All right."

"So we're going steady now?"

"You want to?"

"Yeah. Give me your books."

And now, as if our relationship were not already in the depths of desire, I plunged even deeper by saying, "You wanna go to a movie on Saturday?"

"Why not?"

There might have been reasons. Some people were looking at us now because she was so beautiful, people possibly wondering what she was doing with me; but I knew that I was someone special to be the love of a vision like this, no matter how nearsighted that vision might be.

When we reached her door, I said, "Well, I'll see you Saturday."

"Right," she replied as only she could say it.

"What time?"

"One o'clock."

When this day of days finally arrived, I took her to a theater where I think the admission was a dime. As we took our seats for the matinee, two basic thoughts were in my mind: not to sit in gum and to be a gentleman.

Therefore, I didn't hold her hand. Instead, I put my arm around the top of her seat in what I felt was a smooth opening move. Unfortunately, it was less a move toward love than toward gangrene:[6] With my blood moving uphill, my arm first began to tingle and then to ache. I could not, however, take the arm down and let my blood keep flowing because such a lowering would mean I didn't love her; so I left it up there, its muscles full of pain, its fingertips full of needlepoints.

Suddenly, this romantic agony was enriched by a less romantic one: I had to go to the bathroom. Needless to say, I couldn't let her know about this urge, for great lovers never did such things. The

---

6. **gangrene** *n.*: tissue decay in a part of the body.

DEVELOPING FLUENCY

Activity. Have students re-read the dialogue between Bill and his goddess on this page and the next. Discuss what the characters reveal about themselves in these exchanges. Then, encourage pairs of students to read the dialogue aloud. Afterward, ask the class what additional qualities the readers brought out in the characters.

PAIRED

answer to "Romeo, Romeo, wherefore art thou, Romeo?"[7] was not "In the men's room, Julie."

What a prince of passion I was at this moment: My arm was dead, my bladder was full, and I was out of money too; but I desperately needed an excuse to move, so I said, "You want some popcorn?"

"No," she said.

"Fine, I'll go get some."

When I tried to move, every part of me could move except my arm: It was dead. I reached over and pulled it down with the other one, trying to be as casual as a man could be when pulling one of his arms with the other one.

"What's the matter?" she said.

"Oh, nothing," I replied. "I'm just taking both of my arms with me."

A few minutes later, as I came out of the bathroom, I was startled to meet her: She was coming from the bathroom *too*. How good it was to find another thing that we had in common. With empty bladders and full hearts, we returned to our seats to continue our love.

---

7. **"Romeo . . . Romeo?":** reference to a speech by Juliet in Act II of William Shakespeare's play *The Tragedy of Romeo and Juliet*. The line reads, "O Romeo, Romeo! Wherefore art thou Romeo?" Juliet is actually asking why his name is Romeo.

Meet the Writer

Bill Cosby

While attending college on a football scholarship, **Bill Cosby** (1937–   ) began working as a stand-up comedian for five dollars a night. He became famous for his funny, heartwarming stories about his boyhood in Philadelphia. Bill Cosby has said,

❝You can turn painful situations around through laughter. If you can find humor in anything—even poverty—you can survive it.❞

Cosby's television programs for children include the animated series *Fat Albert and the Cosby Kids*. He also developed programs for *Electric Company* and *Reading Rainbow*.

The Only Girl in the World for Me   **327**

Summary ⬇ *below grade level*

The speaker of this short poem expresses his affection to a girl through a series of metaphors. She is compared to a sunrise, a moonrise, and the spring. After each metaphor, the speaker presents particular circumstances under which each comparison is true. In closing, the speaker claims that he will continue to have feelings for the girl, provided that the purity of her eyes is also reflected in her heart.

DIRECT TEACHING

Ⓐ Literary Focus

❓ **Figurative language.** What connotations does the word *Spring* have? [Possible response: Spring is traditionally the season for courtship and romance.]

Ⓑ Literary Focus

❓ **Theme.** What do you think is the most important word in the poem? [Possible responses: "You"; "if"; "love."] Ask students to think of a theme statement that relates to the most important word. [Possible responses: People look to love for certainty in an ever-changing world; love is often accompanied by conditions that can affect the way lovers feel.]

To a Golden-Haired Girl in a Louisiana Town

Vachel Lindsay

You are a sunrise,
If a star should rise instead of the sun.
You are a moonrise,
If a star should come, in the place of the moon.
5 ⌈ You are the Spring,
Ⓐ If a face should bloom,
⌊ Instead of an apple-bough.
⌈ You are my love
Ⓑ If your heart is as kind
10 ⌊ As your young eyes now.

Girl In A Poppy Field (1891) by Dora Hitz.

DEVELOPING FLUENCY

After students finish the poem, direct them to Meet the Writer on the following page. Have them note Lindsay's unique manner of delivering his poems to the public.
Activity. Have students prepare a dramatic reading of Lindsay's poem. Encourage them to be expressive. Ask students to keep the following questions in mind as they prepare their readings: At which points will I speak softly? At which points will I speak loudly? Which parts will be spoken? Which parts will be sung? What gestures should accompany my reading?

INDIVIDUAL

Meet the Writer

Vachel Lindsay

Poet and Entertainer

Vachel Lindsay (1879–1931) was a modern-day troubador, or wandering poet. He crisscrossed the United States, mostly on foot, seeking audiences who would listen to his poems in exchange for food and lodging.

On his first such journey, Lindsay walked from Jacksonville, Florida, all the way back to Springfield, Illinois, where he had been born and raised. During his tramps, Lindsay not only recited his poems but also spoke out against racial prejudice and other forms of injustice.

Lindsay began a life-long practice of keeping notebooks and diaries as a boy of seven. He had little success getting his poems published until he was thirty-three, when "General William Booth Enters into Heaven," a poem about the founder of the Salvation Army, was published in the journal *Poetry*.

"General William Booth" was widely praised and brought Lindsay instant fame. He became a powerful reciter of this and his other highly rhythmic poems. Rocking on his feet and shaking his arms in the air, Lindsay shouted and sang his poems. His dramatic performances brought him a wide audience of people who had not previously been interested in poetry.

Lindsay sometimes used his fame to help other poets. While on a lecture

tour, he found three poems on his plate in a restaurant in Washington, D.C. Lindsay was so impressed by the poems that he presented them at a reading that night, helping to launch the career of the twenty-three-year-old busboy who had left them there: Langston Hughes (page 566).

For Independent Reading

You might enjoy reading some of Vachel Lindsay's poems on distinctively American subjects, such as "Abraham Lincoln Walks at Midnight," "The Ghosts of the Buffaloes," "The Flower-Fed Buffaloes," and "In Praise of Johnny Appleseed."

Meet the Writer

Vachel Lindsay's father was a doctor who fully expected his son to follow in his footsteps. When Lindsay was a young boy, his father even presented him with a human skeleton and instructed him to put the bones together. Lindsay never succeeded in assembling the skeleton and never developed an interest in medicine. Still, his parents insisted that he enroll in premedical studies in college. After struggling in the medical program for a few years, Lindsay dropped out. He attended art school before achieving recognition for his poetry.

For Independent Reading

If students choose to read Lindsay's poem "Abraham Lincoln Walks at Midnight," ask them to cite lines that explain why Abraham Lincoln is seen walking through Springfield once more.

Writing Workshop

Writing Workshop

Objectives

- Use appropriate prewriting and drafting skills to create a personal narrative.
- Revise the personal narrative by arranging events in a clear order, adding sensory details, and concluding with a statement explaining why the experience was important.
- Reflect on and assess one's writing process and personal narrative.

PRETEACHING

Skills Starter

Motivate. Ask students to share details about how they celebrated their last birthdays. Tell students that though there may be similarities in their experiences, each person has a unique story to tell. Explain that these true stories fall into the category of personal narrative because they are autobiographical in nature.

DIRECT TEACHING

PREWRITING

Choosing a Subject

To help students begin writing, encourage them to jot down ideas about an important event in their lives. Tell students that they can choose an event when they were very happy, very sad, very frightened, extremely embarrassed, or intensely challenged, for example. Have students freewrite for a few minutes about their experiences and refer to their notes when they begin their narratives.

Assignment

Write a narrative about an experience you've had.

Audience

Your teacher, classmates, friends, or family, or anyone who was involved in the event.

R U B R I C
Evaluation Criteria

A good personal narrative

1. focuses on one event
2. grabs the reader's attention
3. includes essential background information
4. relates events in a clear order
5. includes vivid descriptive details
6. may use dialogue to reveal character
7. shows what the incident means to the writer

SKILLS FOCUS

Writing Skills
Write a personal narrative.

NARRATIVE WRITING
Personal Narrative

When you write a personal narrative, you describe an event in your life that has special significance for you. Writing a personal narrative allows you to share that event with others and to take a closer look at yourself. Like a short story, a personal narrative includes a setting, a plot, a point of view, and characters. It may also contain dialogue.

Prewriting

1 Choosing a Subject

Consider the following **prompt:**

> There is one subject about which you are an expert—yourself. Your history is unique—your thoughts, feelings, and experiences belong only to you. Think about an important or memorable event in your life, one that has special meaning for you. Describe what happened, as well as your thoughts and feelings at that time. Explain why this experience is meaningful to you.

To find a subject for your narrative, try listing your favorite objects, places, and activities. Is there an incident involving one of these things that you might write

COLLECTION 3 RESOURCES: WRITING

Planning
- *One-Stop Planner* CD-ROM with ExamView Test Generator

Differentiating Instruction
- *Workshop Resources: Writing, Listening, and Speaking*
- *Supporting Instruction in Spanish*

Writing and Language
- *Workshop Resources: Writing, Listening, and Speaking*
- *Language Handbook Worksheets*
- *Daily Language Activities*

Assessment
- *Holt Assessment: Writing, Listening, and Speaking*
- *One-Stop Planner* CD-ROM with ExamView Test Generator

about? Do you have souvenirs, such as photos, ticket stubs, or letters, that remind you of special times in your life? Explore your ideas by freewriting.

Here are some subjects to consider:

- surprises • conflicts • vacations
- helping others • luck • secrets • sports
- losing a friend • the future • honesty

In choosing a subject to write about, ask yourself these questions:

- Does this incident mean something special to me?
- Do I remember this incident clearly?
- Am I comfortable sharing this incident with my audience?

2 Reflecting on the Importance of the Experience

State in a sentence or two why the experience is important. Such a statement often appears near the end of a personal narrative. For example, the writer of the student model (page 333) concludes his essay with this statement: "I knew right then while I was on the floor that I could never have that feeling again."

As you write your draft, look back at your statement to see if it fits your narrative. If it doesn't, you may need to rewrite your draft or your statement.

Drafting

1 Getting Ideas on Paper

Get the basics of your story down on paper as quickly as you can. Ask the *5W-How?* questions as you write: *Who* was involved in the incident? *What* happened? *When* did it happen? *Where* did it happen? *Why* did it happen? *How* did it happen?

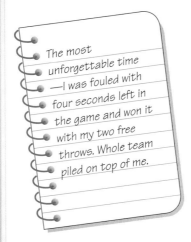

The most unforgettable time —I was fouled with four seconds left in the game and won it with my two free throws. Whole team piled on top of me.

Writing Tips

Methods of Organization
Writers generally use **chronological order** in a personal narrative. They tell about events in the order in which they happened. An alternative pattern of organization is **comparison and contrast.** For example, you might compare and contrast good and bad aspects of your experience.

Transitional Words and Phrases
To show the order of events clearly, use transitional words and phrases, such as *first, then, next, finally,* and *in the meantime.*

Personal Narrative **331**

- *Holt Online Assessment*
- *Holt Online Essay Scoring*

Internet
- go.hrw.com (Keyword: LE5 7-3)
- *Elements of Literature Online*

DRAFTING

Organizing Details

Remind students not to be too concerned with presenting an event *exactly* the way it unfolded—when we remember, we often forget precisely what occurred. Remind them that as long as chronological events and details are presented in a logical and orderly manner, the reader will be able to follow the stream of the narrative.

MODELING

Framework for a Personal Narrative

Help students having difficulty by filling in a sample framework on the chalkboard. For instance, you might use the following example:

What the experience means to me: I am most proud of playing my favorite song for the school talent show.

Introduction (*dialogue, question, statement, or description that grabs the reader's attention*): When I started learning to play the guitar, I never imagined that I would one day perform for a huge audience.

Body (*description of events in chronological order*):

1. My dad played the Beatles' song "Blackbird" when I was very young.

2. It became my favorite song. It took me years to learn to play it on the guitar.

3. I saw the flier for the school talent show and signed up.

4. I practiced the song for weeks. Finally, I played it perfectly for the whole school and won first prize.

Conclusion (*summary expressing the importance of the experience*): Winning the talent show gave me the confidence to pursue my dream of becoming a professional musician.

Framework for a Personal Narrative

What the experience means to me: _____

Introduction (*dialogue, question, statement, or description that grabs the reader's attention*):
_____
_____

Body (*description of events in chronological order*):
1. _____
2. _____
3. _____
4. _____

Conclusion (*summary expressing the importance of the experience*):
_____
_____

Language Handbook
H E L P
_____

To review rules for punctuating dialogue, see the Language Handbook, 14c–k.

---

2 Organizing Details

Organize your details chronologically by filling in a framework like the one shown to the left. Be sure to place events in the correct sequence.

3 Elaborating

Follow the strategies described below, as well as the ones listed on page 333, to come up with descriptive details.

• Replay the experience in your mind as if you were watching it on videotape. What did the people involved say to one another? How did they look? What did they do? Jot down the details.

• To jog your memory about the event and your thoughts and feelings at the time, try returning to the scene.

• Speak to others who were involved in the incident. What details do they remember?

4 Using Dialogue

If you use dialogue, be sure to make it sound the way people really talk. Although slang and sentence fragments are usually avoided in formal writing, it may be natural to use such language in your personal narrative. Here is a passage of dialogue from Borden Deal's "Antaeus" (page 177) that shows realistic use of language:

> T. J. kept looking at the tar under his feet. "You mean you ain't got no fields to raise nothing in?—no watermelons or nothing?"
>
> "Naw," I said scornfully. "What do you want to grow something for? The folks can buy everything they need at the store."

5 Keeping Point of View Consistent

Use first-person pronouns—*I, me, my, we*—in referring to yourself. Keep your point of view consistent throughout your narrative.

Learners Having Difficulty

Tell students having difficulty to begin writing an introduction for their narratives with one of these phrases:

• I never thought I could . . .
• If only I didn't . . .
• Who could have imagined that . . .
• My heart was racing because . . .

English-Language Learners

To help these students elaborate, write the headings *Sounds, Smells, Tastes, Actions,* and *Feelings* on the chalkboard. Have students put appropriate vocabulary words that they might use in their narratives under each heading. It may be helpful for English-language learners to think of vocabulary words in their native languages first and then use a bilingual dictionary to translate them into English.

Student Model

The Clutch Moment

Nine, eight, seven, six, five, four. I was fouled with four seconds left in the game. The fans roared out of their seats, cheering and howling. I couldn't believe it. My dream had come true. These two free throws would decide if we won, lost, or tied.

I stepped up to the free throw line with sweat dripping off my head into my eyes. Chills ran through my body, making my arms feel numb and loose. The only thing I could think of was making these two free throws. I blocked all the cheers out of my head and took a deep breath to relax. I turned the ball in my hands and took four dribbles. I looked at the goal and released the ball. Swish! The game was tied 49–49. The Jefferson Junior fans grew quiet and the Cubs were cheering loudly.

I stepped up to the free throw line for the last time that night. After dribbling again four times I raised my arms to shoot the ball.

It felt like a piece of flab as I released the ball, letting it fly through the air. I knew the ball was not going to miss. I had made the shot of my life to win the game 50–49. It was our ball out of bounds and I threw it in and the time ran out. The game was over! As soon as I raised my hands, I was tackled by Ben Meldrum and the rest of the team. Even the B-team joined in the fun and piled on me.

I knew right then while I was on the floor that I could never have that feeling again.

— Vinnie Merrill
Simonsen Junior High School
Jefferson City, Missouri

A suspenseful opener catches the reader's attention.

The writer supplies necessary background information.

Detailed description of the writer's actions, thoughts, and feelings enable the reader to imagine the scene.

Descriptive details make us feel as if we were there.

A brief conclusion explains why the incident was important.

Strategies for Elaboration

Help your readers see, hear, feel, smell, and even taste what you've experienced by including sensory details in your narrative. Completing these statements may help you remember details:

- I saw . . .
- I heard . . .
- I smelled . . .
- I tasted . . .
- I felt . . .

Photographs of the incident can also help.

- Who's in the picture?
- What expressions do you see on the people's faces?
- What is the year or the season?
- Do any significant objects appear in the photo?

INTERNET

More Writer's Models

Keyword: LE5 7-3

Using Dialogue

To help students write realistic dialogue, tell them to listen to conversations around them and then try to reflect in their narratives the unique way individuals speak. Remind them that they can differentiate among the various people in their narratives by using different vocabulary words or phrases and adding colloquialisms—and even slang.

Student Model

Encourage students to examine the model to see how one student writer catches the reader's attention, elaborates on the event with vivid details, and concludes by stating what the experience meant to him.

Strategies for Elaboration

Encourage students to *show* the reader their experiences through sensory details, rather than just tell the reader about the events. Tell students to jot down as many action details—details that tell what happened and what people did and said—as they recall. Remind students to include vivid details about specific movements, gestures, expressions, and dialogue to make their experiences come alive for the reader.

Special Education Students

To help special education students, suggest that they draw pictures depicting the experiences that they want to write about. Tell students to include specific people, places, and objects in their drawings and then refer to these details when they write their narratives.

Advanced Learners

Enrichment. Encourage advanced learners to experiment with writing brief "What If" versions of their narratives. Have students imagine what *might* have happened if the events they wrote about had a different ending. For example, instead of winning the big game with the final shot, the student misses and his team ends up losing.

DIRECT TEACHING

EVALUATING AND REVISING

Content and Organization Guidelines

Have students form pairs and read their narratives aloud to their partners. Encourage students to close their eyes as their partners read to them. Have students note where details seem vivid and also where they have trouble "seeing" what the writer is describing. Tell students to pay special attention to the events their partner describes in their narrative and to note when they do not understand what is happening. Listeners can then share their impressions with readers.

TECHNOLOGY TIP

Remind students to be careful not to include too much repetition when they use sensory details in their narratives. Suggest that students make use of the thesaurus tool (that is included with most word-processing software) to help them find synonyms for words they use often in their narratives.

Evaluating and Revising

Use the following chart to evaluate and revise your personal narrative.

Personal Narrative: Content and Organization Guidelines

Evaluation Questions	▶ Tips	▶ Revision Techniques
❶ Does your introduction grab the reader's attention and set the scene?	▶ Put stars next to interesting quotations or statements. Circle details that identify the setting.	▶ Add a catchy quotation or statement to the introduction. Add details to make the setting more vivid.
❷ Is the point of view consistent throughout your narrative?	▶ Draw a box around third-person pronouns, such as *they*, *she*, and *himself*. Make sure that these pronouns refer to others, not to yourself.	▶ Use first-person pronouns, such as *I*, *we*, and *my*, to refer to yourself.
❸ Have you arranged events in a clear order?	▶ Number the events as they appear in your paper. Compare this sequence with the actual order of events.	▶ Rearrange any events that are out of order. Add transitional words to link events.
❹ Have you included details that make people, places, and events come to life?	▶ Highlight details that appeal to the senses. In the margin, note which of the senses are involved.	▶ Elaborate with dialogue or sensory details. Delete any irrelevant details.
❺ Have you included your thoughts and feelings?	▶ Put a check mark next to statements of your feelings or thoughts.	▶ Add any other thoughts and feelings you have about what happened.
❻ Does your conclusion state why the experience is memorable?	▶ Underline your statement explaining the importance of the experience.	▶ Add a clear statement explaining why the experience was important.

A revised paragraph from a personal narrative appears on the next page. Read the paragraph; then, answer the questions that follow, which ask you to evaluate the writer's revision.

EVALUATION GUIDELINES

Use these guidelines to quickly assess students' final drafts:	4	3	2	1
	Introduction grabs the reader's attention and provides essential background information.	Introduction grabs the reader's attention and provides essential background information.	Introduction grabs the reader's attention but does not clearly present essential background information.	Introduction does not grab the reader's attention and does not clearly present essential background information.	Introduction does not grab the reader's attention, and essential background information is not provided.
	Point of view is consistent, and events are arranged in a clear order.	Point of view is consistent, and events are arranged in a clear order.	Point of view is consistent, but one or two events are out of order.	Point of view is inconsistent at times, and events are out of order.	Point of view is inconsistent, and events are irrelevant to the narrative.

Revision Model

I have always wanted a brother, and when I learned

that an exchange student from Japan would be living with

us during the summer, I called all my friends and bragged

about it.

suggested
"Maybe he knows judo or karate," my friend Mitch ~~said~~.

imagined
During the last weeks of June, I ~~saw~~ myself with a

black belt like those worn by masters in the martial arts.

I saw myself delivering sharp, quick blows with my hands

ones
and feet, just like the ~~movements~~ I had seen in the movies.

I looked forward to the day we would drive to the airport to

meet Toshiro. I realized that I had jumped to conclusions.

When I picked him out of the crowd of passengers, I

almost gasped in disappointment   *and muscular*
~~was disappointed~~. Instead of being a powerful athlete,

Toshiro was skinny, and he was carrying a violin case!

Evaluating the Revision

1. Where has the writer replaced weak verbs with more expressive verbs?
2. How has the writer rearranged the text to connect the details more clearly?
3. What other changes would you recommend?

PROOFREADING

TIPS

Proofread your work carefully. You might trade papers with a partner and proofread his or her narrative, marking errors in spelling, punctuation, and grammar. If you're working on a computer, use the grammar and spellcheckers. Note, however, that a spellchecker will not catch a word that is used incorrectly.

Communications Handbook
HELP

See Proofreaders' Marks.

PUBLISHING

TIPS

Assemble several personal narratives to create a scrapbook or album. Give your collection a title. Consider illustrating your narrative with photographs or drawings. Share your book with others in your class or your family.

Personal Narrative   **335**

DIRECT TEACHING

Revision Model

To help students grasp the concept of revising with more precise nouns, verbs, and modifiers, present the thought processes of a writer making the changes shown in the Revision Model. Calling students' attention to the end of the second paragraph, you might say, "The writer substitutes the more descriptive phrase 'almost gasped in disappointment' for the simple phrase 'was disappointed.'"

Proofreading Tips

Remind students that their narratives should have a consistent point of view. Tell them that they should use the proper first-person pronouns *I, me, my, we* for most of the narrative, since it is an autobiographical type of writing told from the writer's point of view.

GUIDED PRACTICE

Evaluating the Revision

1. The writer has replaced the weak verbs *said* and *saw* with the more expressive verbs *suggested* and *imagined*.
2. The writer concludes with the sentence that summarizes the lesson he learned from the experience.
3. Possible answer: The writer may want to elaborate on details about Toshiro or include more details about why the experience is memorable to him.

	4	3	2	1
Thoughts, feelings, and vivid descriptive details are included.	Thoughts, feelings, and vivid descriptive details are included.	Thoughts and feelings are included, but there are few descriptive details.	Thoughts and feelings are not included, and there are few descriptive details.	Thoughts, feelings, and descriptive details are not included.
Conclusion clearly states why the experience is memorable.	Conclusion clearly states why the experience is memorable.	Conclusion states why the experience is memorable.	Conclusion vaguely states why the experience is memorable.	There is no conclusion to the narrative.

Collection 3: Skills Review

Literary Skills

SKILLS FOCUS
pp. 336–339

Grade-Level Skills

■ Literary Skills
Analyze theme.

■ Literary Skills
Compare and contrast a story and a poem.

INTRODUCING THE SKILLS REVIEW

Use this review to assess students' grasp of the skills taught in this collection. If necessary, you can use the annotations to guide students in their reading before they answer the questions.

DIRECT TEACHING

Ⓐ Literary Focus

❓ **Recurring themes.** What theme does this opening paragraph suggest? [Possible responses: the importance of home and the love people feel for their homes; the desire people have to make the good times last forever.] **Name another book or story you have read that shares a similar theme.** [Possible responses: *The Wizard of Oz,* the *Little House on the Prairie* series, *The Hobbit.*]

Ⓑ Literary Focus

❓ **Plot.** What is the major problem that the characters face? [They may lose their home if Papa cannot extend the loan.] **Despite what Mama says, how can you tell that they are unlikely to move into a "nice flat"?** [Papa does not have the money to pay off his present loan, yet the flats cost more; flats are "burdens on wages twice the size of Papa's."]

Collection 3: Skills Review

Literary Skills

Test Practice

DIRECTIONS: Read the following story and poem. Then, answer each question that follows.

Home
from Maud Martha
Gwendolyn Brooks

Ⓐ **W**hat had been wanted was this always, this always to last, the talking softly on this porch, with the snake plant in the jardiniere in the southwest corner, and the obstinate slip from Aunt Eppie's magnificent Michigan fern at the left side of the friendly door. Mama, Maud Martha, and Helen rocked slowly in their rocking chairs, and looked at the late afternoon light on the lawn and at the emphatic iron of the fence and at the poplar tree. These things might soon be theirs no longer. Those shafts and pools of light, the tree, the graceful iron, might soon be viewed possessively by different eyes.

Ⓑ Papa was to have gone that noon, during his lunch hour, to the office of the Home Owners' Loan. If he had not succeeded in getting another extension, they would be leaving this house in which they had lived for more than fourteen years. There was little hope. The Home Owners' Loan was hard. They sat, making their plans.

"We'll be moving into a nice flat somewhere," said Mama. "Somewhere on South Park, or Michigan, or in

Washington Park Court." Those flats, as the girls and Mama knew well, were burdens on wages twice the size of Papa's. This was not mentioned now.

"They're much prettier than this old house," said Helen. "I have friends I'd just as soon not bring here. And I have other friends that wouldn't come down this far for anything, unless they were in a taxi."

Yesterday, Maud Martha would have attacked her. Tomorrow she might. Today she said nothing. She merely gazed at a little hopping robin in the tree, her tree, and tried to keep the fronts of her eyes dry.

"Well, I do know," said Mama, turning her hands over and over, "that I've been getting tireder and tireder of doing that firing. From October to April, there's firing to be done."

"But lately we've been helping, Harry and I," said Maud Martha. "And sometimes in March and April and in October, and even in November, we could build a little fire in the fireplace. Sometimes the weather was just right for that."

SKILLS FOCUS

Literary Skills
Analyze theme; compare and contrast a story and a poem.

MINI-LESSON **Reading**

Reviewing Word-Attack Skills
Activity. Display these words. Have students read each word and identify the sound that the letter *i* before another vowel spells or helps to spell.

1. radio [long e]
2. million [y]
3. familiar [y]
4. companion [y]
5. brilliant [y]
6. experience [long e]
7. believe [long e]
8. material [long e]
9. scientists [long i]
10. friends [short e]
11. immediate [long e]
12. senior [y]
13. petunia [y]
14. opinion [y]
15. helium [y]
16. curious [long e]
17. fortieth [long e]
18. genius [long e]
19. union [y]
20. medium [long e]

She knew, from the way they looked at her, that this had been a mistake. They did not want to cry.

But she felt that the little line of white, sometimes ridged with smoked purple, and all that cream-shot saffron would never drift across any western sky except that in back of this house. The rain would drum with as sweet a dullness nowhere but here. The birds on South Park were mechanical birds, no better than the poor caught canaries in those "rich" women's sun parlors.

"It's just going to kill Papa!" burst out Maud Martha. "He loves this house! He *lives* for this house!"

"He lives for us," said Helen. "It's us he loves. He wouldn't want the house, except for us."

"And he'll have us," added Mama, "wherever."

"You know," Helen said, "if you want to know the truth, this is a relief. If this hadn't come up, we would have gone on, just dragged on, hanging out here forever."

"It might," allowed Mama, "be an act of God. God may just have reached down and picked up the reins."

"Yes," Maud Martha cracked in, "that's what you always say—that God knows best."

Her mother looked at her quickly, decided the statement was not suspect, looked away.

Helen saw Papa's coming. "There's Papa," said Helen.

They could not tell a thing from the way Papa was walking. It was that same dear little staccato walk, one shoulder down, then the other, then repeat, and repeat. They watched his progress. He passed the Kennedys', he passed the vacant lot, he passed Mrs. Blakemore's. They wanted to hurl themselves over the fence, into the street, and shake the truth out of his collar. He opened his gate—the gate—and still his stride and face told them nothing.

"Hello," he said.

Mama got up and followed him through the front door. The girls knew better than to go in too.

Presently Mama's head emerged. Her eyes were lamps turned on.

"It's all right," she exclaimed. "He got it. It's all over. Everything is all right."

The door slammed shut. Mama's footsteps hurried away.

"I think," said Helen, rocking rapidly, "I think I'll give a party. I haven't given a party since I was eleven. I'd like some of my friends to just casually see that we're homeowners."

DIRECT TEACHING

C **Literary Focus**

? Characterization. What is Mama complaining about? [Mama is complaining that heating the house is too much work.] **How can you tell that, even so, she is fond of the house?** [Maud Martha says that she made a mistake mentioning a fire in the fireplace because this makes Mama and Helen look like they want to cry. Mama feels sad at the thought of losing the fireplace.]

D **Literary Focus**

? Recurring themes. What theme does this passage suggest? [Possible responses: "Home" is not the house you live in, but the people you are with. "Home" means "wherever the family is together."]

Activity. Display these sets of words. For each set, have students identify the lettered word in which the underlined letter or letters stand for the same sound as in the first word.

1. chord   a. ache   b. choose [a]
2. myth   a. bypass   b. system [b]
3. siphon   a. hyphen   b. haphazard [a]
4. period   a. furious   b. genius [a]
5. architect   a. archery   b. archive [b]
6. cycle   a. plywood   b. symbol [a]
7. radial   a. potential   b. medial [b]
8. graphic   a. sophomore   b. uphold [a]
9. echo   a. achieve   b. orchestra [b]
10. million   a. dandelion   b. onion [b]

Collection 3: Skills Review

DIRECT TEACHING

A Literary Focus

? Recurring themes. What main theme does this poem have in common with "Home"? [Possible responses: "Home" is not just the place where you live and sleep; "home" is where you feel safe and happy. "Home" is a place you love, whether you live there or not.]

Test Practice

Answers and Model Rationales

1. **A** Since the speaker of the poem does not refer to houses, porches, or robins, A is correct.
2. **J** The story states the opposite of F. Helen is concerned about having friends to the house, and Mama complains about work, but all three are upset about the possible loss of the house; J is the best answer.
3. **B** A metaphor is a direct comparison that says one thing is another thing.
4. **H** The poem does not mention a house (G) or a flat (J). The final line of the poem refers to "all this" as home. "All this" includes everything the speaker can see, not just the rock (F).
5. **D** A, B, and C are clearly wrong, as both the characters and the speaker feel happy at the end. Therefore, D is the correct answer.

Test Practice

The word *saguaro* (sə·gwär′ō), in line 8, refers to a huge cactus found in the southwestern United States and northern Mexico.

Gold
Pat Mora

When Sun paints the desert
with its gold,
I climb the hills.
Wind runs round boulders,
    ruffles
5 my hair. I sit on my favorite rock,
lizards for company, a rabbit,
ears stiff in the shade
of a saguaro.
In the wind, we're all
10 eye to eye.

Sparrow on saguaro watches
rabbit watch us in the gold
of sun setting.
Hawk sails on waves of light, sees
15 sparrow, rabbit, lizards, me,
our eyes shining,
watching red and purple sand
    rivers stream down the hill.

A I stretch my arms wide as the sky
like hawk extends her wings
20 in all the gold light of this, home.

1. Maud Martha in "Home" and the speaker of "Gold" share strong feelings about —
   A nature
   B houses
   C robins
   D porches

2. In "Home," Mama, Maud Martha, and Helen are upset because —
   F their house is more expensive than a flat
   G Mama has been working too hard
   H their friends won't come to see them
   J they may be losing their home

3. In "Home," Brooks writes that Mama's "eyes were lamps turned on." This is an example of —
   A a simile
   B a metaphor
   C a definition
   D rhyme

4. What place is home to the speaker of the poem?
   F A favorite rock
   G A house with a porch
   H The desert
   J A nice flat

5. At the end of the story and the poem, the characters and the speaker regard their homes with a feeling of —
   A disappointment
   B anger
   C worry
   D contentment

Using Academic Language

Literary Terms
As part of the review of theme, ask students to look back through the collection to find the meanings of the terms below. Then, have students demonstrate their grasp of theme by citing passages from a story in the collection that illustrate the meanings of the following terms:
Theme (pp. 246, 260, 289); **Topic** (p. 246); **Title** (p. 271); **Recurring Themes** (p. 289); **Comparing Themes** (p. 296).

6. In "Home," Brooks writes that Maud Martha "tried to keep the fronts of her eyes dry." This means that Maud Martha is —

    F near tears

    G cleaning her glasses

    H wet all over from the hose

    J having trouble with her vision

7. Mama says she is tired of doing "that firing." Based on clues in the story, what do you guess that firing means here?

    A Losing a job

    B Starting a fire

    C Cooking

    D Cleaning

8. Brooks describes Mama's eyes as "lamps turned on." Which words from "Gold" mean the same thing?

    F "our eyes shining"

    G "we're all / eye to eye"

    H "sails on waves of light"

    J "I stretch my arms"

9. The following words are in both selections. Which is the **key word** in both selections?

    A purple

    B light

    C sky

    D home

Constructed Response

10. Which statement *best* expresses the **theme** of both the story and the poem?

- Home is a place we associate with special feelings.
- Homelessness is a terrible problem.
- It's a relief to have a nice house of one's own.
- The out-of-doors makes the best kind of home.

Use examples from each to explain why you chose that statement.

6. **F** The meaning of the line reflects the emotion Maud Martha is feeling about the possible loss of her home. G, H, and J in no way reflect this.

7. **B** Clues in the story reveal that the "firing" is done in the winter months. C and D are tasks that are performed year round. A is not relevant to the selection.

8. **F** Eyes being compared to "lamps turned on" suggests eyes that are bright and shiny. Although answers F and G mention eyes, only F accurately reflects the meaning of the phrase. H mentions light, but not in relation to anyone's eyes, and J doesn't make sense in this respect.

9. **D** Because "home" is not simply a structure but a place that evokes great feelings, it is the most significant word in both selections. The other answers are not nearly as significant.

Constructed Response

10. The theme of both the story and the poem is best summed up in the statement *Home is a place we associate with special feelings.* In "Home," Maud Martha and her family are upset that they may be forced out of their home because the times they've shared there have made them feel affection toward it. The speaker in "Gold" feels happy in the desert among the animals.

Test-Taking Tips

Emphasize that students are to select the best option for each multiple-choice question. Point out that a choice that is partly correct or that applies in some cases but not all is not the best option.

   For more instruction on how to answer multiple-choice items, refer students to **Test Smarts,** p. 920.

Collection 3: Skills Review

Informational Reading Skills

SKILLS FOCUS
pp. 340–341

Grade-Level Skills

■ **Reading Skills**
Analyze texts that show cause-and-effect realtionships.

INTRODUCING THE SKILLS REVIEW

Use this review to test students' grasp of cause-and-effect relationships. Use these annotations only if you want to conduct this review orally.

DIRECT TEACHING

Ⓐ Reading Informational Text

❷ Analyze cause and effect.
Why were mongooses brought to Jamaica? What were the initial effects of that action? [*Cause*—Mongooses were imported to kill rats. *Effects*—Mongooses were effective in getting rid of rats; mongooses were bred and sent to other islands.]

Ⓑ Reading Informational Text

❷ Analyze cause and effect.
What caused the mongoose population to sharply increase in the Caribbean? What effects did this increase have? [*Cause*—The mongoose had no natural predators in the Caribbean islands. *Effects*—Mongooses killed livestock and pets, threatened to make endangered species extinct, and spread rabies.]

Test Practice

DIRECTIONS: Read the following article. Then, answer each question that follows.

Mongoose on the Loose
Larry Luxner

Ⓐ In 1872, a Jamaican sugar planter imported nine furry little mongooses from India to eat the rats that were devouring his crops. They did such a good job, the planter started breeding his exotic animals and selling them to eager farmers on neighboring islands.

Ⓑ With no natural predators—like wolves, coyotes, or poisonous snakes—the mongoose population exploded, and within a few years, they were killing not just rats but pigs, lambs, chickens, puppies, and kittens. Dr. G. Roy Horst, a U.S. expert on mongooses, says that today mongooses live on seventeen Caribbean islands as well as Hawaii and Fiji, where they have attacked small animals, threatened endangered species, and have even spread minor rabies epidemics.

In Puerto Rico there are from 800,000 to one million of them. That is about one mongoose for every four humans. In St. Croix, there are 100,000 mongooses, about twice as many as the human population. "It's impossible to eliminate the mongoose population, short of nuclear war," says Horst. "You can't poison them, because cats, dogs, and chickens get poisoned, too. I'm not a prophet crying in the wilderness, but the potential for real trouble is there," says Horst.

According to Horst, great efforts have been made to rid the islands of mongooses, which have killed off a number of species, including the Amevia lizard on St. Croix, presumed extinct for several decades. On Hawaii, the combination of mongooses and sports hunting has reduced the Hawaiian goose, or nene, to less than two dozen individuals. . . .

Horst says his research will provide local and federal health officials with extremely valuable information if they ever decide to launch a campaign against rabies in Puerto Rico or the U.S. Virgin Islands.

SKILLS FOCUS

Reading Skills
Analyze cause and effect.

340 Collection 3 / Living in the Heart

DIFFERENTIATING INSTRUCTION

Advanced Learners
Enrichment. Based on what they have learned about the mongoose in this article and in the story "Rikki-tikki-tavi" (p. 15) students may enjoy inventing a plan for a campaign to control the mongooses on the Caribbean islands.
Activity. Have students read or re-read both the article and "Rikki-tikki-tavi," and

do additional research on the mongoose. Then have them meet in a small group and brainstorm ideas for a campaign. Students might present their plan as a possible chain of causes and effects. Invite them to share their ideas with the class.

Collection 3: Skills Review

1. The following diagram displays information about the **causes and effects** of bringing mongooses to Jamaica.

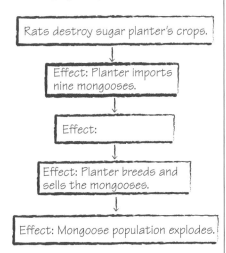

Rats destroy sugar planter's crops.

↓

Effect: Planter imports nine mongooses.

↓

Effect:

↓

Effect: Planter breeds and sells the mongooses.

↓

Effect: Mongoose population explodes.

Which of these events belongs in the third box?

A Mongooses do a good job getting rid of rats.

B Mongooses threaten the Hawaiian goose.

C Mongooses destroy other species.

D Mongooses are difficult to study.

2. In 1872, a Jamaican sugar planter imported nine mongooses to —

F keep snakes away from his farm

G serve as pets for his young children

H eat the rats that were ruining his crops

J breed them for their fur

3. Because the mongooses didn't have any natural predators in that part of the world, their population —

A diminished

B exploded

C fluctuated

D declined

4. You would be *most* likely to find this information about mongooses in a —

F chemistry book

G collection of stories

H travel guide

J magazine on nature

Constructed Response

5. List the **effects** of the mongoose population explosion.

Using Academic Language

Informational Terms

As part of the review of cause and effect, ask students to look back through the collection to find the meanings of the terms and phrases below and to explain cause and effect using these words.

Cause and Effect (pp. 256, 284); **Cause-and-Effect Chain** (p. 284); **Transitions** (p. 284)

Collection 3: Skills Review

Vocabulary Skills

Context Clues

Modeling. Model the thought process of a good reader getting the answer to item 1 by saying: "The juggling act is exciting and the audience is young. I know that the children like the juggling since they are cheering, so *immensely* must mean 'very' or 'hugely.' *Enormously* is a synonym for *hugely,* so C must be the answer."

Test Practice

Answers and Model Rationales

1. **C** See rationale above.

2. **G** A problem that would need hours to solve would be very difficult. Before one could say (F) or measure (J) the solution, one would have to understand (G) the solution.

3. **A** B and C would not hurt anyone's feelings. Forceful comments (D) might annoy someone, but would not necessarily hurt that person's feelings.

4. **H** The words *effort* and *but* suggest that the team tried hard. F and J would suggest that the team didn't try hard and G that they won the game.

5. **D** A favorite meal would make someone feel better. When you feel better, your unhappiness has been reduced.

6. **H** Andy has won often, so he must make the opposing hitters look bad. G means the opposite, and J makes no sense. H is a better choice than F because anemia is a disease that weakens people.

7. **A** Since Brian can't concentrate, he must be troubled.

8. **G** *Sophisticated* must be an antonym or near-antonym of *silly.* Only G comes close to this.

Collection 3: Skills Review

Vocabulary Skills

Test Practice

This Test Practice reviews Vocabulary words you have studied in earlier collections.

Context Clues

DIRECTIONS: Use **context clues** to help you figure out what the underlined words mean. Then, choose the best answer.

1. The exciting juggling act proved to be immensely popular with the young, cheering audience.
   A simply
   B frighteningly
   C enormously
   D immediately

2. Even after hours of careful thought, he still couldn't fathom the solution.
   F say
   G understand
   H hear
   J measure

3. Mary's comments weren't meant to be derisive, but they still hurt my feelings.
   A scornful
   B playful
   C pleasant
   D forceful

4. Our basketball team put in a valiant effort, but it still lost the game.
   F halfhearted
   G overpowering
   H determined
   J adequate

5. Jamal hoped to alleviate his grandmother's unhappiness by cooking her favorite meal.
   A exaggerate
   B ignore
   C notice
   D reduce

6. Andy, a nineteen-game winner, made the opposition's hitters look anemic.
   F lazy
   G challenging
   H weak
   J hungry

7. Brian was so perturbed by his best friend's rude behavior that he couldn't concentrate on his homework.
   A troubled
   B unfazed
   C overjoyed
   D strengthened

8. Mannie wanted to appear sophisticated, but his thin tie and top hat just made him look silly.
   F enthusiastic
   G refined
   H tired
   J unemployed

SKILLS FOCUS

Vocabulary Skills
Use context clues.

Vocabulary Review

This activity can help you see if students have retained the Vocabulary words taught in this collection.

Activity. Have students select the correct word from the box to complete the following sentences.

parched	unrequited	detain
vainly		

1. The police attempted to _____ the suspect. [detain]

2. They _____ searched the premises and found no evidence. [vainly]

3. The candidates spoke so forcefully that their throats became dry and _____. [parched]

4. The young boy's love for the movie star was _____. [unrequited]

Collection 3: Skills Review

Writing Skills

Test Practice

DIRECTIONS: Read the following paragraph from a personal narrative. Then, answer each question that follows.

(1) The day I had been dreading for months finally arrived. (2) It was a wet, cold February morning when I saw the moving vans pull up to our driveway. (3) We were leaving the only home I had ever known, the place where I had built a lifetime of memories. (4) The movers were wearing slickers to keep the rain off. (5) I heard my mother giving instructions to the movers, anxiously telling them to be careful with the baby's crib. (6) As I made a tour of the place, the rooms appeared vacant. (7) All the pictures and curtains had been taken down; the furniture was covered with sheets; the books and breakable objects had been packed away. (8) I knew that I would make new friends and have fun in the years ahead, but nothing would replace my special memories of my first home.

1. What could the writer add to further develop this personal narrative?
   - A The effect of the move on other members of the family
   - B A description of some of the narrator's special memories
   - C Treasured objects broken during the move
   - D The reactions of the neighbors

2. Which of the following sentences is unnecessary and should be deleted?
   - F sentence 3
   - G sentence 4
   - H sentence 7
   - J sentence 8

3. If the narrator were to add dialogue, it would probably come after —
   - A sentence 5
   - B sentence 6
   - C sentence 7
   - D sentence 8

4. Which of the following sentences is the best replacement for sentence 6?
   - F As I entered each room, I found it empty.
   - G As I revisited the rooms, the floorboards creaked.
   - H As I moved around the empty house, I was grief-stricken.
   - J As I walked through the rooms, the house seemed to have lost its life.

5. The **tone** of this story is —
   - A cheerful
   - B reflective and sad
   - C sullen and gloomy
   - D angry and resentful

SKILLS FOCUS

Writing Skills
Analyze a personal narrative.

Skills Review   **343**

Test Practice

Answers and Model Rationales

1. **B** A and D explain the reactions of other people, not the narrator. C, including descriptions of breakable objects might be a descriptive detail to include, but B is the best choice because it explains why this event is important to the narrator.

2. **G** F, H, and J are all sentences crucial to the narrative. G is correct because sentence 4 is an unnecessary detail about what the movers were wearing.

3. **A** Sentence 5 (A) is the best place to insert dialogue because that sentence describes the writer hearing his mother giving anxious instructions to the movers.

4. **J** F is incorrect because it offers no more details than sentence 6 does. G includes an insignificant detail. H explains the narrator's feelings but not the reason for them. J is the best replacement for sentence 6 because it contains a vivid metaphor.

5. **B** The tone of the story is obviously not "cheerful" (A), but it is not quite "sullen and gloomy" (C). There is no hint of the writer being "angry and resentful" (D). B, "reflective and sad," is the best choice to describe the tone of the narrative.

APPLICATION

For homework, have students interview friends or family members who were involved with the events in their personal narratives. Tell students that they can compile quotes, have the interviewees write down reflective paragraphs, and gather photographs of or documents from the event. Students can then present their essays and any accompanying material they've collected.

EXTENSION

Tell students to collect personal narratives written by several people who experienced the same event but have different perspectives on it—for example, survivors of the Holocaust or the bombing of Hiroshima. Tell students to compile these narratives together in a notebook or a computer file and then write down their impressions about these people's stories.

READ ON

For Independent Reading

If students enjoyed the themes and topics explored in this collection, you might recommend these titles for independent reading.

Assessment Options

The following projects can help you evaluate and assess your students' outside reading. Video-tapes or audiotapes of completed projects may be included in students' portfolios.

■ **Design a movie poster.** Have pairs of students work together on a poster for a movie version of *Where the Red Fern Grows.* Remind them that the image on a movie poster should show a central event of the plot or a main theme of the story, without giving away the ending. A poster might show Little Ann nearly drowning, or both dogs fighting the mountain lion, but should not reveal that the two dogs die. Students' posters can be done in any media they like—paints, colored pencils, markers, or even photography or collage. Partners can divide up the tasks however they wish. Display students' completed posters in class.

Fiction

Fast Breaks

Jerome "the Jayfox" is a gifted basketball player and the first African American to attend his North Carolina high school. In *The Moves Make the Man* by Bruce Brooks, Jerome develops an intense friendship with a white teammate, and together they struggle to understand the meaning of truth.

Three's Company

In Wilson Rawls's *Where the Red Fern Grows,* which is set in the Ozark Mountains, Billy Colman works tirelessly through two years of the Great Depression to save money to purchase Old Dan and Little Ann, two hunting dogs. Billy trains the dogs to become the finest raccoon-hunting team in the valley. However, Billy experiences sadness along with his glory. **This title is available in the HRW Library.**

Pen Pals

If you enjoy writing, you may like *Letters to Julia* by Barbara Ware Holmes. Fifteen-year-old Liz Beech dreams of becoming a writer when she begins corresponding with Julia Steward Jones, an editor in New York City. Julia is impressed with Liz's writing ability, and the two become good friends. But when they have a misunderstanding, their relationship becomes strained.

Friends in Need

Mina is not sure if she was kicked out of dance camp because of her rapid growth or because she was the only African American in the class. In the midst of her confusion, she meets Tamer Shipp, a minister who becomes her confidant. Mina and Tamer support each other during traumatic times in Cynthia Voigt's *Come a Stranger.*

344   Collection 3 / Living in the Heart

DIFFERENTIATING INSTRUCTION

Estimated Word Counts of Read On Books:

Fiction		Nonfiction	
The Moves Make the Man	81,000	*Living History:*	
Where the Red Fern Grows	80,000	*Fourteenth-Century Towns*	12,000
Connections to *Where the*		*The New Way Things Work*	93,000
Red Fern Grows	23,000	*Arms and Armor*	16,000
Letters to Julia	47,000	*Montezuma and the Aztecs*	80,000
Come a Stranger	76,000		

Nonfiction

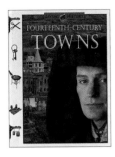

Days of Yore

Have you ever wondered what life was like before malls or television? How did people spend their time? Did they have any fun? John D. Clare brings the past vividly to life in *Living History: Fourteenth-Century Towns*. The book features informative text and photographs reenacting fascinating rituals from the Middle Ages.

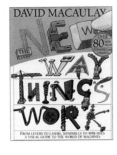

No Myth

Today we don't rely on origin myths to explain how the world operates; scientists provide us with most of the answers. In *The New Way Things Work*, David Macaulay presents "origin myths" of natural phenomena, like the acts of floating and flying. He also tells the stories behind such technological innovations as modems, burglar alarms, and helicopters. The illustrations will guide you through the explanations.

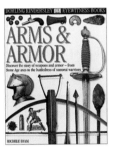

Tools of War

When you look at weaponry from the past, you realize that it can provide valuable insight into the mind-set of a culture. Prehistoric people primarily used stones to hunt. Japanese weapons were highly decorative, to represent the strength of the samurai class. In *Arms and Armor*, Michele Byam looks at weapons from the Stone Age to the Old West.

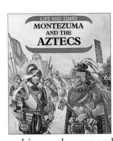

Remembering Montezuma

In 1519, Montezuma was the mighty ruler of the Aztecs. He thought he had nothing to fear. One year later he and his people were ambushed and overcome by a troop of Spanish soldiers led by the cunning Hernán Cortés. In *Montezuma and the Aztecs*, Nathaniel Harris looks at Aztec traditions and discusses Montezuma's leadership of the Aztec Empire before it fell to the Spaniards.

Assessment Options

- **Deliver a valedictory speech.** Have students imagine that Mina from *Come a Stranger* is giving a valedictory speech at her high school graduation. In this speech, she mentions the adults who have influenced her in the course of her life—parents, teachers, and Reverend Shipp. The speech describes the influence each adult has had on Mina and what she has learned from him or her. Students can write this speech and then deliver it to the class. Remind them to use the formal diction appropriate for a graduation ceremony.

- **Stage a leadership debate.** Have students who read *Montezuma and the Aztecs* gather in a small group to debate who was the better and more effective leader, Cortés or Montezuma. Students should use specific examples from the book to support their opinions. A few days in advance of the debate, you may want to organize them into two teams, one team in favor of each leader. Team members can do some further reading on both men, gathering additional evidence to support their side of the argument. Questions students should consider include: What qualities make a good leader? Which leader treated his own people better? Students can stage the debate in class and answer questions from classmates afterwards.

The Read On titles are categorized as shown below:

Collection 4
Point of View: Can You See It My Way?

Literary Focus:
Analyzing Point of View

Informational Focus:
Analyzing an Author's Argument

About Collection 4

In Collection 4, students will master the following skills:

- **Literary Skills:** Analyze first-person, omniscient, objective, and subjective points of view; an autobiography; and a biography.
- **Reading Skills:** Analyze an author's purpose, perspective, and argument; make predictions; find the main idea; distinguish fact from opinion; use the SQ3R system for studying informational texts.
- **Vocabulary Skills:** Clarify word meanings by using definitions and contrast; identify synonyms.
- **Writing Skills:** Develop, write, and revise a descriptive essay.

Informational Text

Each collection of *Elements of Literature* provides a variety of informational texts related to the literature selections by theme or topic.

Minimum Course of Study

Most skills can be taught with a minimum number of selections and features. In the chart to the right, lessons highlighted in green constitute the minimum course of study that provides coverage of the skills taught in Collection 4.

Selection ▪ Feature	Literary Skills
Elements of Literature: Point of View *by* John Leggett	• Understand point of view
Reading Skills and Strategies: Analyzing an Author's Perspective **Canines to the Rescue** *by* Jonah Goldberg ↔ *at grade level*	
After Twenty Years *by* O. Henry ↑ *above grade level* **Informational Text:** **What's *Really* in a Name?** *by* Joan Burditt ↔ *at grade level*	• Analyze point of view
Bargain *by* A. B. Guthrie ↑ *above grade level*	• Analyze first-person point of view
Yeh-Shen *retold by* Ai-Ling Louie ↔ *at grade level* **Informational Text:** **Mirror, Mirror, on the Wall, Do I See Myself As Others Do?** *by* Joan Burditt ↓ *below grade level*	• Understand omniscient point of view
Names / Nombres *by* Julia Alvarez ↔ *at grade level*	• Analyze objective and subjective points of view
An Unforgettable Journey *by* Maijue Xiong ↔ *at grade level* **Informational Text:** **Exile Eyes** *from* National Public Radio, Morning Edition *by* Agate Nesaule ↔ *at grade level*	• Analyze an autobiography

Resource Manager
(pp. 346E–346H)
Lesson and workshop resources are referenced in the Resource Manager on the pages that follow. These resources can be used to reinforce the skills taught in Collection 4, remediate students who are having difficulty, and provide supporting activities for English-language learners.

Reading Skills	Vocabulary Skills	Writing ■ Grammar and Language Skills
• Analyze an author's perspective		
• Make predictions • Analyze an author's perspective	• Clarify word meanings	• Describe events from another point of view • Use end marks correctly
• Make predictions	• Use comprehension strategies	• Write persuasive arguments
• Analyze an author's argument		• Write a story
• Find the main idea	• Clarify word meanings by using definitions	• Write an essay • Avoid dangling modifiers
• Distinguish fact from opinion • Analyze an author's purpose and perspective	• Clarify word meanings by using contrast	• Write up an interview

(continued)

Selection ▪ Feature	Literary Skills	Reading Skills
Elizabeth I *by* Milton Meltzer ↔ *at grade level*	• Analyze a biography • Analyze objective and subjective points of view	• Use the SQ3R system for studying informational texts
Comparing Literature: Mood and Theme **The Last Dinosaur** *by* Jim Murphy ↓ *below grade level* **Buffalo Dusk** *by* Carl Sandburg ↔ *at grade level* **I Was Sleeping Where the Black Oaks Move** *by* Louise Erdrich ↑ *above grade level*	• Analyze mood and theme	• Compare and contrast texts
No Questions Asked: **The Naming of Names** *by* Ray Bradbury ↑ *above grade level*		
Writing Workshop: *Descriptive Writing: Descriptive Essay*		
Skills Review: *Literary Skills* *Informational Reading Skills* *Vocabulary Skills* *Writing Skills*	• Analyze point of view	• Analyze an author's argument

Reading Skills and Strategies

At the beginning of each collection, a **Reading Skills and Strategies** feature written by Kylene Beers offers students strategies to improve their reading skills. Dr. Beers first models the strategy for the students, then guides them through an annotated selection. The questions in her annotations help students apply the strategy to the selection. After the selection, **Practice the Strategy** provides additional tips and practice.

Comparing Literature / Author Study

Each collection has a **Comparing Literature** or **Author Study** feature that focuses on two or more selections that are thematically or topically linked. The selections represent a variety of genres. The features begin with a prereading page that introduces a Literary Focus and a Reading Skill as well as additional information that students may find useful. Each **Comparing Literature** or **Author Study** feature ends with instruction in writing a comparison-contrast essay about the selections they've read or provides a variety of writing, speaking and listening, or other assignments.

Vocabulary Skills	Writing ▪ Grammar and Language Skills
• Clarify word meanings by using definitions	• Write a biographical sketch
	• Research a topic
	• Write a descriptive essay
• Identify synonyms	• Analyze a descriptive essay

No Questions Asked

Each collection ends with a **No Questions Asked** feature that includes one or more selections without accompanying apparatus. These selections allow students to practice reading independently. Annotations for teaching the selections are provided in the **Annotated Teacher's Edition.**

Resource Manager

Selection ■ Feature	Planning	Differentiating Instruction Lesson Plans with ELL Strategies and Practice	Reading Vocabulary
Elements of Literature: Point of View *by John Leggett*	• PowerNotes: Point of View	• Holt Reading Solutions: Lesson Plans, pp. 131–132	• Holt Reading Solutions, pp. 131–132
Reading Skills and Strategies: Analyzing an Author's Perspective Canines to the Rescue *by Jonah Goldberg*			
After Twenty Years *by O. Henry* **Informational Text: What's *Really* in a Name?** *by Joan Burditt*	• One-Stop Planner with ExamView Test Generator	• The Holt Reader, pp. 120–128 • Holt Adapted Reader, pp. 90–99 • Holt Reading Solutions: Lesson Plans, pp. 133–140 • Supporting Instruction in Spanish, p. 13 • Audio CD Library • Audio CD Library, Selections and Summaries in Spanish	• The Holt Reader, pp. 120–128 • Holt Adapted Reader, pp. 90–99 • Holt Reading Solutions, pp. 133–140 • Vocabulary Development, pp. 13–14 • PowerNotes: Making Predictions
Bargain *by A. B. Guthrie*	• One-Stop Planner with ExamView Test Generator	• Holt Adapted Reader, pp. 100–107 • Holt Reading Solutions: Lesson Plans, pp. 141–146 • Supporting Instruction in Spanish, p. 14 • Audio CD Library • Audio CD Library, Selections and Summaries in Spanish	• Holt Adapted Reader, pp. 100–107 • Holt Reading Solutions, pp. 141–146 • PowerNotes: Making Predictions
Yeh-Shen *retold by Ai-Ling Louie* **Informational Text: Mirror, Mirror, on the Wall, Do I See Myself As Others Do?** *by Joan Burditt*	• One-Stop Planner with ExamView Test Generator	• Holt Adapted Reader, pp. 108–113 • Holt Reading Solutions: Lesson Plans, pp. 147–154 • Supporting Instruction in Spanish, pp. 14, 15 • Audio CD Library • Audio CD Library, Selections and Summaries in Spanish	• Holt Adapted Reader, pp. 108–113 • Holt Reading Solutions, pp. 147–154
Names / Nombres *by Julia Alvarez*	• One-Stop Planner with ExamView Test Generator	• The Holt Reader, pp. 129–138 • Holt Adapted Reader, pp. 114–121 • Holt Reading Solutions: Lesson Plans, pp. 155–160 • Supporting Instruction in Spanish, p. 15 • Audio CD Library • Audio CD Library, Selections and Summaries in Spanish	• The Holt Reader, pp. 129–138 • Holt Adapted Reader, pp. 114–121 • Holt Reading Solutions, pp. 155–160 • Vocabulary Development, p. 15
An Unforgettable Journey *by Maijue Xiong* **Informational Text: Exile Eyes** *from National Public Radio, Morning Edition* *by Agate Nesaule*	• One-Stop Planner with ExamView Test Generator	• Holt Reading Solutions: Lesson Plans, pp. 161–165 • Supporting Instruction in Spanish, p. 16 • Audio CD Library • Audio CD Library, Selections and Summaries in Spanish	• Holt Reading Solutions, pp. 161–165 • Vocabulary Development, p. 16 • PowerNotes: Reading Purposes

Writing · Grammar and Language	Assessment
• Daily Language Activities • Language Handbook Worksheets, p. 125	• Holt Assessment: Literature, Reading, and Vocabulary • One-Stop Planner with ExamView Test Generator • Holt Online Assessment
• Daily Language Activities	• Holt Assessment: Literature, Reading, and Vocabulary • One-Stop Planner with ExamView Test Generator • Holt Online Assessment
• Daily Language Activities	• Holt Assessment: Literature, Reading, and Vocabulary • One-Stop Planner with ExamView Test Generator • Holt Online Assessment
• Daily Language Activities • Language Handbook Worksheets, pp. 51–54	• Holt Assessment: Literature, Reading, and Vocabulary • One-Stop Planner with ExamView Test Generator • Holt Online Assessment
	• Holt Assessment: Literature, Reading, and Vocabulary • One-Stop Planner with ExamView Test Generator • Holt Online Assessment

Technology

INTERNET

- go.hrw.com
- Holt Online Assessment
- Holt Online Essay Scoring
- Elements of Literature Online

MEDIA

- One-Stop Planner with ExamView Test Generator
- PowerNotes
- Audio CD Library
- Audio CD Library, Selections and Summaries in Spanish
- Visual Connections Videocassette Program, Segment 4
- Fine Art Transparencies, 5 and 6

 Transparency   Video

 CD-ROM   Audio CD

(continued)

Selection ▪ Feature	Planning	Differentiating Instruction ▪ Lesson Plans with ELL Strategies and Practice	Reading ▪ Vocabulary
Elizabeth I *by* Milton Meltzer	• One-Stop Planner with ExamView Test Generator	• Holt Reading Solutions: Lesson Plans, pp. 169–172 • Supporting Instruction in Spanish, p. 16 • Audio CD Library • Audio CD Library, Selections and Summaries in Spanish	• Holt Reading Solutions, pp. 169–172 • Vocabulary Development, p. 17
Comparing Literature: Mood and Theme **The Last Dinosaur** *by* Jim Murphy **Buffalo Dusk** *by* Carl Sandburg **I Was Sleeping Where the Black Oaks Move** *by* Louise Erdrich		• Holt Reading Solutions: Lesson Plans, pp. 173–176	• Holt Reading Solutions, pp. 173–176
No Questions Asked: **The Naming of Names** *by* Ray Bradbury			
Writing Workshop: *Descriptive Writing:* *Descriptive Essay*	• One-Stop Planner with ExamView Test Generator	• Workshop Resources: Writing, Listening, and Speaking, pp. 34–44 • Supporting Instruction in Spanish, p. 40	
Skills Review: *Literary Skills* *Informational Reading Skills* *Vocabulary Skills* *Writing Skills*			

The Holt Reader

The Holt Reader is a consumable paperback book that can be used alone or to accompany *Elements of Literature*. It offers guided support throughout the reading process and encourages students to become active readers by circling, underlining, questioning, and jotting down responses as they read. *The Holt Reader* works well for homework, students who have missed class, additional instructional time, reteaching, and remediation.

Holt Reading Solutions (HRS)

Holt Reading Solutions pulls together reading resources in the *Elements of Literature* program to create a powerful tool for intervention and whole-class instruction. *HRS* includes diagnostic assessment tools, lesson plans for English-language learners and special education students, adaptations of selected reading selections, vocabulary and comprehension worksheets, information on phonics and decoding, and additional instruction and practice in remedial reading skills.

Writing ■ Grammar and Language	Assessment
	• Holt Assessment: Literature, Reading, and Vocabulary • One-Stop Planner with ExamView Test Generator • Holt Online Assessment
• Workshop Resources: Writing, Listening, and Speaking, pp. 34–44 • Language Handbook Worksheets • Daily Language Activities	• Holt Assessment: Literature, Reading, and Vocabulary • One-Stop Planner with ExamView Test Generator • Holt Online Assessment • Holt Online Essay Scoring
	• Holt Assessment: Literature, Reading, and Vocabulary • One-Stop Planner with ExamView Test Generator • Holt Online Assessment

Technology

INTERNET

- go.hrw.com
- Holt Online Assessment
- Holt Online Essay Scoring
- Elements of Literature Online

MEDIA

 • One-Stop Planner with ExamView Test Generator

 • PowerNotes

 • Audio CD Library

 • Audio CD Library, Selections and Summaries in Spanish

 • Visual Connections Videocassette Program, Segment 4

• Fine Art Transparencies, 5 and 6

 Transparency   Video

 CD-ROM   Audio CD

One-Stop Planner with ExamView Test Generator

The *One-Stop Planner* CD-ROM planning software contains print-based teaching resources, clips from the video program, and valuable assessment tools. The *One-Stop Planner* resources are presented in easy-to-follow, point-and-click menu formats. To preview resources or print out worksheets and tests, you simply make a selection and click.

One-Stop Planner CD-ROM

Collection 4

SKILLS FOCUS

Grade-Level Skills

■ **Literary Skills**
Analyze different points of view, and explain how they affect the overall theme of the work.

■ **Reading Skills**
Analyze an author's argument, purpose, and perspective.

■ **Vocabulary Skills**
Clarify word meanings through the use of definition, example, restatement, and contrast.

Review Skills

■ **Literary Skills**
Identify the speaker, and recognize the difference between first- and third-person narration.

■ **Reading Skills**
Assess the evidence for an author's conclusions.

Upcoming Skills

■ **Literary Skills**
Analyze how a literary work reflects the attitudes and beliefs of its author.

■ **Literary Skills**
Analyze how voice, tone, persona, and choice of narrator affect characterization and plot.

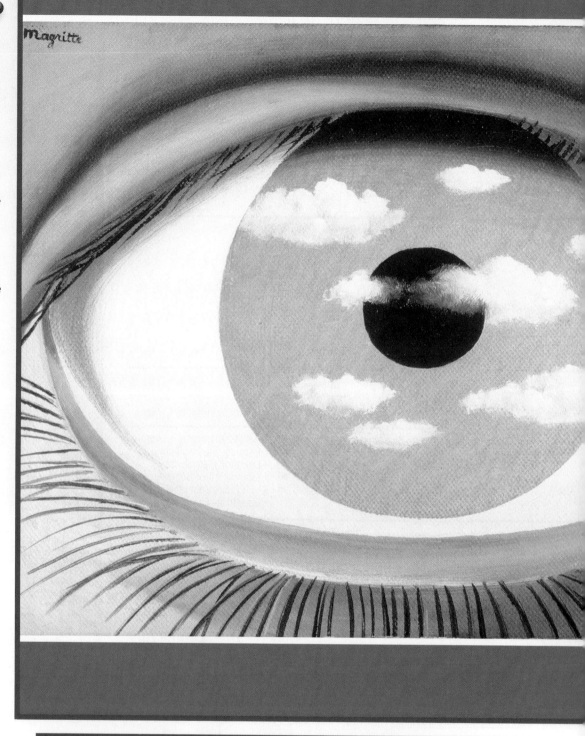

COLLECTION 4 RESOURCES: READING

Planning
■ *One-Stop Planner* CD-ROM with ExamView Test Generator

Differentiating Instruction
■ *The Holt Reader*
■ *Holt Adapted Reader*
■ *Holt Reading Solutions*
■ *Family Involvement Activities in English and Spanish*

■ *Supporting Instruction in Spanish*
■ *Audio CD Library*
■ *Audio CD Library, Selections and Summaries in Spanish*

Vocabulary
■ *Vocabulary Development*

Grammar and Language
■ *Language Handbook Worksheets*
■ *Daily Language Activities*

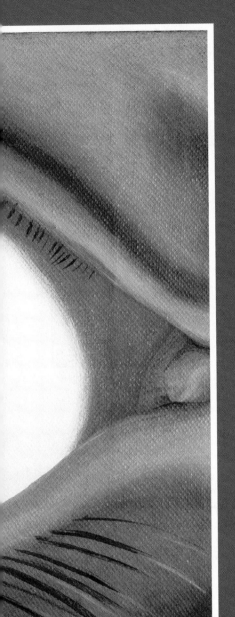

Collection 4

Point of View: Can You See It My Way?

**Literary Focus:
Analyzing Point of View**

**Informational Focus:
Analyzing an Author's
Argument**

INTERNET
Collection
Resources
Keyword: LE5 7-4

Le Faux Miroir (The False Mirror)
(1935) by René Magritte.
Photothèque R. Magritte-ADAGP, © 2005 C. Herscovici,
Brussels/Artists Rights Society (ARS), New York.

347

Grade-Level Skills

■ Literary Skills
Understand point of view.

Review Skills

■ Literary Skills
Identify the speaker, and recognize the difference between first- and third-person narration.

Elements of Literature: Point of View

Bring in a *Peanuts* cartoon showing a typical argument between Linus and Lucy over Linus's blanket. Point out that Linus and Lucy have different views of the events. If Lucy told the story, she would make Linus look childish and insecure. If Linus narrated the same story, he would explain that the blanket makes him feel safe and confident. An omniscient narrator like cartoonist Charles Schulz would show both of their views.

Elements of Literature
Point of View *by* John Leggett
THROUGH WHOSE EYES?

When you were little, you probably imagined at one time or another that there was something terrifying under your bed. Did it ever occur to you that something might find *you* just as terrifying? As the saying goes, "It all depends on your point of view." When you're telling a story, you look at things one way—your way. When someone else tells the story, he or she will put a slightly different spin on the same events.

Novels and short stories are also told from a particular **point of view,** or vantage point. When you're reading, you should ask, "Who is the narrator?" "Can I rely on this narrator to tell the truth?" and "What is the narrator's relationship to the meaning of the story?"

The Big Three

The three most common points of view are the omniscient, the first person, and the third-person limited.

The **omniscient** (äm·nish′ənt) **point of view** is the all-knowing point of view. (In Latin, *omnis* means "all," and *sciens* means "knowing.") You can think of an omniscient narrator as being above the action, looking down on it like a god. This narrator can tell you everything about all the characters, even their most private thoughts.

THE FAR SIDE® By GARY LARSON

"I've got it again, Larry ... an eerie feeling like there's something on top of the bed."

Once upon a time there lived a princess who would have been perfectly happy except for one thing: In a moment of weakness, she had promised to marry a frog. Her father felt sorry for her, but he insisted that she keep her word. (In fact, he was a little nervous—he'd never met a talking frog before.) "After all, a promise is a promise," agreed her mother, who thought the frog was better looking than the princess's last boyfriend. Little did any of the royal family know who the frog really was.

go.
hrw
.com

INTERNET
More About
Point of View
Keyword: LE5 7-4

SKILLS FOCUS

Literary Skills
Understand
point of view.

A story can also be told by one of the characters. In this viewpoint the character speaks as "I." We call this the **first-person point of view.** (*I* is the first-person pronoun.) In this point of view, we know only what this one character can tell us. Sometimes this kind of narrator isn't very reliable.

> I couldn't believe that my parents were actually going to make me marry a slimy, ugly, bulgy-eyed frog! They didn't feel sorry for me at all! All they cared about was a stupid promise I never thought I'd have to keep.

Often a story is seen through the eyes of one character, but the character is *not* telling the story as "I." This is called the **third-person-limited point of view.** In this point of view, a narrator zooms in on the thoughts and feelings of just one character in the story. This point of view helps us share that character's reactions to the story's events.

> The princess tried desperately to get out of her promise. "It was all my parents' fault," she thought. They were so unfair. But she had a nagging feeling that she had only herself to blame— and the frog. "I wonder if the royal chef knows how to cook frogs' legs?" she said to herself.

Point of view is very important in storytelling, and writers love to experiment with it. Someone who wants to tell the frog-and-princess story from a really unusual point of view might choose to let the frog tell it.

Practice

Write three groups of sentences about the situation in the cartoon on page 348.

- In the first group of sentences, write as the **omniscient narrator.** As the omniscient narrator you might want to let your reader know how this unusual situation came about and give some hints about how it will end.

  These people are…

- In the second group of sentences, write from the **first-person point of view** of the monster. Now you will write as "I."

  I am feeling…

- In the third group of sentences, take the **third-person-limited point of view.** This is the hardest. In this point of view, you are going to zoom in and focus on just one character. Concentrate on the boy in the bed.

  This boy is…

Practice

Possible Responses
Omniscient narrator—The boy lay on the bed trying to see through the dark. He kept hearing sounds that made him wonder whether there might be something under the bed. The two monsters lay under the bed, wishing they had more room. Each time the boy stirred, they felt uneasy; there seemed to be something on the bed above them.
First-person point of view—I wished Larry would move over. There wasn't really enough room under this bed for the two of us. But I had to admit it was better than the damp basement we had left behind. My eyes suddenly popped open as I heard a rustling sound over my head. I looked over at Larry, who clearly had heard it too. "I've got it again, Larry," I hissed, " . . . an eerie feeling there's something on top of the bed."
Third-person-limited point of view—The boy lay stiffly on top of the bed, trying vainly to figure out what might be beneath him. He strained to identify the small sounds he kept hearing, telling himself it was only the wind blowing through the window and rustling his sheets. Finally, the suspense got to him; he couldn't keep still any longer.

Apply

Challenge students to retell a familiar tale from different points of view. Students can organize themselves into groups of three. The first student can tell a brief story, such as "Cinderella," from one of the three points of view described in this essay. The next student then tells the story using one of the two remaining points of view, and the third student tells the story using the remaining point of view. Afterward, have each group discuss what this activity taught them about the story and about the importance of point of view.

DIFFERENTIATING INSTRUCTION

Advanced Learners
Enrichment. At the end of this essay, the writer suggests an unusual point of view for the frog and princess story—the frog's point of view. Invite individual students to retell a passage of the story through the eyes of the frog. They can choose either the first-person or the third-person-limited point of view. Have students share their stories with each other in a storytelling group.

English-Language Learners
For additional instruction on point of view for English-language learners and special education students, see *Holt Reading Solutions*.

Grade-Level Skills

■ Reading Skills
Analyze an author's perspective.

OVERVIEW

Purpose. This strategy will help students identify and analyze an author's perspective on a topic by examining textual clues.

Use. This strategy can be used to help students analyze an author's perspective on a topic. It can be particularly useful for nonfiction pieces, such as essays or newspaper editorials, where the writer is trying to convince the reader that his or her argument is justified. It can also be helpful in determining an author's feelings about characters and events in a short story with an omniscient narrator. If students examine the author's word choice, the author's tone, and what the author decides to include or leave out, they will gain a better understanding of the author's perspective. In addition to the pieces in this collection, this strategy can be helpful with "A Mason-Dixon Memory" in Collection 5 and the informational selections in Collection 6.

Reading Skills and Strategies

Analyzing an Author's Perspective

by Kylene Beers

How do the meanings of the two sentences below differ?

Jamal won the race?   Jamal won the *race*?

Although the two sentences include the same words, the difference in emphasis gives them different meanings. Each sentence reveals a different attitude about Jamal's winning the race. As you read an informational text, it's important to understand the author's point of view, or **perspective**. It will help you evaluate his or her ideas.

Tracking Perspective

The reader's job would be much easier if authors would only say, "My point of view on this subject is _____." Of course, that usually doesn't happen. Instead, authors leave hints or clues that reveal their feelings about the topic. You'll find these clues in

- the author's word choice
- the author's tone
- what the author includes
- what the author leaves out

Read the text to the right, and look for these clues. Then, read the article on page 351 and see if you can determine the author's perspective.

SKILLS FOCUS

Reading Skills
Analyze an author's perspective.

Kids' Sports Today

In our wonderful past, kids gathered for pickup baseball games. Anyone could play. Parents watched, or didn't. The point was to have fun. Some kids went on to play high school sports, and that was it. But now four-year-olds try out for the Pee Wee Baseball League. Gym lessons begin at age three. Two-year-olds take soccer class. Ridiculously tennis camps enroll toddlers. By high school, kids are so burned out, lessoned out, and played out that they either drop out or fizzle out. Sports have become too competitive, and too many parents see their child as the next Tiger Woods.

> Words like *wonderful, kids, fun,* and *ridiculously* hint at the author's view of competitive sports.

> Notice what the author tells you; then, notice what isn't mentioned—how sports help develop self-esteem, build leadership, improve social skills.

> Repetition of the word *out* (five times!) creates an insistent **tone** and leads to the author's view that sports are too competitive today.

350   Collection 4 / Can You See It My Way?

DIFFERENTIATING INSTRUCTION

Learners Having Difficulty
Modeling. Students who have difficulty analyzing an author's perspective can use the open-book icons as stopping points to sum up what the author has said so far. Write the following sentences on the chalkboard: "Tara, a golden retriever, is searching for explosives in the rubble of the World Trade Center. Her reward will be a game of fetch." Have students copy the sentences into their notebooks. When they arrive at

each of the other open-book icons, ask them to write one or two similar sentences that summarize what the author has said.

English-Language Learners
To help students understand the author's perspective, write the following statements on the chalkboard:

- Dogs are harder workers than other animals.
- Dogs perform duties only if they receive a reward for their actions.

Using the

Strategy

As you read this article, you'll find this open-book sign at certain points in the story : ![open book]. Stop at these points, and do what the prompts ask.

Canines to the Rescue

Jonah Goldberg

Summary ![arrow] *at grade level*

In this magazine article the author shares his views on the dogs who assisted in the recovery effort in New York City after the destruction of the World Trade Center. The dogs proved willing to sacrifice their own well-being in order to search for possible survivors, as well as for bombs and other dangerous materials. One dog's life was endangered when he fell into a mound of debris while searching for survivors. Upon recovering, he immediately went back to the site to resume his search. The author then explores the dedication of dogs and the loyalty felt between dogs and human beings. While some others feel that dogs can exploit their masters, the author concludes that dogs are genuinely eager to please and will go against their survival instincts to do their duty.

PRETEACHING

Selection Starter

Motivate. Encourage students to share with the class an experience of a pet's loyalty during a time of need. Ask them to consider the following questions as they relate their experiences: Were they surprised by the actions of their pet? Did the pet put itself in danger or discomfort to protect its owner?

- Dogs can stand a high level of pain.
- Relationships between dogs and humans are usually difficult.
- Humans can ask more of their dogs than of other animals.

Ask a student to read each statement aloud. Then, discuss with students whether the author of the selection would agree or disagree with each of these statements. Have students back up their opinions with examples from the text.

Advanced Learners

Enrichment. This article is just one of many portrayals of animals working with human beings in a noble cause to save human lives. **Activity.** Have students research a situation in which an animal worked for the good of human beings. One example is the dolphins who searched the ocean waters for mines during the conflict between the United States and Iraq in 2003. Have students write a brief essay about the situation they chose and present it to the class.

Using the Strategy

I spent the better part of an afternoon about half a mile south of where the World Trade Center[1] stood, with Tara, a three-year-old golden retriever employed by Michael Stanton Associates, a private security firm. Tara's job is to find bombs. Of course, she doesn't know that they are bombs; all she knows is that her human master wants her to find something that smells like plastic explosives, or TNT, or a dozen other dangerous substances. The only payment she will receive for this is a few moments fetching the ball with her boss. ❶

This work ethic is the heart of canine exceptionalism. The dog is the only animal that volunteers for duty. If we want other animals—horses, oxen, mules, falcons, bears, or parrots—to come to our aid, we must either force them or bribe them. You might even call horses our slaves: Their spirit must actually be broken before they will agree to do anything for us. ❷

Long before the rubble settled in downtown New York, German shepherds, Labrador retrievers, and Rottweilers—as well as canines of less aristocratic lineage—were already pulling at their leashes to help with the search-and-rescue efforts. Locating the dead and searching (too often in vain) for the living is obviously an arduous[2] and emotionally draining task for human beings, but it is no picnic for dogs either. The rubble provided unstable footing, was full of glass shards and twisted metal, and sometimes glowed red hot. Dangerous fumes, loud noises, and the equivalent of landslides were constant sources of distraction and peril. Dogs repeatedly had to limp out of the wreckage on bloody paws, the razor-edged debris[3] slicing through even the leather boots distributed to some of them. ❸

---

1. **World Trade Center:** twin towers in New York City that were destroyed on September 11, 2001.
2. **arduous** (är′jσō·əs) *adj.:* hard; difficult.
3. **debris** (də·brē′) *n.:* pieces of stone, wood, glass, or other materials left after something is destroyed.

Worse, the stress associated with not finding survivors was extreme; dogs tasked with this assignment expect—*need*—to find survivors. "They don't like to find bodies. They'll find them, but they don't feel rewarded," veterinarian Douglas Wyler explained. "The dogs are good, they're professionals, but like any professional they can suffer from melancholy and depression. It's hard for the men not to find anyone alive, and the dogs sense that." **4**

But the dogs persevered.[4] Consider Servus, a Belgian Malinois (a smaller version of the German shepherd) who arrived at the Twin Towers site with his owner, police officer Chris Christensen, the day after the disaster. While searching for survivors, Servus fell down a nine-foot hole into a mound of dust and debris. When they pulled him free, "he couldn't breathe," Christensen explained. Servus tried to vomit, to no avail. By the time the convulsions started and Servus's tongue turned purple, between twenty and thirty men were gathered to help an animal they clearly considered a colleague (often, police dogs are given full-dress funerals). The canine was rushed to one of the veterinary MASH units set up to treat the rescue dogs as well as the numerous "civilian" animals and pets injured or abandoned in the surrounding residential areas.

The vets managed to resuscitate[5] Servus, and he was given an IV.[6] (It was not unusual to see rescue humans and rescue dogs lying beside one another, each with his own IV drip.) When the vets unstrapped the dog from the gurney and released him for some doggie R&R,[7] he ran straight from the tent and leapt into the police car assigned to bring dogs to ground zero. "I couldn't believe it," Christensen said. "I told him three times to get out and he just looked at me, so we went to work. We worked for seven hours." **5**

Such dedication has inspired a growing effort in the scientific community to explain this age-old symbiosis between men and dogs. Until fairly recently, the study of dogs has been ignored by scientists more interested in more "authentic" animals—despite the fact that the domestic dog may be the second most successful of all mammal species, after human beings. **6**

More to the point, their success is directly attributable to the fact

---

4. **persevered** (pur·sə·vird′) *v.*: kept trying; persisted.
5. **resuscitate** (ri·sus′ə·tāt′) *v.*: revive; bring back to life.
6. **IV** (abbreviation for *intravenous*) *n.*: medical procedure in which blood plasma, medicine, or nutrients are delivered directly into a vein.
7. **R&R:** abbreviation used in the military, meaning "rest and recuperation."

Using the Strategy

ANALYZE

4 Why do you think the writer includes a quotation from a veterinarian? Remember that the information a writer chooses to include may offer a clue to his or her perspective.

ANALYZE

5 Why do you think the writer included so much information about Servus? (Did you notice that the name sounds like *service*?)

WORD CHOICE

6 You might have seen the word *symbiosis* (sim′bī·ō′sis) in your science class. *Sym–* is a prefix that means "together" and *–bio–* means "life"; the word means "association of members of two species for the benefit of both." In this case the species are humans and dogs. Why do you think the writer uses a scientific term here?

D Reading Skills and Strategies

Analyze. [Possible response to question 4: The author includes a quotation from a veterinarian because this is an expert's opinion that will make the author's argument more credible. The veterinarian supports the author's view that the rescue dogs take their job seriously and experience the failure to find survivors much like humans do.]

E Reading Skills and Strategies

Analyze. [Possible response to question 5: Servus's actions are an excellent example of a dog's selflessness and determination; they support the writer's view that a close link exists between dogs and humans.]

F Reading Skills and Strategies

❓ Express an opinion. Do Servus's actions after his recovery surprise you? Explain your answer. [Possible responses: I'm not surprised because the author has explained that the dogs are taking this job seriously. I am surprised that the dogs have such a strong desire to help people.]

G Reading Skills and Strategies

Word choice. [Possible response to question 6: Using the scientific term provides evidence that the relationship the author is describing can be the subject of a scientific inquiry.]

H Reading Skills and Strategies

❓ Analyze an author's perspective. Do you think the author believes that dogs are "the second most successful of all mammal species"? What information in the article backs up your opinion? [Possible response: Yes, because the article is filled with examples of dogs working hard and selflessly.]

DIRECT TEACHING

Ⓐ Reading Skills and Strategies

Compare and contrast. [He uses the words "con artists" and "pick our pockets."]

Ⓑ Reading Skills and Strategies

❓ **Analyze an author's perspective.** Why does the author include a quotation from someone who disagrees with his views? [Possible response: The author includes the quotation so that he can disprove it with evidence that supports his argument. By doing so, he makes his argument stronger.]

Ⓒ Reading Skills and Strategies

Word choice. [Possible response to question 8: The author distrusts people with overly skeptical views of dogs. "Himself" refers to a dog who is helping with the recovery effort. The crane is above the remains of the World Trade Center.]

Ⓓ Reading Skills and Strategies

Analyze. [Possible response to question 9: The last two paragraphs tell you that the author realizes that dogs have their own reasons for doing the things that humans want them to do. Nevertheless, he admires the desire of dogs to please their human masters even if it means putting their own lives at risk.]

Using the Strategy

COMPARE AND CONTRAST

❼ In this paragraph the writer mentions a legend that explains how the dog became a good friend to humans. He then quotes a nature writer with a very different point of view. What surprising words does Stephen Budiansky use to describe dogs?

WORD CHOICE

❽ *Cynic* (sin'ik) is a harsh word that means "someone who believes that people act only out of self-interest." What does this word choice tell you about the writer's opinion of the people he is describing? Look at the third sentence in this paragraph. Who does "himself" refer to? Where is the crane? (Remember the setting in the first paragraph.)

ANALYZE

❾ Re-read the last two paragraphs of the article. What do they tell you about the author's overall perspective on dogs?

that they have teamed up with human beings. I'm told that according to an American Indian legend, human beings and animals were separated by a great canyon in prehistory. Forced to choose sides, the dog decided to throw in his lot with man and leapt the chasm to live and work with us. The moral of the story is certainly true, though the choice was evolutionary as well as sentimental. Some, like nature writer Stephen Budiansky, take the story too far in the other direction. He argues that canines have mastered an evolutionary strategy that makes us love them: "Dogs belong to that elite group of con artists at the very pinnacle of their profession, the ones who pick our pockets clean and leave us smiling about it." ❼

These cynics would have us believe that dogs—which have, in numerous documented cases, given their lives for human beings—are actually slyly exploiting an emotional glitch in people that makes us love soft, big-eyed furry things. This overlooks the obvious fact that we "con" dogs too; that they, in fact, love us as much as, if not more than, we love them. Allowing himself to be carried by crane hundreds of feet above the ground and then lowered into a smoldering pit of metal and glass defies every instinct a dog has, except one: to be a selfless friend of his ally and master. "Histories are more full of examples of the fidelity[8] of dogs than of friends," observed Alexander Pope. "Heaven goes by favor," remarked Mark Twain. "If it went by merit, you would stay out and your dog would go in." ❽

There's no disputing that dogs do things for canine reasons. Many of their heroic acts can be attributed to misplaced maternal or other instincts. Newfoundlands have saved many people from drowning, but their instinct is just as strong to "save" banana crates and other flotsam. Tara—the ebullient[9] golden retriever I looked for bombs with—doesn't know the details; all she knows is that she wants to please her human master.

And isn't that good enough? ❾

---

8. **fidelity** (fə·del′ə·tē) *n.:* faithfulness.
9. **ebullient** (i·bool′yənt) *adj.:* high-spirited.

FAMILY/COMMUNITY ACTIVITY

Ask students to read the article with their families. Then, have them ask their parents whether they agree with the author's perspective on dogs. Encourage students to ask their parents for reasons why they feel as they do. Perhaps their parents know someone in the community whose dog has displayed similar courage, or perhaps they had a courageous dog when they were younger. Ask students to share their parents' perspectives with the class.

Practice the Strategy 📖

Analyzing an Author's Perspective

As you read "Canines to the Rescue," you examined many of the clues that help reveal the **author's perspective**, or point of view. These clues include word choice, tone, the information included, and the information left out.

PRACTICE

Draw a Perspective Wheel like the one below, and label each section as shown. Then, place the words and phrases listed below in the appropriate sections. Afterward, write a paragraph that describes the author's perspective. Use the wheel to organize your ideas and provide support for your argument. As you read other informational texts, use a wheel like this one to analyze the author's perspective.

Words and Phrases

employed	*volunteers*	*symbiosis*	*selfless*
work ethic	*pulling at their leashes*	*cynics*	*heroic acts*
exceptionalism	*dedication*	*exploiting*	

Quotations and Ideas

Quotation from veterinarian

Story about Servus

American Indian legend

Mark Twain's comment

The expense or effort involved in raising dogs

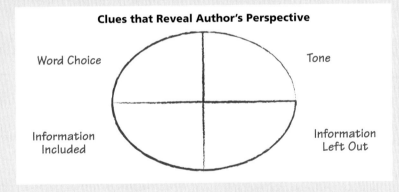

Clues that Reveal Author's Perspective

Word Choice — Tone

Information Included — Information Left Out

 You can use these clues to find the **author's perspective** in all the stories and informational texts you read.

SKILLS FOCUS

Reading Skills
Analyze an author's perspective.

CROSS-CURRICULAR CONNECTIONS

History

Comparing historical documents. After consulting with a history teacher, encourage students to use the Perspective Wheel when comparing historical documents. For example, if students are asked to research differing views on the American Civil War, they can use Perspective Wheels to compare a document that supports the Union with one that supports the Confederacy. By using a Perspective Wheel for each document, students can compare the graphic organizers and gain a better understanding of the perspectives of both sides of the war.

Practice the Strategy

In this feature, students will do the following items: (1) use a graphic organizer to examine the clues that reveal an author's perspective; (2) analyze an author's perspective by examining the author's word choice, tone, and the information the author included and left out; and (3) sum up the author's perspective in a paragraph.

Strategy Tip

When students begin filling out the Perspective Wheel, remind them that words and phrases can be included in more than one portion of the wheel. For example, "pulling at their leashes" could be included for both "Word Choice" (because the phrase conveys the dogs' eagerness to help) and "Tone" (because the writer expresses his admiration of the dogs' selflessness).

PRACTICE

Possible Answers

- *Word Choice*—employed, work ethic, exceptionalism, volunteers, pulling at their leashes, dedication, selfless, heroic acts.
- *Tone*—work ethic, pulling at their leashes, symbiosis, cynics, exploiting, selfless.
- *Information Included*—quotation from veterinarian, story about Servus, American Indian legend, Mark Twain's comment.
- *Information Left Out*—The expense or effort involved in raising dogs.
- Possible paragraph: The author admires the willingness of dogs to sacrifice their well-being to please their masters. He singles out for praise their dedication under great stress in the recovery effort at the World Trade Center. He includes firsthand accounts of dogs' heroism, a scientific quotation, and a comment from Mark Twain to further support his case.

Grade-Level Skills

■ **Literary Skills**
Analyze omniscient point of view.

■ **Reading Skills**
Make predictions.

Review Skills

■ **Literary Skills**
Identify the speaker, and recognize the difference between first- and third-person narration.

Upcoming Skills

■ **Literary Skills**
Analyze the way voice, tone, persona, and choice of narrator affect characterization and plot.

Summary ⬆ *above grade level*

On a cold, rainy night in New York City in the early 1900s, a man explains to an approaching policeman that he is waiting to meet an old friend, Jimmy Wells. Two decades earlier, the pair had agreed to meet at the same spot in exactly twenty years. Assured that the man will stay until Wells arrives, the officer moves on. Soon after, another man arrives, at first pretending to be Wells but then identifying himself as a policeman. He arrests "Silky" Bob, a wanted criminal, and hands him a note revealing that the first patrolman was Wells. Wells could not bring himself to arrest his old friend and "got a plainclothes man to do the job."

Before You Read The Short Story

After Twenty Years

Make the Connection
Quickwrite 🖊

Imagine that you write an advice column for your school newspaper. One day you receive this letter from someone in your school. In a letter, advise "Confused."

> Last Friday I saw my friend Lucy (not her real name) take a wallet that was left on a cafeteria table. I know she needs the money because her dad is between jobs. I don't know what to do! I mean, I want to do what's right—but I don't know how to handle this. She's just never done anything like this before.
>
> Sincerely,
> Confused

INTERNET

Vocabulary
Activity
•
Cross-curricular
Connection
•
More About
O. Henry

Keyword: LE5 7-4

SKILLS FOCUS

Literary Skills
Understand omniscient point of view.

Reading Skills
Make predictions.

Literary Focus
Omniscient Point of View

When you start reading a story, it's a good idea to ask, "Who is telling this story?" When you do this, you are asking about the **point of view.** "After Twenty Years" is told from the **omniscient point of view.** An omniscient narrator knows everything about everybody in a story. This narrator can tell you all about all the characters, their most private feelings, their pasts, even their futures.

Reading Skills 📖
Making Predictions: What Next?

Part of the fun of reading is guessing what will happen next. This process is called **making predictions.** Good readers make predictions without even thinking about it. Here's how to do it:

- Look for clues that **foreshadow,** or hint at, what will happen next.

- As the suspense builds, predict possible outcomes. See if you can guess where the writer is leading you. Revise your predictions as you go.

- Draw on your own experiences— including your other reading experiences—in making your predictions.

As you read "After Twenty Years," look for small open-book signs after some of the paragraphs. Stop at these points to predict what will happen next.

Vocabulary Development

O. Henry loved long, unusual words. Here are some words from "After Twenty Years" that you can add to your own vocabulary:

habitual (hə·bich′ōō·əl) *adj.*: done or fixed by habit. *The officer made his habitual check of the buildings.*

intricate (in′tri·kit) *adj.*: complicated; full of detail. *The officer twirled his club with intricate movements.*

dismally (diz′məl·ē) *adv.*: miserably; gloomily. *People walked dismally through the rainy streets.*

egotism (ē′gō·tiz′əm) *n.*: conceit; talking about oneself too much. *His egotism made him brag about his success.*

simultaneously (sī′məl·tā′nē·əs·lē) *adv.*: at the same time. *Each man looked simultaneously at his friend's face.*

356   Collection 4 / Can You See It My Way?

RESOURCES: READING

Planning
■ *One-Stop Planner* CD-ROM with ExamView Test Generator

Differentiating Instruction
■ *The Holt Reader*
■ *Holt Adapted Reader*
■ *Holt Reading Solutions*
■ *Supporting Instruction in Spanish*
■ *Audio CD Library*

■ *Audio CD Library, Selections and Summaries in Spanish*

Vocabulary
■ *Vocabulary Development*

Grammar and Language
■ *Language Handbook Worksheets*
■ *Daily Language Activities*

After Twenty Years

O. Henry

"We agreed that we would meet here again exactly twenty years from that date and time..."

(Background)
Courtesy of The
Valentine Museum,
Richmond, Virginia.

After Twenty Years

A **Literary Focus**

❓ **Omniscient point of view.** Point out that the omniscient point of view lets the narrator provide information about characters. What information would be missing if the policeman were the narrator? [Readers would not know that he is an impressive figure.]

B **Literary Focus**

❓ **Theme.** Tell students that theme can sometimes depend on the kinds of characters involved. What is your impression of the officer? [Possible responses: He is proud to be a policeman and takes his responsibilities seriously. He believes in law and order.]

C **Vocabulary Development**

Clarify word meanings: Example. Point out the word *reassuringly.* Explain that the man's words—"It's all right, officer"—provide an example that can help readers figure out the meaning of *reassuringly.* Call on volunteers to define the word. [Possible response: *Reassuringly* means "in a way that promotes confidence or says all is well."]

VIEWING THE ART

John Sloan (1871–1951) was a leading social realist. His canvases call forth the exuberance and angst of modern urban life.

Activity. What advantages and disadvantages of city living are suggested by this painting? [Possible responses: *Advantages*—bright lights, tall buildings, excitement. *Disadvantages*—isolation, loneliness, fear of crime.]

The City from Greenwich Village (1922) by John Sloan. Oil on canvas.

A The policeman on the beat moved up the avenue impressively. The impressiveness was habitual and not for show, for spectators were few. The time was barely ten o'clock at night, but chilly gusts of wind with a taste of rain in them had well nigh depeopled the streets.

B Trying doors as he went, twirling his club with many intricate and artful movements, turning now and then to cast his watchful eye down the pacific[1] thoroughfare, the officer, with his stalwart form and slight swagger, made a fine picture of a guardian of the peace. The vicinity was one that kept early hours. Now and then you might see the lights of a cigar store or of an all-night lunch counter, but the majority of the doors belonged to business places that had long since been closed.

When about midway of a certain block, the policeman suddenly slowed his walk. In the doorway of a darkened hardware store a man leaned with an unlighted cigar in his mouth. As the policeman walked up to him, the man spoke up quickly.

C "It's all right, officer," he said reassuringly. "I'm just waiting for a friend. It's an appointment made twenty years ago. Sounds a little funny to you, doesn't it? Well, I'll explain if you'd like to make certain it's all

---

1. **pacific** *adj.:* peaceful.

Vocabulary

habitual (hə·bich′o͞o·əl) *adj.:* done or fixed by habit; customary.

intricate (in′tri·kit) *adj.:* complicated; full of detail.

Learners Having Difficulty
Modeling. Invite learners having difficulty to read "After Twenty Years" in interactive format in *The Holt Reader* and to use the sidenotes as aids to understanding the selection. You can then model the strategy of recognizing points of view. As students read "After Twenty Years," encourage them to ask themselves, "What is the omniscient narrator helping me see about the setting and characters?"

English-Language Learners
Review some of the expressions from the time period: *well nigh* (p. 358) and *chum, chap, pile,* and *call time on him sharp* (p. 359). Also, tell students that a pug nose is short, thick, and turned up at the end and that a Roman nose has a prominent bridge.

straight. About that long ago there used to be a restaurant where this store stands—'Big Joe' Brady's restaurant."

"Until five years ago," said the policeman. "It was torn down then."

The man in the doorway struck a match and lit his cigar. The light showed a pale, square-jawed face with keen eyes and a little white scar near his right eyebrow. His scarf pin was a large diamond, oddly set. ❶

MAKE PREDICTIONS
❶ What could the scar and the large diamond suggest about the man's past?

"Twenty years ago tonight," said the man, "I dined here at 'Big Joe' Brady's with Jimmy Wells, my best chum and the finest chap in the world. He and I were raised here in New York, just like two brothers, together. I was eighteen and Jimmy was twenty. The next morning I was to start for the West to make my fortune. You couldn't have dragged Jimmy out of New York; he thought it was the only place on earth. Well, we agreed that night that we would meet here again exactly twenty years from that date and time, no matter what our conditions might be or from what distance we might have to come. We figured that in twenty years each of us ought to have our destiny worked out and our fortunes made, whatever they were going to be."

"It sounds pretty interesting," said the policeman. "Rather a long time between meets, though, it seems to me. Haven't you heard from your friend since you left?"

"Well, yes, for a time we corresponded," said the other. "But after a year or two we lost track of each other. You see, the West is a pretty big proposition, and I kept hustling around over it pretty lively. But I know Jimmy will meet me here if he's alive, for he always was the truest, staunchest old chap in the world. He'll never forget. I came a thousand miles to stand in this door tonight, and it's worth it if my old partner turns up."

The waiting man pulled out a handsome watch, the lids of it set with small diamonds.

"Three minutes to ten," he announced. "It was exactly ten o'clock when we parted here at the restaurant door."

"Did pretty well out West, didn't you?" asked the policeman.

"You bet! I hope Jimmy has done half as well. He was a kind of plodder, though, good fellow as he was. I've had to compete with some of the sharpest wits going to get my pile. A man gets in a groove in New York. It takes the West to put a razor edge on him." ❷

MAKE PREDICTIONS
❷ What do these boasts suggest about the man's past?

The policeman twirled his club and took a step or two.

"I'll be on my way. Hope your friend comes around all right. Going to call time on him sharp?"

"I should say not!" said the other. "I'll give him half an hour at least. If Jimmy is alive on earth, he'll be here by that time. So long, officer."

"Good night, sir," said the policeman, passing on along his beat, trying doors as he went.

There was now a fine, cold drizzle falling, and the wind had risen from its uncertain puffs into a steady blow. The few foot passengers astir in that quarter hurried dismally and silently along with coat collars turned high and pocketed hands. And in the door of the hardware store the man who had

Vocabulary
dismally (diz′məl·ē) adv.: miserably; gloomily.

Special Education Students
For lessons designed for special education students, see *Holt Reading Solutions*.

D Reading Skills

Make predictions. Remind students that readers make predictions by connecting clues in the text with their own experiences. Ask students the following questions: "In your experience, how do people get scars? What sort of person might wear a large diamond?" [Possible responses: People may get scars in fights or other violent situations. A person who likes to show off his or her wealth might wear a large diamond.]

[Possible response to question 1: The scar and diamond could suggest that the man has had a violent past during which he acquired wealth.]

E Reading Skills

Make predictions. Point out that making predictions means figuring out what the clues in the story reveal about the characters.

[Possible response to question 2: The man's boasts suggest that he has been a hustler, seizing every opportunity to make his "pile."]

F Literary Focus

❷ **Theme.** This appears to be a story about friendship. What is the man saying about Jimmy and friendship? [Possible response: He is saying that Jimmy is very loyal and their friendship is very important to him.]

G Literary Focus

❷ **Omniscient point of view.** How can you tell that the narrator of this story is omniscient, or all-knowing? [Possible response: The narrator describes both the outside setting (the weather) and the inner feelings of the pedestrians (the word *dismally* gives readers insight into their gloomy feelings). The narrator also knows about both the past of the man in the doorway and his present thinking: The friend of his youth is so important to the man that he traveled a thousand miles and is willing to wait for a meeting that may not take place.]

A **Reading Skills**

Make predictions. [Possible response to question 3: It would be unusual for a person to grow two or three inches after the age of twenty. This man may not be Jimmy.]

B **Reading Skills**

Make predictions. [Possible responses to question 4: He is someone who knows Jimmy. He may have been sent in Jimmy's place because Jimmy doesn't want to see Bob, because Jimmy is in trouble, or because Jimmy knows something about Bob and doesn't want to face him.]

C **Advanced Learners**

? **Acceleration.** Situational irony occurs when what happens is different from what is expected to happen. What did you expect to happen? [Possible responses: Bob and Jimmy would have a happy reunion. Something would happen to Jimmy, and he wouldn't be able to make it.]

GUIDED PRACTICE

Monitor students' progress. Guide students in answering these true-false questions. Direct students to locate passages in the text that support their responses.

True-False

1. Bob waits in a doorway to meet his old friend Jimmy Wells. [T]
2. Bob last saw Jimmy ten years ago. [F]
3. Bob recognizes Jimmy as soon as he sees him. [F]
4. The third man in the story is a plainclothes policeman. [T]
5. Jimmy Wells tells the plainclothes policeman where to find Bob. [T]

---

come a thousand miles to fill an appointment, uncertain almost to absurdity, with the friend of his youth, smoked his cigar and waited.

About twenty minutes he waited, and then a tall man in a long overcoat, with collar turned up to his ears, hurried across from the opposite side of the street. He went directly to the waiting man.

"Is that you, Bob?" he asked, doubtfully.

"Is that you, Jimmy Wells?" cried the man in the door.

"Bless my heart!" exclaimed the new arrival, grasping both the other's hands with his own. "It's Bob, sure as fate. I was certain I'd find you here if you were still in existence. Well, well, well!—twenty years is a long time. The old restaurant's gone, Bob; I wish it had lasted, so we could have had another dinner there. How has the West treated you, old man?"

"Bully;[2] it has given me everything I asked it for. You've changed lots, Jimmy. I never thought you were so tall by two or three inches." ❸ 🔖

"Oh, I grew a bit after I was twenty."

"Doing well in New York, Jimmy?"

"Moderately. I have a position in one of the city departments. Come on, Bob; we'll go around to a place I know of and have a good long talk about old times."

The two men started up the street, arm in arm. The man from the West, his egotism enlarged by success, was beginning to outline the history of his career. The other, submerged in his overcoat, listened with interest.

> 🔖 **MAKE PREDICTIONS**
> ❸ What could Jimmy's height signify?

At the corner stood a drugstore, brilliant with electric lights. When they came into this glare, each of them turned simultaneously to gaze upon the other's face.

The man from the West stopped suddenly and released his arm.

"You're not Jimmy Wells," he snapped. "Twenty years is a long time, but not long enough to change a man's nose from a Roman to a pug." ❹ 🔖

"It sometimes changes a good man into a bad one," said the tall man. "You've been under arrest for ten minutes, 'Silky' Bob. Chicago thinks you may have dropped over our way and wires us she wants to have a chat with you. Going quietly, are you? That's sensible. Now, before we go to the station, here's a note I was asked to hand to you. You may read it here at the window. It's from Patrolman Wells."

The man from the West unfolded the little piece of paper handed him. His hand was steady when he began to read, but it trembled a little by the time he had finished. The note was rather short.

> 🔖 **MAKE PREDICTIONS**
> ❹ If the man is not Jimmy Wells, then who do you suppose he is, and why do you think he is sent in Jimmy's place?

> Bob: I was at the appointed place on time. When you struck the match to light your cigar, I saw it was the face of the man wanted in Chicago. Somehow I couldn't do it myself, so I went around and got a plainclothes man to do the job.
>   Jimmy

Vocabulary

egotism (ē′gō·tiz′əm) *n.:* conceit; talking about oneself too much.

simultaneously (sī′məl·tā′nē·əs·lē) *adv.:* at the same time.

---

2. **bully** *interj.:* informal term meaning "very well."

MINI-LESSON **Reading**

Developing Word-Attack Skills
Point out that the letters *c* and *g* have both hard sounds and soft sounds using these words: *cast, gasoline, certain, genuine, city, ginger, compete, good, customer,* and *gust.* Tell students that *c* and *g* stand for the hard sounds /k/ and /g/ before the vowels *a, o,* and *u* and for the soft sounds /s/ and /j/ before the vowels *e* and *i. C* and *g* also stand for their hard sounds when they are followed by another consonant (for example,

crib and *glide*) and when they occur at the end of a word (for example, *panic* and *big*). A final *e* after *c* or *g* makes the sound soft—for example, *police* and *page.* Use *electric* and *electricity* to demonstrate the effect that the vowel *i* has on the letter *c.*
Activity. Write the following items on the chalkboard. Ask a volunteer to read an item aloud and then to call on a classmate, asking him or her to explain why *c* or *g* has a hard or soft sound in each underlined word.

Meet the Writer

O. Henry

"Stories in Everything"

O. Henry (1862–1910) is the pen name of William Sydney Porter, who was born in Greensboro, North Carolina. He left school at fifteen and eventually moved to Texas. There he edited a humor magazine called *The Rolling Stone* and worked for a few years in a bank in Austin. Unfortunately, Porter was a careless record keeper. Two years after he left the bank, he was accused of embezzling its money. Although he was probably innocent, Porter panicked and ran off to Honduras. A year or so later he returned to Austin to be with his dying wife. There he was convicted and spent more than three years in a federal prison in Ohio.

Porter found the plots of many of his stories (including "After Twenty Years") in jail. He may also have found his famous pen name there: The name of a prison guard was Orrin Henry.

After he was released from prison, in 1901, Porter moved to New York. Soon, as O. Henry, he became one of the country's most popular short story writers. His stories are known for their snappy surprise endings. Many of his best-known stories are set in New York's streets and tenements and cheap hotels.

One day while O. Henry was dining with friends at a New York restaurant, a young writer asked him where he got his plots. "Oh, everywhere," replied O. Henry. "There are stories in everything." He picked up the menu on which the dishes of the day were typewritten. "There's a story in this," he said. Then he outlined the story—which he later wrote down and published—called "Springtime à la Carte." (On menus *à la carte* means that each item is priced separately.)

For Independent Reading

"After Twenty Years" is from a collection called *The Four Million and Other Stories.* The title refers to the population of New York City in O. Henry's day. Other O. Henry stories set in New York include "The Gift of the Magi" and "The Last Leaf."

Meet the Writer

Porter drew on a wide range of experiences when he wrote his stories. He had been a ranch hand, land agent, bank teller, magazine publisher, newspaper reporter, cartoonist, druggist, and prison convict. He may even have met a real-life "Silky" Bob while he was in prison.

For Independent Reading

Other collections of O. Henry's stories reflect his varied experiences. *Heart of the West* and *Roads of Destiny* include stories set in the West, while the stories of *Cabbages and Kings* are set in Central America.

---

1. Her <u>pacific</u> nature seemed <u>genuine</u>.
2. His <u>egotism</u> was <u>enlarged</u> by <u>success</u>.
3. <u>Garbage</u> was strewn about the <u>vicinity</u>.
4. An <u>orange</u> flower lay on the <u>cement</u>.
5. The <u>citizen</u> made a <u>gigantic</u> mistake when she <u>forged</u> her birth <u>certificate</u>.

DIFFERENTIATING INSTRUCTION

Advanced Learners

Enrichment. Challenge students to follow O. Henry's method of finding stories "everywhere." Have each student confine his or her search to a single three-square-foot area of the classroom or school. Within that area, the student is to identify something to write a story about. Suggest that each student try to create a surprise ending for his or her story, in the manner of O. Henry's endings.

INDEPENDENT PRACTICE

After You Read

First Thoughts

1. Students may say that they would do what Jimmy did or that they would try to rehabilitate Bob or that they would accept Bob as he is out of loyalty. Students' ideas about their Quickwrite advice will vary.

Thinking Critically

2. The scar near his right eye and the diamond-studded jewelry Bob displays suggest that he may have earned his fortune through illegal means. Bob also implies that he moved around a lot, quite possibly to avoid being arrested.

3. Some students will realize right away that the police officer is Jimmy Wells, especially when they learn that he was "the staunchest, truest old chap"—desirable qualities in a policeman. Other students may not realize who the police officer is until they read the letter.

4. Possible answer: Being honest and true to one's duty is more important than remaining loyal to an old friend.

Extending Interpretations

5. Possible answers: O. Henry's stories are not believable because in real life things usually turn out as expected. O. Henry's stories are believable because the unexpected often happens in real life, as shown by many human-interest stories.

First Thoughts

1. What would you have done if you were Jimmy? Look back at the letter you wrote to "Confused" in your Quickwrite. Would you make any revisions to the advice you gave?

Thinking Critically

2. Several details about Bob's appearance and behavior warn us that he might not be honest or that he is hiding from someone. What clues hint at, or **foreshadow,** something sinister about Bob?

3. When did you realize who the police officer was? Find and explain the first clue to his identity.

4. Both men honor a commitment they made over twenty years ago, but for Jimmy Wells there's one thing more important than even a long friendship. In a sentence or two, state the **theme** of this story. What truth about loyalty versus honesty does the story reveal to you?

Extending Interpretations

5. Some people don't like O. Henry's surprise endings. They think these endings make the stories unbelievable. Do you agree? Explain why or why not.

WRITING

Narrating from Another Point of View

O. Henry chose to tell his story from the **omniscient point of view.** What would we have known—and not known—if he had let Silky Bob tell the story from his own **first-person point of view**? Try retelling one of the scenes from Bob's or Jimmy's point of view. How could the new narrator change the story's **theme**? Is it still about loyalty versus honesty?

go.hrw.com

INTERNET
Projects and Activities
Keyword: LE5 7-4

SKILLS FOCUS

Literary Skills
Analyze point of view.

Reading Skills
Make predictions.

Writing Skills
Describe events from another point of view.

Reading Check

a. Why has the man in the doorway come back to the old neighborhood after twenty years?

b. What does the police officer realize when the man in the doorway lights his cigar?

c. How does the man in the doorway describe Jimmy Wells?

d. What does the police officer do after saying good night to the man in the doorway?

e. What happens to Bob at the end of the story?

362 Collection 4 / Can You See It My Way?

Reading Check

a. He and a boyhood friend agreed to meet there.

b. He realizes the man is wanted by the Chicago police.

c. The man says that Jimmy is the "truest, staunchest old chap in the world" and that he's a good friend but a plodder.

d. He gets a plainclothes policeman to pose as Jimmy Wells and arrest "Silky" Bob.

e. He is arrested by the plainclothes officer.

Clarifying Word Meanings

PRACTICE

To be sure you own the words in the Word Bank, fill out a word web for each word. Clarify the word's meaning through the use of definition, example, restatement, and contrast. The first word has been done for you. Be sure to compare your webs in class.

> **Word Bank**
> habitual
> intricate
> dismally
> egotism
> simultaneously

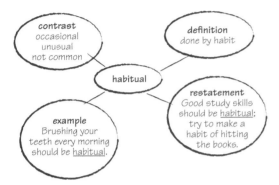

SKILLS FOCUS

Vocabulary Skills
Clarify word meanings.

Grammar Skills
Use end marks correctly.

Grammar Link

End All End-Mark Errors

In written English every sentence must begin with a capital letter and end with one of these **end marks:** a period, a question mark, or an exclamation point. Follow these simple rules:

- Use a period at the end of a statement.
  "It's an appointment made twenty years ago."

- Use a question mark at the end of a question.
  "Is that you, Bob?"

- Use an exclamation point at the end of an exclamation or a command.
  "Bless my heart!"

PRACTICE

Rewrite the following paragraph, adding capitalization and end punctuation marks. (The paragraph contains a total of seven sentences.)

Charlie tried out for the baseball team what did he have to lose it's not as if you have to be Ken Griffey, Jr., to play a position who imagined what would happen it was such a surprise unbelievably, he's hitting leadoff I guess you never know

For more help, see End Marks, 13a–e, in the Language Handbook.

After Twenty Years **363**

Vocabulary Development

PRACTICE

Possible Answers

- *intricate.* Contrast—simple. *Definition*—complicated. *Example*—The plate was decorated with an intricate geometric design. *Restatement*—Mia's music lessons were becoming more intricate, but she enjoyed learning complicated pieces.

- *dismally.* Contrast—cheerfully; happily. *Definition*—miserably; gloomily. *Example*—The chef regarded his ruined dessert dismally. *Restatement*—The hockey fans dismally watched their team regroup after the opposition scored.

- *egotism.* Contrast—selflessness. *Definition*—conceit; thinking too much of oneself. *Example*—Because of his egotism, he monopolized the conversation, telling boring stories about himself. *Restatement*—Raul's egotism is unbearable. His conceit is driving even his closest friends away from him.

- *simultaneously.* Contrast—at different times; in sequence. *Definition*—at the same time. *Example*—The twins simultaneously shouted, "Surprise!" *Restatement*—The audience began shouting out questions simultaneously until the host said that they couldn't be heard if everyone was talking at once.

Grammar Link

PRACTICE

Charlie tried out for the baseball team. What did he have to lose? It's not as if you have to be Ken Griffey, Jr., to play a position. Who imagined what would happen? It was such a surprise! Unbelievably, he's hitting leadoff. I guess you never know.

ASSESSING

Assessment
- *Holt Assessment: Literature, Reading, and Vocabulary*

RETEACHING

For a lesson reteaching point of view, see **Reteaching,** pp. 917G–H.

Grade-Level Skills

■ **Reading Skills**
Analyze an author's perspective.

Summary ⬌ *at grade level*

The author recalls a childhood acquaintance, Patsy, who changed her name when she became an actress. The author says that she was troubled by Patsy's name change because she assumed Patsy was trying to leave her past behind. Though admitting that some people have good reasons for using pseudonyms, the author thinks it important that those who do so hold onto their roots.

PRETEACHING

Selection Starter

Motivate. Ask students if they would change their names if they became entertainers or authors. Let volunteers reveal what names they might choose and why. Then, have students discuss the advantages and drawbacks to changing one's name.

Assign the Reading

Students can read the selection on their own, filling in a chart like the one on this page as they read. Have them answer the Test Practice and Constructed Response questions for homework.

HOMEWORK

Informational Text

LINK TO "AFTER TWENTY YEARS"

Analyzing an Author's Perspective

Reading Focus
Perspective: How We Look at Life

All writers have a perspective on their subjects. O. Henry's perspective is clear in the story "After Twenty Years." He sees life as offering us choices between honest and dishonest behavior. He comes down in favor of honesty, even when friendship is at stake.

Perspective refers to the way we look at a subject. Take the subject of school uniforms. Some people's perspective on that subject is negative. They think children should be free to dress the way they wish. Other people have a positive perspective on school uniforms. They think uniforms help equalize children and do away with clothes competition.

■ After you read "What's *Really* in a Name?," fill out a chart like the one opposite. Doing that should help you identify the writer's perspective on changing names.

"What's *Really* in a Name?"

> The writer doesn't understand why Patsy changed her name.

↓

> The writer tells why some people change their names:
> 1.
> 2.
> 3.
> [and so on]

↓

> The writer states her main concern about changing names:

↓

> Final quotation:

↓

> The writer's perspective on changing names:

SKILLS FOCUS

Reading Skills
Analyze an author's perspective.

It all depends on your point of view.

RESOURCES: READING

Planning
■ *One-Stop Planner* CD-ROM with ExamView Test Generator

Differentiating Instruction
■ *Holt Adapted Reader*
■ *Holt Reading Solutions*
■ *Supporting Instruction in Spanish*
■ *Audio CD Library*

■ *Audio CD Library, Selections and Summaries in Spanish*

Grammar and Language
■ *Daily Language Activities*

Assessment
■ *Holt Assessment: Literature, Reading, and Vocabulary*
■ *One-Stop Planner* CD-ROM with ExamView Test Generator

What's Really in a Name?

Patsy seemed like a movie star before she really became one. She was my sister's friend, and her presence made me hide behind the plants in the living room. I didn't want to talk to her. I just wanted to watch her. She was only in the sixth grade, but she had an air of sophistication that I had never experienced in my seven years.

After we all grew up, Patsy moved to New York and then to Los Angeles. I began to see her on television. Then I saw her in movies. At the end of one movie, I searched the closing credits for her name, but it wasn't there. So I called my sister and said, "I can't believe they left Patsy's name off the credits." My sister said, "They didn't. She changed her name." I hung up the phone feeling confused. To me Patsy would always be Patsy. Why would she need a new name?

Patsy had given herself a pseudonym.° Although it sounds like a bad disease, it's not. A pseudonym is a made-up name. (*Pseudo* comes from a Greek word that means "fake.") For writers a pseudonym is also called a pen name. William Sydney Porter, the famous short story writer, called himself O. Henry (see page 361). Mark Twain's name was really Samuel Clemens.

People have all sorts of reasons for using pseudonyms. It's easy to see why William Sydney Porter had one. He spent more than three years in jail for stealing money from a bank where he had worked. Although the evidence of his crime remains questionable, the damage to his reputation was done. As an ex-convict he might have had a hard time getting his books published. So he changed his name. One story is that the name O. Henry came from his cat.

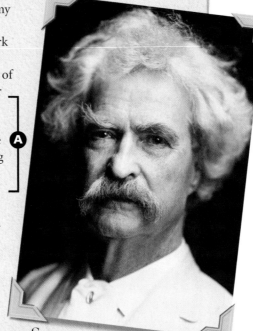

Samuel Clemens/Mark Twain

°**pseudonym** (sōō′də·nim′) *n.*

A **Reading Informational Text**

? **Author's perspective.** What is the author's view of Patsy's name change? [Possible responses: The author doesn't like the change; the author doesn't understand why Patsy needs a new name.]

B **Reading Informational Text**

? **Author's perspective.** What does the author think of William Sydney Porter's changing his name to O. Henry? [She approves of this change, because Porter's reputation was damaged after his conviction for a crime.] **What phrases help you understand the author's views of this name change?** [Possible responses: "People have all sorts of reasons . . .," "It's easy to see . . .," and "He might have had a hard time."]

- *Holt Online Assessment*

Internet
- go.hrw.com (Keyword: LE5 7-4)
- *Elements of Literature Online*

Media
- *Audio CD Library*
- *Audio CD Library, Selections and Summaries in Spanish*

A Reading Informational Text

? Author's perspective. In the author's opinion, what are some good reasons for writers and actors to take pen names and pseudonyms? [Reasons include to help the sale of their books and to make their names more memorable and appealing.]

B Reading Informational Text

? Author's perspective. Though the author approves of other people changing their names, she is still troubled by Patsy's name change. Why? [The author felt that in taking a new name Patsy denied her past, including her connection to the author.] How does the author finally reconcile her mixed feelings about name changes? [She hopes that people who change their names still hold on to a sense of who they are and where they come from.]

GUIDED PRACTICE

Monitor students' progress.
Review students' charts modeled after the one shown on p. 364. [Possible response: *The writer tells why some people change their names*—(1) They want to mask a troubled past; (2) Publishers ask for a pen name; (3) The new name sounds better. *The writer states her main concern about changing names*—People might be trying to get rid of their past. *Final quotation*—"Know from whence you came. If you know from whence you came, there are absolutely no limitations to where you can go." *The writer's perspective on changing names*—Even if you change your name, you should hold on tightly to your true identity.]

When he called the family cat, he yelled, "Oh, Henry." Another story has it that he got it from his prison guard. The guard's name was Orrin Henry.

Sometimes writers give themselves pen names because their publishers ask them to. It might have been hard to sell a shoot 'em-up western if your name was Archibald Lynn Joscelyn. Change that name to Al Cody (think of Cody, Wyoming, and Buffalo Bill Cody), however, and you've got a winner. The romance writer Elaine Carr is really a man named Charles Mason.

The main reason for taking a pseudonym is because it just sounds better. It's more appealing and memorable. Which has a better ring— Charles Lutwidge Dodson or Lewis Carroll? Reginald Kenneth Dwight or Elton John? Ralph Lifshitz or Ralph Lauren? Norma Jean Baker or Marilyn Monroe?

So why am I still troubled today that the beautiful and talented Patsy changed her name? I assumed that by adopting a new name, Patsy was trying to get rid of her past—her old friends, the neighborhood, even the scrawny seven-year-old kid who gazed at her from behind the plants.

Patsy, Norma Jean, Reginald—they probably all had good reasons for choosing new names. I hope when they changed their names, they held on tight to their roots. I agree with writer James Baldwin, who said, "Know from whence you came. If you know from whence you came, there are absolutely no limitations to where you can go."

—Joan Burditt

Reginald Dwight/Elton John

Caryn Elaine Johnson/
Whoopi Goldberg

DIFFERENTIATING INSTRUCTION

Learners Having Difficulty
Have students rest their chins on their desks and notice what they see. Then, have them sit up and look around them. Finally, have students stand and observe their surroundings. Point out that they have just seen the classroom from three different perspectives. Tell students that it's also possible to see things from different mental perspectives. For example, a parent and a teenager might have different views about a movie they've seen together.

Advanced Learners
Enrichment. Invite students to consider how important their own names are to their identities. Have them imagine changing their name to something unusual, attention getting, or exotic. Would they be the same persons they are today if they adopted new names?

Analyzing an Author's Perspective

What's Really in a Name?

Test Practice

1. The writer of this essay believes that —
   - A people should feel free to change their names
   - B it's important to remember where you came from
   - C William Sydney Porter was guilty of stealing money
   - D writers should use pseudonyms if they want to sell books

2. A writer's **perspective** is —
   - F his or her point of view on a subject
   - G a story the writer tells to entertain readers
   - H a sequence of related events
   - J the words a writer chooses

3. This essay was written in order to —
   - A explain a process
   - B describe a place
   - C compare several ideas
   - D express an opinion

4. The writer's **perspective** was *most* influenced by —
   - F Whoopi Goldberg
   - G her sister's friend Patsy
   - H James Baldwin
   - J William Sydney Porter

Constructed Response

1. What is a pseudonym? What is another expression for *pseudonym*?
2. According to this writer, what is the main reason people take pseudonyms?
3. Explain how the quotation from James Baldwin at the end of the essay supports the writer's feelings about pseudonyms.
4. How would you state the **author's perspective** on changing your name? Does she think it is a good idea?

SKILLS FOCUS

Reading Skills
Analyze an author's perspective.

Analyzing an Author's Perspective

Test Practice

Answers and Model Rationales

1. **B** Point out that B is correct because the writer says she agrees with James Baldwin. A is not discussed in the essay. For C and D, students may recall from the text that evidence of Porter's crime is "questionable" and that "sometimes" writers take pen names.

2. **F** Students should recall that the introductory material defines *perspective* as a person's view of something. G, H, and J are not definitions of perspective.

3. **D** Students should quickly recognize that A and B are incorrect. C is incorrect because while several ideas are expressed they are not compared.

4. **G** The writer is mostly influenced by her sister's friend's name change. F is not mentioned in the essay, H is someone who supports her position, and J is an example of someone who adopted a pseudonym.

Constructed Response

1. a made-up name; a pen name
2. The pseudonyms sound better; they're more appealing and memorable.
3. The quote emphasizes the importance of remembering one's roots.
4. Although the author says that there are several good reasons for people to change their name, she thinks it is a bad idea. She believes people should hold on to their roots instead of trying to get rid of them.

ASSESSING

Assessment
- *Holt Assessment: Literature, Reading, and Vocabulary*

RETEACHING

For a lesson reteaching author's argument, see **Reteaching**, p. 917K–L.

Grade-Level Skills

■ **Literary Skills**
Analyze first-person point of view.

■ **Literary Skills**
Understand historical fiction.

■ **Reading Skills**
Make predictions.

Upcoming Skills

■ **Literary Skills**
Analyze the way voice, tone, persona, and choice of narrator affect characterization and plot.

Summary 🔼 *above grade level*

Mr. Baumer, owner of a general store, tries to collect a debt from "Freighter" Slade. This chronic bully and former employee twists Baumer's nose and tosses the bill into the street. Baumer tells Al—the young narrator, who works at the store—that the illiterate Slade resents Baumer, an immigrant who learned to read and owns a business. Baumer, in turn, resents Slade for stealing whiskey he freights by siphoning it out of the barrel. A month later, in a fight over the same bill, Slade breaks Baumer's hand. Baumer then shocks Al by hiring Slade to haul freight. One bitterly cold day during transit, Slade mysteriously freezes to death. Afterward, as Al is unloading a barrel from Slade's wagon, he notices its label: "Wood Alcohol—Deadly Poison." Baumer slyly remarks, "Is good to know to read."

Before You Read | The Short Story

Bargain

Make the Connection
Quickwrite 🖉

With a partner, discuss these questions: What is the difference between justice and revenge? What do these two concepts have in common? What are some examples of each? Jot down your responses so you can refer to them at the end of the story.

Literary Focus
First-Person Point of View

When you are telling a story about something that happened to you, you use *I.* You say, "I was late for practice because the dog got out." You tell your story from the **first-person point of view.** The story "Bargain" is also told from the first-person point of view. It is told by Al, a character in the story who is about thirteen years old.

When a story is told from the first-person point of view, two important things happen. First, we share directly the narrator's thoughts and feelings. Second, we know *only* what the narrator knows. All we learn about the story's events and the other characters comes from the narrator's observations.

Historical Fiction

This story takes place in Moon Dance, a town where we have all been in our imagination. You will recognize Moon

Literary Skills
Understand first-person point of view; understand historical fiction.

Reading Skills
Make predictions.

Dance from TV and movie westerns—its muddy street, its saloon, and its general store. This story is a kind of **historical fiction.** Setting is important in historical fiction. This writer wants you to feel what it was like to live in a rough frontier town. If you took away Moon Dance and all the historical details, you'd have a different story.

Reading Skills 📖
**Making Predictions:
What Will Happen Next?**

Part of the fun of reading is trying to guess what will happen next. This process is called making **predictions.** Here is how you make predictions:

• Look for clues that **foreshadow,** or hint at, what will happen.

• As the suspense builds, predict possible outcomes. See if you can guess where the writer is leading you.

• Ask yourself questions while you read. Revise your predictions as you go.

• Draw on your own experiences and knowledge in making your predictions.

Remember: A good writer often surprises you.

You will find questions in this story that ask about predictions. Look for the open-book signs.

RESOURCES: READING

Planning
■ *One-Stop Planner* CD-ROM with ExamView Test Generator

Differentiating Instruction
■ *Holt Adapted Reader*
■ *Holt Reading Solutions*
■ *Supporting Instruction in Spanish*
■ *Audio CD Library*

■ *Audio CD Library, Selections and Summaries in Spanish*

Grammar and Language
■ *Daily Language Activities*

Assessment
■ *Holt Assessment: Literature, Reading, and Vocabulary*
■ *One-Stop Planner* CD-ROM with ExamView Test Generator

BARGAIN

A. B. Guthrie

He was a man you wouldn't remember from meeting once.

Mr. Baumer and I had closed the Moon Dance Mercantile Company and were walking to the post office, and he had a bunch of bills in his hand ready to mail. There wasn't anyone or anything much on the street because it was suppertime. A buckboard[1] and a saddle horse were tied at Hirsches' rack, and a rancher in a wagon rattled for home ahead of us, the sound of his going fading out as he prodded his team. Freighter[2] Slade stood alone in front of the Moon Dance Saloon, maybe wondering whether to have one more before going to supper. People said he could hold a lot without showing it except in being ornerier[3] even than usual.

Mr. Baumer didn't see him until he was almost on him, and then he stopped and fingered through the bills until he found the right one. He stepped up to Slade and held it out.

Slade said, "What's this, Dutchie?"

Mr. Baumer had to tilt his head up to talk to him. "You know vat it is."

Slade just said, "Yeah?" You never could tell from his face what went on inside his

---

1. **buckboard** *n.*: open carriage.
2. **freighter** *n.* used as *adj.*: here, person who transports goods.

3. **ornerier** (ôr′nər·ē·ər) *adj.*: dialect for "meaner and more stubborn."

Bargain   369

PRETEACHING

Selection Starter

Build background. Tell students that "Bargain" is historical fiction, so the setting plays an important role. Explain that Moon Dance, an imaginary place in the Old West, is like the rugged frontier towns that students have seen in movie westerns.

Assign the Reading

The dialect and the vocabulary related to the Old West will be challenging for many students. You may want to play the audio recording up through the second full paragraph of p. 371 for the class.

DIRECT TEACHING

A Literary Focus

? Point of view. What is this story's point of view? How do you know? [The pronoun *I* indicates that the story is told in the first person.]

B English-Language Learners

Nicknames. Point out that the nickname Dutchie indicates that Baumer is probably a German immigrant. Since the German word for German is *Deutsch,* Americans often called German immigrants "Dutch."

- *Holt Online Assessment*

Internet
- go.hrw.com (Keyword: LE5 7-4)
- *Elements of Literature Online*

Media
- *Audio CD Library*
- *Audio CD Library, Selections and Summaries in Spanish*

A **Reading Skills**

❓ **Predict.** What do you think Slade will do with the bill? Why do you think so? [Possible response: Slade will refuse to pay it and may destroy it. Since Baumer has given him the bill before, he's already failed to pay it at least once. He is described as "ornery," or difficult to manage. He seems rude and threatening.]

B **Reading Skills**

Predict. [Possible response to question 1: Slade will play the part of the bully, intimidating and humiliating Baumer at every turn.]

C **Literary Focus**

❓ **Point of view.** Why does the narrator give this information about himself? [Possible responses: He wants the reader to know who he is. He wants the reader to understand the relationship between himself and Mr. Baumer.]

D **Reading Skills**

Infer. [Possible response to question 2: Mr. Baumer is kind and encouraging. He knows that an education is important, and he tries to make sure that Al understands this. He looks out for Al, who lost his father. Slade is tough, disrespectful, and selfish. He doesn't care about others.]

E **English-Language Learners**

Idiom/metaphor. Explain that mules have a reputation for being stubborn and beavers are known for their tireless activity. The narrator is using a metaphor to say that the townspeople respect Baumer for his determined efforts to succeed.

skull. He had dark skin and shallow cheeks and a thick-growing moustache that fell over the corners of his mouth.

"It is a bill," Mr. Baumer said. "I tell you before, it is a bill. For twenty-vun dollars and fifty cents."

A "You know what I do with bills, don't you, Dutchie?" Slade asked.

Mr. Baumer didn't answer the question. He said, "For merchandise."

Slade took the envelope from Mr. Baumer's hand and squeezed it up in his fist and let it drop on the plank sidewalk. Not saying anything, he reached down and took Mr. Baumer's nose between the knuckles of his fingers and twisted it up into his eyes. That was all. That was all at the time. Slade half turned and slouched to the door of the bar and let himself in. Some men were laughing in there. ❶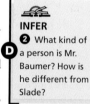

Mr. Baumer stooped and picked up the bill and put it on top of the rest and smoothed it out for mailing. When he straightened up, I could see tears in his eyes from having his nose screwed around.

C He didn't say anything to me, and I didn't say anything to him, being so much younger and feeling embarrassed for him. He went into the post office and slipped the bills in the slot, and we walked on home together. At the last, at the crossing where I had to leave him, he remembered to say, "Better study, Al. Is good to know to read and write and fig-**D**ure." I guess he felt he had to push me a little, my father being dead. ❷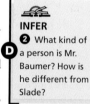

> **PREDICT**
> **B ❶** What part do you suppose Slade will play in this story?

> **INFER**
> **❷** What kind of a person is Mr. Baumer? How is he different from Slade?

I said, "Sure. See you after school tomorrow"—which he knew I would anyway. I had been working in the store for him during the summer and after classes ever since pneumonia took my dad off.

Three of us worked there regularly: Mr. Baumer, of course, and me and Colly Coleman, who knew enough to drive the delivery wagon but wasn't much help around the store except for carrying orders out to the rigs[4] at the hitchpost and handling heavy things like the whiskey barrel at the back of the store which Mr. Baumer sold quarts and gallons out of.

The store carried quite a bit of stuff—sugar and flour and dried fruits and canned goods and such on one side and yard goods and coats and caps and aprons and the like of that on the other, besides kerosene and bran and buckets and linoleum and pitchforks in the storehouse at the rear—but it wasn't a big store like Hirsch Brothers up the street. Never would be, people guessed, going on to say, with a sort of slow respect, **E** that it would have gone under long ago if Mr. Baumer hadn't been half mule and half beaver. He had started the store just two years before and, the way things were, worked himself close to death.

He was at the high desk at the end of the grocery counter when I came in the next afternoon. He had an eyeshade on and black sateen protectors on his forearms, and his pencil was in his hand instead of behind his ear and his glasses were roosted on the nose that Slade had twisted. He didn't hear me open and close the door or hear my feet as I walked back to him, and I saw he wasn't doing anything with the pencil but holding

---

4. **rigs** *n.:* carriages with their horses.

Learners Having Difficulty
Modeling. To help students read "Bargain," model recognizing the first-person point of view. Say: "I notice that the pronoun *I* is used often in the story, referring to the person who is telling the story. This clue tells me that the story is told from the first-person point of view." Encourage students as they read to ask themselves: "What are the narrator's thoughts and feelings?" and "What might the other characters be thinking or

doing that the first-person narrator is not aware of?"

English-Language Learners
Explain that Baumer speaks with a German accent, pronouncing *w* as *v*, and tends to use only the present tenses of verbs. Other characters in the story drop words ("there never was a freighter [who] didn't steal") and use idioms that may be unfamiliar. Assign peer tutors to help students understand the dialogue.

"I think he hate me. That is the thing. He hate me for coming not from this country...."

it over paper. I stood and studied him for a minute, seeing a small, stooped man with a little paunch bulging through his unbuttoned vest. He was a man you wouldn't remember from meeting once. There was nothing in his looks to set itself in your mind unless maybe it was his chin, which was a small pink hill in the gentle plain of his face.

While I watched him, he lifted his hand and felt carefully of his nose. Then he saw me. His eyes had that kind of mistiness that seems to go with age or illness, though he wasn't really old or sick, either. He brought his hand down quickly and picked up the pencil, but he saw I still was looking at the nose, and finally he sighed and said, "That Slade."

Just the sound of the name brought Slade to my eye. I saw him slouched in front of the bar, and I saw him and his string[5] coming down the grade from the buttes,[6] the wheel horses held snug and the rest lined out pretty, and then the string leveling off and Slade's whip lifting hair from a horse that wasn't up in the collar.[7] I had heard it said that Slade could make a horse scream with that whip. Slade's name wasn't Freighter, of course. Our town had nicknamed

---

5. **string** *n.:* here, a group of horses.
6. **buttes** (byo͞ots)*n.:* steep, flat-topped hills that stand alone on a plain.
7. **up in the collar:** pulling as hard as the other horses.

him that because that was what he was.

"I don't think it's any good to send him a bill, Mr. Baumer," I said. "He can't even read."

"He could pay yet."

"He don't pay anybody," I said.

"I think he hate me," Mr. Baumer went on. "That is the thing. He hate me for coming not from this country. I come here, sixteen years old, and learn to read and write, and I make a business, and so I think he hate me."

"He hates everybody."

Mr. Baumer shook his head. "But not to pinch the nose. Not to call Dutchie."

The side door squeaked open, but it was only Colly Coleman coming in from a trip, so I said, "Excuse me, Mr. Baumer, but you shouldn't have trusted him in the first place."

"I know," he answered, looking at me with his misty eyes. "A man make mistakes. I think some do not trust him, so he will pay me because I do. And I do not know him well then. He only came back to town three, four months ago, from being away since before I go into business."

"People who knew him before could have told you," I said.

"A man make mistakes," he explained again.

"It's not my business, Mr. Baumer, but I would forget the bill."

His eyes rested on my face for a long

Bargain 371

Bargain 371

DIRECT TEACHING

F Literary Focus

? Point of view. The narrator can only tell us what he observes about Baumer: that he is holding a pencil but not writing, that his eyes have a "kind of mistiness," and that he carefully feels his nose. What might be going on in Baumer's mind? [Possible responses: Baumer may be thinking about how he can cope with Slade and get him to pay for the injury he has caused and for the money he owes. The "mistiness" of Baumer's eyes may show that he is dreaming of revenge.]

G Learners Having Difficulty

Paraphrase. Ask students to state in their own words what Mr. Baumer is saying here. [Possible responses: Baumer thinks that Slade resents him. Slade is prejudiced against immigrants, particularly an immigrant who has succeeded in learning to read and write and owns a store. Since Slade can't read and write, he cannot feel superior to Baumer, and he hates Baumer for it.]

Special Education Students

For lessons designed for special education students, see *Holt Reading Solutions.*

Advanced Learners

Acceleration. Use the following activity to help advanced learners analyze how the choice of narrator affects characterization and plot.

Activity. After they have read the story, have students discuss the narrator. Point out that Al's version of the events is subjective because he is a participant and has relationships with the other characters. However, his story tends to stick to facts and background. Students should discuss why the writer chose this kind of narrator, what his personality and storytelling methods add to or detract from the story, and how a narration by Baumer or Slade might have been more or less reliable or more or less effective and dramatic.

A Reading Skills

❓ **Infer.** What do you think is really bothering Baumer? [Possible responses: He knows he is in the right; he wants his rights acknowledged more than he wants the money; the principle is important, not the twenty-one dollars and fifty cents. He knows the injustice of Slade's prejudice and, though he can't win in a physical fight with Slade, he wants to stand up to him.]

B Reading Skills

Predict. [Possible responses to question 3: Baumer will figure out a way to get Slade to pay what he owes. Slade will hurt and humiliate Baumer further.]

C Reading Skills

❓ **Predict.** Why do you think the writer includes this information in the story? [Possible responses: It explains how Slade stole whiskey from Baumer. It may be a clue that Slade will try to steal from Baumer again.]

D Reading Skills

Infer. [Possible response to question 4: Baumer is trying to think of a way to get back at Slade. A chiseled jaw is equated with masculinity. Baumer's chin is described as a "little hill," suggesting either that he lacks the strength and toughness to stand up to Slade, or that he has just enough strength in reserve to defeat Slade.]

minute, as if they didn't see me but the problem itself. He said, "It is not twenty-vun dollars and fifty cents now, Al. It is not that anymore."

"What is it?"

He took a little time to answer. Then he brought his two hands up as if to help him shape the words. "It is the thing. You see, it is the thing."

I wasn't quite sure what he meant.

He took his pencil from behind the ear where he had put it and studied the point of it. "That Slade. He steal whiskey and call it evaporation. He sneak things from his load. A thief, he is. And too big for me." ❸

I said, "I got no time for him, Mr. Baumer, but I guess there never was a freighter didn't steal whiskey. That's what I hear."

It was true, too. From the railroad to Moon Dance was fifty miles and a little better—a two-day haul in good weather, heck knew how long in bad. Any freight string bound home with a load had to lie out at least one night. When a freighter had his stock tended to and maybe a little fire going against the dark, he'd tackle a barrel of whiskey or of grain alcohol if he had one aboard consigned to Hirsch Brothers or Mr. Baumer's or the Moon Dance Saloon or the Gold Leaf Bar. He'd drive a hoop out of place, bore a little hole with a nail or bit and draw off what he wanted. Then he'd plug the hole with a whittled peg and pound the hoop back. That was evaporation. Nobody complained much. With freighters you generally took what they gave you, within reason.

"Moore steals it, too," I told Mr. Baumer. Moore was Mr. Baumer's freighter.

"Yah," he said, and that was all, but I stood there for a minute, thinking there might be something more. I could see thought swimming in his eyes, above that little hill of chin. Then a customer came in, and I had to go wait on him. ❹

Nothing happened for a month, nothing between Mr. Baumer and Slade, that is, but fall drew on toward winter and the first flight of ducks headed south and Mr. Baumer hired Miss Lizzie Webb to help with the just-beginning Christmas trade and here it was, the first week in October, and he and I walked up the street again with the monthly bills. He always sent them out. I guess he had to. A bigger store, like Hirsches', would wait on the ranchers until their beef or wool went to market.

Up to a point things looked and happened almost the same as they had before, so much the same that I had the crazy feeling I was going through that time again. There was a wagon and a rig tied up at Hirsches' rack and a saddle horse standing hipshot[8] in front of the harness shop. A few more people were on the street now, not many, and lamps had been lit against the shortened day.

It was dark enough that I didn't make out Slade right away. He was just a figure that came out of the yellow wash of light from the Moon Dance Saloon and stood on the boardwalk and with his head made the little

---

8. **hipshot** *adv.*: with one hip lower than the other.

CROSS-CURRICULAR CONNECTIONS

Culture

The Wild West. Explain to students that the nineteenth-century American frontier was a completely different place from today's United States. Many parts of the West were territories, not states, during the nineteenth century. Justice and customs tended to be rough, and sometimes people took the law into their own hands.

Activity. Have students look up information about the western territories in the nineteenth century. Students can share information about what frontier towns were like, how the laws were enforced, and how individuals settled disputes. Students can then discuss how well "Bargain" presents the setting and the customs of the times.

SMALL GROUP

The Apprentice by Robert Duncan.

Courtesy of the Artist.

motion of spitting. Then I recognized the lean, raw shape of him and the muscles flowing down into the sloped shoulders, and in the settling darkness I filled the picture in—the dark skin and the flat cheeks and the peevish eyes and the moustache growing rank.

There was Slade and here was Mr. Baumer with his bills and here I was, just as before, just like in the second go-round of a bad dream. I felt like turning back, being embarrassed and half scared by trouble even when it wasn't mine. Please, I said to myself, don't stop, Mr. Baumer! Don't bite off anything! Please, shortsighted the way you are, don't catch sight of him at all! I held up and stepped around behind Mr. Baumer and came up on the outside so as to be between him and Slade, where maybe I'd cut off his view.

But it wasn't any use. All along I think I knew it was no use, not the praying or the walking between or anything. The act had to play itself out.

Mr. Baumer looked across the front of me and saw Slade and hesitated in his step and came to a stop. Then in his slow, business way, his chin held firm against his mouth, he began fingering through the bills, squinting to make out the names. Slade had turned and was watching him, munching on a cud of tobacco like a bull waiting.

"You look, Al," Mr. Baumer said without lifting his face from the bills. "I cannot see so good."

Bargain 373

VIEWING THE ART

Robert Duncan, who grew up on a ranch in Utah, often depicts cowboys in his paintings.

Activity. Have students relate the illustration to the story. How does it help them visualize the story's setting and characters?

E Literary Focus

Characterization. What impressions do you form of Slade based on these observations of the narrator? What do the narrator's word choices reveal about the man? [Possible responses: The "lean, raw shape of him and the muscles flowing down . . ." suggest that Slade is physically powerful. The word *peevish* suggests that he is childish and easily annoyed, and the word *rank* suggests that his mustache is thick, coarse, and not very clean.]

F Literary Focus

Point of view. How does the first-person narration help to create suspense? [Possible responses: Readers are inside the mind of the narrator, experiencing his feelings of dread about what will happen. Readers do not know what the other characters may be thinking or planning.]

G Reading Skills

Predict. What do you think Baumer and Slade will do? Why do you think so? [Possible responses: Baumer will give Slade his bill again, because he is stubborn and he knows he is right. Slade will refuse to pay the bill again, because he never pays anyone and he despises Baumer.]

? Interpret. Note that Slade scuffs through the bills after they spill to the ground. Why might he do this? [Possible responses: Slade may want to show his contempt for Baumer's bill. Since Slade cannot read, words on a paper may frustrate him and make him want to lash out.]

B **Literary Focus**

? Point of view. What does Al's comment "I could have hit harder myself" add to this scene? [Possible response: It emphasizes Baumer's physical weakness and helplessness.]

C **Reading Skills**

? Draw conclusions. How do the other characters feel about the fight? How do you know? [Possible responses: No one likes Slade; everyone is on Baumer's side. Everyone is afraid of Slade. Clues that lead to these conclusions are the fact that the characters line up to shield Baumer from Slade; that Al says no one wants to take Slade on; and that McDonald is only friendly because he wants Slade to calm down.]

D **English-Language Learners**

Idioms. Explain to students that "That's the ticket" means "That's the right thing to do."

E **Reading Skills**

Interpret. Ask students why Baumer does not look beaten in spite of losing the fight. [Possible response: Slade's brutality doesn't change the question of right and wrong, and Baumer still knows he is right.]

F **Reading Skills**

Predict. [Possible response to question 5: The narrator reports that Baumer does not look as if he has given up, and Slade angrily threatens Baumer, suggesting Baumer has made a point with him. Baumer will continue to confront Slade until justice is done.]

So I looked, and while I was looking, Slade must have moved. The next I knew, Mr. Baumer was staggering ahead, the envelopes spilling out of his hands. There had been a thump, the clap of a heavy hand swung hard on his back.

Slade said, "Haryu, Dutchie?"

Mr. Baumer caught his balance and turned around, the bills he had trampled shining white between them and at Slade's feet the hat that Mr. Baumer had stumbled out from under.

A Slade picked up the hat and scuffed through the bills and held it out. "Cold to be goin' without a skypiece," he said.

Mr. Baumer hadn't spoken a word. The lampshine from inside the bar caught his eyes, and in them, it seemed to me, a light came and went as anger and the uselessness of it took turns in his head.

Two men had come up on us and stood watching. One of them was Angus McDonald, who owned the Ranchers' Bank, and the other was Dr. King. He had his bag in his hand.

Two others were drifting up, but I didn't have time to tell who. The light came in Mr. Baumer's eyes, and he took a step ahead and **B** swung. I could have hit harder myself. The fist landed on Slade's cheek without hardly so much as jogging his head, but it let the devil loose in the man. I didn't know he could move so fast. He slid in like a practiced fighter and let Mr. Baumer have it full in the face.

Mr. Baumer slammed over on his back, but he wasn't out. He started lifting himself. Slade leaped ahead and brought a boot heel down on the hand he was lifting himself by. I heard meat and bone under that heel and saw Mr. Baumer fall back and try to roll away.

Things had happened so fast that not until then did anyone have a chance to get between them. Now Mr. McDonald pushed at Slade's chest, saying, "That's enough, Freighter. That's enough, now," and Dr. King lined up, too, and another man I didn't know, and I took a place, and we formed a kind of screen between them. Dr. King **C** turned and bent to look at Mr. Baumer.

"Fool hit me first," Slade said.

"That's enough," Mr. McDonald told him again while Slade looked at all of us as if he'd spit on us for a nickel. Mr. McDonald went on, using a half-friendly tone, and I knew it was because he didn't want to take Slade on any more than the rest of us did. "You go on home and sleep it off, Freighter. **D** That's the ticket."

Slade just snorted.

From behind us, Dr. King said, "I think you've broken this man's hand."

"Lucky for him I didn't kill him," Slade answered. "Dutch penny pincher!" He fingered the chew out of his mouth. "Maybe he'll know enough to leave me alone now."

Dr. King had Mr. Baumer on his feet. "I'll take him to the office," he said.

Blood was draining from Mr. Baumer's nose and rounding the curve of his lip and dripping from the sides of his chin. He held **E** his hurt right hand in the other. But the thing was that he didn't look beaten even then, not the way a man who has given up looks beaten. Maybe that was why Slade said, with a show of that fierce anger, "You stay away from me! Hear? Stay clear away, or you'll get more of the same!" **5**

Dr. King led Mr. Baumer away, Slade went back into

PREDICT
5 What clues **F** suggest that Baumer will not give up? How could he get even with Slade?

MINI-LESSON **Reading**

Developing Word-Attack Skills
Display the selection word *ornerier*. Help students analyze the word as the base word *ornery* plus the comparative ending *–er*. Remind students that when suffixes and endings are added to words that end with *y*, the *y* changes to *i*. Recalling this can help them pronounce and decode words.

Then, write the words *mistiness* and *business* on the chalkboard and have students compare their pronunciations. *Mistiness* sounds like the base word *misty* plus *–ness*: /mis′tē·nis/. *Business* is the combination of *busy* and *–ness,* but its pronunciation and meaning have changed over time. The second vowel in *business* is not pronounced: /biz′nis/, and the word has come to mean "work" or "responsibility" instead of "the state of being busy." Share the fact that the word *busyness* (biz′ē·nis) was coined to cover that meaning.

the bar, and the other men walked off, talking about the fight. I got down and picked up the bills, because I knew Mr. Baumer would want me to, and mailed them at the post office, dirty as they were. It made me sorer, someway, that Slade's bill was one of the few that wasn't marked up. The cleanness of it seemed to say that there was no getting the best of him.

Mr. Baumer had his hand in a sling the next day and wasn't much good at waiting on the trade. I had to hustle all afternoon and so didn't have a chance to talk to him even if he had wanted to talk. Mostly he stood at his desk, and once, passing it, I saw he was practicing writing with his left hand. His nose and the edges of the cheeks around it were swollen some.

At closing time I said, "Look, Mr. Baumer, I can lay out of school a few days until you kind of get straightened out here."

"No," he answered as if to wave the subject away. "I get somebody else. You go to school. Is good to learn."

I had a half notion to say that learning hadn't helped him with Slade. Instead, I blurted out that I would have the law on Slade.

"The law?" he asked.

"The sheriff or somebody."

"No, Al," he said. "You would not."

I asked why.

"The law, it is not for plain fights," he said. "Shooting? Robbing? Yes, the law come quick. The plain fights, they are too many. They not count enough."

He was right. I said, "Well, I'd do something anyhow."

"Yes," he answered with a slow nod of his head. "Something you vould do, Al." He didn't tell me what.

Within a couple of days he got another man to clerk for him—it was Ed Hempel, who was always finding and losing jobs—and we made out. Mr. Baumer took his hand from the sling in a couple or three weeks, but with the tape on it, it still wasn't any use to him. From what you could see of the fingers below the tape, it looked as if it never would be.

He spent most of his time at the high desk, sending me or Ed out on the errands he used to run, like posting and getting the mail. Sometimes I wondered if that was because he was afraid of meeting Slade. He could just as well have gone himself. He wasted a lot of hours just looking at nothing, though I will have to say he worked hard at learning to write left-handed.

Then, a month and a half before Christmas, he hired Slade to haul his freight for him. [6]

Ed Hempel told me about the deal when I showed up for work. "Yessir," he said, resting his foot on a crate in the storeroom where we were supposed to be working. "I tell you he's throwed in with Slade. Told me this morning to go out and locate him if I could and bring him in. Slade was at the saloon, o' course, and says to the devil with Dutchie, but I told him this was honest-to-God business, like Baumer had told me to, and there was a quart of whiskey right there in the store for him if he'd come and get it. He was out of money, I reckon, because the quart fetched him."

"What'd they say?" I asked him.

"Search me. There was two or three people in the store and Baumer told me to

G Literary Focus

? Characterization. What does Baumer's practicing writing with his left hand tell you about him? [Possible responses: Baumer is strong-willed, persistent, and courageous. Baumer may believe his right hand has been crippled.]

H Reading Skills

Infer. Point out that Baumer continues to stress the importance of education. Ask why Baumer may have such a strong view about its value. [Possible response: He was able to succeed in business because he learned to read and write English.]

I Reading Skills

? Predict. What do you think Baumer has in mind? Identify clues in the text that support your predictions. [Possible responses: He intends to take matters into his own hands, since he refuses to seek legal help. He intends to use his brains to get even with Slade; he is always talking about the importance of education, and he knows he can't win a fistfight with Slade.]

J Reading Skills

Predict. [Possible responses to question 6: They will confront one another again about the bill. Baumer will take the amount of the bill out of Slade's wages. There will be another fight or showdown between the men. Baumer has a plan to get the better of Slade.]

K Literary Focus

? Point of view. Though the narrator did not witness Baumer's hiring of Slade, he provides a first-hand account of the event. How does he do it? [The narrator repeats the dialogue between himself and Ed Hempel, a character who works at the store and who brought Slade in to see Baumer.]

Activity. Display these words. Have students identify the base word and the suffix or ending.

1. worrisome [worry + –some]
2. compliance [comply + –ance]
3. craziness [crazy + –ness]
4. easiness [easy + –ness]
5. silliness [silly + –ness]
6. hardiness [hardy + –ness]
7. pettiness [petty + –ness]
8. seemliness [seemly + –ness]
9. heaviness [heavy + –ness]
10. heartiest [hearty + –est]
11. happiness [happy + –ness]
12. readiness [ready + –ness]
13. reliant [rely + –ant]
14. wearisome [weary + –some]

VIEWING THE ART

Frederic S. Remington
(1861–1909) left an enduring pictorial record of life on the western frontier. Here, in *The Fall of the Cowboy,* he conjures a wintry image of the loneliness of frontier life.

Activity. Invite students to discuss what this artwork could help them to understand about the lives of the characters in the story. [Possible responses: The work can help readers appreciate how difficult and lonely it must have been for people living on the frontier during the cold days of winter. The possibility of Slade's freezing to death seems more realistic after readers view this wintry scene.]

🅐 Reading Skills

❷ Draw conclusions. Why do you think the narrator mentions Baumer's feeling his broken fingers? [Possible responses: to remind readers that Slade broke Baumer's hand; to show that Baumer is remembering, and perhaps dwelling upon, how Slade harmed him.]

The Fall of the Cowboy (1895) by Frederic S. Remington. Oil on canvas.
© Amon Carter Museum, Fort Worth, Texas (1961.230).

wait on 'em, and he and Slade palavered[9] back by the desk."

"How do you know they made a deal?"

Ed spread his hands out. "'Bout noon, Moore came in with his string, and I heard Baumer say he was makin' a change. Moore didn't like it too good, either."

It was a hard thing to believe, but there one day was Slade with a pile of stuff for the Moon Dance Mercantile Company, and that was

---

9. palavered (pə·lav′ərd) *v.:* talked; met to discuss something.

proof enough with something left for boot.

Mr. Baumer never opened the subject up with me, though I gave him plenty of chances. And I didn't feel like asking. He didn't talk much these days but went 🅐 around absent-minded, feeling now and then of the fingers that curled yellow and stiff out of the bandage like the toes on the leg of a dead chicken. Even on our walks home he kept his thoughts to himself.

I felt different about him now and was sore inside. Not that I blamed him exactly. A hundred and thirty-five pounds wasn't

---

DEVELOPING FLUENCY

Activity. Have students work with partners or in small groups to read sections of the story aloud. One student can read the narration, and others can read the dialogue of the individual characters. Students can help one another with pronunciation of the dialect and of Baumer's German-accented English. Students can compare the dialect to standard English and discuss what the dialect adds to the story.

PAIRED

SMALL GROUP

much to throw against two hundred. And who could tell what Slade would do on a bellyful of whiskey? He had promised Mr. Baumer more of the same, hadn't he? But I didn't feel good. I couldn't look up to Mr. Baumer like I used to and still wanted to. I didn't have the beginning of an answer when men cracked jokes or shook their heads in sympathy with Mr. Baumer, saying Slade had made him come to time.

Slade hauled in a load for the store, and another, and Christmastime was drawing on and trade heavy, and the winter that had started early and then pulled back came on again. There was a blizzard and then a still cold and another blizzard and afterwards a sunshine that was iceshine on the drifted snow. I was glad to be busy, selling overshoes and sheep-lined coats and mitts and socks as thick as saddle blankets and Christmas candy out of buckets and hickory nuts and the fresh oranges that the people in our town never saw except when Santa Claus was coming.

One afternoon, when I lit out from class, the thermometer on the school porch read forty-two degrees below. But you didn't have to look at it to know how cold the weather was. Your nose and fingers and toes and ears and the bones inside you told you. The snow cried when you stepped on it.

I got to the store and took my things off and scuffed my hands at the stove for a minute so's to get life enough in them to tie a parcel. Mr. Baumer—he was always polite to me—said, "Hello, Al. Not so much to do today. Too cold for customers." He shuddered a little, as if he hadn't got the chill off even yet, and rubbed his broken hand with the good one. "Ve need Christmas goods," he said, looking out the window to the furrows that wheels had made in the snow-banked street, and I knew he was thinking of Slade's string, inbound from the railroad, and the time it might take even Slade to travel those hard miles.

Slade never made it at all.

Less than an hour later our old freighter, Moore, came in, his beard white and stiff with frost. He didn't speak at first but looked around and clumped to the stove and took off his heavy mitts, holding his news inside him.

Then he said, not pleasantly, "Your new man's dead, Baumer."

"My new man?" Mr. Baumer said.

"Who do you think? Slade. He's dead."

All Mr. Baumer could say was "Dead!"

"Froze to death, I figger," Moore told him, while Colly Coleman and Ed Hempel and Miss Lizzie and I and a couple of customers stepped closer.

"Not Slade," Mr. Baumer said. "He know too much to freeze."

"Maybe so, but he sure's froze now. I got him in the wagon."

We stood looking at one another and at Moore. Moore was enjoying his news, enjoying feeding it out bit by bit so's to hold the stage. "Heart might've give out, for all I know."

The side door swung open, letting in a cloud of cold and three men who stood, like us, waiting on Moore. I moved a little and looked through the window and saw Slade's freight outfit tied outside with more men around it. Two of them were on a wheel of one of the wagons, looking inside.

"Had a extra man, so I brought your stuff in," Moore went on. "Figgered you'd be glad to pay for it."

"Not Slade," Mr. Baumer said again.

B Literary Focus

? Point of view. How has Al's view of Baumer changed since the start of the story? Why has it changed? [Possible responses: Al has lost respect for Baumer. Al's view has changed because he thinks hiring Slade means that Baumer is weaker and more cowardly than Al had imagined.]

C Advanced Learners

Narrator. Ask students whether they believe Al's interpretation of Baumer's thoughts. [Possible responses: Yes, because Baumer is a good businessman. No, Al can't possibly see inside Baumer's head.] After students have finished the story, return to this passage. Ask what Baumer was really thinking about. [He was wondering whether Slade had taken the bait of the barrel of alcohol.]

DIRECT TEACHING

A **Reading Skills**

❓ Predict. Did you predict this ending? Whether you did or didn't, look for clues in the story that foreshadow it. [Possible response: Guthrie foreshadowed the ending by informing the reader that freighters often steal whiskey to get through cold nights, by saying Baumer didn't look as if he was beaten after the second fight with Slade, and by suggesting that Baumer has something on his mind that Al can't determine.]

B **Reading Skills**

Infer. [Possible response to question 7: Because he was unable to read the warning label, Slade tapped into the barrel of poisonous wood alcohol and drank enough to kill himself.]

GUIDED PRACTICE

Monitor students' progress. Have students answer the following questions.

Short Answer

1. Describe Baumer's appearance. [small, stooped, plain, ordinary-looking, with a stubborn chin]

2. What does Slade call Baumer? [Dutchie]

3. What kind of person is Slade? [a thief, a bully, a drunk, illiterate, mean]

4. What action does Baumer take that surprises Al? [Baumer hires Slade to haul freight.]

5. What skill could Slade have learned that might have kept him alive? [how to read]

"You can take a look at him."

Mr. Baumer answered no.

"Someone's takin' word to Connor to bring his hearse. Anyhow, I told 'em to. I carted old Slade this far. Connor can have him now."

Moore pulled on his mitts. "Found him there by the Deep Creek crossin', doubled up in the snow an' his fire out." He moved toward the door. "I'll see to the horses, but your stuff'll have to set there. I got more'n enough work to do at Hirsches'."

Mr. Baumer just nodded.

I put on my coat and went out and waited my turn and climbed on a wagon wheel and looked inside, and there was Slade piled on some bags of bran. Maybe because of being frozen, his face was whiter than I ever saw it, whiter and deader, too, though it never had been lively. Only the moustache seemed still alive, sprouting thick like greasewood from alkali.[10] Slade was doubled up all right, as if he had died and stiffened leaning forward in a chair.

I got down from the wheel, and Colly and then Ed climbed up. Moore was unhitching, tossing off his pieces of information while he did so. Pretty soon Mr. Connor came up with his old hearse, and he and Moore tumbled Slade into it, and the team, which was as old as the hearse, made off, the tires squeaking in the snow. The people trailed on away with it, their breaths leaving little ribbons of mist in the air. It was beginning to get dark.

Mr. Baumer came out of the side door of the store, bundled up, and called to Colly and Ed and me. "We unload," he said. "Already is late. Al, better you get a couple lanterns now."

We did a fast job, setting the stuff out of the wagons onto the platform and then carrying it or rolling it on the one truck that the store owned and stowing it inside according to where Mr. Baumer's good hand pointed.

A barrel was one of the last things to go in. I edged it up and Colly nosed the truck under it, and then I let it fall back. "Mr. Baumer," I said, "we'll never sell all this, will we?"

"Yah," he answered. "Sure we sell it. I get it cheap. A bargain, Al, so I buy it."

I looked at the barrel head again. There in big letters I saw "Wood Alcohol—Deadly Poison."

"Hurry now," Mr. Baumer said. "Is late." For a flash and no longer I saw through the mist in his eyes, saw, **A** you might say, that hilly chin repeated there. "Then ve go home, Al. Is good to know to read." **❼**

INFER
❼ What happened to Slade? **B**

---

10. **greasewood from alkali:** Greasewood is a thorny desert plant. Alkali is dry, salty soil that might look white and chalky, like Slade's face.

FAMILY/COMMUNITY ACTIVITY

Have students discuss the Quickwrite activity with their families. What do students' families think about the difference between revenge and justice? Can the two be combined? Have students summarize "Bargain" for their families and discuss other ways Mr. Baumer might have taken his revenge or achieved justice.

Meet the Writer

A. B. Guthrie

"Real People in Real Times"

A. B. Guthrie (1901–1991) wanted to portray the West as it was, not create myths about it. He said:

> 66 I want to talk about real people in real times. For every Wyatt Earp or Billy the Kid, there were thousands of people just trying to get along. 99

Most readers agree that Guthrie succeeded. His most famous work, a trilogy about the opening of the West, is noted for its historical accuracy. Guthrie also wrote the screenplay for *Shane,* a famous movie about a western gunslinger. Shane takes justice into his own hands to save a family and pays a bitter price.

Albert Bertram Guthrie, Jr., grew up in the little town of Choteau, Montana. After graduating from college, he traveled extensively and worked at various jobs—ranching in Sonora, Mexico; selling groceries in California; working as a census taker in Montana.

Guthrie became a fiction writer when he took time out from his newspaper job to visit his sick mother. During his visit he had time to write his first novel, *Murders at Moon Dance* (1943). In this book he introduces the setting of "Bargain" and many of his other short stories. In talking about writing, Guthrie said:

> 66 There's no immediate reward in putting words on paper. The reward, great but fugitive, is in having written, in having found the word, the line, the paragraph, the chapter that is as good as ever you can make it. I spent a full day on one line of dialogue and knocked off satisfied. 99

For Independent Reading

Guthrie's novels about the opening of the West are *The Big Sky; The Way West,* which won the Pulitzer Prize; and *These Thousand Hills.*

Meet the Writer

A. B. Guthrie taught creative writing for years at the University of Kentucky. The critic Thomas W. Ford identifies many of the themes of "Bargain" when he offers this summary of Guthrie's vision: "Guthrie sees, as do so many other Americans, East and West, that enormously complex experience called the Western movement as the fundamental American experience. He pictures in the phases of this movement a microcosm of the American character, with all its contradictions and ambiguities: respect for the physical as well as the spiritual, the individual but also the group, innocence and violence, the mean and noble, the practical and the ideal, determinism but also free choice, human limitations along with moments of transcendence, self-destruction, and self-realization."

For Independent Reading

For a different view of the challenges and conflicts of life on the frontier, students may want to read one of the final three volumes of Laura Ingalls Wilder's *Little House* series: *The Long Winter, Little House on the Prairie,* and *These Happy Golden Years.* These autobiographical novels, narrated from the point of view of the teenage heroine Laura, tell of the pioneer life in frontier towns. Wilder's books echo the violence and lawlessness of Guthrie's story, but also examine the more uplifting aspects of life in the Old West.

Advanced Learners

Enrichment. Have students gather for a screening of the famous film *Shane.* Afterward, students can compare the characters, points of view, and themes explored in *Shane* and "Bargain." Which story do students prefer? Which seems more realistic? Which seems more idealistic? Why? What might Shane have done in Baumer's situation? What other actions do students think either Baumer or Shane might have taken to resolve the conflicts they faced?

INDEPENDENT PRACTICE

After You Read

First Thoughts

1. Possible answers: Baumer did nothing to harm Slade except hire him to perform a job. Baumer had a good idea that Slade would steal alcohol from him and therefore is guilty of plotting Slade's murder.

Thinking Critically

2. Students may say that it is about justice because Slade deserved to be punished, or that it is about revenge because Baumer plotted to kill Slade, or that it is about both.

3. Possible answers: Baumer means that the principle of justice must be served. Slade must be made to pay for what he stole and for hurting Baumer.

4. Some students may have predicted that Baumer had something planned for dealing with Slade when he rehired him.

5. Baumer suggests that Slade's death results from Slade's inability to read.

6. Possible answer: Education can be a powerful antidote to those who rely strictly on force.

Extending Interpretations

7. If Baumer had told the story, readers would probably be certain about his plotting Slade's death and the ending wouldn't be a surprise. This would eliminate the fun readers have of figuring things out for themselves. Some students may say that the theme would not change. Others may propose a new theme, such as "a victim of injustice may strike back."

First Thoughts

1. What do you think of what Baumer does to Slade? Does he do the right thing? Why or why not?

Thinking Critically

2. Look again at your Quickwrite notes. Would you say this story is about justice or about revenge? Explain. ✏️

3. When Al suggests that Mr. Baumer forget Slade's bill, Mr. Baumer says that it isn't the money anymore; it is "the thing." What do you think Mr. Baumer means by "the thing"?

4. At what point in the story did you **predict** what was going to happen next? Go back now, and identify the details that provide clues to Slade's fate. 📖

5. Why does Baumer say at the end, "Is good to know to read"?

6. **Theme** sums up what the characters learn or discover in the story and what you learn or discover as you share their experiences. What do you think the theme of "Bargain" is?

Extending Interpretations

7. "Bargain" is written in the **first-person point of view,** from Al's vantage point. What would you have known if Mr. Baumer had told the story himself? Would the story's **theme** change? If so, what might the new theme be?

WRITING

Summarizing the Cases For and Against Mr. Baumer

Imagine that Mr. Baumer is put on trial for causing Slade's death. In one paragraph, **summarize** the case *for* Mr. Baumer. Present evidence to show that Slade is responsible for his own death. This would be the case for the defense. In another paragraph, summarize the case *against* Mr. Baumer. Give reasons and evidence to inform and convince the jury that Mr. Baumer is guilty. This would be the case for the prosecution.

INTERNET
Projects and Activities
Keyword: LE5 7-4

SKILLS FOCUS

Literary Skills
Analyze first-person point of view.

Reading Skills
Make predictions.

Writing Skills
Write persuasive arguments.

> #### Reading Check
> Suppose that Al decides he has to confide to someone what he knows about Baumer's feud with Slade and the likely cause of Slade's death. He chooses to tell the whole story to Dr. King. With a partner, role-play Al and Dr. King. As Al tells what happened, Dr. King should comment and ask questions. Be sure to cover all the **main events** in the story.

Reading Check

Role-play responses will vary. Make sure students cover all the main events in the story, including

- Baumer's encounter with Slade when Slade refuses to pay Baumer's bill and humiliates him

- Al's discussion with Baumer at the store about Slade and his illiteracy

- Baumer's second encounter with Slade, where they get into a fight

- Baumer's decision to hire Slade over the regular freighter

- Slade's death while hauling a load of freight

- Al's discovery of a barrel of poison in Slade's load of freight

Vocabulary Development

Comprehension Strategies: Tips for Word Detectives

When you come across a word you don't know and the nearest dictionary is far, far away, use these tips to unlock its meaning.

- **Look to see if parts of the word are familiar.**
  In "Bargain," Mr. Baumer's store is called the Moon Dance Mercantile Company. In figuring out *mercantile*, you might think of the word *merchant*. A merchant is someone, like Mr. Baumer, who sells goods, or merchandise. *Merchandise, merchant,* and *mercantile* all come from the Latin word *mercari*, which means "to trade."

- **Look at the word's context—the surrounding words and sentences—to see if it helps you figure out what the word means.**
  For example, what if a friend said, "I consigned my old bike to be sold at the bicycle store. They sold it for fifty dollars, kept their fee of twenty dollars, and gave me thirty." The context helps you figure out that the word *consign* means "turn goods over to someone else to sell." Your friend had a storekeeper sell his bike, and he gave the store part of the money.

PRACTICE

1. In "Bargain," Colly carries customers' orders out to carriages waiting at the hitchpost. How would you figure out the meaning of *hitchpost*?

2. Use context clues to figure out the meaning of *screen* in this sentence: "Dr. King lined up, too, and another man I didn't know, and I took a place, and we formed a kind of screen between them [Slade and Mr. Baumer]."

SKILLS FOCUS

Vocabulary Skills
Use comprehension strategies.

Bargain **381**

Vocabulary Development

PRACTICE

Possible Answers

1. To *hitch* means "to tie up," and a *post* is a pole. Since the characters in the story depend on horses for transportation, a *hitchpost* is probably a post to which you can tie your horse while you wait for your order.

2. A *screen* is a kind of protective shield. Dr. King, the other man, and Al make a screen of their bodies; they stand between Slade and Baumer, trying to protect Baumer.

ASSESSING

Assessment
- *Holt Assessment: Literature, Reading, and Vocabulary*

RETEACHING

For a lesson reteaching point of view, see **Reteaching,** pp. 917G–H.

Grade-Level Skills

■ **Literary Skills**
Analyze omniscient point of view.

Review Skills

■ **Literary Skills**
Identify the speaker, and recognize the difference between first- and third-person narration.

Summary 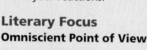 *at grade level*

In this Chinese version of "Cinderella," Yeh-Shen, an orphaned girl, is mistreated by her stepmother and stepsister, and has only one friend: a fish that she feeds every day. The girl grieves deeply when her step-mother catches and eats this fish, but a mysterious old man tells Yeh-Shen that its bones have the power to help her. For some time, she depends upon the bones to provide her with food. When the spring-festival time comes, the girl asks the bones for decent clothes to wear to the feast. She receives a wondrous outfit and is warned not to lose the magical golden shoes. At the festival her stepsister nearly rec-ognizes her, so Yeh-Shen flees, losing a shoe—and with it her ability to communicate with the bones. The lost shoe is presented to the king, who displays it in hopes of finding its owner. No woman can wedge her foot into the tiny shoe except Yeh-Shen; when she does, the king marries her. At the end of the tale, her evil stepmother and stepsister die when their cave home collapses.

Before You Read The Folk Tale

Yeh-Shen

Make the Connection
Talk It Over

What popular story features these characters, object, and theme?

- a hardworking girl
- a wicked stepmother
- a special slipper
- Good is rewarded eventually, and evil is punished.

You probably know those characters and the theme from the fairy tale "Cinderella." "Cinderella" and "Yeh-Shen" are two versions of the same story, about a girl whose dream comes true.

Discussion. People around the world have been telling the Cinderella story for ages. In a small group, talk about why you think the story of "Cinderella" is such a favorite. What do people like about the story? What deep human wishes do you think it expresses? As you read this Chinese folk tale, keep a sheet of paper handy so that you can jot down your reactions.

Literary Focus
Omniscient Point of View

The omniscient (äm·nish′ənt) point of view is probably very familiar to you.

You've heard it in fairy tales since you were young. A narrator who tells a story from the **omniscient point of view** knows everything about the characters and their problems. This omniscient narrator isn't *in* the story. This narrator can't even be seen. In fact, an omniscient, or all-knowing, narrator stands above the action, like a god.

Fish, from an album of twelve studies of flowers, birds, and fish by Tsubaki Chinzan (1801–1854). Watercolor on silk with patterned border.

British Library, London, UK/Bridgeman Art Library.

go.
hrw
.com

INTERNET
Cross-curricular
Connection
Keyword: LE5 7-4

SKILLS
FOCUS

Literary Skills
Understand omniscient point of view.

> **Background**
> **Literature and Literary History**
>
> There are more than nine hundred versions of "Cinderella." Scholars have traced the oldest version back more than a thousand years, to China. The version that you probably know best was collected in 1697 by a French writer named Charles Perrault. His is the first version to include a fairy godmother and a midnight curfew. "Yeh-Shen" is a Chinese version of the Cinderella story.

382   Collection 4 / Can You See It My Way?

RESOURCES: READING

Planning
- *One-Stop Planner* CD-ROM with ExamView Test Generator

Differentiating Instruction
- *Holt Adapted Reader*
- *Holt Reading Solutions*
- *Supporting Instruction in Spanish*
- *Audio CD Library*

- *Audio CD Library, Selections and Summaries in Spanish*

Grammar and Language
- *Daily Language Activities*

Assessment
- *Holt Assessment: Literature, Reading, and Vocabulary*
- *One-Stop Planner* CD-ROM with ExamView Test Generator

Carp (1848) by Taito.

Courtesy of the Board of Trustees of the Victoria and Albert Museum, London.

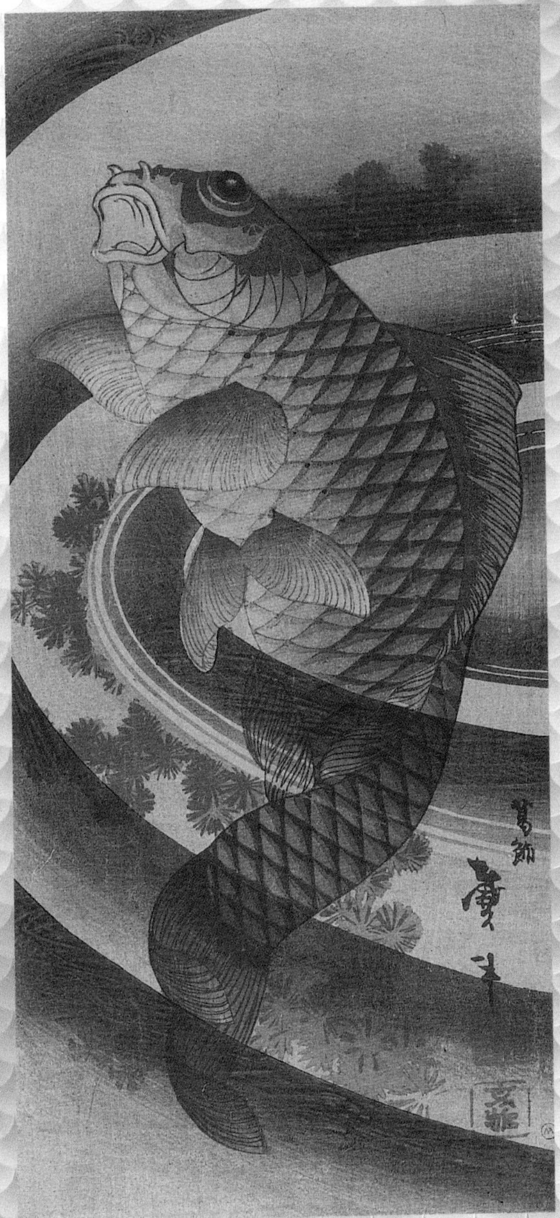

YEH-SHEN

Chinese folk tale,
retold by **Ai-Ling Louie**

THE ONLY FRIEND THAT YEH-SHEN HAD WAS A FISH . . .

In the dim past, even before the Ch'in and the Han dynasties, there lived a cave chief of southern China by the name of Wu. **(A)** As was the custom in those days, Chief Wu had taken two wives. Each wife in her turn had presented Wu with a baby daughter. But one of the wives sickened and died, and not too many days after that Chief Wu took to his bed and died too.

Yeh-Shen, the little orphan, grew to girlhood in her stepmother's home. She was a

- *Holt Online Assessment*

Internet
- go.hrw.com (Keyword: LE5 7-4)
- *Elements of Literature Online*

Media
- *Audio CD Library*
- *Audio CD Library, Selections and Summaries in Spanish*

PRETEACHING

Skills Starter

Build review skills. Remind students that authors can choose one of three points of view from which to narrate their stories. They can choose either the third-person omniscient (the narrator is outside the story and knows what all the characters are doing and thinking), the third-person limited (the point of view character is referred to as "he" or "she," and readers learn only what that character knows), or the first person ("I"). Because many folk and fairy tales are passed down from generation to generation by storytellers, such stories are often told from the third-person omniscient point of view. In addition, since folk and fairy tales often teach a lesson about living, a narrator who knows each character's motives and desires can best convey this lesson.

Assign the Reading

Remind students to recall the features of fairy tales and folk tales they've read in the past. Assign students having difficulty to small groups to read the story.

DIRECT TEACHING

(A) Literary Focus

? Recognize patterns in fairy tales. Point out to students the first four words of the story. What classic fairy-tale beginning does it remind them of? Do they know of any more recent stories or movies that open in the same way? What purpose do such openers serve? [Possible responses: Many fairy tales start with "Once upon a time. . . . " More recently, the first *Star Wars* movie opened with "Long, long ago, in a galaxy far, far away. . . ." Such openers tell readers that the events of the story happened a long time ago and give them a legendary aura.]

? Point of view. Ask students to identify this story's narrative point of view. [omniscient third person] What clues in the first two paragraphs help them figure this out? [Possible responses: These paragraphs tell what Yeh-Shen's stepmother does and why. The narrator also knows Yeh-Shen's only friend is a fish. Therefore, the narrator must know everyone's thoughts and secrets.]

B Literary Focus

Recognize patterns in fairy tales. Remind students of other fairy tales, such as "Snow White," in which a jealous stepmother uses a disguise to trick her victim. Then, ask students to describe the way in which Yeh-Shen's stepmother fools and kills the fish. [She sends Yeh-Shen to get firewood, puts on her stepdaughter's jacket pretending to be Yeh-Shen, and then stabs the fish.]

C Literary Focus

? Recognize character types. Remind students that certain character types such as the wicked stepmother appear often in fairy tales. Who do you think this kind uncle might be? [Possible responses: He might be the spirit of the dead fish or a "fairy godfather" figure.]

---

bright child and lovely too, with skin as smooth as ivory and dark pools for eyes. Her stepmother was jealous of all this beauty and goodness, for her own daughter was not pretty at all. So in her displeasure, she gave poor Yeh-Shen the heaviest and most unpleasant chores.

The only friend that Yeh-Shen had to her name was a fish she had caught and raised. It was a beautiful fish with golden eyes, and every day it would come out of the water and rest its head on the bank of the pond, waiting for Yeh-Shen to feed it. Stepmother gave Yeh-Shen little enough food for herself,

but the orphan child always found something to share with her fish, which grew to enormous size.

Somehow the stepmother heard of this. She was terribly angry to discover that Yeh-Shen had kept a secret from her. She hurried down to the pond, but she was unable to see the fish, for Yeh-Shen's pet wisely hid itself. The stepmother, however, was a crafty woman, and she soon thought of a plan. She walked home and called out, "Yeh-Shen, go and collect some firewood. But wait! The neighbors might see you. Leave your filthy coat here!" The minute the girl was out of sight, her stepmother slipped on the coat herself and went down again to the pond. This time the big fish saw Yeh-Shen's familiar jacket and heaved itself onto the bank, expecting to be fed. But the stepmother, having hidden a dagger in her sleeve, stabbed the fish, wrapped it in her garments, and took it home to cook for dinner.

When Yeh-Shen came to the pond that evening, she found her pet had disappeared. Overcome with grief, the girl collapsed on the ground and dropped her tears into the still waters of the pond.

"Ah, poor child!" a voice said.

Yeh-Shen sat up to find a very old man looking down at her. He wore the coarsest of clothes, and his hair flowed down over his shoulders.

"Kind uncle, who may you be?" Yeh-Shen asked.

"That is not important, my child. All you must know is that I have been sent to tell you of the wondrous powers of your fish."

"My fish, but sir . . ." The girl's eyes filled with tears, and she could not go on.

The old man sighed and said, "Yes, my

Carp with Bogbean by Sadatora (19th century).
British Library, London, UK/Bridgeman Art Library.

DIFFERENTIATING INSTRUCTION

Learners Having Difficulty
Point of view. Be sure students understand that point of view identifies who is telling the story. Encourage students to ask themselves these questions as they read "Yeh-Shen": Is the teller a character in the story, or is the teller someone outside the story who knows everything that's going on? How might the story be different if one of the characters told it?

English-Language Learners
Parents from Africa to Vietnam have told the basic story of Cinderella to their children. Encourage students to share versions of the fairy tale with the class. Then, discuss the similarities and differences among the tales. You might have volunteers create a compare-and-contrast chart on the chalkboard.

Special Education Students
For lessons designed for special education students, see *Holt Reading Solutions*.

child, your fish is no longer alive, and I must tell you that your stepmother is once more the cause of your sorrow." Yeh-Shen gasped in horror, but the old man went on. "Let us not dwell on things that are past," he said, "for I have come bringing you a gift. Now you must listen carefully to this: The bones of your fish are filled with a powerful spirit. Whenever you are in serious need, you must kneel before them and let them know your heart's desire. But do not waste their gifts."

Yeh-Shen wanted to ask the old sage many more questions, but he rose to the sky before she could utter another word. With heavy heart, Yeh-Shen made her way to the dung heap to gather the remains of her friend.

Time went by, and Yeh-Shen, who was often left alone, took comfort in speaking to the bones of her fish. When she was hungry, which happened quite often, Yeh-Shen asked the bones for food. In this way, Yeh-Shen managed to live from day to day, but she lived in dread that her stepmother would discover her secret and take even that away from her.

So the time passed and spring came. Festival time was approaching: It was the busiest time of the year. Such cooking and cleaning and sewing there was to be done! Yeh-Shen had hardly a moment's rest. At the spring festival young men and young women from the village hoped to meet and to choose whom they would marry. How Yeh-Shen longed to go! But her stepmother had other plans. She hoped to find a husband for her own daughter and did not want any man to see the beauteous Yeh-Shen first. When finally the holiday arrived, the stepmother and her daughter dressed themselves in their finery and filled their baskets with sweetmeats. "You must remain at home now and watch to see that no one steals fruit from our trees," her stepmother told Yeh-Shen, and then she departed for the banquet with her own daughter.

As soon as she was alone, Yeh-Shen went to speak to the bones of her fish. "Oh, dear friend," she said, kneeling before the precious bones, "I long to go to the festival, but I cannot show myself in these rags. Is there somewhere I could borrow clothes fit to wear to the feast?" At once she found herself dressed in a gown of azure[1] blue, with a cloak of kingfisher feathers draped around her shoulders. Best of all, on her tiny feet were the most beautiful slippers she had ever seen. They were woven of golden threads, in a pattern like the scales of a fish, and the glistening soles were made of solid gold. There was magic in the shoes, for they should have been quite heavy, yet when Yeh-Shen walked, her feet felt as light as air.

"Be sure you do not lose your golden shoes," said the spirit of the bones. Yeh-Shen promised to be careful. Delighted with her transformation, she bid a fond farewell to the bones of her fish as she slipped off to join in the merrymaking.

That day Yeh-Shen turned many a head as she appeared at the feast. All around her people whispered, "Look at that beautiful girl! Who can she be?"

But above this, Stepsister was heard to say, "Mother, does she not resemble our Yeh-Shen?"

---

1. **azure** (azh'ər) *adj.*: like the color of the sky.

D Literary Focus

Point of view. Ask students how these three sentences show that the narrator is omniscient. [The first tells what Yeh-Shen wants (and hasn't told anyone). The next two tell what her stepmother wants. Only an all-knowing narrator would know both of these things.]

E Correcting Misconceptions

Sweetmeats. Make sure students understand that *sweetmeats* are not meat at all but in fact candy or crystallized fruit.

F Reading Skills

❓ Note descriptive details. What descriptive details does the narrator provide so readers can visualize Yeh-Shen's fine clothes? [Possible responses: azure blue gown; cloak of kingfisher feathers; beautiful slippers with golden threads woven in a fish-scale pattern; glistening, solid-gold soles.]

G Reading Skills

❓ Draw conclusions. Where does the slippers' magic come from? What about their appearance gives you a clue? [Possible response: The magic comes from the spirit of the fish. The clue is their fish-scale pattern.]

CROSS-CURRICULAR CONNECTIONS

Culture

Footbinding. For centuries, Chinese women wanted tiny feet like Yeh-Shen's. A footbinder would bind a young girl's feet so tightly that bones would break and the feet would not grow bigger. Bound feet were considered beautiful, but the procedure was painful and crippling. Footbinding was outlawed in China about one hundred years ago, but the practice continued until very recently.

A Literary Focus

Recognize character types.
How is this king's strategy similar to and different from that of the heroes of Cinderella stories you know? [Possible response: It is like the strategy of the prince in, say, the Disney "Cinderella" in that he wants every woman in the countryside to try on the shoe. It is different in that he doesn't travel around to their homes conducting the search; he puts the slipper on display and waits for the right woman to come claim it.]

B Vocabulary Development

Connotation. Remind students that a word's connotation is the meaning it suggests beyond its denotation (dictionary definition). Point out the word *vigil* and explain that it means a period of watchfulness, especially when others are asleep. It is often connected with religious faith (as in night-long prayer) or military preparedness (as in watching for an expected attack). Ask students for the connotation of the word's use here. [Possible responses: Like a military leader, the king is conducting an exhaustive campaign to find a particular woman. Like a monk or priest, he is faithful to his self-imposed task of finding the shoe's owner.]

C Advanced Learners

Speculate. Ask students why they think Yeh-Shen sneaks into the pavilion at night when she is fairly sure the slipper is hers. Why doesn't she join the crowd trying it on earlier? [Possible responses: She may fear getting into trouble with her stepmother. She is not competing for the king, like the other women. She wants to steal the shoe and return it to the spirit of the fish bones.]

Upon hearing this, Yeh-Shen jumped up and ran off before her stepsister could look closely at her. She raced down the mountainside, and in doing so, she lost one of her golden slippers. No sooner had the shoe fallen from her foot than all her fine clothes turned back to rags. Only one thing remained—a tiny golden shoe. Yeh-Shen hurried to the bones of her fish and returned the slipper, promising to find its mate. But now the bones were silent. Sadly Yeh-Shen realized that she had lost her only friend. She hid the little shoe in her bedstraw and went outside to cry. Leaning against a fruit tree, she sobbed and sobbed until she fell asleep.

The stepmother left the gathering to check on Yeh-Shen, but when she returned home, she found the girl sound asleep, with her arms wrapped around a fruit tree. So, thinking no more of her, the stepmother rejoined the party. Meantime, a villager had found the shoe. Recognizing its worth, he sold it to a merchant, who presented it in turn to the king of the island kingdom of T'o Han.

The king was more than happy to accept the slipper as a gift. He was entranced by the tiny thing, which was shaped of the most precious of metals, yet which made no sound when touched to stone. The more he marveled at its beauty, the more determined he became to find the woman to whom the shoe belonged. A search was begun among the ladies of his own kingdom, but all who tried on the sandal found it impossibly small. Undaunted, the king ordered the search widened to include the cave women from the countryside where the slipper had been found. Since he realized it would take many years for every woman to come to his island and test her foot in the slipper, the

king thought of a way to get the right woman to come forward. He ordered the sandal placed in a pavilion[2] by the side of the road near where it had been found, and his herald[3] announced that the shoe was to be returned to its original owner. Then, from a nearby hiding place, the king and his men settled down to watch and wait for a woman with tiny feet to come and claim her slipper.

All that day the pavilion was crowded with cave women who had come to test a foot in the shoe. Yeh-Shen's stepmother and stepsister were among them, but not Yeh-Shen—they had told her to stay home. By day's end, although many women had eagerly tried to put on the slipper, it still had not been worn. Wearily, the king continued his vigil into the night.

It wasn't until the blackest part of night, while the moon hid behind a cloud, that Yeh-Shen dared to show her face at the pavilion, and even then she tiptoed timidly across the wide floor. Sinking down to her knees, the girl in rags examined the tiny shoe. Only when she was sure that this was the missing mate to her own golden slipper did she dare pick it up. At last she could return both little shoes to the fish bones. Surely then her beloved spirit would speak to her again.

Now the king's first thought, on seeing Yeh-Shen take the precious slipper, was to throw the girl into prison as a thief. But when she turned to leave, he caught a glimpse of her face. At once the king was struck by the sweet harmony of her

---

2. **pavilion** *n.*: large tent or shelter, often highly decorated.
3. **herald** *n.*: the person in a king's court who makes official announcements.

CROSS-CURRICULAR CONNECTIONS

History
The tale's origin. "Yeh-Shen" is set "in the dim past"—centuries before the tale was first recorded. To help students appreciate how old the tale is, explain that the Ch'in Dynasty mentioned in the opening of the story lasted from 221 to 206 B.C. The story was first written down in the T'ang Dynasty some seven hundred years before the first printed Cinderella story appeared in Europe. Ask students how this information helps to confirm that the Cinderella story is an expression of deeply rooted human wishes. [Possible response: The fact that the story has survived for more than a thousand years and appears in many cultures is evidence that it appeals to innate human desires.]

Free Library, Philadelphia, PA./Bridgeman Art Library.

Three Fish (detail) by Belshu.
Color woodblock print.

features, which seemed so out of keeping with the rags she wore. It was then that he took a closer look and noticed that she walked upon the tiniest feet he had ever seen.

With a wave of his hand, the king signaled that this tattered creature was to be allowed to depart with the golden slipper. Quietly, the king's men slipped off and followed her home.

All this time, Yeh-Shen was unaware of the excitement she had caused. She had made her way home and was about to hide both sandals in her bedding when there was a pounding at the door. Yeh-Shen went to see who it was—and found a king at her doorstep. She was very frightened at first, but the king spoke to her in a kind voice and asked her to try the golden slippers on her feet. The maiden did as she was told, and as she stood in her golden shoes, her rags were transformed once more into the feathered cloak and beautiful azure gown.

Her loveliness made her seem a heavenly being, and the king suddenly knew in his heart that he had found his true love.

Not long after this, Yeh-Shen was married to the king. But fate was not so gentle with her stepmother and stepsister. Since they had been unkind to his beloved, the king would not permit Yeh-Shen to bring them to his palace. They remained in their cave home, where one day, it is said, they were crushed to death in a shower of flying stones.

Meet the Writer

Ai-Ling Louie

It Runs in the Family

Ai-Ling Louie (1949–   ) remembers hearing the story "Yeh-Shen," the Chinese version of "Cinderella," from her grandmother. Louie became curious about the origins of this story, which had been told in her family for three generations, so she did some research. She learned that the tale was first written down by Tuan Cheng-shi in an ancient Chinese manuscript during the Tang dynasty (A.D. 618–907) and had probably been handed down orally for centuries before that.

Yeh-Shen   **387**

Advanced Learners

Enrichment. Tell students that many scholars and psychologists believe that the fairy tales we learn as children play important roles in the development of our personalities. They help us to understand our feelings and cope with our problems. They show us how to conquer our fears, set goals for ourselves, form relationships with other people, have faith in goodness, and deal with feelings of being an outsider.

Activity. Have students read an essay on fairy tales by one or more of the following experts: Bruno Bettelheim, Clarissa Pinkola Estes, Verena Kast, Marina Warner, Terri Windling, Jack Zipes. Tell them to examine "Yeh-Shen" or another fairy tale of their choice from that expert's psychological perspective and prepare an oral report for the class.

HOMEWORK

DIRECT TEACHING

VIEWING THE ART

Activity. Point out all the illustrations of carp throughout the story. Explain that in Chinese art, carp specifically symbolize perseverance in the face of difficulties. Why might carp be an appropriate symbol for Cinderella?

GUIDED PRACTICE

Monitor students' progress. Guide the class in answering these comprehension questions. Direct students to locate passages in the text that support their responses.

Short Answer

1. Who gives Yeh-Shen a hard time? Why? [Her stepmother gives her a hard time because she's jealous of Yeh-Shen's beauty and goodness.]

2. Which characters help Yeh-Shen? How? [First, her fish helps her by being her friend. Then, the old man helps her by telling her that the fish's bones house a powerful spirit. Then, the fish's bones help her by providing clothes for the festival.]

Meet the Writer

Ai-Ling Louie always had her nose in a book as a girl. "I remember walking down the crowded, noisy hallway of my junior high school and reading all the while," she says. "I could even climb three flights of stairs and never miss a word."

For Independent Reading

If students are interested in the ways this fairy tale echoes and differs from the "Cinderella" they know, they might enjoy versions from other cultures: *Mufaro's Beautiful Daughters* by John Steptoe (African) or *Jouanah* by Jewell Coburn (Hmong).

After You Read

First Thoughts

1. It expresses our deep wish to be loved for who we are inside, to see justice done, and to have at least one friend we can talk to.

Thinking Critically

2. Possible answer: The theme "goodness is rewarded in the end" is a good theme for today because many people who are suffering may find hope in the future.

3. Possible answer: We would know more about the step-mother's thoughts and motivations if she were the narrator, but we wouldn't know what was troubling Yeh-Shen or why.

Extending Interpretations

4. Possible answer: I disagree with the decision to include the tale. I would rather read a story in which the girl plays a more active role.

ASSESSING

Assessment

■ *Holt Assessment: Literature, Reading, and Vocabulary*

RETEACHING

For a lesson reteaching point of view, see **Reteaching,** p. 917G–H.

After You Read   Response and Analysis

First Thoughts

1. Think about the discussion you had before you read this story. Which of our deepest wishes do you think this story expresses? Is it also about some of our fears? Explain.

Thinking Critically

2. Which of the following statements best sums up the **theme** "Yeh-Shen" reveals?

   • Goodness is rewarded in the end.
   • Bad people are always punished.
   • Love comes to those who deserve it.
   • Jealousy can lead to tragedy.

   Do you think this is a good **theme** for today? Explain.

3. Check the story to see what you learn about Yeh-Shen's step-mother. How would the story change if the stepmother, instead of the **omniscient narrator,** were telling it?

Extending Interpretations

4. Suppose a reviewer of this textbook said, "I don't think the publisher should include this story because it's outdated. Girls don't sit around and wait to be rescued any longer." Do you agree or disagree with the decision to include this story in the textbook? Explain.

WRITING
Writing a Modern Cinderella Story

Imagine a Cinderella/Yeh-Shen story set today in your own community. Who would the underdog be? Who or what would hold the underdog back? Who would rescue the underdog, and how would this happen? With a group of classmates, brainstorm to come up with some ideas. Then, plot out your story. You could act out your modern Cinderella story or videotape the production for your class.

INTERNET
Projects and Activities
Keyword: LE5 7-4

SKILLS FOCUS

Literary Skills
Analyze omniscient point of view.

Writing Skills
Write a story.

> #### Reading Check
> a. Who is Yeh-Shen's only friend?
> b. What does her stepmother do to Yeh-Shen's friend?
> c. A very old man gives Yeh-Shen some advice about the bones of her fish. What is it?
> d. What happens when Yeh-Shen runs away from the festival?
> e. How does the king find Yeh-Shen?

Reading Check

a. Yeh-Shen's only friend is the fish she caught and raised.

b. Her stepmother tricks the fish, kills it, and eats it.

c. He tells her the fish's bones are filled with a spirit that will help her when she is in need.

d. Her golden slipper falls off and her clothes turn to rags. Without the slipper, the fish's bones won't speak.

e. He places the slipper in a pavilion and watches the women who try to put it on until Yeh-Shen finally arrives to claim it.

Tracing an Author's Argument

Reading Focus
Presenting an Argument: Agree with Me

Argument can mean "angry disagreement." Yeh-Shen may have wanted to argue with her nasty stepmother on many occasions. You argue with your friends about all kinds of things, from who should be class president to what music should be played at a dance.

Here the word *argument* is used to mean "debate or discussion." Writers who present an argument are trying to persuade you to think or act in a certain way. They may want you to agree with their opinions, vote for their candidates, buy their products, or support their causes.

Skillful persuaders use solid **evidence** to back up their arguments. They cite **facts** (statements that can be proved true) and **statistics** (number facts).

Skillful persuaders often quote **experts** to convince you that an argument is sound.

When you finish reading a text that presents an argument, ask yourself

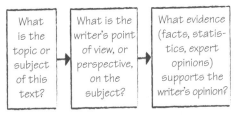

What is the topic or subject of this text? → What is the writer's point of view, or perspective, on the subject? → What evidence (facts, statistics, expert opinions) supports the writer's opinion?

When you read a persuasive essay, you must trace the writer's use of evidence. You want to be certain that the evidence is valid and that it is strong. After all, if you are going to accept someone's argument, you want to be sure it is a good one.

■ The notes beside the selection that follows will help you trace the author's argument.

SKILLS FOCUS

Reading Skills Trace an author's argument.

Mirror, Mirror, on the Wall . . . **389**

A **Reading Informational Text**

? **Trace an author's argument.**
Ask students what the title of the selection leads them to expect. Does it reveal the author's position? [Possible response: Although the author's position is not completely clear from the title, most students will say that the play on the quotation from the evil queen in "Snow White" leads them to believe that the selection will be about self-perception.]

B **Reading Informational Text**

Trace an author's argument.
Ask students if they can guess the author's position at this point. [Most students may infer that the author feels that teens are too critical of their appearance.]

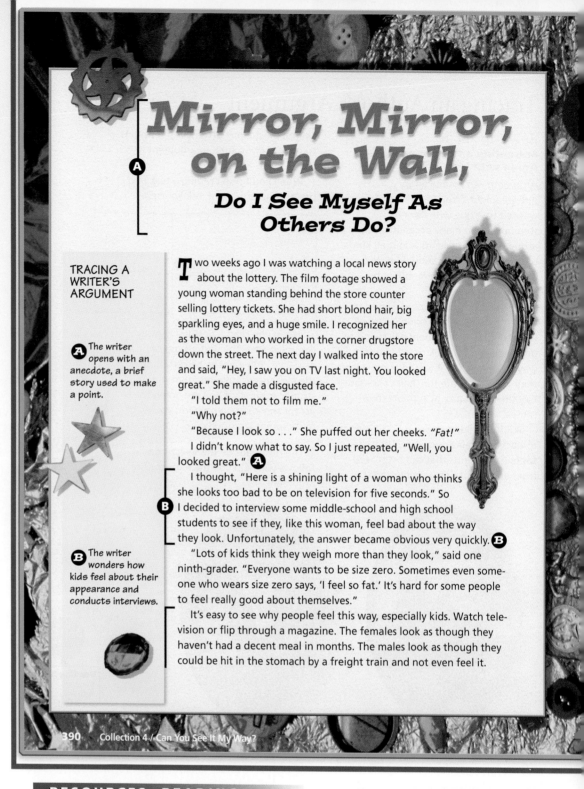

Mirror, Mirror, on the Wall,

Do I See Myself As Others Do?

A

TRACING A
WRITER'S
ARGUMENT

A The writer opens with an anecdote, a brief story used to make a point.

B The writer wonders how kids feel about their appearance and conducts interviews.

Two weeks ago I was watching a local news story about the lottery. The film footage showed a young woman standing behind the store counter selling lottery tickets. She had short blond hair, big sparkling eyes, and a huge smile. I recognized her as the woman who worked in the corner drugstore down the street. The next day I walked into the store and said, "Hey, I saw you on TV last night. You looked great." She made a disgusted face.

"I told them not to film me."

"Why not?"

"Because I look so . . ." She puffed out her cheeks. *"Fat!"*

I didn't know what to say. So I just repeated, "Well, you looked great." **A**

I thought, "Here is a shining light of a woman who thinks she looks too bad to be on television for five seconds." So **B** I decided to interview some middle-school and high school students to see if they, like this woman, feel bad about the way they look. Unfortunately, the answer became obvious very quickly. **B**

"Lots of kids think they weigh more than they look," said one ninth-grader. "Everyone wants to be size zero. Sometimes even someone who wears size zero says, 'I feel so fat.' It's hard for some people to feel really good about themselves."

It's easy to see why people feel this way, especially kids. Watch television or flip through a magazine. The females look as though they haven't had a decent meal in months. The males look as though they could be hit in the stomach by a freight train and not even feel it.

RESOURCES: READING

Internet
- go.hrw.com (Keyword: LE5 7-4)
- *Elements of Literature Online*

Media
- *Audio CD Library*
- *Audio CD Library, Selections and Summaries in Spanish*

I turned every page of a popular teen magazine for girls and counted advertisements for makeup and clothes. Out of 220 pages, 70 were advertisements. That's about one third of the magazine devoted to influencing the way kids dress and look. **C**

Statistics show that models in advertisements are 9 percent taller and 23 percent thinner than the average woman. With the click of a mouse, computers can create a picture of the perfect face by cleaning up a model's complexion, trimming her chin, and getting rid of lines around her eyes. Here's a news flash: She's not a real person, folks. She's an illusion. **D**

Other students I interviewed talked about the importance of wearing certain brands of clothing. These clothes display a brand name somewhere, whether it's plastered in three-inch type across the front or appears on a tiny logo on the sleeve. A middle-school student said, "Sometimes I just want to wear a pair of sweatpants and a T-shirt, but if you do, you're looked down on. The way you dress classifies you—it shows what group you're in. You can walk down the hall and tell who different people hang out with just by looking at their clothes." **E**

If you're thinking I interviewed some pretty insecure kids, you're wrong. A study conducted by the American Association of University Women found that in elementary school 60 percent of girls and 67 percent of boys had high self-esteem—they felt good about themselves. But by the time kids are in high school, self-esteem in girls drops to only 29 percent, compared with self-esteem in boys, which drops to 46 percent. **F**

The good news is that some things may be changing for the better. One middle-school girl reported being on the volleyball and basketball teams. Unlike girls just one generation ago, she can go out for any sport she wants. After an amazing spike or a skillful dribble down the basketball court, however, this beautiful, strong fifteen-year-old still says, "Sometimes you can see yourself as others see you. But if someone says they think I'm pretty, I don't believe them." **G**

Start believing it. Remember what Eleanor Roosevelt said: "No one can make you feel inferior without your consent." **H**

—Joan Burditt

C The writer says that many advertisements in magazines tell kids how they should look.

D The writer says that models don't look like real people—especially when a computer perfects the picture!

E The writer interviewed kids who say that wearing brand-name clothes influences how other kids respond to them.

F The writer cites statistics that show that kids' self-esteem drops in high school.

G The writer says that sports may not help improve girls' self-esteem.

H The writer ends with a quotation that backs up her argument.

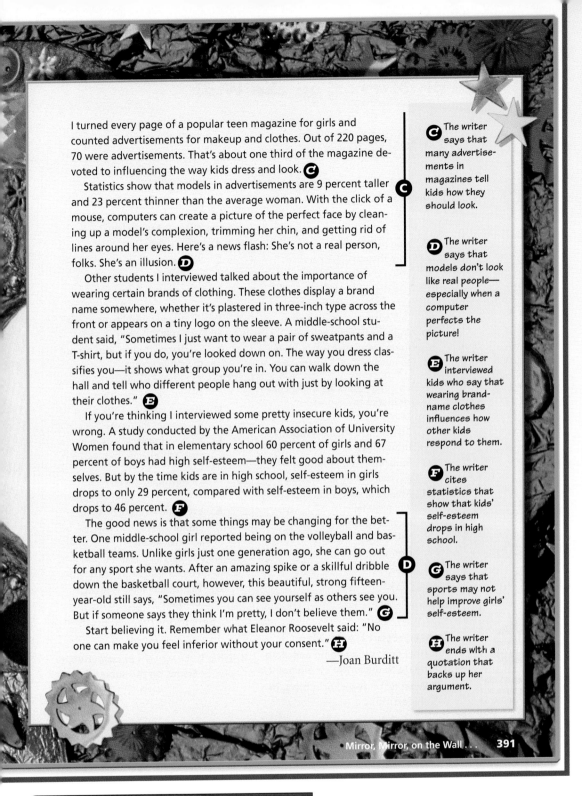

C Reading Informational Text

Trace an author's argument. Ask students if they are persuaded by the author's argument so far. Why or why not? [Some students may be persuaded by her description of the thinness of girls acting on TV and models posing for advertisements. Others may be impressed by her calculation that one teen magazine dedicates a third of its pages to telling girls how to look. Others may say she would be more persuasive if she studied several different magazines.]

D Reading Skills

❓ Express an opinion. Ask students if the author's findings reflect their own feelings or those of their classmates. Are they too critical of themselves? What boosts their self-esteem? [Possible answers: Even students who don't think they are self-critical will probably agree that some of their friends are. Most will agree that excelling in a sport can improve self-esteem, as can being good at music or writing, at building or fixing things, or at playing computer games.]

Monitor students' progress. Have students work in pairs for a think-aloud. First, they should read the selection aloud to each other, taking turns after every few paragraphs. Then, they should discuss their thoughts about the article's content and the author's success in persuading readers to adopt her viewpoint.

DIFFERENTIATING INSTRUCTION

Learners Having Difficulty
Understanding statistics. Some students may have difficulty with the statistics in the article. To help them understand the AAUW study, apply the percentages to your classroom. If there are, say, fifteen girls and fifteen boys in your class, explain that nine of the girls (60 percent) would have felt good about themselves in grade school but only four feel good about themselves now.

By comparison, ten of the boys used to feel good about themselves but seven do now.

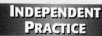
Analyzing an Author's Argument

Test Practice

Answers and Model Rationales

1. **A** Explain that B is the opposite of what the author says and C and D are not addressed in the selection.

2. **H** Remind students that statistics are facts with numbers. G and J don't use numbers and F is an opinion, not a fact.

3. **B** Point out that the author says, "Other students I interviewed . . ." and quotes a student about brand names.

4. **F** Students should realize that G, H, and J are only means to an end. They all contribute to the author's main purpose, F.

5. **B** Students should realize that A, C, and D are all opinions.

Test-Taking Tips

Remind students to pay careful attention to italicized or boldface terms in the questions.

For more instruction on how to answer multiple-choice questions, refer students to **Test Smarts,** p. 920.

Constructed Response

1. The author's opening anecdote shows how a person may be too self-conscious about her appearance when compared with how others perceive her.

2. The topic of this article is how people feel about the way they look.

3. Although many factors contribute to the insecurity people feel about their looks, people should overcome these negative feelings.

Analyzing an Author's Argument

Mirror, Mirror, on the Wall . . .

Test Practice

1. You can tell from this article that the writer believes that —

   A students feel tremendous pressure to look a certain way

   B teen magazines do not influence the way teenagers feel about their appearance

   C parents should keep their children from reading magazines that have models in them

   D students should wear uniforms to school so they won't worry so much about their appearance

2. Which of the following statements uses **statistics** to support a position?

   F I'll bet most students who are thin feel fat.

   G Students feel they have to wear a certain brand of clothing.

   H Models in advertisements are 9 percent taller and 23 percent thinner than the average woman.

   J Computers can change the way people look in photographs.

3. Which type of **evidence** does the writer use to support her point that brand names on clothing are important to many students?

   A An anecdote

   B An interview

   C An expert's opinion

   D A magazine article

4. What is the *most likely* reason the author wrote this essay?

   F To change readers' views about their appearance

   G To tell a story about the woman who works in the drugstore

   H To interview students about the clothes they wear

   J To explain why sports improve girls' self-esteem

5. Which statement is a **fact**—a statement that can be proved true?

   A Everyone wants to be thin.

   B Out of 220 pages, 70 were advertisements.

   C No one can make you feel inferior without your consent.

   D The females look as though they haven't eaten in months.

SKILLS FOCUS

Reading Skills
Analyze an author's argument.

Constructed Response

1. How does the opening anecdote relate to the writer's main point?

2. What is the **topic,** or subject, of this article?

3. What is the writer's **perspective,** or point of view, on this subject?

ASSESSING

Assessment

■ *Holt Assessment: Literature, Reading, and Vocabulary*

RETEACHING

For a lesson reteaching author's argument, see **Reteaching,** pp. 917K–L.

Before You Read | The Essay

Names/Nombres

Make the Connection

Quickwrite ✏️

Write about your given name, family name, or nickname. Explain how you got your name and how you feel about it. Is your name an accurate representation of who you are?

Literary Focus
Point of View: Subjective or Objective?

Has anyone ever said to you, "Don't take it personally"? Well, some writers do take their writing personally. Writers who treat their subject **subjectively** share their own feelings, thoughts, opinions, and judgments. We find **subjective writing** in personal essays and autobiographies and in the editorial pages of a newspaper, where we expect writers to express opinions about news events.

　Objective writing, on the other hand, tends to be unbiased and presents the facts and figures rather than the writer's private feelings. The purpose of objective writing is to inform.

Reading Skills 📖
Discovering the Main Idea: It's in the Details

All the important details in an article or essay add up to a **main idea.** A main idea is the central idea, the one that the writer wants you to remember. In some pieces of writing, like "Names/ Nombres," the writer **implies,** or suggests, the main idea. You have to

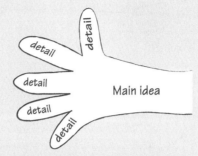

detail · detail · detail · detail · detail — Main idea

infer, or guess, the point that the writer is getting at. To infer a main idea, follow these steps:

- Identify the important details in the selection.
- Think about the point that the important details make.
- Use this information to figure out what the main idea is. State the main idea in your own words.

Vocabulary Development

Practice using these words before you read about Julia Alvarez's problem with her name:

ethnicity (eth·nis′ə·tē) *n.:* common culture or nationality. *Julia's ethnicity was important to her friends.*

exotic (eg·zät′ik) *adj.:* foreign; not native. *At her graduation party, Julia's family served exotic dishes.*

heritage (her′ə·tij) *n.:* traditions that are passed along. *Julia remained proud of her Dominican heritage.*

convoluted (kän′və·lōōt′id) *adj.:* complicated. *The grammar of a new language often seems convoluted.*

go. hrw .com

INTERNET

Vocabulary Activity
•
More About Alvarez

Keyword: LE5 7-4

SKILLS FOCUS

Literary Skills
Understand objective and subjective points of view.

Reading Skills
Find the main idea.

Names / Nombres　**393**

Motivate. Ask students how they would feel if someone mispronounced or misspelled their name. Then, watch the *Visual Connections Videocassette Program* segment "What's in a Name?" After students have shared their thoughts, assign the Quickwrite activity.

Preview Vocabulary

To help students master the Vocabulary words on p. 393, guide them through this exercise.

1. List the <u>ethnicities</u> of yourself and three friends.

2. Name an <u>exotic</u> food you enjoy.

3. List some activities that could be part of a <u>heritage</u> festival.

4. Draw a <u>convoluted</u> invention for turning off your alarm clock.

Assign the Reading

Have members of the class read the story aloud up to the description of the author's sisters on p. 396. Then, allow advanced learners to finish the story independently and answer the After You Read activities as homework. Continue working with readers having difficulty.

HOMEWORK

DIRECT TEACHING

Ⓐ Reading Skills

❓ Predict. Based on the title alone, what do you think this essay is about? [Possible response: It is about someone who has both English and Spanish names and who is bilingual.]

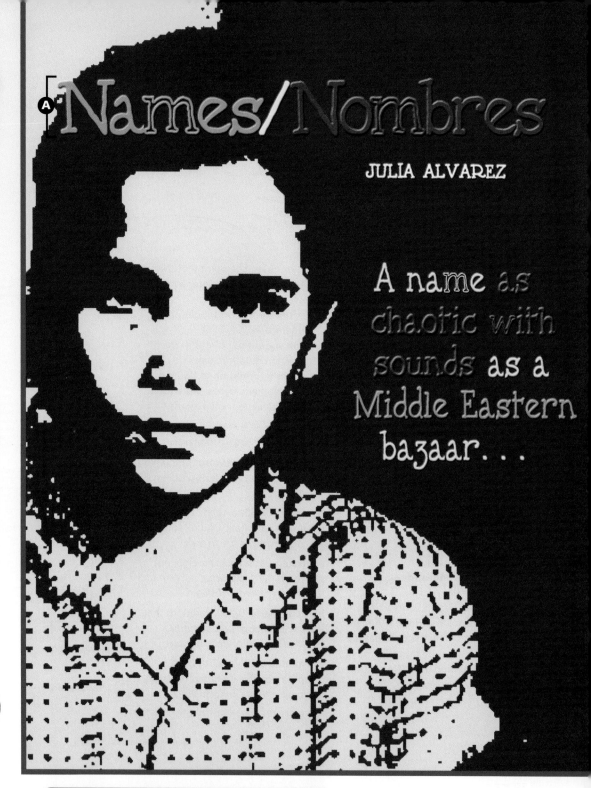

Ⓐ # Names/Nombres

JULIA ALVAREZ

A name as chaotic with sounds as a Middle Eastern bazaar. . .

DIFFERENTIATING INSTRUCTION

Learners Having Difficulty
Modeling. To help students read "Names/Nombres," model the reading skill of discovering the main idea. Say: "When I read an article or essay, I use the important details to figure out the most important single idea that the writer is presenting." Encourage students as they read to ask themselves: "What are the important

details here? What main point do they imply?"

Invite learners having difficulty to read "Names/Nombres" in interactive format in *The Holt Reader* and to use the sidenotes as aids to understanding the selection. The interactive version provides additional instruction, practice, and assessment of the literary skill taught in the Student Edition.

When we arrived in New York City, our names changed almost immediately. At Immigration, the officer asked my father, *Mister Elbures,* if he had anything to declare. My father shook his head no, and we were waved through.

I was too afraid we wouldn't be let in if I corrected the man's pronunciation, but I said our name to myself, opening my mouth wide for the organ blast of the *a,* trilling my tongue for the drumroll of the *r, All-vah-rrr-es!* How could anyone get *Elbures* out of that orchestra of sound?

At the hotel my mother was *Missus Alburest,* and I was *little girl,* as in, "Hey, little girl, stop riding the elevator up and down. It's *not* a toy."

When we moved into our new apartment building, the super called my father *Mister Alberase,* and the neighbors who became mother's friends pronounced her name *Jew-lee-ah* instead of *Hoo-lee-ah.* I, her namesake, was known as *Hoo-lee-tah* at home. But at school I was *Judy* or *Judith,* and once an English teacher mistook me for *Juliet.*

It took a while to get used to my new names. I wondered if I shouldn't correct my teachers and new friends. But my mother argued that it didn't matter. "You know what your friend Shakespeare said, '*A rose by any other name would smell as sweet.*'"[1] My family had gotten into the habit of calling any famous author "my friend" because I had begun to write poems and stories in English class.

By the time I was in high school, I was a popular kid, and it showed in my name. Friends called me *Jules* or *Hey Jude,* and

once a group of troublemaking friends my mother forbade me to hang out with called me *Alcatraz.* I was *Hoo-lee-tah* only to Mami and Papi and uncles and aunts who came over to eat sancocho[2] on Sunday afternoons—old world folk whom I would just as soon go back to where they came from and leave me to pursue whatever mischief I wanted to in America. *JUDY ALCATRAZ,* the name on the "Wanted" poster would read. Who would ever trace her to me?

My older sister had the hardest time getting an American name for herself because *Mauricia* did not translate into English. Ironically, although she had the most foreign-sounding name, she and I were the Americans in the family. We had been born in New York City when our parents had first tried immigration and then gone back "home," too homesick to stay. My mother often told the story of how she had almost changed my sister's name in the hospital.

After the delivery, Mami and some other new mothers were cooing over their new baby sons and daughters and exchanging names and weights and delivery stories. My mother was embarrassed among the Sallys and Janes and Georges and Johns to reveal the rich, noisy name of *Mauricia,* so when her turn came to brag, she gave her baby's name as *Maureen.*

"Why'd ya give her an Irish name with so many pretty Spanish names to choose from?" one of the women asked.

My mother blushed and admitted her baby's real name to the group. Her mother-in-law had recently died, she apologized, and her husband had insisted that the first daughter be named after his mother,

---

1. *"A rose . . . as sweet":* Julia's mother is quoting from the play *Romeo and Juliet.*

2. **sancocho** (sän·kō′chō) *adj.:* stew of meats and fruit.

Names / Nombres 395

DIRECT TEACHING

B Literary Focus
Point of view. Remind students that point of view refers to who is telling the story. In a work with a first-person point of view, the narrator is "I." Personal essays are usually written in the first person. Ask students to identify all the pronouns in this paragraph that reveal its point of view. [we; our; my; I; me. These reveal the first-person narrative point of view.]

C Reading Skills
❓ **Interpret.** When Mrs. Alvarez quotes Shakespeare, what advice about getting along in America is she giving Julia? [Possible response: She is telling Julia that it doesn't matter what name Americans call her because she is still the same person.]

D Reading Skills
❓ **Discover the main idea.** What are the important details in this paragraph? [Possible responses: The author becomes popular and has many nicknames; only her relatives pronounce her name the Spanish way; she doesn't want to spend much time with her uncles and aunts from the Dominican Republic.] **What main idea can you infer from these details?** [Possible response: Julia wants to blend in with the crowd and be a typical American teenager.]

E Cross-curricular Connections
HISTORY
❓ **Alcatraz.** What is Alcatraz? [Alcatraz is an island in San Francisco Bay, once the site of a famous high-security prison.]

English-Language Learners
For lessons designed for intermediate and advanced English-language learners, see *Holt Reading Solutions.*

Special Education Students
For lessons designed for special education students, see *Holt Reading Solutions.*

Advanced Learners
Acceleration. To help students understand point of view, ask them to discuss these questions:
- Is the narrator qualified to write about having a dual identity? Why or why not?
- Would the essay be as effective if it were written from an objective third-person viewpoint? Why or why not?

A Literary Focus

? **Point of view: Subjective versus objective.** Remind students that subjective writing expresses the writer's opinions and feelings. Which two sentences in this paragraph are subjective? [sentences 3 and 4] What makes them subjective? [They describe how the author feels.] What part of this paragraph illustrates objective writing? [The first two sentences present historical facts and give readers the background information they need to understand why Julia just wants to fit in with her classmates.]

B Advanced Learners

? **Speculate.** Why do you think Julia spells *Puerto Rico* as *Portoriko*? [Possible responses: She is showing how the island's name is often mispronounced by North Americans. The misspelling reinforces the idea that many Americans have trouble pronouncing Spanish names, whether of people or places.]

Mauran. My mother thought it the ugliest name she had ever heard, and she talked my father into what she believed was an improvement, a combination of *Mauran* and her own mother's name, *Felicia.*

"Her name is *Mao-ree-shee-ah,*" my mother said to the group of women.

"Why, that's a beautiful name," the new mothers cried. "*Moor-ee-sha, Moor-ee-sha,*" they cooed into the pink blanket. *Moor-ee-sha* it was when we returned to the States eleven years later. Sometimes, American tongues found even that mispronunciation tough to say and called her *Maria* or *Marsha* or *Maudy* from her nickname *Maury.* I pitied her. What an awful name to have to transport across borders!

My little sister, Ana, had the easiest time of all. She was plain *Anne*—that is, only her name was plain, for she turned out to be the pale, blond "American beauty" in the family. The only Hispanic thing about her was the affectionate nicknames her boyfriends sometimes gave her. *Anita,* or, as one goofy guy used to sing to her to the tune of the banana advertisement, *Anita Banana.*

Later, during her college years in the late sixties, there was a push to pronounce Third World[3] names correctly. I remember calling her long distance at her group house and a roommate answering.

"Can I speak to Ana?" I asked, pronouncing her name the American way.

"Ana?" The man's voice hesitated. "Oh! You must mean *Ah-nah!*"

Our first few years in the States, though, ethnicity was not yet "in." Those were the blond, blue-eyed, bobby-sock years of junior

high and high school before the sixties ushered in peasant blouses, hoop earrings, serapes.[4] My initial desire to be known by my correct Dominican name faded. I just wanted to be Judy and merge with the Sallys and Janes in my class. But, inevitably, my accent and coloring gave me away. "So where are you from, Judy?"

"New York," I told my classmates. After all, I had been born blocks away at Columbia-Presbyterian Hospital.

"I mean, *originally.*"

"From the Caribbean," I answered vaguely, for if I specified, no one was quite sure on what continent our island was located.

"Really? I've been to Bermuda. We went last April for spring vacation. I got the worst sunburn! So, are you from Portoriko?"

"No," I sighed. "From the Dominican Republic."

"Where's that?"

"South of Bermuda."

They were just being curious, I knew, but I burned with shame whenever they singled me out as a "foreigner," a rare, exotic friend.

"Say your name in Spanish, oh, please say it!" I had made mouths drop one day by rattling off my full name, which, according to Dominican custom, included my middle names, Mother's and Father's surnames for four generations back.

"Julia Altagracia María Teresa Álvarez Tavares Perello Espaillat Julia Pérez Rochet

---

3. **Third World:** developing countries of Latin America, Africa, and Asia.

4. **serapes** (sə·rä′pēs) *n.:* woolen shawls worn in Latin American countries.

Vocabulary
ethnicity (eth·nis′ə·tē) *n.:* common culture or nationality.
exotic (eg·zät′ik) *adj.:* foreign; not native.

González." I pronounced it slowly, a name as chaotic with sounds as a Middle Eastern bazaar or market day in a South American village.

My Dominican heritage was never more apparent than when my extended family attended school occasions. For my graduation, they all came, the whole lot of aunts and uncles and the many little cousins who snuck in without tickets. They sat in the first row in order to better understand the Americans' fast-spoken English. But how could they listen when they were constantly speaking among themselves in florid-sounding[5] phrases, rococo[6] consonants, rich, rhyming vowels?

Introducing them to my friends was a further trial to me. These relatives had such complicated names and there were so many of them, and their relationships to myself were so convoluted. There was my Tía[7] Josefina, who was not really an aunt but a much older cousin. And her daughter, Aida Margarita, who was adopted, una hija de crianza.[8] My uncle of affection, Tío José, brought my madrina[9] Tía Amelia and her comadre[10] Tía Pilar. My friends rarely had more than a "Mom and Dad" to introduce.

After the commencement ceremony, my family waited outside in the parking lot while my friends and I signed yearbooks with nicknames which recalled our high school good times: "Beans" and "Pepperoni" and "Alcatraz." We hugged and cried and promised to keep in touch.

Our goodbyes went on too long. I heard my father's voice calling out across the parking lot, "*Hoo-lee-tah!* Vámonos!"[11]

Back home, my tíos and tías and primas,[12] Mami and Papi, and mis hermanas[13] had a party for me with sancocho and a store-bought pudín,[14] inscribed with *Happy Graduation, Julie.* There were many gifts—that was a plus to a large family! I got several wallets and a suitcase with my initials and a graduation charm from my godmother and money from my uncles. The biggest gift was a portable typewriter from my parents for writing my stories and poems.

Someday, the family predicted, my name would be well-known throughout the United States. I laughed to myself, wondering which one I would go by.

---

5. **florid-sounding:** flowery; using fancy words.
6. **rococo** (rə·kō′kō) *adj.:* fancy. Rococo is an early-eighteenth-century style of art and architecture known for its fancy ornamentation.
7. **Tía** (tē′ä) *n.:* Spanish for "aunt." *Tío* is "uncle."
8. **una hija de crianza** (ōo′nä ē′hä de krē·än′sä): Spanish for "an adopted daughter." *Crianza* means "upbringing."
9. **madrina** (mä·drē′nä) *n.:* Spanish for "godmother."
10. **comadre** (kô·mä′drä) *n.:* informal Spanish for "close friend." *Comadre* is the name used by the mother and the godmother of a child for each other.

11. **Vámonos!** (vä′mō·nôs): Spanish for "Let's go!"
12. **primas** (prē′mäs) *n.:* Spanish for "female cousins."
13. **mis hermanas** (mēs er·mä′näs): Spanish for "my sisters."
14. **pudín** (pōō·dēn′) *n.:* Spanish cake.

Vocabulary

heritage (her′ə·tij) *n.:* traditions that are passed along.

convoluted (kän′və·lōōt′id) *adj.:* complicated.

C Literary Focus

❓ Point of view: Subjective versus objective. Julia says that her extended Dominican family, with its many complex relationships, differs from the smaller nuclear families of her American friends. As a teenager, how does she feel about this difference? [Possible responses: She finds it slightly embarrassing; she feels a little ashamed of her large, noisy family.]

GUIDED PRACTICE

Monitor students' progress. Guide the class in answering these comprehension questions. Direct students to locate passages in the text that support their responses.

Short Answer

1. Why does the narrator's full name surprise her friends? [It's very long and musical and contains many surnames.]

2. What does Julia do when the immigration officer mispronounces her family name? [She says nothing to him but pronounces the name clearly to herself.]

3. What are some nicknames Julia is given by her friends? [Jules, Hey Jude, and Alcatraz]

4. Where does Julia try to tell her friends she is from? [New York City]

5. What do the students do after the commencement ceremony? [They sign each other's yearbooks and promise to keep in touch.]

FAMILY/COMMUNITY ACTIVITY

Ask for volunteers to play the author in each of her personas—that is, as each version of her name. Have them act out at least one scene involving each name for their families. Each actor should wear a name tag showing which persona she or he is. You might have the persona known as Julia Alvarez tie the scenes together with narration. Help the performers put together a script that is a short version of the essay. Then, help them stage a performance for their families. You might send home a note to parents, explaining how reader's theater works and how the activity benefits students.

Meet the Writer

In her novel *How the Garcia Girls Lost Their Accents,* Julia Alvarez continues where she left off in "Names/Nombres." Like Julia, the character Carla is bilingual and observes both American and Dominican customs. The familiar names of her family and homeland comfort her. In her third novel, *¡Yo!,* Alvarez uses Yolanda Garcia (Yo, for short) as her main character. Yo is now a famous author who writes about characters based on her family and friends. In this novel, however, they talk back. Yo's subjects take turns being highly subjective first-person narrators.

For Independent Reading

- If students are interested in the immigrant experience, they might enjoy *A Long Way from Home,* Maureen Crane Wartski's story of a young Vietnamese refugee.

- If students want to read about another young girl who succeeds, recommend *Maria Tallchief* by Tobi Tobias. This biography tells the story of a girl who puts her heart into dancing and becomes a famous ballerina.

Meet the Writer

Julia Alvarez

Photograph by Cameron Davidson.

"Just Do Your Work and Put in Your Heart"

Born in New York City, **Julia Alvarez** (1950–   ) spent her childhood in the Dominican Republic, returning with her family to New York when she was ten years old. Adjusting to her new surroundings in the early 1960s wasn't easy for young Julia:

> **❝** I can tap into that struggling English speaker, that skinny, dark-haired, olive-skinned girl in a sixth grade of mostly blond and blue-eyed giants. Those tall, freckled boys would push me around in the playground. 'Go back to where you came from!' 'No comprendo!' I'd reply, though of course there was no misunderstanding the fierce looks on their faces. **❞**

Despite the difficulties, being an immigrant gave Julia a special point of view. "We [immigrants] travel on that border between two worlds," she explains, "and we can see both points of view." Later, as a writer, she used those sometimes conflicting perspectives— American and Latino—to describe brilliantly the cultures of the United States and the Dominican Republic.

After college and graduate school, Alvarez taught poetry for twelve years in Kentucky, California, Vermont, Washington, D.C., and Illinois. Now she lives in Vermont, where she writes novels and teaches at Middlebury College.

> **❝** Day to day, I guess I follow my papi's advice. When we first came [to the United States], he would talk to his children about how to make it in our new country. 'Just do your work and put in your heart, and they will accept you!' **❞**

DIFFERENTIATING INSTRUCTION

Advanced Learners
Pen names. Ask students what the names of Mark Twain, Dr. Seuss, Lewis Carroll, M.E. Kerr, and O. Henry have in common. [They are all names writers assumed for the purpose of publishing books.] Invite students to choose one of these names (or any other pen name) and research its origin. Why did the author choose it? What persona was he or she trying to create? Have different students report their findings to the class.

Learners Having Difficulty
Monitoring tip: If students have trouble deciding whether the essay is subjective or objective (question 5), have them re-read the first five paragraphs, looking for the answers to these questions: Who is the narrator? What is her relationship to the author? Are her feelings and opinions included in the essay (either directly or implicitly)? What other viewpoints about names are given?

Writing. You might want to walk students through library research on a specific name, perhaps your own or a volunteer's, before they begin researching and writing on their own. You might also set up a model interview where one student prepares and rehearses questions to ask his or her grandmother, played by another student.

First Thoughts

1. Think back to what you said about your own names in your notes for the Quickwrite. How has reading "Names/Nombres" affected your ideas about your names? ✏️

Thinking Critically

2. As a teenager, why does Julia want to be called Judy? How do you think her attitude has changed since then?

3. Why do you think the writer gave this piece the title "Names/Nombres" instead of just "Names" (or just "Nombres")? What connection do you see between this title and Alvarez's comment about being "on that border between two worlds"?

4. What would you say is the **main idea** of "Names/Nombres"? List three significant details or quotations from the story that you think back up the main idea. 📖

5. Is this essay **subjective** or **objective**? How do you know?

Extending Interpretations

6. "Names/Nombres" includes many Spanish words and phrases. In your opinion, do they make it harder for non-Spanish speakers to read the essay, or do they add something valuable to it? Explain.

WRITING

Writing an Essay

Research all your names to find out what you can about them—first, middle, and last names, plus any other names you've been given as part of your ethnic or religious heritage. You could begin by interviewing your family members to record what they know. Then, check the name books at your library. See if you can learn the origins of all your names. Write about your search and its results in a short essay.

Reading Check

Julia Alvarez has been known by the different names listed below. Explain who uses each name or group of names and what the names mean to Alvarez.

- "little girl"
- Julita (pronounced hōō•lē′tä)
- Judith/Juliet
- Jules/Jude
- Alcatraz
- Judy
- Julia Altagracia María Teresa Álvarez Tavares Perello Espaillat Julia Pérez Rochet González
- Julia Alvarez

INTERNET

Projects and Activities

Keyword: LE5 7-4

SKILLS FOCUS

Literary Skills
Analyze objective and subjective points of view.

Reading Skills
Find the main idea.

Writing Skills
Write an essay.

After You Read

First Thoughts

1. Students may say the essay has strengthened their pride in their names or changed their view of what they want to be called.

Thinking Critically

2. As a teenager, she wanted to blend in. As an adult, she celebrates her heritage by using the Spanish version of her name.

3. The title represents the author's bilingual identity. It encompasses both of her worlds.

4. The main idea is that a name is an important part of a person's identity. Possible details: As a new immigrant, Julia wants her name pronounced correctly; in high school she prefers an American name; as an adult she uses her original name.

5. It's subjective. The author uses "I" and "me" and talks about her experiences and feelings.

Extending Interpretations

6. Possible answer: They add something valuable because they help readers appreciate Julia's bilingual experience and her feelings of being caught between two worlds. They also make the essay more colorful and interesting.

Reading Check

- *"little girl"*—Hotel employees; embarrassment.
- *Julita*—Her parents and family; security.
- *Judith/Juliet*—Her teachers and classmates; loss of identity.
- *Jules/Jude*—Her friends; sense of belonging.
- *Alcatraz*—Troublemakers; rebelliousness.
- *Judy*—People at school; sense of fitting in.
- *Julia Altagracia María Teresa Álvarez Tavares Perello Espaillat Julia Pérez Rochet González*—Family members and possibly her surprised friends; reminder of her Dominican heritage.
- *Julia Alvarez*—The author; her identity as an adult writer.

Possible Answers
1. foreign looking
2. too complicated to understand
3. historical traditions
4. nationality or culture

After You Read Vocabulary Development

Clarifying Word Meanings: Using Definitions

Writers often help us understand difficult words by providing definitions right in the context.

A writer who uses **definition** will explain what a word means right in the sentence or passage. For example, in the following sentence the writer clarifies the meaning of *tía* by defining it later in the sentence.

> "There was my Tía Josefina, who was not really my aunt but a much older cousin."

Be on the lookout for such phrases as *in other words* and *that is* when looking for definitions of words right in context.

PRACTICE

Complete the following sentences, using definition to clarify the meanings of the words from the Word Bank.

1. The dress was definitely exotic—that is, it was _____.

2. Francis's explanation of his science project had grown convoluted. In other words, it was _____.

3. The street festival was planned to introduce visitors to the city's heritage, or _____.

4. Studies have shown that ethnicity, meaning _____ , influences the kinds of programs we watch on television.

Word Bank

ethnicity
exotic
heritage
convoluted

SKILLS FOCUS

Vocabulary Skills
Clarify word meanings by using definitions.

After You Read   Grammar Link

Don't Leave Your Modifiers Dangling

It's easy to make the mistake of "hanging" a modifying phrase on a sentence (usually at the beginning) and forgetting to include the word it modifies:

DANGLING   **Arriving in New York City,** *our names* **changed almost immediately.**

Who arrived in New York City? It sounds as if the names came on their own!

Phrases that hang, or dangle, on a sentence without clearly modifying a word are called **dangling modifiers.** You can correct a dangling modifier by adding, subtracting, or rearranging words:

CLEAR   **Arriving in New York City,** *we* **noticed that our names changed almost immediately.**

The first sentence of "Names/Nombres" shows an even better solution:

CLEAR   **"When** *we* **arrived in New York City, our names changed almost immediately."**

PRACTICE

Find and fix the dangling modifiers in these sentences. You will have to rewrite some of the sentences.

1. Wanting to encourage me, my graduation present was a typewriter.
2. Born in New York City, it was easier for me to adjust to America.
3. Looking back on it now, the incident was funny.

Exchange a sample of your writing with a partner. Then, act as a dangler detector. Read your partner's work carefully to be sure every sentence makes sense and every modifier or phrase modifies something. Your first step should be to identify the modifying phrases (with the permission of the writer, use a colored pen). Dangling modifiers usually appear—or dangle—at the beginning of a sentence.

For more help, see Placement of Modifiers, 5g, in the Language Handbook.

SKILLS FOCUS

Grammar Skills
Avoid dangling modifiers.

SKYWRITING IS VERY TRICKY. YOU HAVE TO KNOW HOW TO FLY, HOW TO SPELL...

AND YOU HAVE TO KNOW THE RULES OF GRAMMAR...

I THINK I GIVE NEW MEANING TO THE TERM "DANGLING PARTICIPLE"...

VOOMP

Names / Nombres   **401**

Grammar Link

PRACTICE

1. Wanting to encourage me, my parents gave me a typewriter as a graduation present.
2. Because I was born in New York City, it was easier for me to adjust to America.
3. Looking back on it now, I can see that the incident was funny.

ASSESSING

Assessment
■ *Holt Assessment: Literature, Reading, and Vocabulary*

RETEACHING

For a lesson reteaching point of view, see **Reteaching,** pp. 917G–H.

DIFFERENTIATING INSTRUCTION

Learners Having Difficulty

Write the following sentences on the chalkboard and have students find and fix the dangling modifiers. (Possible answers are given.)

1. Often having to repeat her last name for people, their puzzled looks were no longer a surprise. [Often having to repeat her last name to people, Julia was no longer surprised by their puzzled looks.]

2. Talking to her friends, they are always astonished to hear her real name. [When talking to her friends, Julia always astonishes them when she tells them her full name.]

3. Signing yearbooks with her friends, the relatives patiently waited for Julia's return to the family celebration. [Because Julia was signing yearbooks with her friends, her relatives waited patiently for her to join them for a family celebration.]

4. Wanting to be accepted, Julia's jokes are often made with her classmates. [Julia, wanting to be accepted, often makes jokes with her classmates.]

Grade-Level Skills

■ **Literary Skills**
Analyze an autobiography.

■ **Reading Skills**
Distinguish fact from opinion.

Review Skills

■ **Literary Skills**
Identify the speaker, and recognize the difference between first- and third-person narration.

Summary 🔁 *at grade level*

Maijue Xiong and her family flee their home in Laos after the Communist takeover of 1975. Taking only a few possessions and as much food as they can carry, the three adults and three children struggle through thick jungle and open fields to the Mekong River on the border of Thailand. There they are forced to pay fishermen everything they have to row them across the river. After the family has waited three years in a Thai refugee camp, the authorities approve their application to emigrate to the United States. There they settle near Los Angeles. Maijue attends school and eventually becomes the first person in her family to attend college.

Before You Read | The Autobiography

An Unforgettable Journey

Make the Connection
Quickwrite ✏️

What do you know about the Vietnam War, which was fought in Southeast Asia from 1957 to 1975? Jot down some of the facts that you know about the war. One fact might have to do with the famous memorial in Washington, D.C.

Literary Focus
Autobiography: Telling You My Story

The most personal kind of writing is autobiographical writing. An **autobiography** is the story of a person's life written by that very person. In this kind of writing, you get inside the writer's mind, and you learn about his or her most personal thoughts, feelings, and ideas. Because of this, autobiographical writing is **subjective** (see page 393).

INTERNET
Vocabulary
Activity
Keyword: LE5 7-4

SKILLS FOCUS

Literary Skills
Understand autobiography.

Reading Skills
Distinguish fact from opinion.

Reading Skills 📖
Distinguishing Fact from Opinion

When you read an autobiography, it's important to be able to tell facts from opinions. A **fact** can be proved true. *The Mekong River flows through Laos* is a fact. It is a statement that can be confirmed by looking at a map.

An **opinion** can be supported by facts, but it can't be proved true or false: *The friendliest people in Southeast Asia are from Laos.* In autobiographical essays, such as "An Unforgettable Journey," writers share their opinions, but they also present facts.

Be careful: People may state an opinion as if it were a fact. If you're in doubt, ask yourself, "Can this statement be proved, or is it someone's personal feeling or belief?"

Vocabulary Development

Knowing these words will make your journey through this autobiography easier:

refuge (ref′yoōj) *n.:* shelter; protection. *Maijue's family sought refuge in the jungle.*

transition (tran·zish′ən) *n.:* change; passing from one condition to another. *The transition from a peaceful village to the jungle was extremely difficult.*

persecution (pʉr′sə·kyoō′shən) *n.:* act of willfully injuring or attacking others because of their beliefs or their ethnic backgrounds. *Because some Hmong worked against the Communists, they faced persecution.*

refugee (ref′yoō·jē′) *n.* used as *adj.:* person who flees home or country to escape war or persecution. *A refugee family may not be welcome anywhere.*

deprivation (dep′rə·vā′shən) *n.:* loss; condition of having something taken away by force. *They suffered from constant deprivation of food.*

RESOURCES: READING

Planning
■ *One-Stop Planner* CD-ROM with ExamView Test Generator

Differentiating Instruction
■ *Holt Reading Solutions*
■ *Supporting Instruction in Spanish*
■ *Audio CD Library*
■ *Audio CD Library, Selections and Summaries in Spanish*

Vocabulary
■ *Vocabulary Development*

Grammar and Language
■ *Daily Language Activities*

Assessment
■ *Holt Assessment: Literature, Reading, and Vocabulary*
■ *One-Stop Planner* CD-ROM with ExamView Test Generator

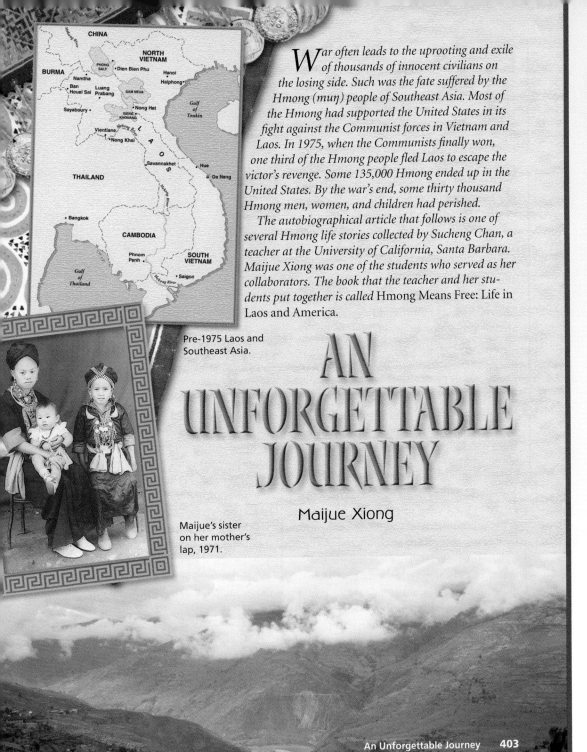

War often leads to the uprooting and exile of thousands of innocent civilians on the losing side. Such was the fate suffered by the Hmong (muŋ) people of Southeast Asia. Most of the Hmong had supported the United States in its fight against the Communist forces in Vietnam and Laos. In 1975, when the Communists finally won, one third of the Hmong people fled Laos to escape the victor's revenge. Some 135,000 Hmong ended up in the United States. By the war's end, some thirty thousand Hmong men, women, and children had perished.

The autobiographical article that follows is one of several Hmong life stories collected by Sucheng Chan, a teacher at the University of California, Santa Barbara. Maijue Xiong was one of the students who served as her collaborators. The book that the teacher and her students put together is called Hmong Means Free: Life in Laos and America.

Pre-1975 Laos and Southeast Asia.

AN UNFORGETTABLE JOURNEY

Maijue Xiong

Maijue's sister on her mother's lap, 1971.

■ Holt Online Assessment

Internet
■ go.hrw.com (Keyword: LE5 7-4)
■ Elements of Literature Online

Media
■ Audio CD Library
■ Audio CD Library, Selections and Summaries in Spanish

Skills Starter

Build skills. As students read Maijue Xiong's autobiography, "An Unforgettable Journey," have them think about how some of the incidents would change if they were told by other characters, such as Maijue's mother, her sister, or a fisherman. Would the facts change or only the opinions?

Preview Vocabulary

Challenge students to substitute a Vocabulary word from p. 402 for the underlined word or phrase in each sentence.

1. They found temporary shelter in a bus station. [refuge]
2. The change from her school in Laos to her school in California bewildered the Hmong child. [transition]
3. Many Hmong families fled Laos to escape harassment. [persecution]
4. The Hmong man became a displaced person when he left Laos. [refugee]
5. The children suffered from the lack of fresh milk and fruit. [deprivation]

Assign the Reading

Tell readers having difficulty to read the selection with a peer tutor as you monitor their progress. Allow advanced learners to read the selection independently and do the After You Read pages as homework.

HOMEWORK

A Reading Skills

? Distinguish fact from opinion. Which of the first three sentences in this paragraph is an opinion? [the third sentence] How can you tell? [It is a statement that cannot be proved or disproved.]

B Literary Focus

Autobiography. Identify the point of view of this autobiography. [first person] Describe the person who wrote this account. [She is an immigrant from Laos who recounts her childhood experiences as a refugee.]

C Cross-curricular Connections

The "Secret War." After gaining its independence from France in 1949, Laos theoretically became a neutral country. However, factions in Laos allied themselves with the North Vietnamese Communists under the direction of Ho Chi Minh, and conflicts between pro- and anti-Communist forces within Laos went on for years. From 1965 on, Americans officially fought the Viet Cong in Vietnam but simultaneously waged a "Secret War" against them in Laos. Xiong's father fought in this war alongside the CIA.

A I was born in a small village called Muong Cha in Laos on April 30, 1972. At the time I was born, my father was a soldier actively fighting alongside the American Central Intelligence Agency° against the Communists. Although a war was in progress, life seemed peaceful. We did not think of ever leaving Laos, but one day our lives were changed forever. We found ourselves without a home or a country and with a need to seek refuge in another country. This period of relocation involved a lot of changes, adjustments, and adaptations. We experienced changes in our language, customs, traditional values, and social status. Some made the transition quickly; others have never fully adjusted. The changes my family and I experienced are the foundation of my identity today.

B After Laos became a Communist country in 1975, my family, along with many others, fled in fear of persecution. Because my father had served as a commanding officer for eleven years with the American Central Intelligence Agency in what is known to the American public as the "Secret War," my family had no choice but to leave immediately. My father's life was in danger, along with those of thousands of others. We were forced to leave loved ones behind, including my grandmother, who was ill in bed the day we fled our village. For a month, my family walked through the dense tropical jungles and rice fields, along rugged trails through many mountains, and battled the powerful Mekong River. We traveled in silence at night and slept in the daytime. Children were very hard to keep quiet. Many parents feared the

---

°**Central Intelligence Agency:** organization that helps protect the United States by gathering information about foreign governments and carrying out secret operations; also known by its initials, CIA.

Maijue Xiong and her parents at her college graduation, June 1995.

The illustrations with this story include examples of traditional Hmong needlework. These items are worn as part of the Hmong traditional costume.

Communist soldiers would hear the cries of their children; therefore, they drugged the children with opium to keep them quiet. Some parents even left those children who would not stop crying behind. Fortunately, whenever my parents told my sisters and me to keep quiet, we listened and obeyed.

I do not remember much about our flight, but I do have certain memories that have been imprinted in my mind. It is all so unclear—the experience was like a bad dream: When you wake up, you don't

---

Vocabulary

refuge (ref'yo͞oj) *n.:* shelter; protection.

transition (tran·zish'ən) *n.:* change; passing from one condition to another.

persecution (pur'sə·kyo͞o'shən) *n.:* act of willfully injuring or attacking (even murdering) others because of their beliefs or ethnic backgrounds.

DIFFERENTIATING INSTRUCTION

Learners Having Difficulty

Modeling. Because autobiography is subjective, students must be able to distinguish fact from opinion. To help them, model the skill by saying, "I read that 'Laos is a country in Asia.' I know that statement is a fact because I can prove it's true by looking it up in an encyclopedia. If I read that 'The food in Laos is delicious,' I know that it's an opinion or personal feeling that can't be proved true." Encourage students as they read to ask themselves: "Can this statement be proved, or is it someone's personal feeling or belief?"

English-Language Learners

For lessons designed for intermediate and advanced English-language learners, see *Holt Reading Solutions.*

Special Education Students

For lessons designed for special education students, see *Holt Reading Solutions.*

Maijue dressed in traditional Hmong costume.

The Xiong family in Lompoc, 1993. Maijue is in the front row, far right.

remember what it was you had dreamed about but recall only those bits and pieces of the dream that stand out the most. I remember sleeping under tall trees. I was like a little ant placed in a field of tall grass, surrounded by dense jungle with trees and bushes all around me—right, left, in the back, and in front of me. I also remember that it rained a lot and that it was cold. We took only what we could carry and it was not much. My father carried a sack of rice, which had to last us the whole way. My mother carried one extra change of clothing for each of us, a few personal belongings, and my baby sister on her back. My older sister and I helped carry pots and pans. My stepuncle carried water, dried meat, and his personal belongings.

From the jungles to the open fields, we walked along a path. We came across a trail of red ants and being a stubborn child, I refused to walk over them. I wanted someone to pick me up because I was scared, but my parents kept walking ahead. They kept telling me to hurry up and to step over the ants, but I just stood there and cried. Finally, my father came back and put me on his shoulders, along with the heavy sack of rice he was carrying. . . .

After experiencing many cold days and rainy nights, we finally saw Thailand on the other side of the Mekong River. My parents bribed several fishermen to row us across. The fishermen knew we were desperate, yet, instead of helping us, they took advantage of us. We had to give them all our valuables: silver bars, silver coins, paper money, and my mother's silver wedding necklace, which had cost a lot of money. When it got dark, the fishermen came back with a small fishing boat and took us across the river. The currents were high and powerful. I remember being very scared. I kept yelling, "We're going to fall out! We're going to fall into the river!" My mom tried to reassure me but I kept screaming in fear. Finally, we got across safely. My family, along with many other families, were picked up by the Thai police and taken to an empty bus station for the night.

After a whole month at this temporary refugee camp set up in the bus station, during which we ate rice, dried fish, roots we dug up, and bamboo shoots we cut down, and drank water from streams, we were in very poor shape due to the lack of

Vocabulary

refugee (ref′yōō·jē′) *n.* used as *adj.:* person who flees home or country to escape war or persecution.

An Unforgettable Journey   **405**

DIRECT TEACHING

D Literary Focus

❓ **Point of view.** The writer describes events that happened when she was a child. How might this account have been different if it had been written by someone who was an adult at the time? [Possible response: Although the adults would also remember the hardships of the trip, they would be much more aware of the danger posed by the Communists.]

E Literary Focus

❓ **Point of view.** How might this passage have been different if it were told from the point of view of the fishermen? [Possible response: The fishermen might explain that they demanded a high price because they were taking a great risk to help the refugees escape—if the Communists caught them, they probably would be executed.]

F Vocabulary Development

Clarify word meanings: Contrast. Ask students to define the word *reassure.* [comfort, soothe, calm] Have them explain how the writer uses contrast to help readers understand the meaning of this word. [The word *but* shows that the child is terrified in spite of the reassurance; so *reassurance* must mean words or gestures designed to calm fears.]

Advanced Learners
Acceleration. To help students analyze the way choice of narrator affects characterization and plot, use the following activity.
Activity. Remind students that because Maijue Xiong lived through these events, her view of them is *subjective.* Students should note sentences or passages that they think reveal the narrator's reliability or unreliability. After reading the excerpt, students should explain why they think her account is or is not trustworthy.

A Reading Skills

❓ Distinguish fact from opinion. Is this paragraph composed mainly of facts or opinions? [facts] How do you know? [Most of the statements can be proven by simple observation.] What opinions does the narrator imply? [Possible responses: The refugees are in a pitiable condition. Children should not have to die because of political conflicts.]

B Literary Focus

❓ Point of view. This autobiography is written by someone who was a child at the time of the events described. How might this account of her parents' arguments have been different if it had been narrated by an unrelated third party such as a refugee camp worker? [Possible responses: It would give more precise reasons for the family's arguments. It would present both the mother's and father's perspectives.]

C Literary Focus

❓ Autobiography. Why do you think the writer never forgot this incident? [Possible responses: She identified with the hungry child because they were the same age and the narrator was always hungry. The hungry child scared her because she realized how easily she might be left alone to beg if something happened to her parents.]

nutrition. Our feet were also swollen from walking. We were then taken to a refugee camp in Nongkhai, where disease was rampant and many people got sick. My family suffered a loss: My baby sister, who was only a few months old, died. She had become very skinny from the lack of milk, and there was no medical care available. The memory of her death still burns in my mind like a flame. On the evening she died, my older sister and I were playing with our cousins outside the building where we stayed. My father came out to tell us the sad news and told us to go find my stepuncle. After we found him, we went inside and saw our mother mourning the baby's death. Fortunately, our family had relatives around to support and comfort us. . . .

Our family life in the camp was very unstable, characterized by deprivation and neglect. My older sister and I were left alone for days while my parents were outside the camp trying to earn money to buy extra food. My parents fought a lot during this period, because we were all under such stress. They knew that if we remained in Thailand, there would be no telling what would become of us. We had to find a better life. Some people in the camp were being sponsored to go to the United States. The news spread that anyone who had served in the military with the CIA could apply to go to America. Since my stepuncle had already gone there two years earlier, he sponsored my family. Because my father had been in the military and we had a sponsor, it took only six months to process our papers when usually it took a year or more. . . .

It took a full day to travel to Bangkok, where we stayed for four nights. The building we stayed in was one huge room. It was depressing and nerve-racking. I especially remember how, when we got off the bus to go into the building, a small child about my age came up to my family to beg for food. I recall the exact words she said to my father, "Uncle, can you give me some food? I am hungry. My parents are dead and I am here alone." My dad gave her a piece of bread that we had packed for our lunch. After she walked away, my family found an empty corner and rolled out our bedding for the night. That night, the same child came around again, but people chased her away, which made me sad.

In the morning, I ran to get in line for breakfast. Each person received a bowl of rice porridge with a few strips of chicken in it. For four days, we remained in that building, not knowing when we could leave for the United States. Many families had been there for weeks, months, perhaps even years. On the fourth day, my family was notified to be ready early the next morning to be taken to the airport. The plane ride took a long time and I got motion sickness. I threw up a lot. Only when I saw my stepuncle's face after we landed did I know we had come to the end of our journey. We had come in search of a better life in the "land of giants."

On October 2, 1978, my family arrived at Los Angeles International Airport, where my uncle was waiting anxiously. We stayed with my uncle in Los Angeles for two weeks and then settled in Isla Vista because there were already a few Hmong families there. We knew only one family in Isla Vista, but later we met other families whom my parents had known in their village and from

---

Vocabulary
deprivation (dep′rə·vā′shən) n.: condition of having something taken away by force.

CROSS-CURRICULAR CONNECTIONS

History

Communism in Laos. Have students research the Communist government of Laos at the time this excerpt takes place. Why did so many Laotians flee when this government came to power? What did the Communists do once they had control of the government? Students can work together on the research and present their information to the class so that everyone will have a better understanding of the historical context of "An Unforgettable Journey."

COLLABORATIVE LEARNING

villages nearby. It was in Isla Vista that my life really began. My home life was now more stable. My mother gave birth to a boy a month after we arrived in the United States. It was a joyous event because the first three children she had were all girls. (Boys are desired and valued far more than girls in Hmong culture.) . . .

I entered kindergarten at Isla Vista Elementary School. The first day was scary because I could not speak any English. Fortunately, my cousin, who had been in the United States for three years and spoke English, was in the same class with me. She led me to the playground where the children were playing. I was shocked to see so many faces of different colors. The Caucasian students shocked me the most. I had never seen people with blond hair before. The sight sent me to a bench, where I sat and watched everyone in amazement. In class, I was introduced to coloring. I did not know how to hold a crayon or what it was for. My teacher had to show me how to color. I also soon learned the alphabet. This was the beginning of my lifelong goal to get an education. . . .

Now that I am older, I treasure the long but valuable lessons my parents tried to teach us—lessons that gave me a sense of identity as a Hmong. "Nothing comes easy . . . ," my parents always said. As I attempt to get a college education, I remember how my parents have been really supportive of me throughout my schooling, but because they never had a chance to get an education themselves, they were not able to help me whenever I could not solve a math problem or write an English paper. Although they cannot help me in my schoolwork, I know in my heart that they care about me and want me to be successful so that I can help them when they can no longer help themselves. Therefore, I am determined to do well at the university. I want to become a role model for my younger brother and sisters, for I am the very first member of my family to attend college. I feel a real sense of accomplishment to have set such an example.

Meet the Writer

Maijue Xiong

A Writer Who Can Never Forget

Maijue Xiong (mī′zhōō·ē sē·ôŋ′) (1972–   ) was a college student in the United States when she wrote this account of her family's flight from Laos. Xiong eventually earned degrees in sociology and Asian American studies at the University of California, Santa Barbara, where she helped found the Hmong Club to promote Laotian culture. An active member of the Asian Culture Committee, Xiong now lives in St. Paul, Minnesota, and teaches at HOPE Community Academy.

An Unforgettable Journey **407**

DIRECT TEACHING

D **Reading Skills**

❷ **Distinguish fact from opinion.** Is this sentence a fact, an opinion, or both? Explain. [It is a fact that the Hmong value boys more than girls. It is the opinion of the Hmong culture that boys are more valuable than girls.]

E **Advanced Learners**

❷ **Speculate.** What do you think the other children thought of Maijue? Why do you think so? [Possible responses: They thought she was strange because she couldn't speak their language and didn't know what to do with crayons. They accepted her because they were used to seeing children from other countries join their class.]

F **Literary Focus**

❷ **Autobiography.** An autobiography will usually explain what a person has learned from his or her life experiences. What does Maijue Xiong say her family's experiences taught her? [She learned that "Nothing comes easy" and that she must work hard to graduate from college and serve as a good role model for her younger brothers and sisters.]

GUIDED PRACTICE

Monitor students' progress. Ask students to review this account looking for incidents that strongly affected the narrator. List the emotions these events aroused in her.

For Independent Reading Advanced students may be interested in reading additional accounts of Hmong refugees and their arrival in America in *Hmong Means Free: Life in Laos and America,* edited by Sucheng Chan.

After You Read

First Thoughts

1. Maijue Xiong probably remembers events that occurred when she was only three years old because they were strenuous and traumatic experiences.

Thinking Critically

2. Possible answers: Subjective—"life seemed peaceful," "the experience was like a bad dream," "the first day was scary." Objective—"I was born in a small village called Muong Cha in Laos on April 30, 1972." "My father's life was in danger. . . ."

3. Possible answer: Fact—Adults drugged children with opium to keep them quiet. Opinion—My parents fought a lot because we were under such stress.

4. Possible answer: When danger threatens, a family must be brave and help one another overcome obstacles to survive.

Extending Interpretations

5. Possible answer: Since a historian would attempt to be objective, a third-person point of view would be adopted rather than the first-person point of view of someone who experienced the events firsthand. The emotional impact of the story would be considerably weaker in the objective third-person point of view than in the first-person point of view.

Reading Check

Time line should include the following events: *April 1972*—birth of Maijue Xiong. *1975*—Xiong family flees Laos; Xiongs cross Mekong River to Thailand. *1975 to 1978*—Xiongs stay in Thai refugee camps; Xiongs apply for permission to move to the United States. *October 1978*—Xiongs move to United States.

After You Read Response and Analysis

First Thoughts

1. Maijue Xiong describes experiences she had when she was only three years old. Often people do not remember events from such a young age. Why do you think Maijue Xiong's memories are so vivid?

Thinking Critically

2. What details in Maijue Xiong's narrative are **subjective**—that is, where does she reveal her feelings? What parts of the story are **objective**—that is, where is there straightforward factual reporting?

3. Maijue Xiong reveals some opinions about having to flee Laos, but she also presents facts. Give an example of a **fact** and an example of an **opinion** in her autobiography.

4. The **main idea** of an article is the most important idea, the one that the writer wants you to remember. Review the last paragraph on page 407. Then, decide what the main idea of this life story appears to be.

Extending Interpretations

5. For an account of the Hmong experiences during the Vietnam War, how would the **point of view** of a historian differ from the point of view of someone who experienced the events firsthand? How might the emotional impact of the story differ?

WRITING

Writing Up an Interview

Interview a family member or neighbor who lived during the Vietnam War. You don't have to interview a veteran of the war—just someone who remembers the period. (Check your Quickwrite notes first.) Before the interview, list the questions you want to ask. Bring pencil and paper to the interview or an audiotape recorder. (If you wish to use a recorder, be sure to ask your subject's permission to do so.) Write up your interview in dialogue form.

Reading Check

Make a time line like the following one, and fill in the main events of Maijue Xiong's life and journey. Be sure to list the events in the sequence in which they occurred:

Maijue Xiong born	Xiong family leaves Laos
1972	1975

SKILLS FOCUS

Literary Skills
Analyze an autobiography.

Reading Skills
Distinguish fact from opinion.

Writing Skills
Write up an interview.

MINI-LESSON Reading

Developing Word-Attack Skills
Write the selection word *central* on the chalkboard. Remind students that when *c* comes before *e, i,* or *y,* it can have the sound /s/. However, the letters *ci* also can have the sound *sh.*

Use the following selection words to demonstrate these rules regarding the letter *c:*

- *process*—c stands for /s/ before *e*
- *accident*—c stands for /s/ before *i*

[Note that in this word, the first *c* stands for /k/ and the second for /s/.]

- *peaceful*—final *ce* stands for /s/
- *appreciate*—c before *i* can also stand for /sh/
- *financially*—ci together can stand for /sh/

Clarifying Meaning Through Contrast

Sometimes writers will clarify the meaning of a word by using **contrast** clues. A writer who uses contrast clues will show how a word is *unlike* another word or another situation. For example, you can get a good idea of what *apprehensive* means in the sentence below because you see it contrasted with *fearless*.

Be on the lookout for signal words that alert you to contrasts: *although, but, yet, still, unlike, not, in contrast, instead, however.*

> The children were extremely <u>apprehensive</u> as they made their way through the dense jungle, <u>but</u> their parents seemed <u>fearless</u>.

> **Word Bank**
>
> refuge
> transition
> persecution
> refugee
> deprivation

PRACTICE

In the following sentences the **contrast** clues point you to the meaning of each underlined word. Use the contrast clues to identify the meaning of each underlined word. All the words are from the Word Bank and are defined in the story.

1. Instead of finding a safe, warm <u>refuge</u>, they suffered exposure to wind and rain.
   Meaning: _____
   Clues: _____

2. In contrast to people who made a <u>transition</u> between cultures, some of the exiles never moved away from their own traditions.
   Meaning: _____
   Clues: _____

3. Although we expected <u>persecution</u> for our beliefs, we found acceptance.
   Meaning: _____
   Clues: _____

4. <u>Refugees</u> are unlike people who have homes and live in their own countries.
   Meaning: _____
   Clues: _____

5. People who have plenty of food and even luxuries cannot understand the <u>deprivation</u> experienced in the refugee camps.
   Meaning: _____
   Clues: _____

SKILLS FOCUS

Vocabulary Skills
Clarify word meanings by using contrast.

An Unforgettable Journey **409**

Vocabulary Development

PRACTICE

Possible Answers

1. *Meaning:* shelter
   Clues: safe, warm

2. *Meaning:* change or shift
   Clue: moved away from

3. *Meaning:* attacks
   Clue: acceptance

4. *Meaning:* someone without a place to live
   Clue: unlike people who have homes and their own countries

5. *Meaning:* without adequate food or supplies
   Clue: plenty of food and luxuries

ASSESSING

Assessment

■ *Holt Assessment: Literature, Reading, and Vocabulary*

Activity. Write these sets of words on the chalkboard. Have volunteers identify the two words in each set in which *c* or *ci* stands for /s/ or /sh/.

1. so<u>c</u>ial   fa<u>c</u>simile   fa<u>c</u>ial
2. ac<u>c</u>ess   ac<u>c</u>ept   ac<u>c</u>urate
3. pro<u>c</u>ess   pro<u>c</u>ure   pre<u>c</u>ise
4. <u>c</u>autious   <u>c</u>ease   <u>c</u>enter

Grade-Level Skills

■ **Reading Skills**
Understand and analyze an author's purpose and perspective.

Summary *at grade level*

Agate Nesaule, once a refugee from Latvia, observes a group of girls and women one day in a beauty salon in Madison, Wisconsin. By their language, their patched clothing, and the look in their eyes, she recognizes them as refugees from Bosnia. In this reminiscence she identifies with their pleasure in their stylish new haircuts and ponders how much time will have to pass before their eyes cease to look haunted.

PRETEACHING

Selection Starter

Build background. Explain that throughout history, people have been forced to leave their countries to escape wars or persecution. Because the United States is a democracy and allows people to openly express their political and religious beliefs, it has always been a popular destination for these exiles, or refugees.

Assign the Reading

Have students read the piece for homework. The next day, have class members discuss their reactions to it. Do they agree with the writer's position? Why or why not?

HOMEWORK

Informational Text

LINK TO "AN UNFORGETTABLE JOURNEY"

Understanding an Author's Purpose and Perspective

Reading Focus
Purpose and Perspective

People write nonfiction with many different purposes in mind. People who write political speeches are trying to **persuade** us to believe or do something. People who write articles in magazines often want to **inform** us about something. People who write personal narratives may want to **reveal a truth about life** or **share an experience.** In "An Unforgettable Journey," Maijue Xiong shares the dramatic experiences she had emigrating from Laos.

All writing reveals some kind of **perspective** on the world. The word *perspective* comes from the Latin *perspicere,* which means "to look at closely." Perspective in writing refers to the writer's point of view toward his or her topic. The writer says, in effect, "Here is what I think about this issue."

■ The personal narrative that follows is by the radio commentator Agate Nesaule. On meeting exiles from Bosnia who had settled in her hometown, Nesaule was reminded of her experiences as a World War II refugee. This piece was written for and broadcast on National Public Radio's *Morning Edition.*

INTERNET
Interactive
Reading Model
Keyword: LE5 7-4

SKILLS FOCUS

Reading Skills
Understand an author's purpose and perspective.

Background
Literature and Social Studies
The War in Bosnia

After World War II, Yugoslavia became a Communist state under the dictatorship of Tito. Bosnia, one of Yugoslavia's republics, was largely made up of three ethnic groups—Slavic Muslims, Croats, and Serbs. In 1980, after Tito died, a government representing the three groups emerged. Muslims and Croats favored independence for Bosnia; Serbs did not. In 1992, Bosnia seceded, or separated, from Yugoslavia. However, the Serbs living in Bosnia resisted. They wished to remain part of Yugoslavia and were backed by the Yugoslav National Army. A bitter struggle resulted, in which Serbs ruth-lessly expelled Muslims and Croats from the areas the Serbs controlled. This practice became known as ethnic cleansing. By late 1995, the conflict had produced an estimated two million refugees, the largest number of refugees in Europe since World War II.

The Commentator

Agate Nesaule fled Latvia during World War II. She was only six years old. Like many exiles from war-torn regions around the world, she found refuge in the United States. Nesaule now lives in Madison, Wisconsin. In this personal narrative she talks about the new exiles she has seen in Madison.

Ⓐ

410 Collection 4 / Can You See It My Way?

RESOURCES: READING

Planning
■ *One-Stop Planner* CD-ROM with ExamView Test Generator

Differentiating Instruction
■ *Holt Reading Solutions*
■ *Supporting Instruction in Spanish*
■ *Audio CD Library*
■ *Audio CD Library, Selections and Summaries in Spanish*

Grammar and Language
■ *Daily Language Activities*

Assessment
■ *Holt Assessment: Literature, Reading, and Vocabulary*
■ *One-Stop Planner* CD-ROM with ExamView Test Generator
■ *Holt Online Assessment*

Exile Eyes

The beauty shop in Wisconsin where I get my hair cut looks very American. The owner is young and energetic; his sideburns remind me of Elvis Presley, and scissors and dryers dangle like guns from his black holster as he moves among the glass-and-chrome shelves. But one afternoon the place is so full of women and girls that I can hardly get in. With the exception of their uniform politeness in offering me their seats, there is nothing unusual about them. Only details of their clothes suggest other places and other times: Europe after World War II; Wisconsin and the Hmong people who settled here after Vietnam; the Baltic countries after the collapse of the Soviet Union.

A summer dress with a snugly fitting dark top has the bottom of ugly checked-brown flannel. A gathered gray polyester skirt is lengthened by a six-inch-wide insert of flowered print. And their shoes are startling in their

Exile Eyes   411

Internet
- go.hrw.com (Keyword: LE5 7-4)
- *Elements of Literature Online*

Media
- *Audio CD Library*
- *Audio CD Library, Selections and Summaries in Spanish*

A **Reading Informational Text**

? **Author's purpose and perspective.** Nesaule says that the women in the beauty parlor all have "exile eyes." What proof does she offer? [She says she has seen "eyes that have lost everything" before, in Latvian, Rwandan, and Chilean refugees. She recognizes their dispossessed, weary, and disillusioned look.]

B **Reading Informational Text**

? **Author's purpose and perspective.** To end her essay, Nesaule enumerates the many challenges the refugee women face. What is her purpose in doing this? [She wants readers to understand how it feels to be a refugee.]

GUIDED PRACTICE

Monitor students' progress. Have the class make a word web with the word *refugee* at its center. On the lines of the web, they can write phrases that describe a refugee. Then, have students write an elaborated definition of the word.

flimsiness. These details speak to me of war and exile as eloquently as words. I'm afraid to look into the women's eyes, and when I finally do, it is as bad as I had expected. **A** They all have exile eyes: eyes that have lost everything and seen the unspeakable but are determined to keep looking, eyes that remain weary and disillusioned even during shy giggles. I have seen those eyes before too, in photographs of the Latvian women who survived Siberia and Rwandan girls being questioned by a journalist, on the Chilean woman doctor who used to clean my house, on my mother. They all have eyes like that.

The owner waits patiently for their consent before he so much as snips a hair. Like them, he is from Bosnia. Under his skilled fingers, their crudely chopped-off tresses take on lovely, sleek shapes. A young woman smiles and makes a playful little bow for her new haircut, but her eyes do not change. I'm glad the Bosnian women are getting more elegant styles than my frizzy permanent at age twelve, when I believed that cutting off my braids would transform me into an American. They will have to do much more even than learn **B** English, live among the poor and desperate, and find new friends and lovers. Acquaintances will ask them questions about their experiences but won't be able to stand hearing honest answers. And their longing for home will be confused with ingratitude to America. So much is ahead of them before their eyes lose their power to disturb.

—Agate Nesaule,
from National Public Radio,
Morning Edition

DIFFERENTIATING INSTRUCTION

Learners Having Difficulty
Since "Exile Eyes" was written for radio, first read the piece aloud for the class. Then, have students choose partners with whom to re-read the narrative. Have them stop at the end of each paragraph to discuss it. Each partner should make sure that the other understands who the refugees are and what their situation is.

English-Language Learners
Be sensitive to the feelings of students who may themselves be refugees. Do not ask them to discuss their experiences. If they wish to do so, they will volunteer.

Advanced Learners
Enrichment. Have students choose one of the historical references in the essay and do a little reading about this group of refugees. Questions for research include the following items: When did this situation occur? Who were the refugees? What were they escaping from? Where did they settle? Students can share their information with the rest of the class.

Analyzing an Author's Purpose and Perspective

Test Practice

1. One reason the writer identifies with the women in the beauty shop is that —
   - A she likes getting her hair cut
   - B she wears the same clothing
   - C they are from her own country
   - D she was an exile as well

2. We can tell from details in this personal narrative that the writer —
   - F is puzzled by the Bosnian women
   - G thinks that the women should wear different clothes
   - H made many mistakes when she was a refugee
   - J sympathizes with the Bosnian women

3. The **purpose** of this commentary is to —
   - A persuade us to support public radio
   - B inform us about current events
   - C persuade us to act in support of exiles
   - D reveal a truth about life

4. Which sentence best describes Nesaule's **perspective** on exiles?
   - F She feels sympathetic toward exiles.
   - G She is critical of the government.
   - H She doesn't understand the problems of exile.
   - J She feels hopeless about exile problems.

5. When the writer says in the last paragraph that she believed cutting off her braids would make her an American, she realizes that —
   - A haircuts make people feel better
   - B becoming an American is easy
   - C beauty is a universal quality
   - D feeling settled in a new country is difficult

Constructed Response

1. What details about the Bosnian women speak to the writer "of war and exile"?

2. How does Nesaule describe the women's "exile eyes"?

3. At the end of the commentary, Nesaule is probably speaking from her own experience when she describes what the Bosnian women will have to do as they transform themselves into Americans. List three things exiles have to do.

SKILLS FOCUS

Reading Skills Analyze an author's purpose and perspective.

Exile Eyes   413

Test Practice

Answers and Model Rationales

1. **D** B and C are not supported by the text. A could be true, but the key word in the question is *identifies*.

2. **J** Nesaule clearly feels a bond with the Bosnian women. She does not mention F, G, or H.

3. **D** A personal narrative usually reveals a truth about life. A, B, and C are not explicitly stated anywhere in the text.

4. **F** G is incorrect because government action is not mentioned, and it is not true that she doesn't understand the problem of exiles (H). J is incorrect because she herself is an example of hope.

5. **D** The writer realizes that the effects of war and displacement are not easily forgotten. A and B suggest such changes are easy, while C is not relevant.

Test-Taking Tips

For instruction on how to answer multiple-choice items, refer students to **Test Smarts,** p. 920.

Constructed Response

1. their patched clothing, flimsy shoes, and the look in their eyes

2. "eyes that have lost everything," "weary and disillusioned," "power to disturb"

3. They will have to learn English, live in poor neighborhoods, and find new friends and lovers.

ASSESSING

Assessment

■ *Holt Assessment: Literature, Reading, and Vocabulary*

Grade-Level Skills

■ **Literary Skills**
Analyze biography.

■ **Literary Skills**
Analyze objective and subjective points of view.

■ **Reading Skills**
Use the SQ3R system for studying informational texts.

Review Skills

■ **Literary Skills**
Identify the speaker, and recognize the difference between first- and third-person narration.

Upcoming Skills

■ **Literary Skills**
Analyze the way voice, tone, persona, and choice of narrator affect characterization and plot.

Summary ⊞ *at grade level*

This biographical narrative of Elizabeth I of England highlights her strengths as a ruler and the unique period in which she ruled. It summarizes many of the ways in which she took England from being a strife-filled, war-torn nation to being one of the great powers of Europe. Exploration, the military, industry, commerce, science, and art all flourished under Elizabeth's leadership. Still, she suffered her share of controversy, most of it springing from religious disputes and assassination attempts.

Before You Read   The Biography

Elizabeth I

Make the Connection
Quickwrite ✏

If you were going to write a biography, what person would you choose? Why? Is your choice based on your feelings about the subject? Jot down some responses to these "biography questions."

Literary Focus
Biography: Telling Lives

The text you're about to read is a **biographical narrative.** In a biography a writer tells the story of another person's life. The word *biography* comes from two Greek words: *bios,* meaning "life" (think of biology), and *graphein,* meaning "to write." Most biographers follow a strictly factual style. They describe events that have been carefully researched.

Objective and Subjective Writing

Writing that presents facts without revealing the writer's feelings and opinions is said to be **objective.** Journalists who report on current events for newspapers usually write in an objective style. Their readers want the facts; they do not want to hear how the reporter feels about the event.

Writing that reveals the writer's feelings and opinions is said to be **subjective.** Biographies often combine objective writing with subjective details. After all, it is hard to write about someone's life without revealing your feelings about that person.

INTERNET
Vocabulary
Activity
Keyword: LE5 7-4

SKILLS
FOCUS

Literary Skills
Understand biography; distinguish objective from subjective writing.

Reading Skills
Use the SQ3R system for studying informational texts.

As you read this biography of Queen Elizabeth I of England, see if you can tell how her biographer feels about his royal subject.

Elizabeth I ruled England for forty-five years, from 1558 to 1603.

Vocabulary Development

These are the words you'll need to know as you read this biography:

monarch (măn′ərk) *n.:* sole and absolute leader. *As monarch, Elizabeth came to the throne of England in 1558.*

alliance (ə·lī′əns) *n.:* pact between nations, families, or individuals that shows a common cause. *Elizabeth's advisor encouraged her to join the alliance against the enemy.*

monopoly (mə·näp′ə·lē) *n.:* exclusive control of a market. *The queen's favorites got rich from a monopoly on imported goods.*

arrogant (ar′ə·gənt) *adj.:* overly convinced of one's own importance. *The queen seemed arrogant, but she did listen to others.*

intolerable (in·täl′ər·ə·bəl) *adj.:* unbearable. *Even though Mary was an enemy, Queen Elizabeth felt it would be intolerable to cut off her cousin's head.*

414   Collection 4 / Can You See It My Way?

RESOURCES: READING

Planning
■ *One-Stop Planner* CD-ROM with ExamView Test Generator

Differentiating Instruction
■ *Holt Reading Solutions*
■ *Supporting Instruction in Spanish*
■ *Audio CD Library*
■ *Audio CD Library, Selections and Summaries in Spanish*

Vocabulary
■ *Vocabulary Development*

Grammar and Language
■ *Daily Language Activities*

Assessment
■ *Holt Assessment: Literature, Reading, and Vocabulary*
■ *One-Stop Planner* CD-ROM with ExamView Test Generator

Reading Skills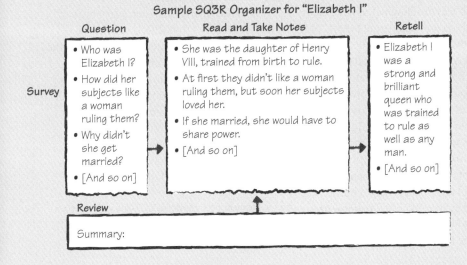

SQ3R: A Study System for Reading Informational Texts

SQ3R stands for *Survey, Question, Read, Retell, Review.* It is a study system that helps readers study texts independently. Below are the SQ3R steps:

S **Survey.** Preview the text. Glance quickly at the headings (if there are any), vocabulary words, and illustrations. Skim the captions, which explain the illustrations, and read the first and last sentence of each paragraph.

Q **Question.** List the questions you'd like to ask about the text, based on your survey.

R **Read.** Read the text carefully to find ideas and information that will answer your questions. Take notes.

R **Retell.** Write responses to your questions in your own words. Try to hit the main points and include important details. You might want to say your answers out loud before you write them down.

R **Review.** Start your review by looking over your completed SQ3R organizer. Try covering up the answers in the "Read and Take Notes" and "Retell" boxes to see if you can answer your questions without looking at your notes. Then, check your memory of the main points and important details by writing a brief summary of the text. If you're shaky on a few details, re-read the parts of the text that contain the information you need.

Sample SQ3R Organizer for "Elizabeth I"

Question	Read and Take Notes	Retell
Survey • Who was Elizabeth I? • How did her subjects like a woman ruling them? • Why didn't she get married? • [And so on]	• She was the daughter of Henry VIII, trained from birth to rule. • At first they didn't like a woman ruling them, but soon her subjects loved her. • If she married, she would have to share power. • [And so on]	• Elizabeth I was a strong and brilliant queen who was trained to rule as well as any man. • [And so on]

Review

Summary:

Elizabeth I **415**

■ *Holt Online Assessment*

Internet
■ go.hrw.com (Keyword: LE5 7-4)
■ *Elements of Literature Online*

Media
■ *Audio CD Library*
■ *Audio CD Library, Selections and Summaries in Spanish*

Skills Starter

Build skills. Point out that to evaluate an author's objectivity, students will need to be able to identify and distinguish between facts and opinions. Remind them that objective facts can be proven true. The statement "Elizabeth I was the queen of England in 1567" is an objective fact. It can be proven true. Opinions are statements that show how someone thinks or feels. They cannot be proven true or false. For example, the statement "Elizabeth I was the greatest queen England has ever had" is an opinion. It shows what someone thinks of Elizabeth I.

Preview Vocabulary

Have students read the definitions of the Vocabulary words on p. 414. Then, to build understanding of the words, have them complete each of the following sentences with the correct Vocabulary word.

1. King George III was the _____ of England during the American Revolution. [monarch]

2. The families interested in saving the wetlands formed an _____ to fight the developers. [alliance]

3. Without any competition, Dingman's Grocery had a _____ of our town's food business. [monopoly]

4. He was so _____ that he didn't think anyone else had a chance of being elected. [arrogant]

5. Connor found the thought of Mariel going to the dance with someone else _____. [intolerable]

Assign the Reading

Have all students do the "Survey" section of their SQ3R organizers at home before reading the biography and completing their organizers in class.

HOMEWORK

A **Literary Focus**

? **Objective writing.** Is this an example of an objective fact or an opinion? Have students explain their answers. [It's an opinion, not a verifiable fact. The example reveals what the author thinks of Elizabeth I.]

B **Literary Focus**

? **Biographical narrative.** How do you know that this selection is biographical and not autobiographical? [The selection is in the third person: Its subject is referred to as "Elizabeth," not as "I."]

C **Reading Skills**

? **Use SQ3R.** What question might you have after reading the last sentence of this paragraph? [Possible questions: How did Elizabeth achieve all of these things? How did England become a great power?]

D **Literary Focus**

? **Objective writing.** How do these details about Elizabeth's youth reveal the objective nature of this biography? [The details are objective facts about Elizabeth's life. Presenting such facts reinforces the author's objectivity.]

E **Literary Focus**

? **Characterization.** What do these details tell you about Elizabeth's character? [Possible responses: She was intelligent and well educated; she was regal, active, and eager.]

ELIZABETH I

Milton Meltzer

"GOOD QUEEN BESS" her people called her. But "good" is a tame word for one of the most remarkable women who ever lived. Elizabeth I came to the throne of England in 1558 at the age of twenty-five. It was not a happy time for a young woman to take the responsibility for ruling a kingdom. Religious conflicts, a huge government debt, and heavy losses in a war with France had brought England low. But by the time of Elizabeth's death forty-five years later, England had experienced one of the greatest periods in its long history. Under Elizabeth's leadership, England had become united as a nation; its industry and commerce, its arts and sciences had flourished; and it was ranked among the great powers of Europe.

Elizabeth was the daughter of King Henry VIII and his second wife, Anne Boleyn. At the age of two she lost her mother when Henry had Anne's head chopped off. Not a good start for a child. But her father placed her in the care of one lord or lady after another, and the lively little girl with the reddish-gold hair, pale skin, and golden-brown eyes won everyone's affection.

Almost from her infancy Elizabeth was trained to stand in for ruling men, in case the need should arise. So she had to master whatever they were expected to know and do. Her tutors found the child to be an eager student. She learned history, geography, mathematics, and the elements of astronomy and architecture. She mastered four modern languages—French, Italian, Spanish, and Flemish[1]—as well as classical Greek and Latin. She wrote in a beautiful script that was like a work of art. The earliest portrait painted of her—when she was thirteen—shows a girl with innocent eyes holding a book in her long and delicate hands, already confident and queenly in her bearing.

She was a strong-willed girl who liked to give orders. She loved to be out on horseback, and rode so fast it frightened the men assigned to protect her. She loved dancing too—she never gave it up. Even in her old age she was seen one moonlit night dancing by herself in the garden.

Elizabeth had a half sister, Mary, born in 1516 of Henry's first wife, Catherine of Aragon. Many years later came Elizabeth, the child of Anne Boleyn, and four years after, her half brother, Edward, the son of Henry's third wife, Jane Seymour. After Henry died, because succession[2] came first through the male, ten-year-old Edward was crowned king. But he lived only another six years. Now Mary took the throne and, soon after, married King Philip II of Spain, a Catholic

---

1. **Flemish:** language spoken in Flanders, a region covering a small part of northern France and Belgium.
2. **succession** *n.*: order in which one succeeds to the throne.

Learners Having Difficulty
Modeling. Before students read "Elizabeth I," suggest that they create a five-column chart to organize important information they will learn as they read. The chart should have the following headings: Dates, Characteristics, Important People, Obstacles or Challenges, Achievements. As students read, encourage them to look for information for their chart. You may want to have students pause every two pages and discuss their findings.

English-Language Learners
The reading level of this selection may present a problem for English-language learners. Make sure students understand how Elizabeth came to be queen. If necessary, encourage students to draw the line of succession, starting with King Henry VIII and then Elizabeth's half brother Edward, continuing with Elizabeth's half sister Mary, and ending with Elizabeth.

HENRY VIII.
Henry VIII, King of England by Hans Holbein the Younger (1497–1543).

QUEEN ELIZABETH I.
Queen Elizabeth I by Henry Bone (1755–1834). Copy of miniature (c. 1592) by Marcus Gheerhaerts. Enamel on copper.

ANNE BOLEYN.

**MARY TUDOR,
QUEEN OF ENGLAND.**

KING PHILIP II.

Ⓐ Literary Focus

Biographical narrative. Make sure students understand that biographies often include quotations from the subject. The use of the first person in such quotations does not indicate that the selection is autobiographical. Students must look at the narration of the text as a whole to accurately identify its form.

Ⓑ Reading Skills

❓ Use SQ3R. A natural question that arises from surveying the first sentence of this paragraph is "Whom did Elizabeth marry?" Ask students if they know or can predict the answer based upon their survey, the first step of SQ3R.

Ⓒ Vocabulary Development

Clarify word meanings: Definition. Point out the phrase *divine right* to students. Then, point out the signal phrase *that is,* which signals to readers that a definition is coming up. Explain that writers of informational materials for students often define unfamiliar words this way within the text. Have students look for more examples of this kind of word definition as they read.

The Granger Collection, New York.

PRINCESS ELIZABETH I.
Elizabeth I of England when a princess (c. 1542–1547).

monarch like herself. He was twenty-seven and she was thirty-eight. But they were rarely together, each ruling their own kingdom. Mary died of cancer at the age of forty-two. That made Elizabeth the monarch.

When she came to the throne on November 17, 1558, it was a day to be marked by celebrations, then and long after. As Her Majesty passed down a London street, an astonished housewife exclaimed, "Oh, Lord! The queen is a woman!" For there were still many who could scarcely believe they were to be ruled by another woman. Elizabeth herself would say with mock modesty that she was "a mere woman." But everyone soon learned

Ⓐ she was a very special woman. "Am I not a queen because God has chosen me to be a queen?" she demanded.

As princess and later as queen, Elizabeth lived in various palaces, with much coming and going; each time she moved, she took along her household staff of 120 people. Often the changes were required because there was no sanitation. The smelly palaces had to be emptied so they could be "aired and sweetened."

Ⓑ Even before Elizabeth came of age, there was much talk of when she would marry, and whom. Marriages among the nobility and royalty were arranged not for love, but for practical reasons—to add land holdings, to strengthen the prestige and power of families, to cement an alliance of nations against a common enemy.

Ⓒ And remember, from the most ancient times, kings claimed that they as men were born to rule by divine right. That is, God had ordained that the crown should pass through the male line of descent. But when the king's wife had no male child, it meant trouble. Who then would rule? That crisis often led to civil war as various factions battled for the

Vocabulary
monarch (män′ərk) *n.:* sole and absolute leader.
alliance (ə·lī′əns) *n.:* pact between nations, families, or individuals that shows a common cause.

DEVELOPING FLUENCY

Activity. Students can use their SQ3R organizers to help them develop fluency with the text. Have students get together with partners to read sections of the selection and fill in their organizers, focusing on the "Retell" and "Review" sections. Partners should encourage each other to read the selection aloud and discuss organizer entries.

Partners may wish to pose the questions from the "Question" section of their organizers to each other. They should identify and read aloud the sections of the text that answer these questions.

PAIRED

power to name a king. Many disputed Elizabeth's right to the throne, and as long as she had neither husband nor successor, her life was in danger.

Ever since Elizabeth was eight, however, she had said again and again, "I will never marry." Did marriage look promising to a girl whose father had had six wives, two of whom, including her own mother, he had beheaded? Yet she liked to hear of people who wanted to marry her.

And there was no shortage of suitors. She continued to insist she wished to live unmarried. No matter how often she said it, men did not believe it. Understandably, since she often made a prince or duke who had come to court her believe she was finally ready to give in—only at the last moment to back out. Once, to a delegation from Parliament come to beg her to marry, she declared, "I am already bound unto a husband, which is the Kingdom of England."

And why should she, the absolute ruler of England, allow a man to sit alongside her as king? The power of husbands over wives in that century—and even now, in many places of this world—was so great that a husband might snatch the reins of power from her and leave her with the title but not the authority she loved to exercise.

Was it fun to be queen? As monarch, she commanded great wealth, inherited from her father, and people who wanted favors were always enriching her with lavish presents. She was no spendthrift, however. She hated to see money wasted, whether her own or the

D "I AM ALREADY BOUND UNTO A HUSBAND, WHICH IS THE KINGDOM OF ENGLAND."

kingdom's. Early on she began keeping careful household account books, and later she would do the same with the royal accounts. Always she urged her counselors to carry out orders as inexpensively as possible.

Above everything else, Elizabeth wanted to have her people think well of her. Her deepest desire was to assure them of peace and prosperity. And why not make a grand personal impression upon them at the same time? In her mature years she gave free rein to her love of jewels and staged brilliant displays for the court and the people. Her dresses were decorated with large rubies, emeralds, and diamonds, and she wore jeweled necklaces, bracelets, and rings. In her hair, at her ears, and around her neck she wore pearls—the symbol of virginity.

During her reign she made many great processions through London, the people wild with excitement, crowding the streets—for the English, like most people, loved spectacle. In the first of them, her coronation, she wore gold robes as she was crowned. Trumpets sounded, pipes and drums played, the organ pealed, bells rang. Then came the state banquet in Westminster Hall. It began at 3:00 P.M., and went on till 1:00 A.M.

Elizabeth was often entertained at house parties. One of them, given by the Earl of Leicester in Kenilworth Castle, lasted for eighteen days in July. Thirty other distinguished guests were invited. The great number of their servants (together with Leicester's) turned the palace into a small

Elizabeth I **419**

DIRECT TEACHING

D **Literary Focus**
Objective writing. Help students see the mix of objective facts and opinion in this paragraph. Students may have trouble identifying the opinion in this paragraph. Point out that it is in the form of a question. The author is offering his speculative opinion that Elizabeth might have been wary of marriage because of her parents' histories.

E **Learners Having Difficulty**
Paraphrase. The author's slightly formal vocabulary—for example, his use of the word *suitors* and the verb *court*—may be difficult for some students. Help students increase their understanding by having an advanced student paraphrase the sentences in this paragraph. [Possible paraphrase: No one believed Elizabeth didn't want to get married. Men constantly asked her to marry them. Sometimes she would lead them on. At one point, she told people that she was already married—to her country.]

F **Advanced Learners**
? **Speculate.** Invite these students to discuss Elizabeth's unique role as a female ruler. How might her situation and feelings about marriage be different if she were ruling today? Would a husband be in the same position to snatch her power away? Then, have students broaden the discussion to include women today. Do they agree with the author that in some places husbands still have absolute power over their wives?

CROSS-CURRICULAR CONNECTIONS

History
The Elizabethan Age. Students' understanding of this biography will be enhanced by a greater knowledge of English history during the reign of Elizabeth. The author makes references to many of the changes and accomplishments that occurred during this time but does not go into detail. If possible, coordinate a mini-unit on Elizabethan history with the social studies teacher.

Activity. Have groups choose an aspect of Elizabethan history mentioned in the text and research it. Groups should write reports of their findings and make presentations to the class. If possible, create a bulletin board or resource center where students can both post and look up information.

SMALL GROUP

A Reading Skills

Use SQ3R. The numerous facts listed here about the Renaissance may lead students to write questions in their organizers that will not be answered by the text itself. Encourage them to use a library, the Internet, and social studies resources to find the answers to these questions.

B Cross-curricular Connections

Elizabethan authors. Many of these names may be unfamiliar to students. Explain that Donne and Spenser were primarily poets, while Marlowe, Jonson, and Shakespeare were poets as well as playwrights.

town. When darkness fell, candles glittered everywhere, indoors and out, creating a fairyland. Musicians sang and played, the guests danced in the garden, and such a great display of fireworks exploded that the heavens thundered and the castle shook. Then came a pleasure relished in those days: the hideous sport of bear baiting. A pack of dogs was let loose in an inner courtyard to scratch and bite and tear at thirteen tormented bears. Still, the happy guests retained their appetite for a "most delicious banquet of 300 dishes."

The tremendous festival at Kenilworth was only one of the highlights of Elizabeth's summer festival. She moved from one great house to another all season long, always at the enormous expense of her hosts. They had little to complain of, however, for their wealth was often the product of the queen's generous bestowal of special privileges. In recognition of his high rank and in return for his support, she granted the duke of Norfolk a license to import carpets from Turkey free of duty. The earl of Essex was favored with the profitable right to tax imported sweet wines. Other pets got rich from a monopoly on the importation of or taxation of silks, satins, salt, tobacco, starch.

England was a small nation at the time she ruled: less than four million people, about as many as live in Arizona today. But the English were a young people, coming to maturity with new worlds opening up to them, in the mind and across the seas. A rebirth of culture—the Renaissance—had begun in the 1400s. With the revival of interest in the literature of the ancient Greek and Roman worlds came the beginning of a great age of discovery. This period marked the transition from medieval to modern times. The arts

and sciences were influenced by changes in economic life. All the nation was swept up in the vast tides of change. Merchants, bankers, the gentry,[3] artisans, seamen, miners—men and women of every class and condition—felt themselves part of the national venture.

At the heart of the change in England was the queen. But no king or queen rules alone, no matter how authoritative or arrogant they may be. They usually look to others for advice, advice they may follow or reject. Elizabeth appointed ministers to handle the various departments of government, and made Sir William Cecil, then thirty-eight, her principal advisor. He was a brilliant, hard-working master of statecraft, devoted to her and England's well-being, and as ruthless as she and the nation's interests required. When he died in old age, his son Robert replaced him at her side.

So great was the queen's role, however, that her time became known as the Age of Elizabeth. Not only did many fine musicians flower, but writers too, such as Christopher Marlowe and John Donne and Ben Jonson and Edmund Spenser. And above all, the incomparable William Shakespeare, whose plays were sometimes performed at court. Astronomers, naturalists, mathematicians, geographers, and architects pioneered in their fields.

Then, too, there were the daring explorers who pushed English expansion overseas.

---

3. **gentry** *n.:* upper class.

Vocabulary

monopoly (mə·năp′ə·lē) *n.:* exclusive control of a market. Monopolies are illegal now because they can control prices.

arrogant (ar′ə·gənt) *adj.:* overly convinced of one's own importance.

WILLIAM SHAKESPEARE.

THE GOLDEN HINDE.
A working replica of the sailing ship *Golden Hinde* used by Drake during the sixteenth century.

SIR FRANCIS DRAKE.
The English explorer Sir Francis Drake (1540?–1596).

One of the queen's favorites, Sir Walter Raleigh, planned the colony of Virginia in America and named it for her, the Virgin Queen. The queen herself put money into several of the great voyages, keeping close watch over the plans and their results. She supported Sir Francis Drake on his three-year voyage around the world, profiting mightily from the immense loot he captured from Spanish ships taken in the Pacific.

For Elizabeth, one of the most urgent problems was the question of religion. Her father had broken with the Catholic Church and launched the English Reformation, creating the Church of England, with himself at its head. When Elizabeth's older half sister, Mary (who remained Catholic), married the Catholic king of Spain, Philip II, she reconciled England with the Church of Rome. In Mary's brief reign she persecuted those Protestants who refused to conform, executing some 270 of them.

When Elizabeth became queen upon Mary's death, she said she hoped religion would not prevent her people from living together in peaceful unity. She did not want to pry into people's souls or question their faith. But in 1570, Pope Pius V excommunicated[4] her, denied her right to the throne, and declared her subjects owed her no allegiance. A directive[5] from the pope's office decreed that the assassination of Queen Elizabeth would not be regarded as a sin. The effect of this directive was to turn practicing Catholics—about half of the English, most of them loyal—into potential traitors.

Though Elizabeth had wanted to pursue a middle way of toleration, circumstances threatened to overwhelm her. She had to beware of several Catholic monarchs of Europe who wished to see a Protestant England overthrown. Philip II of Spain sent ambassadors to England to urge Catholics to rise against

---

4. **excommunicated** *v.*: cast out from a religious community. Strictly speaking, the queen was denied the sacraments of the Catholic Church.
5. **directive** *n.*: order or instructions, especially given by a government.

Elizabeth I **421**

DIRECT TEACHING

C Literary Focus

Biographical narrative. Why do you think the accomplishments and developments of the English are included in this biography? [Possible response: As an absolute monarch, Elizabeth was responsible for allowing or encouraging much of the change that took place in England during her reign.] **Why doesn't the author just present facts about Elizabeth's life?** [Possible response: Biographies of public figures usually include facts about their careers as well as facts about their personal lives.]

D Reading Skills

Compare and contrast. How was Elizabeth a different ruler from her half sister Mary? [Mary persecuted those who were not of her faith, while Elizabeth tried to unify her people regardless of their religion.]

A Learners Having Difficulty

Use context clues. In spite of the footnote, some students may be confused by the presence of two Marys in the text. Help students use context clues to distinguish that this Mary is not the same as Elizabeth's half sister. Point out that the word *cousin* indicates that this Mary is a different person from the one mentioned previously.

B Reading Skills

❓ **Compare and contrast.** Earlier, it seemed that Elizabeth would be a different type of ruler from her half sister, who persecuted Protestants. Has this information about Elizabeth executing Campion made you revise your opinion? [Possible responses: Yes, Elizabeth executed Catholics just as her sister executed Protestants. No, Elizabeth tried to be a uniter, but the circumstances wouldn't let her.]

C Learners Having Difficulty

Break down difficult text. This sentence, with its many clauses, may be confusing for some readers. Have them break the sentence down and make a numbered list of all the actions mentioned. [(1) Elizabeth supervised the high command. (2) She rallied popular support. (3) She sent troops to protect the coasts. (4) She sent Drake's ships to attack the Spanish fleet.] Point out that these actions were happening simultaneously.

D Reading Skills

Use SQ3R. In their organizers, students may have questions about the Spanish Armada that will not be answered by further reading of the selection. Encourage them to do research both in books and on the Internet to find answers to these questions.

A Elizabeth, put her cousin Mary[6] on the throne, and restore Roman Catholicism as the national faith. The line between power, politics, and religion was becoming very thin.

Missionary priests living abroad were sent into England to stir up opposition to the queen. But the English Catholics as a body never rebelled, nor did they ever intend **B** to. Still, missionary priests such as Edmund Campion were convicted of plotting against Elizabeth and executed.

In 1588 a long-threatened invasion of England by Spain was launched by Philip II. He mistakenly believed that the English Catholics were waiting to welcome him. News of his armada of 130 big ships carrying 17,000 soldiers was terrifying. But the queen did not panic. She supervised the high command personally, meanwhile rally-**C** ing popular support for the defense of the realm and sending troops to protect the coasts while Sir Francis Drake's ships set out to attack the Spanish fleet.

The Spanish Armada was defeated in three battles, its ships dispersed. When the news came of the tremendous victory, the citizens took to the streets, shouting for joy.

D The defeat of the Spanish Armada did not end Spain's aggression against England. The Jesuits[7] in England, who were especially identified with Spain, continued to be persecuted. Richard Topcliffe, a notorious hater of

---

6. **Mary:** Mary Stuart (1542–1587) (Mary, Queen of Scots, not Elizabeth's half sister).
7. **Jesuits** (jezh'oo·its): priests who are members of the Roman Catholic Society of Jesus.

HOW DARE STUBBS SAY PUBLICLY SHE WAS TOO OLD TO MARRY?

Catholics, was given authority to track down suspects. He examined them under torture to force information about people who had sheltered them. The treatment of them was so vicious and cruel that the victims welcomed death as a release from their agony.

During Elizabeth's reign several plots to assassinate her were uncovered. Elizabeth managed to give the impression that she was not frightened, but those close to her knew she was. When one of the major plots proved to center around Elizabeth's cousin, Mary, Queen of Scots, Elizabeth found it almost intolerable to put to death a crowned queen. Yet she ordered the use of torture on Mary's co-conspirators, and in the end, Mary was beheaded. A song composed by William Byrd at the time suggests how ominous the news of a monarch's execution was:

The noble famous Queen
who lost her head of late
Doth show that kings as well as clowns
Are bound to fortune's fate,
And that no earthly Prince
Can so secure his crown
but fortune with her whirling wheel
Hath power to pull them down.

When two earls combined forces against her, Elizabeth's troops overcame them. The queen was so enraged she ordered that 800 of the mostly poor rebels be hanged. But she spared the lives of their wealthy leaders so

---

Vocabulary
intolerable (in·täl'ər·ə·bəl) *adj.*: unbearable.

MARY STUART, QUEEN OF SCOTS.
Portrait of Mary Stuart, Queen of Scots (16th century).

SEA BATTLE BETWEEN THE SPANISH ARMADA AND ENGLISH NAVAL FORCES.

DIRECT TEACHING

E **Cross-curricular Connections**
HISTORY

The succession. Although beheaded, Mary, Queen of Scots, had a posthumous "revenge" of sorts. Since Elizabeth never had children, Mary's son James stood next in line to inherit the throne. He became the king of England after Elizabeth's death.

that they might enrich her, either by buying their pardons or by forfeiting[8] their lands.

Elizabeth came down hard on writers who criticized her actions. John Stubbs, a zealous Puritan, wrote a pamphlet expressing horror at the possibility the queen might marry a French Catholic. The queen had Stubbs and his publisher tried and convicted for seditious libel.[9] How dare Stubbs say publicly she was too old to marry, and that the much younger French suitor could not possibly be in love with her? Elizabeth was merciless as she invoked the penalty for libel. With a butcher's cleaver, the executioner cut the right hands off Stubbs and his publisher. Not an uncommon punishment.

How did Elizabeth learn of all these plots and conspiracies? How did she know what

---

8. **forfeiting** (fôr′fit·iŋ) *v.* used as *n.:* giving up, usually because of force of some kind.
9. **seditious libel** (si·dish′əs li′bəl): stirring up discontent about the government (sedition) with false written statements (libel).

plans Philip II of Spain was devising to invade her kingdom? Spies and secret agents—they were her eyes and ears. Crucial to the flow of information was Sir Francis Walsingham. Trained as a lawyer, he lived on the Continent[10] for years, mastering the languages and the ins and outs of European affairs. Upon his return home, he was asked by Sir William Cecil, the queen's right arm, to gather information on the doings and plans of foreign governments. Soon he was made chief of England's secret service. He placed over seventy agents and spies in the courts of Europe. And of course he watched closely the activities of people at home suspected of disloyalty. Letters to and from them were secretly opened, to nip plots in the bud.

Monarchs had absolute power. Elizabeth could arrest anyone, including the topmost ranks of the nobility, and imprison them in the Tower of London even if they had not

---

10. **Continent:** Europe.

Elizabeth I **423**

DIFFERENTIATING INSTRUCTION

Advanced Learners
Enrichment. Encourage students to discuss the idea that even good rulers make some questionable decisions. Does torturing and ordering the execution of people detract from the accomplishments of Elizabeth I? Why or why not?

Activity. Suggest that students create a "Good Queen/Bad Queen" chart, identifying Elizabeth's despotic deeds as well as her achievements. Students might also write an essay expressing their opinion about the belief in the divine right of kings that prevailed in early European history.

HOMEWORK

A Literary Focus

❓ **Characterization.** How do these details about Elizabeth make her come alive for readers? [Possible response: These details allow readers to see Elizabeth as a person as well as a monarch.]

B Literary Focus

❓ **Objective writing.** Overall, would you consider this biography of Elizabeth objective? Have students explain their answers. [Since the biography contains many more facts than opinions, it can be considered objective.]

committed any legal offense. The only thing that held her back was her fear of public opinion. It upset her when a crowd gathered at a public execution and was so disgusted by the butchery that they let out roars of disapproval. Still, like all rulers, Elizabeth said she believed that "born a sovereign princess" she enjoyed "the privilege common to all kings" and was "exempt from human jurisdiction[11] and subject only to the judgement of God."

Despite her blazing nervous energy, Elizabeth was often sick. Her ailments were anxiously reported and discussed. For the English believed her survival was their only guarantee of freedom from foreign invasion and civil war. Once, suffering a raging toothache for the first time, the queen feared the pain of having an extraction. She had never had a tooth pulled and was terrified. To reassure her, an old friend, the Bishop of London, had her watch while the dental surgeon pulled out one of the bishop's own good teeth. And then she consented to have her own taken out.

It was commonly believed then that kings and queens had the magical power to cure disease in their subjects. Eager to demonstrate that she too had the sacred power of royalty, Elizabeth prayed intensely before using the royal touch on people with scrofula, a nasty skin disease. Her chaplain said he watched "her exquisite hands, boldly, and without disgust, pressing the sores and ulcers." In one day it was reported that she

"OLD AGE CAME UPON ME AS A SURPRISE, LIKE A FROST," SHE ONCE WROTE.

A

healed thirty-eight persons. But if she did not feel divinely inspired, she would not try her touch.

Even in the last decade of her life, Elizabeth's energy was astonishing. She was as watchful as always over the affairs of state, though sometimes forgetful. But age made her more irritable; she sometimes shouted at her ladies and even boxed their ears. She was less able to control rival factions out for power, and became so fearful of assassins she rarely left her palaces.

A portrait of her done when she was approaching sixty shows her in a great white silk dress studded with aglets[12] of black onyx, coral, and pearl. She wears three ropes of translucent pearls and stands on a map of England, her England. An ambassador reported that at sixty-three she looked old, but her figure was still beautiful, and her conversation was as brilliant and charming as ever.

There was dancing at court every evening, a pastime she still enjoyed. When it came to displays of gallantry by eager young men, she could act a bit vain and foolish, although never letting any hopeful get out of bounds.

In early 1603 Elizabeth developed a bad cold that led to a serious fever, and then she fell into a stupor[13] for four days. As she lay dying, all of London became strangely silent. On March 24, the life of a rare genius ended. The nation went into mourning.

B

"Old age came upon me as a surprise, like a frost," she once wrote.

---

11. **jurisdiction** (joor′is·dik′shən) *n.:* legal control.

12. **aglets** (ag′lits) *n.:* tips of lace on dresses.
13. **stupor** (stoo′pər) *n.:* loss of sensibility; dullness.

Encourage students to read this selection together with family members. After they complete the selection, students and their families can debate whether or not Elizabeth I was, as Meltzer claims, "one of the most remarkable women who ever lived." Suggest that they discuss the following questions:

• What makes a leader "great" or "remarkable"? Did Elizabeth fit this criteria?

• Were her accomplishments more remarkable because she was a woman?

Meet the Writer

Milton Meltzer

No Shy Guy

The historian **Milton Meltzer** (1915–   ) took an interest in social issues when he was young. After attending Columbia University, he joined the Works Projects Administration, a government agency that provided jobs for workers who were unemployed during the Great Depression of the 1930s. Over time he has written about the Holocaust and the civil rights movement, slavery and immigration. Never one to shy away from controversy, Meltzer writes honestly about injustices that have occurred throughout history.

His biographies cover historic figures, such as George Washington and Mark Twain, as well as others who may not be so well known—like Tom Paine, who battled for America's independence, and Betty Friedan, who fought for women's rights. Throughout most of his work, Meltzer recognizes a common link:

> 66 My subjects choose action.... Action takes commitment, the commitment of dedicated, optimistic individuals. I try to make the readers understand that history isn't only what happens to us. History is what we *make* happen. Each of us. All of us. 99

Meltzer has written over eighty books, many of them award winners. In addition, he has made documentary films and written scripts for radio and television.

For Independent Reading

So much Meltzer to choose from! For more biographies of women like Elizabeth, try *Ten Queens: Portraits of Women of Power.* Or you may prefer *Frederick Douglass: In His Own Words* or *Thomas Jefferson: The Revolutionary Aristocrat.*

Meet the Writer

Although he didn't realize it until it was pointed out to him, Meltzer has fashioned a successful writing career based on championing underdogs. He is a tireless researcher who has revitalized textbooks by including eyewitness accounts and personal documents. He has said that working with the living expression of an era can get one close to reliving the experiences for oneself.

For Independent Reading

Point out that the title of Meltzer's book on Frederick Douglass suggests that much of the material will be autobiographical. Suggest that students who read the book compare it with this biography or others they have read.

After You Read

First Thoughts

1. Possible questions: Why didn't you ever marry? What accomplishments during your reign make you most proud?

Thinking Critically

2. Students should infer that most of Elizabeth's subjects adored her. Evidence to support this inference includes the fact that they called her "Good Queen Bess" and went into mourning when she died. Students may note that some Catholic subjects hated her, since they planned assassination attempts.

3. Possible answers: *Marriage*—wouldn't matter so much for a ruler today. *Executions*—far more troubling today than during Elizabeth's reign. *Intrigues*—struggles for power occur today but may be mitigated by laws. *Processions*—more elaborate during Elizabeth's era. *Parties*—excessive month-long parties would trouble constituents today. *Divine right of kings*—leaders today are generally chosen by popular vote, not as ordained by God. *Separation of church and state*—Elizabeth left religious matters in the hands of people, much like today.

Extending Interpretations

4. Possible answer: Meltzer seems to admire Elizabeth, calling her a "rare genius." His view is balanced; he points out both her good and bad qualities. Yet he tends to be mostly objective—"In early 1603 Elizabeth developed a bad cold. . . ."

After You Read Response and Analysis

First Thoughts

1. If you could ask Elizabeth one question, what would it be?

Thinking Critically

2. What **inferences** can you make about how people felt about Elizabeth? Support your inferences with evidence from the text.

3. Which details in the life of Elizabeth would, and which would not, apply to the life of a ruler today? Consider these topics:
   • the question of marriage
   • the execution of enemies
   • intrigues and plots
   • processions
   • parties
   • the divine right of kings
   • separation of church and state

Extending Interpretations

4. Evaluate this biographer's feelings about Elizabeth. Is his narrative balanced? Is he mostly **objective** as a biographer, or is he very **subjective** in his account of Elizabeth? Find details from the biography to support your answers.

WRITING

Writing a Biographical Sketch

Write a short biographical sketch of the person you chose for your Quickwrite. Before you write, create a character profile by listing facts you know and questions for which you want answers. Use the Internet and library resources to gather information that will answer your research questions. Do you wish to write an **objective** biography—sticking to the facts? Or do you prefer to express some **subjective** feelings?

SKILLS FOCUS

Literary Skills Analyze a biography; analyze objective and subjective points of view.

Reading Skills Use the SQ3R system for studying informational texts.

Writing Skills Write a biographical sketch.

Reading Check

Answer the following questions. Then, complete your SQ3R organizer.

a. What problems did England have when Elizabeth I came to the throne?

b. How did England change during the Renaissance? Who was at the heart of the change?

c. Why didn't Elizabeth want to get married?

d. What was Elizabeth's opinion about her people's religious practices?

e. Why was it always possible that Elizabeth would be assassinated?

Reading Check

a. Religious conflicts, huge government debt, and heavy losses from a war with France

b. Economic changes led to changes in society and to a flowering of artistic and scientific output. Elizabeth promoted many of these changes.

c. Possible answers: She didn't want to give up power to a husband; her parents' experiences had soured her on marriage.

d. Elizabeth hoped religion would not keep her subjects from living together in peace.

e. The struggle for power between Catholics and Protestants continued during her reign, and the pope issued a directive saying that assassinating her would not be a sin.

Clarifying Word Meanings:
Definitions in Context

You may have noticed that the writer of this article helped you out when he used a word that he thought you might not know. He defined the difficult word right there in the sentence or in the next sentence. Writers of textbooks and other materials written for students often do this. It's up to you to be able to recognize a definition when you see it. Here are three examples from "Elizabeth I" in which the writer clarifies word meanings through the use of definition.

In the first example the words *that is* signal a definition coming up.

> "Kings claimed that they as men were born to rule by <u>divine right</u>. That is, God had ordained that the crown should pass through the male line of descent."

In this example, the definition comes before the word:

> "A rebirth of culture—the <u>Renaissance</u>—had begun in the 1400s."

Here the writer defines the word *scrofula* right after the comma:

> "Elizabeth prayed intensely before using the royal touch on people with <u>scrofula</u>, a nasty skin disease."

PRACTICE

Write a sentence for each word in the Word Bank, and define the word by applying one of the methods used in the examples above. Use each method of clarification at least once.

Word Bank

monarch
alliance
monopoly
arrogant
intolerable

Elizabeth I, Queen of England (16th century).

Old London Bridge in 1630 (detail) by Claude de Jong (c. 1610–1663).
The Granger Collection, New York.

SKILLS FOCUS

Vocabulary Skills
Clarify word meanings by using definitions.

Elizabeth I   **427**

Vocabulary Development

PRACTICE

Possible Answers

1. Elizabeth became the monarch of England—that is, the sole and absolute ruler.
2. Spain formed an alliance—a pact—with some of England's missionary priests.
3. It was common for the queen to grant a monopoly, or exclusive control of a commodity or service, to those who were extremely loyal to her.
4. The queen was arrogant, believing that she was so important she could do anything she wanted.
5. Elizabeth found the idea of giving up power to a husband intolerable, that is, unbearable.

ASSESSING

Assessment
■ *Holt Assessment: Literature, Reading, and Vocabulary*

RETEACHING

For a lesson reteaching subjective and objective points of view, see **Reteaching,** pp. 917G–H.

Comparing Literature

OVERVIEW

Purpose. This Comparing Literature feature asks students to compare mood and theme across texts. By exploring details of texts, students will analyze the different ways authors create mood. They will also explore themes related to change and loss by thinking about the meanings of the selections' titles and by identifying and examining key passages.

Use. Direct students' attention to the box on the right. Have them identify words that describe the mood of each selection as they read.

After reading all three selections, students will write an essay comparing and contrasting the selections' moods and themes. Students will fill in comparison-contrast charts, examine the mood and theme in each story, and explain which story they had the most positive response to. Alternatively, students may research and prepare an oral presentation on one of two topics related to the literary selections.

Literary Focus
Mood and Theme

Mood is the overall feeling of a story, poem, or other work of literature. Writers create mood through the words, images, and descriptions they use. Sometimes you can describe the feeling of a work of literature in a single word, such as *dreamy, mysterious, hopeful,* or *sad.* Other times, though, the mood may be more complex and hard to describe. You might need two or three words to convey the mood.

Theme is the truth about life revealed in a work of literature. The story and poems you are about to read are all concerned with change and loss. What each selection reveals about the impact on life of change and loss is its theme. As you read, see if describing the mood of the selection helps you express its theme.

Reading Skills
Comparing and Contrasting

As you read the selections that follow, consider what each reveals about the power of loss and change. Think about whether any of the words in the box at the right can be used to describe the mood of one or more of the texts. A chart at the end of the selections will help you to collect your ideas. You'll use the chart to write a comparison-contrast essay on page 444.

Words for Mood

nostalgic

peaceful

exciting

scary

regretful

angry

joyful

eerie

wistful

proud

Tips for Finding Theme

- Think about the **title** and what it might mean.

- Look for **key passages** in which the writer seems to make important statements about life.

SKILLS FOCUS

Literary Skills
Understand mood and theme.

Reading Skills
Compare and contrast texts.

Before You Read

Dinosaurs ruled the earth for some 160 million years. Why did they vanish? Did a massive asteroid smash into the earth? Did swamps dry up and destroy their habitats? Did drastic changes in temperature kill them off? Here a writer imagines what it might have been like to be the very last dinosaur.

The Last Dinosaur

Jim Murphy

The sun came up slowly, fingers of light poking into and brightening the tangled forest of pine and poplar and hemlock trees. The drone of insects quieted, and the tiny mammals scampered to hide.

In a clearing a small triceratops herd began their day. The female triceratops blinked several times before moving to get the light out of her eyes. Then she went back to the frond she'd ripped from a cycadeoid.[1] **A**

The frond was tough and spiky, but her sharp-edged beak and rows of teeth chopped the plant into easily swallowed pieces. She was about to tug at another frond when a male triceratops began stamping his feet in alarm. **1**

He had been feeding at the base of a tree when his horns became entangled in a mass of grapevines. He shook his head violently to get free. When that didn't work, he backed away, yanking his head

---

1. **cycadeoid** (sī·kad′ē·oid′) *n.:* extinct plant that existed at the time of the dinosaurs. (A frond is the leaf of a palm or fern.)

PREDICT

1 What might be the cause of the male triceratops's alarm? Use your **prior knowledge** to help you make your prediction. **B**

Summary ⬇ *below grade level*

This suspenseful story tells about dinosaurs in an entertaining way and helps students imagine the events that may have led to the extinction of these amazing animals. As three dinosaurs of the *Triceratops* genus search for food, they encounter threats from fire, a mighty tyrannosaur, and the small, swift-moving mammals that are taking over the earth. After the two males are killed and the last triceratops eggs are eaten by mammals, one lone female triceratops remains; her chances for survival are slim.

PRETEACHING

Selection Starter

Build background. Students may believe that dinosaurs died out suddenly, leaving no descendants. Point out to them that dinosaurs, like other species, were already declining before they finally became extinct. Also, tell students that there is evidence suggesting that birds are descended from dinosaurs.

DIRECT TEACHING

A Vocabulary Note
Word origins. So students don't miss it, read aloud the definition of *triceratops* (p. 433). Point out the meaning of the prefix *tri–*, and have students name other words with the same prefix. [Possible responses: *triangle, tricycle, tripod.*]

B Reading Skills
Predict. [Possible response to question 1: The male triceratops is probably alarmed by some threat to himself and the other dinosaurs.]

A **Learners Having Difficulty**

? Find details. What details in this passage support the idea that very few dinosaurs are left in the world? [Possible responses: The herd of triceratopses is made up of only three animals. The three triceratopses have not seen another dinosaur in a long time.]

B **Reading Skills**

Interpret. [Possible responses to question 2: Most students will say that the story's mood is eerie and threatening because of the triceratops's entanglement in the vine, the startling noise that gets the female dinosaur's attention, and the possibility that the dinosaurs may be pursued. Others may view the mood as relatively peaceful since the dinosaurs spend the afternoon eating and wandering.]

INTERPRET

❷ Describe the **mood,** or overall feeling, of the story so far. Find **B** three details to support your interpretation. You may need more than one word to describe the mood.

---

from side to side. Still covered with vines, he halted. His breathing came in short, grunting pants.

Suddenly he lowered his head and charged the tree. He hit it solidly, backed up, and hit it again, and then again. The fourth butt splintered the tree's base, and it leaned over. A few wiggles of his head and the vine slipped off.

He snorted at the vine, challenging it. When it didn't move, he walked around it and left the clearing. He was the largest triceratops and leader of the herd, so the smaller male and the female followed him.

A The three wandered through the forest, always staying near the stream that was their source of water. They did not hurry, and often stopped to nibble at figs or tender tree saplings. On the second day they came to a hillside covered with tasty ferns. The spot was cool and quiet, so they stayed the afternoon, browsing.

A sudden noise made the female jerk up her head to look and listen. They had not seen another dinosaur in a very long time, but she was still wary. A hungry tyrannosaur might have picked up their scent and followed, hoping one of them would stray from the herd. **❷**

DIFFERENTIATING INSTRUCTION

Learners Having Difficulty
Encourage students who are having trouble identifying the theme to ask themselves the following questions: "What does the title tell me about the story? What do I learn about the main characters? What is the main conflict in the story, and how is it resolved? What are the key details in the story?" By asking themselves these questions, students should be able to figure out what point the writer is making about life.

English-Language Learners
Students may be unfamiliar with many of the words that describe the characters and setting in the story. Have them keep track of unfamiliar words by writing down the word and its definition. Then, have students use the word in a sentence. Use the word *sapling* (p. 430) as an example. Tell students that *sapling* means "a young tree." Then, read this sentence to students: "The delicate sapling was eaten by the dinosaur."

The two males sensed her unease and also looked around. A giant dragonfly circled the triceratopses, then flew away. A bird chattered briefly. Then the forest grew still. Was a tyrannosaur out there, watching, waiting? Nothing moved and the noise did not return, but the herd was nervous. They left the hillside and continued their journey.

The next day, the land sloped downward and the stream widened to become a series of falls, pools, and swirling rapids. The path twisted to follow the water and dipped sharply in places. Despite their great size, the triceratopses walked the narrow ledges and leaped boulders with an easy grace.

The female triceratops smelled something. Her sense of sight was very poor, so she turned to face what was causing the strange odor. Wisps of smoke trailed through the trees.

The smoke was from a fire started the night before by heat lightning.[2] The female couldn't see the fire or know that it was advancing toward them. But the smoke was growing thicker and more unpleasant, so the three animals trotted away.

All night they moved quickly to stay clear of the smoke. At dawn, the ground leveled, and the smell seemed to disappear. The two males stopped, exhausted, and bent to drink the cool water. The female continued along the path.

Weeks before, the female triceratops had mated with the leader of the herd. She was hunting now for a spot to build her nest.

The leader stamped his feet and snorted for her to stop, but it did no good. The female would not obey until the nest was completed and her eggs laid. This time, the males followed.

A mile downstream, the forest thinned and the stream emptied into a broad marsh. In the past, dome-headed pachycephalosaurs or armored ankylosaurs would be browsing in the cattails and rushes. Now only the bones of a long-dead anatosaur, half buried in mud, were there to greet the herd. ❸

The female walked the edge of the marsh carefully. The ground was either too wet or too rocky for the nest. On the opposite side of the marsh she found a warm, sandy area with low-growing shrubs.

Immediately she began digging, using the toes of her front and rear feet to shovel out the sand. The hole she dug was six feet across and a foot deep.

2. **heat lightning:** lightning flashes that appear near the horizon on hot nights.

Comparing Literature

INFER

❸ Which details suggest that the dinosaurs are dying out? How do these details affect the **mood** of the story?

DIRECT TEACHING

ⓒ Literary Focus

❓ **Conflict.** What force of nature first threatens the triceratopses? How well are they able to cope with the threat? [Possible response: They're first threatened by fire, and their poor eyesight makes it difficult for them to avoid the fire. However, their sense of smell alerts them to the danger, and because they move quickly, they are able to escape.]

ⓓ Reading Skills

Infer. [Possible response to question 3: Only the bones of one dinosaur remain at the marsh where there used to be many living dinosaurs. These details add to the suspense of the story because they make it clear that dinosaurs are at risk.]

Advanced Learners
Enrichment. Students who enjoy Jim Murphy's approach to teaching animal facts through fiction may like to write their own story about a current endangered species.
Activity. First, have students research facts about an endangered animal species, such as elephants, pandas, or snow leopards. Then, have them incorporate the facts into a short story that takes readers into the minds of the animals.

A Reading Skills

Compare and contrast. [Possible response to question 4: Female triceratopses used to share duties guarding a large group of nests. Now there is only one female triceratops, so she has to guard the nest on her own. The dinosaurs are dying out.]

COMPARE AND CONTRAST

4 How did a female triceratops once care for her eggs? How must she now care for her eggs? What conclusions can you draw from this?

When the hole was finished, she laid fifteen eggs in it to form a circle. Gently she covered the eggs with sand. The sun would warm the sand and eggs, and eventually baby triceratopses would emerge.

The two males were feeding a little distance from the nest. The smaller male approached the nest.

When the female saw him, she placed herself between him and her eggs and lowered her head as a warning. The curious male kept coming, so the female charged him. Only when he backed away did the female stop her charge.

When the herd had been larger, many females would make nests in the same area. They would then take turns guarding the nests or feeding and sleeping. But the female triceratops was alone now. It would be her job to keep clumsy males and egg-eating creatures away from her eggs. The quick shrewlike[3] mammals were especially annoying at night. **4**

Two days later the smell of smoke returned. It was faint, distant, and yet the three triceratopses grew nervous. The female paced near her nest.

---

3. **shrewlike:** resembling a shrew, a small mammal that looks like a mouse.

A Dino Dictionary

Did you know that the names of the dinosaurs come from Greek and Latin words? Read about these terrifying beasts, and look at their pictures. Do they resemble the Greek and Latin words that form their names?

anatosaur (ə•nat′ō•sôr′): two-legged, plant-eating dinosaur with a wide jaw resembling the bill of a duck, webbed feet, and a long tail. The name comes from *anas,* the Latin word for "duck," and *sauros,* the Greek word for "lizard."

ankylosaur (aŋ′kə•lō•sôr′): four-legged, plant-eating dinosaur with thick, leathery skin covered by bony plates. *Ankylos* is Greek for "crooked."

pachycephalosaur (pak′ə•sef′ə•lō•sôr′): two-legged, plant-eating dinosaur with a dome-shaped plate nine inches thick covering its brain. The name comes from Greek: *pachys* (thick) + *kephalē* (head) + *sauros* (lizard).

Science

Activity. Have students work in groups of three to research theories about why dinosaurs became extinct. Each group member should become an expert on one theory, such as the asteroid crash theory, the climate change theory, or the competition with mammals hinted at in Murphy's story. After they do their research, group experts on each topic to share information. Then, have students return to their original groups of three to teach one another what they have learned about their respective theories.

SMALL GROUP

Late in the day, a heavy line of smoke appeared on the other side of the marsh. Flames erupted, reaching into the air.

A flock of birds flew overhead, screeching an alarm. Mammals, made bold by their fear, left their hiding places and ran from the fire. The two males edged away, but the female stayed to guard her eggs.

In the smoke and dark forest shadows, something moved. The shape was big, as big as many of the trees, and had a massive head. Tyrannosaurus rex. The giant flesh eater stepped from the forest, snapping his mouth to reveal seven-inch-long slashing teeth.

Instinctively the two triceratops males rejoined the female and formed a semicircle barrier in front of the nest. The leader lowered his head and stared at his enemy. Neither moved.

Ordinarily, the tyrannosaur would not attack a triceratops, especially near its nest. But a wall of flames and heat had cut off his retreat. Besides, the tyrannosaur had not had a large meal in weeks. **5**

The tyrannosaur darted at the herd, skidded to a sudden halt, then began circling warily, watching for a chance to strike. He hissed and snapped his teeth. At that instant, the largest triceratops charged, his powerful legs driving him directly at the soft belly of his attacker.

Comparing Literature

INFER

5 What details suggest that tyrannosaurs are also in danger?

B **English-Language Learners**

Supply missing words. Ask students what words are missing but implied in the sentence fragment "Tyrannosaurus rex." [Possible response: "*It was a* Tyrannosaurus rex."]

C **Reading Skills**

Infer. [Possible response to question 5: The tyrannosaur hasn't eaten in some time and is willing to attack a triceratops for food. Those details imply that his species is in danger as well.]

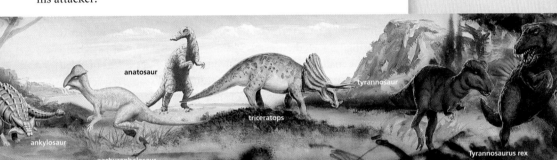

tyrannosaur (tə•ran′ə•sôr′): fierce two-legged meat eater, about forty feet in length. Its name comes from Greek: *tyrannos* (tyrant, or cruel ruler) + *sauros* (lizard).

Tyrannosaurus rex (reks): best-known species of tyrannosaur. In Latin, *rex* means "king."

triceratops (trī•ser′ə•täps′): four-legged, plant-eating dinosaur of North America. The triceratops had three horns on its head, grew to about twenty-five feet in length, and weighed up to four or five tons. Its name comes from Latin and Greek: *tri–* (three) + *kerat–* (horn) + *ōps* (eye, face).

The Last Dinosaur   **433**

Comparing Literature

A Reading Skills

Retell. [Possible response to question 6: The larger triceratops charges the tyrannosaur. The smaller triceratops attacks the tyrannosaur but is killed. The larger triceratops tries to resume the attack, but the tyrannosaur avoids his charge and savagely attacks him.]

B Literary Focus

❓ Mood. What is the result of the battle? How does this add to the suspenseful mood of the story? [Possible response: The tyrannosaur has been defeated, but one of the triceratopses is dead and the other one is injured badly, perhaps fatally. After the battle, the dinosaurs are at even greater risk of attack because they are less able to defend themselves.]

C Reading Skills

❓ Infer. Why is the female reluctant to leave her eggs? What finally forces her to leave them? [Possible response: The female doesn't want to leave her eggs because they may be eaten by other mammals or destroyed by the fire. She finally has to abandon them because the fire is causing her too much pain.]

RETELL

A ❻ Retell the battle between the triceratops herd and the tyrannosaur.

With the aid of his long tail and thickly muscled legs, the tyrannosaur leaped aside to avoid the sharp horns. He spun and dove, mouth wide open, and sank his teeth into the back of the triceratops.

Then the smaller triceratops lunged at the giant, but he was an inexperienced fighter. The tyrannosaur's teeth closed on his neck, and with a quick, deadly yank, he tore a chunk of flesh from the triceratops. The smaller triceratops fell, dying.

The other triceratops tried to charge again, but his right leg was dragging and his movements were slow. Again the tyrannosaur moved aside easily. Using his tail as a spring, the tyrannosaur launched himself for the kill. His teeth sank into the triceratops, while his clawed feet struck him in the stomach. The two rolled, kicking and biting each other.

At this moment, the female triceratops abandoned her eggs and rammed the tyrannosaur full in the side. He bellowed painfully, releasing his hold on the male. The female pushed forward with all her strength, pinning the tyrannosaur against a tree and driving her horns in deeper.

She stepped away and watched her enemy, ready to charge if he got up. His legs and tail flailed weakly, his breathing became labored. Then, with a violent shudder, the great killer died. ❻

B During the battle, the fire had spread, leaping and dancing from tree to tree until it reached the edge of the sandy area. Flames rolled through the reeds.

The male triceratops struggled to get up, but his legs buckled under him. He crawled a few feet but had to stop. His wounds were too severe. A choking wave of smoke surrounded him.

The female triceratops went back to protect her eggs. To one side a tree crashed to the ground, sending up an explosion of sparks. A bush nearby caught fire. The female charged it, slashing at it blindly with her horns.

The roar of the fire became deafening, and the heat and smoke grew painful. Reluctantly the female moved away from her eggs to find air.

C She went only a short distance and turned to go back. The smoke stung her lungs and burned her eyes. She shook her head, but the choking pain would not go away. She backed away some more and lost sight of her nest.

Immediately the tiny mammals pounced on the unguarded nest. Low to the ground the smoke was not so thick. Digging hastily,

they uncovered the eggs and devoured them. Then they scurried from the approaching fire. ❼

The female triceratops hurried through the forest. Several times she stopped to look back toward her eggs. A wall of smoke and flames was all she could see. Finally she gave up.

A tongue of flames reached out at her, and she broke into a gallop. She crashed through branches and vines, leaped over fallen logs heedlessly, with the fire just behind her. At last she came to a rock ledge overlooking a wide river.

The water was dark and deep. Branches and tree roots floated near the banks. The female wanted to find another retreat, but she was surrounded by flames. She hesitated a second, then jumped into the water.

Legs churning frantically, she swam across the river and away from the fire. The river's current caught her, pulling her swiftly along. She struggled to keep her head above water, to breathe, all the while moving her legs. At last her feet touched the river bottom.

Exhausted, her breathing fast, she hauled herself onto solid ground. Across from her, the fire had stopped at the river's edge. She was safe. It was then she noticed the streams of mammals that had also crossed the river to escape the fire.

The light grew dim and the air became chilly. The female's breath gave off thin vapor streams.

COMPARE AND CONTRAST

❼ Think back to the way you described the story's **mood.** Would you change your description now? Why or why not?

The Last Dinosaur 435

D Reading Skills

❓ **Draw conclusions.** Are you surprised by what happens to the triceratops eggs? Why or why not? [Possible responses: Since the threat from the mammals is foreshadowed on p. 432, many students will not be surprised. However, some may have thought that the fire or the tyrannosaur would destroy the eggs.]

E Reading Skills

Compare and contrast. [Possible response to question 7: Earlier the mood was eerie because there were only hints of danger in a relatively peaceful setting. Now the mood is more scary because the dinosaurs are clearly in danger.]

LITERARY CONNECTIONS

Animal Characters
Remind students that they have read another selection that features an animal character as its main protagonist. Have students compare this selection with "Rikki-tikki-tavi" (p. 15). How is Rikki's situation similar to that of the last triceratops? How is it different? Then, ask students to compare and contrast the possible reasons that Kipling and Murphy used animal protagonists. [Possible responses: Both Rikki and the last triceratops are fighting bravely against a threat. However, Rikki is fighting to protect the humans who care for him while the triceratops is fighting for the survival of herself and her species. Kipling may have used animal characters that possess the moral qualities he admired in people. Murphy's purpose may be to tell about real animals in an entertaining, involving way that people can learn from.]

A Advanced Learners

? Challenge the text. Jim Murphy personalizes the fate of the dinosaurs by helping readers understand how it felt to be the last triceratops. Do you think this is a good way to teach science? Why or why not? [Responses will vary. Students may say that appealing to readers' imaginations can be a good way to bring science to life but that not all scientific concepts can be presented in this way.]

B Reading Skills

Predict. [Possible response to question 8: Dinosaurs have been scarce throughout the story, so most students will say that they don't think the triceratops will find another herd.]

Meet the Writer

Jim Murphy grew up in suburban New Jersey and began writing stories and poetry in high school, where he was also a track star. "I thoroughly enjoy my work," he once told an interviewer. "The nonfiction projects let me research subjects that I'm really interested in. . . . The fiction lets me get out some of the thoughts and opinions that rattle around in my head."

For Independent Reading

Students who read Jim Murphy's gripping narrative *Blizzard!: The Storm That Changed America* can discuss the ways that life in the United States was altered by the storm.

PREDICT

B **8** Do you think the female will find another herd to join? Why or why not?

A The triceratops shook her head and snorted. She hadn't eaten much in days and wanted to find some tender plants. And maybe, somewhere deep in the forest, there was another triceratops herd she could join.

Slowly, as the sun went down, the female pushed through the bushes to begin her search. **8**

Meet the Writer

Jim Murphy

Digging Dinosaurs

Jim Murphy (1947–   ) says that dinosaurs have always fascinated him.

  " Our knowledge of them suggests that they were amazing survivors, occupying every corner of the world and adapting to changing climates and food sources for millions of years. "

Murphy feels that studying dinosaurs and finding out how they survived for so long may help humans adapt and survive.

For Independent Reading

Jim Murphy is known for his dramatic re-creations of historical events. *Blizzard!: The Storm That Changed America* is one example of his award-winning historical narratives. In this book, Murphy tells about the Great Blizzard of 1888, a massive snowstorm that devastated the Northeast.

Other books by Murphy that present information in an engaging way are *The Great Fire* and *Across America on an Emigrant Train.*

Music
The Police. The song "Walking in Your Footsteps," written by Sting and performed by the Police, suggests similarities between what happened to the dinosaurs and what could happen to humans. The song explains that dinosaurs (like humans today) were the mightiest creatures on Earth but were doomed to extinction. After students read "The Last Dinosaur," have them listen to the song. The British pop trio the Police

emerged in London in 1976. The trio consisted of bass guitarist and vocalist Gordon Sumner, better known as Sting; lead guitarist Andy Summers; and American-born drummer Stewart Copeland. "Walking in Your Footsteps" is from their acclaimed album *Synchronicity* (1983).
Activity. Ask students what the dinosaur in the song represents [an extinct creature] and what warning the song expresses [what

happened to dinosaurs can happen to humanity if we aren't careful]. Then, have students compare and contrast the theme of the song with the theme of Murphy's story.

First Thoughts

1. Finish this sentence:
   - This story makes me feel . . .

Thinking Critically

2. Think about the **title** of the story. Is the female triceratops the last of her kind? Or is she the last of all dinosaurs? Find evidence in the story that supports one of these interpretations.

3. In telling this story, the writer zooms in on the experiences of a *female* triceratops. Why do you think he decided to focus on a female dinosaur to tell the story of the last dinosaur?

4. Think about how this story makes you feel. What words would you use to describe the **mood**? Find at least three details in the story that help create the mood.

5. What does this story say to you about the topic of loss and change? How would you express its **theme**?

Comparing Literature

6. To gather details for the essay you'll write for the assignment on page 444, fill in information about "The Last Dinosaur" in a chart like the one below. When you write about your response to the text, think about your overall impression of the story. What makes it memorable for you?

> ### Reading Check
>
> Check your comprehension by **retelling** this story. Start with the **title, author,** and **main character.** Next, explain the main **conflict** or problem. Then, review the **plot,** listing the main events in the order in which they occur. Be sure to identify the **climax,** the story's most suspenseful moment, which determines how the conflict is going to turn out. Finally, describe the **resolution,** which tells how the story ends.

Mood and Theme			
	"The Last Dinosaur"	"Buffalo Dusk"	"I Was Sleeping . . ."
Mood			
Theme			
My response to the text			

SKILLS FOCUS

Literary Skills
Analyze mood and theme.

Reading Skills
Compare and contrast texts.

The Last Dinosaur   **437**

First Thoughts

1. Possible answer:
   - This story makes me feel <u>sympathy for the plight of the dinosaurs.</u>

Thinking Critically

2. Possible answer: The female triceratops is the last of her kind because she is no longer able to split egg-guarding duties with other triceratopses.

3. Possible answer: The author focused on a female dinosaur because females play the essential role of the continuation of nearly every species.

4. Students may say that the mood is foreboding, suspenseful, or scary. Details they may cite include the discovery of the dinosaur bones, the attack by the tyrannosaurus rex, and the fire that finally forces the female triceratops to abandon her eggs.

5. Possible answer: The story says that change and loss are usually painful. The theme is that change and loss are inevitable for all species—even one as dominant as the dinosaurs once were.

Comparing Literature

6. Possible answers: *Mood—*frightening, threatening. *Theme—*Any species can become endangered because of threats from nature and other animals. *My response to the text—*I enjoyed the story and felt empathy for the last triceratops.

Reading Check

Possible retelling: In "The Last Dinosaur," Jim Murphy explores what may be the final days of the last triceratops. Although nature and other animals conspire against a female triceratops and her two male allies, she is determined to survive. First, a fire begins to spread. Then a tyrannosaur attacks her companions, hoping for a meal. Even though she kills the enemy, the other two triceratopses are killed in the battle trying to defend the herd. With the fire spreading, mammals swoop in and steal her eggs. The triceratops escapes from the fire but is left on her own, with the hopes of finding a new herd very slim.

PRETEACHING

Summary ↔ *at grade level*

> In this brief poem the speaker laments the disappearance of buffalo from the American plains while recalling with vivid imagery the distinct characteristics they brought to the land.

Selection Starter

Build background. The animals Americans commonly refer to as buffalo are called bison by zoologists. In 1850, there were as many as 20 million of these animals on the Great Plains, but by 1889, only about 500 bison remained alive in the United States. It was around this time that measures were taken to prevent the extinction of the species.

Before You Read

Millions of buffalo once galloped across the Great Plains of North America. Native Americans killed the buffalo for food, and they found uses for all other parts of the animal—from hair to bones. White settlers, however, killed the buffalo nearly to extinction. They killed for food, fur, and leather, but most of all for sport. Today, conservation efforts have succeeded in establishing more than 200,000 head of buffalo. "Buffalo Dusk" was written in 1920, when conservation efforts were just getting started.

CROSS-CURRICULAR CONNECTIONS

Science

Buffalo. Have students build on the background knowledge they've gained about American buffalo to write a brief research report about the history of the animal. Students can find information on the buffalo in an encyclopedia or science book or by using an Internet search engine. They should include details about the appearance of the buffalo, the uses of the buffalo by Native Americans, the factors that led to the species' decline, and the measures that were taken to prevent the buffalo from becoming extinct.

Buffalo Dusk ❶

Carl Sandburg

The buffaloes are gone.
And those who saw the buffaloes are gone.
Those who saw the buffaloes by thousands and how they pawed
    the prairie sod into dust with their hoofs, their great heads
    down pawing on in a great pageant of dusk,
Those who saw the buffaloes are gone.
And the buffaloes are gone. ❷

B

Comparing Literature

INFER

❶ What does the **title** suggest this poem will be about?

A

ANALYZE

❷ What lines, phrases, and words are repeated in this poem? What **mood** does the repetition create?

C

DIRECT TEACHING

Ⓐ Reading Skills

Infer. [Possible response to question 1: Since the word *dusk* refers to the time when day fades and darkness falls, the poem will probably be about the fading away or extinction of the buffalo.]

Ⓑ Comparing Literature

❓ Compare moods. Is this selection's mood similar to or different from the mood of "The Last Dinosaur"? Explain why or why not. [Possible response: Although both selections deal with the extinction of an animal species, the mood is different. The disappearance is actually taking place in "The Last Dinosaur," so the mood is suspenseful and even scary. In "Buffalo Dusk," the buffalo are already gone, so the mood is regretful and sad.]

Ⓒ Reading Skills

Analyze. [Possible response to question 2: The repeated phrases are "the buffaloes are gone" and "those who saw the buffaloes are gone." The repetition creates a mood of resignation, sadness, and possibly disbelief that such an event could have happened.]

DEVELOPING FLUENCY

Activity. Ask students to read the poem to themselves and to think about the mood the poem conveys by its repeated phrases. Then, have students prepare readings based on this mood. Finally, put students into groups and have them discuss why they chose to read the poem the way they did.

INDIVIDUAL

SMALL GROUP

Summary ⬆ *above grade level*

In this poem a speaker living along a river describes a flood that caused destruction to her community. In the first three stanzas the narrator recalls the rising river engulfing the surrounding trees and heron nests. After the flood, the community examines the dead trees while a group of herons fly overhead. The narrator's grandfather says the herons are ghosts of tree people who are pained by the loss. Shifting to the present, the narrator says that the earth shakes the land where the flood took place. She believes the shaking is caused by the elk who have disappeared and are trying to bring the once fruitful land back to life.

DIRECT TEACHING

A Reading Skills

Identify. [Possible response to question 1: The river grows, wrestles with the trees, wraps itself around the trees, and drags off the trees' leaves.]

B Literary Focus

❷ Mood. What is the mood of this stanza? Support your response with details from the text. [Possible response: The dead trees and squawking birds create a mood of sadness and desolation.]

C Reading Skills

Analyze. [Possible responses to question 2: The branches whiten in the "raw sun"; the herons drifting; the herons' hoarse voices.]

Comparing Literature

Before You Read

About sixty-five million years ago, the dinosaurs were destroyed. On the Great Plains of North America in the nineteenth century, the buffalo herds were almost wiped out. In this poem by Louise Erdrich, a flood destroys the landscape along a river. Erdrich is part Chippewa. She often writes about Native Americans and their communities. Besides the landscape, what larger loss could this poem refer to?

I Was Sleeping Where the Black Oaks Move

Louise Erdrich

We watched from the house
as the river grew, helpless
and terrible in its unfamiliar body.
Wrestling everything into it,
5 the water wrapped around trees
until their life-hold was broken.
They went down, one by one,
and the river dragged off their covering. ❶

Nests of the herons, roots washed to bones,
10 snags of soaked bark on the shoreline:
a whole forest pulled through the teeth
of the spillway.° Trees surfacing
singly, where the river poured off
into arteries for fields below the reservation.

15 When at last it was over, the long removal,
they had all become the same dry wood.
We walked among them, the branches
whitening in the raw sun.
Above us drifted herons,
20 alone, hoarse-voiced, broken,
settling their beaks among the hollows. ❷

IDENTIFY

❶ The speaker is describing a flood that she witnessed. She describes the river as if it were alive. What does the river "do" to the trees?

ANALYZE

❷ Re-read lines 15–21. What details help you to see and hear the scene after the flood?

---

12. spillway *n.:* channel around a dam that carries away extra water.

DIFFERENTIATING INSTRUCTION

Learners Having Difficulty
Modeling. If students are having trouble following the action in the poem, remind them to look at the punctuation marks for guidance. Encourage students to separate the poem into individual sentences and then to paraphrase those sentences into more easily understood language. Use the first sentence to model the skill of paraphrasing. Read the sentence, and write the following paraphrase on the chalkboard:

"From our house we saw the river rising dangerously over the land." Then, have students paraphrase the other sentences.

Advanced Learners
Enrichment. Text reformulation is a strategy that allows students to transform a text into another type of text (for example, a student can rewrite a historical document as a personal narrative).

Grandpa said, *These are the ghosts of the tree people,*
moving above us, unable to take their rest.

Sometimes now, we dream our way back to the heron dance.
25 Their long wings are bending the air
into circles through which they fall.
They rise again in shifting wheels.
How long must we live in the broken figures
their necks make, narrowing the sky. ❸

30 Some nights in town's cold winter,
earth shakes.
People say it's a train full of danger
or the plane-broken barriers of sound,
but out there
35 behind the dark trunks of trees
the gone elk have pulled the hide of earth
tight and they are drumming
back the woodland,
tall grass and days we were equal
40 and strong. ❹

INTERPRET

❸ Think about the loss and change caused by the flooding river. What words would you use to describe the **mood** of the poem?

ANALYZE

❹ In the last stanza the speaker describes a mysterious shaking of the earth. What do the townspeople think is causing this shaking? What does the speaker think?

DIRECT TEACHING

Ⓓ Learners Having Difficulty

❓ **Find details.** What shift in the poem takes place at l. 24? [Possible responses: The poem shifts from the past tense to the present tense. The narrator goes from describing a prior incident to reflecting on it currently.]

Ⓔ Reading Skills

Interpret. [Possible response to question 3: The mood of the poem is regretful about the changes the flood brought about and nostalgic for the strength and pride of the community before the flood.]

Ⓕ Reading Skills

Analyze. [Possible responses to question 4: The townspeople think it is some sort of modern disturbance, such as a train or a plane, but the speaker thinks it is the ghosts of elk who drum the land to bring back the fruitful days of the past.]

Activity. Encourage students to rewrite "I Was Sleeping Where the Black Oaks Move" as a newspaper article. Have students write a headline, a lead, and relevant supporting details. Remind students to keep the following questions in mind as they work on the article: What is happening? When and where did the events take place? Who is affected by the action taking place? Invite students to share their articles with the class.

Carl Sandburg was born in the midwestern town of Galesburg, Illinois, to poor, hardworking Swedish immigrants. He left school at age thirteen to help provide income for his family, ultimately traveling the railways in search of work. His companions were the homeless and the unemployed—people who would be given a strong voice in his poetry.

One childhood memory that **Louise Erdrich** clearly keeps may be an early indication of her future as a writer: "My father used to give me a nickel for every story I wrote, and my mother wove strips of construction paper together and stapled them into book covers. . . . At an early age I felt myself to be a published author."

For Independent Reading

- Students who would like to find out more about the midwestern prairie glimpsed in "Buffalo Dusk" can read *Prairie-Town Boy,* Carl Sandburg's narrative of his youth in Illinois.

- Students can also take a look at *The Birchbark House,* a novel rooted in Louise Erdrich's family history. The novel portrays life from the perspective of Omakayas, a young Ojibwa (ō·jib′wā′) girl who faces devastating changes in her life when a smallpox epidemic strikes her community.

Meet the Writers

Carl Sandburg

"I Am the People"
Carl Sandburg
(1878–1967) once defined poetry as "the opening and closing of a door, leaving those who look through to guess about what is seen during a moment." Readers who look through the openings

Sandburg provides in his poetry will see the world from the perspective of the "common folk" of America, whom Sandburg strongly identified with. As he proclaimed in one poem: "I am the people —the mob—the crowd— the mass."

Louise Erdrich

"Someone Believed in Me"
The novels and poems of **Louise Erdrich** (1954–   ) contain powerful themes that reflect her experiences growing up in North Dakota as the daughter of a Chippewa Indian mother and German-American father.

At a young age, Erdrich developed an interest in writing that continued into college. During her junior

year her talent as a poet was recognized: She received a prize from the Academy of American Poets. After graduation, Erdrich decided to "sacrifice all to be a writer." She felt all of her hard work paid off when she won a $5,000 award for one of her short stories. Erdrich notes, "It was like a validation, someone believed in me."

First Thoughts

1. Respond to the poems by completing the following sentences:
   - "Buffalo Dusk" made me feel . . .
   - I would describe the speaker of "I Was Sleeping Where the Black Oaks Move" as . . .

Thinking Critically

2. What changes and losses are mourned in "Buffalo Dusk"? How would you express the poem's **theme**?

3. How might the **mood** of a poem called "Buffalo Dawn" be different from the mood of Sandburg's "Buffalo Dusk"?

4. In "I Was Sleeping. . ." the speaker hints at other changes and losses besides those caused by the flood. What might these changes and losses be? (How does knowing the writer is part Chippewa help answer this question?)

Comparing Literature

5. Now, complete the second and third columns of the chart below. Filling in the chart will help you prepare to write the comparison-contrast essay assignment on page 444.

Mood and Theme			
	"The Last Dinosaur"	"Buffalo Dusk"	"I Was Sleeping . . ."
Mood			
Theme			
My response to the text			

SKILLS FOCUS

Literary Skills
Analyze mood and theme.

Reading Skills
Compare and contrast texts.

Buffalo Dusk / I Was Sleeping Where the Black Oaks Move   443

After You Read

First Thoughts

1. Possible answers:
   - "Buffalo Dusk" made me feel saddened that I'm unable to see buffaloes rambling across plains as they are described in the poem.
   - I would describe the speaker of "I Was Sleeping Where the Black Oaks Move" as someone who is in touch with the history of her people.

Thinking Critically

2. "Buffalo Dusk" mourns the loss of buffaloes and of the people who saw the buffalo. The theme may be that when the buffalo passed away, not only was a species lost, but also a creature that made the world beautiful and wondrous.

3. Possible answer: A poem called "Buffalo Dawn" would probably have a hopeful or joyous mood because it would deal with the arrival of buffaloes on the plains not the extinction of them.

4. Possible answers: The damage done to the land hints at the weakening in modern times of Native American roots and traditions. The trains and planes mentioned in the final stanza hint that members have lost their connection to nature.

Comparing Literature

5. Possible answers: *Mood.* "Buffalo Dusk"—resignation, disbelief. "I Was Sleeping . . ."—sad, nostalgic. *Theme.* "Buffalo Dusk"—When a species becomes extinct, the world loses part of its beauty. "I Was Sleeping . . ."—When damage is done to the natural world, it takes a toll on people as well. *My response to the text.* "Buffalo Dusk"—The imagery of the poem gave me a clear picture of the buffalo before they were extinct. "I Was Sleeping . . ."—I was saddened by the effects the flood had on the people.

After You Read

1. Writing a Comparison-Contrast Essay

Strategy Tip. Some students may think that because the three selections all deal with change and loss, the selections may also have the same theme. Make sure students realize that even though the three pieces deal with the same topic, they treat it in ways that express different themes.

2. Researching a Topic

Strategy Tip. For the assignment to research a topic, encourage students to prepare their presentations on note cards. After they've conducted their research, have them organize their notes according to each question they've answered. Then, have them transfer the essential information onto note cards, using only one note card for each question. Next, students should number each note card in the upper right-hand corner to indicate the order in which they will present the information.

Assignment

1. Writing a Comparison-Contrast Essay

Write a short essay comparing the three texts you've just read. To help plan your essay, review your chart. Write three paragraphs, one about each selection. For each selection, (1) describe the **mood;** (2) express the **theme;** (3) discuss your overall reaction to the text.

In a fourth paragraph, briefly explain which text you had the most positive response to and why. Use details from the texts to support what you say.

> Use the workshop on writing a Comparison-Contrast Essay, pages 772–777, for help with this assignment.

Assignment

2. Researching a Topic

Research and prepare an oral presentation on one of these topics:

- **The Life and Times of the Triceratops**
- **The Life and Times of the North American Buffalo**

Answer the following questions in your report:

- When and for how long did these animals live or thrive?
- What were (are) their eating and mating habits?
- What was their natural habitat?
- What caused the decline of the population? Were the causes human or natural—or both? (If this is not known, what theories explain the decline of the population? Which of these theories seems most likely to you? Why?)

Be sure to report on some questions of your own too!

SKILLS FOCUS

Writing Skills
Write a comparison-contrast essay.

Speaking and Listening Skills
Research and prepare an oral report.

CROSS-CURRICULAR CONNECTIONS

History

Oral presentation. Students are often asked to give oral presentations on noted historical figures. Tell students that they can adapt the strategy tip for oral presentations on other subjects, including history. After they decide on a historical figure to report on, students should ask themselves questions that both they and their audience want to know the answers to, such as "When was the person born? Where did he or she live? What is her or his most notable achievement?" Then, they can organize these questions and answers on note cards as they conduct their research.

NO QUESTIONS ASKED

The Naming of Names

Ray Bradbury

OVERVIEW

The literature in No Questions Asked gives students the chance to read a selection for enjoyment and enrichment as they further explore the themes in this collection. The annotation questions in the margins of the Teacher's Edition should be considered optional. No follow-up questions will appear after the selection.

Summary ⬆ *above grade level*

To escape from the threat of nuclear war on Earth, the Bittering family has traveled to Mars. There Earthling colonists have populated empty Martian cities and given American names to Martian localities. At first, the Bitterings are fearful and homesick, especially the father. When the links between Earth and Mars are cut off, most of the Earthlings accept the changes that are occurring to them; eventually the father begins speaking Martian and acknowledges that he too has been transformed. Five years later, when a rescue mission from Earth arrives, the crew finds abandoned colonies and friendly "natives." Deciding to start over, the crew begins by naming the Lincoln Mountains.

PRETEACHING

Selection Starter

Build background. "The Naming of Names" appeared in 1958, a time when many scientists believed that some form of life might exist on Mars. These beliefs were shattered in 1965, when *Mariner 4*, the first spacecraft to visit the planet, sent back close-up photographs revealing a seemingly lifeless surface on Mars.

A Literary Focus

❓ **Mood.** What details in this description of the setting help create a suspenseful mood? [Possible responses: The description of the wind suggests it could blow away personal identity. The comparison of old cities to dead children's bones suggests abandonment.]

B Reading Skills

❓ **Analyze.** How does Harry feel about his arrival on Mars? [Possible responses: He may be regretting his decision to move there. He may feel that he will not survive long.]

The rocket metal cooled in the meadow winds. Its lid gave a bulging *pop.* From its clock interior stepped a man, a woman, and three children. The other passengers whispered away across the Martian meadow, leaving the man alone among his family.

The man felt his hair flutter and the tissues of his body draw tight as if he were standing at the center of a vacuum.[1] His wife, before him, seemed almost to whirl away in smoke. The children, small seeds, might at any instant be sown to all the Martian climes.[2]

The children looked up at him, as people look to the sun to tell what time of their life it is. His face was cold.

"What's wrong?" asked his wife.

"Let's get back on the rocket."

"Go back to Earth?"

"Yes! Listen!"

The wind blew as if to flake away their identities. At any moment the Martian air might draw his soul from him, as marrow comes from a white bone. He felt submerged in a chemical that could dissolve his intellect and burn away his past.

They looked at Martian hills that time had worn with a crushing pressure of years. They saw the old cities, lost in their meadows, lying like children's delicate bones among the blowing lakes of grass.

"Chin up, Harry," said his wife. "It's too late. We've come over sixty million miles."

The children with their yellow hair hollered at the deep dome of Martian sky. There was no answer but the racing hiss of wind through the stiff grass.

He picked up the luggage in his cold hands. "Here we go," he said—a man standing on the edge of a sea, ready to wade in and be drowned.

They walked into town.

Their name was Bittering. Harry and his wife, Cora; Dan, Laura, and David. They built a small white cottage and ate good breakfasts there, but the fear was never gone. It lay with Mr. Bittering and Mrs. Bittering, a third, unbidden partner at every midnight talk, at every dawn awakening.

"I feel like a salt crystal," he said, "in a mountain stream, being washed away. We don't belong here. We're Earth people. This is

---

1. **vacuum** (vak′yōōm) *n.:* closed space with the air sucked out.
2. **climes** (klīmz) *n.:* regions.

DIFFERENTIATING INSTRUCTION

Learners Having Difficulty
As students read the story, suggest they keep a running list with two headings: *Why Most Colonists Want to Adapt to Martian Ways* and *Why Harry Bittering Wants to Keep Earthling Ways.* Ask students to use the list to keep track of the story's developments, including the conflict between Harry Bittering and the other colonists.

English-Language Learners
Bradbury's use of figurative language and sophisticated vocabulary may make this selection challenging. Students might benefit from reading the story aloud in a group, pausing to discuss any difficult words or sentence structures.

Mars. It was meant for Martians. For heaven's sake, Cora, let's buy tickets for home!"

But she only shook her head. "One day the atom bomb will fix Earth. Then we'll be safe here."

"Safe and insane!"

Tick-tock, seven o'clock, sang the voice-clock; *time to get up.* And they did.

Something made him check everything each morning—warm hearth, potted blood-geraniums—precisely as if he expected something to be amiss.[3] The morning paper was toast-warm from the 6:00 A.M. Earth rocket. He broke its seal and tilted it at his breakfast place. He forced himself to be convivial.[4]

"Colonial days all over again," he declared. "Why, in ten years there'll be a million Earthmen on Mars. Big cities, everything! They said we'd fail. Said the Martians would resent our invasion. But did we find any Martians? Not a living soul! Oh, we found their empty cities, but no one in them. Right?"

> "We don't belong here. We're Earth people. This is Mars."

A river of wind submerged the house. When the windows ceased rattling, Mr. Bittering swallowed and looked at the children.

"I don't know," said David. "Maybe there're Martians around we don't see. Sometimes nights I think I hear 'em. I hear the wind. The sand hits my window. I get scared. And I see those towns way up in the mountains where the Martians lived a long time ago. And I think I see things moving around those towns, Papa. And I wonder if those Martians *mind* us living here. I wonder if they won't do something to us for coming here."

"Nonsense!" Mr. Bittering looked out the windows. "We're clean, decent people." He looked at his children. "All dead cities have some kind of ghosts in them. Memories, I mean." He stared at the hills. "You see a staircase and you wonder what Martians looked like climbing it. You see Martian paintings and you wonder what the painter was like. You make a little ghost in your mind, a memory. It's quite natural. Imagination." He stopped. "You haven't been prowling up in those ruins, have you?"

---

3. **amiss** (ə·mis′) *adj.:* wrong; improper.
4. **convivial** (kən·viv′ē·əl) *adj.:* sociable or friendly.

❓ Point of view. If the narrator were omniscient, or all-knowing, how might this passage change? [Possible response: The reader would be told whether Laura noticed her father's fear and whether she was comforted by her father when he tried to reassure her.]

Ⓑ Literary Focus

Figurative language. Explain to students that Bradbury is using figurative language in this passage: He is comparing rocket travel to a silver web. What meaning is Bradbury conveying through this comparison? [Possible response: When Earth and Mars were linked by rocket travel, Harry and his family could always return to Earth; now that possibility has been removed, and he feels stranded.]

"No, Papa." David looked at his shoes.

"See that you stay away from them. Pass the jam."

"Just the same," said little David, "I bet something happens."

> "A radio flash just came. Atom bombs hit New York! All the space rockets blown up. No more rockets to Mars, ever!"

Something happened that afternoon. Laura stumbled through the settlement, crying. She dashed blindly onto the porch.

"Mother, Father—the war, Earth!" she sobbed. "A radio flash just came. Atom bombs hit New York! All the space rockets blown up. No more rockets to Mars, ever!"

"Oh, Harry!" The mother held on to her husband and daughter.

"Are you sure, Laura?" asked the father quietly.

Laura wept. "We're stranded on Mars, forever and ever!"

For a long time there was only the sound of the wind in the late afternoon.

Alone, thought Bittering. *Only a thousand of us here. No way back. No way. No way.* Sweat poured from his face and his hands and his body; he was drenched in the hotness of his fear. He wanted to strike Laura, cry, "No, you're lying! The rockets will come back!" Instead, he stroked Laura's head against him and said, "The rockets will get through someday."

"Father, what will we do?"

"Go about our business, of course. Raise crops and children. Wait. Keep things going until the war ends and the rockets come again."

The two boys stepped out onto the porch.

"Children," he said, sitting there, looking beyond them, "I've something to tell you."

"We know," they said.

In the following days, Bittering wandered often through the garden to stand alone in his fear. As long as the rockets had spun a silver web across space, he had been able to accept Mars. For he had always told himself: *Tomorrow, if I want, I can buy a ticket and go back to Earth.*

But now: the web gone, the rockets lying in jigsaw heaps of

---

5. **molten girder** (mōlt′'n gur′dər) A girder is a metal beam that helps to support a framework; *molten* means "melted."

molten girder[5] and unsnaked wire. Earth people left to the strangeness of Mars, the cinnamon dusts and wine airs, to be baked like gingerbread shapes in Martian summers, put into harvested storage by Martian winters. What would happen to him, the others? This was the moment Mars had waited for. Now it would eat them.

He got down on his knees in the flower bed, a spade in his nervous hands. *Work,* he thought, *work and forget.*

He glanced up from the garden to the Martian mountains. He thought of the proud old Martian names that had once been on those peaks. Earthmen, dropping from the sky, had gazed upon hills, rivers, Martian seas left nameless in spite of names. Once Martians had built cities, named cities; climbed mountains, named mountains; sailed seas, named seas. Mountains melted, seas drained, cities tumbled. In spite of this, the Earthmen had felt a silent guilt at putting new names to these ancient hills and valleys.

Nevertheless, man lives by symbol and label. The names were given.

Mr. Bittering felt very alone in his garden under the Martian sun, an anachronism[6] bent here, planting Earth flowers in a wild soil.

Think. Keep thinking. Different things. Keep your mind free of Earth, the atom war, the lost rockets.

He perspired. He glanced about. No one watching. He removed his tie. *Pretty bold,* he thought. *First your coat off, now your tie.* He hung it neatly on a peach tree he had imported as a sapling from Massachusetts.

He returned to his philosophy of names and mountains. The Earthmen had changed names. Now there were Hormel Valleys, Roosevelt Seas, Ford Hills, Vanderbilt Plateaus, Rockefeller Rivers, on Mars. It wasn't right. The American settlers had shown wisdom, using old Indian prairie names: Wisconsin, Minnesota, Idaho, Ohio, Utah, Milwaukee, Waukegan, Osseo. The old names, the old meanings.

Staring at the mountains wildly, he thought: *Are you up there? All the dead ones, you Martians? Well, here we are, alone, cut off! Come down, move us out! We're helpless!*

The wind blew a shower of peach blossoms.

He put out his sun-browned hand, gave a small cry. He touched the blossoms, picked them up. He turned them, he touched them again and again. Then he shouted for his wife.

---

6. **anachronism** (ə·nak′rə·niz′əm) *n.:* something out of its proper time in history, like a television in the Middle Ages or penicillin in ancient Rome.

C Cross-curricular Connections
HISTORY
Explain to students that Henry Ford, Cornelius Vanderbilt, and John D. Rockefeller were powerful U.S. industrialists. Point out to students that many localities in the United States have kept the names given to them by Native Americans, while other places have European names. For instance, the name of the state of Minnesota comes from a Native American word, while Louisiana was named by settlers to honor the king of France. Ask students to give additional examples of localities that have Native American names and others that have European names.

? **Infer.** What do you think is happening to the plants and animals? [Possible response: They are undergoing a physical change. Perhaps in the Martian soil and atmosphere they are being affected by the different environment.]

B Vocabulary Note

? **Word choice.** What do "spring violets" and "soft purple" suggest about the Martian lawn? [Possible response: They suggest that the color is familiar and pleasing.] Why might the writer have used these words? [Possible response: He is saying that Mars is different from Earth but just as appealing.]

"Cora!"

She appeared at a window. He ran to her.

"Cora, these blossoms!"

She handled them.

"Do you see? They're different. They've changed! They're not peach blossoms anymore!"

"Look all right to me," she said.

"They're not. They're *wrong*! I can't tell how. An extra petal, a leaf, something, the color, the smell!"

The children ran out in time to see their father hurrying about the garden, pulling up radishes, onions, and carrots from their beds.

"Cora, come look!"

They handled the onions, the radishes, the carrots among them.

"Do they look like carrots?"

"Yes . . . no." She hesitated. "I don't know."

"They're changed."

"Perhaps."

"You know they have! Onions but not onions, carrots but not carrots. Taste: the same but different. Smell: not like it used to be." He felt his heart pounding, and he was afraid. He dug his fingers into the earth. "Cora, what's happening? What is it? We've got to get away from this." He ran across the garden. Each tree felt his touch. "The roses. The roses. They're turning green!"

And they stood looking at the green roses.

And two days later Dan came running. "Come see the cow. I was milking her and I saw it. Come on!"

They stood in the shed and looked at their one cow.

It was growing a third horn.

And the lawn in front of their house very quietly and slowly was coloring itself like spring violets. Seed from Earth but growing up a soft purple.

"We must get away," said Bittering. "We'll eat this stuff and then we'll change—who knows to what? I can't let it happen. There's only one thing to do. Burn this food!"

"It's not poisoned."

"But it is. Subtly, very subtly. A little bit. A very little bit. We mustn't touch it."

He looked with dismay at their house. "Even the house. The wind's done something to it. The air's burned it. The fog at night. The boards, all warped out of shape. It's not an Earthman's house anymore."

CROSS-CURRICULAR CONNECTIONS

Science

The environment. Students might be reminded of the concerns that some people have about breathing, absorbing, or ingesting toxins from the environment. **Activity.** Place students into groups of three, and invite them to research some common toxic materials in the environment and the health problems that these materials cause. Students can present their findings in a chart.

"Oh, your imagination!"

He put on his coat and tie. "I'm going into town. We've got to do something now. I'll be back."

"Wait, Harry!" his wife cried.

But he was gone.

In town, on the shadowy step of the grocery store, the men sat with their hands on their knees, conversing with great leisure and ease.

Mr. Bittering wanted to fire a pistol in the air.

What are you doing, you fools! he thought. *Sitting here! You've heard the news—we're stranded on this planet. Well, move! Aren't you frightened? Aren't you afraid? What are you going to do?*

"Hello, Harry," said everyone.

"Look," he said to them. "You did hear the news, the other day, didn't you?"

They nodded and laughed. "Sure. Sure, Harry."

"What are you going to do about it?"

"Do, Harry, do? What *can* we do?"

"Build a rocket, that's what!"

"A rocket, Harry? To go back to all that trouble? Oh, Harry!"

"But you *must* want to go back. Have you noticed the peach blossoms, the onions, the grass?"

"Why, yes, Harry, seems we did," said one of the men.

"Doesn't it scare you?"

"Can't recall that it did much, Harry."

"Idiots!"

"Now, Harry."

Bittering wanted to cry. "You've got to work with me. If we stay here, we'll all change. The air. Don't you smell it? Something in the air. A Martian virus, maybe; some seed, or a pollen. Listen to me!"

They stared at him.

"Sam," he said to one of them.

"Yes, Harry?"

"Will you help me build a rocket?"

"Harry, I got a whole load of metal and some blueprints. You want to work in my metal shop on a rocket, you're welcome. I'll sell you that metal for five hundred dollars. You should be able to construct a right pretty rocket, if you work alone, in about thirty years."

> "You should be able to construct a right pretty rocket, if you work alone, in about thirty years."

A Literary Focus

? Character. What effect is the setting having on Sam's and Harry's appearances? [Possible response: Sam is losing weight and growing taller. Both Sam's and Harry's eyes are changing from their original color to gold.]

B Reading Skills

? Infer. What does Harry's breaking the mirror suggest about his mental state? [Possible response: He is trying to deny the changes taking place. He is losing self-control.]

C English-Language Learners

Idioms. Explain that the idiom *gave him a hand* means "helped him." Ask students how the idiom might have developed and whether there is a similar expression in their native languages.

D Reading Skills

? Predict. Do you think Harry will succeed in building his rocket? Why or why not? [Some students may predict that he will build the rocket because of his determination. Others may say that he won't be able to because he is already taking on Martian characteristics or because the other settlers may even prevent him from building it.]

Everyone laughed.

"Don't laugh."

Sam looked at him with quiet good humor.

"Sam," Bittering said. "Your eyes—"

"What about them, Harry?"

"Didn't they used to be gray?"

"Well, now, I don't remember."

"They were, weren't they?"

"Why do you ask, Harry?"

"Because now they're kind of yellow-colored."

"Is that so, Harry?" Sam said, casually.

"And you're taller and thinner—"

"You might be right, Harry."

"Sam, you shouldn't have yellow eyes."

"Harry, what color eyes have *you* got?" Sam said.

"My eyes? They're blue, of course."

"Here you are, Harry." Sam handed him a pocket mirror. "Take a look at yourself."

Mr. Bittering hesitated and then raised the mirror to his face.

There were little, very dim flecks of new gold captured in the blue of his eyes.

"Now look what you've done," said Sam a moment later. "You've broken my mirror."

H arry Bittering moved into the metal shop and began to build the rocket. Men stood in the open door and talked and joked without raising their voices. Once in a while they gave him a hand on lifting something. But mostly they just idled and watched him with their yellowing eyes.

"It's supper time, Harry," they said.

His wife appeared with his supper in a wicker basket.

"I won't touch it," he said. "I'll eat only food from our deep freezer. Food that came from Earth. Nothing from our garden."

His wife stood watching him. "You can't build a rocket."

"I worked in a shop once, when I was twenty. I know metal. Once I get it started, the others will help," he said, not looking at her, laying out the blueprints.

"Harry, Harry," she said, helplessly.

"We've got to get away, Cora. We've *got* to!"

The nights were full of wind that blew down the empty moonlit sea meadows past the little white chess cities lying for their twelve-thousandth year in the shallows. In the Earthmen's settlement, the Bittering house shook with a feeling of change.

Lying abed, Mr. Bittering felt his bones shifted, shaped, melted like gold. His wife, lying beside him, was dark from many sunny afternoons. Dark she was, and golden-eyed, burnt almost black by the sun, sleeping, and the children metallic in their beds, and the wind roaring forlorn[7] and changing through the old peach trees, the violet grass, shaking out green rose petals.

7. **forlorn** (fôr·lôrn′) *adj.:* hopeless. *Forlorn* may also mean "deserted" or "abandoned."

The Naming of Names   **453**

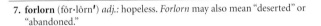

Advanced Learners
Enrichment. Invite students to imagine that they are part of a colony being established on another planet.
Activity. Ask them to work in groups of four to draft guidelines for organizing and governing their settlement. Suggest that they consider such issues as the purpose of the colony, leadership, division of work, interaction with natives of the planet, conflict resolution, and emergency procedures. Have students present their guidelines in pamphlet form.

A **Literary Focus**

❓ Point of view. How do Bittering's thoughts and feelings add suspense to the story? [Possible responses: His thoughts add suspense because he is the only one who is nervous about changing into a Martian. His saying *"Iorrt"* without knowing any Martian words is a concrete way of showing he is becoming a Martian.]

B **Reading Skills**

Retell. At this break in the story, have students retell the changes that have happened to the humans and the environment since rockets stopped coming from Earth. [Possible response: Since the rockets stopped coming from Earth, the flowers, vegetables, animals, and houses on Mars have changed in appearance. The Earthlings are getting taller and thinner. Their eyes are changing color to gold. Bittering has begun to speak Martian words.]

A strange word emerged from Mr. Bittering's lips. *"Iorrt. Iorrt."* He repeated it. It was a Martian word. He knew no Martian.

A The fear would not be stopped. It had his throat and heart. It dripped in a wetness of the arm and the temple and the trembling palm.

A green star rose in the east.

A strange word emerged from Mr. Bittering's lips.

"Iorrt. Iorrt." He repeated it.

It was a Martian word. He knew no Martian.

In the middle of the night he arose and dialed a call through to Simpson, the archaeologist.

"Simpson, what does the word *Iorrt* mean?"

"Why, that's the old Martian word for our planet Earth. Why?"

"No special reason."

The telephone slipped from his hand.

"Hello, hello, hello, hello," it kept saying while he sat gazing out at the green star. "Bittering? Harry, are you there?"

B The days were full of metal sound. He laid the frame of the rocket with the reluctant help of three indifferent men. He grew very tired in an hour or so and had to sit down.

"The altitude," laughed a man.

"Are you *eating,* Harry?" asked another.

"I'm eating," he said, angrily.

"From your deep freezer?"

"Yes!"

"You're getting thinner, Harry."

"I'm not!"

"And taller."

"Liar!"

His wife took him aside a few days later. "Harry, I've used up all the food in the deep freezer. There's nothing left. I'll have to make sandwiches using food grown on Mars."

He sat down heavily.

"You must eat," she said. "You're weak."

"Yes," he said.

He took a sandwich, opened it, looked at it, and began to nibble at it.

"And take the rest of the day off," she said. "It's hot. The children want to swim in the canals and hike. Please come along."

LITERARY CONNECTIONS

Science Fiction

The following comment is from *Space Flight: Imagination and Reality,* by Arthur C. Clarke: "When space travel is achieved, the frontier will merely shift outward, and I think we can rely on the ingenuity of the authors to always keep a few jumps ahead of history. And how much more material they will have on which to base their tales! It should never be forgotten that without some foundation of reality, science fiction would be impossible and that therefore exact knowledge is the friend, not the enemy, of imagination and fantasy. It was only possible to write stories about the Martians when science had discovered that a certain moving point of light was a world. By the time that science has proved or disproved the existence of Martians, it will have provided hundreds of other interesting and less accessible worlds for the authors to get busy with."

"I can't waste time. This is a crisis!"

"Just for an hour," she urged. "A swim'll do you good."

He rose, sweating. "All right, all right. Leave me alone. I'll come."

"Good for you, Harry."

The sun was hot, the day quiet. There was only an immense staring burn upon the land. They moved along the canal, the father, the mother, the racing children in their swimsuits. They stopped and ate meat sandwiches. He saw their skin baking brown. And he saw the yellow eyes of his wife and his children, their eyes that were never yellow before. A few tremblings shook him but were carried off in waves of pleasant heat as he lay in the sun. He was too tired to be afraid.

"Cora, how long have your eyes been yellow?"

She was bewildered. "Always, I guess."

"They didn't change from brown in the last three months?"

She bit her lips. "No. Why do you ask?"

"Never mind."

They sat there.

"The children's eyes," he said. "They're yellow, too."

"Sometimes growing children's eyes change color."

"Maybe *we're* children, too. At least to Mars. That's a thought." He laughed. "Think I'll swim."

They leaped into the canal water, and he let himself sink down and down to the bottom like a golden statue and lie there in green silence. All was water-quiet and deep, all was peace. He felt the steady, slow current drift him easily.

If I lie here long enough, he thought, *the water will work and eat away my flesh until the bones show like coral. Just my skeleton left. And then the water can build on that skeleton—green things, deep-water things, red things, yellow things. Change. Change. Slow, deep, silent change. And isn't that what it is up there?*

He saw the sky submerged above him, the sun made Martian by atmosphere and time and space.

Up there, a big river, he thought, *a Martian river, all of us lying deep in it, in our pebble houses, in our sunken boulder houses, like crayfish hidden, and the water washing away our old bodies and lengthening the bones and—*

He let himself drift up through the soft light.

Dan sat on the edge of the canal, regarding his father seriously.

"*Utha,*" he said.

"What?" asked his father.

The boy smiled. "You know. *Utha's* the Martian word for 'father.'"

C Reading Skills

? Infer. Why can't Cora remember that her eyes were brown just a few months ago? [Possible response: As they become Martians and they lose their Earthling characteristics, the characters forget their past.]

D Reading Skills

? Infer. Why does Bittering suddenly laugh and suggest that they are all children on Mars? [Possible responses: He is becoming too tired to fight. He is changing like the others.]

E Literary Focus

? Point of view. What do Bittering's thoughts indicate about changes in his attitude toward the Martian environment? [Possible responses: He is accepting the environment. He is beginning to see the changes in a positive light.]

Activity. Read the quotation aloud, pausing to explain any parts that students find confusing. Then, ask students to discuss how it affects their understanding of Bradbury's story and the science fiction of the future.

WHOLE CLASS

A Reading Skills

? Compare characters. How is Dan's reaction to his new name similar to or different from that of Julia in "Names/Nombres" (p. 394)? [Possible responses: Just as Julia wants to be accepted by her friends and likes her American identity, Dan wants to feel that he has become part of his new home. Unlike Julia who can communicate with her new friends, Dan has only a vague feeling that he should change.]

B Learners Having Difficulty

? Find details. What do the details in this passage reveal about the way Martians used to live? [Possible responses: The Martian way of life seemed to be unhurried and relaxed. They had an appreciation of beauty in nature and art.]

C Literary Focus

? Point of view. Ask students to re-read passages that reveal Harry's feelings during his picnic in the Martian hills. How do these passages indicate that Harry's view of Martian life has changed? [Possible responses: Harry begins to accept the changes as he lies underwater. He allows Dan to change his name to Linnl. He acknowledges that the Martian villa is lovely. The rocket project is less important to him.]

"Where did you learn it?"

"I don't know. Around. *Utha!*"

"What do you want?"

The boy hesitated. "I—I want to change my name."

"Change it?"

"Yes."

His mother swam over. "What's wrong with Dan for a name?"

Dan fidgeted. "The other day you called Dan, Dan, Dan. I didn't even hear. I said to myself, that's not my name. I've a new name I want to use."

Mr. Bittering held to the side of the canal, his body cold and his heart pounding slowly. "What is this new name?"

"Linnl. Isn't that a good name? Can I use it? Can't I, please?"

Mr. Bittering put his hand to his head. He thought of the silly rocket, himself working alone, himself alone even among his family, so alone.

He heard his wife say, "Why not?"

He heard himself say, "Yes, you can use it."

"Yaaa!" screamed the boy. "I'm Linnl, Linnl!"

Racing down the meadowlands, he danced and shouted.

Mr. Bittering looked at his wife. "Why did we do that?"

"I don't know," she said. "It just seemed like a good idea."

They walked into the hills. They strolled on old mosaic[8] paths, beside still-pumping fountains. The paths were covered with a thin film of cool water all summer long. You kept your bare feet cool all the day, splashing as in a creek, wading.

They came to a small deserted Martian villa with a good view of the valley. It was on top of a hill. Blue marble halls, large murals, a swimming pool. It was refreshing in this hot summertime. The Martians hadn't believed in large cities.

"How nice," said Mrs. Bittering, "if we could move up here to this villa for the summer."

"Come on," he said. "We're going back to town. There's work to be done on the rocket."

But as he worked that night, the thought of the cool blue marble villa entered his mind. As the hours passed, the rocket seemed less important.

---

8. **mosaic** (mō·zā′ik) *adj.*: made of small pieces of colored glass, stone, and so on, often forming a pattern or picture.

In the flow of days and weeks, the rocket receded[9] and dwindled.[10] The old fever was gone. It frightened him to think he had let it slip this way. But somehow the heat, the air, the working conditions—

He heard the men murmuring on the porch of his metal shop.

"Everyone's going. You heard?"

"All going. That's right."

Bittering came out. "Going where?" He saw a couple of trucks, loaded with children and furniture, drive down the dusty street.

"Up to the villas," said the man.

"Yeah, Harry. I'm going. So is Sam. Aren't you, Sam?"

"That's right, Harry. What about you?"

"I've got work to do here."

"Work! You can finish that rocket in the autumn, when it's cooler."

He took a breath. "I got the frame all set up."

"In the autumn is better." Their voices were lazy in the heat.

"Got to work," he said.

"Autumn," they reasoned. And they sounded so sensible, so right.

Autumn would be best, he thought. *Plenty of time, then.*

No! cried part of himself, deep down, put away, locked tight, suffocating. *No! No!*

"In the autumn," he said.

"Come on, Harry," they all said.

"Yes," he said, feeling his flesh melt in the hot liquid air. "Yes, in the autumn. I'll begin work again then."

"I got a villa near the Tirra Canal," said someone.

"You mean the Roosevelt Canal, don't you?"

"Tirra. The old Martian name."

"But on the map—"

"Forget the map. It's Tirra now. Now I found a place in the Pillan mountains—"

"You mean the Rockefeller range," said Bittering.

"I mean the Pillan mountains," said Sam.

"Yes," said Bittering, buried in the hot, swarming air. "The Pillan mountains."

> "You can finish that rocket in the autumn, when it's cooler."

---

9. **receded** (ri·sēd′id) *v.*: withdrew; became more distant.
10. **dwindled** (dwin′dəld) *v.*: shrank.

The Naming of Names   **457**

The Naming of Names   **457**

❓ Predict. What do you think will happen once the Bitterings leave their cottage and move to the Martian villa? [Most students will probably predict that the Bitterings will become completely Martian once they move to the villa.]

B **Reading Skills**

❓ Infer. Why do the Bitterings not look back at the town? [Possible response: The Bitterings have no regrets about leaving the town. They are looking forward to a better life in the villa.]

Everyone worked at loading the truck in the hot, still afternoon of the next day.

Laura, Dan, and David carried packages. Or, as they preferred to be known, Ttil, Linnl, and Werr carried packages.

The furniture was abandoned in the little white cottage.

"It looked just fine in Boston," said the mother. "And here in the cottage. But up at the villa? No. We'll get it when we come back in the autumn."

Bittering himself was quiet.

"I've some ideas on furniture for the villa," he said after a time. "Big, lazy furniture."

"What about your encyclopedia? You're taking it along, surely?"

Mr. Bittering glanced away. "I'll come and get it next week."

They turned to their daughter. "What about your New York dresses?"

The bewildered girl stared. "Why, I don't want them anymore."

They shut off the gas, the water; they locked the doors and walked away. Father peered into the truck.

"Gosh, we're not taking much," he said. "Considering all we brought to Mars, this is only a handful!"

He started the truck.

Looking at the small white cottage for a long moment, he was filled with a desire to rush to it, touch it, say goodbye to it, for he felt as if he were going away on a long journey, leaving something to which he could never quite return, never understand again.

Just then Sam and his family drove by in another truck.

"Hi, Bittering! Here we go!"

The truck swung down the ancient highway out of town. There were sixty others traveling the same direction. The town filled with a silent, heavy dust from their passage. The canal waters lay blue in the sun, and a quiet wind moved in the strange trees.

"Goodbye, town!" said Mr. Bittering.

"Goodbye, goodbye," said the family, waving to it.

They did not look back again.

> The daughter wove tapestries and the sons played songs on ancient flutes and pipes, their laughter echoing in the marble villa.

Summer burned the canals dry. Summer moved like flame upon the meadows. In the empty Earth settlement, the painted houses flaked and peeled. Rubber tires upon which children had swung in backyards hung suspended like stopped clock pendulums[11] in the blazing air.

At the metal shop, the rocket frame began to rust.

In the quiet autumn Mr. Bittering stood, very dark now, very golden-eyed, upon the slope above his villa, looking at the valley.

"It's time to go back," said Cora.

"Yes, but we're not going," he said quietly. "There's nothing there anymore."

"Your books," she said. "Your fine clothes."

"Your *Illes* and your fine *ior uele rre,*" she said.

"The town's empty. No one's going back," he said. "There's no reason to, none at all."

The daughter wove tapestries and the sons played songs on ancient flutes and pipes, their laughter echoing in the marble villa.

Mr. Bittering gazed at the Earth settlement far away in the low valley. "Such odd, such ridiculous houses the Earth people built."

"They didn't know any better," his wife mused. "Such ugly people. I'm glad they've gone."

They both looked at each other, startled by all they had just finished saying. They laughed.

"Where did they go?" he wondered. He glanced at his wife. She was golden and slender as his daughter. She looked at him, and he seemed almost as young as their eldest son.

"I don't know," she said.

"We'll go back to town maybe next year, or the year after, or the year after that," he said, calmly. "Now—I'm warm. How about taking a swim?"

They turned their backs to the valley. Arm in arm they walked silently down a path of clear-running spring water.

Five years later a rocket fell out of the sky. It lay steaming in the valley. Men leaped out of it, shouting.

"We won the war on Earth! We're here to rescue you! Hey!"

But the American-built town of cottages, peach trees, and theaters was silent. They found a flimsy rocket frame rusting in an empty shop.

---

11. **pendulums** (pen′dyo͞o·ləmz) *n.:* hanging weights that swing back and forth; used to regulate the movement of old-fashioned clocks.

C Advanced Learners

? Similes. What does the comparison between the suspended rubber tires and the pendulums of stopped clocks suggest? [Possible responses: The Martian setting has a certain timelessness to it. Time as we know it does not exist on Mars.]

D Reading Skills

? Analyze an author's purpose. What view of life on Mars does Ray Bradbury present? [Possible response: He creates a carefree society in which people remain young and find satisfaction in beauty, music, and laughter.]

E Literary Focus

? Point of view. How has the point of view changed in the story? [The story is no longer being told through Harry's thoughts and feelings because he is no longer in the story.]

A Reading Skills

❓ Predict. What do you think will happen to the rescue crew? [Possible response: They too will eventually change from Earthlings into Martians.]

B Literary Focus

❓ Setting. How does gazing at the surrounding hills affect the lieutenant? [Possible response: He is already becoming attracted to life on Mars.]

The rocket men searched the hills. The captain established headquarters in an abandoned bar. His lieutenant came back to report.

"The town's empty, but we found native life in the hills, sir. Dark people. Yellow eyes. Martians. Very friendly. We talked a bit, not much. They learn English fast. I'm sure our relations will be most friendly with them, sir."

"Dark, eh?" mused the captain. "How many?"

"Six, eight hundred, I'd say, living in those marble ruins in the hills, sir. Tall, healthy. Beautiful women."

"Did they tell you what became of the men and women who built this Earth settlement, Lieutenant?"

"They hadn't the foggiest notion of what happened to this town or its people."

"Strange. You think those Martians killed them?"

"They look surprisingly peaceful. Chances are a plague[12] did this town in, sir."

"Perhaps. I suppose this is one of those mysteries we'll never solve. One of those mysteries you read about."

The captain looked at the room, the dusty windows, the blue mountains rising beyond, the canals moving in the light, and he heard the soft wind in the air. He shivered. Then, recovering, he tapped a large fresh map he had thumbtacked to the top of an empty table.

A "Lots to be done, Lieutenant." His voice droned on and quietly on as the sun sank behind the blue hills. "New settlements. Mining sites, minerals to be looked for. Bacteriological specimens taken. The work, all the work. And the old records were lost. We'll have a job of remapping to do, renaming the mountains and rivers and such. Calls for a little imagination.

"What do you think of naming those mountains the Lincoln Mountains, this canal the Washington Canal, those hills—we can name those hills for you, Lieutenant. Diplomacy. And you, for a favor, might name a town for me. Polishing the apple. And why not make this the Einstein Valley, and further over . . . are you *listening*, Lieutenant?"

B The lieutenant snapped his gaze from the blue color and the quiet mist of the hills far beyond the town.

"What? Oh, *yes,* sir!"

---

12. **plague** (plāg) *n.*: deadly disease that spreads quickly.

Tell students to collaborate on building a time capsule that will await discovery by future explorers from Mars. In the capsule they can store such materials as newspaper articles or headlines, magazine articles, diary entries, drawings and photographs, or simple mementos of life on earth. They can also include lists they prepare of favorite books, movies, and pieces of music that are important to them.

Ray Bradbury

Stories Bite Him on the Leg!

Ray Bradbury (1920–   ) decided at the age of twelve to become a writer. He credits this decision to a circus performer called Mr. Electrico. Bradbury recalls one performance:

> 66Mr. Electrico twitched his blazing sword. He touched me on the right shoulder, the left shoulder, and then gently on my brow and the tip of my nose. I felt the storms jiggling in my eardrums, the blue fire swarming into my brain and down my arms and out my fingertips....99

Bradbury went home and shortly afterward began to write. That idea eventually paid off. Bradbury enjoyed great success with works such as *Fahrenheit 451* (the title refers to the temperature at which book paper burns), *Dandelion Wine, Something Wicked This Way Comes* (its main character is based on Mr. Electrico), and *The Martian Chronicles* (which includes "The Naming of Names").

Bradbury has been called the "world's greatest science fiction writer," but he thinks of himself as an "idea writer." Of the products of his ideas Bradbury says:

> 66My stories have led me through my life. They shout, I follow. They run up and bite me on the leg— I respond by writing down everything that goes on during the bite. When I finish, the idea lets go, and runs off.99

For Independent Reading

In Ray Bradbury's short story collections—such as *The Illustrated Man, R Is for Rocket,* and *The Stories of Ray Bradbury*—you'll find popular stories like "Mars Is Heaven," "The Sound of Summer Running," and "The Flying Machine."

Meet the Writer

Ray Bradbury began his career during the 1940s as a writer for such pulp magazines as *Black Mask, Amazing Stories,* and *Weird Tales.* The publication of *The Martian Chronicles* established Bradbury as an author of sophisticated fantasy stories. This collection of stories, linked by the framing device of the settlement of Mars by Earthlings, features tales of space travel and environmental adaptation. Bradbury's themes, in fact, reflect many of the important issues of the post–World War II era—racism, censorship, technology, and the threat of nuclear war.

For Independent Reading

Students who choose to read selections from one of Bradbury's short story collections can comment on some of the themes that appear throughout Bradbury's work.

The Naming of Names   **461**

Writing Workshop

Objectives

- Use appropriate prewriting and drafting skills to create a descriptive essay.
- Revise the descriptive essay by arranging details in clear order, adding figures of speech and sensory details, and concluding with a statement explaining why the subject is significant to you.
- Review and assess one's writing process and descriptive essay.

PRETEACHING

Skills Starter

Motivate. Ask a volunteer to describe for the class any object of his or her choice (a musical instrument, for example, or a building or exotic animal). The student should describe the object as completely as possible and then call on classmates to guess what the object is. List sensory details on the chalkboard as they are used, and point out to students how the descriptive words and phrases the student uses help listeners to picture the object.

DIRECT TEACHING

PREWRITING

Choosing a Subject

Encourage students to select a subject that they have positive feelings about and would like to share with their readers. Tell students to make a list of descriptive details that could entice readers to want to learn more about the person, place, thing, or event. Have students refer back to their notes when they write their essays.

Assignment
Describe something you've observed.

Audience
Your teacher and classmates.

RUBRIC
Evaluation Criteria

Good descriptive writing

1. clearly identifies the subject being described
2. conveys a strong overall impression of the subject
3. uses sensory details and figures of speech to help readers picture the subject and perhaps hear, smell, taste, and feel it as well
4. presents details in a clear, logical order
5. reveals the writer's thoughts and feelings about the subject

SKILLS FOCUS

Writing Skills
Write a descriptive essay.

DESCRIPTIVE WRITING
Descriptive Essay

Have your ever read a story, or perhaps an autobiography, that was so evocative and richly detailed that you forgot that you were reading and felt like you were really there? In a descriptive essay your goal is to evoke a mood or to create a vivid impression of something through details that appeal to the senses and to the imagination.

Prewriting

1 Choosing a Subject

Read and respond to this prompt:

> When you write a descriptive essay, you write as an observer, not as a participant. You gather details about your subject and arrange them in an essay that lets readers see what you saw, hear what you heard, feel what you felt. A descriptive essay conveys a dominant impression of its subject. Choose a subject—a person, animal, object, place, or experience—and re-create it through detailed description.

Before picking your subject, consider these questions:

- Can I observe this subject directly? If not, can I recall it clearly enough to describe it vividly?
- Do I find the subject interesting? Would it interest a reader?
- Does the subject involve enough sensory details for a good description?

CALVIN AND HOBBES © Watterson. Reprinted with permission of UNIVERSAL PRESS SYNDICATE. All rights reserved.

COLLECTION 4 RESOURCES: WRITING

Planning
- *One-Stop Planner* CD-ROM with ExamView Test Generator

Differentiating Instruction
- *Workshop Resources: Writing, Listening, and Speaking*
- *Supporting Instruction in Spanish*

Writing and Language
- *Workshop Resources: Writing, Listening, and Speaking*
- *Daily Language Activities*
- *Language Handbook Worksheets*

Assessment
- *Holt Assessment: Writing, Listening, and Speaking*

2 Finding More Ideas

For more ideas, freewrite for a few minutes on one or more of these topics:

- activities you can observe (someone cooking dinner; a basketball game)
- people you can observe (your older sister; an athlete)
- animals you can observe (your pet; a monkey at the zoo)
- places and things you can observe (the lunchroom; a tree)
- events you can observe (a scientific experiment; a sunrise)

3 Gathering Details

Gather details about your subject by observing the subject directly or by drawing on your memory. You may find it helpful to use a chart like the one below.

Sensory Details	Events	Impressions
see coconut trees • crickets **hear** airplane • waves **feel** sun • hot air **smell** salt water **taste** lemon candy	dragonflies flutter and glide • trucks haul tons of dirt • ferries race by	This is just the place for me.

Good descriptions are not limited to simple observations and recollections. **Figures of speech,** or imaginative comparisons, can add color to your writing and help your readers picture the subject of your essay. To review figures of speech, see page 464.

4 Organizing

There are three common ways to organize descriptive essays:

Spatial order. Describe details according to location—near to far or far to near, left to right or right to left, top to bottom or bottom to top, clockwise or counterclockwise. Spatial order is often used in descriptions of a place.

Framework for a Descriptive Essay

Introduction (identifies the subject, time, and place and gives background information): _____

_____

Body (presents details in clear order; includes sensory images and figures of speech):

1. _____

Specifics: _____

2. _____

Specifics: _____

3. _____

Specifics: _____

4. _____

Specifics: _____

Conclusion (includes main impression; expresses your feelings; tells why the subject is important): ____

_____

early each morning—smells of baking bread—heat of ovens—long-handled paddles—trays of rolls crisp and hot to touch—delicious taste.

- *One-Stop Planner* CD-ROM with ExamView Test Generator
- *Holt Online Assessment*
- *Holt Online Essay Scoring*

Internet
- go.hrw.com (Keyword: LE5 7-4)
- *Elements of Literature Online*

Gathering Details

If students can directly experience or observe their subjects, tell them to take along a notepad to write down details about the person, place, thing, or event. If students are writing from memory, suggest that they consult photographs that might help them to remember details about their subject.

Modeling

Framework for a Descriptive Essay

Help students having difficulty by filling in a sample framework on the chalkboard. For instance, you might use the following framework:

Introduction (identifies the subject, time, and place and gives background information): I had the chance to visit Buckingham Palace when I went to London this summer.

Body (presents details in clear order; includes sensory images and figures of speech):
1. I walked up the stony path to the gates of Buckingham Palace. Specifics: The black, gold, and marble gates surrounded the palace.
2. Just beyond the gates stood the enormous palace. Specifics: The building had dozens of enormous windows and columns that were more than two stories tall.
3. Guards were posted to my left and right. Specifics: The guards, silent as statues, were dressed in red suits and fuzzy black hats.
4. Across from the palace was St. James's Park. Specifics: The leaves on the lush green trees rustled as the chilly morning air swept through the palace grounds.

Conclusion (includes main impression; expresses your feelings; tells why the subject is important): Ever since I was a little girl, I wanted to visit the home of the British royal family. My trip to London wouldn't have been complete without visiting Buckingham Palace.

Descriptive Essay 463

DIRECT TEACHING

Strategies for Elaboration

When using metaphors, similes, and personification, encourage students to think of colors, shapes, sizes, textures, sounds, tastes, smells, and other qualities that can inspire them to write creative figures of speech—for example, *The setting sun was like a red apple bobbing in the ocean.*

DRAFTING

Focusing on the Main Idea

Point out to students that often one powerful image or detail is more descriptive than many minor images or details piled on top of one another. Challenge students to find one central image or detail that captures the subject of their essays. Students can do this by considering the feeling that is invoked in them by the subject and by choosing an image that might evoke the same feeling in a reader.

Using Transitions

Spatial organization. Tell students that one way to work with spatial organization is to remember how the details appeared to them. Remind them to be specific when describing the location of objects— for example, "Behind me stood a towering wall of granite. I inched closer to the edge of the rocky cliff and beneath me I could see the frothy crashing waves. Far off in the northern horizon, a sailboat dipped in and out of view."

Strategies for Elaboration

Sensory Details
Elaborate with words that appeal to the five senses:

sight   *blinding headlights*

sound   *squish of wet boots*

smell   *fetid odor of decay*

taste   *fiery peppers*

touch   *silky hair*

Figurative Language
Elaborate with vivid figures of speech:

simile
The moon was as bright as the noonday sun.

metaphor
The moon was a butterscotch candy, plump and golden.

personification
The photograph spoke to me of times past.

Language Handbook
HELP

See The Pronoun, 1b; Agreement, 2a–x.

Order of importance. Put the most important details at the beginning or at the end for emphasis. Writers often use order of importance to convey their feelings about a subject. This type of organization works well in descriptions of people and objects.

Chronological order. Arrange details in the order in which they occur or in the order in which you observe them. Chronological order usually works best in description of events, such as a scientific experiment or an approaching storm.

Drafting

1 **Focusing on the Main Idea**

Everything you write needs a focus—a **main idea** that shapes what you put down on paper. To state your main idea clearly, ask yourself: "What is my overall impression of my subject?" or "What is the purpose of my essay?"

2 **Setting the Scene**

Whenever you observe something, you view it from a particular place and at a particular time. By telling readers where you are, you give them a place to "stand" as they observe through your eyes.

3 **Using Transitions**

Use transitional words and phrases to link ideas. Some words that will help you lead the reader from one idea or image to the next are listed below:

Words showing spatial organization: *across from, around, below, beside, between, close to, down, far from*

Words showing order of importance: *first, last, mainly, more important, then, to begin with*

Words showing chronological order: *after, before, eventually, finally, first, now, next, then, when*

DIFFERENTIATING INSTRUCTION

Learners Having Difficulty

Tell students having difficulty to begin writing an introduction for their narratives with one of these phrases:

- If I could be anywhere in the world, I'd be . . .
- The person that inspires me the most is . . .
- My most treasured possession is . . .
- You should have been there! When I . . .
- My mouth waters when I think of . . .

English-Language Learners

To help these students, divide the class into five groups, one for each of the five senses. Ask each group to develop a bank of words that apply to its designated sense. Encourage English-language learners to think of vocabulary words in their native language first and then to translate them into English with the help of a bilingual dictionary. Students can then create posters of their word banks and display them in the classroom for reference.

Student Model

The Nature of Patam

Right now I'm sitting cross-legged on the big gray porch at our Patam beach house. The bright shining sun and hot day make me feel lazy.

The shadowy light-and-dark-green jungle to the left of me has tall, light-brown trunks of trees everywhere. To the right a coconut tree with its palms spread out looks like a parachute. Brown and gray monkeys chatter away as small green crickets sing. Different colored dragonflies flutter and glide so fast in every direction I can't see what color they are!

Lively waves leap to and fro on the pure white beach, while salt water and rock bash noisily together. An airplane rumbles slowly away. Across the bay trucks rattle loudly as they haul tons of brown dirt dark as chocolate.

Boats are all over the water! About three miles out huge tankers loom above the deep, gigantic, calm blue ocean, with ferries racing past them on their way to Singapore. Another boat, a small abandoned tan-brown sampan, bobs gently up and down in the gold sunlit waters that seem like enormous masses of lemon candy. I think Patam is just the place for me.

— Benjamin Bethea
Batam Island Christian Home School
Batam, Indonesia

*The writer introduces his **subject** and tells where he is.*

***Details** of sight, sound, and movement create a vivid picture.*

*The writer uses **spatial organization**; he moves from the trees near him to the plane, trucks, and boats in the distance.*

*The writer tells how he **feels** about this place.*

Writing Tips

Denotation and Connotation
Use words precisely. Let context determine whether a particular word is right. For example, the words *slim* and *skinny* have nearly the same dictionary meaning, but *slim* conveys an impression of strength and health while *skinny* has a connotation of weakness.

Clichés
Avoid expressions that have been used so often that they are stale. Examples are

- *the picture of health*
- *playful as a kitten*
- *red as a rose*

INTERNET
More Writer's Models
Keyword: LE5 7-4

Student Model
Encourage students to examine the model to see how one student writer clearly introduces his subject, elaborates with vivid details, and concludes by revealing his thoughts and feelings about the subject.

Writing Tips

Clichés. Help students avoid clichés by telling them to ask themselves this simple question: "Have I heard this expression before?" Tell students to circle any expression in their drafts that they think might be a cliché. Then, have them ask fellow students if they have heard the phrase used before. If several students respond positively, suggest that students replace the phrase with another figure of speech.

Special Education Students
Have these students describe the room they are in at the moment. Tell them to write down descriptive details about what they see, hear, feel, taste, and smell. Students can then write essays about a particular part of the room or an object in the room.

Advanced Learners
Enrichment. Encourage advanced learners to write a description of a fictional place. Tell them to imagine themselves on a distant planet or in a fantasy world. Encourage students to use vivid details when describing their imagined surroundings.

EVALUATING AND REVISING

Content and Organization Guidelines

Have students form pairs and read their essays aloud to their partners. Tell students to sketch a picture based on the details in their partner's essay. Have students note when they have trouble drawing because the description is unclear or there are not enough details in their partner's essay. Also, have students note where events seem out of order. Tell students to address their partner's comments when they revise their essays.

TECHNOLOGY TIP

If students have access to recording equipment, encourage them to videotape themselves giving oral presentations of their essays. They can then watch the tape and evaluate their essays and how they were presented.

Publishing Tips

If students give oral presentations of their essays, encourage them to make the settings and people come to life for their audience. Remind them to emphasize sensory details and to use gestures, dramatic pauses, and facial expressions to present their descriptions in an exciting manner.

Evaluating and Revising

Use the chart below to help you evaluate and revise your descriptive essay.

Descriptive Essay: Content and Organization Guidelines		
Evaluation Questions	▶ **Tips**	▶ **Revision Techniques**
❶ Does your introduction identify the subject?	▶ **Circle** the subject of the essay.	▶ **Add** a sentence that clearly identifies the subject of your description.
❷ Does your choice of words bring sensory details and figures of speech to life?	▶ **Highlight** sensory details and imaginative comparisons. **Put an S** above sensory details. **Put an F** above sentences that employ figures of speech.	▶ **Elaborate** with additional sensory details. **Delete** irrelevant details.
❸ Are the details arranged in a clear order?	▶ In the margin, **indicate** the mode of organization— spatial, chronological, or order of importance.	▶ **Rearrange** details if necessary. **Add** transitions for greater coherence.
❹ Have you included your thoughts and feelings about the subject?	▶ **Put a check mark** next to any statement of your feelings or thoughts.	▶ **Add** specific details about thoughts and feelings.
❺ Does your conclusion state why the subject is significant to you? Does it convey an overall impression of the subject?	▶ **Underline** the statement that tells why the experience is meaningful. **Bracket** statements that hint at the overall impression.	▶ **Add** a statement explaining why the experience is important or conveying the overall impression.

Read the following descriptive paragraph. Following the model you'll find questions to help you evaluate the writer's revisions.

EVALUATION GUIDELINES	4	3	2	1
Use these guidelines to quickly assess students' final drafts.	**Introduction grabs the reader's attention and clearly identifies the subject.**	Introduction grabs the reader's attention and clearly identifies the subject.	Introduction grabs the reader's attention but does not clearly identify the subject.	Introduction does not grab the reader's attention, and the subject of the essay is unclear.	Introduction does not grab the reader's attention, and essential background information is not provided.
	Word choice brings sensory details and figures of speech to life.	Word choice brings sensory details and figures of speech to life.	Sensory details and figures of speech are included but are clichés.	Sensory details and figures of speech are included but are not vividly presented.	Sensory details and figures of speech are not included.

Revision Model

What is the best food you've ever eaten? For me, it was

a freshly baked roll from my grandparents' bakery.

I discovered this when I visited them last year.
They own a bakery and live upstairs. Every morning I

woke up at about 5 o'clock to the ~~nice~~ smell of newly *delicious* *freshly*

baked bread. I ~~would make~~ my way downstairs where the *made*

bakers were removing bread from the ovens with long- *loaves of*

handled paddles. ~~I was not allowed to touch the trays.~~

One of the bakers would throw me a crisp, well-browned

roll, so hot that I had to keep tossing it from one hand to *sprinkled with poppy seeds*

the other. To this day, I can still recall the smell and taste

of that bread. I ~~went~~ back upstairs, where, all alone in the *ran*

~~gloomy~~ light of early morning, I ~~ate~~ my roll slowly, *dim* *munched*

~~enjoying~~ every bite. *savoring*

Evaluating the Revision

1. What order of organization has the writer used?

2. Which details were added? Do they appeal to different senses?

3. What words were added, deleted, or changed? Do they improve the description?

4. Which sentence concludes the description? Does it explain why the experience was important?

PROOFREADING
TIPS

- Read your final version one sentence at a time to catch and correct mistakes in spelling, punctuation, and grammar conventions.

- You can exchange papers with a partner, but remember that proofreading requires your own close reading.

Communications
Handbook
H E L P
————————
See Proofreaders' Marks.

PUBLISHING
TIPS

Working either alone or in a group, create a brochure, a bulletin-board display, or a multimedia presentation of your essay that uses a variety of visual and auditory aids.

Descriptive Essay **467**

DIRECT TEACHING

REVISING

Revision Model

To help students revise, present the thought processes of a writer making the changes shown in the Revision Model. Calling students' attention to the last sentence, you might say, "The writer replaces *went* with the more active verb *ran*. The word *savoring* is much more descriptive than *enjoying*." After you have finished, ask a volunteer to select another portion of the model and provide a similar rationale for the revisions there.

GUIDED PRACTICE

Evaluating the Revision

1. The writer has used chronological order.

2. The additional phrases "loaves of bread" and "sprinkled with poppy seeds" are vivid sensory details. They both appeal to sight.

3. Possible answer: The sentence "I discovered this when I visited them last year" provides a transition for the details that follow in the essay. The more descriptive words "delicious," "freshly," "ran," "munched," and "savoring" all replace mundane words and improve the description.

4. The sentence "To this day, I can still recall the smell and taste of that bread" is moved to the end to conclude the essay. It expresses why this experience was important to the writer.

	4	3	2	1
Details are presented in a clear and logical order.	Details are presented in a clear and logical order.	Details are presented in order, but transitions are unclear.	Details are presented, but order is hard to follow.	Details are unclear and not in order.
Conclusion includes thoughts and feelings and states why the subject is significant to the writer.	Conclusion includes thoughts and feelings and states why the subject is significant to the writer.	Conclusion includes thoughts and feelings and vaguely states why the subject is significant to the writer.	Conclusion includes thoughts and feelings but does not state why the subject is significant to the writer.	There is no conclusion to the essay.

Collection 4: Skills Review

Literary Skills

SKILLS FOCUS
pp. 468–469

Grade-Level Skills
■ Literary Skills
Analyze point of view.

INTRODUCING THE SKILLS REVIEW

Use this review to assess students' grasp of point of view.

DIRECT TEACHING

Ⓐ Literary Focus
Point of view. Tell students that this article contains objective, or factual, information. Ask students to keep this point of view in mind as they read.

Ⓑ Literary Focus
❓ Point of view. Have students find words and phrases that reveal the narrator's subjective point of view. ["idiot," "not content," "ruin her entire day's work"] **How does this contrast to the news report?** [Here we learn the cook's feelings; the news report is neutral.]

Ⓒ Literary Focus
❓ Point of view. From what point of view is this passage told? [first person] **What might we learn from an omniscient point of view that we do not learn here?** [Possible responses: what takes place outside this narrator's observation; what other characters think and feel.]

Test Practice

Directions: Read the passages. Then, read each question, and write the letter of the best response.

The News of King Midas
from *The Royal News*

Rumors of the so-called Midas touch have been confirmed today. According to sources close to the king, Midas is now unable to eat or drink, as anything he touches turns to gold.

"Serves him right," said one palace insider who asked not to be named. "He could have wished for something sensible, such as a triple-tax-free diversified bond portfolio. Now who knows where the price of gold is heading?"

The king's wife and daughter were unavailable for comment, as they had been turned to gold.

from *Cook to the King: A Novel*

"Sandwich?" the head cook roared. "You want me to fix you a sandwich?" She glared at the king. "With what, may I ask?"

What an idiot he was. Even the smallest servant boy knew what was going to happen by the time dessert was served, but not King Midas. Oh, no. Not content merely to ruin her entire day's work (that perfectly

SKILLS FOCUS

Literary Skills
Analyze point of view.

poached salmon! that lovely macaroni pudding!), he had to come tearing through her kitchen. By the time he was through, there wasn't a crumb that didn't clink and glitter when she swept it up.

from *A Courtier's Memoir*

After all my years serving in the palace, I thought I'd seen it all. When the king, however, started turning everything to gold, you could have knocked me over with a feather. Actually, he nearly *did* knock me over with a feather. An ostrich plume, it was, on my second-best hat! If I do say so myself, I was looking rather spiffy until the king snatched it off and started waving it around. He yelled that he'd turned my hat to gold. It was gold, all right. Solid gold. I've still got the lump on my head to prove it.

King Midas's E-mail

To: gods_helpline@olympus.edu
From: kmidas@palace.org
Subject: My Kingdom for a Burger
OK, point taken. I was greedy and foolish, and I'm sorry. Please, undo my wish before I starve to death!

468 Collection 4 / Can You See It My Way?

DIFFERENTIATING INSTRUCTION

Learners Having Difficulty
In determining point of view, students may be confused by quotations. Explain that in the first article the insider's words express his or her feelings, not those of the narrator. The insider's words are enclosed in quotation marks; the objective, omniscient narrator is simply reporting all the facts. In the second article (third-person limited point of view), explain the difference

between the use of "me" in the dialogue and the use of "she" in the narration.

Advanced Learners
Enrichment. Students may want to try to write another fairy tale or a fable from a few different points of view. Student pairs should check each other's retellings to make certain that the point of view is maintained consistently.

Collection 4: Skills Review

1. In which passage does the narrator use a **third-person-limited point of view**?
    A   *The Royal News*
    B   *Cook to the King*
    C   *A Courtier's Memoir*
    D   King Midas's E-mail

2. The **point of view** in *A Courtier's Memoir* is —
    F   omniscient
    G   first person
    H   third-person limited
    J   second person

3. Which passage is most **objective** in telling what has happened to King Midas?
    A   *The Royal News*
    B   *Cook to the King*
    C   *A Courtier's Memoir*
    D   King Midas's E-mail

4. The **narrator,** or speaker, in *A Courtier's Memoir* is —
    F   the king himself
    G   the cook to the king
    H   an omniscient narrator
    J   a courtier in the king's court

5. The **speaker** in King Midas's E-mail is —
    A   the king himself
    B   the cook to the king
    C   an omniscient narrator
    D   a courtier in the king's court

Constructed Response

6. Briefly describe the differences between the **omniscient, first-person,** and **third-person-limited points of view.**

Answers and Model Rationales

1. **B** Students can eliminate C and D; in both the narrator uses the first-person pronoun *I.* A is not limited to the thoughts and feelings of a single character. Therefore, B is the only possible answer.

2. **G** Students should quickly note the use of the first-person pronoun *I* in the passage and choose G.

3. **A** The other passages have subjective aspects in their reporting. Therefore, A is the only possible answer.

4. **J** The narrator is a courtier in King Midas's court. The title of the passage confirms this.

5. **A** The king is the writer of his own e-mail. Therefore, A is the only correct answer.

Constructed Response

6. The omniscient point of view informs the reader of the thoughts and feelings of all the characters in the story. The first-person point of view tells the story from the viewpoint of a character using the pronoun *I.* The third-person-limited point of view has an outside narrator zooming in on the thoughts and feelings of just one character in the story.

Test-Taking Tips

For more instruction on test taking, refer students to **Test Smarts,** p. 920.

Using Academic Language

Literary Terms

As part of the review of point of view, ask students to look back through the collection to find meanings of the following terms. Then, have students demonstrate their grasp of the terms by citing passages from a story in the collection that illustrate the meanings of the terms.
Point of View (pp. 348, 356); **Omniscient Point of View** (pp. 348, 356, 382);

First-person Point of View (pp. 349, 368);
Third-person-limited Point of View (p. 349);
Subjective Writing (pp. 393, 402, 414);
Objective Writing (pp. 393, 414).

Collection 4: Skills Review

Informational Reading Skills

SKILLS FOCUS
pp. 470–471

Grade-Level Skills
■ Reading Skills
Analyze an author's argument.

INTRODUCING THE SKILLS REVIEW

Use this review to test students' understanding of how an author develops an argument.

DIRECT TEACHING

A **Reading Informational Text**

Analyze the author's argument.
Point out the opening heading and statement. Ask students what argument the author is going to develop based on this information. [The coral reefs are being destroyed and need to be rescued.]

B **Reading Informational Text**

Analyze the author's argument.
Point out that the author uses the expert testimony of scientists to strengthen her argument.

C **Reading Informational Text**

Analyze the author's argument.
Have students identify the cause-and-effect relationship that the author develops. [The destruction of coral reefs would cause the risk of extinction for thousands of species.]

Test Practice

Directions: Read the passage. Then, read each question, and write the letter of the best response.

Can We Rescue the Reefs?
Ritu Upadhyay
from *Time for Kids*

① Time is running out to stop the destruction of coral reefs.

② Under the clear blue sea, bustling communities of ocean creatures live together in brightly colored, wildly stacked structures called coral reefs. These silent, majestic underwater cities are home to four thousand different species of fish and thousands of plants and animals. For millions of years, marine creatures have lived together in reefs, going about their business in their own little water worlds.

③ But danger looms. At an international meeting on coral reefs in October 2000, scientists issued a harsh warning. More than one quarter of the world's reefs have been destroyed. . . . Unless drastic measures are taken, the remaining reefs may be dead in twenty years. "We are about to lose them," says Clive Wilkinson of the Coral Reef Monitoring Network.

Precious Underwater Habitats

④ The destruction of coral reefs, some of which are 2.5 million years old, would have a very serious impact on our oceans. Though coral reefs take up less than 1 percent of the ocean floor, they are home to 25 percent of all underwater species. Wiping them out would put thousands of creatures at risk of extinction. It would also destroy one of our planet's most beautiful living treasures.

⑤ Though it's often mistaken for rock because of its stony texture, coral is actually made up of tiny clear animals called coral polyps. Millions stick together in colonies and form a hard outer shell. When coral die, their skeletons are left behind, and new coral build on top. The colonies eventually grow together, creating large reefs. Reefs grow into complex mazelike structures with different rooms, hallways, holes, and crevices for their inhabitants to live in. Over the years the ancient Great Barrier Reef off Australia's coast has grown to be 1,240 miles long!

SKILLS FOCUS

Reading Skills
Analyze an author's argument.

DIFFERENTIATING INSTRUCTION

Advanced Learners
Enrichment. Invite students to evaluate how effective the author's arguments are in persuading the reader that coral reefs are important, that coral reefs are being destroyed, that something can be done to stop the destruction, and that the reader should take some action to help stop the destruction. Students can discuss these issues in a small group or can write individual reviews expressing their opinions. Urge students to find evidence in the text to support each point they are making. As part of their evaluations, encourage students to point out the most persuasive arguments of the author and to suggest ways in which she could have made an even stronger case.

Collection 4: Skills Review

1. Which of the following statements best summarizes the writer's **perspective** in "Can We Rescue the Reefs?"
   - A The outlook for coral reefs is hopeless.
   - B Global warming is a threat to the whole earth.
   - C Saving endangered coral reefs is very important.
   - D Coral reefs are beautiful little worlds within the oceans.

2. Paragraph 2 contains words and phrases such as "bustling communities," "underwater cities," "home," "going about their business," and "their own little water worlds." The writer uses those words and phrases to —
   - F make coral reefs seem like human societies
   - G describe coral reefs the way a scientist would describe them
   - H tell where coral reefs are located
   - J describe how coral reefs are formed

3. In paragraph 3, the writer supports her position by —
   - A describing her personal fears about the reefs
   - B quoting an expert on the issue
   - C telling a brief story about the development of coral reefs
   - D giving reasons why coral reefs are beautiful

4. Which statement is an example of a **statistic**?
   - F "Time is running out to stop the destruction of coral reefs."
   - G "Coral is actually made up of tiny clear animals. . . ."
   - H "Reefs grow into complex maze-like structures. . . ."
   - J "More than one quarter of the world's reefs have been destroyed. . . ."

5. Which of the following is a statement of **fact**—something that can be proved to be true?
   - A Coral is the most beautiful thing in the sea.
   - B Over the years the ancient Great Barrier Reef has grown to be 1,240 miles long.
   - C Coral reefs must be saved.
   - D Coral reefs are fascinating.

6. The writer's **purpose** in this article is to —
   - F inform
   - G describe
   - H persuade
   - J all of the above

Constructed Response

7. According to the article, why are coral reefs important?

Answers and Model Rationales

1. **C** The word *summarizes* is key. D contains information that is used to develop the author's argument, and B is not mentioned. Only C summarizes the author's point of view. She states that the outlook for reefs is *not* hopeless (A).

2. **F** Students can use the process of elimination to identify the correct choice. The words and phrases are not scientific (G) and do not indicate where the reefs are located or describe how they are formed (H and J). The words and phrases could describe human societies (F).

3. **B** All four statements may be part of the author's argument, but B is the only one that appears in paragraph 3.

4. **J** F is an opinion. Although G and H are true, they are not statistics. J is the only item that includes numerical information.

5. **B** A, C, and D are opinions. Only B includes information that can be proven true.

6. **J** The author informs readers about the coral reefs and their importance, describes the reefs, and tries to persuade readers that the reefs must be saved. J is the best choice.

Constructed Response

7. According to this article, coral reefs are important because they are home to 25 percent of all underwater species.

Using Academic Language

Informational Terms

As part of the review of analyzing an author's argument, ask students to look back through the collection to find the meanings of the following terms. Then, ask students to explain how the terms can be used to analyze the development of an author's argument and perspective in a selection.

Perspective (pp. 350, 364, 410); **Argument** (p. 389); **Evidence** (p. 389); **Facts** (p. 389); **Statistics** (p. 389); **Experts** (p. 389); **Persuade** (p. 410).

Collection 4: Skills Review

Vocabulary Skills

Synonyms

Modeling. Model the thought process of a good reader getting the answer to item 1 by saying, "Something that is described as *exotic* is the opposite of something ordinary in a dull way (A). While things that are exotic may be very desirable to some, they are not very desirable to all (C). In the same way, something that is exotic may be strongly offensive to some but not to all (D). B is the best choice—things that are exotic are different in a fascinating way.

Test Practice

Answers and Model Rationales

1. **B** *Different* and *fascinating* together capture the meaning of *exotic*.

2. **J** *Complicated* is a synonym for *intricate*.

3. **A** The root words *custom* and *habit* are synonyms. Other choices are antonyms.

4. **F** *Complicated* means "hard to untangle," as does *convoluted*.

5. **D** *Transition* implies movement; therefore, *change* is the answer.

6. **G** The prefix *de–* means "reverse of," "opposite of," which is akin to *loss*.

7. **C** *Arrogant* implies a sense of exaggerated self-importance.

8. **J** The base words *tolerate* and *bear* are synonyms.

9. **D** The Latin root *simul* means "at the same time."

10. **G** The idea behind *refuge* is "protection"; *shelter* is the only choice with this meaning.

Test Practice

Synonyms

DIRECTIONS: Choose the word or phrase that means the same, or about the same, as the underlined word.

1. Something that is <u>exotic</u> is —
   A ordinary in a dull way
   B different in a fascinating way
   C very desirable
   D strongly offensive

2. Something that is <u>intricate</u> is —
   F simple
   G inside
   H ancient
   J complicated

3. <u>Habitual</u> is most like —
   A customary
   B irregular
   C occasionally
   D never

4. <u>Convoluted</u> means —
   F complicated
   G ordinary
   H murky
   J strange

5. Someone who is in <u>transition</u> is experiencing —
   A prosperity
   B balance
   C stability
   D change

6. <u>Deprivation</u> is most like —
   F abundance
   G loss
   H privilege
   J growth

7. <u>Arrogant</u> refers to someone who is —
   A overly emotional
   B deeply confused
   C overly self-important
   D easily persuaded

8. <u>Intolerable</u> means —
   F worthwhile
   G unjust
   H infrequent
   J unbearable

9. <u>Simultaneously</u> means —
   A all but one
   B never the same
   C over the top
   D at the same time

10. Someone seeking <u>refuge</u> would be in search of —
    F food
    G shelter
    H clothing
    J garbage

SKILLS FOCUS

Vocabulary Skills
Identify synonyms.

Vocabulary Review

Activity. Have students select the correct word from the box to complete the following sentences.

ethnicity	monarch	refugee
simultaneously		

1. The festival celebrated the group's _____. [ethnicity]

2. After years of war in his country, the doctor found himself a grateful _____ in a new land. [refugee]

3. Both players jumped _____ at the ball that flew by them. [simultaneously]

4. The queen was the last _____ to have absolute rule in the great country. [monarch]

DIRECTIONS: Read the following paragraph from a descriptive essay. Then, answer each question that follows.

(1) The annual book sale, sponsored by our parent-teacher organization, transformed the school gym into an exhibit hall filled with thousands of books, videos, and audiotapes. (2) Tables were covered with brightly colored shawls. (3) The tables were arranged in a horseshoe curve along the walls. (4) At the entrance to the left were works of fiction arranged by subjects such as adventure, romance, and sports. (5) There were tables devoted to ethnic works. (6) At the rear were tables containing works of nonfiction: biographies, histories, essays, and almanacs. (7) Then came nonprint offerings: books on cassette and movies adapted from novels. (8) At the right end of the horseshoe, a group of student volunteers took orders for books. (9) In the center of the gym were tables and chairs that invited browsers to examine books and to chat about them with teachers, librarians, and parents. (10) What one heard was a low buzz of interest, and what one saw were student faces intent on discovering something good to read.

1. The method of organization used in this paragraph is —
A spatial
B chronological
C order of importance
D all of the above

2. What would be the best way to combine sentences 2 and 3?
F Tables were covered with brightly colored shawls, and the tables were arranged in a horseshoe curve along the wall.
G Tables covered with brightly colored shawls were arranged in a horseshoe curve along the walls.
H Tables were covered with brightly colored shawls; also, they were arranged in a horseshoe curve along the walls.
J Tables arranged in a horseshoe curve with brightly colored shawls were along the walls of the gym.

3. Which sentence would be improved by the addition of specific details?
A sentence 4
B sentence 5
C sentence 6
D sentence 7

4. Transitional words or phrases are used in all of the following *except* —
F sentence 3
G sentence 4
H sentence 6
J sentence 7

5. Which of the following would be the *best* replacement for the word *containing* in sentence 6?
A holding
B enclosing
C including
D stacked with

Writing Skills
Analyze a descriptive essay.

Answers and Model Rationales

1. A A is correct because the writer describes the details in relation to their location.

2. G F and H can be edited for clarity. The sentence structure in J is awkward. G is correct because it clearly describes how the tables appeared and how they were arranged.

3. B Sentence 5 (B) would be improved if the writer included examples of specific ethnic works.

4. F Sentence 4 (G) contains the transitional phrase "At the entrance." Sentence 6 (H) contains the phrase "At the rear." Sentence 7 (J) begins with the phrase "Then came." Only sentence 3 (F) does not contain a transitional word or phrase.

5. D The words *holding, enclosing, including,* and *containing* are synonyms. Only D, *stacked with,* is correct because it is a more accurate description of how the books looked on top of a table.

APPLICATION

Anthologies
Have students collect their descriptive essays and publish them in a collection. These anthologies can be separated into sections devoted to topics such as favorite people, places, foods, and objects. Students should write brief introductions for each section and then distribute these anthologies in class.

EXTENSION

Art
For homework, have students create artwork based on their descriptive essays. For a further challenge, students can create art based on another student's essay. Students might choose watercolors, pastels, acrylic paint, or colored pencils to express themselves.

Read On

For Independent Reading

If students enjoyed the themes and topics explored in this collection, you might recommend these titles for independent reading.

Assessment Options

The following projects can help you evaluate and assess your students' outside reading. Videotapes or audiotapes of completed projects may be included in students' portfolios.

- **Make a calendar.** Ask students to create a daily calendar to record Miguel's adventures in *. . . and now Miguel.* In dated boxes on their calendars, ask them to write descriptions of incidents from the story. The calendar covers should contain illustrations of important scenes.

- **Create a commercial.** Ask students to write the script for a television commercial that will advertise a movie based on *The Door in the Wall.* Encourage them to include references to the medieval setting and the mysterious illness of Robin. Explain that they should include instructions about the background music, the order of the scenes in the commercial, and the action.

- **Write a ship's log.** Ask students to suppose that it is part of Jim Hawkins's duty to keep a ship's log on the journey in *Treasure Island.* Have students write log entries that describe the incidents in the story, and ask them to include frequent comments from Jim about what is really happening in the adventure.

Fiction

A Little Patience

Young Miguel Chavez longs for his family to treat him like an adult. For a year he tries to prove that he is ready to make the difficult journey driving sheep into the mountains. It is not until some sheep are missing and a serious letter arrives that Miguel is truly able to prove himself in Joseph Krumgold's Newbery winner *. . . and now Miguel.*

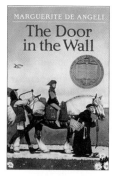

The Faithful Servant

Marguerite De Angeli's *The Door in the Wall* takes place in medieval England. Robin, the son of the great lord Sir John de Bureford, is supposed to become a page—a boy training for knighthood. Unfortunately, he is stricken with a mysterious illness that causes him to lose the movement of his legs. Determined not to disappoint his father, he overcomes his problems and helps to turn back the Welsh invaders who threaten the kingdom.

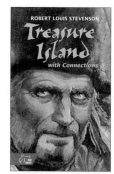

All Aboard!

When Jim Hawkins, an impressionable young cabin boy, discovers a treasure map, he finds himself thrust into an adventure beyond compare. The notorious Long John Silver joins Jim and two of his friends on a ship. Can Hawkins trust this mysterious pirate? Find out in Robert Louis Stevenson's *Treasure Island.*

This title is available in the HRW Library.

In Another Land

Have you ever wondered what it would be like to make your way through India? Anni Axworthy gives you more than a passing glance of the Asian subcontinent in *Anni's India Diary.* Discover Hindu gods and goddesses, learn how to play cricket, and visit the Taj Mahal along with Anni. Lively illustrations accompany the text of Anni's unforgettable journey.

DIFFERENTIATING INSTRUCTION

Estimated Word Counts of Read On Books:

Fiction		Nonfiction	
. . . and now Miguel	59,000	Knots in My Yo-yo String	35,000
The Door in the Wall	33,000	A Samurai Castle	10,000
Treasure Island	70,000	Postcards from France	29,000
Connections to Treasure Island	15,000	Made in China: Ideas and	
Anni's India Diary	3,900	Inventions from Ancient China	20,000

Nonfiction

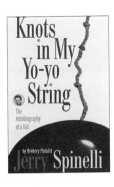

The Way He Was

In *Knots in My Yo-yo String,* Newbery Award–winner Jerry Spinelli touchingly revisits his childhood and growing up. He recalls dreams of becoming a major-league shortstop, hours with comic books, and the only time he received detention in school. Spinelli had no idea he would become a writer, but he recounts in compelling prose the event that inspired him to become one.

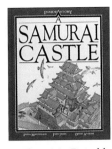

The Customs of Warriors

During the sixteenth and seventeenth centuries, Samurai warriors were the most honored group in Japan. In *A Samurai Castle,* Fiona MacDonald explores the Samurai culture and the conditions that helped shape this distinct group of fighting men. Perceptive illustrations reveal the design of their living arrangements, and MacDonald's narrative tells how the Samurai spent their days, how they trained for battle, and the reasons they were respected and feared.

An Exciting Journey

Megan McNeill Libby had reservations after deciding to spend her junior year in France. When she arrived, she felt out of place in her new surroundings, and she wondered if she would ever learn the customs and language. After a few months she began to make friends and appreciate the fascinating culture. Megan chronicles this exciting time of her life in *Postcards from France.*

A Wealth of Ideas

In *Made in China: Ideas and Inventions from Ancient China,* Suzanne Williams describes some of the many contributions the ancient Chinese made to science and society. From discoveries in astronomy and improvements in irrigation systems to the casting of bronze and the standardization of roads, measurements, and writing, Williams places Chinese invention in a context that helps to break down ethnic and cultural barriers.

Read On 475

The Read On titles are categorized as shown below:

Below Grade Level ⬇
. . . and now Miguel
Anni's India Diary
Made in China: Ideas and
   Inventions from Ancient China

At Grade Level ↔
The Door in the Wall
Knots in My Yo-yo String
A Samurai Castle

Above Grade Level ⬆
Treasure Island
Postcards from France

Collection 5
Worlds of Words: Prose and Poetry

Literary Focus:
Analyzing Prose and Poetry

Informational Focus:
Analyzing Main Idea

About Collection 5

In Collection 5, students will master the following skills:

- **Literary Skills:** Analyze external and internal conflict, an autobiography, a novella, an essay, a lyric poem, a sonnet, an ode, humorous poems and exaggeration, free verse, an elegy, and the sounds of poetry.
- **Reading Skills:** Find the main idea; analyze comparison-and-contrast text structures; distinguish fact from opinion; make generalizations.
- **Vocabulary Skills:** Understand connotation and denotation; complete word analogies; analyze shades of meaning.
- **Writing Skills:** Develop, write, and revise an essay supporting an interpretation.

Informational Text

Each collection of *Elements of Literature* provides a variety of informational texts related to the literature selections by theme or topic.

Minimum Course of Study

Most skills can be taught with a minimum number of selections and features. In the chart to the right, lessons highlighted in green constitute the minimum course of study that provides coverage of the skills taught in Collection 5.

476A

Scope and Sequence

Selection ▪ Feature	Literary Skills
Elements of Literature: Understanding the Forms of Prose *by* Kylene Beers	• Understand forms of prose
Reading Skills and Strategies: Finding the Main Idea **A *Good* Reason to Look Up** *by* Shaquille O'Neal ↓ *below grade level*	
Amigo Brothers *by* Piri Thomas ↔ *at grade level*	• Analyze external and internal conflict
Informational Text: **Right Hook—Left Hook** *by* Joan Burditt ↔ *at grade level*	
from **Barrio Boy** *by* Ernesto Galarza ↔ *at grade level*	• Analyze an autobiography
Song of the Trees *by* Mildred D. Taylor ↔ *at grade level*	• Analyze a novella
Fish Cheeks *by* Amy Tan ↔ *at grade level*	• Analyze an essay
A Mason-Dixon Memory *by* Clifton Davis ↔ *at grade level*	• Analyze an essay
Informational Text: **Buddies Bare Their Affection for Ill Classmate** *from the* Austin American-Statesman ↔ *at grade level*	
Elements of Literature: Painting with Words: **The Elements of Poetry** *by* John Malcolm Brinnin	• Understand images, sounds, and forms in poetry • Understand how to read poetry

Resource Manager

(pp. 476G–476N)

Lesson and workshop resources are referenced in the Resource Manager on the pages that follow. These resources can be used to reinforce the skills taught in Collection 5, remediate students who are having difficulty, and provide supporting activities for English-language learners.

Reading Skills	Vocabulary Skills	Writing ▪ Grammar and Language Skills
• Find the main idea		
• Compare and contrast	• Clarify word meanings	• Write a comparison-contrast essay • Punctuate dialogue correctly
• Analyze comparison-and-contrast text structure		
• Distinguish fact from opinion	• Clarify word meanings by using examples	• Write a brief research report • Use comparative and superlative forms correctly
• Make a generalization	• Understand connotation and denotation	• Explain a theme • Avoid misplaced modifiers
• Identify images	• Complete word analogies	• Write a narrative
• Analyze flashbacks • Summarize a text	• Analyze shades of meaning	• Write a brief persuasive essay • Use commas in a series correctly

(continued)

Selection ▪ Feature	Literary Skills	Reading Skills
I'm Nobody! *by* Emily Dickinson ↓ *below grade level*	• Analyze similes and metaphors	
I Like to See It Lap the Miles *by* Emily Dickinson ↑ *above grade level*	• Analyze an extended metaphor	
I Am of the Earth *by* Anna Lee Walters ↓ *below grade level* **Early Song** *by* Gogisgi/Carroll Arnett ↓ *below grade level*	• Analyze personification	
Madam and the Rent Man *by* Langston Hughes ↔ *at grade level*	• Analyze tone	
Harlem Night Song *by* Langston Hughes ↔ *at grade level* **Winter Moon** *by* Langston Hughes ↔ *at grade level*	• Analyze imagery	
I Ask My Mother to Sing *by* Li-Young Lee ↔ *at grade level*	• Analyze a lyric poem • Analyze a sonnet	
Ode to Family Photographs *by* Gary Soto ↔ *at grade level*	• Analyze an ode	
Elements of Literature: The Sounds of Poetry *by* John Malcolm Brinnin	• Understand sounds of poetry, such as rhythm, rhyme, alliteration, onomatopoeia	
Father William *by* Lewis Carroll ↔ *at grade level* **Sarah Cynthia Sylvia Stout Would Not Take the Garbage Out** *by* Shel Silverstein ↔ *at grade level*	• Analyze humorous poems and exaggeration • Analyze rhythm and meter	
The Runaway *by* Robert Frost ↔ *at grade level*	• Analyze rhyme	
The Pasture *by* Robert Frost ↔ *at grade level* **A Minor Bird** *by* Robert Frost ↔ *at grade level*	• Analyze stanzas • Analyze couplets	• Read a poem

Vocabulary Skills	Writing ▪ Grammar and Language Skills
	• Write a letter to a poet
	• Write a poem
	• Respond to a quotation • Paraphrase a poem
	• Write dialogue • Read a poem aloud
	• Write a poem using imagery
	• Write a poem or description
	• Write an ode
	• Read a poem aloud
	• Write a poem • Prepare a choral reading
	• Imitate a poem • Read a poem aloud

(continued)

Scope and Sequence

Selection ▪ Feature	Literary Skills	Reading Skills
Names of Horses *by* Donald Hall ↑ *above grade level*	• Analyze free verse • Analyze an elegy	
maggie and milly and molly and may *by* E. E. Cummings ↑ *above grade level*	• Analyze exact and slant rhymes	
All in green went my love riding *by* E. E. Cummings ↑ *above grade level*	• Analyze the sounds of poetry	
Arithmetic *by* Carl Sandburg ↔ *at grade level*	• Analyze a catalog poem	
For Poets *by* Al Young ↔ *at grade level*	• Analyze an ars poetica • Analyze figures of speech	• Read a poem
Author Study: Sandra Cisneros **An Interview with Sandra Cisneros** *from* **The Infinite Mind** *by* Marit Haahr ↔ *at grade level* **Salvador Late or Early** *by* Sandra Cisneros ↔ *at grade level* **Chanclas** *by* Sandra Cisneros ↔ *at grade level* **Abuelito Who** *by* Sandra Cisneros ↔ *at grade level* **The Place Where Dreams Come From** *by* Sandra Cisneros ↔ *at grade level*	• Interpret a writer's message	• Make generalizations
No Questions Asked: **The Burning of Books** *by* Bertolt Brecht ↑ *above grade level*		
Writing Workshop: *Persuasive Writing: Supporting an Interpretation*		
Skills Review: *Literary Skills* *Vocabulary Skills* *Writing Skills*	• Analyze forms of prose • Analyze elements of poems	

Vocabulary Skills	Writing ▪ Grammar and Language Skills
	• Write an elegy
	• Write a poem • Write scientific descriptions
	• Write a catalog poem
	• Write a poem giving advice • Read a poem aloud
	• Write an interpretation • Write a poem or short story
	• Write an essay supporting an interpretation
• Use context clues	• Analyze persuasive writing

Selection ▪ Feature	Planning	Differentiating Instruction ▪ Lesson Plans with ELL Strategies and Practice	Reading ▪ Vocabulary
Elements of Literature: Understanding the Forms of Prose *by* Kylene Beers		• Holt Reading Solutions: Lesson Plans, pp. 177–178	• Holt Reading Solutions, pp. 177–178
Reading Skills and Strategies: Finding the Main Idea **A** *Good* **Reason to Look Up** *by* Shaquille O'Neal			
Amigo Brothers *by* Piri Thomas **Informational Text: Right Hook—Left Hook** *by* Joan Burditt	• One-Stop Planner with ExamView Test Generator • PowerNotes: The Short Story	• The Holt Reader, pp. 156–174 • Holt Adapted Reader, pp. 122–129 • Holt Reading Solutions: Lesson Plans, pp. 179–186 • Supporting Instruction in Spanish, p. 17 • Audio CD Library • Audio CD Library, Selections and Summaries in Spanish	• The Holt Reader, pp. 156–174 • Holt Adapted Reader, pp. 122–129 • Holt Reading Solutions, pp. 179–186 • Vocabulary Development, p. 19
from **Barrio Boy** *by* Ernesto Galarza	• One-Stop Planner with ExamView Test Generator • PowerNotes: Nonfiction	• Holt Adapted Reader, pp. 130–135 • Holt Reading Solutions: Lesson Plans, pp. 187–192 • Supporting Instruction in Spanish, p. 17 • Audio CD Library • Audio CD Library, Selections and Summaries in Spanish	• Holt Adapted Reader, pp. 130–135 • Holt Reading Solutions, pp. 187–192 • Vocabulary Development, p. 20
Song of the Trees *by* Mildred D. Taylor	• One-Stop Planner with ExamView Test Generator	• Holt Reading Solutions: Lesson Plans, pp. 193–198 • Supporting Instruction in Spanish, p. 18 • Audio CD Library • Audio CD Library, Selections and Summaries in Spanish	• Holt Reading Solutions, pp. 193–198 • Vocabulary Development, p. 21 • PowerNotes: Making Generalizations
Fish Cheeks *by* Amy Tan	• One-Stop Planner with ExamView Test Generator	• Holt Reading Solutions: Lesson Plans, pp. 199–204 • Supporting Instruction in Spanish, p. 18 • Audio CD Library • Audio CD Library, Selections and Summaries in Spanish	• Holt Reading Solutions, pp. 199–204 • Vocabulary Development, p. 22
A Mason-Dixon Memory *by* Clifton Davis **Informational Text: Buddies Bare Their Affection for III Classmate** *from the* Austin American-Statesman	• One-Stop Planner with ExamView Test Generator	• Holt Adapted Reader, pp. 136–147 • Holt Reading Solutions: Lesson Plans, pp. 205–212 • Supporting Instruction in Spanish, p. 19 • Audio CD Library • Audio CD Library, Selections and Summaries in Spanish	• Holt Adapted Reader, pp. 136–147 • Holt Reading Solutions, pp. 205–212 • Vocabulary Development, p. 23 • PowerNotes: Summarizing a Story
Elements of Literature: Painting with Words: The Elements of Poetry *by* John Malcolm Brinnin	• PowerNotes: Images in Poetry, Sound Effects in Poetry	• Holt Reading Solutions: Lesson Plans, pp. 213–214	• Holt Reading Solutions, pp. 213–214

Writing · Grammar and Language	Assessment
• Daily Language Activities • Language Handbook Worksheets, pp. 136–137	• Holt Assessment: Literature, Reading, and Vocabulary • One-Stop Planner with ExamView Test Generator • Holt Online Assessment
• Daily Language Activities • Language Handbook Worksheets, pp. 47–50	• Holt Assessment: Literature, Reading, and Vocabulary • One-Stop Planner with ExamView Test Generator • Holt Online Assessment
• Daily Language Activities • Language Handbook Worksheets, pp. 51–54	• Holt Assessment: Literature, Reading, and Vocabulary • One-Stop Planner with ExamView Test Generator • Holt Online Assessment
• Daily Language Activities	• Holt Assessment: Literature, Reading, and Vocabulary • One-Stop Planner with ExamView Test Generator • Holt Online Assessment
• Daily Language Activities • Language Handbook Worksheets, pp. 126–131	• Holt Assessment: Literature, Reading, and Vocabulary • One-Stop Planner with ExamView Test Generator • Holt Online Assessment

Technology

INTERNET

- go.hrw.com
- Holt Online Assessment
- Holt Online Essay Scoring
- Elements of Literature Online

MEDIA

- One-Stop Planner with ExamView Test Generator
- PowerNotes
- Audio CD Library
- Audio CD Library, Selections and Summaries in Spanish
- Visual Connections Videocassette Program, Segments 5 and 6
- Fine Art Transparencies, 7, 8, and 9

 Transparency   Video

 CD-ROM   Audio CD

(continued)

Selection ▪ Feature	Planning	Differentiating Instruction ▪ Lesson Plans with ELL Strategies and Practice	Reading ▪ Vocabulary
I'm Nobody! *by* Emily Dickinson	• One-Stop Planner with ExamView Test Generator	• The Holt Reader, pp. 175–178 • Holt Reading Solutions: Lesson Plans, pp. 215–216 • Supporting Instruction in Spanish, p. 20 • Audio CD Library • Audio CD Library, Selections and Summaries in Spanish	• The Holt Reader, pp. 175–178 • Holt Reading Solutions, pp. 215–216
I Like to See It Lap the Miles *by* Emily Dickinson	• One-Stop Planner with ExamView Test Generator	• Holt Reading Solutions: Lesson Plans, pp. 215–216 • Supporting Instruction in Spanish, p. 20 • Audio CD Library • Audio CD Library, Selections and Summaries in Spanish	• Holt Reading Solutions, pp. 215–216
I Am of the Earth *by* Anna Lee Walters **Early Song** *by* Gogisgi/Carroll Arnett	• One-Stop Planner with ExamView Test Generator • PowerNotes: Figures of Speech	• Holt Reading Solutions: Lesson Plans, pp. 217–222 • Supporting Instruction in Spanish, p. 20 • Audio CD Library • Audio CD Library, Selections and Summaries in Spanish	• Holt Reading Solutions, pp. 217–222
Madam and the Rent Man *by* Langston Hughes	• One-Stop Planner with ExamView Test Generator	• Holt Reading Solutions: Lesson Plans, pp. 223–224 • Supporting Instruction in Spanish, p. 21 • Audio CD Library • Audio CD Library, Selections and Summaries in Spanish	• Holt Reading Solutions, pp. 223–224
Harlem Night Song *by* Langston Hughes **Winter Moon** *by* Langston Hughes	• One-Stop Planner with ExamView Test Generator • PowerNotes: Images in Poetry	• Holt Reading Solutions: Lesson Plans, pp. 225–228 • Supporting Instruction in Spanish, p. 21 • Audio CD Library • Audio CD Library, Selections and Summaries in Spanish	• Holt Reading Solutions, pp. 225–228
I Ask My Mother to Sing *by* Li-Young Lee	• One-Stop Planner with ExamView Test Generator	• Holt Reading Solutions: Lesson Plans, pp. 229–232 • Supporting Instruction in Spanish, p. 21 • Audio CD Library • Audio CD Library, Selections and Summaries in Spanish	• Holt Reading Solutions, pp. 229–232
Ode to Family Photographs *by* Gary Soto	• One-Stop Planner with ExamView Test Generator	• Holt Reading Solutions: Lesson Plans, pp. 229–232 • Supporting Instruction in Spanish, p. 22 • Audio CD Library • Audio CD Library, Selections and Summaries in Spanish	• Holt Reading Solutions, pp. 229–232
Elements of Literature: The Sounds of Poetry *by* John Malcolm Brinnin	• PowerNotes: Sound Effects in Poetry	• Holt Reading Solutions: Lesson Plans, pp. 233–234	• Holt Reading Solutions, pp. 233–234

Writing ▪ Grammar and Language	Assessment
• Daily Language Activities	• Holt Assessment: Literature, Reading, and Vocabulary • One-Stop Planner with ExamView Test Generator • Holt Online Assessment
• Daily Language Activities	• Holt Assessment: Literature, Reading, and Vocabulary • One-Stop Planner with ExamView Test Generator • Holt Online Assessment
• Daily Language Activities	• Holt Assessment: Literature, Reading, and Vocabulary • One-Stop Planner with ExamView Test Generator • Holt Online Assessment
• Daily Language Activities	• Holt Assessment: Literature, Reading, and Vocabulary • One-Stop Planner with ExamView Test Generator • Holt Online Assessment
• Daily Language Activities	• Holt Assessment: Literature, Reading, and Vocabulary • One-Stop Planner with ExamView Test Generator • Holt Online Assessment
• Daily Language Activities	• Holt Assessment: Literature, Reading, and Vocabulary • One-Stop Planner with ExamView Test Generator • Holt Online Assessment
• Daily Language Activities	• Holt Assessment: Literature, Reading, and Vocabulary • One-Stop Planner with ExamView Test Generator • Holt Online Assessment

Technology

INTERNET

- go.hrw.com
- Holt Online Assessment
- Holt Online Essay Scoring
- Elements of Literature Online

MEDIA

- One-Stop Planner with ExamView Test Generator
- PowerNotes
- Audio CD Library
- Audio CD Library, Selections and Summaries in Spanish
- Visual Connections Videocassette Program, Segments 5 and 6
- Fine Art Transparencies, 7, 8, and 9

 Transparency   Video

 CD-ROM   Audio CD

(continued)

Selection ▪ Feature	Planning	Differentiating Instruction ▪ Lesson Plans with ELL Strategies and Practice	Reading ▪ Vocabulary
Father William *by* Lewis Carroll **Sarah Cynthia Sylvia Stout Would Not Take the Garbage Out** *by* Shel Silverstein	• One-Stop Planner with ExamView Test Generator	• The Holt Reader, pp. 179–183 • Holt Reading Solutions: Lesson Plans, pp. 235–238 • Supporting Instruction in Spanish, p. 22 • Audio CD Library • Audio CD Library, Selections and Summaries in Spanish	• The Holt Reader, pp. 179–183 • Holt Reading Solutions, pp. 235–238
The Runaway *by* Robert Frost	• One-Stop Planner with ExamView Test Generator	• Holt Reading Solutions: Lesson Plans, pp. 239–240 • Supporting Instruction in Spanish, p. 22 • Audio CD Library • Audio CD Library, Selections and Summaries in Spanish	• Holt Reading Solutions, pp. 239–240
The Pasture *by* Robert Frost **A Minor Bird** *by* Robert Frost	• One-Stop Planner with ExamView Test Generator	• Holt Reading Solutions: Lesson Plans, pp. 241–244 • Supporting Instruction in Spanish, p. 22 • Audio CD Library • Audio CD Library, Selections and Summaries in Spanish	• Holt Reading Solutions, pp. 241–244
Names of Horses *by* Donald Hall	• One-Stop Planner with ExamView Test Generator	• Holt Reading Solutions: Lesson Plans, pp. 245–246 • Supporting Instruction in Spanish, p. 23 • Audio CD Library • Audio CD Library, Selections and Summaries in Spanish	• Holt Reading Solutions, pp. 245–246
maggie and milly and molly and may *by* E. E. Cummings	• One-Stop Planner with ExamView Test Generator	• Holt Reading Solutions: Lesson Plans, pp. 247–251 • Supporting Instruction in Spanish, p. 23 • Audio CD Library • Audio CD Library, Selections and Summaries in Spanish	• Holt Reading Solutions, pp. 247–251
All in green went my love riding *by* E. E. Cummings	• One-Stop Planner with ExamView Test Generator	• Holt Reading Solutions: Lesson Plans, pp. 249–251 • Supporting Instruction in Spanish, p. 23 • Audio CD Library • Audio CD Library, Selections and Summaries in Spanish	• Holt Reading Solutions, pp. 247–251
Arithmetic *by* Carl Sandburg	• One-Stop Planner with ExamView Test Generator	• Holt Reading Solutions: Lesson Plans, pp. 252–255 • Supporting Instruction in Spanish, p. 24 • Audio CD Library • Audio CD Library, Selections and Summaries in Spanish	• Holt Reading Solutions, pp. 252–255
For Poets *by* Al Young	• One-Stop Planner with ExamView Test Generator	• Holt Reading Solutions: Lesson Plans, pp. 252–255 • Supporting Instruction in Spanish, p. 24 • Audio CD Library • Audio CD Library, Selections and Summaries in Spanish	• Holt Reading Solutions, pp. 252–255

Writing · Grammar and Language	Assessment
• Daily Language Activities	• Holt Assessment: Literature, Reading, and Vocabulary • One-Stop Planner with ExamView Test Generator • Holt Online Assessment
• Daily Language Activities	• Holt Assessment: Literature, Reading, and Vocabulary • One-Stop Planner with ExamView Test Generator • Holt Online Assessment
• Daily Language Activities	• Holt Assessment: Literature, Reading, and Vocabulary • One-Stop Planner with ExamView Test Generator • Holt Online Assessment
• Daily Language Activities	• Holt Assessment: Literature, Reading, and Vocabulary • One-Stop Planner with ExamView Test Generator • Holt Online Assessment
• Daily Language Activities	• Holt Assessment: Literature, Reading, and Vocabulary • One-Stop Planner with ExamView Test Generator • Holt Online Assessment
• Daily Language Activities	• Holt Assessment: Literature, Reading, and Vocabulary • One-Stop Planner with ExamView Test Generator • Holt Online Assessment
• Daily Language Activities	• Holt Assessment: Literature, Reading, and Vocabulary • One-Stop Planner with ExamView Test Generator • Holt Online Assessment
• Daily Language Activities	• Holt Assessment: Literature, Reading, and Vocabulary • One-Stop Planner with ExamView Test Generator • Holt Online Assessment

Technology

INTERNET

- go.hrw.com
- Holt Online Assessment
- Holt Online Essay Scoring
- Elements of Literature Online

MEDIA

- One-Stop Planner with ExamView Test Generator
- PowerNotes
- Audio CD Library
- Audio CD Library, Selections and Summaries in Spanish
- Visual Connections Videocassette Program, Segments 5 and 6
- Fine Art Transparencies, 7, 8, and 9

 Transparency   Video

 CD-ROM   Audio CD

(continued)

Selection ■ Feature	Planning	Differentiating Instruction ■ Lesson Plans with ELL Strategies and Practice	Reading ■ Vocabulary
Author Study: Sandra Cisneros **An Interview with Sandra Cisneros** *from* **The Infinite Mind** *by* Marit Haahr **Salvador Late or Early** *by* Sandra Cisneros **Chanclas** *by* Sandra Cisneros **Abuelito Who** *by* Sandra Cisneros **The Place Where Dreams Come From** *by* Sandra Cisneros		• Holt Reading Solutions: Lesson Plans, pp. 256–259 • The Holt Reader, pp. 186–190	• Holt Reading Solutions, pp. 256–259 • PowerNotes: Making Generalizations • The Holt Reader, pp. 186–190
No Questions Asked: The Burning of Books *by* Bertolt Brecht			
Writing Workshop: *Persuasive Writing: Supporting an Interpretation*	• One-Stop Planner with ExamView Test Generator	• Workshop Resources: Writing, Listening, and Speaking, pp. 45–55 • Family Involvement Activities in English and Spanish • Supporting Instruction in Spanish, p. 41	
Skills Review: *Literary Skills* *Vocabulary Skills* *Writing Skills*			

The Holt Reader

The Holt Reader is a consumable paperback book that can be used alone or to accompany *Elements of Literature*. It offers guided support throughout the reading process and encourages students to become active readers by circling, underlining, questioning, and jotting down responses as they read. *The Holt Reader* works well for homework, students who have missed class, additional instructional time, reteaching, and remediation.

Holt Reading Solutions (HRS)

Holt Reading Solutions pulls together reading resources in the *Elements of Literature* program to create a powerful tool for intervention and whole-class instruction. *HRS* includes diagnostic assessment tools, lesson plans for English-language learners and special education students, adaptations of selected reading selections, vocabulary and comprehension worksheets, information on phonics and decoding, and additional instruction and practice in remedial reading skills.

Writing · Grammar and Language	Assessment
• Workshop Resources: Writing, Listening, and Speaking, pp. 45–55 • Language Handbook Worksheets • Daily Language Activities	• Holt Assessment: Literature, Reading, and Vocabulary • One-Stop Planner with ExamView Test Generator • Holt Online Assessment • Holt Online Essay Scoring
	• Holt Assessment: Literature, Reading, and Vocabulary • One-Stop Planner with ExamView Test Generator • Holt Online Assessment

Technology

INTERNET

- go.hrw.com
- Holt Online Assessment
- Holt Online Essay Scoring
- Elements of Literature Online

MEDIA

 • One-Stop Planner with ExamView Test Generator

 • PowerNotes

 • Audio CD Library

 • Audio CD Library, Selections and Summaries in Spanish

• Visual Connections Videocassette Program, Segments 5 and 6

• Fine Art Transparencies, 7, 8, and 9

 Transparency   Video

 CD-ROM   Audio CD

One-Stop Planner with ExamView Test Generator

The *One-Stop Planner* CD-ROM planning software contains print-based teaching resources, clips from the video program, and valuable assessment tools. The *One-Stop Planner* resources are presented in easy-to-follow, point-and-click menu formats. To preview resources or print out worksheets and tests, you simply make a selection and click.

One-Stop Planner CD-ROM

Collection 5

Grade-Level Skills

■ **Literary Skills**
Analyze the characteristics of different forms of prose and poetry.

■ **Reading Skills**
Find the main idea.

■ **Vocabulary Skills**
Clarify word meanings by using definitions, examples, restatements, and contrasts.

Review Skills

■ **Literary Skills**
Analyze different forms of fiction, and describe the main characteristics of each form.

■ **Reading Skills**
Analyze text structures, including comparison and contrast.

■ **Vocabulary Skills**
Understand and explain shades of meaning in related words.

Upcoming Skills

■ **Reading Skills**
Determine whether a summary is an accurate reflection of an original text.

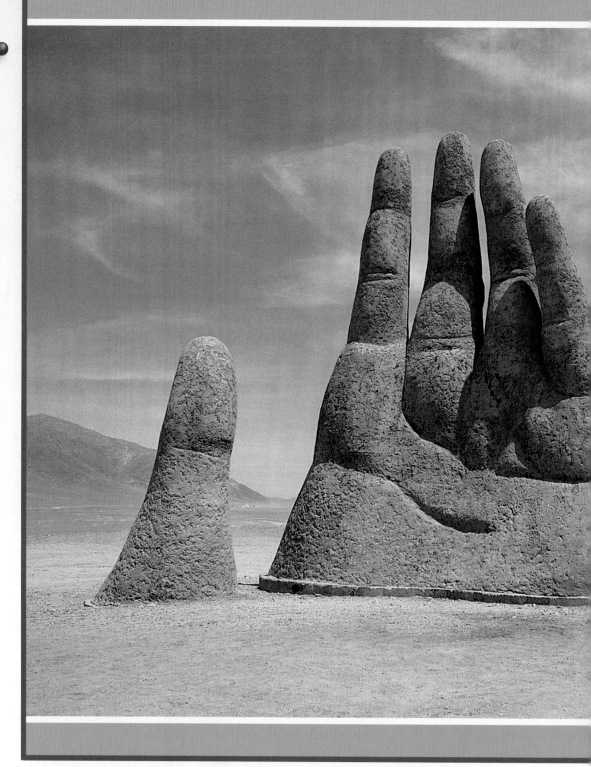

COLLECTION 5 RESOURCES: READING

Planning
■ *One-Stop Planner* CD-ROM with ExamView Test Generator

Differentiating Instruction
■ *The Holt Reader*
■ *Holt Adapted Reader*
■ *Holt Reading Solutions*
■ *Family Involvement Activities in English and Spanish*

■ *Supporting Instruction in Spanish*
■ *Audio CD Library*
■ *Audio CD Library, Selections and Summaries in Spanish*

Vocabulary
■ *Vocabulary Development*

Grammar and Language
■ *Language Handbook Worksheets*
■ *Daily Language Activities*

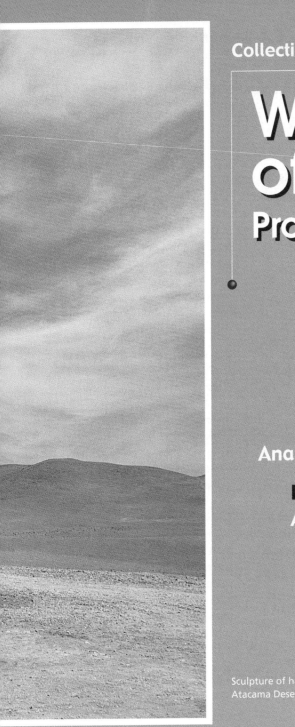

Collection 5

Worlds of Words:
Prose and Poetry

Literary Focus:
Analyzing Prose and Poetry

Informational Focus:
Analyzing Main Idea

INTERNET
Collection Resources
Keyword: LE5 7-5

477

Sculpture of hand,
Atacama Desert, Chile.

Assessment
■ *Holt Assessment: Literature, Reading, and Vocabulary*
■ *One-Stop Planner* CD-ROM with ExamView Test Generator
■ *Holt Online Assessment*

Internet
■ go.hrw.com (Keyword: LE5 7-5)
■ *Elements of Literature Online*

Media
■ *Audio CD Library*
■ *Audio CD Library, Selections and Summaries in Spanish*
■ *Fine Art Transparencies*
■ *Visual Connections Videocassette Program*
■ *PowerNotes*

INTRODUCING THE COLLECTION

Theme: Worlds of words.
Writing can be funny or factual, fantastic or scientific, tender or tragic. It can take many forms—letters, diaries, ballads, song lyrics, and reports, to name just a few. Students will discover the rich variety of choices writers can use to express themselves.

Analyzing prose and poetry.
The collection presents a variety of forms of poetry and prose. As students read the prose selections in this collection, they will learn how to tell whether a narrative is an autobiography, a short story, or a novella and how to recognize such nonfiction forms as the essay, news article, and science report. They will also come to understand the important forms and elements of poetry.

Analyzing main idea. As students read informational pieces tied to the literature in the collection, they will learn how to find the main idea of a piece by identifying and summarizing key details.

VIEWING THE ART

The Atacama Desert, part of the Pacific shoreline of South America, is one of the driest regions in the world. In some parts of the desert, there has never been a recorded instance of rain. In the late nineteenth century, Chile battled Peru and Bolivia for control of the desert, which is a rich source of sodium nitrate deposits. These deposits provided the Chilean government with much of its wealth during the early part of the twentieth century.

Activity. Ask students to consider why the artist may have chosen this location for his hand sculpture. Is he trying to express hope, desperation, or some other emotion? Ask volunteers to share their thoughts with the class.

Grade-Level Skills

■ **Literary Skills**
Understand the characteristics of different forms of prose, including novels, novellas, short stories, and essays.

Upcoming Skills

■ **Literary Skills**
Analyze the characteristics of different forms of dramatic literature, including comedy, tragedy, and dramatic monologue.

Elements of Literature: Forms of Prose

Review the terms *fiction* and *non-fiction.* Then, ask students to volunteer titles of what they have been reading lately—classroom assignments as well as outside reading. Write the titles on the chalkboard, and ask students to identify whether each title is fiction or nonfiction. If students can correctly classify each title, ask them to identify the more specific form of prose the title is—for example, short story, scientific writing, mystery story, or math word problem. This activity will show students that there are many different forms of prose.

Elements of Literature
Reading Like a Wolf *by* Kylene Beers
UNDERSTANDING THE FORMS OF PROSE

A student once asked what I meant when I said his essay was really a short story. "What's the difference?" he wanted to know. "And," he continued, "what does it matter?"

Knowing the Difference Makes a Difference

His question was a good one. Why does knowing the difference between those types of prose make a difference? Well, it's something like knowing the difference in sports terms. If your coach says the team you're playing against uses a one-on-one defense instead of a zone defense, you know what to expect when you hit the basketball court.

Understanding the type of prose you're reading helps you anticipate what you'll find in the text. Once you know that what you are reading is a short story, for example, you'll be expecting characters, conflict, and a theme—you won't be looking for personal opinions or historical accuracy.

You Speak in Prose

You might think of **prose** as everything that isn't poetry. In fact, you've been speaking prose all your life. You also read prose every day—in your textbooks, in novels, in magazines, on the Web, in newspapers, in the notes you pass in the halls, and in the e-mails

you receive. You read each type of prose differently. You read a note from your best friend in one way, and you read the chapter in your science book another way.

Obviously prose covers a lot of ground. It can be generally divided into **fiction**—made-up stories—and **nonfiction,** which relates facts about real people, places, things, and events. Let's look at the different forms that fiction and nonfiction can take.

Fiction: Imagined Events and Characters

A **short story** is just what it sounds like: a short work of **fiction** with a few characters who move through a series of events (the plot) and work through a conflict, which leads to a climax and a resolution.

If all that happens in five to twenty pages, you have a short story. If you find yourself looking at one hundred pages or more, then you've left the short story and headed straight into a **novel.** In a novel you meet lots of characters, probably see subplots unfold within the larger plot, explore many themes, and encounter many conflicts.

If one hundred pages is too long and twenty is too short, then you've got a **novella,** which is simply a short novel.

INTERNET
More About Genres
Keyword: LE5 7-5

Literary Skills
Understand forms of prose.

478   Collection 5 / Worlds of Words: Prose and Poetry

DIFFERENTIATING INSTRUCTION

Learners Having Difficulty
If students are having trouble filling out a prose chart, meet with them individually and go over the differences between essay and short story, novel and novella, or whichever categories are causing confusion.

English-Language Learners
Have students use good unabridged dictionaries to find the origins of the

names for the forms of prose mentioned in this essay. For instance, students will find that the word *fiction* is from the Latin verb *fingere,* meaning "to invent, to make up." This information will help them remember that fiction consists of made-up stories, while nonfiction is the opposite. Students can make glossaries of these terms and keep them in their notebooks for reference.

Nonfiction: Based on Fact

An **essay** is a short piece of prose that discusses a limited topic. Some people write short personal essays about simple things, like eating an ice-cream cone or taking a dog for a walk. Others write longer essays about complex issues, such as freedom, respect, and justice.

Some nonfiction topics are just too big for a short form like the essay. You might read about an Olympic athlete in a magazine article, for example, but if you really wanted to know the whole story of her life, you'd look at a book-length **biography.**

"Is It True?"

Sometimes writers use real-life events in their fiction. Gary Paulsen explains in an essay that he's really been attacked by moose.

When I wrote of the moose attack in *Hatchet* and again in *Brian's Winter,* I used the events from my life in the story. I wrote of what the moose attacks were like. But when it was really happening to me, I didn't think, oh man, this is great, I'm getting creamed by a moose, this will be wonderful to write about in my next book. I just used the memory later in the context of the story.

"Read Like a Wolf Eats"

Whatever type of prose you enjoy the most, remember the important thing is to read. Here's what Gary Paulsen says:

The most, *most* important thing is to read. Read all the time; read when they tell you not to read, read what they tell you not to read, read with a flashlight under the covers, read on the bus, standing on the corner, waiting for a friend, in the dentist's waiting room. Read every minute that you can. Read like a wolf eats. Read.

Practice

To show that you know more about prose than you think you do, work with a partner to fill out a prose chart like the following one. First, copy the chart on a separate piece of paper. Then, think of titles that are examples of each kind of prose. (Notice that there are more types of prose here than we just discussed. You could name even more types if you looked in a bookstore.) You might want to prepare an illustrated "prose group" for your classroom.

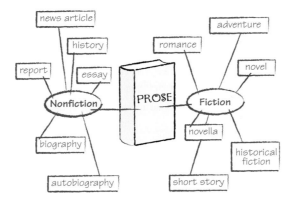

Practice

Go over students' charts with them to be sure they have correctly distinguished between the different forms of prose. You may wish to encourage students to choose works from the class chart for outside or extra-credit reading. [Possible responses: Fiction: adventure—*Treasure Island;* romance—*Sarah, Plain and Tall;* historical fiction—*The Witch of Blackbird Pond;* novella—*Call It Courage;* short story—"Rikki-tikki-tavi"; novel—*The Yearling. Nonfiction:* essay—"Names/Nombres"; history—*Buffalo Hunt;* autobiography—*Barrio Boy;* biography—*Martin Luther King, Jr.*]

Apply

As homework, have students take a walk through a local bookstore or library. Have them note that the bookstore or library is organized by the form of the text—fiction is shelved separately from nonfiction, and the nonfiction is divided into different subject areas, such as history, art, biography, self-help, and so on. Ask students to explain why the books are organized in this way. [Possible responses: Readers are aware of different forms of prose, and these differences are important to them when they choose a book. Books are organized to make it easy for readers to browse and locate what they are interested in.]

HOMEWORK

Advanced Learners
Acceleration. Help students discuss how the same topic might be addressed in different prose forms.
Activity. Have students choose any prose work they have recently read on their own. Each student can write a literary critique that identifies the form of prose of this work, analyzes the form's relationship to the work's overall theme, and discusses how the work might have been different if it had been written in a different form of prose.

Grade-Level Skills
■ **Reading Skills**
Find the main idea.

OVERVIEW

Use. Finding the main idea is especially helpful with informational texts and texts that communicate a powerful message. Ask students to keep track of what they learn about Shaquille O'Neal as they read "A *Good* Reason to Look Up." Then, have them use the facts they learn to find the main idea of the article. (Remind students that main ideas should be expressed in complete sentences.) In addition to the nonfiction selections in Collection 5, "The Power of Music" in Collection 6 and "Three Responses to Literature" in Collection 7 offer students an opportunity to practice finding the main idea.

Summary ⬇ *below grade level*

When he was in high school, Shaquille O'Neal was uncomfortable about his exceptional height. To divert his peers' attention, he played jokes and pranks on his classmates. But O'Neal's parents did not approve of their son's behavior. They encouraged him to follow the Golden Rule— to treat others as he would like to be treated. O'Neal began to follow his parents' advice by using his position as a leading basketball player to set a good example. O'Neal admits that he still makes mistakes but says he keeps looking for ways to set a good example for others.

Reading Skills and Strategies

Finding the Main Idea
by Kylene Beers

Being an Active Reader

While visiting a first-grade classroom during reading time, I watched one boy bounce in his chair as he looked at a storybook. "What are you doing?" I asked. "My teacher said that good readers are active readers, so I'm being active," he replied. While I was sure the teacher had told him that, I was just as sure the activity she had in mind involved thinking rather than bouncing. Good readers *are* active readers, and one important reading activity is finding the main idea.

What the Main Idea *Isn't*

Sometimes figuring out what something *is* can be easier if you start by defining what it *isn't*. The main idea is *not* the plot. It is *not* the theme. It is *not* the topic. It is also *not* a term you use when discussing fiction.

What the Main Idea *Is*

Main idea *is* a term we use when discussing nonfiction. The main idea of a text *is* the idea that is central to the entire text (not just to part of the text). Sometimes the main idea is stated directly; other times it isn't. (If you are talking about fiction, the term for the central idea is *theme*.)

SKILLS FOCUS

Reading Skills
Find the main idea.

As you read the selection on page 481, make a list of what you learn. At the end of the selection, you'll see how to use your list to help you figure out the main idea.

A Model for Finding the Main Idea

Look at the paragraph below. The **topic** is "dogs." What is the **main idea**? (The main idea should be stated in a full sentence.)

> Dogs are very smart animals. You can train them to do many things. They are also friendly and want to be with people and other dogs. They are loyal and quickly forgive you if you forget to play with them for a day. Because of these reasons, dogs are great pets.

The main idea *isn't* that dogs are intelligent, because that is not what the whole paragraph is about.

By the third sentence, you are learning a lot about dogs.

The final sentence reveals the main idea.

DIFFERENTIATING INSTRUCTION

Learners Having Difficulty
Some students may have difficulty identifying the main idea of each paragraph. Work with these students in groups. Have one student read a paragraph aloud. Then, have the student complete this sentence: "That paragraph was about . . ." Have the next student turn the sentence into an "Is the selection *all* about . . . ?" question. Finally, have another student answer the question.

Repeat with the other paragraphs until a student answers yes.

English-Language Learners
Students may not be familiar with the idiom *look up to*. Explain that looking up to someone is admiring him or her. Point out that the phrase applies literally in O'Neal's case— people have to crane their necks to see his face—but that he works hard to make the phrase apply in a figurative sense, too.

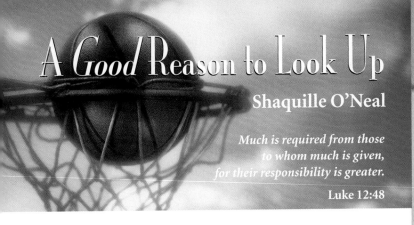

A Good Reason to Look Up

Shaquille O'Neal

*Much is required from those
to whom much is given,
for their responsibility is greater.*

Luke 12:48

Using the Strategy

When I was in junior high school, what my friends thought of me was real important to me. During those years I grew much taller than most of my peers. Being so tall made me feel uncomfortable. In order to keep the focus off of me and my unusual height, I went along with the crowd who would play practical jokes on other kids at school. Being one of the class clowns gave me a way to make sure that the jokes were directed at others, and not at me. ❶

I would pull all kinds of pranks that were hurtful, and sometimes even harmful, to others. Once before gym class, my friends and I put Icy Hot in the gym shorts of one of the kids on the basketball team. Not only was he terribly embarrassed, but he also had to go to the school nurse's office. I thought it was going to be funny, but it ended up that no one thought it was—least of all my father. ❷

My parents didn't always think that my behavior was funny. They reminded me about The Golden Rule: to treat others as I would like to be treated. Many times, I was disciplined for the hurtful way that I was treating others. What I was doing was hurting other kids, and in turn hurting my reputation as someone to be looked up to. My friends were looking up to me because I was tall, but what did they see? ❸

My parents wanted me to be a leader who was a good example to others—to be a decent human being. They taught me to set my own goals, and to do the best at everything that I set out to do. During the lectures I got from my father, he told me over and over again to be the leader that I was meant to be—to be a big man in my heart and actions, as well as in my body. I had to question myself whether or not it was important to be the kind of leader and person my father believed I was inside. I knew in my heart that he was right. So I tried my best to follow my father's advice. ❹

IDENTIFY

❶ Notice the pronoun *I* in the first sentence. This is a first-person account. To find out who the *I* is, check the name of the writer. What have you learned about the writer at this point?

Ⓐ

INFER

❷ This paragraph gives you a specific example of a prank O'Neal pulled. Why do you think O'Neal remembers this specific prank?

Ⓑ

IDENTIFY

❸ O'Neal says that while his pranks were hurting others, they also hurt himself. How did his actions hurt himself?

Ⓓ

INTERPRET

❹ What do you learn about O'Neal's father in this paragraph? What lessons did his father teach O'Neal?

Ⓔ

Ⓒ

A *Good* Reason to Look Up **481**

PRETEACHING

Selection Starter

Motivate. Invite students to share what they know about Shaquille O'Neal. List their responses on the chalkboard. Then, ask students whether they think O'Neal is an admirable person. Encourage students to support their opinions with evidence from the list they've created.

DIRECT TEACHING

Ⓐ Reading Skills and Strategies

Identify. [Possible response to question 1: Shaquille O'Neal is the writer. He was a very tall kid. He played jokes on others to divert attention from himself.]

Ⓑ Reading Skills and Strategies

Infer. [Possible responses to question 2: O'Neal remembers this prank probably because it hurt someone. He remembers it because his father was unhappy with him.]

Ⓒ Reading Skills and Strategies

❓ **Find the main idea.** What do you learn about O'Neal's parents in this paragraph? [Possible response: O'Neal's parents wanted him to treat others as he would like to be treated.]

Ⓓ Reading Skills and Strategies

Identify. [Possible response to question 3: O'Neal's actions hurt his reputation.]

Ⓔ Reading Skills and Strategies

Interpret. [Possible responses to question 4: You learn that O'Neal's father had high standards and expectations. His father taught him to be a leader, to set his own goals, and to do his best at everything he set out to do.]

Other words or phrases that may need clarification include these:
- *class clown*—student known for telling jokes and playing pranks
- *Icy Hot*—ointment that gives the sensation of heat, used to treat sore or cramped muscles
- *to be a big man in my heart and actions*—to have a kind, giving heart and to act accordingly

Advanced Learners

Enrichment. Use the following activity with advanced learners to reinforce and extend the main idea of O'Neal's essay.

Activity. Invite students to write a personal essay modeled on O'Neal's. Have them think of experiences they've had that helped them become better people. Then, have them write about one of these events. Tell students to explain how the event helped shape who they are today.

A Reading Skills and Strategies

? Find the main idea. What is the main idea of the fifth paragraph? [Possible response: When O'Neal concentrated on basketball, he also took on the responsibility of trying to set a good example for others.]

B Reading Skills and Strategies

Find the main idea. [Possible response to question 5: He is talking about the kind of person he is today.]

C Reading Skills and Strategies

Find the main idea. [Possible response to question 6: The word *good* is in italics for emphasis; O'Neal's father is stating that O'Neal should give people a reason to look up to him other than his height. O'Neal is a good leader today because of the advice his father gave him when he was young.]

Meet the Writer

Today, Los Angeles Laker Shaquille Rashaun O'Neal is a star of the basketball scene, but as a child, he was something of a loner. O'Neal and his three siblings grew up on Army bases in the United States and abroad. Always the "new kid," O'Neal had a hard time making friends, and he was especially self-conscious about his height. Once he grew into his body, however, he made his high school's basketball team, and his confidence blossomed. Today, Shaq is known not only for his on-court prowess but for his five rap albums and his appearances on Hollywood's silver screen.

FIND THE MAIN IDEA

5 In this paragraph, O'Neal is no longer telling about what happened to him in junior high. What is he now talking about?

FIND THE MAIN IDEA

6 Why do you think the word *good* is written in italics? What have you learned about why Shaq O'Neal is a good leader today?

A Once I focused on being the best that I could be at basketball and became a leader in the game, I took my responsibility to set a good example more seriously. I sometimes have to stop and think before I act, and I make mistakes occasionally—everyone is human. But I continue to look for opportunities where I can make a difference, and to set a good example because of my father's advice. I now pass it on to you. **5**

"Be a leader, Shaq, not a follower. Since people already have to look up to you, give them a *good* reason to do so." **6**

Meet the Writer

Shaquille O'Neal

"Books Can Take You Anywhere"

Shaquille O'Neal (1972–), also known as Shaq, is one of the most popular players in the National Basketball Association (NBA). He also has the honor of being named one of the NBA's fifty greatest players.

At 7'1", O'Neal's size alone could be intimidating. That size combined with his athletic skill have made him a powerful center for the Los Angeles Lakers.

Basketball isn't O'Neal's only love. He

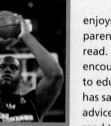

enjoys reading and says his parents motivated him to read. "My parents encouraged me to read and to educate myself," O'Neal has said. "Following their advice, I've always tried to read to better myself."

As a National Advisory Council member of Reading Is Fundamental, an organization that promotes child literacy, O'Neal shares his parents' message with young people. "Books can take you anywhere you want to go," Shaq says. "Follow your dreams and keep reading."

FAMILY/COMMUNITY ACTIVITY

In this essay, O'Neal reflects on important lessons his parents taught him. One of the most important of these is the Bible's Golden Rule—that people should treat others the way they themselves want to be treated. Encourage students to read O'Neal's essay to a parent or another caregiver and then ask the adult to share his or her own Golden Rule. What guiding idea has helped him or her become the person of today?

Practice the Strategy

Finding the Main Idea
PRACTICE 1

Is this selection all about _____?
When it is not stated directly, you can find the main idea of a selection by first identifying the topic and then thinking about what you learned as you read the selection. Next, you take each item on your list and ask yourself, "Is this selection all about _____?" The important word in this question is *all*. Be sure that *all* of the selection is about the item. Once you can answer yes to a question, you're close to figuring out the main idea.

To see how this strategy works, go back to page 480, and re-read the paragraph about the dogs. What did you learn about dogs? You learned they are intelligent, friendly, loyal, and forgiving and they make good pets. Now, ask yourself the "Is this selection all about _____?" question for each of these items:

- Is it all about how dogs are intelligent?
- Is it all about how dogs are friendly?
- Is it all about how dogs are loyal?
- Is it all about how dogs are forgiving?
- Is it all about how dogs make good pets?

The only question you can answer yes to is the last one, because it is the only item that applies to the entire paragraph. You can now use that question to state the main idea. You simply turn the question into a statement: "The main idea of this selection is that dogs make good pets."

Applying the Strategy
PRACTICE 2

Now, try this strategy to find the **main idea** of "A *Good* Reason to Look Up." Here are some questions you might ask yourself about this selection:

- Is this selection all about being tall?
- Is it all about being a prankster?
- Is it all about what his parents wanted O'Neal to be?
- Is it all about how O'Neal became a leader?

What else did you learn? Be sure to ask the "Is this selection all about _____?" question for each thing you learned. When you can answer yes to a question, turn the question into a statement, and you have found the main idea. What is it?

You can use this strategy to find the **main idea** of informational texts in this collection and throughout the book. Just ask yourself, "Is this selection *all* about _____?"

> **Strategy Tip**
> To figure out the **main idea,** re-read the title and the first and last paragraphs. Often something in the title and the first and last paragraphs will give you hints. If there is only one paragraph, read the first and last sentences carefully.

SKILLS FOCUS

Reading Skills
Find the main idea.

Practice the Strategy
In this feature, students practice finding the main idea of an essay by asking "Is it all about . . . ?" questions and by turning one of the questions into a statement.

Strategy Tip
Before students work on identifying the main idea of the essay, remind them that a topic is the subject of a work and can often be stated in one or two words. The main idea, on the other hand, must be expressed in a sentence.

Strategy Tip
In Applying the Strategy, students may have trouble turning one of the "Is it all about . . . ?" questions into a statement. If so, focus their attention on the fourth bulleted question. Help them convert the question into a statement by providing this stem: "O'Neal became a leader by . . . ."

PRACTICE 2

Possible answer: O'Neal became a leader by listening to his parents' advice.

SKILLS FOCUS
pp. 484–495

Grade-Level Skills

■ **Literary Skills**
Understand characteristics of different forms of prose, including the short story.

■ **Reading Skills**
Analyze text structures, including comparison and contrast.

Review Skills

■ **Literary Skills**
Analyze the main conflict of the plot and the way it is resolved.

Summary ↔ *at grade level*

Seventeen-year-old best friends Antonio Cruz and Felix Vargas both dream of becoming lightweight boxing champion of the world. They train together until they find out that they will meet in the ring to determine who will fight in a championship tournament. They pledge to fight to win and agree not to meet until the big night, a week away. Then, before a roaring crowd, the boys trade punishing blows for three furious rounds. In the end, both are still standing. They rush to embrace and leave the ring arm in arm, not waiting to hear who won.

Before You Read The Short Story

Amigo Brothers

Make the Connection

Quickwrite

Conflicts can arise when friends take different sides in a competition. In a group, create a list titled "Rules for Competing Against a Friend."

Literary Focus

The Short Story

A short work of fiction, usually around five to twenty pages, is called a **short story.** (Sometimes a story that's even shorter is called a **short-short story.**) Short stories pack a lot of punch into a few pages. Whatever happens, happens quickly. We meet the **main characters,** get involved in their **problems,** sort out the **complications,** and move speedily to a **climax** and a **resolution.** A good short story can pack a life into a few pages.

Internal and External Conflict

In the story that follows, two best friends competing for a prize must fight each other in a boxing ring. This fight is a perfect example of an **external conflict.** The boys are supposed to knock each other out. Each boy also struggles with an **internal conflict:** How can he do his best without hurting and possibly even losing his closest friend?

go.hrw.com
INTERNET
Vocabulary Activity
Keyword: LE5 7-5

SKILLS FOCUS

Literary Skills Understand forms of prose: the short story; understand internal and external conflict.

Reading Skills Understand comparison and contrast.

Reading Skills

Comparison and Contrast: Finding Similarities and Differences

Piri Thomas begins his story by contrasting the two best friends: "Antonio was fair, lean, and lanky, while Felix was dark, short, and husky." A **comparison** points out similarities between things; a **contrast** points out differences. After you read the story, go back over it, and use a Venn diagram to help identify the ways in which Felix and Antonio are alike and different. Write their likenesses in the space where the circles overlap.

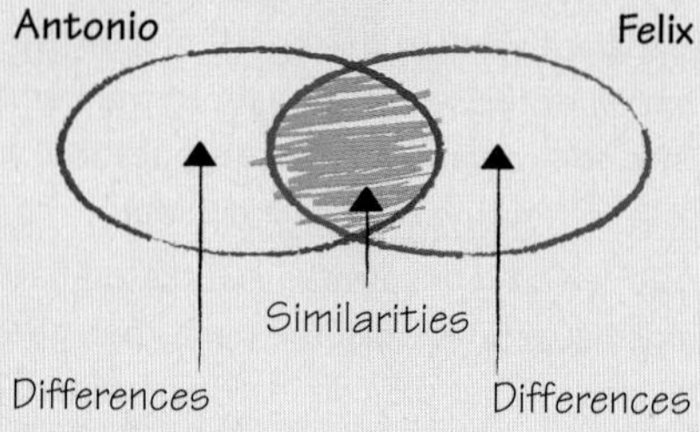

Vocabulary Development

Here are some words to give you a fighting chance:

bouts (bouts) *n.:* matches; contests. *Both boxers had won many bouts.*

pensively (pen′siv·lē) *adv.:* thoughtfully. *Felix nodded pensively as he rested.*

torrent (tôr′ənt) *n.:* flood or rush. *A torrent of emotion left him close to tears.*

dispelled (di·speld′) *v.:* driven away. *All doubt was dispelled the moment Tony made up his mind.*

frenzied (fren′zēd) *adj.:* wild. *The audience's reaction was as frenzied as the battle in the ring.*

RESOURCES: READING

Planning
- *One-Stop Planner* CD-ROM with ExamView Test Generator

Differentiating Instruction
- *The Holt Reader*
- *Holt Adapted Reader*
- *Holt Reading Solutions*
- *Supporting Instruction in Spanish*
- *Audio CD Library*
- *Audio CD Library, Selections and Summaries in Spanish*

Vocabulary
- *Vocabulary Development*

Grammar and Language
- *Language Handbook Worksheets*
- *Daily Language Activities*

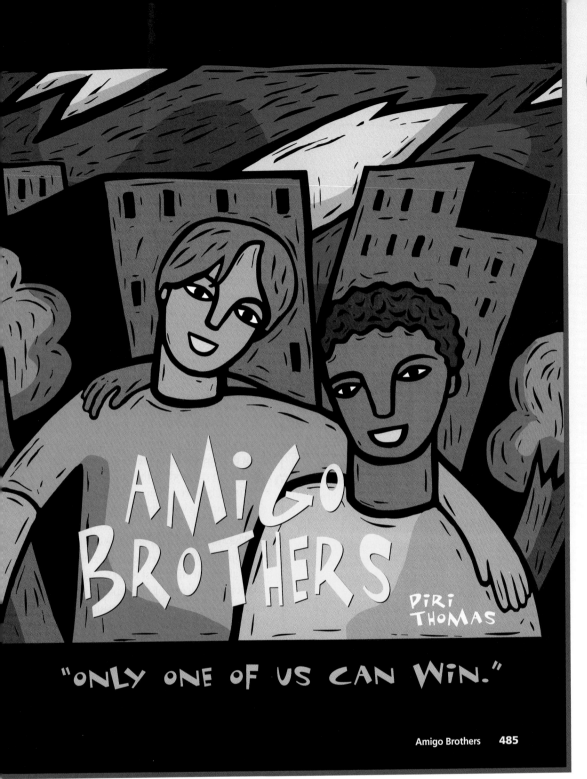

AMIGO BROTHERS

DiRi ThoMAS

"ONLY ONE OF US CAN WIN."

Amigo Brothers   485

Selection Starter

Motivate. Have students think about times when they have competed against friends. Were these situations difficult? Why or why not? How did the competition affect the friendship? Have students discuss these questions in groups and then complete the Quickwrite activity.

Preview Vocabulary

Have students complete each of the following sentences with the correct Vocabulary word.

1. Members of our boxing team fought in three _____. [bouts]
2. After a bloody battle, Angelo sat quietly and _____, wondering whether to fight again. [pensively]
3. A _____ of applause greeted the winner. [torrent]
4. His bruising blows quickly _____ the notion that he couldn't win. [dispelled]
5. The _____ crowd cheered wildly when their favorite knocked out his opponent. [frenzied]

Assign the Reading

You may wish to have students read "Amigo Brothers" together, through "Both fighters had a lot of psyching up to do before the big fight" (p. 488). Most readers can finish the story on their own and answer the Reading Check questions as homework. Readers who have difficulty may complete the story in a group.

HOMEWORK

Assessment
- *Holt Assessment: Literature, Reading, and Vocabulary*
- *One-Stop Planner* CD-ROM with ExamView Test Generator
- *Holt Online Assessment*

Internet
- go.hrw.com (Keyword: LE5 7-5)
- *Elements of Literature Online*

Media
- *Audio CD Library*
- *Audio CD Library, Selections and Summaries in Spanish*

A Reading Skills

? Compare and contrast. How are the boys similar? How are they different? [Possible responses: They are similar in age, background, friendship, dreams, and ambitions. They are different in their appearance.]

B Literary Focus

Internal conflict. Describe the internal conflicts that may result from both boys wanting the same thing. [Since there can't be two champions, the boys will have to balance their friendship for one another against their own desire to succeed.]

C Vocabulary Development

? Clarify word meanings. What is the difference between a boxer and a slugger? How do you know? [Possible responses: Boxers tend to be tall, slim, and quick—tactical fighters. Sluggers tend to be compact and strong—powerful hitters. The writer suggests that each boy's size and build makes him a certain kind of fighter.]

D Literary Focus

? The short story. Remind students that a short story packs a lot into a few pages. How do you know at this point that "Amigo Brothers" is a short story? [Possible response: In the very first page of the story, the two main characters and their major conflict have been introduced.]

Background
Literature and Social Studies

This story is about two friends (*amigos* in Spanish) living on the Lower East Side of New York City. Many boys from the Lower East Side have dreamed of building a better life by winning the New York Golden Gloves, a tournament started in 1927 by Paul Gallico, a newspaper writer. This tournament marks an amateur's entry into the world of big-time boxing.

A ntonio Cruz and Felix Vargas were both seventeen years old. They were so together in friendship that they felt themselves to be brothers. They had known each other since childhood, growing up on the Lower East Side of Manhattan in the same tenement[1] building on Fifth Street between Avenue A and Avenue B.

Antonio was fair, lean, and lanky, while Felix was dark, short, and husky. Antonio's hair was always falling over his eyes, while Felix wore his black hair in a natural Afro style.

Each youngster had a dream of someday becoming lightweight champion of the world. Every chance they had, the boys worked out, sometimes at the Boys' Club on 10th Street and Avenue A and sometimes at the pro's gym on 14th Street. Early morning sunrises would find them running along the East River Drive, wrapped in sweat shirts, short towels around their necks, and handkerchiefs Apache style around their foreheads.

While some youngsters were into street negatives, Antonio and Felix slept, ate, rapped, and dreamt positive. Between them, they had a collection of *Fight* magazines second to none, plus a scrapbook filled with torn tickets to every boxing match they had ever attended, and some clippings of their own. If asked a question about any given fighter, they would immediately zip out from their memory banks divisions, weights, records of fights, knockouts, technical knockouts, and draws or losses.

Each had fought many bouts representing their community and had won two gold-plated medals plus a silver and bronze medallion. The difference was in their style. Antonio's lean form and long reach made him the better boxer, while Felix's short and muscular frame made him the better slugger. Whenever they had met in the ring for sparring sessions,[2] it had always been hot and heavy.

Now, after a series of elimination bouts, they had been informed that they were to meet each other in the division finals that were scheduled for the seventh of August, two weeks away—the winner to represent the Boys' Club in the Golden Gloves Championship Tournament.

The two boys continued to run together along the East River Drive. But even when joking with each other, they both sensed a wall rising between them.

One morning less than a week before their bout, they met as usual for their daily workout. They fooled around with a few jabs at the air, slapped skin, and then took off, running lightly along the dirty East River's edge.

Antonio glanced at Felix, who kept his eyes purposely straight ahead, pausing from time to time to do some fancy leg work

---

1. **tenement** *n.* used as *adj.*: apartment. Tenement buildings are often cheaply built and poorly maintained.

2. **sparring sessions:** practice matches in which boxers use light punches.

Vocabulary
bouts (bouts) *n.*: matches; contests.

DIFFERENTIATING INSTRUCTION

Learners Having Difficulty
Invite learners having difficulty to read "Amigo Brothers" in interactive format in *The Holt Reader* and to use the sidenotes as aids to understanding the selection. The interactive version provides additional instruction, practice, and assessment of the literary skill taught in the Student Edition. Monitor students' responses to the selection, and correct any misconceptions that arise.

English-Language Learners
This story is full of boxing terms that are likely to be unfamiliar. Enlist the help of the gym teacher or boxing coach to help demonstrate terms such as *right cross* and *haymaker*.

Special Education Students
For lessons designed for special education students, see *Holt Reading Solutions*.

while throwing one-twos followed by upper-cuts to an imaginary jaw. Antonio then beat the air with a barrage of body blows and short devastating lefts with an overhead jaw-breaking right.

After a mile or so, Felix puffed and said, "Let's stop a while, bro. I think we both got something to say to each other."

Antonio nodded. It was not natural to be acting as though nothing unusual was happening when two ace-boon buddies were going to be blasting each other within a few short days.

They rested their elbows on the railing separating them from the river. Antonio wiped his face with his short towel. The sunrise was now creating day.

Felix leaned heavily on the river's railing and stared across to the shores of Brooklyn. Finally, he broke the silence.

"Man. I don't know how to come out with it."

Antonio helped. "It's about our fight, right?"

"Yeah, right." Felix's eyes squinted at the rising orange sun.

"I've been thinking about it too, panin.[3] In fact, since we found out it was going to be me and you, I've been awake at night, pulling punches on you, trying not to hurt you."

"Same here. It ain't natural not to think about the fight. I mean, we both are cheverote[4] fighters and we both want to win. But only one of us can win. There ain't no draws in the eliminations."

Felix tapped Antonio gently on the shoulder. "I don't mean to sound like I'm bragging, bro. But I wanna win, fair and square."

Antonio nodded quietly. "Yeah. We both know that in the ring the better man wins. Friend or no friend, brother or no . . ."

Felix finished it for him. "Brother. Tony, let's promise something right here. OK?"

3. **panin** (pä·nēn´) *n.:* Puerto Rican Spanish slang for "pal" or "buddy."
4. **cheverote** (che´ve·rô´tä) *adj.:* Puerto Rican Spanish slang for "the greatest."

THEY WERE SO TOGETHER IN FRIENDSHIP THAT THEY FELT THEMSELVES TO BE BROTHERS. They had known each other since childhood . . .

Amigo Brothers   **487**

Phonetic spellings. Point out that the author sometimes spells words the way the characters would actually pronounce them. Explain that *don't cha* is *don't you* in standard English. Warn students to stay on the alert for other phonetic spellings as they read.

B **English-Language Learners**

Interpret slang. The dialogue is laced with slang, such as *slapped skin, bro, smarts, cooler, split, heavy, dudes.* You might pair English-language learners with readers who can explain the slang. They may point out, for example, that by *heavy* Antonio means "powerful" or "threatening" and that he is warning Felix of troublemakers.

C **Literary Focus**

? **The short story.** What is the purpose of this four-line paragraph? [Possible responses: It moves the action from the day the boys decide to train separately to the night before their fight. It serves as a transition from one main event to the next.] How does the paragraph fit with the short story form? [Possible response: In a short story, things happen quickly. This paragraph speeds the action along.]

D **Cross-curricular Connections**
CULTURE

Film. After acting in summer stock, Issur Danielovitch changed his name to Kirk Douglas and moved to Hollywood in 1946. His brilliant performance in *The Champion* (1949) made him a major star. The film tells the story of Midge Kelly, a ruthless fighter who claws his way to the top of his sport. In this scene, Felix watches Kelly's final fight; he wins but dies afterward. *The Champion* is based on a story by sportswriter Ring Lardner.

"If it's fair, hermano,[5] I'm for it." Antonio admired the courage of a tugboat pulling a barge five times its welterweight size.

"It's fair, Tony. When we get into the ring, it's gotta be like we never met. We gotta be like two heavy strangers that want the same thing and only one can have it. You under-**A** stand, don't cha?"

"Sí, I know." Tony smiled. "No pulling punches. We go all the way."

"Yeah, that's right. Listen, Tony. Don't you think it's a good idea if we don't see each other until the day of the fight? I'm going to stay with my Aunt Lucy in the Bronx. I can use Gleason's Gym for working out. My manager says he got some sparring partners with more or less your style."

Tony scratched his nose pensively. "Yeah, it would be better for our heads." He held out his hand, palm upward. "Deal?"

"Deal." Felix lightly slapped open skin.

"Ready for some more running?" Tony asked lamely.

"Naw, bro. Let's cut it here. You go on. I kinda like to get things together in my head."

"You ain't worried, are you?" Tony asked.

B "No way, man." Felix laughed out loud. "I got too much smarts for that. I just think it's cooler if we split right here. After the fight, we can get it together again like nothing ever happened."

The amigo brothers were not ashamed to hug each other tightly.

"Guess you're right. Watch yourself, Felix. I hear there's some pretty heavy dudes up in the Bronx. Suavecito,[6] OK?"

"OK. You watch yourself too, sabe?"[7]

---

5. **hermano** (er·mä′nô) *n.:* Spanish for "brother."
6. **suavecito** (swä′vä·sē′tô) *adj.:* Puerto Rican Spanish slang for "cool."
7. **sabe** (sä′bā) *v.:* Spanish for "you know."

Tony jogged away. Felix watched his friend disappear from view, throwing rights and lefts. Both fighters had a lot of psyching up to do before the big fight.

The days in training passed much too **C** slowly. Although they kept out of each other's way, they were aware of each other's progress via the ghetto grapevine.

The evening before the big fight, Tony made his way to the roof of his tenement. In the quiet early dark, he peered over the ledge. Six stories below, the lights of the city blinked and the sounds of cars mingled with the curses and the laughter of children in the street. He tried not to think of Felix, feeling he had succeeded in psyching his mind. But only in the ring would he really know. To spare Felix hurt, he would have to knock him out, early and quick.

Up in the South Bronx, Felix decided to take in a movie in an effort to keep Anto-**D** nio's face away from his fists. The flick was *The Champion* with Kirk Douglas, the third time Felix was seeing it.

The champion was getting beaten, his face being pounded into raw, wet hamburger. His eyes were cut, jagged, bleeding, one eye swollen, the other almost shut. He was saved only by the sound of the bell.

Felix became the champ and Tony the challenger.

The movie audience was going out of its head, roaring in blood lust at the butchery going on. The champ hunched his shoulders, grunting and sniffing red blood back into his broken nose. The challenger, confident that he had the championship in the bag, threw a left. The champ countered with

---

Vocabulary
pensively (pen′siv·lē) *adv.:* thoughtfully.

CROSS-CURRICULAR CONNECTIONS

Culture

Boxing films. Boxing is popular not only as a sport but as a subject for films. *The Champion,* which Felix watches in "Amigo Brothers," is one of the great boxing films. Another is Sylvester Stallone's *Rocky* (1976). *When We Were Kings* is an award-winning documentary of Muhammad Ali's 1974 championship fight against George Foreman. **Activity.** Have students gather for a screening of *The Champion, Rocky,* or *When We* *Were Kings.* Students should pay particular attention to the boxing sequences and discuss their reactions afterward. What are the directors' attitudes toward boxing? How can students tell? What is their impression of the fighters and their attitudes toward the sport? What does watching a film about boxing contribute to students' understanding of "Amigo Brothers"?

WHOLE CLASS

a dynamite right that exploded into the challenger's brains.

Felix's right arm felt the shock. Antonio's face, superimposed on the screen, was shattered and split apart by the awesome force of the killer blow. Felix saw himself in the ring, blasting Antonio against the ropes. The champ had to be forcibly restrained. The challenger was allowed to crumble slowly to the canvas, a broken bloody mess.

When Felix finally left the theater, he had figured out how to psych himself for tomorrow's fight. It was Felix the Champion vs. Antonio the Challenger.

He walked up some dark streets, deserted except for small pockets of wary-looking kids wearing gang colors. Despite the fact that he was Puerto Rican like them, they eyed him as a stranger to their turf. Felix did a fast shuffle, bobbing and weaving, while letting loose a torrent of blows that would demolish whatever got in its way. It seemed to impress the brothers, who went about their own business.

Finding no takers, Felix decided to split to his aunt's. Walking the streets had not relaxed him; neither had the fight flick. All it had done was to stir him up. He let himself quietly into his Aunt Lucy's apartment and went straight to bed, falling into a fitful sleep with sounds of the gong for Round One.

Antonio was passing some heavy time on his rooftop. How would the fight tomorrow affect his relationship with Felix? After all, fighting was like any other profession. Friendship had nothing to do with it. A gnawing doubt crept in. He cut negative thinking real quick by doing some speedy fancy dance steps, bobbing and weaving like mercury. The night air was blurred with perpetual motions of left hooks and right

crosses. Felix, his amigo brother, was not going to be Felix at all in the ring. Just an opponent with another face. Antonio went to sleep, hearing the opening bell for the first round. Like his friend in the South Bronx, he prayed for victory via a quick clean knockout in the first round.

Large posters plastered all over the walls of local shops announced the fight between Antonio Cruz and Felix Vargas as the main bout.

The fight had created great interest in the neighborhood. Antonio and Felix were well liked and respected. Each had his own loyal following. Betting fever was high and ranged from a bottle of Coke to cold hard cash on the line.

Antonio's fans bet with unbridled faith in his boxing skills. On the other side, Felix's admirers bet on his dynamite-packed fists.

Felix had returned to his apartment early in the morning of August 7th and stayed there, hoping to avoid seeing Antonio. He turned the radio on to salsa[8] music sounds and then tried to read while waiting for word from his manager.

The fight was scheduled to take place in Tompkins Square Park. It had been decided that the gymnasium of the Boys' Club was not large enough to hold all the people who were sure to attend. In Tompkins Square Park, everyone who wanted could view the fight, whether from ringside or window fire escapes or tenement rooftops.

The morning of the fight Tompkins Square was a beehive of activity with

---

8. **salsa** (säl′sə) *n.* used as *adj.:* Latin American dance music, usually played at fast tempos.

Vocabulary
torrent (tôr′ənt) *n.:* flood or rush.

E Learners Having Difficulty
Clarify understanding. Make sure students realize that Antonio's face doesn't actually appear. Felix is projecting his and Antonio's identities onto the two fighters he is watching on the movie screen.

F Literary Focus
❓ **Internal conflict.** How can you tell that Antonio is trying to resolve an internal conflict? [Possible response: The sentence "A gnawing doubt crept in" suggests that he doesn't really believe that friendship can be left outside the ring.]

G Reading Skills
❓ **Compare and contrast.** Do the friends resolve their internal conflicts in the same way or differently? Explain. [Possible responses: The same way—they both decide to do their best to win; they both decide to think of their opponent as another fighter, not as their friend. Differently—one resolves the conflict by watching a movie, and the other by thinking about the situation.]

H Reading Skills
Compare and contrast. Ask students to identify the phrase that signals the use of a contrast. ["on the other side"] Invite students to name other words or phrases that signal comparison or contrast. [Possible answers: *on the other hand, but, while, instead, like, in the same way.*]

I Literary Focus
❓ **Internal conflict.** Has Felix completely resolved the conflict he feels about fighting Antonio? How do you know? [Possible response: No, because he hopes to avoid seeing him. His friendship for Antonio is so strong that he knows seeing his face will weaken his resolve to fight hard.]

DEVELOPING FLUENCY

Activity. Because of its informal English, which echoes casual speech, this story is an excellent choice for reading aloud. Have students gather in small groups and take turns reading aloud, perhaps one page per turn. Listeners can help readers with pronunciation and flow. After the reading, students can discuss how hearing the story, rather than reading it silently, helped them to visualize the action and the characters' conflicts.

SMALL GROUP

? **Acceleration.** How might this descriptive passage have been different if this short story were told in a different genre—a novel, say, or a film? [Answers will vary. Possible responses: In a novel, the passage would be much longer and might include subplots and minor characters, such as the boys' family members, girlfriends, or managers. In a film, the scene might include bloody moments in the preliminary bouts or someone giving the boys pep talks or suggesting they throw the fight. Either genre could flash back to an earlier time or suggest betrayal as a theme.]

B Reading Skills

? **Predict.** What do you think will happen once the fight begins? Why do you think so? [Students may say that both boys will honor the decision they made and fight hard; or that one boy will throw the fight to the other because he is worried about losing the friendship.]

C Cross-curricular Connections
CULTURE

Boxing. Boxing matches are made up of three-minute rounds. Fighters are given one minute to rest between rounds. If a fighter is knocked down, he or she is given ten seconds to get up and continue fighting. If the fighter cannot get up, he or she is considered knocked out, or down for the count.

---

numerous workers setting up the ring, the seats, and the guest speakers' stand. The scheduled bouts began shortly after noon and the park had begun filling up even earlier.

The local junior high school across from Tompkins Square Park served as the dressing room for all the fighters. Each was given a separate classroom with desk tops, covered with mats, serving as resting tables. Antonio thought he caught a glimpse of Felix waving to him from a room at the far end of the corridor. He waved back just in case it had been him.

The fighters changed from their street clothes into fighting gear. Antonio wore white trunks, black socks, and black shoes. Felix wore sky-blue trunks, red socks, and white boxing shoes. They had dressing gowns to match their fighting trunks with their names neatly stitched on the back.

The loudspeakers blared into the open windows of the school. There were speeches by dignitaries, community leaders, and great boxers of yesteryear. Some were well prepared; some improvised on the spot. They all carried the same message of great pleasure and honor at being part of such a historic event. This great day was in the tradition of champions emerging from the streets of the Lower East Side.

Interwoven with the speeches were the sounds of the other boxing events. After the sixth bout, Felix was much relieved when his trainer, Charlie, said, "Time change. Quick knockout. This is it. We're on."

Waiting time was over. Felix was escorted from the classroom by a dozen fans in white T-shirts with the word "Felix" across their fronts.

Antonio was escorted down a different stairwell and guided through a roped-off path.

As the two climbed into the ring, the crowd exploded with a roar. Antonio and Felix both bowed gracefully and then raised their arms in acknowledgment.

Antonio tried to be cool, but even as the roar was in its first birth, he turned slowly to meet Felix's eyes looking directly into his. Felix nodded his head and Antonio responded. And both as one, just as quickly, turned away to face his own corner.

Bong—bong—bong. The roar turned to stillness.

"Ladies and Gentlemen, Señores y Señoras."

The announcer spoke slowly, pleased at his bilingual efforts.

"Now the moment we have all been waiting for—the main event between two fine young Puerto Rican fighters, products of our Lower East Side."

"Loisaida,"[9] called out a member of the audience.

"In this corner, weighing 134 pounds, Felix Vargas. And in this corner, weighing 133 pounds, Antonio Cruz. The winner will represent the Boys' Club in the tournament of champions, the Golden Gloves. There will be no draw. May the best man win."

The cheering of the crowd shook the window panes of the old buildings surrounding Tompkins Square Park. At the center of the ring, the referee was giving instructions to the youngsters.

"Keep your punches up. No low blows. No punching on the back of the head. Keep your heads up. Understand? Let's have a clean fight. Now shake hands and come out fighting."

---

9. **Loisaida** (loi·sī′dä) *n.:* Puerto Rican English dialect for "Lower East Side."

Developing Word-Attack Skills
Review with students how *e* at the end of a word signals that the preceding vowel sound is long. When final *e* is part of a vowel-consonant-*e* spelling for a long vowel sound, the letter *e* itself is silent. Use these one- and two-syllable words to demonstrate this.

late   rotate   fine   feline

Then, explain that in some words *e* may appear to be part of a vowel-consonant-*e*

pattern, but in fact, it is a syllable on its own. Demonstrate this using the selection word *tenement*. Point out that the word is not pronounced tēn mənt; it is pronounced ten ə mənt. The first *e* has a short *e* sound and the second *e* is a syllable on its own with an unaccented vowel sound. Use the selection word *Apache* to illustrate how in some words final *e* can be a separate syllable pronounced ē.

Activity. Display these pairs of words. Have students tell in which word the underlined *e* is part of the vowel-consonant-*e* pattern [v] and in which *e* is a separate syllable [s].

1. lineage [s]   fineness [v]
2. simile [s]   infantile [v]
3. molehill [v]   molecule [s]
4. lemonade [v]   adequate [s]
5. dateline [v]   category [s]
6. covenant [s]   stovepipe [v]

Both youngsters touched gloves and nodded. They turned and danced quickly to their corners. Their head towels and dressing gowns were lifted neatly from their shoulders by their trainers' nimble fingers. Antonio crossed himself. Felix did the same.

BONG! BONG! ROUND ONE. Felix and Antonio turned and faced each other squarely in a fighting pose. Felix wasted no time. He came in fast, head low, half-hunched toward his right shoulder, and lashed out with a straight left. He missed a right cross as Antonio slipped the punch and countered with one-two-three lefts that snapped Felix's head back, sending a mild shock coursing through him. If Felix had any small doubt about their friendship affecting their fight, it was being neatly dispelled.

Antonio danced, a joy to behold. His left hand was like a piston pumping jabs one right after another with seeming ease. Felix bobbed and weaved and never stopped boring in. He knew that at long range he was at a disadvantage. Antonio had too much reach on him. Only by coming in close could Felix hope to achieve the dreamed-of knockout.

Antonio knew the dynamite that was stored in his amigo brother's fist. He ducked a short right and missed a left hook. Felix trapped him against the ropes just long enough to pour some punishing rights and lefts to Antonio's hard midsection. Antonio slipped away from Felix, crashing two lefts to his head, which set Felix's right ear to ringing.

Bong! Both amigos froze a punch well on its way, sending up a roar of approval for good sportsmanship.

Felix walked briskly back to his corner. His right ear had not stopped ringing. Antonio gracefully danced his way toward his stool none the worse, except for glowing glove burns showing angry red against the whiteness of his midribs.

"Watch that right, Tony." His trainer talked into his ear. "Remember Felix always goes to the body. He'll want you to drop your hands for his overhand left or right. Got it?"

Antonio nodded, spraying water out between his teeth. He felt better as his sore midsection was being firmly rubbed.

Felix's corner was also busy.

"You gotta get in there, fella." Felix's trainer poured water over his curly Afro locks. "Get in there or he's gonna chop you up from way back."

Bong! Bong! Round Two. Felix was off his stool and rushed Antonio like a bull, sending a hard right to his head. Beads of water exploded from Antonio's long hair.

Antonio, hurt, sent back a blurring barrage of lefts and rights that only meant pain to Felix, who returned with a short left to the

Vocabulary
dispelled (di·speld′) v.: driven away.

Amigo Brothers   **491**

DIRECT TEACHING

D Literary Focus

? Conflict. How has the conflict between the two friends changed? [Possible response: The boys seem to have resolved their internal conflicts and are now fully engaged in the external conflict, each fighting to beat his opponent.]

E Learners Having Difficulty

Paraphrase. Have students paraphrase this sentence to make sure they understand it. [Neither boy completed the punch he was throwing, because the bell signaled the end of the round. The crowd cheered the boys' good sportsmanship.]

CROSS-CURRICULAR CONNECTIONS

Culture
Boxing. Boxing may have the longest history of any sport. Boxing was popular in ancient Greece, both for military training and for sport. Romans banned it near the beginning of the Christian era because of its brutality. It returned to prominence during the eighteenth century in England.

Activity. Have students choose partners with whom to research some aspect of the sport of boxing. Possible topics include changes of rules over time; changes of equipment; boxing in a particular country or historical period; famous boxers of the modern era; and boxing in the Olympics. Partners can give class presentations on the results of their research.

PAIRED

DIRECT TEACHING

A Reading Skills

Compare and contrast. Compare and contrast the boys' fighting styles. [Felix always tries to knock Antonio out with hard punches. Antonio is more graceful and light on his feet. Both are fighting hard and trying their best to win.]

B English-Language Learners

Understand idioms. Tell students that an opossum is a small animal that pretends to be dead when it feels threatened, so that predators will leave it alone. Explain that the idiom *playing possum* means "pretending to be dead, hurt, or off one's guard."

C Vocabulary Development

❓ Clarify word meanings.
What is a "haymaker"? How do you know? [Possible response: The context shows that it is a hard punch used in street fighting.]

head followed by a looping right to the body. Antonio countered with his own flurry, forcing Felix to give ground. But not for long.

Felix bobbed and weaved, bobbed and weaved, occasionally punching his two gloves together.

Antonio waited for the rush that was sure to come. Felix closed in and feinted with his left shoulder and threw a right instead. Lights suddenly exploded inside Felix's head as Antonio slipped the blow and hit him with a pistonlike left, catching him flush on the point of his chin.

Bedlam broke loose as Felix's legs momentarily buckled. He fought off a series of rights and lefts and came back with a strong right that taught Antonio respect.

Antonio danced in carefully. He knew Felix had the habit of playing possum when hurt, to sucker an opponent within reach of the powerful bombs he carried in each fist.

A right to the head slowed Antonio's pretty dancing. He answered with his own left at Felix's right eye that began puffing up within three seconds.

Antonio, a bit too eager, moved in too close, and Felix had him entangled into a rip-roaring, punching toe-to-toe slugfest that brought the whole Tompkins Square Park screaming to its feet.

Rights to the body. Lefts to the head. Neither fighter was giving an inch. Suddenly a short right caught Antonio squarely on the chin. His long legs turned to jelly and his arms flailed out desperately. Felix, grunting like a bull, threw wild punches from every direction. Antonio, groggy, bobbed and weaved, evading most of the blows. Suddenly his head cleared. His left flashed out hard and straight, catching Felix on the bridge of his nose.

Felix lashed back with a haymaker, right off the ghetto streets. At the same instant, his eye caught another left hook from Antonio. Felix swung out, trying to clear the pain. Only the frenzied screaming of those along ringside let him know that he had dropped Antonio. Fighting off the growing haze, Antonio struggled to his feet, got up, ducked, and threw a smashing right that dropped Felix flat on his back.

Felix got up as fast as he could in his own corner, groggy but still game. He didn't even hear the count. In a fog, he heard the roaring of the crowd, who seemed to have gone insane. His head cleared to hear the bell sound at the end of the round. He was glad. His trainer sat him down on the stool.

In his corner, Antonio was doing what all fighters do when they are hurt. They sit and smile at everyone.

The referee signaled the ring doctor to check the fighters out. He did so and then gave his OK. The cold-water sponges brought clarity to both amigo brothers. They were rubbed until their circulation ran free.

Bong! Round Three—the final round. Up to now it had been tic-tac-toe, pretty much even. But everyone knew there could be no draw and that this round would decide the winner.

This time, to Felix's surprise, it was Antonio who came out fast, charging across the ring. Felix braced himself but couldn't ward off the barrage of punches. Antonio drove Felix hard against the ropes.

Vocabulary
frenzied (fren′zēd) *adj.:* wild.

The crowd ate it up. Thus far the two had fought with mucho corazón.[10] Felix tapped his gloves and commenced his attack anew. Antonio, throwing boxer's caution to the winds, jumped in to meet him.

Both pounded away. Neither gave an inch and neither fell to the canvas. Felix's left eye was tightly closed. Claret-red blood poured from Antonio's nose. They fought toe-to-toe.

The sounds of their blows were loud in contrast to the silence of a crowd gone completely mute. The referee was stunned by their savagery.

Bong! Bong! Bong! The bell sounded over and over again. Felix and Antonio were past hearing. Their blows continued to pound on each other like hailstones.

Finally the referee and the two trainers

---

10. **mucho corazón** (mōō′chô kô′rä·sôn′): Spanish for "a lot of heart."

pried Felix and Antonio apart. Cold water was poured over them to bring them back to their senses.

They looked around and then rushed toward each other. A cry of alarm surged through Tompkins Square Park. Was this a fight to the death instead of a boxing match?

The fear soon gave way to wave upon wave of cheering as the two amigos embraced.

No matter what the decision, they knew they would always be champions to each other.

BONG! BONG! BONG! "Ladies and Gentlemen. Señores and Señoras. The winner and representative to the Golden Gloves Tournament of Champions is . . ."

The announcer turned to point to the winner and found himself alone. Arm in arm the champions had already left the ring.

Meet the Writer

Piri Thomas

A Survivor from the Mean Streets

Like Antonio and Felix in "Amigo Brothers," **Piri Thomas** (1928–   ) grew up in a rough neighborhood in New York City. Unfortunately, he wasn't as lucky as Antonio and Felix—he didn't have a sport like boxing to help him escape the lures of drugs and crime. As a result, Thomas spent time in prison. While in prison, Thomas discovered he could write, and after his release he published an autobiography called *Down These Mean Streets* (1967). Thomas has worked for many years to help drug addicts give up their addictions and start new lives.

Amigo Brothers **493**

After You Read

First Thoughts

1. Possible answer: I was surprised and glad when I reached the end of the story and found out what Felix and Antonio did. It didn't really matter to me who won the fight.

Thinking Critically

2. Neither wants to injure the other badly, so they both want the fight to end quickly. This shows that they care for one another.

3. They both do their best to win the fight, but they do not sacrifice their friendship for the sake of winning.

4. Possible answers: The external conflict is more important—it causes the internal conflict and is the action-filled heart of the story. The internal conflict is more important—maintaining a long friendship in the face of strong rivalry gives the story its focus and meaning.

Extending Interpretations

5. Students who could not ignore the results may see winning as the most important aspect of the contest. Students who could walk away may believe that winning could threaten a valued friendship.

6. Some students may say that they would not have competed so fiercely.

7. Some students may say that the story is realistic because friendship should be able to survive fair competition. Others may say that it is unrealistic because winning is what competition is all about.

After You Read Response and Analysis

First Thoughts

1. How did you react to the end of the story? Were you surprised by what Felix and Antonio did? Were you disappointed not to find out who won the fight?

Thinking Critically

2. Why do both boys wish for an early knockout? What does this wish show about them and their feelings for each other?

3. The last sentence refers to both boys as "champions." In what sense are they both champions?

4. Which do you think is more important to the story: the **external conflict** (the fight itself) or the **internal conflict** (the feelings the boys struggled with before and during the fight)? Why?

Extending Interpretations

5. Would you be able to walk away from a contest like this fight without finding out if you had won? Why or why not?

6. Look back at your "Rules for Competing Against a Friend" list from your Quickwrite on page 484. How many of them did Antonio and Felix follow? If you had been in their situation, would you have acted differently? Explain. ✏️

7. Did you find this story, particularly its ending, true to life? Do you think two good friends can fight each other and stay friends? Give reasons for your opinion.

INTERNET
Projects and Activities
Keyword: LE5 7-5

SKILLS FOCUS

Literary Skills
Analyze external and internal conflict.

Reading Skills
Compare and contrast.

Writing Skills
Write a comparison-contrast essay.

WRITING

Comparing Characters

In a three-paragraph essay, **compare** and **contrast** the personalities of Felix and Antonio. Start by reviewing the Venn diagram of the boys' similarities and differences that you made after you read the story. In your essay you might want to talk first about their similarities and then about their differences. End by telling which character you like better and why. 📚

Reading Check

a. What dream do both Felix and Antonio have?

b. Why do the boys decide to stop training together?

c. How can you tell that the boys do not "pull punches" in their fight?

d. How does the fight end?

Reading Check

a. Felix and Antonio both dream about becoming the lightweight champion of the world.

b. The boys decide to stop training together because they want to fight without holding back, as if they were strangers.

c. It's clear that the boys have not "pulled their punches" because both are dazed and injured but are still swinging hard at the end of the fight.

d. The fight ends with Felix and Tony hugging and walking arm in arm out of the ring.

Clarifying Word Meanings: Sports Reporting

PRACTICE

1. You're writing a news article about tryouts for the Olympic Games. Write sentences using the words *bouts, frenzied,* and *torrent.*

2. You're a retired tennis player. Write sentences for your autobiography using the words *pensively* and *dispelled.*

3. You're a sportscaster describing the crowd at a hockey game. Write a description using the words *torrent* and *frenzied.*

> **Word Bank**
> bouts
> pensively
> torrent
> dispelled
> frenzied

SKILLS FOCUS

Vocabulary Skills
Clarify word meanings.

Grammar Skills
Punctuate dialogue correctly.

Grammar Link

Punctuate Dialogue Correctly— And Punch Up Your Writing

Dialogue, or conversation, puts a lot of punch into a story. When you include what characters say, your story comes to life. It's important to get the punctuation right when you write dialogue. Just follow these rules:

- Put quotation marks around direct quotations of words spoken aloud:

  Antonio helped. "It's about our fight, right?"

- Begin a quotation with a capital letter:

  After a mile or so, Felix puffed and said, "Let's stop a while, bro. I think we both got something to say to each other."

- Use a comma, a question mark, or an exclamation point (never a period) to set a quotation off from the rest of the sentence:

  "Ready for some more running?" Tony asked lamely.
  "Loisaida," called out a member of the audience.

PRACTICE

Add commas and quotation marks to set off the dialogue in these passages.

1. Felix and Antonio decided they'd each fight to win. Tony said No pulling punches. We go all the way.

2. A woman in the crowd said to her friend with alarm What's going on? It looks as if they're trying to kill each other!

3. Let's have a clean fight said the referee. No low blows. No punching on the back of the head. Got it?

For more help, see Quotation Marks, 14c–k, in the Language Handbook.

Amigo Brothers   **495**

Vocabulary Development

PRACTICE

Possible Answers

1. Of the three bouts fought here tonight, the third was the most frenzied. The torrent of blows exchanged was unbelievable.

2. I looked back pensively over my career. After that first match, my doubts about my ability were dispelled.

3. A torrent of cheers rose from the frenzied fans.

Grammar Link

PRACTICE

1. Felix and Antonio decided they'd each fight to win. Tony said, "No pulling punches. We go all the way."

2. A woman in the crowd said to her friend with alarm, "What's going on? It looks as if they're trying to kill each other!"

3. "Let's have a clean fight," said the referee. "No low blows. No punching on the back of the head. Got it?"

ASSESSING

Assessment
■ *Holt Assessment: Literature, Reading, and Vocabulary*

RETEACHING

For a lesson reteaching interrelated plot events, see **Reteaching,** p. 917D.

DIFFERENTIATING INSTRUCTION

Learners Having Difficulty
Have students work together to answer question 6. They can share their answers to the Quickwrite assignment and then compare and contrast Felix and Antonio's behavior with their answers.
Writing. You may wish to help students fill out their Venn diagrams before they write their essays at home.

HOMEWORK

Advanced Learners
Have students discuss their answers to questions 5 and 7, drawing on actual experiences of competing against friends.
Enrichment. Have students debate their answers to question 4. Remind them to support their arguments with specific details from the story.

Grade-Level Skills

■ **Reading Skills**
Analyze comparison-and-contrast text structure.

Summary 🔄 *at grade level.*

The writer provides an overview of arguments for and against boxing. Arguments against the sport include evidence that boxing causes head injuries, which in turn lead to more serious, chronic conditions. Supporters of boxing believe that it provides certain benefits and opportunities to participants. The sport continues to be popular with both fans and fighters.

PRETEACHING

Selection Starter
Build background. Ask how many students are fans of contact sports like football or boxing. Ask whether any students have seen serious injuries. Take a poll to see how many students think that violent sports should be banned. Ask students to defend their views.

Assign the Reading
Before assigning the reading in class, make sure students understand the difference between the point-by-point and block organizational patterns used for comparing and contrasting.

HOMEWORK

Informational Text

LINK TO "AMIGO BROTHERS"

Understanding Text Structure: Comparison and Contrast

Reading Focus
Compare-and-Contrast Text Structure

Writers who want to present two sides of an issue often use a compare-and-contrast pattern to organize their material. It's a good way to show how two sides might have similar views on some points—**comparing**—and different views on others—**contrasting.**

When writers compare and contrast, they generally arrange their ideas according to one of two organizational patterns: the **point-by-point pattern** or the **block pattern.**

A writer using the point-by-point pattern moves back and forth between the subjects being compared, discussing one feature of each subject at a time.

A writer using the block pattern covers all the points of comparison for the first subject, then all the points of comparison for the second subject, and so on.

■ Notice how "Right Hook–Left Hook: The Boxing Controversy" presents two contrasting views about the sport of boxing, using the block method. First, the writer discusses one view, supported by the American Medical Association. Then she discusses the opposing view.

INTERNET
Interactive
Reading Model
Keyword: LE5 7-5

SKILLS FOCUS

Reading Skills
Understand comparison-and-contrast text structure.

Point-by-Point Method

Feature 1	Subject 1
	Subject 2
Feature 2	Subject 1
	Subject 2

Block Method

Subject 1	Feature 1
	Feature 2
Subject 2	Feature 1
	Feature 2

RESOURCES: READING

Planning
■ *One-Stop Planner* CD-ROM with ExamView Test Generator

Differentiating Instruction
■ *Holt Reading Solutions*
■ *Supporting Instruction in Spanish*
■ *Audio CD Library*
■ *Audio CD Library, Selections and Summaries in Spanish*

Grammar and Language
■ *Daily Language Activities*

Assessment
■ *Holt Assessment: Literature, Reading, and Vocabulary*
■ *One-Stop Planner* CD-ROM with ExamView Test Generator
■ *Holt Online Assessment*

Internet
■ go.hrw.com (Keyword: LE5 7-5)
■ *Elements of Literature Online*

Media
■ *Audio CD Library*
■ *Audio CD Library, Selections and Summaries in Spanish*

Right Hook–Left Hook

THE BOXING CONTROVERSY Ⓐ

A four-year-old gazes at the television screen and laughs as a pig hits a duck over the head with an ironing board. The duck springs back to life, running around in circles with stars spinning around his head. Does this scene sound familiar?

Many doctors believe that as a society we close our eyes to the terrible injuries caused by a tremendous blow to the head. Doctors have expressed deep concern about boxing injuries such as those received by the former heavyweight champion Muhammad Ali. Ali suffers from Parkinson's disease, an illness probably caused by the hits he took in the ring. The symptoms of Parkinson's disease range from slurred speech to difficulty walking. According to doctors and researchers, a blow severe enough to render a person unconscious may result in tearing of nerve fibers and hemorrhaging. In 1984, the American Medical Association came out in support of a complete ban on boxing.

However, the sport of boxing remains popular. Supporters believe that training young people to box instills self-control. They also point out the benefits of fighting according to a set of rules. They believe that boxing provides opportunities for individuals who might otherwise have no chance to achieve financial security. Some doctors disagree with the American Medical Association's position and believe boxing produces few injuries because all major muscle groups are used.

The debate continues, with both sides of the issue verbally slugging it out to try to come to a resolution.

—Joan Burditt

Right Hook–Left Hook   **497**

DIFFERENTIATING INSTRUCTION

Learners Having Difficulty
Have students choose partners with whom to read the article. They should stop at the end of each paragraph to discuss it. Each partner should make sure that the other understands the two points of view being discussed and the reasons for each view.

Advanced Learners
Enrichment. Have students do some reading about Muhammad Ali and other great boxers who sustained serious injuries. Have them gather for a debate about the boxing controversy. Do they think boxing should be banned? If not, why not? Should measures be taken to ensure the fighters' safety? Are changes in the rules advisable? Make sure students support their arguments with details from their research.

Ⓐ Reading Informational Text
❓ Compare and contrast. What does the word *controversy* mean? [It means disagreement or debate.] What does the title lead you to expect about the content of the article? [Possible response: The title, and particularly the word *controversy*, suggest that the writer will contrast two opposing views of boxing.]

Ⓑ Cross-curricular Connections
HISTORY

Muhammad Ali. The boxer Muhammad Ali was originally named Cassius Clay. He won an Olympic gold medal in 1960 and was world heavyweight champion from 1964 to 1968 and from 1974 to 1978. Ali was outspoken on political issues, refusing to fight in Vietnam.

Ⓒ Reading Informational Text
❓ Compare and contrast. What does the first sentence of this paragraph suggest about the article's organizational pattern? [Possible response: The word *however* suggests that the writer has finished discussing one view and will now discuss the contrasting view. This is the block pattern of organization.]

GUIDED PRACTICE

Monitor students' progress. Challenge students to summarize the article. Remind them to include only the main ideas and the most important supporting details. Have partners trade summaries and check that each has not left out anything important or included anything unnecessary. If partners disagree, provide guidance.

Analyzing Text Structure: Comparison and Contrast

Test Practice

Answers and Model Rationales

1. **C** When people close their eyes, they refuse to consider something. C is the best choice.
2. **F** This is a statement of fact from the second paragraph.
3. **D** A and C may be true, but researchers have claimed only D.
4. **F** Though the article explains that some people disagree with the American Medical Association (H) and that some doctors believe that few fighters are seriously injured (G), the article does not take a clear position on these issues. J is not suggested. In the opening sentences of the last two paragraphs, the writer does suggest that the sport is too popular to be banned (F).
5. **C** The sentence clearly states that the debate is continuing and that passions on the subject run high.

Test-Taking Tips

Remind students that some multiple-choice questions, such as question 2, have an answer that students can find by looking back at the text.

For more instruction, refer students to **Test Smarts,** p. 920.

Constructed Response

Possible Answers

■ *Subject 1*—Boxing should be banned (AMA position). *Feature 1*—Boxing may cause severe head injuries. *Feature 2*—Blows to the head may cause serious diseases later in life.

Analyzing Text Structure: Comparison and Contrast
Right Hook–Left Hook

Test Practice

1. When the writer says "we close our eyes" to the devastating effects of head injuries, she means that —
   A head injuries cause blindness
   B people blink when struck on the head
   C people choose not to take the effects of head injuries seriously
   D people take head injuries too seriously

2. According to the article, the former heavyweight champion Muhammad Ali suffers from —
   F Parkinson's disease
   G Alzheimer's disease
   H migraine headache pain
   J Lou Gehrig's disease

3. Researchers say that a knockout blow to the head may result in —
   A an immediate winner of the fight
   B a penalty
   C advances in boxing equipment
   D damage to nerve fibers

4. Even though the dangers of boxing are well known, the sport has not been banned mainly because —
   F it remains popular
   G few fighters are seriously injured
   H the American Medical Association is wrong
   J researchers need to find out more

5. The last sentence of the article implies that the issue is —
   A humorous
   B unimportant
   C controversial
   D settled

Constructed Response

On page 496, a chart shows the block method of organization. Copy the chart, and use it to show the organization of this essay. First, list the views supported by the American Medical Association. Then, list the opposing views.

SKILLS FOCUS

Reading Skills
Analyze comparison-and-contrast text structure.

■ *Subject 2*—Boxing should not be banned. *Feature 1*—Training instills self-control. *Feature 2*—Boxing provides economic opportunities for people. *Feature 3*—Boxing produces few injuries.

ASSESSING

Assessment

■ *Holt Assessment: Literature, Reading, and Vocabulary*

Before You Read   The Autobiography

Barrio Boy

Make the Connection
Quickwrite ✏️

Describe what you would do if you lived in a place where you didn't speak the language well. If you are in this situation now, describe what you are doing to learn the language.

Literary Focus
Autobiography and Biography: Who's Telling?

An **autobiography** is the story of a person's life written by that very person. A **biography** is the story of a person's life told by *another* person. In his autobiography, *Barrio Boy*, Ernesto Galarza tells what it was like to immigrate to Sacramento, California, from a small village in Mexico.

Reading Skills 📖
Distinguishing Fact from Opinion

When you read an autobiography, it's important to be able to tell facts from opinions. A **fact** is a statement that can be proved true. *Sacramento is a city in California* is a fact. An **opinion**, a personal feeling or belief, can't be

proved true or false. In autobiographies, like *Barrio Boy*, writers share their feelings and opinions, but they also present facts.

Don't be fooled: People may state an opinion as if it were a fact. If you're in doubt, ask yourself, "Can this statement be proved, or is it someone's personal feeling or belief?"

Vocabulary Development

Here are some words to learn as you read *Barrio Boy*:

reassuring (rē′ə·shoor′iŋ) *v.* used as *adj.*: comforting. *Ernesto's teachers were kind and reassuring.*

contraption (kən·trap′shən) *n.*: strange machine or gadget. *He was amazed by a contraption that closed the door automatically.*

assured (ə·shoord′) *v.*: promised confidently. *Ernesto's teachers assured him he would enjoy the new school.*

formidable (fôr′mə·də·bəl) *adj.*: awe-inspiring; impressive. *The principal's appearance was formidable.*

INTERNET
Vocabulary Activity
Keyword: LE5 7-5

Background
Literature and Social Studies

Ernesto Galarza was born in 1905 in Jalcocotán, a village in western Mexico. In 1910, when the Mexican Revolution threatened their peaceful mountain home, Ernesto, his mother, and two uncles left their village for Mazatlán, Mexico. Eventually they moved to Sacramento, California, and lived in what Galarza calls a "rented corner of the city"—the *barrio*, or Spanish-speaking neighborhood.

In this part of his life story, Ernesto starts school in America.

SKILLS FOCUS

Literary Skills
Understand forms of prose: autobiography and biography.

Reading Skills
Distinguish fact from opinion.

Grade-Level Skills
- **Literary Skills**
Analyze characteristics of different forms of prose, including autobiography and biography.
- **Reading Skills**
Distinguish fact from opinion.

Summary ↔ *at grade level*

The narrator's family has recently moved to Sacramento, California, from Mazatlán, Mexico, and he must enroll as a first-grader at Lincoln School. Despite his initial anxiety about attending a new school in a new land, Ernesto receives a warm welcome from the principal. His remaining fears are dispelled by his teacher, who guides Ernesto through the "awful idiocies of the English language." At the school, the boy learns that he can be proud of his ethnic heritage while adapting to the language and culture of his new home.

RESOURCES: READING

Planning
- *One-Stop Planner* CD-ROM with ExamView Test Generator

Differentiating Instruction
- *Holt Adapted Reader*
- *Holt Reading Solutions*
- *Supporting Instruction in Spanish*
- *Audio CD Library*
- *Audio CD Library, Selections and Summaries in Spanish*

Vocabulary
- *Vocabulary Development*

Grammar and Language
- *Language Handbook Worksheets*
- *Daily Language Activities*

Assessment
- *Holt Assessment: Literature, Reading, and Vocabulary*
- *One-Stop Planner* CD-ROM with ExamView Test Generator

- *Holt Online Assessment*

Internet
- go.hrw.com (Keyword: LE5 7-5)
- *Elements of Literature Online*

Media
- *Audio CD Library, Selections and Summaries in Spanish*
- *Fine Art Transparencies*
- *Visual Connections Videocassette Program*

Selection Starter

Motivate. Tell students that the narrator of this autobiography goes to his first day of school in the United States not knowing any English. Tell students to imagine how they would cope with going to a school where everyone spoke a different language. English-language learners might share with the class what they have found to be the most difficult aspects of learning English.

Preview Vocabulary

Have students read the Vocabulary words, definitions, and the sample sentences on p. 499. Then, have them fill in the blanks with the word that correctly completes each sentence.

1. Getting our cat Frisky into a carrying case seemed like a _____ task. [formidable]

2. We didn't think Frisky would be eager to jump into that _____. [contraption]

3. To calm Frisky, we spoke in _____ voices. [reassuring]

4. Finally, we _____ ourselves that Frisky would be fine in the carrying case. [assured]

Assign the Reading

Review with students the material on p. 499 about distinguishing fact from opinion before assigning the reading in class. Then, have students note both factual statements and statements of opinion as they read Barrio Boy.

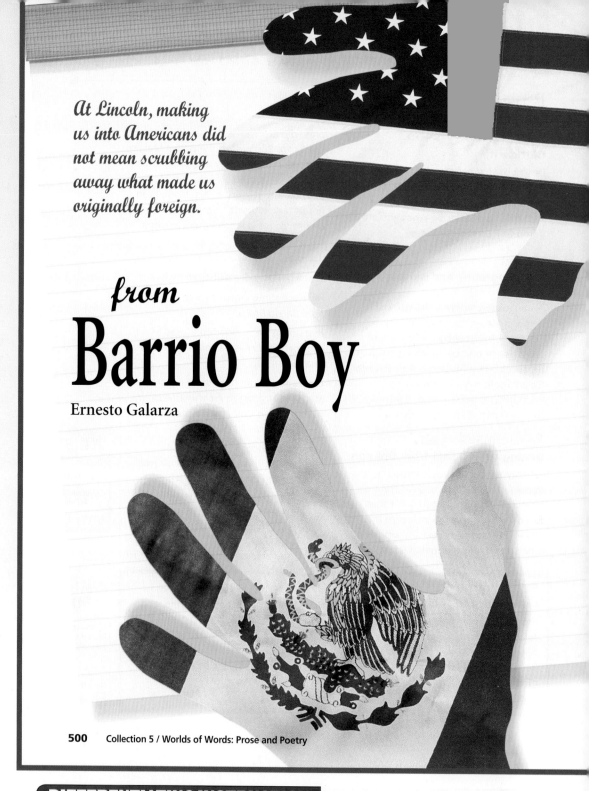

At Lincoln, making us into Americans did not mean scrubbing away what made us originally foreign.

from
Barrio Boy

Ernesto Galarza

Learners Having Difficulty
Modeling. To help students read *Barrio Boy,* model the reading skill of distinguishing fact from opinion. Read the first paragraph aloud. Then, say: "The description of the school is factual. Details about the school's size, structure, color, and roof can be proved to be true. But the last sentence reveals the narrator's opinion or personal feeling: He is not reassured by the school's being different from a familiar Mexican school." Encourage students as they read to ask themselves: "Which words and statements reveal the narrator's opinion?"

English-Language Learners
For lessons designed for intermediate and advanced English-language learners, see *Holt Reading Solutions.*

Special Education Students
For lessons designed for special education students, see *Holt Reading Solutions.*

The two of us [Ernesto and his mother] walked south on Fifth Street one morning to the corner of Q Street and turned right. Half of the block was occupied by the Lincoln School. It was a three-story wooden building, with two wings that gave it the shape of a double T connected by a central hall. It was a new building, painted yellow, with a shingled roof that was not like the red tile of the school in Mazatlán. I noticed other differences, none of them very reassuring.

We walked up the wide staircase hand in hand and through the door, which closed by itself. A mechanical contraption screwed to the top shut it behind us quietly.

Up to this point the adventure of enrolling me in the school had been carefully rehearsed. Mrs. Dodson had told us how to find it and we had circled it several times on our walks. Friends in the barrio explained that the director was called a principal, and that it was a lady and not a man. They assured us that there was always a person at the school who could speak Spanish.

Exactly as we had been told, there was a sign on the door in both Spanish and English: "Principal." We crossed the hall and entered the office of Miss Nettie Hopley.

Miss Hopley was at a roll-top desk to one side, sitting in a swivel chair that moved on wheels. There was a sofa against the opposite wall, flanked by two windows and a door that opened on a small balcony. Chairs were set around a table, and framed pictures hung on the walls of a man with long white hair and another with a sad face and a black beard.

The principal half turned in the swivel chair to look at us over the pinch glasses crossed on the ridge of her nose. To do this, she had to duck her head slightly, as if she were about to step through a low doorway.

What Miss Hopley said to us we did not know, but we saw in her eyes a warm welcome, and when she took off her glasses and straightened up, she smiled whole-heartedly, like Mrs. Dodson. We were, of course, saying nothing, only catching the friendliness of her voice and the sparkle in her eyes while she said words we did not understand. She signaled us to the table. Almost tiptoeing across the office, I maneuvered myself to keep my mother between me and the gringo[1] lady. In a matter of seconds I had to decide whether she was a possible friend or a menace. We sat down.

Then Miss Hopley did a formidable thing. She stood up. Had she been standing when we entered, she would have seemed tall. But rising from her chair, she soared. And what she carried up and up with her was a buxom superstructure, firm shoulders, a straight sharp nose, full cheeks slightly molded by a curved line along the nostrils, thin lips that moved like steel springs, and a high forehead topped by hair

---

1. **gringo** (griŋ′gō) *n.* used as *adj.:* in Latin America, an insulting term for "foreigner"; from the Spanish *griego,* meaning "Greek."

Vocabulary

reassuring (rē′ə·shoor′iŋ) *v.* used as *adj.:* comforting; giving hope or confidence; from the Latin word *securus,* meaning "secure." Look for the related word *assured* on this page.

contraption (kən·trap′shən) *n.:* strange machine or gadget.

assured (ə·shoord′) *v.:* guaranteed; promised confidently.

formidable (fôr′mə·də·bəl) *adj.:* awe-inspiring; impressive.

A Literary Focus

❓ **Autobiography.** Point out that first-person narration is always used in an autobiography. The author/narrator refers to himself as "I" or "me" and to himself and another person as "we" or "us." As the excerpt opens, how does the narrator feel about his first day at school in a new country? [Possible responses: He is a little afraid; he is nervous.]

B Literary Focus

Autobiography. Students may be confused about who Mrs. Dodson is. Remind them that this is an excerpt from a full-length autobiography. Galarza must have introduced her in an earlier part of the book. Have students infer who Mrs. Dodson might be. [Possible response: She might be a Spanish-speaking neighbor who was born in the United States or who has lived in the United States for a long time.]

C Literary Focus

❓ **Autobiography.** Why doesn't the author identify George Washington and Abraham Lincoln by name? [Though Galarza certainly would have known who the two men were when he was writing his autobiography, he describes them as he perceived them as a small boy, unfamiliar with U.S. history.]

D Reading Skills

❓ **Distinguish fact from opinion.** Remind students that feelings are opinions. They are neither true nor false. They reflect one person's experience of a situation. Are these two sentences facts or opinions? Why? [The first statement is an opinion because it reveals Ernesto's awe. The second statement is an observable fact.]

Advanced Learners

Acceleration. Use the following activity to help students analyze a work of literature and show how it reflects the heritage, traditions, attitudes, and beliefs of its author. **Activity.** Have students chart the development of Ernesto Galarza's attitude toward school over time, beginning with his first day of classes, and including his feelings at the end of first grade and later in life. Tell them they may use not only the excerpt but also information from the Meet the Writer feature and from other parts of *Barrio Boy.*

> *Her voice patiently maneuvering me over the awful idiocies of the English language . . .*

gathered in a bun. Miss Hopley was not a giant in body, but when she mobilized it to a standing position she seemed a match for giants. I decided I liked her.

She strode to a door in the far corner of the office, opened it, and called a name. A boy of about ten years appeared in the doorway. He sat down at one end of the table. He was brown like us, a plump kid with shiny black hair combed straight back, **A** neat, cool, and faintly obnoxious.

Miss Hopley joined us with a large book and some papers in her hand. She, too, sat down and the questions and answers began by way of our interpreter. My name was Ernesto. My mother's name was Henriqueta. My birth certificate was in San Blas. Here was my last report card from the Escuela Municipal Numero 3 para Varones[2] of Mazatlán, and so forth. Miss Hopley put things down in the book and my mother signed a card.

As long as the questions continued, Doña Henriqueta could stay and I was secure. Now that they were over, Miss Hopley saw her to the door, dismissed our interpreter, and without further ado took me by the hand and strode down the hall to Miss Ryan's first grade.

Miss Ryan took me to a seat at the front of the room, into which I shrank—the

---

2. **Escuela Municipal Numero 3 para Varones:** Spanish for "Municipal School Number 3 for Boys."

better to survey her. She was, to skinny, somewhat runty me, of a withering height when she patrolled the class. And when I **B** least expected it, there she was, crouching by my desk, her blond, radiant face level with mine, her voice patiently maneuvering me over the awful idiocies of the English language.

During the next few weeks Miss Ryan overcame my fears of tall, energetic teachers as she bent over my desk to help me with a word in the pre-primer. Step by step, she **C** loosened me and my classmates from the safe anchorage of the desks for recitations at the blackboard and consultations at her desk. Frequently she burst into happy announcements to the whole class. "Ito can read a sentence," and small Japanese Ito, squint-eyed and shy, slowly read aloud while the class listened in wonder: "Come, Skipper, come. Come and run." The Korean, Portuguese, Italian, and Polish first-graders had similar moments of glory, no less shining than mine the day I conquered "butterfly," which I had been persistently **D** pronouncing in standard Spanish as boo-ter-flee. "Children," Miss Ryan called for attention. "Ernesto has learned how to pronounce *butterfly*!" And I proved it with a perfect imitation of Miss Ryan. From that celebrated success, I was soon able to match Ito's progress as a sentence reader with "Come, butterfly, come fly with me."

Like Ito and several other first-graders who did not know English, I received private lessons from Miss Ryan in the closet, a narrow hall off the classroom with a door at each end. Next to one of these doors Miss Ryan placed a large chair for herself and a small one for me. Keeping an eye on the class through the open door, she read

DEVELOPING FLUENCY

with me about sheep in the meadow and a frightened chicken going to see the king, coaching me out of my phonetic ruts in words like *pasture, bow-wow-wow, hay,* and *pretty,* which to my Mexican ear and eye had so many unnecessary sounds and letters. She made me watch her lips and then close my eyes as she repeated words I found hard to read. When we came to know each other better, I tried interrupting to tell Miss Ryan how we said it in Spanish. It didn't work. She only said "oh" and went on with *pasture, bow-wow-wow,* and *pretty.* It was as if in that closet we were both discovering together the secrets of the English language and grieving together over the tragedies of Bo-Peep. The main reason I was graduated with honors from the first grade was that I had fallen in love with Miss Ryan. Her radiant, no-nonsense character made us either afraid not to love her or love her so we would not be afraid, I am not sure which. It was not only that we sensed she was with it, but also that she was with us.

Like the first grade, the rest of the Lincoln School was a sampling of the lower part of town, where many races made their home. My pals in the second grade were Kazushi, whose parents spoke only Japanese; Matti, a skinny Italian boy; and Manuel, a fat Portuguese who would never get into a fight but wrestled you to the ground and just sat on you. Our assortment of nationalities included Koreans, Yugoslavs, Poles, Irish, and home-grown Americans.

Miss Hopley and her teachers never let us forget why we were at Lincoln: for those who were alien, to become good Americans; for those who were so born, to accept the rest of us. Off the school grounds we traded the same insults we heard from our elders. On the playground we were sure to be marched up to the principal's office for calling someone a wop, a chink, a dago, or a greaser. The school was not so much a melting pot as a griddle where Miss Hopley and her helpers warmed knowledge into us and roasted racial hatreds out of us.

At Lincoln, making us into Americans did not mean scrubbing away what made us originally foreign. The teachers called us as our parents did, or as close as they could pronounce our names in Spanish or Japanese. No one was ever scolded or punished for speaking in his native tongue on the playground. Matti told the class about his mother's down quilt, which she had made in Italy with the fine feathers of a thousand geese. Encarnación acted out how boys learned to fish in the Philippines. I astounded the third grade with the story of my travels on a stagecoach, which nobody

> *The teachers called us as our parents did, or as close as they could pronounce our names . . .*

else in the class had seen except in the museum at Sutter's Fort. After a visit to the Crocker Art Gallery and its collection of heroic paintings of the golden age of California, someone showed a silk scroll with a Chinese painting. Miss Hopley herself had a way of expressing wonder over these matters before a class, her eyes wide open until they popped slightly. It was easy for me to feel that becoming a proud American, as she said we should, did not mean feeling ashamed of being a Mexican.

DIRECT TEACHING

E English-Language Learners

Understand language differences. Tell students that *bow-wow-wow* is the English way to mimic a dog barking. The words used to mimic animal sounds vary widely from language to language. For example, in Danish, cows make the sound *muh-muh;* in Norwegian, frogs croak *kvekk* and roosters crow *kykkeliky;* in French, cats purr *ron ron.* Ask students to share some English words for animal sounds and the words used in their native languages for the same sounds.

F Reading Skills

❓ **Distinguish fact from opinion.** Why is this statement an opinion and not a fact? [Possible responses: It would be impossible to prove true or false; it expresses Ernesto's feelings about Miss Ryan and his judgment about his performance in first grade.]

G Literary Focus

❓ **Autobiography.** Why do you think Galarza includes these anecdotes about Matti's mother's quilt and his own ride in a stagecoach? [Possible responses: These colorful, personal details make an autobiography come to life; they show us how the school celebrates diversity.]

H Advanced Learners

❓ **Acceleration.** How does Ernesto Galarza's book reflect the attitudes and beliefs he learned at Lincoln School? [Possible response: He learned at the school to be proud of his heritage. Writing a book about his life is one way to express that pride.]

Monitor students' progress.
Guide students in answering these comprehension questions. Direct students to locate passages in the text that support their responses.

Short Answer

1. From what country does Ernesto's family come? [Mexico]

2. What are some of the languages spoken by students at the Lincoln School? [English, Spanish, Japanese, Korean, Portuguese, Italian, and Polish]

3. Why did Ernesto try to interrupt his English lessons with Miss Ryan? [to tell her how a word was said in Spanish]

4. What reasons does Ernesto give for graduating with honors from the first grade? [He had fallen in love with Miss Ryan, and she gave him the confidence to learn.]

Meet the Writer

Tell students that Ernesto Galarza was born in 1905 in a small village in western Mexico with a main street that he says "was just wide enough to park six automobiles hub to hub." In 1910, when the Mexican Revolution threatened their peaceful mountain home, Ernesto, his mother, and two uncles left their village for Mazatlán. Eventually they moved to Sacramento, California, and lived in the *barrio*, or Spanish-speaking neighborhood. Throughout his life, Ernesto Galarza felt a great respect for education, the United States, and his own heritage.

For Independent Reading

Students who enjoyed this selection from *Barrio Boy* might want to check out Lulu Delacre's *Salsa Stories,* about a young girl who fills her notebook with recipes after noticing that food is central to every family story she's ever been told.

Meet the Writer

Ernesto Galarza

"Anecdotes I Told My Family"

For young **Ernesto Galarza** (1905–1984), coming to the United States meant abandoning everything he had ever known—his language, his family, and his customs. He soon discovered that education was the key to making sense of his new life. Eventually he earned his doctorate from Columbia University in New York and then returned to California to teach. Although he was a beloved teacher, Galarza is best remembered for *Barrio Boy,* his bestselling 1971 account of his journey from Mexico to the United States. Galarza explains how he came to write *Barrio Boy:*

> 66 *Barrio Boy* began as anecdotes I told my family about Jalcocotán, the mountain village in western Mexico where I was born. Among this limited public (my wife, Mae, and daughters, Karla and Eli Lu) my thumbnail sketches became bestsellers. Hearing myself tell them over and over, I began to agree with my captive audience that they were not only interesting but possibly good.
>
> Quite by accident I told one of these vignettes at a meeting of scholars and other boring people. It was recorded on tape, printed in a magazine, and circulated among schools and libraries here and there. I received letters asking for reprints, and occasionally a tempting suggestion that I write more of the same, perhaps enough to make a book.
>
> Adding up the three listeners in my family and the three correspondents made a public of six. I didn't need more persuasion than this to link the anecdotes into a story. 99

For Independent Reading

The selection you've read is from one chapter of Galarza's *Barrio Boy.* If you liked the selection, you'll enjoy reading the entire book.

504   Collection 5 / Worlds of Words: Prose and Poetry

Learners Having Difficulty

Monitoring tip: If students have difficulty determining how Lincoln School honored its students' original languages and customs (question e in the Reading Check), refer them to the last paragraph of the selection.
Writing. Before students do the writing assignment for homework, discuss how they might find the facts they need.

Advanced Learners

Encourage students to compare Ernesto Galarza's school experiences with those of other authors of autobiographies, such as Jean Fritz and Helen Keller.
Enrichment. Encourage students to expand their answers to question 5 into an essay that develops an extended metaphor describing U.S. society today.

Response and Analysis

First Thoughts

1. Refer back to your Quickwrite notes (page 499); then, finish one of these sentences:
   - If I went to a school where I did not speak the language, I would . . .
   - I have been in the same situation as Ernesto, and I . . .

Thinking Critically

2. What did you **predict** would happen to Ernesto, and why? How else could his story have ended?

3. In many ways this story is a tribute to Ernesto's teachers. What do you think Galarza means when he says that Miss Ryan was not only "with it" but "with us"?

4. In *Barrio Boy*, Ernesto Galarza reveals some opinions about his life in the United States. Like other writers of **autobiography**, he also presents facts. Give one example of a **fact** and one example of an **opinion** in *Barrio Boy*.

Extending Interpretations

5. The **metaphor** of the melting pot comes from a 1908 play by Israel Zangwill: "America is . . . a great melting pot, where all the races of Europe are melting and reforming!" Ernesto thinks of Lincoln School not as a melting pot—which makes everyone the same—but as a warm griddle. What do you think this means? Which comparison would you use to describe the United States, and why?

WRITING

Writing About Immigration

Ernesto Galarza and many of his classmates were immigrants. What special problems do immigrants face today? How do schools and local governments try to solve these problems? Research these questions in your school library or on the Internet. Then, write two paragraphs giving your responses to the questions. Cite both facts and opinions.

Reading Check

a. How did Ernesto feel about Miss Hopley and Miss Ryan?

b. How was the makeup of Ernesto's class a lot like that of his neighborhood?

c. How did Miss Ryan encourage her students to learn English?

d. According to Miss Hopley and the teachers at Lincoln School, what were the children to remember about *why* they were at school?

e. How did Lincoln School honor its students' original languages and customs?

---

go.hrw.com

INTERNET

Projects and Activities

Keyword: LE5 7-5

SKILLS FOCUS

Literary Skills
Analyze an autobiography.

Reading Skills
Distinguish fact from opinion.

Writing Skills
Write a brief research report.

Barrio Boy   505

First Thoughts

1. Possible Answers
   - If I went to a school where I did not speak the language, I would <u>feel shy and would have a hard time making friends.</u>
   - I have been in the same situation as Ernesto, and I <u>also believe that becoming a proud American doesn't mean feeling ashamed of where I came from.</u>

Thinking Critically

2. Possible answers: I predicted Ernesto would not like the teachers because he couldn't understand them. I predicted Ernesto would succeed at school because autobiographies are usually written by people who have had some success. The story could have ended with Ernesto being unable to learn to read or make friends.

3. Possible answer: Miss Ryan not only is a good teacher but also encourages her students and cares about them.

4. Possible answers: *Fact*—Miss Nettie Hopley was principal of Lincoln School. *Opinion*—The English language contains "awful idiocies."

Extending Interpretations

5. Galarza uses the griddle metaphor to suggest that the students at the Lincoln School retain their individual identities while having knowledge "warmed into" them and racial hatred "roasted out." Another possible metaphor is a tossed salad. Each ingredient of the salad is unique, with its own flavor and characteristics.

Reading Check

a. He liked Miss Hopley. He fell in love with Miss Ryan.

b. The class included people of diverse cultural backgrounds.

c. Miss Ryan helped students individually with patience and praise.

d. Those who were new to the United States were there to become good Americans.

Those who had been born in the United States were there to accept the others.

e. The teachers addressed students by the same names that their parents did. The children could speak their native languages while at play, and they were encouraged to talk about their heritage.

Vocabulary Development

Possible Answers

1. "You did just fine."
2. dishwashers, garbage disposals, and microwave ovens
3. I will always be on your side.
4. Sammy Sosa, Venus Williams, and Tiger Woods

VIEWING THE ART

The Ecuadorian artist **Oswaldo Guayasamín** (1919–1999) was born into poverty, and many of his paintings portray the effects of social injustice in South America and elsewhere. He also did a series of paintings called *The Age of Tenderness* in honor of his mother and all mothers. *My Brother* was painted the year after Guayasamín graduated from the School of Fine Arts in Quito, and he received his first award for it.

Activity. Ask students how the painting illustrates the feelings experienced by Ernesto Galarza on his first day of school in the United States. [Possible response: The eyes and the down-turned mouth suggest the kind of apprehension Galarza described.]

After You Read | Vocabulary Development

Clarifying Word Meanings: Examples

Writers often help readers understand difficult words by using definitions, examples, restatements, or contrasts.

A writer who uses **examples** provides specific instances to show what a word means. Consider the following sentence:

> People came to the meeting from such varied **municipalities** as Sacramento, Oakland, Bakersfield, and San Diego.

Even if you didn't know that a municipality is a city or town, the examples in the sentence give you a clue to the meaning of the word.

Finish the following sentences by using examples to clarify the meanings of the underlined words.

1. The most reassuring words I ever heard were _____.
2. Three contraptions that make life easier today are _____, _____, and _____.
3. I assured my friend I was loyal. I said, "_____."
4. Three formidable figures in sports are _____, _____, and _____.

Word Bank

reassuring
contraption
assured
formidable

SKILLS FOCUS

Vocabulary Skills
Clarify word meanings by using examples.

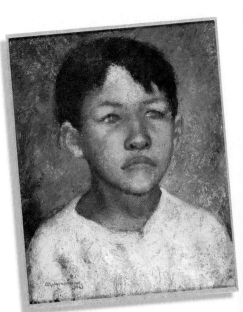

My Brother (1942) by Oswaldo Guayasamín (Oswaldo Guayasamín Calero). Oil on wood (15⅞" × 12¾"). Inter-American Fund (699.1942).

The Museum of Modern Art, New York. Digital Image © The Museum of Modern Art/Licensed by SCALA/Art Resource, NY.

Grammar Link

Making the Most of Comparing Adjectives

The **comparative degree** of an adjective compares two people or things. The **superlative degree** compares more than two people or things.

Comparative Degree	Superlative Degree
Add the ending –er or the word *more* when you compare two items.	Add the ending –est or the word *most* when you compare more than two items.
Example: "The rest of the Lincoln School was a sampling of the <u>lower</u> part of town. . . ."	Example: To the children their beloved Miss Ryan was the <u>most wonderful</u> teacher in the world.

• When comparing, don't use both *more* and *–er,* and don't use both *most* and *–est.*

Ernesto felt ~~more~~ safer when his mother was present.
Matti was the ~~most~~ <u>thinnest</u> boy in the second grade.

• Don't use the superlative form when you compare only two people or things.

         prouder
Do you think Ernesto was ~~proudest~~ of being an American or a Mexican?

         more
Of the two boys, Ito learned ~~most~~ quickly.

PRACTICE

Act as an editor, and show how you'd correct these sentences.

1. Ernesto thought American schools were more stranger than Mexican schools.
2. Ernesto spoke Spanish and English, but his Spanish was best.
3. Was Ernesto proudest of pronouncing *butterfly* or of reading "Little Bo-Peep"?
4. Ernesto did more better in school than he had expected.
5. The most nicest teacher in the Lincoln School was Miss Ryan.
6. Miss Hopley might have been the most tallest person Ernesto had ever seen.

For more help, see Comparison of Modifiers, 5a–f, in the Language Handbook.

SKILLS FOCUS

Grammar Skills
Use comparative and superlative forms correctly.

Grammar Link

PRACTICE

1. Ernesto thought American schools were stranger than Mexican schools.
2. Ernesto spoke Spanish and English, but his Spanish was better.
3. Was Ernesto prouder of pronouncing *butterfly* or of reading "Little Bo-Peep"?
4. Ernesto did better in school than he had expected.
5. The nicest teacher in the Lincoln School was Miss Ryan.
6. Miss Hopley might have been the tallest person Ernesto had ever seen.

Assessment
■ *Holt Assessment: Literature, Reading, and Vocabulary*

For a lesson reteaching forms of prose, see **Reteaching,** p. 917C.

Grade-Level Skills

■ **Literary Skills**
Analyze characteristics of different forms of prose, including the short story, novel, and novella.

■ **Reading Skills**
Make generalizations.

Review Skills

■ **Literary Skills**
Analyze different forms of fiction, and describe the main characteristics of each form.

Upcoming Skills

■ **Literary Skills**
Analyze the importance of the setting to the mood, tone, and meaning of the text.

Summary ⟷ *at grade level*

This moving story is set in Mississippi during the Great Depression. The narrator, eight-year-old Cassie Logan, describes her love for her family's forest, where the trees "sing" to her. While Cassie and her brothers are playing in the woods one day, they learn that Mr. Andersen, a greedy lumber dealer, has been cutting down trees on the Logans' property. If discovered, Andersen plans to pay the Logans a small fee for the forest. The eldest brother, Stacey, rides off to find Papa, who had left home to find work. Papa returns and wires the remaining trees with dynamite, threatening to blow them up unless Mr. Andersen gets off the Logan property. Realizing that Papa is willing to risk his life to defend his family and his trees, Mr. Andersen backs down.

Before You Read   The Novella

Song of the Trees

Make the Connection
Quickwrite ✏
Agree? Disagree?
disagree 0 1 2 3 4 agree

1. People gain self-respect by standing up for their beliefs.

2. Given the chance, most people will never take advantage of another person.

3. Some people are treated unfairly because of the color of their skin.

4. Nobody owns the earth.

Rate each of those statements with a number from 0 to 4. (Zero means that you completely disagree; 4 means you completely agree.) Then, discuss these issues with the rest of the class.

SKILLS FOCUS

Literary Focus
Novels and Short Stories

A **short story** usually has just one main plot line, one or two major characters, one important conflict, and one main theme. With a **novel**—which is a book-length work of fiction—a lot more will happen. More characters will appear, the conflicts will multiply, subplots will develop, and several themes will be operating at once. Settings may also become more numerous. A short story usually takes place within a limited time frame, but a novel can span many generations.

Occasionally a writer will find that a narrative is too long for a short story and too short for a novel. The story that results, which may run from twenty to one hundred pages, is known as a **novella.** Mildred Taylor's *Song of the Trees* was first published in a small book by itself, as a forty-eight-page novella.

Reading Skills 📖
Making Generalizations: Putting It All Together

A **generalization** is a broad statement that tells about something in general. A statement about a story's **theme** is a kind of generalization. From specific evidence in the story, you make a broad universal statement about life. To make a statement about the theme of *Song of the Trees,* you have to

• think about the main events and conflicts in the story

• decide what the characters have discovered by the end of the story

• think about how the story relates to your experiences

Background
Literature and Social Studies

The depression referred to in this story is the Great Depression, the severe economic decline in the United States that lasted from 1929 to 1942. During the Depression many banks and businesses closed. People lost their jobs, their savings, and even their homes. Many people had barely enough food to eat. This was also a time when the segregation of African Americans was still a sad reality in parts of the United States.

508   Collection 5 / Worlds of Words: Prose and Poetry

Vocabulary Development

Study the following words from *Song of the Trees:*

finicky (fin′ik·ē) *adj.:* fussy and extremely careful. *Little Man was finicky when it came to his appearance.*

dispute (di·spyo͞ot′) *n.:* argument. *Mama settled the dispute between the two brothers.*

ambled (am′bəld) *v.:* walked without hurrying. *They ambled through the forest, listening to the song of the trees.*

delved (delvd) *v.:* searched. *Cassie delved into the bowl of blackberries and grabbed the biggest one.*

curtly (kurt′lē) *adv.:* rudely, using few words. *The man spoke curtly to Mama, showing his lack of respect.*

skirting (skurt′iŋ) *v.:* avoiding. *Instead of speaking to the point, Mr. Andersen was skirting the issue.*

elude (ē·lo͞od′) *v.:* escape cleverly. *The children hoped to elude punishment for their bold behavior.*

incredulously (in·krej′oo·ləs·lē) *adv.:* unbelievingly. *Mr. Andersen stared incredulously at Papa when Papa ignored him.*

ashen (ash′ən) *adj.:* pale. *He turned ashen with fright.*

sentries (sen′trēz) *n.:* guards. *The sentries stood guard over the quiet landscape.*

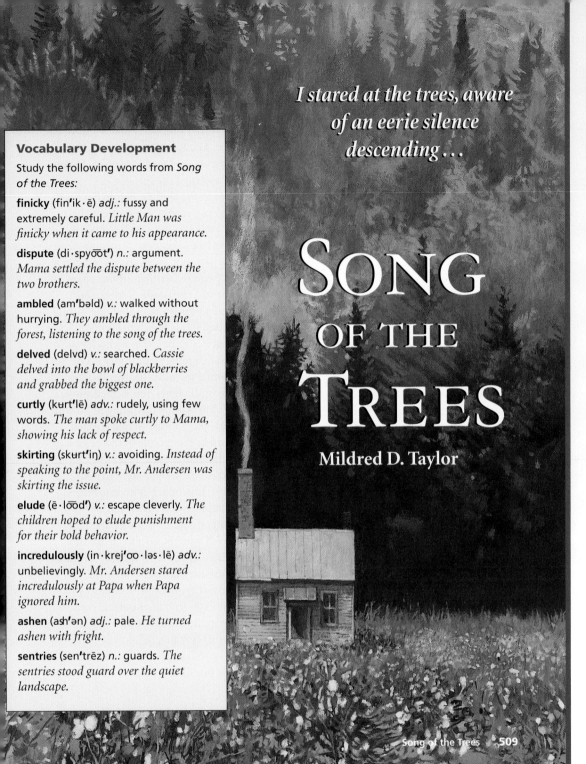

I stared at the trees, aware of an eerie silence descending...

SONG OF THE TREES

Mildred D. Taylor

Song of the Trees **509**

Build background. To help students visualize what people experienced during the Depression, display photographs taken during the period by such photographers as Dorothea Lange, Walker Evans, and Eudora Welty. Find out if your library has one of these noted collections: *You Have Seen Their Faces,* by Erskine Caldwell and Margaret Bourke-White; *12 Million Black Voices,* by Richard Wright; and *One Time, One Place,* by Eudora Welty. Encourage students to share whatever they may have learned about the Depression from family members or friends.

Preview Vocabulary

Have students pair up to read the definitions of the Vocabulary words and to quiz each other about the meanings of the words. Afterward, have them work together on the following exercises:

- Pantomime the meanings of the words *ambled*, *delved*, *finicky*, *incredulously*, and *sentries.* Have your partner guess which word you are pantomiming.
- Role-play a *dispute*. One will speak *curtly*, and the other will chatter.
- Draw pictures that show prey trying to *elude* its hunter, a motorcycle *skirting* an obstacle, and a person with an *ashen* complexion.

- *One-Stop Planner* CD-ROM with ExamView Test Generator
- *Holt Online Assessment*

Internet
- go.hrw.com (Keyword: LE5 7-5)
- *Elements of Literature Online*

Media
- *Audio CD Library*
- *Audio CD Library, Selections and Summaries in Spanish*
- *Fine Art Transparencies*

A **Cross-curricular Connections**
CULTURE

Family names. "Big Ma" is Cassie's name for her grandmother. Ask students if they use similar names for their grandparents or older family members. Ask students where the names come from. Some may be non-English words; some may be nicknames.

B **Literary Focus**

Theme. Point out the connection between this paragraph and the title of the novella. Tell students that this connection suggests that a theme may grow out of this idea, and encourage them to watch for further references to the singing trees.

C **Reading Skills**

Make generalizations. Suggest to students that Mama is trying to teach Christopher-John an important lesson. Help them turn the specific content of Mama's scolding into a generalization by giving them two sentence stems to complete. First, have them complete this sentence about the specific situation:

■ Times are hard, Christopher-John, so _____. [Possible response: eat only when you are hungry.]

Then, give them this generalization to complete:

■ When times are hard, family members _____. [Possible response: must share and make sacrifices for one another.]

Cassie. Cassie, child, wake up now," Big Ma called gently as the new sun peeked over the horizon.

I looked sleepily at my grandmother and closed my eyes again.

"Cassie! Get up, girl!" This time the voice was not so gentle.

I jumped out of the deep, feathery bed as Big Ma climbed from the other side. The room was still dark, and I stubbed my toe while stumbling sleepily about looking for my clothes.

"Shoot! Darn ole chair," I fussed, rubbing my injured foot.

"Hush, Cassie, and open them curtains if you can't see," Big Ma said. "Prop that window open, too, and let some of that fresh morning air in here."

I opened the window and looked outside. The earth was draped in a cloak of gray mist as the sun chased the night away. The cotton stalks, which in another hour would glisten greenly toward the sun, were gray. The ripening corn, wrapped in jackets of emerald and gold, was gray. Even the rich brown Mississippi earth was gray.

Only the trees of the forest were not gray. They stood dark, almost black, across the dusty road, still holding the night. A soft breeze stirred, and their voices whispered down to me in a song of morning greeting.

"Cassie, girl, I said open that window, not stand there gazing out all morning. Now, get moving before I take something to you," Big Ma threatened.

I dashed to my clothes. Before Big Ma had unwoven her long braid of gray hair, my pants and shirt were on and I was hurrying into the kitchen.

A small kerosene lamp was burning in a corner as I entered. Its light reflected on seven-year-old Christopher-John, short, pudgy, and a year younger than me, sitting sleepily upon a side bench drinking a large glass of clabber milk.[1] Mama's back was to me. She was dipping flour from a near-empty canister, while my older brother, Stacey, built a fire in the huge iron-bellied stove.

"I don't know what I'm going to do with you, Christopher-John," Mama scolded. "Getting up in the middle of the night and eating all that cornbread. Didn't you have enough to eat before you went to bed?"

"Yes'm," Christopher-John murmured.

"Lord knows I don't want any of my babies going hungry, but times are hard, honey. Don't you know folks all around here in Mississippi are struggling? Children crying cause they got no food to eat, and their daddies crying cause they can't get jobs so they can feed their babies? And you getting up in the middle of the night, stuffing yourself with cornbread!"

Her voice softened as she looked at the sleepy little boy. "Baby, we're in a depression.

_____
1. **clabber milk:** thickly curdled sour milk.

Learners Having Difficulty
Modeling. To help students read "Song of the Trees" and understand its themes, model the reading skill of making generalizations. Have students read the second column on p. 511. Then, write on the chalkboard: "Parents often try to protect their children from difficult problems." Explain that this is a generalization or broad statement about life that is based on specific

evidence in "Song of the Trees" and that connects to the experiences of many people. Encourage students to ask themselves as they read, "What discoveries about life do the characters make? What general ideas about living am I getting from the story?"

English-Language Learners
Explain to students that Mildred Taylor is re-creating in the dialogue the spoken language of many African Americans in

Mississippi in the 1930s. Translate dialect such as "Darn ole chair" into "Darn old chair," "No'm" into "No, Ma'am," "Them trees ain't singing" into "Those trees aren't singing," and so on. Once students have read a page or two, they should have no trouble getting the drift of the dialect.

Special Education Students
For lessons designed for special education students, see *Holt Reading Solutions.*

Why do you think Papa's way down in Louisiana laying tracks on the railroad? So his children can eat—but only when they're hungry. You understand?"

"Yes'm," Christopher-John murmured again, as his eyes slid blissfully shut.

"Morning, Mama," I chimed.

"Morning, baby," Mama said. "You wash up yet?"

"No'm."

"Then go wash up and call Little Man again. Tell him he's not dressing to meet President Roosevelt[2] this morning. Hurry up, now, cause I want you to set the table."

Little Man, a very small six-year-old and a most finicky dresser, was brushing his hair when I entered the room he shared with Stacey and Christopher-John. His blue pants were faded, but except for a small grass stain on one knee, they were clean. Outside of his Sunday pants, these were the only pants he had, and he was always careful to keep them in the best condition possible. But one look at him and I knew that he was far from pleased with their condition this morning. He frowned down at the spot for a moment, then continued brushing.

"Man, hurry up and get dressed," I called. "Mama said you ain't dressing to meet the president."

"See there," he said, pointing at the stain. "You did that."

"I did no such thing. You fell all by yourself."

"You tripped me!"

"Didn't!"

"Did, too!"

"Hey, cut it out, you two!" ordered Stacey, entering the room. "You fought over that stupid stain yesterday. Now get moving, both of you. We gotta go pick blackberries before the sun gets too high. Little Man, you go gather the eggs while Christopher-John and me milk the cows."

Little Man and I decided to settle our dispute later when Stacey wasn't around. With Papa away, eleven-year-old Stacey thought of himself as the man of the house, and Mama had instructed Little Man, Christopher-John, and me to mind him. So, like it or not, we humored him. Besides, he was bigger than we were.

I ran to the back porch to wash. When I returned to the kitchen, Mama was talking to Big Ma.

"We got about enough flour for two more meals," Mama said, cutting the biscuit dough. "Our salt and sugar are practically down to nothing and—" She stopped when she saw me. "Cassie, baby, go gather the eggs for Mama."

"Little Man's gathering the eggs."

"Then go help him."

"But I ain't set the table yet."

"Set it when you come back."

I knew that I was not wanted in the kitchen. I looked suspiciously at my mother and grandmother, then went to the back porch to get a basket.

Big Ma's voice drifted through the open window. "Mary, you oughta write David and tell him somebody done opened his letter and stole that ten dollars he sent," she said.

"No, Mama. David's got enough on his

---

2. **President Roosevelt:** Franklin Delano Roosevelt (1882–1945) was president of the United States from 1933 to 1945.

Vocabulary
finicky (fin′ik·ē) *adj.:* fussy and extremely careful.
dispute (di·spyo͞ot′) *n.:* argument.

D Literary Focus

? Characterization. What two different methods of characterization does the author use to reveal something about Little Man? [The author has Cassie, the narrator, tell readers that Little Man is finicky and then shows Little Man acting finicky.]

E Learners Having Difficulty

Use graphic aids. Help students recall the names and ages of the four children by having them create a chart with the children's names and ages from oldest to youngest.

F Literary Focus

? Novella: Exposition. What do you learn about the family through this conversation? [The family is low on money, and while they can eat garden foods, Mama needs money to buy her medicine. Someone has stolen money that the father had sent in the mail.]

G Cross-curricular Connections
ECONOMICS/HISTORY

The value of a dollar. Ten dollars may seem like a small amount to students unless they understand the effect of inflation on the value of a dollar. Inflation occurs when the amount of money in circulation increases relative to the amount of goods for sale. As a result, prices rise and the value of a dollar declines. Over the course of U.S. history, the general trend has been toward a decline in the value of the dollar. According to one inflation calculator, the amount of goods that could be bought for $10 in 1935 would have cost $121.04 in 1999.

Advanced Learners
Acceleration. Use the following activity to help students analyze the relevance of the setting to the mood, tone, and meaning of the text.
Activity. Have students consider the effect of the setting on the mood and theme of the story by filling in this chart after they have finished reading the story.

Setting	Effect on Mood	Effect on Theme
Time:		
Place:		
Customs:		
Attitudes of People:		

Ⓐ Reading Skills

Make generalizations. Point out that the reactions of Cassie and Stacey to the trees represent two different ways that people often respond to nature. Ask students to make a generalization about these two ways of responding. [Possible response: Some people may respond emotionally and imaginatively to nature, while others respond in a logical, literal, and matter-of-fact way.]

Ⓑ Reading Skills

Make generalizations. Point out that in large families the children often assume different roles with one another. Have students discuss the relationships they have observed among the children. Ask them to make generalizations about the different roles siblings may assume. [Possible responses: The oldest child is often the leader and takes responsibility for the others. Younger siblings may need to be prompted to do their chores. Cassie, as the next to oldest and the only girl, worries about her mother and takes her worries to her older brother.]

Ⓒ English-Language Learners

Idioms. Some students may be unfamiliar with the idiom *Last one to it's a rotten egg.* Tell them that children use this phrase to challenge others to a race. Have students share special phrases from their own childhood games.

---

mind. Besides, there's enough garden foods so we won't go hungry."

"But what 'bout your medicine? You're all out of it and the doctor told you good to—"

"Shhhh!" Mama stared at the window. "Cassie, I thought I told you to go gather those eggs!"

"I had to get a basket, Mama!" I hurried off the porch and ran to the barn.

After breakfast, when the sun was streaking red across the sky, my brothers and I ambled into the coolness of the forest, leading our three cows and their calves down the narrow cow path to the pond. The morning was already muggy, but the trees closed out the heat as their leaves waved restlessly, high above our heads.

"Good morning, Mr. Trees," I shouted. They answered me with a soft, swooshing sound. "Hear 'em, Stacey? Hear 'em singing?"

"Ah, cut that out, Cassie. Them trees ain't singing. How many times I gotta tell you that's just the wind?" He stopped at a sweet alligator gum, pulled out his knife, and scraped off a glob of gum that had seeped through its cracked bark. He handed me half.

As I stuffed the gooey wad into my mouth, I patted the tree and whispered, "Thank you, Mr. Gum Tree."

Stacey frowned at me, then looked back at Christopher-John and Little Man walking far behind us, munching on their breakfast biscuits.

"Man! Christopher-John! Come on, now," he yelled. "If we finish the berry picking early, we can go wading before we go back."

Christopher-John and Little Man ran to catch up with us. Then, resuming their leisurely pace, they soon fell behind again.

A large gray squirrel scurried across our path and up a walnut tree. I watched until it was settled amidst the tree's featherlike leaves; then, poking one of the calves, I said, "Stacey, is Mama sick?"

"Sick? Why you say that?"

"Cause I heard Big Ma asking her 'bout some medicine she's supposed to have."

Stacey stopped, a worried look on his face. "If she's sick, she ain't bad sick," he decided. "If she was bad sick, she'd been in bed."

We left the cows at the pond and, taking our berry baskets, delved deeper into the forest looking for the wild blackberry bushes.

"I see one!" I shouted.

"Where?" cried Christopher-John, eager for the sweet berries.

"Over there! Last one to it's a rotten egg!" I yelled, and off I ran.

Stacey and Little Man followed at my heels. But Christopher-John puffed far behind. "Hey, wait for me," he cried.

"Let's hide from Christopher-John," Stacey suggested.

The three of us ran in different directions. I plunged behind a giant old pine and hugged its warm trunk as I waited for Christopher-John.

Christopher-John puffed to a stop, then, looking all around, called, "Hey, Stacey! Cassie! Hey, Man! Y'all cut that out!"

I giggled and Christopher-John heard me.

"I see you, Cassie!" he shouted, starting toward me as fast as his chubby legs would carry him. "You're it!"

Vocabulary

ambled (am′bəld) *v.:* walked easily, without hurrying.

delved (delvd) *v.:* searched.

DIRECT TEACHING

D Reading Skills

❷ **Draw conclusions.** Why does the sudden silence in the forest worry Cassie? [Possible responses: She likes to imagine that the trees respond to her. Usually when she is in the woods, the trees "sing" to her and seem to echo her own happy mood. The silence suggests to her that something is wrong.]

"Not 'til you tag me," I laughed. As I waited for him to get closer, I glanced up into the boughs of my wintry-smelling hiding tree, expecting a song of laughter. But the old pine only tapped me gently with one of its long, low branches. I turned from the tree and dashed away.

"You can't, you can't, you can't catch me," I taunted, dodging from one beloved tree to the next. Around shaggy-bark hickories and sharp-needled pines, past blue-gray beeches and sturdy black walnuts I sailed, while my laughter resounded through the ancient forest, filling every chink. Overhead, the boughs of the giant trees hovered protectively, but they did not join in my laughter.

Deeper into the forest I plunged.

Christopher-John, unable to keep up, plopped on the ground in a pant. Little Man and Stacey, emerging from their hiding places, ran up to him.

"Ain't you caught her yet?" Little Man demanded, more than a little annoyed.

"He can't catch the champ," I boasted, stopping to rest against a hickory tree. I slid my back down the tree's shaggy trunk and looked up at its long branches, heavy with sweet nuts and slender green leaves, perfectly

D

CROSS-CURRICULAR CONNECTIONS

Literature
"Trees." Joyce Kilmer's poem "Trees" (1913) begins with this rhyming couplet:
  "I think that I shall never see
  A poem lovely as a tree."
Activity. Have students find and read "Trees" in its entirety. Ask them to relate the sentiments expressed in the poem to Cassie's thoughts and feelings in *Song of the Trees.*

INDIVIDUAL

History/Literature
African American writers and the Great Depression. This story is set in Mississippi during the Great Depression, but it was written by the contemporary author Mildred Taylor.
Activity. Have students work in pairs to research an African American writer who worked during the years of the Depression. Some well-known figures include Arna Bontemps, Zora Neale Hurston, Langston

Hughes, and Margaret Walker. One of the students in each pair should write a brief overview of the writer's life to read to the class; the other should read a poem, story, or section of a longer work by the writer and give a brief summary of it to the class. Ask students to discuss briefly how these writers' portrayals of African American life during the Depression compare with the portrayal in Mildred Taylor's story.

PAIRED

DIRECT TEACHING

A Reading Skills

Predict. Have students read up to this point. Then, ask if they can tell what the *X*'s on the trees might mean. [Possible response: They may mean that the trees are to be cut down.] Have students read on to check their predictions.

B Advanced Learners

❓ Appreciate setting's effect on mood. Ask students to recall when and where this story is set and what type of relationship young African Americans would have with white men at this time and in this place. Given this setting, what mood does the appearance of two white men evoke? [Possible response: a mood of fear and potential danger.]

C Literary Focus

Novella: Conflict. This passage introduces the conflict that will be the central struggle in the rest of the story. Ask students to describe the opposing forces in the conflict. [Possible response: Mr. Andersen wants to cut down the trees that belong to Cassie's family. The conflict is between a dishonest logger and Cassie's family.]

D Literary Focus

❓ Characterization. Even though readers have not yet seen David, they can get some ideas about his character from what other characters say and do. What do you think of David from Tom and Mr. Andersen's words and actions? [Possible response: He is a proud, courageous man.]

still. I looked around at the leaves of the other trees. They were still also. I stared at the trees, aware of an eerie silence descending over the forest.

Stacey walked toward me. "What's the matter with you, Cassie?" he asked.

"The trees, Stacey," I said softly, "they ain't singing no more."

"Is that all?" He looked up at the sky. "Come on, y'all. It's getting late. We'd better go pick them berries." He turned and walked on.

"But, Stacey, listen. Little Man, Christopher-John, listen."

The forest echoed an uneasy silence.

"The wind just stopped blowing, that's all," said Stacey. "Now stop fooling around and come on."

I jumped up to follow Stacey, then cried, "Stacey, look!" On a black oak a few yards away was a huge white *X*. "How did that get there?" I exclaimed, running to the tree.

"There's another one!" Little Man screamed.

"I see one too!" shouted Christopher-John.

Stacey said nothing as Christopher-John, Little Man, and I ran wildly through the forest counting the ghostlike marks.

"Stacey, they're on practically all of them," I said when he called us back.

"Why?"

Stacey studied the trees, then suddenly pushed us down.

"My clothes!" Little Man wailed indignantly.

"Hush, Man, and stay down," Stacey warned. "Somebody's coming."

Two white men emerged. We looked at each other. We knew to be silent.

"You mark them all down here?" one of the men asked.

"Not the younger ones, Mr. Andersen."

"We might need them, too," said Mr. Andersen, counting the *X*'s. "But don't worry 'bout marking them now, Tom. We'll get them later. Also them trees up past the pond toward the house."

"The old woman agree to you cutting these trees?"

"I ain't been down there yet," Mr. Andersen said.

"Mr. Andersen . . ." Tom hesitated a moment, looked up at the silent trees, then back at Mr. Andersen. "Maybe you should go easy with them," he cautioned. "You know that David can be as mean as an ole jackass when he wanna be."

"He's talking about Papa," I whispered.

"Shhhh!" Stacey hissed.

Mr. Andersen looked uneasy. "What's that gotta do with anything?"

"Well, he just don't take much to any dealings with white folks." Again, Tom looked up at the trees. "He ain't afraid like some."

Mr. Andersen laughed weakly. "Don't

CROSS-CURRICULAR CONNECTIONS

History

FDR, the New Deal, and African Americans. When Franklin Delano Roosevelt took office in 1933, he promised a "new deal" and went about setting up government programs to counteract the effects of the Depression. Aware that the economic downturn had hit African Americans harder than other groups, FDR invited some prominent African Americans to advise him on programs. Although discrimination against African Americans continued to be widespread in the United States, Eleanor Roosevelt (FDR's wife) and cabinet members Harry Hopkins and Harold Ickes tried to combat discrimination against minorities in the relief and job programs of the New Deal. During Roosevelt's administration, more African Americans than ever before were appointed to higher-level government positions.

worry 'bout that, Tom. The land belongs to his mama. He don't have no say in it. Besides, I guess I oughta know how to handle David Logan. After all, there are ways. . . .

"Now, you get on back to my place and get some boys and start chopping down these trees," Mr. Andersen said. "I'll go talk to the old woman." He looked up at the sky. "We can almost get a full day's work in if we hurry."

Mr. Andersen turned to walk away, but Tom stopped him. "Mr. Andersen, you really gonna chop all the trees?"

"If I need to. These folks ain't got no call for them. I do. I got me a good contract for these trees and I aim to fulfill it."

Tom watched Mr. Andersen walk away; then, looking sorrowfully up at the trees, he shook his head and disappeared into the depths of the forest.

"What we gonna do, Stacey?" I asked anxiously. "They can't just cut down our trees, can they?"

"I don't know. Papa's gone. . . ." Stacey muttered to himself, trying to decide what we should do next.

"Boy, if Papa was here, them ole white men wouldn't be messing with our trees," Little Man declared.

"Yeah!" Christopher-John agreed. "Just let Papa get hold of 'em and he gonna turn 'em every which way but loose."

"Christopher-John, Man," Stacey said finally, "go get the cows and take them home."

"But we just brought them down here," Little Man protested.

"And we gotta pick the berries for dinner," said Christopher-John mournfully.

"No time for that now. Hurry up. And stay clear of them white men. Cassie, you come with me."

We ran, brown legs and feet flying high through the still forest.

By the time Stacey and I arrived at the house, Mr. Andersen's car was already parked in the dusty drive. Mr. Andersen himself was seated comfortably in Papa's rocker on the front porch. Big Ma was seated too, but Mama was standing.

Stacey and I eased quietly to the side of the porch, unnoticed.

"Sixty-five dollars. That's an awful lot of money in these hard times, Aunt Caroline," Mr. Andersen was saying to Big Ma.

I could see Mama's thin face harden.

"You know," Mr. Andersen said, rocking familiarly in Papa's chair, "that's more than David can send home in two months."

"We do quite well on what David sends home," Mama said coldly.

Mr. Andersen stopped rocking. "I suggest you encourage Aunt Caroline to sell them trees, Mary. You know, David might not always be able to work so good. He could possibly have . . . an accident."

A Literary Focus

? Theme. Why is Mama standing up to Mr. Andersen? [Possible responses: She wants him to know that she won't give in to his threats and bullying. She is acting as her husband would if he were there.]

B Literary Focus

? Characterization. What do Mr. Andersen's words reveal about his character? [Possible response: He is greedy, a bully, racist, sexist, and potentially violent. He threatens David in order to scare the family into giving him what he wants—the right to cut down and sell their trees for profit.]

C Literary Focus

? Novella: Plot. Point out to students that this is a turning point in the novella. It is not the climax, leading to the resolution of the conflict, however. Because a novella is longer than a short story, it can have more than one turning point. In what way is this turning point significant? [Possible response: Before this point, Mr. Andersen had to be sneaky about his plans. Now that Big Ma has been intimidated into agreeing to his price, he can openly cut the trees.]

D Learners Having Difficulty

Summarize. Read aloud this important scene in which Stacey is sent off to bring his father home. Have students visualize the scene as you read. Then, have them summarize what has just taken place. [Possible summary: Cassie wakes up when she hears voices outside in the night. She sees her mother and grandmother outside in their nightclothes and Stacey mounted on a horse. She goes outside to find out what is going on and learns that Stacey is secretly being sent to bring their father home.]

Big Ma's soft brown eyes clouded over with fear as she looked first at Mr. Andersen, then at Mama. But Mama clenched her fists and said, "In Mississippi, black men do not have accidents."

"Hush, child, hush," Big Ma said hurriedly. "How many trees for the sixty-five dollars, Mr. Andersen?"

"Enough 'til I figure I got my sixty-five dollars' worth."

"And how many would that be?" Mama persisted.

A Mr. Andersen looked haughtily at Mama. "I said I'd be the judge of that, Mary."

"I think not," Mama said.

Mr. Andersen stared at Mama. And Mama stared back at him. I knew Mr. Andersen didn't like that, but Mama did it anyway. Mr. Andersen soon grew uneasy under that piercing gaze, and when his eyes swiftly shifted from Mama to Big Ma, his face was beet red.

B "Caroline," he said, his voice low and menacing, "you're the head of this family and you've got a decision to make. Now, I need them trees and I mean to have them. I've offered you a good price for them and I ain't gonna haggle over it. I know y'all can use the money. Doc Thomas tells me that Mary's not well." He hesitated a moment, then hissed venomously, "And if something should happen to David . . ."

C "All right," Big Ma said, her voice trembling. "All right, Mr. Andersen."

"No, Big Ma!" I cried, leaping onto the porch. "You can't let him cut our trees!"

Mr. Andersen grasped the arms of the rocker, his knuckles chalk white. "You certainly ain't taught none of your younguns how to behave, Caroline," he said curtly.

"You children go on to the back," Mama said, shooing us away.

"No, Mama," Stacey said. "He's gonna cut them all down. Me and Cassie heard him say so in the woods."

"I won't let him cut them," I threatened. "I won't let him! The trees are my friends and ain't no mean ole white man gonna touch my trees—"

Mama's hands went roughly around my body as she carried me off to my room.

"Now, hush," she said, her dark eyes flashing wildly. "I've told you how dangerous it is . . ." She broke off in midsentence. She stared at me a moment, then hugged me tightly and went back to the porch.

Stacey joined me a few seconds later, and we sat there in the heat of the quiet room, listening miserably as the first whack of an ax echoed against the trees.

D That night I was awakened by soft sounds outside my window. I reached for Big Ma, but she wasn't there. Hurrying to the window, I saw Mama and Big Ma standing in the yard in their nightclothes and Stacey, fully dressed, sitting atop Lady, our golden mare. By the time I got outside, Stacey was gone.

"Mama, where's Stacey?" I cried.

"Be quiet, Cassie. You'll wake Christopher-John and Little Man."

"But where's he going?"

"He's going to get Papa," Mama said. "Now be quiet."

"Go on, Stacey, boy," I whispered. "Ride for me, too."

As the dust billowed after him, Mama said, "I should've gone myself. He's so young."

Vocabulary

curtly (kurt′lē) *adv.*: rudely and with few words.

MINI-LESSON Reading

Developing Word-Attack Skills

Remind students that vowel digraphs such as *ai* and *ea* usually stand for long vowel sounds. Illustrate this by using the selection words *stain* and *clean*. The digraph *ai* stands for the long *a* in *stain*, and the digraph *ea* stands for the long *e* in *clean*. Ask students to identify other examples of words in the selection in which *ai* stands for the long *a* and *ea* stands for the long *e*. (Possibilities for *ai*: braid, exclaimed, wait, afraid, remained; for *ea*: streaking, eat, heat, eager, easy, mean)

Point out that there are some words in which these two digraphs do not stand for the long vowel sounds. For instance, in the selection word *against*, *ai* stands for the short *e*.

Big Ma put her arm around Mama. "Now, Mary, you know you couldn't've gone. Mr. Andersen would miss you if he come by and see you ain't here. You done right, now. Don't worry, that boy'll be just fine."

Three days passed, hot and windless.

Mama forbade any of us to go into the forest, so Christopher-John, Little Man, and I spent the slow, restless days hovering as close to the dusty road as we dared, listening to the foreign sounds of steel against the trees and the thunderous roar of those ancient loved ones as they crashed upon the earth. Sometimes Mama would scold us and tell us to come back to the house, but even she could not ignore the continuous pounding of the axes against the trees. Or the sight of the loaded lumber wagons rolling out of the forest. In the middle of washing or ironing or hoeing, she would look up sorrowfully and listen, then turn toward the road, searching for some sign of Papa and Stacey.

On the fourth day, before the sun had risen, bringing its cloak of miserable heat, I saw her walking alone toward the woods. I ran after her.

She did not send me back.

"Mama," I said. "How sick are you?"

Mama took my hand. "Remember when you had the flu and felt so sick?"

"Yes'm."

"And when I gave you some medicine, you got well soon afterward?"

"Yes'm."

E

"Well, that's how sick I am. As soon as I get my medicine, I'll be all well again. And that'll be soon, now that Papa's coming home," she said, giving my hand a gentle little squeeze.

The quiet surrounded us as we entered the forest. Mama clicked on the flashlight, and we walked silently along the cow path to the pond. There, just beyond the pond, pockets of open space loomed before us.

"Mama!"

"I know, baby, I know."

On the ground lay countless trees. Trees that had once been such strong, tall things. So strong that I could fling my arms partially around one of them and feel safe and secure. So tall and leafy green that their boughs had formed a forest temple.

And old.

So old that Indians had once built fires at their feet and had sung happy songs of happy days. So old they had hidden fleeing black men in the night and listened to their sad tales of a foreign land.

F

In the cold of winter, when the ground lay frozen, they had sung their frosty ballads of years gone by. Or on a muggy, sweat-drenched day, their leaves had rippled softly, lazily, like restless green fingers strumming at a guitar, echoing their epic tales.

But now they would sing no more. They lay forever silent upon the ground.

Those trees that remained standing were like defeated warriors mourning their fallen dead. But soon they, too, would fall, for the white *X*'s had been placed on nearly every one.

517

DIRECT TEACHING

E **Literary Focus**

❓ **Characterization.** What can you tell about Mama's character from this conversation? [Possible responses: She is warm and affectionate with her children. She is honest but makes an effort to reassure Cassie that all will be well.]

F **Literary Focus**

❓ **Theme.** Cassie says that the trees had once made her "feel safe and secure," not only because of their strength but also because of their age. What scenes from the past does she connect with the trees? How did the trees offer comfort to other people? [Possible response: She associates the trees with other groups of "outsiders"—people who have lost their lands. She imagines Native Americans sitting around fires, telling happy tales of their past, and fugitive slaves hiding in the forest, thinking of their faraway homelands.]

Use the selection words *threatened, heavy,* and *head* as examples of words in which *ea* stands for the short *e* instead of the long *e*.
Activity. Display these sentences and have volunteers underline the two words that contain *ai* or *ea*. Have them tell which word has a long vowel sound.
1. The family was about to eat breakfast. [eat]

2. Uneasiness hung heavy in the air. [uneasiness]
3. The children were afraid to go against their parents' wishes. [afraid]
4. Mean greed threatened the woods. [mean]
5. Men were ready to steal the trees. [steal]

A Literary Focus

❓ Novella: Plot. Point out to students that the scene that ends here is not strictly necessary to advance the plot. Why might the author have included it? [Possible response: Since a novella is longer than a short story, the author can include more scenes to develop characters and help establish the theme.]

B Reading Skills

❓ Infer. What personal qualities does Little Man seem to share with his parents? [Possible response: Like his father and mother, he does not let himself be pushed around or treated with disrespect.]

C Reading Skills

❓ Make generalizations. Cassie defends Little Man, and Christopher-John defends Cassie. What do their actions say about close families in general? [Possible response: Family members pull together when someone threatens one of them.]

"Oh, dear, dear trees," I cried as the gray light of the rising sun fell in ghostly shadows over the land. The tears rolled hot down my cheeks. Mama held me close, and when I felt her body tremble, I knew she was crying too.

A When our tears eased, we turned sadly toward the house. As we emerged from the forest, we could see two small figures waiting impatiently on the other side of the road. As soon as they spied us, they hurried across to meet us.

"Mama! You and Cassie was in the forest," Little Man accused. "Big Ma told us!"

"How was it?" asked Christopher-John, rubbing the sleep from his eyes. "Was it spooky?"

"Spooky and empty," I said listlessly.

"Mama, me and Christopher-John wanna see too," Little Man declared.

"No, baby," Mama said softly as we crossed the road. "The men'll be done there soon, and I don't want y'all underfoot."

"But, Mama—" Little Man started to protest.

"When Papa comes home and the men are gone, then you can go. But until then, you stay out of there. You hear me, Little Man Logan?"

"Yes'm," Little Man reluctantly replied.

But the sun had been up only an hour when Little Man decided that he could not wait for Papa to return.

"Mama said we wasn't to go down there," Christopher-John warned.

"Cassie did," Little Man cried.

"But she was with Mama. Wasn't you, Cassie?"

"Well, I'm going too," said Little Man. "Everybody's always going someplace 'cepting me." And off he went.

Christopher-John and I ran after him. Down the narrow cow path and around the pond we chased. But neither of us was fast enough to overtake Little Man before he reached the lumbermen.

"Hey, you kids, get away from here," Mr. Andersen shouted when he saw us. "Now, y'all go on back home," he said, stopping in front of Little Man.

"We are home," I said. "You're the one who's on our land."

"Claude," Mr. Andersen said to one of the black lumbermen, "take these kids home." **B** Then he pushed Little Man out of his way. Little Man pushed back. Mr. Andersen looked down, startled that a little black boy would do such a thing. He shoved Little Man a second time, and Little Man fell into the dirt.

Little Man looked down at his clothing covered with sawdust and dirt and wailed, "You got my clothes dirty!"

C I rushed toward Mr. Andersen, my fist in a mighty hammer, shouting, "You ain't got no right to push on Little Man. Why don't you push on somebody your own size—like me, you ole—"

The man called Claude put his hand over my mouth and carried me away. Christopher-John trailed behind us, tugging on the man's shirt.

"Put her down. Hey, mister, put Cassie down."

CROSS-CURRICULAR CONNECTIONS

History

Local history. Point out how Cassie associates the trees and the history of the peoples who have lived in the forest (p. 517). She paints a vivid picture of Native Americans celebrating beneath the trees and later of African Americans seeking safety under the trees' cover. Only small areas of old-growth forest such as the one Cassie loves survive outside of national parks. Ask students if they have ever visited such forests.

Activity. Have students research the natural history of their local area and write an imaginative description of some aspect of the place as it was in the past. Then ask them to draw a sketch of what they described.

INDIVIDUAL

A Literary Focus

❓ Characterization. What type of person is Tom? [Possible response: He has a sense of humor. He doesn't seem to like or respect Mr. Andersen.] Ask students to go back and find other details about Tom that show him to be sympathetic to the Logans. Remind students that, because this is a novella, the author has space to develop minor characters like Tom.

B Literary Focus

❓ Theme. Why do Cassie and Christopher-John risk being hurt even though they probably know that they can't win against grown men? [Possible responses: They will take any risk to try to protect a family member; they have learned to stand up for themselves.]

The man carried me all the way to the pond. "Now," he said, "you and your brothers get on home before y'all get hurt. Go on, get!"

As the man walked away, I looked around. "Where's Little Man?"

Christopher-John looked around too.

"I don't know," he said. "I thought he was behind me."

Back we ran toward the lumbermen.

We found Little Man's clothing first, folded neatly by a tree. Then we saw Little Man, dragging a huge stick and headed straight for Mr. Andersen.

"Little Man, come back here," I called.

But Little Man did not stop.

Mr. Andersen stood alone, barking orders, unaware of the oncoming Little Man.

"Little Man! Oh, Little Man, don't!"

It was too late.

Little Man swung the stick as hard as he could against Mr. Andersen's leg.

Mr. Andersen let out a howl and reached to where he thought Little Man's collar was. But, of course, Little Man had no collar.

"Run, Man!" Christopher-John and I shouted. "Run!"

"Why, you little . . ." Mr. Andersen cried, grabbing at Little Man. But Little Man was too quick for him. He slid right through Mr. Andersen's legs. Tom stood nearby, his face crinkling into an amused grin.

"Hey, y'all!" Mr. Andersen yelled to the lumbermen. "Claude! Get that kid!"

But sure-footed Little Man dodged the groping hands of the lumbermen as easily as if he were skirting mud puddles. Over tree stumps, around legs, and through legs he dashed. But in the end, there were too many lumbermen for him, and he was handed over to Mr. Andersen.

For the second time, Christopher-John and I went to Little Man's rescue.

"Put him down!" we ordered, charging the lumbermen.

I was captured much too quickly, though not before I had landed several stinging blows. But Christopher-John, furious at seeing Little Man handled so roughly by Mr. Andersen, managed to elude the clutches of the lumbermen until he was fully upon Mr. Andersen. Then, with his mightiest thrust, he kicked Mr. Andersen solidly in the shins, not once, but twice, before the lumbermen pulled him away.

Mr. Andersen was fuming. He slowly took off his wide leather belt. Christopher-John, Little Man, and I looked woefully at the belt, then at each other. Little Man and Christopher-John fought to escape, but I closed my eyes and awaited the whining of the heavy belt and its painful bite against my skin.

Vocabulary

skirting (skurt'in) *v.:* narrowly avoiding.

elude (ē·lood') *v.:* escape by quickness or cleverness.

What was he waiting for? I started to open my eyes, but then the zinging whirl of the belt began and I tensed, awaiting its fearful sting. But just as the leather tip lashed into my leg, a deep, familiar voice said, "Put the belt down, Andersen."

I opened my eyes.

"Papa!"

"Let the children go," Papa said. He was standing on a nearby ridge with a strange black box in his hands. Stacey was behind him, holding the reins to Lady.

The chopping stopped as all eyes turned to Papa.

"They been right meddlesome," Mr. Andersen said. "They need teaching how to act."

"Any teaching, I'll do it. Now, let them go."

Mr. Andersen looked down at Little Man struggling to get away. Smiling broadly, he motioned our release. "Okay, David," he said.

As we ran up the ridge to Papa, Mr. Andersen said, "It's good to have you home, boy."

Papa said nothing until we were safely behind him. "Take them home, Stacey."

"But, Papa—"

"Do like I say, son."

Stacey herded us away from the men. When we were far enough away so Papa couldn't see us, Stacey stopped and handed me Lady's reins.

"Y'all go on home now," he said. "I gotta go help Papa."

"Papa don't need no help," I said. "He told you to come with us."

"But you don't know what he's gonna do."

"What?" I asked.

"He's gonna blow up the forest if they don't get out of here. So go on home where y'all be safe."

"How's he gonna do that?" asked Little Man.

"We been setting sticks of dynamite since the middle of the night. We ain't even been up to the house cause Papa wanted the sticks planted and covered over before the men came. Now, Cassie, take them on back to the house. Do like I tell you for once, will ya?" Then, without waiting for another word, he was gone.

"I wanna see," Little Man announced.

"I don't," protested Christopher-John.

"Come on," I said.

We tied the mare to a tree, then belly-crawled back to where we could see Papa and joined Stacey in the brush.

"Cassie, I told you . . ."

"What's Papa doing?"

The black box was now set upon a sawed-off tree stump, and Papa's hands were tightly grasping a T-shaped instrument which went into it.

"What's that thing?" asked Little Man.

"It's a plunger," Stacey whispered. "If Papa presses down on it, the whole forest will go *pfffff*!"

Our mouths went dry and our eyes went wide. Mr. Andersen's eyes were wide, too.

"You're bluffing, David," he said. "You ain't gonna push that plunger."

"One thing you can't seem to understand, Andersen," Papa said, "is that a black man's always gotta be ready to die. And it don't make me any difference if I die today or tomorrow. Just as long as I die right."

Mr. Andersen laughed uneasily. The lumbermen moved nervously away.

"I mean what I say," Papa said. "Ask anyone. I always mean what I say."

"He sure do, Mr. Andersen," Claude said, eyeing the black box. "He always do."

"Shut up!" Mr. Andersen snapped. "And

Song of the Trees **521**

DIRECT TEACHING

C Learners Having Difficulty

Find details. Ask students to find details suggesting that Mr. Andersen is afraid of Papa but considers himself superior to Papa. [Possible response: Mr. Andersen obeys Papa's demand to let the children go, but then he calls Papa "boy," a deliberate insult to a grown African American man.]

D Literary Focus

? Novella: Conflict. What advantage does Papa have in his conflict with Mr. Andersen? [Possible responses: Papa is holding the plunger and seems ready to carry out his threat; Mr. Andersen can't be sure that David is bluffing.]

E Literary Focus

? Theme. What do you think David means when he says "Just as long as I die right"? [Possible responses: He means that he can accept death if it comes as the result of his doing the right thing and defending something he loves. He means that he will not let himself back down out of fear or cowardice.]

DEVELOPING FLUENCY

Activity. Have the whole class take turns reading the climactic scene aloud, starting on p. 521 with the paragraph that begins "'Let the children go,' Papa said." When a student has read as much as he or she wants, that student stops and the person next to him or her picks up where the story was left off.

WHOLE CLASS

A Literary Focus

Novella: Climax. In what way is this the high point of the novella's action? [Possible response: Until this point Mr. Andersen has bullied and threatened the Logans in order to get his way. David Logan has figured out a way to stop Mr. Andersen, but it could come at a great price. Readers wonder which way the conflict will be resolved.]

B Literary Focus

Theme. How has David won his self-respect? [Possible response: He has stood up to Mr. Andersen's threats.]

C Literary Focus

Novella: Resolution. Does this resolution of the conflict seem realistic, based on the characters of Mr. Andersen and David Logan? [Possible responses: Yes, Mr. Andersen is a bully and a coward. It seems realistic that he would back down. No, it would be more realistic for Mr. Andersen to call David's bluff.]

Monitor students' progress.
Guide students in answering these comprehension questions. Direct students to locate passages in the text that support their responses.

Short Answer

1. Why is Papa away at the beginning of the story? [He has gone where there is work.]

2. How does Cassie know that something is wrong in the forest? [She suspects something because the trees stop "singing." Then she sees the mysterious white X's.]

3. What does Mr. Andersen want to do with the trees? [He wants to cut them down and sell the lumber]

4. How does Papa save the forest? [He threatens to blow it up.]

---

the rest of y'all stay put." Then turning back to Papa, he smiled cunningly. "I'm sure you and me can work something out, David."

"Ain't nothing to be worked out," said Papa.

"Now, look here, David, your mama and me, we got us a contract. . . ."

"There ain't no more contract," Papa replied coldly. "Now, either you get out or I blow it up. That's it."

"He means it, Mr. Andersen," another frightened lumberman ventured. "He's crazy and he sure 'nough means it."

"You know what could happen to you, boy?" Mr. Andersen exploded, his face beet red again. "Threatening a white man like this?"

Papa said nothing. He just stood there, his hands firmly on the plunger, staring down at Mr. Andersen.

Mr. Andersen could not bear the stare. He turned away, cursing Papa. "You're a fool, David. A crazy fool." Then he looked around at the lumbermen. They shifted their eyes and would not look at him.

"Maybe we better leave, Mr. Andersen," Tom said quietly.

Mr. Andersen glanced at Tom, then turned back to Papa and said as lightly as he could, "All right, David, all right. It's your land. We'll just take the logs we got cut and get out." He motioned to the men. "Hey, let's get moving and get these logs out of here before this crazy fool gets us all killed."

"No," Papa said.

Mr. Andersen stopped, knowing that he could not have heard correctly. "What you say?"

"You ain't taking one more stick out of this forest."

"Now, look here—"

"You heard me."

"But you can't sell all these logs, David," Mr. Andersen exclaimed incredulously.

Papa said nothing. Just cast that piercing look on Mr. Andersen.

"Look, I'm a fair man. I tell you what I'll do. I'll give you another thirty-five dollars. An even hundred dollars. Now, that's fair, ain't it?"

"I'll see them rot first."

"But—"

"That's my last word," Papa said, tightening his grip on the plunger.

Mr. Andersen swallowed hard. "You won't always have that black box, David," he warned. "You know that, don't you?"

"That may be. But it won't matter none. 'Cause I'll always have my self-respect."

Mr. Andersen opened his mouth to speak, but no sound came. Tom and the lumbermen were quietly moving away, putting their gear in the empty lumber wagons. Mr. Andersen looked again at the black box. Finally, his face ashen, he too walked away.

Papa stood unmoving until the wagons and the men were gone. Then, when the sound of the last wagon rolling over the dry leaves could no longer be heard and a hollow silence filled the air, he slowly removed his hands from the plunger and looked up at the remaining trees standing like lonely sentries in the morning.

"Dear, dear old trees," I heard him call softly, "will you ever sing again?"

I waited. But the trees gave no answer.

Vocabulary
incredulously (in·krej′ōō·ləs·lē) *adv.:* unbelievingly.
ashen (ash′ən) *adj.:* pale.
sentries (sen′trēz) *n.:* guards.

FAMILY/COMMUNITY ACTIVITY

Have students work in small groups to research what life was like in their community during the Great Depression. Guide them to several local resources, such as a historical society or a city resource and information office. They may also be able to conduct interviews with local residents who can give them firsthand information. Afterward, they can present their findings to the class. Encourage students to find photographs or make drawings for their presentations.

Meet the Writer

Mildred D. Taylor

We Could Be Anything

Mildred D. Taylor (1943–) grew up in Toledo, Ohio. In high school she was an honor student, a newspaper editor, and a class officer—but, she says, she wasn't able to do what she really wanted: be a cheerleader.

Every summer she and her family visited Mississippi relatives, and she listened to their stories. By the time she was nine or ten, she knew that she wanted to write. "I wanted to show a Black family united in love and pride, of which the reader would like to be a part."

Her first effort, *Song of the Trees*, introduced the Logan family and won first prize in the African American category of a competition for children's books. In 1977, when she accepted the Newbery Award for her second work about the Logan family, *Roll of Thunder, Hear My Cry*, Taylor talked about her father:

❝ Throughout my childhood he impressed upon my sister and me that we were somebody, that we were important and could do or be anything we set our minds to do or be. He was not the kind of father who demanded A's on our report cards. He was more concerned about how we carried ourselves, how we respected ourselves and others, and how we pursued the principles upon which he hoped we would build our lives. He was constantly reminding us that how we saw ourselves was far more important than how others saw us.... Through David Logan have come the words of my father, and through the Logan family the love of my own family. ❞

For Independent Reading

You can rejoin Cassie Logan and her family in the novels *Let the Circle Be Unbroken* and *The Road to Memphis*.

Meet the Writer

Many authors choose personal lessons as the subjects for their work. Mildred Taylor is no exception. "From as far back as I can remember," she says, "my father taught me a different history from the one I learned in school. . . . There was often humor in his stories, sometimes pathos, and frequently tragedy; but always the people were graced with a simple dignity that elevated them from the ordinary to the heroic."

For Independent Reading

- Students who choose to read *Roll of Thunder, Hear My Cry; Let the Circle Be Unbroken;* or *The Road to Memphis* may be interested to know that the three books, all narrated by Cassie Logan, take her from age nine to seventeen.
- For a story about Cassie Logan's father as a young boy, students can read Mildred Taylor's *The Well.*
- The Oklahoma Dust Bowl during the Great Depression is the setting for Karen Hesse's *Out of the Dust;* the story is about fourteen-year-old Billie Jo's attempts to cope with life after her mother's tragic death.
- *Bud, Not Buddy,* by Christopher Paul Curtis, shows the Depression through the eyes of a ten-year-old orphan in Flint, Michigan.

Advanced Learners
Enrichment. Have students find out more about Mildred Taylor. Suggest that they enter *Mildred Taylor* as a key word in a search engine. Students can also find information about Taylor in the encyclopedias *Something About the Author* and *Something About the Author Autobiography Series.*

After You Read

First Thoughts

1. Possible answer: The most vivid scene for me is the last scene, in which the father stands in a clearing, holding a dynamite plunger and threatening Mr. Andersen.

Thinking Critically

2. Possible passages: Cassie and her mother's going to see the damage to the forest (p. 517); the end of the story when Papa speaks to the trees (p. 522). Possible answer: Cassie loves the trees because they are beautiful and old. She thinks of them as friends.

3. "Hissed venomously" suggests a snake. Students might feel he is evil or dangerous.

4. Possible answers: Since Cassie's father is away from home, he would not have firsthand knowledge of many of the events. However, readers would know more about the father's inner thoughts and feelings.

Extending Interpretations

5. Possible answers: Students may agree more with statement 1 because of David's behavior, with 2 and 3 because of Mr. Andersen's behavior and words, and with 4 because of Cassie's musings about the trees.

6. Possible answers: The characters are believable because they all have individual characteristics and interact with one another realistically. Some may think Mr. Andersen seems too evil to be real.

First Thoughts

1. What scene from the story do you remember most vividly?

Thinking Critically

2. Cassie describes the trees as if they could talk and sing. Find two passages in the story in which the trees seem human. Why do you think Cassie loves her trees so much?

3. When you read on page 516 that Mr. Andersen "hissed venomously," what are you reminded of? How do you feel about Mr. Andersen's behavior?

4. *Song of the Trees* is told by Cassie. How would the story be different if it were told by her father?

Extending Interpretations

5. Go back to the statements you rated on page 508. Individually and with the class, rate the four statements again, using the same scale. Have any of your opinions changed now that you've read the story? ✎

6. Taylor says that in writing *Song of the Trees*, "[I] drew upon people and places I had known all my life." In creating the character of Cassie, for example, she drew on the personalities of her sister and an aunt. How believable did the characters seem to you? Explain.

INTERNET
Projects and Activities
Keyword: LE5 7-5

SKILLS FOCUS

Literary Skills
Analyze a novella.

Reading Skills
Make a generalization.

Writing Skills
Explain a theme.

WRITING

Writing About Theme

Theme, as you learned earlier (pages 236–237), is the *meaning* of a story. Theme points to what the main characters learn in the story and to what *you* learn as you share their experiences. In a paragraph, explain what you think the theme of this story is.

Reading Check

Create a story map for the **plot** of *Song of the Trees*. Copy and fill in the following diagram:

Characters:

Conflicts:

Event:

Event:

Event:

Event: [Add as many event boxes as you need.]

Resolution of conflict:

Reading Check

Possible answers: *Characters*—Cassie, Big Ma, Mama, Papa, Stacey, Christopher-John, Little Man, Mr. Andersen. *Conflicts*—The Logans versus Mr. Andersen. *Event*—The Logan children hear Mr. Andersen and Tom talking about cutting down trees on the Logan property. *Event*—Mr. Andersen offers Big Ma sixty-five dollars for the trees. *Event*—Big Ma and Mama send Stacey to fetch Papa. *Event*—Papa threatens to dynamite the whole forest. *Resolution of conflict*—Mr. Andersen backs off and leaves.

Connotations: What's the Difference Between . . .

Would you rather be described as *curious* or *nosy*? The two words have the same basic meaning, or **denotation,** but they have different connotations. **Connotations** are the feelings and associations that have come to be attached to certain words. Most people wouldn't mind being called curious: It suggests that you are interested in the world around you and want to learn about it. *Nosy* has negative connotations: It suggests that you are someone who puts your nose into other people's business.

Word Bank

finicky
dispute
ambled
delved
curtly
skirting
elude
incredulously
ashen
sentries

PRACTICE

Test your skills at recognizing shades of meaning. (Use a dictionary to check your answers.) What's the difference between the following words and phrases? It would help if you go back and read the word in its context in the story.

1. *careful* and *finicky*
2. a *brawl* and a *dispute*
3. *walked* and *ambled*
4. *looked for* and *delved*
5. *matter-of-factly* and *curtly*
6. *passing* and *skirting*
7. *escape* and *elude*
8. *doubtfully* and *incredulously*
9. *creamy* and *ashen*
10. *watchers* and *sentries*

SKILLS FOCUS

Vocabulary Skills
Understand connotation and denotation.

Song of the Trees **525**

Vocabulary Development

PRACTICE

Possible Answers
1. *Careful,* meaning "thoughtful and painstaking," has a positive connotation; *finicky* implies being overly fussy.
2. *Brawl* suggests a violent conflict, while *dispute* suggests a reasonable disagreement.
3. *Walked* suggests a normal pace, while *ambled* suggests a slow, leisurely stroll.
4. *Delved* implies a deeper investigation than *looked for.*
5. *Matter-of-factly* suggests no emotion, while *curtly* implies rude impatience.
6. *Passing* means going by somebody or something, while *skirting* means narrowly avoiding somebody or something.
7. *Elude* suggests a clever *escape* or avoidance.
8. *Doubtfully* means having doubts, while *incredulously* suggests disbelief.
9. *Ashen* suggests an unhealthy, gray pallor, while *creamy* suggests a healthy cream color.
10. *Watchers* simply observe, while *sentries* stand guard for security.

DIFFERENTIATING INSTRUCTION

Learners Having Difficulty
Have students fill out the story map diagram in class. Help students recall that a conflict is a struggle between two opposing sides. Remind them to include only those events directly related to the major conflict.

Advanced Learners
Have students discuss this question: What makes some people able to resist a bully, while others seem unable to stand up for themselves? Have them infer what kind of upbringing David Logan might have had, and then suggest that they read Mildred Taylor's *The Well,* which shows David as a boy.

Enrichment. Have students answer question 4 by writing an interior monologue for David Logan as he rides back to Mississippi with Stacey.

HOMEWORK

Grammar Link

PRACTICE

1. The final conversation between Mr. Logan and Mr. Andersen is a key scene in this story.
2. We often watched Little Man fidgeting with his clothing in front of the mirror.
3. I understood almost every word of the story.
4. Stacey saw a man named Mr. Andersen near the tree.
5. The children, who were weeping softly, looked at the trees.
6. The trees, with their leafy boughs, whispered to the children.
7. Mr. Andersen's car, with its shiny fenders, was already parked in the driveway.
8. Other books by Mildred Taylor are about the Logans.
9. In this book, there's a story about a mongoose who kills snakes.
10. There's also a story called "A Rice Sandwich" about a girl named Esperanza.

ASSESSING

Assessment

■ *Holt Assessment: Literature, Reading, and Vocabulary*

RETEACHING

For a lesson reteaching forms of prose, see **Reteaching**, p. 917C.

After You Read Grammar Link

All Modifiers! Places, Please!

To work well, modifiers have to be in the right place. A modifier that seems to modify the wrong word in a sentence is called a **misplaced modifier.** Here's an example of a misplaced modifier:

MISPLACED   Today I read a story about a forest that was almost blown up <u>in my literature book.</u>

Did the forest blow up in the book? No, the phrase *in my literature book* is misplaced. To fix the sentence, place the modifier as close as possible to the word it modifies—*read.*

CORRECT   Today I read <u>in my literature book</u> a story about a forest that was almost blown up.

MISPLACED   Cassie heard the men say they were going to cut down the forest <u>with her own ears.</u>

CORRECT   Cassie heard <u>with her own ears</u> the men say they were going to cut down the forest.

CORRECT   <u>With her own ears,</u> Cassie heard the men say they were going to cut down the forest.

Grammar Skills
Avoid misplaced modifiers.

PRACTICE

Move the misplaced modifiers in these sentences to the right place.

1. The final conversation is a key scene in this story between Mr. Logan and Mr. Andersen.
2. Fidgeting with his clothing, we often watched Little Man in front of the mirror.
3. I almost understood every word of the story.
4. Stacy saw a man near the tree named Mr. Andersen.
5. The children looked at the trees who were weeping softly.
6. The trees whispered to the children with their leafy boughs.
7. Mr. Andersen's car was already parked in the driveway with its shiny fenders.
8. Other books are about the Logans by Mildred Taylor.
9. There's a story about a mongoose who kills snakes in this book.
10. There's also a story about a girl named Esperanza called "A Rice Sandwich."

For more help, see Placement of Modifiers, 5g, in the Language Handbook.

Before You Read   The Essay

Fish Cheeks

Make the Connection
Quickwrite ✏️

A girl is walking down the hall at school. Coming toward her is a boy she's been dying to meet. They are almost next to each other when she slips, loses her balance, and falls to the floor in a clumsy heap. How could a moment like this possibly have a positive outcome?

Jot down your responses to that question. Then, in a group, share your possible outcomes.

Literary Focus
Humorous Essays: Tickling Your Funny Bone

An **essay** is a short piece of nonfiction prose that looks at one subject in a limited way. Though essays can be formal and logical, many of the essays we enjoy today are relaxed, informal writings that reveal a great deal about the writer's feelings. Most essays—like this one by Amy Tan—are published in popular magazines.

Writers of **humorous essays** are something like stand-up comics: They entertain us by putting a funny spin or twist on odd or embarrassing moments from everyday life.

Writers of humorous essays aren't always just out for laughs, however. They often have other, more serious purposes in mind. As you read the following essay, see if you think the writer intends to do more than tickle your funny bone (but first, read the essay just for fun).

Reading Skills 📖
Describing Images: Appealing to the Senses

When writers describe things, they create **images**—pictures drawn with words. To help readers imagine places, events, and characters, they use language that appeals to the senses, as Amy Tan does in this true story. When you read descriptions, notice that

- most images are visual, but they often appeal to several senses at once
- writers often choose details that show how they *feel* about what they describe

Vocabulary Development

Learning the following words will help you appreciate the vividness of Amy Tan's writing:

appalling (ə·pôl′iŋ) *adj.*: horrifying. *The amount of food on the dinner table was simply appalling.*

wedges (wej′iz) *n.*: pie-shaped slices. *The tofu was cut into bite-sized wedges.*

clamor (klam′ər) *n.*: loud, confused noise. *The clamor in the dining room probably could have been heard down the hall.*

rumpled (rum′pəld) *v.* used as *adj.*: wrinkled and untidy. *Amy was embarrassed by her uncle's rumpled gifts.*

muster (mus′tər) *v.*: call forth. *She couldn't even muster up a smile for her mother after dinner.*

INTERNET

Vocabulary Activity
•
Cross-curricular Connection
•
More About Tan

Keyword: LE5 7-5

Literary Skills
Understand forms of prose: the essay.

Reading Skills
Understand images.

Fish Cheeks   **527**

SKILLS FOCUS
pp. 527–532

Grade-Level Skills

■ **Literary Skills**
Analyze characteristics of different forms of prose, including the essay.

■ **Reading Skills**
Understand images.

Summary ↔ *at grade level*

At age fourteen, Amy Tan has a crush on the minister's son. Her parents invite the minister's family to dinner for Christmas Eve. Amy is embarrassed by the Chinese food her mother serves and by her relatives' Chinese table manners. But Amy's mother reminds her to be proud that she is Chinese. Years later, Amy realizes just how sensitive her mother was to her feelings; she served all of Amy's favorite foods for that dinner.

Selection Starter

Motivate. Ask students to think about whether their families have ever embarrassed them in front of their friends. Have they ever wished they could just sink right through the floor? Ask for volunteers to share embarrassing moments that they can now look back on calmly or even with humor.

Preview Vocabulary

After students read the definitions and sample sentences on p. 527, have them do the following exercises.

1. Describe a food that you think tastes <u>appalling</u>.

2. Draw a picture of an apple cut into <u>wedges</u>.

3. Tell about a time that you and your friends raised a <u>clamor</u>.

4. List ways to make sure your clothes aren't <u>rumpled</u>.

5. Tell about a time that you were not able to <u>muster</u> a sound.

Assign the Reading

You might read the entire essay aloud. Then, assign advanced students the After You Read activities for homework. Review the essay with small groups of readers having difficulty.

HOMEWORK

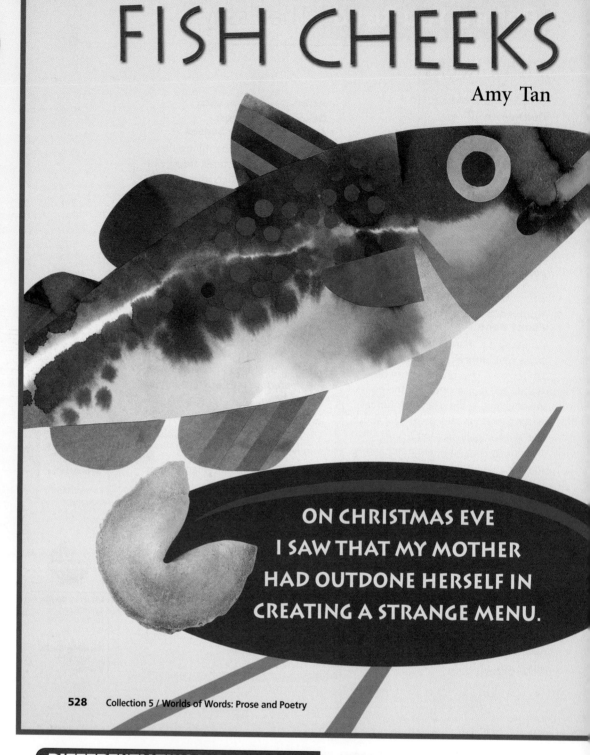

FISH CHEEKS

Amy Tan

ON CHRISTMAS EVE
I SAW THAT MY MOTHER
HAD OUTDONE HERSELF IN
CREATING A STRANGE MENU.

528   Collection 5 / Worlds of Words: Prose and Poetry

DIFFERENTIATING INSTRUCTION

Learners Having Difficulty
Modeling. To help students read humorous descriptions such as those in "Fish Cheeks," model the skill of recognizing sensory language. Say: Suppose you read a description such as the following: "slimy rock cod with bulging fish eyes." You can tell that a fish is slimy if you touch it, so the word *slimy* appeals to the sense of touch. You can both see and touch something that is bulging, so that word appeals to your senses of sight and touch." Encourage students as they read to ask themselves, "What senses does this description appeal to?"

English-Language Learners
You might display pictures from magazines or newspapers of some of the Chinese foods described in this essay and some foods found at typical American Christmas

I fell in love with the minister's son the winter I turned fourteen. He was not Chinese, but as white as Mary in the manger. For Christmas I prayed for this blond-haired boy, Robert, and a slim new American nose.

When I found out that my parents had invited the minister's family over for Christmas Eve dinner, I cried. What would Robert think of our shabby *Chinese* Christmas? What would he think of our noisy *Chinese* relatives who lacked proper American manners? What terrible disappointment would he feel upon seeing not a roasted turkey and sweet potatoes but *Chinese* food?

On Christmas Eve I saw that my mother had outdone herself in creating a strange menu. She was pulling black veins out of the backs of fleshy prawns. The kitchen was littered with appalling mounds of raw food: a slimy rock cod with bulging fish eyes that pleaded not to be thrown into a pan of hot oil. Tofu, which looked like stacked wedges of rubbery white sponges. A bowl soaking dried fungus back to life. A plate of squid, their backs crisscrossed with knife markings so they resembled bicycle tires.

And then they arrived—the minister's family and all my relatives in a clamor of doorbells and rumpled Christmas packages. Robert grunted hello, and I pretended he was not worthy of existence.

Dinner threw me deeper into despair. My relatives licked the ends of their chopsticks and reached across the table, dipping them into the dozen or so plates of food. Robert and his family waited patiently for platters to be passed to them. My relatives murmured with pleasure when my mother brought out the whole steamed fish. Robert grimaced. Then my father poked his chopsticks just below the fish eye and plucked out the soft meat. "Amy, your favorite," he said, offering me the tender fish cheek. I wanted to disappear.

At the end of the meal my father leaned back and belched loudly, thanking my mother for her fine cooking. "It's a polite Chinese custom to show you are satisfied," explained my father to our astonished guests. Robert was looking down at his plate with a reddened face. The minister managed to muster up a quiet burp. I was stunned into silence for the rest of the night.

After everyone had gone, my mother said to me, "You want to be the same as American girls on the outside." She handed me an early gift. It was a miniskirt in beige tweed. "But inside you must always be Chinese. You must be proud you are different. Your only shame is to have shame."

And even though I didn't agree with her then, I knew that she understood how much I had suffered during the evening's dinner. It wasn't until many years later—long after I had gotten over my crush on Robert—that I was able to fully appreciate her lesson and the true purpose behind our particular menu. For Christmas Eve that year, she had chosen all my favorite foods.

Vocabulary

appalling (ə·pôl′iŋ) *adj.:* shocking; horrifying.

wedges (wej′iz) *n.:* pie-shaped slices.

clamor (klam′ər) *n.:* loud, confused noise.

rumpled (rum′pəld) *v.* used as *adj.:* wrinkled and untidy.

muster (mus′tər) *v.:* call forth.

Fish Cheeks   **529**

Meet the Writer

Meet the Writer

Amy Tan published three adult novels and two children's books in just six years and was much in demand as a speaker. Then both her mother and her best friend fell seriously ill, forcing Tan to cut back on public appearances to help care for them. During this time, she wrote *The Bonesetter's Daughter.*

Tan writes, "I write because there is a lot I don't understand about life and death, myself and the world and the great in-between. . . . I write to find the questions that I should ask."

For Independent Reading

■ If students like Amy Tan's writing, they might enjoy her children's books *The Moon Lady* and *The Chinese Siamese Cat.*

■ If students want to read more about a Chinese American childhood, they might like Laurence Yep's *Child of the Owl,* in which the heroine of the story moves in with her Chinese grandmother.

Amy Tan

Finding Answers in Stories

"I was the only Chinese girl in class from third grade on. I remember trying to belong and feeling isolated. I felt ashamed of being different and ashamed of feeling that way. When I was a teenager, I rejected everything Chinese. . . . The only people I could think I wanted to be like were fictional characters. In part, that is one of the reasons I began to write. You're looking for answers in your life, and you can't find them in anyone else. You end up finding them in stories."

Amy Tan (1952–   ) found her friends in books—fairy tales, the *Little House* novels of Laura Ingalls Wilder, and later, the British novels of the Brontë sisters. Later still she began to write books of her own, about a life half a world away from America's prairies and Britain's moors.

Tan spent her childhood in Oakland, California, where her parents had settled after leaving China. When she was fifteen, both her father and her brother died from brain tumors. After these losses her mother revealed a long-kept secret: Amy had three half sisters still living in China. These upheavals in her family changed Amy Tan's sense of who she was. Suddenly her Chinese heritage became important to her. She began to read whatever she could about China, later taking college courses in Chinese literature and history. Most of all, Tan became fascinated by her mother's stories about her experiences in China during the war-torn 1930s and 1940s.

In recent years, Amy Tan has made several trips to China, where she has come to know the sisters who once seemed lost to her forever. She now loves the Chinese culture she once tried so hard to reject.

530 Collection 5 / Worlds of Words: Prose and Poetry

DIFFERENTIATING INSTRUCTION

Learners Having Difficulty
Question 5 focuses on the main idea of the essay. Work on this question with students before asking them to answer the other items. *Monitoring tip:* If students have trouble finding images that appeal to different senses (question 3), have them re-read paragraphs three through six. Tell them to ask themselves, "What would I see and smell if I were in that kitchen?" and

"What would I hear when the guests arrived?"
Writing. Remind students to list sensory details before they begin writing. Encourage them to picture the event as a scene from a movie or TV show and to describe the sights, sounds, smells, tastes, and touch sensations they experienced.

HOMEWORK

After You Read Response and Analysis

First Thoughts

1. Have you ever felt the way Amy does? What would you have done that Christmas Eve if you had been Amy?

Thinking Critically

2. Why do you think Amy is ashamed of her family's Chinese traditions? What does her mother mean when she says, "Your only shame is to have shame"?

3. Find one **image** in the story that creates a vivid picture in your mind. Find three other images that help you feel you can touch, smell, taste, or hear details of the dinner.

4. Why do you suppose it isn't until many years later that Amy realizes her mother chose all of Amy's favorite foods for the Christmas Eve dinner? What do you think are her mother's "lesson" and "true purpose" in preparing those foods?

5. Is this **essay** about a strange menu, or is it really about something else? In one or two sentences, state what you think is Tan's **main idea.**

Extending Interpretations

6. Amy's mother tells her that she can be an American girl on the outside but must always be Chinese on the inside. Do you think that is possible? Is it a good idea? Explain your answer.

7. Where does the **title** "Fish Cheeks" come from? Do you think it's a good title? Tell why or why not.

WRITING

Writing a Narrative

Have you ever been in an embarrassing situation that somehow ended with a positive outcome (like the one you wrote about for the Quickwrite)? Write about that experience, or write about a time when you were anxious about making a good impression. Think about your **purpose:** Will you be writing only to entertain, or will your narrative have a point? Include images in your story that will help readers share your experience.

Reading Check

Imagine that it is Christmas Eve twenty years later. With a partner, retell the main events of "Fish Cheeks." Let one person play the role of Amy and the other person play her mother. Let Amy retell the story. Let her mother add details.

INTERNET
Projects and Activities
Keyword: LE5 7-5

SKILLS FOCUS

Literary Skills
Analyze an essay.

Reading Skills
Identify images.

Writing Skills
Write a narrative.

Fish Cheeks   **531**

Reading Check

Role-play responses will vary. Make sure students cover all the main events in the story, including these:

• Amy falls in love with Robert.

• Amy cries with shame when her parents invite Robert's family to Christmas Eve dinner.

• Amy's mother cooks an elaborate Chinese meal.

• Amy's father offers Amy a fish cheek during dinner.

• Amy's father belches at the end of the meal.

• After dinner, Amy's mother gives Amy a miniskirt.

• Amy's mother tells Amy to take pride in being Chinese.

After You Read

First Thoughts

1. Like Amy, many English-language learners may experience a conflict about their dual identity. Invite these students to share their experiences.

Thinking Critically

2. She is ashamed because their traditions are so different from the "American" ones that Robert follows. Her mother means that Amy should be ashamed only of not being proud of her heritage.

3. Possible answers: "A slimy rock cod with bulging fish eyes" is a vivid image that appeals to the senses of touch and sight. The relatives' licking and dipping their chopsticks appeals to taste and sight, the murmuring over steamed fish appeals to hearing and smell, and the burping appeals to hearing.

4. Young Amy is too self-conscious to realize what her mother is doing. As an adult, she realizes that her mother wanted to show her how much her family loved her and how proud she should be of her heritage.

5. The main idea is that it's best to be true to yourself and your heritage.

Extending Interpretations

6. Possible answer: Yes, it's possible and a good idea. Being from two cultures can lead to confusion or conflict, but it can also make a person more interesting and more understanding of others' ways.

7. Amy's father offers her fish cheeks, her favorite food, but she cringes in embarrassment. Because the dish represents Amy's mixed feelings about her Chinese background, it provides a good title for this essay.

Vocabulary Development

PRACTICE

1. appalling
2. rumpled
3. clamor
4. muster
5. wedges

ASSESSING

Assessment

■ *Holt Assessment: Literature, Reading, and Vocabulary*

RETEACHING

For a lesson reteaching forms of prose, see **Reteaching,** p. 917C.

After You Read | Vocabulary Development

Word Analogies: Pairs of Pairs

A **word analogy** begins with a pair of items that are related in some way. You figure out that relationship, and then complete another pair that has a similar relationship. For example,

Sweet is to *sour* as _____ is to *short.*
   a. small   b. bitter   c. tall   d. round

The relationship of *sweet* to *sour* is one of opposites. *Tall,* the opposite of *short,* is the best way to complete the analogy.

Try this one:

Kitten is to *cat* as _____ is to *dog.*
   a. poodle   b. puppy   c. fur   d. bark

A kitten is a young cat, so the correct answer is *puppy,* which is a young dog. Once you figure out the relationship, completing the analogy should be a snap.

Word Bank

appalling
wedges
clamor
rumpled
muster

PRACTICE

Complete the following analogies. First, figure out the relationship between the words in the first pair. Then, choose a Word Bank word that has a similar relationship to the last word in the sentence. Here's a hint for the first item:

1. *Sad* is to *happy* as _____ is to *delightful.*
The relationship between *sad* and *happy* is one of opposites. What word in the Word Bank is the opposite of *delightful*?

2. *Pressed* is to *neat* as _____ is to *sloppy.*

3. *Whisper* is to *soft* as _____ is to *loud.*

4. *Receive* is to *get* as _____ is to *summon.*

5. *Slices* is to *pizza* as _____ is to *cheese.*

SKILLS FOCUS

Vocabulary Skills
Complete word analogies.

A Mason-Dixon Memory

Make the Connection
Quickwrite 🖉

How far would you go to do the right thing? Think of something you really care about. It could be a possession or an event you're looking forward to—anything you'd hate to give up. Can you imagine a situation in which doing the right thing might mean giving up the thing you want so much? For example, what if going to a party means you have to break a date with a friend who wasn't invited? Jot down your thoughts on how you might handle such a situation.

Literary Focus
The Essay

One form of nonfiction you'll often be asked to read—and write—is the **essay,** a short piece of nonfiction prose that focuses on a single topic. An essay can be about anything, from "The Meaning of Life" to "How I Feel About My Cat."

An essay can be formal in tone and highly structured, with statements laid out in careful order and evidence supporting each one. An essay can also be personal and even humorous, as if the writer were sitting down with us for a chat. An essay's tone and structure will depend on its **purpose**—does the writer want to inform us? persuade us? entertain us? or do something else?

Reading Skills 📖
Recognizing Text Structures

Essays, like other pieces of writing, are often structured in ways that help make their meaning clear. This essay is structured around **flashbacks**—the narrator twice goes back to an earlier time to tell a story that relates to the first story he is telling. Like many essayists, the writer uses his final paragraph to sum up his main idea. As you read the essay, look for the open-book signs. These alert you to the essay's structure. (If you miss the flashbacks, you may be hopelessly lost in time!)

Vocabulary Development

Here are some words you'll learn as you read this selection:

predominantly (prē·däm′ə·nənt·lē) *adv.:* mainly. *The story is predominantly about the meaning of friendship.*

forfeit (fôr′fit) *v.:* lose the right to compete. *Dondré's teammates would forfeit the tournament.*

resolve (ri·zälv′) *v.:* decide. *In tough situations, people can resolve to do the right thing.*

ominous (äm′ə·nəs) *adj.:* threatening. *The look on the chaperone's face was ominous.*

erupted (ē·rup′tid) *v.:* burst forth. *Applause erupted from the audience after Dondré's speech.*

INTERNET
Vocabulary Activity
Keyword: LE5 7-5

SKILLS FOCUS

Literary Skills
Understand forms of prose: the essay.

Reading Skills
Recognize text structures: flashback.

SKILLS FOCUS
pp. 533–542

Grade-Level Skills
■ Literary Skills
Analyze forms of prose: the essay.
■ Reading Skills
Analyze flashbacks.

Summary ⬌ *at grade level*

This essay interweaves two real-life incidents to examine how people respond to bigotry. In 1991, Dondré Green, the only African American on the high school golf team in Monroe, Louisiana, was barred from playing in a tournament at a whites-only country club. His teammates forfeited the tournament rather than play without Dondré. This incident reminds the author of an episode that took place in 1959, when he was thirteen years old. On a school trip to Washington, D.C., Clifton Davis and his white classmates were scheduled to visit an amusement park in Maryland. The morning of the visit, a chaperone informed Clifton that the amusement park, south of the Mason-Dixon line, would not admit blacks. When the tearful Clifton broke the news to his roommate Frank, Frank vowed not to go either, and soon all their classmates joined the boycott.

Selection Starter

Build background. Share with students an example of alleged racism or sexism recently reported in a newspaper. Who claims to have been discriminated against? What is the evidence? Then, remind students that during the 1950s many African Americans in the South faced segregation in schools, buses, housing, and employment. The civil rights movement of the 1950s and 1960s slowly eroded these Jim Crow laws, even though some forms of racial discrimination continue today.

Preview Vocabulary

Have students read the definitions of the Vocabulary words on p. 533. Then, have students match each word with one of the following definitions.

1. most often or commonly [predominantly]
2. lose [forfeit]
3. broke out [erupted]
4. foreshadowing evil [ominous]
5. make a decision [resolve]

Assign the Reading

Have volunteers read the essay aloud to the end of the first flashback ("But above all, I was filled with pride"). Then, pair advanced students with learners having difficulty. Have these pairs work together, reading to find out how the two separate incidents, one in 1959 and the other in 1991, are related.

A Mason-Dixon Memory

Clifton Davis

Sponsor: Fred Matte

Dondré Green

Brad Coenen

Damon Marsala

Jeff McNew

David Elias

DIFFERENTIATING INSTRUCTION

Learners Having Difficulty
Modeling. To help students read "A Mason-Dixon Memory," model the reading skill of recognizing text structures. Say: "When you know that a story is set at a certain time, such as the year 1991, but the author breaks the time order to describe events that occurred earlier (say, in 1959), you know the author is using a text structure called flashback." Encourage students as they read to ask themselves: "When did these events occur in relation to the main time setting of the story?"

English-Language Learners
Flashbacks. To be sure English-language learners understand the flashback structure, have them mark the sections about Dondré with a self-sticking note of one color and then mark the sections about Clifton Davis

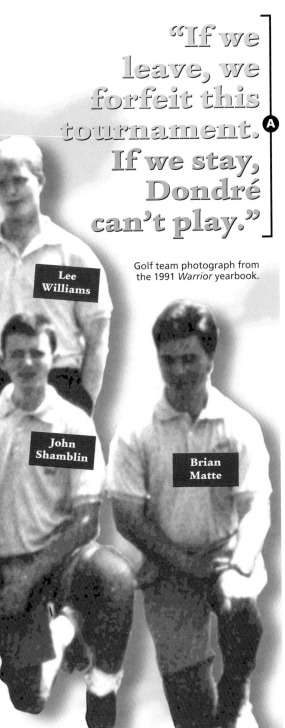

"If we leave, we forfeit this tournament. If we stay, Dondré can't play."

Golf team photograph from the 1991 *Warrior* yearbook.

Lee Williams

John Shamblin

Brian Matte

Dondré Green glanced uneasily at the civic leaders and sports figures filling the hotel ballroom in Cleveland. They had come from across the nation to attend a fundraiser for the National Minority College Golf Scholarship Foundation. I was the banquet's featured entertainer. Dondré, an eighteen-year-old high school senior from Monroe, Louisiana, was the evening's honored guest.

"Nervous?" I asked the handsome young man in his starched white shirt and rented tuxedo.

"A little," he whispered, grinning.

One month earlier, Dondré had been just one more black student attending a <u>predominantly</u> white Southern school. Although most of his friends and classmates were white, Dondré's race had never been an issue. Then, on April 17, 1991, Dondré's black skin provoked an incident that made nationwide news.

"Ladies and gentlemen," the emcee[1] said, "our special guest, Dondré Green."

As the audience stood applauding, Dondré walked to the microphone and began his story. "I love golf," he said quietly. "For the past two years, I've been a member of the St. Frederick High School golf team. And though I was the only black member, I've always felt at home playing at the mostly white country clubs across Louisiana."

The audience leaned forward; even the waiters and busboys stopped to listen. As I listened, a memory buried in my heart since childhood began fighting its way to life.

---

1. **emcee** (em′sē′) *n.:* master of ceremonies.

Vocabulary
predominantly (prē·däm′ə·nənt·lē) *adv.:* mainly.

DIRECT TEACHING

A Reading Skills
Predict. Have the class read the call-out quotation aloud. Point out that it sets forth an either-or situation: Either the team leaves or it stays. It also describes specific causes and effects: Leaving will cause a forfeit, but staying will result in discrimination against one player.

B Literary Focus
❓ The essay. What is the principal difference between an essay and a short story? [Essays are nonfiction containing factual information; short stories are fiction.] What facts do you learn about Dondré Green and the author in this opening paragraph? [Dondré Green is an eighteen-year-old golfer from Louisiana. The author, presumably an older person, is an entertainer. They are both attending a fundraiser in Cleveland for the National Minority College Golf Scholarship Foundation.]

C Reading Skills
❓ Text structure. Point out to students that this paragraph contains the first hint that a flashback is coming. What is that hint? [Possible response: The author mentions a long-buried memory, which readers may expect him to share.]

in another color. Move around the classroom making sure the notes are in the correct positions.

Special Education Students
For lessons designed for special education students, see *Holt Reading Solutions*.

Text structure. Tell students that extra space often, but not always, indicates a flashback or a switch in time.

[Possible response to question 1: The words "thirty-two years ago" indicate a flashback. The events of the flashback take place in 1959.]

B **Literary Focus**

❓ The essay. Based on what you have read so far, is this essay a formal, structured essay on a specific topic or a personal essay? [Possible response: This essay is a personal essay because the writer shares his life's experiences; it is not a formal examination of a subject.]

C **Vocabulary Development**

Clarify word meanings. Explain that a mimeographed letter was a letter that had been "run off" or reproduced many times on a mimeograph machine, an old-style copier.

D **Learners Having Difficulty**

❓ Find details. How can you tell that the trip was very important to the author? [Possible responses: He worked hard to earn the money for it. He was "trembling with excitement."]

"Our team had driven from Monroe," Dondré continued. "When we arrived at the Caldwell Parish Country Club in Columbia, we walked to the putting green."

Dondré and his teammates were too absorbed to notice the conversation between a man and St. Frederick athletic director James Murphy. After disappearing into the clubhouse, Murphy returned to his players.

"I want to see the seniors," he said. "On the double!" His face seemed strained as he gathered the four students, including Dondré.

"I don't know how to tell you this," he said, "but the Caldwell Parish Country Club is reserved for whites only." Murphy paused and looked at Dondré. His teammates glanced at each other in disbelief. "I want you seniors to decide what our response should be," Murphy continued. "If we leave, we forfeit this tournament. If we stay, Dondré can't play."

As I listened, my own childhood memory from thirty-two years ago broke free. **❶**

> **📖 TEXT STRUCTURE**
> **❶** The writer adds extra space here. What words indicate a **flashback**? What year are we now in?

In 1959 I was thirteen years old, a poor black kid living with my mother and stepfather in a small black ghetto on Long Island, New York. My mother worked nights in a hospital, and my stepfather drove a coal truck. Needless to say, our standard of living was somewhat short of the American dream.

Nevertheless, when my eighth-grade teacher announced a graduation trip to Washington, D.C., it never crossed my mind that I would be left behind. Besides a complete tour of the nation's capital, we would visit Glen Echo Amusement Park in Maryland. In my imagination, Glen Echo was Disneyland, Knott's Berry Farm, and Magic Mountain rolled into one.

My heart beating wildly, I raced home to deliver the mimeographed letter describing the journey. But when my mother saw how much the trip would cost, she just shook her head. We couldn't afford it.

After feeling sad for ten seconds, I decided to try to fund the trip myself. For the next eight weeks, I sold candy bars door-to-door, delivered newspapers, and mowed lawns. Three days before the deadline, I'd made just barely enough. I was going!

The day of the trip, trembling with excitement, I climbed onto the train. I was the only nonwhite in our section.

Our hotel was not far from the White House. My roommate was Frank Miller, the son of a businessman. Leaning together out of our window and dropping water balloons on passing tourists quickly cemented our new friendship.

Every morning, almost a hundred of us loaded noisily onto our bus for another adventure. We sang our school fight song dozens of times—en route[2] to Arlington National Cemetery and even on an afternoon cruise down the Potomac River.

We visited the Lincoln Memorial twice, once in daylight, the second time at dusk. My classmates and I fell silent as we walked in the shadows of those thirty-six marble columns, one for every state in the Union that Lincoln labored to preserve. I stood next to Frank at the base of the nineteen-

---

2. **en route** (än rōōt′): on the way.

Vocabulary
forfeit (fôr′fit) v.: lose the right to something.

CROSS-CURRICULAR CONNECTIONS

History
Racial discrimination in sports. Racial discrimination against athletes has often made headlines. The best-known example is probably Jackie Robinson. In 1947, he was the first African American to break the color barrier in major league baseball. Playing for the Brooklyn Dodgers, Robinson endured insults, threats, and physical abuse, but he paved the way for other African American baseball players. In more recent years, the golf star Tiger Woods faced similar incidents of prejudice.

Activity. Ask students to work in pairs to research examples of racial prejudice in sports and present a brief oral report to the class.

PAIRED

foot seated statue. Spotlights made the white Georgian marble seem to glow. Together, we read those famous words from Lincoln's speech at Gettysburg, remembering the most bloody battle in the War Between the States: "We here highly resolve that these dead shall not have died in vain—that this nation, under God, shall have a new birth of freedom. . . ."

As Frank motioned me into place to take my picture, I took one last look at Lincoln's face. He seemed alive and so terribly sad.

The next morning I understood a little better why he wasn't smiling. "Clifton," a chaperone said, "could I see you for a moment?"

The other guys at my table, especially Frank, turned pale. We had been joking about the previous night's direct water-balloon hit on a fat lady and her poodle. It was a stupid, dangerous act, but luckily nobody got hurt. We were celebrating our escape from punishment when the chaperone asked to see me.

"Clifton," she began, "do you know about the Mason-Dixon line?"

"No," I said, wondering what this had to do with drenching fat ladies.

"Before the Civil War," she explained, "the Mason-Dixon line was originally the boundary between Maryland and Pennsylvania—the dividing line between the slave and free states." Having escaped one disaster, I could feel another brewing. I noticed that her eyes were damp and her hands shaking.

"Today," she continued, "the Mason-Dixon line is a kind of invisible border between the North and the South. When you cross that invisible line out of Washington, D.C., into Maryland, things change."

There was an ominous drift to this conversation, but I wasn't following it. Why did she look and sound so nervous?

"Glen Echo Amusement Park is in Maryland," she said at last, "and the management doesn't allow Negroes inside." She stared at me in silence.

I was still grinning and nodding when the meaning finally sank in. "You mean I can't go to the park," I stuttered, "because I'm a Negro?"

She nodded slowly. "I'm sorry, Clifton," she said, taking my hand. "You'll have to stay in the hotel tonight. Why don't you and I watch a movie on television?"

I walked to the elevators feeling confusion, disbelief, anger, and a deep sadness. "What happened, Clifton?" Frank said when I got back to the room. "Did the fat lady tell on us?"

Without saying a word, I walked over to my bed, lay down, and began to cry. Frank was stunned into silence. Junior-high boys didn't cry, at least not in front of each other.

It wasn't just missing the class adventure that made me feel so sad. For the first time in my life, I was learning what it felt like to be a "nigger." Of course there was discrimination in the North, but the color of my skin had never officially kept me out of a coffee shop, a church—or an amusement park.

"Clifton," Frank whispered, "what is the matter?"

"They won't let me go to Glen Echo Park tonight," I sobbed.

Vocabulary

resolve (ri·zälv′) v.: decide; make a formal statement.

ominous (äm′ə·nəs) adj.: threatening, like a bad sign; warning of something bad.

A Mason-Dixon Memory **537**

Learners Having Difficulty
Map reading. A spatial aid may make the text more accessible for students who have trouble picturing the places Clifton and his friends visit in Washington, D.C.
Activity. Provide maps of the Washington, D.C. area. Have students locate the landmarks mentioned in the text: the White House, the Lincoln Memorial, the Potomac River, and Arlington National Cemetery (in Virginia). Explain the significance of each place. If someone has visited the cemetery, for instance, have them tell about the flame that burns twenty-four hours a day at President Kennedy's grave, and the Tomb of the Unknowns, which honors those who died anonymously in battle. Also have them locate the Mason-Dixon line, the border between Washington, D.C. and the southern states of Maryland and Virginia.

E **Cross-curricular Connections**
HISTORY
The Lincoln Memorial. The Lincoln Memorial was built to commemorate Abraham Lincoln (1809–1865), the sixteenth president of the United States. Lincoln is revered for saving the Union and issuing the Emancipation Proclamation of 1863, which ended slavery in the United States. The Lincoln Memorial, one of the most beautiful buildings in Washington, D.C., is modeled on the Parthenon in Greece. Behind its thirty-six marble pillars looms a huge statue of Lincoln, sculpted by Daniel Chester French. The words about freedom that Clifton reads suggest Lincoln's hopes for a new society based on equality after the Civil War. Many historic events in the civil rights era took place on the steps of the Lincoln Memorial, including Martin Luther King, Jr.'s famous "I Have a Dream" speech of 1963.

F **Advanced Learners**

? **Interpret the title.** Given the facts about the Mason-Dixon line that you learn from this dialogue, why do you think the author chose this phrase as the title for his essay? [Possible response: He chose it to evoke thoughts about segregation and prejudice in the minds of his readers.]

G **Literary Focus**
Foreshadowing. Remind students that foreshadowing is the use of clues to suggest events that will happen later in the work. Ask them to identify passages earlier in the essay where Davis foreshadows the chaperone's announcement that the amusement park is segregated. [Possible response: Clifton's observation at the Memorial that Lincoln looks sad suggests that Lincoln's dream of equality has not been fully realized.]

"Because of the water balloon?" he asked. "No," I answered, "because I'm a Negro."

"Well, that's a relief!" Frank said, and then he laughed, obviously relieved to have escaped punishment for our caper with the balloons. "I thought it was serious!"

Wiping away the tears with my sleeve, I stared at him. "It *is* serious. They don't let Negroes into the park. I can't go with you!" I shouted. "That's pretty serious to me."

I was about to wipe the silly grin off Frank's face with a blow to his jaw when I heard him say, "Then I won't go either."

For an instant we just froze. Then Frank grinned. I will never forget that moment. Frank was just a kid. He wanted to go to that amusement park as much as I did, but there was something even more important than the class night out. Still, he didn't explain or expand.

The next thing I knew, the room was filled with kids listening to Frank. "They don't allow Negroes in the park," he said, "so I'm staying with Clifton."

"Me too," a second boy said.

"Those jerks," a third muttered. "I'm with you, Clifton." My heart began to race. Suddenly, I was not alone. A pint-sized revolution had been born. The "water-balloon brigade," eleven white boys from Long Island, had made its decision: "We won't go." And as I sat on my bed in the center of it all, I felt grateful. But above all, I was filled with pride. ❷

> 📖 **TEXT STRUCTURE**
> ❷ The writer uses extra space again. Where are we now in time?

Dondré Green's story brought that childhood memory back to life. His golfing teammates, like my childhood friends, had an important decision to make. Standing by

their friend would cost them dearly. But when it came time to decide, no one hesitated. "Let's get out of here," one of them whispered.

"They just turned and walked toward the van," Dondré told us. "They didn't debate it. And the younger players joined us without looking back."

Dondré was astounded by the response of his friends—and the people of Louisiana. The whole state was outraged and tried to make it right. The Louisiana House of Representatives proclaimed a Dondré Green Day and passed legislation permitting lawsuits for damages, attorneys' fees, and court costs against any private facility that invites a team, then bars any member because of race.

As Dondré concluded, his eyes glistened with tears. "I love my coach and my teammates for sticking by me," he said. "It goes to show that there are always good people who will not give in to bigotry. The kind of love they showed me that day will conquer hatred every time."

Suddenly, the banquet crowd was standing, applauding Dondré Green. ❸

> 📖 **TEXT STRUCTURE**
> ❸ Again, extra space. How do you know the writer has flashed back again?

My friends, too, had shown that kind of love. As we sat in the hotel, a chaperone came in waving an envelope. "Boys!" he shouted. "I've just bought thirteen tickets to the Senators-Tigers game. Anybody want to go?"

The room erupted in cheers. Not one of

Vocabulary

erupted (ē·rup′tid) *v.*: exploded or burst forth.

FAMILY/COMMUNITY ACTIVITY

Encourage students and their families to hold family echo readings at home, using students' favorite parts of "A Mason-Dixon Memory." In an echo reading, each student pairs off with a younger sibling or perhaps a family member who is less fluent in English. The student reads a section of the essay (ranging from a paragraph to a page, depending on both partners' comfort levels). Then, the partner reads along and repeats what the first reader read aloud. This allows the younger or less fluent partner to read a piece of literature successfully. You might send home a note to parents, explaining how the echo reading works and how the activity benefits students.

us had ever been to a professional baseball game in a real baseball park.

On the way to the stadium, we grew silent as our driver paused before the Lincoln Memorial. For one long moment, I stared through the marble pillars at Mr. Lincoln, bathed in that warm yellow light. There was still no smile and no sign of hope in his sad and tired eyes.

"We here highly resolve . . . that this nation, under God, shall have a new birth of freedom . . ."

In his words and in his life, Lincoln had made it clear that freedom is not free. Every time the color of a person's skin keeps him out of an amusement park or off a country-club fairway, the war for freedom begins again. Sometimes the battle is fought with fists and guns, but more often the most effective weapon is a simple act of love and courage. ❹

Whenever I hear those words from Lincoln's speech at Gettysburg, I remember my eleven white friends, and I feel hope once again. I like to imagine that when we paused that night at the foot of his great monument, Mr. Lincoln smiled at last. As Dondré said, "The kind of love they showed me that day will conquer hatred every time."

📖 **MAIN IDEA**
❹ The writer reflects on both stories, his and Dondré Green's. What sentence in this paragraph states the **main idea** of this essay?

F

Meet the Writer

Clifton Davis

A Man of Many Talents

Clifton Davis (1946–   ) may be better known for writing tunes than for writing prose. He wrote the song "Never Can Say Goodbye," which sold two million records. He's still involved with music today, as a composer, recording artist, and host of a gospel-music radio program.

Clifton Davis is also an actor. He has appeared in several plays on Broadway and received a Tony nomination for his performance in *Two Gentlemen of Verona*. Davis has also appeared in movies and on TV shows. The role he is best known for is Rev. Reuben Gregory on the television series *Amen*. The curious thing about casting Davis in the role of the minister is that he really *is* a minister, in the Seventh-Day Adventist Church.

Davis believes it's important to do what's right, even if you're making a living amid the glitz and glamour of Hollywood.

A Mason-Dixon Memory   **539**

DIRECT TEACHING

F **Reading Skills**

Main idea. [Possible response to question 4: The main idea is contained in this sentence: "Sometimes the battle is fought with fists and guns, but more often the most effective weapon is a simple act of love and courage."]

GUIDED PRACTICE

Monitor students' progress. Guide the class in answering these comprehension questions. Direct students to locate passages in the text that support their responses.

Short Answer

1. What problem does Dondré's team face at the country club? [Only whites can play golf at the club, so Dondré can't play with his team.]

2. What changes occur because of the country club's treatment of Dondré? [The Louisiana House of Representatives proclaimed Dondré Green Day and authorized lawsuits against private facilities that invite a team and then bar a team member from playing because of race.]

For Independent Reading

■ Students who would like to learn more about the struggle against racism might be interested in *Martin Luther King: The Peaceful Warrior* by Edward Clayton.

■ If students would like to read more about an athlete who overcomes bigotry, they might enjoy *Tiger: A Biography of Tiger Woods* by John Strege.

DIFFERENTIATING INSTRUCTION

Advanced Learners
Point out how rare it is for one person to succeed as a singer, composer, radio host, actor, writer, and minister. Ask students to think about the common link among all those talents—creativity.

Enrichment. Have students research an artist who is talented in more than one field—for example, Paul McCartney (singer, songwriter, painter), Queen Latifah (singer, actress, talk-show host), or Bill Cosby (comedian, author, actor). Have them compile a list of that person's accomplishments. Suggest that they write a letter to the artist asking how his or her talents complement each other.

HOMEWORK

After You Read

First Thoughts

1. Possible Answers
   - If I were a teammate of Dondré Green's or a classmate of Clifton Davis's, I would have stood by my friend's side.
   - Being a friend means offering support during times of trouble.

Thinking Critically

2. The flashback begins at the space in column 1 on p. 536, breaks off near the end of column 1 on p. 538, and continues in column 2 on p. 538 to the end of the selection. The flashback is a personal memory that illustrates the central point of the essay—solidarity in the face of bigotry.

3. Possible answer: They were outraged. Dondré may have been astounded that so many people cared about what had happened to him and about racial inequity in their state.

4. Possible answers: "doing the right thing," "sticking by your friend," or "acting on your deepest principles."

Extending Interpretations

5. After reading the essay, students may have changed the way they feel about personal sacrifice for a worthy cause.

6. Some students may say that love and courage may work on a personal level; others may say that it takes new laws to combat bigotry.

First Thoughts

1. Finish these sentences:
   - If I were a teammate of Dondré Green's or a classmate of Clifton Davis's, I would . . .
   - Being a friend means . . .

Thinking Critically

2. The narrator, Clifton Davis, starts one story and then flashes back to another story, one that happened to him. Where does the **flashback** begin and end? What does it have to do with Davis's main story?

3. How did Dondré Green's teammates and the people of Louisiana react to the fact that he had been barred from the tournament? Why do you think Dondré was astounded by this response?

4. The narrator says there was "something even more important" than going to the amusement park. Frank never explained what that something was. How would you explain it?

Extending Interpretations

5. Look back at your Quickwrite notes. Did reading this story change the way you look at choices that might force you to give up something you value? If so, explain how and why.

6. Green and Davis both believe that a simple act of love and courage is the most effective weapon against prejudice. Do you agree? Explain.

WRITING

Supporting a Position

Many people devote their lives to fighting for important causes, such as civil rights. Write a brief **persuasive essay** on an issue that *you* really care about. First, identify the issue and state your opinion of it. Then, list evidence that supports your opinion.

go.
hrw
.com

INTERNET
Projects and
Activities
Keyword: LE5 7-5

SKILLS
FOCUS

Literary Skills
Analyze an
essay.

Reading Skills
Analyze
flashbacks.

Writing Skills
Write a brief
persuasive essay.

Reading Check

How were the experiences of Dondré Green and Clifton Davis alike? Fill in a chart like the one below to compare their experiences:

	Experience	Friends' Response
Green		
Davis		

Reading Check
Possible answer:

	Experience	Friends' Response
Green	A country club would not admit him because of his race.	His teammates refused to play if Green couldn't and forfeited the tournament.
Davis	An amusement park would not admit him because of his race.	His classmates refused to go to the park if Davis couldn't.

Synonyms: Shades of Meaning

Words with the same or almost the same meaning are called **synonyms.** Synonyms usually have different shades of meaning. *Rigid* and *firm* are synonyms, but most people would rather be called *firm* than *rigid.* A dictionary or a thesaurus, a book of synonyms, can help you pick exactly the word you need.

PRACTICE

Make a word map like the following one for the rest of the Word Bank words. Find at least one synonym for each word, and put it in the word map. Then, write at least one sentence using each word. Discuss the synonyms and their shades of meaning, if any.

Word Bank

predominantly
forfeit
resolve
ominous
erupted

forfeit

synonym
lose

synonym
give up

You can <u>forfeit</u> a vacation to help a friend.

SKILLS FOCUS

Vocabulary Skills
Analyze shades of meaning.

A Mason-Dixon Memory **541**

Vocabulary Development

PRACTICE

1. *forfeit. Synonyms*—lose (implies they tried but failed), give up (implies they failed to try).
2. *predominantly. Synonyms*—mostly, largely.
3. *resolve. Synonyms*—intend (less strong than *resolve*), determine (less precise than *resolve* because it could mean "find out" instead).
4. *ominous. Synonyms*—sinister (suggests evil or danger), foreboding (suggests imminent evil or danger).
5. *erupted. Synonyms*—exploded (always suggests an action that results from a pressured or tense situation), broke out (weaker than *erupted*).

Student-written examples will vary.

DIFFERENTIATING INSTRUCTION

Learners Having Difficulty

Monitoring tip: If students have trouble seeing the relationship between the flashback and Dondré Green's story, have them reread the last two paragraphs. Then, ask them to think about the following question: The Union soldiers fought (with guns) to end slavery. How did Davis's and Green's friends fight to end discrimination? [by sticking together and refusing to patronize places that enforced segregation]

Writing. You might encourage students to brainstorm issues they care about (e.g., protecting the environment, helping homeless people, or rescuing abused animals) before they begin writing their persuasive essays at home. Remind them to provide statistics that back up the reasons for their opinions.

HOMEWORK

Grammar Link

PRACTICE

1. Davis sold candy bars, delivered newspapers, and mowed lawns.
2. Lincoln's sad, wise, tired face impressed them.
3. Sincere, courageous acts of love can conquer hatred.
4. They saw many famous national landmarks in Washington, D.C.

ASSESSING

Assessment

■ *Holt Assessment: Literature, Reading, and Vocabulary*

RETEACHING

For a lesson reteaching forms of prose, see **Reteaching,** p. 917C.

After You Read   Grammar Link

Commas Make Sense of a Series

- Use commas to separate words, phrases, or clauses in a series.

INCORRECT	Davis felt "confusion disbelief anger and a deep sadness."
CORRECT	Davis felt "confusion, disbelief, anger, and a deep sadness."

- In most cases, use commas to separate two or more adjectives that come before a noun.

INCORRECT	It was a stupid dangerous act.
CORRECT	It was a stupid, dangerous act.

- Do not place a comma between an adjective and a noun that immediately follows it.

INCORRECT	Green's teammates made a fast, important, costly, decision.
CORRECT	Green's teammates made a fast, important, costly decision.

- If the last adjective in a series is closely connected in meaning to the noun that follows it, do not use a comma before that adjective.

INCORRECT	"Spotlights made the white, Georgian marble seem to glow."
CORRECT	"Spotlights made the white Georgian marble seem to glow."

To decide whether a comma is needed, add the word *and* between the adjectives. If the *and* sounds strange, don't use a comma. (*White* and *Georgian marble* sounds strange, so don't use a comma there.)

SKILLS FOCUS

Grammar Skills
Use commas in a series correctly.

542   Collection 5 / Worlds of Words: Prose and Poetry

PRACTICE

Copy the sentences below. Add commas where necessary to separate the items in a series. Compare your answers with a partner's.

1. Davis sold candy bars delivered newspapers and mowed lawns.
2. Lincoln's sad wise tired face impressed them.
3. Sincere courageous acts of love can conquer hatred.
4. They saw many famous national landmarks in Washington, D.C.

For more help, see Commas: Items in a Series, 13f–g, in the Language Handbook.

No comma between an adjective and a noun that immediately follows it!

TO A GREAT, MAYOR WHO

DIFFERENTIATING INSTRUCTION

Learners Having Difficulty
Some learners may have trouble deciding where commas belong. For them, extra practice may be helpful.
Activity. Have students add or delete commas where needed in the following sentences.

1. It was a clear sunny hot, day at the golf course. [It was a clear, sunny, hot day at the golf course.]

2. The White House, and the Lincoln Memorial are both found in the nation's beautiful, capital city. [The White House and the Lincoln Memorial are both found in the nation's beautiful capital city.]

3. They pass the time on the bus by talking singing and playing games. [They pass the time on the bus by talking, singing, and playing games.]

4. His roommate, and the ten, other boys support Clifton Davis. [His roommate and the ten other boys support Clifton Davis.]

Summarizing

Reading Focus
Summarizing: Putting It All in a Nutshell!

Have you ever found yourself rambling on and on about something that's happened to you or about something you read, such as "A Mason-Dixon Memory," and your patient-but-now-frustrated listener finally says, "Enough already—just give it to me in a nut-shell"? What your friend's asking for is a summary.

A **summary** restates the main events or main ideas of a text in a much shorter form than the original.

Summaries are useful because they can help you remember the most important points in material you've just read. They're especially handy if you're doing research from a number of sources. Reviewing your summaries will show you how one source differs from another.

Before you write a summary, read the text carefully to decide what details to include and what to leave out. The main events will probably be easy to recognize, but the **main ideas**—the central or most important ideas in a text—can be harder to discover. Sometimes the writer states a main idea directly, but usually you have to infer, or guess, what it is. One way to discover the main ideas is by identifying important details and then thinking about what point they make.

■ Use a graphic organizer like the one below to collect information for a summary of the newspaper article "Buddies Bare Their Affection for Ill Classmate." Part of the organizer has been completed for you. Add as many boxes as you need for the main events. Then, fill in the writer's **main idea.**

Main Events

> Doctors remove tumor from Ian O'Gorman.

↓

> He starts chemotherapy.

↓

> [ ]

↓

> [ ]

The Writer's Main Idea

> [ ]

SKILLS FOCUS

Reading Skills
Understand how to summarize; understand main idea.

Buddies Bare Their Affection for Ill Classmate **543**

SKILLS FOCUS
pp. 543–545

Grade-Level Skills
■ **Reading Skills**
Summarize a text.
■ **Reading Skills**
Understand main idea.

Summary ⬌ at grade level

Thirteen boys shaved their heads to support their classmate, Ian O'Gorman, who suffered from lymphoma, a type of cancer. Because he had to start chemotherapy treatment, Ian decided to shave his head before his hair fell out. His friend Kyle suggested that the other boys in class shave their heads too, so Ian wouldn't feel as if he stuck out. Their teacher, Mr. Alter, touched by the classmates' show of support, also shaved his head. When Ian was released from the hospital, he was eager to play sports again with his friends.

PRETEACHING

Selection Starter
Motivate. Ask students how far they would go to help a sick friend. Would they send him or her a card? Visit him or her in the hospital? If their friend lost his or her hair, would they shave their heads in a gesture of solidarity?

Assign the Reading
Allow advanced students to read this article on their own while you work with the rest of the class, using the medical definitions in this Teacher's Edition on p. 544.

RESOURCES: READING

Planning
■ *One-Stop Planner* CD-ROM with ExamView Test Generator

Differentiating Instruction
■ *Holt Adapted Reader*
■ *Holt Reading Solutions*
■ *Supporting Instruction in Spanish*
■ *Audio CD Library*

■ *Audio CD Library, Selections and Summaries in Spanish*

Grammar and Language
■ *Daily Language Activities*

Assessment
■ *Holt Assessment: Literature, Reading, and Vocabulary*
■ *One-Stop Planner* CD-ROM with ExamView Test Generator

■ *Holt Online Assessment*

Internet
■ go.hrw.com (Keyword: LE5 7-5)
■ *Elements of Literature Online*

Media
■ *Audio CD Library*
■ *Audio CD Library, Selections and Summaries in Spanish*

A Reading Informational Text

? Main idea. What sentence contains the main idea of this paragraph? [The third sentence: "Thirteen of them shaved their heads so a sick buddy wouldn't feel out of place."]

B Reading Informational Text

Summarize. Ask students to summarize this paragraph in twenty words or less. Remind them to concentrate on the most important details. [Possible response: Doctors removed a tumor from Ian O'Gorman's small intestine, and he started chemotherapy to treat lymphoma.]

C Reading Skills

? Interpret. Why do you think Ian was surprised that his friends got their heads shaved too? [Possible responses: He didn't realize how much they cared about him. He wouldn't have chosen to be hairless if he weren't sick, and he probably knew his friends didn't like being bald, so he appreciated their sacrifice.]

D Advanced Learners

? Extend the text. Is it easier for people to do the right thing when they are acting alone or when they are part of a group? Why? [Some students may say that it's easier when acting alone because the individual isn't dependent on other people's approval. Others may say it's easier in a group because the members give each other support and encouragement.]

Buddies Bare Their Affection for Ill Classmate

OCEANSIDE, CAL., MAR. 19 (Associated Press) — In Mr. Alter's fifth-grade class, it's difficult to tell which boy is undergoing chemotherapy. Nearly all the boys are bald. Thirteen of them shaved their heads so a sick buddy wouldn't feel out of place.

"If everybody has their head shaved, sometimes people don't know who's who. They don't know who has cancer and who just shaved their head," said eleven-year-old Scott Sebelius, one of the baldies at Lake Elementary School.

For the record, Ian O'Gorman is the sick one. Doctors recently removed a malignant tumor from his small intestine, and a week ago he started chemotherapy to treat the disease, called lymphoma.

"Besides surgery, I had tubes up my nose. I had butterflies in my stomach," said Ian, who'll have eight more weeks of chemotherapy in an effort to keep the cancer from returning.

Ian decided to get his head shaved before all his hair fell out in clumps. To his surprise, his friends wanted to join him.

"The last thing he would want is to not fit in, to be made fun of, so we just wanted to make him feel better and not left out," said ten-year-old Kyle Hanslik.

Kyle started talking to other boys about the idea, and then one of their parents started a list. Last week, they all went to the barbershop together.

"It's hard to put words to," said Ian's father, Shawn, choking back tears as he talked about the boys. "It's very emotional to think about kids like that who would come together, to have them do such a thing to support Ian."

The boy's teacher, Jim Alter, was so inspired that he, too, shaved his head.

Ian left the hospital March 2. Although he has lost twenty pounds and is pale, he is eager to get back to the business of being an eleven-year-old playing baseball and basketball. "I think I can start on Monday," he said.

—from the *Austin American-Statesman*

Ian O'Gorman (center), who is undergoing chemotherapy for cancer, is surrounded by his classmates, who shaved their heads as a show of support.

DIFFERENTIATING INSTRUCTION

Learners Having Difficulty
Medical terms. Some students may be put off or even frightened by the medical terms in the article. Help them create a vocabulary list and look up the words together.

- *chemotherapy*—a therapy (medical treatment) that uses chemicals to fight disease
- *cancer*—a disease in which malignant tumors expand and crowd out healthy body tissue

- *malignant*—tending to produce deterioration or even death
- *tumor*—an abnormal mass of tissue in the body
- *lymphoma*—a tumor in the tissue of the lymph nodes

Summarizing a Text

Buddies Bare Their Affection for Ill Classmate

Test Practice

1. According to the opening paragraph, what's difficult to tell about the boys in Mr. Alter's class is who —
   A is the brightest student
   B is undergoing chemotherapy
   C once had the longest hair
   D Ian O'Gorman is

2. The main reason the boys shaved their heads was to —
   F look unusual
   G show individuality
   H act original
   J show support

3. Kyle Hanslik got the idea of shaving his head because —
   A he liked the way Ian looked
   B he didn't want Ian to be made fun of
   C he was protesting Ian's illness
   D he wanted to confuse the teacher

4. Who else was surprisingly inspired to shave his head?
   F Mr. Alter
   G Ian's dad
   H Kyle's dad
   J Ian's doctor

Constructed Response

A good **summary** of an informational text covers the main events or main points, not every single detail. That is why a summary is always much shorter than the original piece. Use the information you collected in your graphic organizer (page 543) to write a summary of the news story about Ian and his friends. Here are some tips for writing a good summary:

- Cite the author and title of the article you are summarizing.
- Cite the topic of the article in a few words.

- Retell the main events or main points of the article, using your own words. Include only key events or key points.
- Sum up the writer's message or **main idea.**

After you have written your summary, read it over and ask yourself: Would a person who has not read the article understand what it is about? If your answer is negative, go back and revise your summary.

SKILLS FOCUS

Reading Skills
Summarize a text.

Summarizing a Text

Test Practice

Answers and Model Rationales

1. **B** Explain that A and C are irrelevant. Point out that if you can't tell who's undergoing chemotherapy, you can't tell who Ian O'Gorman is.

2. **J** Direct students to the fifth and sixth paragraphs of the article. The boys shaved their heads so Ian wouldn't stand out, so F, G, and H are wrong.

3. **B** The sixth paragraph describes Kyles's motivation. A is clearly incorrect. D is not mentioned in the text. B is better than C because the article states Ian does not want to stand out.

4. **F** Point out the article's next-to-last paragraph, which says the teacher shaved his head, too. The hair of the boys' fathers and Ian's doctor is not mentioned, so G, H, and J are wrong.

Test-Taking Tips

For more instruction on how to answer multiple-choice questions, refer students to **Test Smarts** on p. 920.

Assessment

■ *Holt Assessment: Literature, Reading, and Vocabulary*

Constructed Response

Possible summary: This newspaper article, "Buddies Bare Their Affection for Ill Classmate," by an unnamed writer, tells about thirteen boys who shaved their heads to support their friend, Ian O'Gorman, after doctors removed a tumor from his small intestine. Because he had to undergo chemotherapy, Ian shaved his head before his hair fell out. His friend Kyle suggested that the other boys in class shave their heads too, so Ian wouldn't stand out. Their teacher, Mr. Alter, shaved his head also. When Ian got out of the hospital, his spirits were high—he looked forward to playing sports again.

The author's message is that a group of boys sacrificed their hair to show their sick friend that they cared about him.

Grade-Level Skills

■ **Literary Skills**
Understand figures of speech, images, sounds, and forms in poetry.

■ **Literary Skills**
Understand how to read poetry.

Upcoming Skills

■ **Literary Skills**
Understand and explain the characteristics of different forms of poetry.

**Elements of Literature:
The Elements of Poetry**

Have students discuss their favorite songs and explain what they like about them (e.g., melody, rhythm, lyrics). Encourage them to be specific when they describe these elements. For example, is the beat joyful, soothing, exciting, stormy? Do the lyrics rhyme? Do they describe a commonplace emotion in a striking way? Explain that poets are like songwriters and also like visual artists in many ways. Review the terms *images, figures of speech, rhythm, rhyme,* and *stanza.* To reinforce the guidelines for reading a poem, choose a poem from this collection and read it aloud for the class.

Elements of Literature
Painting with Words
by John Malcolm Brinnin

THE ELEMENTS OF POETRY

People rarely see poets at work. Even if you could watch a poet writing, you would not be able to notice much action. The making of a poem is mostly a solitary, mental activity. The only activity you might notice is the poet's use of speech—poets are not usually silent while they work. They often test what they write by saying it out loud.

To begin to understand what elements go into the making of a poem, it might help to think of the poet as an artist who is creating something with words.

INTERNET
More About Imagery
Keyword: LE5 7-5

Literary Skills
Understand images, sounds, and forms in poetry; understand how to read poetry.

Creating Images

A poet uses words the way a painter uses colors. Like painters, poets want to share a special, personal vision of the world. To do that, poets create **images,** or pictures. Poets also use **figures of speech**—language that helps make startling connections between dissimilar things. Like a painter's colors, a poet's words can put your imagination to work; they can make you see the world in new, unexpected ways.

Creating Sounds

Like musicians, poets are also concerned with sounds. Imagine a composer of music trying various patterns of notes on a piano in order to create a pleasing melody. That will give you a good idea of what poets try to do with words. Poets choose their words with great care. They revise them repeatedly, trying to find the combination that will produce just the right sound— perhaps a harsh sound, a musical sound, or a sound that matches the gallop of a horse. A poet's goal is to create sounds that will match the feelings and ideas they want to share with us.

Deciding on Forms

Like sculptors, poets are also concerned with shape, or form. When they write and revise, poets are chiseling their words to create the shapes you see on the page. Poets think about such things as how long their lines should be and whether they should group them into units (called **stanzas**). Some poets use forms based on strict rules that may be hundreds of years old. Other poets may experiment with freer forms. Whatever form a poet chooses to use, his or her purpose is to give the words a pleasing shape on the page and to help convey meaning.

546   Collection 5 / Worlds of Words: Prose and Poetry

DIFFERENTIATING INSTRUCTION

Learners Having Difficulty
Elements of poetry. Play recordings of several popular songs. Point out elements such as images, figures of speech, rhythms, rhymes, and refrains in each song.
Activity. Have students meet in small groups to listen to a recording of a popular song. After listening, ask the groups to use a scale of one to five to rate the following elements of the song: images, figures of speech, rhymes, and rhythm. Then, have them rate the overall song based on its elements.

Advanced Learners
Acceleration. In order to help advanced learners recognize the characteristics of different forms of poetry, point out that two forms of poetry with strict rules are the ballad and the sonnet.

How to Read Poetry

Follow these guidelines as you read the poems in this collection:

1. Read the poem aloud at least once. A poem's sense is linked to its sound.

2. Look for sentences, and pay attention to **punctuation.** Stop briefly at semicolons or after periods. Pause at commas. Look for sudden shifts in thought after dashes. If a line does not end with punctuation, do not make a full stop; pause only very briefly, and continue to the end of the sentence.

3. Always read a poem in a normal voice, as if you were speaking to a friend. If the poem has a steady beat, let the music emerge naturally. Do not force the poem's music by reading in a singsong way.

4. Look up unfamiliar words. Poets choose words carefully. Sometimes words in a poem are used to mean more than one thing.

5. Poets often describe one thing in terms of another. For example, a poet might describe snowflakes as if they were insects. Be alert for comparisons. Let them work on your imagination.

6. After a first reading, think about the poem. Especially think about its images and sounds, its flow of emotions and ideas. Then, read the poem a second or even a third time. With each re-reading you will discover something new.

7. Think about the poem's meaning— what message is being transmitted from the poet to you? You'll find that your response to many poems will be "It tells me something I always knew, but I never thought of it that way before."

Practice

Many years ago schoolchildren often memorized and recited poems. A poem's **rhymes** and **rhythms** help to make it fairly easy to memorize. If you would like to memorize a poem, try these techniques on one of the poems in this chapter, or memorize part of a long poem like "The Highwayman" (page 247) or "Annabel Lee" (page 261). Once you have your poem memorized, recite it for the class.

1. Read the poem aloud three or four times.

2. Look for rhymes. Rhyming words help your memory.

3. Memorize two lines at a time. Say the lines aloud several times; then cover them up, and try to recite them from memory.

4. Try to picture the words of the poem on the page.

Practice

One easy poem for memorizing and reciting is Emily Dickinson's "I'm Nobody!" (p. 549). Read the poem aloud to the class, and then invite pairs of students to memorize and recite it together, perhaps taking turns on alternating lines.

Apply

Other short, humorous poems that students may enjoy memorizing and reciting are William Jay Smith's "The Toaster," Charles Malams's "Steam Shovel," Richard LeGallienne's "I Meant to Do My Work Today," Lewis Carroll's "How Doth the Little Crocodile," and Ogden Nash's "The Germ" or "The Pig." Ask your school librarian to locate copies of these poems, and have students memorize them for homework.

HOMEWORK

Activity. Have students find several examples of ballads and sonnets. In a small group, have them compare and contrast the stanzas, rhythms, and rhyme schemes of the two forms, as well as the purposes the poets may have had for using the particular form they did.

Grade-Level Skills

■ Literary Skills
Analyze figures of speech in poetry, such as simile and metaphor.

Upcoming Skills

■ Literary Skills
Identify the literary devices that define a writer's style.

Summary ⬇ *below grade level*

In this famous eight-line poem, the speaker shares the pleasure of being a "Nobody" who values privacy and feels a kinship with other "Nobodies." Using a vivid simile and metaphor, the speaker shows disdain for public figures and the crowds who idolize them, comparing the celebrities to a croaking frog and their admirers to a bog.

I'm Nobody!

Make the Connection
Pair and Share

"In the future everyone will be world-famous for fifteen minutes." With a partner, discuss that famous statement, which was made by the artist Andy Warhol. Do you agree with Warhol? Why or why not? What do you feel are the privileges and pitfalls of fame?

Quickwrite

Imagine that you become a celebrity overnight. Fill in a chart like the one below, showing how sudden fame might change you and your private life.

Fame

Pluses (+)	Minuses (−)
_____	_____
_____	_____
_____	_____
_____	_____

INTERNET

More About Dickinson

Keyword: LE5 7-5

SKILLS FOCUS

Literary Skills
Understand figures of speech, such as simile and metaphor.

Literary Focus
Figures of Speech

In "I'm Nobody!" Emily Dickinson throws a spotlight on her ideas by using **figures of speech.** Figures of speech compare things that at first glance seem very different. Thinking about these unusual comparisons lets you see familiar things in a new light. The comparisons in figures of speech are imaginative and are not meant to be understood as literally true.

The most common figures of speech are similes and metaphors. A **simile** compares two unlike things, using a specific word of comparison such as *like* or *as*:

The sleeping calico cat is *like* a cushion.

A **metaphor** directly compares two unlike things without the use of a specific word of comparison:

The sleeping calico cat *is* a cushion.

548   Collection 5 / Worlds of Words: Prose and Poetry

Senecio (1922) by Paul Klee. Oil on gauze on cardboard (40.5 cm × 38 cm).

I'm Nobody!

Emily Dickinson

I'm Nobody! Who are you?
Are you Nobody too?
Then there's a pair of us!
Don't tell! they'd banish us, you know!

A

How dreary to be Somebody!
How public—like a Frog—
To tell your name the livelong June
To an admiring Bog!

B

PRETEACHING

Skills Starter
Build skills. Write these examples on the chalkboard:

The pass receiver runs like the wind.

The tackle is as powerful as a freight train.

The quarterback is a giant in the history of the game.

Ask students what two things are being compared in each sentence. Then, ask how the two things being compared are alike and how they are different. Underline the words *like* and *as* in the first two sentences, and explain that such comparisons are called similes. Then, ask if the third comparison includes the word *like* or *as*. Explain that a figurative comparison without the word *like* or *as* is called a metaphor.

DIRECT TEACHING

A **Reading Skills**

? Interpret. Why does the speaker say "I'm Nobody"? [Possible response: The speaker is a very private, unknown person.] Why does the speaker welcome another "Nobody"? [Possible response: Even private, unknown people need friends who understand them and share their values.]

B **Literary Focus**

? Figures of speech. The speaker compares the "Somebody" to a frog. Is this comparison a simile or a metaphor? Explain. [It is a simile because it contains the word *like*.] The speaker compares the Somebody's admirers to a bog. Is this comparison a simile or a metaphor? Explain. [It is a metaphor because it does not contain *like* or *as*.]

DIFFERENTIATING INSTRUCTION

Learners Having Difficulty
You may wish to have students work in pairs. Play the audio recording and have them read the poem silently while they listen. Then, monitor students as one partner reads a line of the poem and the other paraphrases what it means. Then, invite the pairs to prepare an oral reading of the poem, speaking some lines in unison and others solo. Invite students to share their readings of the poem with the class.

English-Language Learners
Explain that the word *banish* means "drive out" and that the word *livelong* means "entire." Point out that *bog* means a low-lying, wet area that's often considered unpleasant or unhealthy. Students might be familiar with the metaphorical expression *bogged down*, meaning "stuck in a difficult or unpleasant situation."

After You Read

First Thoughts

1. The speaker seems to prefer self-reliance and privacy to fame. Students can discuss whether they agree with the speaker, giving reasons to support their views.

Thinking Critically

2. "Nobody" may be a person who does not care what others think and does not seek public recognition. "Somebody" may be a person who is famous or sought after by others.

3. "They" might be society in general or a current, popular social group. "They" might banish the speaker for not fitting in or caring about fame.

4. Possible answers: Both a frog and a public person could be viewed as making noise to attract attention. Some frogs puff up with air to attract the attention of a potential mate, just as popular people may puff themselves up to attract attention in their social world. To be compared to a croaking frog is not flattering; the speaker seems to ridicule such people.

5. Possible answer: Since a bog may be a dismal place and a croaking frog is hardly worthy of admiration (except, perhaps, to another frog), the speaker seems to have a low opinion of people who idolize celebrities.

6. The "you" in the poem is not identified, but it may be someone the speaker feels close to; perhaps "you" is a reader who shares the speaker's values.

Extending Interpretations

7. Possible details include Dickinson's decision to live reclusively and her refusal to attach her name to her published poetry.

After You Read   Response and Analysis

First Thoughts

1. How do you think the speaker feels about fame? Do you agree? (Be sure to check your notes for the Quickwrite on page 548.) ✏

Thinking Critically

2. What does "Nobody" mean in this poem? What does "Somebody" mean?

3. Who are "they" in line 4? Why would "they" banish the speaker?

4. The **simile** in the second stanza compares a celebrity to a frog. How could a frog and a public person be similar? Is this a flattering comparison?

5. In the **metaphor** in the last line, admirers of famous people are compared to creatures in a bog (a marshy place) that admire a croaking frog. How do you think the poet feels about people who idolize celebrities?

6. Whom do you think the speaker is talking to?

Extending Interpretations

7. What details in the biography of the poet (page 553) might explain her feelings about fame?

INTERNET

Projects and Activities

Keyword: LE5 7-5

SKILLS FOCUS

Literary Skills
Analyze similes and metaphors.

Writing Skills
Write a letter to a poet.

Art Skills
Design a cover.

WRITING

A Letter to the Poet

If you could talk to Emily Dickinson, what would you want to tell her? What would you want to ask her? Write a letter to Dickinson, letting her know what you think of her poem and what you wonder about her life.

ART

Designing a Cover

Sometimes you *can* judge a book by its cover. Design a cover for a collection of Emily Dickinson's poetry, titled *I'm Nobody and Other Selected Poems*. Using "I'm Nobody!" as your inspiration, decide what art you want to put on the front cover to give readers an idea of what's inside. On the back cover, create more art, or draw a picture of the author.

550   Collection 5 / Worlds of Words: Prose and Poetry

ASSESSING

Assessment

■ *Holt Assessment: Literature, Reading, and Vocabulary*

DIFFERENTIATING INSTRUCTION

Advanced Learners

Enrichment. Encourage students to reflect on popular attitudes toward "Somebodies" and "Nobodies" in magazines, tabloid newspapers, and on television talk shows.

Activity. Have students create similes and metaphors to express their attitudes toward the "Somebodies" and "Nobodies" in society today.

HOMEWORK

I Like to See It Lap the Miles

Make the Connection
Quickwrite ✏️

Before the coming of the railroad, people depended on horses to take them where they wanted to go. When the poet Emily Dickinson was young, trains were still so new that people often called them iron horses. It's not surprising then that she compares a train's movements to those of a horse.

Take a moment to think about how trains are similar to horses. Jot down your ideas in a chart like this one:

	Horse	Train
What it does		
Its speed		
Its sounds		

Literary Focus
Extended Metaphor

Most writing (and most conversation) would be a lot less interesting without metaphors. A **metaphor** is an imaginative comparison between two things that are basically not alike at all. A metaphor makes a comparison directly, without using words such as *like* or *as*. We use these imaginative comparisons to bring our ideas alive. Metaphors help us to see or understand a subject in a new way. For example, when you read that a person has a heart of stone, you do not think that the person's heart is made of rock. Instead, you use what you already know or feel about stones to realize how cold, hard, and uncaring the person is.

An **extended metaphor** is a metaphor that is developed, or extended, through several lines of writing or even throughout an entire poem. "I Like to See It Lap the Miles" uses an extended metaphor to compare a train to a horse throughout the whole poem. You may have to read the poem several times before you catch all of Dickinson's comparisons.

go.
hrw
.com

INTERNET

More About Dickinson
Keyword: LE5 7-5

SKILLS FOCUS

Literary Skills
Understand metaphor and extended metaphor.

551

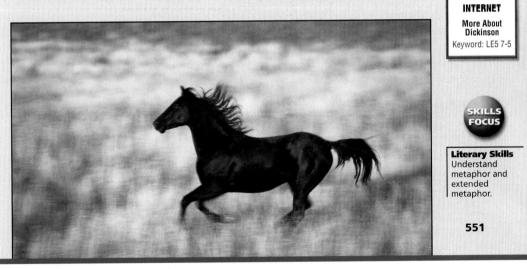

SKILLS FOCUS
pp. 551–554

Grade-Level Skills
■ **Literary Skills**
Analyze figures of speech in poetry, such as metaphor and extended metaphor.

Upcoming Skills
■ **Literary Skills**
Identify the literary devices that define a writer's style.

Summary ⬆ *above grade level*

In this poem, the speaker describes the movement of a train in terms more often associated with that of a powerful, fast-running horse. She sees the iron horse "lick" through valleys, "stop to feed" at tanks, "step" around mountains, "peer" in shacks along the roadside, and "chase itself" downhill to stop at its "own stable door."

RESOURCES: READING

Planning
■ *One-Stop Planner* CD-ROM with ExamView Test Generator

Differentiating Instruction
■ *Holt Reading Solutions*
■ *Supporting Instruction in Spanish*
■ *Audio CD Library*
■ *Audio CD Library, Selections and Summaries in Spanish*

Assessment
■ *Holt Assessment: Literature, Reading, and Vocabulary*
■ *One-Stop Planner* CD-ROM with ExamView Test Generator
■ *Holt Online Assessment*

Internet
■ go.hrw.com (Keyword: LE5 7-5)
■ *Elements of Literature Online*

Media
■ *Audio CD Library*
■ *Audio CD Library, Selections and Summaries in Spanish*

Selection Starter

Motivate. Have students close their eyes and imagine a train moving through a landscape in the American West. Next, have them imagine a powerful stallion covering the same ground. Then, invite them to read the poem and discover how Dickinson's visual images compare with their own.

DIRECT TEACHING

A Literary Focus

❷ Metaphor and extended metaphor. In stanza 1, what words or phrases compare the movements or actions of the train to those of a horse? ["lap," "lick," "stop to feed itself," "step"]

B Literary Focus

❷ Metaphor and extended metaphor. What two things are being compared in line 15? [A star is being compared to a train or a horse.]

C Reading Skills

❷ Read poetry. How can a train or a horse be docile (tame) and omnipotent (all-powerful) at the same time? Explain this seeming contradiction. [Possible response: Both a train and a horse are large and powerful, but they can be controlled by a driver or a rider.]

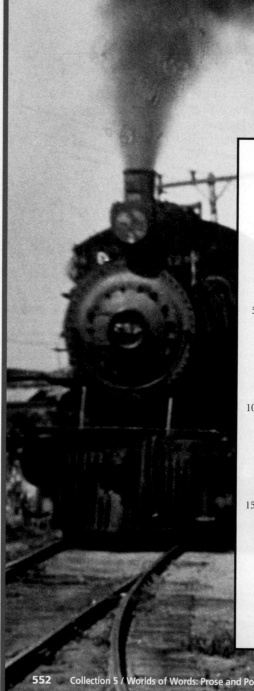

I Like to See It Lap the Miles

Emily Dickinson

A
I like to see it lap the Miles—
And lick the Valleys up—
And stop to feed itself at Tanks—
And then—prodigious° step

5   Around a Pile of Mountains—
And supercilious° peer
In Shanties—by the sides of Roads—
And then a Quarry pare

To fit its sides
10   And crawl between
Complaining all the while
In horrid—hooting stanza—
Then chase itself down Hill—

And neigh like Boanerges°—
15 **B** Then—prompter than a Star
C Stop—docile and omnipotent
At its own stable door—

4. **prodigious** (prō·dij'əs) *adj.:* enormous.
6. **supercilious** (sōō'pər·sil'ē·əs) *adj.:* haughty; stuck-up.
14. **Boanerges** (bō'ə·nur'jēz): biblical name meaning "sons of thunder." In Dickinson's time it had come to mean a preacher who gave thunderous sermons.

DIFFERENTIATING INSTRUCTION

Learners Having Difficulty
Before students read the poem, make the comparison between train and horse explicit. Point out the words that are specific references to a horse ["feed itself," "neigh," "stable door"]. Then, have students provide parallel concepts that apply to a train. [A train does not feed itself, but it does fill up on fuel; a train does not neigh, but it does whistle; a train does not stay overnight in a stable, but it is put in a depot when not in use.]

English-Language Learners
To help students understand and remember the definitions of *prodigious, supercilious, peer, pare, prompt, docile,* and *omnipotent,* first explain the definitions. Then, read the poem while students pantomime the definitions as they apply to the train.

Special Education Students
To help students focus their attention and comprehend written material, have them listen with headphones to an audiotape of the poem and highlight the words "lap," "lick," "feed," "crawl," "chase," and "neigh" as they hear them. Ask them to explain what these words refer to in the poem.

Meet the Writer

Emily Dickinson

Who Is That Mysterious Woman in White?

Today **Emily Dickinson** (1830–1886) ranks as one of America's—and the world's—greatest poets. During her lifetime, however, she was anything but famous. Of the seventeen hundred poems she wrote, only seven were published while she was alive—and she refused to have her name put on any of them.

After a normal, sociable childhood and adolescence, Dickinson seemed to retreat into the world of her own household at the age of twenty-six. By the time she was forty, she dressed only in white and rarely left her family's house in Amherst, Massachusetts. Except for family and a few old friends, she saw no one. Why? No one knows for sure. Her poems often deal with the relationship between her inner self and the outer world. Perhaps she had to draw back from the world and study it from a distance in order to write about it.

Many successful poets in the nineteenth century used regular rhymes and dum-de-dum rhythms. Emily Dickinson did not. Her rhythms were irregular and her rhymes slightly off. More important, she chose strong images to express her bold ideas. All in all, she was a true American original.

After Emily Dickinson died, her sister discovered in a locked box seven or eight

The Granger Collection, New York.

hundred poems written on envelopes, paper bags, and scraps of paper, all neatly sewn into little packets. It looked as if the poet had been hoping someone would find the poems and publish them. Yet in her lifetime no one had really understood what poetry meant to Emily Dickinson. Here is how she once defined it:

> ❝ If I read a book and it makes my whole body so cold no fire can ever warm me, I know that is poetry. If I feel physically as if the top of my head were taken off, I know that is poetry. These are the only ways I know it. Is there any other way? ❞

Meet the Writer

Although Emily Dickinson was a recluse for much of her life, she did maintain a lively correspondence with family members and friends. Excerpts from her letters were included in the Tony Award–winning one-woman show *The Belle of Amherst,* starring actress Julie Harris. Recordings of the show are available on videotape and on the Internet. In one letter to her mentor, Thomas Wentworth Higginson, Dickinson included the following description of her isolated life:

"You ask of my companions. Hills, sir, and the sundown, and a dog large as myself, that my father bought me. They are better than beings because they know, but do not tell. . . .

"I have a brother and sister; my mother does not care for thought, and father, too busy with his briefs to notice what we do. He buys me many books, but begs me not to read them, because he fears they joggle the mind."

Although Dickinson avoided adults, she did welcome neighborhood children to her yard. She often baked treats for them and lowered the goodies down in a basket from her window. She even joined the children in their games but would disappear "in a flash" at the approach of adults.

For Independent Reading

■ For students who would like to read more of Dickinson's poetry, recommend *Emily Dickinson: Poetry for Young People,* edited by Frances Schoonmaker Bolin and illustrated by Chi Chung.

■ Students interested in the theme of solitude versus popularity may enjoy the anthology *Pierced by a Ray of Sun: Poems About the Times We Feel Alone,* edited by Ruth Gordon.

DIFFERENTIATING INSTRUCTION

Advanced Learners
Enrichment. Tell students that Emily Dickinson's short, quirky, intensely emotional poems are favorites with many poets writing today and that readings of her work have been recorded and are available online.
Activity. Have students search the Internet for readings of Emily Dickinson's poems. Encourage them to listen to several

readings and then select their favorites to play for a classroom Emily Dickinson festival.

After You Read

First Thoughts

1. Students' pictures will vary but should share some common elements, such as a train (or a horse), a valley, mountains, shacks, quarry walls, a hill, and a stable (or station).

Thinking Critically

2. Words such as "Tanks" and "hooting" suggest that the poem is about a train, along with the fact that so many miles are covered in a short span of time. Words such as "lap," "lick," "feed," "step," "neigh," and "stable" tell you that the train is being compared to a horse. Students familiar with the Christian tradition may say that the poem also refers to Jesus, who is both "docile and omnipotent" and was born under a star, in a stable.

3. Adjectives include *prodigious, supercilious, prompter, docile,* and *omnipotent.* Dickinson likes the train. She is amazed by its power and freedom.

4. Possible answer: I found reading the poem aloud to be most helpful because the rhythm reminded me of a train hurtling down the tracks.

Extending Interpretations

5. Possible answers: A train's billowing smokestack resembles a horse's flying mane; a train's pumping wheels resemble a horse's galloping legs; the hard, solid sides of a train resemble a horse's muscular torso.

6. Possible answers include computers, satellites, robots, and space shuttles.

Assessment

■ *Holt Assessment: Literature, Reading, and Vocabulary*

After You Read Response and Analysis

First Thoughts

1. Let someone read the poem aloud to you. Draw a picture of what you see as you listen to the poem. Be sure to compare what *you* see in the poem with what other listeners see.

Thinking Critically

2. Although Emily Dickinson uses an **extended metaphor** in this poem, she never says directly what she is describing or what she is comparing that thing to. What clues in the poem tell you that she is writing about a train and comparing it to a horse? Could this poem be about two other things?

3. List all the adjectives Dickinson uses to describe the train. Think about these adjectives as well as the opening line of the poem. How do you think Dickinson feels about this train?

4. Look back at the strategies for "How to Read Poetry" on page 547. Which of these suggestions did you find most helpful? Pick one and explain how it helped you to understand "I Like to See It Lap the Miles."

Extending Interpretations

5. Look back at the chart you made for the Quickwrite on page 551. Did you find any comparisons between a train and a horse that Dickinson missed?

6. What machine would be as awesome today as the train was in Emily Dickinson's time?

WRITING

Extending a Metaphor

Choose a mechanical object (car, vacuum cleaner, lawn mower, blow-dryer, electric shaver, helicopter, spaceship), and write a brief poem comparing it to something living. Try to keep the mechanical object and the living object unnamed, as Dickinson does. Hint at the identity of your mystery items by including the sounds, smells, feel, appearance, and actions of the objects.

SKILLS FOCUS

Literary Skills
Analyze an extended metaphor.

Writing Skills
Write a poem.

DIFFERENTIATING INSTRUCTION

English-Language Learners

Work with students in a group to help them complete the Thinking Critically questions. As students look for clues and adjectives that extend Dickinson's metaphor, provide synonyms or definitions as needed. Help students understand that some words in the poem, such as "feed" and "docile," are often used in reference to work animals or livestock.

Before You Read — The Poems

I Am of the Earth *and* Early Song

Make the Connection
Quickwrite ✏️

Think of all the ways in which you are connected to the earth. To begin, fill in a chart like the one below:

Planet Earth

| Gifts we receive from the earth: | Gifts we give back to the earth: |

What is the most important gift the earth gives to you? What is the most important thing you give the earth? Briefly explain your answers.

Literary Focus
Personification

Common sense tells us that a cloud can't cry and a river can't get angry. They can in the imagination of writers, though. When writers give human or living qualities to nonhuman or nonliving things, they are using **personification.** In "I Am of the Earth," the speaker uses personification when she speaks of the earth as a mother cradling a child.

Chochiti Pueblo jar (c. 1885).
Museum of Fine Arts, Houston, Texas.
USA/Gift of Miss Ima Hogg.

SKILLS FOCUS

Literary Skills
Understand personification.

SKILLS FOCUS
pp. 555–559

Grade-Level Skills
■ **Literary Skills**
Analyze figures of speech in poetry, such as personification.

Upcoming Skills
■ **Literary Skills**
Identify the literary devices that define a writer's style.

Summary ⬇ *below grade level*

In these short poems, two poets of Native American descent describe their love for and gratitude toward the earth. The speaker of "I Am of the Earth" personifies the earth as a mother: The maternal earth has raised, fed, and cared for the speaker and will eventually embrace the speaker in death. The speaker of "Early Song" gives thanks for a beautiful day, for the people the speaker considers brothers and sisters, for the earth, and for the blood that links humanity to the earth.

RESOURCES: READING

Planning
■ *One-Stop Planner* CD-ROM with ExamView Test Generator

Differentiating Instruction
■ *Holt Reading Solutions*
■ *Supporting Instruction in Spanish*
■ *Audio CD Library*
■ *Audio CD Library, Selections and Summaries in Spanish*

Assessment
■ *Holt Assessment: Literature, Reading, and Vocabulary*
■ *One-Stop Planner* CD-ROM with ExamView Test Generator
■ *Holt Online Assessment*

Internet
■ go.hrw.com (Keyword: LE5 7-5)
■ *Elements of Literature Online*

Media
■ *Audio CD Library*
■ *Audio CD Library, Selections and Summaries in Spanish*

Build skills. Write the following sentence on the chalkboard: *The weary old car groaned and complained as I turned the key, and soon it began coughing out black smoke.*

Ask students why a writer might use such words to describe an old car. [By comparing the car to a weary person who smokes, the writer vividly conveys how old and run-down it is.]

DIRECT TEACHING

A Literary Focus

? Personification. In "I Am of the Earth," what does the earth do that makes it like a mother? [Possible response: The earth bears, cares for, nourishes, rewards, punishes, and embraces the speaker.]

B Cross-curricular Connections
CULTURE

Prayer. The four prayers mentioned in l. 6 are addressed to the north, south, east, and west. Each direction is associated with a color and with specific plants, animals, and religious symbols. In addition, each direction is believed to have specific powers and to offer distinct types of protection.

C Reading Skills

? Analyze imagery. What beliefs do you think the speaker is conveying with this image? [Possible responses: The speaker comes from and will return to the earth; all living things, including the earth, are connected.]

I Am of the Earth
Anna Lee Walters

I am of the earth
She is my mother
She bore me with pride
She reared me with love
5   She cradled me each evening
She pushed the wind to make it sing
She built me a house of harmonious colors
She fed me the fruits of her fields
She rewarded me with memories of her smiles
10   She punished me with the passing of time
And at last, when I long to leave
She will embrace me for eternity

Early Song
Gogisgi/Carroll Arnett

As the sun rises
high enough to
warm the frost
off the pine needles,

5   I rise to make
four prayers of
thanksgiving for
this fine clear day,

for this good brown
10   earth, for all
brothers and sisters,
for the dark blood

that runs through me
in a great circle
15   back into this
good brown earth.

DIFFERENTIATING INSTRUCTION

English-Language Learners
You may need to help students interpret ll. 3 and 4 of "I Am of the Earth." Make sure students understand that in the context of the poem the word *bore* is used as the past tense of the verb *bear* and means "gave birth." The word *reared* in this context means "brought up a child." Have students discuss attitudes toward the earth that are prevalent in their own cultures.

For lessons designed for intermediate and advanced English-language learners, see *Holt Reading Solutions*.

VIEWING THE ART

Pueblo pottery. The Pueblo pottery shown in the photograph is part of a centuries-old tradition. These useful pots and jars are made from materials of various colors, which are dug from the ground in the villages where the pottery is created. Other materials, such as the glaze and the fuel for the fire, are also gathered from the earth. Pottery making involves several steps, including drying the clay, soaking it to remove impurities, and modeling it by hand. The pottery is often painted with geometric patterns or designs of birds, flowers, or deer.

557

For Independent Reading

- For students who would like to explore visions of the earth expressed by poets from other Native American cultures, you might recommend the anthology *The Trees Stand Shining: Poetry of the North American Indians,* selected by Hettie Jones and illustrated by Robert Andrew Parker.

- Another fine anthology of Native American poetry is *In the Trail of the Wind: American Indian Poems and Ritual Orations,* edited by John Bierhorst.

Meet the Writers

Anna Lee Walters

"Words Poured Out"
At the age of sixteen, **Anna Lee Walters** (1947–   ) left home to attend a boarding school in New Mexico. In the Southwest, Walters began to discover her roots in the Pawnee and Otoe cultures—and in the process unlocked her voice as a writer. She recalls:

> 66 Words poured out, page after page. I am still amazed by it, by the torrent of thoughts deposited there. . . . Today my occupation as a writer

is related to what my grandfather and grandmother did when they repeated family history in the manner of their elders, leading the family all over this sacred land, this continent most recently called America in the last five hundred years, in their retelling of the Otoe journey from the dawn of time until they came to rest at Red Rock Creek a little over a century ago. 99

Gogisgi/Carroll Arnett

"What It Feels Like to Be Alive"
Gogisgi/Carroll Arnett (1927–   ), an American of Cherokee descent, was born in Oklahoma City. He has published more than three hundred poems and stories in magazines, sometimes under his Cherokee name, Gogisgi.

> 66 I write poems because it seems sensible to do so and wasteful not to. A poem has a use insofar as it shows what it feels like to be alive. 99

DIFFERENTIATING INSTRUCTION

Advanced Learners
Enrichment. Tell students that the earth is personified as a mother in the mythology of many cultures around the world, including the mythology of many Native American cultures.
Activity. Have students search the Internet for stories and information about the idea of the earth as a mother in different cultures. Suggest that they begin by using the search term *mythology* and then refine their search within those results, using the search term *earth mother* or *Gaia* (the earth goddess of Greek mythology). You may want to preview Web sites in advance before assigning this activity.

After You Read Response and Analysis

First Thoughts

1. How does each speaker connect to the earth? Do you share any of these connections? Check your notes for the Quickwrite on page 555.

Thinking Critically

2. **Tone** refers to the way a writer feels about a subject. Tone is communicated by word choice, including figures of speech. What words tell you how each of these speakers feels about the earth?

3. What words in the poem tell you that Walters **personifies** the earth as her mother? What message or feeling about our world does this comparison convey?

4. What does Arnett mean by the "great circle" (line 14)? How does Walters get at the same idea?

Extending Interpretations

5. Are people always grateful children of the earth? How do some people show that their feelings about the earth are very different from the feelings of these two poets?

WRITING

Responding to a Quotation

The following quotations use features of the earth to teach lessons. Choose one that you like, and write a paragraph or a brief essay about what the words mean to you. Include any of your own experiences to illustrate the lesson.

"There is no hill that never ends." —Masai proverb

"Do you have the patience to wait till your mud settles and the water is clear?" —Tao-te Ching

Paraphrasing

Write a paraphrase of one of the poems you have just read. (When you **paraphrase** something, you put it in your own words, making sure to keep the writer's meaning.) Paraphrasing can help you understand and recall a text. Follow these rules: (1) Read the poem line by line. (2) Rewrite each line or sentence in clear and simple prose. (3) Restate each figure of speech in your own words—that is, explain the comparison, and describe its emotional effect on you.

SKILLS FOCUS

Literary Skills
Analyze personification.

Writing Skills
Respond to a quotation; paraphrase a poem.

I Am of the Earth / Early Song   **559**

After You Read

First Thoughts

1. Possible answers: These speakers consider the earth a family member. Students may view the earth as a generous force or a useful resource.

Thinking Critically

2. Words that suggest a positive tone include "love," "cradled," "fed," and "embrace" from the Walters poem and "thanksgiving" and "good" from the Arnett poem.

3. Possible answer: Words include "bore," "reared," and "cradled." The comparison suggests love for the earth. It also conveys the power of the earth to nurture or punish its children.

4. Possible answers: Arnett refers to the eternal cycle of birth and death. In the last line of her poem, Walters speaks of death as the eternal "embrace" of mother earth.

Extending Interpretations

5. Possible answer: People who litter, pollute the air and water, and plunder natural resources without restoring them show no respect for the earth as a living thing.

ASSESSING

Assessment
- *Holt Assessment: Literature, Reading, and Vocabulary*

DIFFERENTIATING INSTRUCTION

Learners Having Difficulty

Have students meet in small groups to answer the questions orally. *Monitoring tip:* If students have difficulty answering question 4, point out that a circle has no beginning and no end. Have them consider the meaning of comparing life on earth to a circle. Then, point out the word *eternity* in the last line of the Walters poem, and tell students that it means "forever" or "time

without end." Finally, have the groups share their answers to question 5 in a class discussion.

Writing. You might want to read aloud the quotations and discuss their meanings with the class before asking students to write their responses at home. The Masai proverb suggests that all troubles or difficulties (like climbing a hill) come to an end. The quotation from the Tao-te Ching suggests that the process of discovering one's

true self or destiny takes time.

Grade-Level Skills

■ Literary Skills

Analyze how tone is conveyed in a text through word choice and rhythm.

Summary *at grade level*

> A rental agent tries to collect rent from a tenant. The tenant refuses to pay, complaining about the broken sink and other problems that have not been fixed. The agent retorts that maintenance isn't his job. The two are at an impasse.

PRETEACHING

Skills Starter

Build skills. Remind students that a synonym for the word *tone* is *attitude*. Challenge students, one after another, to say, "You're a big help," each with a different tone of voice. After each student speaks, have listeners try to define the tone. Was it sarcastic? sincere? neutral? This exercise will help students see that tone significantly affects meaning.

Before You Read The Poem

Madam and the Rent Man

Make the Connection
Quickwrite 🖉

"Grin and bear it."

"Stand up for yourself."

What does "grin and bear it" mean? Have you ever been in a situation where you had to grin and bear it? What does "stand up for yourself" mean? When do people have to stand up for themselves?

Write down your thoughts in response to the following questions:

- Which is harder—to grin and bear it or to stand up for yourself?

- Can you stand up for yourself and still be polite? and still be popular?

- Will people respect you if you always deal with situations you don't like by grinning and bearing it?

Literary Focus
Tone

Has anyone ever said to you, "Don't use that tone of voice with me"? Your tone can change the meaning of what you say. Tone can turn a statement like "You're a big help" into a genuine compliment or a cruel, sarcastic remark.

Poems and stories have tones too. As you read "Madam and the Rent Man," listen for the **tone,** or the writer's attitude, toward his no-nonsense speaker.

Background
Literature and Place

This poem is set in Harlem, a section of New York City where many people live in rented apartments. The speaker of the poem is a woman who has reason to be angry with her landlord.

go.hrw.com

INTERNET
More About
Hughes
Keyword: LE5 7–5

SKILLS FOCUS

Literary Skills
Understand
tone.

The poet Langston Hughes in Harlem.

560 Collection 5 / Worlds of Words: Prose and Poetry

Hunter Museum of American Art, Chattanooga, Tennessee. Museum purchase with funds provided by the Benwood Foundation and the 1982 Collectors' Group. HMA 1982.10. © 2005 Gwendolyn Knight Lawrence/Artists Rights Society (ARS), New York.

The Apartment (1943) by Jacob Lawrence. Gouache on paper (21¼" × 29¼").

Madam and the Rent Man

Langston Hughes

The rent man knocked.
He said, Howdy-do?
I said, What
Can I do for you? **Ⓐ**
5 He said, You know
Your rent is due.

I said, Listen,
Before I'd pay
I'd go to Hades°
10 And rot away! **Ⓑ**

The sink is broke,
The water don't run,
And you ain't done a thing
You promised to've done.

15 Back window's cracked,
Kitchen floor squeaks,
There's rats in the cellar,
And the attic leaks.

He said, Madam,
20 It's not up to me.
I'm just the agent,
Don't you see?

I said, Naturally,
You pass the buck.
25 If it's money you want
You're out of luck.

He said, Madam,
I ain't pleased!
I said, Neither am I. **Ⓒ**

30 So we agrees!

---

9. Hades (hā′dēz′): in Greek mythology, the underworld, or world of the dead.

Ⓐ Literary Focus

❓ **Tone of voice.** What tone of voice does the rent man use? Explain your answer. [He is polite. "Howdy-do" is a casual, friendly expression meant to put the tenant at ease.]

Ⓑ Literary Focus

❓ **Tone of voice.** What tone of voice does the tenant use? Explain your answer. [She is angry. The place is in bad shape, and she thinks the rent man doesn't care.] Have two students try reading the dialogue aloud, trying out different tones of voice until they find the tones that the class agrees fit the characters best. Have students define these tones of voice.

Ⓒ Literary Focus

Tone. After students have finished reading, have them sum up the poem's tone in one or two words. Challenge them to explain how the rhythms and rhyme scheme affect the tone. [The poem has a definite "swing" rhythm and regular rhyme scheme, which make the tone more humorous or cynical than it would be otherwise.]

VIEWING THE ART

Jacob Lawrence (1917–2000) was an eminent painter of African American life. His distinctive expressionist style features flat, angular lines and forceful colors. *The Apartment* is part of a cycle of paintings of daily life in Harlem.

Activity. Ask students how this picture makes them feel—sad, angry, happy, or frightened? How do the colors and shapes combine to create a mood in the painting?

Learners Having Difficulty
Have students form pairs and use copies of the poem to help them follow the verbal battle and sort out which character speaks which lines. Suggest that they underline the poem's words with two different colors, one for the tenant and one for the rent man. Students may be confused by the fact that the tenant is both narrating the poem and reporting her speech verbatim. If necessary, point out that every line not spoken by the rent man is, in fact, spoken by the tenant. However, not all of her words are spoken to the rent man. Have students circle the tenant's words that are not addressed to the rent man.

After You Read

First Thoughts

1. Ask students what specific details in the poem led them to choose their responses.

Thinking Critically

2. The speaker is a female tenant in run-down housing.

3. She doesn't want to pay her rent because agreed-upon repairs to her place haven't been done.

4. It means "shift the blame." The rent man tries to shift the blame for not making the repairs away from himself.

5. The poem suggests that people should fight for their rights and that they should not neglect their responsibilities. It also suggests that a little give-and-take is necessary to resolve a standoff.

6. The underlying tone is angry, or cynical, but the swing of the rhythm gives the poem a feeling of humor and liveliness.

Extending Interpretations

7. Students should agree that there are times when one has to speak bluntly. Since the rent man had already promised to see about the repairs, the tenant is perfectly right to express her displeasure.

Assessment

■ *Holt Assessment: Literature, Reading, and Vocabulary*

After You Read Response and Analysis

First Thoughts

1. Which of the following would you say to Madam, and why?
   - "Wait a minute, Madam—you might be evicted."
   - "Why are you picking on the agent? It's not his fault."
   - "You tell him, Madam!"

Thinking Critically

2. Who is the **speaker** in this poem?

3. What is her argument with the rent man?

4. What does "pass the buck" mean? How has the rent man passed the buck?

5. Do you think this poem has a **message**? Explain.

6. What **tones** do you hear expressed in this poem? Think of both the speaker and the rent man.

Extending Interpretations

7. The woman in the poem speaks plainly and bluntly. Do you think she is right to speak this way? Explain. Compare her attitude with those in your Quickwrite notes. ✏️

WRITING

Writing Dialogue

Write a dialogue between two people who disagree about something—perhaps money, noise, or food. The dialogue can be funny or serious. Use the vocabulary and speech patterns of everyday conversation to make your characters sound real.

SPEAKING AND LISTENING

Reading Dialogue

Prepare a read-aloud of "Madam and the Rent Man" in which you and a partner (as Madam and the rent man) read the dialogue. Practice changing the **tone** of your voice as the argument intensifies. Perform your read-aloud for the class. Afterward, ask your listeners to analyze your interpretation of the poem. Did they notice anything new about the poem as they heard it read aloud?

INTERNET

Projects and Activities

Keyword: LE5 7-5

SKILLS FOCUS

Literary Skills
Analyze tone.

Writing Skills
Write dialogue.

Speaking and Listening Skills
Read a poem aloud.

DIFFERENTIATING INSTRUCTION

Learners Having Difficulty
Have partners work together to answer question 6. Remind them that a single poem can have many different tones. Then, direct students to ll. 9–10, l. 22, and ll. 28–30. These lines reveal key shifts in tone, or attitude, in the poem.

Advanced Learners
Enrichment. Have students consider how the argument might be resolved. Challenge them to write another stanza or two of the poem, in which the tenant and rent man come to an agreement.

HOMEWORK

Before You Read The Poems

Harlem Night Song *and* Winter Moon

Make the Connection
Quickwrite ✏️

How does the night make you feel? Do you find it mysterious? Is it a time for dreaming? Or does the night make you fearful? Do you worry that dangerous creatures might be lurking in the dark? Take a moment, and jot down the first five words that come into your mind when you think of the night.

Literary Focus
Imagery

Imagery is language that appeals to the senses. When you read "The Highwayman" on page 247, for example, you might have *pictured* the moonlit highway. You might have *heard* the horse galloping down that moonlit highway. You might have *felt* the wind blowing through the trees. You might even have *smelled* the moldy hay in the stable. Poets hope their imagery will unlock storehouses of memory and stir our imaginations. They hope their images will make us say, "Oh yes, I see what you mean."

Look for sensory images in "Harlem Night Song" and "Winter Moon." Which of your senses—sight, hearing, touch, taste, smell—do the images appeal to?

INTERNET
More About Hughes
Keyword: LE5 7-5

New building going up. Madison Avenue and 113th Street, New York City (1947).

SKILLS FOCUS

Literary Skills
Understand imagery.

Grade-Level Skills
■ **Literary Skills**
Analyze imagery in poetry.

Upcoming Skills
■ **Literary Skills**
Identify the literary devices that define a writer's style.

Summary ⬌ *at grade level*

"Harlem Night Song" is a love poem delivered by a speaker to an implied lover. First, the speaker invites the beloved to wander through the night with him. Then he describes the glow of the moon on the rooftops, the color of the night sky, the radiance of the stars, and the sound of distant music. He concludes as he began with an invitation to "roam the night together / Singing."

In "Winter Moon," the speaker marvels at the color and shape of a crescent moon in the winter sky.

RESOURCES: READING

Planning
■ *One-Stop Planner* CD-ROM with ExamView Test Generator

Differentiating Instruction
■ *Holt Reading Solutions*
■ *Supporting Instruction in Spanish*
■ *Audio CD Library*
■ *Audio CD Library, Selections and Summaries in Spanish*

Assessment
■ *Holt Assessment: Literature, Reading, and Vocabulary*
■ *One-Stop Planner* CD-ROM with ExamView Test Generator
■ *Holt Online Assessment*

Internet
■ go.hrw.com (Keyword: LE5 7-5)
■ *Elements of Literature Online*

Media
■ *Audio CD Library*
■ *Audio CD Library, Selections and Summaries in Spanish*

Motivate. On the chalkboard, write *Sight, Hearing, Smell, Taste,* and *Touch.* Ask students to imagine taking a walk in their neighborhood on a summer night. What might they see, hear, smell, taste, or feel? List their responses in the appropriate columns. This exercise will help students respond to the sensory images in Hughes's two "nighttime" poems.

DIRECT TEACHING

A Literary Focus

Imagery. Remind students that an image appeals to one or more of the five senses—sight, hearing, touch, taste, and smell. Then, have students identify two images in the poem that appeal to sight and two that appeal to hearing. [Possible responses: sight—the glow of the moon, the blue sky; hearing—the lovers' song, the music of the band.]

B Literary Focus

❷ Speaker. To whom is the speaker speaking? [He is speaking to someone he loves.] How would you describe the speaker? [Possible responses: loving, romantic, poetic.]

C Literary Focus

❷ Imagery. Which qualities of the moon have the strongest impact on the speaker? How can you tell this? [The repetition of the words "thin and sharp," as well as the use of "slim," suggests that the speaker is most struck by the moon's thin shape, which he imagines would be sharp to the touch.]

D Reading Skills

Paraphrase. Ask students to describe what the speaker sees in their own words. [Possible response: He sees an eerie, white sliver of a moon, shining in the night sky.]

Harlem Night Song

Langston Hughes

Come,
Let us roam° the night together
Singing.

I love you.

5 Across
A The Harlem roof-tops
Moon is shining.
Night sky is blue.
Stars are great drops
10 Of golden dew.

Down the street
A band is playing.

I love you.

B Come,
15 Let us roam the night together
Singing.

Winter Moon

Langston Hughes

C How thin and sharp is the moon tonight!
How thin and sharp and ghostly white
D Is the slim curved crook of the moon tonight!

---

2. **roam** (rōm) *v.*: wander.

DIFFERENTIATING INSTRUCTION

Learners Having Difficulty
To reinforce their understanding of "Harlem Night Song," invite students to draw a picture or make a collage of the scene described in the poem. Have them write a line or two from the poem next to appropriate parts of their pictures, such as "Moon is shining" or "Night sky is blue."

English-Language Learners
Students will gain a greater understanding of Hughes's rhythms and cadences by hearing the poems read aloud. First, read each poem in its entirety, emphasizing the central images. Then, read the poems again, pausing to have students echo you. Finally, ask individuals to take turns reading the entire poem aloud.

Rooftops, Midtown Manhattan (1944) by Brett Weston.

Meet the Writer

Langston Hughes wrote about the everyday people of Harlem during the Depression, the "people up today and down tomorrow, working this week and fired the next." However, he was determined to present the problems of people like Madam and the rent man with wit and humor. He commented, "The race problem in America is serious business, I admit, but must it *always* be written about seriously?" In addition, Hughes was committed to writing in the dialect that he heard around him in Harlem. He advised himself and other poets to "Hang yourself, poet, in your own words. Otherwise, you are dead."

For Independent Reading

■ Hughes said that the two poets who influenced him the most were Walt Whitman and Carl Sandburg. Students may enjoy dipping into Whitman's *Leaves of Grass* and *Rainbows Are Made: Poems by Carl Sandburg*.

■ Students can enjoy jazz poems by Hughes and others in *Moment's Notice* (1993), edited by Art Lange and Nathaniel Mackey, and *The Jazz Poetry Anthology* (1991), edited by Sascha Feinstein and Yusef Komunyakaa.

Meet the Writer

Langston Hughes

"Just Singing"

Langston Hughes (1902–1967) was one of the first African American writers to win worldwide favor. Still, he never lost his popularity with the people he wrote about. Hughes once said:

> ❝I knew only the people I had grown up with, and they weren't people whose shoes were always shined, who had been to Harvard, or who had heard of Bach.❞

Langston Hughes was born in Joplin, Missouri, and worked at many different jobs in various cities while writing poetry in his spare time. For two years he worked as a busboy at a hotel in Washington, D.C. During this time he wrote many poems, among them blues poems, which he would make up in his head and sing on his way to work.

> ❝One evening, I was crossing Rock Creek Bridge, singing a blues I was trying to get right before I put it down on paper. A man passing on the opposite side of the bridge stopped and looked at me, then turned around and cut across the roadway.

> He said 'Son, what's the matter? Are you ill?'
>
> 'No,' I said. 'Just singing.'
>
> 'I thought you were groaning,' he commented. 'Sorry!' And he went on his way.
>
> So after that I never sang my verses aloud in the street anymore.❞

Hughes became a major literary figure in what is now known as the Harlem Renaissance of the 1920s. His poems often echo the rhythms of blues and jazz.

For Independent Reading

You can find some of Hughes's best poems in a collection called *The Dream Keeper and Other Poems*.

566   Collection 5 / Worlds of Words: Prose and Poetry

DIFFERENTIATING INSTRUCTION

Advanced Learners

Enrichment. Have students read more of Langston Hughes's poetry. Each student can choose a poem that he or she responds to and read or perform it for the class. Students can briefly introduce the poem, give any background information they can about when and why Hughes wrote it, and read or recite it. Then, have a class discussion about all of the Hughes poems shared. What is the tone of each? Do some share the same tone? How does the biographical information about Hughes in the text inform their understanding of the poems?

After You Read Response and Analysis

First Thoughts

1. Which **image** in Hughes's poems stands out most clearly in your mind? Why?

Thinking Critically

2. Poems, like songs, often repeat lines, stanzas, or words. What sentences are repeated in "Harlem Night Song"? Describe the **tone** you hear in these lines.

3. Explain the **sensory images** in "Harlem Night Song."

4. What do the images in "Harlem Night Song" reveal about the speaker?

5. Draw a picture of the moon the speaker sees in "Winter Moon." Which words in particular help you visualize the moon?

WRITING

Writing a Poem

Write a poem about the night. Your poem can be as short as "Winter Moon" or as long as you like. Be sure to use **imagery** in your poem. See how many of the five senses you can appeal to. You may want to use some of the words you jotted down in your Quickwrite response.

Footer

SKILLS FOCUS

Literary Skills
Analyze imagery.

Writing Skills
Write a poem using imagery.

After You Read

First Thoughts

1. Possible images from "Harlem Night Song" include moonlight on the rooftops, the blue night sky, the golden starlight, and a band playing. Possible images from "Winter Moon" include the thinness, sharpness, and curvature of the moon.

Thinking Critically

2. "Come, / Let us roam the night together / Singing" and "I love you" are repeated. The speaker's tone may be described as loving, romantic, urgent, or passionate.

3. Moonlight on the rooftops, the blue night sky, and the golden starlight help the reader visualize the action in the poem. The mention of singing and a band playing help the reader hear what is happening.

4. Possible answer: The images in "Harlem Night Song" reveal that the speaker feels excited by and drawn to the sensual beauty of the night.

5. Possible words include "thin," "sharp," "ghostly white," and "slim curved crook."

Assessment

■ *Holt Assessment: Literature, Reading, and Vocabulary*

DIFFERENTIATING INSTRUCTION

Learners Having Difficulty

If students have trouble answering question 2, remind them that tone is the attitude or feeling of a writer toward his or her subject. If they find question 4 difficult, have them talk about the characteristics of gold and dew and how the sight and touch of "golden dew" would make them feel.

Advanced Learners

Enrichment. Challenge these students to include in the night poems they write images that appeal to all five of their senses.

I Ask My Mother to Sing

SKILLS FOCUS
pp. 568–571

Grade-Level Skills

■ **Literary Skills**

Analyze and explain the characteristics of different forms of poetry, including lyric poems and sonnets.

Summary ⟷ *at grade level*

In response to the implied question in the poem's title, the speaker's mother—and then grandmother—break into song. The speaker, inspired by the women's song, imagines a scene from his relatives' past in China, a place he has never been. In his mind's eye, he sees summer rain falling on a lake and picnickers scurrying for shelter as he listens to the song. He also imagines waterlilies, brimming with rainwater, tipping over, and righting themselves only to be filled with water again. The women cry as they sing, but neither stops singing.

Make the Connection
Quickwrite ✏

Do you have any memories that are both happy and sad at the same time? Do you know some older people who tell stories that make them smile and weep? Jot down the bittersweet memories or stories that come to mind.

Literary Focus
Lyric Poem

There are two basic types of poems: A **narrative poem** tells a story, and a **lyric poem** expresses an emotion. The word *lyric* comes from the Greek language. In ancient Greece lyric poems were sung to the music of a stringed instrument called a lyre. Today we call the words to all kinds of songs lyrics.

Most of the poems in this collection are lyric poems. As you read these poems, you'll discover that lyric poems come in many shapes and sizes and express a wide range of feelings.

Sonnet

Some lyric forms are simple, but many, like the sonnet, are complex. The challenge to the lyric poet using a complex form is to express his or her thoughts and feelings within the restrictions of the form—somewhat like playing a game with strict rules.

Li-Young Lee's "I Ask My Mother to Sing" is a sonnet. A **sonnet** is a lyric poem of fourteen lines. There are several different types of sonnets. In the one this poet follows, the lines are divided into three quatrains (a quatrain is four lines of verse). Each quatrain focuses on one aspect of a subject. The sonnet ends with a couplet (two lines that usually rhyme). As you will see, Li-Young Lee varies this structure a bit.

SKILLS FOCUS

Literary Skills
Understand lyric poems; understand sonnets.

Background
Literature and Social Studies

Li-Young Lee's mother was a member of the Chinese royal family. His family fled China when the Communists took control of the country. The Summer Palace is where the royal family would go to escape the heat. The palace is located in the hills outside the capital city of Peking (now called Beijing) and consists of many beautiful buildings situated around Kuen Ming Lake. One of these buildings is a large teahouse made of stone in the shape of a boat. When an emperor ruled China, the palace was visited only by the royal family and their attendants. Today it is a museum, open to tourists from around the world.

RESOURCES: READING

Planning
■ *One-Stop Planner* CD-ROM with ExamView Test Generator

Differentiating Instruction
■ *Holt Reading Solutions*
■ *Supporting Instruction in Spanish*
■ *Audio CD Library*
■ *Audio CD Library, Selections and Summaries in Spanish*

Assessment
■ *Holt Assessment: Literature, Reading, and Vocabulary*
■ *One-Stop Planner* CD-ROM with ExamView Test Generator
■ *Holt Online Assessment*

Internet
■ go.hrw.com (Keyword: LE5 7-5)
■ *Elements of Literature Online*

Media
■ *Audio CD Library*
■ *Audio CD Library, Selections and Summaries in Spanish*

I Ask My Mother to Sing

Li-Young Lee

She begins, and my grandmother joins her.
Mother and daughter sing like young girls.
If my father were alive, he would play
his accordion and sway like a boat.

5   I've never been in Peking, or the Summer Palace,
nor stood on the great Stone Boat to watch
the rain begin on Kuen Ming Lake, the picnickers
running away in the grass.

But I love to hear it sung;
10   how the waterlilies fill with rain until
they overturn, spilling water into water,
then rock back, and fill with more.

Both women have begun to cry.
But neither stops her song.

I Ask My Mother to Sing   **569**

PRETEACHING

Selection Starter

Motivate. Ask students if they have ever written an acrostic poem. In an acrostic poem certain letters, such as the initial letter of each line, spell out a word or phrase when the letters are read from top to bottom. Ask them whether they enjoyed writing such a poem, and why. Explain that writing poems that fit a certain pattern or follow certain rules can be both challenging and fun.

DIRECT TEACHING

A Literary Focus

? Sonnets. Remind students that a sonnet is a fourteen-line poem that is divided into several subsections or groups of lines. How is this sonnet divided? What is the subject matter of each section of the sonnet? [This sonnet is made up of three quatrains, or groups of four lines, and one couplet, or pair of two lines. The first two quatrains tell who is singing and what they are singing about. The third quatrain tells how the speaker feels about what he is hearing. The final couplet tells how the women feel about their singing.]

B Literary Focus

? Lyric poems. What competing feelings do the last two lines express? [Possible response: The women's love for their Chinese homeland and the happy memories of times spent there compete with their present sense of loss and longing.]

DIFFERENTIATING INSTRUCTION

English-Language Learners

To help students understand the long compound sentence that makes up the second stanza, work with them to break the sentence down into four parts: (1) "I've . . . Palace," (2) "nor . . . Stone Boat," (3) "to watch . . . Kuen Ming Lake," and (4) "the picnickers . . . grass." Write these four parts on the board. Students should easily understand the first part. For the second part, circle "nor," and tell students that it connects l. 5 to ll. 6–8. Explain that the words *have I* are implied, or left out, in l. 6. Read ll. 5–6 with the implied words filled in—"*I've never been in Peking . . . nor [have I] stood . . . to watch.*" Finally, guide students to understand that the last two parts of the long sentence ("to watch . . . Kuen Ming Lake" and "the picnickers . . . grass") tell the reader that the speaker has never watched "rain begin on Kuen Ming Lake" and "picnickers running away in the grass."

Meet the Writer

When Li-Young Lee was a child, his father read to him from the King James Version of the Bible and quoted from three hundred Chinese poems he knew from memory. Lee was enchanted by the poetry, but it wasn't until college that he realized that living human beings—not angels or long-dead poets—wrote poems. It was then that Lee began to write poems about his own experiences.

Lee's family all still live together because they feel they have lost one family home and do not wish to lose another. Lee writes of the past to preserve the family's memories and create an imaginative link to a lost homeland.

For Independent Reading

If students enjoy this poem, you might recommend these other works by Li-Young Lee: "A Story" from *The City in Which I Love You* and "Early in the Morning" and "The Gift" from *Rose.*

Meet the Writer

Li-Young Lee

"Beautiful Stories"

Li-Young Lee (1957–   ) once made the following comment:

> ❝ I think immigrants have beautiful stories to tell. But the problem is to make art out of it. ❞

Lee succeeded in using art to tell his family's story in the award-winning memoir *The Winged Seed: A Remembrance.* An important part of the narrative is based in Jakarta, Indonesia, Lee's birthplace. His family had moved to Indonesia from China, where Lee's father had been the Communist leader Mao Tse-tung's physician. The family was forced to flee Indonesia in 1959, after anti-Chinese sentiment resulted in the jailing of Lee's father. After spending time in Hong Kong and Japan, the family settled in America in 1964.

When asked how he became a poet, Lee recalls the following:

> ❝ That was when I first started to learn the English language. . . . Words like *yarn* or *bird* or *tree* felt . . . saturated with meaning. I think

that's when I really was taken with the English language. I started writing little things to my mother. . . . My brother and I caught a fish once . . . and I wrote a poem. 'Here is a fish. Make a nice dish.' . . . I safety-pinned it through the gill of the fish and gave it to our mother. It seemed that the word *fish* and the thing we gave her were one and the same. ❞

DIFFERENTIATING INSTRUCTION

Advanced Learners

Acceleration. Explain that more traditional forms of the sonnet typically follow a rhyme scheme, or fixed pattern of rhyme. **Activity.** Provide an example of a rhyming sonnet, such as one written by Shakespeare. As a group, decipher the rhyme scheme of the sonnet (usually *abab cdcd efef gg*), and discuss the subject matter of each quatrain. Finally, ask students why Lee may have

chosen to write a nonrhyming sonnet. How does the absence of rhyme affect the sound and the mood of a sonnet?

After You Read   Response and Analysis

First Thoughts

1. Why do you think the mother and grandmother cry when they sing this song?

Thinking Critically

2. Take a look at how the poet fits his thoughts into the structure of a **sonnet**. What is the topic of each of the first three quatrains? How do the last two lines sum up the point of the poem?

3. It might seem at first that the speaker changes the subject in the second stanza. What **inference** do you have to make in order to understand how the second stanza connects to the first?

4. A **lyric poem** expresses the speaker's thoughts and feelings. How does the speaker react to the song his mother and grandmother sing?

5. What **images** do you see as the two women sing? Make a list of at least five images from the poem, and explain which senses the images appeal to.

6. The last two lines of the poem say: "Both women have begun to cry. / But neither stops her song." Compare this experience of the mother and grandmother with the story or experience you described in your Quickwrite notes.

WRITING

Describing a Song

Write a poem or a descriptive paragraph about a song that makes you especially happy or sad. Be sure to tell who sings the song, what it says, and what it makes you think about. Try to create some images to describe your responses to the song.

SKILLS FOCUS

Literary Skills
Analyze a lyric poem; analyze a sonnet.

Writing Skills
Write a poem or description.

I Ask My Mother to Sing   **571**

ASSESSING

Assessment

■ *Holt Assessment: Literature, Reading, and Vocabulary*

Grade-Level Skills

■ Literary Skills
Analyze the characteristics of
different forms of poetry,
including odes.

Summary ⬌ *at grade level*

As if he were flipping through
an old photo album, the poet
describes what he sees in a series
of childhood snapshots: his feet
near a pond, his sister posing
with a giraffe, his brother standing on one foot. The poet comments that his mother wasn't
very skilled at taking pictures—
she cut off people's heads or
photographed them with their
eyes closed. Still, he says, it was
fun to have Mamá behind the
camera—as the photos of laughing loved ones prove.

Before You Read The Poem

Ode to Family Photographs

Make the Connection
Quickwrite 🖉

What do you think is worth celebrating
in your life? It might be a favorite person,
place, or thing. It might even be an
idea, like peace or patriotism. List five
subjects that you would like to praise.

Literary Focus
Ode

There are many ways to commemorate
important people, things, or events. You
might have a parade in their honor, as
we sometimes do for baseball teams or
astronauts. You might give them an
award, as we do for great writing or
acting. What people in ancient Greece
often did was write an ode. An **ode** is a
poem that pays tribute to someone or
something of great importance to the
poet.

The first odes, written in honor of
famous people, were long, complex, and
elegant. Over the centuries, many odes
have been written in a formal style to
praise lofty subjects, such as beauty, joy,
and freedom.

Today's odes tend to be more
informal. Some are even humorous.
Many have been written about
everyday objects, such as tomatoes,
frogs, and socks. Gary Soto's ode
celebrates something most people have
in their homes—family photos.

Literary Skills
Understand
odes.

RESOURCES: READING

Planning
■ *One-Stop Planner* CD-ROM with
ExamView Test Generator

Differentiating Instruction
■ *Holt Reading Solutions*
■ *Supporting Instruction in Spanish*
■ *Audio CD Library*
■ *Audio CD Library, Selections and
Summaries in Spanish*

Assessment
■ *Holt Assessment: Literature, Reading,
and Vocabulary*
■ *One-Stop Planner* CD-ROM with
ExamView Test Generator
■ *Holt Online Assessment*

Internet
■ go.hrw.com (Keyword: LE5 7-5)
■ *Elements of Literature Online*

Media
■ *Audio CD Library*
■ *Audio CD Library, Selections and
Summaries in Spanish*

Ode to Family Photographs

Gary Soto

This is the pond, and these are my feet.
This is the rooster, and this is more of my feet.

Mamá was never good at pictures.

This is a statue of a famous general who lost an arm,
5   And this is me with my head cut off.

This is a trash can chained to a gate,
This is my father with his eyes half-closed.

This is a photograph of my sister
And a giraffe looking over her shoulder.

10   This is our car's front bumper.
This is a bird with a pretzel in its beak.
This is my brother Pedro standing on one leg on a rock,
With a smear of chocolate on his face.

Mamá sneezed when she looked
15   *Behind the camera: the snapshots are blurry,*
The angles dizzy as a spin on a merry-go-round.

But we had fun when Mamá picked up the camera.
How can I tell?
Each of us laughing hard.
20   Can you see? I have candy in my mouth.

PRETEACHING

Selection Starter
Motivate. Ask students if they have an old photo that they particularly enjoy looking at from time to time. Then, have them write a description of the picture and tell why it appeals to them.

DIRECT TEACHING

A Reading Skills
? Make generalizations. What generalization can you make about the photographs the poet describes? [Possible responses: The photographs are not very artistic. They show a variety of everyday objects and scenes.]

B Literary Focus
? Style. Why do you think Soto uses italics for some of his lines? [to distinguish between his descriptions of the photos and his comments about them]

C Literary Focus
? Ode. The poem's title tells you that this poem celebrates family photographs. What else does the poem celebrate? [It celebrates the poet's mother and her unique style of photography.]

DIFFERENTIATING INSTRUCTION

Special Education Students
These students may have difficulty making a connection between the poem's title and its content. To help them see that the poem describes a series of photos, have students look for two words that are repeated often in the poem. ["This is"] Explain that each time students see these words, they can be sure that a description of a photograph will come next. You may want to make rough sketches of each photo described. Then as you read aloud each "This is . . ." statement, hold up the corresponding sketch.

Writing poems and stories is not all Soto has accomplished. He directed *The Pool Party,* an award-winning television film; and he wrote the libretto, or words, for an opera titled *Nerd-landia!*

For Independent Reading

If students enjoy this poem, you might recommend a collection of Soto's poems *A Fire in My Hands* or his book of short stories about growing up, titled *Baseball in April and Other Stories.*

Meet the Writer

Gary Soto

"I Began to Feel Like I Was Doing Something Valuable"

Gary Soto (1952–) first discovered poetry in college, where he had originally planned to major in geography:

> 66 I know the day the change began, because it was when I discovered in the library a collection of poems . . . called *The New American Poetry.* . . . I discovered this poetry and thought, This is terrific: I'd like to do something like this. So I proceeded to write my own poetry, first alone, and then moving on to take classes. 99

Soto obviously made the right decision when he chose to be a writer—his award-winning fiction and poetry are loved by people of all ages.

Although Soto's work contains elements from his Mexican American heritage, as well as aspects of his experiences as a migrant laborer, he also manages to address universal themes. When Soto started receiving fan mail from Mexican American teenagers in response to the work he had published for adults, he was inspired to write works specifically for young readers, including the award-winning collection *Baseball in April and Other Stories.* Soto shared these thoughts about his decision to write for young readers:

> 66 I began to feel like I was doing something valuable. I thought I might be able to make readers and writers out of this group of kids. 99

For Independent Reading

In *Neighborhood Odes,* which "Ode to Family Photographs" is taken from, Gary Soto presents poems that capture the pleasures of childhood.

FAMILY/COMMUNITY ACTIVITY

Encourage students to spend time with friends or family members looking at old photographs and discussing what the photos show, when they were taken, and who took them. Invite volunteers to bring their favorite "mistake" photos to class and to tell the stories behind them.

After You Read Response and Analysis

First Thoughts

1. Did you imagine yourself or anyone you know in Soto's pictures? (Maybe you saw yourself as the photographer.) Which **images** in this ode made you smile?

Thinking Critically

2. What details in the poem tell you that the poet's *mamá* was not a very good photographer?

3. **Odes** are written in praise of something. What do you think this poet is praising? (It's not just family photographs!)

WRITING

Celebrating in an Ode

Write an **ode** celebrating something on the list you wrote for the Quickwrite on page 572. Try to convey your feelings for all aspects of your subject. For example, if you write "An Ode to My Baseball Bat," you might praise its weight, balance, and power; the comfortable grip on the rubber; the way it swings through the air; the satisfying *whonk* when it hits the ball; how you got it; how long you have had it; and how it helps you win games. When you write your ode, you can talk directly to the reader, as Gary Soto does, or you can talk to the object you are celebrating ("Bat, you are . . .").

SKILLS
FOCUS

Literary Skills
Analyze an ode.

Writing Skills
Write an ode.

Ode to Family Photographs **575**

After You Read

First Thoughts

1. Students may be reminded of relatives and other loved ones by Soto's descriptions of his family. Images that made students smile could include "me with my head cut off," "my father with his eyes half-closed," and "Pedro standing on one leg on a rock, / With a smear of chocolate on his face."

Thinking Critically

2. Possible answers: One photo shows only the poet's feet; in another, the poet's head is cut off; another shows a trash can; another catches the poet's father with his eyes closed.

3. The poet is praising his mother as well as the family photographs.

ASSESSING

Assessment

■ *Holt Assessment: Literature, Reading, and Vocabulary*

DIFFERENTIATING INSTRUCTION

Learners Having Difficulty

Before students answer question 3, have them think of a friend or family member who has a habit or a tendency that amuses them. Discuss whether such traits make the person more or less endearing, and why.

Elements of Literature
The Sounds of Poetry
by John Malcolm Brinnin

Poets use many techniques to make music out of words. The most common **sound effects** used in poetry are also used in the songs you love to listen to.

Rhythm: The Rise and Fall of Our Voices

Rhythm refers to the rise and fall of our voices as we use language. As in music, a poem's rhythm can be fast or slow, light or solemn. A poem might also sound just like everyday speech.

Poetry that is written in **meter** has a regular pattern of stressed and unstressed syllables. Poetry that is written in **free verse** does not have a regular pattern of stressed and unstressed syllables. Free verse sounds like ordinary speech.

When poets write in meter, they count out the number of stressed syllables (or strong beats) and unstressed syllables (weaker beats) in each line. Then they repeat the pattern throughout the poem. To avoid a singsong effect, poets usually vary the basic pattern from time to time. Try reading aloud the following lines from a famous poem called *The Rime of the Ancient Mariner* by Samuel Taylor Coleridge. Can you hear that each line has four stressed syllables alternating with four unstressed syllables?

INTERNET
More About the Sounds of Poetry
Keyword: LE5 7-5

SKILLS FOCUS

Literary Skills
Understand sounds of poetry, such as rhythm, rhyme, alliteration, onomatopoeia.

Day after day, day after day,
We stuck, nor breath nor motion;
As idle as a painted ship
Upon a painted ocean.

A poem's rhythm can be shown by using accent marks: (′) for stressed syllables and (˘) for unstressed syllables. This marking is called **scanning.**

Day after day, day after day

Rhyme: Chiming Sounds

Rhyme is the repetition of the sound of a stressed syllable and any unstressed syllables that follow: *sport* and *court*; *smother* and *another*; *sputtering* and *muttering*. The echoing effect of rhyme gives us pleasure. It makes us look forward to hearing certain chiming sounds throughout the poem. In the verse from *The Rime of the Ancient Mariner,* the rhyming words are *motion* and *ocean*.

Rhymes like *motion/ocean* in Coleridge's verse are called **end rhymes** because they occur at the ends of lines. **Internal rhymes** occur within lines, as in this line from the same poem:

The fair breeze blew, the white foam flew . . .

576   Collection 5 / Worlds of Words: Prose and Poetry

Poets will often use a pattern of rhymes, called a **rhyme scheme.** To describe a rhyme scheme, assign a new letter of the alphabet to each new end rhyme. The rhyme scheme of Coleridge's verse is *abcb*.

Alliteration: Repeating Consonants

Another way poets create sound effects is through the use of alliteration (ə·lit′ər·ā′shən). **Alliteration** is the repetition of consonant sounds in words that are close together. Read this tongue twister of a poem aloud to hear all the repeated *t* sounds:

A Tutor

A tutor who tooted the flute
Tried to tutor two tooters to toot.
   Said the two to the tutor,
   "Is it harder to toot, or
To tutor two tooters to toot?"
       —Carolyn Wells

"A Tutor" is a **limerick,** a humorous five-line poem. Limericks have a definite rhythm and rhyme scheme. Try scanning the poem and describing the rhyme scheme now that you've tooted through it.

Onomatopoeia: Sound Echoes Sense

Onomatopoeia is a long word that is pronounced like this: än′ō·mat′ō·pē′ə. It is the use of words with sounds that echo their sense. *Crash, bang, boom, hiss,* and *toot* are all examples of onomatopoeia.

To see how sounds alone can suggest sense, read aloud this famous nonsense poem. You will not find all the words in a dictionary, but the sounds will help you guess what is going on. (What *is* going on?)

Jabberwocky

'Twas brillig, and the slithy toves
   Did gyre and gimble in the wabe;
All mimsy were the borogoves,
   And the mome raths outgrabe.
"Beware the Jabberwock, my son!
   The jaws that bite, the claws that catch!
Beware the Jubjub bird, and shun
   The frumious Bandersnatch!"
He took his vorpal sword in hand:
   Long time the manxome foe he sought—
So rested he by the Tumtum tree,
   And stood awhile in thought.
And, as in uffish thought he stood,
   The Jabberwock, with eyes of flame,
Came whiffling through the tulgey wood,
   And burbled as it came!
One, two! One, two! And through and through
   The vorpal blade went snicker-snack!
He left it dead, and with its head
   He went galumphing back.
"And hast thou slain the Jabberwock?
   Come to my arms, my beamish boy!
O frabjous day! Callooh! Callay!"
   He chortled in his joy.
'Twas brillig, and the slithy toves
   Did gyre and gimble in the wabe;
All mimsy were the borogoves,
   And the mome raths outgrabe.
       —Lewis Carroll

The Sounds of Poetry   **577**

Have students collaborate on creating a dictionary for the nonsense words in "Jabberwocky." Students can read the poem aloud and discuss the meanings suggested by the sounds. You might also encourage students to use context clues to help them decide on definitions. After the dictionary is completed, ask students how helpful sound was in determining a nonsense word's meaning.

Apply

Point out to students that sound effects are just as important to playwrights as they are to poets. Since the dialogue in a play is meant to be spoken aloud, playwrights have to pay close attention to effects like onomatopoeia, alliteration, and repetition. In verse plays like those by Shakespeare, sound effects are even more important. The next time students attend a play or watch a movie, have them listen closely for sound effects in the dialogue.

SKILLS FOCUS
pp. 578–585

Grade-Level Skills

■ Literary Skills
Analyze humorous poems and exaggeration.

■ Literary Skills
Analyze sound effects in poetry, including rhythm and meter.

Summary ⬄ *at grade level*

"Father William" records a "non-sense" conversation between a young man and his old father. In it, the young man poses three questions about how the old man manages to perform some strenuous physical feats at his advanced age. The father has an answer for each question, but his answers do not give the son any satisfaction. Both father and son seem to be hiding their true feelings about each other behind their questions and answers. Finally, the old man refuses to answer any more of his son's questions and threatens to throw him down the stairs.

In "Sarah Cynthia Sylvia Stout," Shel Silverstein humorously explores the consequences of putting off unpleasant tasks. In spite of her father's repeated requests, Sarah Cynthia refuses to take out the garbage. As a result, the kitchen is piled high with food scraps and rotten remains of all kinds—a mess that eventually extends out of her home and clear across the country. At last, Sarah Cynthia agrees to take out the garbage, but it is too late. The girl meets an unwelcome (though unspecified) fate.

Father William *and* Sarah Cynthia Sylvia Stout Would Not Take the Garbage Out

Make the Connection
Quickwrite ✏️

What makes you laugh? Do you like wild and crazy physical actions? Do you prefer clever wordplay? Jot down some of the things in TV shows and songs that you find funny.

Literary Focus
Humorous Poems

Many poems are written to make you laugh—or at least smile. That doesn't mean they don't have a point to make. They just make their point with humor. One element that many humorous poems share is **exaggeration**—that is, describing something as bigger or smaller, or worse or better than it really is. As you read the two humorous poems that follow, notice what they exaggerate. Then, ask yourself: Were the poems written to make a serious point, or were they written just for fun?

Rhythm

In English and other languages, **rhythm** is a musical quality produced by the repetition of stressed and unstressed syllables or by the repetition of words and phrases or even whole lines or sentences. When the stressed and unstressed syllables are arranged in a regular pattern, we call the pattern **meter.**

SKILLS FOCUS

Literary Skills
Understand humorous poems and exaggeration; understand rhythm and meter.

You can discover the meter of a line by reading it aloud and exaggerating the stressed syllables. For example, in the line *The girl is walking to the store*, you can sound out the meter like this: The GIRL is WALKing TO the STORE. You can also show the poem's meter by using accent marks (') over stressed syllables and (˘) over unstressed syllables. This marking is called **scanning.** It looks like this:

˘ ′ ˘ ′ ˘ ′ ˘ ′
The girl is walking to the store.

There are many different kinds of meter. You can hear another pattern if you read this line aloud: *In the morning we go for a ride*. It sounds like this: In the MORning we GO for a RIDE. Here's how it looks with scanning:

˘ ˘ ′ ˘ ˘ ′ ˘ ˘ ′
In the morning we go for a ride.

As you can hear in these examples, a regular beat is often found in ordinary speech as well as in poetry. In a poem written in meter, the meter supplies the underlying beat. But just as you wouldn't want to exaggerate the stressed syllables when you talk to your friends, you also don't want to overemphasize them when you read a poem.

Read "Father William" aloud, and listen for its beat.

RESOURCES: READING

Planning
■ *One-Stop Planner* CD-ROM with ExamView Test Generator

Differentiating Instruction
■ *The Holt Reader*
■ *Holt Reading Solutions*
■ *Supporting Instruction in Spanish*
■ *Audio CD Library*

■ *Audio CD Library, Selections and Summaries in Spanish*

Assessment
■ *Holt Assessment: Literature, Reading, and Vocabulary*
■ *One-Stop Planner* CD-ROM with ExamView Test Generator
■ *Holt Online Assessment*

Internet
■ go.hrw.com (Keyword: LE5 7-5)
■ *Elements of Literature Online*

Media
■ *Audio CD Library*
■ *Audio CD Library, Selections and Summaries in Spanish*

Father William

Lewis Carroll

"You are old, Father William," the young man said,
    "And your hair has become very white;
And yet you incessantly° stand on your head—
    Do you think, at your age, it is right?"

5 "In my youth," Father William replied to his son,
    "I feared it might injure the brain;
But now that I'm perfectly sure I have none,
    Why, I do it again and again."

"You are old," said the youth, "as I mentioned before,
10   And have grown most uncommonly fat;
Yet you turned a back somersault in at the door—
    Pray, what is the reason of that?"

"In my youth," said the sage, as he shook his gray locks,
    "I kept all my limbs very supple°
15 By the use of this ointment—one shilling the box—
    Allow me to sell you a couple."

---

3. **incessantly** (in·ses′ənt·lē) *adv.*: without ceasing; continually.
14. **supple** (sup′əl) *adj.*: easily bent; flexible.

(Pages 579–580)
Illustrations by
John Tenniel
(1820–1914), the
original illustrator
of Carroll's *Alice's
Adventures in
Wonderland*

PRETEACHING

Selection Starter
Motivate. On the chalkboard, write *It will take me three years to complete this assignment!* Ask students if they have ever made such a comment to their friends when they were facing a difficult task. Then, challenge them to explore why we exaggerate or overstate in situations like this one. Guide students to see that underneath the humor of exaggerated statements can lurk very real concerns.

DIRECT TEACHING

A Literary Focus
Humorous poems. At what point do you know that this poem is meant to be humorous? [The poem becomes obviously humorous in l. 3, when we learn that Father William is continuously standing on his head.]

B Literary Focus
Rhythm and meter. Point out that the reader is carried through the poem by its strong, regular rhythm. Have a volunteer read ll. 9 and 10 aloud, exaggerating the stressed syllables. Then, have students use the *da-DUM* method to discover the meter of the two lines. Write it on the board. [da da DUM da da DUM da da DUM da da DUM / da da DUM da da DUM da da DUM]

DIFFERENTIATING INSTRUCTION

Learners Having Difficulty
The poem's strict question-and-answer format and rather formal tone and word choice—especially in contrast to its silly subject matter—heighten its humor. Students may be unable to discern the contrast between the form and content. To illustrate, give some examples of how very ordinary comments and requests can be voiced in such formal language that they become silly. *Please deposit your dispensables in the rubbish receptacle,* for instance, is a silly, pretentious way to say *Put your trash in the garbage can.*

Father William **579**

A Literary Focus

? **Exaggeration.** Find one example of exaggeration in these stanzas. Why is it humorous? [Possible responses: How much the old man eats (a whole goose) and the strength of his jaws (he crushes the goose's bones and beak) are exaggerated. Each example is funny because it runs contrary to what we expect of older people.]

B Literary Focus

? **Humorous poems.** What is funny about the question Father William poses in l. 31? [Possible responses: He asks whether he can listen all day to "such stuff," when he is the one who has been serving up the tall tales. If he has the ability to do so many amazing things, he should certainly have the ability to answer a young man's questions.]

"You are old," said the youth, "and your jaws are too weak
　　　　For anything tougher than suet°;
Yet you finished the goose, with the bones and the beak;
　　　　Pray, how did you manage to do it?"

20 **A**

"In my youth," said his father, "I took to the law,
　　　　And argued each case with my wife;
And the muscular strength which it gave to my jaw,
　　　　Has lasted the rest of my life."

25　"You are old," said the youth; "one would hardly suppose
　　　　That your eye was as steady as ever;
Yet you balanced an eel on the end of your nose—
　　　　What made you so awfully clever?"

　　"I've answered three questions, and that is enough,"
30　　　　Said his father; "don't give yourself airs!
B Do you think I can listen all day to such stuff?
　　　　Be off, or I'll kick you downstairs!"

---

18. **suet** (soo′it) *n.:* a kind of fat.

DIFFERENTIATING INSTRUCTION

English-Language Learners
Some of the idioms and multiple-meaning words in the poem may present a challenge for these students. Before they read, review the meanings of the following words and phrases:
• *Turned a back somersault* (l. 11) means to roll over backward.
• The word *locks* (l. 13) refers to long strands of hair.

• A *shilling* (l. 15) was a unit of British currency, or money.
• The word *pray* (l. 20) means "please, tell me."
• *Argued each case* (l. 22) means talked in favor of one side of an issue.
• To *give yourself airs* (l. 30) is to act in a self-important manner.
• To *be off* (l. 32) is to go away.

Advanced Learners
Enrichment. Explain to students that "Father William" is a parody, or humorous imitation, of a poem by Robert Southey called "The Old Man's Comforts."
Activity. Provide students with a copy of Southey's poem. Then, have them write a paragraph that compares and contrasts the original text with Carroll's parody.

Meet the Writer

Lewis Carroll

"He Was One of Us"

Lewis Carroll (1832–1898) had two separate careers. Under the pseudonym Lewis Carroll, he was the author of *Alice's Adventures in Wonderland* and its sequel, *Through the Looking Glass.* Under his real name, he was Rev. Charles Lutwidge Dodgson, a teacher of mathematics and a clergyman.

Carroll had seven sisters and three brothers. As a child, he was always in charge of family entertainment, inventing and performing magic tricks, puppet plays, and clever games.

Carroll was educated at home until he was twelve, then sent to boarding school, which he disliked intensely. The other boys teased him because he preferred reading to sports. He also stammered when he was nervous, a condition that bothered him all of his life.

As a student at Oxford University, Carroll received a grant that provided him with an income for the rest of his life. Two conditions of the grant were that he remain unmarried and that he take holy orders, which would qualify him to become a priest in the Church of England. Although his stammer made preaching difficult, he managed to deliver a sermon occasionally. Interestingly, the stutter disappeared when he was around children, who loved to hear the stories he told.

Carroll spent many days in the company of children, writing nonsense verse and creating puzzles. As one of his young friends said:

> 66 He was one of us, and never a grown-up pretending to be a child in order to preach at us. . . . 99

Once Carroll went on a picnic with three young girls, one of whom was named Alice. He told them a story he made up about a girl named Alice, who went down a rabbit hole into a fabulous wonderland. That was the beginning of *Alice's Adventures in Wonderland,* from which the poems "Jabberwocky" (page 577) and "Father William" (page 579) are taken.

Meet the Writer

Charles Dodgson (pronounced *Dod*-son) was a man of many talents and interests. When he wasn't creating imaginative worlds for children, he could be found taking photographs or studying anatomy and medical science. About his profession, mathematics, Dodgson once said that it was the true wonderland, "for nothing is impossible" there.

DIFFERENTIATING INSTRUCTION

Advanced Learners
Enrichment. Because this poem clearly indicates each speaker and sets off the dialogue in quotation marks, students can easily develop a script for a dramatic performance.
Activity. Invite pairs of students to plan and perform a dramatic reading of the poem for the class. As they plan, encourage students to experiment with different tones of voice (for example, amazement, sarcasm, skepticism) and discuss how shifts in tone create shifts in meaning. Allow students to use costumes and props to accentuate the poem's humor.

As an alternative, you may want to have students locate and perform dramatic selections from *Alice's Adventures in Wonderland* or *Through the Looking Glass.*

PAIRED

? **Humorous poems.** What common tendency of young people does this poem poke fun at? [their tendency to not clean up after themselves or to postpone unpleasant chores]

B Learners Having Difficulty

Find details. Like Sarah Cynthia's garbage, the details in this poem pile up rather quickly—and its strong rhythms tend to propel the reader rapidly through the mess. Slow students down by asking them to identify seven things that the garbage *did*. [It filled the can, covered the floor, cracked the window, and blocked the door (ll. 11–12); it rolled down the hall, lifted the roof, and broke the wall (ll. 21–22).]

C Literary Focus

Rhythm and meter. Have students read ll. 23–24 aloud in unison, exaggerating the rhythm. Then, help them identify the lines' rhythm. [DA da DA da DA da DA / DA da DA da DA da DA] Ask how this steady beat affects their reading rate. [It speeds it up.]

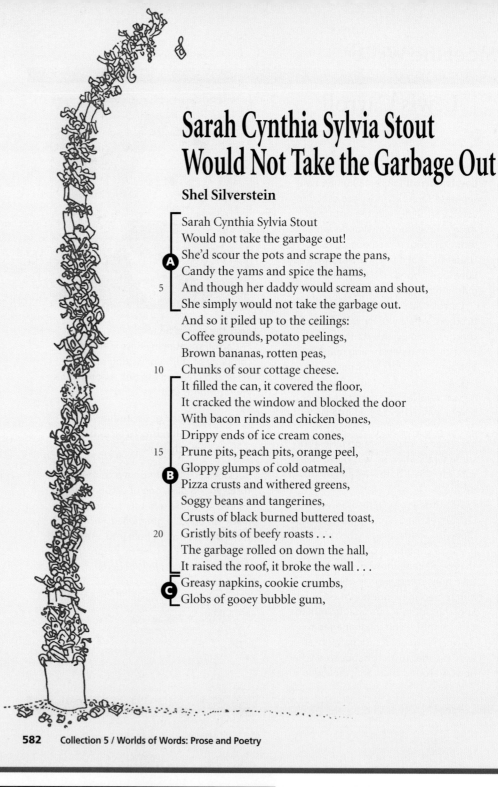

Sarah Cynthia Sylvia Stout Would Not Take the Garbage Out

Shel Silverstein

A
  Sarah Cynthia Sylvia Stout
  Would not take the garbage out!
  She'd scour the pots and scrape the pans,
  Candy the yams and spice the hams,
5 And though her daddy would scream and shout,
  She simply would not take the garbage out.
  And so it piled up to the ceilings:
  Coffee grounds, potato peelings,
  Brown bananas, rotten peas,
10 Chunks of sour cottage cheese.
  It filled the can, it covered the floor,
  It cracked the window and blocked the door
  With bacon rinds and chicken bones,
  Drippy ends of ice cream cones,
15 Prune pits, peach pits, orange peel,
B Gloppy glumps of cold oatmeal,
  Pizza crusts and withered greens,
  Soggy beans and tangerines,
  Crusts of black burned buttered toast,
20 Gristly bits of beefy roasts . . .
  The garbage rolled on down the hall,
  It raised the roof, it broke the wall . . .
C Greasy napkins, cookie crumbs,
  Globs of gooey bubble gum,

DIFFERENTIATING INSTRUCTION

Learners Having Difficulty
Students intimidated by the poem's dense texture and abundant details may enjoy listening to an audio recording of "Sarah Cynthia Sylvia Stout" before reading it on their own. Before playing the recording, encourage students to listen not only for what happens in the poem but also for its more striking details. After listening, ask students to share some of the images they remember and discuss what makes the poem funny.

English-Language Learners
For lessons designed for English-language learners, see *Holt Reading Solutions*.

Special Education Students
For lessons designed for special education students, see *Holt Reading Solutions*.

D Literary Focus

? **Exaggeration.** What exaggeration does the poet make about the piles of garbage in ll. 33 and 34? [The garbage reached the sky.]

E Literary Focus

? **Humorous poems.** What serious message underlies the poem's comic tone? [Possible response: Untidiness or procrastination can have very unpleasant consequences.]

25 Cellophane from green baloney,
    Rubbery blubbery macaroni,
    Peanut butter, caked and dry,
    Curdled milk and crusts of pie,
    Moldy melons, dried-up mustard,
30 Eggshells mixed with lemon custard,
    Cold french fries and rancid meat,
    Yellow lumps of Cream of Wheat.
    At last the garbage reached so high
    That finally it touched the sky.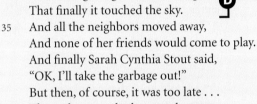
35 And all the neighbors moved away,
    And none of her friends would come to play.
    And finally Sarah Cynthia Stout said,
    "OK, I'll take the garbage out!"
    But then, of course, it was too late . . .
40 The garbage reached across the state,
    From New York to the Golden Gate.
    And there, in the garbage she did hate,
    Poor Sarah met an awful fate,
    That I cannot right now relate
45 Because the hour is much too late.
    But children, remember Sarah Stout
    And always take the garbage out!

Sarah Cynthia Sylvia Stout Would Not Take the Garbage Out   **583**

Meet the Writer

In addition to creating whimsical poems and illustrations for children, Silverstein also composed musical scores for movies, and in 1988, he coauthored, with David Mamet, the screenplay for *Things Change*. Although some critics find his work superficial, others consider it equal to that of the famous children's book writer Theodor "Dr. Seuss" Geisel (1904–1991).

Meet the Writer

Shel Silverstein

"I Couldn't Dance. . . . So I Started to Draw and Write."

Shel Silverstein (1932–1999) began drawing and writing when he was a young boy growing up in Chicago. He wrote:

> ❝When I was a kid—12, 14 around there—I would much rather have been a good baseball player or a hit with the girls. But I couldn't play ball. I couldn't dance. Luckily, the girls didn't want me; not much I could do about that. So I started to draw and write. I was also lucky I didn't have anyone to copy, be impressed by. I . . . developed my own style.❞

When Silverstein grew up, he became a writer of children's books, a poet, a cartoonist, and a songwriter. He created and illustrated two of the world's most popular collections of poems for children: *Where the Sidewalk Ends* (1974), which includes "Sarah Cynthia Sylvia Stout," and *A Light in the Attic* (1981). Silverstein said:

> ❝I would hope that people, no matter what age, would find something to identify with in my books, pick one up and experience a personal sense of discovery.❞

First Thoughts

1. What did you find funny in these poems? Did either of the poems include any of the sources of humor that you listed in your Quickwrite notes? Explain.

Thinking Critically

2. One element of humor is **exaggeration**—describing something as bigger, smaller, better, or worse than it is. List three examples of exaggeration in "Sarah Cynthia Sylvia Stout." Explain which is your favorite example.

3. Read "Father William" aloud, and identify its **meter.** To show your answer, write out a line of the poem, and use the **scanning** method described on page 578. Use the same method to show the meter in line 3 of "Sarah Cynthia Sylvia Stout."

4. Part of the humor of these poems comes from their clever **rhymes.** Silverstein has even found a rhyme for *macaroni.* (Can you think of any other words that rhyme with *macaroni*?) Take one group of rhyming words from one of the poems, and see how far you can extend the list with other rhyming words.

5. Silverstein's poem is full of **alliteration**—the repetition of similar consonant sounds in nearby words. Sarah's entire name is an example of alliteration. Find three other examples of alliteration in Silverstein's poem. Which sounds are repeated in each of your examples?

Extending Interpretations

6. What do you think is the main point of each poem? Do you think these poets are serious about their points, or are they just having fun?

7. In "Sarah Cynthia Sylvia Stout," the poet says, "Poor Sarah met an awful fate, / That I cannot right now relate." What do you think that fate might be?

SPEAKING AND LISTENING

Reading Aloud

Work with a partner to prepare an oral reading of one of these poems. First, decide who should read which lines. Then, practice reading aloud until you are satisfied you have given the poem the expression you want. Decide where you will read slowly, where you will speed up, and where you will change your tone of voice.

SKILLS FOCUS

Literary Skills
Analyze humorous poems and exaggeration; analyze rhythm and meter.

Speaking and Listening Skills
Read a poem aloud.

ASSESSING

Assessment

- *Holt Assessment: Literature, Reading, and Vocabulary*

First Thoughts

1. Students will probably be amused by the poems' exaggerations, unexpected turns, and descriptive details.

Thinking Critically

2. Possible examples include the garbage breaking down walls, lifting the roof, reaching the sky, extending across the country, and mysteriously ending the life of Sarah Cynthia. Ask students to provide reasons why they selected an example as their favorite.

3. The meter of "Father William" is da da DUM da da DUM da da DUM da da DUM. The meter of "Sarah Cynthia Sylvia Stout" is da DA da DA da DA da DA. For whichever lines students choose, make sure students have accent marks over stressed syllables and cups over unstressed syllables.

4. Students' rhyming lists should reflect a significant (and perhaps humorous) effort to extend them as far as possible.

5. Possible answers: "*scour the pots and scrape the pans*" (l. 3); "It filled the can, it covered the floor, / It *cracked* the window and *blocked* the door" (ll. 11–12); "Prune *pits, peach pits,* orange *peel*" (l. 15); "Globs of *gooey* bubble *gum*" (l. 24); "Peanut butter, *caked* and dry, / *Curdled* milk and *crusts* of pie" (ll. 27–28).

Extending Interpretations

6. Possible answers: The main point of "Father William" is that older people do not always act in the ways young people expect. The main point of "Sarah Cynthia Sylvia Stout" is that people who fail to fulfill their responsibilities will face the consequences. Most students will agree that both poets use humor to convey weightier messages.

7. Possible answers: Sarah may have been crushed or smothered by her own garbage, or she may have been lost in its mountainous piles.

Grade-Level Skills
■ **Literary Skills**
Analyze sound effects in poetry, including rhyme and rhyme scheme.

Upcoming Skills
■ **Literary Skills**
Identify the literary devices that define a writer's style.

Summary *at grade level*

> This short rhyming poem is set in a rural area during a snowfall. The poem's speaker and a friend stop to wonder at the strange behavior of a colt that seems terrified by the snow. They attribute human feelings to the colt, which appears to be "running away" from this new reality it has just encountered. In the end the speaker and the friend seem to feel the colt's anguish and angrily wonder why no one has come to put the poor little creature back into its stall.

Before You Read | The Poem

The Runaway

Make the Connection
Quickwrite ✏

In "The Runaway," Robert Frost introduces us to a colt who's never seen snow before. Even if the only horses you've met are in the movies, you can probably identify with the colt in this poem, because he is behaving the way most of us act when we encounter something new and strange.

Take a few notes on what you think the title of the poem refers to.

Literary Focus
Rhyme and Rhyme Scheme: Sound Decisions

Which words rhyme with
- *star*
- *peaches*
- *mice*
- *stopping*

Maybe your answer came automatically. There's something about **rhyme** that just comes naturally to people.

In a poem, rhymes at the ends of lines are called **end rhymes.** End rhymes determine a poem's **rhyme scheme,** or pattern of rhymes. To find out a poem's rhyme scheme, you can assign a different letter of the alphabet to each new end rhyme. The rhyme scheme of "The Runaway" begins with *abacbc*.

INTERNET
More About Frost
Keyword: LE5 7-5

SKILLS FOCUS

Literary Skills
Understand rhyme and rhyme scheme.

Background
Literature and Science

The subject of "The Runaway" is a Morgan colt. Morgans are a breed of swift, strong horses named for Justin Morgan (1747–1798), a Vermont schoolteacher who owned the stallion that founded the line. Morgans are small, sturdy horses that excel at weight-pulling contests. Today they are used mostly for riding and in herding cattle.

586 Collection 5 / Worlds of Words: Prose and Poetry

Planning
- *One-Stop Planner* CD-ROM with ExamView Test Generator

Differentiating Instruction
- *Holt Reading Solutions*
- *Supporting Instruction in Spanish*
- *Audio CD Library*
- *Audio CD Library, Selections and Summaries in Spanish*

Assessment
- *Holt Assessment: Literature, Reading, and Vocabulary*
- *One-Stop Planner* CD-ROM with ExamView Test Generator
- *Holt Online Assessment*

Internet
- go.hrw.com (Keyword: LE5 7-5)
- *Elements of Literature Online*

Media
- *Audio CD Library*
- *Audio CD Library, Selections and Summaries in Spanish*

The Runaway

Robert Frost

Once when the snow of the year was beginning to fall,
We stopped by a mountain pasture to say, "Whose colt?"
A little Morgan had one forefoot on the wall,
The other curled at his breast. He dipped his head
5   And snorted at us. And then he had to bolt.
We heard the miniature thunder where he fled,
And we saw him, or thought we saw him, dim and gray,
Like a shadow against the curtain of falling flakes.
"I think the little fellow's afraid of the snow.
10   He isn't winter-broken. It isn't play
With the little fellow at all. He's running away.
I doubt if even his mother could tell him, 'Sakes,
It's only weather.' He'd think she didn't know!
Where is his mother? He can't be out alone."
15   And now he comes again with clatter of stone,
And mounts the wall again with whited eyes
And all his tail that isn't hair up straight.
He shudders his coat as if to throw off flies.
"Whoever it is that leaves him out so late,
20   When other creatures have gone to stall and bin,
Ought to be told to come and take him in."

The Runaway   **587**

After You Read

First Thoughts

1. Possible answers:
   - As he faced his first snowfall alone, the colt felt <u>scared and abandoned</u>.
   - As I read about the colt, I felt <u>sad for him</u>.

Thinking Critically

2. *Winter-broken* means "used to the realities of winter."
3. Possible answer: The speaker feels angry at the person's insensitivity to the colt's fear.
4. The colt is trying to run away from the snow, a new experience that frightens him. Ask students to defend their guesses with details from the text.
5. The rhyme scheme is *abacbc defddef gg hihi jj.*
6. Possible answer: Yes, I agree with this interpretation because the speaker refers to the colt as "he" and "the little fellow" and imagines what the colt's mother would "tell" him and how the colt might react to his mother's words (ll. 11–13).

Extending Interpretations

7. Possible answers: Other runaways include teenagers who run away from home or refugees who leave their nation of origin. Lines 9–14 and 19–21 could apply to these people.

Assessment

- *Holt Assessment: Literature, Reading, and Vocabulary*

First Thoughts

1. How would you complete each of these sentences?
   - As he faced his first snowfall alone, the colt felt . . .
   - As I read about the colt, I felt . . .

Thinking Critically

2. To break a colt is to get a young horse used to being ridden. What do you think the expression "winter-broken" (in line 10) means?
3. How do you think the speaker feels about the person who has left the colt alone in the pasture?
4. Why do you think Frost called the poem "The Runaway"? (What is the colt running away from? What did you guess the **title** meant?)
5. Read the poem aloud to hear its conversational rhythms and rhyming sounds. Make a list of its **rhyming** words. Then, work out its **rhyme scheme.**
6. Some people think that the colt **symbolizes** a lost child or someone who is too young or too innocent to understand what he or she is experiencing. Do you agree with this interpretation, or do you have another one? Support your interpretation with details from the poem.

Extending Interpretations

7. The term *runaway* can refer to people too. What other runaways are found in our world? What lines from the poem could apply to them?

go.hrw.com

INTERNET
Projects and Activities
Keyword: LE5 7-5

SKILLS FOCUS

Literary Skills
Analyze rhyme and rhyme scheme.

Speaking and Listening Skills
Prepare a choral reading.

Writing Skills
Write a poem.

SPEAKING AND LISTENING
Choral Reading

With several classmates, prepare a group reading of "The Runaway." Decide which lines you will assign to a chorus and which lines you'll assign to a single voice. Practice reading aloud until the conversational speech rhythms come through.

WRITING
Writing a Poem

In five lines or more, tell how you would feel if you were this little horse. How would you feel about the weather, about your mother, and about the people watching you?

Learners Having Difficulty

Monitoring tip: If students have difficulty answering question 3, read the poem aloud to them again, emphasizing the speaker's emotional identification with the colt and the anger he expresses in ll. 19–21.

Choral reading. Suggest that students assign an individual to read the dialogue in the poem (ll. 9–14 and 19–21) and that they read the rest of the poem as a group.

Advanced Learners

Acceleration. Encourage advanced learners to focus on the symbolism of the poem—how the colt's panic might represent young children left on their own.

Activity. In response to question 6, have students create a collage to illustrate ll. 9–11. The collage might feature photographs of children reacting to new experiences.

The Pasture *and* A Minor Bird

Make the Connection
Quickwrite ✎

Robert Frost's poetry often focuses on connections between human life and the world of nature. Even if you live in a city, nature is all around you, from the sun and moon in the sky to the grass at your feet to the birds chirping in your ear. Make a list of the aspects of nature you notice as you move through your day.

Literary Focus
Stanza

In a poem a group of lines that form a unit is called a **stanza.** Like a paragraph in prose, a stanza often expresses a unit of thought. Stanzas can be of any length; they can even be a single line. In the poems that follow, "The Pasture" has two stanzas of four lines each, and "A Minor Bird" has four stanzas of two lines each.

Couplet

Each two-line stanza in "A Minor Bird" is a couplet. A **couplet** is two consecutive lines of poetry that rhyme and express a complete thought.

Reading Skills
Reading a Poem 📖

Robert Frost writes in an easy, conversational tone, which is how *you* should sound when you read his poems aloud. Here is an important tip that will help you read poems—for both their meaning and their sound:

Pay attention to punctuation.

Most poems are written in sentences, but the sentences may not end at the ends of lines. Don't stop reading at the end of a line of poetry unless you see some punctuation there. Make a full stop for a period, but pause just briefly for a comma, colon, semicolon, or dash. If the poem has no punctuation at all (and some don't), you'll have to figure out where to pause based on the thought groups you find in the poem.

INTERNET
More About Frost
Keyword: LE5 7-5

Background
Literature and Music

In the title "A Minor Bird," Robert Frost plays with two meanings of the word *minor. Minor* can mean "less important or lesser in rank." (Think of minor leagues in baseball.) *Minor* also refers to a type of key in music. A musical key is a sequence of related tones that form a scale. Most Western music is written in major keys. To some people, songs written in major keys sound happy. Minor keys, to the Western ear, tend to sound sad or haunting.

SKILLS FOCUS

Literary Skills
Understand stanzas; understand couplets.

Reading Skills
Read a poem.

The Pasture / A Minor Bird **589**

The Pasture

Robert Frost

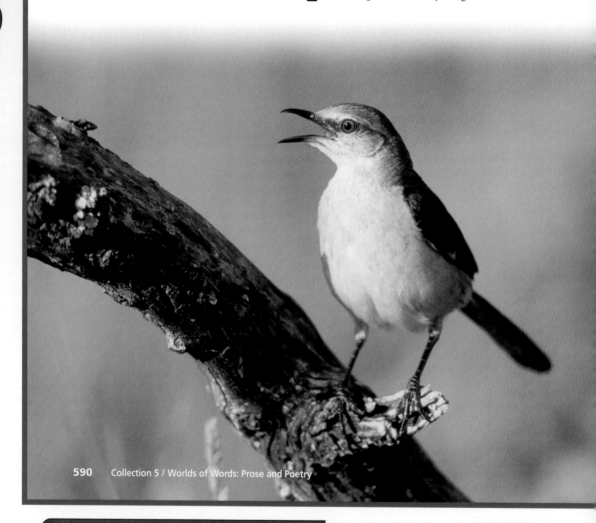

A I'm going out to clean the pasture spring;
I'll only stop to rake the leaves away
(And wait to watch the water clear, I may):
I shan't be gone long.—You come too.

I'm going out to fetch the little calf
That's standing by the mother. It's so young
It totters when she licks it with her tongue.
I shan't be gone long.—You come too.

A Minor Bird

Robert Frost

B I have wished a bird would fly away,
And not sing by my house all day;

Have clapped my hands at him from the door
When it seemed as if I could bear no more.

The fault must partly have been in me.
The bird was not to blame for his key.

C And of course there must be something wrong
In wanting to silence any song.

Selection Starter

Motivate. Have students think about times when they have an important—but pleasant—task to do. Ask them whether they like to do such activities alone or with others. If the task is an unpleasant one, do they prefer to do it alone or with someone else? Why?

DIRECT TEACHING

A **Literary Focus**

❓ **Stanza.** What single thought does the first stanza express? [The speaker is going out to clean the pasture spring and welcomes the listener to join him.]

B **Literary Focus**

❓ **Couplet.** What specific thing does the speaker do in the first couplet? (Hint: Look for the main verb.) [wish the bird would fly away] What does the speaker do in the second couplet? [clap his hands] What common goal do these actions have? [to get the bird to go away]

C **Reading Skills**

❓ **Read poetry.** If you were saying this sentence to a friend, would you pause after "wrong" or not? [Possible response: yes, briefly.] Tell students that when reading a poem, the natural rhythms of language—in addition to the poem's punctuation—can help them decide when to pause.

Learners Having Difficulty
In "The Pasture," Frost uses a variety of punctuation marks to help create a conversational tone. To help students recognize this tone, review the function of some or all of the following punctuation:

- The semicolon (;) is used to connect two independent clauses that are related to each other.

- Parentheses ((...)) are used to set off comments that aren't directly related to the subject at hand.
- The colon (:) is used to introduce a list, a quotation, a summary, or a formal declaration.
- The dash (—) is used to indicate a sudden change in thought or to introduce a summary statement.

Have students locate each punctuation mark in the poem and explain how it functions.

Meet the Writer

Robert Frost

"A Lump in the Throat"

While in high school in Lawrence, Massachusetts, **Robert Frost** (1874–1963) decided to become a poet. Not only did he succeed, but for a time he was America's most celebrated living poet.

He was the first poet ever to read a poem for a presidential inauguration, that of John F. Kennedy in 1961. On his seventy-fifth birthday, the U.S. Senate passed a resolution in his honor stating, "His poems have helped to guide American thought and humor and wisdom, setting forth to our minds a reliable representation of ourselves and of all men."

"Rob" Frost lived most of his life on farms in Vermont and New Hampshire. There he grew corn, taught, and raised a family. Frost filled his poems with images of the people of New England and their haybarns, farmhouses, pastures, apple orchards, and woods. His work speaks to people everywhere because it springs from intense feelings.

Frost says this about poetry:

> ❝ A poem . . . begins as a lump in the throat, a sense of wrong, a homesickness, a lovesickness. . . . It finds the thought and the thought finds the words. ❞

Frost felt that "it is most important of all to reach the heart of the reader."

For Independent Reading

If you enjoy poetry, read more of Frost's poems in *You Come Too: Favorite Poems for Young Readers.*

After You Read

First Thoughts

1. Possible answers:
   • When I finished reading "The Pasture," I felt <u>happy and uplifted</u>.
   • When I finished reading "A Minor Bird," I thought <u>of a time when I spoiled something good</u>.

Thinking Critically

2. Possible answer: The poem makes a good starting point because it invites the reader to join the poet in his experience.

3. Most students will say that the speaker's soothing tone and gentle nature make them feel like accepting his invitation.

4. The "you" might be the speaker's spouse, friend, or other loved one; it might also be the reader. The "I" may be a farmer or the poet himself.

5. Possible answers: Couplet 1— The speaker is annoyed by the bird's singing and wishes it would go away. Couplet 2—He claps his hands to scare the bird away. Couplet 3—He realizes he is partly to blame; the bird does not choose its song. Couplet 4—There is something wrong in trying to stop what is natural or beautiful.

6. Some students will agree that nature's beauty is a gift to be cherished and protected. Others will disagree, saying there is a time for song and a time for silence.

7. Possible answer: When we treat the gifts of nature harshly (or when we destroy beauty of any kind), we diminish or lessen ourselves.

After You Read   Response and Analysis

First Thoughts

1. Respond to the poems by finishing these sentences:
   • When I finished reading "The Pasture," I felt . . .
   • When I finished reading "A Minor Bird," I thought . . .

Thinking Critically

2. Frost asked that "The Pasture" be printed at the front of all collections of his poetry. Why do you think it would make a good starting point for a book of poems?

3. The speaker in "The Pasture" offers an invitation. As you read the poem, did you feel like accepting the invitation? Why or why not?

4. Who could the "you" be in "The Pasture"? Who might "I" be?

5. The **stanzas** in "A Minor Bird" are all **couplets.** Explain the main idea of each couplet.

6. Do you agree with the last two lines of "A Minor Bird"? Why or why not?

7. How would you express the **theme,** or message, of "A Minor Bird"? (You might find a hint in the two meanings of the word *minor*.)

WRITING

Imitating "The Pasture"

Write a one-stanza poem of your own that keeps the last sentence of "The Pasture." In your first three lines, tell about something you are about to do outdoors. Start your poem with the words "I'm going out to . . . ," and try to create one striking visual image. Your Quickwrite notes might give you some ideas.

SPEAKING AND LISTENING

Reading Aloud Alone

Choose one of these poems to read aloud. As you practice reading it, don't forget this tip for reading a poem: *Pay attention to the punctuation.* When you have practiced enough to read the poem smoothly, perform it for your class.

SKILLS FOCUS

Literary Skills
Analyze stanzas; analyze couplets.

Reading Skills
Read a poem.

Writing Skills
Imitate a poem.

Speaking and Listening Skills
Read a poem aloud.

ASSESSING

Assessment

■ *Holt Assessment: Literature, Reading, and Vocabulary*

DIFFERENTIATING INSTRUCTION

Learners Having Difficulty

Have students write answers to questions 1–3. Then, have them work in pairs to answer questions 4–7. Review with students the definitions of *couplet* and *stanza* as necessary. To help students develop a theme statement for question 7, remind them to re-read the last two lines of the poem and work together to paraphrase the couplet.

Before You Read   The Poem

Names of Horses

Make the Connection
Quickwrite ✏️

"Names of Horses" describes the life of a farm horse in the days before machinery took over the work. Think about an animal you once knew and loved, and jot down some of the memorable things that animal did in the course of a lifetime. The animal may be one you lived with or one you learned about through books or nature shows on television.

Literary Focus
Free Verse

"Names of Horses" is written in free verse. **Free verse** does not follow a regular rhyme scheme or meter, but it does make use of many other elements of poetry, including

- **imagery**—language that appeals to any of the five senses, most often sight, but also hearing, touch, taste, and smell

- **alliteration** (ə·lit′ər·ā′shən)— repetition of consonant sounds in words close to each other (*marvelous memories of mangoes and melons*)

- **onomatopoeia** (än′ō·mat′ō·pē′ə)— the use of words that sound like what they mean (the goose's *honk*)

- **rhythm**—a musical quality produced by repetition

Elegy

"Names of Horses" is an **elegy** (el′ə·jē), a poem that mourns the passing of something—a person, an animal, a way of life, a season of the year—that is important to the writer. There are many important elegies in literature. Walt Whitman wrote a heartfelt elegy mourning the death of Abraham Lincoln. Oliver Goldsmith wrote a comic elegy about a cat who was drowned in a goldfish bowl. The most famous elegy is probably Thomas Gray's "Elegy Written in a Country Churchyard." Gray mourns the anonymous people buried in a rural graveyard.

Once you've read "Names of Horses," you may agree with this reader's response:

> When someone asks me why I love poetry, I read "Names of Horses" to them, and they always say, "Oh, I didn't know poetry could be like that." And then they, too, say they love poetry.
>
> —Mary Shannon
> Kagel Canyon, California

SKILLS FOCUS

Literary Skills
Understand free verse; understand elegy.

SKILLS FOCUS
pp. 593–597

Grade-Level Skills
- **Literary Skills**
Analyze free verse.
- **Literary Skills**
Analyze an elegy.

Upcoming Skills
- **Literary Skills**
Analyze the characteristics of different forms of poetry.

Summary ⬆ *above grade level*

In this celebration of horses' lives, the speaker imagines the life of a horse who lived 150 years ago. He describes the horse's winter labor hauling wood; his spring labor pulling manure; his summer labor mowing the fields and harvesting the hay; and his Sunday work of carrying churchgoers. The speaker then imagines the day the horse was led, old and lame, to the pasture of dead horses, where he was mercifully shot and buried. There, the speaker muses, the horse's bones have for many years mingled with the roots of trees and flowers— and with the bones of other laborers like himself.

RESOURCES: READING

Planning
- *One-Stop Planner* CD-ROM with ExamView Test Generator

Differentiating Instruction
- *Holt Reading Solutions*
- *Supporting Instruction in Spanish*
- *Audio CD Library*
- *Audio CD Library, Selections and Summaries in Spanish*

Assessment
- *Holt Assessment: Literature, Reading, and Vocabulary*
- *One-Stop Planner* CD-ROM with ExamView Test Generator
- *Holt Online Assessment*

Internet
- go.hrw.com (Keyword: LE5 7-5)
- *Elements of Literature Online*

Media
- *Audio CD Library*
- *Audio CD Library, Selections and Summaries in Spanish*

Skills Starter

Build skills. To review the literary elements that may appear in free-verse poems, write the following items on the chalkboard:

The warm summer sand soothed my winter-weary feet.
Have you ever heard the screech of hungry sea gulls at the beach?

Then, have students identify in them examples of imagery, alliteration, onomatopoeia, and rhyme. [The first sentence contains examples of alliteration and imagery. The second sentence contains rhyme and onomatopoeia.]

DIRECT TEACHING

Ⓐ Literary Focus

❓ Free verse. What consonant sound is repeated throughout this stanza? [/s/]

Ⓑ Literary Focus

Free verse. Ask students to find an example of onomatopoeia in these lines. ["clacketing" (line 8)]

Ⓒ Literary Focus

Free verse. Explain that free-verse poets sometimes use *internal rhyme,* or rhyme within a single line, to give their poems a musical quality. Have students find two examples of internal rhyme in the third stanza. ["hayrack back" (l. 11), "hay a day" (l. 12)]

Ⓓ Literary Focus

❓ Free verse. To what does the poet compare the wood of the window sill? [glass smoothed by the sea] To which of the five senses does this image appeal? [touch]

Names of Horses

Donald Hall

Ⓐ
All winter your brute shoulders strained against collars, padding
and steerhide over the ash hames,° to haul
sledges of cordwood for drying through spring and summer,
for the Glenwood stove next winter, and for the simmering range.

5   In April you pulled cartloads of manure to spread on the fields,
dark manure of Holsteins,° and knobs of your own clustered with oats.
Ⓑ
All summer you mowed the grass in meadow and hayfield, the mowing machine
clacketing beside you, while the sun walked high in the morning;

Ⓒ
and after noon's heat, you pulled a clawed rake through the same acres,
10   gathering stacks, and dragged the wagon from stack to stack,
and the built hayrack back, uphill to the chaffy° barn,
three loads of hay a day, hanging wide from the hayrack.

Sundays you trotted the two miles to church with the light load
of a leather quartertop buggy, and grazed in the sound of hymns.
Ⓓ
15   Generation on generation, your neck rubbed the window sill
of the stall, smoothing the wood as the sea smooths glass.

---

2. **hames** (hāmz) *n.:* rigid pieces along a horse's collar, to which lines connecting the collar to a wagon are attached.
6. **Holsteins** (hōl′stēnz′) *n.:* members of a breed of large, black-and-white dairy cattle.
11. **chaffy** (chaf′ē) *adj.:* full of chaff (hay or straw).

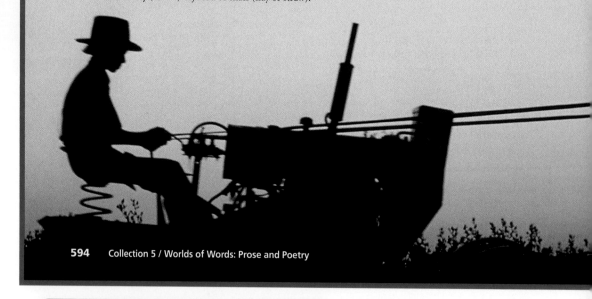

594   Collection 5 / Worlds of Words: Prose and Poetry

DIFFERENTIATING INSTRUCTION

Learners Having Difficulty

To help students mentally organize this poem, tell them that the speaker is imagining what a workhorse of long ago might have done on four different days: a winter day, a spring day, a typical Sunday, and a day when he was very old. As they read, have them stop periodically to write down in their own words what the horse did on each of the four days.

English-Language Learners

Help students find the action of the poem by having them look for the main verbs in each stanza. (For example, in stanza 1, the main verbs are *strained* and *haul*; in stanza 2, they are *pulled* and *mowed;* and so on.) After students identify these verbs, work with them to identify the objects or prepositional phrases that follow the verbs. (For example, *strained against collars* and

When you were old and lame, when your shoulders hurt bending to graze,
one October the man who fed you and kept you, and harnessed you every morning,
led you through corn stubble to sandy ground above Eagle Pond,
20 and dug a hole beside you where you stood shuddering in your skin,

and lay the shotgun's muzzle in the boneless hollow behind your ear,
and fired the slug into your brain, and felled you into your grave,
shoveling sand to cover you, setting goldenrod upright above you,
where by next summer a dent in the ground made your monument.

25 For a hundred and fifty years, in the pasture of dead horses,
roots of pine trees pushed through the pale curves of your ribs,
yellow blossoms flourished above you in autumn, and in winter
frost heaved your bones in the ground—old toilers, soil makers:

O Roger, Mackerel, Riley, Ned, Nellie, Chester, Lady Ghost.

Names of Horses **595**

E **Reading Skills**

Predict. How does the action of this stanza differ from that of the others? [Possible responses: It is more specific; it is more storylike; it introduces a human being; the horse becomes passive rather than active.] **What do you think will happen next?** [The horse will get shot.]

F **Literary Focus**

Elegy. What does this poem mourn? [Possible responses: an imagined horse; all workhorses who lived and died like the one described; a long-ago time when both animals and people were closely tied to the earth and to each other.] **When does the reader first realize that this poem is an elegy?** [in the last full stanza]

G **Reading Skills**

Draw conclusions. What do the names in the poem's last line signify? [They are the names of horses who are buried in the pasture.]

haul . . . cordwood.) Have students jot down each verb/object pair as a way of summarizing the poem's main points.

Meet the Writer

As a firm follower of his grand-father's advice—"work, work, work"—Hall himself can probably relate to the laborious life of the horse he describes. The poet begins his workday at 4:30 A.M., writes until 10:00 A.M., and then reads and rewrites for the rest of the day. His huge literary output includes twelve books of poetry, four plays, twenty-two books of prose, and dozens of magazine publications. His own advice to aspiring writers? "Don't show it to anybody until you've revised it a lot."

For Independent Reading

Students who like this poem may also enjoy the following children's books by Donald Hall: *I Am the Dog, I Am the Cat, The Farm Summer 1942, When Willard Met Babe Ruth,* and *Lucy's Christmas.*

Meet the Writer

Donald Hall

"I Fell in Love with Poetry"

Donald Hall (1928–   ) started writing at a young age. When he was only sixteen years old, he was accepted to the Bread Loaf Writers' Conference, one of the oldest writers' conferences in the United States. Hall's first work was also published that same year. About his early fascination with poetry, Hall has said:

> ❝ I fell in love with poetry. When I was twelve I started writing poetry; when I was fourteen I got serious. I began to work a couple of hours every day on my poems. And when I finished working on a poem, I would go back to the beginning and start writing it over again.... When I was fourteen I really wanted to do in my life what I in fact have ... ended up doing, which is astounding. ❞

Born in New Haven, Connecticut, Hall spent a childhood full of poetry. His mother read poems to him, and his grandfather, during Hall's summers at his New Hampshire farm, recited poems "all day long without repeating himself."

For many years, Hall was an instructor at the University of Michigan at Ann Arbor. In 1975, he moved to the family farm in New Hampshire, where he currently devotes his time to writing. From 1984 to 1989, Hall served as poet laureate of New Hampshire.

For Independent Reading

Hall has edited numerous anthologies, including *The Oxford Book of Children's Verse in America*, a collection that includes well-known poems as well as less-familiar verses.

DIFFERENTIATING INSTRUCTION

Advanced Learners

Enrichment. Have students research the broad range of works Donald Hall has produced over the course of his career. Then, invite them to create a Donald Hall sampler that includes examples of the writer's work from at least four different genres, such as poetry, children's literature, essay, and short story. Challenge students to include works that share a common theme or topic.

First Thoughts

1. Respond to "Names of Horses" by finishing these sentences:

- This poem made me feel . . .
- The **image** I remember most vividly is . . .

Thinking Critically

2. This **free verse** poem is rich in **imagery.** Take your favorite **image,** and draw or describe what it helps you visualize.

3. Study lines 7 and 8. In these lines, find and explain one example of each of these devices: imagery, alliteration, and onomatopoeia.

4. Why do you think the speaker calls the horses "old toilers, soil makers" in line 28?

5. How do you think the speaker feels about the horses he names in line 29? Use examples from the poem to support your response.

6. How does the last line of the poem reflect the **title**?

Extending Interpretations

7. Re-read Mary Shannon's comment about this poem on page 593. Why do you think she reads someone "Names of Horses" when she wants to explain why she loves poetry? Explain the effect the poem had on you.

WRITING

Writing an Elegy

Review your Quickwrite notes, and then write an **elegy** for the animal you described. You may want to try writing in **free verse.** Be sure to use vivid **imagery** in describing the life of your animal. Try also to include some of the other poetic elements you learned about on page 593. (If you prefer, address your **elegy** to *many* cats, dogs, dinosaurs, or whatever type of animal you have chosen, and title your elegy "Names of . . .")

SKILLS FOCUS

Literary Skills
Analyze free verse; analyze an elegy.

Writing Skills
Write an elegy.

Names of Horses   **597**

Grade-Level Skills

■ **Literary Skills**

Analyze sound effects in poetry, including the use of exact and slant rhymes.

Upcoming Skills

■ **Literary Skills**

Identify the literary devices that define a writer's style.

Summary ⬆ *above grade level*

Four girls go to the beach one day. Maggie finds a shell, milly a starfish, and may a stone. Molly is frightened by a crab. Each girl has an experience that reveals her individuality.

PRETEACHING

Selection Starter

Motivate. Ask how many students have ever been to the beach. What did they do there? Why do people enjoy going to the beach so much? Tell students that they will read a poem in which four girls find four different things at the beach.

Before You Read | The Poem

maggie and milly and molly and may

Make the Connection
Quickwrite ✏

"Maggie and milly and molly and may" make some discoveries at the sea. What do you associate with the sea? Close your eyes and let sights, sounds, smells, and feelings fill your mind.

In any "ocean shape" that inspires you, such as a starfish, an octopus, or a series of waves, write down the sensory details you associate with the sea. Here's an example:

salty air

Literary Focus
Kinds of Rhymes

E. E. Cummings is famous for the ways he plays with sounds and punctuation. This poem is filled with rhyming sounds. Some of the rhymes are **exact** (*may/day*, *stone/alone*, *me/sea*), but some catch us by surprise because they are slightly off. These near rhymes are called **slant rhymes.** *Milly* and *molly*, for example, form a slant rhyme: Their sounds almost rhyme—but not exactly.

Background
Literature and Language

Editors are probably itching to capitalize the *m*'s in the title of this poem, but they'd better keep their pencils to themselves. E. E. Cummings did not use standard punctuation (or any punctuation, in many cases), and he stopped capitalizing early in his writing career. These quirks of **style** are trademarks of his poetry.

SKILLS FOCUS

Literary Skills
Understand exact and slant rhymes.

RESOURCES: READING

Planning
■ *One-Stop Planner* CD-ROM with ExamView Test Generator

Differentiating Instruction
■ *Holt Reading Solutions*
■ *Supporting Instruction in Spanish*
■ *Audio CD Library*
■ *Audio CD Library, Selections and Summaries in Spanish*

Assessment
■ *Holt Assessment: Literature, Reading, and Vocabulary*
■ *One-Stop Planner* CD-ROM with ExamView Test Generator
■ *Holt Online Assessment*

Internet
■ go.hrw.com (Keyword: LE5 7-5)
■ *Elements of Literature Online*

Media
■ *Audio CD Library*
■ *Audio CD Library, Selections and Summaries in Spanish*

maggie and milly and molly and may

E. E. Cummings

maggie and milly and molly and may
went down to the beach(to play one day) **A**

and maggie discovered a shell that sang
so sweetly she couldn't remember her troubles,and

5   milly befriended a stranded star
whose rays five languid° fingers were; **B**

and molly was chased by a horrible thing
which raced sideways while blowing bubbles:and **C**

may came home with a smooth round stone
10   as small as a world and as large as alone.

For whatever we lose(like a you or a me)
it's always ourselves we find in the sea

6. **languid** (laŋ′gwid) *adj.:* drooping; weak; slow.

maggie and milly and molly and may   **599**

After You Read

First Thoughts

1. Possible answers: We sometimes can literally see our reflections in the sea; figuratively, the sea is a place where we can discover or reconnect with ourselves as individuals.

Thinking Critically

2. Possible answer: Maggie finds comfort in something that lets her forget; Milly helps a stranded creature and thus finds a friend; Molly finds a creature that makes her fearful and troubled; May finds a stone that inspires reflection and philosophical thoughts.

3. Exact rhymes—*may/day, troubles/bubbles, stone/alone,* and *me/sea.* Slant rhymes— *milly/molly, star/were,* and *sang/thing.* The poem's couplet form might have led students to expect more exact rhymes.

4. Possible answer: The poem has a gentle, playful, caring tone. The poem's alliteration and rhymes keep the tone from being too serious.

Extending Interpretations

5. Some students will say that Cummings's unusual style makes the poem interesting, while others may say it makes the poem difficult and confusing.

Assessment

■ *Holt Assessment: Literature, Reading, and Vocabulary*

After You Read   Response and Analysis

First Thoughts

1. What do the last lines of the poem mean to you?

Thinking Critically

2. Cummings writes that "it's always ourselves we find in the sea." How does each girl find herself in the sea?

3. What **exact rhymes** do you hear in the poem? What **slant rhymes** do you hear? (What sounds did you expect to hear?)

4. Read the poem aloud. What **tone** do you hear as you read about maggie, milly, molly, and may? How do the sounds of the poem contribute to its tone?

Extending Interpretations

5. What do you think of E. E. Cummings's use of lowercase letters and his unusual punctuation? Does this style affect your understanding of the poem?

WRITING
Writing a Poem

Create your own poem about the ocean or another place you've visited. (You might get ideas about the ocean from the notes you made for the Quickwrite on page 598.) Try out any techniques that pleased you in Cummings's poem. You might want to adopt trademarks of Cummings's style: no capitalization, not much punctuation, and words bumping into punctuation marks.

Here's how one writer began a poem about the ocean:

The beach was milk,

the air sheer as silk,

the sun kissed the shore.

ART AND WRITING
Writing Scientific Descriptions

Create a museum display that shows the objects maggie, milly, molly, and may find on the beach. Include pictures and scientific information about shells, starfish, crabs (or whatever you think the "horrible thing" is), and stones.

go.
hrw
.com

INTERNET
Projects and Activities
Keyword: LE5 7-5

SKILLS FOCUS

Literary Skills
Analyze exact and slant rhymes.

Writing Skills
Write a poem; write scientific descriptions.

DIFFERENTIATING INSTRUCTION

Learners Having Difficulty
Have partners discuss their answers to question 1. Then, have them think about their own visits to the seashore and what they find at the beach. What do they learn about themselves from these discoveries?

English-Language Learners
Because there can be enormous variations in sounds between English and other languages, some students may have difficulty understanding or identifying slant rhymes. Pair English-language learners up with fluent partners to answer question 3.

All in green went my love riding

Make the Connection
Quickwrite ✏

E. E. Cummings wrote this in the twentieth century, but he imitates the style and subject matter of songs and poems of centuries ago. In those old songs and poems, a man or woman often told a story about love, death, and betrayal. Certain images were frequently used over and over again. Deer, for example, were often used to symbolize women; hunters were the men who wished to conquer the wild deer.

Think about songs that are popular today. What is one of the most common subjects? Are most songs tragic or comic? How do they deal with love? Jot down your responses.

Literary Focus
The Sounds of Poetry

"All in green went my love riding" is a haunting poem. Read the poem aloud at least once, and listen for all these sounds:

- **rhyme**—exact rhymes (*riding / smiling*) and slant rhymes (*down / dawn*)

- **repetition** of words (*riding, smiling, deer*) and lines (*All in green went my love riding*)

- **alliteration**—the repetition of consonant sounds in nearby words (*the lean lithe deer, the sleek slim deer*)

A stag hunt and a king, possibly Dagobert I (632–639), on his throne (detail), from *The Life and Miracles of St. Denis* by French School. Vellum.
Bibliotheque National, Paris, France (Ms Fr 1098).

Background
Literature and Literary History

This poem describes a romantic scene from a time when royalty hunted deer, using bows and arrows and many hunting dogs (often fast, muscular dogs that looked like greyhounds). The deer were hunted for food but also for sport.

SKILLS FOCUS

Literary Skills
Understand the sounds of poetry, such as rhyme, repetition, and alliteration.

SKILLS FOCUS
pp. 601–605

Grade-Level Skills

■ Literary Skills
Analyze the sounds of poetry, such as rhyme, repetition, and alliteration.

Upcoming Skills

■ Literary Skills
Identify the literary devices that define a writer's style.

Summary ⬆ *above grade level*

The speaker of this poem can be imagined as either a woman or a deer—or both. In it, the speaker tells of a hunter who sets out early one morning, dressed in green and riding a golden horse. With the help of four hounds, the hunter pursues a group of fleet-footed deer across meadows, through valleys, and finally into the mountains. There, the hunter takes aim and shoots— and the heart of the speaker (and presumably of the deer) stops dead.

RESOURCES: READING

Planning
■ *One-Stop Planner* CD-ROM with ExamView Test Generator

Differentiating Instruction
■ *Holt Reading Solutions*
■ *Supporting Instruction in Spanish*
■ *Audio CD Library*
■ *Audio CD Library, Selections and Summaries in Spanish*

Assessment
■ *Holt Assessment: Literature, Reading, and Vocabulary*
■ *One-Stop Planner* CD-ROM with ExamView Test Generator
■ *Holt Online Assessment*

Internet
■ go.hrw.com (Keyword: LE5 7-5)
■ *Elements of Literature Online*

Media
■ *Audio CD Library*
■ *Audio CD Library, Selections and Summaries in Spanish*

All in green went my love riding

E. E. Cummings

All in green went my love riding
on a great horse of gold
into the silver dawn.

four lean hounds crouched low and smiling
5   the merry deer ran before.

A
Fleeter be they than dappled dreams
the swift sweet deer
the red rare deer.

Four red roebuck at a white water
10   the cruel bugle sang before.

B
Horn at hip went my love riding
riding the echo down
into the silver dawn.

four lean hounds crouched low and smiling
15   the level meadows ran before.

Softer be they than slippered sleep
the lean lithe deer
the fleet flown deer.

Four fleet does at a gold valley
20   the famished arrow sang before.

C
Bow at belt went my love riding
riding the mountain down
into the silver dawn.

four lean hounds crouched low and smiling
25   the sheer peaks ran before.

Paler be they than daunting death
the sleek slim deer
the tall tense deer.

Four tall stags at a green mountain
30   the lucky hunter sang before.

PRETEACHING

Selection Starter

Motivate. Give students examples of rhyme, repetition, and alliteration. Help them to see that each of these effects involves repeated elements: either sounds, words, or entire sentences. Then, ask them why repetition might be a good device to use in a poem about a hunt or a chase. [Possible response: A hunt is characterized by the repetitive sounds of a horse's galloping and hounds barking.]

DIRECT TEACHING

A Literary Focus

Alliteration, assonance, and repetition. Explain that the repetition of a vowel sound is called *assonance.* Have students identify one example each of assonance, alliteration, and repetition in these lines. [assonance—the repeated long /e/ sound in "fleeter," "dreams," "sweet," and "deer"; alliteration—the repeated /d/ sound in "dappled," "dreams," and "deer"; repetition—the repeated word "deer".]

B Literary Focus

❷ Rhyme. What is the slant rhyme in this stanza? [*down/dawn*] How does this rhyme illustrate what it describes? [The word *dawn* echoes the word *down,* which mimics the sound of the horn echoing across the landscape.]

C Literary Focus

❷ Repetition. What lines or phrases are repeated throughout the poem? ["went my love riding"; "into the silver dawn"; and "four lean hounds crouched low and smiling"] What mood or feeling do these repeated lines give the poem? [Possible response: a feeling of awe, tension, inevitability, hopelessness.]

DIFFERENTIATING INSTRUCTION

Learners Having Difficulty

Lines 4–5, 9–10, 14–15, 19–20, 24–25, 29–30, and 34–35 of this poem are inverted sentences. To help students untangle the syntax, have them read each pair of lines aloud, reversing the order in which they appear. For example, ll. 4–5 would read: *The merry deer ran before four lean hounds crouched low and smiling.* After students invert the first, second, fourth, and sixth of these sentences, ask them to comment on the adjective used in each independent clause (that is, "merry," "cruel," "famished," and "lucky"). What noun does each adjective modify? What does each adjective suggest about the speaker's point of view?

All in green went my love riding
on a great horse of gold
into the silver dawn.

four lean hounds crouched low and smiling
35   my heart fell dead before.

A stag hunt and a king, possibly Dagobert I (632–639), on his throne,
from *The Life and Miracles of St. Denis* by French School. Vellum.
Bibliotheque National, Paris, France (Ms Fr 1098).

D Reading Skills

❷ Analyze. What is unclear or ambiguous in the ending of the poem? [Possible responses: The speaker announces that her heart has fallen dead. It is unclear whether she literally has been killed by her lover or just emotionally deadened by his cruelty. His literal prey, the deer, is surely dead.]

DEVELOPING FLUENCY

Activity. Have groups of students of varying abilities prepare a dramatic reading of this poem. Suggest that each student read lines that are repeated or that very closely echo one another. Encourage readers to alter the speed and the tone of their reading over the course of the poem as the content suggests. (Early in the poem, for example, the deer are "merry"; later, they are "tense.") After all groups perform, discuss as a class the readings' similarities and differences.

MIXED ABILITY

Meet the Writer

E. E. Cummings gave this advice to young poets struggling to find their own voices: "As for expressing nobody-but-yourself in words, that means working just a little harder than anybody who isn't a poet can possibly imagine. Why? Because nothing is quite so easy as using words like somebody else. We all of us do exactly this nearly all of the time—and whenever we do it, we're not poets.

"If, at the end of your first ten or fifteen years of fighting and working and feeling, you find you've written one line of one poem, you'll be very lucky indeed."

For Independent Reading

- Students who enjoy Cummings's style may want to dip into his *Complete Poems.*

- Students who are interested in learning more about Cummings may want to read his autobiographical work *i: six nonlectures.* These speeches were first given as a series of lectures at Harvard University and later published in book form. They are a mix of prose and poetry, including Cummings's own poetry and some of his favorites by other writers. As students can see by the excerpt of Cummings's prose on this page, his prose shows the same hallmarks of style as his poetry.

Meet the Writer

E. E. Cummings

"you and I are not snobs."
E. E. Cummings (1894–1962) started writing poetry as a student at Harvard University. After he read some ancient classical poetry, suddenly, as he put it, "an unknown and unknowable bird started singing."

During World War I, Cummings was an ambulance driver in France. He was mistakenly arrested for treason and clapped into detention for three months. That experience was a turning point in his life. In prison, Cummings discovered his passion for freedom and personal growth. Over the next four decades he celebrated these passions.

The following quotation is from the preface to a book of Cummings's poems. The words appear here just as he wrote them.

B The poems to come are for you and for me and are not for mostpeople
—it's no use trying to pretend that mostpeople and ourselves are alike. Mostpeople have less in common with ourselves than the squarerootofminusone. You and I are human beings;mostpeople are snobs....

you and I are not snobs. We can never be born enough. We are human beings;for whom birth is a supremely welcome mystery,the mystery of growing:the mystery which happens only and whenever we are faithful to ourselves. B

In his writing, Cummings liked to use lowercase letters, unusual word spacing (words often bump together), and his own brand of punctuation. Even though his style is new, his themes are familiar. Cummings, like lyric poets throughout the ages, celebrates the joy and wonder of life and the glory of the individual.

DIFFERENTIATING INSTRUCTION

Advanced Learners
Acceleration. To help students identify literary devices that define a writer's style, have them form small groups to read and share more of Cummings's poems. Encourage the group to define and discuss Cummings's style. How does his style contribute to the meaning in his poems? Do students find Cummings's style distracting? charming? compelling? Suggest that students pay particular attention to Cummings's use of parentheses. What might he be trying to imply with the parentheses in his poems?

First Thoughts

1. What do you think happens to the speaker at the end of the poem?

Thinking Critically

2. Who do you think the speaker is? a woman or a deer? Explain.

3. Why do you think the lover's bugle is called "cruel" (line 10) and his arrow is described as "famished" (line 20)?

4. Look at the words used to describe the hounds. Are the hounds sinister in any way? Explain your answer.

5. If this is a poem about love, what message do you think it delivers about love? How does it compare with popular songs today? Check your Quickwrite responses for ideas.

6. This poem is full of color. List all the colors you see in the poem.

7. Fill in a chart like the one below with examples showing how the poem uses the **sounds of poetry.** To remind yourself of the definitions for these terms, refer to page 601.

Sounds of Poetry	Details from the Poem
Rhyme	
Repetition	
Alliteration	

ART

Illustrating the Poem

Draw or paint a picture of a scene described in this very visual poem. If you prefer, cut pictures out of magazines or newspapers, and create a collage of images from the poem. A collage (which comes from a French word meaning "glue") is a collection of items pasted on a flat surface. A collage can contain pictures, flowers, pebbles, string, and so on.

SKILLS FOCUS

Literary Skills
Analyze the sounds of poetry.

Art Skills
Illustrate the poem.

All in green went my love riding   **605**

SKILLS FOCUS
pp. 606–608

Grade-Level Skills
■ Literary Skills
Analyze a catalog poem.

Summary ⬌ *at grade level*

This free-verse poem lists nine comments about arithmetic. Six of the comments are humorous definitions, based on the kind of concrete associations that a child might make. The speaker describes arithmetic as having numbers flying in your head; knowing how many you've won or lost; reciting counting rhymes; squeezing numbers from your head to your pencil; getting right or wrong answers; memorizing multiplication tables. The other three items in the list all begin with "If." They are far-fetched and elaborate puzzles, which make fun of actual math problems ("If you have two animal crackers, . . . and you eat one and a striped zebra . . . eats the other, how many animal crackers will you have if . . .").

VIEWING THE ART

Activity. Make sure students realize that the number seven is placed into a seven-sided figure. Ask pairs of students to collaborate on a drawing that incorporates numbers, shapes, and other facets of mathematics.

Arithmetic

Make the Connection
Quickwrite

You've been studying arithmetic in school ever since kindergarten, maybe even since nursery school. You might love or hate your math classes, but you probably use information you learned there in your life every day when you tell time or make purchases. How do you use math? Jot down five ways you use arithmetic when you're not in school.

Literary Focus
Catalog Poem

"Arithmetic" is a **free-verse poem**—a poem without rhyme or a regular meter. It's also a **catalog poem.** A catalog is a list. You've probably looked through lots of catalogs, perhaps from toy stores or electonics stores. Museums also create catalogs of all the artworks displayed in an exhibit. In "Arithmetic," Carl Sandburg doesn't list items for sale or on exhibition. Instead, he lists his thoughts on the subject of arithmetic.

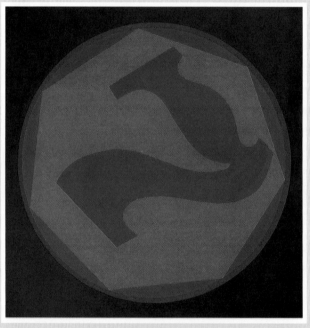

SKILLS FOCUS

Literary Skills
Understand catalog poems.

The *X-7* by Robert Indiana (1998).
Morgan Art Foundation Limited, Private Collection. © 2003 Morgan Art Foundation Ltd./
Artist Rights Society (ARS), New York.

606 Collection 5 / Worlds of Words: Prose and Poetry

RESOURCES: READING

Planning
■ *One-Stop Planner* CD-ROM with ExamView Test Generator

Differentiating Instruction
■ *Holt Reading Solutions*
■ *Supporting Instruction in Spanish*
■ *Audio CD Library*
■ *Audio CD Library, Selections and Summaries in Spanish*

Assessment
■ *Holt Assessment: Literature, Reading, and Vocabulary*
■ *One-Stop Planner* CD-ROM with ExamView Test Generator
■ *Holt Online Assessment*

Internet
■ go.hrw.com (Keyword: LE5 7-5)
■ *Elements of Literature Online*

Media
■ *Audio CD Library*
■ *Audio CD Library, Selections and Summaries in Spanish*

ARITHMETIC

Carl Sandburg

1   Arithmetic is where numbers fly like pigeons in and out of your head.

2   Arithmetic tells you how many you lose or win if you know how many you
    had before you lost or won.

3   Arithmetic is seven eleven all good children go to heaven—or five six
    bundle of sticks.

4   Arithmetic is numbers you squeeze from your head to your hand to your
    pencil to your paper till you get the answer.

5   Arithmetic is where the answer is right and everything is nice and you can
    look out of the window and see the blue sky—or the answer is wrong and
    you have to start all over and try again and see how it comes out this time.

6   If you take a number and double it and double it again and then double it a
    few more times, the number gets bigger and bigger and goes higher and
    higher and only arithmetic can tell you what the number is when you
    decide to quit doubling.

7   Arithmetic is where you have to multiply—and you carry the multiplication
    table in your head and hope you won't lose it.

8   If you have two animal crackers, one good and one bad, and you eat one and a
    striped zebra with streaks all over him eats the other, how many animal
    crackers will you have if somebody offers you five six seven and you say
    No no no and you say Nay nay nay and you say Nix nix nix?

9   If you ask your mother for one fried egg for breakfast and she gives you two
    fried eggs and you eat both of them, who is better in arithmetic, you or your
    mother?

For a biography of Carl Sandburg, see Meet the Writers on page 442.

Arithmetic   607

INDEPENDENT PRACTICE

After You Read

First Thoughts

1. Possible answers:
   - The speaker's idea about arithmetic that I liked best is <u>the good feeling people get when they answer a question correctly.</u>
   - I think arithmetic is <u>more challenging than the poem makes it seem.</u>

Thinking Critically

2. Possible answer: The tone of the poem is playful, amused, even nostalgic. Although the speaker seems to find learning arithmetic a bit frustrating or senseless at times, he seems to enjoy it, mostly.
3. "Arithmetic is" (ll. 1, 3, 4, 5, and 7); "If you" (ll. 6, 8, and 9); "double it," "bigger," "higher" (l. 6); "no," "nay," "nix" (l. 8).
4. Students are likely to say that in their experience, some numbers (or formulas) stay in their heads, or minds, while others slip away.
5. Possible answer: *six/sticks* (l. 3); *head/hand* (l. 4); *striped/streaks, No/Nay/Nix* (l. 8).

Extending Interpretations

6. Some students may feel as affectionate toward arithmetic as Sandburg does. Others may feel differently.

First Thoughts

1. Finish these sentences:
   - The speaker's idea about arithmetic that I liked best is . . .
   - I think arithmetic is . . .

Thinking Critically

2. How would you describe the **tone** of this poem? Do you think Sandburg likes arithmetic? Explain.
3. The writer of a **free-verse poem** often creates **rhythm** through repetition. What repeated words or phrases give "Arithmetic" its rhythm?
4. In the first line of the poem, a **simile** compares the way you remember numbers to "pigeons flying in and out of your head." How does this figure of speech reflect what you know about numbers?
5. List three or four examples of **alliteration**—the repetition of consonant sounds in nearby words—in this poem.

Extending Interpretations

6. Look back at your Quickwrite notes, and think about something you can say about arithmetic based on your own experiences. Write your thoughts in a form that could be added to the end of Carl Sandburg's poem.

WRITING

Writing a Catalog Poem

Catalog poems can be fun to write. Think of a topic that you care about. Then, list your ideas or feelings about your topic in the form of a catalog poem. Open your poem the way Sandburg opens his:

   "[My topic] is . . ."

Maybe you want to write about another school subect:

   "History is . . ."

   "Grammar is . . ."

SKILLS FOCUS

Literary Skills
Analyze a catalog poem.

Writing Skills
Write a catalog poem.

608   Collection 5 / Worlds of Words: Prose and Poetry

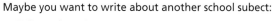

ASSESSING

Assessment

■ *Holt Assessment: Literature, Reading, and Vocabulary*

DIFFERENTIATING INSTRUCTION

Learners Having Difficulty
The title of this poem may be off-putting to some students. Before they begin reading, explain that the poem takes a playful, whimsical look at the "work" of mathematics. Have students read the poem aloud in a group. Afterward, have each student tell which line most closely describes his or her own experience with or feelings about math.

English-Language Learners
Tell students that the activities humorously described in the poem under the title *arithmetic* are part of the study of mathematics, or "math" for short. The word *arithmetic* is not as widely used in schools as it once was, but, when used, it refers to the simpler computational skills that are taught to children in the early grades.

Before You Read The Poem

For Poets

Make the Connection
Quickwrite 🖉

The poem you are about to read, "For Poets," is written especially for poets. By now you've read many poems, and you've probably even written a few. From your own poetry reading and writing experiences, what advice do you have for poets? Jot down your suggestions.

Literary Focus
Ars Poetica

As you already know from its title, "For Poets" is written for poets. That makes it an **ars poetica**—a poem about poetry. *Ars poetica* is Latin for "art of poetry."

Figures of Speech

We all use figures of speech every day. A **figure of speech** compares one thing to something else, something very different. A figure of speech is not literally true. When we say someone is "cool," we are using a figure of speech. The person is not literally "cool"—his or her temperature is not below normal. Instead, when we say someone is "cool," we are comparing that person's

style and attitude to weather that is not blazing hot. We are saying the person is not bothered by things.

Metaphors and **similes** are examples of figures of speech. Here are some common figures of speech we use every day:

> *He's built like a tank.*
> *This party's a bust.*
> *Those plans are down the tube.*

Reading Skills 📖
Reading a Poem

Remember the tip that helps you both to understand a poem and to read it aloud? *Pay attention to the punctuation.* But "For Poets" has no punctuation, so how will you know when to pause or when to keep on reading? Here's the answer: You'll have to decide for yourself. Here's another tip, though, that can help you decide:

> *Pay attention to the thoughts.*

Think about what the poet is saying, and then determine when a thought begins and when it ends. When you read "For Poets," you might want to pause at the end of most—but not all—lines. It's up to you.

SKILLS FOCUS

Literary Skills
Understand ars poetica; understand figures of speech.

Reading Skills
Read a poem.

For Poets **609**

SKILLS FOCUS
pp. 609–612

Grade-Level Skills
■ **Literary Skills**
Analyze ars poetica.
■ **Literary Skills**
Analyze figures of speech in poetry.
■ **Reading Skills**
Read a poem.

Summary ↔ *at grade level*

In the first two lines the speaker boldly advises poets to "stay beautiful / but dont stay down underground too long." Then, in the rest of the poem, he restates that advice, using concrete images from nature. He warns against becoming a "mole," "worm," "root," or "stone." Instead, he urges an active moving "out into the sunlight." Using verbs like *breathe, knock, poke, blink, walk, swim,* and *fly,* he challenges poets not only to connect with nature but to transcend it.

PRETEACHING

Skills Starter

Build review skills. As you review similes and metaphors, remind students that a simile uses a signal word such as *like* or *as* to compare one thing to another, unlike thing, whereas a metaphor simply describes one thing in terms of another without the use of a comparing word. Have students identify each figure of speech in the list at the top of the second column.

RESOURCES: READING

Planning
■ *One-Stop Planner* CD-ROM with ExamView Test Generator

Differentiating Instruction
■ *Holt Reading Solutions*
■ *Supporting Instruction in Spanish*
■ *Audio CD Library*
■ *Audio CD Library, Selections and Summaries in Spanish*

Assessment
■ *Holt Assessment: Literature, Reading, and Vocabulary*
■ *One-Stop Planner* CD-ROM with ExamView Test Generator
■ *Holt Online Assessment*

Internet
■ go.hrw.com (Keyword: LE5 7-5)
■ *Elements of Literature Online*

Media
■ *Audio CD Library*
■ *Audio CD Library, Selections and Summaries in Spanish*

Ⓐ Literary Focus

❓ Figures of speech. What qualities do some poets share with moles, worms, roots, and stones? [Possible response: Poets sometimes become loners or bookworms, living in their minds and losing touch with life and people.]

Ⓑ Literary Focus

❓ Figures of speech. What might it mean to "breathe in trees"? [Possible response: to experience the beauty of nature directly.]

Ⓒ Reading Skills

Read poetry. Privately instruct one student to read the third stanza aloud as if there were a period after "blink" and another to read it as if there were a comma. Have the class listen and discuss the differences in meaning suggested by each reading.

Ⓓ Literary Focus

❓ Ars poetica. What is the speaker advising when he tells poets to "swim upstream"? [Possible responses: Think for yourself; don't follow the crowd.]

For Poets

Al Young

Stay beautiful
but dont stay down underground too long
Dont turn into a mole
or a worm
5   or a root
or a stone

Come on out into the sunlight
Breathe in trees
Knock out mountains
10   Commune with snakes
& be the very hero of birds

Dont forget to poke your head up
& blink
Think
15   Walk all around
Swim upstream

Dont forget to fly

Three Doves and a Snake
by Andrea Eberbach.

DIFFERENTIATING INSTRUCTION

English-Language Learners
The absence of punctuation may make this poem difficult for students to read and understand. Provide students with photocopies of the poem, and work with them to supply logical punctuation marks—for example, periods at the end of ll. 2, 6, 7, 11, 13, 16, and 17 and commas at the end of ll. 1, 8, 9, 10, 14, and 15. Then, have students read the poem aloud, pausing or stopping as the introduced punctuation indicates.

Meet the Writer

Al Young

"A Keen Observer of the Human Comedy"

Al Young (1939–) has been called "a gifted stylist and a keen observer of the human comedy." He was born in Ocean Springs, Mississippi, and spent the first ten years of his life in the South. His next ten years were spent in and near Detroit, Michigan.

As a teenager, Young's poems and stories were published in local publications, providing an indication of his future career. Young attended the University of Michigan at Ann Arbor, where he was co-editor of the school's literary magazine, and the University of California at Berkeley, from which he graduated in 1969.

Between the ages of eighteen and twenty-five, Young played the guitar and flute and sang professionally throughout the United States. He also

worked as a disc jockey, a writing teacher, a language consultant, and a screenwriter.

"For Poets" appears in Young's poetry collection titled *Heaven: Collected Poems 1956–1990.*

Meet the Writer

As both a poet and a human being, Al Young has taken his own advice: He has tried to live as full a life as possible. In addition to writing, playing music, and teaching, Young has also worked as a medical photographer, a warehouseman, a clerk-typist, a railroad worker, an interviewer for the California Department of Employment, and a film narrator. He has written numerous screen-plays, in addition to poetry, fiction, and essays. His work has been translated into more than a dozen languages.

CROSS-CURRICULAR CONNECTIONS

Culture

Poetry and the piano. Al Young once said that "poetry is to the rest of writing what the piano is to all of music." Ask students what they think this statement means. Then, read them Young's own explanation: "By this I mean that some knowledge of poetry or skills acquired by composing poetry can put any writer in an advantageous position." Ask students to discuss whether they agree or disagree with Young, and why. Then, have them think of other *Poetry is to the rest of writing as _____ is to _____* analogies, drawn from their own areas of knowledge or expertise.

SMALL GROUP

First Thoughts

1. Possible answer:
   - I think the best advice in this poem is <u>to avoid staying inside too long.</u>

Thinking Critically

2. Possible answer: Poets run the risk of becoming too withdrawn from the world or uninvolved in life. Like moles, worms, and roots, poets can live out of the light of day in a solitary world of their own; like stones, they can become fixed and deadened, mentally and emotionally.

3. Possible answer: In the second stanza the speaker advises poets to "knock out mountains," meaning poets should be ambitious, vigorous, and courageous. In stanza three the speaker advises poets to "poke your head up / & blink," meaning to look at the world with fresh eyes.

Extending Interpretations

4. Most students will agree that Young has offered sound advice to poets. Students may say too that Young's advice applies to the act of living as well as writing.

Assessment

- *Holt Assessment: Literature, Reading, and Vocabulary*

First Thoughts

1. Respond to "For Poets" by finishing this sentence:
   - I think the best advice in this poem is . . .

Thinking Critically

2. This poem is made up of a series of **figures of speech,** in which certain behaviors are compared to things in nature. What do you think the speaker means when he says "dont stay down underground too long"? What behaviors of poets are being compared to the behaviors of a mole, a worm, a root, and a stone?

3. In the second and third stanzas, choose two lines and explain what advice the speaker is giving to poets through the **figures of speech.**

Extending Interpretations

4. Do you think that Young has offered good advice to poets? How does his advice compare to the advice you wrote about in your Quickwrite on page 609?

WRITING
An Ars Poetica

Write down your advice to poets in the form of a poem or **ars poetica.** You might imitate the structure of this poem and open three verses with the words *Stay, Come,* and *Don't forget.*

SPEAKING AND LISTENING
An Oral Interpretation

Work together with a partner to decide how to read "For Poets" aloud. Decide when you should pause and when you should keep on reading. Take turns reading the poem aloud until you both feel you are reading smoothly and well. Then, perform the poem for the class.

SKILLS FOCUS

Literary Skills
Analyze an ars poetica; analyze figures of speech.

Reading Skills
Read a poem.

Writing Skills
Write a poem giving advice.

Speaking and Listening Skills
Read a poem aloud.

DIFFERENTIATING INSTRUCTION

Learners Having Difficulty

Before students answer question 2, have them write the words *mole, worm, root,* and *stone* down the left side of a sheet of paper. Have them list characteristics or actions of the creature or object named by each word. Students can then refer to the list to see which characteristics or actions might be shared, in one sense or another, with poets.

Author Study Sandra Cisneros

Literary Focus
A Writer's Messages

Sandra Cisneros writes about feelings we can all understand. She writes with humor about life's joys and frustrations. She writes about being lonely and afraid. She writes about wanting what we can't have. She describes the fear of not fitting in—as well as the feeling that maybe we don't really want to fit in. These feelings are close to her heart and often come from her own experiences. Her writing also explores the lives of people who belong to two cultures and speak two languages. Many of her works celebrate her memories of her Mexican American childhood.

Reading Skills
Making Generalizations

A **generalization** is a broad statement about something. In making a generalization, you combine evidence in the text with what you already know. After you read the selections by Cisneros, you'll have a chance to make generalizations about her work. To make a generalization about a work of literature, ask yourself these questions:

- What is the work's **conflict,** or problem?
- What **message** about life does the work reveal?
- How does the work relate to your experience?

Key Elements of Cisneros's Writing

- **Everyday language,** including slang and sentence fragments, gives the feeling of people speaking aloud.
- **Strong images** and **metaphors** bring the work alive.
- **Spanish words** mixed with English words reflect the heritage of the characters and of the writer.
- **Messages** often focus on family relationships and learning how to fit into the world around us.

SKILLS FOCUS

Literary Skills
Interpret a writer's message.

Reading Skills
Make generalizations.

Author Study: Sandra Cisneros **613**

Grade-Level Skills
- **Literary Skills**
Interpret a writer's message.
- **Reading Skills**
Make generalizations.

Upcoming Skills
- **Grade-Level Skills**
Analyze how a literary work reflects the attitudes and beliefs of its author.

OVERVIEW
Purpose. This Author Study feature on Sandra Cisneros gives students the opportunity to read several works by a well-known writer, to analyze a writer's message, and to make generalizations about the writer's work. The feature contains an interview with Cisneros and a biographical time line, as well as two stories, one poem, and an essay by the author. Postselection questions and charts help students identify the message of each selection. Students will have the opportunity to compare and contrast Cisneros's messages in a final essay.

Use. Direct students' attention to the box identifying the key elements of Cisneros's writing. If you wish, draw a chart on the chalkboard with four columns labeled *Everyday Language, Strong Images, Spanish Words,* and *Messages.* Ask students to provide items to fill in the chart as they read the selections.

DIFFERENTIATING INSTRUCTION

Learners Having Difficulty
If students have trouble with the concept of a writer's message, explain that the message of a story is the writer's main idea or belief about life. Read the information about making generalizations aloud to students. Explain that the message of a story is usually implied, rather than directly stated. Then, encourage small groups of students to identify the writer's message in a story with which they are already familiar.

English-Language Learners
Although Cisneros's stories typically use everyday language, devices such as figurative language and dialogue run into the text may be challenging for students. As students read the selections in this feature, monitor their comprehension with frequent reading checks. Pair English-language learners with students who are proficient speakers. Have them work together to paraphrase challenging paragraphs or sections.

Advanced Learners
Enrichment. Advanced students might be encouraged to maintain an "interview log" as they read the selections. Have them use the opening interview of the feature as a prototype. After they read each work, have students enter in their logs questions for Cisneros about the characters, main conflicts, or message of the work. When they have finished reading the feature, have students present their questions to the class.

Summary ⬄ *at grade level*

After a short biographical introduction, the interviewer, Marit
Haarh, invites Sandra Cisneros to
read the brief story "Salvador
Late or Early." First conceived as
a poem, "Salvador Late or Early"
describes a boy named Salvador
who made a strong impression
on Cisneros during her childhood. He was in her class at
school and always showed up in
tattered, disheveled clothes.
Cisneros goes on to discuss the
values of responsibility, consideration, and hard work that she
learned while growing up poor
in a large family. Running
beneath the interview is a time
line showing highlights of
Cisneros's career.

PRETEACHING

Selection Starter

Motivate. Invite students to share
prior knowledge about interviews
and interview techniques. For
example, students can identify
and describe interviews they have
heard or seen recently on radio or
television. Ask students what kind
of information an interviewer
hopes to gain from a writer being
interviewed. [Possible response: They
might hope to gain insight into the
writer's methods or influences.]

DIRECT TEACHING

Ⓐ Vocabulary Note

Prefixes. Explain that the prefix
in– often means "not." The word
infinite comes from the Latin root
word *finis,* meaning "end" or
"limit." Ask students what they
think *infinite* means. [*Infinite* means
"without end" or "limitless."]

Author Study
Sandra Cisneros

Before You Read

Ⓐ Lichtenstein Creative Media's Marit Haahr interviewed Sandra
Cisneros on the public radio program *The Infinite Mind.* During
the broadcast, she asks Cisneros to read her short story
"Salvador Late or Early" to the listeners. The two then talk about
the story and the way it relates to Cisneros's life. From their
conversation we learn something about how writers draw from
their own experiences to create literature.

Ⓑ # AN INTERVIEW WITH SANDRA CISNEROS

from *The Infinite Mind*

Marit Haahr. Writer Sandra Cisneros was born in Chicago in the
1950s, the third child and only daughter of seven. Her books include *The House on Mango Street* and *Woman Hollering Creek.* She's
won numerous awards, including the MacArthur Foundation Fellowship, which is often called the genius grant. Her latest novel,
Caramelo, [was] published in September [2002].

Haahr. You were recently published in an anthology entitled *Growing Up Poor.* With that in mind, I'd actually like to begin with a
reading from your short story collection *Woman Hollering Creek.*
Can you describe this story, "Salvador Late or Early," for our listeners?

Ⓒ **Sandra Cisneros.** I didn't intend it to be a story. I thought perhaps
it'd be a poem. I was remembering a classmate of mine I couldn't
forget. So it began from that place of not being able to forget. ❶ 📖

Cisneros now reads the story.

(continued on page 616)

(Opposite) Sandra Cisneros at her
home in San Antonio, Texas.

IDENTIFY

Ⓓ ❶ What four things
have you just learned
about the story Cisneros
is going to read?

614   Collection 5 / Worlds of Words: Prose and Poetry

B Learners Having Difficulty

Italics. Make sure students understand that italics have several common uses. In the introduction and the first part of the interview, italics are used for the title of a radio show and for the titles of four books written by Cisneros. Ask students to identify a title for which italics are not used. [Italics are not used for the story title "Salvador Late or Early."] Tell students that in general, the titles of full-length works, newspapers, magazines, and radio and television shows appear in italics. Titles of shorter works, such as stories, poems, and articles, generally do not appear in italics. Remind students that italics may also be used to emphasize a word or phrase or to signal that a word has been borrowed from a foreign language.

C Reading Skills

❷ Infer. Why do you think Cisneros might have first planned "Salvador Late or Early" as a poem rather than a story? [Possible response: Cisneros felt that she could best convey what Salvador was like through the figurative language of poetry rather than through narrative prose in a story.]

D Reading Skills

Identify. [Possible response to question 1: Cisneros based the story on memories of a classmate of hers; she started out thinking the story would be a poem; the story is part of a collection of stories called *Woman Hollering Creek;* and Cisneros began the story because she could not forget this particular classmate.]

An Interview with Sandra Cisneros 615

DIRECT TEACHING

Ⓐ Reading Skills

Read aloud. Point out Cisneros's use of rhythm, repetition, parallelism, compression, figurative language ("the color of caterpillar," "homes are the color of bad weather"), and imagery ("the dim dark of the morning"). Explain to students that these devices give Cisneros's prose a poetic cast. Be sure students observe the punctuation as they read.

Ⓑ Reading Skills

Identify. [Possible responses to question 3: Images include "shakes the sleepy brothers awake" (sight), "feeds them milk and cornflakes from a tin cup" (taste), "dim dark of the morning" (sight), "the string of younger brothers" (sight), "Tugs the arms" (sight, touch), and "the hundred little fingers of red, green, yellow, blue, and nub of black sticks" (sight).]

Ⓒ Reading Skills

Read a time line. Explain that this time line shows the highlights of Cisneros's career. Point out that the time line covers a little more than fifty years and is divided into ten-year intervals.

Meet the Writer

In a lecture given at a junior high school in California, Sandra Cisneros commented as follows on her vocation as a writer: "I am the first woman in my family to pick up a pen and record what I see around me, a woman who has the power to speak and is privileged enough to be heard. That is a responsibility. I don't know when I first said to myself I am going to be a writer. Perhaps that first day my mother took me to the public library when I was five, or perhaps again when I was in high school and my English teacher forced me to read a poem out loud, and I became **entranced** with the sounds, or perhaps when I enrolled in the creative writing class in college, not knowing it would lead to other creative writing workshops and graduate school. Perhaps."

READ ALOUD

❷ Cisneros says that she first thought this story would be a poem. Read this paragraph aloud to hear how her prose is like poetry. Remember to pause at the punctuation marks as you read.

IDENTIFY

❸ Cisneros uses strong **images** to describe Salvador and what he does to help his mama. List three images, and tell what sense each appeals to.

Salvador Late or Early

Salvador with eyes the color of caterpillar, Salvador of the crooked hair and crooked teeth, Salvador whose name the teacher cannot remember, is a boy who is no one's friend, runs along somewhere in that vague direction where homes are the color of bad weather, lives behind a raw wood doorway, shakes the sleepy brothers awake, ties their shoes, combs their hair with water, feeds them milk and cornflakes from a tin cup in the dim dark of the morning. ❷

Salvador, late or early, sooner or later arrives with the string of younger brothers ready. Helps his mama, who is busy with the business of the baby. Tugs the arms of Cecilio, Arturito, makes them hurry, because today, like yesterday, Arturito has dropped the cigar box of crayons, has let go the hundred little fingers of red, green, yellow, blue, and nub of black sticks that tumble and spill over and beyond the asphalt puddles until the crossing-guard lady holds back the blur of traffic for Salvador to collect them again. ❸

Ⓒ A CISNEROS TIME LINE

She begins a series of sketches about her family and childhood while at the University of Iowa Writers' Workshop program in 1977.

In 1966, Cisneros's parents buy a house on Campbell Avenue in Chicago.

1950   **1960**   **1970**

Born on December 20, 1954, in Chicago, Illinois.

Attends Loyola University from 1972 to 1976. Takes a creative-writing class, in which she begins to write seriously.

Salvador inside that wrinkled shirt, inside the throat that must clear itself and apologize each time it speaks, inside that forty-pound body of boy with its geography of scars, its history of hurt, limbs stuffed with feathers and rags, in what part of the eyes, in what part of the heart, in that cage of the chest where something throbs with both fists and knows only what Salvador knows, inside that body too small to contain the hundred balloons of happiness, the single guitar of grief, is a boy like any other disappearing out the door, beside the schoolyard gate, where he has told his brothers they must wait. Collects the hands of Cecilio and Arturito, scuttles off dodging the many schoolyard colors, the elbows and wrists crisscrossing, the several shoes running. Grows small and smaller to the eye, dissolves into the bright horizon, flutters in the air before disappearing like a memory of kites. **4**

Haahr. Thank you. It's certainly clear that the image that Salvador left in your mind was very strong. Why do you think that was?

Cisneros. Because he sat in front of me and his shirts were always wrinkled and the collars were dirty. I thought, "Doesn't his mama

Author Study

Sandra Cisneros

INTERPRET

4 How do you think Salvador feels as he hurries through his busy day? What details in the story support your interpretation?

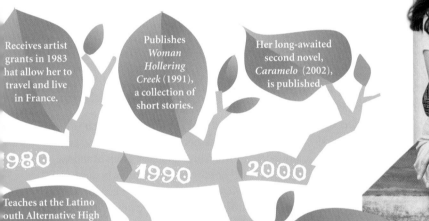

Receives artist grants in 1983 that allow her to travel and live in France.

Publishes *Woman Hollering Creek* (1991), a collection of short stories.

Her long-awaited second novel, *Caramelo* (2002), is published.

1980   1990   2000

Teaches at the Latino Youth Alternative High School in Chicago, 1978–1980.

Publishes *The House on Mango Street* (1984), based on sketches she began in Iowa.

Buys a house of her own in San Antonio, Texas, which she later paints purple.

In 1995, receives a MacArthur Foundation genius grant. *The House on Mango Street* is translated into Spanish.

DIRECT TEACHING

D Reading Skills

? Infer. What does Cisneros suggest about Salvador when she calls his body "too small to contain the hundred balloons of happiness, the single guitar of grief"? [Possible response: Growing up in a poor family and shouldering many responsibilities, Salvador has little time to consider whether he is happy or sad. He focuses on getting through the day and doing what his family expects him to do.]

E Reading Skills

Interpret. [Possible responses to question 4: Salvador most likely feels harassed, apprehensive, and hurried, but nevertheless he carries out his duties with skill and a sense of responsibility and loyalty to his family. Details supporting such an interpretation include Cisneros's physical description of Salvador, as well as her references to his body's "history of hurt" and "geography of scars" and to the throbbing inside his chest.]

DIFFERENTIATING INSTRUCTION

Learners Having Difficulty
Encourage students to break down difficult text, such as the first sentence in the last paragraph of the story. Tell students to pay attention to key repetitions in the story, such as the preposition *inside,* as well as parallel structures, such as the phrase *in what part.* Suggest to students that Cisneros's style—her choice of words, images, and sentence structure—is designed to convey a variety of messages about

Salvador. One message may be that Salvador is a caring person who knows firsthand the meaning of suffering and deprivation.

Advanced Learners
Enrichment. Discuss with students the literary form of the prose poem—a brief work in prose that uses many poetic devices. Cisneros may be considered one of the masters of this genre, especially in such vignettes as "Salvador Late or Early" and

those in *The House on Mango Street* (such as "Chanclas," p. 620).
Activity. Have students meet in small groups to sketch out a prose poem of their own. Groups should carefully consider a limited scene or subject for their work. Students may then suggest poetic elements, such as images and sound effects, to add to their work. Have each group appoint a spokesperson to report the results of the group's work.

DIRECT TEACHING

A Reading Skills

? Interpret. [Possible response to question 5: She means that she realizes that Salvador was growing up in a family setting very much like her own. She knows what it is like to be compelled to assume responsibility for others at an early age. Cisneros uses her own memories to imagine how Salvador must have felt.]

B Reading Skills

? Make generalizations. From the evidence in this passage, what skills or gifts do you think a writer needs to bring a character such as Salvador to life? [Possible response: A writer needs powers of observation, curiosity, self-knowledge, and empathy, the ability to identify with others.]

C Reading Skills

? Identify. [Possible responses to question 6: Cisneros learned the value of money and hard work. At a deeper level, she learned about the responsibilities of a youngster in a loving and close-knit family.]

D Reading Skills

? Interpret. How is Cisneros's concluding remark about Harvard ironic? [Possible response: Cisneros ironically stresses that some of the most important lessons about life and values, such as responsibility and the importance of hard work, are taught not at Harvard but rather in a family setting.]

INTERPRET

5 What does Cisneros mean when she says Salvador "was me"? How does this feeling of hers enable her to know her character Salvador so well?

INTERPRET

6 What lesson did Cisneros learn from her family?

---

love him?" I thought about him a lot, and I remembered him so clearly. I remember walking down streets visiting my aunt and thinking, "Now that kind of building must be the kind that Salvador lives in." I knew him intimately, perhaps more than he knew himself, and he stayed with me all the years. I realized when I finished writing the story that he was me. That's why I could know what he did and what kind of house he lived in and who his younger brothers were and who he had to wait for—all the things that a tiny being like that knew and the remarkable things that perhaps he had to take care of that he never thought of as remarkable. **5**

Haahr. I know that one of the defining features of your childhood was growing up without much money. What were the physical circumstances of your childhood like?

Cisneros. Well, you know, it came [to me] at a very young age that we just didn't have money for everything. My older brother was the one that would always pull me aside and say, "Don't ask for anything. Papa doesn't have any money." or "Don't shame him by asking for something that he can't give you or that he'll give you and that'll hurt us later in the week." So there was the sense of being responsible for the others. I was very conscious of it when I went to Catholic school, because there was a class difference between myself and the majority of the students in the school that I went to.

Haahr. How did being conscious of that affect you?

Cisneros. It made you responsible. It made you want to be protective of your mother and father and not ask for too many things. It made you, sometimes, I think, value money in a way that perhaps your classmates did not, because you had to save for the things that you really wanted. When my father died, he was sad and cried and said he wished he could have given us more. And I said he gave us just enough, because we valued what we had, and we worked for what we had. That was a lesson you can't learn in Harvard. **6**

FAMILY/COMMUNITY ACTIVITY

Encourage students to share this story, as well as Cisneros's reflections on her memories of Salvador, with friends or family members. They might read the story together and then discuss the way the writer feels about Salvador and her recollections of her own family life. They might also consider questions like these: "How do members of our family stick up for one another? What makes family relationships special or different from the relationships we have with other people?"

First Thoughts

1. Describe your reaction to "Salvador Late or Early."

Thinking Critically

2. "Salvador Late or Early" includes powerful **metaphors**—comparisons of unlike things. Choose one metaphor from each paragraph, and explain what it helps you to understand about Salvador and his life.

3. Strong **images** are another poetic element in this story. Draw or describe one of the visual images that especially appeals to you.

4. What is the **mood** of this story? What does the mood tell you about the writer's attitude toward Salvador?

5. Do you agree with Cisneros that Salvador is "a boy like any other"? Cite details in the story to support your interpretation.

Cisneros's Message

6. Think about why Cisneros wrote this story. Use her responses in the interview to help you decide on the story's **message.** Some possible messages of the story are

   • Remarkable people come from all walks of life.
   • Life without much money can still be rich.
   • It's important to make sacrifices for the good of others.

Choose one of these messages, or come up with another of your own. Write the message in a chart like the one below, and then explain why you chose it and what you think about it.

> Cisneros's message in "Salvador Late or Early":
>
>
> My response to the message:

Reading Check

a. What chores does Salvador do before and after he goes to school?

b. What does Salvador look like? Use details from the story to describe him.

c. In the interview, what reasons does Cisneros give for remembering Salvador all her life?

SKILLS FOCUS

Literary Skills
Interpret a writer's message.

Reading Skills
Make generalizations.

An Interview with Sandra Cisneros   **619**

After You Read

First Thoughts

1. Possible answers: I think Salvador is a boy who has no time to be happy or sad because he is so busy taking care of his younger brothers. I feel sorry for him, but I also admire him for his loyalty.

Thinking Critically

2. Possible answers: Paragraph 1—"homes are the color of bad weather" suggests the dreariness of Salvador's surroundings. Paragraph 2—"the hundred little fingers of red, green, yellow, blue" suggests the anxiety Salvador feels as he picks up the crayons from the street while the traffic waits. Paragraph 3—"limbs stuffed with feathers and rags" stresses Salvador's fragility and suggests that he does not get enough to eat.

3. Images may include "crooked hair and crooked teeth," "raw wood doorway," and "the elbows and wrists crisscrossing.

4. Possible answer: The mood might be described as hectic and pressured because Salvador has to take care of his brothers and does not have time to play. The mood suggests that the author has compassion for Salvador, because she understands his responsibilities.

5. Some students may agree, saying that any boy must cope with the needs and demands of loved ones and school. Other students may disagree, pointing out that Salvador exhibits a rare degree of selflessness for his age.

Cisneros's Message

6. Possible response: *Cisneros's message in "Salvador Late or Early"*—Salvador has too much responsibility for a boy his age. *My response to the message*—I don't think I could be as responsible as Salvador has to be. I find his dedication admirable.

Reading Check

a. Salvador cares for his younger brothers. He feeds them, dresses them, takes them to school, and makes sure they get home safely.

b. Details include eyes the "color of caterpillar," crooked hair and teeth, wrinkled shirts, and forty-pound, fragile-looking body.

c. She identifies with Salvador. She knows what it's like to grow up poor and assume a lot of responsibility at an early age.

The narrator, a young girl named Esperanza, tells of the embarrassment she feels at a family party when she has to wear a pair of old saddle shoes that make her feel clumsy and awkward. She shyly declines an invitation from a boy to dance. Esperanza's mood changes when her uncle Nacho tells her she's the prettiest girl at the party and insists on dancing with her. She forgets all about her shoes, and she notices that the boy who showed interest in her has been watching her dance.

PRETEACHING

Selection Starter

Build background. For many people, a baptism, or christening, serves as the occasion for a special party that brings together family members. People attending these celebrations often wear festive clothing—such as Esperanza's new pink-and-white dress in "Chanclas"— and enjoy a feast, music, and dancing. Ask students to notice how Cisneros appeals to several of the senses as she describes the party held to celebrate the baptism of the narrator's little cousin.

A Reading Skills

Interpret. [Possible response to question 1: Esperanza asks her mother, "What about the shoes?" Her mother answers, "I forgot. Too late now. I'm tired. Whew!"]

B Reading Skills

? Analyze. How does the narrator hint at her disappointment and frustration in this passage? [Possible response: by emphasizing how late it is and how long she has waited for her mother to come home.]

C Reading Skills

Identify. [Possible response to question 2: The narrator has been waiting for the party celebrating her little cousin's baptism. She is going to Precious Blood Church, where the party is being held.]

Author Study
Sandra Cisneros

Before You Read

"Chanclas"[1] is a story from Cisneros's well-loved book *The House on Mango Street*. Her novel takes the form of a series of very short stories linked by the voice of a narrator, a girl named Esperanza, who is growing up in a Latino neighborhood in Chicago. In this particular story, Cisneros writes about a feeling we've probably all experienced—the embarrassment of not having the right clothes, of not looking good enough. What happens to the narrator's embarrassment by the end of the story?

Chanclas

Sandra Cisneros

It's me—Mama, Mama said. I open up and she's there with bags and big boxes, the new clothes and, yes, she's got the socks and a new slip with a little rose on it and a pink-and-white striped dress. What about the shoes? I forgot. Too late now. I'm tired. Whew! ❶

Six-thirty already and my little cousin's baptism is over. All day waiting, the door locked, don't open up for nobody, and I don't till Mama gets back and buys everything except the shoes.

Now Uncle Nacho is coming in his car, and we have to hurry to get to Precious Blood Church quick because that's where the baptism party is, in the basement rented for today for dancing and tamales and everyone's kids running all over the place. ❷

Mama dances, laughs, dances. All of a sudden, Mama is sick. I fan her hot face with a paper plate. Too many tamales, but Uncle Nacho says too many this and tilts his thumb to his lips.

---

1. **chanclas** (chän′kläs) *n.:* Spanish slang for "old, worn-out shoes."

INTERPRET

Ⓐ ❶ The first paragraph ends with a little conversation. Who asks the question? Who responds?

IDENTIFY

Ⓒ ❷ What has the narrator been waiting for? Where is the narrator going?

DIFFERENTIATING INSTRUCTION

Learners Having Difficulty

Cisneros's stylistic device of running the dialogue into the narrative and her omission of quotation marks may challenge some students. Have students read the first, fourth, and seventh paragraphs aloud, and make sure they can identify the quotations and the speakers in the dialogue. Then, ask students why Cisneros might have used this

stylistic device. [Possible response: It keeps the narrative moving and suggests both the narrator's childish impatience and her acute embarrassment.]

Special Education Students

For lessons designed for special education students, see *Holt Reading Solutions*.

Everybody laughing except me, because I'm wearing the new dress, pink and white with stripes, and new underclothes and new socks and the old saddle shoes I wear to school, brown and white, the kind I get every September because they last long and they do. My feet scuffed and round, and the heels all crooked that look dumb with this dress, so I just sit. ❸

Meanwhile that boy who is my cousin by first communion or something asks me to dance and I can't. Just stuff my feet under the metal folding chair stamped Precious Blood and pick on a wad of brown gum that's stuck beneath the seat. I shake my head no. My feet growing bigger and bigger.

Then Uncle Nacho is pulling and pulling my arm and it doesn't matter how new the dress Mama bought is because my feet are ugly until my uncle who is a liar says, You are the prettiest girl here, will you dance, but I believe him, and yes, we are dancing, my Uncle Nacho and me, only I don't want to at first. My feet swell big and heavy like plungers, but I drag them across the linoleum floor straight center where Uncle wants to show off the new dance we learned. And Uncle spins me, and my skinny arms bend the way he taught me, and my mother watches, and my little cousins watch, and the boy who is my cousin by first communion watches, and everyone says, wow, who are those two who dance like in the movies, until I forget that I am wearing only ordinary shoes, brown and white, the kind my mother buys each year for school. ❹

And all I hear is the clapping when the music stops. My uncle and me bow and he walks me back in my thick shoes to my mother who is proud to be my mother. All night the boy who is a man watches me dance. He watched me dance. ❺

INTERPRET

❸ What great problem, or **conflict,** does the narrator face? **D**

IDENTIFY

❹ Cisneros is famous for using **figurative language,** such as similes. What simile does the narrator use to describe her feet? (A **simile** compares two different things, using a word of comparison, such as *like* or *as*.) **F**

COMPARE AND CONTRAST

❺ How have the narrator's feelings changed by the end of the story? Use details to explain the change. **H**

Chanclas **621**

D Reading Skills

❓ **Interpret.** [Possible response to question 3: Esperanza wants to enjoy herself at the party, but she is ashamed of her old, scuffed shoes.]

E Reading Skills

❓ **Interpret.** How would you characterize Uncle Nacho, judging from the details in this passage? [Possible response: He is cheerful, fun loving, generous, and caring.]

F Reading Skills

❓ **Identify.** [She compares her feet to large, heavy plungers.]

G Reading Skills

❓ **Interpret.** What is the effect of the writer's use of repetition ("watches me dance. He watched me dance") at the end of the story? [Possible response: It reaffirms the change in Esperanza's mood from embarrassment to joy, and it suggests that she is happy knowing that the boy is watching her.]

H Reading Skills

❓ **Compare and contrast.** [Possible response to question 5: Her embarrassment and frustration have changed to exhilaration and pride. Details showing the change include the reactions of the crowd, Esperanza's comment about her mother's pride, and her delight that the boy who "is a man"—probably because he is somewhat older—has watched her with admiration.]

After You Read

First Thoughts

1. Possible answer:
   - I think the narrator of this story is <u>lucky to have a relative like Uncle Nacho who can make her feel good about herself.</u>

Thinking Critically

2. She is embarrassed to dance with the boy because she thinks her shoes look awkward and clumsy; she agrees to dance with Uncle Nacho because he compliments her and insists that they show off the new dance they have learned together. She feels safe with him.

3. Students should identify passages in the first, fourth, and seventh paragraphs. In the first paragraph, the speakers are Esperanza and her mother; in the fourth paragraph, the speakers are Esperanza's mother and Uncle Nacho; in the seventh paragraph, the speaker is Uncle Nacho.

4. She overcomes the conflict between her desire to have fun at the party and her embarrassment over her scuffed, clumsy shoes.

5. Possible answers: "Plungers" (noun) is a powerful word Cisneros uses to explain what the narrator felt her feet looked like; "swell" (verb) describes how the narrator perceives her feet; "crooked" (adjective) describes the narrator's heels and provides a strange and unflattering picture of her feet.

Cisneros's Message

6. Possible answers: *Cisneros's message in "Chanclas"*—The beauty in people often emerges through their actions rather than from their appearance. *My response to the message*—I agree; people I'm close to are beautiful to me because of the things they do, not the way they look.

After You Read "Chanclas"

First Thoughts

1. Finish this sentence:
   - I think the narrator of this story is . . .

Thinking Critically

2. Explain why the narrator refuses to dance with the boy who asks her, but dances with her uncle.

3. In this story, the **dialogue** runs into the text rather than being set off with quotation marks. Re-read the story, and identify the passages that represent actual conversations. If you want, read the dialogue aloud.

4. What **conflict**, or challenge, does the narrator overcome?

5. Cisneros uses vivid words to make her **images** come alive. Pick out a noun, a verb, and an adjective that you think are particularly powerful. Explain why you chose them.

Cisneros's Message

6. Choose a message that you think is important in "Chanclas." Write it in a chart like the one below, and record your responses to the message.

   Here are some possibilities:

   - There are more important things in life than clothes.
   - Certain kinds of beauty lie beneath the surface.
   - You may find pleasure in a situation when you least expect to.

Cisneros's message in "Chanclas":
My response to the message:

Reading Check

Retell this story to a partner. Start with the title and author. Who is the main character, and what is her problem, or **conflict**? Tell the main events in the order in which they occur. Now, describe the story's **climax,** which is the moment when the conflict ends. Finally, what is the **resolution,** or ending, of the story?

SKILLS FOCUS

Literary Skills
Interpret a writer's message.

Reading Skills
Make generalizations.

Reading Check
Retellings should include the name of the main character (Esperanza), the conflict (her desire to enjoy the party versus her embarrassment at having to wear old, ugly shoes), the climax (the crowd's admiration for her dancing with Uncle Nacho), and the resolution (the narrator's delight that the boy who asked her to dance is watching her).

Before You Read

"Abuelito Who" is a collection of memories of the poet's grandfather. *Abuelito* (ä·bwä·lē′tō) is Spanish for "granddaddy." Read the poem aloud twice.

Abuelito Who

Sandra Cisneros

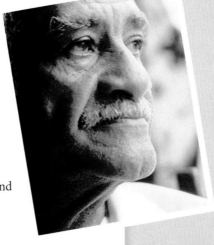

Abuelito who throws coins like rain
and asks who loves him
who is dough and feathers
who is a watch and glass of water
5 whose hair is made of fur
is too sad to come downstairs today ❶
who tells me in Spanish you are my diamond
who tells me in English you are my sky
whose little eyes are string
10 can't come out to play
sleeps in his little room all night and day
who used to laugh like the letter *k*
is sick
is a doorknob tied to a sour stick
15 is tired shut the door
doesn't live here anymore
is hiding underneath the bed ❷
who talks to me inside my head
is blankets and spoons and big brown shoes
who snores up and down up and down up and down
20   again
is the rain on the roof that falls like coins ❸
asking who loves him
who loves him who? ❸

Abuelito Who   623

Summary ◀▶ *at grade level*

In the poem "Abuelito Who," the speaker lovingly recalls details of her grandfather's appearance and personality. She also remembers the changes she saw in Abuelito as he grew old and sick. In the essay "The Place Where Dreams Come From," Sandra Cisneros discusses memories from her childhood that inspired the poem.

PRETEACHING

Selection Starter

Motivate. Have students write quickly about their memories of an older relative or neighbor. Then, ask students to consider how Cisneros feels about her grandfather as they read the poem.

DIRECT TEACHING

Ⓐ Reading Skills

Identify. [Details include "throws coins like rain," "dough and feathers," and "hair . . . made of fur." In l. 6, we learn that Abuelito is too sad to come downstairs.]

Ⓑ Reading Skills

Infer. [Possible response to question 2: Abuelito has changed because he has grown old and sick.]

Ⓒ Reading Skills

Identify. Find the metaphor and the simile in l. 21. ["Rain . . . that falls like coins" is the simile and "[Abuelito] is the rain" is the metaphor. Be sure students notice the metaphors Abuelito himself uses, in ll. 7–8.]

Ⓓ Reading Skills

Infer. [Possible response to question 3: The speaker would say that she loves Abuelito because she writes of him in a sympathetic way.]

CROSS-CURRICULAR CONNECTIONS

Foreign Languages

Spanish. Like English, the Spanish language has many suffixes, or syllables added to the ends of words to change their meanings. The *–ito* suffix in Spanish, for example, is used to indicate smallness or express affection. Thus, *gato* means "cat"; *gatito* means "kitty." Similarly, *abuelo* means "grandfather," *abuelito* means "little grandpa" or "granddaddy." In Spanish the word for "grandmother" is *abuela.* Can you guess what the word for "little grandma" is? [*abuelita*] The *–ito* or *–ita* suffix is often added to a child's name. *Juan* (pronounced "hwän"), the Spanish equivalent of *John,* becomes *Juanito* ("Johnny"); *Juana,* which is equivalent to *Joan* or *Joanna,* becomes *Juanita* ("Joanie").

DIRECT TEACHING

A Reading Skills

❓ **Identify.** What metaphor did Abuelito use for the children's allowance? [He referred to it as their *domingo,* or "Sunday," because that was the day he distributed their allowance.]

B Reading Skills

Analyze. [Possible response to question 1: This paragraph explains ll. 1–2 in the poem—the description of Abuelito throwing coins like rain and asking who loves him.]

C Reading Skills

Analyze. [Images that might refer to a time when Abuelito was sick and cranky include "little eyes are string" (l. 9), "sleeps in his little room all night and day" (l. 11), "is a doorknob tied to a sour stick" (l. 14), "is tired shut the door" (l. 15), and "is hiding underneath the bed" (l. 17).]

ANALYZE

❶ Look back at "Abuelito Who" (page 623). Which lines in the poem does this paragraph explain?

ANALYZE

❷ Look again at "Abuelito Who." Find four **images** that might refer to the time when Abuelito was "sick and cranky."

Before You Read

Cisneros grew up speaking both Spanish and English. She writes in English but often uses Spanish words in her writing. She says, "I think that incorporating the Spanish, for me, allows me to create new expressions in English—to say things in English that have never been said before." In this essay, Cisneros talks about what inspired her to write "Abuelito Who."

La Mulita (1923) by Abraham Angel.
Artese Historia Mexico.

The Place Where Dreams Come From

Sandra Cisneros

When I was little, my grandpa—my Abuelito, that is, which is sort of like Granddaddy, only sweeter—my Abuelito used to love to give all his grandchildren their *domingo* (literally "Sunday," because that's the day children receive it), that is, their allowance. But my Abuelito loved the ritual of asking in a loud voice, "Who loves Grandpa?" and we would answer, also in a loud voice, "We do!" Then he would take a handful of change he'd been saving all week for this purpose, Mexican coins which are thick and heavy, and toss them up in the air so that they'd fall like rain, like a *piñata* (pē·nyä′tä), and we'd scramble all over each other picking up as many coins as we could. To me it was much more fun to get our *domingo* this way instead of having it placed in our hands. ❶

Well, it's this fun grandpa that this poem is about. And about the coins falling like rain, and rain falling like coins, that at times makes me think of him and miss him. I recall he became rather sick and cranky in his last years. I suppose that's what some of the images refer to, but I was grown and gone already, and my Abuelito in faraway Mexico City. ❷

I'm not sure what exactly all the images refer to, and I'm not sure I ever knew. But that's what's so wonderful about poetry. It comes from some deep and true place inside you, the place where dreams come from. We don't always know what dreams mean, do we, and we don't have to always know to enjoy and experience them. That's how it is with poetry, too. When I write, I don't question where images are coming from. I write dictated by sound and directed by my heart. And these images—"dough and feathers," "little eyes are string," and "doorknob tied to a sour stick"—felt right then and still feel right as I read them now. "Dough and feathers" I suppose has to do with how he felt when I held him and he held me. He was soft and squishy as dough or feathers. But it could also mean the color of his skin and hair. The texture of his skin. The silliness of his being. They're all "right." **3**

"Little eyes are string" is harder to pinpoint. Did I mean like a spiral of string, like when we are sick? Maybe. But then again, perhaps it's the way he looked at me when he was sick. And "doorknob tied to a sour stick." I recall a cane he had and how he changed when he was very old and cranky and waved it when he wanted to make a point. So I suppose he had "soured." Why tied to a doorknob? Who knows?

A few biographical tidbits. My grandfather *did* laugh like the letter *k*. A kind of "kkkk" sound when he chuckled, which, surprisingly, I've inherited. **4**

And. He was very proud that he could speak English, even though he lived in Mexico City most of his life. And so he liked to show off his English to his grandchildren from the United States when they came to visit. "You are my diamond," my grandpa would say in typical Mexican fashion. But then he would mistranslate "You're my heaven" and instead come out with "You're my sky," because "sky" and "heaven" are the same word in Spanish. I remember thinking even as a child that it sounded wonderful— "You're my sky." How much better than *heaven*. All, all of that! Imagine. I've always been much more partial to sky and clouds, and am even now. **5**

Finally, the older we grow, the younger we become as well, don't you think? That is, our Abuelito had to take naps, and he liked to play games, like the one with the coins, and he talked to us in a way that other adults didn't, and he couldn't climb the stairs very well, like my baby brothers. So in a way he was getting younger and younger and younger until he wasn't anymore.

INTERPRET

3 According to Cisneros, what makes poetry "wonderful"? **D**

INTERPRET

4 According to Cisneros, which details in "Abuelito Who" are biographical? Which details from the poem remain mysterious to Cisneros? **F**

INTERPRET

5 Think about Cisneros's comment about combining a knowledge of Spanish and English to create something new (see Before You Read, page 624). According to this paragraph, where has she combined languages in "Abuelito Who"? Look back at the poem to find the exact lines. **G**

E

H

D **Reading Skills**
Interpret. [Possible answer to question 3: Poetry is wonderful because it comes from "some deep and true place" inside a person—what Cisneros calls "the place where dreams come from."]

E **Reading Skills**
❓ Identify. According to Cisneros, how might the phrase "sour stick" have originated? [It might have been suggested by Abuelito's cane or by his sour mood.]

F **Reading Skills**
Identify. [Possible response to question 4: Biographical details include the references to the coins, the "sour stick," and the laugh that sounded like the letter *k*. Details from the poem that remain mysterious are "little eyes are string" (l. 9) and "doorknob tied to a sour stick" (l. 14).]

G **Reading Skills**
Interpret. [Possible response to question 5: She has combined languages in ll. 7–8, where she refers to Abuelito's use of Spanish and his mistranslation of a Spanish phrase into English—a mistake that Cisneros thought actually resulted in a more loving expression.]

H **Reading Skills**
❓ Evaluate. Is the final paragraph an effective conclusion to this essay, in your opinion? Why or why not? [Possible response: Yes, it is effective because Cisneros explains that as Abuelito grew older, he became more and more childish. The details in the paragraph clearly convey the writer's love and sympathy for Abuelito.]

Learners Having Difficulty
Have students paraphrase the anecdote that Cisneros tells in the essay's first paragraph. Then, have them discuss why they think she found it more fun to get her allowance this way instead of having it placed directly in her hand. Finally, have students identify the changes in Abuelito that are described in the second paragraph.

INDEPENDENT PRACTICE

After You Read

First Thoughts

1. Possible answer:
   - If I could ask Sandra Cisneros one question, I would ask her <u>why she became a writer.</u>

Thinking Critically

2. The last three lines echo the first two lines by mentioning coins, rain, and love.

3. Possible answer: The speaker feels tender and sympathetic but also a little sad, since she misses her grandfather.

4. Possible answer: "who is dough and feathers" (Abuelito feels soft and squishy but is also fragile); "who is a watch and glass of water" (perhaps refers to Abuelito's taking medicine at certain times); "whose little eyes are string" (perhaps refers to Abuelito's being ill); "is a doorknob tied to a sour stick" (perhaps refers to Abuelito's cane and to his cranky moods); "is blankets and spoons and big brown shoes" (perhaps refers to objects the speaker associates with Abuelito); "is the rain on the roof" (suggests Abuelito's comforting nature).

5. Possible answer: Students may say they understand the poem better after reading Cisneros's essay because in it she explains her use of metaphors.

Cisneros's Message

6. Possible answers: *Cisneros's message in "Abuelito Who"*— It is often the small details that we remember most about our loved ones. *My response to the message*—I found Cisneros's depiction of Abuelito touching but sad as well, because he is not the energetic person he once was. This poem made me want to pay more attention to the details of people's characters.

First Thoughts

1. Finish this sentence:
   - If I could ask Sandra Cisneros one question, I would ask her . . .

Thinking Critically

2. Re-read the first two lines and the last three lines of "Abuelito Who." How does the poem circle back to its beginning?

3. Explain the speaker's feelings for her grandfather.

4. In the poem, Cisneros uses many **metaphors** to describe her grandfather. List three such metaphors, and explain what you think they mean. Cisneros's essay "The Place Where Dreams Come From" may give you some ideas.

5. In the essay, Cisneros describes her inspiration for the poem. How do you feel about the poem now? Do you understand it better? Explain.

Cisneros's Message

6. State the message from "Abuelito Who" in a chart like the one below, and then jot down your response to that message.

   Think of your own message statement, or choose one of these possibilities:

   - People change with the passing of time.
   - Memories of everyday life offer lasting inspiration.
   - Family ties strengthen over the years.

Cisneros's message in "Abuelito Who":
My response to the message:

Reading Check

List the **similarities** and **differences** between the grandfather in "Abuelito Who" and the grandfather that Cisneros describes in "The Place Where Dreams Come From."

SKILLS FOCUS

Literary Skills
Interpret a writer's message.

Reading Skills
Make generalizations.

Reading Check

Similarities—Abuelito distributes the children's allowance; he laughs with a sound like the letter *k;* he becomes ill and cranky as he grows old. *Differences*—The poem's speaker recalls firsthand Abuelito's declining health and cranky moods; in the essay the writer says that she had grown up and gone away during Abuelito's last years, which he spent in far-off Mexico City.

Author Study: Sandra Cisneros

Assignment

1. Writing About a Writer's Message

Write an essay in which you discuss Cisneros's **messages** in the stories and poem you have just read. Before you write, review the charts you filled in after you read "Salvador Late or Early," "Chanclas," and "Abuelito Who." Write three paragraphs. In the first paragraph, write a **generalization** about Sandra Cisneros's writing based on the messages in each work and on what she says about her writing in the interview and essay. In the second paragraph, state the messages in the stories and poem. In the third paragraph, describe your responses to the selections and their messages. You may want to use quotations to support your interpretations.

Assignment

2. Writing About a Writer's Language

Write an essay in which you discuss how Cisneros uses everyday language, strong images, metaphors, and Spanish words in "Salvador Late or Early," "Chanclas," and "Abuelito Who." After writing an introductory paragraph, you can organize your essay in one of two ways.

1. You can write a paragraph about each work and describe its examples of the four elements.
2. You can write a paragraph about each element and describe how it is used in the three works.

Write a final paragraph describing your responses to Cisneros's writing.

Assignment

3. Writing a Poem or Story

Cisneros often turns her life experiences into stories and poems by paying attention to the details that make people and situations unique. Try your hand at writing either a poem or a story.

- Write a poem based on your memories of a relative or good friend. If you want, use Cisneros's basic structure in "Abuelito Who"— begin with the person's name, and add descriptive details, starting each line with the pronoun *who*.
- Using "Chanclas" as a model, write a short story about an autobiographical incident. Begin with your memories, and then use vivid words and images to describe the setting, characters, and events.

Use the workshop on Supporting an Interpretation, pages 630–635, for help with the first two assignments.

SKILLS FOCUS

Writing Skills
Write an interpretation; write a poem or short story.

After You Read

1. Writing About a Writer's Message

Strategy tip. To help students get started, have them review the charts they made about Cisneros's message after reading each selection. Encourage students to think about the similarities between these messages. How do the themes of the selections relate to one another?

2. Writing About a Writer's Language

Strategy tip. Urge students having difficulty to write about the literary selections in order, devoting a paragraph to each one. This approach is easier because it involves less moving back and forth between subjects.

3. Writing a Poem or Story

Strategy tip. Suggest to students that they find ideas or springboards for their poem or story by interviewing family members. Alternatively, they may want to look through old family photographs for inspiration.

Author Study: Sandra Cisneros **627**

OVERVIEW

The poem in No Questions Asked gives students the chance to read for enjoyment. The annotations in the margins of the Teacher's Edition are optional. No follow-up questions will appear after this poem.

Summary ⬆ *above grade level*

The poem tells of an eminent poet who learns that his books are not among those being condemned and burned by the government. Furious, the poet dashes off a letter to those in power, imploring them to burn his works—or, in the poet's words, "Burn me!"

PRETEACHING

Selection Starter

Motivate. Ask students to discuss the topic of censorship. Ask if they know whether any of their favorite movies, songs, or books have been censored or condemned by the government. Have them explain whether they believe censorship is ever necessary or justified.

DIRECT TEACHING

Ⓐ Reading Skills

❓ **Analyze.** What is surprising about the poet's reaction to the news of the book burning? [You would expect a writer *not* to want his or her books to be burned.]

Ⓑ Advanced Learners

Irony. Ask students to explain what is ironic, or unexpected, about the narrator saying he is being treated like a liar because his books are not being burned. [Possible response: If books were to be destroyed, one would expect that the books contained falsehoods. However, the narrator states that the condemned works contain the truth, while books that contain lies are being spared.]

Before You Read

Sometimes governments and even individuals with strong opinions try to control what people think by destroying the books of those who disagree with them. For example, in 1933, thousands of Nazi students and some of their professors ransacked university libraries and bookstores in thirty German cities, and burned books written by Jews and by those opposed to Nazi ideas. Bertolt Brecht's books were among those tossed on the bonfires.

The Burning of Books

Bertolt Brecht

When the Regime ordered that books with dangerous teachings
Should be publicly burnt and everywhere
Oxen were forced to draw carts full of books
To the funeral pyre, an exiled poet,
5 One of the best, discovered with fury, when he studied the list
Of the burned, that his books
Ⓐ ⎡ Had been forgotten. He rushed to his writing table
     ⎢ On wings of anger and wrote a letter to those in power.
     ⎣ Burn me, he wrote with hurrying pen, burn me!
10 Ⓑ ⎡ Do not treat me in this fashion. Don't leave me out. Have I not
      ⎢ Always spoken the truth in my books? And now
      ⎢ You treat me like a liar! I order you:
      ⎣ Burn me!

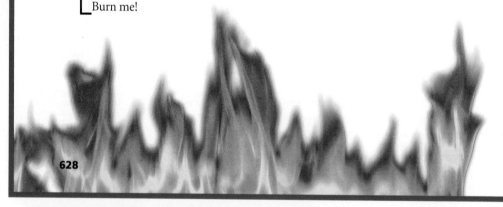

628

DIFFERENTIATING INSTRUCTION

English-Language Learners

Explain to students that a writer's name is often used to stand for his or her body of work. For example, the question *Have you read Shakespeare?* means "Have you read Shakespeare's works?" Point out that in this poem, the statement "Burn me" is used in a similar way, to mean "Burn my works." The poet's choice of words also shows how closely he identifies himself with his work, as if he and his ideas were one.

Advanced Learners

Enrichment. Explain to students that an exile is someone who is forced to leave his or her homeland, usually for political reasons.

Activity. Have each student research modern-day writers in exile, choose one, and prepare a brief oral report about him or her. The presentation should include a sample of the writer's work and comments the writer made about living and working

Meet the Writer

Bertolt Brecht

His Reputation Caught Fire

Bertolt Brecht (1898–1956) began studying medicine in 1917 at the University of Munich in Germany, while working at the same time as a drama critic and playwright. He eventually left his university studies to concentrate on literature and drama. In 1922, Brecht became famous for his play *Drums in the Night*, for which he received Germany's notable Kleist prize. During this period he wrote operas with music by Kurt Weill. "Mack the Knife," a song from one of those operas—*The Threepenny Opera*—was made popular in the United States and throughout the world by Louis Armstrong and other singers.

In 1933, Brecht left his homeland because the Nazis had come to power and he had been targeted as an enemy. During that year, thousands of Nazi sympathizers ransacked bookstores and libraries throughout Germany and threw tens of thousands of "anti-Nazi" books into raging bonfires. Unlike the works of the speaker in the poem "The Burning of Books," Brecht's works were among those destroyed by the Nazis.

The burning of his books did not destroy Brecht's reputation, however. He went on to receive international acclaim for his significant and innovative plays. While in exile (mostly in Denmark and the United States), Brecht produced some of his finest works, including *Mother Courage and Her Children* and *The Life of Galileo*.

Brecht is also recognized as a great poet. Some critics even consider his poetry to be his finest work.

Meet the Writer

Throughout his writing career, Brecht experimented with a wide range of styles and drew on a large number of sources. In his later dramatic works (including *Mother Courage and Her Children*) he introduced a technique called the "alienation effect." In these plays, Brecht strove to keep his audience emotionally distant from his characters. He wanted his audience to *think* rather than to *feel*. Although *Mother Courage* was a great success, it was in some ways a failure for the playwright: Audiences were moved by his main character, a stubborn old woman facing overwhelming odds.

For Independent Reading

Students can find other poems by the same author in *Bertolt Brecht: Poems 1913–1956*.

away from home. Students may also want to report on exiled writers who returned home and how their return affected their lives and work.

Writing Workshop

Objectives

- Use appropriate prewriting and drafting skills to develop a persuasive essay supporting an interpretation of a work.
- Revise the essay by adding precise nouns, verbs, adjectives, details, and quotations and other references to make the argument more convincing.
- Reflect on and assess one's writing process and interpretative essay.

PRETEACHING

Skills Starter

Motivate. Point out that when they identified the author's message for the works in the Author Study feature on Sandra Cisneros, students were interpreting a writer's theme. Call on volunteers to comment on a recent occasion when they discussed the message of a film or television program with family members or peers. What differences in interpretation emerged in the discussion? How did the participants support their views about the work's message?

DIRECT TEACHING

PREWRITING

Choosing a Subject

Help students see that each example cited in the prompt focuses on a literary element: symbolism, theme, and characterization, respectively. Remind students that freewriting is often an effective way to generate ideas for an essay.

Assignment

Write an essay supporting your interpretation of a literary work.

Audience

Your teacher, classmates, or other students in your school.

RUBRIC
Evaluation Criteria

A good interpretation of a literary work

1. identifies the work by title and author
2. states the interpretation clearly
3. supports the interpretation with evidence such as details, examples, and reasons
4. has a clear organization
5. restates or reinforces the interpretation in a strong conclusion

SKILLS FOCUS

Writing Skills
Write an essay supporting an interpretation.

PERSUASIVE WRITING

Supporting an Interpretation

In discussing a story or a poem, you and your classmates have probably differed at times in your views of a character's actions or your analyses of a theme. Good literature often stimulates readers to think and to respond in a variety of ways. This is not to say that *any* response to a literary work is valid, however. An interpretation of a work's meaning has to be supported by evidence. In this workshop you will write an essay interpreting some aspect of a literary work that interests you.

Prewriting

1 Choosing a Subject

Read and respond to this **prompt:**

> When you analyze something, you take it apart to see how it works. When you interpret, you reveal what you've discovered through your analysis. A literary interpretation often begins with a problem you wish to solve. For example, what is the symbolic meaning of the roof garden in "Antaeus" (page 175)? What does the story "A Day's Wait" (page 191) say about courage? How does Cummings differentiate the girls in "maggie and milly and molly and may" (page 599)? Choose some aspect of a work that you would like to explore, and write an essay interpreting its significance.

Brainstorm a list of ideas with your classmates. Here are some literary topics to consider:

- how a specific literary element (such as setting, imagery, or tone) is used in a selection
- why a character is (or isn't) convincing
- what is the main idea in a story, poem, or essay

630   Collection 5 / Worlds of Words: Prose and Poetry

COLLECTION 5 RESOURCES: WRITING

Planning
- *One-Stop Planner* CD-ROM with ExamView Test Generator

Differentiating Instruction
- *Workshop Resources: Writing, Listening, and Speaking*
- *Family Involvement: Activities in English and Spanish*
- *Supporting Instruction in Spanish*

Writing and Language
- *Workshop Resources: Writing, Listening, and Speaking*
- *Daily Language Activities*
- *Language Handbook Worksheets*

Assessment
- *Holt Assessment: Writing, Listening, and Speaking*
- *One-Stop Planner* CD-ROM with ExamView Test Generator

2 Developing a Thesis

Writing about a literary work is a way of getting to know it better. In putting your thoughts down on paper, you become more fully involved with the work. You may have to read a work several times before you determine what your focus will be.

Jot down your thoughts, even if they are random at first. One graphic organizer that can help you sort out your thoughts and reach conclusions is a cluster diagram such as the one on the right. Freewriting for several minutes will also allow you to explore ideas.

Aim for a manageable topic. In a short paper you may have time and space to discuss only one aspect of a work. You need to formulate a **thesis,** or controlling idea, about the topic. Here are some examples to guide you:

Selection: "The Dinner Party" (page 118)
Topic: The plot of the story
Thesis: The plot is carefully designed to overturn stereotypes about gender differences.

Selection: "Rikki-tikki-tavi" (page 15)
Topic: The character of the hero
Thesis: In his treatment of Rikki, Kipling combines animal characteristics with human motives.

Selection: "The Smallest Dragonboy" (page 147)
Topic: The theme of the story
Thesis: Through courage and determination a boy overcomes obstacles to fulfilling his dream.

Selection: "Jabberwocky" (page 577)
Topic: Making sense of the poem
Thesis: The sounds of real and invented words help to tell the story of a battle and its victory.

Selection: *The Monsters Are Due on Maple Street* (page 59)
Topic: Explaining a title
Thesis: *Monsters* in the title refers to the mob of humans as well as to the aliens.

Cluster Diagram "maggie and milly and molly and may"

maggie finds a singing seashell and forgets her troubles.

milly makes friends with a starfish by helping it.

All the girls respond individually at the beach.

molly is frightened by a creature like a crab.

may finds a stone that makes her thoughtful.

INTERNET
More Writer's Models
Keyword: LE5 7-5

Language Handbook
HELP

See The Pronoun, 1b;
Agreement, 2a–x.

Supporting an Interpretation **631**

Developing a Thesis

Be sure students understand the difference between a topic and a thesis. For example, if writers want to discuss the plot of "The Dinner Party," they must analyze this literary element to find a controlling idea or thesis. One such idea focuses on the overturning of stereotypes. To help students gather more ideas for a thesis, suggest they review their responses to the After You Read questions following each selection.

Graphic Organizers

You may wish to review a range of graphic organizers that can help students in their prewriting: for example, flow charts for plot sequence, Venn diagrams for comparison and contrast, and two- or three-column charts for figurative language.

■ *Holt Online Assessment*
■ *Holt Online Essay Scoring*
Internet
■ go.hrw.com (Keyword: LE5 7-5)
■ *Elements of Literature Online*

DIRECT TEACHING

Presenting Evidence

Depending on students' interest and prior reading, you may wish to challenge them to identify one or two items of evidence for the sample thesis presented for each selection. For example, students could cite specific words from the poem "Jabberwocky" that support the thesis claim about telling the story of a battle. As students identify each item of evidence, invite the class to evaluate its persuasive weight or effectiveness.

Strategies for Elaboration

Explain to students that some of the elements listed for poetry can be used for fiction as well: for example, imagery, figurative language, and tone.

DRAFTING

Writing the Essay

Remind students to keep their audience in mind when writing their essays. You may want to advise students that as a rule, an interpretive essay should not devote a great deal of space to plot summary—especially when it may be assumed that the audience is already familiar with the work. However, specific items of evidence require references to a work's language and details. Incorporating these references smoothly and clearly into a persuasive essay should be an important goal for every student writer.

Framework for an Interpretive Essay

Introduction (includes title, author, and thesis statement): _____
_____

Body (presents evidence in support of thesis): _____
_____

Main Ideas:
1. _____
2. _____

Conclusion (restates thesis, revealing insights into the work): _____
_____

Strategies for Elaboration

Note specific details that provide supporting evidence. Provide explanations or commentaries that draw connections for the reader.

In **fiction,** describe
• actions
• thoughts
• words
• others' behavior
• direct comments by writer

In **poetry,** comment on
• imagery
• figurative language
• sound effects
• tone

---

3 Presenting Evidence

In an interpretive essay the evidence you present in support of a thesis may include direct quotations; paraphrased lines or short passages; details such as images, actions, and dialogue; and explanations or reasons. Select evidence carefully, choosing the best or most persuasive examples to back up your conclusions.

Drafting

1 Organizing the Essay

Organize your essay to include an introduction, the body of the text, and a conclusion. In your **introduction,** identify the work, author, and the problem you will write about. Also include a statement of your thesis.

The **body** of your essay should present the evidence supporting your thesis. Each paragraph in the body should focus on a major supporting idea.

The **conclusion** should bring together your main ideas and restate your thesis. You may add a personal comment or extend the conclusion to cover related works.

In an interpretive essay the type of organization that is most effective is **order of importance.** Put the most important details at the beginning or at the end for emphasis.

2 Writing the Essay

Use language that is appropriate for your purpose and audience. Remember that your purpose is to convey ideas clearly and that you are writing for your teacher or other students.

Make the order of your ideas clear by using **transitional expressions,** such as *first, last, mainly, more important, then,* and *to begin with.*

DIFFERENTIATING INSTRUCTION

Learners Having Difficulty

Characterization. Analyzing a character in fiction may be the most manageable topic for some student writers. Remind students that the personality of a character is usually suggested through indirect means, such as actions, thoughts, dialogue, and the reactions of other characters. Also stress that the most successful characters in fiction are *round* rather than *flat;* that is,

they incorporate a variety of character traits that make them realistic and three-dimensional.

English-Language Learners

Some students may gather information about the literary element they will focus on in their essay by listening to a recording of the literary work they chose. Suggest that students listen for relevant details and that they stop the tape while they compile

examples of the literary element in a chart of evidence.

Advanced Learners

Enrichment. Encourage advanced students to incorporate comparison and contrast into their interpretations. For example, an analysis of the story "Antaeus" might refer to another story with teenage characters and a similar theme.

Student Model

A Boy's Struggle with Courage

The story "A Day's Wait" by Ernest Hemingway suggests that courage is often a difficult thing to have. For a whole day, Schatz believes that he will die from a fever of 102 degrees because he misunderstood information that schoolmates told him.

The boy shows his courage by holding back his emotions. Instead of listening to the story that his father is reading, Schatz looks at the foot of the bed, thinking. While he could be crying like a baby because he believes he is going to die, he braves the reality and doesn't react. It seems that it's difficult to keep his cool and show courage because he doesn't talk much to anyone, but instead has a staring contest with the foot of the bed.

Schatz struggles with his fear. While staring at the foot of the bed, he is thinking very hard and barely listens to anything that his father tells him. Instead of giving in to his disease, he holds on and stays alive. This is proved when Schatz refuses to sleep for fear of dying while doing so. It probably took a lot of struggle to decide if he should just give up or if he should give his life a chance. Schatz decides to brave the possible consequences with courage instead of giving in. When he finally tells his father what he has been thinking and learns that he will not die, Schatz is able to relax.

"A Day's Wait" suggests that courage is difficult to deal with. I agree but think that Schatz should have asked his father in the beginning of the story to clarify his sickness instead of assuming the worst. If Schatz hadn't brought up the subject of his death near the end of the story, he might have just given up before realizing that he wasn't going to die. Instead of fighting to get better, he might not have done anything and made it worse. "A Day's Wait" certainly proves that it is hard to have courage.

—Rochelle BaRoss
George Washington Middle School
Ridgewood, NJ

*The writer's **thesis** is clearly stated in the first sentence.*

***Details** of Schatz's behavior in the story are used to support the writer's thesis.*

*More **details** from the story support the thesis.*

*The writer **contrasts** Schatz's behavior with her own opinions.*

*The last sentence **restates** the writer's thesis, or main idea.*

DIRECT TEACHING

Student Model

Encourage students to examine the model to see how the student writer identifies the work, the author, and the topic for analysis and states the thesis.

Writing Tips

Be sure students understand the importance of using quotations from the literary work in their persuasive interpretations. Quotations are a good source of support for an interpretation of a writer's main ideas. However, students should avoid quoting excessively in their essay.

DIRECT TEACHING

EVALUATING AND REVISING

Content and Organization Guidelines

Suggest that students read their revised essays aloud to a peer editor, who will check for a clear thesis statement, appropriate paragraphing, effective organization, adequate elaboration of details, and an effective conclusion. Have students record the peer editor's suggestions for improvement on their drafts with a colored pencil. They can then decide whether to make the recommended changes.

TECHNOLOGY TIP

Remind students who use word processors to save a copy of their first drafts before they begin revising. If they aren't happy with their revisions, they can go back to the original and revise it again.

Evaluating and Revising

Use the following chart to evaluate and revise your essay.

Supporting an Interpretation: Content and Organization Guidelines

Evaluation Questions	▶ Tips	▶ Revision Techniques
❶ Are the author and the title named in your introduction?	▶ **Highlight** the author and the title.	▶ **Add** a sentence or phrase naming the author and the title.
❷ Does your introduction have a clear thesis?	▶ **Underline** the thesis statement.	▶ **Add** a sentence that clearly states the thesis.
❸ Is the main idea of each paragraph clear, and does it support the thesis?	▶ **Bracket** the main idea discussed in each paragraph of the body.	▶ **Revise** the body paragraphs so that each deals with a main idea.
❹ Is the main idea of each body paragraph supported with evidence?	▶ **Draw a box** around each supporting detail or quotation. **Draw a wavy line** under elaborations.	▶ **Add** details or quotations to support your thesis. **Elaborate** on details or quotations with commentary.
❺ Does your conclusion restate the thesis and summarize your main points? Does it leave readers with something to consider?	▶ **Highlight** the sentence in the conclusion that restates the thesis. **Circle** the summary of key points.	▶ **Add** a sentence restating the thesis. **Add** a sentence that applies the thesis to a broader experience or connects it with other works.

On the next page you'll find an excerpt from an interpretive essay that has been revised. Following the model are questions to help you evaluate the writer's revisions.

634   Collection 5 / Worlds of Words: Prose and Poetry

EVALUATION GUIDELINES

	4	3	2	1
Use these guidelines for quick assessment of students' final drafts.	**Beginning introduces author and work, identifies topic or problem, and presents a thesis.**	Beginning identifies author and work, clearly states topic or problem, and presents a clear thesis for the analysis.	Beginning identifies author and work incompletely, refers vaguely to topic or problem, and fails to present a clear thesis.	Beginning merely names author and work and hints at topic of essay.	Beginning does not introduce author, work, or topic or problem and includes no thesis statement.
	All evidence in the body of the essay supports the thesis, and each paragraph focuses on a major supporting idea.	The evidence in the body of the essay is clear and persuasive, and each paragraph contains a main idea supporting the thesis.	Some of the evidence in the body of the essay is repetitive or irrelevant to the thesis.	The evidence presented is not especially persuasive, and paragraphs lack unity and coherence.	Very little evidence is presented to support the thesis, and the essay is poorly organized.

Revision Model

Who are the monsters in ~~the~~ teleplay <u>The Monsters</u>
Rod Serling's

<u>Are Due on Maple Street</u>? The title suggests that the

monsters ~~are~~ nonhuman, perhaps aliens from
might be

another planet. At the end of the play, we see ~~them~~.
two figures in a spacecraft.

However, as the events of the play ~~show~~, the real
unfold

monsters are the ~people, whose panic ~~turns~~ them into
ordinary   *transforms*

a ~mob, ready to turn on one another. As the narrator
self-destructive

says, "The tools of conquest do not necessarily come

with bombs and explosions~." The weapons can be
and fallout

prejudice and fear. The teleplay shows that lives can be

destroyed by irrational suspicions.

Evaluating the Revision

1. Do you agree with the additions and deletions the writer
   has made? Explain.
2. Where has the writer changed the order of material? Does
   this change improve clarity?
3. What additional changes would you recommend to
   improve the content or organization of this essay excerpt?

PROOFREADING
TIPS
- Pay particular attention
  to your punctuation of
  the title of the work.
- Use quotation marks at
  the beginning and at the
  end of material quoted
  directly. Indented
  quotations, however, do
  not need quotation
  marks.
- Proofread your work at
  least twice. Ask another
  student to work with
  you, checking for errors
  in grammar, spelling, and
  punctuation.

**Communications
Handbook
HELP**
―――――――
See proofreaders' marks.

PUBLISHING
TIPS
- Publish your interpretation on a Web site that
  accepts student writing.
- Tape-record a reading of
  your essay for a class
  audio library.

DIRECT TEACHING

Revision Model
To help students grasp the concept
of improving clarity, present the
thought processes of a writer
making the changes shown in the
Revision Model. Calling students'
attention the insertion of the last
sentence into l. 7, you might say,
"The last sentence is more effective in the middle of the essay
because it sums up the action of
the characters in the teleplay and
serves as a bridge to a specific
quotation from *The Monsters Are
Due on Maple Street.*"

GUIDED PRACTICE

Evaluating the Revision
Possible Answers
1. Most students will recognize the
   logic of the changes. For example, the writer has substituted a
   stronger verb, *transforms,* for
   the vague word *turns* in l. 6. In
   the following line, the mob is
   described, more specifically, as
   "self-destructive."
2. The writer has inserted the last
   sentence in the draft into l. 7 in
   order to improve clarity.
3. Have students support their
   suggestions with reasons and
   examples.

	4	3	2	1
The conclusion brings main ideas together and restates the thesis.	The conclusion concisely restates the writer's thesis and contains an appropriate personal comment or response.	The conclusion fails to echo or restate the writer's thesis.	The conclusion contains no summary of the writer's main ideas and is awkwardly phrased.	The essay lacks any clear or appropriate conclusion.
Evidence from the work is smoothly and clearly introduced to support the writer's interpretation.	Supporting evidence, including quotations in proper format, is skillfully woven into the body of the essay.	Evidence for the writer's thesis is present, but it is presented in awkward or incorrect form.	The writer includes very little evidence to support the thesis, and the essay consists largely of plot summary and repetition.	The writer fails to include any evidence from the work to support the thesis.

Collection 5: Skills Review

Literary Skills

Test Practice

DIRECTIONS: Read the following list. Then, read each question, and decide which is the best answer.

A Prose Reading List

Key to Abbreviations

E = easy	A = average	C = challenging
F = fiction	NF = nonfiction	

- Caselli, Giovanni. *The Renaissance and the New World.* **C, NF** The author looks at the Renaissance advancements in commerce and technology that became the foundation of eighteenth-century life in England and America.

- Cosby, Bill. "Lessons." **A, NF** In this humorous essay, Cosby writes about how he and his daughter dealt with her poor performance on a test.

- Dahl, Roald. *Boy.* **C, NF** With a humorous touch the renowned author tells about his childhood years in England.

- Fritz, Jean. *Stonewall.* **E, NF** Fritz tells the life of Thomas "Stonewall" Jackson from his boyhood years to his Civil War achievements.

- George, Jean Craighead. *My Side of the Mountain.* **E, F** In this novel, Sam Gribley runs away to the Catskill Mountains, where challenges from humans and nature await.

- Hansen, Joyce. *Which Way Freedom?* **E, F** In this novel set at the beginning of the Civil War, Obi sets out to find his mother after a long separation.

- Saint-Exupéry, Antoine de. *The Little Prince.* **E, F** In this fable a stranded pilot meets a little boy who recounts his fantastic adventures on various planets.

- Soto, Gary. *Baseball in April.* **E, F** A collection of short stories. In one story, Michael and Jesse fail to make the Little League team but still find a way to play the game they love.

- Taylor, Mildred D. *Song of the Trees.* **A, F** In this novella the Logan family must prevent a businessman from destroying the forest that has brought joy to their lives.

- Zindel, Paul. *The Pigman.* **C, F** In this prize-winning novel, John and Lorraine are dissatisfied with their lives until they meet Mr. Pignati, who teaches them to cherish every moment.

SKILLS FOCUS

Literary Skills Analyze forms of prose.

Collection 5: Skills Review

Literary Skills

SKILLS FOCUS
pp. 636–637

Grade-Level Skills

■ Literary Skills
Analyze the characteristics of different forms of prose.

INTRODUCING THE SKILLS REVIEW

Use this review to assess students' grasp of the skills taught in this collection. You may wish to use the annotations to go over elements of the skills orally with the class.

DIRECT TEACHING

Ⓐ Literary Focus

Forms of prose. Go over this key to the abbreviations. Ask students to identify the categories of prose in the key. [fiction, nonfiction] Ask them to give examples of each category. [Possible responses: *Fiction*—novel, short story. *Nonfiction*—biography, history, essay.]

Ⓑ Literary Focus

❓ Forms of prose. How do you know that this book is a biography and not a historical novel? [The abbreviation *NF* means nonfiction, so Stonewall Jackson must have been a real person.]

Ⓒ Literary Focus

❓ Forms of prose. What does the word *novella* tell you about this book? [It is longer than a short story but shorter than a novel.]

Using Academic Language

Have students look back through the collection to find the meanings of the following terms. Then, have students demonstrate their understanding of these terms by citing passages from selections in the collection that illustrate their meanings.
Short story (pp. 484, 508); **Internal conflict** (p. 484); **External conflict** (p. 484); **Autobiography** (p. 499); **Biography** (p. 499); **Novel** (p. 508); **Essay** (pp. 527, 533).

Collection 5: Skills Review

1. Which one of the following statements is true of both fiction and nonfiction?
   A It cannot be based on actual events.
   B It cannot be longer than one hundred pages.
   C It often reveals important truths.
   D It must have resolution.

2. Which book on the reading list is an **autobiography**?
   F *The Little Prince*
   G *The Pigman*
   H *My Side of the Mountain*
   J *Boy*

3. Which book on the reading list is a **biography**?
   A *Which Way Freedom?*
   B *Stonewall*
   C *Song of the Trees*
   D *The Renaissance and the New World*

4. Which book on the reading list is a collection of **short stories**?
   F *The Little Prince*
   G *The Renaissance and the New World*
   H *Baseball in April*
   J *Boy*

5. Which item on the reading list is an **essay**?
   A "Lessons"
   B *Stonewall*
   C *Boy*
   D *Baseball in April*

6. Which two books on the list are **novels**?
   F *Which Way Freedom?* and *Song of the Trees*
   G *The Little Prince* and *Baseball in April*
   H *Boy* and *Stonewall*
   J *The Pigman* and *My Side of the Mountain*

7. Which book on the reading list is **historical fiction**?
   A *Which Way Freedom?*
   B *My Side of the Mountain*
   C *Stonewall*
   D *The Little Prince*

Constructed Response

8. In what ways are fiction and nonfiction different?

9. How can you tell the difference between a short story, a novel, and a novella?

Skills Review **637**

Test-Taking Tips

Point out that each entry in the list has both abbreviations and a written description. If students don't find the answer in one element, they should look at the other.

For more instruction on taking tests, refer students to **Test Smarts,** p. 920.

Answers and Model Rationales

1. **C** A, B, and D are true of neither fiction nor nonfiction. Fiction is often based on actual events, and no genre is limited in length. Works of prose may or may not come to a resolution. C is the only choice left.

2. **J** An autobiography is nonfiction, so F, G, and H are incorrect—they are fiction. Since *Boy* tells about the author's childhood, it is an autobiography.

3. **B** A and C cannot be correct because they are works of fiction. D doesn't tell the life story of an individual. B is the story of Stonewall Jackson; the abbreviation *NF* shows that he was a real person.

4. **H** *Baseball in April* is described as a short story collection and is coded as fiction. G and J are nonfiction, and F is one long story.

5. **A** B, C, and D are incorrect because B and C are longer than an essay, and D is a collection of short stories. "Lessons" is identified as an essay.

6. **J** F is incorrect because *Song of the Trees* is a novella. G is incorrect because *Baseball in April* is a book of short stories. H is incorrect because the selections are nonfiction.

7. **A** D is a fantasy novel. C is nonfiction. B doesn't appear to be about a particular historical period or event. A is correct; it is fiction with a Civil War setting.

Constructed Response

8. Fiction is based on imaginary events, whereas nonfiction deals with real people, places, things, and events.

9. Short stories are no longer than twenty pages, novels are longer than one hundred pages, and novellas are between twenty and one hundred pages.

Literary Skills

SKILLS FOCUS
pp. 638–639

Grade-Level Skills
- Literary Skills

Analyze elements of poems.

INTRODUCING THE SKILLS REVIEW

Use this review to assess students' grasp of poetic elements.

DIRECT TEACHING

Ⓐ Literary Focus

❓ Metaphor. To what is the sea compared in this poem? [a hungry dog] Name two things the "dog" does. [Possible responses: rolls on the beach; clashes his teeth; gnaws the stones; moans "Bones, bones, bones!"; licks his paws.]

Ⓑ Literary Focus

Rhyme. Remind students that a stanza's rhyme scheme is marked by labeling the sound at the end of each line with a letter of the alphabet, starting with *a*; sounds that rhyme with each other are labeled with the same letter. Ask students to identify the rhyme scheme of stanza 2. [*abccb*]

Ⓒ Literary Focus

❓ Alliteration. What consonant sound is repeated in the last line? [/s/] Why do you think the poet chose to repeat this sound? [to suggest the sound of a dog's snoring.]

Test Practice

DIRECTIONS: Read the following poem. Then, answer each question.

The Sea

James Reeves

The sea is a hungry dog,
Giant and gray.
He rolls on the beach all day.
With his clashing teeth and shaggy jaws
5 Ⓐ Hour upon hour he gnaws
The rumbling, tumbling stones,
And "Bones, bones, bones!"
The giant sea dog moans,
Licking his greasy paws.

10 And when the night wind roars
And the moon rocks in the stormy cloud,
Ⓑ He bounds to his feet and snuffs and sniffs,
Shaking his wet sides over the cliffs,
And howls and hollos long and loud.

15 But on quiet days in May or June,
When even the grasses on the dune
Play no more their reedy tune,
With his head between his paws
He lies on the sandy shores,
20 Ⓒ So quiet, so quiet, he scarcely snores.

638   Collection 5 / Worlds of Words: Prose and Poetry

MINI-LESSON   Reading

Reviewing Word-Attack Skills
Activity. Display these sets of words without underlines. Have students identify the word in each set in which *s* stands for /z/.

1. sea	<u>bones</u>	cliffs
2. stormy	sniffs	<u>days</u>
3. <u>rolls</u>	rocks	shaking
4. sandy	<u>paws</u>	scarcely
5. <u>howls</u>	so	shaggy

Collection 5: Skills Review

1. In which of the following sets do *all* the words **rhyme**?

   A dog / gray / day

   B stones / bones / moans

   C sniffs / cliffs / loud

   D paws / shores / snores

2. The **rhyme scheme** of the last **stanza** of the poem is —

   F *aabbcc*

   G *abcabc*

   H *abcdef*

   J *aaabcc*

3. Which of the following is an example of a **metaphor**?

   A "The rumbling, tumbling stones"

   B "But on quiet days in May or June"

   C "The sea is a hungry dog"

   D "Giant and gray"

4. Which of the following lines contains **alliteration,** or the repetition of consonant sounds?

   F "The giant sea dog moans"

   G "Licking his greasy paws"

   H "But on quiet days in May or June"

   J "So quiet, so quiet, he scarcely snores"

5. Which of the following lines contains **onomatopoeia,** or words that sound like what they mean?

   A "And howls and hollos long and loud"

   B "Hour upon hour he gnaws"

   C "Licking his greasy paws"

   D "He lies on the sandy shores"

6. What **tone** is evoked by the repetition and word choices in the last stanza?

   F a quiet, peaceful tone

   G a sad and lonely tone

   H a lively and happy tone

   J a rough and angry tone

Constructed Response

7. List three different ways in which the poem compares the sea to a dog.

8. Find **images** in the poem that appeal to each of the following senses: sight, hearing, touch, and taste.

Literary Skills
Analyze elements of poems.

Skills Review   **639**

Test Practice

Answers and Model Rationales

1. **B** Remind students that rhyming words have the same end sounds.

2. **J** Point out that "June," "dune," and "tune" all rhyme (*a*); that "paws" has a different end sound (*b*); and that "shores" and "snores" rhyme (*c*).

3. **C** In this metaphor, the sea is compared to a dog.

4. **J** The /s/ sound is repeated in "so," "scarcely," and "snores."

5. **A** Students should understand that the sounds of the words *howls* and *hollos* suggest the words' meanings.

6. **F** The repetition of the word *quiet* and the lazy, lulling sounds of the stanza's words create a tranquil mood.

Constructed Response

7. Possible answers: The "giant sea dog" rolls on the beach, gnaws on the stones, moans, bounds, shakes his wet sides, howls, rests.

8. Possible answer: *Sight*—The hungry dog is "giant and gray" (l. 2); *Hearing*—"clashing teeth" (l. 4); *Touch*—"Shaking his wet sides" (l. 13); *Taste*—"Licking his greasy paws" (l. 9).

Using Academic Language

Literary Terms
Have students look back through the collection to find the meanings of the terms listed at the right. Then, have students demonstrate their understanding of these terms by citing passages from selections in the collection that illustrate their meaning.

Metaphor (p. 551); **Extended metaphor** (p. 551); **Personification** (p. 555); **Tone** (p. 560); **Imagery** (p. 563); **Rhythm** (p. 578); **Rhyme** (pp. 586, 598, 601); **Repetition** (p. 601); **Alliteration** (p. 601).

Collection 5: Skills Review

Vocabulary Skills

Context Clues

Modeling. Model the thought process of a good reader getting the answer to item 1 by saying: "*Contagious* can't be right, because it means 'spreading' or 'catching'; the fighters' 'flurry of punches' wouldn't spread to the crowd. The fighters' blows are hard, but it doesn't make sense for that to be the crowd's reaction. Fighters throwing punches are not being deceptive. *Frenzied* means excited and crazy or wild, just like a fast series of punches; A is correct."

Test Practice

Answers and Model Rationales

1. **A** See rationale above.
2. **G** An average, small, or unremarkable size would not impress the children. That leaves G.
3. **D** The words *they couldn't agree* suggest that *argument,* a synonym for *disagreement,* is the best choice.
4. **G** The phrase "do everything in her power" makes G the best choice.
5. **D** Because the children are frightened, D seems to make the most sense.
6. **J** If the ground is behaving like "choppy water," it must be moving; J is correct.
7. **B** The word *matches* suggests a boxing contest, or a tennis match, both of which are contests.
8. **J** A mountain range has no single top for a climber to stand on. G and H do not fit the context. J is the only answer that makes sense.

Test Practice

Context Clues

DIRECTIONS: As you read each sentence, use the other words in the sentence to help you figure out what the underlined word means. Then, choose the best answer.

1. The crowd's reaction was as <u>frenzied</u> as the flurry of punches being thrown by the fighters.
   A wild
   B contagious
   C hard
   D deceptive

2. The children were impressed by the <u>formidable</u> size of their huge school.
   F average
   G awesome
   H small
   J unremarkable

3. They couldn't agree on much, but this <u>dispute</u> promised to drive them even further apart.
   A problem
   B outrage
   C situation
   D argument

4. She had to do everything in her power to <u>muster</u> the energy to be nice to her brother after what he had done.
   F forgive
   G summon
   H forget
   J receive

5. The darkening sky cast an <u>ominous</u> shadow, which frightened the children.
   A cold
   B dismal
   C fearful
   D threatening

6. Without warning the ground began <u>churning</u> like the choppy waves of a lake.
   F sinking
   G glistening
   H bending
   J stirring

7. Of the many matches scheduled for the night, the last <u>bout</u> would be most thrilling.
   A choice
   B contest
   C bridge
   D draw

8. The climber stood at the top of the <u>bluff</u> and surveyed the valley below with her binoculars.
   F mountain range
   G river bottom
   H ship
   J steep cliff

SKILLS FOCUS

Vocabulary Skills
Use context clues.

Vocabulary Review

Use the following activity to find out whether your students have retained the Vocabulary words taught in this collection.
Activity. Have students complete each sentence with the correct word from the pair given in parentheses.

1. The champion boxer fought many _____ in the ring. (bouts, contraption) [bouts]
2. Mandy's clothes were _____ because she had stuffed them into the suitcase. (buckled, rumpled) [rumpled]
3. Mama was angry, so she spoke _____. (curtly, incredulously) [curtly]
4. The blood drained from Charley's face, leaving her cheeks _____. (ashen, finicky) [ashen]
5. Ernesto was scared by the _____ of many strange voices. (clamor, resolve) [clamor]

Collection 5: Skills Review

Writing Skills

Test Practice

DIRECTIONS: Read the following paragraph from an essay supporting an interpretation. Then, answer each question that follows.

(1) Why do we admire the robber in Alfred Noyes's poem "The Highwayman"? (2) Obviously, he is a criminal who holds up stagecoaches and steals passengers' money and jewels at gunpoint. (3) If King George's men had not shot him down on the highway, he might have ended his career on the gallows. (4) Yet, the poet's skill makes us admire the highwayman because he is a romantic figure—daring and fearless. (5) The poet depicts the highwayman as a romantic hero. (6) He is handsomely dressed, like a gentleman. (7) He wears a stylish hat, lace at his chin, a coat of velvet, and pants of doeskin (lines 7–8). (8) He rides with "a jeweled twinkle," his weapons reflecting the starlight. (9) He is also a faithful lover. (10) The redcoats are unable to catch him until he is betrayed by a rival for his love.

1. Which sentence contains the **thesis,** or main idea, of the essay?
   A sentence 1
   B sentence 3
   C sentence 4
   D sentence 6

2. Which sentence is repetitive and should be deleted?
   F sentence 2
   G sentence 5
   H sentence 7
   J sentence 8

3. A **paraphrase,** or restatement, of specific lines from the poem appears in—
   A sentence 4
   B sentence 7
   C sentence 9
   D sentence 10

4. Which sentence does *not* contain a transitional word?
   F sentence 2
   G sentence 4
   H sentence 7
   J sentence 9

5. Sentences 6–9 all begin with the pronoun *he.* How might you introduce variety into these sentences?
   A Substitute "the highwayman" for "he" in one or more sentences.
   B Add transitional expressions such as *moreover* or *in addition.*
   C Combine the ideas in sentences 6 and 7 into one sentence.
   D All of the above

SKILLS FOCUS

Writing Skills
Analyze persuasive writing.

Skills Review   641

Test Practice

Answers and Model Rationales

1. **C** Only sentence 4 contains the controlling idea of the passage. A asks a question, and B presents a speculation. D contains a subordinate detail.

2. **G** Sentence 5 essentially repeats sentence 4; note the occurrence of the word *romantic* in both sentences. F, H, and J present various facts about the highwayman, but none of these sentences is repetitive.

3. **B** Sentence 7 offers a paraphrase, which is signaled by the details themselves and by the inclusion of a line reference. A presents the thesis statement, which is not a paraphrase. C presents an evaluation of the hero, while D gives a plot detail.

4. **H** F contains the transition word "Obviously"; G opens with "Yet"; J contains the transition word "also." Only H lacks a transitional expression.

5. **D** All the alternatives presented would result in increased variety in these sentences.

APPLICATION

Compile a Critical Anthology

Encourage students to pool their essays to create a critical anthology of literary interpretations. Have student groups select writers to compose a table of contents, a brief preface, and an index for the anthology.

EXTENSION

Write a Critical Biography

Tell students that many biographers of literary figures interweave literary criticism with biographical details. The premise for such writing is that experiences in real life have an important effect on a writer's choice of subjects and also on his or her individual style. Have each student select a writer who interests him or her, research the writer's life and works, and present an outline for a critical biographical sketch linking biographical data with critical interpretation of one or more works by the author.

READ ON

For Independent Reading

If students enjoyed the themes and topics explored in this collection, you might recommend these titles for independent reading.

Assessment Options

The following projects can help you evaluate and assess your students' outside reading. Videotapes or audiotapes of completed projects may be included in students' portfolios.

- **Keep a diary.** Have students pretend they are Jimmy in *Somewhere in the Darkness*, keeping a diary of his brief time with his father so that he can share it with his own children someday. Diary entries should cover the main events of Jimmy's time with Crab and describe the boy's changing feelings for his father.

- **Stage a medieval fair.** Have students who read *Adam of the Road* gather in a small group to stage a medieval fair like the one in which Adam might have performed. Entertainment can include juggling acts, musical performances, and a brief play. Encourage students to use their imaginations to create costumes and acts. Remind them that Adam and other strolling players of the Middle Ages were very poor; they had to get the most from slender resources to achieve an effect. Students should do the same. Set aside a class period for students to enjoy the fair.

Fiction

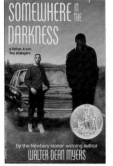

Sentimental Journey

Suffering from a kidney disease and confined to a prison hospital, Cephus "Crab" Little decides to make up for lost time with his son Jimmy in *Somewhere in the Darkness* by Walter Dean Myers. Together they journey to Crab's hometown in Arkansas, where Jimmy's growing understanding of his father's past helps him come to terms with his father and himself.

Women of Valor

In *Cut from the Same Cloth: American Women of Myth, Legend, and Tall Tale*, Robert D. San Souci takes a look at women characters in American legends with a talent for adventure. You'll find stories about Molly Cotton-Tail, Brer Rabbit's clever wife, and Sister Fox, the brains behind Brother Coyote. The stories are entertaining, and they often offer up a few lessons as well.

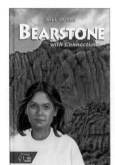

Helping Hand

Fourteen-year-old Cloyd never knew his parents and never went to school. After being on his own for so long, he has trouble accepting the kindness of an old rancher from Colorado. In Will Hobbs's novel *Bearstone*, Cloyd embraces his Native American heritage, begins to respect others, and learns what it takes to be an adult.

This title is available in the HRW Library.

On the Road Again

It's the summer of the year 1294. Adam, an eleven-year-old minstrel boy who loses contact with his father, is confounded by another minstrel named Jankin, who steals his dog, Nick. In this Middle Ages adventure, Adam scours the English countryside in search of the two things that mean the most to him—his father and his lovable dog. Of course, along the way he learns a few lessons and meets some interesting friends in Elizabeth Janet Gray's Newbery Award–winning historical novel, *Adam of the Road*.

642 Collection 5 / Worlds of Words: Prose and Poetry

DIFFERENTIATING INSTRUCTION

Estimated Word Counts of Read On Books:

Fiction		Nonfiction	
Somewhere in the Darkness	45,500	Amos Fortune: Free Man	36,000
Cut from the Same Cloth:		Shrinking Forests	37,000
American Women of Myth,		Volcano and Earthquake	21,000
Legend and Tall Tale	38,000	The Great Depression	5,000
Bearstone	40,000		
Connections to Bearstone	8,800		
Adam of the Road	59,000		

Nonfiction

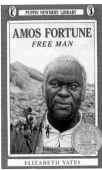

Roots of Prejudice

In Africa in 1710, Amos Fortune was born to a king. At the age of fifteen, he was captured by slave traders and transported in chains to the colony of Massachusetts. Despite the horrors of captivity, Fortune never gave up hope in securing his personal freedom. When he finally became a free man at the age of sixty, he dedicated the remainder of his life to freeing others like him. Find out more about this remarkable man in Elizabeth Yates's Newbery winner, *Amos Fortune: Free Man.*

Take Care of the Earth

Forests play an important role in the earth's environment; yet we cut them down at an alarming rate, threatening the well-being of animals, plants, and ourselves. In *Shrinking Forests,* Jenny Tesar explains how essential it is to preserve rain forests. If you enjoy this book, you may enjoy other books in the Our Fragile Planet series; each examines an environmental problem.

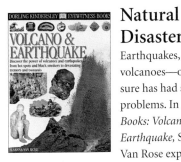

Natural Disasters

Earthquakes, floods, volcanoes—our planet sure has had some problems. In *Eyewitness Books: Volcano & Earthquake,* Susanna Van Rose explains how these problems occur. The book also covers the most famous disasters in world history, from the eruption of Mount Vesuvius during the first century to the San Francisco earthquake of 1989.

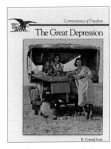

Heartbreaking Times

During the 1920s, the United States was enjoying prosperity. Then, on October 29, 1929, the New York Stock Exchange crashed. The country fell into the Great Depression; as a result, jobs were scarce, banks were closing, and families were starving. In *The Great Depression,* R. Conrad Stein looks back on this bleak period in American history.

Read On   643

The Read On titles are categorized as shown below:

Below Grade Level ⬇
Somewhere in the Darkness
Shrinking Forests

At Grade Level ⬌
Cut from the Same Cloth: American Women of Myth, Legend, and Tall Tale
Bearstone
Volcano and Earthquake
The Great Depression

Above Grade Level ⬆
Adam of the Road
Amos Fortune: Free Man

Collection 6
Our Literary Heritage: Greek Myths and World Folk Tales

Literary Focus:
Analyzing Myths and Folk Tales

Informational Focus:
Summarizing

About Collection 6

In Collection 6, students will master the following skills:

- **Literary Skills:** Understand and analyze Greek and Roman myths and folk tales; analyze an origin myth, the superhero motif, metamorphosis, taboos, the motif of wishes, and the origin motif.
- **Reading Skills:** Analyze Greek and Latin roots and affixes; summarize a myth, an article, and main ideas.
- **Vocabulary Skills:** Understand Greek prefixes, word origins, figurative language, and allusions; use onomatopoeia and descriptive and specific words.
- **Writing Skills:** Develop, write, and revise a comparison-contrast essay.

Informational Text

Each collection of *Elements of Literature* provides a variety of informational texts related to the literature selections by theme or topic.

Minimum Course of Study

Most skills can be taught with a minimum number of selections and features. In the chart to the right, lessons highlighted in green constitute the minimum course of study that provides coverage of the skills taught in Collection 6.

Scope and Sequence

Selection ▪ Feature	Literary Skills
Elements of Literature: The Myths of Greece and Rome *by* David Adams Leeming	• Understand Greek and Roman myths
Reading Skills and Strategies: Becoming Word-Wise *by* Kylene Beers **Greek and Latin Roots and Affixes** ↔ *at grade level*	
The Origin of the Seasons *retold by* Olivia Coolidge ↔ *at grade level*	• Analyze an origin myth
Orpheus, the Great Musician *retold by* Olivia Coolidge ↔ *at grade level*	• Identify elements of myth: the Underworld • Analyze a myth
Informational Text: The Power of Music *from* **Nadja on My Way** *by* Nadja Salerno-Sonnenberg ↔ *at grade level*	
The Flight of Icarus *retold by* Sally Benson ↔ *at grade level*	• Analyze the moral of a myth
King Midas and the Golden Touch *retold by* Pamela Oldfield ↔ *at grade level*	• Analyze irony
Informational Text: The Funeral Banquet of King Midas *by* John Fleischman ↔ *at grade level*	
Elements of Literature: Folk Tales *by* Virginia Hamilton	• Understand folk tales

Resource Manager
(pp. 644E–644J)

Lesson and workshop resources are referenced in the Resource Manager on the pages that follow. These resources can be used to reinforce the skills taught in Collection 6, remediate students who are having difficulty, and provide supporting activities for English-language learners.

Reading Skills	Vocabulary Skills	Writing ▪ Grammar and Language Skills
• Analyze Greek and Latin roots and affixes		
• Analyze cause and effect	• Understand Greek prefixes • Use descriptive words	• Write a myth
• Summarize a myth	• Clarify word meanings • Understand figurative language	• Compare myths
• Analyze facts and opinions • Analyze anecdote		
• Make a generalization	• Understand word origins	• Write an analysis of three myths • Distinguish between adjectives and adverbs
• Use prior knowledge • Summarize an article	• Understand word origins • Understand allusions • Clarify word meanings by context	• Write a play

(continued)

Scope and Sequence

Selection ▪ Feature	Literary Skills	Reading Skills
Oni and the Great Bird *retold by* Abayomi Fuja ↔ *at grade level*	• Analyze the superhero motif	• Summarize
Master Frog *retold by* Lynette Dyer Vuong ↑ *above grade level*	• Analyze metamorphosis	• Make predictions
The Crane Wife *told by* Sumiko Yagawa *translated from the Japanese by* Katherine Paterson ↑ *above grade level*	• Analyze taboos	• Draw conclusions
Aunty Misery *by* Judith Ortiz Cofer ↔ *at grade level*	• Analyze the motif of wishes	• Analyze cause and effect
The Hummingbird King *retold by* Argentina Palacios ↔ *at grade level*	• Analyze the origin motif	• Retell the story
Informational Text: **The Search Goes On** *from* **The Mystery of the Ancient Maya** *by* Carolyn Meyer *and* Charles Gallenkamp ↑ *above grade level*		• Summarize the main ideas
Comparing Literature: The Cinderella Story **Aschenputtel** *retold by* Jakob *and* Wilhelm Grimm *translated by* Lucy Crane ↑ *above grade level* **Dinorella** *by* Pamela Duncan Edwards ↔ *at grade level* **Interview** *by* Sara Henderson Hay ↔ *at grade level*	• Analyze the Cinderella story	• Compare and contrast texts
No Questions Asked: **The Dream of Good Fortune** *from* **The Arabian Nights** *dramatized by* Paul Sills ↓ *below grade level*		
Writing Workshop: *Expository Writing: Comparison-Contrast Essay*		
Skills Review: *Literary Skills* *Vocabulary Skills* *Writing Skills*	• Analyze a fable	

Vocabulary Skills	Writing ▪ Grammar and Language Skills
• Clarify word meanings	• Write a summary • Use *they're*, *their*, and *there* correctly
• Clarify word meanings • Use specific words	• Write a personal essay
• Use onomatopoeia	• Write a folk tale • Use *good* and *well* correctly
	• Write a story about a wish
• Clarify word meanings	• Write a story • Recognize irregular verbs
	• Write a comparison-contrast essay • Write a new Cinderella story • Write from another point of view
	• Write a comparison-contrast essay
• Identify synonyms	• Analyze a comparison-contrast essay

Resource Manager

Selection ▪ Feature	Planning	Differentiating Instruction ▪ Lesson Plans with ELL Strategies and Practice	Reading ▪ Vocabulary
Elements of Literature: The Myths of Greece and Rome *by* David Adams Leeming	• PowerNotes: The Myths of Greece and Rome	• Holt Reading Solutions: Lesson Plans, pp. 261–262	• Holt Reading Solutions, pp. 261–262
Reading Skills and Strategies: Becoming Word-Wise *by* Kylene Beers **Greek and Latin Roots and Affixes**			
The Origin of the Seasons *retold by* Olivia Coolidge	• One-Stop Planner with ExamView Test Generator	• The Holt Reader, pp. 198–208 • Holt Adapted Reader, pp. 148–153 • Holt Reading Solutions: Lesson Plans, pp. 263–267 • Supporting Instruction in Spanish, p. 25 • Audio CD Library • Audio CD Library, Selections and Summaries in Spanish	• The Holt Reader, pp. 198–208 • Holt Adapted Reader, pp. 148–153 • Holt Reading Solutions, pp. 263–267
Orpheus, the Great Musician *retold by* Olivia Coolidge **Informational Text: The Power of Music** *from* **Nadja on My Way** *by* Nadja Salerno-Sonnenberg	• One-Stop Planner with ExamView Test Generator	• Holt Reading Solutions: Lesson Plans, pp. 268–273 • Supporting Instruction in Spanish, pp. 25, 26 • Audio CD Library • Audio CD Library, Selections and Summaries in Spanish	• Holt Reading Solutions, pp. 268–273 • Vocabulary Development, p. 25 • PowerNotes: Summarizing a Story
The Flight of Icarus *retold by* Sally Benson	• One-Stop Planner with ExamView Test Generator	• Holt Adapted Reader, pp. 154–157 • Holt Reading Solutions: Lesson Plans, pp. 274–278 • Supporting Instruction in Spanish, p. 26 • Audio CD Library • Audio CD Library, Selections and Summaries in Spanish	• Holt Adapted Reader, pp. 154–157 • Holt Reading Solutions, pp. 274–278 • PowerNotes: Making Generalizations
King Midas and the Golden Touch *retold by* Pamela Oldfield **Informational Text: The Funeral Banquet of King Midas** *by* John Fleischman	• One-Stop Planner with ExamView Test Generator	• Holt Reading Solutions: Lesson Plans, pp. 279–284 • Supporting Instruction in Spanish, p. 27 • Audio CD Library • Audio CD Library, Selections and Summaries in Spanish	• Holt Reading Solutions, pp. 279–284 • Vocabulary Development, p. 26
Elements of Literature: Folk Tales *by* Virginia Hamilton	• PowerNotes: Folk Tales	• Holt Reading Solutions: Lesson Plans, pp. 285–286	• Holt Reading Solutions, pp. 285–286
Oni and the Great Bird *retold by* Abayomi Fuja	• One-Stop Planner with ExamView Test Generator	• The Holt Reader, pp. 209–220 • Holt Reading Solutions: Lesson Plans, pp. 287–291 • Supporting Instruction in Spanish, p. 28 • Audio CD Library • Audio CD Library, Selections and Summaries in Spanish	• The Holt Reader, pp. 209–220 • Holt Reading Solutions, pp. 287–291 • Vocabulary Development, p. 27

Writing Grammar and Language	Assessment
• Daily Language Activities	• Holt Assessment: Literature, Reading, and Vocabulary • One-Stop Planner with ExamView Test Generator • Holt Online Assessment
• Daily Language Activities	• Holt Assessment: Literature, Reading, and Vocabulary • One-Stop Planner with ExamView Test Generator • Holt Online Assessment
• Daily Language Activities • Language Handbook Worksheets, p. 9	• Holt Assessment: Literature, Reading, and Vocabulary • One-Stop Planner with ExamView Test Generator • Holt Online Assessment
• Daily Language Activities	• Holt Assessment: Literature, Reading, and Vocabulary • One-Stop Planner with ExamView Test Generator • Holt Online Assessment
• Daily Language Activities	• Holt Assessment: Literature, Reading, and Vocabulary • One-Stop Planner with ExamView Test Generator • Holt Online Assessment

Technology

INTERNET

- go.hrw.com
- Holt Online Assessment
- Holt Online Essay Scoring
- Elements of Literature Online

MEDIA

 • One-Stop Planner with ExamView Test Generator

• PowerNotes

• Audio CD Library

• Audio CD Library, Selections and Summaries in Spanish

• Fine Art Transparencies, 10

 Transparency

 CD-ROM   Audio CD

(continued)

Resource Manager

Selection ■ Feature	Planning	Differentiating Instruction ■ Lesson Plans with ELL Strategies and Practice	Reading ■ Vocabulary
Master Frog *retold by* Lynette Dyer Vuong	• One-Stop Planner with ExamView Test Generator	• Holt Reading Solutions: Lesson Plans, pp. 292–296 • Supporting Instruction in Spanish, p. 28 • Audio CD Library • Audio CD Library, Selections and Summaries in Spanish	• Holt Reading Solutions, pp. 292–296 • Vocabulary Development, p. 28 • PowerNotes: Making Predictions
The Crane Wife *told by* Sumiko Yagawa *translated from the Japanese by* Katherine Paterson	• One-Stop Planner with ExamView Test Generator	• Holt Reading Solutions: Lesson Plans, pp. 297–302 • Supporting Instruction in Spanish, p. 29 • Audio CD Library • Audio CD Library, Selections and Summaries in Spanish	• Holt Reading Solutions, pp. 297–302
Aunty Misery *by* Judith Ortiz Cofer	• One-Stop Planner with ExamView Test Generator	• Holt Reading Solutions: Lesson Plans, pp. 303–305 • Supporting Instruction in Spanish, p. 29 • Audio CD Library • Audio CD Library, Selections and Summaries in Spanish	• Holt Reading Solutions, pp. 303–305
The Hummingbird King *retold by* Argentina Palacios **Informational Text: The Search Goes On** *from* **The Mystery of the Ancient Maya** *by* Carolyn Meyer *and* Charles Gallenkamp	• One-Stop Planner with ExamView Test Generator	• Holt Reading Solutions: Lesson Plans, pp. 306–310 • Supporting Instruction in Spanish, p. 30 • Audio CD Library • Audio CD Library, Selections and Summaries in Spanish	• Holt Reading Solutions, pp. 306–310 • Vocabulary Development, p. 29 • PowerNotes: Discovering the Main Idea
Comparing Literature: The Cinderella Story Aschenputtel *retold by* Jakob *and* Wilhelm Grimm, *translated by* Lucy Crane **Dinorella** *by* Pamela Duncan Edwards **Interview** *by* Sara Henderson Hay		• Holt Reading Solutions: Lesson Plans, pp. 311–314	• Holt Reading Solutions, pp. 311–314

Writing Grammar and Language	Assessment
• Daily Language Activities	• Holt Assessment: Literature, Reading, and Vocabulary • One-Stop Planner with ExamView Test Generator • Holt Online Assessment
• Daily Language Activities	• Holt Assessment: Literature, Reading, and Vocabulary • One-Stop Planner with ExamView Test Generator • Holt Online Assessment
• Daily Language Activities	• Holt Assessment: Literature, Reading, and Vocabulary • One-Stop Planner with ExamView Test Generator • Holt Online Assessment
• Daily Language Activities • Language Handbook Worksheets, pp. 27–30	• Holt Assessment: Literature, Reading, and Vocabulary • One-Stop Planner with ExamView Test Generator • Holt Online Assessment

(continued)

Technology

INTERNET

- go.hrw.com
- Holt Online Assessment
- Holt Online Essay Scoring
- Elements of Literature Online

MEDIA

 • One-Stop Planner with ExamView Test Generator

 • PowerNotes

 • Audio CD Library

• Audio CD Library, Selections and Summaries in Spanish

• Fine Art Transparencies, 10

Transparency

CD-ROM   Audio CD

Selection ■ Feature	Planning	Differentiating Instruction ■ Lesson Plans with ELL Strategies and Practice	Reading ■ Vocabulary
No Questions Asked: The Dream of Good Fortune *from* **The Arabian Nights** *dramatized by* Paul Sills			
Writing Workshop: *Expository Writing: Comparison-Contrast Essay*	• One-Stop Planner with ExamView Test Generator	• Workshop Resources: Writing, Listening, and Speaking, pp. 56–66 • Supporting Instruction in Spanish, p. 42	
Skills Review: *Literary Skills* *Vocabulary Skills* *Writing Skills*			

The Holt Reader

The Holt Reader is a consumable paperback book that can be used alone or to accompany *Elements of Literature*. It offers guided support throughout the reading process and encourages students to become active readers by circling, underlining, questioning, and jotting down responses as they read. *The Holt Reader* works well for homework, students who have missed class, additional instructional time, reteaching, and remediation.

Holt Reading Solutions (HRS)

Holt Reading Solutions pulls together reading resources in the *Elements of Literature* program to create a powerful tool for intervention and whole-class instruction. *HRS* includes diagnostic assessment tools, lesson plans for English-language learners and special education students, adaptations of selected reading selections, vocabulary and comprehension worksheets, information on phonics and decoding, and additional instruction and practice in remedial reading skills.

Writing Grammar and Language	Assessment
• Workshop Resources: Writing, Listening, and Speaking, pp. 56–66 • Language Handbook Worksheets • Daily Language Activities	• Holt Assessment: Literature, Reading, and Vocabulary • One-Stop Planner with ExamView Test Generator • Holt Online Assessment • Holt Online Essay Scoring
	• Holt Assessment: Literature, Reading, and Vocabulary • One-Stop Planner with ExamView Test Generator • Holt Online Assessment

One-Stop Planner with ExamView Test Generator

The *One-Stop Planner* CD-ROM planning software contains print-based teaching resources, clips from the video program, and valuable assessment tools. The *One-Stop Planner* resources are presented in easy-to-follow, point-and-click menu formats. To preview resources or print out worksheets and tests, you simply make a selection and click.

One-Stop
Planner CD-ROM

Technology

INTERNET

• go.hrw.com

 • Holt Online Assessment

• Holt Online Essay Scoring

• Elements of Literature Online

MEDIA

 • One-Stop Planner with ExamView Test Generator

 • PowerNotes

 • Audio CD Library

• Audio CD Library, Selections and Summaries in Spanish

 • Fine Art Transparencies, 10

Transparency

CD-ROM   Audio CD

Collection 6

SKILLS FOCUS

Grade-Level Skills

■ **Literary Skills**
Analyze elements of Greek and Roman myths.

■ **Literary Skills**
Analyze world folk tales.

■ **Reading Skills**
Summarize texts.

■ **Reading Skills**
Analyze text structures, including cause and effect.

■ **Vocabulary Skills**
Analyze Greek and Latin roots and affixes.

Review Skills

■ **Reading Skills**
Recognize differences between facts, supported inferences, and opinions.

■ **Vocabulary Skills**
Use context clues to determine meanings of unknown words.

Upcoming Skills

■ **Literary Skills**
Analyze recurring themes across traditional and contemporary works.

■ **Reading Skills**
Determine whether a summary is an accurate reflection of an original text.

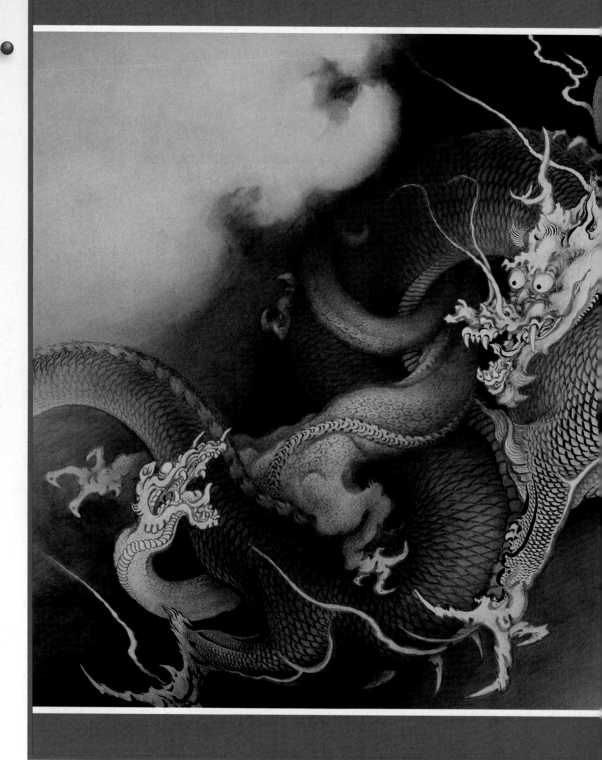

COLLECTION 6 RESOURCES: READING

Planning
■ *One-Stop Planner* CD-ROM with ExamView Test Generator

Differentiating Instruction
■ *The Holt Reader*
■ *Holt Adapted Reader*
■ *Holt Reading Solutions*
■ *Family Involvement Activities in English and Spanish*

■ *Supporting Instruction in Spanish*
■ *Audio CD Library*
■ *Audio CD Library, Selections and Summaries in Spanish*

Vocabulary
■ *Vocabulary Development*

Grammar and Language
■ *Language Handbook Worksheets*
■ *Daily Language Activities*

Collection 6

Our Literary Heritage
Greek Myths and World Folk Tales

Literary Focus:
Analyzing Myths and Folk Tales

Informational Focus:
Summarizing

INTERNET
Collection Resources
Keyword: LE5 7-6

Two Dragons in Clouds (detail) by Hogai Kano I.
© Philadelphia Museum of Art.

645

INTRODUCING THE COLLECTION

Theme: Our literary heritage. Explain to students that the ancient myths in this collection were told by people to explain their origins and the natural world around them. Point out that many modern words and ideas have their roots in the interactions and motifs found in these stories.

Analyzing myths and folk tales. Many aspects of myths and folk tales are discussed in Collection 6. As students read the Greek and Roman myths in the collection, remind them to look for similarities between these myths and the stories people tell today to explain the modern world. As students read world folk tales, encourage them to think about the cultures that shaped the various versions of familiar tales—and about how they might learn more about these cultures.

Summarizing. Students will read informational selections connected topically to the literature. These informational texts will teach students how to accurately summarize a text by including main ideas and key details.

VIEWING THE ART

Hogai Kano I (1828–1888) was one of the last practicing members of the esteemed Kano school of artists. His unique blend of the Japanese aesthetic and Western techniques contributed to the rise of modern Japanese-style painting.

Activity. Have students closely examine Kano's painting of the two dragons. Ask students to list other characters, creatures, places, and things that they associate with mythology and folk tales. [Possible answers: Zeus, Mount Olympus, unicorns, and gold.]

Grade-Level Skills

■ **Literary Skills**
Understand elements of Greek and Roman myths.

Upcoming Skills

■ **Literary Skills**
Analyze recurring themes across traditional and contemporary works.

Elements of Literature: The Myths of Greece and Rome

This feature discusses the continuing influence of Greece and Rome in the Western world, reflected even today in art, literature, and other aspects of our culture. The essay goes on to describe why and how Greek myths first arose; how they were influenced by the Roman conquest; and how myths are used. The essay concludes by naming some of the major gods and goddesses of Greek and Roman mythology.

Elements of Literature
The Myths of Greece and Rome *by* David Adams Leeming

INSIGHTS INTO OUR WORLD

It is hard to imagine what our civilization would be like without the mythology of ancient Greece and Rome. The ancient immortals are still around us in spirit. If you go to any one of the great museums of Europe or America, you will find statues and paintings of classical gods and heroes. If you read poetry in English classes, you will come across references to ancient places such as Troy and Carthage, monsters such as the Sirens and the Cyclops, and gods and heroes such as Poseidon, Odysseus (whose Roman name is Ulysses), Athena, and Hercules. These are all names from mythology—names that poets and artists expect us to recognize.

What Is a Myth?

Myths are stories that represent the deepest wishes and fears of human beings. They explained to the ancient people the mysterious and sometimes frightening forces of the universe— forces such as seasonal changes, fire, lightning, drought, floods, and death.

INTERNET
More About Myths
Keyword: LE5 7-6

SKILLS FOCUS

Literary Skills
Understand Greek and Roman myths.

Makers of Myths

The myths you will read here originated in the area around the Mediterranean Sea (see the inset of the map on pages 648–649). These old myths were passed on orally from generation to generation.

By the second century B.C., the Romans had conquered the Greeks and had adopted the Greek myths. The Romans added a new, cynical tone to the old stories. This tone reflected the fact that the Romans were less serious about religion than the Greeks were.

The Uses of Mythology

Myths are not merely ancient tales. Like all true art, the great myths give us insights into the nature of our world.

Myths are used for these purposes:

1. to explain the creation of the world
2. to explain natural phenomena
3. to give story form to ancient religious practices
4. to teach moral lessons
5. to explain history
6. to express, as dreams do, the deepest fears and hopes of the human race

---

Learners Having Difficulty
Before students read this feature, write the words and names from classical mythology on the chalkboard, pronounce them for the class, and ask students to repeat them after you. Also, briefly describe each monster, hero, god, and goddess. If possible, show students pictures of any characters who are not already depicted in the illustrations provided in the collection.

English-Language Learners
English-language learners will also benefit from hearing classical names read aloud.

Advanced Learners
Enrichment. Assign each student a different Greek or Roman mythological character. Ask students to research the following information:

- character's special talents
- place(s) associated with character
- character's relationship to other mythological characters

Have students share their research by making pocket-size trading cards with a picture of the character on the front and data about the character on the back. Allow class time for students to trade cards.

A Family Affair: Gods and Goddesses

According to the Greek myths, the divinities lived on Mount Olympus. Many of them traveled down to spend time with ordinary people. To the myth makers, a god or goddess was a powerful being, often identified with a force of nature.

Practice

The chart below shows some of the Greek and Roman gods and goddesses and their special powers. List the names of the divinities that you recognize. Can you think of any other Greek and Roman gods and goddesses you can add to your list? Now, write down whatever prior knowledge you have about the gods and goddesses on your list.

Greek Name	Roman Name	Area of Power
Zeus (zyo͞os)	Jupiter	king of the gods; sky; weather
Apollo (ə·päl′ō)	Apollo	the sun; youth; music; archery; healing; prophecy
Artemis (är′tə·mis)	Diana	twin sister of Apollo; the moon; hunting
Hades (hā′dēz′)	Pluto	king of the underworld
Poseidon (pō·sī′dən)	Neptune	ruler of the seas
Hera (hēr′ə)	Juno	wife of Zeus; queen of gods; women; marriage
Dionysus (dī′ə·nī′səs)	Bacchus	wine; fertility; music
Athena (ə·thē′nə)	Minerva	wisdom; war; crafts
Hephaestus (hē·fes′təs)	Vulcan	craftsman for the gods; fire
Hermes (hur′mēz)	Mercury	messenger god; secrets; tricks
Demeter (di·mēt′ər)	Ceres	agriculture; earth; corn
Persephone (pər·sef′ə·nē)	Proserpine	daughter of Demeter; queen of Hades

CROSS-CURRICULAR CONNECTIONS

Art
Illustrating the myths. As students read the myths in this collection, have them work in groups to create bumper stickers, comic strips, or posters for mythological characters.

SMALL GROUP

Drama
Performing the myths. If you have used the teaching idea in Apply, at right, students may wish to take one of the ideas for a modern myth and improvise a scene to perform for the class.

SMALL GROUP

Practice

After students have read the essay, ask them to name additional words, images, or expressions from Greek and Roman myths and epics that survive today. [Possible responses: the word *democracy*, which comes from the Greek word *dēmokratia* meaning "rule of the people"; the names of the planets and the months; the signs of the zodiac; the figure of Cupid on Valentine's Day cards; and expressions such as *Trojan horse* and *Achilles' heel*.]

Apply
To help students internalize the purposes of myths, have them plan "Myths for Today." Divide students into six small groups. Assign each group a different one of the six uses of mythology listed on p. 646. Ask students to provide examples for each use.

- Group 1 should specify whose point of view is being presented; for example, a kindergartner's explanation of creation.
- Group 2 should choose a phenomenon, such as a hurricane or a hailstorm.
- Group 3 should choose one custom, such as throwing rice during a wedding.
- Group 4 should select a moral or a practical lesson, such as "Crime doesn't pay."
- Group 5 should choose a historical topic, such as the causes of the Civil War, or an event such as the first moon landing.
- Group 6 should define the hope or fear expressed, such as the fear of being alone.

Then, have students brainstorm to come up with ideas for modern-day myths that could be used for their assigned purpose. When the brainstorming slows down, ask each group to reach a consensus on the idea it likes best. Encourage students to follow up by actually writing new myths.

HOMEWORK

The literary map on these pages presents the major geographical sites for the myths in this collection. The place names are real, but some of the events or characters that are named exist only in mythology. For example, Lydia, in modern Turkey, is identified as the region where King Midas rules. King Midas is a character in classical mythology, but there was also a real King Midas. (See p. 688.) Notice that the map also contains two insets:

- The inset at the lower left, on p. 648, shows the island of Sicily, which lies off the "toe" of Italy's "boot." (This part of Italy is visible at the far-left edge of the map.) The inset identifies Sicily as the mythical home of Persephone.

- The small inset midway on the right side of p. 649 shows where Greece lies in relation to the rest of the world as represented in world maps today.

The World of Classical Mythology

CROSS-CURRICULAR CONNECTIONS

Geography
Three-dimensional maps. As students read the myths in this collection, you might have them create their own dioramas or relief maps of the locale involved in a specific myth. They might use clay or papier-mâché and brightly color their dioramas or relief maps with tempera or watercolor paints.

INDIVIDUAL

Art
Compass rose. Note that the illustration on p. 649 that gives the directions *north, east, south,* and *west* is called a compass rose. Artistically inclined students might wish to create a compass rose of their own, employing design elements that appeal to their imaginations.

INDIVIDUAL

Propontis

Troy

ASIA MINOR

Lesbos

Orpheus buried

Chios

LYDIA
King Midas rules

Zeus and Hera
married here

Icaria

SAMOS

Icarus drowns

LEBINTHUS

Naxos

Rhodes

Greece

King Minos rules

Palace of Cnossus

Mount Ida

Childhood home
of Zeus

Apply

Have students find Sicily on the map and tell what mythic event takes place there. [Hades kidnaps Persephone.] Then, ask them to find the place where Hercules is born. [Thebes]

Next, give students five minutes to study the map. When time is up, have students close their books and try to answer questions such as the following three:

- Where were Zeus and Hera married? [Samos]
- Where is the Oracle of Delphi located? [near Mount Parnassus]
- Who rules the region known as Lydia? [King Midas]

Alternatively, you may want to have students work in pairs. Each student can ask his or her partner three questions before reversing roles.

Apply

Have students locate a map of modern Greece. Then, ask them to identify old place names that are still in use. [Ionian Sea, Aegean Sea, Gulf of Corinth, Sparta, Athens, Mount Olympus, Mount Parnassus]

HOMEWORK

The Myths of Greece and Rome: Insights into Our World   **649**

SKILLS FOCUS
pp. 650–653

Grade-Level Skills

■ **Reading Skills**
Analyze Greek and Latin roots and affixes.

OVERVIEW

Purpose. Learning the meanings of Greek and Latin word parts will help students decode unfamiliar words they encounter in their reading.

Use. Students can use this lesson on Latin and Greek roots and affixes to help determine meanings of unfamiliar words in any text. Also, students will find this lesson helpful when completing the Vocabulary Development activities in Collection 7.

Summary ⬌ *at grade level*

> This feature begins by providing students with an example of pig Latin and then explaining how to decode it. Students are then introduced to the process of decoding English words with Greek and Latin origins. Once students learn what certain Greek and Latin word parts mean, they can decipher a range of English words that use those parts.

Becoming Word-Wise

by Kylene Beers

Can you read the following sentence?

> **Ifay ouyay ancay eadray isthay, enthay ouyay ancay eadray igpay atinlay.**

Well, how did you do? If you know Pig Latin, then you probably did just fine. Pig Latin—not at all related to the Latin the ancient Romans spoke—requires you to take off the first letter (or sometimes letters) of a word, put that letter at the end of the word, and then add the long *a* sound (ā). So, *pig* becomes *igpay*. Once you figure out how words work in Pig Latin (owhay ordsway orkway inay igpay atinlay), then you can speak it, write it, read it, and understand it.

Building Your Vocabulary

Figuring out the meaning of words and how they work to make meaning is the key to mastering any language. Since many English words can be traced to Greek and Latin, if you can learn what **Greek** and **Latin roots** and **affixes** mean, you have a key to understanding many English words.

For instance, if you know that the Latin prefix *dis–* means "not" or "the opposite," you can figure out that the word *dislocate* means "put out of place" or "locate in a different place" (as in "dislocate a shoulder"). If you know that the Latin root *–aud–* means "hear," then you can guess that *audible* has something to do with hearing.

SKILLS FOCUS

Reading Skills
Understand Greek and Latin roots and affixes.

On the next pages are lists of common roots and affixes from Greek and Latin. Note their meanings. Note examples of how these roots and affixes are used to build English words. (*L* in the chart stands for "Latin"; *G* stands for "Greek.")

Remember . . .

Roots are the fundamental parts of a word. *–Loc–* is a Latin root for "place." *Locate* is based on the Latin root *–loc–*.

Affixes are word parts added to a root to alter its meaning.

Prefixes are affixes added to the front of a word (*dis*locate).

Suffixes are affixes added to the end of a word (loca*tion*).

DIFFERENTIATING INSTRUCTION

Learners Having Difficulty

Before they begin studying the charts on pp. 651–652, review with students the meanings of *root, prefix,* and *suffix.* Then, write the following words on the chalkboard, underlining the indicated word parts:

re<u>play</u> [prefix]   <u>magni</u>fy [suffix]
<u>excite</u>ment [suffix]   <u>instruc</u>tor [root]
<u>review</u> [root]   <u>reveng</u>e [root]
<u>trans</u>late [prefix]   <u>suit</u>able [suffix]
<u>im</u>pact [prefix]

Have students identify each underlined word part as a root, a prefix, or a suffix. Then, challenge them to identify the other parts of each word. For example, the first word on the list, *replay,* contains the root *–play–* as well as the prefix *re–*.

English-Language Learners

Students' native languages may contain some of the Greek and Latin roots listed on p. 651. For example, the Spanish word for *hand* is *mano,* which is derived from the

Latin root *–man–*. Have students review the list, considering each root in turn. Invite them to share with the rest of the class words from their languages of origin that contain any of the roots and also to explain the meanings of those words.

Advanced Learners

Enrichment. Tell students that the history of a word—how it got from its original form to the form we use today—is called a

GREEK AND LATIN ROOTS AND AFFIXES

Commonly Used Roots Ⓐ

Root	Meanings	Examples
–act– (L)	act	action, actor, react, transact, enact
–aud– (L)	hear	audience, auditorium, audible, audition
–bio– (G)	life	biology, biography, biofeedback, bionics
–cred– (L)	believe; trust	credit, discredit, credible, credulous
–dem– (G)	people	democracy, Democrat, demographics
–dic– (L)	speak; say	dictate, predict, contradict, verdict, diction
–geo– (G)	earth	geography, geology
–graph– (G)	write; draw;	autograph, paragraph, phonograph, photograph, telegraph
–loc– (L)	place	allocate, locate, location
–man– (L)	hand	manual, manufacture, manuscript, manipulate
–ped– (L)	foot	pedal, pedestrian, pedestal
–pop– (L)	people; nation	population, popular, populace
–port– (L)	carry	import, export, portable, porter, transport
–sign– (L)	mark; sign	insignia, signal, significant, signature
–spec– (L)	see; look at	inspect, respect, spectacle, spectator, suspect
–tract– (L)	pull; drag	attract, detract, contract, subtract, traction, tractor
–vid– (L)	see; look	evidence, video, provide, providence
–volv– (L)	roll	evolve, involve, revolve, revolver, revolution

---

PRETEACHING

Selection Starter

Motivate. Ask students if they have ever seen a film or a video of an automobile being manufactured. If so, have them describe what they remember about the process. Point out that cars of a similar model all begin with the same frame. Added to that frame are the mechanical parts (the engine, gas tank, and so on), the interior pieces (seats, dashboard components, floorboards, and so on), and the exterior pieces (fenders, antennas, windshield wipers, and so on). Depending on the kinds of parts added, frames that are identical in the beginning can be turned into very different cars with very different personalities and capabilities.

Next, explain that words are built in a similar fashion. You can begin with a basic word part called a root, which is like the frame of a car. To that root you can then add different parts called affixes. As with cars, these extra parts can change identical roots into words with different meanings and functions.

DIRECT TEACHING

Ⓐ Vocabulary Note

Greek and Latin roots. Have students use dictionaries to locate other words that contain the roots on p. 651. For example, if students look up *bio–*, they will find the words *biohazard, biome,* and *biotechnology.* As students identify additional words, have them explain how each word's meaning relates to the meaning of its root.

Ⓑ Reading Skills and Strategies

Identify. [Roots can go in the beginning ("activate"), middle ("attraction"), or end ("transact") of the new words they help form.]

---

word's etymology. Write the following sample etymology for the word *democracy* on the board:

[Fr. *démocratie* < ML *democratia* < Gr *dēmokratia* < *dēmos,* the people + *kratein,* to rule < *kratos,* strength]

Guide students to see that English inherited the word *democracy* from French, which in turn inherited its form of the word from Latin, which in turn inherited its form of the word from Greek.

Activity. Have students choose one of the example words listed in the third column of the chart on this page, or assign a different word to each student. Using a dictionary, students can then prepare an etymology of their word using the same format as the one for *democracy* at the left. Have students translate the etymology into "regular English" by writing two or three sentences explaining it. Students can then share their etymologies in small groups.

DIRECT TEACHING

A Reading Skills and Strategies

Identify. [A prefix would be found at the beginning of a word.]

B Vocabulary Note

Word parts. Point out that the prefix *in–* or *im–* can also mean "not," as in the words *insensitive* and *impassable.* Have students tell which meaning applies to the prefix in each of the following words: *immeasurable* [not]; *insincere* [not]; *intrude* [into]; *inject* [into].

C Reading Skills and Strategies

Identify. [A suffix would be found at the end of a word.]

A **IDENTIFY**

In what part of a word would you find a **prefix**? Hint: The meaning for the prefix *pre–* will give you the answer.

C **IDENTIFY**

In what part of a word would you find a **suffix**?

Commonly Used Prefixes

Prefix	Meanings	Examples
anti– (G)	against; opposing	antiwar, anticlimax
bi– (L)	two	bisect, bimonthly
co– (L)	with; together	coexist, codependent
de– (L)	away from; off; down	debrief, debug
dia– (G)	through; across; between	diameter, diagonal
in–, im– (L)	in; into; within	introduce, imprison
inter– (L)	between; among	interpersonal, intersect
non– (L)	not	nonprofit, nonfat
post– (L)	after; following	postnasal, postgraduate
pre– (L)	before	prepayment, preview
re– (L)	back; backward; again	reverse, return, recur
sub– (L)	under; beneath	submarine, substandard
syl–, sym–, syn–, sys– (G)	together; with	syllable, symmetric, synthesis, system
trans– (L)	across	transplant, translate

Commonly Used Suffixes

Suffix	Meanings	Examples
–able (L)	able; likely	readable, lovable
–ance, –ancy (L)	act; quality	admittance, constancy
–ate (L)	to become; to cause; to be	captivate, activate
–fy (L)	to make; to cause; to be	liquefy, simplify
–ible (L)	able; likely	flexible, digestible
–ity (L)	state; condition	reality, sincerity
–ize (L)	to make; to cause; to be	socialize, motorize
–ment (L)	result; act of; state of being	judgment, fulfillment
–ous (L)	characterized by	dangerous, malicious
–tion (L)	action; condition	rotation, election

CROSS-CURRICULAR CONNECTIONS

Culture

Romance languages. Explain to students that when the Romans conquered much of the Western world (including what is now Europe, North Africa, and the Middle East), they also imposed their language on the inhabitants of these places. During the years of Roman control, the Latin language that was spoken in different regions gradually evolved into separate but similar languages. Today these languages—French, Spanish, Portuguese, Italian, and Romanian—are called Romance languages, meaning "from the Roman."

Although English is not a Romance language, about 60 percent of its vocabulary comes from Latin. This is due largely to an important historical event known as the Norman Conquest. When William the Conqueror invaded England from Normandy, in France, he brought the French language with him. As a result, French—and its parent language, Latin—greatly influenced the formation of the modern English we speak today.

Practice the Strategy 📖

Building Your Vocabulary

You can increase your vocabulary by building "vocabulary trees" from the root up. For an example of a vocabulary tree, look below at the tree a student made using the root *–cred–*. Here are the steps you can follow to create your own vocabulary tree:

1. On a piece of paper, draw a tree like the one below, and put a word root from the chart on page 651 in the root section of the tree.

2. In the trunk, put one word from the "Examples" column that uses that root, and define the word.

3. In the branches, put other words that you hear or read or use in your own writing that come from that root.

4. On the twigs of the branches, explain how you used that word or where you read it.

5. Add as many branches as possible to your vocabulary tree.

📖 In whatever you read, use your knowledge of Greek and Latin roots and affixes to help you figure out the meaning of unfamiliar words.

Strategy Tip

To figure out the meaning of an unfamiliar word when a dictionary is not nearby:

- **Say the word aloud.** Once you hear it, you may recognize it.

- **Break the word apart.** What is the root? Does it have a prefix or suffix?

- **Think about the context.** Look for clues to the word's meaning in the surrounding words.

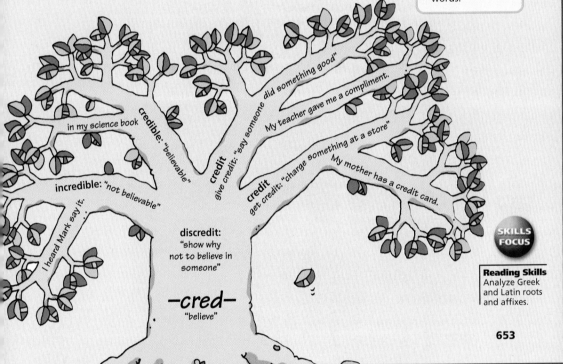

credible: "believable"
in my science book
incredible: "not believable"
I heard Mark say it...
credit: give credit: "say someone did something good"
My teacher gave me a compliment.
credit: get credit: "charge something at a store"
My mother has a credit card.
discredit: "show why not to believe in someone"

–cred–
"believe"

SKILLS FOCUS

Reading Skills
Analyze Greek and Latin roots and affixes.

653

Practice the Strategy

Strategy Tip

You may want to have students create two trees: one containing a common root that is used in many words they know, and another containing a less common root that is used in fewer words they know. Creating the first tree will familiarize them with the process, and creating the second tree will help them extend their vocabulary.

Strategy Tip

Remind students to draw trees with roots, trunks, branches, and twigs large enough to write in.

Strategy Tip

As an alternative to step 4, students can write sentences that contain the word and that provide clues to its meaning.

MINI-LESSON **Reading**

Reviewing Word-Attack Skills

Activity. Have students choose the correct word in each pair to complete the sentence. Then, have them identify the word's prefix or suffix and tell what it means.

1. When Jill flies to Paris next month, it will be her third (transatlantic / subatlantic) trip. [transatlantic; *trans–* is a prefix meaning "across"]

2. If you sleep in class, you will (infurify / infuriate) the teacher. [infuriate; *–ate* is a suffix meaning "to become" or "to cause"]

3. In order to finish the project, we must all (cooperate / deoperate). [cooperate; *co–* is a prefix meaning "together"]

4. Football fans usually enjoy watching the (pregame / postgame) show before the Super Bowl. [pregame; *pre–* is a prefix meaning "before"]

5. Her actions were (couragement / courageous). [courageous; *–ous* is a suffix meaning "characterized by"]

Grade-Level Skills

■ **Literary Skills**
Analyze origin myths.

■ **Reading Skills**
Analyze text structures, including cause and effect.

Review Skills

■ **Literary Skills**
Identify different forms of fiction, and describe the main characteristics of each form.

Summary ⇄ *at grade level*

This is a modern retelling of an ancient Greek origin myth explaining why the earth has seasons. Demeter is goddess of the harvest. The laughter of her daughter, Persephone, resounds even in the ears of gloomy Hades, who presides over the land of the dead. Hades goes to Zeus on Olympus and asks if he can have Persephone for his wife. When Zeus agrees, Hades whisks Persephone away to his bleak domain. Grief-stricken at her daughter's disappearance, Demeter neglects her harvest duties, and the earth is threatened by famine. Zeus sends Hermes to Hades to arrange for Persephone's release. The crafty Hades coaxes Persephone to eat seven pomegranate seeds before she departs. For the seven seeds eaten, Persephone must spend seven months of every year in Hades. But during the other five months, the earth rejoices at her presence in verdant splendor.

Before You Read The Myth

The Origin of the Seasons

Make the Connection
Quickwrite ✏️

Ancient people looked to myths for answers to questions about the natural world, just as we look to science today. The ancients wondered, for example, why there were seasons. What do you know about the seasons in the area where you live? Is there anything about the seasons you don't understand? Write down your responses.

Literary Focus
Origin Myths

The ancient Greeks did not possess the scientific knowledge we have today. Still, they were as curious about their natural surroundings as we are about ours. They longed for explanations. Why do we have so many different kinds of flowers? Why is there night and day? Why do the seasons change? For answers to their questions, the ancient people turned to their myth makers.

They believed these storytellers were directly in touch with the source of all knowledge—the gods. The myth makers were the guardians of a tradition with the same purpose as science: to provide explanations of how the world works. **Origin myths** are the special type of myths that give an explanation for how something came to be.

Reading Skills 📖
Understanding Cause and Effect

Since origin myths explain how something came about, they tell about causes and their effects. Often, the gods do something that causes an effect on Earth. Sometimes the cause-and-effect chain begins on Earth: People do something that causes the gods to react. The way the gods react then has an effect on Earth. As you read the myth "The Origin of the Seasons," notice the chain of cause and effect that results in the cycle of seasons on Earth.

Literary Skills
Understand origin myths.

Reading Skills
Understand cause and effect.

Pomegranates.

The Origin of the Seasons

retold by Olivia Coolidge

Demeter, the great earth mother, was goddess of the harvest. Tall and majestic was her appearance, and her hair was the color of ripe wheat. It was she who filled the ears with grain. In her honor white-robed women brought golden garlands of wheat as first fruits to the altar. Reaping, threshing, winnowing,[1] and the long tables set in the shade for the harvesters' refreshment—all these were hers. Songs and feasting did her honor as the hard-working farmer gathered his abundant fruit. All the laws which the farmer knew came from her: the time for plowing, what land would best bear crops, which was fit for grapes, and which to leave for pasture. She was a goddess whom men called the great mother because of her generosity in giving. Her own special daughter in the family of the gods was named Persephone. ❶

>
> **CAUSE AND EFFECT**
> ❶ As goddess of the harvest, what **effects** does Demeter have on the Earth?

1. **reaping:** cutting and gathering the grain; **threshing** and **winnowing:** two ways of separating the grain from the husks.

Persephone was the spring maiden, young and full of joy. Sicily was her home, for it is a land where the spring is long and lovely, and where spring flowers are abundant. Here Persephone played with her maidens from day to day till the rocks and valleys rang with the sound of laughter, and gloomy Hades heard it as he sat on his throne in the dark land of the dead. Even his heart of stone was touched by her young beauty, so that he arose in his awful majesty and came up to Olympus to ask Zeus if he might have Persephone to wife. Zeus bowed his head in agreement, and mighty Olympus thundered as he promised. ❷

Thus it came about that as Persephone was gathering flowers with her maidens in the vale of Enna, a marvelous thing happened. Enna was a beautiful valley in whose meadows all the most lovely flowers of the year grew at the same season. There were wild roses, purple crocuses, sweet-scented violets, tall iris, rich

> **INFER**
> ❷ Who is Persephone? What season might she represent? Why do you think Hades wants her to be his bride?

The Origin of the Seasons **655**

❓ **Descriptive language.** Which words in this passage help you to picture the action? Find three nouns, three verbs, and three adjectives. [Possible responses: Nouns—*meadow, narcissus, root, blossoms, chariot, roses, lilies, turf;* Verbs—*picking, calling, strayed, beheld, sprang, stretched, shrieked, cascaded, swept;* Adjectives—*blossoming, marvelous, beautiful, sweet, precious, dark-eyed, golden, coal-black, rumbling, wild, grassy*]

B Reading Skills

Retell. [Possible response to question 3: Gathering flowers in a meadow, Persephone strays from her companions. She sees a strange, beautiful flower with a hundred blooms and reaches out to pluck it, but it transforms into a stranger and traps her within its embrace. The stranger is Hades who sweeps Persephone into his chariot and carries her away to the underworld before her companions know what has happened.]

C Literary Focus

Origin myths. Point out that the reference to Phoebus Apollo's chariot connects with another myth. Ancient Greeks believed that Phoebus Apollo (sometimes identified with Helios, the sun god) drove his chariot across the heavens, giving light to the world.

D Reading Skills

Retell. [Possible response to question 4: Phoebus Apollo tells Demeter that Hades abducted Persephone.]

E Reading Skills

❓ **Identify cause and effect.** What effect does Persephone's abduction have on Demeter? [Possible response: Demeter falls into deep despair and takes on the form of an old woman.]

---

narcissus,[2] and white lilies. All these the girl was gathering, yet fair as they were, Persephone herself was fairer far.

As the maidens went picking and calling to one another across the blossoming meadow, it happened that Persephone strayed apart from the rest. Then, as she looked a little ahead in the meadow, she suddenly beheld the marvelous thing. It was a flower so beautiful that none like it had ever been known. It seemed a kind of narcissus, purple and white, but from a single root there sprang a hundred blossoms, and at the sweet scent of it the very heavens and earth appeared to smile for joy. Without calling to the others, Persephone sprang forward to be the first to pick the precious bloom. As she stretched out her hand, the earth opened in front of her, and she found herself caught in a stranger's arms. Persephone shrieked aloud and struggled, while the armful of flowers cascaded down to earth. However, the dark-eyed Hades was far stronger than she. He swept her into his golden chariot, took the reins of his coal-black horses, and was gone amid the rumbling sound of the closing earth before the other girls in the valley could even come in sight of the spot. When they did get there, nobody was visible. Only the roses and lilies of Persephone lay scattered in wild confusion over the grassy turf. ❸ 📖

Bitter was the grief of Demeter when she heard the news of her daughter's mysterious fate. Veiling herself

RETELL
❸ **Retell** the story of Persephone's disappearance.

with a dark cloud, she sped, swift as a wild bird, over land and ocean for nine days, searching everywhere and asking all she met if they had seen her daughter. Neither gods nor men had seen her. Even the birds could give no tidings, and Demeter in despair turned to Phoebus Apollo, who sees all things from his chariot in the heavens.

"Yes, I have seen your daughter," said the god at last. "Hades has taken her with the consent of Zeus, that she may dwell in the land of mist and gloom as his queen. The girl struggled and was unwilling, but Hades is far stronger than she." ❹ 📖

When she heard this, Demeter fell into deep despair, for she knew she could never rescue Persephone if Zeus and Hades had agreed. She did not care any more to enter the palace of Olympus, where the gods live in joy and feasting and where Apollo plays the lyre while the Muses sing. She took on her the form of an old woman, worn but stately, and wandered about the earth, where there is much sorrow to be seen. At first she kept away from the homes of people, since the sight of little children and happy mothers gave her pain. One day, however, as she sat by the side of a well to rest her weary feet, four girls came down to draw water. They were kind hearted and charming as they talked with her and concerned themselves about the fate of the homeless stranger-woman who was sitting at their

RETELL
❹ What news does Phoebus Apollo, the sun god, give to Demeter?

---

2. **narcissus** (när·sis′əs): family of lilies including daffodils and jonquils. "Echo and Narcissus" (page 290) gives the ancient Greeks' explanation of how this flower came to be.

La Primavera: Flora (detail) (1477) by Sandro Botticelli. Uffizi Gallery, Florence, Italy. Erich Lessing/Art Resource, NY.

VIEWING THE ART

Sandro Botticelli (1444–1510) of Florence helped to define the Italian Renaissance. Born Alessandro di Mariano Filipepi, he came under the early influence of Andrea del Verrocchio and Antonio Pollaiuolo. Less concerned with a precise representation of space and perspective than other Italian painters of the period, he created work notable for its boldly imaginative, free-flowing approach. He portrayed subjects drawn from ancient mythology with lush sensuality, as in this detail from *La Primavera: Flora.*

Activity. Have students study the details from Botticelli's work on pp. 657 and 659–660. Ask them to cite specific details that relate the painting to "The Origin of the Seasons." [Possible response: The young woman could easily be Persephone, the personification of spring, and the detail showing flowers could be the field from which Hades abducts her.] You might also have students collect other artistic representations of the four seasons and compare

DEVELOPING FLUENCY

Activity. Have students work together in small groups to write and perform sketches based on scenes from the story. The sketches may be based on passages of dialogue or action. Suggest that the groups choose one member to act as a narrator who introduces and explains the sketch, while the other members take individual or choral parts. Encourage students to include sound effects and background music when they present their sketches to the class.

SMALL GROUP

A **Reading Skills**

❓ **Infer.** How does the baby Demophoon affect Demeter? [Possible response: The baby helps her temporarily forget her sadness about the loss of Persephone.]

B **Reading Skills**

Cause and effect. [Possible responses to question 5: The baby's charm convinces Demeter to become his nurse. His good nature causes Demeter to want to care for him and keep him as her own.]

C **Vocabulary Note**

Word origins. Point out that the word *ambrosia* as used in mythology means "food and ointment of the gods." Today the word describes any food that is especially delicious. It is also the name of a dessert made from coconut and oranges.

D **Learners Having Difficulty**

❓ **Use prior knowledge.** How is it possible for Demeter to place Demophoon in the fire without burning him? [She is one of the goddesses from Olympus, and she uses her divine powers to protect, strengthen, and transform the baby.]

gates. To account for herself, Demeter told them that she was a woman of good family from Crete, across the sea, who had been captured by pirates and was to have been sold for a slave. She had escaped as they landed once to cook a meal on shore, and now she was wandering to find work.

A The four girls listened to this story, much impressed by the stately manner of the strange woman. At last they said that their mother, Metaneira,[3] was looking for a nurse for their new-born brother, Demophoon.[4] Perhaps the stranger would come and talk with her. Demeter agreed, feeling a great longing to hold a baby once more, even if it were not her own. She went therefore to Metaneira, who was much struck with the quiet dignity of the goddess and glad to give her charge of her little son. For a while thereafter Demeter was nurse to Demophoon, and his smiles and babble consoled her in some part for her own darling daughter. She began to make plans for Demophoon: He should be a great hero; he should become an immortal, so that when he grew up she could keep him with her. **5**

📖 **CAUSE AND EFFECT**

B **5** Explain what **causes** Demeter to become Demophoon's nurse.

C Presently the whole household was amazed at how beautiful Demophoon was growing, the more so as they never saw the nurse feed him anything. Secretly Demeter would anoint him with ambrosia,[5] like the gods, and from her breath, as he lay in her lap, he would draw his

nourishment. When the night came, she would linger by the great fireside in the hall, rocking the child in her arms while the embers burned low and the people went off to sleep. Then, when all was still, she would stoop quickly down and put the baby into the fire itself. All night long the child would sleep **D** in the red-hot ashes, while his earthly flesh and blood changed slowly into the substance of the immortals. In the morning when people came, the ashes were cold and dead, and by the hearth sat the stranger-woman, gently rocking and singing to the child.

Presently Metaneira became suspicious of the strangeness of it all. What did she know of this nurse but the story she had heard from her daughters? Perhaps the woman was a witch of some sort who wished to steal or transform the boy. In any case it was wise to be careful. One night, therefore, when she went up to her chamber, she set the door ajar and stood there in the crack silently watching the nurse at the fireside crooning over the child. The hall was very dark, so that it was hard to see clearly, but in a little while the mother beheld the dim figure bend forward. A log broke in the fireplace, a little flame shot up, and there clear in the light lay the baby on top of the fire.

Metaneira screamed loudly and lost no time in rushing forward, but it was Demeter who snatched up the baby. "Fool that you are," she said indignantly to Metaneira, "I would have made your son immortal, but that is now impossible. He shall be a great hero, but in the end he will have to die. I, the goddess Demeter, promise it." With that

---

3. **Metaneira** (met′ə·nē′rə).
4. **Demophoon** (de·mäf′ō·än′).
5. **ambrosia** (am·brō′zhə): food of the gods.

La Primavera: Flora (detail) (1477) by Sandro Botticelli.
Uffizi Gallery, Florence, Italy. © Erich Lessing/Art Resource, NY.

Learners Having Difficulty
Some students may have difficulty following the story's multiple plot threads. To help them connect the subplot about Demophoon with the main plot about Persephone, tell them ahead of time to watch for a smaller story within the main story. Draw a story map on the chalkboard, and indicate where Demophoon's tale

begins and ends. After students have read the story, discuss how the tale of Demophoon relates to the main story.

English-Language Learners
For lessons designed for English-language learners, see *Holt Reading Solutions.*

VIEWING THE ART

Remind students that the illustrations on pp. 657, 659, and 660 are details from a larger painting by **Sandro Botticelli,** titled *La Primavera.* If possible, display a print of the whole painting to help students see how the pieces fit into it. They may be familiar with another of Botticelli's works, *Birth of Venus.*

Activity. Here are some questions you might ask students about the painting:

- Which details in the painting strike you the most?
- Whom does the portrait remind you of?
- Does the woman in the detail of the painting look as if she represents or is part of the natural world?

Special Education Students

Special education students who are having trouble with the story within the story may be better able to focus on the main events of the plot if they read the frame story about Persephone first. When they reach the end of the last full paragraph on page 656, provide a brief summary of what has happened. Then, have students resume their reading with the first full paragraph on page 661.

old age fell from her and she grew in stature. Golden hair spread down over her shoulders so that the great hall was filled with light. She turned and went out of the doorway, leaving the baby on the ground and Metaneira too amazed and frightened even to take him up. **6**

A

CAUSE AND EFFECT
6 What **causes** Metaneira to become suspicious of Demeter? What is the **effect** of Metaneira's suspicion?

All the while that Demeter had been wandering, she had given no thought to her duties as the harvest goddess. Instead she was almost glad that others should suffer because she was suffering. In vain the oxen spent their strength in dragging the heavy plowshare[6] through the soil. In vain did the sower with his bag of grain throw out the even handfuls of white barley in a wide arc as he strode. The greedy birds had a feast off the seed corn that season; or if it started to sprout, sun baked it and rains washed it away. Nothing would grow. As the gods looked down, they saw threatening the earth a famine such as never had been known. Even the offerings to the gods were neglected by despairing men who could no longer spare anything from their dwindling stores. **7**

B

CAUSE AND EFFECT
7 Demeter is no longer acting as goddess of the harvest. List some **effects** of her neglect.

At last Zeus sent Iris, the rainbow, to seek out Demeter and

---

6. **plowshare:** cutting blade of a plow.

La Primavera: Flora (detail) (1477) by Sandro Botticelli.

Uffizi Gallery, Florence, Italy. © Erich Lessing/Art Resource, NY.

appeal to her to save mankind. Dazzling Iris swept down from Olympus swift as a ray of light and found Demeter sitting in her temple, the dark cloak still around her and her head bowed on her hand. Though Iris urged her with the messages of Zeus and offered beautiful gifts or whatever powers among the gods she chose, Demeter would not lift her head or listen. All she said was that she would neither set foot on Olympus nor let fruit grow on the earth until Persephone was restored to her from the kingdom of the dead.

At last Zeus saw that he must send Hermes of the golden sandals to bring back Persephone to the light. The messenger found dark-haired Hades sitting upon his throne with Persephone, pale and sad, beside him. She had neither eaten nor drunk since she had been in the land of the dead. She sprang up with joy at the message of Hermes, while the dark king looked gloomier than ever, for he really loved his queen. Though he could not disobey the command of Zeus, he was crafty, and he pressed Persephone to eat or drink with him as they parted. Now, with joy in her heart, she should not refuse all food. Persephone was eager to be gone, but since the king entreated her, she took a pomegranate[7] from him to avoid argument and delay. Giving in to his pleading, she ate seven of the seeds. Then Hermes took her with him, and she came out into the upper air.

When Demeter saw Hermes with her daughter, she started up, and Persephone too rushed forward with a glad cry and flung her arms about her mother's neck. For a long time the two caressed each other, but at last Demeter began to question the girl. "Did you eat or drink anything with Hades?" she asked her daughter anxiously, and the girl replied:

"Nothing until Hermes released me. Then in my joy I took a pomegranate and ate seven of its seeds."

"Alas," said the goddess in dismay, "my daughter, what have you done? The Fates have said that if you ate anything in the land of shadow, you must return to Hades and rule with him as his queen. However, you ate not the whole pomegranate, but only seven of the seeds. For seven months of the year, therefore, you must dwell in the underworld, and the remaining five you may live with me."

Thus the Fates had decreed, and even Zeus could not alter their law. For seven months of every year, Persephone is lost to Demeter and rules pale and sad over the dead. At this time Demeter mourns, trees shed their leaves, cold comes, and the earth lies still and dead. But when, in the eighth month, Persephone returns, her mother is glad and the earth rejoices. The wheat springs up, bright, fresh, and green in the plowland. Flowers unfold, birds sing, and young animals are born. Everywhere the heavens smile for joy or weep sudden showers of gladness upon the springing earth. ⑧

CAUSE AND EFFECT
⑧ What **effect** did Persephone's eating seven pomegranate seeds have on the Earth?

---

7. **pomegranate** (päm′ə·gran′it): round, red fruit containing many seeds that can be eaten. Pomegranates are pictured on page 654.

After You Read

First Thoughts

1. Possible answer: They seem self-centered and spoiled. They are more powerful than humans, but they are not more kind.

Thinking Critically

2. Demeter's mood guides the seasons. When Persephone is with her, Demeter's joy brings both spring and summer; when Persephone is in the underworld, Demeter's sorrow brings fall and winter.

3. Because her own child is gone, Demeter may want another child to care for.

4. Possible answer: Without her generosity, all people will starve, so even the king of the gods must respect her wishes. She is a powerful force.

Extending Interpretations

5. Possible answer: I feel sorriest for Persephone, because Hades kidnaps her and then tricks her into staying with him in the underworld for more than half of every year.

6. Possible answers: "Hansel and Gretel," "Goldilocks and the Three Bears," and the story of Adam and Eve from the Book of Genesis in the Bible.

After You Read Response and Analysis

First Thoughts

1. What are your first impressions of the gods and goddesses in this myth? What do you think of the way they treat one another and the people on Earth?

Thinking Critically

2. How does this story of the kidnapping of a young girl and her mother's grief explain the change of seasons on Earth?

3. Why do you think Demeter spends so much time with the baby Demophoon, even planning to make him immortal?

4. Demeter is able to force Zeus to change his mind about the marriage of Hades and Persephone. What does this tell you about "the great earth mother"?

Extending Interpretations

5. Which character in this myth do you feel the most sympathy for? Why?

6. What other stories do you know of in which someone eats a forbidden food—or breaks a taboo (a rule strictly prohibiting something) and pays dearly for it?

WRITING

Writing an Origin Myth

Throughout the world, people have told imaginative stories to explain the cycle of seasons. Write your own origin myth explaining why the seasons change as they do in your part of the world. If you live in a region where the weather rarely changes, tell how this came to be. You may find ideas for your myth in your Quickwrite notes.

Reading Check

Many events in this ancient myth are connected by **cause and effect.** Describe the effect of each event listed below:

a. Gloomy Hades falls in love with beautiful young Persephone.

Effect:

b. Unhappy about the loss of her daughter, Demeter gives no thought to her duties as the harvest goddess.

Effect:

c. Demeter vows that she will not let fruit grow on the earth until Persephone is returned.

Effect:

d. While in the land of the dead, Persephone eats seven seeds from a piece of fruit.

Effect:

Reading Check

a. Hades kidnaps Persephone and takes her to the underworld.

b. Nothing will grow; famine threatens; humans stop making offerings to the gods.

c. The gods become upset; Zeus sends Hermes to the underworld to arrange for the return of Persephone.

d. Persephone must spend seven months of each year in the underworld.

English Prefixes Derived from Greek

A **prefix** is a word part that is added to the beginning of a word to change the word's meaning. Many prefixes that we use today come from ancient Greek. Some common ones appear in the first column of the chart below. The first row of the chart is filled in for you.

PRACTICE

Use a dictionary to complete the rest of the chart.

	Meaning	Example
anti-	against	antidote: something that acts against a poison
auto-		
hydro-		
meta-		
sym- or syn-		

Descriptive Words

In "The Origin of the Seasons," Hades drives Persephone into a hole in the ground. Here's how Coolidge describes the scene:

"He swept her into his golden chariot, took the reins of his coal-black horses, and was gone amid the rumbling sound of the closing earth. . . ."

This sentence creates a rich picture because it uses **descriptive words.** In good descriptive writing you find

- *concrete, specific nouns:* It isn't just a *vehicle*—it's a *chariot.*

- **precise verbs:** He didn't just *put* her in—he *swept* her in.

- **vivid adjectives** that appeal to the senses: The horses are *coal-black;* the earth makes a *rumbling* sound.

PRACTICE

Rewrite each of the sentences below, using descriptive language. Remember to use specific nouns, precise verbs, and vivid adjectives.

1. Persephone lived in a perfectly nice place.

2. Some horses went by, making a lot of noise.

3. Poor Persephone sat on a throne.

SKILLS FOCUS

Vocabulary Skills
Understand Greek prefixes; use descriptive words.

Vocabulary Development

English Prefixes

PRACTICE

Possible Answers

- *auto*– *Meaning*—"self"; *Example*—autobiography: a self-told life story
- *hydro*– *Meaning*—"water"; *Example*—hydroelectricity: energy from water power
- *meta*– *Meaning*—"change"; *Example*—metamorphosis: change in form
- *sym*– or *syn*– *Meaning*—"same"; *Example*—synonyms: words with the same meaning

Descriptive Words

PRACTICE

Possible Answers

1. Persephone played on a flower-covered island in a blue sea.
2. Four black stallions came thundering up out of the earth.
3. Sorrowful Persephone slumped on her silver throne.

ASSESSING

Assessment

- *Holt Assessment: Literature, Reading, and Vocabulary*

DIFFERENTIATING INSTRUCTION

Learners Having Difficulty
To reinforce students' facility with descriptive language, have them replace each of the underlined words in the sentences below with a more specific noun, precise verb, or a vivid adjective. [Possible responses are in brackets.]

1. When she flipped the switch, the rocket <u>went</u> into the air. [blasted, roared]

2. This restaurant serves curry that is really <u>hot</u>. [fiery]

3. Because she was a queen, she lived in a huge, beautiful <u>house</u>. [palace, mansion]

4. I watched helplessly as the ball <u>broke</u> the window. [shattered]

5. A <u>faint</u> sound surged softly through the crowd when the lights dimmed. [murmuring]

Summary *at grade level*

In this Greek myth the hero, Orpheus, produces music no being can resist. He is madly in love with the nymph Eurydice. On their wedding day she is bitten by a snake and dies. Grieving, Orpheus descends into Hades to find her. His song so mesmerizes the denizens of the underworld that even Hades is moved. He tells Orpheus to flee the underworld while its guardians remain entranced. Hades will permit Eurydice to follow—unless Orpheus looks back. Orpheus cautiously ascends, torn by inner conflict and worried about trickery. Just as he approaches daylight, he swirls to look back, and as he reaches for Eurydice, she vanishes in a puff of smoke. He hurries down again, but the guardians bar his way. For seven days he grieves in silence on the banks of the river Styx, and then he ascends to earth. Sorrow lends his music even greater power, but he scorns all listeners. At last, angered by the god Dionysus, the women of Thrace kill him. His spirit is united with that of Eurydice in the daffodil meadows of Elysium, where they walk together forever.

Orpheus, the Great Musician

Make the Connection
Quickwrite ✏️

"Great music can pull you right out of your chair. It can make you cry, or laugh, or feel a way you've never felt before."
—Nadja Salerno-Sonnenberg

Think of a time when music touched your life. Write briefly about the experience.

Literary Focus
The Underworld of Myth

You don't have to read many myths before you find yourself in that frightful place called the underworld. As you know from "The Origin of the Seasons," the underworld is a dark and gloomy place ruled by the stern god Hades. To reach Hades' home, you cross the River Styx (stiks) on a ferryboat rowed by Charon (ker′ən). Then you pass through gates guarded by Cerberus (sur′bər·əs), a three-headed dog. Normally only the souls of the dead go to Hades. Sometimes, however, living people attempt the dangerous journey, usually to reach someone who has died.

INTERNET
Vocabulary
Activity
Keyword: LE5 7-6

Reading Skills
Summarizing

SKILLS FOCUS

Literary Skills
Identify elements
of myth: the
underworld.

Reading Skills
Summarize.

In a summary, you mention only the most important information in a text.

The tricky part of **summarizing** is deciding what to include and what to leave out. When you summarize a myth, be sure to include:

- the title
- the author (the one who retells the myth)
- the main characters
- the conflict
- the main events
- the resolution

Vocabulary Development

Here are some of the words you'll learn as you read the myth.

inconsolable (in′kən·sōl′ə·bəl) *adj.:* unable to be comforted; brokenhearted. *Orpheus was inconsolable and could not be comforted when his true love died.*

ghastly (gast′lē) *adj.:* horrible; ghostlike. *People shudder in fear when they enter the ghastly halls of the underworld.*

reluctance (ri·luk′təns) *n.:* unwillingness. *His reluctance to live without his love led him to brave the underworld.*

ascended (ə·send′id) *v.:* moved up. *They ascended the long narrow path up the mountain.*

RESOURCES: READING

Planning
■ *One-Stop Planner* CD-ROM with ExamView Test Generator

Differentiating Instruction
■ *Holt Reading Solutions*
■ *Supporting Instruction in Spanish*
■ *Audio CD Library*
■ *Audio CD Library, Selections and Summaries in Spanish*

Vocabulary
■ *Vocabulary Development*

Grammar and Language
■ *Daily Language Activities*

Assessment
■ *Holt Assessment: Literature, Reading, and Vocabulary*
■ *One-Stop Planner* CD-ROM with ExamView Test Generator

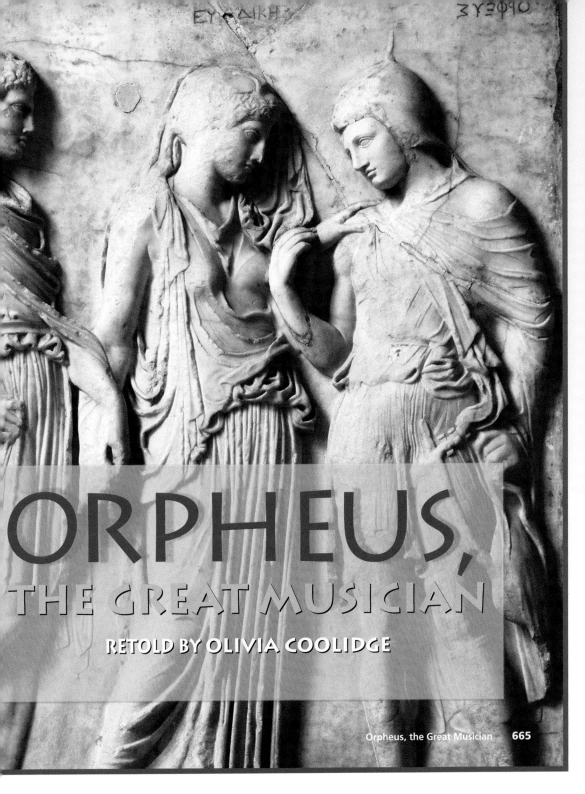

ORPHEUS, THE GREAT MUSICIAN

RETOLD BY OLIVIA COOLIDGE

Orpheus, the Great Musician **665**

VIEWING THE ART

Orpheus, Eurydice, and Hermes, the Roman sculpture shown on this page, is a relief—a form of sculpture in which figures are set off from a flat background. Rome's military conquest of Greece, in the second century B.C., was counterbalanced by Greece's, cultural conquest of Rome. The educated Greek slaves who filled teaching posts in Roman schools instilled in their students a love for Homer's epics and made the Greek language essential to Roman aristocrats and scholars. Greek influence swept over the arts. Many Roman sculptors churned out precise replicas of Greek classics, like this one.

Activity. After students have read the story of Orpheus, ask them to identify the figures in the relief. They should note facial expressions, gestures, garments, and ornamentation.

PRETEACHING

Skills Starter

Build skills. Point out that a good summary includes all of the major events that make up a story's plot and that a plot usually contains the following elements:

- an **introduction,** which gives background information
- a **conflict,** or problem that the characters face
- a **climax,** or high point
- a **resolution,** or ending

After reviewing these terms, have students identify each plot element in a well-known tale, such as "The Three Little Pigs." Then, tell them to be on the lookout for the same plot elements as the read the myth of Orpheus.

Preview Vocabulary

Have students read the Vocabulary words and definitions on p. 664. Then, direct them to choose the correct synonym for each word from the following list:

horrifying   [*ghastly*]
brokenhearted   [*inconsolable*]
rose   [*ascended*]
unwillingness   [*reluctance*]

Orpheus, The Great Musician   **665**

■ *Holt Online Assessment*

Internet
■ go.hrw.com (Keyword: LE5 7-6)
■ *Elements of Literature Online*

Media
■ *Audio CD Library*
■ *Audio CD Library, Selections and Summaries in Spanish*

PRETEACHING

Assign the Reading
Have students read the selection aloud in small groups and then complete the After You Read questions and activities as homework.

HOMEWORK

DIRECT TEACHING

A Reading Skills

? Summarize. What important background information about Orpheus is given at the beginning of the story? [Orpheus produces powerful music; he is in love with Eurydice, who inspires his music.]

B Reading Skills

? Summarize. What conflict, or problem, does Orpheus face? [Eurydice dies.] How does he begin to try to solve this problem? [He decides to journey to the underworld in search of her.]

VIEWING THE ART

Another example of a relief appears on this page. In high reliefs, sculptured figures rise from the background to at least half of their natural depth; shallower forms, like the sculpture of the lyre player, are called low reliefs, or bas-reliefs. The lyre was the favorite instrument of the god Apollo, who embodied the virtues of wisdom, harmony, and restraint.

In the legend of Orpheus, the Greek love of music found its fullest expression. Orpheus, it is said, could make such heavenly songs that when he sat down to sing, the trees would crowd around to shade him. The ivy and vine stretched out their tendrils. Great oaks would bend their spreading branches over his head. The very rocks would edge down the mountainsides. Wild beasts crouched harmless by him, and nymphs[1] and woodland gods would listen to him, enchanted.

Orpheus himself, however, had eyes for no one but the nymph Eurydice.[2] His love for her was his inspiration, and his power sprang from the passionate longing that he knew in his own heart. All nature rejoiced with him on his bridal day, but on that very morning, as Eurydice went down to the riverside with her maidens to gather flowers for a bridal garland, she was bitten in the foot by a snake, and she died in spite of all attempts to save her.

Orpheus was inconsolable. All day long he mourned his bride, while birds, beasts, and the earth itself sorrowed with him. When at last the shadows of the sun grew long, Orpheus took his lyre[3] and made his way to the yawning cave which leads down into the underworld, where the soul of dead Eurydice had gone.

THE EARTH ITSELF SORROWED WITH HIM.

---

3. **lyre** (līr): small harp.

Vocabulary
inconsolable (in′kən·sōl′ə·bəl) *adj.:* unable to be comforted; brokenhearted.

---

1. **nymphs:** minor goddesses of nature, usually young and beautiful, living in mountains, rivers, or trees.
2. **Eurydice** (yoo·rid′i·sē′).

Lyre player. Greece.

DIFFERENTIATING INSTRUCTION

Learners Having Difficulty
Have students study the layout of the story, examining the illustrations and the pullout quotes displayed on pp. 666 and 668. Invite students to reflect on these elements and write questions about them, such as *How will the story involve a lyre?* and *Why is the earth sad?* Such reflecting and questioning will give them a head start in understanding the content before they read the myth.

Advanced Learners
As students read the myth, have them copy words and phrases that Coolidge uses to describe Orpheus's music, such as "heavenly songs" and "marvelous voice." After they have read the myth, ask them to imagine that they are among the denizens of the underworld who have just heard Orpheus's music for the first time.

Even gray Charon, the ferryman of the Styx, forgot to ask his passenger for the price of crossing. The dog Cerberus, the three-headed monster who guards Hades' gate, stopped full in his tracks and listened motionless until Orpheus had passed. As he entered the land of Hades, the pale ghosts came after him like great, uncounted flocks of silent birds. All the land lay hushed as that marvelous voice resounded across the mud and marshes of its dreadful rivers. In the daffodil fields of Elysium, the happy dead sat silent among their flowers. In the farthest corners of the place of punishment, the hissing flames stood still. Accursed Sisyphus,[4] who toils eternally to push a mighty rock uphill, sat down and knew not he was resting. Tantalus, who strains forever after visions of cool water, forgot his thirst and ceased to clutch at the empty air.

The pillared[5] hall of Hades opened before the hero's song. The ranks of long-dead heroes who sit at Hades' board looked up and turned their eyes away from the pitiless form of Hades and his pale, unhappy queen. Grim and unmoving sat the dark king of the dead on his ebony throne, yet the tears shone on his rigid cheeks in the light of his ghastly torches. Even his hard heart, which knew all misery and cared nothing for it, was touched by the love and longing of the music.

At last the minstrel[6] came to an end, and a long sigh like wind in pine trees was heard from the assembled ghosts. Then the king spoke, and his deep voice echoed through his silent land. "Go back to the light of day," he said. "Go quickly while my monsters are stilled by your song. Climb up the steep road to daylight, and never once turn back. The spirit of Eurydice shall follow, but if you look around at her, she will return to me."

Orpheus turned and strode from the hall of Hades, and the flocks of following ghosts made way for him to pass. In vain he searched their ranks for a sight of his lost Eurydice. In vain he listened for the faintest sound behind. The barge of Charon sank to the very gunwales[7] beneath his weight, but no following passenger pressed it lower down. The way from the land of Hades to the upper world is long and hard, far easier to descend than climb. It was dark and misty, full of strange shapes and noises, yet in many places merely black and silent as the tomb. Here Orpheus would stop and listen, but nothing moved behind him. For all he could hear, he was utterly alone. Then he would wonder if the pitiless Hades were deceiving him. Suppose he came up to the light again and Eurydice was not there! Once he had charmed the ferryman and the dreadful monsters, but now they had heard his song. The second time his spell would be less powerful; he could never go again. Perhaps he had lost Eurydice by his readiness to believe.

Every step he took, some instinct told him that he was going farther from his bride. He toiled up the path in reluctance and despair, stopping, listening, sighing, taking a few slow steps, until the dark

---

4. **Sisyphus** (sis′ə·fəs).
5. **pillared:** having pillars (columns).
6. **minstrel:** singer.

7. **gunwales** (gun′əlz): upper edges of the sides of a boat.

Vocabulary
ghastly (gast′lē) *adj.:* horrible; ghostlike.
reluctance (ri·luk′təns) *n.:* unwillingness.

C Literary Focus

? The underworld of myth. These paragraphs provide a guide to the underworld. What beings and places are mentioned? [Charon, ferryman of the Styx; Cerberus, monstrous three-headed guard dog; "pale ghosts," spirits of the dead; "dreadful rivers," haunt of the ghosts; "daffodil fields of Elysium," realm of the "happy dead"; "farthest corners . . . hissing flames," place of punishment; Sisyphus, spirit eternally pushing a rock uphill; Tantalus, spirit forever reaching for cool water; "pillared hall," throne room of King Hades and his queen.]

D Vocabulary Note

Figurative language. Remind students that figurative language describes one thing in terms of another. Then, ask students what the ghosts' sigh is compared to in this passage. [wind in pine trees] Point out that because this comparison uses the word *like,* it is considered a simile.

E Reading Skills

? Predict. Recall how Hades tricked Persephone in "The Origin of the Seasons." Do you think Hades will really allow Eurydice to leave the underworld with Orpheus? Explain. [Possible responses: Yes, if Orpheus doesn't look back, Hades will keep his word. No, even if Orpheus doesn't look back, Hades will have another trick up his sleeve.]

F Reading Skills

? Summarize. How would you summarize the action in this paragraph? [Possible response: Orpheus heads back toward daylight, but he is tormented by the thought that Eurydice is not really following him.]

CROSS-CURRICULAR CONNECTIONS

Music
Orpheus, composed. Franz Liszt (1811–1886) was one of nineteenth-century Europe's greatest pianists. He was also a talented composer, known for piano pieces such as the *Hungarian Rhapsodies* and for orchestral music such as his twelve symphonic poems, the most famous of which is *Les Préludes.* Writing in a very different style was the Russian composer Igor Stravinsky (1882–1971), whose best-known work, *The Rite of Spring,* helped usher in the modernist experimentation of the early twentieth century. Many of Stravinsky's works—*Orpheus* among them—were originally composed for ballets.
Activity. Have students listen to "Orpheus" from *Symphonic Poems* by Franz Liszt and *Orpheus* by Igor Stravinsky and discuss which piece they feel better captures the qualities they associate with Orpheus and his music.

A **Reading Skills**

❓ **Summarize.** What happens at the story's climax? [Possible response: Orpheus turns around, sees Eurydice, and tries to embrace her, but she disappears.]

B **Literary Focus**

❓ **Descriptive language.** What are some of the precise verbs, specific nouns, and vivid adjectives that the writer uses in this passage? [Verbs—*shrank, stumbled, mourned;* Nouns—*mud banks, wailing, nightingale;* Adjectives—*gray, flitting, steep.*]

C **Literary Focus**

❓ **The underworld of myth.** How do Orpheus and Eurydice's actions reflect those of other beings who reside in the underworld? [Possible response: They walk together eternally. This fate resembles that of Sisyphus, who eternally rolls a rock uphill, and Tantalus, who eternally chases visions of cool water.]

GUIDED PRACTICE

Monitor students' progress. To check their comprehension, have students answer the following questions:

1. What is Orpheus's great talent? [making beautiful music]

2. How and when does Eurydice die? [She dies after being bitten by a snake on her wedding day.]

3. After Eurydice dies, where does Orpheus go? [into the underworld]

4. What does Hades tell Orpheus? [that Orpheus may lead Eurydice out of the underworld if he doesn't look back at her]

5. Why is Eurydice unable to return to daylight? [because Orpheus looks back at the last minute]

thinned out into grayness. Up ahead a speck of light showed clearly the entrance to the cavern.

A At that final moment Orpheus could bear no more. To go out into the light of day without his love seemed to him impossible. Before he had quite ascended, there was still a moment in which he could go back. Quick in the grayness he turned and saw a dim shade at his heels, as indistinct as the gray mist behind her. But still he could see the look of sadness on her face as he sprung forward saying, "Eurydice!" and threw his arms about her. The shade dissolved in the circle of his arms like smoke. A little whisper seemed to say "Farewell" as she scattered into mist and was gone.

The unfortunate lover hastened back again down the steep, dark path. But all was in vain. This time the ghostly ferryman was deaf to his prayers. The very wildness of his mood made it impossible for him to attain the beauty of his former music. At last, his despair was so great that he could not even sing at all. For seven days he sat huddled together on the gray mud banks, listening to the wailing of the terrible river. The flitting ghosts shrank back in a wide circle from the living man, but he paid them no attention. Only he sat with his eyes on Charon, his ears ringing with the dreadful noise of Styx.

B Orpheus arose at last and stumbled back along the steep road he knew so well by now. When he came up to earth again, his song was pitiful but more beautiful than ever. Even the nightingale who mourned all night long would hush her voice to listen as Orpheus sat in some hidden place singing of his lost Eurydice. Men and women he could bear no longer, and when they came to hear him, he drove them away. At last the women of Thrace, maddened by Dionysus and infuriated by Orpheus's contempt, fell upon him and killed him. It is said that as the body was swept down the river Hebrus, the dead lips still moved faintly and the rocks echoed for the last time, "Eurydice." But the poet's eager spirit was already far down the familiar path.

C In the daffodil meadows he met the shade of Eurydice, and there they walk together, or where the path is narrow, the shade of Orpheus goes ahead and looks back at his love.

> THE SHADE DISSOLVED IN THE CIRCLE OF HIS ARMS LIKE SMOKE.

Vocabulary
ascended (ə·send′id) *v.:* moved up.

DIFFERENTIATING INSTRUCTION

Learners Having Difficulty
Have students return to the prereading questions they wrote for the Differentiating Instruction activity on page 666. Working in groups, students can read their questions aloud one by one while other group members take turns answering them.

English-Language Learners
For lessons designed for English-language learners, see *Holt Reading Solutions.*

Special Education Students
For lessons designed for special education students, see *Holt Reading Solutions.*

Meet the Writer

Olivia Coolidge

"I Write Because . . . I Almost Have To"

Olivia Coolidge (1908–   ) developed an interest in storytelling at an early age. She recalls:

> My sister and I used to make up fairy stories and tell them to each other . . . . One day we decided that we would make a book out of them, but there was a drawback. . . . [N]either of us [was] very good at our copybooks, and we did not see how we could ever write one whole story, let alone a collection, down on paper.

Although Coolidge didn't succeed in writing down her childhood stories, she began to write later in life and received awards and recognition for her work.

Coolidge has used her storytelling gifts mainly to make mythology and history exciting for young readers. She believes strongly in the power of the story:

> A good book should excite, amuse and interest. It should give a sense of seeing as a movie does. In other words, a good book needs imagination and the gift of a good storyteller. I write because I like writing, because I want to write, and because I almost have to. I have a great many things I want to say, ideas I want to express and pictures I want to convey to other people.

For Independent Reading

For more myths and ancient stories by Olivia Coolidge, look for *Greek Myths and Legends of the North*. To explore the ancient world from which these stories emerged, check out *The Golden Days of Greece*.

Meet the Writer

Olivia Coolidge was born in England, and she graduated from Oxford University. She taught Latin, Greek, and English in England and the United States. Besides retelling Greek and Norse myths, she has also written about historical figures such as Abraham Lincoln. Her books include *The Maid of Artemis* and *The Apprenticeship of Abraham Lincoln*.

For Independent Reading

Tell students who enjoy Coolidge's writing that this author has written books on a wide range of historical and biographical topics, including *Caesar's Gallic War, The Trojan War, Gandhi,* and *Lives of Famous Romans*. Encourage students to use the Internet or a library catalog to locate other works by Coolidge.

INDEPENDENT PRACTICE

After You Read

First Thoughts

1. Possible answers: Yes, because Hades tricked Persephone; therefore, he cannot be trusted. No; even if Hades had lied, there was nothing to be gained by looking back.

Thinking Critically

2. The ancient Greeks pictured the afterlife as both sad and happy. Some of the dead are tortured souls; others, who dwell in the fields of Elysium, are happy.

3. Possible answer: Orpheus's love for Eurydice causes him to risk a trip to the underworld, but it also causes him to look back to check for her presence.

4. Possible answers: Love and death may be at odds. Love is more powerful than death because, in the end, Orpheus and Eurydice are reunited.

Extending Interpretations

5. Possible answers: Both my notes and the story say that music can make people forget their troubles and help them to overcome obstacles.

6. Possible answers: Yes, Hades made a promise and would have kept it. No, Hades was not fair; he knew Orpheus would look back. If I were a god or a goddess, I might let Eurydice go back with Orpheus as a way of thanking him for his beautiful music.

First Thoughts

1. If you were Orpheus, would you have looked back? Why or why not?

Thinking Critically

2. On the basis of this myth, how do you think the ancient Greeks pictured the afterlife?

3. Explain how the same feeling that prompted Orpheus's descent into the underworld also caused him to fail.

4. What lessons about love and death does this myth seem to teach? In this story, which is more powerful, love or death? Why?

Extending Interpretations

5. What does this myth say about the power of music? How does this message compare with your own feelings about music? Be sure to check your Quickwrite notes.

6. Do you think Hades was fair to Orpheus and Eurydice? Tell how you might change the outcome if you were a god or goddess.

WRITING

Comparing Myths

Use a chart like the one below to compare this myth with "The Origin of the Seasons."

	"Orpheus"	"The Origin of the Seasons"
How the character faces the mystery of death		
How nature responds to the character's grief or joy		
The effect of breaking a taboo or rule		

go.hrw.com

INTERNET
Projects and Activities
Keyword: LE5 7-6

SKILLS FOCUS

Literary Skills
Analyze a myth.

Reading Skills
Summarize a myth.

Writing Skills
Compare myths.

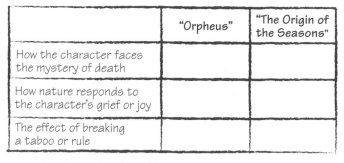

Reading Check

Summarize the main events of the myth you have just read by filling in a diagram like the one below. Write two or three sentences in each box.

Beginning

Middle

End

Reading Check

- **Beginning:** Orpheus's music charms all beings. He himself is madly in love with Eurydice, but she dies.

- **Middle:** Orpheus's music charms everyone in the underworld. Hades tells him that Eurydice may leave while the guardians of the underworld are entranced, as long as Orpheus does not look back at her on their way out.

- **End:** Orpheus distrusts Hades and looks back, and Eurydice vanishes. Orpheus's music still charms people, but he scorns them, and the women of Thrace kill him. He joins Eurydice in the daffodil meadows of the underworld.

Clarifying Word Meanings

PRACTICE

Each numbered sentence contains a word from the Word Bank. After reading the sentence, make up a reasonable answer to the question that follows. Write your answer.

Word Bank
inconsolable
ghastly
reluctance
ascended

1. The queen was inconsolable. What just happened to the queen?
2. The king saw a ghastly sight. What did the king see?
3. He ate the meal with some reluctance. What explains his reluctance?
4. The golden cloud ascended. Where was the cloud after it ascended?

Figurative Language

Figurative language describes one thing in terms of something else. Figurative language is not meant to be taken as literally true.

A **simile** is a comparison between two unlike things, using a word such as *like, as, resembles,* or *than.*

EXAMPLE "...a long sigh like wind in pine trees was heard from the assembled ghosts." [The sigh of the ghosts is compared to the wind in the pines.]

Personification is figurative language in which a nonhuman thing is talked about as if it were human.

EXAMPLE "...when he sat down to sing, the trees would crowd around to shade him." [The trees are given the human ability to crowd around someone.]

PRACTICE

Find the figurative language in each sentence. Tell what is compared to what. Then, tell if the comparison is a simile or personification.

1. "All day long he mourned his bride, while birds, beasts, and the earth itself sorrowed with him."
2. "The shade dissolved in the circle of his arms like smoke."

SKILLS FOCUS

Vocabulary Skills
Clarify word meanings; understand figurative language.

Orpheus, the Great Musician   **671**

Vocabulary Development

Clarifying Word Meanings

PRACTICE

Possible Answers
1. Rumpelstiltskin had threatened to take her firstborn child away if she could not guess his name.
2. The king saw the ghost of his father.
3. He hates squash, and the main dish was squash casserole.
4. The cloud was high in the sky.

Figurative Language

PRACTICE

1. "birds, beasts, and the earth . . . sorrowed"—nonhumans and nonliving things given human characteristics; personification
2. "The shade dissolved . . . like smoke"—disappearance of the spirit compared to smoke; simile

ASSESSING

Assessment
■ *Holt Assessment: Literature, Reading, and Vocabulary*

DIFFERENTIATING INSTRUCTION

Learners Having Difficulty
Reinforce students' understanding of figurative language by having them complete the following items. Direct students to find the example of figurative language in each sentence and then to state whether it is a simile or personification.

1. When Orpheus sang a happy song, nature smiled. ["nature smiled"—personification]
2. Orpheus's words poured down on the forest like a soft spring rain. ["words poured . . . like a soft spring rain"—simile]
3. As his song grew stronger, the woods began to dance with the breeze. ["woods began to dance"—personification]
4. For Tantalus, Orpheus's song was as soothing as a drink of cool water. ["song was as soothing as a drink of cool water"—simile]
5. Orpheus sang in a voice like sunshine after a storm. ["a voice like sunshine after a storm"—simile]

Grade-Level Skills

■ **Reading Skills**
Analyze anecdote.

Review Skills

■ **Reading Skills**
Recognize differences between facts and opinions.

Summary ⟷ *at grade level*

In this excerpt from her autobiography, the violinist Nadja Salerno-Sonnenberg reflects on the power of music in her life. Music, she claims, is one of life's most noble pursuits—and one of humanity's most indispensable sources of beauty and inspiration.

PRETEACHING

Selection Starter

Motivate. Have students write an ending to this sentence stem: *Music is . . . .* Then, invite students to read their sentence aloud and explain whether it is a fact or an opinion, and why.

Assign the Reading

Read the selection aloud as a class. Have students complete the Test Practice independently, giving help as needed to readers having difficulty.

Informational Text   LINK TO "ORPHEUS, THE GREAT MUSICIAN"

Understanding Autobiography

Reading Focus
Distinguishing Fact from Opinion

The power of music is timeless. In the ancient Greek myth, even the trees and rocks gathered around to listen to Orpheus sing. In the following selection, a modern-day violinist describes the importance of music in her life.

When you read an autobiography (the story of a person's life, written by that person), it is important to distinguish facts from opinions. What is stated as a fact by the writer might really be an opinion.

- A fact is a statement that can be proved true. *The myth of Orpheus tells the story of the great musician's love for Eurydice.* You can prove this statement is true by reading the myth. *The story of Orpheus is a myth from ancient Greece.* You can prove this statement is true by referring to a reliable source such as an encyclopedia or a text about mythology.

- An opinion is a belief, judgment, or conclusion based on what the writer

INTERNET
Interactive
Reading Model
Keyword: LE5 7-6

SKILLS
FOCUS

Reading Skills
Distinguish fact
from opinion;
understand
anecdote.

thinks. Opinions cannot be proved or disproved. *People have always enjoyed the story of Orpheus.* This opinion is supported by the fact that the story has been retold for hundreds of years; it is not a fact because it cannot be proved that the story was always enjoyed. *Orpheus is the greatest myth in the world.* This is an opinion because it cannot be proved which myth is the greatest. It is not supported by any facts at all.

Anecdote

Personal writing such as an autobiography often includes anecdotes. An **anecdote** is a very brief story told to make a point.

■ In "The Power of Music," Nadja Salerno-Sonnenberg bases her statements on her own experiences and emotions. As you read, notice where she uses facts, opinions, and anecdotes. For example, in her first sentence Nadja says: "This is something I know for a fact: . . ." When you finish the sentence, decide if you agree that it is indeed a fact.

Background

Nadja Salerno-Sonnenberg is a violinist who appears in concert in the United States and throughout the world. She was born in Rome, Italy, and moved to the United States with her family in 1969. She writes about her love of music and her career in her autobiography, *Nadja on My Way.*

---

672   Collection 6 / Our Literary Heritage: Greek Myths and World Folk Tales

---

RESOURCES: READING

Planning

■ *One-Stop Planner* CD-ROM with ExamView Test Generator

Differentiating Instruction

■ *Holt Reading Solutions*
■ *Supporting Instruction in Spanish*
■ *Audio CD Library*
■ *Audio CD Library, Selections and Summaries in Spanish*

Assessment

■ *Holt Assessment: Literature, Reading, and Vocabulary*
■ *One-Stop Planner* CD-ROM with ExamView Test Generator
■ *Holt Online Assessment*

Internet

■ go.hrw.com (Keyword: LE5 7-6)
■ *Elements of Literature Online*

Media

■ *Audio CD Library*
■ *Audio CD Library, Selections and Summaries in Spanish*

The Power of Music

from **Nadja on My Way**

Nadja Salerno-Sonnenberg

This is something I know for a fact: You have to work hardest for the thing you love most. And when it's music that you love, you're in for the fight of your life.

It starts when your blood fills with music and you know you can't live without it. Every day brings a challenge to learn as much as possible and to play even better than you did the day before.

You may want to achieve fame and glory, or you may want to play for fun. But whenever you fall in love with music, you'll never sit still again.

Music is more important than we will ever know. Great music can pull you right out of your chair. It can make you cry, or laugh, or feel a way you've never felt before. It can make you remember the first person you loved. . . Music has that power.

Just imagine a world without music. What would you whistle when you walked down the street? How could you make a movie?

How could you have a ball game without an organist leading the crowd when you're down by a run in the ninth?

You could be the most successful doctor in the world, but if you never turn on the radio, never go to a concert, never sing in the shower, never see *The King and I*[1]—then you can't be a total, fulfilled human being. It's impossible.

When you realize how vital music is, you realize a musician's fight is quite a noble, heroic endeavor. It didn't always seem that way to me. There was a time, years ago, when I felt discouraged and it seemed selfish to put so much time into music. Being a musician didn't seem as useful to others as being a surgeon, or even a good politician.

But I came to understand that it's a great, great gift to help people forget their everyday life and be uplifted. And better than uplifted, to be inspired; that's what music can do. It's important to us all, and I'm proud to put mind and muscle into recording, concerts, teaching, and studying: into being a musician.

Emotionally, music has brought me an enormous amount of joy and an enormous amount of despair and frustration. Because of music, I have learned what a battle is. I've won most, but not all—not by a long shot.

1. *The King and I:* well-known American musical and one of the most widely performed shows in the musical theater. A movie version was made in the 1950s.

The Power of Music **673**

The Power of Music **673**

Analyzing Autobiography

Test **Practice**

Answers and Model Rationales

1. **A**   B is incorrect because the author claims the opposite in paragraphs 1 and 2; C is incorrect because literature is never mentioned; and D is incorrect because the author is speaking for herself, not for all people.

2. **J**   Students should understand that the statement expresses a conclusion drawn from the writer's experience, but there is no way to prove this conclusion.

3. **C**   Students should recall that an anecdote is a brief story told to illustrate an important point.

4. **H**   This statement can be proved, and so it is a fact.

Test-Taking Tips

For more information on how to answer multiple-choice items, refer students to **Test Smarts,** p. 920.

Constructed Response

Possible Answers

1. Music has been a part of human culture for thousands of years. There are many different kinds of music. I can play two musical instruments.

2. Country music is the best kind of music there is.

3. I was feeling anxious one afternoon because I had so much to do. I had two tests the next day; I had to watch my younger brother for an hour; and I had to help Dad clean up the dinner dishes. After dinner I went to my room and put in my favorite Bob Dylan CD. It helped me clear my mind, calm down, focus on my studying—and earn two A's!

Analyzing Autobiography
The Power of Music

Test **Practice**

1. Which of the following statements best expresses the **main idea** of the selection?

   A   Music is vitally important in life.

   B   It is easy to learn music.

   C   Music is more important than literature.

   D   Everyone loves music.

2. "You could be the most successful doctor in the world, but if you never turn on the radio, never go to a concert . . . then you can't be a total, fulfilled human being." This statement is —

   F   a fact

   G   a lie

   H   an anecdote

   J   an opinion

3. Which of the following statements is an **anecdote**?

   A   "It starts when your blood fills with music and you know you can't live without it."

   B   "Great music can pull you right out of your chair."

   C   "There was a time, years ago, when I felt discouraged and it seemed selfish to put so much time into music."

   D   "It's impossible."

4. Which of the following statements is a **fact**?

   F   "Just imagine a world without music."

   G   "How could you make a movie?"

   H   "[Great music] can make you cry or laugh, or feel a way you've never felt before."

   J   "When you realize how vital music is, you realize a musician's fight is quite a noble, heroic endeavor."

Constructed Response

SKILLS FOCUS

Reading Skills
Analyze facts and opinions; analyze anecdote.

1. List three **facts** you know about music.

2. Write one **opinion** about music.

3. Tell a personal **anecdote** about music.

ASSESSING

Assessment

■ *Holt Assessment: Literature, Reading, and Vocabulary*

The Flight of Icarus

Make the Connection
Quickwrite ✏️

Long before the invention of the airplane, people yearned to fly. They dreamed of climbing through the air, dipping, floating, plummeting—as free as birds. They wanted to escape the earth and soar above all its problems. Today, of course, flight is an everyday reality. We travel through the air in everything from helicopters to jumbo jets, from hot-air balloons to space shuttles.

Express your feelings about flying by completing one of these sentences:

- I long to fly like a seagull because . .
- If we couldn't fly . . .

Literary Focus
Morals of Myths

When a young bird flies from the nest for the first time, we say that it is "trying its wings." As you read this myth, notice what happens when a young boy tries his wings. If you think about what the boy attempts to do, what he ignores, and what happens to him as a result, you'll find the morals in the story. A **moral** is a lesson about the right way to behave. The morals in many Greek myths were used to teach children values.

Reading Skills 📖
Making Generalizations

When you make a generalization, you look at evidence and make a broad statement about what it tells you. Someone who says, "All stories contain conflicts" is making a generalization from experience with many stories. As you read these myths, think of generalizations you might make about myths and the kinds of stories they tell.

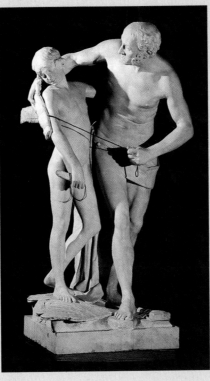

Daedalus and Icarus by Antonio Canova.

Museo Correr, Venice, Italy. © Alinari/Art Resource, NY.

go.hrw.com

INTERNET
Cross-curricular Connection
Keyword: LE5 7-6

SKILLS FOCUS

Literary Skills
Understand morals in myths.

Reading Skills
Make generalizations.

SKILLS FOCUS
pp. 675–681

Grade-Level Skills
- **Literary Skills**
Analyze morals in myths.
- **Reading Skills**
Make generalizations.

Summary ⬌ *at grade level*

Minos, the king of Crete, locks the designer of his labyrinth, Daedalus, in a tower for helping the Greek hero Theseus escape from the maze. Aided by his son, Icarus, Daedalus escapes from the tower and devises a plan to leave the island by air. After Icarus gathers feathers, Daedalus fashions a set of artificial wings. In a cautious test, Daedalus achieves momentary flight. Then he makes wings for his son, and both of them take to the air. Daedalus warns Icarus not to fly too low, where moisture will damage the wings, nor too high, where the sun will melt the wax holding them together. As the two rise toward freedom, Daedalus is alarmed to see Icarus soaring ever closer to the sun. The story reaches its climax as the wax melts, Icarus's wings disintegrate, and he plunges into the sea. Daedalus buries the boy in a land he names Icaria, in memory of his son. Then, Daedalus flies to Sicily, where he hangs up his own wings as an offering to Apollo. The story of Icarus highlights a moral lesson—the danger of ambition unchecked by caution.

RESOURCES: READING

Planning
- *One-Stop Planner* CD-ROM with ExamView Test Generator

Differentiating Instruction
- *Holt Adapted Reader*
- *Holt Reading Solutions*
- *Supporting Instruction in Spanish*
- *Audio CD Library*

- *Audio CD Library, Selections and Summaries in Spanish*

Grammar and Language
- *Language Handbook Worksheets*
- *Daily Language Activities*

Assessment
- *Holt Assessment: Literature, Reading, and Vocabulary*
- *One-Stop Planner* CD-ROM with ExamView Test Generator

- *Holt Online Assessment*

Internet
- go.hrw.com (Keyword: LE5 7-6)
- *Elements of Literature Online*

Media
- *Audio CD Library*
- *Audio CD Library, Selections and Summaries in Spanish*

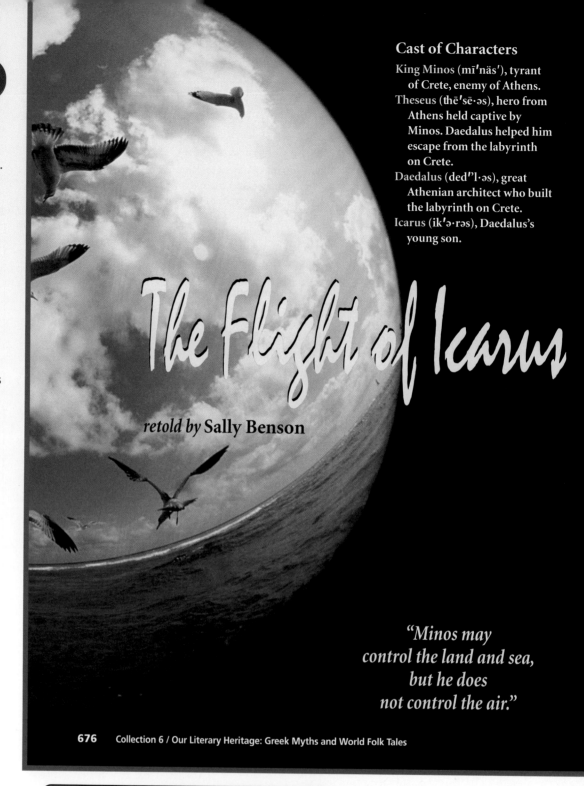

Selection Starter

Motivate. Have students think of a time when they were given good advice but chose to ignore it. As volunteers share their stories, encourage them to describe both the negative and the positive consequences of their actions. For example, did not following the advice harm them in any way? On the other hand, did it help them learn any important lessons?

Assign the Reading

Read the myth aloud as a class. Then, allow students to work in groups to complete items 1–5 on the After You Read page. Students can complete the Reading Check and items 6–7 independently.

Cast of Characters

King Minos (mī′näs′), tyrant of Crete, enemy of Athens.

Theseus (thē′sē·əs), hero from Athens held captive by Minos. Daedalus helped him escape from the labyrinth on Crete.

Daedalus (ded″l·əs), great Athenian architect who built the labyrinth on Crete.

Icarus (ik′ə·rəs), Daedalus's young son.

The Flight of Icarus

retold by **Sally Benson**

"Minos may control the land and sea, but he does not control the air."

676   Collection 6 / Our Literary Heritage: Greek Myths and World Folk Tales

DIFFERENTIATING INSTRUCTION

English-Language Learners
To help students tackle difficult vocabulary, give them this list of words from the story: *ingenious* (p. 677); *skirted, misgivings, prowess* (p. 678); *exaltation* (p. 679). Read aloud the sentences from the story in which the words occur. Point out the context clues in the sentences and the surrounding paragraphs. Discuss each sentence, and ask students to write definitions of the words. Finally, ask students to look up dictionary definitions of the words and to compare them with the definitions they wrote.

Special Education Students
For lessons designed for special education students, see *Holt Reading Solutions*.

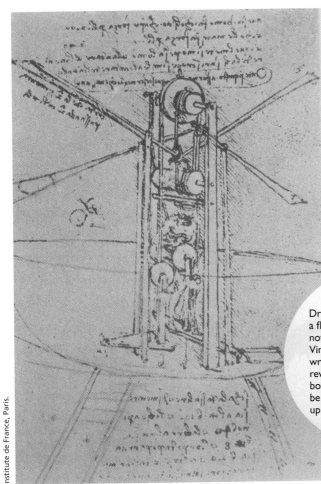

Drawing of a man operating a flying machine, from a notebook of Leonardo da Vinci (1452–1519). Da Vinci wrote backward and in reverse to keep his notebooks secret; his words can be read by holding the page up to a mirror.

Institute de France, Paris.

When Theseus escaped from the labyrinth, King Minos flew into a rage **A** with its builder, Daedalus, and ordered him shut up in a high tower that faced the lonely sea. In time, with the help of his young son, Icarus, Daedalus managed to escape from the tower, only to find himself a prisoner on the island. Several times he tried by bribery to stow away on one of the vessels sailing from Crete, but King Minos kept strict watch over them, and no ships were allowed to sail without being carefully searched.

Daedalus was an ingenious artist and was not discouraged by his failures. "Minos may control the land and sea," he said, "but he does not control the air. I will try that way." **B**

He called his son, Icarus, to him and told the boy to gather up all the feathers he could find on the rocky shore. As thousands of gulls soared over the island, Icarus soon collected a

The Flight of Icarus **677**

Predict. Ask students who are encountering the story for the first time to write predictions of what they think Daedalus will do with the feathers. After they have read the story, have them compare their predictions with what actually happens.

B **Reading Skills**

? **Interpret.** Why do Daedalus's eyes fill with tears? [Possible response: Daedalus feels joy and pride at the beautiful spectacle of his son and the finished wings. His tears are tears of joy.]

huge pile of feathers. Daedalus then melted some wax and made a skeleton in the shape of **A** a bird's wing. The smallest feathers he pressed into the soft wax and the large ones he tied on with thread. Icarus played about on the beach happily while his father worked, chasing the feathers that blew away in the strong wind that swept the island and sometimes taking bits of the wax and working it into strange shapes with his fingers.

It was fun making the wings. The sun shone on the bright feathers; the breezes ruffled them. When they were finished, Daedalus fastened them to his shoulders and found himself lifted upwards, where he hung poised in the air. Filled with excitement, he made another pair for his son. They were smaller than his own, but strong and beautiful.

Finally, one clear, wind-swept morning, the wings were finished, and Daedalus fastened them to Icarus's shoulders and taught him how to fly. He bade him watch the movements of the birds, how they soared and glided overhead. He pointed out the slow, graceful sweep of their wings as they beat the air steadily, without fluttering. Soon Icarus was sure that he, too, could fly and, raising his arms up and down, skirted over the white sand and even out over the waves, letting his feet touch the snowy foam as the water thundered and broke over the sharp rocks. Daedalus watched him proudly but with misgivings. He called Icarus to his side and, putting his arm round the boy's shoulders, said, "Icarus, my son, we are about to make our flight. No human being has ever traveled through the air before, and I want you to listen carefully to my instructions. Keep at a moderate height, for if you fly too low, the fog and spray will clog your wings, and if you

fly too high, the heat will melt the wax that holds them together. Keep near me and you will be safe."

He kissed Icarus and fastened the wings more securely to his son's shoulders. Icarus, standing in the bright sun, the shining wings drooping gracefully from his shoulders, his golden hair wet with spray, and his eyes bright and dark with excitement, looked like a lovely bird. Daedalus's eyes filled with tears, **B** and turning away, he soared into the sky, calling to Icarus to follow. From time to time, he looked back to see that the boy was safe and to note how he managed his wings in his flight. As they flew across the land to test their prowess before setting out across the dark wild sea, plowmen below stopped their work and shepherds gazed in wonder, thinking Daedalus and Icarus were gods.

Father and son flew over Samos and Delos, which lay on their left, and Lebinthus,° which lay on their right. Icarus, beating his wings in joy, felt the thrill of the cool wind on his face and the clear air above and below him. He flew higher and higher up into the blue sky until he reached the clouds. His father saw him and called out in alarm. He tried to follow him, but he was heavier and his wings would not carry him. Up and up Icarus soared, through the soft, moist clouds and out again toward the glorious sun. He was bewitched by a sense of freedom and beat his wings frantically so that they would carry him higher and higher to heaven itself. The blazing sun beat down on the wings and softened the wax. Small feathers fell from the wings and floated softly down, warning Icarus to stay his flight and glide to earth. But the enchanted boy did not notice them until

° **Samos** (sā′mäs), **Delos** (dē′läs), and **Lebinthus** (lə·bin′thəs): Greek islands in the Aegean Sea.

CROSS-CURRICULAR CONNECTIONS

Music

The Beatles' "Flying." Spearheading the British invasion of the American pop charts in the 1960s, the Beatles—John Lennon, Paul McCartney, George Harrison, and Ringo Starr—are often called the greatest rock band ever. The Liverpool-based group, which took its name in 1960 and broke up a decade later, gradually moved from innocuous songs to more creative ventures, including its innovative 1967 concept album

Sgt. Pepper's Lonely Hearts Club Band. The follow-up, *Magical Mystery Tour,* on which "Flying" first appeared, was written in part for a late-1967 TV film of the same name. "Flying" is atypical of Beatles' songs in that it is credited to all four Beatles instead of just one or two.

Activity. Have students listen to "Flying" after they have read "The Flight of Icarus." Ask students to jot down words to describe the images and moods the music evokes.

Then, have them work individually or in groups to change the ending of the song in order to make it reflect the ending of the myth. Have them perform their changed versions in the same humming (or da-dumming) style that the Beatles use in "Flying."

INDIVIDUAL

SMALL GROUP

the sun became so hot that the largest feathers dropped off and he began to sink. Frantically he fluttered his arms, but no feathers remained to hold the air. He cried out to his father, but his voice was submerged in the blue waters of the sea, which has forever after been called by his name.

Daedalus, crazed by anxiety, called back to him, "Icarus! Icarus, my son, where are you?" At last he saw the feathers floating from the sky, and soon his son plunged through the clouds into the sea. Daedalus hurried to save him, but it was too late. He gathered the boy in his arms and flew to land, the tips of his wings dragging in the water from the double burden they bore. Weeping bitterly, he buried his small son and called the land Icaria in his memory.

Then, with a flutter of wings, he once more took to the air, but the joy of his flight was gone and his victory over the air was bitter to him. He arrived safely in Sicily, where he built a temple to Apollo and hung up his wings as an offering to the god, and in the wings he pressed a few bright feathers he had found floating on the water where Icarus fell. And he mourned for the birdlike son who had thrown caution to the winds in the exaltation of his freedom from the earth.

Meet the Writer

Sally Benson

Stories That Have Rounded Ends

Sally Benson (1900–1972) never studied writing. She didn't have to: It came naturally. After high school she skipped college and went directly to work, first for a bank and then for newspapers. In 1930, she was reviewing thirty-two movies a month for a daily paper when she got an idea for a short story. She sat down, typed it out, and sold it to *The New Yorker*. Dazed by her good fortune, she stopped writing for nine months. But when her money ran out, she wrote another story and sold that one, too. From then on she poured stories out. Benson published one book

of Greek and Roman myths, but most of her stories tell the amusing adventures of a thirteen-year-old girl named Judy Graves.

66 I like stories that have rounded ends and don't rise to climaxes; that aren't all wrapped up in a package with plot. I like them, that's why I write them. 99

The Flight of Icarus **679**

Invite students to read the story of Icarus aloud with a parent or another parental figure. Afterward, each can tell about a time when he or she acted or felt like Icarus or Daedalus. Next, each can explain whether, in retrospect, he or she would have done something differently or whether the experience was too valuable to miss.

After You Read

First Thoughts

1. Possible answers: *I long to fly . . .* because I'll be free. *If we couldn't fly,* we would be prisoners forever.

Thinking Critically

2. Icarus also suffers because he forgets or ignores a warning.

3. Icarus tries to be like a bird. The story's moral is that people should know and accept their limitations.

4. Some students may have known the outcome before they started reading. For others, the most obvious moment of foreshadowing probably occurs when Daedalus warns Icarus not to fly too low or too high.

Extending Interpretations

5. Icaria is the name of the land where Daedalus buries Icarus, and the sea into which Icarus falls is called the Icarian Sea. The Greek island of Icaria still bears that name; the Icarian Sea is an arm of the Aegean Sea between the coast of Asia Minor and the islands of Patmos and Leros.

6. Possible answers: Icarus is a lot like teenagers today who take thoughtless risks when they attempt something like a high dive before they really know how. Teenagers can identify with Icarus. Like Icarus, they need to take off on their own.

7. Possible answer: Taking a chance is a good thing when people reach for challenging goals, such as learning a skill or applying to a top college. Taking chances can be dangerous when people expose themselves to harm, as in driving fast in hazardous weather conditions.

After You Read Response and Analysis

First Thoughts

1. Look back at the sentence you completed for the Quickwrite on page 675. How might Daedalus and Icarus have completed those sentences? ✎

Thinking Critically

2. The myths of Persephone and Orpheus include warnings that the characters fail to listen to. How is the story of Icarus like those myths?

3. How does Icarus try to be something he is not? What **moral lesson** can you learn from his failure?

4. When did you first guess the outcome of the myth? What hints in the story helped you make this prediction?

Extending Interpretations

5. Like other myths, this one explains the names of some geographical features in Greece. What are they, and how did they get there?

6. How do you feel about Icarus? Do you think teenagers today can identify with him? Why or why not?

7. This story seems to suggest that people shouldn't try to "fly too high." We often hear the opposite advice: "Reach for the stars." From your own experience, when do you think taking chances is a good thing? When can it be dangerous?

WRITING
Analyzing the Myths

Skim through the three myths you have read so far. Take notes on the fantasy elements, the moral lessons, and the explanations of natural phenomena in each myth. Then, use your notes to make a **generalization** about myths. Open your general statement with the words "Myths are stories that . . ." Support your generalization with details from the myths. 📖

Reading Check

You're a news reporter on the scene, eager to interview Daedalus when he lands. Write a lead paragraph for the news story, telling what happened, why it happened, whom it happened to, when and where it happened, and how it happened.

go. hrw .com

INTERNET
Projects and Activities
Keyword: LE5 7-6

SKILLS FOCUS

Literary Skills
Analyze the moral of a myth.

Reading Skills
Make a generalization.

Writing Skills
Write an analysis of three myths.

Reading Check

Possible answer: Daedalus, the designer of the famed labyrinth in Crete, alit here today, mourning the death of his son, Icarus. Strapped to the ingenious wings his father had fashioned, Icarus flew so high that the sun melted the wax holding the feathers in place, and the boy plunged into the sea. On landing, Daedalus moaned, "My son, Icarus! O Icarus, my son!" He vowed to name this land Icaria in his honor.

After You Read — Vocabulary Development

Place Names from Greece and Rome

When the first Europeans settled in the land that became the United States, they needed names for their towns and cities. They often looked to ancient Rome and Greece for ideas.

PRACTICE

Use the index in an atlas or other geographical reference book to identify the following:

1. the state or states in which the following American cities are located
2. the location of the original Greek or Roman place known by that name

| Athens | Delphi | Olympia |
| Rome | Syracuse | Sparta |

The Fall of Icarus (detail). Copper engraving. The Bettmann Archive.

Grammar Link

Adjective Versus Adverb

Many adverbs end in -*ly.* Such adverbs are generally formed by adding the ending -*ly* to adjectives.

EXAMPLES   **proud** + **ly:** "Daedalus watched him proudly but with misgivings."

secure + **ly:** "He . . . fastened the wings more securely to his son's shoulders."

In some sentences, however, it's hard to know which word to use—the adjective or the adverb.

He arrived safe/safely in Sicily.

To solve this problem, ask yourself which word the modifier describes. An adverb modifies a verb, an adjective, or another adverb.

EXAMPLE   "He arrived safely in Sicily. . . ."

An adjective modifies a noun or a pronoun.

EXAMPLE   He had a safe arrival in Sicily.

For more help, see The Adjective, 1c, and The Adverb, 1h, in the Language Handbook.

PRACTICE

Choose the correct word from each underlined pair.

1. Daedalus flew rapid/rapidly to lift his son from the sea.
2. The accident had happened so sudden/suddenly.
3. Mourning his son, Daedalus sat listless/listlessly on the sand.
4. Icarus was confident/confidently that he could fly higher.

SKILLS FOCUS

Vocabulary Skills
Understand word origins.

Grammar Skills
Distinguish between adjectives and adverbs.

Vocabulary Development

PRACTICE

Possible Answers

- Athens: 1. Alabama, Georgia, Ohio, Tennessee, Texas; 2. ancient city-state in Greece, center of Greek culture in fifth century B.C.
- Rome: 1. Georgia, New York; 2. capital of ancient Roman Empire
- Delphi: 1. Indiana; 2. home of famous oracle of Apollo in ancient Greece
- Syracuse: 1. Kansas, New York, Utah; 2. ancient city-state in Sicily
- Olympia: 1. Washington; 2. a plain and sanctuary in Greece, site of ancient festival in honor of Zeus
- Sparta: 1. Georgia, Illinois, Tennessee, Wisconsin; 2. military city-state in ancient Greece

Grammar Link

PRACTICE

1. rapidly
2. suddenly
3. listlessly
4. confident

ASSESSING

Assessment

- *Holt Assessment: Literature, Reading, and Vocabulary*

DIFFERENTIATING INSTRUCTION

Learners Having Difficulty
Reinforce students' understanding of adjectives and adverbs by having them choose the correct word from each underlined pair:

1. Icarus thought that flying was wonderful/wonderfully. [wonderful]
2. He felt that he was going unbelievable/unbelievably high. [unbelievably]

3. He flapped his wings more powerful/powerfully to rise even higher. [powerfully]
4. His slow/slowly climb continued. [slow]
5. Final/Finally, he could go no higher; he was losing control. [Finally]

To extend the activity, have students identify the word that is modified by each adverb or adjective.

Grade-Level Skills

■ Literary Skills
Analyze irony.

■ Reading Skills
Use prior knowledge.

Upcoming Skills

■ Literary Skills
Identify the literary devices (such as irony) that define a writer's style.

Summary  *at grade level*

> King Midas of Lydia, already steeped in good fortune, wants to be the most powerful and envied man in the world. One day he finds the satyr Silenus lying drunk in his garden. When Midas returns Silenus to his master, Dionysus, the grateful god offers to grant the king any wish. Midas asks to have anything he touches turn to gold. The granted wish ironically turns into a curse. The desolate king begs Dionysus to repeal the power, and he follows the god's instruction to bathe in the river Pactolus. Midas emerges relieved to find his golden touch gone.

Before You Read · The Myth

King Midas and the Golden Touch

Make the Connection
Quickwrite ✎

Greed is a powerful emotion—it can disrupt friendships, spark wars, and topple empires. What happens to greedy people who value money above everything else? Write briefly about a modern-day situation in which greed led to unhappiness or suffering.

Literary Focus
Irony

Irony is the difference between what you say and what you mean or between what's supposed to happen and what does happen. When you say "How graceful" to someone who's just fallen flat on his face, you're using irony. When a firehouse burns down, that's irony. It's a contrast between expectation and reality. This myth is about an ironic situation: There's a big difference between what Midas expects to happen and what does happen.

Reading Skills 📖

Using Prior Knowledge: Building on What You Know

Get together with a group of classmates. Brainstorm to find answers to the questions about greed on the map below. You may want to add questions—and answers—of your own.

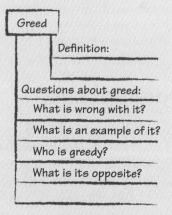

Greed

Definition:

Questions about greed:

What is wrong with it?

What is an example of it?

Who is greedy?

What is its opposite?

SKILLS FOCUS

Literary Skills
Understand irony.

Reading Skills
Use prior knowledge.

One of a pair of bracelets with ram's-head finials (c. 330–300 B.C.). Greek. Said to be from near Thessaloniki. Gold, rock crystal (8 cm wide x 7.8 cm high).
The Metropolitan Museum of Art, Harris Brisbane Dick Fund, 1937 (37.11.11-.12). Photograph © 1993 The Metropolitan Museum of Art.

682   Collection 6 / Our Literary Heritage: Greek Myths and World Folk Tales

---

RESOURCES: READING

Planning
■ *One-Stop Planner* CD-ROM with ExamView Test Generator

Differentiating Instruction
■ *Holt Reading Solutions*
■ *Supporting Instruction in Spanish*
■ *Audio CD Library*
■ *Audio CD Library, Selections and Summaries in Spanish*

Grammar and Language
■ *Daily Language Activities*

Assessment
■ *Holt Assessment: Literature, Reading, and Vocabulary*
■ *One-Stop Planner* CD-ROM with ExamView Test Generator
■ *Holt Online Assessment*

Internet
■ go.hrw.com (Keyword: LE5 7-6)
■ *Elements of Literature Online*

Media
■ *Audio CD Library*
■ *Audio CD Library, Selections and Summaries in Spanish*

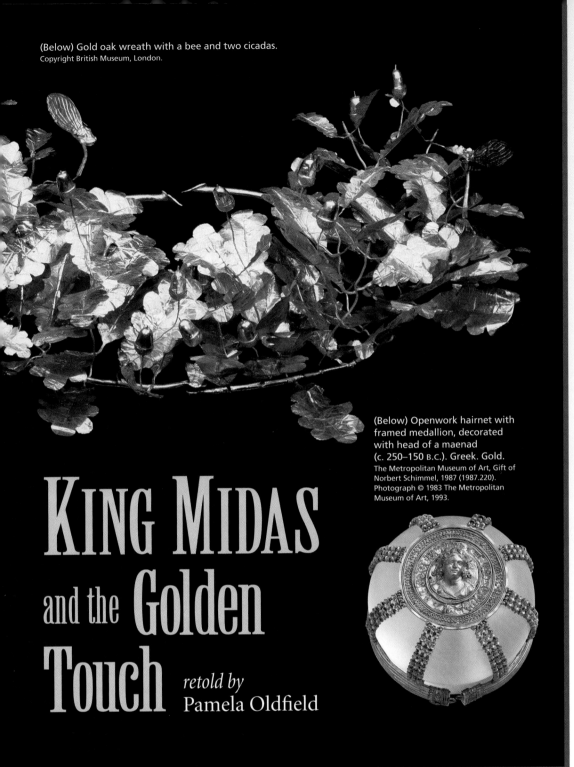

(Below) Gold oak wreath with a bee and two cicadas.
Copyright British Museum, London.

(Below) Openwork hairnet with framed medallion, decorated with head of a maenad (c. 250–150 B.C.). Greek. Gold.
The Metropolitan Museum of Art, Gift of Norbert Schimmel, 1987 (1987.220). Photograph © 1983 The Metropolitan Museum of Art, 1993.

KING MIDAS
and the Golden
Touch
retold by
Pamela Oldfield

PRETEACHING

Selection Starter
Motivate. Have students complete this old adage: "Be careful for what you ask for, ..." [You just might get it!] Then, ask students if they have ever wanted something very badly, gotten that thing, and then discovered that having it was more of a curse than a blessing. Allow a few volunteers to share their stories. Then, explain that these stories describe ironic situations, or situations in which expectations do not match reality.

Assign the Reading
Read the story aloud as a class. Then, have advanced learners complete the After You Read questions independently while you continue working with readers having difficulty.

DIFFERENTIATING INSTRUCTION

English-Language Learners
Before students read, give them this list of words from the story: *discontented, peered, trespassing* (p. 684), and *jubilant* (p. 685). Read aloud the sentences in which they occur, pointing out context clues. Ask students to write definitions of the words. Then, ask them to compare their definitions with those in a dictionary.

For lesson plans designed for English-language learners, see *Holt Reading Solutions.*

Special Education Students
For lesson plans designed for special education students, see *Holt Reading Solutions.*

Advanced Learners
Invite students to research literary connections—more on the satyr Silenus or the god Dionysus, for example. Or ask them to

compare the cure of Midas in the river Pactolus with the cure of Naaman the Syrian in the river Jordan in the Bible (2 Kings 5:1–27). Have students focus on characters, motivations, and resolutions in the two stories. Ask students to comment on the ironic final twist, involving the greed of the character Gehazi, in the Naaman story.

A Cross-curricular Connections
HISTORY

King Midas. Tell students there was a real king named Midas who ruled territories in Phrygia, now western Turkey, in the eighth century B.C.

B Literary Focus

❓ **Character.** Does King Midas sound like a bad person? Why or why not? [Possible responses: Yes, the narrator calls him greedy, so he must be bad. No, the narrator comments that he is no better or worse than anyone else.]

C Literary Focus

Myth. Point out that unusual creatures play key parts in myths. Some of these creatures are dangerous, such as the Minotaur, who has the body of a man and the head of a bull. Others, like Silenus, play comic roles. Explain that satyrs are usually represented as creatures with the body of a man, small horns, pointed ears, and goat legs with hooved feet.

VIEWING THE ART

As metalworking advanced into the Bronze Age, gold and other precious metals were increasingly common materials for jewelry. In the classical Greek period (fifth and fourth centuries B.C.), miniature foliage, animals, and birds were common motifs in exquisitely filigreed necklaces, pendants, and earrings, as shown in the gold jewelry pictured on pp. 682–683 and on this page.

Activity. Have students engage in an observation project in which they collect, photograph, draw, or write descriptions of ornamental objects in stores, friends' homes, or their own homes. Ask them to identify each object as essentially decorative, functional, or religious.

Brooch in the form of a pediment with Pegasus figures (c. 340–320 B.C.). Greek. Gold (length: 7.8 cm).
The Metropolitan Museum of Art, Rogers Fund, 1906 (06.11.59).
Photograph © 1993 The Metropolitan Museum of Art.

A Many years ago in the land of Lydia, there was a beautiful garden. Roses of every shade grew there, and on warm summer nights the air was heavy with their fragrance. The garden belonged to a palace, and the palace was the home of a king whose name was Midas. He was, it is true, **B** rather greedy, but on the whole no better and no worse than any other man. Midas had a loving wife and a daughter he adored, but he was still discontented. He wanted to be the most powerful king in the world; he wanted everyone to envy him.

One day as he was walking through the palace garden, he was startled to see a pair of legs sticking out from beneath his favorite rosebush. The strange thing about these legs was that they had hoofs instead of feet. The king stared at them for a moment and then called for the gardener's boy.

"What do you make of that?" he asked. The boy parted the branches of the rosebush and peered through.

C "It's a satyr, Your Majesty," he reported, trying not to laugh. "I think it's Silenus."

The satyrs were strange, mischievous creatures—half man, half beast—who roamed the world in search of adventure. Midas frowned, angry that somebody should be sleeping in his garden.

The boy ran off to fetch the gardener, and between them they dragged Silenus from under the rosebush and pulled him to his feet. Silenus grinned foolishly. He was holding an empty wine jar.

"You are trespassing in my garden," Midas told him severely. "What have you to say for yourself?" The old satyr shrugged.

"I got lost, so I sat down for a drink," he told the king, looking quite unrepentant.

"Disgraceful," said Midas. "I shall send word to your master at once." Silenus began to look worried, for his master was the god Dionysus, who was not only powerful but also quick-tempered.

"I beg you not to do that," he cried. "He will be angry with me. Suppose I make a bargain with you? If you will overlook my foolishness, I will entertain you with strange and wonderful tales, better than any you have heard before."

Midas agreed and the satyr stayed on in the palace, delighting the king with wonderful accounts of his adventures. At the end of the

684   Collection 6 / Our Literary Heritage: Greek Myths and World Folk Tales

MINI-LESSON   Reading

Developing Word-Attack Skills
Review these sounds represented by the letter *y*:
- *y* stands for the consonant sound /y/ in *yellow* and *you*
- *y* stands for /ī/ in *fly* and *shyness*
- final *y* stands for /ē/ in words like *cherry* and *baby* and in words with the suffix *–ly*

Use the selection word *Lydia* to introduce another use for the letter *y*. Point out that in *Lydia* the letter *y* stands for short *i*. Explain that the word *Lydia* is a Greek place name and that *y* commonly stands for short *i* in words with Greek origins.
Activity. Have students categorize the following words into four groups according to the sound represented by the letter *y*:

week, Midas sent the satyr back to Dionysus. The god was very fond of Silenus, despite his many faults, and was pleased to see him safe and sound. He wanted to thank Midas for taking care of the old satyr and offered the king any gift he cared to name.

Any gift he cared to name! What a marvelous opportunity! He pondered for a whole day and a night and then asked Dionysus if he could make a wish. The god agreed and Midas asked for the power to turn whatever he touched into gold. The god granted his wish, and Midas was jubilant.

"Imagine a king with a golden touch!" he cried. "I shall be the wealthiest and most powerful king in the world."

The king began to experiment with his new gift. He hurried into the garden and touched one of the flowers. At once, the whole bush turned to gold. He went from bush to bush, touching all the blooms, until the entire garden had turned to gold. Then he looked around him. Suddenly Midas felt doubtful. Gone were the colors and the glorious perfume. The garden was still and lifeless.

Inside the palace, the king called for a goblet of wine. As soon as it touched his lips the wine turned to gold and he could not drink.

A terrible thought occurred to him.

"What will happen when I eat?" he wondered. With trembling fingers he reached out to take an apple from a bowl of fruit. As soon as he touched it, the apple turned to gold.

"What have I done?" he whispered. "If I cannot eat or drink I shall die!" He knew that he had made a terrible mistake and decided to beg Dionysus to take back his gift. "I will go to him at once," he cried, but his decision came too late. At that very moment his daughter ran into the room.

"Stay away from me!" Midas shouted, but she took no notice. She threw her arms around him—and was turned to gold. His daughter was now a gleaming but lifeless statue. The king stared at her in horror.

"What have I done to you?" he cried, kneeling beside her. His grief was so great that nobody could console him. He hurried to the palace of Dionysus and threw himself at the god's feet.

"Forgive my stupid greed!" he begged. "Tell me what I must do to save my child. I will do anything you say."

Dionysus told him to find the river Pactolus and wash himself in its waters. Midas set off at once. He went alone and walked for many miles over rough and stony ground.

When he reached the river he found it flowing deep and strong. Midas waded straight in. He was instantly swept away by the current. When at last he managed to reach the shore, he wondered if the curse had indeed been washed from him. Looking back, he saw that the river now gleamed and sparkled in the sun. On the riverbed tiny nuggets of gold lay among the pebbles. Dionysus had spoken truthfully, and the terrible power had left him. Joyfully Midas made his way home.

As he approached the palace, Midas's daughter ran to greet him. He lifted her into his arms and carried her into the garden. Midas was overjoyed to hear her laughter once again, and he sighed happily as he breathed in the fragrance of the flowers.

"I have learned my lesson," he said softly, "and I am content."

King Midas and the Golden Touch   685

mystified	majesty	typing
gymnasium	clarity	bypass
yesterday	youth	irony
syntax	truthfully	envy

[Consonant sound /y/—yesterday, youth. Long *i*—typing, bypass. Short *i*—mystified, gymnasium, syntax. Long *e*—majesty, clarity, irony, truthfully, envy]

After You Read

First Thoughts

1. Possible answers:
   • If I were Midas, I would have thought more before I made my wish.
   • I was surprised when Midas's food turned into gold.

Thinking Critically

2. Possible answers: Midas learns that his family is more important than wealth and power. Midas learns to value other things he has taken for granted.

3. Possible answer: I wish that if I *want* something to turn to gold, it will turn to gold when I touch it.

4. Possible answer: Midas expects to become wealthier and more powerful, but instead he loses the things he values most.

Extending Interpretations

5. Possible answer: The lesson of the story of Midas is "Appreciate the good things in life without being greedy for more."

6. Saying that someone had the "Midas touch" would mean that the person was successful at making money. It would probably be a compliment.

After You Read Response and Analysis

First Thoughts

1. Finish these sentences:
   • If I were Midas, I . . .
   • I was surprised when . . .

Thinking Critically

2. At the end of the myth, Midas says, "I have learned my lesson. . . . I am content." What lesson do you think Midas has learned? What makes him content?

3. How would you word the wish for the golden touch in order to avoid Midas's problem?

4. **Irony** is the difference between what you expect to happen and what actually does happen. What irony do you see in Midas's story?

Extending Interpretations

5. How would you connect the lesson in "King Midas and the Golden Touch" to life today? Look back at your map of the word *greed* on page 682 for ideas.

6. What would we mean if we said someone had the "Midas touch"? Would it be a compliment? Before responding, look back at your Quickwrite notes.

WRITING

Writing a Play

"King Midas and the Golden Touch" is a story rich enough to share. With a group of classmates, write a play version of the story, and act it out for a group of younger students in your school. You'll need actors to play the roles of King Midas, Silenus, Midas's daughter, and Dionysus. As you work on the dialogue for your play, think of a dramatic way to show the change from girl to golden statue.

---

go.hrw.com

INTERNET
Projects and Activities
Keyword: LE5 7-6

SKILLS FOCUS

Literary Skills
Analyze irony.

Reading Skills
Use prior knowledge.

Writing Skills
Write a play.

Reading Check

The diagram below shows the first **cause** and the final **effect** in the tale of King Midas. Fill in the chain of events that leads from one to the other. Add as many boxes as you need.

> Midas is greedy.
>
> ↓
>
> [ ]
>
> ↓
>
> [ ]
>
> ↓
>
> Midas is content.

Reading Check

- Midas is greedy.
- Midas finds the satyr Silenus.
- Midas returns Silenus to Dionysus.
- Dionysus offers the king "any gift."
- Midas asks Dionysus for the power to change anything he touches into gold.
- When Midas's food and drink turn into gold, he cannot eat.
- Midas decides to ask Dionysus to take back the golden touch.
- Midas accidentally turns his daughter into a gold statue.
- Midas begs Dionysus to help him save his daughter.
- Midas washes in the river Pactolus, as Dionysus tells him to do.
- The golden touch leaves Midas, and his daughter is restored to life.
- Midas is content.

Vocabulary Development

Words from Mythology: Making Up Names

People over the ages have often turned to the ancient myths when they've wanted to name something new (such as a planet, a missile, a business, a disease).

PRACTICE

Work with a small group to see if you can use your knowledge of the myths and the chart of gods and goddesses on page 647 to make up imaginative names for these things:

1. a disco
2. a fishery
3. a sheet-metal shop
4. a messenger service
5. a cereal
6. a high school
7. a health club or spa
8. a winery

Using Allusions

An **allusion** is a reference to a work of literature or to an actual event, person, or place. When a speaker or writer makes an allusion, he or she expects the audience to recognize the reference and understand its meaning. For example, if you were to say that a stockbroker has "the golden touch," you would expect people to know you are alluding to the Midas myth. As you can see, a simple allusion can say a great deal in very few words.

PRACTICE

For each sentence, identify the allusion to mythology and explain its meaning. Research any allusions you don't recognize.

1. I feel sorry for Teresa, packed off to boarding school for half the year like poor Persephone.
2. When the power failed, the subway station became a dark and dismal underworld.
3. A modern-day Orpheus, the cellist played so beautifully he lifted the spirits of his audience.

SKILLS FOCUS

Vocabulary Skills
Understand word origins; understand allusions.

King Midas and the Golden Touch **687**

Vocabulary Development

Words from Mythology: Making Up Names

PRACTICE

Students should show knowledge of the special talents of particular characters. Possible answers follow:

1. The Orpheum
2. Neptune's Nets
3. Vulcan's Forge
4. Wings of Mercury
5. Demeter's Choice
6. The Atheneum
7. Pool of Narcissus
8. Dionysus's Vineyard

Using Allusions

PRACTICE

1. Persephone spends part of every year in the kingdom of Hades; the allusion compares a student's time in boarding school to Persephone's time in the underworld.
2. The underworld is gloomy and sad; the allusion suggests that the station becomes foreboding.
3. Orpheus's music is so beautiful that it has a positive effect on everyone and everything around him; the allusion suggests that the cellist's playing was similarly moving.

ASSESSING

Assessment
■ *Holt Assessment: Literature, Reading, and Vocabulary*

DIFFERENTIATING INSTRUCTION

Learners Having Difficulty

Reinforce students' knowledge of the mythological characters in this collection by having them name a Greek god or goddess with whom each of the people described below could be associated. Have students use the chart on p. 647 and also draw from information provided in the myths they have read. Students may use either the Roman or the Greek name of the god or goddess.

1. A person who loves the ocean. [Neptune, Poseidon]
2. A person who is very powerful. [Jupiter, Zeus]
3. A person who grows her own vegetables. [Ceres, Demeter]
4. A person who relays messages. [Mercury, Hermes]
5. A person who is hardhearted, sad, and gloomy. [Pluto, Hades]

Grade-Level Skills

■ **Reading Skills**
Summarize an article.

Upcoming Skills

■ **Reading Skills**
Determine whether a summary
is an accurate reflection of an
original text.

Summary *at grade level*

In 1957, archaeologists discovered in modern-day Turkey the
2,700-year-old tomb of Midas,
king of Phrygia. Resting within
the tomb were the remains of
the king, who had been buried
in a wooden coffin atop countless
layers of fine-woven linens. Also
discovered in the tomb were
cups and cauldrons containing
a dry, powdery sludge. The
sludge was packaged and stored
at the University of Pennsylvania
for forty years. Recently,
though, analyses showed that
the powdery substances are
actually the remains of Midas's
funeral banquet. The menu
included a meat-and-bean stew
and a punch made of wine,
beer, and mead.

PRETEACHING

Selection Starter

Build background. Explain to
students that the King Midas in the
article they are about to read was
an actual king who ruled territories in the ancient country Phrygia,
now part of Turkey. The article
explains how today's scientists
learned about him.

Preview Vocabulary

To build students' familiarity with
the Vocabulary words on p. 688,
have them work with a partner to
write a sentence using each word.

Informational Text

Summarizing a Text

Reading Focus
Summarizing

To **summarize** "King Midas and the Golden
Touch," you might write this:

King Midas is very rich, but he is greedy and is
not content with what he has. One day Midas
helps a follower of the god Dionysus, and in
return the god says that Midas can have any gift
he wants. King Midas asks that anything he
touch be turned to gold. He is delighted with
his new power until he turns his beloved
daughter into a gold statue. Midas begs Dionysus to forgive his greed, undo the gift, and restore his daughter. The god agrees, and King
Midas learns to be content with what he has.

A **summary** is a short restatement of the major
events or main ideas of a text. A summary of a
text is much shorter than the original, and it is
generally not as interesting. To summarize a
story, such as the myth of King Midas, you retell
all the main events and explain cause and effect.
To summarize an informational text, such as the
magazine article that follows, you restate the
main ideas and important details that support
those main ideas.

■ As you read "The Funeral Banquet of King
Midas," jot down anything you think might be a
main idea. These notes will help you summarize
the article when you have finished reading it.

SKILLS FOCUS

Reading Skills
Summarize
a text.

Checklist for a Summary of Informational Texts

1. Begin the summary with the
   title and **author** of the text.

2. State the **topic** of the text.

3. List the **main ideas,** in the
   order in which they occur.

4. Include important **supporting
   details** for the main ideas.

5. Put **quotation marks**
   around any words from the
   text that are quoted exactly.

Vocabulary Development

You'll learn these words as you read the
magazine article.

archaeologists (är′kē·äl′ə·jists) *n.:* scientists who study the culture of the past,
especially by excavating ancient sites.
*After years of digging, the archaeologists
were thrilled to find the hidden tomb.*

excavating (eks′kə·vāt′iŋ) *v.* used as *n.:*
uncovering or exposing by digging.
*It was his seventh season excavating the
burial site.*

avalanche (av′ə·lanch′) *n.:* mass of
loosened snow, earth, rocks, and so on,
suddenly and swiftly sliding down a
mountain. *They did not want their
digging to cause an avalanche that would
again bury the tomb.*

interior (in·tir′ē·ər) *n.:* inner part of
anything. The opposite of *interior* is
*exterior. They were amazed at the condition
of the objects in the interior of the tomb.*

RESOURCES: READING

Planning
■ *One-Stop Planner* CD-ROM with
ExamView Test Generator

Differentiating Instruction
■ *Holt Reading Solutions*
■ *Supporting Instruction in Spanish*
■ *Audio CD Library*
■ *Audio CD Library, Selections and
Summaries in Spanish*

Vocabulary
■ *Vocabulary Development*

Grammar and Language
■ *Daily Language Activities*

Assessment
■ *Holt Assessment: Literature, Reading,
and Vocabulary*
■ *One-Stop Planner* CD-ROM with
ExamView Test Generator

from Muse *magazine*

THE FUNERAL BANQUET OF KING MIDAS

John Fleischman

Hercules, they say, could kill a lion with his bare hands. The great Achilles, the story goes, could only be wounded on the heel. And King Midas turned everything he touched to gold. Well, Hercules and Achilles may have been myths, but there really was a King Midas. Recently we even found out what they served at his funeral.

The real King Midas lived in what is now central Turkey 2,700 years ago, in a kingdom called Phrygia. We know there was a King Midas because his neighbors, the mighty Assyrian kings to the east, wrote about him.

They called him Mita. The Greeks, who lived west of Phrygia, also knew about him. The Greek historian Herodotus said Midas was the first "barbarian" (or non-Greek) to dedicate an offering to Apollo at his shrine at Delphi. After he died, the Greek poets turned the man into a legend, giving him the curse of a golden touch and a shameful pair of donkey's ears.[1] But we were

---

1. **donkey's ears:** In the Greek myth, sometime after King Midas recovers from his golden touch, the god Apollo gets angry at him for foolish behavior and gives him donkey's ears.

The Funeral Banquet of King Midas **689**

■ *Holt Online Assessment*
Internet
■ go.hrw.com (Keyword: LE5 7-6)
■ *Elements of Literature Online*
Media
■ *Audio CD Library*
■ *Audio CD Library, Selections and Summaries in Spanish*

A Reading Informational Text

❓ **Use context clues.** What words give you a clue about what archaeologists do? ["dug up his tomb"]

B Reading Informational Text

❓ **Summarize.** What is the main idea of this paragraph? [Possible response: In 1957, archaeologists discovered the tomb of King Midas.]

C Vocabulary Development

Antonyms. Have students use *interior* as an adjective in a sentence. Then, ask what an antonym for *interior* might be. [*exterior*]

A reintroduced to the real King Midas when archaeologists dug up his tomb in 1957.

Rodney Young, an archaeologist at the University of Pennsylvania Museum, was searching for Midas's tomb in the ruins of Gordion, the ancient capital of Phrygia. It was Young's seventh season excavating the city, and he was exploring the base of a massive burial mound. To explore the mound without destroying it, he brought in **B** Turkish coal miners to dig a horizontal shaft. After tunneling 68 meters (about as far as 68 people holding hands would reach), the miners struck a smooth stone wall. When they broke through, a wave of rubble spilled out, blocking the tunnel. Young had them clear as much as they could without bringing down the clay ceiling. Beyond the rubble was a rough wall of heavy logs. The men sliced through that and unleashed another stone avalanche. Once it was cleared

away, they found an inner wall of beautifully crafted boxwood and cedar.

Young carefully sawed open a hatch, pushed his light into the interior, and found **C** himself staring into the eye sockets of King Midas. The king was facing him, laid out on what Young thought was a bed (it turned out to be an open coffin carved from a single tree) in a tomb stuffed with ancient textiles, wooden furniture, iron tripods, and bronze vessels—but not a speck of gold.

Vocabulary

archaeologists (är′kē·äl′ə·jists) *n.:* scientists who study the culture of the past, especially by excavating ancient sites.

excavating (eks′kə·vāt′iŋ) *v.* used as *n.:* uncovering or exposing by digging.

avalanche (av′ə·lanch′) *n.:* mass of loosened snow, earth, rocks, and so on, suddenly and swiftly sliding down a mountain.

interior (in·tir′ē·ər) *n.:* the inner part of anything. The opposite of *interior* is *exterior*.

The 49-meter (about 160 feet) tall burial mound of Midas. It was almost 3,000 years before anyone bothered to check if there was anything inside.

690 Collection 6 / Our Literary Heritage: Greek Myths and World Folk Tales

DIFFERENTIATING INSTRUCTION

Learners Having Difficulty
Before students read, have them write *Who?, What?, When?, Where?,* and *How?* down the left side of each of two sheets of paper. After *Who?* on the first sheet, have them write *Rodney Young and his team.* After *Who?* on the second sheet, have them write *Elizabeth Simpson.* Then, as they read the article, have students locate and record information that answers the remaining

questions on each sheet. When they are done, students can use the information to write a brief summary of the article.

English-Language Learners
Have students use context clues to determine the meanings of difficult words such as *massive, horizontal, unleashed, textiles,* and *astounded.*

Inside the Tomb

This drawing of the inside of the tomb was made before anything was moved, and all the objects were photographed in place.

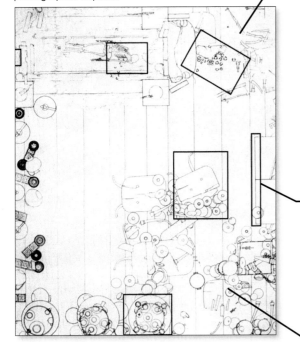

Near the front of Midas's collapsed sarcophagus, some bronze fibulae pour out of a torn sack. (Fibulae are sort of like ancient safety pins.) People must have thought they'd come in handy in the underworld, since Midas's sack held about 100 of them.

Carved wooden panels from the front of the buffet tables. On the right is a fallen bronze bowl.

Archaeologist Ellen Kohler, who also worked on the dig, says the skeleton of King Midas rested on what looked "like a million blankets," with a cover of thick felt over uncounted layers of fine-woven linens in purple, white, and pink. When the tomb was first opened, there was a strong, clean smell of freshly cut wood. "It smelled like the inside of a cedar chest," she says. "The wood still looked freshly cut."

The archaeologists were astounded to find cloth and wood in such good condition because these materials usually rot quickly. Amazingly, the cloth and wood in Midas's

No, it's not an elephant tusk. It's the wooden leg of a table that has collapsed, spilling more bronze bowls onto the floor.

A Reading Informational Text

Summarize. Summarize the process that kept the textiles and the wood in such good condition. [Possible response: The tomb was almost airtight. Therefore, the bacteria that worked on the body used up almost all of the oxygen. Without oxygen, the decaying process slowed almost to a stop.]

B Learners Having Difficulty

❷ Find details. How did scientists prove that this was King Midas's tomb? [The tree rings in the tomb's wooden walls showed that the trees were cut down no later than 718 B.C., which was when the Assyrians said Midas ruled.]

C Reading Informational Text

❷ Summarize. The article's focus shifts in these paragraphs. What new topic or question is introduced? [Possible response: What was the sludge in all of those cups and cauldrons?]

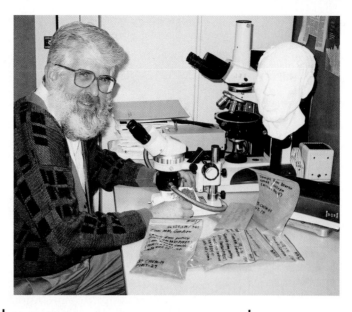

Patrick McGovern with bags of sludge from Midas's tomb. In front of him is a white plaster bust of the king—a reconstruction based on the shape of his skull.

tomb were saved by the decaying body of the king. Midas had been sealed under a burial mound of clay 49 meters high, making the tomb both dry and nearly airtight. As the bacteria that cause decay worked on his body, they also used up nearly all the oxygen in the tomb. Lack of oxygen slowed down the decay process so much that the textiles and wooden furniture were preserved for centuries. Unfortunately, once moist outside air entered the tomb, the textiles crumbled and turned a muddy brown within days.

But how could anyone be sure this was the tomb of Midas and not of some other Phrygian big shot? The answer has to do with that inner wall of boxwood and cedar. You could still see tree rings in the wood—wide ones the tree added in good years and narrow ones the tree added in bad years. Peter Kunihom of Cornell University was able to match the pattern of wide and narrow rings to the patterns in trees whose

age was known. In 1996, he said that the timbers were cut no later than 718 B.C., which was when the Assyrians said King "Mita" ruled in Phrygia.

But something had been overlooked in the excitement of the big discovery. At the bottom of all those bronze cauldrons and cups there was a dry, powdery sludge.[2] The powder was poured into paper bags, which were rolled shut, labeled, and shipped back to the University of Pennsylvania Museum of Archaeology in Philadelphia. There they sat on a shelf for 40 years.

Recently, Elizabeth Simpson of the Bard Graduate Study Center in New York, an expert on the Midas-tomb furniture, wondered what had happened to the sludge. She called Patrick McGovern, an archaeo-chemist at the Penn museum. Could he find

---

2. **sludge** *n.:* any heavy, muddy, or slimy deposit or waste.

Developing Word-Attack Skills
Review the typical spellings for the sound /ch/ using these selection words:
- *ch* for initial /ch/: *chest*
- *ch* for final /ch/ after consonants or vowel digraphs: *punch, touch, searching*
- *tch* for final /ch/ after short vowel sounds: *hatch*

Then, remind students that the digraph *ch* can also be pronounced /k/. Illustrate this alternative sound-letter correspondence using these selection words:
- *Achilles, archaeologist, archaeochemist, chemical, technology*—the letters *ch* stand for /k/

Activity. Have students identify the sound that the digraph *ch* represents in each of the following words:
change [/ch/]   *chilly* [/ch/]
choir [/k/]   *scratch* [/ch/]
Then, write these sentences on the board. Have students identify what sound the digraph *ch* stands for in each example.

the bags and run modern tests on their contents?

McGovern climbed the museum stairs and found the bags on a bookshelf in Ellen Kohler's office. Examining the powdery remains, he realized that there were two different kinds of sludge, one from the tomb's big cauldrons and pots and another from the drinking vessels. He guessed that the cauldrons were used for meat, and the vessels for alcoholic beverages. Both sludges had thoroughly dried over the centuries, but there was a good chance the food molecules hadn't broken down and could still be identified.

McGovern did some of the analysis himself, but also sent samples to several chemical laboratories that had more advanced equipment. The chemists used technology that wasn't available to Rodney Young in 1957. When the results of the tests came back, McGovern had the menu for Midas's funeral banquet.

They started with barbecue, either sheep or goat roasted over an open fire and basted with olive oil, honey, and spices. Part of the barbecued meat was for sacrifice, probably to the Phrygians' most powerful goddess, Matar. The rest became the main ingredient of a stew. The Phrygians added beans (probably lentils), more olive oil and honey, wine, anise or fennel, and more spices. The second sludge turned out to be from an alcoholic drink called a *kykeon* by the Greeks; we'd call it a punch. It's a mixture of grape wine, barley beer, and a fermented honey drink known as mead. Part of this punch would have been poured out on the ground or an altar stone as an offering to Matar. All the cauldrons, bowls, and dishes that were packed away so carefully inside the tomb were used for offerings to the goddess. The food and drink were part of the religious ceremony for the dead king.

So how did Midas end up with a golden touch? "I think Greek myth is really hard to fathom," says archaeologist Elizabeth Simpson. She believes that any king who was as wealthy as Midas would have been seen as a great man, especially by the poorer Greeks along the coast. Long after his death, his great burial mound at Gordion would have impressed them. "It took a long time and a lot of precise engineering to build that," says Dr. Simpson. "I say the Gordion earthwork is the counterpart of an Egyptian pyramid."

But great monuments don't guarantee great fame. Aside from King Tut, how many pharaohs can you name? How many of the great kings of Assyria? How many emperors of Persia? But if you were asked for the kings of little Phrygia, you would remember at least one "golden" name.

The Funeral Banquet of King Midas **693**

1. <u>Archaeologists</u> found many interesting objects in the tomb. [/k/]
2. They found a king's remains, some cauldrons, some cups, and a <u>bunch</u> of ancient "safety pins" called fibulae. [/ch/]
3. Luckily, <u>chemists</u> were able to date many of the items found in the tomb. [/k/]

DIRECT TEACHING

D Reading Informational Text

? Summarize. What main idea does this paragraph present? [Possible response: It tells what was served at King Midas's funeral banquet—namely, a meat-and-bean stew and an alcoholic punch.]

E English-Language Learners

Idioms. Remind students that the phrase *golden touch* alludes, or refers, to the wish, that King Midas was granted in the myth—that everything he touch turn to gold. Explain that the phrase is also used today as a figure of speech referring to a person's ability to make everything he or she "touches," or is associated with, successful or valuable.

F Reading Informational Text

? Summarize. Read this paragraph, and sum up its main idea. In other words, how is the question at the beginning of the paragraph answered? [Possible response: Midas became such a legend because he was extraordinarily rich.]

GUIDED PRACTICE

Monitor students' progress. To check students' understanding of the selection, have them state in a sentence the main ideas of the article. [Possible response: In 1957, archaeologists discovered the remains from a funeral banquet in King Midas's tomb.]

Summarizing a Text

Answers and Model Rationales

1. **C** The evidence of Midas's existence is based on writings from his neighbors. A and D are only rumors or legends. B does not support the case for King Midas's existence, even though it is true.

2. **F** Neither pictures of King Midas (G) nor the kinds of food King Midas liked (J) are mentioned in the article. Item H is negated on p. 690, which states that "not a speck of gold" was found in the tomb.

3. **D** Remind students that the cloth was preserved by the absence of oxygen and that once the tomb was opened, oxygen reentered the chamber and caused the cloth to deteriorate.

4. **F** Point out that this detail is important because it explains why King Midas became a mythological character.

Test-Taking Tips

For more information on how to answer multiple-choice items, refer students to **Test Smarts,** p. 920.

Constructed Response

Possible Answer
In 1957, a group of archaeologists discovered the tomb of Midas, who ruled territories in the small kingdom of Phrygia about 2,700 years ago. The king's body had decayed, but many of the other objects in the tomb were well preserved. These objects included bronze bowls, wooden furniture, and metal fasteners called fibulae. Midas's coffin was carved out of a single tree trunk. Scientists analyzed trees rings in the tomb's wooden walls to date the tomb

---

Summarizing a Text

THE FUNERAL BANQUET OF KING MIDAS

1. How do we know there really was a King Midas?
   - **A** The Greeks made him into a legend.
   - **B** He lived 2,700 years ago in Phrygia.
   - **C** His neighbors, the Assyrians, wrote about him.
   - **D** He turned everything he touched into gold.

2. Why do scientists think they found the tomb of King Midas, and not of someone else?
   - **F** Tree rings in the wood date the tomb to the time of King Midas's rule.
   - **G** The skeleton looks just like pictures we have of King Midas.
   - **H** The tomb is filled with lots and lots of gold.
   - **J** The tomb contains the kinds of food that King Midas liked to eat.

3. What happened to the cloth in King Midas's tomb once the tomb was opened?
   - **A** It was preserved in a museum.
   - **B** It was worn in a play based on the myth.
   - **C** Historians used it to learn about customs of the time.
   - **D** It crumbled and turned brown within days.

4. How do scientists think the myth of the "golden touch" might have developed?
   - **F** King Midas was a wealthy king and impressed his neighbors.
   - **G** King Midas had a palace made entirely of gold.
   - **H** The kingdom of Phrygia was famous for its gold mines.
   - **J** The sand in Phrygia glows golden in the sunlight.

Constructed Response

Look back at the notes you took while reading "The Funeral Banquet of King Midas." Then, write a brief **summary** of the magazine article. List only the main ideas and the most important supporting details.

SKILLS FOCUS

Reading Skills
Summarize an article.

---

and to prove that it was, in fact, that of King Midas. Later, scientists analyzed a powdery substance that was found in some of the tomb's vessels. These tests showed that a meat-and-bean stew and an alcoholic punch were part of Midas's funeral ceremony. Scholars believe that Midas became famous because he was such a wealthy king—a theory that, in spite of the absence of gold, his tomb tends to support.

Using Context Clues

When you don't understand a word, you can often find clues to its meaning in the surrounding passages. For an example, here is a passage from "The Funeral Banquet of King Midas" that includes a word from the Word Bank.

> **"After he died, the Greek poets turned [King Midas] into a legend, giving him the curse of a golden touch and a shameful pair of donkey's ears. But we were reintroduced to the real King Midas when archaeologists dug up his tomb in 1957."**

The word *but* is a context clue that lets you know two things are being contrasted. Poets tell "legends," but archaeologists tell about the "real" king; therefore, archaeologists are probably scientists. Since archaeologists *dug* up the tomb of an ancient king, you could figure out that they are scientists who dig up things buried in the ground.

PRACTICE

For each passage below from "The Funeral Banquet of King Midas," give the meaning of the underlined word, identify the context clues, and explain how they reveal that meaning.

1. "It was Young's seventh season <u>excavating</u> the city, and he was exploring the base of a massive burial mound. To explore the mound without destroying it, he brought in Turkish coal miners to dig a horizontal shaft."

2. "When they broke through, a wave of rubble spilled out, blocking the tunnel. Young had them clear as much as they could without bringing down the clay ceiling. Beyond the rubble was a rough wall of heavy logs. The men sliced through that and unleashed another stone <u>avalanche</u>."

3. "Once [the rubble] was cleared away, they found an inner wall of beautifully crafted boxwood and cedar.
   "Young carefully sawed open a hatch, pushed his light into the <u>interior</u>, and found himself staring into the eye sockets of King Midas."

Word Bank

archaeologists
excavating
avalanche
interior

SKILLS FOCUS

Vocabulary Skills
Clarify word meanings by context.

Vocabulary Development

PRACTICE

Possible Answers

1. *Excavating* means "digging something up." *Context clues*—"exploring the base of a massive burial mound"; "dig a horizontal shaft." The clues reveal the word's meaning by suggesting that *excavate* means "to uncover" or "to dig."

2. An *avalanche* is a large quantity of material that comes down suddenly. *Context clues*—"wave of rubble"; "bringing down"; "unleashed." The clues tell you that the rubble moves in a downward motion and that it can easily be let loose.

3. *Interior* means "the inside of something." *Context clues*— "inner wall"; "sawed open a hatch"; "pushed his light [into the interior]." The clues tell you that the archaeologists were probing into a previously closed inner chamber.

ASSESSING

Assessment

■ *Holt Assessment: Literature, Reading, and Vocabulary*

Grade-Level Skills
■ Literary Skills
Understand folk tales.

Upcoming Skills
■ Literary Skills
Analyze recurring themes across traditional and contemporary works.

Elements of Literature: Folk Tales

In this feature, Virginia Hamilton—a folklorist and a skilled writer of original stories—uses recollections of folk-tale storytelling in her family to explore folk tales as "self-portraits" of their tellers and as a global vehicle for sharing dreams, frustrations, and values.

Elements of Literature
Folk Tales *by* Virginia Hamilton

TELLING TALES

Who tells stories where you live? Is it your mother or father? Is it your uncle or aunt? your cousin or your friend? Is it you?

"Nobody I know tells stories," I answered when my English teacher asked that question. "At my house, everybody just talks."

Now I realize that both my father and mother were storytellers. I simply did not recognize that what they were "talking" were stories.

Mother would begin a story with "That reminds me" or "I remember when." Once she began, "That reminds me of the time all of the Boston ivy fell from Mrs. Pinton's house."

"All of it? All at once—when did that happen?" my oldest sister, Nina, asked. And Mother was off and running with the tale about "the day the ivy fell."

My mom and dad loved telling stories and remembering their pasts. We don't know for certain, but perhaps folk tales—"tells"—began in a similar way.

How Folk Tales Grow

Literary Skills
Understand folk tales.

Folk tales are stories passed on by word of mouth, often over many centuries. Each time the tale is told, it is changed a bit because no two people tell a story exactly the same way.

Some of these folk tales travel; that is, as they are told and retold, they move out of their original environments into other times and other places. Although traditional folk tales reflect the particular culture and people that created them, common features, called **motifs,** can be found in folk stories from many parts of the world. You'll find that many folk tales include motifs like grateful beasts, tests of the hero, magic, false parents, fairy godmothers, and brave youngest sons and daughters.

Handed down from generation to generation, told over and over again, these "tells" become familiar stories—"They say the people could fly . . ."; "Once upon a time . . ." They have become tales of the folks.

American Folk Tales: Keeping Cultures Alive

When the first Europeans came with their folk tales, the Native Americans already had an elaborate and rich folklore tradition. Other folk tales traveled to the New World from other countries. For example, Africans who were brought to America as slaves carried with them their unique "folk-telling" traditions. Over generations they passed on tales about their lives on the plantations and about their relationships with the white men and women who held them as slaves.

In fact, the African American storyteller developed the animal tale into a

696 Collection 6 / Our Literary Heritage: Greek Myths and World Folk Tales

DIFFERENTIATING INSTRUCTION

Learners Having Difficulty
Students may find it helpful to have a set of questions on which to focus as they read. Turn the subheadings in the feature into questions: How do folk tales grow? How have American folk tales kept cultures alive? What do folk tales have to do with a sense of "community"? Why are "tells" and storytellers important? Then have students discuss the answers to these questions.

English-Language Learners
This feature offers culturally diverse students many opportunities to participate. Have volunteers describe occasions when old stories are told within the family and tell how those stories are family "self-portraits." Ask other volunteers to summarize a tale they think reflects their cultural background; then discuss elements from Hamilton's essay that apply to it.

highly individual form. In this animal tale the social order of the plantation is broken down into animal elements, which symbolize the people in the plantation community. The African folk-tale tellers who were slaves fantasized about freedom and so developed another kind of folk tale, an **escape story,** about flying away from slavery.

In America, people from Ireland, Denmark, Germany, France, Italy, Poland, Turkey, the Middle East, Russia, China, Japan, Korea, Vietnam, Cambodia, the Philippines, Brazil, Haiti, Puerto Rico, Nigeria, Jamaica, and practically everywhere else have told their children folk tales from their old homelands. These stories, as well as their dances, songs, and folk art, help these people stay together and keep their beliefs and cultures alive.

Folk Tales and Community

Some folk tales are simple stories and others are complex. But the basic situation of the tale teller weaving his or her magic for a community of listeners is found everywhere, in every society.

For generation after generation, folk tales keep alive and close what we regard as important. They reveal who we are. As they instruct us in living, they show us our weaknesses and strengths, our fears and joys, our nightmares and wishes. Folk tales are our self-portraits.

"Tells" and Tale Givers

All over America there are folk-tale-telling festivals, in which tale tellers stand up and give "tells" to the listeners. In fact, storytelling festivals take place every year all around the world—from Scotland to South Africa. In the United States, festivals occur in more than thirty states.

Storytelling is an ancient and wonderful custom. I have grown out of the tale-giving tradition and so, perhaps, have some of you. As you read these folk tales from around the world, think about those early folk-tale tellers who committed tales to memory in order to tell them aloud. Try to picture what those early tellings must have been like—imagine the smoky underground kivas of the Pueblos, the dusty village squares in Nigeria.

Sitting or standing there, surrounded by the community of listeners, the teller calls softly, "Time was when the animals could talk . . ." The listeners respond. They lean forward, absolutely quiet now, eager to hear, to be entertained, to learn.

Practice

All cultures have their own folk tales. Do you have any favorites? Maybe you are familiar with "Little Red Riding Hood" or "Cinderella." Make a list of all the folk tales you can remember. What makes these tales memorable?

Practice

Use this essay to help students review some elements of folk tales. Ask the following questions:

- **According to Hamilton, what is a "tell," or folk tale?** [It is a story that is passed along by word of mouth, often over generations.]
- **Name two motifs that are common in folk tales.** [Possible answers: grateful beasts, heroic tests, magic, false parents, fairy godmothers, brave youngest children.] **Why, then, are stories with the same motif not the same in every way?** [As folk tales traveled beyond their places of origin, they changed to reflect and meet the needs of new listeners. Storytellers also changed other elements of the tales to satisfy their own desire for creativity.]
- **What two types of folk tales were associated with enslaved African Americans?** [animal tales and escape stories] **Why were such stories told?** [Escape stories captured the people's desire to get away from the conditions of slavery. Animal tales helped symbolize the interaction of people in the plantation community.]

Apply

After students have read this feature, allow them to experience the pleasure of being the audience of a storyteller. Arrange to have a storyteller come to class; secure an audiotape (or, preferably, a videotape) of a storytelling session; or prepare to perform your favorite tale for the class. Suggest that students take notes on the performance and see if they can find evidence of any of the elements, such as motifs or metamorphoses, that Hamilton mentions. Follow up with a class discussion, inviting students to name their favorite aspects of the experience and to share other comments.

Advanced Learners

Enrichment. Some of Virginia Hamilton's tales appear in *The People Could Fly: American Black Folktales*. Have students read stories in that collection (or listen to them read by James Earl Jones on the audiotape edition), summarize them for the class, and explain how Hamilton puts into practice the things that she notes in this feature.

Grade-Level Skills

■ **Literary Skills**
Analyze elements of folk tales, including the superhero motif.

■ **Reading Skills**
Summarize.

Upcoming Skills

■ **Literary Skills**
Analyze recurring themes across traditional and contemporary works.

Summary ⟷ *at grade level*

In this Yoruban folk tale, the main character, Oni, is born wearing boots that grow as he grows. The boots later prove to make him invulnerable to enemy arrows. Oni's peers fear this and banish him from the village. He wanders to the village of Ajo and offers to help its people by vanquishing Anodo, a giant eagle that menaces the village. Oni kills the monstrous bird but gets trapped beneath a cotton tree that snaps in half when Anodo crashes to earth. Oni wriggles free, leaving one of his magic boots behind. The next day, when a local warrior takes credit for the kill, Oni asserts his claim. The boot is retrieved, Oni shows that it fits only his own foot, and he receives half the kingdom as his reward.

Before You Read The Folk Tale

Oni and the Great Bird

Make the Connection
Quickwrite ✏️

Superman, Wonder Woman, and Batman are popular action heroes. What makes these characters superheroes? How are they different from real-life heroes? Write briefly about what you think makes someone a hero in real life.

Literary Focus
Motifs in Folk Tales: Superheroes

Features that are repeated in stories throughout the world are called **motifs** (mō·tēfs′). From your reading, you may remember the evil witch, the poor stepdaughter, the man-eating monster, the quest to save a kingdom. All these are popular motifs in storytelling. Another popular motif—the larger-than-life **superhero**—appears in the Yoruban folk tale you are about to read.

Reading Skills
Summarizing

A lot happens in the next story. After you read it, you'll be asked to write a summary. To prepare for your summary, as you read take notes on the main characters, the conflict, the time and place, the main events, and the resolution.

INTERNET
Vocabulary
Activity
•
Cross-curricular
Connection
Keyword: LE5 7-6

SKILLS FOCUS

Literary Skills
Understand motifs.

Reading Skills
Summarize.

Vocabulary Development

You'll learn these words as you read "Oni and the Great Bird."

implored (im·plôrd′) *v.*: asked or begged. *The old man implored Oni to do nothing dangerous.*

commenced (kə·menst′) *v.*: began. *Oni commenced to sing only when the eagle flew near.*

invincible (in·vin′sə·bəl) *adj.*: unbeatable. *No one could beat invincible Oni.*

hovered (huv′ərd) *v.*: hung in the air. *The great bird flew in and hovered above them.*

impostor (im·päs′tər) *n.*: person who pretends to be someone or something that he or she is not. *The hunter who claimed to have done Oni's deeds was an imposter.*

Background
Literature and Music

"Oni and the Great Bird" is a folk tale of the Yoruba, a West African people known for their storytelling and musical talents. In the tale, short songs, or chants, are set off from the rest of the story. When Yoruban stories are told in ritual gatherings, these lines are chanted to the accompaniment of drums called gangans. These drums are used to imitate the sounds and patterns of Yoruban speech.

698 Collection 6 / Our Literary Heritage: Greek Myths and World Folk Tales

---

RESOURCES: READING

Planning
■ *One-Stop Planner* CD-ROM with ExamView Test Generator

Differentiating Instruction
■ *The Holt Reader*
■ *Holt Reading Solutions*
■ *Supporting Instruction in Spanish*
■ *Audio CD Library*

■ *Audio CD Library, Selections and Summaries in Spanish*

Vocabulary
■ *Vocabulary Development*

Grammar and Language
■ *Daily Language Activities*
■ *Language Handbook Worksheets*

Oni and the Great Bird

Yoruban, retold by
Abayomi Fuja

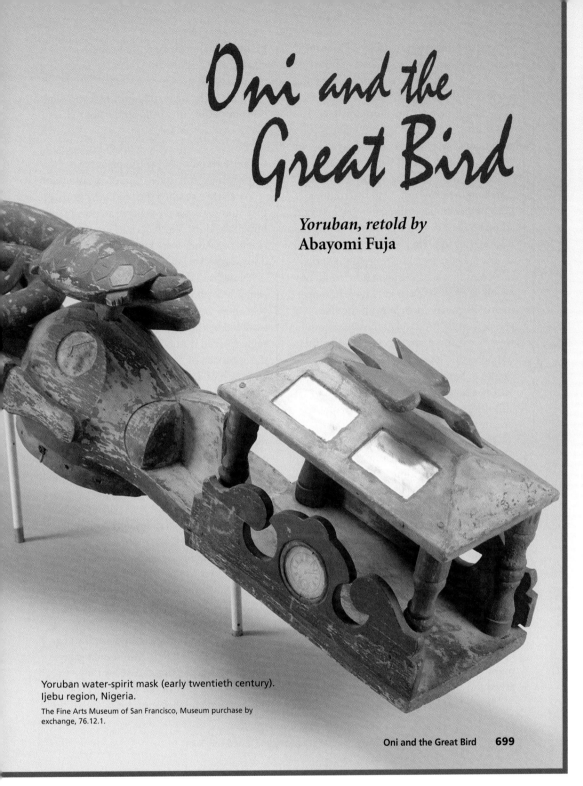

Yoruban water-spirit mask (early twentieth century).
Ijebu region, Nigeria.

The Fine Arts Museum of San Francisco, Museum purchase by
exchange, 76.12.1.

Oni and the Great Bird   **699**

Assessment

■ *Holt Assessment: Literature, Reading,
and Vocabulary*
■ *One-Stop Planner* CD-ROM with
ExamView Test Generator
■ *Holt Online Assessment*

Internet

■ go.hrw.com (Keyword: LE5 7-6)
■ *Elements of Literature Online*

Media

■ *Audio CD Library*
■ *Audio CD Library, Selections and
Summaries in Spanish*

Selection Starter

Motivate. Have students name some superheroes they've met in books, in movies, and on television. Discuss what makes these superheroes exceptional.

Preview Vocabulary

Have students read the definitions of the Vocabulary words on p. 698. Then ask them to explain their answers to the following questions:

1. "I implored Mom to let me go," your friend says, "but she refused." How hard did your friend try?
2. If a vehicle hovered, what was it doing?
3. What would you do if you discovered an imposter?
4. You enter the theater as the movie commences. How late are you?
5. Would you want to undertake a dangerous expedition with someone who thought he was invincible? Why or why not?

Assign the Reading

Have the class read the first two pages of the selection aloud. Then, have students finish reading the story independently. Assign the After You Read activities as homework.

HOMEWORK

VIEWING THE ART

Nigerian art is characterized by diverse styles. One prevalent artistic tradition is the mask. Some masks are carved from wood and boast bold figures; others resemble skulls and human heads; others depict animal features and geometric shapes.

Activity. Call on volunteers to name adjectives that they think describe this mask. [Possible responses: *detailed, noble, mysterious*]

Oni and the Great Bird   **699**

A Literary Focus

? Superhero motif. What makes Oni different from other people? [Possible responses: He was born wearing boots that grow as he grows; he is unaffected by the arrows of enemies.]

B Reading Skills

? Summarize. After students have read the first paragraph, challenge them to recap Oni's biography, up to his banishment, in no more than two sentences. [Possible response: Oni, who was born wearing magical boots, is not hurt by enemy arrows. Afraid of his strangeness, some villagers make a false charge against him and have him banished.] Students might save their summaries for the summary activity on p. 705.

C Cross-curricular Connections CULTURE

Yoruba. The Yoruba, who live chiefly in southwestern Nigeria, are one of more than 250 tribal groups in Nigeria. The name *Yoruba* identifies both the people and one of Nigeria's regional languages. When Oni left his village, it is quite possible that he met a group of people with a different language and set of customs.

D Learners Having Difficulty

Find details. Point out that the speaker is giving background information. Ask students to list the important details that are presented. [The village has been menaced for years by a giant eagle. The bird arrives at dusk and stays until dawn. It kills anyone who is not safely indoors. The bells are rung as a warning to villagers to return home. No one knows where the eagle comes from or where it goes when it leaves at dawn.]

There was once a strange boy called Oni who was born wearing a pair of boots. As Oni grew, the boots grew also. When he was a boy of eighteen years of age, war broke out between his people and another village. It was during the battle that Oni made a second discovery about himself, which separated him from his fellow men and made him different. The enemy arrows did not seem to harm him. Many pierced his body, which in the ordinary course of events should have slain him. The other young men noticed this too. They already regarded Oni as strange because of his wonderful boots, but when they discovered that he could not be killed, they were afraid to have him near them. When he returned from the war, several people tried to kill him in various ways but without any success. Finding this did not work, it was decided to find an excuse to banish him. He was accused of setting a house on fire in the village, and although Oni had nothing to do with the fire, he was found guilty and banished.

Oni wandered alone on foot for a long time. One afternoon he came to the banks of a great river, and finding an empty canoe and feeling tired of walking, he got into the boat and made his way downstream. Towards evening, when it was growing dark, Oni reached a town and decided to pull into the bank and spend the night there. There were the sounds of many bells being rung and people seemed to be in a hurry. Oni tied up the canoe and climbed the bank, and as he did so, he met an old man. "Good evening, my friend. My name is Oni. I am a stranger to your town and have nowhere to spend the night. Will you take me to your house?" Oni asked the old man.

"Yes, certainly, come along with me, but we must go quickly because the bells are ringing and it is growing dusk," replied the old man.

"What is the name of your town and why do your people ring bells on the approach of darkness?" asked Oni.

"People call this place Ajo, but hurry up, we must get indoors. I will explain the bells to you when we are inside," replied the old man.

When they reached the old man's house, they found his people waiting anxiously for him at the door. The bells had now stopped ringing and they were hurried inside and the door was securely fastened.

"Now," said the old man, "sit down and eat with us and I will explain. For many years now we, the people of Ajo, have been troubled by the nightly arrival of a giant eagle. We call it Anodo. It always appears on the approach of darkness and stays until the approach of dawn. Anybody who is unfortunate enough to be out of doors at the time of its appearance is sure to be killed by it. You were very fortunate, young man, to reach Ajo before darkness. Our king has ordered the ringing of bells to warn the people to return to their homes and lock the doors. None of us knows where the eagle comes from or where it goes when it leaves us at dawn. It is a terrible curse, and in the past it has killed many of our people."

The old man had hardly finished speaking when Oni heard the sound of great wings flapping over the house. It sounded like a great wind, and the windows and doors shook in their frames.

"It must be a very great bird," remarked Oni. After Oni had fed, the old man gave him a mat and a cloth and he lay down to sleep in the corner of the room. Sleep would not come to Oni, however, for he heard the

---

DIFFERENTIATING INSTRUCTION

Learners Having Difficulty
Read the story aloud to students. Pause at the following points, and have students tell what has happened:
- " . . . he was found guilty and banished." (p. 700)
- " . . . as it flew to and fro over Ajo." (p. 701)
- " . . . ordered Oni to lie down on his mat and keep quiet." (p. 702)

- " . . . then Oni fainted again." (p. 703)
- " . . . the streets were full of happy, dancing people." (p. 704)

English-Language Learners
After students have read the account of Oni's battle against the fearsome Anodo (p. 702), invite them to share stories from their own cultural traditions about heroes who confront monstrous beings.

constant noise of the great eagle's wings as it flew to and fro over Ajo.

When morning had come and the eagle had departed, Oni thanked the old man for his kindness and set out to find the king of Ajo and to ask for an audience.[1] It was granted.

"My name is Oni and I am a stranger to your town. I have come to offer my services in helping to rid this town of the eagle Anodo," said Oni.

"And what makes you think you will succeed where so many others have tried and failed?" asked the king.

"I have certain powers and juju,"[2] said Oni.

"So had the others. One by one all my hunters have tried and have been killed or carried off by Anodo. Strangers have come from time to time to offer their services, but they too have perished. It is some time now since anybody has tried to kill Anodo, and I have issued orders to my remaining hunters not to try, as enough of them have been killed already," said the king.

"Have you ever offered a reward to anybody who could succeed in killing the bird?" asked Oni.

"Indeed, yes. The man who succeeds will have half my kingdom. I made that offer long ago," replied the king.

---

1. **audience** *n.:* here, formal interview with a person of high rank.
2. **juju** *n.:* magic charm used by some West African peoples; the magic of such charms.

Yoruban mounted-warrior veranda post, carved by Olowe of Ise (twentieth century).
New Orleans Museum of Art: Museum Purchase: Ella West Freeman Foundation Matching Fund 70.20.

Oni and the Great Bird   701

Oni and the Great Bird   701

A Reading Skills

❓ Identify cause and effect.
The villagers are obviously afraid of the eagle. Why, then, are they so upset that Oni plans to try to kill it? [Possible responses: They probably doubt that Oni will succeed. They may fear that Anodo will retaliate, taking out its vengeance on them.]

B Literary Focus

❓ Figurative language. What does Oni mean when he sings about "the knives of nature and man"? [The "knives of nature" are Anodo's sharp talons; the "knives of man" are Oni's weapons.]

C Literary Focus

Action verbs. Have students identify the action verbs (or verb forms) in this sentence [*threw, swooped, seizing, drew*] and discuss how they help set the battle in vivid motion. Ask students to find and comment on other action verbs in the account of the battle. [Examples include *pecked, buried, beat, rolled, swept,* and *plunged.*]

"Then I will try tonight," answered Oni, and he paid his respects to the king and departed.

Oni returned to the old man's house and told him what had happened and of his intention to challenge Anodo. The old man was very frightened and implored him to give up the idea, for he would only perish and perhaps all those in the house too. But Oni was not frightened. He took his bow and arrows and knives and examined them carefully.

It seemed ages to Oni before he heard the bells ringing. Never had he known a longer day in his life. The old man was uneasy and his people were almost hostile towards Oni. When they heard the bells ringing at last, they lost no time in fastening the doors and windows and ordered Oni to lie down on his mat and keep quiet.

Presently they heard the noise of a great wind, which heralded the approach of Anodo. Soon the great wings were above the house. Oni waited till the great bird was overhead and then he commenced to sing:

> Tonight Oni will be at war with Anodo,
> The eagle whose talons are sharper than
>   knives,
> For now the knives of nature and man will
>   meet.
> Oni is invincible; his knife is sharp.

Anodo heard the challenge as he hovered over the house, and circling slowly round, he came back and sang:

> Ah, fortune, I have found a victim
>   tonight,
> I have lived many months without a kill,
> Will the singer come out and feel the
>   sharpness

Of my talons and of my beak? It will
   take me
A moment to tear him to pieces. Come out.

All the people in the house were terrified. They seized Oni and threw him out of the house, fearing the vengeance of Anodo on them all.

As they threw Oni out into the road, Anodo swooped down and, seizing him in his talons, drew him upwards. Oni slashed the eagle in the chest with his knife and the eagle dropped him with a scream. Oni fell to the ground, dazed. He picked himself up as the huge bird descended once again. He had time to use his bow and discharge an arrow into Anodo before the wounded bird beat him to the ground with his great wings and pecked him severely. Again Oni's knife tore at the eagle, and he buried it twice in Anodo. Slowly the eagle beat his great wings and rose slowly into the air; then he hovered for a last terrible dive on Oni. Oni watched him and, putting an arrow in his bow, took aim. The great bird hovered; then with a terrible noise he tore down on the boy, gathering speed as he came. There was a great roar of wind as he came down. Oni discharged a second arrow, then another and another in quick succession, but still the bird came on. A moment later it had hit Oni and knocked him over. The boy rolled over, a thousand lights dancing before his eyes; then all went blank, and he felt himself sinking down and down into a bottomless pit. He was knocked unconscious and had not seen that the great

---

Vocabulary
implored (im·plôrd') *v.:* asked or begged.
commenced (kə'·menst') *v.:* began.
invincible (in·vin'sə·bəl) *adj.:* unbeatable.
hovered (huv'ərd) *v.:* hung in the air.

CROSS-CURRICULAR CONNECTIONS

Geography
Nigeria. Ask students to find Nigeria on a map and to locate a river along which Oni could have traveled to find the village of Ajo. Next, provide them with pages from an almanac that contain information on the country (or have them find such information on their own), and ask them to create a travel brochure using facts about the Yoruba people or Nigeria.

INDIVIDUAL

bird was already dead before it struck him. Its great wings swept the boy to one side, and it plunged on into a cotton tree, which snapped like a twig and came crashing down to bury the eagle and Oni under a mass of leaves.

When Oni recovered, he felt very weak, and it was all he could do to free himself from the great wing of the dead Anodo and the cotton tree leaves. As he struggled, one **D** of his magic boots came off and remained stuck beneath the dead bird. He was very weak and with great difficulty staggered along till he reached the edge of the river; then Oni fainted again. **E**

Early next morning the people came out to see the dead Anodo lying in the broken cotton tree. There was great rejoicing and drumming and the king soon appeared with his chiefs to view the wonderful sight. "Who is the great man who killed Anodo?" he asked. One of his hunters stepped forward and, prostrating[3] himself on the ground, claimed that he was responsible for the deed.

"Then you will be rewarded generously, for I have promised to give half my kingdom to the man who killed Anodo and it is yours," replied the king.

There was great rejoicing and dancing and the hunter was carried to the king's palace and feasted. A very bedraggled figure then appeared; his clothes were torn and one of his boots was missing. It was Oni.

"Ah," said the king, "here is the stranger who calls himself Oni and who came yesterday to announce his intention of killing the eagle. You come too late, my friend, I fear."

"I killed Anodo. This man is an impostor and a liar," said Oni.

There was whispering between the king and his chiefs. At last he said, "Very well, you claim to have killed Anodo. What proof have you got to offer?"

Epa cult mask.
Founders Society Purchase, Friends of African Art Fund. Photograph © 1995 The Detroit Institute of Arts Accession number 77.71.

---

3. **prostrating** (präs′trāt′iŋ) *v.* used as *adj.*: throwing oneself on the ground to show humility and submission, a traditional gesture of respect toward rulers in many cultures.

Vocabulary
impostor (im·päs′tər) *n.*: person who pretends to be someone or something that he or she is not.

Oni and the Great Bird   **703**

MINI-LESSON   Reading

Developing Word-Attack Skills
Point out that there's a mnemonic to help people remember whether a word is spelled with *ie* or *ei*:
   I before *e* except after *c*
   And when sounded like *a*
   As in *neighbor* and *weigh.*
When one is reading, however, the problem is how to pronounce *ie.* These words from the selection illustrate some of the possibilities:

a. In *pierce, ie* stands for short *i.*
b. In *pieces* and *chiefs, ie* stands for long *e.*
c. In *view, ie* is followed by *w,* producing a *y* sound and a long *u.*
d. In *quiet, ie* stands for two vowel sounds: long *i* and the unstressed vowel sound schwa.
e. In *audience, ie* also stands for two different vowel sounds, but in this word the sounds are long *e* and schwa.

Activity. Have students determine the sound of *ie* in each of these words and identify the type of sound, using the lettered list on the right.
1. field [b]
2. client [d]
3. fierce [a]
4. obedient [e]
5. review [c]

a. short *i*
b. long *e*
c. long *u*
d. long *i* and schwa
e. long *e* and schwa

Oni and the Great Bird   **703**

? **Compare and contrast.** How is Oni's situation similar to that of another folk-tale character? [Possible response: Oni loses his boot and must prove his identity by showing that he is the only one who can fit into it, just as Cinderella has to prove her identity by fitting into the slipper that she lost.] Tell students that they will read several other stories with the same motif later in this collection.

GUIDED PRACTICE

Monitor students' progress. Use these questions to check students' comprehension of the tale.

1. What is strange about Oni's birth? [He is born wearing boots.]

2. Why do people fear him? [He cannot be harmed by enemy arrows in battle.]

3. Why does the bell ring in the town of Ajo? [to warn people to get indoors before darkness and the arrival of Anodo]

4. What weapons does Oni use to kill the bird? [a knife and a bow and arrow]

5. What is Oni's reward for killing the bird? [half of the kingdom]

Meet the Writer

In his stories, Abayomi Fuja attempts to maintain the spirit of Yoruban storytelling by including phrases that are traditionally chanted as free verse. The Yoruba, who live mainly in Nigeria, are estimated to number more than five million. For centuries they have been known for their drum-based storytelling and oratory.

"You see my condition," replied Oni, "but if you require further proof, send your men out to clear away the dead eagle and the broken cotton tree. Somewhere underneath you will find one of my boots."

The king ordered his men to go at once and search for the boot. After some little time the men returned. They carried Oni's magic boot. "We found it underneath the dead eagle's wing," they announced to the king.

"Now if you are still undecided and disbelieve my story, will you ask everybody to try on the boot and see if it fits," said Oni.

The king ordered everybody to try to see if they could fit the boot to their feet. Strange to relate, although it looked a perfectly normal boot, nobody could manage to put it on. When they had all tried without success,

the boot was placed before the king and Oni stepped forward and said:

Boot from Heaven—boot from Heaven, Go on to your master's foot.

Immediately, the boot started to move from before the king and fitted itself onto Oni's foot of its own accord. The people and the king were convinced of the truth of Oni's claims and marveled greatly and were very delighted and grateful for his brave deed. The dishonest hunter was taken out and executed, and Oni received the promised reward.

That night, for the first time for many years, the bells of Ajo did not sound the curfew. Instead, the streets were full of happy, dancing people.

Meet the Writer

Abayomi Fuja

At Home in Two Worlds

Abayomi Fuja, a Yoruban, was born in Nigeria. When he was growing up, Fuja was taught by British missionaries, so he learned English and studied European stories at school. As an adult he decided to celebrate his Yoruban heritage by collecting the traditional folk tales of his people. He devoted six years to recording tales like "Oni and the Great Bird." Though written in English, they remain true to the style and spirit of the original Yoruban folk tales. By retelling these traditional African stories in English, Fuja brings together the two worlds in which he grew up.

For Independent Reading

If you liked "Oni and the Great Bird," you might want to explore the other stories in *Fourteen Hundred Cowries,* the book it's taken from. (A cowrie is a glossy shell that the Yoruba use to signal certain ideas. For instance, two shells placed together means friendship; two shells placed apart means hostility.)

CROSS-CURRICULAR CONNECTIONS

Culture

West African storytellers. In West Africa the word *griot* (grē′ō) is the name for a person who is an expert in oral performance. In Africa today a griot may be a professional storyteller, singer, or entertainer. In the past, the griot's role was chiefly that of preserving tradition. Griots were skilled at creating and transmitting the many forms of African oral literature. Many also memorized their nation's histories and laws.

Rather than consulting books or libraries, people in Africa's kingdoms consulted griots. Elsewhere on the African continent, storytellers, bards, town criers, and oral historians also preserved and continued the oral traditions.

Activity. Ask students to do more research on griots and present their findings to the rest of the class.

First Thoughts

1. Do you think Oni is a hero? Be sure to check your notes for the Quickwrite on page 698. 🖋

Thinking Critically

2. Look back at Oni's song to Anodo before the fight (page 702). What do you think the song shows about Oni's **character**?

3. What makes Oni an example of the **super-hero motif** in folk tales? How is Oni like the action heroes in comics and movies?

4. The magic boots set Oni apart, making him "strange" and "different." What lesson might this tale teach Yoruban children about how to behave toward people who are different from them?

5. Think about what happens to the hunter who tries to take credit for killing Anodo. What does his fate tell you about the beliefs of the Yoruba?

Extending Interpretations

6. Oni was an outsider—even among his own people. Do you think that heroes in real life are usually outsiders, or are they usually part of the group? Give examples to support your point of view.

7. In this story Oni saves the people from the threat of a giant eagle. If the story were set in modern times, what dangerous force might Oni have to save the people from?

WRITING

Writing a Summary

In a **summary** you restate the most important events of a story. Refer to the notes you took while you read, and write a summary of "Oni and the Great Bird." Tell about each major event in a complete sentence. Use transitional words like *then, after,* and *as a result* to indicate when and where events happened and what caused the events to happen. 📖

Reading Check

a. Why must Oni leave his village?

b. How does the king of Ajo react to Oni's offer to fight Anodo?

c. What happens when Oni fights Anodo?

d. How does Oni prove that the hunter who claims to have killed Anodo is an impostor?

INTERNET
Projects and Activities
Keyword: LE5 7-6

Literary Skills
Analyze the superhero motif.

Reading Skills
Summarize.

Writing Skills
Write a summary.

After You Read

First Thoughts

1. Possible answer: Oni can be physically hurt and he can experience emotions such as impatience and uncertainty—just like the rest of us. But he is heroic because he is able to overcome adversity.

Thinking Critically

2. The song reveals Oni's confidence and belief in his own power.

3. Oni is an example of the superhero motif because he has superhuman powers. Like action heroes, Oni fights against a dangerous enemy and must use his physical strength to prevail.

4. Yoruba children might learn to respect differences in people and to understand that differences may be good.

5. The execution of the dishonest hunter suggests that the Yoruba disapprove of lying.

Extending Interpretations

6. Students may suggest that fictional heroes such as Superman are often outsiders but that real-life heroes, such as Mohandas Gandhi or Abraham Lincoln, are usually supported and praised by most of the people whom they attempt to help.

7. Answers might include such natural disasters as a hurricane, an earthquake, or a tornado.

Reading Check

a. Oni is banished after being declared guilty of setting a villager's house on fire—a false accusation made by villagers who fear him.

b. The king seems doubtful, for he tells Oni that many others have tried but failed to kill Anodo.

c. In a fierce battle, Oni shoots Anodo from the sky. As the bird crashes to the ground, it plunges into a cotton tree, which buries both Anodo and Oni.

d. While freeing himself, Oni loses one of his boots. It is found beneath Anodo's body. Oni invites everyone to try it on, but it fits only his foot.

Vocabulary Development

PRACTICE

Students should demonstrate their knowledge of the meanings of the Vocabulary words defined on p. 698.

Grammar Link

PRACTICE

Invite students to comment on what they learn from preparing a test such as the following:

1. Are you going _____ tomorrow? [there]
2. Do you know if _____ going too? [they're]
3. Please put _____ books on the desk for me. [their]
4. _____ going to the movie with me Saturday. [They're]
5. _____ supposed to hang _____ coats _____.
[They're, their, there]

ASSESSING

Assessment

■ *Holt Assessment: Literature, Reading, and Vocabulary*

After You Read · Vocabulary Development

Clarifying Word Meanings

PRACTICE

Imagine that you work for an animation production company that is launching a cartoon about a new superhero. Use the words in the Word Bank to write a summary of the cartoon superhero's first adventure. (You may make the verbs any tense you wish.)

> **Word Bank**
> implored
> commenced
> invincible
> hovered
> impostor

(Left) Spider-Man.
(Right) Superman.

Grammar Link

They're, Their, There

Many words in English sound like other words but have very different meanings and functions. Three words often confused are *they're, their,* and *there*:

they're: a contraction of "they are."

their: a personal possessive pronoun.

there: a word that means "at that place" or that begins a sentence such as "There was once a strange boy called Oni who was born wearing a pair of boots."

EXAMPLES

When the people of the town hear the bells, they're very frightened. [They are very frightened.]

" 'Our king has ordered the ringing of bells to warn the people to return to their homes and lock the doors.' " [*Their* is a possessive pronoun modifying *homes*.]

Tonight there will be much celebrating in the town.

When you find one of these confusing words in your writing, ask yourself:

1. Can I substitute the words *they are*? If so, use *they're*.
2. Does the word answer the question *whose*? If so, use *their*.

PRACTICE

Be a test maker. Write five sentences that ask for a choice between *there*, *their*, and *they're*. Exchange tests with a partner, and then grade your partner's paper.

SKILLS FOCUS

Vocabulary Skills
Clarify word meanings.

Grammar Skills
Use *they're*, *their*, and *there* correctly.

706   Collection 6 / Our Literary Heritage: Greek Myths and World Folk Tales

---

DIFFERENTIATING INSTRUCTION

Learners Having Difficulty
To give students extra practice using *they're, their,* and *there,* have them choose the word that correctly completes each sentence.

1. They're/There were many people who wanted to try on Oni's boot. [There]
2. Oni thought, "These people— they're/there all impostors." [they're]
3. "There/Their attempts will fail." [Their]

4. "There/Their is my boot, and now I will prove that their/they're liars." [There, they're]
5. Soon the people of Ajo were dancing around the fire, singing the praises of their/there new hero. [their]

Before You Read   The Folk Tale

Master Frog

Make the Connection
Quickwrite ✎

The main character of this Vietnamese folk tale is just like other boys except for his unusual appearance. People who judge him only by his looks are missing all the special qualities and talents that lie beneath the surface. There's more to all of us than what appears on the surface. What are your special qualities and talents? List some of the things you're good at.

Literary Focus
Motifs in Folk Tales: Metamorphosis

This story involves a **metamorphosis** (met′ə·môr′fə·sis)—a fantastic transformation, or change, from one shape to another. Shape changes are common motifs in comics, myths, and fairy tales. In numerous folk tales, for example, a frog with bulging eyes turns into a handsome prince when someone loves him despite his ugly appearance. In this story a frog changes shape; however, the metamorphosis has an unusual twist.

Reading Skills
Making Predictions

There are so many surprises in "Master Frog" that it is a good story to use for making **predictions,** or guessing what will happen next.

Before you read, follow these steps:
- Think about your prior experience with folk tales.
- Remember what you've learned about **metamorphosis.**
- Preview the quotations on pages 708, 710, 713, and 714. Then, write a sentence predicting what will happen in this story.

While you read, follow these steps:
- Adjust your original prediction, if necessary.
- Write a new prediction before you begin each page.

Vocabulary Development

Pay attention to these words as you read "Master Frog."

admonished (ad·män′isht) *v.:* warned or urged. *The teacher admonished the other students to be more like Master Frog.*

entreaties (en·trēt′ēz) *n.:* earnest requests. *All his mother's entreaties couldn't change Master Frog's mind.*

charade (shə·rād′) *n.:* obvious pretense or act. *The king got mad at Master Frog's proposal, which he thought was a charade.*

presumptuous (prē·zump′chōō·əs) *adj.:* too bold; arrogant. *The king ordered the presumptuous frog out of his sight.*

cowered (kou′ərd) *v.:* crouched and trembled in fear. *When the tigers roared, everyone cowered in fear.*

INTERNET
Vocabulary Activity
Keyword: LE5 7-6

SKILLS FOCUS

Literary Skills
Understand metamorphosis.

Reading Skills
Make predictions.

SKILLS FOCUS
pp. 707–717

Grade-Level Skills

■ **Literary Skills**
Analyze elements of folk tales, including metamorphosis.

■ **Reading Skills**
Make predictions.

Summary ⬆ *above grade level*

After her husband dies, Giang Dung gives birth to a frog. The creature grows up as a clever, affectionate boy. When he asks to marry the king's daughter, the astonished king curtly dismisses him; Master Frog counters by causing a magical stampede of wild animals in the palace. Princess Kien Tien offers to marry him, and the pair soon settle into a happy marriage. One day Kien Tien is horrified to find her husband dead. Her mourning is interrupted by the appearance of a handsome young man. It is the new incarnation of Master Frog, a prince of Fairyland, who has come to earth in search of adventure. The prince warns his bride that his frog skin must be preserved or he will have to return to Fairyland. Kien Tien's jealous sisters destroy the skin, and Master Frog dies. The sisters then drug Kien Tien, throw her into the sea, and tell their father that the princess has committed suicide. Returning to earth, Master Frog dashes to the watery depths to rescue his beloved, and they live happily ever after.

Master Frog   **707**

Selection Starter

Motivate. Write the word *metamorphosis* on the board. Ask students to identify the word's root [–*morph*–] and then underline it. Tell students that this Greek root means "form." Then, ask them what they think the prefix *meta*– means. ["change"] Finally, have students explain why a frog is an appropriate choice for a character who changes form. [because tadpoles undergo metamorphosis to become frogs]

Preview Vocabulary

Have students consider the definitions of the Vocabulary words on p. 707 and think about the intensity of each word. Have pairs or small groups of students suggest at least two synonyms or near-synonyms for each word (using a thesaurus if they wish). [Possible responses: *admonished*—cautioned, advised, scolded; *entreaties*—wishes, petitions, demands; *charade*—make-believe, trickery, deceit; *presumptuous*—confident, egotistical, audacious; *cowered*—cringed, groveled]

Assign the Reading

In class, read the first three pages of the story aloud while students follow along in their books. Stop at the end of each page and have students make predictions about what will happen next. Then have students finish reading and jotting down their predictions independently. Assign the After You Read activities as homework.

A Reading Skills

Draw conclusions. How do these townspeople seem to feel about physical beauty? Explain. [Possible response: They seem to value it highly, because they gossip about why anyone would marry a girl as plain as Giang Dung. After she is widowed, they speculate that she will not find another husband.]

Master Frog

Vietnamese, retold by
Lynette Dyer Vuong

Except for his strange appearance, Master Frog was really quite an ordinary boy . . .

One of a pair of belt buckles. Eastern Inner Mongolia
Asian Art Museum of San Francisco, The Avery Brundage Collection, B60B1082/1083.
Used by permission.

Giang Dung[1] was a plain girl, so plain in fact that all the townspeople marveled when her parents finally found her a husband. Then they nodded their heads knowingly and whispered to one another that the young man must have been after her father's money. He had plenty of it, it was true, and Giang Dung was his only child. The day of the wedding came and passed, and the people found more interesting things to gossip about until a few months later, when Giang Dung's husband died.

"It's fortunate that she's expecting a child," one person said, and the rest agreed. "At least she'll have someone to look after her in her old age. It's certain she'll never find anyone else to marry her."

But when the child was born, instead of being a boy to carry on her husband's name or at least a girl to give her some comfort and companionship, it was only a frog. And the people's tongues wagged again until they tired of the subject. "What would you expect? Giang Dung almost looks like a frog herself, she's so ugly."

Poor Giang Dung cried for days until she had no tears left. Then she resigned herself to her fate and determined to raise the frog as well as she could. If she was being punished for some unknown evil she had

1. **Giang Dung** (zäng′ zōōm′): Vietnamese for "pretty face," an ironic name for a plain girl.

DIFFERENTIATING INSTRUCTION

Learners Having Difficulty
You may want to model the reading skill of making predictions for these students. After you read the short paragraph at the top of p. 709 (" . . . won't cause you any trouble"), say: "I have already learned that the frog is an active, helpful, intelligent boy. People with these qualities are usually good students. Even though the teacher doesn't expect him to do well, I predict that the frog will become a model student." As they read, encourage students to ask themselves, "From what I already know, what do I predict will happen next?"

English-Language Learners
Although "Master Frog" is an old story, Vuong uses modern dialogue to tell it. As you discuss passages of dialogue in the story, invite students to contrast various

committed, she would have to make the best of it and serve her sentence. But on the other hand, Heaven sometimes worked in mysterious ways, and it was just possible that some great destiny lay ahead for her son. ❶

⛵ PREDICT
❶ Do you think Giang Dung is being punished, or is the frog marked for greatness? Give reasons for your prediction.

But as the years passed, Giang Dung forgot both of these theories. Except for his strange appearance, Master Frog was really quite an ordinary boy—now mischievous, now helpful, but always affectionate. He followed her around the house as she went about her daily tasks, helping her to care for the silkworms.[2] He gathered mulberry leaves for her to chop and place in their trays; he watched them as they began to spin their cocoons, fascinated at the way they swung their heads down and round and then up again to surround themselves with the fine strands. He often perched beside her as she sat at the loom and thought it great fun to take the shuttle in his mouth and wriggle his small body in and out among the warp threads. Sometimes, as she was cooking, he would hop up on the stove to stir the soup, or if he was sure she was not watching him, to snap up some tasty tidbit with his long, sticky tongue. But, like other children, he was often bored with being indoors and went out to play hide-and-seek and hopscotch with the boys of the neighborhood. All in all, he was both a good-natured and an intelligent little fellow, and his mother decided at last that something must be done about his education.

2. **silkworms:** moth caterpillars that produce cocoons of silk fiber. Some silkworms are grown and cultivated as the source of silk.

"A frog? In my class?" the teacher demanded when Giang Dung brought him to the school. "Impossible! I would be the laughingstock of the town."

"Then at least let him sit at the back and listen," she pleaded with him. "I promise you he won't cause you any trouble."

As the weeks went by, Master Frog proved himself such a model student that at last the teacher moved him up to the head of the class and often admonished the others to follow his example. At first he had tried to grasp the brush with his front feet but later found that he could form more graceful characters if he held it in his mouth. Generally he was the first to commit a passage to memory, and if none of the others could correctly interpret a line of the reading, the teacher would call on Master Frog. Finally, Master Frog completed his education and grew to young froghood.

"It's time to think of learning some trade," Giang Dung suggested to him one day. "Tomorrow I will go to town and talk to some of the craftsmen. Perhaps one of them would be willing to take you on as an apprentice."

But Master Frog shook his head. "Mother, first I would like to get married."

"G . . . get married!" she stammered, almost unable to believe her ears. "I . . . is there any particular girl you have in mind?"

"Yes, Mother. Princess Kien Tien,[3] the king's youngest daughter."

Giang Dung drew back in alarm. "Son, you must be out of your mind! How could

3. **Kien Tien** (kē·'n′ tē·en′).

Vocabulary
admonished (ad·män′isht) *v.:* warned or urged.

Master Frog   **709**

DIRECT TEACHING

ⓑ Reading Skills
Predict. [Possible response to question 1: Giang Dung's frog son is probably marked for greatness because Giang Dung has never done anything deserving of punishment.]

ⓒ English-Language Learners
Context clues. If students are not familiar with the word *laughingstock*, ask if they can figure out its meaning from the context. [A laughingstock is an object of ridicule.]

ⓓ Reading Skills
❷ Analyze character. What do Giang Dung's attitude toward her son and her actions on his behalf reveal about her character? [Possible response: She is a loving and attentive mother who accepts the child as he is.]

ⓔ Vocabulary Note
Suffixes. Students already may know that the suffix *–ly* usually signals adverbs. Use this sentence to point out that the adverbs formed by *–ly* sometimes signal expressions of time (*generally*), sometimes expressions of manner (*correctly*), and sometimes other information.

characters' manners of speaking (the king's daughters, for example). For additional strategies to supplement instruction for English-language learners, see *Holt Reading Solutions.*

Special Education Students
For lessons designed for special education students, see *Holt Reading Solutions.*

Advanced Learners
In her introduction to *The Brocaded Slipper,* from which this tale comes, Lynette Dyer Vuong says that for Master Frog, "winning the princess did not automatically rid him of his ugly skin. In Vietnamese fairy tales one usually must work hard to deserve to 'live happily ever after.'" Challenge students to support Vuong's comment by citing specific details from the story.

A Reading Skills

Predict. [Possible response to question 2: Yes, Master Frog will probably marry Kien Tien. Frogs in folk tales and fairy tales usually end up marrying princesses. Also, Master Frog has been successful at everything else he has tried so far.]

B Advanced Learners

❷ Verbal irony. What does the king mean when he comments on the "noble air" of Master Frog? [He is being sarcastic, making fun of Master Frog.] After Master Frog's transformation, return to this comment, pointing out that the king had no idea that Master Frog's nobility actually was greater than his own.

C Learners Having Difficulty

Break down difficult text. The length of this sentence need not derail readers. Have them read aloud the description of the first daughter, ending at the phrase *fell to the floor.* Explain that the semi-colon indicates a break in thought. Then have them continue with the two remaining descriptions. Ask students to restate in their own words what each description reveals about the king's daughters. Emphasize that punctuation can assist readers by breaking down lengthy passages into manageable units of thought.

you ever hope to marry the king's daughter?"

"Nevertheless I shall marry her." Master Frog planted all four feet on the table in a stance of determination. "Tomorrow I shall go to the king to ask for her hand." ❷

A

> **📖 PREDICT**
> ❷ Think about what you know about folk tales. Do you think Master Frog will marry Princess Kien Tien?

All Giang Dung's protests—all her entreaties —were in vain. Master Frog had made up his mind, and

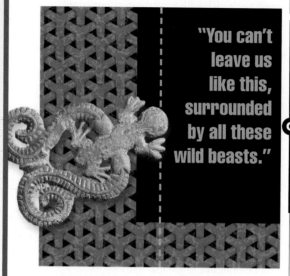

"You can't leave us like this, surrounded by all these wild beasts."

nothing could change it. And so the next morning he and Giang Dung set off for the palace.

Giang Dung set him down as they entered the audience hall, and he hopped straight up to the king, bowing respectfully as he neared the throne. The king stared at him in astonishment as he made his request and then burst out laughing.

"So you want to marry my daughter," he said. "Well, I have three daughters. Which one is it you want? But don't be in a hurry to

make up your mind." His lips twisted in amusement as he motioned to one of the courtiers.[4] "Bring their royal highnesses here."

"Come here, my dears," he beckoned to them as they entered the hall. "A suitor has presented himself to request the hand of one of you." With a grand sweep of his forearm he indicated Master Frog at the foot of the throne. "He has not yet told me the extent of his kingdom or the number of vassals[5] who pay him tribute, but does he not have a noble air?" He turned back to Master Frog. "Allow me to introduce my daughters to your highness: Kim Chau,"[6] he pointed to the first, who cast a contemptuous[7] glance in Master Frog's direction, then gave her head such a violent toss that one of her pearl hairpins slipped from its place and fell to the floor; "Bich Ngoc,"[8] he indicated the second, who made a face at him and stuck out her tongue; "and Kien Tien," he presented the last of the three, who had stood the whole time, her hands folded in her long sleeves and her eyes on the floor. "Now would you please tell me which of the three pleases you?"

Kim Chau's chin rose a trifle higher. "I won't marry him, Father."

"I'll kill myself if you force me to marry him," Bich Ngoc declared with a stamp of her foot.

4. **courtiers** (kôrt'ē·ərz) *n.:* royal attendants.
5. **vassals** *n.:* subjects.
6. **Kim Chau** (kim' chō'): Kim is Vietnamese for "gold" and *chau* for "pearl or precious stone."
7. **contemptuous** (kən·temp'ch'o͞o·əs) *adj.:* scornful, snobbish.
8. **Bich Ngoc** (bik' näp'): *Ngoc* is Vietnamese for "emerald."

Vocabulary
entreaties (en·trēt'ēz) *n.:* earnest requests.

Science
Frog findings. Have students work in pairs to gather information about frogs and to share their findings with the class (using visuals to illustrate, if possible). That information might include facts related to the following topics:
• types of frogs
• scientific names
• physical characteristics
• environment
• behavior
• eating habits
Consider allowing a volunteer to bring a frog to class for observation.

PAIRED

"Your Majesty," Master Frog interrupted them, "it is Kien Tien whose hand I have come to seek."

"Enough of this charade." The king's face had grown angry. "We have carried this joke far enough." He motioned to the guards. "Take this presumptuous creature out of my sight at once and execute him."

As the king finished speaking, Master Frog croaked in a loud voice. Suddenly the building began to shake as lightning flashed and thunder roared. On all sides the doors flew open, and the guards cowered in terror as wild beasts of every description burst into the hall. Elephants trumpeted as they stampeded in, tigers roared, leopards and panthers growled as they sprang from one corner to another.

"A few minutes ago Your Majesty inquired about my vassals," Master Frog's croak rose above the uproar. "They have come. I will leave them here to answer any questions you may have about the extent of my kingdom. Until we meet again, Your Majesty." Master Frog turned and hopped toward the exit.

"Wait! Wait!" the king shouted after him as a tiger leapt over his throne, pursuing a panther in a game of tag. "You can't leave us like this, surrounded by all these wild beasts." But Master Frog only hopped over their backs, one after another, as he made his way to the door. "Daughters, what shall we do?"

"I wouldn't marry a frog if he were the son of Jade Emperor!" Kim Chau's voice was as haughty as ever, though she winced[9] as a leopard brushed past her.

Bich Ngoc covered her face as a bear lumbered toward her. "I'd rather be torn limb from limb!" she screeched.

---

9. **winced** (winst) *v.*: drew back in fear, making a face.

"Father, I'll marry him." Kien Tien squeezed between two elephants to the king's side. "It's not right for us to think only of ourselves when the whole kingdom may be in danger. And the frog cannot be such a bad sort. He's obviously an individual of great power, yet he does not appear to be cruel. With all these beasts surrounding us, not one of us has been harmed." ❸

📖 **INFER**
❸ What do Kien Tien's words tell you about her **character**?

As she finished speaking, the uproar ceased, and one by one the beasts filed from the hall. Master Frog stood alone before the king.

"I will send the engagement gifts tomorrow," he said as he, too, turned and hopped from the room.

A few days later the wedding was celebrated with great pomp and ceremony. Kings and dignitaries[10] of all the surrounding countries came to pay their respects, and no one dared to laugh at Master Frog or the princess, for the tales of his great power had spread far and wide.

During the weeks that followed, Master Frog and Kien Tien lived together happily as the two came to understand each other better and to care for each other more deeply. In spite of his ugliness, Kien Tien found him such an intelligent and such a pleasant companion that as the days went by,

---

10. **dignitaries** *n.*: people holding high, dignified positions.

Vocabulary

charade (shə·rād′) *n.*: obvious pretense or act.
presumptuous (prē·zump′cho͞o·əs) *adj.*: too bold; arrogant.
cowered (kou′ərd) *v.*: crouched and trembled in fear.

D Reading Skills

❓ **Make judgments.** Up until now, there was no indication that Master Frog had supernatural powers or that he would take violent action. What do you think of his response to the king? [Many students may feel that his response is out of character. Others may say that since this is a fairy tale—in which anything can happen—the usual rules about character and predictability do not apply.]

E Cross-curricular Connections
LITERATURE

Jade Emperor. In tales from Vietnamese mythology the Jade Emperor (in Vietnamese, Ngoc Hoang), a celestial being, was the chief god of Taoism and the king of the gods and fairies. Ironically, the frog that Kim Chau so despises turns out to be exactly what she mentions—a son of Jade Emperor.

F Reading Skills

Infer. [Possible response to question 3: Kien Tien's words tell me that she is selfless, insightful, and generous.]

G Reading Skills

❓ **Extend the text.** How do Kien Tien's feelings about Master Frog change? [Possible response: She goes from being somewhat afraid of Master Frog to having genuine affection for him.]

CROSS-CURRICULAR CONNECTIONS

Culture
Vietnam and China. The culture of Vietnam has been heavily influenced by that of China. Indeed, Vietnam ("the Smaller Dragon") was annexed to the Han empire and was ruled for a thousand years by China ("the Greater Dragon"). Vietnam had its own culture, but much of its formal expression in art and literature took place through Chinese forms (such as using an adaptation of Chinese characters for writing).

INDIVIDUAL

A Reading Skills

Predict. [Possible response to question 4: The man will turn out to be the frog, in a new form.]

B Literary Focus

? Metamorphosis. What do you think has caused this change? [Possible responses: Master Frog's successes in life and love; Kien Tien's love for Master Frog.]

C Reading Skills

? Predict. What can you guess from the young man's warning? [Possible response: His warning may indicate that something will happen to the skin later on.]

D English-Language Learners

Idioms. Explain to English-language learners that a white elephant was a prized possession, often worshipped in southeastern Asia. The term *white elephant* also refers to a possession no longer wanted by its owner. This definition refers to a custom of the kings of Siam, who would express displeasure with a member of the court by giving him a white elephant. The expense of the elephant's upkeep would bring the courtier to financial ruin.

E Reading Skills

? Infer. Why is Bich Ngoc so interested in seeing the frog skin? [Possible responses: She wants to see if perhaps Master Frog is still a frog and the prince is a hoax; she wants to harm the frog skin because she is jealous.]

she grew genuinely fond of him. Then one morning she awoke to find the frog lying dead on the pillow beside her.

With a cry she lifted her husband's body to her lips, kissing it again and again as her tears wet the mottled[11] green skin. Someone called her name, and she looked up to see a handsome young man standing next to the bed, his arms outstretched as if to embrace her. **④**

PREDICT

④ Many folk tales involve a **metamorphosis**, or shape change. Who do you predict the handsome young man will turn out to be?

She backed away from him, crying out in alarm. "How dare you come here?" she demanded. "Can't you see my husband is dead and I am mourning him?" Suddenly her eyes narrowed. "Or was it you who killed him, you miserable creature!" She burst into fresh tears. "You shall surely die for your crime!"

The man smiled. "No, Kien Tien. I am Master Frog. What you are holding there is only my skin, which I shed during the night." He sat down beside her. "I am a fairy, a heavenly mandarin,[12] one of the sons of Jade Emperor. I was bored with the life in Fairyland and wanted to seek adventure in the world below. But when I asked my father's permission, he was angry with me. He said he would grant my request but that I must be born as a frog. Only if I could succeed in that form would I be able to resume my true shape. Now I have proved myself and am allowed to shed the frog's skin. But you must put the skin away carefully where no harm

can come to it because if it should ever be destroyed, I would have to return immediately to Jade Emperor's palace."

Overjoyed at her good fortune, Kien Tien did as he said. The days that followed were full of joy for the newlyweds. The king was filled with pride at the handsomeness and intelligence of his son-in-law, which matched so well the beauty and talent of his youngest daughter. He took them wherever he went to show them off. On every trip that he made to the surrounding countries, they accompanied him in his golden palanquin,[13] and when he rode through the streets of the capital, they sat beside him on the back of his white elephant, cheered by all who watched them pass.

"Why didn't he tell us who he was in the first place?" Kim Chau grumbled to her sister as they watched the parade from the palace balcony. "Was it fair to come in that ugly old frog skin and then change into a handsome prince after he'd married Kien Tien?"

"If she was dumb enough to marry a frog, he should have stayed a frog," Bich Ngoc grunted in agreement.

"He should be punished for his deception. What right did he have to ask for Kien Tien anyway? I'm the oldest."

"Kien Tien says he's a son of Jade Emperor, but I don't believe it. He's probably nothing but an ordinary frog. Why don't we see if we can find his skin and have a look at it?"

The sisters went to Kien Tien's room, searching through chest after chest and shelf after shelf till at last, among a pile of her

---

11. **mottled** (mät′ld) *adj.*: spotted or streaked.
12. **mandarin** *n.*: member of any powerful group.

13. **palanquin** (pal′ən·kēn′) *n.*: covered structure enclosing a couch. A palanquin is carried by long poles resting on the shoulders of two or more men.

712   Collection 6 / Our Literary Heritage: Greek Myths and World Folk Tales

DIFFERENTIATING INSTRUCTION

Advanced Learners

Activity. Have students work in groups of three to present a television literary review show about "Master Frog." A host should introduce, moderate, and wrap up as reviewers summarize the story, tell what they did or did not like about it, and give it a thumbs-up or a thumbs-down rating. If possible, videotape the presentations for student review and enjoyment.

SMALL GROUP

most precious silks, they found what they were looking for. ⑤

"She hid it well enough," Kim Chau sniffed. "No wonder. It's an ugly old thing, isn't it?"

Bich Ngoc reached for it, turning it over in her hands. "It certainly is. And just as I thought, nothing but an ordinary frog skin." She squinted her eyes thoughtfully. "Who knows but what, if we caught a couple of frogs for ourselves, they might shed their skins for us? There might be a handsome

📖 **PREDICT**
⑤ What do you think the two sisters will do with the frog skin? How might their actions affect Master Frog?

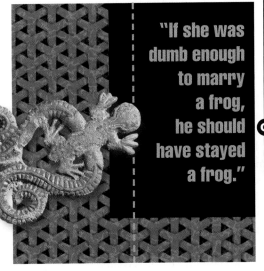

"If she was dumb enough to marry a frog, he should have stayed a frog."

prince in any one of them if we could just get him to come out." She stuffed Master Frog's skin into her sash as the two of them hurried out to the pond.

Day by day Kim Chau and Bich Ngoc watched their chosen frogs, waiting for the hoped-for transformation. They fed them on the most delicious foods; petted them; cooed endearments and whispered promises of fame, fortune, and riches in their ears. And each night they gently laid them on the pillow next to them, certain that the coming morning would bring the answer to their dreams. But nothing happened; both frogs remained as they were when they had fished them from the pond.

"There has to be a prince in there!" Bich Ngoc cried one morning in exasperation. "And I'm not going to wait any longer to find him." She picked up a knife and began to skin the poor creature alive.

Kim Chau snatched up her own frog and followed her example. But before they were finished, it was plain that no prince was to be found. In disgust the sisters threw the corpses into the fireplace.

Bich Ngoc jerked Master Frog's skin from her belt. "I don't know what I'm still carrying this around for," she grunted as she tossed it into the fire.

Meanwhile in Kien Tien's room, she and Master Frog were just getting out of bed. Suddenly he gave a cry of pain.

"My chest, my arms, my legs are burning!" he cried. "My whole body is on fire."

As Kien Tien rushed to his side, he fell to the floor, writhing in agony. Moments later he lay lifeless in her arms. Kien Tien pressed him close to her, weeping bitterly.

"It must be because you burned his old frog skin," Kim Chau whispered to Bich Ngoc when they heard what had happened. "What are we going to do? Sooner or later she'll discover the skin is missing, and if she finds out we took it and tells Father . . ."

Bich Ngoc clapped her hand over her sister's mouth. "We aren't going to sit around and wait for that to happen!"

Together they went to Kien Tien's room, where she lay on the bed weeping. They sat down beside her, stroking her hair to comfort her.

Master Frog **713**

DIRECT TEACHING

F Reading Skills
Predict. [Possible response to question 5: They may keep the skin or destroy it. Their actions might cause Master Frog to lose all that he has worked so hard to gain.]

G Literary Focus
❓ **Specific words.** What are some of the specific words that help us imagine Bich Ngoc and her plan? [Specific words include *squinted, caught, stuffed,* and *sash.*]

H Reading Skills
❓ **Predict.** What do you think the sisters are going to do next? [Possible response: They seem desperate to keep their sister from finding out why her husband has died—so desperate, perhaps, that they may try to kill her.]

CROSS-CURRICULAR CONNECTIONS

Industrial Arts
Diorama. Have students work in teams to create a diorama of the Crystal Palace as they imagine it. Remind students to use details from the story as well as their own imaginations to create the scene.

SMALL GROUP

A **Literary Focus**

❓ **Metamorphosis.** In what sense has Master Frog undergone another metamorphosis? [He has come back to life.]

B **Reading Skills**

❓ **Infer.** How does Bich Ngoc try to deceive her brother-in-law and hide her guilt? [Possible response: She weeps false tears of grief, repeats to him the lie about Kien Tien's suicide, and offers to help in any way she can.]

C **Cross-curricular Connections**
LITERATURE

The Crystal Palace. In Vietnamese mythology, the Crystal Palace was the underwater home of the Dragon King (Hai Long Vuong), ruler of the seas. "Master Frog" presents the Dragon King as the brother of Jade Emperor.

D **Reading Skills**

Predict. [Possible responses to question 6: The couple will live happily ever after. Kien Tien's sisters may have to pay a price for their selfish behavior.]

E **Reading Skills**

❓ **Compare and contrast.** How does the ending of this tale remind you of other stories in this collection? [Possible response: The main characters live happily ever after and are rewarded for their good deeds, while the troublemakers suffer the consequences of their evil deeds.]

"Come, little sister, it's a terrible tragedy, but you mustn't spend the whole day lying here crying." Bich Ngoc poured some tea from the teapot on the table, dropping a little sleeping powder into the cup as she carried it back to the bed. "Here, drink something warm. It'll make you feel better."

Kien Tien raised her head, sipping the hot liquid as Bich Ngoc held it to her lips. Then she lay down again and was soon fast asleep.

Quickly the sisters lifted her and carried her outside to the carriage. As fast as they could make the horses go, they rode out of town to the seaside. Then, making sure that no one was around, they shoved their sister out of the carriage, watching with satisfaction as she hit the surface of the water and sank beneath the waves. Then they rushed home

As Master Frog rose, a company of shrimps and turtles entered the hall.

to tell their father that Kien Tien had committed suicide.

"We tried to stop her," Bich Ngoc sobbed into her handkerchief. "But she wouldn't listen to us. She was so miserable at the thought of never seeing Master Frog again that

she threw herself into the sea. The waves carried her away before we could call for help."

Suddenly gasps rose throughout the audience hall. Master Frog had entered the room.

He approached the throne, bowing respectfully. "Jade Emperor has allowed me to return to the earth to complete my lifetime," he told the king. "But why is everyone crying? What has happened?" He gazed from one person to another, seeking an answer.

"Dear brother-in-law, our sister is dead." Bich Ngoc wiped the tears from her eyes as she spoke. "She was so overcome with sorrow at losing you that she threw herself into the sea." She stepped closer to him, laying her hand on his arm. "I know what a shock it is for you. But Kim Chau and I will do everything we can to help. Either one of us would be willing to take our sister's place."

But Master Frog was already running toward the door. At his order a horse was saddled, and he leapt on its back, riding at top speed toward the sea. Fearlessly he dove in, letting his body sink to the bottom. Swiftly he ran across the ocean floor to the Crystal Palace and, bursting through the gates, prostrated himself before the Dragon King of the Waters.

The Dragon King gazed down at him kindly. "Stand up, nephew. What you are seeking may be behind you."

As Master Frog rose, a company of shrimps and turtles entered the hall. One of them bore Kien Tien in his arms.

"My soldiers have found your wife," the Dragon King told him. "I would have let her live here in my palace, but since you've come for her, you may take her home with you."

Master Frog rushed toward her joyfully. As he lifted her from the turtle-soldier's arms, she opened her eyes and smiled up at him. Then both of them fell at the Dragon

---

DEVELOPING FLUENCY

Students may enjoy reading this story aloud as if it were a script. Assign readers the following parts: narrator, villager 1, villager 2, villager 3, Giang Dung, teacher, Master Frog (in frog form), the king, Kim Chau, Bich Ngoc, Kien Tien, Master Frog (in human form), the Dragon King. Give students time to review their lines before they read aloud. Encourage them to familiarize themselves with the lines that come right before their own and to listen for these lines as cues.

King's feet to thank him for his mercy.

Master Frog led Kien Tien out of the Crystal Palace and up through the water to the shore, where his horse was waiting. Together they rode back to the palace. **6** 🏊

Kim Chau glanced down from her balcony to see Master Frog reining his horse below. She drew back in alarm and called to her sister.

"We're done for," she trembled, grabbing Bich Ngoc's arm and pulling her after her. "Kien Tien will tell Father everything."

🏊 **PREDICT**
6 How do you think the story will end?

The two of them raced down the stairs and out a back way. "We'll hide in the forest," Bich Ngoc decided. "No one will find us there."

And the two were never seen or heard of again. But as for Kien Tien and Master Frog, they lived happily ever after, loved and respected by all for their kind deeds. Before many days had passed, they had Giang Dung brought to the palace, where she lived in comfort and happiness to a ripe old age. In due time Master Frog became king and, with Kien Tien as his queen, ruled their people in peace and prosperity for many long years.

Meet the Writer

Lynette Dyer Vuong

Taking a Chance on Love

Lynette Dyer Vuong (1938–   ) believes in love at first sight because that's what happened when she met a young Vietnamese man who was studying in the United States. Love led her to follow him back to Vietnam, marry him, and stay there with him for thirteen years—the country was then in the midst of the Vietnam War.

As Vuong learned Vietnamese, she began to follow another love—the world of folklore and fairy tales. She was amazed to discover that Vietnam has its own versions of five stories she loved as a child—"Cinderella," "Thumbelina," "The Frog Prince," "Rip Van Winkle," and "Goose Girl." She remembers:

66 Five familiar faces in an unfamiliar land; it is fascinating that similar ideas have arisen and then developed into different stories under the influence of two such diverse cultures as East and West. Perhaps it is a testimony to the fact that we are each uniquely individual, . . . yet bound together by a common humanity. 99

Vuong fled Vietnam with her husband and children in 1975. She continues to work on retelling the fairy tales she had grown to love.

For Independent Reading

If you'd like to read the other fairy tales Vuong discovered during her stay in Vietnam, look for her book *The Brocaded Slipper*.

Monitor students' progress.
Use these questions to assess students' comprehension.

1. What do people think about Master Frog's mother? [They find her plain and ugly.]
2. Whom does Master Frog want to marry? [Princess Kien Tien, the king's youngest daughter]
3. Why does Master Frog have to protect his frog skin after he becomes human? [If it is destroyed, he will have to return to Jade Emperor's palace.]
4. What causes the prince to die? [Bich Ngoc throws his skin into the fire.]
5. Where do the prince and Kien Tien find each other again? [at the Crystal Palace, on the ocean floor]

Meet the Writer

When Lynette Dyer Vuong was seven years old, her father built her an area that she thought of as a castle; there, she began composing and illustrating fantasy stories of adventure. At the age of ten, she wrote her first historical novel—a fifty-page tale that taught her the importance of research.

For Independent Reading

In addition to *The Brocaded Slipper*, Vuong has published two other collections of Vietnamese folklore, *The Golden Carp* and *Sky Legends of Vietnam*.

Master Frog **715**

After You Read

First Thoughts

1. Students may mention the appearance of wild animals in the king's hall or the lovers' reunion in the Crystal Palace.

Thinking Critically

2. Kim Chau and Bich Ngoc show their disgust in their faces; Kien Tien, however, reacts politely to Master Frog. This behavior shows the youngest sister's generous character and the shallowness of her sisters' characters.

3. Kien Tien admires Master Frog's good nature and intelligence.

4. The sisters discover that Master Frog is a very handsome prince and are angry that he has fooled them. They are jealous of their sister as well. Their change of heart shows the selfishness of these two young women.

5. One important lesson this story teaches is that character is more important than physical appearance.

6. Some students may have been surprised to see that the princess survives being thrown into the ocean, because the sisters' evil act seems so final. Others may not have been surprised, because folk-tale characters often come back to life.

Extending Interpretations

7. Possible answers: In "Rumpelstiltskin," Rumpelstiltskin causes straw to turn into gold. In "Cinderella," Cinderella's tattered clothing is transformed into a beautiful ball gown. Each of these transformations is a reward to a character who has suffered throughout the story.

8. Answers should be based on students' own experiences, stories that they have read, or films or television programs that they have seen.

After You Read   Response and Analysis

First Thoughts

1. Which scene in the story do you remember most vividly? Why?

Thinking Critically

2. What is different about the ways Kien Tien, Kim Chau, and Bich Ngoc first react to Master Frog? What does this tell you about each sister's **character**?

3. What qualities does Kien Tien admire in Master Frog even before she realizes that he is a prince?

4. How do Kim Chau's and Bich Ngoc's feelings about Master Frog change after his **metamorphosis**? What does their sudden change of heart tell you about their **character**?

5. What lessons do you think this story teaches?

6. Think about the **predictions** you made as you read "Master Frog." Were you surprised by the twist this story takes at the end? Explain why or why not.

Extending Interpretations

7. What other stories do you know in which a **metamorphosis** takes place? In each case, what caused the metamorphosis—is the change a reward or a punishment?

8. Kien Tien can look beyond Master Frog's appearance and see the person within, but her sisters can't. Do you think most people are like Kien Tien, or are they like her sisters? Why do you think so?

WRITING

Writing a Personal Essay

Refer back to your Quickwrite notes, and write a paragraph or two in which you describe your good qualities and talents. Be sure to explain why your special talents are important to you.

INTERNET
Projects and Activities
Keyword: LE5 7-6

SKILLS FOCUS

Literary Skills
Analyze metamorphosis.

Reading Skills
Make predictions.

Writing Skills
Write a personal essay.

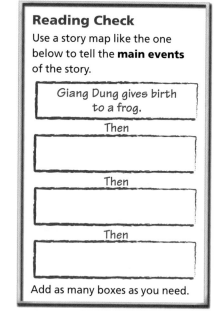

Reading Check
Use a story map like the one below to tell the **main events** of the story.

> Giang Dung gives birth to a frog.

Then

Then

Then

Add as many boxes as you need.

Reading Check
Giang Dung gives birth to a frog. *Then* the frog grows up to be a smart, helpful young frog. *Then* he marries the king's youngest daughter, Kien Tien. *Then* Master Frog is transformed into a human being. *Then* the princess's jealous sisters burn his frog skin and Master Frog dies. *Then* they drug Kien Tien and throw her in the ocean, claiming that she has committed suicide. *Then* Master Frog and Kien Tien are reunited at the underwater palace of the Dragon King. *Then* they return home and live happily ever after.

After You Read · Vocabulary Development

Clarifying Word Meanings

PRACTICE

1. Use two words from the Word Bank to write a statement about a student who's been grounded for two weeks.
2. Use three words from the Word Bank to write a few sentences urging students to challenge an unfair rule.

> **Word Bank**
> admonished
> entreaties
> charade
> presumptuous
> cowered

Using Specific Words

No two words have exactly the same meaning. Some words, like *sit*, have a general meaning but do not paint a vivid picture. Other words, like *perch* or *settle*, describe specific kinds of sitting. Each paints a different picture.

The author of "Master Frog" helps us imagine the creature's froggy behavior by using specific words to describe him. For example, she says that he *perched* beside his mother as she sat at the loom and would *wriggle* his body in and out of the threads on the loom.

SKILLS FOCUS

Vocabulary Skills
Clarify word meanings; use specific words.

PRACTICE

Rewrite the following sentences, replacing the underlined words with more exact ones. Be sure to compare your revisions in class.

1. Kien Tien's tears wet the <u>greenish</u> skin of her dead husband's body.
2. When Master Frog said he wanted to marry the king's daughter, the king <u>looked</u> at him.
3. When Master Frog croaked, tigers, leopards, and panthers <u>came</u> into the room.

B.C. By permission of Johnny L. Hart FLP, and Creators Syndicate, Inc.

Vocabulary Development

Clarifying Word Meanings

PRACTICE

Possible Answers
1. After her mother <u>admonished</u> her for being so late, Rosa made several <u>entreaties</u> that she be allowed to go to the game.
2. Fellow seventh-graders, we must not <u>cower</u> under this rule. It is not <u>presumptuous</u> to challenge a rule that we think is unfair. We may be <u>admonished</u> for our views, but let's stand up for our rights.

Using Specific Words

PRACTICE

Possible Answers
1. emerald, jade
2. stared, glared
3. flew, bounded

ASSESSING

Assessment
■ *Holt Assessment: Literature, Reading, and Vocabulary*

DIFFERENTIATING INSTRUCTION

Learners Having Difficulty
Have students rewrite the following sentences, replacing the underlined words with more specific ones. [Possible replacements for the underlined words are shown.]

1. People thought it was <u>good</u> that Giang Dung had a child so that someone would look after her when she was older. [fortunate]
2. Master Frog and his wife lived together <u>well</u>. [blissfully]
3. What <u>mean</u> sisters Kim Chau and Bich Ngoc were! [malicious]
4. Kien Tien <u>walked</u> slowly through the woods, <u>sad</u> for her lost love. [wandering; grieving]
5. At last, the young <u>people</u> left the Crystal Palace and <u>went</u> home. [lovers; galloped]

Grade-Level Skills

■ **Literary Skills**
Analyze elements of folk tales, including taboos.

■ **Literary Skills**
Recognize onomatopoeia.

■ **Reading Skills**
Draw conclusions.

Summary ⬆ *above grade level*

In this folk tale, a peasant named Yohei encounters a wounded crane. Yohei tends to the creature's wing. Later a beautiful woman asks to be Yohei's wife and begins serving him faithfully. When Yohei's money dwindles, the woman offers to weave some cloth but warns Yohei not to look in on her while she weaves. After three days and three nights she emerges with a bolt of fine material. The couple live comfortably on the earnings from the cloth. When the money is nearly gone, the woman offers to weave once more. Again the cloth brings in enough money to enable them to get by. Then a neighbor encourages Yohei to sell his wife's cloth for larger sums, and Yohei presses his wife to weave yet again. She agrees, this time taking longer than before. Overcome by curiosity, Yohei peeks into her room. He sees a blood-smeared crane plucking out its own feathers and weaving them. Horrified, Yohei faints. He awakens to find only a bolt of beautiful cloth. A distant voice whispers a farewell, and Yohei spots a crane flying away.

Before You Read The Folk Tale

The Crane Wife

Make the Connection
Quickwrite ✎

Sometimes you may have been told that if you do—or don't do—something, there will be terrible consequences. *Don't eat too much candy all at once. Don't play with matches.* Some of these warnings may seem silly or senseless at first, but if you were to disobey them, you might be sorry. Jot down other warnings you remember and the consequences that could result if the warnings are not obeyed.

Literary Focus
Motifs in Folk Tales: Taboo

This Japanese folk tale is about the breaking of a taboo. A **taboo** is a prohibition of something. Some societies, for example, forbid the eating of certain foods. A taboo is a common motif in myths as well as folk tales. In "Orpheus, the Great Musician" (page 665), for example, Orpheus is allowed to lead his wife up and out of the Land of the Dead as long as he doesn't look back at her. If you remember what happens when he does look back, you may predict that something bad will happen involving a broken taboo in this story too. As you read "The Crane Wife," watch for the taboo, and think about whether you would have behaved as Yohei did.

Literary Skills
Understand taboo; recognize onomatopoeia.

Reading Skills
Draw conclusions.

Onomatopoeia

The translator of this tale gives us the flavor of its original language by using some Japanese words. The words are examples of **onomatopoeia** (än′ō·mat′ō·pē′ə), or words whose sounds echo their meanings. (In English, *boom, growl,* and *swish* are onomatopoetic words.) In the first paragraph of the folk tale, the Japanese word *basabasa* is how the original storyteller thought rustling wings would sound. When you come across the Japanese words in the story, say them out loud. They are pronounced the way they look.

Reading Skills 📖
Drawing Conclusions

Anytime you read, you probably draw many **conclusions** about what is happening in the text. You decide whether the characters are good or bad, whether their decisions are wise or stupid, whether an outcome is fair or unfair. You base your conclusions on

• your own prior knowledge, experience, and beliefs

• details in the text

Keep a list of the conclusions you draw as you read "The Crane Wife."

RESOURCES: READING

Planning
■ *One-Stop Planner* CD-ROM with ExamView Test Generator

Differentiating Instruction
■ *Holt Reading Solutions*
■ *Supporting Instruction in Spanish*
■ *Audio CD Library*
■ *Audio CD Library, Selections and Summaries in Spanish*

Grammar and Language
■ *Language Handbook Worksheets*
■ *Daily Language Activities*

Assessment
■ *Holt Assessment: Literature, Reading, and Vocabulary*
■ *One-Stop Planner* CD-ROM with ExamView Test Generator
■ *Holt Online Assessment*

Cranes on folding screen by Ogata Korin (1658).

THE CRANE WIFE

told by **Sumiko Yagawa**

translated from the Japanese
by **Katherine Paterson**

In a faraway mountain village, where the snow falls deep and white, there once lived all alone a poor young peasant named Yohei. One day, at the beginning of winter, Yohei went out into the snow to run an errand, and, as he hurried home, suddenly *basabasa* he heard a rustling sound. It was a crane, dragging its wing, as it swooped down and landed on the path. Now Yohei could see that the bird was in great pain, for an arrow had pierced its wing. He went to where the crane lay, drew out the arrow, and very carefully tended its wound.

Late that night there came a tapping *hoto-hoto* on the door of Yohei's hut. It seemed very peculiar for someone to be calling at that time of night. When he slid open the door to look out, there before him stood a beautiful young woman.

"I beg you, sir," she said in a voice both delicate and refined, "please allow me to become your wife."

Yohei could hardly believe his ears. The more closely he looked, the more noble and lovely the woman appeared. Gently he took her hand and brought her inside.

The Crane Wife   **719**

Internet
■ go.hrw.com (Keyword: LE5 7-6)
■ *Elements of Literature Online*
Media
■ *Audio CD Library*
■ *Audio CD Library, Selections and Summaries in Spanish*

A Reading Skills

? Predict. Do you think Yohei's happiness will last? Explain. [Possible response: His happiness will probably not last because Yohei is under pressure to find work and make more money.]

B Literary Focus

? Taboo. What request does Yohei's wife make before she begins weaving? [She asks Yohei not to look in on her while she is working.] What do you think would happen if Yohei broke this taboo? [Possible responses: He might see something terrible. His wife might die.]

C Literary Focus

? Onomatopoeia. What words are used to represent the sound of the loom? [*Tonkara tonkara*]

Needlework hanging with cranes, cycads, and wisteria (textile) by Japanese School (19th century). Ashmolean Museum, Oxford, UK.

"Yohei has got some fine wife at his house," the villagers gossiped among themselves.

And it was true. The young woman was modest and kind, and she served Yohei faithfully. He could no longer recognize the cold, cold dreary hut where he had lived all alone, his house had become so bright and warm. The simple Yohei was happier than he could have ever dreamed.

In reality, however, with two mouths to feed instead of one, poor Yohei became poorer than he was before. And, since it was winter and there was no work to be found, he was very quickly coming to the bottom of what he had stored away.

At this point the young woman had a suggestion. "The other women of the village have looms upon which to weave cloth," she said. "If you would be so kind as to allow it, I should like to try my hand at weaving too."

In the back room of the hut, the young woman set up a loom and closed it off with sliding paper doors. Then she said to Yohei, "Please, I beg you, I beg you, never look in upon me while I am weaving."

Tonkara tonkara. For three days and three nights the sound of the loom continued. Without stopping either to eat or drink, the young woman went on weaving and weaving. Finally, on the fourth day, she came out. To Yohei she seemed strangely thin and completely exhausted as, without a word, she held out to him a bolt of material.

And such exquisite cloth it was! Even Yohei, who had absolutely no knowledge of

720 Collection 6 / Our Literary Heritage: Greek Myths and World Folk Tales woven goods, could only stare in astonishment at the elegant, silken fabric.

Yohei took the cloth and set out for town. There he was able to sell it for such a high price that for a while the two of them had enough money to live quite comfortably and pleasantly.

The winter, however, stretched on and on until, finally, there was very little money left. Yohei hesitated to say anything, so he kept quiet, but at last the young woman spoke up. "I shall weave on the loom one more time. But, please, let this be the last." And, once more, having been warned not to look in on the woman as she wove, the simple Yohei settled down to wait outside just as she asked.

This time the weaving took four days and four nights. A second time the young woman appeared carrying a bolt of cloth, but now she seemed thinner and more pathetic than before. The fabric, moreover, was lighter and even more beautiful. It seemed almost to glow with a light all its own.

Yohei sold the material for an even higher price than the first time. "My," he marveled, "what a good wife I have!" The money bag he carried was heavy, but Yohei's heart was light, and he fairly skipped as he hurried home.

Now, the man next door had noticed that Yohei seemed to be living far more grandly than he had in the old days, and he was most curious. Pretending to be very casual about it all, he made his way through the snow and began to chat. Yohei, being a simple and innocent fellow, told the neighbor how his wife's woven goods had brought a wonderful price.

The man became more curious than ever. "Tell me," he said, "just what kind of thread does your wife use? My woman's cotton cloth never fetched a price like that. If your wife's stuff is as marvelous as you say, you ought to take it to the capital, to the home of some noble. You could probably sell it for ten times—for a hundred times more. Say, how about it? Why don't you let me do it for you? We'd split the profits right down the middle. Just think of it! We could live out the rest of our lives doing nothing but sitting back and fanning ourselves."

Before Yohei's very eyes, gold coins great and small began to dazzle and dance. If only he could get his wife to relent, if only he could persuade her to weave again, they could seize such a fortune as had never been known before.

When Yohei presented her with this idea, the young woman seemed quite perplexed. "Why in the world," she asked, "would anyone need so much money as that?"

"Don't you see?" he answered. "With money like that a man's problems would all disappear. He could buy anything he liked. He could even start his own business."

"Isn't it plenty to be able to live together, just the two of us?"

When she spoke this way, Yohei could say no more. However, from that time on, whether asleep or awake, all he could do was think about money. It was so painful for the young woman to see Yohei in this state that her eyes filled with tears as she watched him, until finally, unable to bear it another day, she bowed to his will.

"Very well then," she said. "I will weave one more time. But truly, after this, I must never weave again." And once more she warned the now joyful Yohei, saying, "For the sake of heaven, remember. Do not look in on me."

Yohei rubbed his hands together in his eagerness and sat down to wait.

Tonkara tonkara. The sound of the loom continued on and on into the fifth day. The

DIRECT TEACHING

D Reading Skills

❓ **Draw conclusions.** How has Yohei's wife changed? [She is thinner and seems exhausted.] **What conclusion can you draw from this change?** [Possible response: The weaving is demanding work and takes a lot out of the woman.]

E Literary Focus

❓ **Conflict.** What conflict does Yohei face? [He wants his wife to weave again, but she does not want to do so.]

F Literary Focus

Motifs. Note that this is the third time the woman weaves, and that the number three has long been regarded as a powerful, even magical number. The number three is a common motif in folk tales, which often deal with supernatural or magical occurrences. There are three bears in "Goldilocks," three pigs in "The Three Little Pigs," three fairy godmothers in "Sleeping Beauty," and three wicked stepsisters in "Cinderella." Have students name other stories or myths they know that contain this motif.

A Reading Skills

❓ **Draw conclusions.** What is the bright crimson running through the cloth? [the crane's blood]

B Vocabulary Development

Context clues. Ask students to consider the context of the passage to determine the meaning of *entreaty*. [They should realize that *entreaty* means "request" because Yohei insisted on looking in on his wife while she wove even though she had asked him not to.]

Monitor students' progress. To assess students' comprehension of the story, have them write a *First, Next, Last* synopsis of the story's plot. Encourage them to write as many *Nexts* as they need to cover all of the story's main events.

work in the back room seemed to be taking longer than ever.

Yohei, no longer the simple fellow that he had once been, began to wonder about certain peculiar things. Why did the young woman appear to grow thinner every time she wove? What was going on in there behind those paper doors? How could she weave such beautiful cloth when she never seemed to buy any thread?

The longer he had to wait, the more he yearned to peep into the room until, at last, he put his hand upon the door.

"Ah!" came a voice from within. At the same time Yohei cried out in horror and fell back from the doorway.

What Yohei saw was not human. It was a crane, smeared with blood, for with its beak it had plucked out its own feathers to place them in the loom.

At the sight Yohei collapsed into a deep faint. When he came to himself, he found, lying near his hand, a bolt of fabric, pure and radiantly white, through which was woven a thread of bright crimson. It shone with a light this world has never known.

From somewhere Yohei heard the whisper of a delicate, familiar voice. "I had hoped," the voice said sorrowfully, "that you would be able to honor my entreaty. But because you looked upon me in my suffering, I can no longer tarry in the human world. I am the crane that you saved on the snowy path. I fell in love with your gentle, simple heart, and, trusting it alone, I came to live by your side. I pray that your life will be long and that you will always be happy."

"Wai-t!" Yohei stumbled in his haste to get outside.

It was nearly spring, and, over the crest of the distant mountains, he could barely discern the tiny form of a single crane, flying farther and farther away.

Snow. Print from the Tokaido series (c. 1830s) by Hiroshige Utugawa.

DIFFERENTIATING INSTRUCTION

Advanced Learners
Enrichment. Write the following question on the chalkboard, and have students answer it in a paragraph or two: "Is it possible for a storyteller to create a compelling story in which a taboo is introduced but remains unbroken? If so, outline the plot of such a story. If not, explain your reasoning."

English-Language Learners
For lessons designed for English-language learners, see *Holt Reading Solutions.*

Special Education Students
For lessons designed for special education students, see *Holt Reading Solutions.*

Meet the Writer

Katherine Paterson

"Searching for a Place to Stand"

Katherine Paterson (1932–   ) was born in China, where both of her parents served as missionaries. Of the early years of her life, when her family moved frequently, she has written:

> I remember the many schools I attended in those years mostly as places where I felt fear and humiliation. I was small, poor, and foreign.... I was a misfit both in the classroom and on the playground. Outside of school, however, I lived a rich, imaginative life.

Paterson has also reflected on the effect that this background had on her writing:

> When I look at the books I have written, the first thing I see is the outcast child searching for a place to stand.

Paterson has drawn upon both her rich inner life and her difficult childhood experiences in writing her highly acclaimed young adult novels.

© Samantha Loomis Paterson.

For Independent Reading

Paterson lived in Japan as well as in China. Three novels set in Japan during feudal times are *The Sign of the Chrysanthemum, Of Nightingales That Weep,* and *The Master Puppeteer.* Other popular novels by Paterson you may enjoy are *Bridge to Terabithia, Jacob Have I Loved, The Great Gilly Hopkins, Lyddie,* and *Flip-Flop Girl.*

Meet the Writer

Although Paterson's family moved frequently—they had moved fifteen times by the time she was fifteen years old—Paterson managed to make close friends. "I always knew I was worth something," she once commented, "because I had many wonderful friends who knew all my faults and failings and they still cared for me." Paterson also read and wrote stories as a way of dealing with her loneliness. She believes it is important for young people to read fiction because it allows them to experience life at a safe distance. In this way, she says, young readers can prepare for the challenges they will face later in life.

CROSS-CURRICULAR CONNECTIONS

Science

Cranes. Divide the class into two groups. Have one group gather scientific information about cranes, including their habitat, their anatomy and appearance, and their behavior. Have the other group gather cultural information about cranes, including how they are regarded in Japanese and other Asian societies; how they are represented in the arts; and what they are thought to symbolize. Instruct each group to present their findings in an oral report that includes at least two visuals. Then, have the members of both groups identify and discuss any interesting correlations (or contradictions) in their findings.

SMALL GROUP

INDEPENDENT PRACTICE

After You Read

First Thoughts

1. Possible answer: If I were Yohei I would have not asked my wife to weave a third time.

Thinking Critically

2. She admires his gentle personality. His weakness is his greed.

3. The crane becomes a woman. Other stories that involve shape changes include "Medusa" and "Cinderella."

4. Some students may conclude that it is fair that Yohei loses his wife, because he is greedy. Others will conclude that Yohei should not have lost his wife because he is a kind, compassionate man at heart.

Extending Interpretations

5. Possible answer: Students may say that smoking cigarettes is a taboo. The consequence of breaking taboos can range from getting into trouble to developing serious health problems.

Reading Check

a. The crane turns into a beautiful woman who wants to be Yohei's wife.

b. After each weaving session she appears thinner.

c. He wants to amass a fortune so that he will be able to buy anything he likes and so that he might start a business.

d. He looks in on his wife while she is weaving. In order to weave the cloth, the wife—who is actually the crane—plucks out her feathers to use as thread. As she does so, she becomes increasingly pale and thin.

After You Read Response and Analysis

First Thoughts

1. Finish the following sentence:
   • If I were Yohei . . .

Thinking Critically

2. What **character traits** does the young woman admire in Yohei? What weakness does he display when he asks her to weave a third time?

3. In many folk tales, a marvelous change of form, or **metamorphosis,** takes place. What metamorphosis takes place in this story? What other stories do you know that involve shape changes?

4. What **conclusions** can you draw about this tale? (Was it fair that Yohei lost his wife? Does the story have a useful message for today?) Discuss the reasons for your conclusions.

Extending Interpretations

5. The motif of a **taboo** is common in myths and folklore. People in real life are also often told not to do something, but do it anyway. What are some taboos you know of? What are the consequences of breaking them? Check your Quickwrite notes for ideas.

WRITING

Writing a Folk Tale

Write your own folk tale that includes a **metamorphosis** and a **taboo** that is broken. First, think about where and when you want the story to take place. Will it be today? once upon a time? Second, think about your characters—are they young? old? Where do they live? Then, decide on the kind of shape change you'll include. Will it be a reward or punishment? Finally, choose a taboo that your character will break.

Reading Check

a. How is Yohei rewarded for his kindness to the wounded crane?

b. What makes Yohei suspect that something is strange about his wife?

c. Why does Yohei ask his wife to weave one last time?

d. What **taboo** does Yohei break? How does Yohei lose his wife?

SKILLS FOCUS

Literary Skills
Analyze taboos.

Reading Skills
Draw conclusions.

Writing Skills
Write a folk tale.

724 Collection 6 / Our Literary Heritage: Greek Myths and World Folk Tales

DIFFERENTIATING INSTRUCTION

Learners Having Difficulty
As students answer question 3, help them to see that the transformation of the crane into the woman and back again is not the only transformation that takes place in the story. Point out that Yohei also changes. Have students discuss the transformation Yohei undergoes—for example, from a gentle, simple person to a greedy, aggressive one.

After You Read Vocabulary Development

Onomatopoeia

In "The Crane Wife" the reader can hear what is happening in the story through **onomatopoeia,** or the use of words with sounds that echo their meanings. Some examples of onomatopoeia in English are *honk, beep,* and *meow.*

PRACTICE

In place of the Japanese words in each passage below from the story, think up your own example of onomatopoeia in English.

1. ". . . as he hurried home, suddenly *basabasa* he heard a rustling sound."

2. "Late that night there came a tapping *hotohoto* on the door of Yohei's hut."

3. "*Tonkara tonkara.* For three days and three nights the sound of the loom continued."

Grammar Link

Using *Good* and *Well* Correctly

Choosing between *good* and *well* may sometimes seem very hard. Here are a few simple rules to help you get the job done right:

- *Good* is an adjective. Use it to modify a noun; never use it to modify a verb. (*Yohei was a good man.*)

- *Well* is usually an adverb. Use it to modify a verb. (*Yohei's wife wove well.*)

- Although it is usually an adverb, *well* is also used as an adjective to mean "healthy." (*Yohei's wife felt well when she recovered from weaving.*)

Note: *Feel good* and *feel well* mean different things. *Feel good* means "feel happy or pleased." (*Yohei felt good when the young woman asked to be his wife.*) *Feel well* simply means "feel healthy." (*Yohei didn't feel well when he didn't have enough to eat.*)

PRACTICE

Choose the correct word in each of the following sentences:

1. Yohei did (*good/well*) when he got a wife.

2. Yohei could not provide (*good/well*) for his small family.

3. Yohei's wife did not feel (*good/well*) when she wove the cloth.

4. The loom worked very (*good/well*).

5. Yohei did not feel (*good/well*) about his wife's leaving him.

SKILLS FOCUS

Vocabulary Skills
Use onomatopoeia.

Grammar Skills
Use *good* and *well* correctly.

PRACTICE

Possible Answers
1. *shrish-shresh*
2. *rap-rap-rap*
3. *floomp-flump floomp-flump*

Grammar Link

PRACTICE

1. well
2. well
3. good
4. well
5. good

ASSESSING

Assessment
- *Holt Assessment: Literature, Reading, and Vocabulary*

Grade-Level Skills
■ **Literary Skills**
Analyze elements of folk tales, including the motif of wishes.
■ **Reading Skills**
Analyze cause and effect.

Review Skills
■ **Literary Skills**
Identify themes as conveyed through characters, actions, and images.

Upcoming Skills
■ **Literary Skills**
Analyze recurring themes across traditional and contemporary works.

Summary 🔁 *at grade level*

An old woman known as Aunty Misery lives alone, with nothing but a pear tree for company. Day after day the local children climb the tree, shake loose its fruit, and run off with armfuls of pears. One night Aunty Misery gives shelter to a stranger. In return, the stranger—really a sorcerer in disguise—offers Aunty Misery a single wish. She wishes that anyone who climbs her pear tree will not be able to come down until she allows it. Years pass, and Death comes to the old woman's door at last. Aunty Misery tricks him into climbing the pear tree to fetch her a few last pieces of fruit. With Death safely stowed in the tree, people stop dying. Doctors, pharmacists, and undertakers start to go out of business. Finally, Aunty Misery makes a deal with Death: She will let him descend if he promises never to come for her again. He agrees. As a result, both misery and death are still present in the world.

Before You Read · The Folk Tale

Aunty Misery

Make the Connection
Quickwrite 🖉

Why do people have to face misery and death? What would happen if, for a period of time, no one in the whole world could die? How would people feel about that? Jot down your responses to these questions; then, see how this folk tale from Puerto Rico answers them.

Literary Focus
Motifs in Folk Tales: Wishes

Many folk tales are about a gift of **wishes**—often as a result of someone doing a good deed. This **motif** (mō·tēf′)—a feature repeated in tales throughout the world—appears in the myth on page 683, when a god grants King Midas any gift he wants. As it turns out, the gift King Midas wishes for causes him great unhappiness. In the tale you are about to read, Aunty Misery is also granted a wish. Do you think she will be happy with the consequences, or results, of her wish?

INTERNET
More About Cofer
Keyword: LE5 7-6

SKILLS FOCUS

Literary Skills
Understand the motif of wishes.

Reading Skills
Follow a cause-and-effect chain.

Reading Skills 📖
Following a Cause-and-Effect Chain

Events in a story often follow a **cause-and-effect chain:** Something happens that causes something else to happen. This event then causes another event to happen. And so on and so on to the end of the story. As you read "Aunty Misery," fill in a chart like the one below to show the story's cause-and-effect chain.

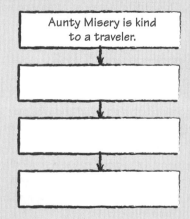

Add as many boxes as you need to tell the story.

RESOURCES: READING

Planning
■ *One-Stop Planner* CD-ROM with ExamView Test Generator

Differentiating Instruction
■ *Holt Reading Solutions*
■ *Supporting Instruction in Spanish*
■ *Audio CD Library*
■ *Audio CD Library, Selections and Summaries in Spanish*

Grammar and Language
■ *Daily Language Activities*

Assessment
■ *Holt Assessment: Literature, Reading, and Vocabulary*
■ *One-Stop Planner* CD-ROM with ExamView Test Generator
■ *Holt Online Assessment*

Aunty Misery

Judith Ortiz Cofer

This is a story about an old, a very old woman who lived alone in her little hut with no other company than a beautiful pear tree that grew at her door. She spent all her time taking care of this tree. The neighborhood children drove the old woman crazy by stealing her fruit. They would climb her tree, shake its delicate limbs, and run away with armloads of golden pears, yelling insults at *la Tia Miseria*,[1] Aunty Misery, as they called her.

One day, a traveler stopped at the old woman's hut and asked her for permission to spend the night under her roof. Aunty Misery saw that he had an honest face and bid the pilgrim come in. She fed him and made a bed for him in front of her hearth. In the morning the stranger told her that he would show his gratitude for her hospitality by granting her one wish.

"There is only one thing that I desire," said Aunty Misery.

"Ask, and it shall be yours," replied the stranger, who was a sorcerer in disguise.

"I wish that anyone who climbs up my pear tree should not be able to come back down until I permit it."

"Your wish is granted," said the stranger,

---

1. **la Tia Miseria** (lä tē′ə mĕ′ze·rē′ə).

A Literary Focus

❓ Figurative language. How does the author describe Death's voice? [She says that he sounds as if he had just swallowed a desert.] Explain that this comparison, which includes the phrase *as if,* is a simile. Then, have students find another example of a simile in the story. [Both the children and Death get stuck to the tree "as if with glue"; Death lets out a sigh "like wind through a tomb."]

B Reading Skills

❓ Cause and effect. What is the effect of Death's decision to fetch Aunty Misery some pears? [He gets stuck in the tree.]

C Reading Skills

❓ Cause and effect. What are some of the effects of Death's predicament? [Possible responses: No one dies for a time. Doctors, pharmacists, and undertakers lose business. Old people grow impatient to depart this world.]

D Reading Skills

❓ Cause and effect. What is the permanent effect of Aunty Misery's deal with Death? [Misery and death will both be forever in the world.]

E Literary Focus

❓ The wish motif. How does this story's ending differ from that of other stories with the wish motif? [Possible response: In this story the person who makes the wish ends up getting exactly what she wants—and more. In other stories with the wish motif, the wishes, which are often motivated by greed, lead to the wishers' doom.]

touching the pear tree as he left Aunty Misery's house.

And so it happened that when the children came back to taunt the old woman and to steal her fruit, she stood at her window watching them. Several of them shimmied up the trunk of the pear tree and immediately got stuck to it as if with glue. She let them cry and beg her for a long time before she gave the tree permission to let them go on the condition that they never again steal her fruit, or bother her.

Time passed and both Aunty Misery and her tree grew bent and gnarled with age. One day another traveler stopped at her door. This one looked untrustworthy to her, so before letting him into her home the old woman asked him what he was doing in her village. He answered her in a voice that was dry and hoarse, as if he had swallowed a desert: "I am Death, and I have come to take you with me."

Thinking fast, Aunty Misery said, "All right, but before I go I would like to pluck some pears from my beloved tree to remember how much pleasure it brought me in this life. But I am a very old woman and cannot climb to the tallest branches where the best fruit is. Will you be so kind as to do it for me?"

> "I am Death, and I have come to take you with me."

With a heavy sigh like wind through a tomb, Señor Death climbed the pear tree. Immediately he became stuck to it as if with glue. And no matter how much he cursed and threatened, Aunty Misery would not allow the tree to release Death.

Many years passed and there were no deaths in the world. The people who make their living from death began to protest loudly. The doctors claimed no one bothered to come in for examinations or treatments anymore, because they did not fear dying; the pharmacists' business suffered too because medicines are, like magic potions, bought to prevent or postpone the inevitable; priests and undertakers were unhappy with the situation also, for obvious reasons. There were also many old folks tired of life who wanted to pass on to the next world to rest from miseries of this one.

La Tia Miseria was blamed by these people for their troubles, of course. Not wishing to be unfair, the old woman made a deal with her prisoner, Death: if he promised not ever to come for her again, she would give him his freedom. He agreed. And that is why there are two things you can always count on running into in this world: Misery and Death: *La miseria y la muerte.*[2]

---

2. **y la muerte** (ē lä mwer′tä).

Learners Having Difficulty

If students are having trouble identifying causes and effects, be sure they understand that effects can themselves become causes of other events. Write these statements on the chalkboard, and have students copy them as reminders: *A cause makes something happen. An effect is what happens.* To help students identify causes and effects in "Aunty Misery," write *Aunty Misery takes in a stranger for the night* next to the definition of *cause* on the chalkboard. Then, ask them what effect follows. [The stranger grants Aunty Misery a wish.] Write their response next to the definition of *effect* on the board. Then, have students refer to the examples of causes and effects for guidance as they read.

Monitor students' progress.
Write the following sentences on the board, and have students list their numbers in the correct cause-and-effect order.

1. Aunty Misery makes a deal with Death: He will never come for her again. [3]

2. Misery and death remain in the world forever. [4]

3. Aunty Misery is able to trap Death in a tree. [2]

4. Aunty Misery is granted a wish. [1]

Meet the Writer

Cofer, who teaches at the University of Georgia, began writing creatively when she was in graduate school. At that time, Cofer says, "I decided . . . to set aside a time to write, the hours between five and seven A.M. That is the discipline I still follow. . . . I call it a room of my own."

For Independent Reading

Students interested in the writing process may wish to read essays from Cofer's collection, *Woman in Front of the Sun: On Becoming a Writer.*

Meet the Writer

Judith Ortiz Cofer

Bridging Between Two Cultures

Judith Ortiz Cofer (1952–   ) grew up surrounded by storytellers, so it was almost inevitable that she would also tell stories herself. As she points out:

> In an extended family, the family story, gossip, or myth becomes something that is repeated so often and used in so many ways to teach lessons or to make a point that I couldn't help but be trained in [storytelling] as I grew up.

Cofer was born in Puerto Rico but moved with her family to Paterson, New Jersey, when she was two years old. Her father had joined the U.S. Navy and was stationed in the Brooklyn Naval Yard. But whenever her father was sent to sea, Cofer returned to Puerto Rico with the rest of the family. As a result, Cofer found herself divided between two very different worlds. Fortunately she was able to take refuge in books.

> I absorbed literature . . . as a creature who breathed ink. Each writer . . . taught me that language could be tamed. I realized that I could make it perform. I had to believe the work was important to my being: to use my art as a bridge between my cultures. . . . I began crossing the bridge, traveling back and forth without fear and confusion.

For Independent Reading

In the short story collection *An Island Like You: Stories of the Barrio,* Cofer vividly portrays the experiences of teenagers growing up in a Puerto Rican community in New Jersey.

DIFFERENTIATING INSTRUCTION

English-Language Learners

After students read the Meet the Writer feature about Judith Ortiz Cofer, suggest that they look for interviews or autobiographical sources in which writers discuss the rewards and difficulties of "crossing the bridge" between cultures. Have students share the information they find by posting it on a classroom bulletin board.

Encourage students to look on the Internet for information about

- the age at which the authors began writing
- the inspiration the writers took from people in their own communities
- the degree to which the writers emphasize similarities or differences between cultures

After You Read   Response and Analysis

First Thoughts

1. Would people be happier if there were no death in the world? Discuss your responses to the moral of this folk tale. Be sure to check your Quickwrite notes. ✏

Reading Check

Complete the chart showing a **cause-and-effect chain** (see page 726). 📖

Thinking Critically

2. How does Aunty Misery show she is a clever woman in the ways she uses her wish?

3. According to the folk tale, what happens in the world when there is no death? What other effects can you imagine if there were no death?

4. How does the folk tale explain why we can always count on running into misery and death?

WRITING

Writing a Story About a Wish

Write your own story about a person who is granted a wish in reward for doing something generous. Is the wish a wise wish or a foolish one? Does the person learn something as a result of what happens when the wish is granted? Before you write your story, you might gather your details in a chart like the one to the right.

	Wish Story
Setting	
Characters	
Good deed	
Wish	
Consequences	
Ending	

ART

Drawing a Graphic Story

Create a graphic story based on this folk tale. (A **graphic story** is one told in pictures, like a comic strip.) You will have to decide how many panels you will need. You can tell the story by using dialogue bubbles to show what the characters are saying. If you wish, you can also explain what is happening in brief captions under the panels.

SKILLS FOCUS

Literary Skills
Analyze the motif of wishes.

Reading Skills
Analyze cause and effect.

Writing Skills
Write a story about a wish.

Art Skills
Draw a graphic story.

Aunty Misery   **731**

DIFFERENTIATING INSTRUCTION

Advanced Learners

Enrichment. Have students work in groups to create an original folk tale using a cause-and-effect chain. On a sheet of paper, one student writes down the name of a character who might appear in a folk tale, along with a brief description of that character. The student then passes the paper to another person in the group, who writes down a wish that the character might be granted. The second student passes the paper on to a third student, who writes down an effect, or result, of that wish. Students continue passing the paper around until all the group members have contributed. Then, after one student reads aloud the entire cause-and-effect chain, the group members work together to come up with a logical ending for their folk tale.

INDEPENDENT PRACTICE

After You Read

First Thoughts

1. Possible answer: People would be happier without death because they wouldn't have to worry about their health.

Thinking Critically

2. She shows she is clever by tricking Death into climbing the pear tree and then using the power granted by the wish to trap him.

3. In a world without death, people complain about its absence. Students may say that if death no longer existed, people would behave more and more recklessly.

4. In the folk tale, Misery and Death agree to leave each other alone. As a result, both are free to go about their business in the world.

Reading Check
Possible Answers

- Aunty Misery is kind to a traveler.

- The traveler grants her one wish.

- She asks for the power to keep anyone who climbs her pear tree from getting down without her permission.

- Years later Aunty Misery tricks Death into climbing the tree when he comes to call for her.

- People stop dying.

- People begin to complain.

- Death agrees to leave Aunty Misery alone if he can come down.

- Misery and death continue to exist in the world.

ASSESSING

Assessment
- *Holt Assessment: Literature, Reading, and Vocabulary*

Grade-Level Skills

■ **Literary Skills**
Analyze elements of folk tales, including origin motifs.

■ **Reading Skills**
Retell a story.

Review Skills

■ **Literary Skills**
Identify themes as conveyed through characters, actions, and images.

Upcoming Skills

■ **Literary Skills**
Analyze recurring themes across traditional and contemporary works.

Summary ⬌ at grade level

At the opening of this story, the wife of a chief gives birth to a son. When an extraordinarily large and colorful hummingbird attends the birth, the high priest determines that the baby, too, will be extraordinary. He gives the baby boy a bright red feather as a protective charm; the boy is named Kukul, after the feather. Kukul grows to be handsome and clever, and he is invulnerable in battle. He has an enemy, however—Chirumá, his uncle, who would have become chief if Kukul had not been born. When Chirumá fails to undermine Kukul's claim as chief, he steals Kukul's charm and then kills him. Kukul's body, however, is transformed into a beautiful, wise bird—a quetzal. The people make the quetzal their symbol of freedom.

Before You Read The Folk Tale

The Hummingbird King

Make the Connection
Quickwrite ✏️

If you could have an animal as a protector, what would the animal be? Would you choose your animal for its strength, wisdom, cleverness, comfort, beauty, speed, faithfulness—or just because you like it? Jot down your ideas for your own personal protector.

Literary Focus
Motifs in Folk Tales: Origins

Myths and folk tales often explain the origin of something in nature or human life. The Greek myth of Demeter and Persephone explains the origin of the seasons (page 655). The Puerto Rican folk tale "Aunty Misery" explains how misery came into the world (page 727). "The Hummingbird King," a Mayan folk tale, also explains the origin of something, but you may not be able to figure out what that is until the very end.

Reading Skills ✍️
Retelling

A good way to be sure you understand and remember all the key events in a story is to **retell** the story when you have finished reading it. As you read this story, jot down the story's key events. When you have finished reading, you will have everything you need to retell the story.

Literary Skills
Understand the origin motif.

Reading Skills
Retell a story.

Background
Literature and Social Studies

Today you can see the beautiful ruined temples and pyramids of the great Mayan civilization in Mexico, Guatemala, Belize, and Honduras. The Maya dominated this region for about 650 years, from about A.D. 250 to A.D. 900. At their peak the Maya ruled about two million people and had a vast network of trade. One of the items they traded was the shimmering tail feather of the bird called quetzal (ket•säl'), from the highlands of Guatemala.

What happened to the Maya? Scholars are not sure. One by one their cities were abandoned, and by 1200, the Maya were absorbed by the Toltecs. In the mid-1500s, almost all the Maya were conquered by Spain.

The character Kukul in this tale was a real person, called Kukulcán. His symbol was the quetzal. You can still see images of the bird in the great temple dedicated to Kukulcán at Chichén Itzá in Mexico's Yucatán Peninsula.

RESOURCES: READING

Planning
■ *One-Stop Planner* CD-ROM with ExamView Test Generator

Differentiating Instruction
■ *Holt Reading Solutions*
■ *Supporting Instruction in Spanish*
■ *Audio CD Library*
■ *Audio CD Library, Selections and Summaries in Spanish*

Grammar and Language
■ *Daily Language Activities*

Assessment
■ *Holt Assessment: Literature, Reading, and Vocabulary*
■ *One-Stop Planner* CD-ROM with ExamView Test Generator
■ *Holt Online Assessment*

THE HUMMINGBIRD KING

Mayan, retold by **Argentina Palacios**

© Justin Kerr.

Pyramids, palaces, and temples of stone stand silent and abandoned, hidden by dense rain forests. But that was not always so. Long, long ago, great cities built by the Mayan people were centers of activity.

In one of those cities—one whose name has long been forgotten—there lived an old *halac uinic*, or chief. Since he had no son to succeed[1] him, he knew that his younger brother, Chirumá, would one day take his place.

But the chief's wife wanted a child. Each day, she prayed with all her heart. And, one day, her prayers were answered. She gave birth to a son. The child was born on the thirteenth day of the month, a lucky day. For the number thirteen reminded the Mayan people of their thirteen heavens.

Just as the baby was being born, another sign appeared. A beautiful hummingbird perched on a tree branch in front of the stately residence. It was not an ordinary bird, but the largest and most brightly colored hummingbird anyone had ever seen. No one had ever remembered a bird of its kind standing still for so long.

The high priest determined that this was an omen. "The messenger of the gods has come," he said. "He is telling us that this child will be extraordinary, just like this hummingbird."

In the days that followed, a special naming ceremony took place. The high priest gave the chief and his wife a bright red feather he'd found beneath the tree branch where the hummingbird perched.

"We shall name our son Kukul," the chief's wife proclaimed. "That name means 'beautiful feather.'"

"And so shall this feather protect the boy as long as he carries it with him," the priest said.

A great celebration took place in the public plaza. Everyone joined the festivities.

---

1. **succeed** *v.*: follow into a position (here, the position is that of *halac uinic*, or chief).

The Hummingbird King   **733**

Internet
- go.hrw.com (Keyword: LE5 7-6)
- *Elements of Literature Online*

Media
- *Audio CD Library*
- *Audio CD Library, Selections and Summaries in Spanish*

The Hummingbird King   **733**

A Reading Skills

❓ **Compare characters.** How is Kukul like Oni in "Oni and the Great Bird"? [Both have a power that protects them from their enemies—and both have enemies.]

VIEWING THE ART

Activity. Invite students to comment on the artifacts shown on pp. 734–735. In particular, encourage them to talk or write about the sense of determination in the figures—and how an evil determination drives the plot of "The Hummingbird King."

Mayan tripod vase from the Valley of Ulúa (10th century).
Musée d'ethnographie, Geneva, Switzerland. © Scala/Art Resource, New York.

Everyone was happy, except Chirumá. He knew that, because of this child, he would never become *halac uinic*.

Kukul grew into a handsome young man with jet-black hair and skin the color of cinnamon. He was quick of mind and excelled at any task he was given. As a young boy, he spent long hours with his father. Together, they would study the stars.

Like all Mayan boys, Kukul learned the art of warfare from his elders. He made his own spears, bows, and arrows—straight and strong as the boy himself.

Soon the time came for Kukul to take his place among the men of his nation. A nomad[2] tribe was attempting a raid. Kukul,

2. **nomad** *n.* used as an *adj.:* wandering, with no permanent home. Nomadic peoples move about constantly in search of food, pasture, and so on.

Chirumá, and the others went to war. Showers of spears and arrows rained down. Kukul fought bravely, at times at the very front. But wherever he was, not a single weapon fell on him.

Chirumá observed this. "The gods must watch out for Kukul," he thought to himself.

All at once, Kukul saw an arrow flying straight toward Chirumá, and Kukul positioned himself like a shield in front of his uncle. The arrow changed its course and fell to the ground without harming anyone. The enemy fled in astonishment and Kukul turned toward the wounded.

"How could it be that Kukul never gets hurt?" Chirumá wondered. "He must have a strong charm. I will find out."

That night, as Kukul slept on his straw mat, Chirumá came upon him. He carefully

DIFFERENTIATING INSTRUCTION

Learners Having Difficulty
Before students begin reading the story, remind them that they often can focus their reading by setting a "let's find out" goal for themselves. Encourage students to do so by taking a few moments to reflect and build on clues that the story provides. Then ask students to write their own prereading questions and predictions for "The Hummingbird King," based on the title of the story.

[Responses might resemble the following:
• Question: Who is the hummingbird king?
• Predictions: A man, not a woman, will be the hero of this story. The story will feature a bird character or a person who becomes ruler of the birds.]
After students have finished the story, ask them to compare their questions and predictions with the events described in the story. Invite comments.

Mayan plate depicting
ballgame of pelota
(c. A.D. 590).
The Granger Collection,
New York.

B Reading Skills

❓ **Infer.** Why does Chirumá say
such things about his nephew?
[Possible responses: Chirumá is jealous
of Kukul and wants to make him look
bad. Chirumá wants the priest to
choose him as the new chief.]

searched Kukul's sleeping body but found
nothing. Then he saw it—a large red feather
barely sticking out of the straw mat.

"His charm!" Chirumá said cheerfully
to himself, as he carefully lifted the feather
from its hiding place.

When Kukul awoke, he saw that the feather
was gone. He searched everywhere, but he
could not find it. Nor could he remember the
words of the priest on the day he was born.
Without realizing it, Kukul had lost the charm
and all the protection it provided.

It came to pass that the old chief went to
the afterlife. Upon his death, all the high
priests prepared to meet in council to
choose a new chief. Chirumá knew that the
priests would favor his nephew. He looked
for the youngest priest, the one he knew
could be easily swayed.

"Kukul is not a hero," he said. "Arrows
never fall where he places himself. He is
afraid to fight."

"No, he is not," said the priest. "Kukul is
using his intelligence to win."

Chirumá would find any opportunity to
talk to that priest about Kukul. Another day,
he told him, "Kukul is reckless. He stops to
take care of the wounded and puts his men
in danger."

"Kukul is compassionate," replied the
priest.

"He is inexperienced," countered
Chirumá, as he sowed the seeds of doubt.

Now according to custom, a new *halac
uinic* could be anyone in the departed chief's
family. The high priests met.

"It should be Kukul, without a doubt,"
said the oldest priest.

B

The Hummingbird King   **735**

English-Language Learners
For activities designed for English-language
learners, see *Holt Reading Solutions.*

Special Education Students
For activities designed for special education
students, see *Holt Reading Solutions.*

Advanced Learners
Like "The Hummingbird King," many classical
Greek myths tell of humans who are

transformed into animals or objects from
the natural world. Challenge students to
read about any of the following characters
from Greek mythology and to compare
their fates with that of Kukul:

- Arachne
- Ceyx and Alcyone
- Baucis and Philemon
- Daphne
- Callisto

Ask students why they think transformation
stories exist in virtually all cultures of the
world. [Possible response: Such stories express
a basic human desire to become better in
some way.]

A Reading Skills

❓ Speculate. Do you think that the young priest's opinion will have much influence? Why or why not? [Possible response: Probably not; he is the youngest and perhaps the least experienced of the priests, and the other priests want Kukul to become the chief.]

B Reading Skills

❓ Retell. What major events that have happened so far might you include in a retelling of this story? [Possible response: Kukul, the son of the chief, is protected from enemy attacks by a red hummingbird feather. Kukul's jealous uncle, Chirumá, finds and steals the charm. When Kukul's father dies, Chirumá tries to dissuade the priests from choosing Kukul as their next chief—but to no avail. Kukul proves to be a fine leader.]

C Literary Focus

❓ Onomatopoeia. Why are words like *rustling, flurry,* and *fluttered* effective in describing this movement? [Possible response: They sound like the sounds that they name and help make the description vivid.]

D Reading Skills

❓ Draw conclusions. About whom is the hummingbird warning Kukul? Explain. [He is probably warning Kukul about Chirumá. Chirumá has reason to resent Kukul; he has also tried already to undermine the choice of Kukul as chief and has gained possession of the charm that protects Kukul.]

E Literary Focus

Fantasy. Students have read about several amazing transformations in the stories in this collection. Discuss students' thoughts about this one, especially as it occurs after Kukul dies. [Possible response: It is sad that Kukul dies before the transformation takes place; nevertheless, he changes into something extremely beautiful, and in his new form he becomes a symbol of one of his culture's highest values.]

"It should be Kukul," the second priest chimed in.

"Yes, without a doubt," the third priest added.

[A] There was silence. "It should be Chirumá," said the youngest. "Kukul is too young and inexperienced."

They argued about the merits of each man. In the end, no one changed his vote and Kukul was chosen as *halac uinic*.

[B] Under his rule, there was peace throughout the land. In time, even Chirumá's friend came to appreciate that Kukul had been a good choice.

Kukul spent much time studying the stars. He made mathematical calculations. He could tell the farmers the best times to plant to reap the richest crops. Everybody was happy with Kukul, except Chirumá.

[C] One day, Kukul was hunting in the forest. He heard the rustling of leaves and raised his bow and arrow. With a flurry, a magnificent hummingbird, larger than any hummingbird Kukul had ever seen, fluttered next to him. The hummingbird spoke these words, "I am your guardian, Kukul. My job is to warn you. Beware. Death is circling you. Beware of a man."

[D] "Magnificent hummingbird, my guardian, what man should I beware of?" asked Kukul.

"Someone very close to you. Be careful, Kukul," said the bird. Then it flew away.

Kukul walked on through the forest. As he came to a thicket, he heard the faint rustling of leaves. He pointed his arrow, but saw nothing. Kukul crouched low to the ground and moved slowly. He had not gone far when . . . *sssss* . . . it came. An arrow pierced his chest.

In pain, Kukul pulled out the arrow and headed for the river to wash his wound. "Surely, it is not deep," he tried to convince himself, but his strength began to fade as his chest turned scarlet with blood.

A few more steps and Kukul had to lean against a tree. "It is so dark," he moaned. He fell onto a sea of emerald grass and there he died. Alone. Betrayed.

Then, something extraordinary happened. Slowly, Kukul's body changed to the color of the grass, but his chest remained scarlet. His skin became feathers, and his hair a gorgeous crest.

[E] By the time Chirumá came out of the thicket, Kukul's arms had turned into wings. All Chirumá could see was a glowing green bird with a scarlet chest and a long, long tail, flying off into the sunlight.

Mayan seated figure of a priest or nobleman. Hardwood.
The Granger Collection, New York.

LITERARY CONNECTIONS

Heroes

The setting of this folk tale differs from others in this collection; furthermore, only "Oni and the Great Bird" matches this tale in its focus on conflicts between men. Nevertheless, students will see the theme of personal action or reward repeated in Kukul's story.

Activity. Work with students to make a summary chart of the "hero" characters from the stories in this collection. Have them chart the rewards each character receives (if known). Use these notes as a springboard to a discussion about topics such as these:

- the differences between external and internal beauty
- the nature of heroism
- the ways folk tales can teach readers about the values of a particular culture

WHOLE CLASS

The people mourned the loss of Kukul, but after a time, Chirumá was chosen to be the new chief. Chirumá was a cruel and warlike king, and soon after, enemies again attacked the city and in fierce battle took Chirumá prisoner. Everybody watched while his body was painted black and white, the colors of a slave. He was taken away from the city, never to be seen again.

Today, a most beautiful green bird with a scarlet chest, a long, long tail, and a gorgeous crest perches high up on the trees in the deep, cool cloud forest, watching everything and listening for the rustling of leaves.

The Mayan of old called this bird *kukul*. They carved its image into stone and placed it on their temples and palaces. Today this wise and peaceful bird—a symbol of freedom to all its people—is known as the *quetzal*.

Meet the Writer

Argentina Palacios

Quetzal Tales

Argentina Palacios grew up in Panama. As an adult living in Texas, Palacios at first became a teacher, like her mother. Little by little, though, she discovered the rewards of writing and telling stories. "The Hummingbird King" is one of the stories she tells children and adults at schools, museums, zoos, and even jails around the country.

"The Hummingbird King" tells the story of the origin of the quetzal (ket·säl'). The quetzal is a brilliantly colored bird found only in the cloud forests of the highlands of Guatemala. The bird's head and back are emerald green; its chest is bright red. There is a wide crest of gold-and-green hairlike feathers on its head. The upper tail feathers are very large—up to three feet long.

Palacios says:

> **Legends say the quetzal loves its freedom so much that it will die in captivity. But the cloud forests that are its natural habitat are disappearing from the earth. Happily, scientists have had some success breeding the quetzal in zoos and nature parks, preserving the Mayan ideal of people living in harmony with nature.**

The Hummingbird King   **737**

MINI-LESSON **Reading**

Developing Word Attack Skills
Activity. Display these sets of words. Have students decide what sound the letters *qu* stand for in the first word and underline the other word that has the same sound. Remind students that the sound may be spelled differently in the other word.

1. quetzal   queen   <u>carrot</u>
2. quart   <u>liquid</u>   cover
3. conquer   <u>kettle</u>   quick
4. inquire   bunk   <u>equate</u>
5. lacquer   <u>bicker</u>   quaint

F Reading Skills

Make judgments. Do you think that Chirumá deserves his fate? Why or why not? [Possible responses: Yes; Chirumá was a murderer and a cruel and warlike leader. No; slavery is too horrible a fate to wish on anyone.]

G Literary Focus

The origin motif. What does this story explain the origin of? [the quetzal] Why is the quetzal seen as a symbol of freedom? [Under Kukul's leadership the people were free and prosperous, whereas under Chirumá's they were attacked and conquered.]

H Reading Skills

Retell. Review the events of the story, beginning with the scene in which Kukul is hunting in the forest. Then, retell these events to a partner. [Possible response: Kukul receives a warning from his guardian, a hummingbird. Soon after, Chirumá shoots and kills Kukul. Kukul is transformed into a beautiful bird, a quetzal. Chirumá becomes chief but is eventually taken prisoner in battle and led into slavery. The quetzal becomes a symbol of freedom for the Mayan people.]

GUIDED PRACTICE

Monitor students' progress. Have the class retell the story. Begin the retelling with the following sentence: *Long ago, a little boy was born to a Mayan chief and his wife.* Then, call on a student to supply the next event and then in turn, call on another student, and so on. Prompt students as needed.

After You Read

First Thoughts

1. Some students may like the folk tale because of the suspense created by the dynamic between Kukul and Chirumá. Others may dislike it because of the cruel fate that befalls Chirumá.

Thinking Critically

2. He is born on the thirteenth; a magnificent hummingbird attends his birth.
3. The jealousy of Kukul's uncle, Chirumá, poses the greatest danger to the boy.
4. Kukul is immune to the attacks of enemies.
5. It can be called an origin story because it explains the origin of the bird known as the quetzal.
6. Possible answers: The Mayan people built great cities. They were eventually conquered by the Spanish. The Maya carved images of the quetzal and placed them in their temples. The quetzal is still a symbol of freedom.

Extending Interpretations

7. When Kukul dies, he is transformed into a bird: His skin becomes feathers, his hair becomes a crest, and his arms become wings. Other metamorphoses in this collection include Master Frog's transformation into a human being and the crane wife's transformation from a crane into a woman and back into a crane.
8. Answers could include the story of Moses from the Bible and the story of Superman.

Assessment

■ *Holt Assessment: Literature, Reading, and Vocabulary*

First Thoughts

1. How would you evaluate this folk tale? To answer, complete one of these sentences:
   - I liked the folk tale because . . .
   - I disliked the tale because . . .

Thinking Critically

2. In many hero stories a baby's birth is accompanied by extraordinary events. What omens indicate that the baby Kukul will be a special person?
3. In such hero stories the baby's life is often endangered by people jealous of his or her power. Who or what threatens this baby's life?
4. What supernatural events demonstrate that Kukul has a special protector?
5. Why can this folk tale be called an **origin** story?
6. This story tells about a real person, but it mixes historical events with fantasy. What historical events do you find in the story?

Extending Interpretations

7. What supernatural events happen when Kukul dies? What other marvelous **metamorphoses,** or changes in form, have you read about in this collection of folk tales?
8. What other hero stories do you know of—from other cultures—that share some of the features of this story? (Be sure to consider stories you've seen in comics and movies.)
   - The birth of a hero accompanied by extraordinary omens
   - The threat of a jealous family member or other person
   - Supernatural events that take place in the hero's life
   - Metamorphoses at the hero's death

SKILLS FOCUS

Literary Skills Analyze the origin motif.

Reading Skills Retell the story.

Writing Skills Write a story.

WRITING

A Story About an Animal Protector

Refer to your Quickwrite notes, and choose an animal who could act as your personal protector in a time of trouble. Write a brief story describing your animal and how you found it, how the animal protects you, and what happens to you and the animal at the end.

Reading Check

Retell the main events of the story to a partner. You will find help in retelling a story on page 4. You will also find a rating sheet on page 13 that your partner can use to evaluate your retelling.

Reading Check

Possible retelling: The wife of a Mayan chief gives birth to a boy, Kukul, who is protected by the red feather of a magnificent hummingbird. The feather keeps the boy safe from enemy attacks. Jealous, Kukul's uncle, Chirumá, steals the feather and tries to keep the priests from naming Kukul as his father's successor. When his attempts fail, the uncle shoots Kukul with an arrow. No longer protected by the feather, Kukul dies and is transformed into a beautiful bird, a quetzal. Chirumá becomes chief at last but is taken prisoner in battle soon after. The quetzal has become a symbol of freedom.

Summarizing the Main Ideas

Reading Focus
Summarizing the Main Ideas

When you did a retelling of "The Hummingbird King," you included all the main events of that ancient Mayan folk tale. The article that follows tells about the search to discover ancient Mayan objects and buildings buried in the jungles of Guatemala. When you finish reading the article, you will be asked to **summarize** it. In summarizing informational texts such as this article, you do a brief retelling of the **main ideas** and only the most important supporting details. (For more help in summarizing informational texts, see page 688).

■ To prepare for your summary, write down the main idea in each paragraph you read. When you finish reading, decide how important each of those ideas is to the entire article. Include only the most important ones in your final summary.

Quetzal.

Vocabulary Development

Studying these words will help you understand the article.

decipher (dē·sī′fər) *v.*: interpret; find the meaning of. *Scientists try to decipher the meaning of the ancient Mayan writing.*

ransacked (ran′sakt′) *v.*: searched thoroughly for goods to steal; looted, robbed. *Grave robbers have ransacked many ancient Mayan tombs.*

artifacts (ärt′ə·fakts′) *n.*: objects made by people or adapted for human use. *Many important artifacts have been stolen from the tombs.*

connoisseurs (kän′ə·sʉrz′) *n.*: people who are experts on something. *The connoisseurs declared the "ancient" sculpture a fake.*

unscrupulous (un·skrōō′pyə·ləs) *adj.*: dishonest. *Stolen Mayan treasures may be bought by unscrupulous collectors.*

SKILLS FOCUS

Reading Skills
Summarize the main ideas.

The Search Goes On   **739**

SKILLS FOCUS
pp. 739–745

Grade-Level Skills
■ **Reading Skills**
Summarize the main ideas.

Summary ⬆ *above grade level*

> To make the point that the world still holds undiscovered treasures—and mysteries—the writers recount a 1984 discovery at Río Azul, the ruins of an ancient Maya town. The authors describe the surprise of finding a mysterious, untouched tomb there. Along the way, they also discuss the looting of archaeological sites and measures that the United States has taken to stop the trade in stolen national treasures.

PRETEACHING

Skills Starter

Motivate. Have students read the title, and then ask what question it implies. [The search for what?] Next, have students survey the visuals and captions on pp. 741 and 743. Then, ask them what kind of search the article will most likely describe. [the search for ancient artifacts]

Preview Vocabulary

Have students study the Vocabulary words on this page. Then have them answer each of the following questions using one of the words.

1. Your little sister has torn through your room, looking for her favorite socks. What has she done? [ransacked it]

2. If you find an arrowhead once used by American Indians, what have you found? [an artifact]

3. Your cousin knows everything a person can possibly know about gourmet popcorn. What is he? [a popcorn connoisseur]

4. You find a five-dollar bill in the cafeteria and keep it—even when you overhear a girl say she lost it. Your action is what? [unscrupulous]

Assign the Reading

Have students read the selection and complete the Test Practice questions independently. Review the questions in class, using each item as a topic for discussion.

A Reading Informational Text

? Summarize. Give a one-sentence summary of each of the article's first two paragraphs. [Possible response: Paragraph 1— Many remnants of Mayan civilization have yet to be discovered and analyzed. Paragraph 2—Scientists discovered a Mayan ruin in 1962, but did not have the money to excavate it.]

B Reading Informational Text

? Connect with the text. If you were thinking about a career in archaeology, would this information make you more eager about it—or less? Explain. [The possibility of danger might prove a discouragement to some and an incentive to others.]

C Cross-curricular Connections
CULTURE

Protecting the past. Posting guards at archaeological sites is just one way in which Guatemala is trying to prevent the theft of Mayan artifacts. Looters often are willing to risk an armed confrontation with such guards, however, because dealing in this stolen treasure is very profitable. In fact, it is estimated that this "business" earns its participants about $120 million each year.

D Reading Informational Text

? Hypothesize. Why do you think some people might want to have private collections of illegally collected artifacts? [Possible responses: They take pride in having something that other people do not have.]

The Search Goes On
from *The Mystery of the Ancient Maya*

Carolyn Meyer and Charles Gallenkamp

Brilliant achievements, exciting revelations, and countless unsolved mysteries—this is the legacy left by the ancient Maya. Huge areas remain to be explored, dozens of key sites to be investigated. There are hieroglyphic inscriptions[1] to decipher and mountains of data to analyze. And so there are always new projects, new digs, new studies—and new breakthroughs.

In 1962 a geologist prospecting for an oil company in the jungle of Guatemala came across a cluster of ruins. He got in touch with Richard E. W. Adams, a young archaeologist who was on a dig in another part of the country. At that time all the two could do was to map the Río Azul site, named for a river nearby. There was no money then to excavate the ruins they had found.

Over the next twenty years thieves dug trenches around the pyramids, tunneled into them, and even split them open to get at the treasures inside. The looters ransacked at least twenty-eight tombs in this and the surrounding area, smuggling jewelry and other priceless objects into the United States, where they were sold to art collectors for huge sums of money.

When Adams returned to Río Azul in 1981, he heard about the looting and saw the deep trenches and the scattered rubble. On one occasion he and another scientist surprised armed looters at work. Shots were fired and one of the thieves was wounded, but they all got away. After the incident Guatemalan government troops swept the area, and guards with automatic weapons have remained on duty ever since to prevent further looting.

There are tragic consequences to looting: When artifacts are stolen and sold, all the valuable information they could provide is lost forever. The whole historical and archaeological context of each piece of remarkable pottery and exquisite jade jewelry is destroyed. A stolen artifact becomes merely a prized object in a private collection that is often kept secret or shared with only a few connoisseurs.

But unscrupulous collectors are willing to pay enormous sums for

---

1. **hieroglyphic** (hī′ər·ō·glif′ik) **inscriptions:** engraved hieroglyphics (writing in which pictures, rather than letters, are used).

Vocabulary

decipher (dē·sī′fər) *v.:* interpret; find the meaning of.

ransacked (ran′sakt′) *v.:* searched thoroughly for goods to steal; looted, robbed.

artifacts (ärt′ə·fakts′) *n.:* objects made by people or adapted for human use.

connoisseurs (kän′ə·surz′) *n.:* people who are experts on something.

unscrupulous (un·skroo′pyə·ləs) *adj.:* dishonest.

RESOURCES: READING

Planning
- *One-Stop Planner* CD-ROM with ExamView Test Generator

Differentiating Instruction
- *Holt Reading Solutions*
- *Supporting Instruction in Spanish*
- *Audio CD Library*
- *Audio CD Library, Selections and Summaries in Spanish*

Vocabulary
- *Vocabulary Development*

Grammar and Language
- *Daily Language Activities*

Assessment
- *Holt Assessment: Literature, Reading, and Vocabulary*
- *One-Stop Planner* CD-ROM with ExamView Test Generator

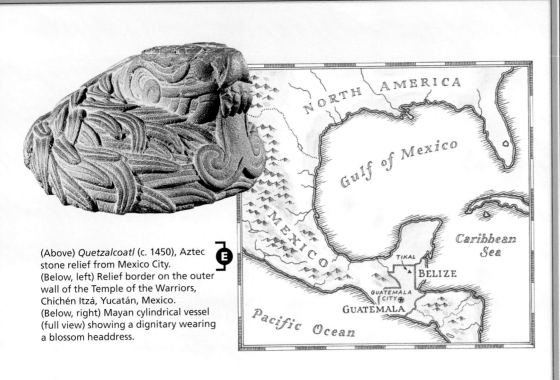

(Above) *Quetzalcoatl* (c. 1450), Aztec stone relief from Mexico City.
(Below, left) Relief border on the outer wall of the Temple of the Warriors, Chichén Itzá, Yucatán, Mexico.
(Below, right) Mayan cylindrical vessel (full view) showing a dignitary wearing a blossom headdress.

E **Cross-curricular Connections**
CULTURE

Quetzalcoatl. Quetzalcoatl, the Feathered Serpent, was an important god of the Aztecs, the people who dominated Mexico after the decline of the Maya. The Maya did not worship Quetzalcoatl, but they did worship a closely related god whom they called Kukulcan.

The Search Goes On   **741**

- *Holt Online Assessment*

Internet
- go.hrw.com (Keyword: LE5 7-6)
- *Elements of Literature Online*

Media
- *Audio CD Library*
- *Audio CD Library, Selections and Summaries in Spanish*

A Reading Informational Text

? Summarize. How might you summarize this paragraph? [Possible response: Dishonest collectors are willing to pay a price for illegally acquired artifacts.] Would you include this idea in a summary of the entire article? Explain. [Possible response: Yes, I would include it, because the paragraph identifies one of the greatest threats to the gathering and analyzing of important historical data.]

B Reading Informational Text

? Infer. Why do you think the United States has committed itself so strongly to stopping archaeological looting? [Possible responses: The United States holds that a country has a right to the national treasures found within its borders. The United States appreciates the importance of giving historians and scientists, as well as collectors, access to such artifacts.]

C Reading Informational Text

? Identify cause and effect. How do the workers know they have found a tomb before they reach its entrance? [The workers discover that there is a secret chamber cut into the rock below the ground surface. The fact that it is painted suggests that it is a tomb containing valuable artifacts.]

D Advanced Learners

? Irony. Irony occurs when something is the opposite of what you expect it to be. What is ironic about the workers' entry into the tomb? [Possible response: Instead of using high-tech gear to lower themselves into the chambers, they make a ladder that was probably much like the ones the Maya themselves used.]

treasures for their private collections. The possibility of such profit drives looters to search out and plunder as-yet undiscovered sites. Once they've taken what they want, the looters use smuggling networks to get the ancient jars and jewels out of the jungle and into the hands of collectors all over the world.

Adams and other archaeologists used the incident at Río Azul to convince Congress to pass a law to stop national treasures looted in other countries from being brought into the United States. In addition, the United States signed an agreement that commits this country to recover and return stolen cultural and archaeological objects from Mexico and Central America.

Meanwhile, Adams raised the money to begin excavating the ruin in a race against the looters. The ancient city of Río Azul was probably a small center under the control of the bigger city of Tikal, a few miles to the south. It covers about 470 acres and contains four major temple pyramids and adjoining smaller buildings. Adams and his team had been working on the site for several weeks in the spring of 1984, hoping to get as much accomplished as possible before the rainy season began. Then on May fifteenth a workman's leg plunged through rock-and-dirt fill and down through the roof of a secret chamber, a cave cut into the rock some 13 feet below the surface of the ground.

Hidden by a wing of a temple built on top of it, the cave had gone undetected by looters—and until then by archaeologists as well.

One of the expedition leaders peered in. "It's painted!" he yelled; whoops of excitement greeted the announcement. They began working furiously to clear the rubble from the entrance to what they knew was a tomb. Next they lowered a miniature video camera into the opening. And finally, using vines and saplings from the jungle—traditional Maya building materials—they climbed down into the chamber.

The skeleton of a nobleman in his thirties, his shroud nothing more than dust, lay on a wooden bier.[2] Elaborate and mysterious wall paintings and fifteen pieces of pottery surrounded his body. One of the pieces was a beautifully made jar with an unusual screw-top lid. On top of the skeleton lay a stingray spine used in bloodletting rituals. Parrots chattered overhead and Guatemalan government guards with rifles and machetes stood by as the contents of Tomb 19, as it was now designated, were recorded and labeled and then transported to the National Museum of Anthropology in Guatemala City.

---

2. **bier** (bir) *n.:* platform on which a corpse is placed.

DIFFERENTIATING INSTRUCTION

Learners Having Difficulty

If students have trouble summarizing the main idea of any given paragraph, have them use the following sentence stem to spur their thinking: *This paragraph tells all about . . .* Once students complete the sentence stem, have them use the information they supply as the subject of a new sentence that summarizes the paragraph's main idea. For example, if students say that the last paragraph on this page tells all about

the tomb scientists discovered, they might then form the following statement of the paragraph's main idea: *The tomb scientists discovered may have belonged to the relative of an important ruler.*

English-Language Learners

Students may find the reading level of this feature somewhat challenging. Before you begin, ask students to think of action-adventure movies about finding a treasure.

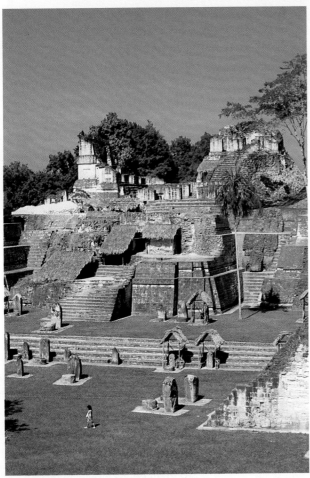

North Acropolis and Central Plaza (c. A.D. 700), Mayan ruins, Tikal, Guatemala.

The date of the tomb is about A.D. 420 to 470, the height of the Classic period.[3] Adams, who calls it "a moment frozen in time," believes that the tomb was built for a relative of a ruler buried in a large pyramid nearby, already looted and stripped of its wall paintings. All that could be read of the hieroglyphics on the walls and pottery were the words *great son*.

---

3. **Classic period:** the period, beginning around A.D. 250 and ending around 900, during which Mayan civilization reached its peak.

The Search Goes On   **743**

DIRECT TEACHING

E ● **Reading Informational Text**

❓ **Interpret.** At the beginning of this feature, the authors say that the Maya have left "countless unsolved mysteries." How does the information at the end of the feature support this statement? [Possible response: The authors share what little is known of the occupant of Tomb 19—that he seems to have been a nobleman and that perhaps he has something to do with an inscription that reads *great son*. His actual identity is, for now, a mystery.]

GUIDED PRACTICE

Monitor students' progress. To assess students' understanding of the article and of its main ideas, have them tell whether each of the following ideas should be included in a summary of the article.

1. Many Mayan artifacts remain undiscovered. [should]
2. One archaeological site in Guatemala was named the Río Azul site. [should not]
3. When sites are looted, invaluable information is lost. [should]
4. Smuggling networks are used to get ancient jars out of the jungle. [should not]
5. Back at the Guatemala site, an ancient tomb was discovered by accident. [should]

(The opening sequence of *Raiders of the Lost Ark* may be an ideal discussion starter.) Have students draw on their knowledge of such films as they offer comments about various kinds of treasure and the lengths to which treasure hunters might go to reach their goals. Work with students to make a master list of scenes that they might expect in a film about treasure hunting. As they read "The Search Goes On," ask them to make notes about any details that remind them of such scenes. Invite comments, filling in any important details that may have been missed.

Advanced Learners
Enrichment. At the end of this feature, students learn a little about a nobleman buried at the Río Azul site. Who is he, and what does the inscription *great son* have to do with him? Could he possibly be Kukul?

Activity. Invite students to respond to these questions by creating a tribute to this nobleman in a format of their own choosing (for example, a fictitious obituary or a portrait). Have students share and discuss their tributes.

Summarizing the Main Ideas

Answers and Model Rationales

1. **B** If students identify item C as the correct answer, clarify that looters ransacked the ruins *in spite of* the presence of government troops.

2. **F** Refer students to paragraph 4 of the article. Clarify that the "historical and archaeological context" of an artifact means how, when, where, and why an artifact was created and used.

3. **D** Students should recall that the tomb was discovered by accident as workmen probed the site.

4. **H** The last paragraph of the article confirms the possible identity of the tomb's occupant.

Test-Taking Tips

For more information on how to answer multiple-choice items, refer students to **Test Smarts,** p. 920.

Constructed Response

Possible Answers

1. They are sold to private collectors who illegally purchase the artifacts for exorbitant prices.

2. Scientists are upset because once an object is taken from a site, information about its origins is lost forever.

3. Many remnants of Mayan civilization have yet to be discovered. In 1962, some scientists found an ancient Mayan ruin in Guatemala, but they did not have the money to excavate it. Over the next two decades, thieves looted the site and government troops were brought in to protect it. Still, the ancient artifacts continued

---

Summarizing the Main Ideas

The Search Goes On

1. What happened to the Río Azul site because there was no money to excavate the ruins?
   - A The site was destroyed by an earthquake.
   - B The treasures were stolen by looters.
   - C The treasures were saved by government troops.
   - D The site disappeared into the jungle.

2. What do scientists hope to discover from the objects in the ancient Mayan tombs?
   - F the history and customs of the people
   - G gold and precious stones in the jewelry
   - H great art for private collections
   - J the identity of the thieves

3. How did the scientists discover Tomb 19?
   - A They saw it on a map.
   - B They figured out where it was from ancient writings.
   - C They dug and dug and dug.
   - D A workman's leg broke through the roof.

4. Who do scientists think is buried in Tomb 19?
   - F the ruler of Tikal
   - G the ruler of the Río Azul site
   - H a relative of a ruler
   - J a common man

Constructed Response

1. **What happens to the objects stolen from the ancient Mayan tombs?

2. **Why are scientists upset when objects are stolen from the tombs?

3. **Summarize** the article by describing its **main ideas.** Include only the most important supporting details.

SKILLS FOCUS

Reading Skills
Summarize the main ideas.

---

to fetch high prices on the black market. Scientists convinced the U.S. government to help protect the national treasures of foreign countries. Meanwhile, scientists returned to the Guatemala site and discovered an ancient tomb. The tomb dates to about A.D. 450 and may belong to an important relative of a ruler buried nearby.

Clarifying Word Meanings

PRACTICE

Use words from the Word Bank to fill in the blanks in the following sentences. Use each word only once.

> **Word Bank**
>
> decipher
> ransacked
> artifacts
> connoisseurs
> unscrupulous

1. His mother was furious when Bobby _____ the house looking for his baseball mitt.

2. The teacher gave Alicia a poor grade on her composition because he couldn't _____ the handwriting.

3. As candy _____ , Maria and Miguel knew how to pick the best chocolates from the box.

4. On a class trip to the museum, the students examined the _____ from ancient Egypt.

5. The _____ salesperson lied when he said the old jalopy had been given new brakes.

Grammar Link

Irregular Verbs

Many people have trouble with irregular verbs. You don't form the past tense of irregular verbs by adding –*d* or –*ed*, as you do with regular verbs. The only way to be sure you know the various forms of irregular verbs is to memorize them. Reading this list aloud several times will help you remember these odd verb forms.

Base Form	Past	Past Participle
am/is/are	was/were	(has/have) been
begin	began	(has/have) begun
break	broke	(has/have) broken
bring	brought	(has/have) brought
do	did	(has/have) done
find	found	(has/have) found
go	went	(has/have) gone
see	saw	(has/have) seen

PRACTICE

Act as an editor: Provide the correct irregular verb forms in the paragraph below.

We had went to the jungle and had began searching for ruins. We brung axes and machetes to clear the thick growth. We finally breaked through and seen a temple covered with vines. I been surprised that we done such a good job!

For more help, see Irregular Verbs, 3c, in the Language Handbook.

SKILLS FOCUS

Vocabulary Skills
Clarify word meanings.

Grammar Skills
Recognize irregular verbs.

Vocabulary Development

PRACTICE

1. ransacked
2. decipher
3. connoisseurs
4. artifacts
5. unscrupulous

Grammar Link

PRACTICE

We had *gone* to the jungle and had *begun* searching for ruins. We *brought* axes and machetes to clear the thick growth. We finally *broke* through and *saw* a temple covered with vines. I *was* surprised that we *had* done such a good job!

ASSESSING

Assessment

■ *Holt Assessment: Literature, Reading, and Vocabulary*

Comparing Literature

OVERVIEW

Purpose. This Comparing Literature feature explores the common elements of two Cinderella stories and one Cinderella poem. An understanding of these elements will help students appreciate the universal human concerns and desires expressed in the selections.

Use. Direct students' attention to the box identifying the features of a typical Cinderella story, and tell them to look for these elements as they read "Aschenputtel," "Dinorella," and "Interview." As they read, students will fill in charts showing similarities and differences in the stories' characters, plots, tones, and themes. After reading the stories, students will write an essay comparing and contrasting them.

Literary Focus
The Cinderella Story

When you read "Yeh-Shen" (page 383), you learned that there are more than nine hundred versions of the Cinderella story from all around the world and that "Yeh-Shen" comes from China. You are about to read three other versions of this popular tale. "Aschenputtel" is a traditional folk tale from Germany. "Dinorella" is a lively contemporary version. "Interview" is a short poem that suggests the story of Cinderella would be very different if it were told by another character. As you read each selection, compare it to the typical Cinderella story. Think about: Who are the **characters**? What is the **plot**? What is the **tone** (serious, humorous, sad)? What is the **theme,** or message?

Reading Skills
Comparing and Contrasting

These three selections offer different versions of the same story. As you read each one, think about how the stories are the same and how they are different. When you have finished reading all three selections, you will be asked to write an essay comparing the stories. A chart at the end of each selection will help you gather details for your essay.

SKILLS FOCUS

Literary Skills
Analyze the Cinderella story.

Reading Skills
Compare and contrast texts.

Features of a Typical Cinderella Story

Characters:
- a young girl
- a wicked stepmother and jealous stepsisters
- a handsome prince
- magical characters who help the girl

Plot:
- The girl lives in poverty yet longs to go to the prince's ball.
- Magical characters help the girl.
- The prince falls in love with the girl, but she runs off and he has to find her.
- The girl and the prince live happily ever after.

You probably know the story of Cinderella. "Aschenputtel" is the German version of that story. In both tales a young girl's mother dies and her father remarries. The girl is then mistreated by her stepmother and stepsisters, but in the end, she marries the handsome prince. As you read, think about how this version of the Cinderella story is the same as or different from any other version you may know.

Aschenputtel

German, retold by
Jakob *and* **Wilhelm Grimm,**
translated by **Lucy Crane**

747

Summary ⬆ *above grade level*

A rich widower, the father of a virtuous girl, remarries. The girl's stepmother and stepsisters ridicule her and force her to perform chores. Having no bed to sleep in, the girl is forced to rest in the cinders of the hearth, so her family calls her Aschenputtel ("Cinder-fool"). At her request, her father brings her a hazel twig when he returns from the fair. Aschenputtel plants it on her mother's grave, and a hazel tree springs up. Whenever she goes to the tree to weep and pray, a white bird appears and brings her anything she wishes for.

The king announces a festival at which his son will choose a bride. Aschenputtel's stepmother devises a chore to keep her at home. Aschenputtel calls on the birds for assistance. She then goes to the tree and asks for garments of silver and gold, which she wears to the festival. The prince stays by her side all evening. He tries to follow her home, but she eludes him. These events are repeated the following two nights, but on the third evening, Aschenputtel loses a shoe as she flees. The prince vows to marry whomever the shoe fits. The two stepsisters cut off parts of their feet in a vain attempt to fit into the shoe. Aschenputtel is then summoned. She slips the shoe on with ease, and the prince declares her his bride and rides off with her on his horse. At Aschenputtel's wedding, pigeons peck out the stepsisters' eyes.

PRETEACHING

Selection Starter

Motivate. Ask students why they think the story of Cinderella is a favorite. Use these questions as a springboard for discussion:

• What do people like about this story?
• What universal wishes does this story express?
• What universal fears does it express?

If you were going to write a modern-day Cinderella story, where would it be set? Who would its main characters be?

DIRECT TEACHING

A Reading Skills

❓ **Predict.** What prediction can you make from the mother's words? [Possible response: After her mother's death, Aschenputtel may face problems that will make it hard for her to remain "pious and good"; her mother's spirit will help Aschenputtel deal with her problems.]

B Reading Skills

Identify. [Possible response to question 1: The tone is serious.]

C Literary Focus

❓ **The Cinderella story.** What feature of the typical Cinderella story is introduced here? [the wicked stepmother and stepsisters]

D Reading Skills

Compare and contrast. [Possible response to question 2: The daughter is kind and devoted, while the stepsisters are jealous and wicked. The tone has changed to a more exaggerated one, because the stepsisters are so mean.]

E Reading Skills

❓ **Speculate.** Why do you think the only character who is given a name is Aschenputtel? [Possible response: In folk tales, character types are more important than individuals, because what is emphasized is a fixed pattern of behavior.]

IDENTIFY

❶ Re-read the first three paragraphs. How would you describe the **tone** of the folk tale?

COMPARE AND CONTRAST

❷ From what you have read so far, how is the daughter different from her stepsisters? How has the **tone** changed?

There was once a rich man whose wife lay sick, and when she felt her end drawing near, she called to her only daughter to come near her bed and said,

"Dear child, be pious and good, and God will always take care of you, and I will look down upon you from heaven and will be with you."

And then she closed her eyes and expired.[1] The maiden went every day to her mother's grave and wept and was always pious and good. When the winter came, the snow covered the grave with a white covering, and when the sun came in the early spring and melted it away, the man took to himself another wife. **❶**

The new wife brought two daughters home with her and they were beautiful and fair in appearance but at heart were wicked and ugly. And then began very evil times for the poor stepdaughter.

"Is the stupid creature to sit in the same room with us?" said they. "Those who eat food must earn it. Out with the kitchen maid!"

They took away her pretty dresses and put on her an old gray kirtle[2] and gave her wooden shoes to wear.

"Just look now at the proud princess, how she is decked out!" cried they, laughing, and then they sent her into the kitchen. There she was obliged to do heavy work from morning to night, get up early in the morning, draw water, make the fires, cook, and wash. Besides that, the sisters did their utmost to torment her—mocking her and strewing peas and lentils among the ashes and setting her to pick them up. In the evenings, when she was quite tired out with her hard day's work, she had no bed to lie on but was obliged to rest on the hearth among the cinders. And as she always looked dusty and dirty, they named her Aschenputtel. **❷**

It happened one day that the father went to the fair, and he asked his two stepdaughters what he should bring back for them.

"Fine clothes!" said one.

"Pearls and jewels!" said the other.

"But what will you have, Aschenputtel?" said he.

"The first twig, Father, that strikes against your hat on the way home; this is what I should like you to bring me."

---

1. **expired** (ek·spīrd′) *v.:* died. In Latin, *exspirare* means "to breathe out"; to breathe out one's last breath is to die.
2. **kirtle** *n.:* old-fashioned word for "dress."

748   Collection 6 / Our Literary Heritage: Greek Myths and World Folk Tales

---

DIFFERENTIATING INSTRUCTION

Learners Having Difficulty
Remind these students that there are significant differences between this version of the story and the Cinderella story they probably know. Have students create a two-column chart in which they list similarities and differences between the familiar tale and the one they are reading now. After they finish reading and taking notes, discuss students' findings in a small group. Have

students add to their charts any similarities or differences they overlooked.

English-Language Learners
Students may be confused by the mix of poetry and prose in "Aschenputtel." Discuss what is being requested or announced in each example of poetry. Students should see that the poetry is reserved for the birds and the tree that help Aschenputtel. For

"Is the stupid creature to sit in the same room with us?"

So he bought for the two stepdaughters fine clothes, pearls, and jewels, and on his way back, as he rode through a green lane, a hazel twig struck against his hat; and he broke it off and carried it home with him. And when he reached home, he gave to the stepdaughters what they had wished for, and to Aschenputtel he gave the hazel twig. She thanked him and went to her mother's grave, and planted this twig there, weeping so bitterly that the tears fell upon it and watered it, and it flourished and became a fine tree. Aschenputtel went to see it three times a day and wept and prayed, and each time a white bird rose up from the tree, and, if she uttered any wish, the bird brought her whatever she had wished for. ❸

Now it came to pass that the king ordained³ a festival that should last for three days and to which all the beautiful young women of that country were bidden so that the king's son might choose a bride from among them. When the two stepdaughters heard that they too were bidden to appear, they felt very pleased, and they called Aschenputtel and said,

"Comb our hair, brush our shoes, and make our buckles fast, we are going to the wedding feast at the king's castle."

Aschenputtel, when she heard this, could not help crying, for she too would have liked to go to the dance, and she begged her stepmother to allow her.

"What, you Aschenputtel!" said she. "In all your dust and dirt, you want to go to the festival! You that have no dress and no shoes! You want to dance!"

But since she persisted in asking, at last the stepmother said,

"I have scattered a dish full of lentils in the ashes, and if you can pick them all up again in two hours, you may go with us."

Then the maiden went to the back door that led into the garden and called out,

---

3. **ordained** (ôr·dānd′) *v.*: ordered or decreed.

INTERPRET

❸ How does Aschenputtel's request for a twig prove to be a good choice?

G

F

H

DIRECT TEACHING

F **Reading Skills**

Interpret. [Possible response to question 3: The twig ends up producing a tree in which lives a bird who grants Aschenputtel's wishes.]

G **Literary Focus**

❓ The Cinderella story. What typical Cinderella-story character appears at this point in the story? [the handsome prince]

H **Literary Focus**

❓ Motifs in folk tales. How long is the festival supposed to last? [three days] How do the stepsisters' demands reflect the motif of the number three? [The stepsisters demand that Aschenputtel do three things to help them get ready for the festival.]

---

additional strategies to supplement instruction for English-language learners, see *Holt Reading Solutions.*

Special Education Students
For lessons designed to help special education students, see *Holt Reading Solutions.*

DIRECT TEACHING

Ⓐ Cross-curricular Connections

CULTURE

Animal symbolism. Point out that Aschenputtel calls the doves gentle and that in many cultures, doves symbolize peace. (They may also symbolize the mother's soul at peace in heaven.) Invite students to explain how various birds are viewed in their cultures (as symbols of wisdom or strength or as omens of trouble, for example).

Ⓑ Reading Skills

Infer. [Possible response to question 4: She calls them gentle. The way she addresses them suggests that she herself is gentle.]

Ⓒ Literary Focus

❓ The Cinderella story. What typical elements of the Cinderella story do these birds supply? [They are magical and they help the girl.]

Ⓓ English-Language Learners

Break down difficult text. Long sentences like this one, in which thoughts are connected by a series of *ands,* appear frequently in this story. Have students break this sentence down into three or more short ones. [Possible response: So there came to the kitchen two white doves. Then some turtledoves came, followed by a crowd of all the other birds under heaven, chirping and fluttering. They alighted among the ashes. The doves nodded with their heads and began to pick, peck, pick, peck. Then the other birds joined in and put all the good grains into the dish.]

INFER

❹ How does Aschenputtel show consideration for the birds in the way she calls them? What does this tell you about her **character**?

Ⓐ
O gentle doves, O turtledoves,
And all the birds that be,
The lentils that in ashes lie
Come and pick up for me!
⠀⠀⠀The good must be put in the dish,
⠀⠀⠀The bad you may eat if you wish. ❹

Ⓒ Then there came to the kitchen window two white doves, and after them some turtledoves, and at last a crowd of all the birds under heaven, chirping and fluttering, and they alighted among the ashes; and the doves nodded with their heads and began to pick, peck, pick, peck, and then all the others began to pick, peck, pick, peck and put all the good grains into the dish. Before an hour was over, all was done, and they flew away. Then the maiden brought the dish to her stepmother, feeling joyful and thinking that now she should go to the feast; but the stepmother said,

"No, Aschenputtel, you have no proper clothes, and you do not know how to dance, and you would be laughed at!"

And when Aschenputtel cried for disappointment, she added,

"If you can pick two dishfuls of lentils out of the ashes, nice and clean, you shall go with us," thinking to herself, "for that is not possible." When she had strewed two dishfuls of lentils among the ashes, the maiden went through the back door into the garden and cried,

"She is my partner," said the prince.

O gentle doves, O turtledoves,
And all the birds that be,
The lentils that in ashes lie
Come and pick up for me!
⠀⠀⠀The good must be put in the dish,
⠀⠀⠀The bad you may eat if you wish.

Ⓓ So there came to the kitchen window two white doves, and then some turtledoves, and at last a crowd of all the other birds under heaven, chirping and fluttering, and they alighted among the ashes, and the doves nodded with their heads and began to pick, peck, pick, peck, and then all the others began to pick, peck, pick, peck and put all the good grains into the dish. And before half an hour was over, it was all done, and they flew away. Then the maiden took the dishes to the stepmother, feeling joyful and thinking that now she should go with them to the feast. But her stepmother said, "All this is of no good to you; you cannot come with us, for you have no proper clothes and cannot dance; you would put us to shame."

E

Then she turned her back on poor Aschenputtel and made haste to set out with her two proud daughters.

F

And as there was no one left in the house, Aschenputtel went to her mother's grave, under the hazel bush, and cried,

> Little tree, little tree, shake over me,
> That silver and gold may come down
>   and cover me.

Then the bird threw down a dress of gold and silver and a pair of slippers embroidered with silk and silver. And in all haste she put on the dress and went to the festival. But her stepmother and sisters did not know her and thought she must be a foreign princess, she looked so beautiful in her golden dress. Of Aschenputtel they never thought at all and supposed that she was sitting at home, picking the lentils out of the ashes. The King's son came to meet her and took her by the hand and danced with her, and he refused to stand up with anyone else so that he might not be obliged to let go her hand; and when anyone came to claim it, he answered,

"She is my partner." **5**

And when the evening came, she wanted to go home, but the prince said he would go with her to take care of her, for he wanted to see where the beautiful maiden lived. But she escaped him and jumped up into the pigeon house. Then the prince waited until her father came along, and told him that the strange maiden had jumped into the pigeon house. The father thought to himself, "It cannot surely be Aschenputtel" and called for axes and hatchets and had the pigeon house cut down, but there was no one in it. And when they entered the house, there sat Aschenputtel in her dirty clothes among the cinders, and a little oil lamp burnt dimly in the chimney; for Aschenputtel had been very quick and had jumped out of the pigeon house again and had run to the hazel bush; and there she had taken off her beautiful dress and had laid it on the grave, and the bird had

COMPARE AND CONTRAST

5 Explain how people treat Aschenputtel differently depending on what she's wearing. **G**

Aschenputtel **751**

E Vocabulary Note

? **Multiple meanings.** What does the stepmother mean by "proper clothes"? What else can *proper* mean? [Possible responses: Here, *proper* means "suitable." Other meanings of *proper* include "polite; respectable" and "belonging to a specific individual."]

F Literary Focus

? **The Cinderella story.** Which elements of the Cinderella story appear in this passage? [a poor girl who longs to go to the prince's ball; the wicked stepmother and stepsisters; magical characters who help the girl.]

G Reading Skills

Compare and contrast. [Possible response to question 5: When Aschenputtel is dressed in her ordinary, shabby clothes, she is treated with scorn. When she is dressed in beautiful clothes, others admire her and seek her company.]

H Reading Skills

? **Compare and contrast texts.** Do these details differ from those in the Cinderella story you're familiar with? If so, how? [Possible response: Yes; in the story I know, Cinderella travels to and from the ball in a pumpkin that has been transformed by a fairy godmother into a carriage. The fairy godmother also dresses Cinderella for the ball and changes mice into footmen. That story does not include a pigeon house, a mother's grave, or a magic tree and birds. In addition, in that story the ball lasts a single evening, whereas this one continues the next day.]

CROSS-CURRICULAR CONNECTIONS

Art
Illustrate a scene. Ask students to illustrate their favorite scene from "Aschenputtel" and to come up with a caption for their illustration. Work with students to create a display of the finished illustrations, arranged in chronological order, for the class and others to enjoy. Encourage students to discuss their reasons for choosing their particular scenes and depictions.

WHOLE CLASS

Language Arts
Write a letter in character. Have students assume the persona of a character in "Aschenputtel" and write a letter to another character. Remind students to use thoughts and language consistent with their chosen characters. Invite students to exchange letters.

INDIVIDUAL

DIRECT TEACHING

A Reading Skills

? Make judgments. What do you make of Aschenputtel's father's decision to cut down the tree? [Students will probably say that it is a strange thing for a father to do, especially if his child might be in the tree.] What can you conclude about the father from his behavior? [Possible responses: He is a thoughtless or careless father; he wishes his daughter ill.]

B Literary Focus

? Motifs in folk tales. How does this time period relate to the story's motif? Explain. [This is another example of the "charmed" number three; it is the third day of the festival.]

C Vocabulary Note

Synonyms. Aschenputtel's dress is described as unmatched in "splendor and brilliancy." Ask students to suggest synonyms for *splendor* and *brilliancy*. [Possible responses: grandeur, magnificence, radiance.]

carried it away again, and then she had put on her little gray kirtle again and had sat down in the kitchen among the cinders.

The next day, when the festival began anew, and the parents and stepsisters had gone to it, Aschenputtel went to the hazel bush and cried,

> Little tree, little tree, shake over me,
> That silver and gold may come down
> and cover me.

Then the bird cast down a still more splendid dress than on the day before. And when she appeared in it among the guests, everyone was astonished at her beauty. The prince had been waiting until she came, and he took her hand and danced with her alone. And when anyone else came to invite her, he said,

"She is my partner."

And when the evening came, she wanted to go home, and the prince followed her, for he wanted to see to what house she belonged; but she broke away from him and ran into the garden at the back of the house. There stood a fine large tree, bearing splendid pears; she leapt as lightly as a squirrel among the branches, and the prince did not know what had become of her. So he waited until her father came along, and then he told him that the strange maiden had rushed from him, and that he thought she had gone up into the pear tree. The father thought to himself,

A "It cannot surely be Aschenputtel" and called for an axe and felled the tree, but there was no one in it. And when they went into the kitchen, there sat Aschenputtel among the cinders, as usual, for she had got down the other side of the tree and had taken back her beautiful clothes to the bird on the hazel bush and had put on her old gray kirtle again.

B On the third day, when the parents and the stepchildren had set off, Aschenputtel went again to her mother's grave and said to the tree,

> Little tree, little tree, shake over me,
> That silver and gold may come down
> and cover me.

C Then the bird cast down a dress the likes of which had never been seen for splendor and brilliancy, and slippers that were of gold.

And when she appeared in this dress at the feast, nobody knew what to say for wonderment. The prince danced with her alone, and if anyone else asked her, he answered,

---

CROSS-CURRICULAR CONNECTIONS

Music

Rodgers and Hammerstein's *Cinderella*. Richard Rodgers (1902–1979), composer, and Oscar Hammerstein II (1895–1960), lyricist, together created a string of memorable musicals, including *Oklahoma!*, *Carousel*, *South Pacific*, *The King and I*, and *The Sound of Music*. Somewhat lesser known is their musical version of the Cinderella story. *Cinderella* was well received as a 1957 television production and was remade successfully in 1965 and 1997.

Activities.

• After students have read "Aschenputtel," play a few songs from *Cinderella*—for example, "In My Own Little Corner," "The Prince is Giving a Ball," and "Ten Minutes Ago." Ask students how well they think these songs capture the story as the Grimms told it. (You might point out that the musical is based on Perrault's version, not on the Grimms'.)

• Have students work in pairs (like Rodgers and Hammerstein) to write a song based on "Aschenputtel" or "Dinorella." Students may fit new words to a familiar melody or create a song that is wholly their own. Invite volunteers to perform their songs.

PAIRED

He turned his horse round and took the false bride home.

"She is my partner." ⑥

And when it was evening, Aschenputtel wanted to go home, and the prince was about to go with her when she ran past him so quickly that he could not follow her. But he had laid a plan and had caused all the steps to be spread with pitch,[4] so that as she rushed down them, her left shoe remained sticking in it. The prince picked it up and saw that it was of gold and very small and slender. The next morning he went to the father and told him that none should be his bride save the one whose foot the golden shoe should fit. Then the two sisters were very glad, because they had pretty feet. The eldest went to her room to try on the shoe, and her mother stood by. But she could not get her great toe into it, for the shoe was too small; then her mother handed her a knife, and said,

"Cut the toe off, for when you are queen, you will never have to go on foot." So the girl cut her toe off, squeezed her foot into the shoe, concealed the pain, and went down to the prince. Then he took her with him on his horse as his bride and rode off. They had to pass by the grave, and there sat the two pigeons on the hazel bush and cried,

There they go, there they go!
There is blood on her shoe;
The shoe is too small,
—Not the right bride at all!

Then the prince looked at her shoe and saw the blood flowing. And he turned his horse round and took the false bride home again, saying she was not the right one and that the other sister must try on the shoe. So she went into her room to do so and got her toes comfortably in, but her heel was too large. Then her mother handed her the knife, saying, "Cut a piece off your heel; when you are queen, you will never have to go on foot."

---

4. **pitch** (pich) *n.:* here, black, sticky tar.

IDENTIFY

⑥ A common **motif** in folk tales is the number three. What events have happened three times in this story?

D Reading Skills

Identify. [Possible response to question 6: The stepmother has refused to let Aschenputtel to go the festival, the magical birds have produced a beautiful gown for Aschenputtel, and Aschenputtel has enjoyed the prince's company.]

E Reading Skills

❓ **Respond to the text.** What do you think of the prince's plan? [Some students may consider it a clever plan; others may propose alternatives.]

F Literary Focus

❓ **The Cinderella story.** What do the details in this passage reveal about the characters of the stepmother and stepsisters? [Possible response: They are greedy, dishonest, and devious.]

DIRECT TEACHING

A Reading Skills

Predict. [Possible response to question 7: Aschenputtel—the third sister—will try on the shoe, and it will fit.]

B Literary Focus

❼ Motifs of folk tales. How do the pigeons' cries illustrate the motif of the number three in this story? [The pigeons cry out three times before the prince and Aschenputtel come together.]

So the girl cut a piece off her heel and thrust her foot into the shoe, concealed the pain, and went down to the prince, who took his bride before him on his horse and rode off. When they passed by the hazel bush, the two pigeons sat there and cried,

> There they go, there they go!
> There is blood on her shoe;
> The shoe is too small,
> —Not the right bride at all!

Then the prince looked at her foot and saw how the blood was flowing from the shoe and staining the white stocking. And he turned his horse round and brought the false bride home again.

"This is not the right one," said he. "Have you no other daughter?" ❼

"No," said the man, "only my dead wife left behind her a little stunted[5] Aschenputtel; it is impossible that she can be the bride." But the King's son ordered her to be sent for, but the mother said,

"Oh, no! She is much too dirty; I could not let her be seen."

But he would have her fetched, and so Aschenputtel had to appear.

First she washed her face and hands quite clean and went in and curtseyed to the prince, who held out to her the golden shoe. Then she sat down on a stool, drew her foot out of the heavy wooden shoe, and slipped it into the golden one, which fitted it perfectly. And when she stood up and the prince looked in her face, he knew again the beautiful maiden that had danced with him, and he cried,

"This is the right bride!"

The stepmother and the two sisters were thunderstruck and grew pale with anger, but the prince put Aschenputtel before him on his horse and rode off. And as they passed the hazel bush, the two white pigeons cried,

> There they go, there they go!
> No blood on her shoe;
> The shoe's not too small,
> The right bride is she after all.

And when they had thus cried, they came flying after and perched on Aschenputtel's shoulders, one on the right, the other on the left, and so remained.

---

5. **stunted** (stunt′id) *v.* used as *adj.:* not properly grown.
6. **curry favor:** try to win approval by flattering and fawning.

PREDICT

❼ Two times a sister has tried on the shoe that was too small. What do you predict will happen next?

CROSS-CURRICULAR CONNECTIONS

Culture

Social norms. Several details in the Grimm brothers' telling of this story might be handled differently by a storyteller from another culture.

Activity. Invite students to research and report on how some other cultures might address these matters:

• the status of a widower's children following his remarriage

• relations between siblings

• romance between members of different social classes

INDIVIDUAL

And when her wedding with the prince was appointed to be held, the false sisters came, hoping to curry favor[6] and to take part in the festivities. So as the bridal procession went to the church, the eldest walked on the right side and the younger on the left, and the pigeons picked out an eye of each of them. And as they returned, the elder was on the left side and the younger on the right, and the pigeons picked out the other eye of each of them. And so they were condemned for the rest of their days because of their wickedness and falsehood. **❽**

C

INTERPRET

❽ Throughout the story white pigeons (or doves) right the wrongs done to Aschenputtel. What do you think the birds might represent?

D

Aschenputtel **755**

C Literary Focus

❓ The Cinderella story. The stepsisters are "condemned because of their wickedness and falsehood." Why is Aschenputtel rewarded? [Possible response: She is not like her stepsisters. She finds love because she has remained "pious and good," despite the hardships she has faced.]

D Reading Skills

Interpret. [Possible responses to question 8: The birds may represent justice. They may represent the soul of Aschenputtel's mother.]

DIFFERENTIATING INSTRUCTION

Advanced Learners
Enrichment. Aschenputtel is given tasks that seem impossible; fortunately, she has the doves to help her. Students may never face a situation like hers, but they face other challenges and problems on a daily basis.
Activity. Have students, working in groups of three or four, form a "problem patrol" and decide how to handle a difficult task. Here is one situation that students might

consider, along with a problem-solution chart they may find helpful:
• Before you are allowed to go to the movies, you must complete your chores. The movie begins in one hour, but it will take you at least two hours to finish your chores. What will you do?

Problem	Solution
How to complete chores and still see the movie?	Ask for help; try to see a later movie.

Meet the Writers

Jakob and Wilhelm Grimm lived at a time when the German states were struggling to achieve a unified constitutional government. The brothers supported this movement by gathering folk tales from people throughout Germany and by preparing a massive dictionary of the German language. Jakob was the bolder and more experimental of the two, and he was good with words. He kept rigidly to his work schedule but also could take time to be a loving uncle. Wilhelm was the gentler, more poetic brother; he also had a gift for popular speech.

For Independent Reading

Invite students to bring collections of Grimms' fairy tales to class and to read (or, if the tales are long, summarize) some of the more compelling ones for the class.

Meet the Writers

Jakob and Wilhelm Grimm

The Granger Collection, New York.

Two Brothers with a Dream

Before the 1800s, most fairy tales were not written down. They existed only in the memories of people who had heard them from their elders. **Jakob** (1785–1863) and **Wilhelm** (1786–1859) **Grimm** decided that the traditional stories of Germany ought to be written down in one book before they were forgotten. Jakob wrote:

> 66 It is high time that these old traditions were collected and rescued before they perish like dew in the hot sun or fire in a stream and fall silent forever in the unrest of our days. 99

The two brothers wandered from farm to village, looking for good storytellers who knew the old tales. They listened patiently and wrote the stories down. By the time the last edition of their stories was published, in 1857, the brothers had collected about two hundred tales. Some of the best-known ones are "Little Red Riding Hood," "Rumpelstiltskin," "Hansel and Gretel," "Sleeping Beauty," and, of course, "Aschenputtel," or "Cinderella."

For Independent Reading

If you browse through *The Complete Grimm's Fairy Tales,* you will find some truly grim stories. These German tales are filled with acts of cruelty and murder. In the United States, retellers of the tales have sometimes toned them down, producing storybook versions that are much less terrifying.

DIFFERENTIATING INSTRUCTION

Learners Having Difficulty

Before students begin working on the After You Read questions, make sure they can correctly answer the following:

1. With whom does Aschenputtel live, and why? [She lives with her father, her stepmother, and her two stepsisters; her own mother has died.]

2. What happens to the twig that Aschenputtel plants? [It grows into a tree that is home to a magic bird.]

3. How is Aschenputtel able to go to the ball? [The bird in the tree brings her lovely clothes.]

4. Where does Aschenputtel go the first time she leaves the prince? [She escapes into a pigeon house.]

5. What does each stepsister do to try to convince the prince that she is the true bride? [Each cuts off part of her foot to make it fit into the shoe.]

After You Read "Aschenputtel"

First Thoughts

1. Which of our deepest wishes do you think this story expresses? Do you think it is also about some of our fears? Explain.

Thinking Critically

2. Which of the following statements do you think best sums up the lesson "Aschenputtel" seems to teach?

   • Goodness is rewarded in the end.
   • Bad people are always punished.
   • Love conquers all.

   Do you think this is a good lesson for today's world? Explain.

3. How is the **motif** of the number three used in this folk tale? Explain how it helps to build suspense.

4. Many modern versions of this story do not punish the wicked stepsisters. What do you think of this version's ending? Did the stepsisters deserve their fate? Do such cruel details belong in a story for children? Explain your responses.

Comparing Literature

5. After you've read all three selections, you'll be asked to compare the way each presents the typical Cinderella story. You can begin to prepare for your essay now by filling out the "Aschenputtel" column in a chart like the one below. Continue to fill in your chart after you finish reading each of the other selections.

Reading Check

a. What does Aschenputtel do with the twig her father gives her?

b. What does the stepmother do to stop Aschenputtel from attending the feast?

c. Who helps Aschenputtel complete her tasks?

d. How does the prince manage to get one of Aschenputtel's golden slippers?

e. What happens to the stepsisters on Aschenputtel and the prince's wedding day?

Comparing Cinderella Stories			
	"Aschenputtel"	"Dinorella"	"Interview"
Characters			
Plot			
Tone			
Theme			

INTERNET
Projects and Activities
Keyword: LE5 7-6

SKILLS FOCUS

Literary Skills
Analyze the Cinderella story.

Reading Skills
Compare and contrast texts.

After You Read

4. Some students will find the story's ending disturbing. They may say that graphic details should be removed from versions of the story meant for little children, who are not ready to learn from a story that may scare them. Other students may say that the story's ending should not be altered because it shows the stepsisters being justly punished, because children will know that the story is only a fantasy, or because the stronger images will make a more lasting impression.

Comparing Literature

5. Possible answers: *Characters*—young girl, wicked stepmother and stepsisters, handsome prince, magical birds. *Plot*—Young girl treated cruelly by stepmother and stepsisters; is helped by magical birds to go to the prince's festival, which lasts three days; is ultimately identified by the prince (by means of a lost shoe) and becomes his wife. *Tone*—grim; formal. *Theme*—True beauty is not external; good behavior is rewarded, and bad behavior is punished.

Reading Check

a. She plants the twig on her mother's grave, and it grows into a hazel tree.

b. The stepmother makes her ashamed of her appearance and has her separate lentils from the ashes.

c. All the birds in the area help Aschenputtel complete her tasks.

d. The prince has the steps coated with pitch so that her shoe will stick as she runs away.

e. Their eyes are plucked out by the pigeons.

First Thoughts

1. Possible answer: The story reflects desires to find love and happiness, to be rewarded for virtuous behavior, and to see evil punished. The story may reflect the fear of losing a loved one or of not being accepted as part of a family.

Thinking Critically

2. Students should be encouraged to present solid arguments to support their choices. The best answer is probably "Goodness is rewarded in the end," because Aschenputtel is eventually rewarded with marriage to the prince and escape from her horrible situation.

3. The stepmother sets three impossible tasks; the festival lasts three days; Aschenputtel asks for dresses three times; she flees from the prince three times; and three sisters try on the slipper. The motif helps build suspense by making the reader curious about how the third time will be different.

Summary ⇄ *at grade level*

The "dainty and dependable" dinosaur Dinorella is abused by her stepsisters, Dora and Doris. When they receive an invitation to a dance at the den of Duke Dudley, the stepsisters ridicule Dinorella's appearance and lack of dinosaur jewels. Left alone, Dinorella is visited by Fairydactyl, who provides her with dinosaur jewels. As she approaches the dance, Dinorella sees a deinonychus abducting the duke, so she hurls insults and dirt balls at him. The predator, thinking that Dinorella's jewels are the eyes of a demon, is frightened. When Dinorella throws one of her diamonds at him, he drops the duke and runs away. Duke Dudley vows to marry the dinosaur to whom the jewel belongs. As Doris and Dora clamor for his attention, Fairydactyl summons Dinorella, who has the matching jewel. The duke declares his love, and the happy pair dance off.

DIRECT TEACHING

Ⓐ Literary Focus

❓ **Alliteration.** Alliteration can help establish a mood or emphasize certain words. What is the effect of the alliteration in the first sentence? [The repetition adds humor to the story.]

Ⓑ Comparing Literature

Compare Cinderella stories. Call on volunteers to describe how Dora and Doris fit the character type of the "wicked stepsisters." [Like Aschenputtel's sisters, Dora and Doris are demanding and cruel. They enjoy tormenting their stepsister.]

Ⓒ Reading Skills

Compare and contrast. [Possible response to question 1: This story is humorous, whereas the traditional story is serious. Both feature an ill-treated young girl and two wicked stepsisters, but here the characters are dinosaurs.]

Before You Read

This is a delightful dinosaur version of the Cinderella story. It deals with dreadful stepsisters, a dance till dawn, a distracting disturbance, dangling diamonds, a dashing duke, and darling, adorable Dinorella. Do you discern a pattern here? This repetition of the same or similar consonant sounds is called **alliteration.** See if you can read the story aloud without tripping over your tongue.

DINORELLA

Pamela Duncan Edwards

Ⓐ   Dora, Doris, and Dinorella lived down in the sand dunes in a dinosaur den.

Dora and Doris did nothing all day. They dumped debris around the den. They never did the dusting or the dishes. Dinorella was dainty and dependable. Dora and Doris were dreadful to Dinorella. All day they demanded . . .

Ⓑ   "**DINORELLA**, dig the garden.

"**DINORELLA**, fetch us drinks.

"**DINORELLA**, start the dinner."

"She's a dingbat," sniggered Dora.

"She's a dumbhead," giggled Doris. ❶

COMPARE AND CONTRAST

Ⓒ ❶ How is this version of the story different from the traditional story of Cinderella so far? How is it the same?

758   Collection 6 / Our Literary Heritage: Greek Myths and World Folk Tales

DIFFERENTIATING INSTRUCTION

Learners Having Difficulty
Students will enjoy hearing this story read aloud. Before you begin reading, have students write the following words down the left side of a sheet of paper: *Cinderella, wicked stepsister 1, wicked stepsister 2, prince, fairy godmother.* As you read, have them write each "Dinorella" character's name next to the name or title of the corresponding character in the traditional tale. After you read, review the list with students.

Have them name the one character in "Dinorella" that has no counterpart in the traditional tale. [deinonychus] Extend the activity by having students recall and list the names of corresponding characters from "Aschenputtel."

English-Language Learners
After students read "Dinorella," point out the importance of jewels—particularly, Dinorella's diamond—to this story. Explain

One day a card was delivered to the den:

Dinosaur Dance
Duke Dudley's Den
At Dusk
Hors d'oeuvres, Dandelion Cola
Dancing Until Dawn

Duke Dudley was the most dashing dinosaur in the dunes. ❷

"I would die for a date with the duke," said Dora, decorating herself with dinosaur jewels.

"Definitely," sighed Doris, dolling up for the dance.

"A dance," said Dinorella diffidently. "How divine."

"**YOU** can't go to the dance," said Doris. "**YOU'RE** too dowdy."

"**YOU'RE** too dull," agreed Dora. "And **YOU** don't have decent dinosaur jewels. Of course **YOU** can't go to the dance."

Poor Dinorella felt down in the dumps as she watched her stepsisters depart.

Suddenly, Dinorella heard a droning noise.

"Don't be dismal," cried Fairydactyl. "You **SHALL** go to the dance."

"But I'm so drab," said Dinorella, "and I don't have decent dinosaur jewels."

"I'll soon deal with that," declared Fairydactyl. "These will outdazzle all other dinosaur jewels."

"**DARLING** Fairydactyl!" exclaimed Dinorella in delight. With her diamonds dangling, she set out for the dance. ❸

Dusk had fallen when Dinorella heard a deafening disturbance coming from the direction of Duke Dudley's Den.

A DASTARDLY DEED WAS TAKING PLACE!

A deinonychus[1] was dragging off the duke.

"**I'M DONE FOR!**" cried the duke. "He will **DEVOUR** me!" ❼

"Indeed I will!" laughed the deinonychus. "I'll be digesting you by daybreak."

---

1. **deinonychus** (dī·nän′i·kəs) *n.:* small, swift, meat-eating dinosaur.

INTERPRET

❷ Why do you think this story has a duke instead of a prince? (Could it have something to do with **alliteration**—the use of similar consonant sounds in nearby words?)

COMPARE AND CONTRAST

❸ Fairydactyl saves the day. Who saves the day in "Aschenputtel"?

D Reading Skills
Interpret. [Possible response to question 2: The author uses a duke instead of a prince in the story because *duke* starts with *d* and thus extends the story's alliteration.]

E Reading Skills
❷ **Determine an author's purpose.** Is the author's purpose chiefly to inform or to entertain? [The author intends the story to be entertaining.] You might want to introduce the term *parody*, which refers to a humorous imitation of a work or of characteristics of style.

F Reading Skills
Compare and contrast. [Possible response to question 3: the magical hazel tree and its resident bird.]

G Comparing Literature
❼ **Compare Cinderella stories.** How does this story differ from the traditional tale? [The duke must be rescued from an evil character.] Point out that the deinonychus has no counterpart in the traditional tale.

that in English, the word *jewel* can also refer to a person with admirable qualities. Ask students to draw a jewel-shaped outline and fill it in with words, ideas, or images that they think show how Dinorella is a "jewel" of a character.

Special Education Students
For lessons designed for special education students, see *Holt Reading Solutions.*

Advanced Learners
Enrichment. "Dinorella" is a spoof of the Cinderella tale. Have students hold a panel discussion on the function of humor in this story. For example, does humor help make a familiar tale seem fresher, or does it mock the traditional tale? Do the moral lessons conveyed by the original tale still come across when humor is added? You

may want to assign certain positions to students and have them gather supporting evidence to use during the discussion.

A Comparing Literature
Compare Cinderella stories.
How could Aschenputtel's lovely gowns also be considered "weapons" to be used against an evil foe (or foes)? [Possible response: The gowns serve as weapons that help Aschenputtel escape from the grip of her wicked stepsisters.] **How are Dinorella's "weapons" differently used?** [She uses them to liberate a potential suitor rather than to liberate herself.]

B Reading Skills
Compare and contrast. [Possible response to question 4: Both characters display courage in the face of difficulties. Dinorella, though, is more aggressive than the long-suffering, somewhat passive Aschenputtel. The characters' motives differ too: Dinorella acts to save another, whereas Aschenputtel acts to save herself.]

C English-Language Learners
Understand slang. *Dumped* (instead of *dropped*) and *double-quick* (instead of *rapidly*) are just two examples of slang in this story. Ask students to share similar expressions from their first languages.

D Reading Skills
❷ **Respond.** What do you think of the dinosaurs' panicked response? [The image of dinosaurs, usually depicted as fierce and lumbering, "dashing about in distress" is funny.] **What do you think of Duke Dudley's response?** [Students may admire his calmness and cool-headedness.]

COMPARE AND CONTRAST

B ❹ How is Dinorella's behavior similar to or different from that of Aschenputtel?

Dinorella was not a daring dinosaur, but something drastic had to be done.

"I may become dessert, but I'm determined to drive away that dreaded carnivore."

Dinorella climbed to the top of the dune.

"YOU DISGUSTING DUMMY," she roared. "DROP THE DUKE!"

Dinorella began to hurl dirtballs at the deinonychus.

The dumbfounded deinonychus stopped in disbelief. "Who called me a dummy?" he demanded.

The moon's light caught Dinorella's dangling diamonds. Dots and dabs of light darted toward the deinonychus.

A "A DEVIL!" cried the deinonychus. "See its dreadful demon eyes!"

Dinorella detached a diamond and directed it toward the deinonychus.

The diamond hit the deinonychus HARD in his dentures. ❹

C "The devil will destroy me with its deadly eyes," bellowed the distraught deinonychus. He dumped Duke Dudley and departed double-quick.

The den was dense with dinosaurs dashing about in distress. "A demon," they cried. "WE'RE DOOMED."

D "DIMWITS!" roared Duke Dudley through the din. "Demons don't throw diamonds. It was a damsel who defended me with her dazzling dinosaur jewel.

"When I discover her, I shall ask her to be my darling."

CROSS-CURRICULAR CONNECTIONS

Science
Deinonychus antirropus. Duke Dudley has good reason to fear, for his abductor is a dinosaur known as *Deinonychus antirropus* (literally, "terrible claw"). Standing about five feet tall and ten feet long, *Deinonychus* was known for its speed, agility, and intelligence. These traits, along with its powerful jaws, sharp teeth, and clawed feet, made it a frighteningly efficient killer.

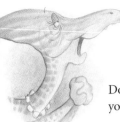

All the dinosaur dames were delirious. "The jewel is mine!" they each declared.

"MINE!" cried Doris.

"NO, DEFINITELY MINE," bellowed Dora, giving Doris a dig. "I am the damsel you desire."

"i DOUBT iT," declared Duke Dudley. "Your dinosaur jewels don't match." ❺

Just then, Fairydactyl arrived at the dance. She quickly saw the dilemma.

"WHERE iS DINORELLA?" she demanded.

"Dinorella!" scoffed Dora, "that dopey domestic."

"Dinorella!" laughed Doris. "She's back at the den."

But Fairydactyl spied Dinorella dodging behind the dune.

"DINORELLA," she directed, "come down."

So down came Dinorella, looking distracted.

Cried the duke, "She wears but one dazzling jewel!"

"Dinorella, you are adorable. You're definitely quite a dish. I beg you to be my dearest."

"DREAMY!" said Dinorella as they danced off into the dawn.

"DRAT!" said Dora and Doris. ❻

COMPARE AND CONTRAST

❺ How is this part of the story similar to "Aschenputtel"? How is it different? ❻

EVALUATE

❻ Which version of the Cinderella story— "Dinorella" or "Aschenputtel"—do you like best? Why? ❽

DIRECT TEACHING

ⓔ Vocabulary Note

Connotations. Words can have suggested meanings (connotations) as well as literal meanings (denotations). What connotations are suggested by *delirious*? [Possible response: The female dinosaurs are wildly excited and behave as if they were feverish.] **by *bellowed*?** [Possible response: A bull bellows, so the sound Dora makes is powerful, loud, and ridiculous.] **What other words might you use in their place?** [Possible responses, respectively: *thrilled, excited; shouted, yelled*]

ⓕ Reading Skills

Compare and contrast. [Possible response to question 5: As in "Aschenputtel," the wicked stepsisters both try to claim the prized object as their own. Here, though, the step-sisters bicker childishly; and, unlike Aschenputtel's gullible prince, this skeptical duke dismisses the heroine's stepsisters without delay.]

ⓖ Literary Focus

❼ Analyze the Cinderella story. How do the endings of both "Aschenputtel" and "Dinorella" fulfill the requirements of a Cinderella story? [In both stories, the prince and the Cinderella character live happily ever after.]

ⓗ Reading Skills

Evaluate. [Some students will prefer "Dinorella" because of its humor, playful tone, and contemporary language.]

Pamela Duncan Edwards

A Unique Character

About her story "Dinorella," **Pamela Duncan Edwards** has said:

> 66 I knew children loved fairy stories, and I also knew—because I taught for so long—that children love dinosaurs. And I thought, what a great thing to do, to put together two of the things that children like so much—put together a dinosaur and put together a fairy story. However, I didn't want to make Dinorella the same type of character as Cinderella. 99

Edwards was born and raised in England, where she was a preschool teacher. When she moved to the United States, she started her career as a children's librarian at a school in Virginia. When Edwards attended a children's literature conference with illustrator Henry Cole, they first discussed ideas for children's books. The partnership they later developed resulted in many highly praised storybooks.

The first book Edwards wrote was, like "Dinorella," focused on a single consonant. She has said:

> 66 I do like writing alliterative books. I have great fun writing them because I get my thesaurus out. I have to find a word that begins with that letter that will say what I want to say. It's such good fun. And as I'm reading in my thesaurus, I'm finding other words. . . . So it's a great expansion of my vocabulary, as well as the child's vocabulary. 99

For Independent Reading

For other funny alliterative stories by Pamela Duncan Edwards, try *Some Smug Slug* and *Four Famished Foxes and Fosdyke.*

DIFFERENTIATING INSTRUCTION

Advanced Learners

Enrichment. Students will enjoy the chance to write their own Cinderella spoofs modeled on this one. First, have students choose an animal species to use for their cast of characters. Then, challenge students to use the initial consonant sound of that animal's name as the dominant consonant sound in their story. (For example, the *f* sound would dominate in a story about ferrets; the *s* sound would dominate in a story about snakes; and so on.) Before students begin writing, they may want to brainstorm a list of names, nouns, and verbs that begin with their consonant sound. After students finish, invite volunteers to read their stories to the class.

After You Read "Dinorella"

First Thoughts

1. Finish the following sentence:
   - The part of "Dinorella" I liked best (or least) was . . .

Thinking Critically

2. What new story elements does "Dinorella" add to the traditional Cinderella story, such as "Aschenputtel"? (Think about the characters, the plot, and the setting.)

3. "Aschenputtel" has a serious **tone**, which means that the storyteller takes the characters and their problems very seriously. This indicates that the teller has a serious message for the reader. What is the tone of "Dinorella"? Is it serious, comical, satiric, bitter, or something else?

4. Do you think the writer has a serious message for the reader? Explain how you would express the message, or **theme,** of "Dinorella."

5. "Dinorella" tells the Cinderella story through **alliteration** with the sound of *d*. Retell at least part of the story using another consonant. Perhaps Kittenella could cut a caper with the King of Cats, for example. You'll find lots of inspiration, as Edwards says she did, in a thesaurus.

Comparing Literature

6. Fill in the "Dinorella" column in a chart like the one below. Your finished chart will help you complete the assignment on writing a comparison-contrast essay on page 767.

Comparing Cinderella Stories			
	"Aschenputtel"	"Dinorella"	"Interview"
Characters			
Plot			
Tone			
Theme			

SKILLS FOCUS

Literary Skills
Analyze the Cinderella story.

Reading Skills
Compare and contrast texts.

Reading Check

Summarize "Dinorella." Start with the title and author. Then, name the main characters and their **conflict,** or problem. As you describe the main events, see how many words you can use that begin with *d*. Finally, state the **resolution** of the problem.

After You Read

First Thoughts

1. Possible answer:
   - The part of "Dinorella" I liked best was <u>when Duke Dudley sees Dinorella's diamond.</u>

Thinking Critically

2. Possible answer: "Dinorella" adds a villain (in the form of the deinonychus) and a Cinderella figure who saves her prince from a terrible fate.

3. The tone of "Dinorella" is humorous.

4. Possible answer: Yes, the underlying message of "Dinorella" is serious. It could be expressed this way: *Those who take positive action will be rewarded.*

5. Students' retellings should contain repetitions of their chosen consonant sound.

Comparing Literature

6. Possible answers: *Characters*— young female dinosaur, wicked stepsisters, handsome duke, Fairydactyl, the evil deinonychus. *Plot*—Young Dinorella is bossed around and mocked by her stepsisters; is helped by Fairydactyl to go to Duke Dudley's dance; saves the duke's life on the way; is ultimately identified by the duke (through her lost jewel) and is taken as his wife. *Tone*—comical. *Theme*—Good behavior will be rewarded.

Reading Check

Possible summary: "Dinorella" was written by Pamela Duncan Edwards. In this story, Dinorella lives with her two stepsisters, Dora and Doris, in a den in the dunes. The sisters dump all the housework on Dinorella, who leads a dreary life. When they are invited to Duke Dudley's dance, the sisters are delighted. Dinorella desires to dance, too, but doesn't have any suitable duds. Fairydactyl drops some diamonds on the depressed dino, and Dinorella digs them. Delirious with delight, she departs for the dance. On the way, she discovers the duke in the grips of the dastardly deinonychus. Directing one of her jewels at the evil dinosaur, Dinorella demonstrates her dependability, and the deinonychus ducks away on the double. The duke doesn't know who did the deed, but he does know it was a damsel with diamonds. He dismisses the stepsister's declarations, and is delighted to discover, with the aid of Fairydactyl, that his daring darling is Dinorella herself.

Summary ⬌ *at grade level*

In this poem, Cinderella's "wicked stepmother" is asked by a member of the press to describe her award-winning daughter's early life. In response, the stepmother praises her own daughters, who, she says, are well-behaved and fortunate not to be petty and dishonest, like Cinderella is—even if they lack her beauty and marital status.

PRETEACHING

Selection Starter

Motivate. Ask students this question: "If you were going to retell the Cinderella story from the point of view of a character other than Cinderella, who would it be? Why?"

DIRECT TEACHING

Ⓐ Vocabulary Note
Multiple-meaning words. Read the definition of *biddable* in the footnote. In this context, what else might *biddable* mean? [Capable of being bid—i.e., for purchase or for marriage.]

Ⓑ Reading Skills
Identify. [Response to question 1: The speaker is Cinderella's stepmother. She refers to her own two daughters and to Cinderella herself.]

Before You Read

This poem uses a modern-day event—an interview with the press—to present an unexpected point of view on the story of Cinderella. As you read the poem, decide who the speaker is. What **tone** do you hear in the poem; that is, what is the speaker's attitude or feeling toward Cinderella? Do you believe the speaker?

Anjelica Huston as the stepmother in *Ever After: A Cinderella Story.*

INTERVIEW

Sara Henderson Hay

Yes, this is where she lived before she won
The title Miss Glass Slipper of the Year,
And went to the ball and married the king's son.
You're from the local press, and want to hear
5 About her early life? Young man, sit down.
These are my *own* two daughters; you'll not find
Ⓐ Nicer, more biddable° girls in all the town,
And lucky, I tell them, not to be the kind ❶

---

7. **biddable** (bid'ə·bəl) *adj.:* obedient.

IDENTIFY

Ⓑ ❶ Who is the speaker of the poem? How can you tell?

DIFFERENTIATING INSTRUCTION

Learners Having Difficulty
To review the concept of tone with students, read the poem aloud twice. First, read the poem in a gentle tone. Next, read the poem in an angry, vindictive tone. After you read, ask students which voice seemed more appropriate, given what they know about Cinderella stories. Then, have them suggest words that describe the tone of voice you used for each reading. [Possible responses: sweet, gentle; bitter, angry]

That Cinderella was, spreading those lies,
10 Telling those shameless tales about the way
    We treated her. Oh, nobody denies
    That she was pretty, if you like those curls.
    But looks aren't everything, I always say. ❷
    Be sweet and natural, I tell my girls,
15 And Mr. Right will come along, someday.

COMPARE AND CONTRAST

❷ What does the speaker tell you about Cinderella's **character**? How does her character differ from the characters of "Aschenputtel" and "Dinorella"? **D**

Meet the Writer

Sara Henderson Hay

A Dedicated Poet

Sara Henderson Hay (1906–1987) was born in Pittsburgh and lived there and in the South for most of her life. Hay's first published poem, which was about golf, appeared in a publication titled *Judge Magazine* when she was ten years old. Hay also received encouragement to write when her work was published in her hometown newspaper while she was in high school and when her poems were published in the school magazine at Columbia University in New York City. Hay went on to win awards for her poems and to publish six poetry collections.

For Independent Reading

Read Hay's poetry collection *Story Hour,* which "Interview" is taken from, and enjoy the author's surprising and often humorous twists on several old tales.

Interview 765

DIRECT TEACHING

C Literary Focus

❓ The Cinderella story. In what way might these words illustrate a traditional element of the Cinderella story? [They might show how vindictive and cruel the stepmother really is.]

D Reading Skills
Compare and contrast. [Possible response to question 2: According to the speaker, Cinderella is a self-interested liar—quite a different character from the obedient, uncomplaining Aschenputtel or the selfless Dinorella.]

Meet the Writer
After graduating from Columbia University, Hay took a secretarial job at the publishing company Charles Scribner's and Sons, working her way from the editorial offices to the rare book department. At the same time, she was writing her own poems and working as a freelance editor. Within a few years, Hay's poems had begun to appear in journals and anthologies. In 1935—just before World War II—she accompanied journalist Gladys Baker on a tour of Europe to help with a series of interviews for the *New York Times.*

For Independent Reading
Students who like poetry may enjoy reading Hay's "small son" series, first published in the 1939 collection *This, My Letter.* The poems so skillfully depict a fictional little boy that many people believed him to be real.

INDEPENDENT PRACTICE

After You Read

First Thoughts

1. Possible answer:
   • What surprised me most about this poem was <u>the characterization of Cinderella as a shameless liar.</u>

Thinking Critically

2. The speaker is Cinderella's stepmother. She is talking to a news reporter who has come to her home to conduct an interview. The speaker says, "Yes, this is where she lived" (line 1), and asks her guest to "sit down" (line 5).

3. Possible answer: The speaker's attitude is bitter and vindictive. She might feel this way because Cinderella actually was a liar or she might feel this way because Cinderella was chosen by the prince to be his wife instead of one of her own daughters.

4. Possible answer: I tend to believe Cinderella's story, because in this poem the speaker's words and tone provide further evidence that the stepmother is petty, jealous, and biased toward her own daughters.

5. Possible answers: No, she doesn't believe what she is saying; she is only saying bad things about Cinderella to make herself and her daughters look better. Yes, she does believe what she is saying; it is only natural to love and trust one's own children more than someone else's. Students should deduce from the speaker's words (i.e., "looks aren't everything," line 13) that the daughters are homely.

6. Some students will agree that stepmothers and stepsisters are often represented unfairly in fairy tales, and will admire this poem for trying to even the score. Others may agree while also believing that in this case the stepmother's reputation is further damaged. Still others will disagree, saying that such characters are only types and are not meant to represent stepmothers and stepsisters in the actual world.

7. Possible answers: serious, defeated, bitter, jealous, resentful, impatient, pandering, cloying, and so on.

Comparing Literature

8. Possible answers: *Characters*—Speaker (Cinderella's stepmother), her two daughters, a news reporter. *Plot*—A reporter comes to Cinderella's former home for an interview. The stepmother invites the reporter to come in and sit down. Next, she introduces her own two daughters and comments on their eligibility. She points out that they are quite unlike the dishonest Cinderella, and insists that, in spite of their looks, they will one day meet Mr. Right. *Tone*—spiteful. *Theme*—A person can't help but show his or her true colors.

After You Read   "Interview"

First Thoughts

1. Finish the following sentence:
   • What surprised me most about this poem was . . .

Thinking Critically

2. Who is the speaker in this poem? Whom is the speaker talking to? Where do the events in this poem take place? How do you know?

3. What is the speaker's **attitude** toward Cinderella? Why would she feel this way?

4. Perhaps the **message** in this poem is that there are two sides to every story. Whose side of this story do you tend to believe? Explain why.

5. Do you think that the speaker really believes what she is saying about Cinderella and her own girls? What do you suppose her own girls look like?

6. One idea in this poem might be that stepmothers and stepsisters are portrayed unfairly in fairy tales. What are your responses to this idea?

7. **Tone** refers to the speaker's attitude toward a subject. Tone can be admiring, serious, critical, sarcastic, comic, bitter, disrespectful, and so on. What tone do you hear in this version of the Cinderella story? (Maybe you hear more than one.)

Comparing Literature

8. Fill in the "Interview" column to complete the chart you started after you read the first two Cinderella stories.

Comparing Cinderella Stories			
	"Aschenputtel"	"Dinorella"	"Interview"
Characters			
Plot			
Tone			
Theme			

SKILLS FOCUS

Literary Skills
Analyze the Cinderella story.

Reading Skills
Compare and contrast texts.

Assignment

1. Writing a Comparison-Contrast Essay

To help you write a comparison-contrast essay on the three selections, refer back to the charts you filled in after you read "Aschenputtel," "Dinorella," and "Interview." You can organize your essay in two ways.

1. You can write three paragraphs—one paragraph for each selection. In this case, you would describe the characters, the plot, the tone, and the theme, selection by selection.

2. Or, you could write four paragraphs—one on the characters in each selection, one on the plot of each selection, one on the tone of each selection, and one on the theme of each selection.

Whichever method of organization you use, be sure to include a final paragraph in which you describe your responses to the selections.

Use the workshop on writing a Comparison-Contrast Essay, pages 772–777, for help with this assignment.

Assignment

2. Writing a New Cinderella Story

What might happen if a princess rescues a boy from a life of drudgery? Create a version of the Cinderella story with this role reversal. Before you write, decide who your characters will be, when and where they will live, what their problem is, and what happens to them. Illustrate your story, if you wish, and read it aloud to the class.

Assignment

3. Writing Another Character's Side of the Story

In "Interview" you heard from one of the major characters in the Cinderella story. Let another character speak and tell his or her side of the story. Let us hear from one of the stepsisters, the prince, the dove, the king, the fairy godmother—or even another guest at the ball. Write as "I." Will your speaker be answering questions in an interview, or will there be some other occasion for the speaker to speak up?

SKILLS FOCUS

Writing Skills
Write a comparison-contrast essay; write a new Cinderella story; write from another point of view.

After You Read

1. Writing a Comparison-Contrast Essay

Strategy tip. Urge students having difficulty to write about first one story and then the other. This approach is easier because it involves less moving back and forth between subjects. Students can then use the concluding paragraph to note key similarities and differences between the three Cinderella stories.

2. Writing a New Cinderella Story

Strategy tip. As they complete their prewriting for this assignment, have students consider the different tones their story might have. Are they aiming for a light, romantic mood; a comic-book mood; or a serious, instructive mood? Knowing this will help students design a plot, setting, and characters to match.

3. Writing Another Character's Side of the Story

Strategy tip. Have students present dramatic readings of their poem for the class without first revealing their character's identity. Audience members can then guess the identity of the speaker based on clues the poem provides.

DIFFERENTIATING INSTRUCTION

Learners Having Difficulty
If students have difficulty organizing their essays, allow them to choose and compare one or two rather than all four elements (characters, plot, tone, and theme) of these Cinderella stories.

English-Language Learners
Before students begin writing, be sure they have correctly registered the tone of each story. If necessary, point out key passages that give clues to the stories' tones; for example, her mother's advice to Aschenputtel early in that story; Dora and Doris's first spoken lines in "Dinorella"; and lines 9 and 10 of "Interview." Alternatively, you may want to allow students to compare the stories' characters, plots, and themes only.

OVERVIEW

The literature in No Questions Asked gives students the chance to read for enjoyment. The annotations in the margins of the Teacher's Edition are optional. No follow-up questions will appear after this play.

Summary ⬇ *below grade level*

When the story opens, Luqman Ali, a poor man who lives in Baghdad in the valley of the potters, is told by an angel to go to Cairo to seek his fortune. In Cairo he is mistaken for a thief, arrested, and beaten. The Chief of Police tells him that dreams mean nothing; he himself ignored a dream to go to Baghdad, where he would find buried treasure under a stove in a shack in the alley of the potters. Luqman Ali dances home to his shack. He and his wife move the stove, find the treasure, and revel in the jewels.

PRETEACHING

Selection Starter

Build background. This tale is from *The Arabian Nights*—also called *The Arabian Nights' Entertainment* or *A Thousand and One Nights.* The device that binds the stories together is their narration by Scheherazade. In order to delay her execution, she tells the sultan a new tale each night. The story-telling so intrigues the sultan that he spares her life.

DIRECT TEACHING

Ⓐ Reading Skills

❓ Compare and contrast.

Which of the folk tales or classical Greek myths you read could have had this same title? ["Aschenputtel" and "King Midas and the Golden Touch" are the most likely responses; accept others if students can explain their reasoning.]

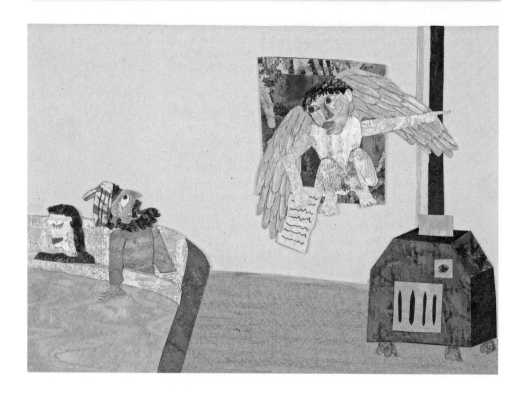

Ⓐ The Dream of Good Fortune

from The Arabian Nights,
dramatized by Paul Sills

Characters

Luqman Ali	The Chief of Police
His Wife	A Thief
An Angel	The Lieutenant

768 Collection 6 / Our Literary Heritage: Greek Myths and World Folk Tales

DIFFERENTIATING INSTRUCTION

Learners Having Difficulty
Assign each student a part and have them read the story aloud as a group. Before they begin reading, discuss the name of the main character, Luqman (LUKE-mahn). Direct students' attention to the abbreviation preceding each of that character's lines. Ask them what English word the abbreviation looks like. [luck] Have students read to find out how Luqman's bad luck turns into good luck.

Advanced Learners
In many myths and legends, language that at first seems perfectly clear turns out to be ambiguous or have unexpected significance. In classical Greek mythology, proclamations of the oracle of Apollo at Delphi are notorious for their ambiguity. In Shakespeare's *Macbeth,* the "impossible" predictions of the three Weird Sisters nevertheless come to pass. In Luqman Ali's case, we expect him to find his fortune in Cairo. Instead, he

Luq. Luqman Ali, a poor but honest dung sweeper, lived in the alley of the tanners, off the street of the potters, in the heart of the great city of Baghdad.[1]

Wife. He and his wife had nothing in the world but an old iron stove, and barely enough to eat.

Luq. But still they did not despair in the mercy of the Almighty. One night Luqman Ali and his wife lay down to sleep, and he had a dream.

Angel. An angel appeared with a message: "Luqman Ali, alley of the tanners, off the street of the potters, in the city of Baghdad—Dear Luq, Go to Cairo,[2] and there you will find your fortune."

Luq. Luqman Ali awoke his wife and told her of his strange dream.

Wife. Go back to sleep, my love, it was only a dream.

---

1. **Baghdad:** ancient Middle Eastern city, the center of Islamic civilization during the period in which many of the *Arabian Nights* stories are set. Today Baghdad is the capital of Iraq.
2. **Cairo** (kī′rō): capital of Egypt.

DIRECT TEACHING

B **English-Language Learners**
Build background knowledge. Explain that a *tanner* is a person who turns animals' hides into leather by treating them with a special chemical.

C **Literary Focus**

? **Author's style.** What is unusual about the lines spoken by these characters? [The characters refer to themselves in the third person, as if they were narrators.] **Why do you think the author decided to write these lines (and others throughout the play) in such a way?** [Possible response: to give the drama a slightly comical feel or a modern feel]

finds the key to a fortune in the words of the Chief of Police.

Activity. Ask students to recall myths or legends they know from any culture that feature promises or predictions made by supernatural beings—gods, genies, angels, tricksters, or spirits. What is misleading or ambiguous about the words themselves or unexpected about the way in which the predictions are fulfilled?

A Literary Focus

? Motifs. What other mythical or magical stories do you know in which things come in threes? [Responses may range from "Goldilocks and the Three Bears" to "Cinderella" to stories from many cultures in which a genie or similar being grants someone three wishes.]

B Reading Skills

Predict. Pause and ask students to predict what will come of Luqman Ali's dream. [Some students will predict wealth, but may anticipate an outcome like that in the Midas story, where the wealth is harmful. Others may believe that some trickery was involved in the way the angel phrased its directions.] Advise students to save their predictions for comparison with the actual outcome of the story.

C Reading Skills

Read a map. Have students consult a map of the Middle East to determine the distance between the two cities of this story, both of which still exist today: Baghdad in Iraq and Cairo in Egypt.

Angel. Luqman Ali, go to Cairo, and there you will find your fortune.

Luq. Wife, wake up; the angel came again and told me to go to Cairo, to seek my fortune.

Wife. If it happens a third time, you'll have to go.

Angel. Luqman Ali, are you still here? Go to Cairo! Your fortune awaits you there.

Luq. I go! I go! Wife, awaken—I must go to Cairo. And so Luqman Ali set off on the road to Cairo. Through hot desert winds—sand-storms—cold nights. Luqman Ali traveled the road until, weary and sore, in the shimmering heat, he saw the great city of Cairo. Tired and not knowing where to go, he took refuge in the courtyard of a great mosque,[3] where he lay down to sleep.

Thief. That night, a thief entered the courtyard and broke through the wall of an adjoining house.

[*A woman screams offstage. The* THIEF *returns to the courtyard, hits* LUQ, *and runs off.*]

Luq. Stop, thief! Stop, thief!

Chief of Police. The chief of police . . .

Lieutenant. And his lieutenant . . .

Chief of Police. Arrived at the scene, and they found Luqman Ali, and thinking him to be the thief . . .

Lieutenant. They beat him with their clubs and dragged him off to jail.

Chief of Police. Who are you?

Luq. Luqman Ali.

Chief of Police. Where do you come from?

Luq. Baghdad.

Chief of Police. What brings you to Cairo?

Luq. I had a dream . . .

[*The* LIEUTENANT *squeezes* LUQ'*s nose, sending him to his knees.*]

Chief of Police. What are you doing in Cairo?

Luq (*rises*). I had a dream . . .

[*The* LIEUTENANT *squeezes his head.*]

Chief of Police (*waving the* LIEUTENANT *away*). What brings you to Cairo?

---

3. **mosque** (mäsk) *n.:* Muslim house of worship.

Music

Violin solo from *Scheherazade* by Nicholas Rimsky-Korsakov. With Modest Mussorgsky, Aleksandr Borodin, and two others, Nicholas Rimsky-Korsakov (1844–1908) was a member of the group of composers nicknamed the Russian (or Mighty) Five. The group's aim was to rid classical music of its strong German and French influences and instead produce compositions of a distinctly Russian nature.

Nevertheless, Rimsky-Korsakov's two best-known works draw on other cultures as well: His *Capriccio espagnol* tries to capture the flavor of Spain, and his orchestral suite *Scheherazade* attempts to retell in music four different episodes from *The Arabian Nights.*

Activity. Before students read the selection, play for them the opening portion of *Scheherazade,* which includes the famous violin solo. Explain that the violin music,

which recurs throughout, represents Scheherazade spinning her thousand and one tales for the sultan. Ask students to predict the kind of story Scheherazade tells by what the music suggests. Then have students read the selection to see if their predictions are correct.

WHOLE CLASS

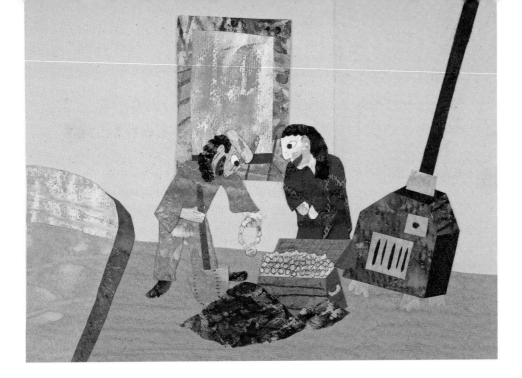

Luq (*again on his knees*). I had a dream. An angel appeared to me three times in a row and told me to go to Cairo, where I would find my fortune.

Chief of Police. And what did you find?

Luq. I got arrested and beat up.

Chief of Police. It hurts too, doesn't it? Dreams mean nothing. We all have dreams. You fool! That's the trouble with you people. Superstitious. I had a dream only last night: An angel came to me and told me to go to Baghdad, to the alley of the potters, off the street of the tanners, to a little old shack, and there under an old iron stove I would find a treasure. Did I go? No! I stayed here doing my job. Here, take these dinars[4] and get out of here.

[*So* LUQ *sets off to his home in Baghdad. He "dances" back to Baghdad, calling "Wife, wife." They move the stove, find the treasure, and adorn each other with jewels. She kisses his nose.—"Owww!!!"— Fade Out.*]

---

4. **dinars** (di·närz') *n.*: kind of money used in many Middle Eastern countries.

DIRECT TEACHING

D Literary Focus

? Irony. Dramatic irony occurs when the audience or a character knows something that another character does not. **What is ironic about this speech?** [We and Luqman Ali understand something the Police Chief does not. It appears that Luqman had to go far away to discover the treasure that lay under his own stove. The scorn of the rational policeman for "superstitious" people allows Luqman and his wife to benefit from their belief in dreams.]

E Reading Skills

? Interpret. How would you state the moral, or lesson about life, that the story teaches? Remember that many interpretations are possible, as long as they are supported by the details of the story. [Possible responses: Good fortune begins at home. Believe your dreams. Good things happen to honest people who work for their good fortune.]

DEVELOPING FLUENCY

Activity. The brevity of this dramatization; its simple, repetitive language; and its humorous tone make it ideal for classroom performance. Organize students in groups of six and have them plan, rehearse, and perform the play for the class. If some groups consist of seven members, challenge them to assign certain lines to a narrator. While the narrator speaks, the characters can act out what is being said. Encourage students to enhance their productions with one or two simple—but significant—props.

SMALL GROUP

Writing Workshop

Writing Workshop

Objectives

- Use appropriate prewriting and drafting skills to write a comparison-contrast essay.
- Revise the essay by rearranging sentences, adding transitional expressions, and providing additional supporting details and examples.
- Reflect on and assess one's writing process and essay.

PRETEACHING

Skills Starter

Motivate. Have students think of a time when they were trying to decide which of two movies to see. Then, ask how they made that decision. Did they consider the time each movie started? Where each movie was showing? Which actors appeared in each? Which story sounded more interesting? Tell them that when they went through this process, they were comparing and contrasting different aspects of the movies. Tell them that in this workshop, they will use a similar process to compare and contrast two literary works.

DIRECT TEACHING

PREWRITING

Choosing a Topic

As students look for texts to compare and contrast, encourage them to choose works that have basic similarities as well as differences.

Assignment

Write an essay comparing and contrasting two literary elements, subjects, or works.

Audience

Your teacher and classmates

RUBRIC
Evaluation Criteria

A good comparison-contrast essay

1. identifies the topic and the thesis of the essay in its introduction

2. discusses at least two similarities or differences

3. includes specific details and examples to support statements

4. brings the essay to a close with a summary or restatement of the main idea

SKILLS FOCUS

Writing Skills
Write a comparison-contrast essay.

EXPOSITORY WRITING
Comparison-Contrast Essay

In this collection you have seen that there are some stories, like the tale about Cinderella, that exist in many versions. While there are similarities in all these versions, there are also differences.

The technique of comparison and contrast can help you increase your understanding of two or more things. When you **compare,** you look for similarities. When you **contrast,** you look for differences. Comparison-and-contrast writing is useful in any field of study. It is particularly useful in analyzing literary elements, characters, or works. In this workshop you will write a comparison-contrast essay on a topic of your choice.

Prewriting

1 Choosing a Topic

Read and respond to this **prompt:**

> In reading literature, you often compare and contrast different works. One folk tale or myth may recall another you have read; characters in two stories may choose different solutions to a similar problem; two poems may express different points of view on the same topic. When you compare two subjects, you may find that you get a clearer view of each one. Choosing two works that you have read in this anthology or elsewhere, write a comparison-contrast essay that discusses similarities and differences in both works.

One way to find a topic is to look through some of the collections in this book. For example, the selections in Collection 1 focus on the element of **plot;** those in Collection 2 focus on the element of **characterization.** The works you

772   Collection 6 / Our Literary Heritage: Greek Myths and World Folk Tales

---

COLLECTION 6 RESOURCES: WRITING

Planning
- *One-Stop Planner* CD-ROM with ExamView Test Generator

Differentiating Instruction
- *Workshop Resources: Writing, Listening, and Speaking*
- *Supporting Instruction in Spanish*

Writing and Language
- *Workshop Resources: Writing, Listening, and Speaking*
- *Daily Language Activities*
- *Language Handbook Worksheets*

Assessment
- *Holt Assessment: Writing, Listening, and Speaking*

---

choose don't have to be the same type; however, they must have something in common. Here are some possibilities for your comparison-contrast essay:

- Two similar fables, folk tales, or myths
- Characters who face a similar problem
- Two poems with a common theme
- Two versions of a work—a novel and a movie or TV adaptation

Identify a pair of selections or features for your essay. Then, freewrite, jotting down similarities in one column and differences in another.

2 Finding Similarities and Differences

In deciding which features to compare and contrast, compare like with like. If you choose to compare and contrast two poems, focus on the same elements of both works: imagery, rhythm and theme, for example. If you choose two characters, discuss each character's actions, appearance, thoughts, and feelings. A **Venn diagram** can help you collect ideas about how your subjects are alike and different. Similarities appear where the two circles overlap; differences appear where they don't overlap. Here is a Venn diagram for the Student Model on page 775.

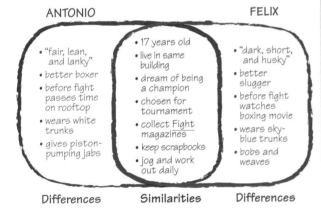

ANTONIO   FELIX

Differences   Similarities   Differences

Comparison-Contrast Essay **773**

Writing Tip

The word *compare* can be used broadly to mean "compare and contrast." Whenever you see the word *compare* on a test or essay assignment, find out if you're expected to both compare and contrast.

Block Method

Subject 1: Antonio
Feature 1: behavior
Feature 2: characteristics
Feature 3: feelings

Subject 2: Felix
Feature 1: behavior
Feature 2: characteristics
Feature 3: feelings

Point-by-Point Method

Feature 1: behavior
Subject 1: Antonio
Subject 2: Felix

Feature 2: characteristics
Subject 1: Antonio
Subject 2: Felix

Feature 3: feelings
Subject 1: Antonio
Subject 2: Felix

DIRECT TEACHING

Finding Similarities and Differences

Remind students that their freewriting will not be graded for content, spelling, or grammar. Tell them to keep writing until they run out of ideas and then to review their chart. Does one side contain far fewer ideas than the other? If so, have students re-read parts of their texts, looking for additional similarities or differences and then listing these in the chart. Explain that they will not have to use every idea they list; nor will they have to limit their ideas to those they think of now.

MODELING

Venn Diagram

Help learners having difficulty by filling in the Venn diagram on the board with an example. For instance, you might compare and contrast the main characters of "Aschenputtel" and "Dinorella":

Similarities—both stories feature wicked stepsisters; the main character in each wants to go to a big party but doesn't have anything appropriate to wear; the main characters get help from a character with magic powers.

Differences—Dinorella is a dinosaur, while Aschenputtel is a girl; Dinorella succeeds because she takes action, while Aschenputtel succeeds because she is humble and virtuous; Dinorella rescues her prince, whereas Aschenputtel is rescued by hers.

- *One-Stop Planner* CD-ROM with ExamView Test Generator
- *Holt Online Assessment*
- *Holt Online Essay Scoring*

Internet
- go.hrw.com (Keyword: LE5 7-6)
- *Elements of Literature Online*

Organize Your Information

Ask students, "When you're getting dressed, do you put on a sock and a shoe on one foot and then a sock and a shoe on the other? Or do you put on both socks and then both shoes?" Tell students that the block method is like dressing one foot first, then dressing the other, while the point-by-point method is like putting on both socks, and then both shoes. Explain that in this comparison, each foot represents a text, and each shoe and sock represents a point of comparison (such as plot and characters).

DRAFTING

Developing Your Draft

Suggest that when drafting, students jump straight to the body of their essay. Tell them to use the method they have chosen to write paragraphs that compare and contrast the two texts, and that they can reorder their paragraphs later on if necessary. Explain that it will be easier to formulate a thesis statement and an introductory paragraph after they see what the body of their essay actually says.

Transitional Expressions

Tell students that if they are using the point-by-point method, they will need transitional expressions within each paragraph; for example, *Both stories contain the figure of the prince. However, in "Aschenputtel" the prince is a traditional prince, while in "Dinorella" the prince is a duke.* Students who use the block method will probably use more transitional expressions when they discuss their second text. This is because later in the essay they will occasionally want to refer back to their first text, as in this example: *Like Aschenputtel, Dinorella lacks the proper attire for a ball.* Remind students that no matter how their essays are organized, using transitional expressions is always helpful when they're going from one paragraph to the next.

Writing Tip

A good conclusion should be more than just a summary of your ideas. Expand the main idea that you stated in your introduction. One possibility is to connect the works with your own or your readers' experiences. Another possibility is to extend the discussion to other works or to broader topics related to the works you have chosen.

Transitional Expressions

Transitional words that show similarities

also	just as
another	like
as well as	neither
both	not only
in addition	similarly
in the same way	too

Transitional words that show differences

although	nor
but	on the other
ever	hand
in contrast	otherwise
instead	still
in spite of	unlike
nevertheless	yet

---

3 Organize Your Information

The details in a comparison-contrast essay are usually arranged in one of two patterns: **block method** or **point-by-point method.** Block style focuses on all points of comparison for one subject at a time. The point-by-point method alternates between subjects, explaining how both are alike and different for each point of comparison. These patterns are shown in the column to the right on page 773.

Drafting

1 Developing Your Draft

Construct your essay in three parts.

- **Introduction:** Identify the topic of your paper, giving the titles of the works and the names of the authors. Include one or two sentences that summarize your **thesis,** or main idea, about the similarities and differences of your subjects. Add any background information that your readers might need.

- **Body:** Discuss two or three of the most important similarities or differences. Choose either the block method or the point-by-point method of organization.

- **Conclusion:** Restate your main idea. Summarize all the points you have made in the body of your paper. If you wish, add a personal response or direct the reader to other related works.

2 Guiding Your Reader

Help your reader out by giving clues to when you are comparing and contrasting. You can do this by using transitional words and phrases. The box in the left column lists some **transitional expressions** that show similarities and some that show differences.

774 Collection 6 / Our Literary Heritage: Greek Myths and World Folk Tales

---

Learners Having Difficulty

Work with students to create two possible outlines for the body of an essay comparing and contrasting two well-known fairy tales (such as "The Three Little Pigs" and "The Three Billy Goats Gruff"), one using the block method and the other using the point-by-point method. For example, an outline for the block method might look like this:
Body Paragraph 1: Discuss characters and plot of "The Three Little Pigs."

Body Paragraph 2: Discuss characters and plot of "The Three Billy Goats Gruff."

An outline using the point-by-point method might look like this:
Body Paragraph 1: Discuss characters in "The Three Little Pigs" and "The Three Billy Goats Gruff."
Body Paragraph 2: Discuss plot in "The Three Little Pigs" and "The Three Billy Goats Gruff."

Student Model

Amigo Brothers

Piri Thomas's story "Amigo Brothers" is about two best friends named Felix and Antonio who love boxing. Although they are different in appearance and have different styles of boxing, the two boys share many similarities, which is probably why they are best friends. They are faced with a challenge. They will have to compete against each other for the Golden Gloves Championship Tournament, and only one can win.

Thesis statement

Both boys have shared many experiences growing up. Both are seventeen years old. Each one dreams of someday being lightweight champion of the world. They have grown up on the Lower East Side of Manhattan and live in the same tenement building. They sleep, eat, and dream positive. Between them, they have a collection of Fight magazines and also "a scrapbook filled with torn tickets to every boxing match they had ever attended." Both boys have decided that no matter what happens in the tournament fight, they will always be champions to each other!

Topic sentence

Point-by-point method

Direct quotation

During the big fight both boys show good sportsmanship and play by the rules. They fight a good clean match, and at the end of the fight they embrace. It seems obvious that they care more about their close friendship than about who actually wins the fight. Just as the announcer turns to point out the winner, he finds himself alone in the ring. The two champions, Felix and Antonio, have already left the ring, arm in arm.

Topic sentence

Conclusion

—Melissa Spechler
Weber Middle School
Port Washington, New York

Strategies for Elaboration

Elaborate on the main points of your paper by using these strategies:

- Use **specific details** and **examples** to support your general statements. Search for relevant passages to quote or paraphrase.

- Show understanding of the subject matter by using terms accurately. Check definitions of any literary elements referred to in your essay.

INTERNET
More Writer's Models
Keyword: LE5 7-6

775

DIRECT TEACHING

EVALUATING AND REVISING

Content and Organization Guidelines

Suggest that students re-read their essays, using a highlighter of one color to mark parts of the essay that show how the two texts are similar, and a highlighter of another color to mark parts that show how the two texts are different. If, after they do this, one color appears significantly less often than the other, students will then know what kind of information they need to add to create a better balance.

TECHNOLOGY TIP

If students who use word processors decide to change the format of their essay (for example, from block to point-by-point), remind them that the cut-and-paste function will help them move blocks of text from one location to another.

Evaluating and Revising

Use the following chart to evaluate and revise your comparison-contrast essay.

Comparison–Contrast Essay: Content and Organization Guidelines

Evaluation Questions	▶ Tips	▶ Revision Techniques
① Does your introduction state the thesis of your essay? Do you identify works by title and author?	▶ **Underline** the thesis statement. **Circle** titles and authors.	▶ **Add** a sentence that states the main idea of the essay. **Add** titles of works and authors' names.
② Do you discuss two or more similarities or differences?	▶ **Put a check mark** next to each example of comparison or contrast.	▶ **Add** examples of comparison or contrast. **Delete** irrelevant statements.
③ Is the body of your essay organized by either the block method or the point-by-point method?	▶ In the margin **label** the method of organization. **Put the letter A** above each point about the first subject. **Put the letter B** above each point for the second subject.	▶ **Rearrange** sentences into either block order or point-by-point order.
④ Does your essay contain transitional expressions to show comparison or contrast?	▶ **Highlight** transitional words and phrases.	▶ **Add** transitional words that show similarities or differences.
⑤ Do you provide specific details and examples to back up your general statements?	▶ **Underline** supporting details and examples.	▶ **Elaborate** with specific details and examples.
⑥ Does your conclusion restate and expand on the main idea stated in the introduction?	▶ **Bracket** the restatement of your main idea. **Underline** statements that expand your main idea.	▶ **Elaborate** on statements that summarize or evaluate.

The following paragraph is from an essay about two classical myths with some points of similarity and difference. Use the questions following the model to evaluate the writer's revisions.

EVALUATION GUIDELINES

	4	3	2	1
Use these guidelines to quickly assess students' final drafts.	**Introduction states the thesis of the essay and identifies two works by title and author.**	Introduction clearly states the essay's thesis and identifies the works' titles and authors.	Introduction includes a vague thesis statement and identifies the works' titles and authors.	Introduction does not include a thesis statement, but does identify the works' titles and authors.	Introduction does not include any of these elements.
	Body discusses two or more similarities and differences and is organized by the block method or the point-by-point method.	Body discusses two or more similarities and differences and is organized using a block or a point-by-point method.	Body discusses two or more similarities and differences but does not use one of the prescribed methods of organization.	Body discusses one similarity and one difference and is poorly organized.	Body does not discuss any similarities or differences.

Revision Model

Descent to the underworld appears as a common

theme in *several* classical myths. In "The Origin of the

Seasons," *retold by Olivia Coolidge,* Demeter, the goddess of the harvest,

grieves for her daughter, Persephone, who was

snatched away *by the lord of the underworld*. In "Orpheus, the Great Musician,"

also retold by Coolidge, Orpheus ~~shows courage in~~ *braves a journey*

~~descending~~ to the underworld to bring back his

beloved wife, Eurydice. *Whereas* Demeter succeeds in

keeping her daughter on Earth for part of the year, ~~but~~

Orpheus fails the test set by the gods and loses

Eurydice forever. He is reunited with his wife only after

his death. In both cases, there are conditions set for the

return of the young women.

Evaluating the Revision

1. Which details have been added for greater precision or clarity?

2. Where has the writer deleted or replaced text to make the writing more concise?

3. Why has the writer rearranged the order of sentences? Does this change improve the writing?

Comparison-Contrast Essay **777**

PROOFREADING TIPS

- Carefully read through your paper at least twice. Exchange papers with a partner to find and correct any other errors.

- Check the spelling of authors' names and of titles.

- Underline or italicize the titles of books and longer works. Enclose the titles of short works, like poems and essays, in quotation marks.

Communications
Handbook
H E L P

See Proofreaders' Marks.

PUBLISHING TIPS

- Copies of your essays can be filed in the school library or media center for other students' reference.

- Create a bulletin board for student essays. The class can choose the essays to be displayed.

DIRECT TEACHING

Revision Model

To help students grasp the concept of revising to add important information, present the thought process of a writer making the changes shown on the Revision Model. Calling students' attention to its second sentence, you might say, "I forgot to add the name of the person who retold this myth, so I'll insert it after the title. The sentence also ends rather abruptly. I'll add a phrase that identifies who snatched Persephone away."

Proofreading Tips

To help students check their punctuation of the texts' titles, tell them that their opening paragraph should include either two underlines (for titles of books and longer works) or two sets of quotation marks, or one of each.

GUIDED PRACTICE

Evaluating the Revision
Possible Answers

1. The author's name and the identity of Persephone's kidnapper were added.

2. In the third sentence, the writer replaced "shows courage in descending" with "braves a journey."

3. The writer rearranged the sentences to introduce more clearly a comparison of the two myths.

	4	3	2	1
Essay contains transitional expressions to show comparison or contrast and includes details and examples to back up general statements.	Essay contains appropriate transitional expressions and ample support for its general statements.	Essay contains some transitional expressions and some support for its general statements.	Essay contains few transitional phrases and little support for its general statements.	Essay contains no transitional phrases and no support for its general statements.
Conclusion restates and expands on the main idea stated in the introduction.	Conclusion restates the essay's thesis in and expands on it with additional information or insights.	Conclusion restates the main idea (perhaps verbatim) and expands on it somewhat.	Conclusion either does not restate the main idea or does not expand on it.	Conclusion neither restates the main idea nor expands on it.

Literary Skills

SKILLS FOCUS
pp. 778–779

Grade-Level Skills

■ Literary Skills
Analyze a fable.

INTRODUCING THE SKILLS REVIEW

Use this review to assess students' grasp of fables.

DIRECT TEACHING

Ⓐ Literary Focus

❓ **Fables.** What common elements of fables are present in this story? [Possible responses: animal characters; a main problem; an enemy or fearsome creature.]

Ⓑ Literary Focus

❓ **Character.** Why do you think the author makes a point of stating that the mouse who suggests the plan is "very young," while the mouse who points out its flaw is "old"? [The author seems to think that young people are foolish and rash and that old people are sensible and wise.] **How do you feel about these concepts of youth and age?** [Possible responses: On the whole, they are fairly accurate. The concepts are unfair; some young people are wise, and some old people are foolish.]

Ⓒ Literary Focus

❓ **Fable.** What is the more common way of expressing this moral in English? ["Easier said than done."]

Test Practice

DIRECTIONS: Read the fable. Then, answer each question that follows.

Belling the Cat
Aesop

Ⓐ The Mice once called a meeting to decide on a plan to free themselves of their enemy, the Cat. At least they wished to find some way of knowing when she was coming so they might have time to run away. Indeed, something had to be done, for they lived in such constant fear of her claws that they hardly dared stir from their dens by night or day.

Ⓑ Many plans were discussed, but none of them was thought good enough. At last a very young Mouse got up and said:

"I have a plan that seems very simple, but I know it will be successful. All we have to do is to hang a bell about the Cat's neck. When we hear the bell ringing, we will know immediately that our enemy is coming."

All the Mice were much surprised that they had not thought of such a plan before. But in the midst of the rejoicing over their good fortune, an old Mouse arose and said:

"I will say that the plan of the young Mouse is very good. But let me ask one question: Who will bell the Cat?"

Ⓒ *It is one thing to say that something should be done, but quite a different matter to do it.*

---

1. What **problem** is dealt with in this fable?
   - **A** The mice want to help a cat.
   - **B** A silly young mouse has captured a cat.
   - **C** The mice want to know when the cat is approaching.
   - **D** The cat wants to befriend the mice.

2. What plan is proposed to solve the problem?
   - **F** A bell should be put on the cat.
   - **G** The cat should be killed.
   - **H** The mice should put a bell in their den.
   - **J** The cat should be welcomed.

3. What is wrong with the plan?
   - **A** It is too easy and won't work.
   - **B** The mice are too old to act.
   - **C** No one wants to do it because it is dangerous.
   - **D** It was a silly mouse's idea.

4. Which of the following is the best restatement of the **moral** of this fable?
   - **F** A good plan is hard to find.
   - **G** It is easier to propose plans than it is to carry them out.
   - **H** People are basically cowards.
   - **J** If you won't take a chance, nothing will get done.

LITERARY CONNECTIONS

Fables from Other Cultures
Suggest that students check school and local libraries for books containing fables or animal stories from other cultures. One good source from India is the *Panchatantra*, a collection of fables that dates back to the second century B.C. or later. Like European fables, these stories can be entertaining as well as instructive.

Activity. Have students bring in the books they find, and ask them to read passages aloud. Discuss the cross-cultural similarities students find.

WHOLE CLASS

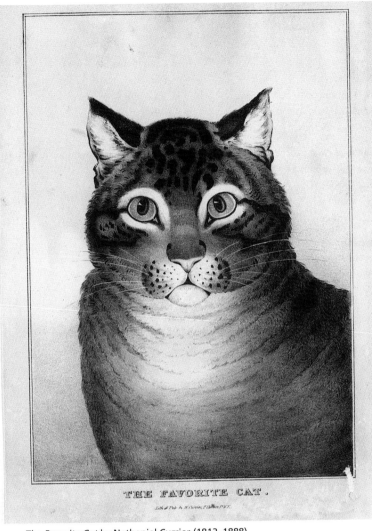

THE FAVORITE CAT.

The Favorite Cat by Nathaniel Currier (1813–1888).
Lithograph, hand-colored (12⅞'' high x 8¾'' wide).
The Metropolitan Museum of Art, Bequest of Adele S. Colgate, 1962.
(63.550.159). Photograph © 1983 The Metropolitan Museum of Art.

Literary Skills
Analyze a fable.

Skills Review   **779**

VIEWING THE ART

Nathaniel Currier (1813–1888) led a team of outstanding graphic artists who produced some seven thousand lithographs that captured life in nineteenth-century America: rustic farms, mushrooming cities, military triumphs and defeats, steam and sailing ships, domestic animals like the one shown here, and sporting events.

Activity. Ask students what this cat's expression communicates to them—curiosity, caution, anger, fear, contentment, alertness, affection, or some mixture of emotions.

Test Practice

Answers and Model Rationales

1. **C** Paragraph 1, sentence 2 provides a direct statement of the mice's problem.

2. **F** The mention of a bell in option H may mislead some students. Remind them that the story's title provides a clue about where (or on whom) the bell should be hung.

3. **C** Although this factor is not stated directly in the text, it is implied by the final question posed by the old Mouse.

4. **G** Options F, H, and J may all be secondary morals of the fable, but they do not restate the moral provided at the end of the text.

Test-Taking Tips

For more instruction on how to answer multiple-choice items, refer students to **Test Smarts,** p. 920.

Using Academic Language

Literary Terms
As part of the review of myths and folk tales, ask students to look back through the collection to find the meanings of the following terms. Then, have students demonstrate their grasp of the terms by citing passages from a selection that illustrate the meanings of the terms.

Myth (pp. 646, 654, 664, 675); **Origin Myth** (p. 654); **Underworld** (p. 664); **Morals** (p. 675); **Irony** (p. 682); **Folk Tales** (pp. 696, 698, 707, 718, 726, 732); **Motif** (pp. 698, 707, 718, 726, 732); **Superhero** (p. 698); **Metamorphosis** (p. 707); **Taboo** (p. 718); **Wishes** (p. 726); **Origin** (p. 732).

Collection 6: Skills Review

Vocabulary Skills

Synonyms

Modeling. Model the thought process of finding the answer to item 1 by saying, "I know that to *console* is to comfort. I also know that the prefix *in–* can mean 'not.' The word *inconsolable* must mean 'not able to be comforted.' Answer A sounds right, because it is difficult to comfort someone who is *heartbroken.* B, C, and D have nothing to do with being comforted. The answer must be A, *heartbroken.*"

Test Practice

Answers and Model Rationales

1. **A** *Inconsolable* means "not able to be consoled." A is the only word that means nearly the same thing.

2. **H** Since to climb something is to go up it, the answer is H.

3. **B** To arrive at B, students will need prior knowledge of the phrase *in vain,* which means "without effect."

4. **F** Point out that love is often spoken of in terms of giving and receiving or of returning; therefore, B is correct.

5. **C** Students should recall that *implore* means "to beg."

6. **F** The prefix and suffix of *invincible* offer clues to help students choose the correct answer.

7. **B** Answer B, *urged,* is the only word that can be logically substituted for *admonished.*

8. **H** Point out that one who presumes many things is often overconfident, or *arrogant.*

9. **A** The word *cowered* suggests a cowardly action.

10. **J** Point out that the word *intently* is related to the word *intense,* which means "concentrated."

Test Practice

Synonyms

DIRECTIONS: Choose the word or phrase that means the same, or about the same, as the underlined word.

1. A person who is inconsolable is —
   - A heartbroken
   - B curious
   - C hardworking
   - D unconscious

2. Climbers who ascended a mountain —
   - F went around it
   - G discovered it
   - H went up it
   - J went down it

3. When someone vainly loves another, he or she loves —
   - A foolishly
   - B uselessly
   - C successfully
   - D passionately

4. If a person's love is unrequited, it is —
   - F not returned
   - G not required
   - H not respectable
   - J not reliable

5. If you implored someone to do something, you —
   - A dared
   - B forced
   - C begged
   - D insisted

6. An invincible army is —
   - F unbeatable
   - G not strong
   - H in retreat
   - J on attack

7. A teacher who admonished students to behave —
   - A argued
   - B urged
   - C praised
   - D threatened

8. A presumptuous person is —
   - F pretty
   - G fortunate
   - H arrogant
   - J fair

9. A dog that cowered —
   - A crouched and trembled
   - B barked and growled
   - C jumped up and down
   - D cried and yelped

10. When you study intently, you —
    - F watch TV while you work
    - G work halfheartedly
    - H are not at all interested
    - J work with great concentration

SKILLS FOCUS

Vocabulary Skills
Identify synonyms.

Vocabulary Review

Use the following activity to find out whether your students have retained the Vocabulary words taught in this collection. **Activity.** Have students choose the correct words from the box to complete the sentences.

commenced	deciphered
hovered	ransacked

1. The whistle blew, and the race _____ . [commenced]

2. Maura _____ her drawers, looking for the lost bracelet. [ransacked]

3. The hot air balloon _____ above the park. [hovered]

4. Have you ever _____ a secret code? [deciphered]

Collection 6: Skills Review

Writing Skills

Test Practice

DIRECTIONS: Read the following paragraph. Then, read the questions below it. Choose the best answer to each question, and mark your answers on your paper.

(1) Although myths and folk tales are often grouped together as forms of folklore, there are significant differences between them. (2) Like all forms of folklore, myths and folk tales reflect the traditional beliefs and customs of the cultures that created them. (3) Both myths and folk tales have been passed from one generation to another by word of mouth. (4) Their original authors are unknown. (5) Myths, however, usually involve gods and other supernatural beings. (6) Myths may explain some natural event, and they may teach moral lessons. (7) Folk tales also reflect the particular culture that created them. (8) Folk tales often contain legendary elements, and they may include magic and fantasy.

1. The **thesis,** or main idea, of this paper is stated in —
   A sentence 1
   B sentence 2
   C sentence 3
   D sentence 7

2. Which sentence is unnecessary and should be deleted?
   F sentence 1
   G sentence 3
   H sentence 5
   J sentence 7

3. Transitional expressions are used in all of the following *except* —
   A sentence 1
   B sentence 2
   C sentence 4
   D sentence 5

4. Which type of text structure is used in this passage?
   F chronological
   G cause and effect
   H comparison and contrast
   J step by step

5. Which of these statements is accurate?
   A Sentence 1 contains a definition of folklore.
   B Sentence 2 focuses on a difference between myths and folk tales.
   C Sentence 5 focuses on a similarity between myths and folk tales.
   D Sentence 6 identifies purposes of some myths.

SKILLS FOCUS

Writing Skills
Analyze a comparison-contrast essay.

Skills Review **781**

Test Practice

Answers and Model Rationales

1. **A** Only answer A (sentence 1) expresses the thesis of this passage. B and C (sentences 2 and 3) each identify similarities between myths and folk tales, and D (sentence 7) describes a characteristic of folk tales.

2. **J** This sentence contains the word *also,* which should (but does not) relate the sentence to something that came before. It should therefore be eliminated.

3. **C** Sentence 1 contains the transitional word *Although.* Sentence 2 contains the transitional word *Like.* Sentence 5 contains the transitional word *however.*

4. **H** The passage compares and contrasts myths and folk tales; that is, it tells how they are similar and how they are different.

5. **D** Sentence 1 provides the thesis of the passage. Sentence 2 focuses on a similarity between myths and folk tales. Sentence 5 focuses on one characteristic of myths.

APPLICATION

Supporting Details
Have students imagine that they are revising the passage that appears on this page. Direct them to return to the myths and folk tales they have read in this collection and to find examples and details that would support sentences 2, 5, 6, and 8.

EXTENSION

Evaluating Articles
Have students look through newspapers or magazines to find an article that compares and contrasts two topics, such as summer movies or kinds of exercise. Then have them read and evaluate that article using the following criteria:

- Does the article tell how the two topics are similar and different?
- Does the article provide sufficient examples and details to illustrate the similarities and differences?
- Is the article well-organized?

After students complete their evaluations, ask them how they might use the information they gained by reading this article. [Possible responses: to make a choice; to decide on a course of action]

READ ON

For Independent Reading

If students enjoyed the themes and topics explored in this collection, you might recommend these titles for independent reading.

Assessment Options

The following projects can help you evaluate and assess your students' outside reading. Videotapes and audiotapes of completed projects may be included in students' portfolios.

- **Tell a story with drums.** Invite students who read *Patakin: World Tales of Drums and Drummers* to retell one of the stories using drums to help convey punctuation, rhythm, or mood.

- **Illustrate a character's transformation.** Have students who read *The Samurai's Tale* create a series of illustrations that show how Taro changes over time. Encourage them to draw some pictures that show Taro's different stations in life, and others that show the actions he takes to achieve his goals. Have them select quotations from the story to use as captions for their illustrations.

- **Create a book of tales.** Ask students to create their own book filled with stories like the ones Linda Fang retells in *The Chi-Lin Purse.* Allow students to include stories told to them by friends and relatives, stories from TV shows or movies they have seen, retellings of stories from other books they have read, and stories they have written themselves.

Fiction

The Beat of the Drums

Listen to the powerful and inspiring language of drums. Experience the different rhythms of drumming for protection, freedom, and transformation. The ten tales of *Patakin: World Tales of Drums and Drummers* by Nina Jaffe celebrate a variety of drums and their special roles in storytelling.

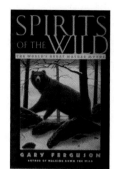

Nature's Mysteries

If you like exploring nature, you'll love reading about it in Gary Ferguson's book, *Spirits of the Wild.* Stories from around the globe in this entertaining collection reveal the magical and often mysterious quality of the world around us.

Samurai Code of Honor

After being orphaned as a young boy, Taro becomes a servant to a great warrior lord. Join Taro as he rises through the ranks from kitchen cook to samurai warrior. Eventually, Taro is asked by his lord to infiltrate an enemy's castle. Will he accomplish the mission? Will he make it back home to marry the woman he loves? *The Samurai's Tale* by Erik C. Haugaard brings sixteenth-century Japan to life with samurai, shoguns, ninjas, and more.

Tales from Ancient China

Linda Fang's *The Chi-Lin Purse* is a collection of stories derived from ancient Chinese folklore, operas, and novels. The stories are from the Warring States Period in China (770–221 B.C.) and range in style from classic folktales to grand operas. Each tale is accompanied by a beautiful, black-and-white illustration, which shows the styles from that story's time period.

DIFFERENTIATING INSTRUCTION

Estimated Word Counts of Read On Books:

Fiction		Nonfiction	
Patakin: World Tales of Drums and Drummers	24,500	*Gods, Goddesses, and Monsters*	51,000
Spirits of the Wild	21,000	*Life in a Medieval Castle*	69,000
The Samurai's Tale	69,800	*Explorers of the Ancient World*	10,000
The Chi-Lin Purse	25,000	*The Incas*	15,000

Nonfiction

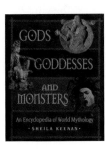

A Rich Resource

Learn about mythical figures from around the globe in *Gods, Goddesses, and Monsters*, by Sheila Keenan. Spider Woman, a powerful North American spirit who is both wise and kind, and the mighty Thor, who makes the heavens shake whenever he raises his hammer, are two of the major mythological characters from fifteen different cultures detailed in this fascinating encyclopedia.

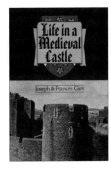

Living in a Castle

Have you ever wondered how people lived in the Middle Ages? What did the lord of a castle have for breakfast? What did boys and girls do when school ended for the day? How did people bathe? Find the answers to these questions and more when you read *Life in a Medieval Castle* by Joseph and Frances Gies.

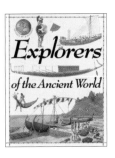

Sail Away!

Imagine heading off into an unknown world without any maps! In *Explorers of the Ancient World*, Anthony Brierley tells how the Egyptians, Phoenicians, and Greeks all courageously explored the Mediterranean world and the coasts of Africa. The book discusses and illustrates the tools and ships the explorers used on their journeys. Pictures of artifacts are included to make this exciting history come alive.

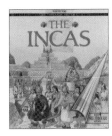

Inca Life

In *The Incas*, Tim Wood takes you on a tour of the Inca empire. You visit inside a typical Inca house, a temple to the sun god, an emperor's palace, and more. If you enjoy this book, you may want to read other titles in the See Through History series.

Assessment Options

- **Show and tell.** Have students who read *Gods, Goddesses, and Monsters* choose their favorite figure and impersonate him or her for the class, in costume, if possible. After a brief dramatic performance, have students identify the character by name, special talents, and culture of origin.

- **Write a schedule.** Have students who read *Life in a Medieval Castle* write a one-day schedule for a typical medieval teenager (or child, or adult). Have students copy the schedule onto the board or onto a transparency and read it to the class, answering questions and providing background information as necessary.

- **Chart the waters.** Have students who read *Explorers of the Ancient World* create a chart containing information about the Egyptian, Phoenician, and Greek explorers' ships, tools, and destinations. When they are finished, have them use the chart to draw some conclusions about the similarities and differences among the three groups of explorers. Challenge students to make a generalization or two about exploration in the ancient world.

The Read On titles are categorized as shown below:

Below Grade Level ⬇
The Chi-Lin Purse
Explorers of the Ancient World
The Incas

At Grade Level ↔
Patakin: World Tales of Drums and Drummers
Spirits of the Wild
Gods, Goddesses, and Monsters

Above Grade Level ⬆
The Samurai's Tale
Life in a Medieval Castle

Collection 7
Literary Criticism: Where I Stand

Literary Focus:
Criticizing Literature

Informational Focus:
Evaluating Evidence

About Collection 7

In Collection 7, students will master the following skills:

- **Literary Skills:** Understand and analyze literary criticism; analyze a legend, the qualities of a hero, and a quest story; evaluate responses to a literary work.
  Reading Skills: Evaluate evidence; analyze stereotypes and bias; compare and contrast heroes.
  Vocabulary Skills: Understand Latin and Anglo-Saxon word origins and prefixes; Greek roots, prefixes, and suffixes; and French word origins.
  Writing Skills: Develop, write, and revise an informative report.

Informational Text

Each collection of *Elements of Literature* provides a variety of informational texts related to the literature selections by theme or topic.

Minimum Course of Study

Most skills can be taught with a minimum number of selections and features. In the chart to the right, lessons highlighted in green constitute the minimum course of study that provides coverage of the skills taught in Collection 7.

Scope and Sequence

Selection ■ Feature	Literary Skills
Elements of Literature: Literary Criticism *by* Madeline Travers Hovland	• Understand literary criticism
Reading Skills and Strategies: Evaluating Evidence **Letter to the Editor** ↔ *at grade level*	
King Arthur: The Sword in the Stone *by* Hudson Talbott ↑ *above grade level*	• Analyze a legend
Three Responses to Literature ↔ *at grade level*	• Analyze and evaluate responses to a literary work
Informational Text: **He's No King** ↔ *at grade level*	
Merlin and the Dragons *by* Jane Yolen ↔ *at grade level*	• Analyze the qualities of a hero
Sir Gawain and the Loathly Lady *retold by* Betsy Hearne ↑ *above grade level*	• Analyze a quest story
Comparing Literature: Real Heroes *from* **Long Walk to Freedom** *by* Nelson Mandela ↔ *at grade level*	• Analyze heroes
Rosa Parks *by* Rita Dove ↔ *at grade level*	
No Questions Asked: **The Impossible Dream** *lyrics by* Joe Darion ↔ *at grade level*	
Writing Workshop: *Expository Writing: Informative Report*	
Skills Review: *Literary Skills* *Informational Reading Skills* *Vocabulary Skills* *Writing Skills*	• Analyze literary criticism

Resource Manager
(pp. 784C–784F)

Lesson and workshop resources are referenced in the Resource Manager on the pages that follow. These resources can be used to reinforce the skills taught in Collection 7, remediate students who are having difficulty, and provide supporting activities for English-language learners.

Reading Skills	Vocabulary Skills	Writing Grammar and Language Skills
• Evaluate evidence		
	• Understand Latin and Anglo-Saxon word origins	• Write a letter
	• Understand Latin and Anglo-Saxon prefixes	• Write a critical response to literature
• Analyze stereotype and bias	• Understand Greek roots	
	• Understand prefixes and suffixes • Clarify word meanings by using examples	• Write a literary analysis
	• Understand French word origins	• Write a critical response to literature • Use *its* and *it's* and *your* and *you're* correctly
• Compare and contrast heroes		• Write a comparison-contrast essay • Write a biographical sketch • Present an oral report
		• Write an informative report
• Evaluate evidence	• Understand multiple-meaning words	• Analyze an informative report

Selection ▪ Feature	Planning	Differentiating Instruction ▪ Lesson Plans with ELL Strategies and Practice	Reading ▪ Vocabulary
Elements of Literature: Literary Criticism *by* Madeline Travers Hovland		• Holt Reading Solutions: Lesson Plans, pp. 315–316	• Holt Reading Solutions, pp. 315–316
Reading Skills and Strategies: Evaluating Evidence *by* Sheri Henderson **Letter to the Editor**			
King Arthur: The Sword in the Stone *by* Hudson Talbott **Three Responses to Literature** **Informational Text: He's No King**	• One-Stop Planner with ExamView Test Generator	• The Holt Reader, pp. 232–254 • Holt Reading Solutions: Lesson Plans, pp. 317–328 • Supporting Instruction in Spanish, p. 31 • Audio CD Library • Audio CD Library, Selections and Summaries in Spanish	• The Holt Reader, pp. 232–254 • Holt Reading Solutions, pp. 317–328 • Vocabulary Development, p. 31
Merlin and the Dragons *by* Jane Yolen	• One-Stop Planner with ExamView Test Generator	• Holt Reading Solutions: Lesson Plans, pp. 329–333 • Supporting Instruction in Spanish, p. 32 • Audio CD Library • Audio CD Library, Selections and Summaries in Spanish	• Holt Reading Solutions, pp. 329–333 • Vocabulary Development, p. 32
Sir Gawain and the Loathly Lady *retold by* Betsy Hearne	• One-Stop Planner with ExamView Test Generator	• The Holt Reader, pp. 255–268 • Holt Adapted Reader, pp. 158–165 • Holt Reading Solutions: Lesson Plans, pp. 334–339 • Supporting Instruction in Spanish, p. 37 • Audio CD Library • Audio CD Library, Selections and Summaries in Spanish	• The Holt Reader, pp. 255–268 • Holt Adapted Reader, pp. 158–166 • Holt Reading Solutions, pp. 334–339 • Vocabulary Development, p. 33
Comparing Literature: Real Heroes *from* **Long Walk to Freedom** *by* Nelson Mandela **Rosa Parks** *by* Rita Dove		• Holt Reading Solutions: Lesson Plans, pp. 340–343	• Holt Reading Solutions, pp. 340–343

Writing ▪ Grammar and Language	Assessment
• Daily Language Activities	• Holt Assessment: Literature, Reading, and Vocabulary • One-Stop Planner with ExamView Test Generator • Holt Online Assessment
• Daily Language Activities	• Holt Assessment: Literature, Reading, and Vocabulary • One-Stop Planner with ExamView Test Generator • Holt Online Assessment
• Daily Language Activities • Language Handbook Worksheets, pp. 140–142	• Holt Assessment: Literature, Reading, and Vocabulary • One-Stop Planner with ExamView Test Generator • Holt Online Assessment

Technology

INTERNET
- go.hrw.com
- Holt Online Assessment
- Holt Online Essay Scoring
- Elements of Literature Online

MEDIA

 • One-Stop Planner with ExamView Test Generator

 • Audio CD Library

 • Audio CD Library, Selections and Summaries in Spanish

 • Fine Art Transparencies, 11 and 12

Transparency

CD-ROM   Audio CD

(continued)

Selection ▪ Feature	Planning	Differentiating Instruction ▪ Lesson Plans with ELL Strategies and Practice	Reading ▪ Vocabulary
No Questions Asked: The Impossible Dream *lyrics by* Joe Darion			
Writing Workshop: *Expository Writing: Informative Report*	• One-Stop Planner with ExamView Test Generator	• Workshop Resources: Writing, Listening, and Speaking, pp. 67–79 • Family Involvement Activities in English and Spanish • Supporting Instruction in Spanish, p. 43	
Skills Review: *Literary Skills* *Informational Reading Skills* *Vocabulary Skills* *Writing Skills*			

The Holt Reader

The Holt Reader is a consumable paperback book that can be used alone or to accompany *Elements of Literature*. It offers guided support throughout the reading process and encourages students to become active readers by circling, underlining, questioning, and jotting down responses as they read. *The Holt Reader* works well for homework, students who have missed class, additional instructional time, reteaching, and remediation.

Holt Reading Solutions (HRS)

Holt Reading Solutions pulls together reading resources in the *Elements of Literature* program to create a powerful tool for intervention and whole-class instruction. *HRS* includes diagnostic assessment tools, lesson plans for English-language learners and special education students, adaptations of selected reading selections, vocabulary and comprehension worksheets, information on phonics and decoding, and additional instruction and practice in remedial reading skills.

Writing · Grammar and Language	Assessment
• Workshop Resources: Writing, Listening, and Speaking, pp. 67–79 • Language Handbook Worksheets • Daily Language Activities	• Holt Assessment: Literature, Reading, and Vocabulary • One-Stop Planner with ExamView Test Generator • Holt Online Assessment • Holt Online Essay Scoring
	• Holt Assessment: Literature, Reading, and Vocabulary • One-Stop Planner with ExamView Test Generator • Holt Online Assessment

Technology

INTERNET

- go.hrw.com
- Holt Online Assessment
- Holt Online Essay Scoring
- Elements of Literature Online

MEDIA

 • One-Stop Planner with ExamView Test Generator

• Audio CD Library

• Audio CD Library, Selections and Summaries in Spanish

• Fine Art Transparencies, 11 and 12

One-Stop Planner with ExamView Test Generator

The *One-Stop Planner* CD-ROM planning software contains print-based teaching resources, clips from the video program, and valuable assessment tools. The *One-Stop Planner* resources are presented in easy-to-follow, point-and-click menu formats. To preview resources or print out worksheets and tests, you simply make a selection and click.

One-Stop Planner CD-ROM

 Transparency

 CD-ROM   Audio CD

Collection 7

SKILLS FOCUS

Grade-Level Skills

■ **Literary Skills**
Criticize literature.

■ **Reading Skills**
Evaluate the quality of the author's evidence to support claims, noting instances of bias and stereotyping.

■ **Vocabulary Skills**
Use affixes and word origins to understand vocabulary.

Review Skills

■ **Literary Skills**
Analyze archetypes and symbols that are found in legends.

■ **Reading Skills**
Assess the evidence for an author's conclusions.

■ **Reading Skills**
Recognize unsupported inferences, fallacious reasoning, persuasion, and propaganda.

Upcoming Skills

■ **Reading Skills**
Evaluate the logic, consistency, and structural patterns of informational texts.

■ **Vocabulary Skills**
Use word origins to determine historical influences on English word meanings.

COLLECTION 7 RESOURCES: READING

Planning
■ *One-Stop Planner* CD-ROM with ExamView Test Generator

Differentiating Instruction
■ *The Holt Reader*
■ *Holt Adapted Reader*
■ *Holt Reading Solutions*
■ *Family Involvement Activities in English and Spanish*

■ *Supporting Instruction in Spanish*
■ *Audio CD Library*
■ *Audio CD Library, Selections and Summaries in Spanish*

Vocabulary
■ *Vocabulary Development*

Grammar and Language
■ *Language Handbook Worksheets*
■ *Daily Language Activities*

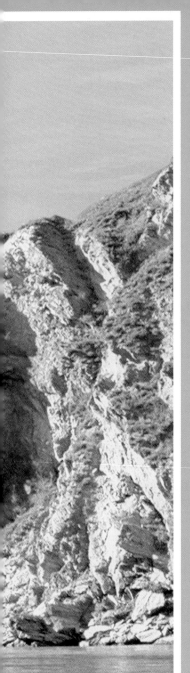

Literary Criticism: Where I Stand

Literary Focus:
Criticizing Literature

Informational Focus:
Evaluating Evidence

INTERNET
Collection
Resources
Keyword: LE5 7-7

The Argonauth that guards the entrance to the Falls of Rauros. From *The Lord of the Rings: The Fellowship of the Ring.*

785

INTRODUCING THE COLLECTION

Theme: Where I stand. When students read stories, they develop strong opinions about the effectiveness of plots and characters and the overall quality of the works. In this collection, students will learn to express opinions about literature and back them with reasons and solid evidence.

Criticizing literature. Students will learn how to critically discuss works of literature by examining common literary elements, such as plot, character, and theme in Arthurian legends. Students will also have the opportunity to compare characterizations of two modern-day heroes, Nelson Mandela and Rosa Parks.

Evaluating evidence. Students will read literary criticism and other informational pieces and discuss whether the evidence the authors use to support their opinions is adequate, accurate, and appropriate. Students will also evaluate sources and assess evidence they have gathered to write an informational report at the end of the collection.

VIEWING THE ART

Activity. Most students will probably recognize the art as a scene from the film *The Lord of the Rings: The Fellowship of the Ring.* Ask a student familiar with the film to summarize it for the class. Then, introduce students to the concept of criticism by asking them to state whether they liked or disliked the movie and to explain why they feel as they do.

Review Skills

■ Literary Skills
Critique the credibility of characterization and plot.

**Elements of Literature:
Literary Criticism**

Ask students how they liked a recent movie or television show that most of them have seen. If they respond with vague statements such as "It was great" or "I didn't like it," ask them specific questions like these:

• Were the characters believable?

• Did the plot seem realistic or far-fetched?

• What message did you get from the movie or TV show?

After the discussion, point out that they have been critiquing the movie or TV show using the same kinds of criteria they can use to evaluate works of literature.

Elements of Literature
Literary Criticism

HOW DID YOU LIKE IT?

by Madeline Travers Hovland

You're leaving a movie with a friend—or you've played a new computer game a classmate has lent you—or you've read a story for homework. Your friend asks, "How'd you like it?" Suppose you give one of these answers:

"Great!"

"It was OK. I've seen better."

"That was pretty bad."

Your friend comes back at you with "How come?" You're going to feel pretty silly if all you come up with is "Uh, I dunno." Backing up your opinions of what you read gets easy once you've learned the language of literature. The fact is, you've been learning how to talk about literature as you've been reading this book. Each collection has challenged you to think, talk, and write intelligently about literary works that you've read.

Learning the Language

After you read something, you respond to it with an overall impression. You liked it, or maybe you didn't. Fine—but look a little closer. Why did you respond that way, and how can you communicate that response to others?

Chances are your response had something to do with the way the writer used the **literary elements**.

INTERNET

More About
Literary Criticism
Keyword: LE5 7-7

Literary Skills
Understand
literary criticism.

The terms for the literary elements have been in **boldface** throughout this book. Literary elements are things like **character, plot,** and **theme.** Using these terms, or **academic language,** helps all of us share our thoughts about what we read.

Talking About Stories

1 **Character.** When you respond to a story, you almost always want to talk about its characters. Here are some questions about characters that you can consider:

• Are the characters believable?

• Are they totally unrealistic?

• Are the causes, or **motivation,** of the characters' actions clear?

• How did you *feel* about the main character?

• What connections can you make between the characters and others you've met—including characters in stories, movies, and TV shows?

• Did you identify with any of the characters—that is, did any of them seem to share your values, dreams, worries, opinions, or background?

2 **Plot.** When critics talk about plot, they talk about what happened in a story. Did the writer hold your attention? Was the story

786 Collection 7 / Literary Criticism: Where I Stand

Learners Having Difficulty
Before students read the essay, review the definitions of character, plot, and theme, and have them identify examples of each from recently read selections. After students have read the essay, model for them, applying the questions in the essay to a type of reading they enjoy, such as comic books or sports biographies.

Advanced Learners
Acceleration. Use this activity to help advanced learners analyze how a work reveals its author's heritage. Point out that every work of literature is the product of an author writing at a particular time and from a particular point of view. Tell them that in addition to examining literary elements, they can analyze a work by

believable? Was the plot clear—did you understand the series of causes and effects that make up a plot?

3 **Theme.** When most people finish reading a novel or a short story, they want to talk about meaning, or **theme.** What did the story mean? Did the story say something important about life, or did it leave you thinking, "So what?" Did it say something new, fresh, and meaningful to you? Was its theme old and tired, something you've heard many times before, like "Crime doesn't pay" or "True love wins in the end"?

Talking About a Poem

When you're dealing with poems, the important literary elements you'll want to talk about are things such as **figurative language, imagery,** and **sound effects.** You'll talk about meaning with poetry, too—that is, as with short stories, you'll talk about **theme,** and how you respond to that theme.

Talking About Nonfiction

When you read a work of nonfiction, such as a biography or an autobiography, you'll want to talk about the writer's **objectivity.** You'll also want to ask about the **primary sources** the writer used for historical data. You'll want to talk about the writer's **accuracy** on historical details. Biography and autobiography are full of **characters.** You'll want to evaluate the characters and decide if the writer has made them seem alive.

The Mirror on the Page

When we talk about literary elements in a story, a poem, or a piece of nonfiction, we're not just learning about literature. We're learning about ourselves—what fascinates us, what inspires us, what we think of ourselves, what we believe in with all our hearts. The works of literature we read become a mirror. As we understand and learn to communicate our responses to them, we learn a little more about who we are.

Practice

Divide the class into three groups. Then, choose one story or one poem that you all have read in class. Each group will discuss the same story or poem for about five minutes. For your discussions, select a question from the ones cited in this essay, and focus your discussion on that question. When your discussions are completed, after five minutes, each group should report on its discussion. What responses were expressed? Were the responses affected by a particular literary element (for example, did a group feel strongly that a character was not believable and so rejected the whole story)? What did members of the group learn from the discussion?

Practice

Help students organize themselves into three groups. Then, encourage each group to choose one story or poem for discussion and choose one question from the essay to discuss.

Possible responses for *Song of the Trees,* based on the question "Are the characters believable?":

Discussion report—Group members agreed that the children were completely believable, but there was disagreement about the father. While some found him believable, others felt that it was unrealistic that a father would endanger himself and his family by incurring the wrath of a white man in the South at that time.

What group members learned from the discussion—People with different opinions may have valid reasons for their opinions. An opinion that is supported with details from the text is more convincing than one that is not.

Apply

Encourage students to choose one of the questions in the essay and use it as the basis for a family discussion about a television show that everyone has watched. Allow time for students to report on their family discussions.

HOMEWORK

exploring how it reflects the author's background and beliefs.

Activity. Ask students to draw up a list of questions that could be used to prompt a discussion of a literary work based on the author's background and how it is revealed in the work.

Grade-Level Skills

■ **Reading Skills**
Evaluate the quality of the author's evidence to support claims.

OVERVIEW

Purpose. Evaluating evidence helps readers make judgments about the quality of an author's writing in informational texts.

Use. Students should evaluate evidence when they read pieces in which the author makes a claim or expresses an opinion. With "Letter to the Editor," students can identify the author's support for the claim that violent video games are not harmful to children and then determine whether the evidence presented actually supports the claim. Evaluating evidence will be helpful with the other informational pieces in this collection as well.

Summary at grade level

A letter to a newspaper editor disputes the suggestion made in an editorial that video games cause children to behave violently. The writer states that the Barbie Game she and her sister played did not shape their values and that her brother's childhood hours with a plastic rifle didn't make him violent. She believes that kids today are "playing make-believe," just as she did. She notes, however, that the National Institute on Media and the Family, which assesses the content of video games, reports a link between fighting and "an increased appetite for violence in video games." What troubles the author is the possibility that video games foster isolation, since they are played alone.

Reading Skills and Strategies

Evaluating Evidence

by Sheri Henderson

The Triple A's of Evidence: Adequate, Accurate, Appropriate

When you read informational texts, you expect a writer's evidence to be adequate, accurate, and appropriate. Don't simply take evidence for granted. Evidence doesn't always make sense. You need to **evaluate,** or judge, the evidence for yourself.

Evidence should be **appropriate.** *Appropriate* means "suitable, relevant; right for the purpose." Appropriate evidence is to the point. Appropriate evidence is not inflammatory. Appropriate evidence is not based on a stereotype. When you read a statement and think to yourself, "What does that have to do with anything?" you're probably looking at **inappropriate** evidence.

Evidence should be **accurate.** *Accurate* means "free from mistakes or errors." If a writer states an opinion using words such as *all, each,* and *every,* you're probably looking at evidence that is **inaccurate.**

Evidence should be **adequate.** *Adequate* means "enough for what is needed; sufficient." If you have to trust a person's feelings instead of relying on facts, the evidence is most likely **inadequate.**

Practice your ability to evaluate evidence as you read "Letter to the Editor" on page 789.

SKILLS FOCUS

Reading Skills
Evaluate evidence.

Tips for Evaluating Evidence

• Look for **facts.** Plenty of facts usually means the information you're reading is **adequate.**

• Look for **reliable sources** in support of **accurate** information. Does the writer cite quotations, statistics, case studies?

• Are opinions backed up with facts? **Opinions** not supported by facts are examples of **inappropriate** evidence.

DIFFERENTIATING INSTRUCTION

Learners Having Difficulty

Modeling. To help students read "Letter to the Editor," model evaluating evidence. Have students read the first six paragraphs. Then, say, "The author is responding to an editorial on video games by discussing games that she and her siblings played as children. She uses evidence from her own life to support a claim that childhood games do not influence behavior. I would say that the evidence is biased because the author has an emotional view of herself and her upbringing. The evidence is appropriate for supporting a claim about past behavior but not as evidence about behavior today. Also, a few personal examples do not constitute adequate support." Encourage students as they read on to ask themselves, "Do these facts and opinions provide adequate support for the author's claim?"

English-Language Learners

Be sure students are familiar with the popular Barbie doll. Call on volunteers

Letter to the Editor

Regarding your recent editorial, "Violent Video Games Cause Violence in Children":

My sisters and I used to play the Barbie Game for hours, duking it out for the chance to be "Queen of the Prom." The object of the game was to be the first player to get a dress and, of course, a date. There were four boys and four dresses to compete for. The one who drew "Poindexter" as a date was totally humiliated. The dress didn't matter as much, just so long as you had something to wear to the big event.

I suppose one could say that the Barbie Game made us care more about boys and clothes than our own brains and souls. But it did none of those things. We knew it was all fiction. We didn't care if we were competing for dresses or expensive property. We were just competing. ❶

Today some people would proclaim that games like this one made us into empty-headed weaklings. They would get a quick-witted and firm reaction from one of my sisters.

My brother, possibly the nicest guy I've ever known, spent his childhood in army fatigues wielding a plastic rifle. Outside my window I would hear the battles going on. ❷

So what is all this hysteria today about video games? Isn't it the same thing? Kids are just playing make-believe. They know it's not real.

The National Institute on Media and the Family would respond that the issue of the impact of video and computer games is no child's play. The Institute has developed "KidScore," an evaluation system that rates the amount of violence, the portrayal of violence, fear, illegal or harmful content, language, nudity, and sexual content. Not exactly things that were on my old Barbie game board nor in my brother's war games.

David Walsh, president of the Institute, reports, among many other findings, "Youth who report an increased appetite for violence in video games are more likely to have gotten into physical fights in the previous year." ❸

Letter to the Editor **789**

Using the Strategy

As you read, you'll find this open-book sign at certain points in the text: . Stop at these points, and think about what you've just read. Do what the prompt asks you to do.

INTERPRET

❶ Why do you think the writer tells about playing the Barbie Game with her sisters? What statement in the third paragraph does this evidence support? **A**

EVALUATE

❷ What evidence does the writer give for her claim that playing army games is not harmful? Is this evidence **appropriate**? Why or why not? **B**

INTERPRET

❸ Does this **expert testimony** support the writer's claim that games are *not* harmful? Or does it support the opposite point of view? Explain. **C**

PRETEACHING

Selection Starter

Motivate. Ask students to describe some of the games they play (such as computer games, board games, or outdoor sports). Lead a class discussion on whether students think there is any connection between the games they play and the way they behave. Tell them that they are going to read a letter expressing an opinion on this issue.

DIRECT TEACHING

A Reading Skills and Strategies

Interpret. [Possible responses to question 1: The writer tells about playing the Barbie Game to bolster support for her argument by describing her personal experience of playing games. This evidence supports the statement "But it did none of those things."]

B Reading Skills and Strategies

Evaluate. [Possible response to question 2: The writer supports her claim by stating that her brother is "possibly the nicest guy I've ever known." This evidence is inappropriate because it is an unsupported opinion about someone whom the writer is close to.]

C Reading Skills and Strategies

Interpret. [Possible response to question 3: The expert testimony does not support the writer's claim. The correlation between the desire for violence in video games and the participation in physical fights suggests that violent video games are harmful for children, a view that the writer opposes.]

---

to describe Barbie and her outfits. Then, explain to English-language learners that the selection is written in informal English. Point out sentence fragments, and define slang terms such as *duking it out* ("fighting") and idioms such as *empty-headed* ("stupid; ignorant").

Advanced Learners

Enrichment. Have students write letters expressing their own opinions in response to the following question: "Do games played in childhood affect people's later behavior?" Remind students to support their opinions with accurate, appropriate, and adequate evidence. Suggest that they find statistics and expert opinions (perhaps by researching on the Internet) and use personal examples. Afterward, have them meet to discuss and debate the issue.

A Reading Skills and Strategies

Interpret. [Possible response to question 4: The positive aspects of video games are that they provide practice in problem solving and logic, introduce children to technology, and teach children to follow directions. The writer gets the information from the Institute's report.]

B Reading Skills and Strategies

❷ Evaluate evidence. How do you feel about the Institute's statement? Is this a reasonable concern about video games? [Some students will share the writer's concern about children playing games alone. Others will say it's good to have a game to play by oneself.]

C Reading Skills and Strategies

Compare and contrast. [Possible response to question 5: The writer finds that video games are frequently played alone and thus foster social isolation. The writer and her brother and sisters played together.]

Using the Strategy

INTERPRET

❹ What are the positive aspects of video games? Where does the writer get this information?

COMPARE AND CONTRAST

❺ What problem with playing video games does the writer find in the Institute's report? Explain the difference between video games and the games her brother and sisters played.

It turns out there are positive aspects of video games. They provide practice in problem solving and logic. They introduce children to technology. Games give children a chance to practice following directions. ❹

But as I read the Institute's findings, I notice one tiny sentence that sends a chill up my spine. "Games could foster social isolation as they are often played alone." Sure, my sisters were a pain when they won the game. Yes, I got tired of listening to arguments between my brother and his friends about exactly who got hit in battle. But we all had a connection to one another. We fought some, laughed a lot, and without knowing it, helped one another grow up. ❺

I'm not sure you can do that with a computer. Technology can do a lot of things, but it still can't do that.

—A Concerned Reader

Practice the Strategy

Evaluating Evidence

When you evaluate evidence, you judge whether it is

- **adequate**—Is there enough evidence to back up the claim?
- **accurate**—Is it free from mistakes or errors?
- **appropriate**—Is it to the point and free from emotional appeals?

PRACTICE 1

Here are some examples of poor evidence from an essay about the dangers of the Internet. Decide whether each italic statement is **inadequate**, **inaccurate**, or **inappropriate**.

1. *Every teenager in America uses the Internet, and test scores have gone down all over the country.* This statement is _____ because not *every* teenager uses the Internet. No information supports the connection.

2. *My son's grades fell at the time he was allowed to use the Internet for a month.* This evidence is _____ because it is one person's experience, which is not enough to support the claim. There may be other reasons for the son's poor performance.

3. *The Internet stifles the imagination because anyone who spends a lot of time with machines becomes antisocial and mean.* This is _____ evidence because it is based only on an emotional appeal.

> Whenever you read informational texts—in this collection and in your life outside of school—evaluating the evidence to be sure it is adequate, accurate, and appropriate will make you a smart reader.

PRACTICE 2

In the blanks on the left, write the letter from the description on the right that best fits each statement.

___**1.** My brother, who knows a lot, says bugs are helpful.

___**2.** There are fifty stars on the United States flag.

___**3.** Studying math is more valuable than studying art.

___**4.** The almanac gives facts about all fifty states.

a. fact

b. opinion

c. reliable source

d. unreliable source

SKILLS FOCUS

Reading Skills
Evaluate evidence.

Evaluating Evidence **791**

INDEPENDENT PRACTICE

Practice the Strategy

In the first part of this feature, students will determine whether evidence is inadequate, inaccurate, or inappropriate. In the second part they'll determine whether statements are facts or opinions and whether they're from reliable or unreliable sources.

Strategy Tip

Remind students to think about the source of a piece of evidence when they are determining whether it is adequate. If the evidence is based on one person's experience, it is probably inadequate. If it is the result of a survey or a study of a number of people, it is more likely to be adequate.

PRACTICE 1

1. inaccurate
2. inadequate
3. inappropriate

PRACTICE 2

1. d
2. a
3. b
4. c

DIFFERENTIATING INSTRUCTION

Learners Having Difficulty

Students having difficulty distinguishing facts from opinions should form small groups and re-read "Letter to the Editor" together. Have a student in each group read the first sentence of the selection aloud. Then, have the groups discuss whether the statement is a fact or opinion. Students should continue taking turns reading the selection aloud. Finally, bring the class together to discuss their overall opinions of the quality of the author's evidence.

SMALL GROUP

Summary ⬆ *above grade level*

Uther Pendragon, high king of Britain, gives up his firstborn son, Arthur, to the sorcerer Merlin, who gives the child to Sir Ector to raise. After Uther's death plunges Britain into chaos for sixteen years, Merlin decides it is finally time for Arthur to become king. The magician inserts a sword in an anvil on top of a block of white marble and places this sword in a stone in a London churchyard. An engraving says that whoever pulls the sword from the anvil is the rightful king of England. Sir Ector, his son Sir Kay, and Arthur travel to London to attend a festival. When Arthur can't find Sir Kay's sword for a tournament, he "borrows" the one stuck in the anvil. Upon learning of this feat, Sir Ector has Arthur return the sword to the anvil. The next day at a contest, no one can pull the sword from the anvil. Then Merlin presents Arthur, who once again easily dislodges the sword. Because of opposition from other lords, Arthur must do this several more times before being crowned high king.

Before You Read   The Legend

King Arthur: The Sword in the Stone

Make the Connection
Quickwrite 🖉

Some people living today could be so famous that stories about them will be made up and told for years. Think about the qualities that might turn someone into a legend. Write down the names and deeds of some people who could be legends a hundred years from now.

Literary Focus
Legend: A Little Fact, a Lot of Story

A **legend** is a very old story, passed down from one generation to the next, which usually has some connection to a real historical person or event. Legends combine historical facts with made-up events, which are often fantastic. Perhaps

Vocabulary Development

Preview these words from the story:

turbulent (tur′byə·lənt) *adj.*: wild; disorderly. *King Arthur restored peace to a turbulent land.*

tournament (toor′nə·mənt) *n.*: series of contests. *Sir Kay hoped to show his bravery during the tournament.*

integrity (in·teg′rə·tē) *n.*: honesty; uprightness. *A knight's integrity kept him from wrongdoing.*

congregation (käŋ′grə·gā′shən) *n.*: gathering. *The king spoke to a congregation of villagers.*

the most famous hero of legend in Western literature is the king called Arthur.

INTERNET

Vocabulary Activity

Keyword: LE5 7-7

SKILLS FOCUS

Literary Skills
Understand legends.

Background
Literature and Social Studies

The hero behind the legend of King Arthur probably lived about 500 A.D. The real Arthur is believed to have been a military leader of people called the Britons.

In the first century B.C., the Romans invaded Britain and they ruled for about four hundred years. After the armies of Rome pulled out of England in 410 A.D., several peoples tried to seize control. According to the earliest legends, a leader named Arthur united the Britons and led them to victory against one of those invading peoples, the Saxons.

After Arthur's death the Saxons and the Angles, another people, conquered the Britons, but stories about the warrior king's unusual courage and goodness lived on among his people.

For hundreds of years, minstrels traveled from castle to castle throughout Europe, singing stories about Arthur. The legend became a series of stories about noble knights who rode out to do battle with evil wherever they found it.

Perhaps Arthur continues to live in the imagination because he represents the leader who will return someday, in time of darkness and need, to save his people.

RESOURCES: READING

Planning
■ *One-Stop Planner* CD-ROM with ExamView Test Generator

Differentiating Instruction
■ *The Holt Reader*
■ *Holt Reading Solutions*
■ *Supporting Instruction in Spanish*
■ *Audio CD Library*

■ *Audio CD Library, Selections and Summaries in Spanish*

Vocabulary
■ *Vocabulary Development*

Grammar and Language
■ *Daily Language Activities*

Assessment
■ *Holt Assessment: Literature, Reading, and Vocabulary*

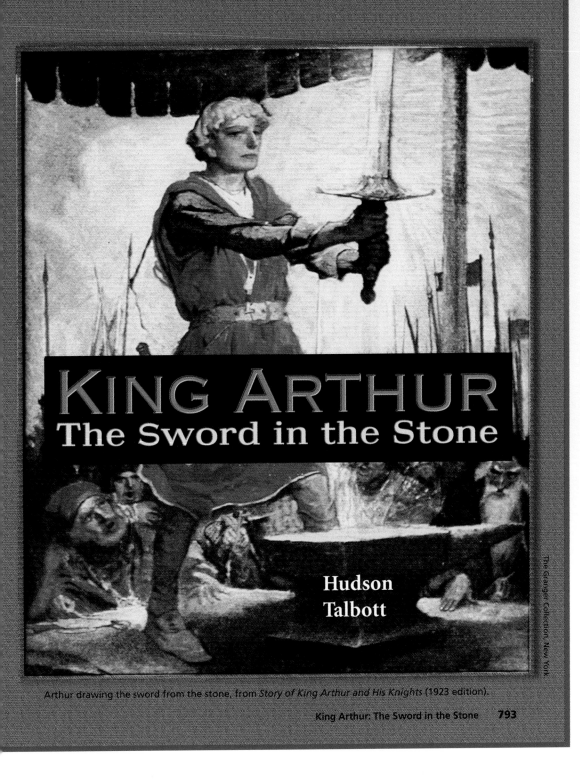

KING ARTHUR
The Sword in the Stone

Hudson
Talbott

The Granger Collection, New York.

Arthur drawing the sword from the stone, from *Story of King Arthur and His Knights* (1923 edition).

King Arthur: The Sword in the Stone **793**

Selection Starter

Motivate. Ask students what they think of when they hear the name King Arthur. Can they recall some other names associated with his legend? Some may have seen the Disney video of *The Sword in the Stone*. Tell them that they are going to read a story about Arthur as a teenager. Then, ask them to predict what this legendary figure might have been like as a young man. After the discussion, have students complete the Quickwrite.

Preview Vocabulary

To help students master the Vocabulary words on p. 792, have them write their responses to the following questions. (Possible responses are given.)

1. What would you do if you saw a turbulent crowd headed toward you? [I would walk in the opposite direction.]

2. At what kind of modern tournament might you see kings, queens, knights, and bishops? [at a chess tournament]

3. If a person with integrity found a wallet containing two hundred dollars, what would she do? [She would return it to the owner.]

4. Where in your community would you expect to see a congregation of students? [at a basketball game]

Assign the Reading

You might wish to read the first five paragraphs aloud to students, up to the point when the great dragon appears in the sky. Advanced students can continue reading on their own and do the After You Read activities for homework while you continue to work with small groups of readers having difficulty.

HOMEWORK

- *One-Stop Planner* CD-ROM with ExamView Test Generator
- *Holt Online Assessment*

Internet
- go.hrw.com (Keyword: LE5 7-7)
- *Elements of Literature Online*

Media
- *Audio CD Library*
- *Audio CD Library, Selections and Summaries in Spanish*
- *Fine Art Transparencies*

A Literary Focus

❓ Legend. Point out that a character who is a sorcerer is probably not based on historic fact. Which parts of this story could have a basis in reality? [Possible responses: A king might have chosen a trusted advisor to act as a go-between and help him win the hand of his dead enemy's wife. A king might have agreed to have his son raised by others to keep him from harm.]

B Cross-curricular Connections
SCIENCE

Constellation. The reference here is probably to the constellation known as Draco, the dragon. It includes the North Star.

C Reading Skills

Retell. [Possible response to question 1: Merlin agrees to help Uther secure the hand of Lady Igraine, for which Uther agrees to give Merlin their firstborn son.]

The Granger Collection, New York.

Medieval knight on horseback.

I n ancient times, when Britain was still a wild and restless place, there lived a noble king named Uther.[1] After many years of turmoil, Uther defeated the invading barbarians and drove them from the land. For this triumph, his fellow British lords proclaimed him their high king, or Pendragon, meaning "Dragon's Head."

Soon after his coronation,[2] Uther Pendragon met and fell in love with the beautiful Lady Igraine,[3] a widow whose husband Uther had killed in battle. Uther married Igraine and adopted her two young daughters, Margaise[4] and Morgan le Fay. The price for this love was a high one, however. In his passion, the king had asked for the help of his sorcerer, Merlin, in winning the hand of Lady Igraine. In return Uther had agreed to give up their firstborn son. Merlin had foreseen great evil descending upon the king and felt that he alone could protect a young heir in the dangerous times ahead.

Before long, a beautiful boy child was born. But the joy surrounding the birth was brief, for Merlin soon appeared to take the child away.

"But the child was just born!" exclaimed Uther. "How did you find out so quickly?"

Silently, the old sorcerer led the king to a balcony and pointed upward. There overhead was a great dragon formed by the stars. Its vast wings arched over the countryside, and its tail swept north beyond the horizon. "You see by this sign, my lord, that it is not I who calls for your son, but destiny."

Sadly, the king gave up his son, for Merlin convinced him that the child's great future was threatened. Indeed, Uther Pendragon died within a year from a traitor's poison and Britain was once again plunged into darkness. ❶ 📖

After the death of the high king, the struggle for leadership tore Britain to pieces. The great alliance King Uther had forged was shattered into dozens of quarreling, petty kingdoms—leaving no united force to oppose foreign invasion. Barbarians swept in once again and order gave way to chaos. Marauding knights roamed the countryside, taking what they wanted and burning the rest. No one was safe at home, and travel was even more dangerous, with outlaws ruling the roads. Fear was a constant companion of those who managed to stay alive.

After sixteen turbulent years, the archbishop of Canterbury[5] summoned Merlin

📖 RETELL

❶ What deals are made between Uther and Merlin?

---

1. **Uther** (yo͞o′thər).
2. **coronation** *n.:* ceremony for crowning a king or a queen.
3. **Igraine** (ē·grān′).
4. **Margaise** (mär·gāz′).

5. **archbishop of Canterbury:** even today, the highest-ranking bishop of the Church of England.

Vocabulary
turbulent (tur′byə·lənt) *adj.:* wild; disorderly.

Learners Having Difficulty
Invite learners having difficulty to read *King Arthur: The Sword in the Stone* in interactive format in *The Holt Reader* and to use the sidenotes as aids to understanding the selection. The interactive version provides additional instruction, practice, and assessment of the literary skill taught in the Student Edition. Monitor students' responses to the selection, and correct any misconceptions that arise.

English-Language Learners
Introduce students to these words from the world of knights: *knight, squire, jousting, lance, charger, armor, tourney.* Also, make sure they know what an anvil is. If possible, show them pictures of knights in battle that illustrate some of these words, as well as the words *chain mail, halberd, mace,* and *bludgeon,* which are defined in footnotes.

Merlin the Magician (1903) by Howard Pyle.
The Granger Collection, New York.

to help restore order. Although the two men were of different faiths, they had great respect for each other and shared much wisdom between them.

"I am at a loss, Sir Wizard!" confided the archbishop. "I don't know how to help the people, and they are suffering more each day. If only Uther Pendragon were here!"

"I share your concerns, my lord, but I have good news," said Merlin. "Although the end of King Uther's reign left us in the dark for many years, it is at last time for the sun to return to Britain. A brilliant sun, my lord. Perhaps the brightest that Britain will ever know."

"But the sun was out this morning, sire," said the archbishop. "What has the weather to do with this?"

"I speak of the son of Uther Pendragon, the true heir of royal blood who lives in a distant land and must now be summoned forth to keep his date with destiny."

"His date with who?" asked the archbishop. "But the king had no heirs! Alas, that is our problem!"

"I wish to prove otherwise, my lord," replied Merlin. "If I have your leave to use my magic, I shall create an event to bring forth this young heir and prove to the world that he is the true and rightful **D** high king of Britain."

The delighted archbishop agreed immediately, and Merlin withdrew to devise his scheme. ❷ 📖

On a Sunday morning in late November the great cathedral of London was filled to capacity. As Mass was being said, a sudden murmur rippled through the crowd on the cathedral steps. Turning to see the cause of the commotion, the archbishop stopped in midprayer and walked toward the door. In the churchyard he discovered a block of white marble with an anvil sitting on top. Driven into the anvil, gleaming in the pale winter sun, was a sword. Its blade was of flawless blue-white steel, and the hilt was of highly wrought gold, inlaid with rubies, sapphires, and emeralds. Engraved in the marble block were these words:

WHOSO PULLETH OUT THIS SWORD FROM THIS STONE AND ANVIL IS RIGHTWISE KING BORN OF ENGLAND.

📖 **ANALYZE**
❷ How does Merlin use the words *sun* and *son* in his discussion with the archbishop? What does Merlin promise the archbishop?

King Arthur: The Sword in the Stone 795

A Reading Skills

Retell. [Possible response to question 3: Using his magic, Merlin has buried a beautifully wrought sword in an anvil and a block of marble. Whoever can pull the sword free from the stone and anvil will be declared king.]

Ah, so this is Merlin's plan! thought the archbishop, smiling to himself. A group of barons and knights suddenly pushed their way through the crowd, each stating loudly that he should be the first to try. A few managed to leap onto the stone and give the sword an unsuccessful yank before the archbishop stopped them.

"Order! Order!" he shouted, raising his hands to quiet the crowd. "I hereby proclaim that on Christmas morning, one month from today, all those who consider themselves worthy of attempting to pull this sword from the stone and anvil will be given the opportunity. He who wins the sword, thereby wins the kingdom." ❸

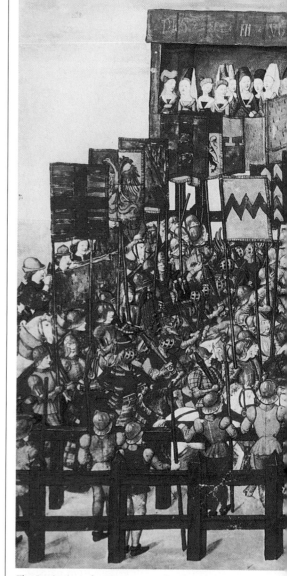

The Beginning of a Tournament, from French manuscript (14th century).
The Granger Collection, New York.

A 📖 **RETELL**
❸ What test will prove who the rightful king is?

A mighty roar of approval rose from the crowd. Some even danced and stomped their feet. Noticing how pleased they were, the archbishop went further. "And to celebrate this momentous occasion, a <u>tournament</u> shall be held on Christmas Eve."

With this, the delighted parishioners swept the flustered archbishop onto their shoulders and carried him jubilantly around the stone several times before setting him down. They hadn't had such cause for celebration in a long, long time.

To all parts of the kingdom, messengers rushed out, carrying the archbishop's proclamation.[6] Every castle and village was alerted, from Sussex to Cornwall and, finally, to the dark forest of Wales. There lived a certain gentle knight by the name of Sir Ector Bonmaison[7] with his two sons. The

---

6. **proclamation** *n.*: official public announcement.
7. **Bonmaison** (bōn′mā·zōn′): This name is French for "good house."

Vocabulary
tournament (tʊr′nə·mənt) *n.*: series of contests.

796   Collection 7 / Literary Criticism: Where I Stand

History
The Middle Ages. The legends surrounding King Arthur are set in the High Middle Ages, the period between roughly A.D. 1000 and 1400. This was the time of feudalism, Crusades, knights, and chivalry. However, the time of the historical Arthur, sometimes called the Dark Ages or the Early Middle Ages (roughly A.D. 500–1000), was a period of frequent warfare. Urban life all but disappeared. In England, it was the time of the Anglo-Saxon invasion.

Though frequently portrayed as barbarians, the Anglo-Saxons possessed a complex culture. Archaeological digs at their burial mounds at Sutton Hoo have yielded such skillfully wrought treasures as scepters, swords, shields, and rings. Anglo-Saxon culture also produced scholars (the Venerable Bede) and poets (the *Beowulf* poet).

elder was a handsome, robust youth, recently knighted and now known as Sir Kay. The younger was a gentle blond lad of about sixteen whom Sir Ector and his wife had adopted as an infant. His name was Arthur.

Although Arthur was not of his blood, Sir Ector loved both sons equally and devoted himself to their upbringing. ❹

📖 INFER

❹ Who do you guess this adopted son is?

B

King Arthur: The Sword in the Stone   **797**

Still, warfare was the dominant activity, and loyalty to leaders was a virtue. Anglo-Saxon families lived in dwellings built around a courtyard or a chieftain's hall. For security, a fence surrounded all of the buildings. This living arrangement strengthened the bonds between leader and followers.

Activity. Have groups of students research the differences between Anglo-Saxon

England and the High Middle Ages described in this legend.

SMALL GROUP

B Reading Skills

Infer. [Possible response to question 4: Because Arthur is adopted and the sound of his name is similar to that of the deceased king (Uther), it is likely that Arthur is really King Uther's son.]

VIEWING THE ART

Manuscript illumination. Prior to the invention of the printing press around 1450–1455, books were produced manually by highly skilled artisans.

The process began with the preparation of parchment, or vellum, made of specially treated animal skin. Trained scribes handwrote the text onto the vellum in calligraphy, or stylized and ornamental lettering.

Next, artists painstakingly decorated the text with hand-applied pigments and gold or silver. (The term *illuminated manuscript* owes its name to these reflective metals, which catch the light and cause the page to seem illuminated.) Artists usually specialized in one of three areas of illumination: *miniatures, initial letters,* and *borders.* Miniatures are tiny scenes painted in the margins of texts or larger ones filling entire pages, such as the tournament scene shown at left. Initial letters are the embellished, oversized first letters of text passages, elaborately decorated and often including tiny figures or even narrative scenes. Borders are fanciful decorative motifs that adorn the margins of manuscripts.

Activity. Supply felt-tipped calligraphy pens, wide-ruled paper, and colored pencils, and divide students into small groups. Help each group decide who will be their scribe and who will create the artwork. Then, have each group choose a short dramatic passage from *King Arthur: The Sword in the Stone* and create their own illuminated manuscript page.

? Characterization. What qualities of the young Arthur are described here? [Possible response: He is dutiful and humble, and he has a strong attachment to animals.] Are these qualities promising ones for a future hero? [Possible responses: Yes, a hero needs to attend to responsibilities and not be excessively proud. No, a hero should command others and be proud of himself.]

B Reading Skills

Compare and contrast. [Possible response to question 5: Sir Kay is excited about the tournament and the prospect of proving himself as a knight. He is ambitious and somewhat arrogant. Although Arthur has thought about riding alongside Sir Kay in battle, he is more modest and content to serve as Sir Kay's squire.]

C Literary Focus

? Plot. Arthur has not heard about the contest. Is this lack of knowledge a realistic plot device? [Possible responses: Yes, it is realistic that he hasn't heard about it because Sir Kay is not interested in the contest, and they left in a hurry. No, it is not realistic because Kay and Ector certainly would have talked about the reason for the tournament.]

Sir Kay was the first to hear the news of the great events in London, for as usual, he was in the courtyard polishing his helmet when the messenger arrived.

"A tournament! At last, a tournament!" he shouted. "We must set out for London at once! Father, you know what this means to me."

"Yes, son, I do," said Sir Ector, bringing the weary messenger a bowl of food. "I was young and hotblooded once, too, and eager to show the world my worthiness of knighthood. But this sword-pulling contest—do you wish to be king, as well?" he asked Kay with a smile.

"I make no pretense about that, sir. To prove myself on the field of battle is my dream."

"Please remember that, my son," said Sir Ector. "Pursuing one's goals with integrity is all that matters. Now go find Arthur so that we may prepare to leave. London is a long way off."

(A) Arthur had wandered off alone, as he often did after finishing his chores. He was as devoted as ever to being a good squire for his brother. But, after all, Kay was *Sir* Kay now, and he rarely had anything to say to his younger brother except to bark orders at him. Arthur didn't mind, though. He was happy just to watch Kay practice his jousting and to dream of someday riding beside him in battle. In the meantime, he had to content himself with his other companions—Lionel and Jasper, his dogs; Cosmo, his falcon; the orphaned fox cubs he kept hidden in the hollow log; and the deer that came to the edge of the woods when he whistled. He was in the woods now, patiently holding out a handful of oats for the deer, when Kay came bounding through the meadows to find him.

"Arthur, come quickly!" he shouted. "We're leaving for London at once! There's a big tournament. Here's your chance to show me what a good squire you can be! Hurry!"

Arthur stood silently for a moment. He had never been more than a few miles from his home. Was he daydreaming? Or was he really going to London to help Sir Kay bring honor and glory to their family as the whole world looked on? He ran back home, doubting his own ears until he reached the courtyard and saw Sir Ector preparing their horses for the journey. **⑤**

All of Britain seemed to be making its way to London Town that Christmas. Kings and dukes, earls and barons, counts and countesses funneled into the city gates for the great contest. Sir Ector was pleased to see old friends and fellow knights. Sir Kay was eager to register for the jousting. And Arthur was simply dazzled by it all.

(C) As Sir Ector and his sons made their way through the city streets, a glint of sunlight on steel caught Arthur's eye. How odd, he thought. A sword thrust point first into an anvil on top of a block of marble, sitting in a churchyard—surrounded by guards! London is so full of wonders!

Dawn arrived with a blare of trumpets, calling all contestants to the tournament. In Sir Ector's tent, Arthur buckled the

> **COMPARE AND CONTRAST**
> **⑤** Now you've **(B)** met Arthur and his brother, Kay. How are they different from each other?

Vocabulary
integrity (in·teg′rə·tē) *n.*: honesty; uprightness.

DEVELOPING FLUENCY

Activity. The story of young Arthur appeals to all ages. Invite a class from a nearby elementary school for a read-aloud session. Have groups of three or four of your students take turns reading the story aloud to small groups of younger students. Then, have the groups discuss what they think of various characters, including Arthur, Kay, Ector, Merlin, and Urien and Lot.

CROSS AGE

chain mail[8] onto Sir Kay and slipped the tunic of the Bonmaison colors over his brother's head. Sir Ector stood and watched until the preparation was complete and his son stood before him in all his knightly glory. Silently they embraced, mounted their horses, and headed for the tournament grounds.

The stadium for the event was the grandest ever built. Never had there been such a huge <u>congregation</u> of lords and ladies in the history of England. The stands surrounded a great meadow, swept clean of all snow, with the combatants' tents at either end. In the central place of honor sat the archbishop. Patiently, he greeted each king and noble as they came forth to kiss his hand. "I should do this more often," he chuckled to himself.

The first event was the mock battle, or *mêlée*. The contestants were divided into two teams—the Reds and the Greens. Sir Kay was with the Reds, who gathered at the southern end of the field, while their opponents took the north. They all readied their lances and brought down their helmet visors in anticipation of combat. Everyone looked to the archbishop for a signal. Slowly, he raised his handkerchief, paused, and let it flutter to the ground. From either end of the field, the thunder of thousands of horse hooves rolled forward, shaking the earth, rattling the stands—louder and louder until a terrifying crash of metal split the air. A shower of splintered lances rained down in all directions. The audience gasped, and a few ladies fainted. Nothing had prepared them for this scale of violence.

D

Illustration from a 14th-century German manuscript.
The Granger Collection, New York.

Sir Kay performed admirably, for he charged ahead of his teammates and unseated two of the Greens. He was already winning accolades[9] as he wheeled his charger around to aid a fellow Red.

As the teams withdrew, they revealed a battleground strewn with fallen warriors, some struggling to rise under the weight of their armor, others lying ominously still. Bits and pieces of armor and broken lances littered the field.

E

---

9. **accolades** *n.:* words of praise.

Vocabulary
congregation (käŋ′grə·gā′shən) *n.:* gathering.

---

8. **chain mail** *n.:* flexible armor made of thousands of tiny metal links.

D **Vocabulary Development**
Latin and Anglo-Saxon roots. Tell students that *combatants* comes from the same Latin root as *combat.* Ask students to consult a dictionary to find a synonym for *combatants* that has an Anglo-Saxon root. [fighters]

E **Reading Skills**

? **Respond to literature.** The violent combat of mock battle was a form of sport as well as training for warfare. Armed combat is no longer viewed as sport. How are sports in our society today like the mock battles of medieval times? [Possible responses: In sports today, such as football, two teams line up against each other and clash on the field. Players may be injured. Audiences cheer on the teams and thrill at the sight of aggressive conflicts viewed from a safe distance.]

MINI-LESSON **Reading**

Developing Word-Attack Skills
To explore silent letters, write these words from the selection on the chalkboard. Have a volunteer read the words aloud and underline the consonant letter whose sound is not heard.

sword	[*w* is silent]
heir	[*h* is silent]
dumbstruck	[*b* is silent]
solemnly	[*n* is silent]
knights	[*k* is silent]

Write these sentences on the chalkboard. Have volunteers read them aloud and identify in each sentence the word with a silent letter.
1. The candidates formed a column. [column]
2. Arthur answered the challenge. [answered]
3. Merlin knew who Arthur was. [knew]
4. When all had failed, Arthur climbed onto the block. [climbed]
5. His claim to the throne was honest. [honest]

Activity. Have students identify the word in each set in which the underlined letter is silent. Answers are checked.

1.	knowledge√	humankind	frankness
2.	crumble	humbly	numbness√
3.	solemnity	autumn√	grimness
4.	forsworn	swelter	answer√
5.	lumber	plumber√	cumbersome

A Reading Skills

Analyze. Make sure students understand the significance of Arthur's actions by having them look back in the text to find what is written on the stone.

[Possible response to question 6: The engraving on the marble block states that anyone who pulls the sword from the stone will become the rightful king of Britain. Arthur has done just that, but he doesn't yet realize how significant his action is.]

The next charge was to be undertaken with swords. Sir Kay was appointed captain of his team for having done so well in the first round. He trotted over to Arthur and handed down his lance.

"Kay! You were magnificent!" gushed Arthur, wiping down the steaming war horse. "You've brought great honor to our house this day!"

"I need my sword, Arthur," said Sir Kay, struggling to take his helmet off.

"Your sword, of course!" said Arthur brightly. He turned to get it, but then stopped suddenly. Where was the sword? His eyes scanned the little tent with its collection of weaponry. Spear, halberd, mace, bludgeon[10] . . . but no sword.

"Excuse me, Kay," said Arthur, "could you use a battle axe?"

"Arthur, please! My sword!" said Sir Kay. "We haven't much time."

"Of course, Kay! But just a moment—I'll finish polishing it," said Arthur, slipping out through the slit in their tent. With one great leap, he landed on his pony's back and galloped madly through the deserted streets, rushing back to their camp.

"Sword. Sword. Where did I put that *sword*?" he muttered, desperately searching through the chests and bags. But to no avail.

How could this happen? he thought. Kay without a sword . . . and the whole world watching!

He paced back and forth, and then a thought struck him: Kay will not be without a sword today. I know where I can get one!

A few minutes later, he trotted into the churchyard where the sword in the anvil stood on the marble block. There wasn't a guard in sight—even they had gone to the tourney. Quietly, he brought his pony up to the stone and tugged on the reins.

"OK, Blaze. . . . We'll just see if this sword can be unstuck," he whispered. He stretched out his arm until his fingers touched the hilt.

"Hey, it's looser than I thought. . . . Steady, Blaze! Steady, boy!" As the pony stepped back a few paces, the sword glided out of the anvil's grip, unbalancing Arthur. He regained his seat and looked down in wonder at the mighty blade in his hand. 6 📖

ANALYZE

6 Remember Merlin's test. What is the significance of what has just happened?

"This isn't just *any* sword. . . . Perhaps it's something the church provides for needy strangers. Yes, that must be it! Well, I'll return it after the tournament. Someone else may need it. Thank you, sword, for saving me," he said, pressing its cross to his lips. "Wait until Kay sees this!"

He flung his cloak around the great sword and drove his little horse back to the tournament with lightning speed.

By now, Sir Kay had dismounted and was rather chafed.[11]

"Arthur, where have you been?" he shouted. "You . . ."

He caught himself as Arthur dropped to one knee and opened the cloak.

"Your sword, my lord," Arthur said confidently. But his smile quickly disappeared when he saw Sir Kay's reaction. Frozen in place, his face white as milk, Sir Kay stared at the sword. Finally, he spoke.

---

10. **halberd** (hal′bərd), **mace** (mās), **bludgeon** (bluj′ən): weapons.

11. **chafed** (chāft) *v.* used as *adj.*: annoyed.

CROSS-CURRICULAR CONNECTIONS

History

Tournaments and jousting. In medieval times, tournaments were celebrated occasions on which knights fought one another to display their skill and courage to their king. Early medieval tournaments consisted of melees—mock battles between two bodies of armed horsemen—but in the fifteenth century the joust superseded the melee. Jousting was also a mock form of battle, but it involved two mounted knights charging each other with leveled lances, each attempting to unhorse the other. Although jousting was considered a mock form of combat, it was still extremely dangerous and fell out of favor in the sixteenth century. It was replaced by tilting, in which a horseman rides at full gallop and attempts to insert his lance through small suspended metal rings.

Activity. Point out to students that even though jousting has slipped in popularity since medieval times, it is far from a dead sport and is, in fact, the state sport of Maryland. Lead the class in a discussion of where they might encounter jousting in the modern world. Some students may have seen the film *A Knight's Tale*, and others may have seen tilting or jousting exhibitions at medieval or renaissance fairs.

WHOLE CLASS

"Where did you get this?" he asked Arthur, although he knew the answer.

Arthur confessed that he had searched in vain for Sir Kay's sword and had borrowed this one instead.

"Get Father at once, and tell no one of this!" said Sir Kay sternly.

Arthur thought he must be in terrible trouble. Surely he could return the sword without his father knowing. Why did Father have to be told? Nevertheless, he obeyed his brother and returned quickly with Sir Ector.

Sir Kay closed the curtains of the tent and opened the cloak, revealing the sword to his father.

Sir Ector gasped when he saw it. "How can this be?"

"Father, I am in possession of this sword," said Sir Kay nervously. "That is what matters. Therefore, I must be king of all Britain."

"But how came you by it, son?" asked Sir Ector.

"Well, sire, I needed a sword . . . and we couldn't find mine . . . so, I decided to use this one!" said Sir Kay. Beads of sweat formed on his brow.

"Very well, lad. You drew it out of the stone. I want to see you put it back. Let's go," said Sir Ector.

"But *I have the sword*!" said Sir Kay. "Isn't that enough?"

"No," replied Sir Ector, as he mounted his horse and headed toward the cathedral. Arthur rode close behind and, ever so slowly, Sir Kay mounted and followed.

The churchyard was still deserted when the three arrived. "Put the sword back in the anvil," said Sir Ector bluntly. "I must see it."

"Father, I . . ."

"Just do it, Kay, and you shall be king. If that's what you want." Sir Kay climbed onto the block. Sweat was now pouring off him. He raised the mighty sword over his head and plunged it downward. But the sharp point skidded across the surface of the anvil, causing Sir Kay to fall headfirst off the block.

"Now, son, tell me. How came you by this sword?" asked Sir Ector again.

"Arthur brought it to me," said Sir Kay, dusting himself off. "He *lost* my other one."

Suddenly a fear gripped Sir Ector's heart. "Arthur, my boy," he said quietly, "will you try it for us?"

"Certainly, Father," said Arthur, "but do we have to tell anyone about this? Can't we just . . ."

"Son, please," said Sir Ector solemnly. "If you can put the sword in that anvil, please do so now."

With a pounding heart, the lad took the sword from Sir Kay's hand and climbed slowly onto the block of marble. Raising it with both hands over his head, he thrust it downward, through the anvil, burying the point deep within the stone. Effortlessly he pulled it out again, glanced at his stunned father, and shoved the sword into the stone, even deeper this time.

Sir Ector shrieked and sank to his knees. His mouth moved, but no words came out. He put his hands together as in prayer. Silently, Sir Kay knelt and did the same.

"Father! What are you doing?" cried Arthur, leaping down from the stone. "Please! Get up! Get up! I don't understand!"

"Now I know!" sputtered Sir Ector, choking back tears. "Now I know who you are!" 7

INFER

7 What does Sir Ector now know about his adopted son?

B **Literary Focus**

? **Characterization.** What do you learn about Sir Kay from his actions? [He is not above stretching the truth to get something he wants.] How does his behavior affect your appreciation of the story? [Possible responses: By adding conflict, it makes the story more interesting. Sir Kay's behavior contrasts, or serves as a foil for, Arthur's behavior.]

C **Reading Skills**

? **Speculate.** Why might Sir Ector be fearful? [Possible responses: If Arthur is the rightful king, their quiet lives will change greatly. He may fear that he will lose the affection of his adopted son. He may fear that danger lies ahead for Arthur, whom he loves.]

D **Reading Skills**

Infer. [Possible response to question 7: Sir Ector now knows that Arthur is the son of King Uther Pendragon and Lady Igraine.]

A Literary Focus

? **Characterization.** How is Arthur's behavior consistent with what you have learned about his character so far? [Possible response: In the past he has shown himself to be humble and content with his life as a younger son. His behavior is consistent because he still values his family and does not seek glory.]

B Advanced Learners

? **Acceleration.** Since little is known of the historical figure on whom the Arthur legend is based, the characteristics attributed to Arthur must reflect the values of the storytellers who created the legend. From this passage, what can you infer about those values? [Possible response: The storytellers valued humility, love of family, and a sense of duty.]

C Literary Focus

? **Theme.** What message is Merlin giving Arthur? [Only you can decide what your future will be. No outside force controls it.] Is this a meaningful message for readers today? [Possible responses: Yes, people need to be reminded to take charge of their lives. No, most people today believe they are in charge of their destiny.]

"I'm your son, Father!" said the bewildered lad, crouching down by his father and putting his head to Sir Ector's chest.

After a few deep breaths, Sir Ector regained his composure. He smiled sadly down at Arthur and stroked his head.

"Fate would have it otherwise, my boy. Look there behind you." He pointed to the gold lettering on the marble block, which stated the purpose of the sword and the anvil.

Arthur sat in silence and stared at the words in the marble.

"Although you were adopted, I've loved you like my own child, Arthur," said Sir Ector softly. "But now I realize you have the blood of kings in you. To discover your birthright is the true reason we came to London. You are now our king and we your faithful servants."

At this, Arthur broke into tears. "I don't want to be king. Not if it means losing my father!" he sobbed.

"You have a great destiny before you, Arthur. There's no use avoiding it," said Sir Ector.

Arthur wiped his eyes with his sleeve. He straightened up so he could look Sir Ector in the eyes. A few minutes passed.

"Very well," Arthur finally said slowly. "Whatever my destiny may be, I am willing to accept it. But I still need you with me."

"Then so it shall be, lad. So it shall be," said Sir Ector.

They sat quietly for a time, comforting each other, until they felt another presence. From across the yard a hooded figure quietly floated into the fading light of the winter afternoon and knelt down beside them.

"Merlin," said Sir Ector, bowing his head to the famous enchanter.

"I've been waiting for you, Arthur," said the wizard.

"You know me, my lord?" asked Arthur.

"I put you in this good man's care many years ago and have kept an eye on you ever since."

"How did you do that, sire? We live far from here."

"Oh, I have my ways," replied Merlin. "But you still managed to surprise me. The sword-pulling contest isn't until tomorrow, and you pulled it out today!" he said with a chuckle.

"But what is to become of me now?" asked Arthur.

"Well, let us start with tomorrow," replied the old sorcerer. "We must still have the contest to prove to the world that you are the rightful heir. I will come for you when the time is right."

"But after that, sire, what is my future?" asked the boy.

Merlin weighed this question carefully. He wasn't at all sure whether the boy was prepared for his answer. Finally, he spoke. "I can tell you only what my powers suggest—and they point to greatness. Greatness surrounds you like a golden cloak. Your achievements could inspire humankind for centuries to come. But you alone can fulfill this destiny and then only if you wish it. You own your future. You alone."

Arthur breathed deeply and cast his eyes downward. He thought of all the goodbyes he would have to say. He thought of his fishing hole, and the birds that ate seeds from his hand. He thought of the deer that came when he called them.

"What time tomorrow, sire?" he asked.

"After all have tried and failed, whenever that may be," replied Merlin.

Morgan le Fay, Queen of Avalon by Anthony Frederick Augustus Sandys (1829–1904).

"I will be ready, sire," said Arthur. Then he rose, bade Merlin farewell, and silently returned to his tent.

On Christmas morning, the archbishop said Mass for the largest gathering he had seen in years. The grounds surrounding the cathedral were also filled—with those seeking to make history or watch it being made.

As soon as the service ended, those who wished to try for the throne formed a line next to the marble block.

Leading the line was King Urien of Gore, husband to Margaise, Uther Pendragon's adoptive daughter. Ever since the high king's death, Urien had claimed loudly that he was the rightful heir. Indeed, he took his position on the marble block with a great sense of authority and gave the sword a confident tug, then another, and another. Urien was sweating and yanking furiously when finally asked to step down.

Next came King Lot of Orkney, husband to Morgan le Fay. King Lot felt certain that his wife's magical powers would assure his victory. But pull and tug as he might, he couldn't move the sword. After that, King Mark of Cornwall, King Leodegrance of Cameliard, and King Ryence of North Wales all took their place on the stone—and failed. The dukes of Winchester, Colchester, Worcester, and Hamcester did not fare any better. Some thought the longer they waited, the looser the sword would become, thereby improving their chances. But this wasn't the case, for the sword never budged, not even slightly. Kings, dukes, earls, counts, and knights all left that marble block empty-handed. Finally, as the day waned and the line neared its end, the crowd grew impatient for a winner. Merlin went for Arthur. 8

📖 **INFER**

8 How are all these men who try to pull the sword out of the anvil different from Arthur?

Sir Ector and Sir Kay opened the curtains of their tent when they saw Merlin approaching.

"Your hour has come, my lord," said the old wizard to Arthur, who was standing

King Arthur: The Sword in the Stone **803**

DIRECT TEACHING

D **Reading Skills**

❓ **Compare and contrast.**
Compare and contrast the attitudes of Urien and Lot with that of Arthur. [Possible response: All three are confident that they can do the deed. Urien and Lot feel they deserve the kingship, which Arthur does not.] What theme does the contrast suggest? [Possible response: The best person for a job may not be the one who wants it the most.]

E **Reading Skills**

Infer. [Possible responses to question 8: The men who attempt to pull the sword from the stone are ambitious—they all want to be the next king of Britain. Arthur does not. Their titles suggest that they are royalty or part of the ruling class. Arthur is merely a squire. They all seem to be grown men with experience. Arthur is only sixteen years old.]

VIEWING THE ART

Frederick Sandys (1829–1904) was both a painter and a highly regarded book illustrator. Critics always noted Sandys's skilled draftsmanship and his penchant for choosing as his subjects *femmes fatales*, or alluring but dangerous women.

Morgan le Fay, Arthur's sister, appears throughout the Arthurian romances in a number of varied roles. Sometimes she is a fairy enchantress and ruler of Avalon, the island Arthur would retire to, where Morgan would tend to his wounds. Other versions represent her as a malevolent troublemaker, bent on stirring up conflict between Arthur and his queen, Guinevere.

Activity. Ask students to study the painting and discuss whether Morgan le Fay appears hostile or benevolent. Do they think she might qualify as a *femme fatale*?

The ruling class. The concept that all human beings are equal is a relatively recent one. At the time when this story takes place, only those of noble birth were considered fit to rule. Thus, this contest is not open to everyone, but only to those with credentials.

B Literary Focus

? Legend. In legends and hero tales, the hero must often perform three difficult tasks before winning the prize. In this story, Arthur performs the same deed three times. How is each time different? [The first time, he is alone and unaware of what he has done. The second time, he becomes aware of his feat. The third time, he is publicly acknowledged.]

---

alone in the center of the tent. Silently, the boy walked forth as one in a dream.

The crowd made way for them as they entered, for Merlin was still revered by all. But who could these other people be? Especially that young blond lad dressed all in red. What was he doing here?

Merlin brought Arthur before the archbishop and bowed deeply. Arthur dropped to one knee.

"My lord," said Merlin, "I present to you a most worthy candidate for this contest. Has he your permission to attempt to pull yonder sword from the stone?"

The archbishop gazed down at the handsome lad. "Merlin, we are not familiar with this youth, nor with his credentials. By what right does he come to this place?"

"By the greatest right, my lord," said Merlin. "For this is the trueborn son of King Uther Pendragon and Queen Igraine."

The crowd broke into a loud clamor at hearing this. The startled archbishop raised his hands, but order was not easily restored.

"Merlin, have you proof of this?" asked the archbishop.

"With your permission, sire," blurted Arthur suddenly, "perhaps I can prove it by handling yonder sword in the anvil."

"Very well then, lad," said the archbishop, admiring Arthur's youthful boldness. "You have my permission. If what Merlin says is true, may God be with you."

Arthur rose and stepped up onto the marble block. He grabbed hold of the mighty golden hilt with both hands. A surge of sparkling warmth traveled up his arms, across his shoulders, and throughout his body. With one mighty tug, he freed the sword from the anvil and lifted it heavenward. The blade flashed like lightning as he

swung it around his head for all to see. Then, turning the point downward again, he drove it back into the anvil with equal ease.

The entire gathering stood dumbstruck for a long moment, trying to comprehend what they had just seen. Arthur looked about for reassurance. He looked to Sir Ector, then Merlin, and then the archbishop. They all simply stared at him, with eyes wide in amazement. A child giggled and clapped his hands in glee, then so did another, and another. Cheers began to ring out as people found their voices again. Suddenly, a thunder of shouting and clapping rose up around Arthur. Amidst the tumult, he closed his eyes and whispered, "Thank you, Father."

Then he grabbed the sword's hilt for a second time and withdrew it. As he brought it above his head, a thousand swords throughout the crowd were raised in solidarity.[12] Arthur drove the sword back into the anvil and pulled it out once again. This time, as he lifted the great blade to the sky, more swords and halberds were raised, along with brooms, rakes, and walking sticks, as counts and common folk alike saluted their newfound king.

Not everyone was overjoyed at this turn of events, however. Although all had seen the miracle performed, several kings and dukes were unwilling to recognize Arthur's right to the throne. Loudest among the grumblers were King Lot and King Urien, Arthur's brothers-in-law. "How dare this

---

12. **solidarity** (säl′ə·dar′ə·tē) *n.:* unity among a group.

(Opposite) *Arthur Drawing Forth the Sword* (1903) by Howard Pyle.
The Granger Collection, New York.

VIEWING THE ART

Howard Pyle (1853–1911) was one of the foremost book illustrators of his day, as well as an influential teacher, painter, and writer. He wrote and illustrated a number of books, including a four-volume work of Arthurian legends, in which this image first appeared. Much of Pyle's work, like *Arthur Drawing Forth the Sword*, is done in a sedate, traditional pen-and-ink style that harked back to the wood engravings that were popular during his childhood. Yet Pyle, along with artists such as William Morris, N. C. Wyeth, and Maxfield Parrish, helped revolutionize book illustration at the turn of the century. Whereas nineteenth-century illustrations for adventure stories had been almost uniformly flat, two-dimensional, and woodenly staged, Pyle and others used innovative styles and vivid depictions of characters in action.

Activity. Encourage interested students to enter into a search engine the names of any of the above-mentioned artists, as well as the terms *Arts and Crafts movement* and *Brandywine school*, to learn more about turn-of-the-century book illustration.

Predict. [Possible response to question 9: King Lot and King Urien may try to stir unrest among those who do not yet know of Arthur's victory. They may try to overthrow Arthur by waging war on him.]

B Literary Focus

Legend. As legends are passed on from one generation to the next, new elements are added, and the story becomes very long. Although the story of how Arthur became king ends here, the ending allows for the possibility of many further episodes.

GUIDED PRACTICE

Monitor students' progress.
Check students' comprehension by asking them to imagine that they are going to film the story. Before starting, they must write a one- or two-sentence summary of each major scene. [Possible summaries for first three scenes: *Scene 1*—Merlin takes the baby Arthur from his father, the king. *Scene 2*—Many years later, Merlin tells the archbishop of Canterbury he will devise a way to bring forth the true king. He sets a sword in an anvil on a stone that says whoever pulls out the sword is the rightful king of England. *Scene 3*—Sir Ector and his sons Kay and Arthur (who is adopted), set out for the tournament at which the sword-pulling contest will be held.]

---

beardless, unknown country boy think he can be made high king to rule over us!" they said. "Obviously, Merlin is using the boy to promote himself!"

But these malcontents[13] gained no support from those around them and were quickly shouted down. So they gathered themselves together and stormed away in a huff of indignation.[14] 9

To everyone else, the day belonged to Arthur. All the other kings and nobles rushed forth to show their acceptance, for they trusted Merlin and were grateful to have a leader at last. They hoisted the young king-to-be above their heads to parade him through the streets of London.

As the noisy procession flowed out of the churchyard, the archbishop hobbled over to Merlin to offer congratulations for a successful plan.

"Thank you, my lord, but I think we are not yet finished," said the wizard.

The archbishop looked puzzled.

"I fear that King Lot and King Urien and those other discontented souls will leave us no peace until they have another chance at the sword," continued Merlin. "We must offer them a new trial on New Year's Day."

And so they did. But again, no one could budge the sword but Arthur. These same troublesome kings and dukes still refused to acknowledge his victory, though. So another trial took place on Candlemas,[15] and yet another on Easter.

> **PREDICT**
> 9 Based on their actions here, what do you predict King Lot and King Urien will do?

---

13. **malcontents** (mal′kən·tents′) *n.*: discontented or unhappy people.
14. **indignation** *n.*: righteous anger.
15. **Candlemas** (kan′dəl·məs): church feast on February 2.

By now, the people had grown impatient, for they had believed in Arthur all along and had grown to love him. The idea of having a fresh young king inspired hope and optimism. The world suddenly felt young again.

Finally, after the trial held on Pentecost,[16] they cried out, "Enough! Arthur has proven himself five times now! We will have him for our king—and no other!"

The archbishop and Merlin agreed. There was proof beyond dispute at this point. So the coronation was set for May Day in the great cathedral of London.

Upon arriving that morning, Arthur stepped up on the block and pulled the sword from the anvil for the last time. With the blade pointing heavenward, he entered the church, walked solemnly down the central aisle, and laid the sword upon the altar. The archbishop administered the holy sacraments[17] and finally placed the crown upon Arthur's head.

Ten thousand cheers burst forth as the young king emerged from the cathedral. At Merlin's suggestion, Arthur stepped up on the marble block to speak to the people. A hush fell over the masses as he raised his hands to address them.

"People of Britain, we are now one. And so shall we remain as long as there is a breath in my body. My faith in your courage and wisdom is boundless. I ask now for your faith in me. In your trust I shall find my strength. For your good I dedicate my life. May this sword lead us to our destiny."

---

16. **Pentecost** (pen′tə·kôst′): Christian festival on the seventh Sunday after Easter, celebrating the "birthday" of the Christian Church.
17. **sacraments** *n.*: rituals instituted by the church, such as baptism, Holy Communion, and penance.

FAMILY/COMMUNITY ACTIVITY

Encourage students to retell the legend to a group of younger family members or neighbors. They might then organize the group to act out the story, adding costumes and props, if they want, and perform it for a group of adults.

Meet the Writer

Hudson Talbott

Time Traveler

The first highly successful series of books written and illustrated by **Hudson Talbott** (1949–) featured a gang of talking, time-traveling dinosaurs. *We're Back: A Dinosaur's Story,* the first of Talbott's dinosaur tales, was later adapted into a feature-length movie produced by Steven Spielberg.

Some of Talbott's readers, hoping for more humorous stories about dinosaurs, were surprised by the next subject he chose. *King Arthur: The Sword in the Stone* is the first book in his ongoing series, *Tales of King Arthur.* Before he started writing his King Arthur books, Talbott traveled through England and Wales researching the legends.

❝ Even I was surprised by what this project released in me—an untapped love of history and legend and a passion for the classics. Seemingly random occurrences in my own past—from collecting knights and horses as a child to my years in Europe wandering through castles and cathedrals—all began to make sense as they coalesced [came together] and helped inspire this work. ❞

Writing and illustrating books for young people is actually Talbott's second career. He supported himself first as an artist, freelance illustrator, and designer. He says that creating books for children feels "more rewarding, more permanent" than anything else he has done. "After all, a good children's book can have a lifetime effect on people."

For Independent Reading

If you especially enjoy paintings of war scenes, don't miss Talbott's *King Arthur and the Round Table.* It tells of Arthur's wars to unite his kingdom, his fateful meeting with Guinevere, and the gift of the Round Table. In Talbott's *Excalibur,* Arthur acquires a magical sword and begins to face the responsibilities of being king.

Meet the Writer

Even when he isn't time traveling, Hudson Talbott is often on the go. In fact, he says that travel is one of his "greatest joys—whether it's by land, sea, air—or cyberspace." Many of his books reflect this wanderlust. A trip to Amsterdam led to his book *Forging Freedom,* the true story of a boy from Amsterdam who forged official documents so Jews could escape the Nazis during World War II. *Amazon Diary* resulted from a trip into the heart of the Amazon rainforest, where Talbott and others made contact with the Stone-Age Yanomami people. Talbott posts travel diaries of his recent trips on his Web site.

For Independent Reading

- If students choose to read books about King Arthur by Hudson Talbott, ask them to compare and contrast the young Arthur in *King Arthur: The Sword in the Stone* with the mature Arthur of his other books.

- For a legend about an Anglo-Saxon hero in the period just after the historic Arthur, students might read *Beowulf: A New Telling,* by Robert Nye. In this legend, after many adventures, the hero Beowulf destroys the monster Grendel.

- Another tale of King Arthur and his knights is told in *The Sword and the Circle,* by Rosemary Sutcliff.

After You Read

First Thoughts

1. Possible answer: Yes, because it is a compelling story that combines the factual and the fantastic.

Thinking Critically

2. ■ Arthur is sent to live in an obscure place.
   ■ When Arthur is growing up, his parentage is unknown.
   ■ Merlin foresees danger for Arthur.
   ■ Arthur pulls the sword from the anvil.
   ■ Arthur is a likely person to be king by birth but unlikely to be king by his upbringing.

3. He lies about the sword, thus showing he lacks the integrity to be king.

4. He becomes self-confident and willing to assume the great responsibility of leading his people.

5. Possible answers: A king's son could have been sent away to be raised in a safer place. A king's death could have plunged a land into chaos. A sword could not be placed so that only one person could move it. A person could not pull a sword from an anvil.

Extending Interpretations

6. Comparisons should point out similarities and differences between the student's legendary hero and Arthur. Possible answers: All heroes have similar characteristics, such as courage and integrity. A society's values determine whether a hero is a warrior, an intellectual, an artist, or a politician, for example.

After You Read   Response and Analysis

First Thoughts

1. Do you think Arthur's story deserves to be a legend? Explain.

Thinking Critically

2. The chart at the lower right shows the pattern of a typical hero tale. How well does Arthur's story fit the pattern? Fill out the chart and see.

3. How does Sir Kay, Arthur's brother, show that he doesn't have what it takes to be king?

4. How does Arthur change during the story? What evidence suggests that he will be a great king?

5. **Legends** are based on historical facts. The stories become exaggerated as they are passed down from one generation to the next. List two events in this story that could have happened in real life. List two fantastic, supernatural events that could not have happened in real life.

Extending Interpretations

6. Look back at your Quickwrite notes. Compare Arthur with the future legendary hero you described. Do a society's values determine the heroes it admires, or are all heroes alike in certain ways? Explain.

WRITING

Write a Letter to Merlin

Imagine this: You're Arthur, and you've just been crowned king. You love Sir Ector and Sir Kay, but now you want to find out what happened to your father and mother. Write a letter to Merlin as if you were Arthur. What questions do you want to ask? How do you feel about the fact that you were never told you were adopted by Sir Ector? End your letter by confiding to Merlin how you feel about being king.

Reading Check

a. What does Uther agree to give Merlin in return for the sorcerer's help in getting Uther married to Lady Igraine?

b. Why does Merlin make the bargain with Uther?

c. What happens to Britain after Uther's death?

d. How does Arthur prove he is the rightful king of England?

e. How do King Lot and King Urien feel about Arthur as king?

Hero's Story	Arthur's Story
Hero is born in an obscure place.	
Hero is of unknown parentage.	
Hero is threatened as a child.	
Hero passes a test to prove he is king.	
Hero is an unlikely person to be king.	

Reading Check

a. He agrees to give Merlin his firstborn son.

b. Merlin, having foreseen danger, thinks that only he can protect the child.

c. The many kingdoms quarrel, leaving the country open to foreign invasion. No one is safe from violence.

d. He pulls the sword from the anvil.

e. They are unhappy and unwilling to recognize Arthur as king.

After You Read Vocabulary Development

Latin and Anglo-Saxon Word Origins

You've learned that, after Arthur's death, the Angles and the Saxons conquered the Britons. At that point, Anglo-Saxon words began coming into the language we now call English. Anglo-Saxon words tend to be short, one-syllable, simple words: *deer, pig, cow, man, wife, foot.* It's hard to make up an English sentence without using at least one Anglo-Saxon word. Words like *the, for, in,* and *is,* for instance, come from Anglo-Saxon.

In 1066, the Norman-French conquered Britain. Some of the longer, "fancier" words in English today tend to be words that were once French. In the opening sentence of *King Arthur: The Sword in the Stone,* you read the word *ancient,* which comes from a French word, *ancien.* Before it came into French, the root of *ancient* came from Latin, *ante,* "before." The Anglo-Saxon word meaning the same thing is a very different word: *old.*

PRACTICE

In each of the following sentences, find two words that come from Anglo-Saxon (also called Old English) and two words that come from French and Latin. You will have to use a dictionary. In most dictionaries you will find brackets, like these [ ], that show where the word comes from. For words from Anglo-Saxon, you'll find this: **[ME], [AS],** or **[OE].** For words from Latin or French, you'll find these: **[L]** and **[Fr].** One of the words you pick for each sentence should be the Word Bank word. Don't bother with place names or proper names. Write the Anglo-Saxon or Latin root of each word you choose.

1. After sixteen turbulent years the archbishop of Canterbury asked Merlin for help.
2. "And to celebrate this momentous occasion, a tournament shall be held on Christmas Eve."
3. "Pursuing one's goals with integrity is all that matters."
4. Never had there been such a huge congregation of lords and ladies.

> **Word Bank**
> turbulent
> tournament
> integrity
> congregation

The Granger Collection, New York.

King Arthur of Britain (detail) (14th century). French tapestry.

SKILLS FOCUS

Vocabulary Skills
Understand Latin and Anglo-Saxon word origins.

King Arthur: The Sword in the Stone **809**

Vocabulary Development

PRACTICE

Possible Answers

1. *Anglo-Saxon* years (*yere*), asked (*askien*); *French/Latin* turbulent (*turba*), archbishop (*archebishop*).
2. *Anglo-Saxon* this (*this*), held (*held*); *French/Latin* celebrate (*celebraten*), tournament (*tournement*).
3. *Anglo-Saxon* goals (*gol*), with (*wither*); *French/Latin* pursuing (*poursuir*), integrity (*integrite*).
4. *Anglo-Saxon* never (*nevere*), lords (*hlaford*); *French/Latin* congregation (*gregare*), huge (*ahuge*).

ASSESSING

Assessment

■ *Holt Assessment: Literature, Reading, and Vocabulary*

Grade-Level Skills

■ Literary Skills
Analyze responses to a literary work.

Review Skills

■ Literary Skills
Evaluate how the author uses various techniques (such as credible plots and settings) to influence readers' perspectives.

Summary ⟷ *at grade level*

This selection consists of three essays that respond to *King Arthur: The Sword in the Stone*. The essayists analyze the character of Arthur and answer the question "Does Arthur have the potential for greatness?"

PRETEACHING

Selection Starter

Motivate. Ask students if they have ever attended a movie with friends and then argued afterward about how good the movie was, what the roles of the characters revealed, or what the movie really meant. Point out that just as viewers have different ideas about movies, so readers respond in different ways to literature. Explain that students are now going to learn what three readers thought of Arthur in *King Arthur: The Sword and the Stone*. After reading the essays, students will decide which of these readers makes the most convincing case.

Before You Read The Essays

Three Responses to Literature

Make the Connection
Quickwrite

Have you ever done peer editing in writers' workshop groups, where you've given constructive criticism about another student's work? Make a list of the criteria you use to evaluate a partner's writing.

Literary Focus
Literary Criticism: Responding to Literature

In this lesson you will read and evaluate three responses to a literary work. The three essays answer a question about the character of Arthur in *King Arthur: The Sword in the Stone* (page 793). It will be your job to evaluate each response as if you were a teacher or a critic. How well has each writer answered the question? How well are the ideas about Arthur supported?

Analyzing a Response to Literature

A response should be focused. A focused response sticks to the topic. In this case the question asks whether or not Arthur has the potential for greatness. As you read each essay, ask yourself:

• Does it answer the question?
• Does it answer the question in a convincing way?
• Does it stick to the topic of Arthur's character?

A response must provide textual support. A supported response will offer details from the text—or from the writer's own experience—to support major ideas. Ask yourself:

• Does the writer clearly define the qualities necessary for greatness?
• Does the writer prove or disprove that Arthur has these qualities?

The most **successful responses** will offer specific, concrete examples from the text to support each main idea. An analysis of character should focus on the character's actions and words and on how other people respond to that character.

The following three essays all answer the same question about Arthur's character. The side notes with the first essay show you how well the writer responds to the question. Read the other two essays carefully to see how well they do the same.

King Arthur of Britain by Howard Pyle.
The Granger Collection, New York.

SKILLS FOCUS

Literary Skills Analyze responses to a literary work.

Three Responses to Literature

> **Question:** Does Arthur have the potential for greatness? Analyze the character of Arthur in your response.

Essay 1

In *King Arthur: The Sword in the Stone*, the writer uses important contrasts between Sir Kay and Arthur to show how Arthur is different from most youths his age. In the choices he makes and in the way he lives, Arthur shows that he is capable of greatness.

To fulfill his destiny of greatness, Arthur has to have wisdom. Although nobody sixteen years old has lived long enough to have a lot of wisdom, the writer shows us that Arthur is already gaining it. Arthur has found and protected orphaned fox cubs. He has tamed birds and deer. This requires patience and the ability to look and listen. In contrast, Kay, a more typical boy, spends most of his time polishing his helmet. Today, it would be a car, but we get the idea. How many teens today would choose to tame wild creatures for the joy of it? Arthur is unusual in a good way, a way that will bring wisdom to him.

There is a more important contrast between Arthur and Kay. Kay ignores the truth and forgets his dream when he sees a chance to be king. Before they leave for London, Kay tells his father, "To prove myself on the field of battle is my dream." Yet, when the sword falls into Kay's hand the next day, Kay forgets all of that. He sees a chance to be the king, and he tries to claim it even though he knows he didn't earn it. In contrast to Kay, Arthur thinks of others. He goes to London hoping to "help bring honor and glory to his family." He takes the sword only to meet Kay's need. He says nothing while Kay claims the kingship as his own. When he is forced to admit that he took the sword, he sees right away that being king will force him to say goodbye to many things he loves: the deer, his birds, fishing. This shows how Arthur is different from most youths. Most would see only the glory of being a king; Arthur sees past that to the sacrifices it will require. He realizes that he will never be able to live for himself only. It is a future he does not want. It is his destiny, though, and he has the courage to see that too. "Very well, whatever my destiny may be, I am willing to accept it." This combination of insight and courage also shows his potential for greatness.

A

> Answers the question directly.

> States first main idea.

> Supports main idea with examples from the text.

> Sums up main idea.

B

> States second main idea.

> Supports second main idea with examples from the text.

Assign the Reading

You may want to have students having difficulty meet in small groups to read the first essay together and then find in the essay the points raised in the side notes. Encourage students, as they read the next two essays, to determine whether each essay answers the question about Arthur's potential for greatness and supports its ideas with examples from the story.

DIRECT TEACHING

A Reading Skills

? Compare and contrast. What details does the writer use here to contrast the characters of Arthur and Kay? [Arthur has the patience to protect and tame animals, while Kay spends most of his time polishing his helmet.]

B Learners Having Difficulty

? Find details. What details does the writer use to support the idea that Arthur is willing to make sacrifices for others? [Possible responses: The writer quotes Arthur's desire to "help bring honor and glory to his family" and also explains how Arthur takes the sword only for Kay and allows Kay to claim the kingship. Finally, the writer points out that Arthur accepts the kingship even though he knows he will have to give up many things he loves in order to be king.]

Internet
- go.hrw.com (Keyword: LE5 7-7)
- *Elements of Literature Online*

Media
- *Audio CD Library*
- *Audio CD Library, Selections and Summaries in Spanish*

A Literary Focus

❓ **Analyze a response to literature.** What evidence is provided here to support the idea that Arthur is kind? [Arthur rescues and tames wild animals. He is nice to his brother Kay. He is willing to let Kay have the crown.] **Do you find this evidence convincing? Why or why not?** [Possible response: Some details are convincing, but the detail about the crown is not, because Arthur's behavior is not motivated by kindness.]

B Reading Skills

❓ **Express an opinion.** Do you agree with the writer that kindness is an important quality of a "great" leader? [Possible responses: Yes, because greatness entails more than just leadership ability and intelligence; a great leader must be a virtuous person who inspires his or her subjects. No, in order to lead effectively, a great leader must sometimes disregard the concerns of some of the people so that the majority may benefit.]

C Learners Having Difficulty

❓ **Find details.** What details does the writer give to support the idea that Arthur is honest? [Possible responses: Arthur does not lie to his father about pulling the sword out of the stone; he honestly says that he does not want to be king.]

D Literary Focus

❓ **Analyze a response to literature.** Did this essay convince you that Arthur has the potential for greatness? Which idea or detail did you find the most convincing? [Accept any responses that students can justify with details from the essay. Encourage students to use the information under "Analyzing a Response to Literature" on p. 810.]

When Arthur asks Merlin what his future will be, Merlin replies, "Greatness surrounds you like a golden cloak. Your achievements could inspire humankind for centuries to come. But you alone can fulfill this destiny and then only if you wish it. You own your future. You alone." How many of us are told that, if we fail ourselves, we will fail humankind? Arthur gives it all he has. He faces the archbishop, the crowds, the jealous kings who will now be his enemies. When Arthur tells the people at his coronation, "For your good I dedicate my life," somehow, we know he will not fail them . . . or himself.

Uses a direct quote to support third main idea.

Ends with a key quote from Arthur himself.

Essay 2

Arthur possesses the potential to be a great king. Throughout the story, Arthur shows kindness, honesty, a good heart, and courage. These are qualities any great person should have.

A **B** First, Arthur is kind. He rescues and tames wild animals. If he was not kind, would he do that? He is also nice to his brother, Sir Kay, even when his brother is full of himself. He is also willing to let Kay have the crown, but this might not be a kindness, since Arthur doesn't really want it. A great king must be kind to others in order to keep the love of the people. Arthur will succeed in this way.

C Second, Arthur is honest. He does not lie to his father about pulling out the sword. At that point he thinks he is in trouble for it, so that is a courageous thing for him to do. Arthur is also truthful when he says he doesn't want to be a king but will do it if he has to. Arthur would rather stay at home with his animals in the woods and his family. A great person must be honest, and Arthur will succeed in this way, too.

Third, Arthur has a good heart. He tries his hardest in everything he does. He might mess things up, like when he loses Kay's sword, but he still tries his best. A great person cannot ever give up.

D Fourth, Arthur is courageous. He stands up and faces all those people to pull out the sword. He is just sixteen years old, and now he will have to be a king of a country that many people want to take over. All in all, Arthur will fulfill his destiny by showing kindness, honesty, a good heart, and courage.

Arthur Drawing the Sword from the Stone by Louis Rhead (1857–1926).
The Granger Collection, New York.

DIFFERENTIATING INSTRUCTION

Learners Having Difficulty
If students need help evaluating the essays, review "Analyzing a Response to Literature" on p. 810. Help students to formulate questions such as the following that they can answer as they read each essay.

- Does the response answer the question about Arthur's potential for greatness?
- Does the response stick to the subject of Arthur's character?

- Does the response offer evidence to support its main ideas?
- Does the response offer examples of Arthur's behavior and of how others react to him?

English-Language Learners
Pair English-language learners with fluent readers. Assign each pair to read one of the sample essays aloud together, stopping after each paragraph to evaluate how well it

Essay 3

Arthur is the son of King Uther Pendragon and Queen Igraine. On the night he is born, the stars form the shape of a dragon to foreshadow Arthur's greatness. Merlin takes him away to keep him safe. Arthur's father is poisoned a year later, so it is a good decision to take the baby away. When Arthur is sixteen, his country needs him. The years while he has been growing up were lawless and dark. Merlin devises a way to make the people accept Arthur. He puts a sword in an anvil outside the church, with a note that says that whoever could pull out the sword is the rightful king of England. The archbishop declares a contest on Christmas morning to see who is the rightful king, and a tournament on Christmas Eve. Arthur goes along to London to be squire for his bossy brother, Sir Kay. Kay is an annoying character, but Arthur doesn't mind being bossed around by Kay. He spends the time on the way to the tournament thinking of how to be a good squire and bring honor to his family. When they get to London, Arthur is amazed to see a sword in an anvil on a large block of marble with soldiers standing around it. He thinks London is full of wonders. Kay does a really good job in the first part of the tournament. He has just enough time to rest and change before the next event, and he asks Arthur for his sword. Arthur can't find it! He leaps on his pony to go back to their tent, but it isn't there. Arthur decides to borrow the one he saw from the anvil, and he goes to see about getting it. It comes out pretty easily, and Arthur takes it to Sir Kay. Kay tells Arthur to get their father. Then Kay wants to claim he's king. Their father makes him prove it. Of course, Kay cannot put the sword back, but Arthur can. Their father, Sir Ector, is overcome when he realizes who Arthur really is. He tells Arthur he can't avoid his destiny. Merlin comes along and tells Arthur he is going to be a great king, but he will have to fulfill his destiny. It will be Arthur's choice. He has to want it. Arthur is sad to give up the life he loves, but he says he will accept whatever his destiny is. Then he pulls the sword out on five different occasions to prove his worth. The people love him, and he is crowned King of England.

Illustration from an early-14th-century manuscript.

The Granger Collection, New York.

Three Responses to Literature 813

E Reading Skills

Compare and contrast. How is the beginning of this essay different from the beginnings of Essays 1 and 2? [Unlike Essays 1 and 2, this essay does not begin by identifying the qualities of Arthur's character that show he has the potential for greatness.]

F Literary Focus

Analyze a response to literature. What literary element does this essay focus on? [plot] What literary element did the question prompt ask the writer to focus on? [character]

G Learners Having Difficulty

Re-read. Re-read the ending of the essay. Does the writer mention any qualities of Arthur's character that show he has the potential for greatness? [no] Why is this a problem? [Possible response: The question prompt asks writers to analyze the character of Arthur. This essay does not do that.]

GUIDED PRACTICE

Monitor students' progress. Ask students to identify the essay that was the most persuasive and the essay that was the least persuasive in showing Arthur's potential for greatness. Have students give reasons for their choices.

fulfills the requirements under "Analyzing a Response to Literature" on p. 810. Afterward, bring the pairs together to share and compare their analyses.

PAIRED

Advanced Learners

Enrichment. These students may have good suggestions for improving the essays to better match the requirements on p. 810

Activity. Have pairs of students discuss and evaluate Essay 1 or Essay 2 and make a list of suggested revisions. Then, have each student write a revision of the essay. Students can share and compare their revised essays.

PAIRED

After You Read

First Thoughts

1. All three essay writers admired him.

Thinking Critically

2. Arthur is already gaining wisdom at the age of sixteen: "[Arthur] has tamed birds and deer. This requires patience and the ability to look and listen." Arthur thinks about others before himself: "He goes to London hoping to 'help bring honor and glory to his family.'" Arthur possesses insight and courage: "'Very well, whatever my destiny may be, I am willing to accept it.'"

3. Possible answer: Comparing and contrasting Arthur and Kay is an effective way of answering the essay question because it allows the writer to list the qualities that make someone great and show that Arthur possesses those qualities.

4. The detail about Arthur's kindness to Sir Kay is not clearly supported by the story, because the writer suggests that Arthur had a motivation other than kindness for his treatment of Kay.

5. Possible answer: "The essay does not answer the question" is a valid criticism because the essay says nothing about the qualities of Arthur's character or his potential for greatness. The only evidence of Arthur's potential for greatness presented by the writer is the reference to Arthur's ability to pull the sword out of and put it back into the anvil.

6. Students' ratings will vary, but most will give Essay 1 the highest rating, Essay 2 a midlevel rating, and Essay 3 the lowest rating. Students' Quickwrite responses will vary. Make sure that they understand the basic criteria for evaluating literature presented in "Analyzing a Response to Literature."

First Thoughts

1. How do you think each writer felt about the character of Arthur?

Thinking Critically

2. Essay 1 provides specific details from the text to support its analysis of Arthur's **character.** List three of these supporting details.

3. Essay 1 uses **comparison and contrast** to make its points. Is this an effective way to answer the question about Arthur's character? Why or why not?

4. Essay 2 lists four qualities of greatness that the writer thinks Arthur possesses. Which of these qualities is *not* clearly supported in the story?

5. Analyze the following criticisms of Essay 3, and decide which one is valid. Explain the reasons for your choice.

   • The writer should have summarized the plot.

   • The essay does not answer the question.

   • The writer should have quoted some of Arthur's exact words to support the main points about his character.

   • The writer doesn't put quotation marks around Arthur's exact words.

6. On a scale of 0 to 5, with 0 being the lowest rating and 5 the highest, how would you rate each essay? Base your evaluation on the tips for "Analyzing a Response to Literature" on page 810. How do these tips compare with the list of criteria you wrote in your Quickwrite response?

SKILLS FOCUS

Literary Skills
Analyze and evaluate responses to a literary work.

Writing Skills
Write a critical response to literature.

WRITING

Literary Criticism: Responding to Literature

Write a paragraph discussing the literary element of *King Arthur: The Sword in the Stone* that stood out for you. Was it the plot? the characters? the unusual setting? the theme of the rightful ruler becoming king? Be sure to support your response with details from the legend.

> **Reading Check**
>
> a. Which essay states the answer to the question about Arthur in the opening sentence?
>
> b. Which essay uses direct **quotations** from the text to support its main ideas?
>
> c. Which essay contains a plot **summary** rather than a character analysis?

Reading Check

a. Essay 2

b. Essay 1

c. Essay 3

Vocabulary Development

Latin and Anglo-Saxon Prefixes

The English language spoken during the time when the real King Arthur lived (around 500 A.D.) used a great many words from Latin and Anglo-Saxon. The Latin words in the English language have come from many sources.

- Some came into English when Roman soldiers occupied Britain for about 450 years, beginning in 55 B.C.
- Other Latin words came into English after the Normans invaded England in 1066. The Normans brought French words with them, which in turn had come from Latin.
- Other Latin words came from the Catholic Church, which was very important in Britain for centuries.

In the box are some prefixes from the Latin language and from the old form of the English language called Anglo-Saxon. English speakers have found all of these prefixes to be very useful. A **prefix** is a word part added to the front of another word to change its meaning: When you add the prefix *un–* to the word *digested,* for example, you get the word *undigested,* meaning "not digested." If you add the prefix *pre–* to *digested,* you get *predigested,* meaning "digested beforehand."

A Box of Prefixes
(*L* means the prefix is from Latin. *AS* means it is from Anglo-Saxon.)

contra–	against (L)
mis–	badly (AS)
over–	above; excessively (AS)
post–	after (L)
pre–	before (L)
pro–	favoring; forward (L)
retro–	backward (L)
semi–	half (L)
sub–	under (L)
un–	not (AS)

PRACTICE

Answer each question below. Refer to the box of prefixes to help you figure out the meanings of any words you do not already know.

1. If a rocket <u>misfires</u>, what has happened to it?
2. If a medical test is <u>unfavorable</u>, why would you be upset?
3. What does it mean to say that someone is <u>overstating</u> a case?
4. If a food is <u>contraindicated</u> by the doctor, should you eat it or avoid it?
5. If someone is <u>postoperative</u>, has the surgery already been performed or is it about to begin?
6. Why shouldn't a juror <u>prejudge</u> a case?
7. If a politician is <u>pro–social security</u>, is she for it or against it?
8. If your pay is <u>retroactive</u>, are you being paid for past work or for future work?
9. What would you expect to find if someone is <u>semiconscious</u>?
10. Does a <u>subway</u> run aboveground or underground?

SKILLS FOCUS

Vocabulary Skills
Understand Latin and Anglo-Saxon prefixes.

Three Responses to Literature **815**

Vocabulary Development

PRACTICE

1. The rocket has fired badly.
2. An unfavorable test is not favorable, which means it offers bad news.
3. Overstating a case means to make too strong a case, to be excessively sure of oneself in relation to the evidence.
4. You would avoid a food that is contraindicated, because the doctor has advised against it.
5. The surgery has already been performed, since *post–* means "after."
6. A juror is supposed to judge a case based on evidence presented during a trial, rather than making a judgment before the trial begins.
7. She is for it or favoring it.
8. Retroactive pay is for past work because *retro–* means "backward."
9. You would expect to find someone who is half conscious—a person who is drifting into and out of consciousness.
10. Since *sub–* means "under," a subway must run underground.

ASSESSING

Assessment
- *Holt Assessment: Literature, Reading, and Vocabulary*

RETEACHING

For a lesson reteaching literary criticism, see **Reteaching**, p. 917I.

Grade-Level Skills

■ **Reading Skills**
Evaluate the quality of an author's evidence, noting instances of stereotype and bias.

Review Skills

■ **Reading Skills**
Recognize unsupported inferences, fallacious reasoning, persuasion, and propaganda.

Summary ↔ *at grade level*

> The sons-in-law of Uther Pendragon, the deceased king, protest Arthur's being crowned king. They object on the grounds of his youth, inexperience, and unknown origins and show their bias against Arthur, calling him "a nobody" and "a weakling." They express stereotypical views of boys who love animals and show their bias in favor of royalty and the military. They suggest that Merlin engineered Arthur's victory and demand a new contest to choose a worthy king.

PRETEACHING

Skills Starter

Build skills. Challenge students to define the terms *bias* and *stereotype.* What is the difference between the two? How might a politician use bias and stereotyping in a speech about a political opponent?

Evaluating Evidence: Understanding Stereotype and Bias

Reading Focus

Stereotype: No Room for Individuality

Imagine you're sitting on a bench in a shopping mall, waiting for your ride to show up. You begin hearing bits of conversations from shoppers as they walk by. You hear these comments:

"People who drive sports cars are reckless."

"All politicians are dishonest."

"Boys are better than girls at math."

"Teenagers aren't concerned with world issues."

"All teenagers drive recklessly."

"Football players aren't good at schoolwork."

"Smart kids are geeky."

"Rich kids are selfish."

You've just heard people express their opinions of others using **stereotypes.** That means they are using unfair, fixed ideas about groups of people. Stereotypes don't allow for any individuality. They brand every member of a group with the same characteristics. Stereotypes are very hurtful. They are often used to persuade you to do or believe something.

Bias: An Inclination to Favor Someone or Something

If you've ever watched your favorite sports team on the opposing team's host TV channel, you've probably noticed that the broadcasters favor the home team with their comments and calls. What you're really noticing is something called **bias**—attitudes and beliefs that shape a person's thinking in spite of the facts. Of course, your bias is evident also—you want your team to win!

■ As you read editorials, letters to the media (such as the one that follows), or any kind of political or social commentary, be on the lookout for expressions that suggest the writer has already made up his or her mind about something or someone. Think of bias as an inclination to think a certain way. In its worst form, bias becomes prejudice.

INTERNET
Interactive Reading Model
Keyword: LE5 7-7

SKILLS FOCUS

Reading Skills
Understand stereotype and bias.

Arthur and his knights setting out on the quest for the Holy Grail (c. 1380–1400) by Italian School. Vellum.

816   Collection 7 / Literary Criticism: Where I Stand

RESOURCES: READING

Planning
■ *One-Stop Planner* CD-ROM with ExamView Test Generator

Differentiating Instruction
■ *Holt Reading Solutions*
■ *Supporting Instruction in Spanish*
■ *Audio CD Library*
■ *Audio CD Library, Selections and Summaries in Spanish*

Grammar and Language
■ *Daily Language Activities*

Assessment
■ *Holt Assessment: Literature, Reading, and Vocabulary*
■ *One-Stop Planner* CD-ROM with ExamView Test Generator
■ *Holt Online Assessment*

Internet
■ go.hrw.com (Keyword: LE5 7-7)
■ *Elements of Literature Online*

Media
■ *Audio CD Library*
■ *Audio CD Library, Selections and Summaries in Spanish*

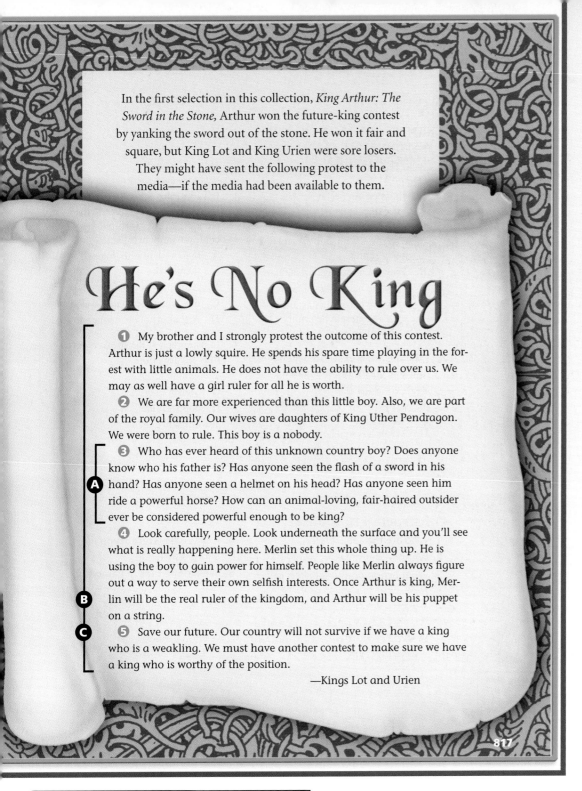

In the first selection in this collection, *King Arthur: The Sword in the Stone*, Arthur won the future-king contest by yanking the sword out of the stone. He won it fair and square, but King Lot and King Urien were sore losers. They might have sent the following protest to the media—if the media had been available to them.

He's No King

1 My brother and I strongly protest the outcome of this contest. Arthur is just a lowly squire. He spends his spare time playing in the forest with little animals. He does not have the ability to rule over us. We may as well have a girl ruler for all he is worth.

2 We are far more experienced than this little boy. Also, we are part of the royal family. Our wives are daughters of King Uther Pendragon. We were born to rule. This boy is a nobody.

3 Who has ever heard of this unknown country boy? Does anyone know who his father is? Has anyone seen the flash of a sword in his hand? Has anyone seen a helmet on his head? Has anyone seen him ride a powerful horse? How can an animal-loving, fair-haired outsider ever be considered powerful enough to be king?

4 Look carefully, people. Look underneath the surface and you'll see what is really happening here. Merlin set this whole thing up. He is using the boy to gain power for himself. People like Merlin always figure out a way to serve their own selfish interests. Once Arthur is king, Merlin will be the real ruler of the kingdom, and Arthur will be his puppet on a string.

5 Save our future. Our country will not survive if we have a king who is a weakling. We must have another contest to make sure we have a king who is worthy of the position.

—Kings Lot and Urien

817

DIRECT TEACHING

A Reading Informational Text

? Assess evidence: Bias and stereotyping. What bias do the speakers show? [Possible response: They show a bias against people who love animals, people from the country, and people of unknown parentage, and a bias in favor of the military.]

B Reading Skills

? Evaluate. Ask students to evaluate the speakers' arguments. Are any of their arguments convincing? Why or why not? [Some students may say that all the arguments are unconvincing. Other students may say that the speakers' concern about Arthur's youth and physical weakness is a convincing argument.]

C Reading Informational Text

? Assess evidence: Bias and stereotyping. What attitudes and beliefs shape the speakers' opinion that Arthur is not fit to rule? [Possible response: In their world, physical strength is the means to take and hold power. Their attitude is that a physically strong warrior will make the best king, not a young boy.]

GUIDED PRACTICE

Monitor students' progress. Ask students to write a one-paragraph news report that summarizes the speech.

DIFFERENTIATING INSTRUCTION

Learners Having Difficulty
To help students understand stereotype and bias, write these statements on the chalkboard:
- Stay away from big dogs; they are vicious and dangerous.
- Teenagers just play with computers; we need someone more reliable to work in our office.

Elicit from students examples showing that the statements are unfair. Discuss the first statement as an example of stereotyping and the second statement as an example of bias.

Advanced Learners
Enrichment. Ask students how Arthur and Merlin might have responded to this protest.
Activity. Challenge students to write the statement that Arthur and Merlin might

have released in answer to this plea for another contest. Suggest that they use the same structure, stating their opinion in the first paragraph and then explaining their reasons. Remind students to consider any biases Arthur and Merlin might possess.

Analyzing Stereotype and Bias

Test Practice

Answers and Model Rationales

1. **A** Students can eliminate B, C, and D because these statements are not suggested in paragraph 1. Only the details of A are mentioned.

2. **J** The question suggests respect for those who have been tested in battle. Though F and G may seem to be logical choices, they are not supported by details in the paragraph.

3. **A** B expresses a bias of the speakers but not their main focus. C and D are apparent reasons, but the overall tone of the speech suggests that A provides the speakers' main motive.

4. **G** The speakers object to the possibility that Merlin, not King Arthur, will be the true power in England.

Test-Taking Tips

Remind students not to rely totally on their memories. After they read a question, they should go back to the text to look for the answer. Point out that multiple-choice questions, such as the ones to the right, often indicate a paragraph or section, so students will not have to re-read the entire text.

For more information on how to answer multiple-choice questions, refer students to **Test Smarts,** p. 920.

Analyzing Stereotype and Bias

He's No King

Test Practice

1. Which statement best describes the speakers' **bias** in paragraph 1?
   - **A** They are biased against a boy who plays with animals and is a lowly squire.
   - **B** They are biased against animals.
   - **C** They are biased against kings.
   - **D** They are biased against using such a contest to determine who will be king.

2. "Has anyone ever seen the flash of a sword in his hand?" is a **biased** question suggesting that —
   - **F** Arthur lied about pulling the sword out of the stone
   - **G** Arthur has said he hates fighting
   - **H** kings need quick reflexes
   - **J** kings have to be tested in battle

3. It is clear that King Lot and King Urien, the speakers, protest the outcome of the sword-pulling contest mainly because —
   - **A** they wish to rule England themselves
   - **B** Arthur is good with animals
   - **C** they think the contest was fixed
   - **D** Arthur is not old enough to lead

4. In paragraph 4, the speakers reveal **bias** against —
   - **F** Arthur
   - **G** Merlin
   - **H** puppet rulers
   - **J** kings in general

Constructed Response

1. Who are the speakers?
2. What do the speakers want?
3. What action do the speakers call for?
4. Analyze the **stereotype** in paragraph 1.
5. Explain the **bias** in paragraph 2.

SKILLS FOCUS

Reading Skills
Analyze stereotype and bias.

Constructed Response

1. The speakers are Kings Lot and Urien.
2. The speakers want to oust Arthur as king and rule themselves.
3. They call for a new contest.
4. The speakers compare Arthur to a "girl ruler," expressing the stereotype that females are unfit to rule.
5. The speakers are biased in favor of those who share their family background. They believe that only members of the royal family should rule.

After You Read Vocabulary Development

Greek Roots

Many English words have long histories—many words have been borrowed from the French, who borrowed them from the Romans, who in turn borrowed them from the Greeks. Knowing what a Greek word root means can help you figure out the meaning of other words that come from the same or similar roots.

PRACTICE

Below you will find five Greek roots and their definitions. Use context clues and the root definitions to figure out the modern words and fill in the blanks in each sentence.

GREEK ROOTS		
Root	Definition	Also Used As . . .
–astron–	"star"	–astro–
–chronos–	"time"	–chron–
–decem– –deka–	"ten"	–dec–
–helios–	"sun"	–heli–

1. If you are really in a hurry, you can charter a heli _ _ _ _ er to fly you there.
2. Events that are recorded in sequence of time are said to be chron _ _ _ _ _ _ al.
3. Some say that when our stars are crossed, _ _ _ aster strikes.
4. In ancient Rome the tenth month was Dec _ _ _ _ _ .
5. Astro _ _ _ _ s may one day visit other planets.
6. Diseases that extend over a long period of time are said to be chron _ _ .
7. A person who can compete in ten athletic events is called a dec _ _ _ _ ete.
8. Astro _ _ _ _ is the scientific study of the stars and the planets.
9. A dec _ _ _ is a period of ten years.
10. Heli _ _ is a light gas used to make balloons float.

ASTRO'S USES

SKILLS FOCUS

Vocabulary Skills
Understand Greek roots.

Vocabulary Development

PRACTICE

1. helicopter
2. chronological
3. disaster
4. December
5. astronauts
6. chronic
7. decathlete
8. astronomy
9. decade
10. helium

ASSESSING

Assessment
■ *Holt Assessment: Literature, Reading, and Vocabulary*

Grade-Level Skills

■ Literary Skills
Analyze the qualities of a hero.

Summary *at grade level*

Yolen's tale features a story within a story. In the frame story, a young King Arthur is spending a restless night, troubled by bad dreams. He seeks out Merlin, who tells him a story.

Merlin's story takes place in a small Welsh village. A fatherless boy named Emrys dreams of dragons and a stone tower. The dreams come true when Vortigern, a false king, appears, bearing flags emblazoned with red dragons and demanding that the townspeople build him a stone battle tower. After the tower is built and mysteriously destroyed three times, Emrys tells Vortigern that he has dreamed about two dragon eggs under the tower. The eggs are then uncovered, and they soon hatch. A red dragon and a white dragon emerge and fight each other to the death. The victory of the white dragon, Emrys coura-geously explains to Vortigern, foretells the false king's own defeat by an army bearing flags of white dragons. The army, led by Uther, arrives and defeats Vortigern.

As the frame story resumes, Arthur learns that he, the son of Uther, is the true king and that Merlin is the boy, Emrys. Arthur returns to bed, confident in his new kingship.

Before You Read The Legend

Merlin and the Dragons

Make the Connection
Quickwrite ✏️

Everybody loves a hero, but just what is a hero? Is it a comic book superhero with special powers? Is it an astronaut who lands on the moon? Is it a firefighter who rescues people from a burning building? Is it a freedom fighter who goes to jail in the cause of justice? Is it a librarian who helps children develop a love of learning? Jot down your ideas on what makes someone a hero.

Literary Focus
Heroes and Quests

Throughout the world and throughout literature, we find stories of great heroes who have saved their people from terrible threats. The plots of many of these stories follow a typical pattern.

Heroes in such tales are often born in unusual circumstances, often in secret. Sometimes their true parents are unknown. The hero is often trained by a wise, older man. When his time comes, the young hero proves himself (these old stories were always about masculine heroes) through some fantastic feat of strength or intellect.

The hero then gathers a band of followers and embarks on a **quest** to save his people from some threat—a monster, perhaps, or a false leader.

You have seen part of this pattern in the story of King Arthur you just read, *King Arthur: The Sword in the Stone.* As you read "Merlin and the Dragons," look for events that also match the pattern of the hero tale.

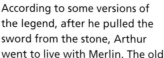
INTERNET
Vocabulary Activity
Keyword: LE5 7-7

SKILLS FOCUS
Literary Skills Understand heroes.

Vocabulary Development

Here are some words you'll need to know to understand the story:

ruthless (rōōth′lis) *adj.*: without pity. *A ruthless army destroyed the village.*

bedraggled (bē·drag′əld) *adj.*: hanging limp and wet; dirty. *The bedraggled horses needed rest.*

insolence (in′sə·ləns) *n.*: disrespect. *The rebels were punished for their insolence.*

recognition (rek′əg·nish′ən) *n.*: knowing again. *Merlin was pleased at Arthur's recognition of his past.*

Background
Literature and Legend

According to some versions of the legend, after he pulled the sword from the stone, Arthur went to live with Merlin. The old wizard was to teach the boy the lessons of being a good ruler.

In the story you are about to read, Arthur knows he is king, but he doesn't yet know his true parentage.

820   Collection 7 / Literary Criticism: Where I Stand

RESOURCES: READING

Planning
■ *One-Stop Planner* CD-ROM with ExamView Test Generator

Differentiating Instruction
■ *Holt Reading Solutions*
■ *Supporting Instruction in Spanish*
■ *Audio CD Library*
■ *Audio CD Library, Selections and Summaries in Spanish*

Vocabulary
■ *Vocabulary Development*

Grammar and Language
■ *Daily Language Activities*

Assessment
■ *Holt Assessment: Literature, Reading, and Vocabulary*
■ *One-Stop Planner* CD-ROM with ExamView Test Generator

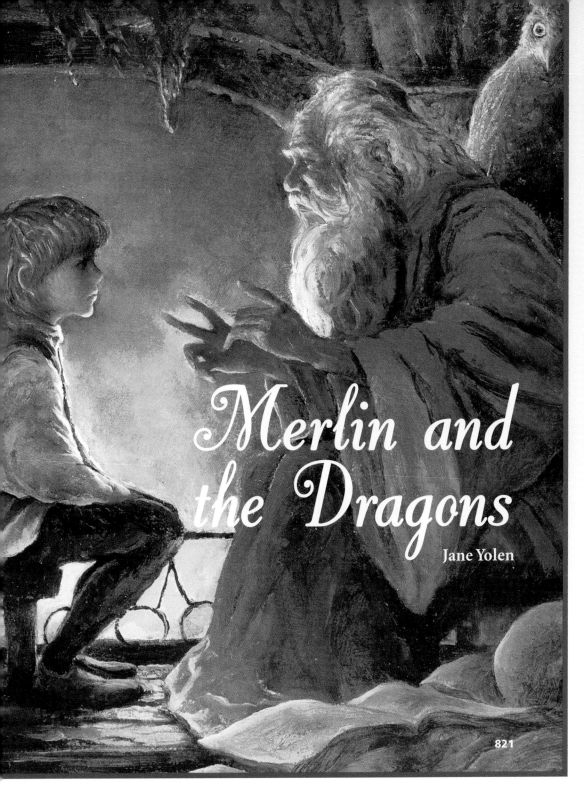

Merlin and the Dragons

Jane Yolen

821

Selection Starter

Build background. Tell students that this selection includes a story within a story. The selection opens and closes with a frame story, which introduces the main story—a kind of flashback. Students may have seen this technique used in movies such as *Titanic* and *The Princess Bride*.

Preview Vocabulary

Have students complete each sentence with a Vocabulary word.

1. A cutthroat cardplayer might make a _____ move. [ruthless]

2. A _____ dog might need a shampoo and brushing. [bedraggled]

3. A naughty child might behave with _____. [insolence]

4. Detectives use their powers of _____ to identify clues. [recognition]

- *Holt Online Assessment*

Internet
- go.hrw.com (Keyword: LE5 7-7)
- *Elements of Literature Online*

Media
- *Audio CD Library*
- *Audio CD Library, Selections and Summaries in Spanish*
- *Fine Art Transparencies*

? Find details. What details
show that Arthur does not feel
ready to be king? [Possible responses:
He is scared, has trouble sleeping, has
bad dreams; he had tossed his crown
angrily under his bed; the crown feels
"too heavy for his head."]

B Literary Focus

? A story pattern: Character.
What does the dialogue tell you
about the characters of Merlin and
Arthur and their relationship?
[Possible responses: Arthur is not com-
fortable asserting his authority as king.
Merlin, who is older and wiser, speaks
to Arthur like a father to a young boy.]

C Literary Focus

? A story pattern: Hero. What
characteristic of a typical would-be
hero is revealed about Emrys in
this passage? [He does not know
who his father is.]

D English-Language
Learners

Interpret invented and
multiple-meaning words.
Explain that *flutterby* and *wriggletail* are words invented by Emrys
to describe butterflies and lizards.
Have students break down the
compound words and explain why
the names fit these animals. Also,
clarify that the word *spell* has a
special meaning in this context,
referring to magical words spoken
by a wizard or a witch.

The night was dark and storm clouds
marched along the sky. Rain beat against
the gray castle walls. Inside, in a bedroom
hung with tapestries, the young King Arthur
had trouble sleeping. Awake, he was frightened. Asleep, he had disturbing dreams.

At last he climbed out of bed, took a candle to light his way, and started out the
door. Suddenly remembering his crown, he
turned back and found it under the bed
where he'd tossed it angrily hours before. It
felt too heavy for his head, so he carried it,
letting it swing from his fingers.

As he walked along the hall, strange shadows danced before him. But none were as
frightening as the shadows in his dreams.

He climbed the tower stairs slowly, biting
his lip. When he reached the top, he pushed
open the wooden door. The old magician
was asleep in his chair, but woke at once,
his eyes quick as a hawk's.

"What is it, boy?" the old man asked.
"What brings you here at this hour?"

"I am the king," Arthur said, but softly as
if he were not really sure. "I go where I will."
He put the crown on Merlin's desk.

"You are a boy," Merlin replied, "and boys
should be in their beds asleep."

Arthur sighed. "I could not sleep," he
said. "I had bad dreams."

"Ah . . ." Merlin nodded knowingly.
"Dreams." He held out a hand to the boy,
but Arthur didn't dare touch those long,
gnarled fingers. "Let me read your dreams."

"It is one dream, actually," Arthur said.
"And always the same: a fatherless boy who
becomes king simply by pulling a sword
from a stone."

"Ah . . ." Merlin said again, withdrawing
his fingers. "I know the very child. But if
you cannot tell me more of your dream, I

shall have to tell you one of mine. After all,
a dream told is a story. What better than a
story on a rainy night?"

Arthur settled onto a low stool and gazed
up at the wizard. A story! He hadn't known
he wanted a story. He'd come seeking
comfort and companionship. A story was
better than both.

He listened as Merlin began.

In a small village high up in the rugged
mountains of Wales lived a lonely, fatherless
boy named Emrys. Dark-haired he was, and
small, with sharp bright eyes, and a mouth
that rarely smiled. He was troubled by
dreams, sleeping and waking. Dreams of
dragons, dreams of stone.

His mother was the daughter of the local
king and tried to be both mother and father
to him. But a princess is only taught lute
songs and needlework and prayers. She'd
never once climbed a tree after a bird's egg
or skinned her knee pursuing a lizard, or
caught a butterfly in a net. Emrys had to
invent that part of growing up himself. And
a lonely inventing it turned out to be.

The other boys in the village teased him
for not knowing who his father was.
"Mother's babe," they cried, chasing him
from their games.

So Emrys went after birds' eggs and
lizards, butterflies and frogs by himself,
giving them names both odd and admiring,
like "flutterby" and "wriggletail," and
making up stories of their creation. And he
chanted strange-sounding spells because he
liked the sounds, spells that sometimes
seemed to work, most times did not.

But he never told his dreams aloud.
Dreams of dragons, dreams of stone.

Now in the village lived an old man who

Learners Having Difficulty
Some students may need help identifying the
pattern of the hero as they read "Merlin and
the Dragons." Review the Literary Focus section on p. 820, and have students list the common characteristics of literary heroes: an
unusual birth; unknown parents; being
trained by a wise, older man; performing a
fantastic feat; and embarking on a quest to
save people. Then, as students read the

story, encourage them to match items on the
list with events in the plot.

English-Language Learners
You may wish to review words that are
associated with the world of fantasy, such
as *dragons, dreams, magic, magicians,
prophecies, spell, vision,* and *wizard.* Be sure
students understand the relationship
between *magic* and *magicians* and the
differences in their pronunciation. Explain

knew all sorts of things, from reading and writing to how birds speak and why leaves turn brown in autumn. And because Emrys was the son of a princess, the grandson of a king, the old man taught him all he knew.

It was this learning that brought the village boys to him, not in friendship but in curiosity. They would ask Emrys to show them some trick with the birds, or to tell them stories. Glad for the company, Emrys always obliged. He even took to making up harmless predictions to amuse them.

"The rain will soon fall," he would say. And often it did.

"The first spring robin will arrive." And soon after, it came.

Now any farmer's son could have made the same right guesses and after awhile the village boys were no longer impressed. However, one day Emrys found a book of seasons and planetary movements in the old man's cottage and read it cover to cover. Then he went out and announced to the astonished boys: "Tomorrow the sun will disappear."

The next day at noon, just as the calendar had foretold, an eclipse plunged the countryside into darkness. The boys and their parents were equally horrified and blamed Emrys. From then on he was called "demon's son" and avoided altogether.

Years went by and Emrys grew up, terribly alone, dreaming dreams he did not understand: dreams of a shaking tower, dreams of fighting dragons.

One day when Emrys was twelve, a cruel and ruthless man named Vortigern came to the valley. Vortigern had unjustly declared himself High King over all Britain. But the country was at last in revolt against him and he had been forced to flee, riding ever farther north and west. At last he had

arrived at the foot of Dinys Emrys, the mountain which towered above the village, with a bedraggled army on tired horses, bearing tattered banners emblazoned with red dragons. A handful of court magicians rode with them.

Vortigern pointed to the jagged mountain peak. "There," he said in a voice hard and determined. "There I will build my battle tower, so that I may see my enemies when they approach."

He turned to his soldiers. "Gather the people of this village and bring them to me, for they will be the hackers and haulers. They will make me a tower of stone."

Vocabulary

ruthless (rōōth′lis) *adj.*: without pity.
bedraggled (bē·drag′əld) *adj.*: hanging limp and wet; dirty.

DIRECT TEACHING

E Literary Focus

❓ A story pattern: Hero. What feature of the typical hero's story does this passage reveal? [Emrys, the fatherless boy, is trained by a wise old man.]

F Cross-curricular Connections
SCIENCE

Eclipses. A solar eclipse occurs when the moon passes between the earth and the sun. The moon's shadow covers the light from the sun and creates darkness on the earth. Since the movements of these bodies are predictable, scientists know when eclipses will occur.

G Vocabulary Development

Use affixes to understand words. Have students break down the word *unjustly* into its prefix (*un–*, "not"), base word (*just,* "fair, legitimate"), and suffix (*–ly,* "in the way of") and use these word parts to tell the word's meaning ("in a way that is not legitimate or fair").

---

that *spell* in this context means "a charm" or "words believed to have magical powers" and is a different word from the verb *spell,* which means "to name or write the letters of a word correctly." You might help students relate the words *spell* and *spellbind* ("to fascinate; to hold as if under a spell").

Special Education Students
For lessons designed for special education students, see *Holt Reading Solutions.*

Advanced Learners
Acceleration. Use this activity to help advanced learners identify and analyze themes that recur in traditional and contemporary works.
Activity. In the stories about the boyhoods of Arthur and Merlin, have students note character traits, situations, and themes that remind them of those from contemporary stories, TV shows, and movies about heroes.

A Literary Focus

Recurring themes. Point out to students that the tower is built and destroyed three times before Vortigern turns to his magicians for help. Explain that in traditional folk tales events often happen in threes. Have students name some of these tales. Then, ask if they can think of any contemporary stories in which events happen in threes.

B Literary Focus

? A story pattern: Plot. Why do the magicians tell Vortigern to look for a fatherless child spawned by a demon? [They fear Vortigern, so to protect their own reputations they propose a solution that they think cannot be proved wrong.] **What unintended effect does their advice have?** [Emrys is arrested because he fits the description.]

Young Emrys looked on in amazement. Banners sewn with red dragons? A tower of stone? Such things had been in his dreams. What could it all mean?

The Welsh stonecutters began their work under the watchful eyes of the soldiers. For many days they mined the stone, cutting huge pieces from the sides of Dinys Emrys. They swore they could hear the cries of the mountain at each cut.

Next they hauled the stones with ropes, their little Welsh ponies groaning with the effort. Finally, came the day when they built the tower up on the mountainside, stone upon stone, until it rose high above the valley.

That night Emrys went to bed and dreamed once again his strange dreams. He dreamed that the tower—the very one built by Vortigern—shook and swayed and tumbled to the ground. And he dreamed that beneath the tower slept two dragons, one red as Vortigern's banners, and one white.

That very night the High King's tower began to shudder and shake and, with a mighty crash, came tumbling down. In the morning, when he saw what had happened, Vortigern was furious, convinced the villagers had done it on purpose.

"Your work is worthless," he bellowed at the Welshmen. "You will be whipped, and then you will get to work all over again."

So the Welshmen had to go back to their stonework, great welts on their backs. They hacked and hauled, and once again the tower rose high above the valley. But the night they were finished, it was the same. The tower shook and tumbled to the ground. By morning there was only a jumble of stones.

Vortigern drove the villagers even harder, and by the following week the tower was once again rebuilt. But a third time, in the night, a great shudder went through the mountain and the work once again lay in ruins. Vortigern's rage could not be contained. He called for his magicians. "There is some dark Welsh magic here. Find out the cause. My tower must stand."

Now these magicians had neither knowledge nor skill, but in their fear of Vortigern they put on a good show. They consulted the trees, both bark and root; they threw the magic sticks of prophecy; they played with the sacred stones of fate. At last they reported their findings.

"You must find a fatherless child," they said. "A child spawned by a demon. You must sprinkle his blood on the stones. Only then will the gods of this land let the stones stand." They smiled at one another and at Vortigern, smiles of those sure that what they ask cannot be done.

Vortigern did not notice their smiles. "Go find me such a child."

The magicians stopped smiling and looked nervous. "We do not know if any such child exists," they said. "We do not know if your tower can stand."

Furious, Vortigern turned to his soldiers. "Gold to whomever brings me such a child," he roared.

Before the soldiers could move, a small voice cried out. "Please, sir, we of the village know such a boy." The speaker was a spindly lad named Gwillam.

"Come here, child," said Vortigern. "Name him."

Gwillam did not dare get too close to the High King. "His name is Emrys, sir. He was spawned by a demon. He can cry the sun from the sky."

Vortigern turned to the captain of his

guards. "Bring this demon's son to me."

At that very moment, Emrys was on the mountain with the old man, absorbed in a very strange dream. Under the ruins of the tower he saw two huge stone eggs breathing in and out. Just as he emerged from his dream, he was set upon by Vortigern's soldiers. "What shall I do?" he cried.

The old man put a hand on his shoulder. "Trust your dreams."

The soldiers quickly bound Emrys and carried him to the High King, but Emrys refused to show any fear. "You are the boy without a father, the boy spawned by a devil?" Vortigern asked.

"I am a boy without a father, true," Emrys said. "But I am no demon's son. You have been listening to the words of frightened children."

The villagers and soldiers gasped at his impudence, but Vortigern said, "I will have your blood either way."

"Better that you have my dream," Emrys said. "Only my dream can guide you so that your tower will stand."

The boy spoke with such conviction, Vortigern hesitated.

"I have dreamed that beneath your tower lies a pool of water that must be drained. In the mud you will find two hollow stones. In each stone is a sleeping dragon. It is the breath of each sleeping dragon that shakes the earth and makes the tower fall. Kill the dragons and your tower will stand."

Vortigern turned to his chief magician. "Can this be true?"

The chief magician stroked his chin. "Dreams *can* come true. . . ."

Vortigern hesitated no longer. "Untie the boy, but watch him," he said

to his soldiers. "And you—Welshmen—do as the boy says. Dig beneath the rubble."

So the Welshmen removed the stones and dug down until they came to a vast pool of water. Then the soldiers drained the pool. And just as Emrys had prophesied, at the pool's bottom lay two great stones. The stones seemed to be breathing in and out, and at each breath the mud around them trembled.

"Stonecutters," cried Vortigern, "break open the stones!"

Two men with mighty hammers descended into the pit and began to pound upon the stones.

Once, twice, three times their hammers rang out. On the third try, like jets of lightning, cracks ran around each stone and they broke apart as if they had been giant eggs. Out of one emerged a dragon white as

DIRECT TEACHING

C **Literary Focus**

❓ **A story pattern: Hero.**
How does Emrys's behavior with Vortigern fit the behavior expected of a hero? [Possible responses: Emrys is only twelve, but he is not afraid to contradict and challenge a powerful king. He has the courage and confidence to confront injustice.]

D **Literary Focus**
Recurring themes. Have students discuss other stories, both traditional and contemporary, in which the power of dreams and their interpretations is a major theme.

A Learners Having Difficulty

Read aloud. To maintain students' interest and to increase comprehension, have a fluent reader read this exciting climactic scene aloud.

new milk. Out of the other a dragon red as old wine.

Astonished at the power of his dreaming, Emrys opened and closed his mouth, but could not speak. The men in the pit scrambled for safety.

The High King Vortigern looked pleased. "Kill them! Kill the dragons!"

But even as he spoke, the dragons shook out their wings and leapt into the sky.

"They are leaving!" cried the chief magician.

"They are away!" cried the soldiers.

"They will not go quite yet," whispered Emrys.

No sooner had he spoken than the dragons wheeled about in the sky to face one another, claws out, belching flame. Their battle cries like nails on slate echoed in the air.

Advancing on one another, the dragons clashed, breast to breast, raining teeth and scales on the ground. For hour after hour they fought, filling the air with smoke.

First the red dragon seemed to be winning,

826 Collection 7 / Literary Criticism: Where I Stand

CROSS-CURRICULAR CONNECTIONS

Culture
Dragons in folklore and art. In European legends from the Middle Ages, dragons are represented as evil beasts that the hero must destroy in order to save his people. In Chinese legends, however, the dragon is often portrayed as a protective animal, one of the four guardian spirits of the world. Over the centuries the dragon became a symbol of the Chinese emperors and a popular figure in Chinese arts and crafts.

Activity. Have students explore legends and images of dragons from folk tales, art, and rituals in countries around the world. Have them present their findings in a multimedia Dragon Festival for the class.

WHOLE CLASS

B Reading Skills

❓ **Predict.** How do you think Vortigern will be defeated in the end? [Possible response: Another king bearing the emblem of a white dragon may bring his army to fight Vortigern's army.]

then the white. First one drew blood, then the other. At last, with a furious slash of its jaws, the white dragon caught the red by the throat. There was a moment of silence, and then the red dragon tumbled end over end until it hit the ground.

The white dragon followed it down, straddling its fallen foe and screaming victory into the air with a voice like thunder.

"Kill it! Kill the white now!" shouted Vortigern.

As if freed from a spell, his soldiers readied their weapons. But before a single arrow could fly, the white dragon leapt back into the air and was gone, winging over the highest peak.

"Just so the red dragon of Vortigern shall be defeated," Emrys said, but not so loud the High King could hear.

Cursing the fleeing dragon, Vortigern ordered the tower to be built again. Then he turned to Emrys. "If the tower does not stand this time, I *will* have your blood."

That night young Emrys stared out his

Merlin and the Dragons   **827**

A **Literary Focus**

A story pattern: Character.
What does this scene with the hawk contribute to your knowledge of Emrys? [Possible responses: It shows his close connection with nature; it offers a new, dramatic way for Emrys to foretell the future; it demonstrates his fantastic ability. Very perceptive readers may recall that Merlin was described as having "eyes quick as a hawk's" and may suspect a connection between Emrys and Merlin.]

B **Reading Skills**

Draw conclusions. Why do you think Emrys tells Vortigern about the coming attack? [Possible responses: He knows there is nothing Vortigern can do to avoid defeat, so the warning will do him no good; he wants Vortigern to know that he is doomed.]

window, past the newly built tower. A hawk circled lazily in the sky. Suddenly the hawk swooped down, landing on his window ledge. There was a moment of silent communion between them, as if Emrys could read the hawk's thoughts, as if the **A** hawk could read his. Then away the hawk flew.

Mountains, valleys, hillsides, forests gave way beneath the hawk's wings until, far off in the distance, it spied thousands of flickering lights coming up from the south. As if in a dream, Emrys saw these things, too.

Emerging from his vision, Emrys turned from the window and went downstairs. He found King Vortigern by the foot of the tower.

"I have seen in a vision that your fate is linked with the red dragon's," Emrys cried. **B** "You will be attacked by thousands of soldiers under the white dragon's flag— attacked and slain."

Vortigern drew his sword, angry enough to kill the boy for such insolence. But at that very moment, a lookout atop the tower shouted: "Soldiers, my lord! Thousands of them!"

Vortigern raced to the top of the tower stairs and stared across the valley. It was true. And as he watched further, one of the knights leading the army urged his horse forward and raced along to the tower foot, shouting: "Come and meet your fate, murderous Vortigern!"

Vortigern turned to his own men. "Defend me! Defend my tower!"

But when they saw the numbers against them, the men all deserted.

"Surrender, Vortigern!" cried a thousand voices.

"Never!" he called back. "Never!"

Vocabulary
insolence (in′sə·ləns) n.: disrespect.

Advanced Learners
Enrichment. Some students may be aware that the Arthurian legend has inspired many writers and filmmakers to create variations on the original story. Encourage students to evaluate Jane Yolen's embellishment of the legend in comparison to the embellishments of other stories and films that have dealt with this ever-popular subject.

Activity. Have a group of students screen videos based on the Arthurian legend. Possibilities include Hollywood classics such as *Knights of the Round Table* and *A Connecticut Yankee in King Arthur's Court;* the cartoons *The Sword in the Stone* and *Quest for Camelot;* and the live-action time-travel comedy *A Kid in King Arthur's Court.* Have students select one or two of the works for the whole class to view.

The old wizard stopped speaking.

"Well?" Arthur asked. "What happened to Vortigern? You cannot end a story there."

Merlin looked at him carefully. "What do *you* think happened?"

"Vortigern was slain, just as Emrys said."

"Is that the boy speaking?" asked the wizard. "Or the king?"

"The boy," admitted Arthur. "A king should forgive his enemies and make them his chiefest friends. You taught me that, Merlin. But what did happen?"

"The men of the white dragon defeated Vortigern all right. Burned him up in his own tower."

"And that knight, the one who rode up to the tower first. What became of him?"

"His name was Uther Pendragon and he eventually became the High King," Merlin said.

"Uther," mused Arthur. "He was the last High King before me. But then he was a hero. He was fit to rule. Perhaps one of his sons will come to claim my throne."

"Uther had only one son," Merlin said softly, "though only I knew of it." He looked steadily at the boy. "That son was you, Arthur."

"Me?" For a moment Arthur's voice squeaked. "Uther was my father? Then I am not fatherless? Then I am king by right and not just because I pulled a sword from a stone."

Merlin shook his head. "Don't underestimate your real strength in pulling that sword," Merlin cautioned. "It took a true and worthy king to do what you did."

Arthur gave a deep sigh. "Why did you not tell me this before?"

The old wizard's hawk eyes opened wide. "I could not tell you until you were ready.

There are rules for prophets, just as there are rules for kings."

"So now I am king in truth."

Merlin smiled. "You were always king in truth. Only you doubted it. So you can thank your dreams for waking you up."

"What of Emrys?" Arthur asked. "What happened to him?"

"Oh—he's still around," replied the wizard. "Went on dreaming. Made a career of it." He rummaged around in some old boxes and crates by the desk until he found what he was looking for. "I still have this. Saved it all this time." He tossed a large yellowed dragon's tooth across to Arthur.

Sudden recognition dawned on Arthur's face. "You? You saved this? Then you were the boy named Emrys!"

"Surely you guessed that before," Merlin teased. "But now perhaps we can both go back to sleep."

"Thank you, Merlin," Arthur said. "I don't think I shall dream any more bad dreams."

Merlin's gnarled fingers caged the boy's hand for a moment. "But you shall dream," he said quietly. "Great men dream great dreams, and I have dreamed your greatness." He plucked the crown from the desktop. "Don't forget this, my lord king."

Arthur took the crown and placed it carefully on his head. Then he turned, went out the door, and down the tower stairs.

Merlin watched for a moment more, then sank back down in his chair. Closing his eyes, he fell immediately to sleep, dreaming of knights and a Round Table.

Vocabulary
recognition (rek′əg·nish′ən) *n.:* knowing again.

Merlin and the Dragons   **829**

Meet the Writer

Jane Yolen is an experienced folksinger as well as a storyteller, so she is very conscious of the sounds and rhythms of the words in her stories. "I read all of my stuff out loud," she says, "because it's very important for me to please the ear as well as the eye. . . . I write a sentence and then read it out loud before going on to the next. Then the paragraph is read aloud. Finally, the entire book is read and re-read to the walls, to the bathtub, to the blank television, to my long-suffering husband."

For Independent Reading

- For another tale of adventure and fantasy based on Arthurian legends, students might enjoy *The Grey King,* Susan Cooper's Newbery Award–winning story of an epic struggle fought by two boys and a dog against the powers of darkness.
- For students who enjoy fantasy-adventures, recommend *The Hero and the Crown* by Robin McKinley, the story of a king's daughter who battles dragons to become a hero and save her father's kingdom.

Meet the Writer

Jane Yolen

"Empress of Thieves"

When you click on the name *Yolen, Jane* in the computerized author index at your school or public library, you'll find screen after screen after screen of book titles. **Jane Yolen** (1939–   ) has written more than two hundred books for young people, plus dozens more for adults.

Yolen has said that she was raised on the tales of King Arthur, so it is not surprising that the King Arthur legend is one of her favorite subjects. She is considered an expert in the study and research of Arthurian legends. The character of Merlin seems to fascinate her especially, and she has written several books about him.

Yolen grew up surrounded by books and the tradition of storytelling. Both her parents were writers. One of her great-grandfathers was a storyteller in a Russian village. Yolen was in the eighth grade when she wrote her earliest books: a work about pirates and a seventeen-page historical novel about a trip by covered wagon. Since then Yolen has written many kinds of books, but she says that her primary sources of inspiration are the legends, tales, and myths of folklore.

> ❝ As a writer I am the empress of thieves, taking characters like gargoyles off Parisian churches, the *ki-lin* (or unicorn) from China, swords in stones from the Celts, landscapes from the Taino people. I have pulled threads from magic tapestries to weave my own new cloth. ❞

For Independent Reading

If you want to read more of Yolen's novels about Merlin, look for her Young Merlin series: *Passager, Hobby,* and *Merlin.* You might also enjoy *The Dragon's Boy,* a novel about Arthur before he knew he would be king. If you share Yolen's fascination with dragons, don't miss her Pit Dragon trilogy: three fantasy novels —*Dragon's Blood, Heart's Blood,* and *A Sending of Dragons*—set in another world.

DIFFERENTIATING INSTRUCTION

Advanced Learners

Enrichment. Tell students that, in addition to writing her own stories based on legendary heroes, Jane Yolen has collected folk tales of many cultures, including Irish, Chinese, Native American, and Australian. **Activity.** Have a group of students read stories from the chapter "Heroes: Likely and Unlikely" in Jane Yolen's book *Favorite Folktales from Around the World.* Then, have them compare and contrast the characteristics of heroes from different cultures. Encourage them to make a presentation to the class.

After You Read Response and Analysis

First Thoughts

1. Do you think Emrys is a hero? In your answer, explain what you think a hero is. Check your Quickwrite notes from page 820 for ideas. ✏️

Thinking Critically

2. What details in the **plot** of this story give Emrys some of the qualities of a hero?

3. Explain what Arthur learns about the identity of Emrys at the end of the story.

4. Merlin taught Arthur that "A king should forgive his enemies and make them his chiefest friends." What do you think of this as advice for any ruler?

Extending Interpretations

5. The tales of King Arthur say little about the childhood of Arthur and even less about Merlin's childhood. Think about your responses to this story, which presents new, made-up details for an old legend. How do you feel about Jane Yolen inventing details to fill in the gaps?

WRITING

Analyzing Two Legends

Briefly summarize the plots of *King Arthur: The Sword in the Stone* (page 793) and "Merlin and the Dragons" (page 821). Tell which story you liked better, and give two or three reasons for your preference. Explain which literary elements in the work—plot, character, setting, theme—shaped your responses. Compare your responses with the responses of several classmates.

Reading Check

a. It is important that you notice the **structure** of this story. This is a story-within-a-story. What is happening in the **frame story**—the story that starts at the beginning?

b. Where does the story-*within*-the-story start? Where does it end?

c. Who is telling that story—the story about Emrys and the dragons?

d. Why is that storyteller telling Arthur the story about Emrys and the dragons?

e. Why do the boys call Emrys "demon's son"?

f. Where does Emrys get his special knowledge about nature? How does he know about the dragons in the stones?

g. Why has Vortigern fled to the valley where Emrys lives? Why does he want to have Emrys killed?

h. What happens when Vortigern's men pound on the stones beneath the tower?

i. Who leads the attack against Vortigern? How is Vortigern's conqueror related to Arthur?

SKILLS FOCUS

Literary Skills
Analyze the qualities of a hero.

Writing Skills
Write a literary analysis.

Merlin and the Dragons **831**

After You Read

First Thoughts

1. Possible answer: Yes, I think Emrys is a hero. He has many qualities of the typical hero: His true father is unknown; he is trained by a wise old man; and he has special powers, the ability to make prophecies and to see visions.

Thinking Critically

2. Emrys does not know who his father is and is trained by a wise old man. When he is twelve, Emrys saves his people and proves himself by confronting an unjust king and displaying his powers of prophecy.

3. Emrys is Merlin as a boy.

4. Possible answers: It is good advice because the king can thus make sure that his former enemies don't conspire against him. It is bad advice because it might lull the king into trusting an enemy.

Extending Interpretations

5. Some students may say that new details keep the old legend fresh and appealing. Others may say that the original stories should be passed on intact, preserving the past.

Reading Check

a. The boy Arthur has just been crowned king, and he can't sleep because he's worried. He goes to talk to Merlin about his bad dreams, and Merlin starts to tell him a story.

b. It begins after the sentence "He listened as Merlin began" (p. 822). It ends with "The old wizard stopped speaking" (p. 829).

c. Merlin is telling the story.

d. Merlin is reassuring Arthur that he is the rightful king, the son of Uther, to help the boy relax and sleep.

e. They think he has magical powers after he predicts a solar eclipse.

f. An old man who can read and write teaches Emrys about nature. The dragons in the stones appear in Emrys's dream.

g. Vortigern flees after the people revolt when he unjustly declares himself king. He wants Emrys killed because magicians say that only the blood of "a fatherless child . . . spawned by a demon" will let his tower stand.

h. The stones break open, and a white dragon and a red dragon emerge.

i. The attack is led by Uther Pendragon, the rightful king of Britain. Uther is Arthur's father.

Vocabulary Development

- *be–. Meaning*—"make or cause to be," "on," or "thoroughly." *Possible words*—becalmed, befuddled, befriend.
- *un–. Meaning*—"not." *Possible words*—unknown, unwise, unlock.
- *ex–. Meaning*—"out." *Possible words*—exhale, exclude, extract.
- *–less. Meaning*—"without." *Possible words*—hopeless, fatherless, careless.
- *in–. Meaning*—"not" or "in." *Possible words*—inaccurate, inactive, include.
- *–tion. Meaning*—"the act of," "the state of." *Possible words*—celebration, ignition, prediction.

PRACTICE 2

Possible Answers
1. Adolf Hitler, Attila the Hun, Joseph Stalin
2. a stray cat, campers caught in the rain, a marathon runner at the end of a race
3. respect
4. winning a sports championship, recording a hit CD, winning an election

ASSESSING

Assessment
- *Holt Assessment: Literature, Reading, and Vocabulary*

After You Read   Vocabulary Development

Prefixes and Suffixes: Useful Additions

PRACTICE 1

The Word Bank words contain several useful prefixes and suffixes. A **prefix** is a word part added to the front of a word to change its meaning; a **suffix** is a word part added to the end of a word to change its meaning.

Using a dictionary, make word maps for these useful prefixes and suffixes:

    be–   ex–   in–
    un–   –less   –tion

Use the word map opposite as a model. The prefix *non–* is shown as an example.

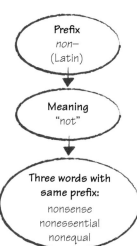

Word Bank
ruthless
bedraggled
insolence
recognition

Prefix
non–
(Latin)

↓

Meaning
"not"

↓

Three words with same prefix:
nonsense
nonessential
nonequal

Clarify Word Meanings by Using Examples

PRACTICE 2

1. Name three <u>ruthless</u> people in history.
2. Name three things that could be described as <u>bedraggled</u>.
3. Name an attitude that would be the opposite of <u>insolence</u>.
4. Name three achievements that would win someone <u>recognition</u>.

SKILLS FOCUS

Vocabulary Skills
Understand prefixes and suffixes; clarify word meanings by using examples.

Before You Read The Legend

Sir Gawain and the Loathly Lady

Make the Connection
Quickwrite 🖉

Imagine you're in a life-or-death situation. Your survival depends on giving the correct answer to one of these questions:

> What do men want most in the world? What do women want most in the world?

In your journal, write three answers to each question. Circle the one that you think gives you your best shot at survival.

Literary Focus
The Quest

A **quest** is a long and perilous journey taken in search of something of great value: a treasure, a kingdom, the hand of a fair maiden, or the answer to an important question. During the quest, heroes of folk tales and legends face temptations and difficult tasks—they may be called on to slay a dragon or solve a riddle.

Centuries ago riddles were used often in stories, as a sort of test. A **riddle** is a puzzling question or problem. The hero usually had to answer the riddle correctly before going on with the quest. In the old days, riddles were important in real life, too. A riddle contest sometimes grew into a battle of wits with great rewards for the winner and exile or death for the loser.

Vocabulary Development

As you begin this quest, here are some words you'll need to arm yourself. The last word may be the most important word in the story.

chivalry (shiv′əl·rē) *n.:* code that governed knightly behavior, such as courage, honor, and readiness to help the weak. *Chivalry required knights to help those in need.*

countenance (koun′tə·nəns) *n.:* face; appearance. *The knight's countenance revealed his fear.*

loathsome (lōth′səm) *adj.:* disgusting. *Dame Ragnell's appearance was loathsome.*

sovereignty (sǎv′rən·tē) *n.:* control; authority. *Arthur had sovereignty over all of Britain.*

A knight and his lady feeding a falcon, from a German manuscript (detail) (c. 14th century).

The Granger Collection, New York.

SKILLS FOCUS

Literary Skills
Understand the quest.

SKILLS FOCUS
pp. 833–844

Grade-Level Skills
■ Literary Skills
Analyze a quest story.

Summary ⬆ *above grade level*

During a hunt, King Arthur meets Sir Gromer, a knight who wants revenge for old wrongs. Sir Gromer offers Arthur a bargain: They will meet in one year, and if Arthur can answer the riddle "What do women most desire?" Gromer will spare his life. Arthur and his knight Sir Gawain ride through the kingdom seeking the answer to the riddle. A hideous hag agrees to give the king the answer in exchange for marriage to Gawain. When Gawain agrees, the hag answers the riddle, saying that women desire to rule men. Gawain and the hag—Dame Ragnell—marry. When they are alone, Ragnell becomes beautiful. She explains that she is under a spell, which Gawain has half broken by marrying her. Now she will remain ugly only half the time. She asks Gawain to choose when he would rather have her ugly—by day or by night. When Gawain tells her that *she* must decide, the spell is completely broken— her ugliness is gone for good.

Skills Starter

Build background. Review what students already know about the legends of King Arthur and the knights of the Round Table. Explain that a key aspect of the Arthurian code of chivalry was courtesy to all women, regardless of class or age.

Preview Vocabulary

Point out to students that the word *loathly* in the title has the same meaning as *loathsome.* Then, discuss the model sentences on p. 833 and have students match each Vocabulary word with its synonym.

1. chivalry [d]   **a.** face
2. countenance [a]   **b.** rule
3. loathsome [c]   **c.** hateful
4. sovereignty [b]   **d.** courtesy

Assign the Reading

Use the Quickwrite activity on p. 833 as the springboard for a class discussion. Next, have students read the story up to the introduction of the riddle. Students can then revise their guesses and finish the legend for homework.

HOMEWORK

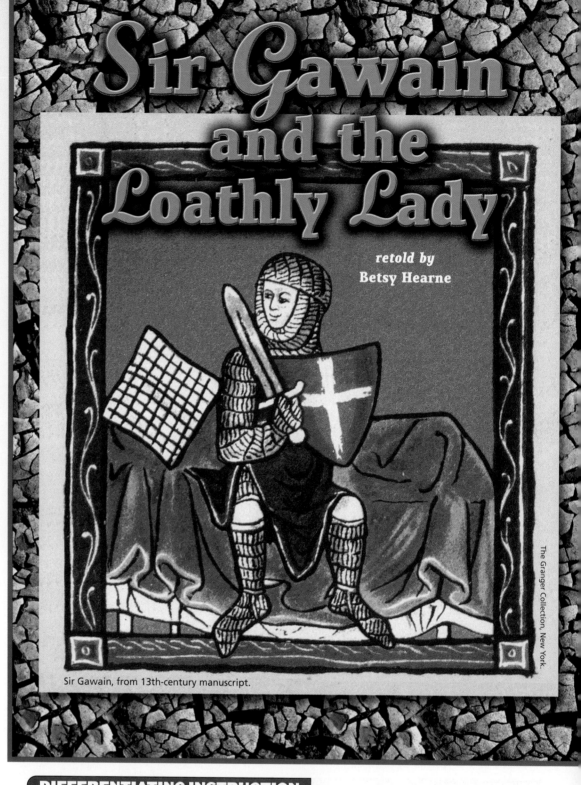

Sir Gawain and the Loathly Lady

retold by **Betsy Hearne**

Sir Gawain, from 13th-century manuscript.

The Granger Collection, New York.

DIFFERENTIATING INSTRUCTION

Learners Having Difficulty
To help students read "Sir Gawain and the Loathly Lady," discuss some familiar fairy tales, such as "Beauty and the Beast," "Cinderella," and "Jack and the Beanstalk," and the motifs that occur in such stories: the hero or heroine, the villain, the transformation, the quest, and so on. Write the motifs on the chalkboard, and encourage students to look for similar characters and events in the story.

English-Language Learners
This legend is filled with common vocabulary words used in unusual ways. For instance, consider the word *charged* in "he charged me I should not escape him" or the word *heat* in "would have slain me with great heat." Have students note unfamiliar uses of common words as they go through the selection. Afterward, they can compare lists with partners and work together to define the words.

Now if you listen awhile I will tell you a tale of Arthur the King and how an adventure once befell him.

Of all kings and all knights, King Arthur bore away the honor wherever he went. In all his country there was nothing but chivalry, and knights were loved by the people.

One day in spring King Arthur was hunting in Ingleswood with all his lords beside him. Suddenly a deer ran by in the distance and the king took up chase, calling back to his knights, "Hold you still every man, I will chase this one myself!" He took his arrows and bow and stooped low like a woodsman to stalk the deer. But every time he came near the animal, it leapt away into the forest. So King Arthur went a while after the deer, and no knight went with him, until at last he let fly an arrow and killed the deer. He had raised a bugle to his lips to summon the knights when he heard a voice behind him.

"Well met, King Arthur!"

Though he had not heard anyone approach, the king turned to see a strange knight, fully armed, standing only a few yards away.

"You have done me wrong many a year and given away my northern lands," said the strange knight. "I have your life in my hands—what will you do now, King Alone?"

"Sir Knight, what is your name?" asked the king.

"My name is Gromer Somer Joure."[1]

"Sir Gromer, think carefully," said the king. "To slay me here, unarmed as I am, will get you no honor. All knights will refuse you wherever you go. Calm yourself—come to Carlyle and I shall mend all that is amiss."

1. Gromer Somer Joure (grō·mer′ sō·mer′ zhoor′).

"Nay," said Sir Gromer, "by heaven, King! You shall not escape when I have you at advantage. If I let you go with only a warning, later you'll defy me, of that I'm sure."

"Spare my life, Sir Gromer, and I shall grant you whatever is in my power to give. It is shameful to slay me here, with nothing but my hunting gear, and you armed for battle."

"All your talking will not help you, King, for I want neither land nor gold, truly." Sir Gromer smiled. "Still . . . if you will promise to meet me here, in the same fashion, on a day I will choose . . ."

"Yes," said the king quickly. "Here is my promise."

"Listen and hear me out. First you will swear upon my sword to meet me here without fail, on this day one year from now. Of all your knights none shall come with you. You must tell me at your coming what thing women most desire—and if you do not bring the answer to my riddle, you will lose your head. What say you, King?"

"I agree, though it is a hateful bargain," said the king. "Now let me go. I promise you as I am the true king, to come again at this day one year from now and bring you your answer."

The knight laughed, "Now go your way, King Arthur. You do not yet know your sorrow. Yet stay a moment—do not think of playing false—for by Mary[2] I think you would betray me."

"Nay," said King Arthur. "You will never

2. **by Mary:** a mild oath.

Vocabulary
chivalry (shiv′əl·rē) n.: code that governed knightly behavior, which demanded courage, honor, and readiness to help the weak.

A **Literary Focus**

? **Heroic quests.** What will King Arthur have to do during the upcoming year because of his bargain with Sir Gromer? [Possible response: He will have to search for the answer to Sir Gromer's riddle.] **How does this particular quest involve the reader?** [Possible response: The reader will also try to guess the answer to the riddle.]

Special Education Students
For lessons designed for special education students, see *Holt Reading Solutions.*

Advanced Learners
Acceleration. Use the following activity to help advanced learners examine the recurring theme of good versus evil across traditional and contemporary works.
Activity. After they have finished reading "Sir Gawain and the Loathly Lady," have students discuss the characters in the story. Which characters are wholly evil? wholly good? Who wins in the end? Then, have students choose a contemporary work that involves the struggle of good versus evil, and ask the same questions. What differences between the classical and the contemporary work emerge?

A Literary Focus

Legends. Help students to see that King Arthur's statement beginning "Farewell, Sir Knight . . ." sets up two typical character types in legends. There is Sir Gromer, the evil knight, and King Arthur, the hero who, as indicated in this statement, always keeps his word, even if it means death.

B English-Language Learners

Understand archaic diction. Ask two students to read this brief dialogue aloud. Point out that the characters in this story don't speak today's English. They use few contractions, some of their words are now archaic, and their phrasing is old-fashioned. Explain that in her retelling, Betsy Hearne is trying to give the reader a flavor of the Old English spoken more than one thousand years ago.

C Literary Focus

❓ **Heroic quests.** Explain that King Arthur and Sir Gawain plan to travel around asking people the riddle in hopes that a consensus about the correct answer will emerge. Do you think this is a good plan? What do you think will happen? [Possible responses: Many students will think this plan is a logical first step to solving the riddle; others will predict that no consensus will emerge.]

D Literary Focus

❓ **Respond to literature.** How do you respond to the description of the lady? What makes you respond this way? [Students may be horrified by her looks, especially her "pushed-in nose" or her "yellowing tusks," but impressed by her evident good spirits and her sweet voice.]

---

find me an untrue knight. Farewell, Sir Knight, and evil met. I will come in a year's time, though I may not escape." The king began to blow his bugle for his knights to find him. Sir Gromer turned his horse and was gone as quickly as he had come, so that the lords found their king alone with the slain deer.

"We will return to Carlyle," said the king. "I do not like this hunting."

The lords knew by his countenance that the king met with some disturbance, but no one knew of his encounter. They wondered at the king's heavy step and sad look, until at last Sir Gawain[3] said to the king, "Sire, I marvel at you. What thing do you sorrow for?"

"I'll tell you, gentle Gawain," said Arthur. "In the forest as I pursued the deer, I met with a knight in full armor, and he charged me I should not escape him. I must keep my word to him or else I am foresworn."[4]

"Fear not my lord. I am not a man that would dishonor you."

"He threatened me, and would have slain me with great heat, but I spoke with him since I had no weapons."

"What happened then?" said Gawain.

"He made me swear to meet him there in one year's time, alone and unarmed. On that day I must tell him what women desire most, or I shall lose my life. If I fail in my answer, I know that I will be slain without mercy."

"Sire, make good cheer," said Gawain. "Make your horse ready to ride into strange country, and everywhere you meet either man or woman, ask of them the answer to

---

3. **Gawain** (gä′wān).
4. **foresworn** *adj.*: untrue to one's word; shown to be a liar.

---

the riddle. I will ride another way, and every man and woman's answer I will write in a book."

"That is well advised, Gawain," said the king. They made preparations to leave immediately, and when both were ready, Gawain rode one way and the king another—each one asked every man and woman they found what women most desire.

Some said they loved beautiful clothes; some said they loved to be praised; some said they loved a handsome man; some said one, some said another. Gawain had so many answers that he made a great book to hold them, and after many months of traveling he came back to court again. The king was there already with his book, and each looked over the other's work. But no answer seemed right.

"By God," said the king, "I am afraid. I will seek a little more in Ingleswood Forest. I have but one month to my set day, and I may find some good tidings."

"Do as you think best," said Gawain, "but whatever you do, remember that it is good to have spring again."

King Arthur rode forth on that day, into Ingleswood, and there he met with a lady. King Arthur marveled at her, for she was the ugliest creature that he had ever seen. Her face seemed almost like that of an animal, with a pushed-in nose and a few yellowing tusks for teeth. Her figure was twisted and deformed, with a hunched back and shoulders a yard broad. No tongue could tell the foulness of that lady. But she rode gaily on a palfrey[5] set with gold and precious stones,

---

5. **palfrey** (pôl′frē) *n.*: gentle riding horse.

Vocabulary
countenance (koun′tə·nəns) *n.*: face; appearance.

MINI-LESSON **Reading**

Developing Word-Attack Skills

Write the selection word *preparation* and the base word *prepare* on the chalkboard. Compare the pronunciations of the two words. Help students recognize that the stress pattern changes when the suffix *–tion* is added to *prepare*. The second syllable, which is the stressed syllable in *prepare,* becomes an unstressed syllable in *preparation.* Stress shifts to the first and third syllables: prep′ə·rā′shən.

Repeat the procedure with *attraction* and *attract.* Help students recognize that the stress pattern does not change in these words. The second syllable has the greatest stress in both words.

Activity. Have volunteers read these pairs of words and tell if the stress shifts when the suffix is added. Using these words, encourage students to make a generalization about when stress shifts and when it doesn't.

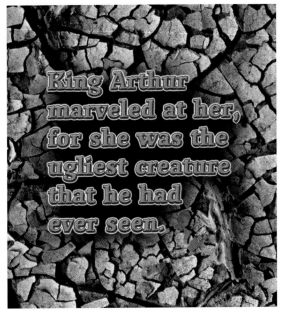

King Arthur marveled at her, for she was the ugliest creature that he had ever seen.

and when she spoke her voice was sweet and soft.

"I am glad that I have met with you, King Arthur," she said. "Speak with me, for your life is in my hand. I know of your situation, and I warn you that you will not find your answer if I do not tell you."

"What do you want with me, lady?" said the king, taken aback by the lady's boldness.

"Sir, I would like to speak with you. You will die if I do not save you, I know it very well."

"What do you mean, my lady, tell me," stammered the king. "What is your desire, why is my life in your hand? Tell me, and I shall give you all you ask."

"You must grant me a knight to wed," said the lady slowly. "His name is Sir Gawain. I will make this bargain: If your life is saved another way, you need not grant my desire. If my answer saves your life, grant

me Sir Gawain as my husband. Choose now, for you must soon meet your enemy."

"By Mary," said the king, "I cannot grant you Sir Gawain. That lies with him alone—he is not mine to give. I can only take the choice to Sir Gawain."

"Well," she said. "Then go home again and speak to Sir Gawain. For though I am foul, yet am I merry, and through me he may save your life or ensure your death."

"Alas!" cried the king. "That I should cause Gawain to wed you, for he will not say no. I know not what I should do."

"Sir King, you will get no more from me. When you come again with your answer I will meet you here."

"What is your name, I pray you tell me?"

"Sir King, I am the Dame Ragnell, that never yet betrayed a man."

"Then farewell, Dame Ragnell," said the king.

Thus they departed, and the king returned to Carlyle again with a heavy heart. The first man he met was Sir Gawain. "Sire, how did you fare?" asked the knight.

"Never so ill," said the king. "I fear I will die at Sir Gromer's hand."

"Nay," said Gawain. "I would rather die myself I love you so."

"Gawain, I met today with the foulest lady that I ever saw. She said she would save my life, but first she would have you for her husband."

"Is this all?" asked Gawain. "Then I shall wed her and wed her again! Though she were a fiend, though she were as foul as Beelzebub,[6] her I shall marry. For you are my king and I am your friend—it is my part to save your life, or else I am a false knight

---

6. **Beelzebub** (bē·el′zə·bub′): the devil; Satan.

DIRECT TEACHING

E Reading Skills

❓ Speculate. Who do you think this woman is? Why do you think she might know the answer to the riddle? [Possible responses: She is a witch or a sorceress who plans to trap Arthur; she is a woman who can use her magic powers to help Arthur. In legends, characters often appear mysteriously with exactly the items or information that the hero or heroine needs.]

F Literary Focus

❓ Respond to literature. Point out that King Arthur was forced to make a bargain with Sir Gromer. Now, in his quest to find the answer to the riddle, he is again presented with a bargain. How does Arthur's response to this bargain affect your opinion of him? [Possible response: By allowing Sir Gawain to make his own decision about marrying the lady, Arthur shows he is not a tyrant but a good king.]

G Learners Having Difficulty

Paraphrase. The archaic vocabulary and phrasing of some of the story's lengthy speeches may hinder some students. Have students work with partners to paraphrase any dialogue they don't understand. They should start by finding the main subject and verb of each sentence. They then should deal with the subordinate clauses.

---

1. explore   exploration [shift]
2. exhaust   exhaustion
3. complete   completion
4. invite   invitation [shift]
5. inspire   inspiration [shift]
6. animate   animation
7. combine   combination [shift]
8. suffocate   suffocation
9. reserve   reservation [shift]
10. inform   information [shift]

A Literary Focus

? **Respond to literature.** Do you think Ragnell gives Arthur the correct answer to the riddle? Why or why not? [Most students will think the answer is right because no one else has suggested it and Arthur thought all the other answers were wrong. Other students might think Dame Ragnell is setting a trap for King Arthur.]

B Reading Skills

? **Infer.** Why do you think Arthur offers Gromer the books first, instead of Ragnell's answer? [Possible response: He wants to save Gawain from having to keep his promise.] **What does this show about King Arthur's character?** [Possible responses: He is truly a good friend; he thinks of others first.]

and a great coward. If she were the most loathsome woman that ever a man might see, for your love I would spare nothing."

"Thank you, Gawain," said King Arthur then. "Of all knights that I have found, you are the finest. You have saved my life, and my love will not stray from you, as I am king in this land."

The day soon came when the king was to meet the Dame Ragnell and bear his answer to Sir Gromer. Gawain rode with him to the edge of Ingleswood Forest, but there the king said, "Sir Gawain, farewell. I must go west, and you must go no further."

"God speed you on your journey. I wish I rode your way," said Gawain.

The king had ridden but a mile or so more when he met the Dame Ragnell. "Ah, Sir King, you are welcome here bearing your answer."

"Now," said the king, "since it can be no other way, tell me your answer, save my life, and Gawain shall you wed; so he has promised. Tell me in all haste. Have done, I may not tarry."[7]

"Sire," said the Dame Ragnell, "now you will know what women desire most, high and low. Some men say we desire to be fair, or to wed, or to remain fresh and young, or to have flattery from men. But there is one thing that is every woman's fantasy: We desire of men, above all other things, to have sovereignty, for then all is ours. Therefore go on your way, Sir King, and tell that knight what I have said to you. He will be angry and curse the woman who told you, for his labor is lost. Go forth—you will not be harmed."

The king rode forth in great haste until

_____
7. **tarry** *v.:* linger; delay.

he came to the set place and met with Sir Gromer.

"Come, come, Sir King," said the knight sternly. "Now let me have answer, for I am ready."

The king pulled out the two books for Sir Gromer to see. "Sir, I dare say the right one is there."

Sir Gromer looked over them, every one, and said at last, "Nay, nay, Sir King, you are a dead man."

"Wait, Sir Gromer," said the king. "I have one more answer to give."

"Say it," said Sir Gromer, "or so God help me you shall bleed."

"Now," said the king, "here is my answer and that is all—above all things, women desire sovereignty, for that is their liking and their greatest desire; to rule over any man. This they told me."

Sir Gromer was silent a moment with rage, but then he cried out, "And she that told you, Sir Arthur, I pray to God I might see her burn in a fire, for that was my sister, Dame Ragnell. God give her shame—I have lost much labor. Go where you like, King Arthur, for you are spared. Alas that I ever saw this day, for I know that you will be my enemy and hunt me down."

"No," said King Arthur, "you will never find me an attacker. Farewell." King Arthur turned his horse into the forest again. Soon he met with the Dame Ragnell, in the same place as before. "Sir King," she said. "I am glad you have sped well. I told you how it would be, and now since I and none other have saved your life, Gawain must wed me."

_____
Vocabulary
loathsome (lōth'səm) *adj.:* disgusting.
sovereignty (säv'rən·tē) *n.:* control; authority.

"I will not fail in my promise," said the king. "If you will be ruled by my council, you shall have your will."

"No, Sir King, I will not be ruled," said the lady. "I know what you are thinking. Ride before, and I will follow to your court. Think how I have saved your life and do not disagree with me, for if you do you will be shamed."

The king was ashamed to bring the loathly lady openly to the court, but forth she rode till they came to Carlyle. All the country wondered when she came, for they had never seen so foul a creature, but she would spare no one the sight of her. Into the hall she went, saying, "Arthur, King, fetch in Sir Gawain, before all the knights, so that you may troth[8] us together. Set forth Gawain my love, for I will not wait."

C

Sir Gawain stepped forward then, and said, "Sir, I am ready to fulfill the promise I made to you."

"God have mercy," said the Dame Ragnell when she saw Gawain. "For your sake I wish I were a fair woman, for you are of such goodwill." Then Sir Gawain wooed her[9] as he was a true knight, and Dame Ragnell was happy.

"Alas!" said the Queen Guinevere, and all the ladies in her bower.[10] "Alas!" said both king and knights, that the beautiful Gawain should wed such a foul and horrible woman.

She would be wedded in no other way than this—openly, with announcements in every town and village, and she had all the ladies of the land come to Carlyle for the

---

8. **troth** (trôth) *v.:* engage to marry.
9. **wooed her:** said romantic things; spoke of love.
10. **bower** (bou′ər) *n.:* old-fashioned word for a private room.

"Alas!" said the Queen Guinevere, and all the ladies in her bower.

Queen Guinevere (1858) by William Morris.
Oil on canvas.
The Granger Collection, New York.

feast. The queen begged Dame Ragnell to be married in the early morning, as privately as possible. "Nay," said the lady. "By heaven I will not no matter what you say. I will be wedded openly, as the king promised. I will

Sir Gawain and the Loathly Lady 839

C Vocabulary Development

Understand Anglo-Saxon roots. Explain that *troth* is an Anglo-Saxon word. Have students guess its meaning from the context, without looking at the footnote. [promise to marry, to wed] Explain that until relatively modern times, a betrothal, or agreement to marry, was considered almost as binding as a wedding itself. Today people use the word *engagement* rather than *betrothal*.

VIEWING THE ART

William Morris was born in Essex, England, in 1834, and enjoyed a comfortable, affluent childhood. He originally intended to take holy orders, but when his schooling was done he decided to devote his life to art. After studying painting (*Queen Guinevere* is his only surviving oil painting), Morris determined that his creative future lay in the field of decorative arts. He and the artists who worked under him at Morris & Co. were most renowned for their stained glass work, characterized by its delightful foliage patterns. His most enduring accomplishment, however, was in the field of textile and wallpaper design. His elegant designs, marked by subtle color combinations and balanced compositions, were influenced by medieval art and his own observation of natural forms. Apart from achievements in fine art and design, the multitalented Morris was a very highly regarded poet and prose writer, a successful publisher, and one of the most active propagandists for the socialist cause in England.

Activity. Invite students to compare Morris's painting of Queen Guinevere with Sandys's painting of Morgan le Fay, on p. 803. How are the settings similar? How does the woman's posture affect the mood of each painting?

A Reading Skills

? Predict. What choice will Gawain make? Why do you think so? [Possible responses: Fair by day, so that other people will treat her well instead of avoiding her and so that he will be known as husband to a beautiful wife; fair by night, so that he can enjoy her beauty himself.]

B Literary Focus

? Respond to literature. Point out that Arthur had to answer a riddle for high stakes, and now Gawain's future happiness depends on his choosing correctly. Do you think his decision is the right one? Explain. [Possible response: Yes; Gawain has given Ragnell her own choice, which is what she told Arthur all women want.]

GUIDED PRACTICE

Monitor students' progress. Have students complete each sentence.

Short Answer

1. _____ wants to kill King Arthur to revenge a wrong. [Sir Gromer]

2. _____ helps the king in his quest to find the riddle's answer. [Sir Gawain]

3. _____allows Gawain to decide whether or not to marry Dame Ragnell. [King Arthur]

4. _____ gives King Arthur the correct answer to the knight's riddle. [Dame Ragnell]

5. _____ turns into a beautiful woman in the wedding chamber. [Dame Ragnell]

not go to the church until High Mass time,[11] and I will dine in the open hall, in the midst of all the court."

At the wedding feast there were lords and ladies from all estates, and Dame Ragnell was arrayed in the richest manner—richer even than Queen Guinevere. But all her rich clothes could not hide her foulness. When the feasting began, only Dame Ragnell ate heartily, while the knights and squires sat like stones. After the wedding feast, Sir Gawain and the Lady Ragnell retired to the wedding chamber that had been prepared for them.

"Ah, Gawain," said the lady. "Since we are wed, show me your courtesy and come to bed. If I were fair you would be joyous—yet for Arthur's sake, kiss me at least."

Sir Gawain turned to the lady, but in her place was the loveliest woman that he had ever seen.

"By God, what are you?" cried Gawain.

"Sir, I am your wife, surely. Why are you so unkind?"

"Lady, I am sorry," said Gawain. "I beg your pardon, my fair madam. For now you are a beautiful lady, and today you were the foulest woman that ever I saw. It is well, my lady, to have you thus." And he took her in his arms and kissed her with great joy.

"Sir," she said, "you have half-broken the spell on me. Thus shall you have me, but my beauty will not hold. You may have me fair by night and foul by day, or else have me fair by day, and by night ugly once again. You must choose."

"Alas!" said Gawain. "The choice is too

hard—to have you fair on nights and no more, that would grieve my heart and shame me. Yet if I desire to have you fair by day and foul by night, I could not rest. I know not in the world what I should say, but do as you wish. The choice is in your hands."

"Thank you, courteous Gawain," said the lady. "Of all earthly knights you are blessed, for now I am truly loved. You shall have me fair both day and night, and ever while I live as fair. For I was shaped by witchcraft by my stepmother, God have mercy on her. By enchantment I was to be the foulest creature, till the best knight of England had wedded me and had given me the sovereignty of all his body and goods. Kiss me, Sir Gawain—be glad and make good cheer, for we are well." The two rejoiced together and thanked God for their fortune.

King Arthur came himself to call them to breakfast the next day, wondering why Gawain stayed so late with his loathly bride. Sir Gawain rose, taking the hand of his lady, and opened the door to greet the king.

The Dame Ragnell stood by the fire, with her pale lovely skin and red hair spilling down to her knees. "Lo," said Gawain to the king, "this is my wife the Dame Ragnell, who once saved your life." And Gawain told the king the story of the lady's enchantment.

"My love shall she have, for she has been so kind," said the king. And the queen said, "You will have my love forever, Lady, for you have saved my Lord Arthur." And from then on, at every great feast, that lady was the fairest, and all his life Gawain loved the Lady Ragnell.

Thus ends the adventure of King Arthur and of the wedding of Sir Gawain.

---

11. **High Mass time:** main Mass of Sunday morning. People of the highest class would attend High Mass.

Meet the Writer

Betsy Hearne

Transforming a Beast

Betsy Hearne (1942–   ) includes "Sir Gawain and the Loathly Lady" in her collection of twenty-seven Beauty and the Beast folk tales from storytellers around the world. She writes that this story "is striking in its emphasis on the importance of a woman's power to control her own choices. The horrific but heroic female saves a king's life, outwits a sorcerer, wins a husband worthy of her, and reforms him even as he transforms her."

Hearne's work in collecting and connecting various types of Beauty and the Beast tales began with her studies in graduate school. She believes that:

❝ All of the stories . . . are about journeys in which the heroine or hero is transformed not through winning battles but through love for another being. . . . Beauty and the Beast tales suggest, among other things, that love is as powerful as force in coming to terms with what we fear. ❞

Hearne has worked as a children's librarian, and she is a highly respected critic, reviewer, writer, and university professor. She has edited both essay and folklore collections. She has also written four novels for young people and two volumes of poetry.

For Independent Reading

If you're interested in more Beauty and the Beast tales, be sure to read Hearne's collection, *Beauties and Beasts.* Another remarkable book by Hearne is *Seven Brave Women.* In it she describes the achievements of seven of her female ancestors, "unsung heroes," each of whom made history in her own way.

Meet the Writer

In *Beauty and the Beast: Visions and Revisions of an Old Tale,* Hearne examines how the same basic tale of a transformation from ugliness to beauty has changed over time and across cultures.

For Independent Reading

Students who especially enjoyed the quest and the riddle game may be interested in *The Hobbit.* J.R.R. Tolkien's classic tale of a quest for lost treasure includes a climactic riddle game between the hero, Bilbo, and a wicked creature named Gollum.

LITERARY CONNECTIONS

Geoffrey Chaucer

Geoffrey Chaucer was an English writer of the late fourteenth century. He wrote the stories that make up his famous work, *The Canterbury Tales,* between 1380 and 1400. In that work, a diverse group of pilgrims traveling to the shrine at Canterbury agrees to tell stories to pass the time. Chaucer's Wife of Bath tells a version of "Sir Gawain and the Loathly Lady" under the title "Sir Gawain and the Green Knight."

Activity. Have interested students locate and read "The Wife of Bath's Tale" from *The Canterbury Tales.* Tell them to find a modern edition, as they will have trouble understanding the Middle English of the original. Students can gather together to discuss the tale and compare and contrast it with "Sir Gawain and the Loathly Lady." Point out that the two versions of the story were written nearly six hundred years apart. Ask students how they think the times in which each version was written affect the way the story is told.

After You Read

First Thoughts

1. Students who agree with the answer will say that all human beings want to have their own way and to control their lives. Students who disagree may suggest that each individual wants something different. Students will probably say that goals and desires do not depend on gender.

Thinking Critically

2. Dame Ragnell changes from an ugly hag into a beautiful woman. Gawain breaks the spell that made her look ugly by marrying her and giving her free choice.

3. By reminding Gromer of the code of chivalry and by pledging his own honor, the unarmed Arthur was able to persuade Gromer not to kill him immediately. Chivalry also made the king behave politely to Ragnell instead of running away at the sight of her. Chivalry made him give Gawain the choice of whether to wed Ragnell or not.

4. Gawain shows chivalry and respect for Ragnell, allowing her to make her own decision rather than making it for her.

Reading Check

- The knight agrees to spare Arthur if the king can tell him in one year what women most desire.

- Dame Ragnell offers to give Arthur the answer to the riddle in exchange for marriage to Sir Gawain.

- Dame Ragnell tells Arthur the answer to the riddle.

- Dame Ragnell and Gawain marry. Gawain allows her to choose whether to be beautiful by day or by night, and the spell is broken. Dame Ragnell turns from a hag into a perpetual beauty.

After You Read   Response and Analysis

First Thoughts

1. Do you agree with the answer to the riddle, or do you like your own Quickwrite answer better? Tell why you think men and women are the same or different in what they want most in life. ✏

Thinking Critically

2. Myths, legends, and folk tales are full of **metamorphoses** (met′ə·môr′fə·sēz′)—marvelous changes from one shape or form to another one. A metamorphosis can be a punishment or a reward. What metamorphosis takes place in this story? What causes it?

3. King Arthur goes on a **quest** to find the answer to a riddle. Find three places on the quest where he could have made a big mistake—but managed to stay on the right path. How did the code of **chivalry** help him make the right decision each time?

4. What did you think of the choice presented to Gawain on his wedding night? Gawain makes the correct choice and is rewarded for it. What values are shown by Gawain in the choice he makes?

Reading Check

This tightly plotted story is a series of **causes** and **effects.** Some of the key events in the story are listed in the boxes that follow. Write down the missing plot links (the empty boxes) in your notebook.

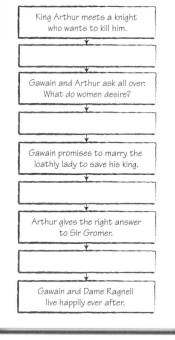

King Arthur meets a knight who wants to kill him.

↓

↓

Gawain and Arthur ask all over: What do women desire?

↓

↓

Gawain promises to marry the loathly lady to save his king.

↓

↓

Arthur gives the right answer to Sir Gromer.

↓

↓

Gawain and Dame Ragnell live happily ever after.

WRITING

SKILLS FOCUS

Literary Skills
Analyze a quest story.

Writing Skills
Write a critical response to literature.

Literary Criticism: Respond to the Legend

Find one aspect of this story you had a strong response to. Maybe you felt that the plot was not believable. Maybe you especially love stories set long ago. Maybe you didn't like the way the story treated ugliness. Maybe you disagree with the main idea of the story. Discuss the story in a small group, focusing on the aspect you had a strong response to. Then, write a brief essay describing your response to the story and explaining why you feel this way.

DIFFERENTIATING INSTRUCTION

Learners Having Difficulty

Students having trouble identifying key events for the Reading Check can work in small groups to fill in the missing plot links. After they complete the organizer, have them discuss how each event leads into the next one, creating a series of causes and effects. Suggest that they ask themselves the following questions: What does Arthur's meeting with Sir Gromer cause him to do?

What effect does Gawain's decision about his wife have on the outcome of the story?

Advanced Learners

Enrichment. Point out to students that "Beauty and the Beast" tales always involve a metamorphosis from ugliness to beauty, and that implied in this metamorphosis is a change from evil or imperfection to goodness.

After You Read Vocabulary Development

French Word Origins

In 1066, the Normans, who lived in France, invaded England, led by William the Conqueror. As you may have guessed from his name, William and his Normans conquered England. Within a few years the language spoken by important people in England started to be French. Words used in government, by the church, and by people at court were French.

In fact, the stories about King Arthur and his knights include many stories from France. You can spot some French influence in this story of the loathly lady:

- The angry knight's name is Gromer Somer Joure, a French name.
- *Palfrey,* meaning "gentle horse," is from the French language.

> **Word Bank**
> chivalry
> countenance
> loathsome
> sovereignty

PRACTICE 1

Use a dictionary to look up the Word Bank words. Most dictionaries tell you in brackets the history of a word, followed by the word's definition. Which words are from the French language? Which word is English?

PRACTICE 2

This reteller of the King Arthur legend has tried to give the story an old-fashioned flavor. Translate the following sentences into the kind of English you and your friends speak today.

1. In all his country there was nothing but chivalry, and knights were loved by the people.
2. The lords knew by his countenance that the king met with some disturbance, but no one knew of his encounter.
3. "If she were the most loathsome woman that ever a man might see, for your love I would spare nothing."
4. "We desire of men, above all other things, to have sovereignty, for then all is ours."

La Belle Dame sans Merci (1893) by John William Waterhouse.

Vocabulary Skills
Understand French word origins.

Vocabulary Development

PRACTICE 1

Sovereignty, chivalry, and *countenance* are French. *Loathsome* is Anglo-Saxon.

PRACTICE 2

Possible Answers
1. Everyone in the country had good manners, and all the people admired the knights.
2. The look on the king's face told the lords that he was upset, but no one knew what had happened.
3. "I love you so much that I would do this for you even if she were the ugliest woman the world has ever seen."
4. "More than anything, we would like men to let us control our own lives."

Activity. Have students form small groups to discuss the problems inherent in linking beauty and goodness. Are beautiful people always good and ugly people always bad? What messages—especially about women— do tales like this send readers? Students may wish to focus their essay on this issue.

SMALL GROUP

Grammar Link

PRACTICE

1. It's

2. you're

3. its

4. your

5. its, your

ASSESSING

Assessment

- *Holt Assessment: Literature, Reading, and Vocabulary*

After You Read Grammar Link

Words Often Confused

The different forms of two small words in English give writers a lot of trouble. The two simple words are from Old English; they are *you* and *it. You* comes from the Old English word *eow,* and *it* comes from the Old English word *hit.*

The problems come with different forms of the words. Read these words aloud: *its* and *it's,* and *your* and *you're.* The words in each pair sound alike, but they have different uses.

- The personal possessive pronouns *its* and *your* show that something belongs to someone or something. Possessive pronouns should not have apostrophes.

  "Sir Knight, what is your name?" [The name belongs to the knight.]

  The palfrey was a gentle horse, its halters studded with jewels. [The halters belong to the horse.]

- The contractions *you're* and *it's* are both shortened combinations of a personal pronoun and the verb *is, has,* or *are.* A contraction has an apostrophe to show where letters are omitted.

  It's [it is] **easy to lose yourself in a good story.**

  You're [you are] **going to love the loathly lady story.**

SKILLS FOCUS

Grammar Skills
Use *its* and *it's* and *your* and *you're* correctly.

King Arthur on His Throne Surrounded by Counselors (14th century).

PRACTICE

Write each sentence below, choosing the correct form of the underlined words. A tip: If you are unsure which word is correct, try substituting two words, such as *it is* or *you are.* If the sentence makes sense, you need the apostrophe because letters are omitted.

1. Its/It's clear that the author uses old-fashioned words.

2. Her style makes you feel as if your/you're reading the original.

3. King Arthur set up the Round Table; it's/its purpose was to make every knight equal.

4. For your/you're research paper, look up the Holy Grail.

5. The quest was it's/its own re-ward. What quest stories are told in you're/your tradition?

For more help, see Apostrophes, 15a–c, in the Language Handbook.

844 Collection 7 / Literary Criticism: Where I Stand

DIFFERENTIATING INSTRUCTION

Learners Having Difficulty
Some students may need additional practice in using *its/it's* and *your/you're* correctly. In each sentence below, have them choose the correct form of the italicized words.

1. On King Arthur's quest, *its/it's* his task to find the answer to a riddle. [it's]

2. Arthur admitted to the woman, "*Your/You're* the only one who knows the truth!" [You're]

3. The spell had cast *its/it's* evil influence on Dame Ragnell. [its]

4. *Your/You're* not alone in thinking that this story is similar to "Beauty and the Beast." [You're]

5. In *your/you're* book, the story is beauti-fully illustrated. [your]

Comparing Literature

Literary Focus
Real Heroes

In this book you have read about the deeds of many literary **heroes.** One great hero was Orpheus, who braved the underworld to rescue the woman he loved. Another was King Arthur, who used might to conquer evil in the world. Now you are going to read about two real-life heroes: Nelson Mandela and Rosa Parks. Both of these great people lived under legal systems that discriminated against people of color. For Mandela it was apartheid (ə·pär′tāt′), or racial segregation, in South Africa. For Parks it was racial segregation in the United States. Both took actions to right what they believed was wrong, and their actions helped thousands of people to know real freedom. Nelson Mandela recounts his experiences in his autobiography *Long Walk to Freedom*. Rosa Parks's story is told by the poet Rita Dove.

> ### Characteristics of a Hero
>
> - bravery
> - inner strength
> - honesty
> - sense of justice
> - loyalty to ideals
> - helpfulness to others
> - willingness to make personal sacrifices
>
> What other characteristics might a person need in order to be a hero?

Reading Skills
Comparing and Contrasting

As you read these two accounts, think about what makes these two people heroic. Consider

- the choices they make
- what happens to them
- how they respond to setbacks
- the effects of their actions

When you finish the selections, you will write an essay on heroism, focusing on Nelson Mandela and Rosa Parks.

Literary Skills
Understand heroes.

Reading Skills
Compare and contrast heroes.

Comparing Literature **845**

Grade-Level Skills

■ Literary Skills
Analyze heroes.

■ Reading Skills
Compare and contrast heroes.

OVERVIEW

Purpose. This Comparing Literature feature explores the characteristics of the literary hero by presenting two real-life heroes, Nelson Mandela and Rosa Parks. An appreciation of these heroes will deepen students' understanding of legends, myths, and epics.

Use. Direct students' attention to the box identifying characteristics of a hero, and tell them to look for these elements in the actions and descriptions of Nelson Mandela and Rosa Parks. After they read the selections, they will examine the actions of both figures by filling out a Comparing and Contrasting Real Heroes chart. They will then use the information they've gathered to write a comparison-contrast essay.

Summary ⬌ at grade level

In this excerpt from his memoir, Nelson Mandela explains how his understanding of freedom evolved during the course of his life. He describes the conflict he experienced between his desire to fulfill his obligations to his family and his commitment to the struggle for justice and freedom in South Africa. Mandela explains that as a child he felt free, but as a young man he came to believe that his freedom was an illusion. He joined the African National Congress to fight for freedom and equal rights for all South Africans. While serving time in prison for his anti-apartheid activities, Mandela came to the conclusion that in denying freedom to others, his oppressors were robbing themselves of their own freedom. He ends his essay by describing the road to freedom as a long one, one that has not yet ended.

PRETEACHING

Selection Starter

Motivate. Have students think of someone they admire. Then, have them look at the "Characteristics of a Hero" box on p. 845. Ask students to think of incidents that illustrate these characteristics in the person they admire. Encourage students to share their descriptions in class.

Nelson Mandela at the prison on Robben Island, South Africa, where he had been incarcerated (1994).

Before You Read

Nelson Mandela was born and raised in a tribal village in South Africa. After graduating from college and law school, Mandela joined the African National Congress to fight against apartheid, the government policy of racial segregation. He was arrested and, from 1962 till 1990, spent nearly twenty-eight years in prison, where he fought apartheid from his prison cell. In 1993, Mandela was awarded the Nobel Peace Prize. He served as the first democratically elected state president of South Africa from May 1994 until June 1999. Although now retired from public office, Mandela continues to work for democracy, freedom, and justice throughout Africa and the world. In this excerpt from his autobiography, he describes his "long walk to freedom."

846   Collection 7 / Literary Criticism: Where I Stand

DIFFERENTIATING INSTRUCTION

Learners Having Difficulty

Tell students that there is a great deal of information in this selection. Suggest that they read it slowly and take notes about Nelson Mandela's "walk to freedom." Then, pair students and have them discuss their notes.

PAIRED

English-Language Learners

You may want to review vocabulary with these students before they read the selection. Provide students with definitions of the following words: *apartheid, comrades, obligations, inclinations, potential, law-abiding.* For lessons designed for intermediate and advanced English-language learners, see *Holt Reading Solutions.*

FROM LONG WALK TO FREEDOM

Nelson Mandela

The policy of apartheid created a deep and lasting wound in my country and my people. All of us will spend many years, if not generations, recovering from that profound hurt. But the decades of oppression and brutality had another, unintended effect, and that was that it produced the Oliver Tambos, the Walter Sisulus, the Chief Luthulis, the Yusuf Dadoos, the Bram Fischers, the Robert Sobukwes[1] of our time—men of such extraordinary courage, wisdom, and generosity that their like may never be known again. Perhaps it requires such depth of oppression to create such heights **A** of character. My country is rich in the minerals and gems that lie beneath its soil, but I have always known that its greatest wealth is its people, finer and truer than the purest diamonds. ❶

It is from these comrades in the struggle that I learned the meaning of courage. Time and again, I have seen men and women risk and give their lives for an idea. I have seen men stand up to attacks and torture without breaking, showing a strength and resiliency that defies the imagination. I learned that courage was not the absence of fear, but the triumph over it. I felt fear myself more times than I can remember, but I hid it behind a mask of boldness. The brave man is not he who does not feel afraid, but he who conquers that fear. ❷

I never lost hope that this great transformation would occur. Not only because of the great heroes I have already cited, but because of the courage of the ordinary men and women of my country. I always knew that deep down in every human heart, there is mercy and generosity. No one is born hating another person because of the color of his skin, or his background, or his religion. People must learn to hate, and if they can learn to hate, they can be taught to love, for love comes more naturally to the human heart than its opposite. Even in the grimmest times in prison, when my comrades and I were pushed to our limits, I would see a glimmer of humanity

---

1. **Oliver Tambos ... Robert Sobukwes:** freedom fighters against South African apartheid.

INTERPRET

❶ What qualities does Nelson Mandela admire in his fellow freedom fighters? Why do you think he says they are "finer and truer than the purest diamonds"? **B**

COMPARE AND CONTRAST

❷ How is Mandela's definition of courage the same as or different from your own? **C**

Ⓐ Comparing Literature

❓ **Compare heroes.** Ask students to think about this statement by Mandela. Does it call to mind any of the literary characters they have read about in this collection? **Explain.** [Students may be reminded of King Arthur, who becomes a hero only after Britain has descended into chaos.]

Ⓑ Reading Skills

Interpret. [Possible responses to question 1: Mandela admires their courage, wisdom, and generosity. He says they are "finer and truer" than diamonds because he values these qualities more than material wealth.]

Ⓒ Reading Skills

Compare and contrast. [Possible response to question 2: My definition is similar to Mandela's: I also believe that showing courage involves overcoming fear.]

Special Education Students
For lessons designed for special education students, see *Holt Reading Solutions.*

Advanced Learners
Acceleration. Use this activity to help students compare and contrast historical figures from different places and eras.
Activity. Have students read about another prominent figure who fought for freedom, such as Martin Luther King, Jr. or Aung San

Suu Kyi. Then, have students compare facts they learn about the person with facts about Nelson Mandela that are presented in this selection. Have students discuss similarities and differences in the circumstances of the two figures and the way they responded to the challenges they faced.

Comparing Literature

DIRECT TEACHING

A Reading Skills

Interpret. [Possible response to question 3: Mandela says that it is more natural for humans to love than to hate and that people must be taught to hate. A brief glimpse of humanity was enough to give Mandela hope that people had not been completely taken over by hatred.]

B Reading Skills

Interpret. [Possible response to question 4: Mandela states that every man has an obligation to his family and to his community. Under apartheid a South African man who tried to fulfill his obligations to his country was punished and inevitably forced to neglect his family.]

C Literary Focus

❓ Heroes. Do you believe Mandela is exhibiting heroic behavior in making this commitment to his people? Explain. (Refer students to the box listing characteristics of a hero on p. 845 if they have difficulty.) [Possible response: Mandela's willingness to make sacrifices for the struggle is heroic.]

INTERPRET

❸ What does Mandela say about hate? Why do you think that a brief glimpse of a guard's humanity was enough to reassure Mandela about "man's goodness"?

INTERPRET

❹ According to Mandela, what two obligations does every man have? Why was it "almost impossible" for a man of color to meet those obligations in South Africa?

---

in one of the guards, perhaps just for a second, but it was enough to reassure me and keep me going. Man's goodness is a flame that can be hidden but never extinguished. **❸**

We took up the struggle with our eyes wide open, under no illusion that the path would be an easy one. As a young man, when I joined the African National Congress, I saw the price my comrades paid for their beliefs, and it was high. For myself, I have never regretted my commitment to the struggle, and I was always prepared to face the hardships that affected me personally. But my family paid a terrible price, perhaps too dear a price for my commitment.

In life, every man has twin obligations—obligations to his family, to his parents, to his wife and children; and he has an obligation to his people, his community, his country. In a civil and humane society, each man is able to fulfill those obligations according to his own inclinations and abilities. But in a country like South Africa, it was almost impossible for a man of my birth and color to fulfill both of those obligations. In South Africa, a man of color who attempted to live as a human being was punished and isolated. In South Africa, a man who tried to fulfill his duty to his people was inevitably ripped from his family and his home and was forced to live a life apart, a twilight existence of secrecy and rebellion. I did not in the beginning choose to place my people above my family, but in attempting to serve my people, I found that I was prevented from fulfilling my obligations as a son, a brother, a father, and a husband. **❹**

In that way, my commitment to my people, to the millions of South Africans I would never know or meet, was at the expense of the people I knew best and loved most. It was as simple and yet as incomprehensible as the moment a small child asks her father, "Why can you not be with us?" And the father must utter the terrible words: "There are other children like you, a great many of them . . ." and then one's voice trails off.

I was not born with a hunger to be free. I was born free—free in every way that I could know. Free to run in the fields near my mother's hut, free to swim in the clear stream that ran through my village, free to roast mealies[2] under the stars and ride the broad backs of slow-moving bulls. As long as I obeyed my father and

---

2. **mealies** (mē'lēz) *n.:* in South Africa, ears of corn.

848   Collection 7 / Literary Criticism: Where I Stand

CROSS-CURRICULAR CONNECTIONS

History

Apartheid. *Apartheid* refers to a policy of strict racial segregation adopted in South Africa by the National Party when they took power in 1948. Under apartheid more than 80 percent of South Africa's land was set aside for the exclusive use of whites. Black and mixed-race South Africans faced discrimination in education and employment and were denied representation in the national government. Opposition to

apartheid existed from its beginnings. South Africans engaged in strikes, civil disobedience, marches, and, finally, armed struggle to overturn the policy. This resistance, together with an international campaign of trade sanctions, helped bring apartheid to an end. In 1991, the South African government repealed most of the laws that made up the legal framework of apartheid. In 1994, the first all-race

national elections in the country's history were held. The African National Congress won most of the seats in the National Assembly, and Nelson Mandela became president of South Africa.

Activity. Ask students to research race relations in South Africa today. Have students share their findings with the class.

848   **Collection 7**   Literary Criticism: Where I Stand

Nelson Mandela greets Soweto children in South Africa (1990).

abided by the customs of my tribe, I was not troubled by the laws of man or God.

It was only when I began to learn that my boyhood freedom was an illusion, when I discovered as a young man that my freedom had already been taken from me, that I began to hunger for it. At first, as a student, I wanted freedom only for myself, the transitory[3] freedoms of being able to stay out at night, read what I pleased, and go where I chose. Later, as a young man in Johannesburg, I yearned for the basic and honorable freedoms of achieving my potential, of earning my keep, of marrying and having a family—the freedom not to be obstructed in a lawful life.

But then I slowly saw that not only was I not free, but my brothers and sisters were not free. I saw that it was not just my freedom that was curtailed,[4] but the freedom of everyone who looked like I did. That is when I joined the African National Congress, and that is when the hunger for my own freedom became the greater hunger for the freedom of my people. It was this desire for the freedom of my people to live their lives with dignity and self-respect that animated my life, that transformed a frightened young man into a bold one, that drove a law-abiding attorney to become a criminal, that turned a family-loving husband into a man

---

3. **transitory** (tran′sə·tôr′ē) *adj.*: passing; temporary.
4. **curtailed** (kər·tāld′) *v.* used as adj.: cut short.

DIRECT TEACHING

D Literary Focus

❓ Character. What words would you use to describe the young Nelson Mandela? [Possible responses: ambitious; eager to enjoy life.] **Do these words call to mind your idea of a hero? Explain.** [Most students will probably say no. The freedom Mandela wanted as a young man involved only himself: He wanted the freedom to do as he pleased and to establish himself and enjoy success.]

E Reading Skills

❓ Analyze cause and effect. What are two effects of Mandela's realization that he *and* his people were not free? [Possible responses: He joined the African National Congress; his desire for his own freedom developed into a desire for freedom for all black South Africans.]

A **Reading Skills**

Retell. [Possible response to question 5: Mandela's attitude changed when he saw that it was not only his own freedom but also that of his country-men that was limited. He became even bolder and more determined, realizing that even if he himself attained freedom, he would never be satisfied until all of his people were free as well.]

B **Literary Focus**

❓ Heroes. What heroic character-istics does Mandela display in this paragraph? [Possible responses: determination; concern for others; a sense of justice.]

C **Reading Skills**

Identify. [Possible response to question 6: To be free, people must live in a way that respects the rights of all people to be free.]

RETELL

❺ Retell the way that Mandela's attitude toward freedom changes in this paragraph.

IDENTIFY

❻ Mandela says that ending apartheid is not enough to create freedom. What else does he say is necessary for people to be free?

---

without a home, that forced a life-loving man to live like a monk. I am no more virtuous or self-sacrificing than the next man, but I found that I could not even enjoy the poor and limited freedoms I was allowed when I knew my people were not free. Freedom is indivisible; the chains on any one of my people were the chains on all of them, the chains on all of my people were the chains on me. **❺**

It was during those long and lonely years that my hunger for the freedom of my own people became a hunger for the freedom of all people, white and black. I knew as well as I knew anything that the oppressor must be liberated just as surely as the oppressed. A man who takes away another man's freedom is a prisoner of hatred, he is locked behind the bars of prejudice and narrow-mindedness. I am not truly free if I am taking away someone else's freedom, just as surely as I am not free when my freedom is taken from me. The oppressed and the oppressor alike are robbed of their humanity.

When I walked out of prison, that was my mission, to liberate the oppressed and the oppressor both. Some say that has now been achieved. But I know that that is not the case. The truth is that we are not yet free; we have merely achieved the freedom to be free, the right not to be oppressed. We have not taken the final step of our journey, but the first step on a longer and even more difficult road. For to be free is not merely to cast off one's chains, but to live in a way that respects and enhances the freedom of others. The true test of our devotion to freedom is just beginning. **❻**

I have walked that long road to freedom. I have tried not to falter; I have made missteps along the way. But I have discovered the secret that after climbing a great hill, one only finds that there are many more hills to climb. I have taken a moment here to rest, to steal a view of the glorious vista that surrounds me, to look back on the distance I have come. But I can rest only for a moment, for with freedom come responsibilities, and I dare not linger, for my long walk is not yet ended.

FAMILY/COMMUNITY ACTIVITY

Ask students to discuss Mandela's memoir with a parent, grandparent, or caregiver. Encourage students to ask about similarities and differences between Mandela's situation in South Africa and life for African Americans in the South during the 1950s and 1960s. Ask students to discuss their conversations in class.

Meet the Writer

Nelson Mandela

A Cherished Ideal

Nelson Mandela (1918–   ) has dedicated his life to ending racial oppression in South Africa. Before his historic release from prison, Mandela endured nearly three decades as a political prisoner in his native land.

Mandela joined the African National Congress (ANC), an organization promoting black liberation, in 1944. In 1960, the South African government outlawed the ANC. As a result, Mandela went into hiding and secretly continued to work for the group. He was eventually caught and received a five-year prison sentence.

In 1963, the police discovered Mandela's involvement with the military unit of the ANC, and he was put on trial for treason and other charges. During the trial, Mandela delivered a powerful speech illustrating his commitment to the struggle for racial equality. At the end of his speech, Mandela declared:

❝ I have cherished the ideal of a democratic and free society. . . . It is an ideal which I hope to live for and to achieve. But if needs be, it is an ideal for which I am prepared to die.❞

The court sentenced Mandela to life in prison.

Both at home and abroad, the South African government faced pressure to release Mandela. In 1990, F. W. de Klerk (who served as South Africa's president until 1994) ordered Mandela's release from prison.

Following Mandela's release, the two leaders worked together to bring peace to South Africa. In 1993, they were jointly awarded the Nobel Peace Prize in recognition of their efforts.

One historic reform that both men worked for was the establishment of South Africa's first democratic election, which took place in 1994. For the first time in the country's history, citizens of all races were allowed to vote in a national election. As a result, Mandela became the country's first black president, a position he held until 1999.

Meet the Writer

During Nelson Mandela's tenure as president of South Africa, he worked tirelessly to uphold the ideal of freedom. In 1996, he signed into law a constitution for the country that provided for majority rule, with protections for minorities' rights, and guaranteed freedom of expression to all citizens. He also sought to improve South Africans' standard of living by allotting government money to create jobs and develop healthcare.

For Independent Reading

Students who want to learn more about Nelson Mandela's life may want to try the biographies *Nelson Mandela: No Easy Walk to Freedom* by Barry Denenberg and *Nelson Mandela* by Reggie Finlayson.

INDEPENDENT PRACTICE

After You Read

First Thoughts

1. Possible answer:
   • Nelson Mandela is a courageous man who fights for his convictions.

Thinking Critically

2. The people Mandela knows and loves most are his family. Mandela's commitment to the South African people prevented him from fulfilling his obligations to his family because anti-apartheid activists had to go underground.

3. Possible answer: Mandela means that people cannot be lovers of freedom as long as they are denying freedom to others. He points out that oppressors themselves are prisoners "of prejudice and narrow-mindedness."

4. Some students will say that most people would find the ability within themselves to act bravely when faced with dire circumstances. Others will say that few people have Mandela's courage or ability to lead.

5. Possible answer: Mandela was able to endure because of his dedication to the cause of freedom and his willingness to make sacrifices for that ideal.

Comparing Literature

6. Possible answers: *Challenge to authority*—Mandela took part in the struggle against apartheid. *Effects of actions*—Mandela was put on trial and then imprisoned for almost twenty-eight years; his efforts helped end apartheid. *My responses to actions*—I admire Mandela for his courage. *Feeling about freedom*—Mandela feels that freedom is worth making sacrifices for.

First Thoughts

1. Complete the following sentence:
   • Nelson Mandela is . . .

Thinking Critically

2. Explain why Mandela's commitment to the people of South Africa came at the expense of the people he knew and loved most. Who are those people?

3. What does Mandela mean when he says "the oppressor must be liberated just as surely as the oppressed" (page 850)? Use details from the text to support your response.

4. Mandela says he is no more virtuous or self-sacrificing than anyone else. Do you think someone else could have accomplished what he did? Or do you think it took someone with his special qualities or powers? Explain your position.

5. What personal strengths and beliefs enabled Mandela to devote his life to fighting injustice and to endure nearly twenty-eight years in prison without losing his dignity or humanity?

Comparing Literature

6. After you read the next selection, you will write an essay on heroism, in which you compare and contrast the heroic qualities of two people who helped to improve the world we live in—Nelson Mandela and Rosa Parks. To prepare for that essay, fill in the column on Nelson Mandela in a chart like the one below.

Comparing and Contrasting Real Heroes		
	Nelson Mandela	Rosa Parks
Challenge to authority		
Effects of actions		
My responses to actions		
Feeling about freedom		

SKILLS FOCUS

Literary Skills
Analyze heroes.

Reading Skills
Compare and contrast heroes.

Reading Check

Explain how Nelson Mandela felt about **freedom**

a. as a child
b. as a student
c. as a young lawyer
d. when he was in prison
e. after he got out of prison

Reading Check
Possible Answers

a. Mandela did not hunger for freedom because he was free in every way he knew.

b. He realized that he was not free in some ways, but he was concerned only about freedom for himself.

c. He could not enjoy what freedoms he had knowing that his fellow South Africans were not free.

d. Mandela wanted freedom for all people and came to believe that oppressors are in need of liberation, along with the oppressed.

e. Mandela believes that the struggle for freedom cannot end until people live in such a way that other people's right to freedom is respected.

Before You Read

While Nelson Mandela fought injustice in South Africa, on the other side of the globe, Rosa Parks stood against injustice in the United States—by refusing to give up her seat on a Montgomery, Alabama, bus in 1955. Both helped to end discrimination in their countries, and both have come to symbolize for the world the triumph of the human spirit over injustice.

Rosa Parks

Rita Dove

Rosa Parks arrives at a Montgomery, Alabama, courthouse with civil rights leader E. D. Nixon (center).

Rosa Parks 853

Summary ⬄ *at grade level*

In this essay, Rita Dove describes Rosa Parks's famous encounter with a Montgomery bus driver, an event that played a key part in the struggle to end segregation. On December 1, 1955, Rosa Parks was arrested for refusing to give up her seat on a Montgomery bus to a white man. The African American population of Montgomery staged a one-day boycott of the buses to protest Parks's arrest and trial. That day a group called the Montgomery Improvement Association was founded to continue the battle against segregation. Martin Luther King, Jr., who was the minister of a local church, was elected president. Public transportation in Montgomery was integrated a year later.

PRETEACHING

Selection Starter

Build background. Explain to students that racial segregation is a policy requiring people of different races to live in separate areas and use separate facilities. Segregation was widespread across the American South by the middle of the twentieth century. Tell students that the following article is about one woman who chose to stand up to the unjust policy of racial segregation.

DIRECT TEACHING

A Reading Skills

? Ask questions. Ask students why they think the writer decided to open this piece with a quotation. Tell them to consider the following questions to clarify the meaning of the quotation: What time and place does the text refer to? Why was the time right and the place wrong? [Possible responses: The time was 1955; the place was a bus in Montgomery, Alabama. The time was right because African Americans felt they could no longer endure segregation and were ready to demand an end to it. The place was wrong because many injustices had been committed against African Americans living there.]

B Comparing Literature

? Compare heroes. What similarities do you find between Rosa Parks as she is described here and Nelson Mandela? [Possible response: Both Parks and Mandela contested authority when they felt that an injustice was being done.]

C Reading Skills

Compare and contrast. [Possible response to question 1: Parks, David, and the boy with his finger in the dike all confronted a formidable force or opponent alone.]

D Reading Skills

Retell. [Possible response to question 2: African Americans had to pay their fare at the main entrance, then re-enter through a back entrance. They were required to give up their seats to white people and could not even sit across from them.]

> How she sat there, the time
> right inside a place so wrong it
> **A** was ready.
> —From "Rosa," in *On the Bus
> with Rosa Parks* by Rita Dove

We know the story. One December evening, a woman left work and boarded a bus for home. She was tired; her feet ached. But this was Montgomery, Alabama, in 1955, and as the bus became crowded, the woman, a black woman, was ordered to give up her seat to a white passenger. When she remained seated, that simple decision eventually led to the disintegration[1] of institutionalized segregation in the South, ushering in a new era of the civil rights movement.

This, anyway, was the story I had heard from the time I was curious enough to eavesdrop on adult conversations. I was three years old when a white bus driver warned Rosa Parks, "Well, I'm going to have you arrested," and she replied, "You may go on and do so." As a child, I didn't understand how doing nothing had caused so much activity, but I recognized the template:[2] David slaying the giant **B** Goliath, or the boy who saved his village by sticking his finger in the dike. And perhaps it is precisely the lure of fairy tale retribution[3] that colors the lens we look back through. Parks was forty-two years old when she refused to give up her seat. She has insisted that her feet were not aching; she was, by her own testimony, no more tired than usual. And she did not plan her fateful act: "I did not get on the bus to get arrested," she has said. "I got on the bus to go home." **①**

Montgomery's segregation laws were complex: Blacks were required to pay their fare to the driver, then get off and reboard through the back door. Sometimes the bus would drive off before the paid-up customers made it to the back entrance. If the white section was full and another white customer entered, blacks were required to give up their seats and move farther to the back; a black person was not even allowed to sit across the aisle from whites. These humiliations were compounded by the fact that two thirds of the bus riders in Montgomery were black. **②**

Parks was not the first to be detained for this offense. Eight months earlier, Claudette Colvin, fifteen, refused to give up her seat

---

COMPARE AND CONTRAST

C ① How is Rosa Parks's action like David slaying Goliath or the boy with his finger in the dike?

RETELL

D ② Explain Montgomery's segregation laws.

---

1. **disintegration** (dis·in′tə·grā′shən) *n.:* the breaking up of something.
2. **template** (tem′plit) *n.:* pattern.
3. **retribution** (re′trə·byo͞o′shən) *n.:* punishment for evil or reward for good.

DIFFERENTIATING INSTRUCTION

Learners Having Difficulty
Modeling. To help students read this essay, model the reading skill of tracing cause and effect. Point out to students that the first paragraph ends with a statement saying that Rosa Parks's decision to remain seated on the bus in Montgomery led to the repeal of segregation laws. Ask students to trace the chain of causes and effects that led to Parks's arrest and to the desegregation of Montgomery buses. Begin by referring students to the fourth paragraph of the selection and stating, "Because they refused to give up their seats on a bus, Claudette Colvin and Mary Louise Smith were arrested." Ask students to trace the events in the essay from there.

English-Language Learners
For lessons designed to help intermediate and advanced English-language learners, see *Holt Reading Solutions*.

A statue of
Rosa Parks at the
Birmingham Civil
Rights Institute
in Birmingham,
Alabama.

DIRECT TEACHING

VIEWING THE ART

Activity. Have students look
carefully at the depiction of Rosa
Parks in this illustration. What
emotions does Parks seem to be
feeling? [Possible responses: Parks
looks calm but determined; the grip
of her hand on her purse suggests
tension.] Suggest to students that
they study the other photographs
that accompany this selection.

Rosa Parks   855

Special Education Students
For lessons designed to help special education students, see *Holt Reading Solutions.*

Advanced Learners
Enrichment. Encourage students to
research other major figures and events in
the battle for racial equality in the United
States. Have them note key phrases and
images they come across in their research.

Activity. Ask each student to bring in three
photographs or phrases clipped from newspapers or magazines that relate to the
fight against racial injustice. Then, have the
whole class collaborate on a collage that
depicts the history of racial injustice from
the civil rights movement to the present
day. Afterward, display the collage in the
classroom.

WHOLE CLASS

A Reading Skills

? Infer. Why do you think it was a good idea for Parks not to frown, struggle, or shout? [Possible response: By behaving in a calm, restrained manner, Parks would avoid provoking the authorities and help keep the focus of attention on the injustice she was challenging instead of herself.]

The bus on which Rosa Parks refused to give up her seat, on exhibit at the Henry Ford Museum in Dearborn, Michigan.

and was arrested. Black activists met with this girl to determine if she would make a good test case—as secretary of the local N.A.A.C.P.,[4] Parks attended the meeting—but it was decided that a more "upstanding" candidate was necessary to withstand the scrutiny of the courts and the press. And then in October, a young woman named Mary Louise Smith was arrested; N.A.A.C.P. leaders rejected her too as their vehicle, looking for someone more able to withstand media scrutiny. Smith paid the fine and was released.

Six weeks later, the time was ripe. The facts, rubbed shiny for retelling, are these: On December 1, 1955, Mrs. Rosa Parks, seamstress for the Montgomery Fair department store, boarded the Cleveland Avenue bus. She took a seat in the fifth row—the first row of the "Colored Section." The driver was the same one who had put her off a bus twelve years earlier for refusing to get off and reboard through the back door. ("He was still mean looking," she has said.) Did that make her stubborn? Or had her work in the N.A.A.C.P. sharpened her sensibilities so that she knew what to do—or more precisely, what not to do: Don't frown, don't struggle, don't shout, don't pay the fine?

At the news of the arrest, local civil rights leader E. D. Nixon exclaimed, "My God, look what segregation has put in my hands!" Parks was not only above moral reproach (securely married, reasonably employed) but possessed a quiet fortitude as well as

4. **N.A.A.C.P.:** National Association for the Advancement of Colored People, an organization in existence since 1909.

DEVELOPING FLUENCY

Activity. Dove's conversational tone makes this selection an excellent choice for reading aloud. Group students in pairs, and have them read sections of the article to each other. Encourage students to make suggestions about inflection, pronunciation, and tone as they listen. Afterward, have students discuss whether hearing the article helped them imagine the events it describes.

PAIRED

political savvy—in short, she was the ideal plaintiff [5] for a test case. **❸**

She was arrested on a Thursday; bail was posted by Clifford Durr, the white lawyer whose wife had employed Parks as a seamstress. That evening, after talking it over with her mother and husband, Rosa Parks agreed to challenge the constitutionality of Montgomery's segregation laws. During a midnight meeting of the Women's Political Council, 35,000 handbills were mimeographed for distribution to all black schools the next morning. The message was simple:

"We are . . . asking every Negro to stay off the buses Monday in protest of the arrest and trial. . . . You can afford to stay out of school for one day. If you work, take a cab, or walk. But please, children and grownups, don't ride the bus at all on Monday. Please stay off the buses Monday." **❹**

Monday came. Rain threatened, yet the black population of Montgomery stayed off the buses, either walking or catching one of the black cabs stopping at every municipal bus stop for ten cents per customer—standard bus fare. Meanwhile, Parks was scheduled to appear in court. As she made her way through the throngs at the courthouse, a demure figure in a long-sleeved black dress with white collar and cuffs, a trim black velvet hat, gray coat and white gloves, a girl in the crowd caught sight of her and cried out, "Oh, she's so sweet. They've messed with the wrong one now!"

Yes, indeed. The trial lasted thirty minutes, with the expected conviction and penalty. That afternoon, the Montgomery Improvement Association was formed. So as not to ruffle any local activists' feathers, the members elected as their president a relative newcomer to Montgomery, the young minister of Dexter Avenue Baptist Church: the Rev. Martin Luther King, Jr. That evening, addressing a crowd gathered at the Holt Street Baptist Church, King declared in that sonorous, ringing voice millions the world over would soon thrill to: "There comes a time that people get tired." When he was finished, Parks stood up so the audience could see her. She did not speak; there was no need to. Here I am, her silence said, among you.

And she has been with us ever since—a persistent symbol of human dignity in the face of brutal authority. The famous U.P.I. [6]

---

5. **plaintiff** (plān′tif) *n.*: person who brings a suit, or complaint, into a court of law.
6. **U.P.I.**: United Press International, a service that supplies articles and photographs to newspapers around the world.

Comparing Literature

COMPARE AND CONTRAST

❸ Why did civil rights leaders think Rosa Parks was the ideal person to bring a test case against the bus segregation laws? Whom else did they consider?

INTERPRET

❹ How do you think the bus boycott supported Rosa Parks's case against segregation laws?

DIRECT TEACHING

B **Reading Skills**
Compare and contrast. [Possible response to question 3: Rosa Parks was the ideal person because she was brave, politically active, and respected in her community. The other people they considered were Claudette Colvin and Mary Louise Smith.]

C **Reading Skills**
Interpret. [Possible response to question 4: Since the majority of people who rode on the buses were African American, there was probably a sharp decrease in income for the city that day. The boycott testified to the collective strength of Montgomery's African American population.]

D **Literary Focus**
❓ Heroes. Would you describe the African Americans who boycotted the buses as heroic? Why or why not? [Some students will say that they were heroic because they stayed true to their ideals and supported a member of their community. Others may say that taking part in the boycott did not require as much courage as acting alone.]

E **Advanced Learners**
❓ Cause and effect. In what ways did Rosa Parks's conviction prove to be ironic? [Possible response: Since convictions for this violation occurred with some frequency, those who supported segregation probably expected that life would go on as usual. However, the "victory" in the courts led to the formation of the Montgomery Improvement Association and increased pressure to overturn the segregation laws.]

A Reading Skills

? Use context clues. What point is the writer making by contrasting these images of grandiose figures and dramatic events with acts like Parks's? [Possible response: Seemingly insignificant acts by little-known people may have momentous consequences.]

B English-Language Learners

Idioms. Explain to English-language learners that *crunch time* is a slang expression that refers to a critical point in a given situation.

C Reading Skills

Compare and contrast. [Possible responses to question 5: Like Nelson Mandela, Rosa Parks took actions that helped bring about major changes in society. Both Mandela and Parks helped people realize that the capacity for bravery and heroism is within everyone.]

Rosa Parks on her way to jail after her trial.

photo (actually taken more than a year later, on December 21, 1956, the day Montgomery's public transportation system was legally integrated) is a study of calm strength. She is looking out the bus window, her hands resting in the folds of her checked dress, while a white man sits, unperturbed, in the row behind her. That clear profile, the neat cloche[7] and eyeglasses and sensible coat—she could have been my mother, anybody's favorite aunt.

A History is often portrayed as a string of arias in a grand opera, all baritone intrigues and tenor heroics. Some of the most tumultuous events, however, have been provoked by serendipity[8]—the assassination of an inconsequential archduke spawned World War I, a kicked-over lantern may have sparked the Great Chicago Fire. One cannot help wondering what role Martin Luther King, Jr. would have played in the civil rights movement if the opportunity had not presented itself that first evening of the boycott—if Rosa Parks had chosen a row farther back from the outset, or if she had missed the bus altogether.

At the end of this millennium (and a particularly noisy century), it is the modesty of Rosa Parks' example that sustains us. It is no less than the belief in the power of the individual, that cornerstone of the American Dream, that she inspires, along with the hope that all of us—even the least of us—could be that brave, that serenely **B** human, when crunch time comes. **5**

COMPARE AND CONTRAST

C 5 How are Rosa Parks's actions and goals similar to Nelson Mandela's?

---

7. **cloche** (klōsh) *n.:* tight-fitting women's hat.
8. **serendipity** (ser′ən·dip′ə·tē) *n.:* accident, usually accidental luck.

FAMILY/COMMUNITY ACTIVITY

Have students interview a parent, grandparent, or caregiver about Rosa Parks and the Montgomery bus boycott. Tell students to ask their interviewees how they felt when they first learned of Rosa Parks's actions. Also tell students to ask questions about the way Parks was perceived then and to draw comparisons to the way she is perceived now.

Meet the Writer

Rita Dove

An Award-Winning Poet

Rita Dove (1952–   ) discovered that she wanted to be a poet during her college years. She recalls:

> ❝I took creative writing courses and I began to write more and more, and I realized I was scheduling my entire life around my writing courses, and I said, 'Well maybe you need to figure out if this is what you want to do.'❞

Dove decided to pursue her interest in poetry and received a master's degree from the University of Iowa Writers' Workshop in 1977.

Dove had already achieved recognition for her work when her first poetry collection, *The Yellow House on the Corner,* was published in 1980. In 1987, she was awarded the Pulitzer Prize for the collection *Thomas and Beulah,* which was inspired by the lives of her grandparents.

In 1993, Rita Dove was named poet laureate, one of America's highest literary honors. She became the youngest person and first African American to be appointed to this position.

Dove, who is currently an English professor at the University of Virginia, shares these feelings about writing poetry:

> ❝I know that every time that I write a poem . . . I try to remember . . . the reader that I was . . . the moment of opening a book and absolutely having my world fall away and entering into another one and feeling there was one other voice that was almost inside of me, we were so close.❞

Meet the Writer

Although she is known mainly for her poetry, Rita Dove has produced works in other genres. She published a collection of short stories, *Fifth Sunday,* in 1985. She has also written a novel, *Through the Ivory Gate,* and a full-length play, *The Darker Face of Earth.*

After You Read

First Thoughts

1. Possible answer:
   - I think Rosa Parks is <u>a brave, dignified, and inspirational figure.</u>

Thinking Critically

2. Most students will say Rosa Parks did the right thing by breaking the law because this particular law was unjust. Explain to students who believe that Parks should have obeyed the law that Parks, through her action, challenged an injustice and helped bring about a positive change in American society.

3. Possible answer: People who have experienced injustice—such as members of a persecuted group—are the most likely to take a stand.

Comparing Literature

4. Possible answers: *Challenge to authority*—Rosa Parks refused to give up her seat on a bus to a white passenger. *Effects of actions*—She helped end segregation in Montgomery. *My responses to actions*—I admire Rosa Parks for standing up to authority to fight for her convictions. *Feeling about freedom*—Rosa Parks valued freedom highly because she fought against seemingly impossible odds to gain hers.

Reading Check

Possible answers: (1) Rosa Parks refuses to give up her seat. (2) Rosa Parks is arrested. (3) She challenges the constitutionality of Montgomery's segregation laws. (4) African Americans boycott buses to show their support. (5) Parks is tried and found guilty. (6) The Montgomery Improvement Association is formed. (7) Montgomery's public transportation system is desegregated.

After You Read "Rosa Parks"

First Thoughts

1. Complete the following sentence:
   - I think Rosa Parks is . . .

Thinking Critically

2. Do you think that Rosa Parks did the right thing by refusing to give up her seat on the bus, or do you think people should always obey the law? Explain your opinion.

3. What do you think causes a person to take a stand against injustice, even when it involves a personal sacrifice?

Comparing Literature

4. To plan your essay comparing and contrasting heroes, fill in the column on Rosa Parks in a chart like the one below.

Reading Check

To **retell** the story of Rosa Parks, fill in a sequence chart like the one below.

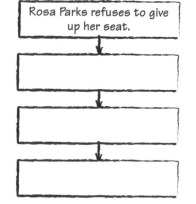

Add as many boxes as you need.

Comparing and Contrasting Real Heroes		
	Nelson Mandela	Rosa Parks
Challenge to authority		
Effects of actions		
My responses to actions		
Feeling about freedom		

SKILLS FOCUS

Literary Skills
Analyze heroes.

Reading Skills
Compare and contrast heroes.

Comparing *Long Walk to Freedom* with "Rosa Parks"

Assignment
1. Writing a Comparison-Contrast Essay

Write a comparison-contrast essay about the heroism of Nelson Mandela and Rosa Parks. For ideas, refer to the chart you filled in after each selection and to the "Characteristics of a Hero" on page 845. You can organize your essay in two ways:

a. You can begin with a paragraph describing your idea of a hero. Then you can write a paragraph that explains why you think Mandela and Parks are heroes. Use information from your chart to support your ideas.

b. Or you can write two paragraphs—one about Mandela and one about Parks—in which you discuss the ways they stood up for their beliefs. You might end your essay with a paragraph describing how these two people represent (or don't represent) your idea of a real hero.

Assignment
2. Biographical Sketch

Write a biographical sketch of either Nelson Mandela or Rosa Parks. Base your sketch on

- what you learned from the selection about the person you chose
- information in the Meet the Writer (if you chose Nelson Mandela)
- additional information you find in the library or on the Internet

Place the sketches from your class into a folder to serve as a resource in your school library. Or, if possible, make a display for a bulletin board to share your information with other students in your school.

Assignment
3. Celebrating Heroes

Plan a class day to celebrate heroes. Individually or with a partner, pick a person you think is a hero. This can be someone you know or someone you have read about. Gather as much information as you can about your hero, and present it to the class. If possible, add a multimedia component to your presentation: Photos, slides, and video or audio clips can help to make your hero come alive for your audience.

SKILLS FOCUS

Writing Skills
Write a comparison-contrast essay; write a biographical sketch.

Speaking and Listening Skills
Present an oral report.

After You Read

1. Writing a Comparison-Contrast Essay

Strategy tip. Urge students having difficulty to write one paragraph about Mandela and a second paragraph about Parks. Then, have them write a third paragraph in which they outline similarities between the two people.

Strategy tip. Students may find it helpful to work with a partner on developing the points they want to present in their essays.

2. Biographical Sketch

Strategy tip. Tell students that this biographical sketch can be written in an informal style. Advise students to include their own thoughts about their essay's subject. Have them review their answers to the After You Read questions on p. 852 and p. 860 to get ideas for their sketches.

3. Celebrating Heroes

Strategy tip. If students choose to do a presentation about someone they know personally, suggest that they use photographs taken at different points in their subject's life. Encourage them to use the photos to describe their hero's development and the effect he or she had on them.

CROSS-CURRICULAR CONNECTIONS

History
Multimedia presentation. Suggest to students that they create a multimedia presentation on a historical figure they admire. Have them ask their parents if they saved any newspaper clippings about the person from the time when he or she was alive. Also advise them to search the Internet for images of their subject. Encourage students to prepare audio or video recordings of any speeches given by their subject.

OVERVIEW

OVERVIEW

The selection in No Questions Asked gives students the chance to read for enjoyment. The annotations in the margins of the Teacher's Edition are optional. No follow-up questions will appear after this selection.

Summary ↔ *at grade level*

> In the first two verses of the song, the singer speaks of doing what is thought to be impossible, like "reach[ing] the unreachable star." The singer declares that he will not give up on his quest. Only by continually striving for the impossible throughout his lifetime will he be satisfied.

DIRECT TEACHING

A Literary Focus

❓ Heroes. Which characters in the other selections from this collection have dreamed of attaining seemingly unreachable goals? Use evidence from the texts to support your opinions. [Possible responses: Arthur overcame adversity to become king. Nelson Mandela and Rosa Parks overcame racial barriers to help make society more just.]

B Literary Focus

Heroes. Ask students what the image of someone "scorned and covered with scars" says about the nature of heroism. [Possible response: Heroes must endure hardships— including, sometimes, the contempt of others.]

Before You Read

"The Impossible Dream" was originally written for the musical *Man of La Mancha,* where it is sung by the character Don Quixote (kē·hōt′ē). The song has since been recorded and performed by many popular singers, including Elvis Presley and Frank Sinatra.

The Impossible Dream

Lyrics by Joe Darion

To dream the impossible dream,
To fight the unbeatable foe,
To bear with unbearable sorrow,
To run where the brave dare not go.

To right the unrightable wrong,
To love pure and chaste from afar,
To try when your arms are too weary,
To reach the unreachable star!

This is my quest, to follow that star,
No matter how hopeless, no matter how far;
To fight for the right without question or pause,
To be willing to march into hell for a heavenly cause!

And I know, if I'll only be true to this glorious quest,
That my heart will lie peaceful and calm when I'm laid to my rest.

And the world will be better for this;
That one man, scorned and covered with scars,
Still strove with his last ounce of courage,
To reach the unreachable stars.

862   Collection 7 / Literary Criticism: Where I Stand

CROSS-CURRICULAR CONNECTIONS

Literature / Theater

Don Quixote. The musical *Man of La Mancha* is based on one of the most popular, influential, and enduring novels in all of literature—*Don Quixote* by Miguel de Cervantes. It is rumored that the idea for the novel came to Cervantes while he was in jail for failure to pay his debts. The title character of the novel is an aging landowner who reads only courtly romances. He comes to believe that he is a knight-errant, destined to fight for justice and to triumph over evil. In the course of his adventures, he mistakes windmills for giants, a roadside inn for a castle, and the inn's servant girl as a fair maiden whom he will serve as a knight.

Although *Don Quixote* is generally regarded as a parody of the tales of chivalry, some readers see it as the story of a truly heroic man. This view of Don Quixote prevailed in *Man of La Mancha,* a musical

Don Quixote (1955) by Pablo Picasso (1881–1973).
Musee d'Art et d'Histoire, St. Denis, France, © 2003 Estate of Pablo Picasso/Artist Rights Society (ARS), New York.

VIEWING THE ART

The Spanish painter, sculptor, printmaker, and writer **Pablo Ruiz y Picasso** (1881–1973) is one of the most highly acclaimed and widely exhibited artists of the twentieth century. Picasso produced art in a range of styles, but he is probably best known for the radical abstract style of his cubist paintings.

Picasso's drawing of Don Quixote and Sancho Panza under a blazing sun is an iconic image of one of the most enduring literary creations of all time.

Activity. Have students closely examine Picasso's drawing. What details in the work make Don Quixote appear heroic? What details make him appear foolish? [Possible responses: His sword and shield give him a heroic appearance. Both he and his horse look somewhat malnourished, which make him appear foolish.]

adaptation of the novel, which opened on Broadway in 1965. Richard Kiley's Quixote was a valiant hero who fought for what he believed was just. The show ran for more than five years, and Kiley won a Tony Award for his performance.

Activity. Ask students to think of other literary works, plays, or films, in which the main character is both a comic figure and an idealistic hero. Then, have them discuss their ideas with the class.

Writing Workshop

Objectives

- Use appropriate prewriting and drafting skills to create an informative report centered on a thesis.
- Revise the informative report to include documented and organized information and a conclusion that summarizes ideas.
- Reflect on and assess one's writing process and informative report.

PRETEACHING

Skills Starter

Motivate. Tell students that finding, locating, and reporting information is part of everyday life. Ask students to think of a question that puzzles them. It might be a question with a concrete answer, such as "Why is the sky blue?" It might be more abstract, such as "Why is music so important to teenagers?" Have students record their questions and brainstorm for a few minutes about sources they might consult to find answers.

DIRECT TEACHING

PREWRITING

Choosing a Subject

Remind students that they should choose a subject that they will enjoy researching. Encourage them to think about what interests them, such as their favorite hobbies or sports. As long as they can find reliable sources of information for their reports, they can choose to write about any subject.

Assignment

Write an informative report on a topic of your choice.

Audience

Your teacher, classmates, and other students in your school

RUBRIC
Evaluation Criteria

A successful informative report

1. centers on a thesis, or controlling idea, supported by evidence
2. includes accurately documented information from several sources
3. organizes information in a logical way
4. ends by summarizing ideas or drawing an overall conclusion

SKILLS FOCUS

Writing Skills
Write an informative report.

864   Collection 7 / Literary Criticism: Where I Stand

Writing Workshop

EXPOSITORY WRITING
Informative Report

In this workshop you'll find, organize, and present facts in an informative report that will add to your readers' knowledge of a topic. Your success will depend upon how well you select and use evidence to support your **thesis,** the controlling idea of your paper.

Prewriting

1   Choosing a Subject

Read and respond to the following **prompt:**

> A research project often begins with a question or a topic that interests the writer. The selections in this collection, for example, may have raised questions about the Arthurian legend. What evidence exists for a historical King Arthur? What kind of training did a medieval knight receive? How has the Arthurian legend been treated in the movies or on television?

For your report, choose a subject you would like to investigate, such as some aspect of conservation, space travel, coed sports, or animal communication. Then, frame a question that will guide your research. To keep your subject focused and manageable, check an encyclopedia or another general source. If the entry is lengthy, your topic may be too broad. See the inverted pyramid on the next page for an example of how to narrow a topic.

2   Finding and Evaluating Sources

Most informative reports are based on several sources. Plan to consult at least three sources. Whenever possible, use **primary sources,** such as diaries, letters, and maps. You can also use **secondary sources,** which are interpretations of primary materials. They include magazine and newspaper articles, encyclopedia entries, and TV and video documentaries. You can access both primary and secondary sources in a library or on the Internet, and you may be able to get additional information from museums, colleges, and interviews with experts. Be sure to evaluate every source by asking the questions that appear in the Research Tips box to the right.

3 **Taking Notes**

Use these guidelines as you take notes:
- Write your notes on three-by-five-inch note cards. On each card, write the source of the information. Include the title and the page number where you found the information.
- Write your notes in your own words, summarizing information carefully. If you copy anything word for word, put quotation marks around it in your notes. Using someone else's words without crediting your source is **plagiarism,** a form of stealing. Generally, you should **paraphrase,** or restate information in your own words.

4 **Writing a Thesis Statement**

Your **thesis statement** tells what the point of your paper will be. It usually appears in your introductory paragraph. Your thesis statement should include both the topic of your paper and the most important conclusion you've drawn from your research.

5 **Organizing the Report**

Making an outline is a good way to plan and organize the information you'll put in your report.
- Decide how you will organize the information in your report—by **order of importance** or **chronological** (time) **order.**

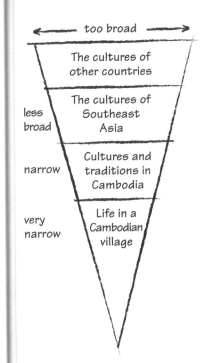

too broad

The cultures of other countries

The cultures of Southeast Asia — less broad

Cultures and traditions in Cambodia — narrow

Life in a Cambodian village — very narrow

Research Tips

Evaluate sources by asking these questions:
- Who is the author? What is the author's background?
- How trustworthy is the information? What are the author's sources?
- Is the information up-to-date? If you use a Web site, check when the site was developed or last revised.

Informative Report **865**

Taking Notes

Tell students to keep their notes and the source information they have gathered in a folder. Explain that having a central location for research materials will make it easier for them to refer to their findings when they're writing their reports.

Writing a Thesis Statement

Once they begin writing their research reports, students may find that they have either too much or too little information in their outlines and must refine their thesis statements. For example, a student writing about the causes of pollution might change a broad thesis statement like "Pollution from nearby factories and increased traffic has created an unhealthy environment" to "Pollution from nearby factories has caused Fisher Pond to become contaminated."

Organizing the Report

Tell students that if they use chronological order to organize their reports, they should begin by creating a time line of events. Instruct them to list events on the time line in the order in which they occur and refer to it as they write.

- *One-Stop Planner* CD-ROM with ExamView Test Generator
- *Holt Online Assessment*
- *Holt Online Essay Scoring*

Internet
- go.hrw.com (Keyword: LE5 7-7)
- *Elements of Literature Online*

DIRECT TEACHING

DRAFTING

Getting Started

Have students review their research notes to find a fact that they find particularly interesting. Suggest that they use this fact in the introduction to grab readers' attention.

Listing Sources

Tell students that it is important that they record bibliographical information accurately so that readers can verify data and find additional information from the sources themselves.

TECHNOLOGY TIP

Remind students that almost anyone can publish on the World Wide Web. Tell them to check the credentials of the author and the Web site. If the writer has a degree in the field about which he or she writes or if the Web site is affiliated with a credible organization, the information is more likely to be reliable.

Outline

A Typical Day in a Cambodian Village

Organization: time order

I. Morning
  A. Rooster instead of alarm clock
  B. Go outside to wash
    1. Brush teeth with finger and sand
    2. Water in barrel
  C. Breakfast not customary
II. Daytime
  A. Long walk to school . . .

Main point: Customs are different in Cambodia.

Framework for an Informative Report

- **Introduction:** Hooks reader's interest; clearly identifies subject of report

- **Body:** Discusses each main idea in one or more paragraphs; supports each main idea with facts, examples, and quotations

- **Conclusion:** Summarizes or restates main idea(s); draws conclusions

---

- Decide which facts and examples from your notes you'll use to support each part of your report. Arrange your note cards in the order of the points in your outline.

- Include a sentence that sums up the main point of your report.

The box to the left shows part of an outline for the Student Model.

Drafting

1 Getting Started

To capture your readers' attention, offer an unusual piece of information or set a surprising scene. Make your topic and main point clear.

2 Drafting the Body

Write at least one paragraph for each main heading in your outline. As you write, you may decide to rearrange your ideas, take out information, or add new information. Keep referring to your notes, and go back to your sources if you need more information.

3 Wrapping Up

Bring your report to a close by tying your ideas together. Sum up your main point or reflect on the information. Consider closing with a vivid image or quotation.

4 Listing Sources

At the end of your paper, list your sources of information. Follow the guidelines in the Communications Handbook or a style guide, such as the Modern Language Association (MLA) guide, your teacher selects. Look carefully at the punctuation, capitalization, and order of information in your guide. Follow it exactly.

866 Collection 7 / Literary Criticism: Where I Stand

DIFFERENTIATING INSTRUCTION

Learners Having Difficulty

Suggest that students use index cards to create their outlines, writing each main heading of the outline on a separate index card. Subheadings and details can go on other cards and can then be placed behind the corresponding main heading. Students can lay out the cards and arrange them in the correct order. Suggest that students use different-colored cards for the different sections of the outline.

English-Language Learners

Some students may find that sources are difficult to understand because they contain complex ideas and vocabulary. Suggest that they restrict sources to print media. To help students clarify basic concepts or understand vocabulary, suggest that they first consult simple texts that are heavily illustrated.

Student Model

This is the beginning of a report on Africanized honeybees.

The Invasion of the Killer Bees

They were once the subject of science fiction movies. Now that they have traveled over five thousand miles and left more than one thousand deaths in their wake, Africanized or "killer" honeybees are a frightening reality to people from South America to Nevada. Today scientists warn that the bees are here to stay and urge people to learn how to coexist with these sometimes hostile creatures.

Africanized honeybees are very different from the native honeybees that live in the United States. Native bees, also called European honeybees, live mostly in hives and hollow trees. They have few enemies and are usually gentle. In warm regions of Africa, honeybees build their nests in the open and protect them fiercely.

Killer bees are extremely nervous, and they are also fighters. Native bees chase people for a few yards when they are bothered. Africanized bees, however, will chase an intruder for as much as half a mile. Their poison is not different from the poison of ordinary bees, but they come after people in a big swarm, sometimes leaving their victims with more than one thousand stings. According to one expert, a human can't survive more than six stings per pound of body weight (Horiuchi).

—Adel Habib
Austin, Texas

The title states the **topic** *clearly but in a way that grabs the reader's attention.*

The writer presents the history of the bees in **chronological order.**

The writer **contrasts** *Africanized bees with native bees.*

The writer supports the **main point**—*that Africanized bees are a dangerous invasion—with* **facts** *and an* **expert opinion.**

The writer follows the MLA style guide for his **source citations.**

Strategies for Elaboration

Elaborate on the main points of your paper by using these strategies:

- Use **specific details** and **examples** to support your general statements. Search for relevant passages to quote or paraphrase.

- Show understanding of the subject matter by using terminology accurately. Check definitions of any literary elements referred to in your essay.

go.hrw.com

INTERNET
More Writer's Models
Keyword: LE5 7-7

Student Model

Encourage students to examine the model to see how one student writer grabs the reader's attention with an interesting introduction, elaborates on details, uses factual information, and properly cites the source material.

Strategies for Elaboration

Suggest to students that they include definitions of any specialized terms in their reports. Remind students to check their sources and dictionaries for the correct usage of scientific terminology and any other specialized vocabulary they encounter.

Informative Report   867

Special Education Students

Students may be tempted to write a rough draft and feel that creating an outline is too difficult or time-consuming. Others may feel that moving from an outline to a rough draft is an overwhelming prospect. Encourage them by explaining that they can create a first draft by simply fleshing out their outlines.

Advanced Learners

Enrichment. Challenge advanced learners who have access to video recording equipment to make a short documentary film about their subjects. Remind them that they can use props to re-enact scenes if they cannot directly observe their subjects. Tell them to ask for adult supervision when making their films.

DIRECT TEACHING

EVALUATING AND REVISING

Content and Organization Guidelines

Have students form pairs to discuss and revise their reports. Tell students to exchange papers with their partners and read them. Then, have students jot down questions that they have about their partners' reports. Remind students to note whether enough supporting details are presented and whether the reports are clearly organized. Students should share their suggestions with their partners and take their partners' comments into consideration when they revise.

Works Cited

Horiuchi, Vince. "Yes, the Bees Are Coming. No, Don't Panic Yet." *The Salt Lake Tribune* 11 Nov. 1999. 25 Mar. 2000
http://www.sltrib.com/1999/nov/11111999/science/46004.htm.

Schoenmann, Joe. "Valley Buzz." *Las Vegas Review-Journal* 13 Feb. 2000. 25 Mar. 2000
http://www.lvrj/com/lvrj home/2000/Feb-13-Sun-000/news/12954791.html.

Evaluating and Revising

Use the following chart to revise and evaluate your informative report.

Informative Report: Content and Organization Guidelines

Evaluation Questions	▶ Tips	▶ Revision Techniques
❶ Does your introduction identify both the topic and the main point of your report?	▶ **Underline** your statement of the report's topic and main idea.	▶ **Add** a thesis statement, or the main point you are making about the topic.
❷ Does each paragraph in the body of your report develop one subtopic?	▶ In the margin, **label** the subtopic of each paragraph.	▶ **Delete** unrelated ideas. **Rearrange** information into specific paragraphs. **Link** ideas with transitional words and phrases.
❸ Does each paragraph contain supporting evidence such as facts, examples, and direct quotations?	▶ **Highlight** the facts, examples, and quotations that elaborate each subtopic.	▶ **Elaborate** with additional facts and examples from notes.
❹ Does your conclusion sum up your overall findings?	▶ **Put a check mark** next to your final statement or summary.	▶ **Add** a question that your research did not answer, or revise your conclusion for clarity.
❺ Have you included at least three sources in the *Works Cited* list?	▶ **Number** the sources listed.	▶ **Add** sources to the *Works Cited* list, and add information from those sources to your report.

The following Revision Model is from an informative report. Use the questions below the model to evaluate the writer's changes.

EVALUATION GUIDELINES

	4	3	2	1
Use these guidelines to quickly assess students' final drafts.	**Introduction contains a thesis statement that identifies the topic and main point.**	Introduction has a clear thesis statement that identifies the topic and main point.	Introduction contains a thesis statement but it does not clearly identify the topic and main point.	Introduction has a vague thesis statement that does not clearly identify the topic and main point.	Introduction does not contain a thesis statement.
	Each paragraph develops a subtopic, and supporting evidence is presented.	Each paragraph clearly develops a subtopic, and ample supporting evidence is presented.	Each paragraph develops a subtopic, but supporting evidence is insufficient.	Paragraphs do not develop subtopics, and supporting evidence is insufficient.	Paragraphs are not organized, and no supporting evidence is provided.

Revision Model

The education of a medieval knight was quite rigorous.

from a noble household

At the age of seven, a boy ∧ would be taken to the court

of an overlord

or castle. There, as a page, he performed menial tasks

received instruction in

but also ~~learned many things:~~ dancing, playing musical

instruments, hunting, falconry, wrestling, tilting with

spears, and riding a horse. At fourteen, the page became

mount

a squire. He then had to learn how to ~~get on~~ a horse

while wearing armor, use a battle-axe, and perform

other military skills. His education usually ended at

when

twenty-one, ∧ ~~and~~ he was initiated into the order of

knighthood. Knighthood was conferred by an "accolade."

According to The Columbia Encyclopedia, this was "a blow,

usually with the flat of sword, on the neck or shoulder."

He first fasted and spent whole nights at prayer.

Evaluating the Revision

1. What details have been added? Do these details add important information? Tell why or why not.

2. Where has the writer rearranged material? Do you agree with these changes? Explain.

PROOFREADING
TIPS

- Be sure to check carefully the spelling and capitalization of names of people, places, and events.

- Carefully check your list of sources.

- Exchange papers with a classmate and proofread each other's work for errors in grammar, spelling, and mechanics.

Communications Handbook HELP

See Proofreaders' Marks.

PUBLISHING
TIPS

Present a multimedia report to your class, using an oral reading with an audio or visual accompaniment. You might tape-record relevant background music and play it as you read, or you might show slides and illustrations.

DIRECT TEACHING

Proofreading Tips

Have students read their drafts over at least twice. On the first reading, tell students to pay close attention to the content of their reports, especially for the accuracy of the facts they have presented. On the second reading, have students examine their reports for punctuation and grammar errors.

Publishing Tips

Remind students that when giving oral presentations of their reports, they will need more organizational clues, or signposts, for listeners than they do in written reports. They should use guiding words such as *three main points* or *first, second, third* to help listeners follow their ideas.

GUIDED PRACTICE

Evaluating the Revision

1. Possible answer: The writer adds the details "from a noble household" and "of an overlord." These details add essential background information and improve the clarity of the writing.

2. The writer moves the sentence "He first fasted and spent whole nights at prayer" up to the correct position in the chronological order of events presented in the report.

	4	3	2	1
Conclusion sums up overall findings.	Conclusion coherently sums up overall findings.	Conclusion adequately sums up overall findings.	Conclusion vaguely sums up overall findings.	There is no conclusion to the report.
At least three sources are used in the report and documented in the *Works Cited* list.	At least three sources are used in the report, and all are properly documented in the *Works Cited* list.	At least three sources are used in the report, but they are not properly documented in the *Works Cited* list.	Fewer than three sources are used in the report and documented in the *Works Cited* list.	No sources used or cited.

Collection 7: Skills Review

Literary Skills

SKILLS FOCUS
pp. 870–871

Grade-Level Skills

■ **Literary Skills**
Analyze literary criticism.

INTRODUCING THE SKILLS REVIEW

Use this review to assess students' grasp of the skills taught in this collection. If necessary, you can use the annotations to guide students in their reading before they answer the questions.

DIRECT TEACHING

Ⓐ Literary Focus

❓ Analyze literary criticism.
How does theme affect the writer's response to "Sir Gawain and the Loathly Lady"? [The writer admires Arthur and Sir Gawain for keeping promises that go against their own interests because they are doing the right thing, which is the story's theme.]

Ⓑ Literary Focus

❓ Analyze literary criticism.
What is the writer's opinion of the King Arthur stories? [The writer disapproves of the scarcity of women characters and their portrayal.] How does the writer use "Sir Gawain and the Loathly Lady" to support this opinion? [by pointing out the passive role of the main female character]

Test Practice

DIRECTIONS: Read the essays. Then, answer each question that follows.

Essay 1

Themes in Arthurian Legends

There are many themes in the stories of King Arthur and his knights. The themes all speak to our deepest wishes: We all wish for a leader who will come and save us in our hour of need; we all wish that might will be used for right; we all wish that goodness will always be rewarded. The Arthur stories are also about doing the right thing, even when the cost of such action is great.

In *King Arthur: The Sword in the Stone,* Arthur is only sixteen when he is faced with a destiny that fills him with unhappiness: to be king of England. Yet he shoulders the burden because it is his fate. It is the right thing to do.

"Sir Gawain and the Loathly Lady" is the best story built around the theme of doing the right thing. Arthur and Gawain must make horrible choices, and they both choose to do the right thing. Sir Gromer makes Arthur promise to return unarmed one year from that day. Arthur will not break his word to save his life, even when the bargain he was forced to make is most unfair. Sir Gawain must make a truly horrifying choice. He weds the loathly lady because, for him, it is the right thing to do. He gave his word.

The end of each story shows that characters are rewarded for choosing to do the right thing. We wish that were always true in real life.

Essay 2

Women Characters in the King Arthur Stories

The three selections, *King Arthur: The Sword in the Stone,* "Merlin and the Dragons," and "Sir Gawain and the Loathly Lady," all reveal the way women are portrayed in the King Arthur stories. In *King Arthur: The Sword in the Stone* and "Merlin and the Dragons," there are no women characters at all. All of the characters are male, and all of them are heroic because they are strong and brave. They earn the reader's approval by pulling swords out of stones and stabbing people in battle. In "Sir Gawain and the Loathly Lady," one of the main characters is a lady changed by magic into a beast. She is doomed to stay in this state until a man loves her for herself alone. She is freed from her enchantment when a man agrees to marry her, although the truth is that Sir Gawain marries her only because he has agreed to in order to save King Arthur.

SKILLS FOCUS

Literary Skills
Analyze literary criticism.

MINI-LESSON   **Reading**

Reviewing Word-Attack Skills
Activity. Write the following words on the chalkboard. Have students read these words and decide which contain silent consonants. If a word contains silent consonants, have a student volunteer underline them.

1. autumn [n]
2. honorary [h]

3. swarm [none]
4. heritage [none]
5. knight [k, g, h]
6. doubtful [b]
7. sword [w]
8. kindred [none]
9. troublesome [none]
10. solemn [n]

Collection 7: Skills Review

None of these stories show women or girls in active roles. I prefer to read *Harriet the Spy*. At least there is a character girls can identify with.

1. What **literary element** is the focus of Essay 1?
   - A Plot
   - B Character
   - C Setting
   - D Theme

2. What **literary element** is the focus of Essay 2?
   - F Plot
   - G Character
   - H Setting
   - J Theme

3. Which of these **generalizations** is supported by details in the essays?
   - A The writer of Essay 1 wishes that people were rewarded for doing the right thing in real life.
   - B The writer of Essay 1 hates the King Arthur stories.
   - C The writer of Essay 2 dislikes male characters.
   - D The writer of Essay 2 likes the women characters in the King Arthur stories.

4. Which **criticism** would you apply to Essay 1?
   - F The writer does not mention *King Arthur: The Sword in the Stone.*
   - G The writer does not mention "Merlin and the Dragons."
   - H The writer does not supply any details to support the main idea.
   - J The writer talks about too many literary elements.

Constructed Response

5. What is the **main idea** in Essay 1?
6. What is the **main idea** in Essay 2?

Test Practice

Answers and Model Rationales

1. **D** The title and first sentence of the essay make the focus clear.
2. **G** The title and references to character throughout the essay show that the focus is character.
3. **A** This choice is stated in the final paragraph of Essay 1. Students can eliminate B, because the writer shows a liking for the stories; C, because the writer seems to approve of male characters; and D, because the writer seems to have no affection for the women characters.
4. **G** Students can eliminate F, because the writer mentions *King Arthur: The Sword in the Stone;* H, because the writer provides supporting details; and J, because the writer discusses only theme. Only G is left.

Constructed Response

5. The main idea in Essay 1 is that doing the right thing is a recurring theme in the King Arthur stories.
6. The main idea in Essay 2 is that the three selections reveal the way women are portrayed in the King Arthur stories.

Test-Taking Tips

For more information on test taking, refer students to **Test Smarts,** p. 920.

Using Academic Language

As part of the review of literary criticism, ask students to look back through the collection to find the meanings of the following terms. Then, have students demonstrate their understanding of the terms by citing passages from stories in the collection that illustrate the meanings of the terms.
Literary Criticism (pp. 786, 810); **Literary Elements** (p. 786); **Character** (p. 786); **Plot** (p. 786); **Theme** (p. 787); **Legend** (p. 792); **Heroes** (pp. 820, 845); **Quest** (pp. 820, 833).

Collection 7: Skills Review

Reading Skills

SKILLS FOCUS
pp. 872–873

Grade-Level Skills
- Reading Skills
Evaluate evidence.

INTRODUCING THE SKILLS REVIEW

Use this review to test students' ability to assess the adequacy, accuracy, and appropriateness of evidence to support an author's assertions. Use these annotations only if you want to conduct the review orally.

DIRECT TEACHING

A Reading Skills

? Evaluate evidence. What unstated assertion does this paragraph suggest? [There are no heroes in today's world.] **Is the evidence given adequate to support this conclusion? Explain.** [No. No facts, statistics, or examples are given. The statements are sweeping generalizations. None can be proved.]

B Reading Skills

? Evaluate evidence. Does this paragraph give accurate and appropriate evidence to support the writer's assertion? Explain. [Yes. It gives facts that can be proven and provides an example of a World War II hero.]

Test Practice

DIRECTIONS: Read the speech. Then, answer each question that follows.

Looking for Heroes

A Speech to the Graduating Class of Lakeville Middle School

A Our world, freshly beginning a new age, is a long way from the time of King Arthur. We have no fighting knights, no daring rescues of damsels, no more brave souls who think only of others above all else. We have no loyalty, no honor, no chivalry. All we have are the stories and thus, some distant memories of what the world used to be and will never be again.

If you believe that, I've got some oceanfront property in Oklahoma to sell you.

We have to change the way we think about heroes. We've just been looking in all the wrong places. Let's dismiss King Arthur and the knights of the Round Table for just a moment and go on our own quest to find our own heroes.

So, turn off the TV. Shut down the computer. Put away the magazines. Just watch life with me for a few moments.

First, we'll journey to Abilene, Texas. As we walk down the sidewalk, I want you to notice that elderly man walking toward his car. He's just an ordinary man, and it seems as if there is nothing special about him. But over fifty years

Reading Skills
Evaluate evidence.

B ago on his forty-third Air Force mission escorting bombers over occupied Europe, his plane's engine quit at thirty thousand feet. The plane plunged 26,000 feet before he could get the engine started again. He eventually had to bail out and spent six months in hiding. He was then turned over to the Gestapo and spent three months in prison. This pilot, Bill Grosvenor, is one of about 93,000 American prisoners of war who returned alive from Europe after World War II.

Next, we fly to Seattle, Washington. As we pull up to St. Joseph's Catholic Church, I want you to notice the woman carrying a large bag and hurrying up the steps. Her name is Jeannie Jaybush, and she created the Baby Corner, an organization that last year gave away about $1,000,000 worth of baby items to families in need. About 12 percent of Seattle's homeless population is made up of children who are five years old and younger, according to the City of Seattle's Human Services Department. Because of the efforts of Jaybush, these children now have some of the basic

---

DIFFERENTIATING INSTRUCTION

Advanced Learners
Enrichment. Have each student write a brief definition of the word *hero* and then think of a modern hero who fits this description. As "Looking for Heroes: A Speech to the Graduating Class of Lakeville Middle School" indicates, heroes are not limited to famous people. Students can also look for heroes in the people that they know.

Activity. Each student can write a brief speech in praise of his or her hero. Speeches should include accurate, adequate, and appropriate evidence to persuade listeners that this person deserves to be called a hero. Students can deliver their speeches in class. Encourage listeners to consider the evidence and ask questions.

necessities that are needed to grow and be healthy.

If we had more time, we could fly to Duluth to visit a woman who is caring for her husband, one of the fourteen million Americans who have Alzheimer's disease. We could stop in Chicago, where a child with cancer lives each day fully. We could also land in Los Angeles, where a bilingual child is teaching his parents to read in English.

We'll stop our search for now, but let yours continue. Keep looking, and let your heart lead you to the heroes of today. I'll promise you, they're a lot easier to find than oceanfront property in Oklahoma.

1. The main **assertion** in this speech is —
   A there were more heroes in the old days
   B our world is full of heroes
   C we need more heroes like King Arthur
   D it is impossible to find heroes in today's world

2. Which of the following statements from the speech is an **accurate** piece of evidence that can be proven?
   F "About 12 percent of Seattle's homeless population is made up of children who are five years old and younger."
   G "We have to change the way we think about heroes."
   H "We have no loyalty, no honor, no chivalry."
   J "We've just been looking [for heroes] in all the wrong places."

3. Suppose a listener responded to this speech by saying, "Heroes are usually males who are recognized by most of the population." This would be an example of —
   A accurate evidence
   B appropriate evidence
   C adequate evidence
   D stereotyping

4. The speech supports its assertion mainly with —
   F statistics
   G quotes from experts
   H examples of people considered heroic
   J stereotypes

Constructed Response

5. Do you think the evidence in this speech is **adequate** to support its assertion? Why or why not?

DIRECT TEACHING

C **Reading Informational Text**

? **Evaluate evidence.** Has the writer made a convincing case for modern heroes? Explain. [Possible response: Yes, the specific examples of modern heroes are appropriate, adequate evidence, which can be checked for accuracy.]

Test Practice

Answers and Model Rationales

1. **B** Students can eliminate A and C because the writer says we can dismiss heroes like King Arthur and find our own. The writer claims the opposite of D.

2. **F** This is the only choice that gives factual evidence and the source for it. G, H, and J express opinions only.

3. **D** The listener's statement is an inaccurate generalization about a group of people. A, B, and C are incorrect because the listener's response offers no evidence.

4. **H** Most of the speech discusses specific examples that support the writer's assertion. Students can eliminate F, because there is only one statistic in the speech; G, because there are no quotes from experts; and J, because the writer doesn't use any stereotypes.

Constructed Response

5. Possible answer: Yes, the speech contains adequate evidence to support its assertion. It gives many different examples of everyday heroes, and it provides some empirical evidence that can be checked for accuracy.

Test-Taking Tips

For more information on taking tests, refer students to **Test Smarts,** p. 920.

Collection 7: Skills Review

Vocabulary Skills

Multiple-Meaning Words

Modeling. Model the thought process of a good reader getting the answer to item 1 by saying: "The block of marble has an anvil sitting on top of it, just as the wooden block has a statue on top of it. In A, *block* is used as a verb and therefore could not be the resting place of an object. Though the *blocks* in B and D are nouns, neither means a solid piece that could hold an object. Therefore, C is correct."

Test Practice

Answers and Model Rationales

1. **C** See the rationale above.

2. **H** In the quotation and in H, the noun *scale* means "a system of grouping by degrees." In F, *scale* refers to a weighing machine. In G, it refers to a sequence of musical tones. In J, *scale* is an adjective meaning "proportional."

3. **A** In the quotation and in A, *line* means "a row of persons waiting to do something." In B, the word refers to a long cord used in fishing. In C, *line* means "a speech in a play." In D, it means "border."

4. **J** In the quotation and in J, *present* is a verb (pronounced differently from the noun or adjective) meaning "to formally introduce." In F, the word means "in attendance." In G, it means "gift." In H, *present* refers to the current time.

5. **C** In the quotation and in C, *point* refers to a sharp tip. In A, it is a verb meaning "to direct one's finger at something." In B, *point* means "a particular time." In D, *point* means "main idea."

Collection 7: Skills Review

Vocabulary Skills

Test Practice

Multiple-Meaning Words

DIRECTIONS: Choose the answer in which the underlined word is used the same way it is used in the quotation from *King Arthur: The Sword in the Stone.*

1. "In the churchyard he discovered a block of white marble with an anvil sitting on top."
   - **A** The football player tried to block his opponent's kick.
   - **B** They walked one block to the bus stop.
   - **C** The statue was placed on a large wooden block.
   - **D** Our class bought a block of tickets for the performance.

2. "Nothing had prepared them for this scale of violence."
   - **F** Weigh yourself on the scale in the bathroom.
   - **G** The pianist practiced each scale twenty times.
   - **H** The scale of talent at this year's gymnastic competition was quite impressive.
   - **J** On this scale model, one inch represents three feet.

3. "As soon as the service ended, those who wished to try for the throne formed a line next to the marble block."
   - **A** The line to buy tickets was longer than we expected.
   - **B** The fisherman attached the hook to his line.
   - **C** The actor had only one line to memorize.
   - **D** The truck crossed the state line at six o'clock.

4. "'My lord,' said Merlin, 'I present to you a most worthy candidate for this contest.'"
   - **F** When the teacher called my name, I said, "Present."
   - **G** For my birthday I was given the present of my dreams.
   - **H** Don't dwell on the past; focus on the present.
   - **J** The emcee at the wedding reception finally said, "I now present the bride and groom."

5. "Then, turning the point downward again, he drove it back into the anvil with equal ease."
   - **A** It's not polite to point.
   - **B** At a certain point in the discussion, the group felt it would be a good time to take a break.
   - **C** The warrior sharpened the point of his spear before going into battle.
   - **D** "Get to the point," she said impatiently.

SKILLS FOCUS

Vocabulary Skills
Understand multiple-meaning words.

Vocabulary Review

Use this activity to assess students' retention of the collection Vocabulary.
Activity. Have students select the correct word from the box to complete each of the following sentences.

| countenance | sovereignty | ruthless |
| bedraggled | turbulent | |

1. On a _____ night, a lone rider approached the castle. [turbulent]

2. Despite his _____ appearance, he had an air of authority. [bedraggled]

3. The _____ expression on his _____ betrayed his evil intentions. [ruthless; countenance]

4. "Your enemies surround you," he announced. "You are now under the _____ of the all-powerful King Lorgan." [sovereignty]

Collection 7: Skills Review

Writing Skills

Test Practice

DIRECTIONS: Read the following passage from an informative report. Then, read the questions below it. Choose the best answer to each question.

(1) One place connected with the legend of King Arthur is Glastonbury, in Somerset, England. (2) Around 1190, monks claimed they had found Arthur's grave in Glastonbury Abbey's cemetery. (3) An excavation turned up a lead cross with Arthur's name inscribed on it. (4) A coffin was also found. (5) It contained the bones of a man and a woman. (6) They were presumed to be the remains of King Arthur and Queen Guinevere. (7) These remains were moved to a tomb in the abbey church, but everything disappeared after the monasteries were dissolved in 1539. (8) No one knows what became of the cross. (9) Modern excavation has shown that there had indeed been an earlier burial at Glastonbury. (10) No evidence exists of whose grave it was. (11) Some storytellers identify Glastonbury with Avalon, King Arthur's final resting place.

1. This is an excerpt from an informative report. What is the most likely topic of the complete essay?
   A The beginnings of the Arthurian legend
   B Important excavations
   C Places connected with the Arthurian legend
   D Historical events and the legend of Arthur

2. Which of the following sources would be appropriate to consult in writing this informative report?
   F *The New Arthurian Encyclopedia*
   G *The Early History of Glastonbury*
   H *The Arthurian Handbook*
   J All of the above

3. Which two sentences could best be combined to improve the flow of the passage?
   A sentences 2 and 3
   B sentences 4 and 5
   C sentences 6 and 7
   D sentences 8 and 9

4. Which of the following words could *best* be used to connect sentences 9 and 10?
   F and
   G so
   H however
   J therefore

5. Where could sentence 11 be moved to improve the logical flow of the passage?
   A after sentence 1
   B after sentence 4
   C after sentence 7
   D after sentence 9

SKILLS FOCUS

Writing Skills
Analyze an informative report.

APPLICATION

Classroom Talk Show

Have students form small groups to prepare a presentation for the class. Then, have one student from each group volunteer to be the host of their group's talk show. The rest of the students will play guests with expertise in their subject. Each student will have time to present on their subject as the host asks them questions (that the students have discussed beforehand) and provides transitions between students.

Collection 7: Skills Review

Writing Skills

Test Practice

Answers and Model Rationales

1. **C** A and D are not mentioned in the excerpt, and B only addresses a detail contained in the excerpt. Only C, "Places connected with the Arthurian legend" could be the topic of the report.

2. **J** All of the sources listed could be useful in finding information about the subject of the report.

3. **B** Sentences 4 and 5 could easily be combined: "A coffin was also found that contained the bones of a man and a woman."

4. **H** Only *however* (H) is a transitional word that signals the differences between sentence 9 and 10—that even though there was a burial at the site, there is no proof that it was King Arthur's grave.

5. **A** Sentence 11 would best be moved to follow sentence 1 because it contains the main idea that should be introduced at the beginning of the paragraph.

EXTENSION

Artwork

For homework, have students create artwork that depicts a particular aspect of their reports. Students may choose to create sculptures, figurines, dioramas, paintings, sketches, or posters.

READ ON

For Independent Reading

If students enjoyed the themes and topics explored in this collection, you might recommend these titles for independent reading.

Assessment Options

The following projects can help you evaluate and assess your students' outside reading. Videotapes or audiotapes of completed projects may be included in students' portfolios.

- **Tell a tale at the Round Table.** Have several students each choose one of the legendary figures whose tale is told in *The Arthurian Legends: An Illustrated Anthology.* Have students pretend that they are authors famous for their vivid and exciting versions of Arthurian legends. Each of the writers should tell a tale of the legendary figure they have chosen—in prose, poetry, or song. Tell students that they must be true to the original legends but that they can add details and embellishments.

- **Hold a debate.** Have students work in pairs to stage a debate about the desirability of living forever. One partner should play the role of the man in the yellow suit from *Tuck Everlasting.* The other should play the part of a member of the Tuck family.

Fiction

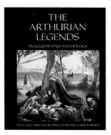

All Sides of Arthur

Richard Barber has compiled the most exciting stories about King Arthur in *The Arthurian Legends: An Illustrated Anthology.* You will learn about the social and historical contexts of the legends and how the stories have changed over time. But the focus of the book is King Arthur himself: his daring rescues, his heroic deeds, and his greatest challenges. You will find out why these tales still resonate with readers of all ages.

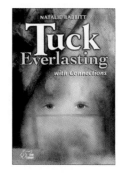

The Water of Life

Have you ever wished you could live forever? In Natalie Babbitt's *Tuck Everlasting,* the members of the Tuck family are granted eternal life when they drink from a hidden stream. Then they find out that living forever isn't what it's cracked up to be. This novel is also published in Spanish as *Tuck para siempre.*
This title is available in the HRW Library.

More than They Can Chew?

Four young lives are changed one summer by the discovery of a coin. Not just any coin, but a coin that grants wishes—or rather, *half* wishes. In Edward Eager's novel, *Half Magic,* Jane, Katherine, Mark, and Martha accidentally make themselves *half* invisible, ship themselves to the Sahara Desert, and finally transport themselves back to King Arthur's court. Then they think that maybe *double* wishing can solve all their problems—but will it really?

Payback

As Myles Falworth undergoes rigorous training for knighthood, he learns that his blind father was wrongfully accused of treason and stripped of his lands. Now that he has grown up, Myles attempts to restore honor to his father by challenging his father's toughest enemies. In *Men of Iron,* Howard Pyle weaves a dramatic tale of suspense and bravery.

DIFFERENTIATING INSTRUCTION

Estimated Word Counts of Read On Books:

Fiction		Nonfiction	
The Arthurian Legends: An Illustrated Anthology	170,000	Heroic Stories	70,000
		Life in a Medieval Village	21,000
Tuck Everlasting	28,000	The World of King Arthur and His Court	24,000
Connections to Tuck Everlasting	16,000		
Half Magic	40,000	Queen Eleanor: Independent Spirit of the Medieval World	38,000
Men of Iron	75,000		

Nonfiction

Leaders by Example

Anthony Masters looks at the lives of twenty-four exceptional people in *Heroic Stories*. You've probably heard of some of these heroes, such as Martin Luther King, Jr., and Anne Frank. Do you know about Christy Brown, who overcame a troubling disability to become a writer, or Pauline Cutting, who worked tirelessly in hospitals in Beirut? All of the people profiled in the book embody a heroic ideal.

Things Have Changed

Gwyneth Morgan takes you back to thirteenth-century England in *Life in a Medieval Village*. In vivid detail, Morgan explores the everyday life of a peasant family, a lord and his manor, and the role of the church during this unique period in history. You may be surprised by the food people ate, the clothes they wore, and what they did for a living.

The Historical Arthur

Kevin Crossley-Holland's *The World of King Arthur and His Court* examines the ideals and customs of Arthurian times. You'll learn how a boy became a knight and was schooled in the specifics of courtly love. Crossley-Holland also compares the legends of King Arthur to actual history. Was Arthur real or fictional? The answer may surprise you.

A Heroic Woman

Eleanor of Aquitaine (ak'wə·tān') was queen of France and later England in the 1100s. During her lifetime she supported the arts and helped establish the courtly manners you've read about in the Arthurian tales. Her strength of character brought her trouble—she was held in confinement for fifteen years by her husband. Find out the whole story in Polly Schoyer Brooks's biography *Queen Eleanor: Independent Spirit of the Medieval World.*

The Read On titles are categorized as shown below:

Collection 8
Reading for Life

Informational Focus:
Analyzing Information in Public, Workplace, and Consumer Documents
Following Technical Directions

About Collection 8
In Collection 8, students will master the following skills:

- **Reading Skills:** Analyze information in public documents, workplace documents, and consumer documents; follow technical directions.
- **Speaking and Listening Skills:** Develop, write, revise, and present a public-service announcement.

Informational Text
Each collection of *Elements of Literature* provides a variety of informational texts related to the literature selections by theme or topic.

Minimum Course of Study
Most skills can be taught with a minimum number of selections and features. In the chart to the right, lessons highlighted in green constitute the minimum course of study that provides coverage of the skills taught in Collection 8.

Resource Manager
(pp. 878C–878D)
Lesson and workshop resources are referenced in the Resource Manager on the pages that follow. These resources can be used to reinforce the skills taught in Collection 8, remediate students who are having difficulty, and provide supporting activities for English-language learners.

Scope and Sequence

Selection ▪ Feature	Literary Skills
Reading Informational Texts: Reading for Life *by* Sheri Henderson	
Reading Skills and Strategies: **Reading for Information** **From Page to Film** *by* Kathryn R. Hoffman ↓ *below grade level*	
Informational Texts: **Casting Call** ↔ *at grade level* **Hollywood Beat** ↔ *at grade level* **Application for Permission to Work in the Entertainment Industry** ↔ *at grade level*	
Informational Texts: **Letter from Casting Director** ↔ *at grade level* **Talent Instructions: On Location** ↔ *at grade level* **E-mail Memo** ↔ *at grade level* **E-mail Directory** ↔ *at grade level*	
Informational Texts: **BART System Map** ↔ *at grade level* **BART's Bicycle Rules** ↔ *at grade level* **BART Ticket Guide** ↔ *at grade level* **BART Schedule** ↔ *at grade level*	
Informational Text: **How to Change a Flat Tire** ↔ *at grade level*	
Writing Workshop: *Multimedia Presentation: Public-Service Announcement*	
Skills Review: *Speaking and Listening Skills*	

Reading Skills	Vocabulary Skills	Writing – Grammar and Language Skills
• Understand consumer, workplace, and public documents		
• Read for information		
• Analyze information in public documents		
• Analyze information in workplace documents		
• Analyze information in consumer documents		
• Follow technical directions		
		• Deliver a public-service announcement
		• Analyze a public-service announcement

Resource Manager

Selection ■ Feature	Planning	Differentiating Instruction ■ Lesson Plans with ELL Strategies and Practice	Reading ■ Vocabulary
Reading Informational Texts: Reading for Life *by* Sheri Henderson		• Holt Reading Solutions: Lesson Plans, pp. 345–346	• Holt Reading Solutions, pp. 345–346
Reading Skills and Strategies: Reading for Information From Page to Film *by* Kathryn R. Hoffman			
Informational Texts: Casting Call **Hollywood Beat** **Application for Permission to Work in the Entertainment Industry**	• One-Stop Planner with ExamView Test Generator	• The Holt Reader, pp. 286–291 • Holt Reading Solutions: Lesson Plans, pp. 347–351 • Supporting Instruction in Spanish, p. 38 • Audio CD Library • Audio CD Library, Selections and Summaries in Spanish	• The Holt Reader, pp. 286–291 • Holt Reading Solutions, pp. 347–351
Informational Texts: Letter from Casting Director **Talent Instructions: On Location** **E-mail Memo** **E-mail Directory**	• One-Stop Planner with ExamView Test Generator	• Holt Adapted Reader, pp. 166–169 • Holt Reading Solutions: Lesson Plans, pp. 352–356 • Supporting Instruction in Spanish, p. 38 • Audio CD Library • Audio CD Library, Selections and Summaries in Spanish	• Holt Adapted Reader, pp. 166–169 • Holt Reading Solutions, pp. 352–356
Informational Texts: BART System Map **BART's Bicycle Rules** **BART Ticket Guide** **BART Schedule**	• One-Stop Planner with ExamView Test Generator	• Holt Reading Solutions: Lesson Plans, pp. 357–361 • Supporting Instruction in Spanish, p. 38 • Audio CD Library • Audio CD Library, Selections and Summaries in Spanish	• Holt Reading Solutions, pp. 357–361
Informational Text: How to Change a Flat Tire	• One-Stop Planner with ExamView Test Generator	• Holt Reading Solutions: Lesson Plans, pp. 362–364 • Supporting Instruction in Spanish, p. 38 • Audio CD Library • Audio CD Library, Selections and Summaries in Spanish	• Holt Reading Solutions, pp. 362–364
Writing Workshop: *Multimedia Presentation: Public-Service Announcement*	• One-Stop Planner with ExamView Test Generator	• Workshop Resources: Writing, Listening, and Speaking, pp. 80–90	
Skills Review: *Speaking and Listening Skills*			

Writing Grammar and Language	Assessment
	• Holt Assessment: Literature, Reading, and Vocabulary • One-Stop Planner with ExamView Test Generator • Holt Online Assessment
	• Holt Assessment: Literature, Reading, and Vocabulary • One-Stop Planner with ExamView Test Generator • Holt Online Assessment
	• Holt Assessment: Literature, Reading, and Vocabulary • One-Stop Planner with ExamView Test Generator • Holt Online Assessment
	• Holt Assessment: Literature, Reading, and Vocabulary • One-Stop Planner with ExamView Test Generator • Holt Online Assessment
• Workshop Resources: Writing, Listening, and Speaking, pp. 80–90 • Daily Language Activities • Language Handbook Worksheets	• Holt Assessment: Writing, Listening, and Speaking • One-Stop Planner with ExamView Test Generator • Holt Online Assessment • Holt Online Essay Scoring
	• Holt Assessment: Writing, Listening, and Speaking • One-Stop Planner with ExamView Test Generator • Holt Online Assessment

Technology

INTERNET

- go.hrw.com
- Holt Online Assessment
- Holt Online Essay Scoring
- Elements of Literature Online

MEDIA

 • One-Stop Planner with ExamView Test Generator

• Audio CD Library

• Audio CD Library, Selections and Summaries in Spanish

 CD-ROM   Audio CD

Collection 8

SKILLS FOCUS

Grade-Level Skills

■ **Reading Skills**
Analyze information in consumer, workplace, and public documents.

■ **Reading Skills**
Follow technical instructions in order to understand the use of a simple mechanical device.

■ **Reading Skills**
Read for information.

Review Skills

■ **Reading Skills**
Use the structural features of newspapers, magazines, and online data to obtain information.

Upcoming Skills

■ **Reading Skills**
Use consumer, workplace, and public documents to solve problems and explain situations.

COLLECTION 8 RESOURCES: READING

Planning
■ *One-Stop Planner* CD-ROM with ExamView Test Generator

Differentiating Instruction
■ *The Holt Reader*
■ *Holt Adapted Reader*
■ *Holt Reading Solutions*
■ *Family Involvement Activities in English and Spanish*

■ *Supporting Instruction in Spanish*

Assessment
■ *Holt Assessment: Literature, Reading, and Vocabulary*
■ *One-Stop Planner* CD-ROM with ExamView Test Generator
■ *Holt Online Assessment*

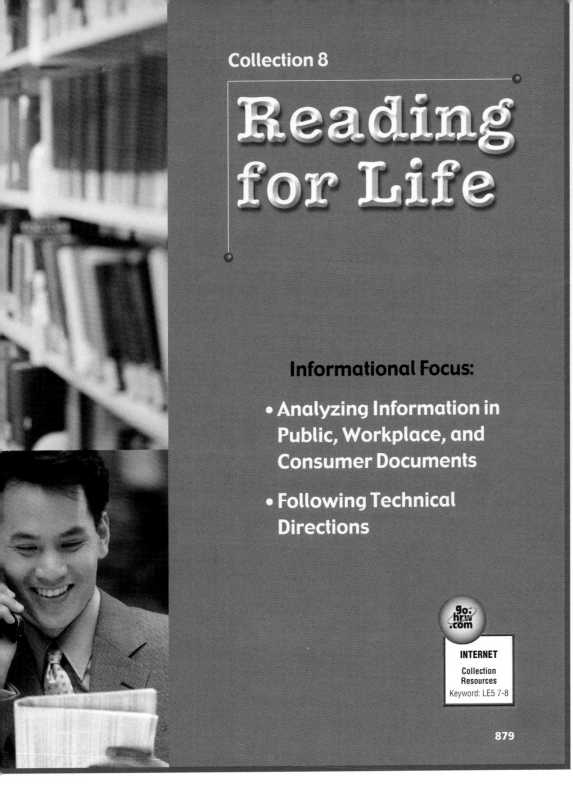

Collection 8

Reading for Life

Informational Focus:

- **Analyzing Information in Public, Workplace, and Consumer Documents**

- **Following Technical Directions**

go.
hrw
.com

INTERNET

Collection
Resources
Keyword: LE5 7-8

879

Theme: Reading for life. The selections in this collection mimic real-life reading experiences that students may face now or in the future. The selections are set in a narrative context that will appeal to every student who has ever dreamed of being in a movie: a twelve-year-old learning about, applying for, and working at a job in a motion picture.

Analyzing information in public, workplace, and consumer documents. In the public documents section, students will read a casting call, a magazine article, and an application form. The section on workplace documents includes a business letter, on-the-job instructions, an e-mail memo, and an e-mail directory. Consumer documents explain how to get around on a public transit system.

Following technical directions. Students will follow technical directions by learning how to change a flat tire.

VIEWING THE ART

Activity. Have students look at the pictures of the different types of reading on pp. 878–879. Have students done any of these activities today? What other types of informational reading have they done this week? [Possible responses: read a magazine; read an encyclopedia for research; looked at a map.]

Internet
- go.hrw.com (Keyword: LE5 7-8)
- *Elements of Literature Online*

Media
- *PowerNotes*

Grade-Level Skills

■ **Reading Skills**
Understand information in consumer, workplace, and public documents.

Upcoming Skills

■ **Reading Skills**
Use consumer, workplace, and public documents to solve problems and explain situations.

Reading Informational Texts: Reading for Life

Ask students to suggest different situations in which they must read to get information. Have a volunteer write students' ideas on the board. Remind students that reading informational texts involves skills that are different from but as important as the skills needed to read literature. Ask students as they read the essay to notice which informational texts mentioned in the essay do not appear on their class list.

Reading Informational Texts
Reading for Life *by* Sheri Henderson

Getting the Job Done

The purpose of consumer, workplace, and public documents is to provide information. These documents are everywhere, and that is a *good* thing. Without them a society as complex as ours would not be able to function well. Since these documents contain information that is important to all of us, they deserve—and require—our close attention and careful reading. The information they contain can be as simple as advertising for a new movie or as complex as warnings about your prescription medication. Whether simple or complex, though, consumer, workplace, and public documents cannot do their job of providing information if we do not do our job, which is reading them carefully.

Consumer Documents

Most days you probably look to consumer documents for all sorts of information. **Advertisements** tell you what is available to buy and how much it costs, what movie is just out on video, and when your favorite store is having a sale. Providers of services publish **schedules** of movie showtimes, school lunch menus, TV programs, and bus or train or plane timetables. **Labels** on the goods you buy give you, the consumer, information about what you are buying. Labels on packaged food list the food's ingredients and nutritional value. Labels on shoes declare which parts are synthetic and which parts are not. Labels on your clothing tell you what your shirt is made of and how to care for it.

Mechanical and electronic equipment come with **warranties, contracts, instructional manuals,** and **technical directions.** These guide you in the safe and proper use of products. Whenever you encounter consumer information, especially technical directions, it is a good idea to read it through slowly and carefully. The seller is required only to include the information. It's up to you to read and understand it. As many consumers have found out too late, "I didn't understand it" will not get you your money back if the item does not work because you didn't read the directions. Informed consumers know that it's better to read consumer documents *before* they use the product.

Workplace Documents

As their name suggests, workplace documents are those you encounter in a job. Your first communication with a possible employer may be through a **business letter,** in which you state your qualifications and request a job interview. However, a business letter isn't always necessary. You may merely be asked to complete an **application.** When you are hired, you may be asked to sign an **employment contract,** which spells out what is expected of

SKILLS FOCUS

Reading Skills
Understand consumer, workplace, and public documents.

DIFFERENTIATING INSTRUCTION

Learners Having Difficulty
Have available a sampling of the different kinds of documents mentioned in the essay: for example, a clothing advertisement, a bus schedule, the nutritional label from an item of packaged food, a job application, a printout of information from your community's Web site. Go over each of these with students, pointing out how the information in each could be useful to students.

Advanced Learners
Acceleration. Point out that people often read informational texts when they need to make decisions or solve problems.
Activity. Ask students to find two examples of the same type of informational text. For example, they might find two different movie advertisements or two sets of laundering instructions from shirts or pants made of different fabrics. Have students explain how reading and comparing the two informational pieces might help them make a decision.

you as an employee and what you can expect in return from your employer. You may need to provide a Social Security number, a **work permit,** and a **tax form** for your employer to use when calculating taxes to deduct from your wages. You may also be given **insurance forms** to fill out and sign. To help you succeed in your job, your employer may provide an **employee manual,** a set of rules and instructions related to the job.

When workers need to communicate with one another, they usually do so through **memorandums,** often called memos. Businesses frequently use **e-mail memos** to communicate because e-mail is fast, convenient, and easily retrieved. Of course, the number and types of workplace documents you encounter will depend on the kind of work you do. However, one thing is certain: Whatever kind of work you do, workplace documents will play an important role in helping you succeed.

Public Documents

If there were a chemical spill on a road near your house, would you be told about it? If you wanted to learn about sports programs at local parks before you moved into a new neighborhood, could you do it? If you wanted to know how much the mayor earns in your community, could you find out? The answer to all of these questions is *yes!* The answers can be found in public documents. Public documents supply citizens with information that may be of interest to them. Public documents can relate to schools, churches, government agencies, the courts, libraries, and fire and police departments, to name just a few.

Typically most citizens do not read the public documents put out by the government, the military, and nonprofit agencies or groups. Instead, they read **newspaper articles** that report on the documents. Whether you read a document itself or a newspaper account of its contents, public documents exist to tell you what is happening in your world.

Reading Ahead

The following pages will give you some practice reading various kinds of consumer, workplace, and public documents. You'll also get a chance to follow some technical directions. Challenge yourself as you read to see how well you can locate the important information in all the documents.

Grade-Level Skills

■ **Reading Skills**
Read for information.

OVERVIEW

Use. The tips for reading informational texts can be particularly useful with magazine and newspaper articles, Web pages, and technical directions. With "From Page to Film," have students use the tips for reading informational texts to identify the main points of each section of the article. In addition to the selections in this collection, reading for information will be useful for students when they read advertisements, letters, and other writings in their day-to-day life.

Summary ⬇ *below grade level*

The writer of this informational article provides an overview on how some popular young-adult literary works became movies. The process can be difficult because movies require more action than books, which can spend pages discussing characters' thoughts. Also, the literary works being adapted are sometimes too long or too short to be turned easily into a film. Consequently, the movie's creators may take away or add scenes and characters to the film, which audiences can find problematic. Finally, the writer notes that movies can have an impact on an audience that some books may not have because of the input many people contribute when working on a movie.

Reading Skills and Strategies

Reading for Information
by Kylene Beers

In one basic way, reading informational materials differs from reading stories. Can you figure out what that difference is?

It's *not* that stories are usually fiction and informational texts are usually nonfiction. With both fiction and nonfiction you have to

- process information
- think about what the text is saying
- compare and contrast
- predict what will happen next
- summarize what has happened already
- understand the sequence of events
- recognize the writer's point of view
- connect what you already know with what you are reading
- note cause-and-effect relationships
- make inferences
- draw conclusions

The basic difference is that most fiction uses a narrator to tell you what is happening, but in most informational materials there is no narrator to guide you along. This lack of a guide may slow down some readers. You can guide yourself through informational texts, though, by following the tips on the right.

SKILLS FOCUS

Reading Skills
Read for
Information.

Tips for Reading Informational Texts

1. **Numbered steps** in a text tell you, "First, do this. Next, do that."

2. **Headings** call out, "Look here! This is a new topic you're about to meet."

3. **Boldface** and *italic* words or phrases alert you, "This is an important word or definition. Pay attention!"

4. **Graphics,** such as maps, charts, graphs, and illustrations, also tell you, "Step right up! Important information can be found here."

5. Phrases such as *on the other hand, by comparison, by contrast,* or *still others believe* often introduce the **opposite** of what's come before. The information may conflict with what you've already read.

6. Phrases and words such as *consequently, as a result, this results in,* or *therefore* explain the **effects** of something.

DIFFERENTIATING INSTRUCTION

Learners Having Difficulty
After students have discerned the subject of the article, they may have trouble organizing all the information that follows. Call students' attention to the headings on pages 884 and 886. Remind them that headings usually introduce new information related to the subject of the article. Have students sum up in a sentence the main idea of the paragraphs after each heading.

Have volunteers share their responses with the class.

English-Language Learners
Some English-language learners may have trouble with the terminology the writer uses to describe filmmaking. Explain that a screenplay is the script that is used when making a movie.

What's the next big movie? It just might be at the bottom of your book bag! ❶ 📖

From Page to Film

Kathryn R. Hoffman
from Time for Kids

Ron Weasley, Stuart Little, Shrek, Jesse Tuck: What do they have in common? All have made the move from the small, printed page to the big silver screen—and all with a good deal of success! ❷ 📖

Children's books can make blockbuster movies. The film based on J. K. Rowling's first Harry Potter book made more money than any film the year it came out. *Harry Potter*'s success has sent movie producers to their kids' bookshelves in search of the next big hit. *Ella Enchanted, Holes, The Cat in the Hat,* and Lemony Snicket's *The Bad Beginning* are just a few of the books that have made it to the movies.

Using the Strategy

As you read, you'll find this open-book sign at certain points in the story: 📖. Stop at these points, and think about what you've just read. Do what the prompt asks you to do.

PREDICT

❶ The **boldface headline** above the title draws you in and hints at what the article is about. What do you think the subject of the article will be?   Ⓐ

IDENTIFY

❷ The **title** and the **first paragraph** make the subject of the article clear. What is it?   Ⓑ

PRETEACHING

Selection Starter
Motivate. Ask students to think of short stories they've read that they think would be entertaining as movies. Encourage students to share their choices with the class and explain their reasons. Open up the topic for group discussion.

DIRECT TEACHING

Ⓐ Reading Skills and Strategies
Predict. [Possible responses to question 1: The article will deal with movies made from children's books. The article will be about popular children's movies.]

Ⓑ Reading Skills and Strategies
Identify. [Possible response to question 2: The subject of the article is children's books that have been made into popular movies.]

Ⓒ Reading Skills and Strategies
❓ Read for information. What information does the author provide about the subject of the essay in the second paragraph? [Possible response: She gives examples of successful movies that are based on children's books.]

Advanced Learners
Enrichment. Ask students if they've read a novel, such as *Holes* or *Tuck Everlasting,* that was made into a movie they've seen.
Activity. Ask students to write a movie review in which they point out the differences between the movie and the book. Have students keep the following questions in mind as they write:

- What events occur in the movie that did not exist in the book?
- What events were omitted from the movie?
- Are the characters portrayed differently in the movie from the way they're portrayed in the book?

Students can close their review by expressing an opinion about whether the movie was an improvement on the book.

A Reading Skills and Strategies

Analyze. [Possible responses to question 3: The subhead "Great Expectations" is unclear, as it could refer to the expectations of the original author of the book, those of the audience, or even the novel *Great Expectations.* "Write and Rewrite" is clearer; it is apparent that this section will be about the difficulties a screenwriter faces when turning a book into a movie.]

B Reading Skills and Strategies

Read for information. Sum up the information the author conveys in this paragraph. [Possible response: Filmmakers often have difficulty translating an author's original vision into a good film.]

C Reading Skills and Strategies

Read for information. Name two differences between movies and books that might cause difficulty for writers like Sachar. [Possible response: Books can be as long or short as an author would like them to be, whereas movies are generally about two hours long. The writing in books needs to be detailed so readers can imagine scenery, while the scenery is provided in films.]

Using the Strategy

ANALYZE

A ❸ **Subheads** alert you to the subject of the text that follows. Do the red subheads on this page make the subject of each section clear? Explain.

Great Expectations ❸ 📖

Movie versions of kids' books have been around for a long time. Some favorite family films—*The Wizard of Oz* and *Willy Wonka and the Chocolate Factory*— are loved just as much as the books they were based on.

B But making movies from beloved books isn't easy. Filmmakers have a hard time living up to the images in readers' minds. "When you read, you translate what the author says into your own personal movie that runs in your head," says Natalie Babbitt, the author of *Tuck Everlasting.* It can be hard to accept another version.

Write and Rewrite

C Screenwriters don't set out to ruin the work of a great author. Sometimes they are the same person! Louis Sachar not only wrote the bestseller *Holes,* he penned the screenplay too. Movies are so different from books, he says, "I had to figure out the story all over again."

LITERARY CONNECTIONS

Children's Literature

Some students may not even realize that *The Wizard of Oz* and *Willy Wonka and the Chocolate Factory* are films adapted from literature.

Buoyed by the success of his previous picture book called *Father Goose: His Book,* L. Frank Baum (1856–1919) wrote *The Wonderful Wizard of Oz.* When the book was published in 1900, children greeted Dorothy's journey from Kansas to the magical land of Oz with much enthusiasm. In addition to being a gripping tale, the story contains innovations in children's literature. The story combines the mystical elements of fairy tales with familiar images such as cornfields and scarecrows. Baum later adapted it into a hit stage musical. He continued to produce more Oz books throughout his life, due both to popular demand and to his own increasing debts, but none have remained as popular as his first.

Pacing is a big issue. Films usually move faster than books and require more action. The book *Tuck Everlasting,* for example, devotes many pages to an emotional struggle in a character's head. Says Jeffrey Lieber, who wrote the *Tuck* screenplay: "I kept asking myself, 'What's the image on the screen?'"

Length is an issue too. When film-makers take a four-hundred-page book, something has to go. While working on the second film, *Harry Potter* director Chris Columbus realized he had to cut the Death Day Party scene—a ghostly celebration. "I had some heated discussions with my kids," Columbus says. Over their objections, he sacrificed the scene for the good of the movie. ❹

At the other extreme, the creators of *Shrek, Jumanji,* and *The Cat in the Hat* movies have had to turn short stories into ninety minutes of big-screen action. To do so, they added characters and plot details. The donkey that almost stole the show in *Shrek* barely existed in the book. **E** **F**

INFER

❹ **Paragraph breaks** indicate that the writer is beginning a new subject. What is the **main idea** of this paragraph?

D

DIRECT TEACHING

D **Reading Skills and Strategies**

Infer. [Possible response to question 4: At times, filmmakers must cut out scenes from the book to keep the movie at a reasonable length.]

E **Reading Skills and Strategies**

❷ **Read for information.** What does the phrase "at the other extreme" mean? [Possible response: The phrase means that what will follow will express the opposite of what's come before.] **What type of information about turning books into films will follow? Explain.** [Possible response: Since the previous paragraph dealt with having to cut scenes out of books to make a movie, this paragraph will probably deal with having to add scenes to already existing texts.]

F **English-Language Learners**

Idioms. Have a volunteer point out to English-language learners that "stole the show" means "was the most popular performer in a show."

Roald Dahl (1916–1990) gained recognition for his short stories for adults and his memoir *Boy: Tales of Childhood.* However, he is best known for his children's books, including *Charlie and the Chocolate Factory.* Partially inspired by his real-life experiences with a grouchy candy-store owner, the book has sold over one million hardcover copies in the United States alone. Dahl pointed out that kids are attracted to his books because of the sense of justice in his stories—mean people always get their comeuppance.

Activity. Have students read either *The Wonderful Wizard of Oz* or *Charlie and the Chocolate Factory* and then watch the film adaptation of the book they read. Then, have them write a brief essay comparing the book to the film upon which it was based.

A Reading Skills and Strategies

? Read for information. What is the main idea of the closing paragraph? [Possible response: Authors have only themselves to rely on when writing a book, while many people contribute to the making of a movie.]

B Reading Skills and Strategies

Analyze. [Possible response to question 5: The sidebar calls attention to recent information on a few more books that are being made into movies. The illustrations show readers examples of popular books and their translations onto the big screen.]

Using the Strategy

ANALYZE

5 This **sidebar** repeats information that appears in the text. Why do you think it is included here? What additional information do you learn from the **illustrations** that appear with the article?

It Takes Teamwork

Authors who have helped turn their books into films are struck by the team effort. "The book is just me alone in my room," says Sachar. Movies draw on the talents of actors, set and costume designers, and musicians, among others. They have tools that no writer has. "A safe, faithful telling of the book, I think that's a failure," says *Jumanji* author Chris Van Allsburg. "You haven't used the magic of filmmaking."

A Few Recent Books That Made It to the Movies

The Polar Express
The book is reported to be a favorite of Tom Hanks, who plays the conductor.

The Cat in the Hat
The cat from the books has a Hollywood look. Mike Myers plays the cat.

The Bad Beginning
This is the first book in Lemony Snicket's book series *A Series of Unfortunate Events* to make it to the screen. Others may soon follow. **5**

Practice the Strategy

Reading for Information

Similarities to Reading Stories

When you read informational texts, you use most of the same reading skills that you need for reading a story. For example, you compare and contrast, predict what will happen next, make inferences, connect the text with what you know already, and draw conclusions.

Differences from Reading Stories

When you read a story, a narrator guides you through what is happening by recounting the events, usually in chronological order. When you read informational texts, there is usually no narrator to guide you. However, you can use some common informational text features as your guides.

PRACTICE

In a chart like the one below, give examples and explain how you were able to use each text feature to help you read and understand "From Page to Film."

Informational Text Features	Examples and Explanations
Headings	
Boldface or italic words and phrases	
Graphics (maps, charts, illustrations)	
Sidebar	
Paragraph breaks	

Whenever you read for information, you can use these **text features** to help guide you through the documents.

SKILLS FOCUS

Reading Skills
Read for information.

Practice the Strategy

In this feature, students will use a chart to help organize the information they gained from various text features in the article.

Strategy Tip

Remind students that they can use their answers to some of the callout questions as a basis for filling out the chart.

PRACTICE

Possible answers: *Headings*—The heading "Write and Rewrite" lets me know that I'm about to read about revising a text into a screenplay usable for filmmaking. *Boldface or italic words and phrases*—The boldface and italic headlines at the beginning of the article tell me that the article is about popular children's movies. *Graphics (maps, charts, illustrations)*—The graphics provide the reader with covers of popular children's books and images from movies based on those books. *Sidebar*—The sidebar in this article gives me information about more kids' books that are being made into movies. *Paragraph breaks*—The first paragraph break on page 884 indicates that information about the difficulties of making these films will follow.

CROSS-CURRICULAR CONNECTIONS

Science

Reading a science textbook. After you consult with their science teacher, remind students that they can use the chart in this feature when studying their science textbooks. Science textbooks generally contain all of the text features listed in the chart. Encourage students to use the chart when they encounter difficult sections of the texts or when they need to make notes for a science exam.

Grade-Level Skills

■ **Reading Skills**
Analyze information in public documents.

Review Skills

■ **Reading Skills**
Use the structural features of newspapers, magazines, and online data to obtain information.

Summary ⬌ *at grade level*

In a biking magazine, twelve-year-old Sam reads a casting call announcement for a new movie. She is interested, so she finds an online article about the project and learns that the movie is going to be a version of *The Hobbit,* with the hobbits riding bikes as they battle the "baddies." Before trying out, Sam wants to make sure she will qualify for a work permit, so she downloads an application that explains how to get permission to work in a movie.

PRETEACHING

Selection Starter

Motivate. Ask how many students would like to be in a movie. If anyone knows how nonprofessionals find work in films, have them share this information. Then, tell students that the selection will describe how one girl got a small part in a movie.

Assign the Reading

Have advanced learners read the selection independently while you monitor other students. Define important words, such as *casting* and *audition,* as necessary.

Informational Text

Analyzing Information in Public Documents

Reading Focus
Public Documents

All **public documents** have one thing in common: They inform people (you) about things you might need or want to know. Public documents are all about information. Let's follow one person's experience in finding information she needs by using some public documents.

Locating Information: An Announcement

Meet Sam (Miss Samantha Sallyann Lancaster, and don't even think about calling her anything but Sam, thank you very much). Anyone who knows Sam for five minutes knows two things about her: She's smart, and she can beat anyone, anytime, anywhere on her BMX bike. So imagine Sam's excitement when she comes across this **announcement** in her favorite biking magazine:

SKILLS FOCUS

Reading Skills
Analyze information in public documents.

Casting Call

A If you've been looking for the right break to get into motion pictures, this may be your chance. StreetWheelie Productions is casting fresh talent for an upcoming action movie.

? What?

To audition, you must

- be a charismatic, awesome, off-the-wall male or female individualist

- be an expert at making your BMX-type bike do whatever you want it to do

? Who?

- have your own bike

B
- look like you're between the ages of twelve and fifteen

- meet the requirements for a permit to work in the entertainment industry if you are under age eighteen

- be living in or near San Francisco during July and August 2004

Auditions will be held in

C **Golden Gate Park, San Francisco**
Saturday, May 25, 2004
10:00 A.M. to 5:00 P.M.

? When and where?

Bring your bike.

See you in the movies!

RESOURCES: READING

Planning
■ *One-Stop Planner* CD-ROM with ExamView Test Generator

Differentiating Instruction
■ *The Holt Reader*
■ *Holt Reading Solutions*
■ *Supporting Instruction in Spanish*

Assessment
■ *Holt Assessment: Literature, Reading, and Vocabulary*
■ *One-Stop Planner* CD-ROM with ExamView Test Generator
■ *Holt Online Assessment*

Internet
■ go.hrw.com (Keyword: LE5 7-8)
■ *Elements of Literature Online*

889

A Reading Informational Text

? Locate information. Public documents may employ attention-grabbing techniques to pull readers in. What is this casting call announcement trying to "sell" and to whom? [Possible response: It is trying to "sell" the idea of coming to the casting call to the kind of people the film company wants in the movie.]

B Reading Informational Text

? Locate information. Since public documents can be read by anybody, the organizers of a casting call must find some way of limiting the responses to a manageable number. This section explains what kind of people the movie company is looking for. Which of these requirements strictly limit who can respond? [Possible responses: be an expert BMX-type bike rider; have your own bike; meet the requirements for a permit to work in the entertainment industry if under age 18; live in or near San Francisco during July and August 2004.]

C Reading Informational Text

? Locate information. From this, would Sam know exactly when and where to appear for the auditions? [Possible responses: The time is clear, but some students may realize that a more specific location than Golden Gate Park should be provided.]

DIFFERENTIATING INSTRUCTION

Learners Having Difficulty
Students may need help focusing on the details in informational texts. Suggest that as they read "Casting Call" they look for answers to these questions: "Would I be the kind of person the production company is looking for at the audition? Why or why not?" "What would I have to do to go to the audition?" You might write these questions on the chalkboard to help students focus on finding the details as they read.

English-Language Learners
You may want to assign peer tutors to help students who are learning English to understand the article from *Hollywood Beat*. The article has a breezy informal style and is filled with slang terms, such as *radical, out-of-sight, dudes, baddies,* and *big talent,* as well as references to pop culture figures (Batman, Mr. Rogers) that may be unfamiliar to some students. Have peer tutors read the article aloud and answer their partners' questions.

Special Education Students
For lessons designed for special education students, see *Holt Reading Solutions.*

A Reading Informational Text

? Locate information. When you are looking for information from a public document, you sometimes have to sift fact from opinion. What fact does this paragraph contain? [Possible response: StreetWheelie Productions is developing a new movie version of J.R.R. Tolkien's *The Hobbit*.]

B Reading Informational Text

Locate information. Point out to students that if they want to be sure that the information in a public document is accurate, they must check that the sources of the information are reliable. In this case, unnamed "sources close to the production" may or may not be reliable.

Locating Information: An Article

Sam thinks, "Cool!" This may be for her, but she wants more information. An **Internet search** using the key words *StreetWheelie Productions* and *San Francisco* yields this **article** from *Hollywood Beat,* a newsmagazine:

Hollywood Beat

Shhhhhh!

A Here's a little secret for you. Remember Bilbo Baggins, the lovable little hobbit who saved Middle Earth from the Powers of Darkness in J.R.R. Tolkien's classic novel? Well, that little hobbit's about to get radical. *Hollywood Beat* has discovered that StreetWheelie Productions is developing an out-of-sight version of this tale, and Middle Earth will never be the same.

? What's the topic?

Set in San Francisco, the hobbits are bike-riding dudes who, in order to save their world, oppose an endless stream of baddies who ride BMX bikes. The principal character, Bilbo, is a nerdy innocent who finds himself at the center of (Middle) Earth–shaking events. The result? Batman meets Mr. Rogers.

? Why a bike?

B Sources close to the production say that there is some big talent interested in the project. As of yet, nobody's talking, but remember . . . you'll hear all about it first on *Hollywood Beat.*

J.R.R. Tolkien

Professor J.R.R. Tolkien was correcting an examination paper when he turned to find a blank page. On impulse he wrote on it, "In a hole in the ground there lived a Hobbit." Compelled to follow this impulse, Tolkien asked himself, "What is a hobbit?" The answer led him to create a vivid fantasy world, which he used as the basis for bedtime stories for his children. Eventually he wrote them down. Published in 1937, *The Hobbit* became an instant classic.

Activity. Explain to students that in Tolkien's book, hobbits are described as being about half as tall as human beings, with fat stomachs, curly brown hair, and a cheerful appearance. Their fingers are long and nimble, and their laughter is deep and rich. They wear bright colors, mainly green and yellow. Ask students to form small groups and discuss how a filmmaker might put these characters into a live-action movie set in contemporary San Francisco. What would the hobbitlike characters look like? What would they wear? Students might write or draw their descriptions.

SMALL GROUP

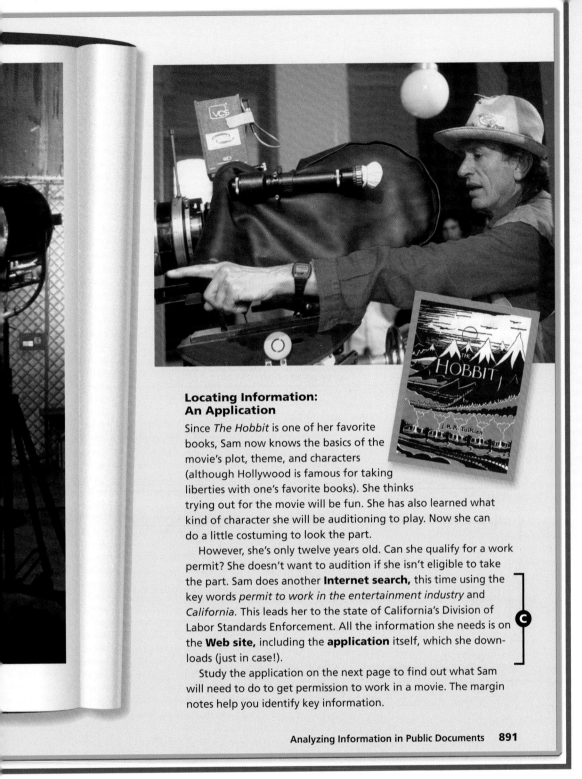

Locating Information: An Application

Since *The Hobbit* is one of her favorite books, Sam now knows the basics of the movie's plot, theme, and characters (although Hollywood is famous for taking liberties with one's favorite books). She thinks trying out for the movie will be fun. She has also learned what kind of character she will be auditioning to play. Now she can do a little costuming to look the part.

However, she's only twelve years old. Can she qualify for a work permit? She doesn't want to audition if she isn't eligible to take the part. Sam does another **Internet search,** this time using the key words *permit to work in the entertainment industry* and *California.* This leads her to the state of California's Division of Labor Standards Enforcement. All the information she needs is on the **Web site,** including the **application** itself, which she downloads (just in case!).

Study the application on the next page to find out what Sam will need to do to get permission to work in a movie. The margin notes help you identify key information.

Analyzing Information in Public Documents   891

C Reading Informational Text

? Locate information. To do an efficient search for information on the Internet, it's important to choose useful key words. How did Sam know what key words to use? [In the casting call she found the phrase *permit to work in the entertainment industry.* Then, knowing the work would be in California, she used the additional key word to narrow the search.]

A Reading Informational Text

? Locate information. Point out that the statement "This is not a permit" informs applicants that filling out an application does not guarantee receiving a permit. Why is this statement important to applicants? [Possible responses: It lets them know that they cannot start working until they receive a permit. It prevents applicants from assuming that the completed form is, in itself, a permit.]

B Reading Informational Text

? Locate information. What steps must Sam take to apply for a work permit? [Provide information on the form about herself, including her address and her school; get her parent or guardian to sign the form; get a school official to certify that she meets the school district's requirements; mail or take the completed application to an office of the Division of Labor Standards Enforcement.]

C Reading Informational Text

? Locate information. For an applicant to be issued a work permit, who must agree to it? [A parent or guardian must sign the document, indicating that he or she approves of the child's having a permit. A school official at the school the child attends must also indicate agreement.]

D Reading Informational Text

? Locate information. Does Sam have to fill out the last portion of the application? [She does not have to fill it out unless she is specifically instructed to do so.]

STATE OF CALIFORNIA
Division of Labor Standards Enforcement

APPLICATION FOR PERMISSION TO WORK IN THE ENTERTAINMENT INDUSTRY

A THIS IS NOT A PERMIT ☐ NEW ☐ RENEWAL

PROCEDURES FOR OBTAINING WORK PERMIT

1. Complete the information required below.
2. School authorities must complete the School Record section below.
3. For minors 15 days through kindergarten, please attach a certified copy of the minor's birth certificate. See reverse side for other documents that may be accepted.
4. Mail or present the completed application to any office of the Division of Labor Standards Enforcement for issuance of your work permit.

What does the first section require?

Name of Child					Professional Name, if applicable	

Permanent Address Number Street   City   State   Zip Code   Home Phone No.

School Attending   Grade

Date of Birth	Age	Height	Weight	Hair Color	Eye Color	Sex

Statement of Parent or Guardian: It is my desire that an Entertainment Work Permit be issued to the above-named child. I will read the rules governing such employment and will cooperate to the best of my ability in safeguarding his or her educational, moral, and physical interest. I hereby certify, under penalty of perjury, that the foregoing statements are true and correct.

Name of Parent or Guardian (print or type)   Signed   Daytime phone #

SCHOOL RECORD

☐ I certify that the above-named minor meets the school district's requirements with respect to age, school record, attendance, and health.

☐ Does not meet the district's requirements and permit should not be issued.

What does the second section require?

Authorized School Official   Date

School Address   School Telephone

[School Seal or Stamp]

HEALTH RECORD

COMPLETE THIS SECTION IF INSTRUCTED TO DO SO OR IF INFANT UNDER ONE MONTH OF AGE

Name of Doctor   Address   Telephone Number

I certify that I am Board Certified in pediatrics and have carefully examined

and, in my opinion: He/She is physically fit to be employed in the production of motion pictures and television. If less than one month, infant is at least 15 days old, was carried to full term, and is physically able to perform.

Signature   M.D.   Date

Approved DLSE 277 Rev. 03/99

What does the last section require?

Sam's happy. She knows she'll qualify for a work permit, and she decides to go to the audition. Before she goes, test yourself. In reading these documents, have you been able to find all the information Sam needs?

892   Collection 8 / Reading for Life

FAMILY/COMMUNITY ACTIVITY

Encourage students to talk with their families about different types of public documents that family members have consulted for information. Family members might discuss how they assess the accuracy of these public documents, especially information found on the Internet. You may want to have students bring to class an assortment of public documents, to help everyone get a sense of the many kinds of information that are available.

Analyzing Information in Public Documents

Test Practice

1. The fact that the advertisement appeared in Sam's favorite biking magazine suggests that the casting agents are especially interested in kids who can —
   A read magazines
   B act a little crazy
   C follow directions
   D ride a bike

2. If Sam is hired to play a part, she will be working during —
   F May and June
   G June and July
   H July and August
   J August and September

3. Sam is probably auditioning to play —
   A a hobbit
   B Mr. Rogers
   C a baddie
   D Bilbo Baggins

4. Sam is confident that she will qualify for a **work permit.** To do so, she will need all of the following *except* —
   F the full support and help of her parent or guardian
   G a statement of good health from a doctor
   H a statement from her school that she has met the district's requirements for her grade level
   J permission from her school to be absent when necessary

5. If Sam wanted to find out more about StreetWheelie Productions, her *best* choice would be to —
   A search the Internet using the key words *StreetWheelie Productions*
   B look in an encyclopedia under "Film Industry"
   C read *The Hobbit* again
   D post a question on her school's electronic bulletin board

Constructed Response

1. What is the most important purpose of a **public document**?

2. Where and when will the auditions be held?

3. What special talent must people have to audition for this part?

4. What will the movie be about?

SKILLS FOCUS

Reading Skills
Analyze information in public documents.

Analyzing Information in Public Documents

Test Practice

Answers and Model Rationales

1. **D** Students should realize that not every reader of a biking magazine acts crazy or can follow directions, so B and C are not logical choices. The ad was placed in a magazine for a specific audience—bikers—so A is incorrect.

2. **H** Students should note that the casting call requires actors to be living in the San Francisco area during July and August.

3. **A** Students should realize that the article says the hobbits are "bike-riding dudes" and that the casting call says being able to ride a bike is a requirement for the part. C is incorrect because no "baddie" is mentioned; D is incorrect because the leading role would be reserved for the interested "big talent"; and Mr. Rogers, B, is not in the movie.

4. **J** J is the best answer, although some students may argue that G is possible because the application says it may not be required. F and H are required.

5. **A** Students should recognize that an encyclopedia has general, not current, information; *The Hobbit,* a novel written many years ago, would not tell about the production company; and the school's electronic bulletin board would, at best, yield hearsay from unqualified sources. Thus, B, C, and D are not good choices.

Test-Taking Tips

For more information on how to answer multiple-choice questions, refer students to **Test Smarts** on p. 920.

Constructed Response

1. Public documents inform people of things they may need or want to know.

2. The auditions will be held in Golden Gate Park, San Francisco, on Saturday, May 25, 2004, from 10:00 A.M. to 5:00 P.M.

3. They must be very good at riding and perhaps doing tricks on their BMX-type bikes.

4. The movie will be based on J.R.R. Tolkien's *The Hobbit* but will be set in San Francisco, and the hobbits will ride bikes as they battle the "baddies."

Grade-Level Skills

■ **Reading Skills**
Analyze information in workplace documents.

Upcoming Skills

■ **Reading Skills**
Use workplace documents to solve problems and explain situations.

Summary *at grade level*

Sam auditions for the movie. She soon receives a business letter offering her a part in the production and outlining the main points covered in her contract. When she reports for her first day of work, she receives a list of workplace instructions. As shooting progresses, Sam understands why she was instructed to check the filming schedule daily—it changes constantly. When Sam misplaces her most recent schedule, she locates it in her e-mail directory.

PRETEACHING

Selection Starter

Build background. Tell students that workers are often expected to read and remember written information. Tell them that this lesson will give them experience with different forms of documents used in the workplace.

Informational Text

Analyzing Information in Workplace Documents

Reading Focus
Workplace Documents

Whether you work in a small business with only one other person or in a huge corporation with offices all over the world, your working life will depend on many types of **workplace documents.** Businesses put important information in writing so that agreements, decisions, and requirements are clear to everyone involved. Let's look at some of the workplace documents that Sam encounters after her audition.

Locating Information:
A Business Letter

The audition has gone really well. Everyone is as nice as he or she can be, and someone takes down all of Sam's information and talks with her and her mother for quite a while. Pretty soon Sam receives the **business letter** shown on the next page.

SKILLS FOCUS

Reading Skills
Analyze information in workplace documents.

RESOURCES: READING

Planning
■ *One-Stop Planner* CD-ROM with ExamView Test Generator

Differentiating Instruction
■ *Holt Adapted Reader*
■ *Holt Reading Solutions*
■ *Supporting Instruction in Spanish*

Assessment
■ *Holt Assessment: Literature, Reading, and Vocabulary*

■ *One-Stop Planner* CD-ROM with ExamView Test Generator
■ *Holt Online Assessment*

Internet
■ go.hrw.com (Keyword: LE5 7-8)
■ *Elements of Literature Online*

STREETWHEELIE PRODUCTIONS

2323 South Robertson Boulevard
Beverly Hills, CA 90210

June 7, 2004
Miss Samantha Lancaster
1920 Ygnacio Valley Road
Walnut Creek, CA 94598

Dear Sam:

On behalf of StreetWheelie Productions, it is my pleasure to offer you a part in our production. Attached is your contract. I know that contracts can be difficult to read and understand, so it is important that before you sign it, you and your parents understand it thoroughly. The items in the contract spell out the issues we discussed last Saturday, as follows:

- You are responsible for your own transportation to and from filming. Pay attention to scheduled dates, times, and locations.
- Check your e-mail first thing each morning and last thing each night. If you are experiencing trouble with your e-mail and are unsure of the next day's schedule, call Alonsa anytime, 24/7.
- You must report to makeup, hair, and wardrobe two hours before your first call.
- You may *not* change your hairstyle or hair color during filming. We all admired the brightness of the lime green you have achieved and the way your hair flows from under your helmet when you're riding.
- Unless otherwise noted, you must report with your bike for all calls. You may not wash or otherwise clean all that great grunge off your bike.
- Because you are not yet age sixteen, a parent or guardian must be present whenever you are working. As we discussed with your mother, your grandfather will be an appropriate guardian as long as he has with him at all times a written document signed by your parents, authorizing him to act as your guardian.
- Nonprofessional actors are paid a minimum hourly wage. You will receive a check at the end of each week. Your eight-hour maximum workday will begin when you arrive each day and end when you leave each day. By law you may not work more than eight hours a day. One paid hour of rest and recreation will be part of your eight-hour workday, but the thirty-minute lunch, also paid, will *not* be part of the workday. You will always have twelve hours or more between the end of one workday and the makeup call for the next.
- In addition to the above hourly wage, you will receive a bonus at the end of your filming schedule. This bonus will be paid on your last day of work, on the condition that you have fulfilled all aspects of your contract with regard to attendance, punctuality, and appearance. This bonus will equal the total of all your previous hourly checks. It will, in effect, double your earnings.

If you have any questions, call Juanita Diaz, our lawyer. Her phone number is on the contract. We look forward to having you on the project.

Sincerely,

Cassandra Rice

Cassandra Rice, Casting Director

Responsibility 1: transportation.

Responsibility 2: work schedule.

Responsibility 3: arrival time.

Responsibility 4: appearance.

Responsibility 5: equipment.

Responsibility 6: parental supervision.

Wages.

Contact for questions.

A Reading Informational Text

❓ **Locate information.** Point out that a business letter always contains the address of the sender. Often the name, address, and phone number of the organization are preprinted on the stationery. Why is this part of the letter important? [It lets the recipient know who the letter is from and how to get in touch with the sender.]

B Reading Informational Text

❓ **Locate information.** Why is it important to understand the contract before signing it? [Possible response: A contract is a legal document; once it is signed, the parties are legally bound by the terms of the contract.]

C Reading Informational Text

❓ **Locate information.** Point out that Sam has now received the same information three times, twice in writing. Why would the film company summarize in the letter the main points of a contract that is attached? [Possible response: It is very important that Sam and her parents understand the terms of the contract, which "can be difficult to read and understand."]

D Reading Informational Text

❓ **Locate information.** What is the maximum number of hours per day that Sam would actually be working? [seven] What is the total number of hours a day that she may be at the workplace? [eight and a half]

DIFFERENTIATING INSTRUCTION

Advanced Learners
Acceleration. Use the following activity with advanced learners to help them use workplace documents to explain decisions and solve problems.
Activity. After students have read the first two workplace documents, suggest that they make a list of things that they would take to work each day if they were Sam. Be sure they discuss the reasons for their choices.

A Reading Informational Text

Locate information. Explain that Sam doesn't need an employee manual because her job is temporary and limited. Tell students that an employee manual usually contains company policies about such topics as sick days, vacation time, and dress codes. It may also spell out grounds for dismissal. In some ways it is similar to a school's student handbook.

B Reading Informational Text

❓ **Infer.** Tell students that the word *horseplay* means "loud, rough fun." Why would horseplay not be permitted? [Possible response: Horseplay would be disruptive and potentially dangerous on a movie set.]

C Reading Informational Text

❓ **Locate information.** Point out that italic type is used to emphasize certain words. In what other ways might words, phrases, or sections be emphasized? [Possible responses: through the use of boldface type, all-capital letters, underscoring, colors.]

D Reading Informational Text

❓ **Locate information.** Point out that the rules are as complete as possible to avoid the need for a lot of questions. According to this rule, can a worker use a pager or cell phone in the call or food area any time he or she wishes? [No. Even in those areas a call cannot be made or a pager used if it would interfere with filming.]

Locating Information: Workplace Instructions

Sam thinks, "Wow! I'm going to be in a movie!" Before she knows it, her first day arrives. As soon as Sam gets to the location, she is introduced to a whole new set of friends . . . *and* to a whole new set of rules. Everyone in the crew is nice, but they all make it clear that everyone is there to work, and they expect Sam to understand that fun movies are just as hard to make as serious ones. Sam's job doesn't require an employee manual, but she does receive a list of **workplace instructions.**

Talent Instructions: On Location

What to do and what not to do.

1. No horseplay is permitted.

2. When you arrive, sign in with Jim, and pick up a call pager.

3. Report *immediately* to makeup, hair, and wardrobe.

4. Movies require a lot of waiting. Bring something that you can do *quietly* while you wait. Music players are fine if the headphones do not interfere with makeup, hair, or costume. Electronic games are popular; their sound effects *must* be turned off. You *could* even read a book. People do.

5. When you are ready, report to the call area, and stay there. *Always* keep your call pager with you.

6. Personal cell phones, pagers, etc., may be used only in the call or food areas and only if they do not interfere with filming. Ringers must be set to "off" or "silent alert."

7. Leave all personal belongings in your assigned locker when on the shooting site.

8. You may talk in nonfilming areas, but there is *no talking* on the shooting site.

Locating Information: E-mail Memos and Directory

Sam finds out she loves being involved in making movies. The work is fun and interesting. Many of the other kids complain about having to wait for hours just to do a short scene, but Sam is interested in everything going on and so is never bored. Since she knows how to be quiet and stay out of the way, she is allowed to watch the filming all day long. The days just fly by.

As time goes on, Sam understands why she is required to check her e-mail every morning and night. It's hard to remember which schedule is the most recent one. Luckily, Sam can always look it up on her saved mail. At the right is one of Sam's **e-mail memos.**

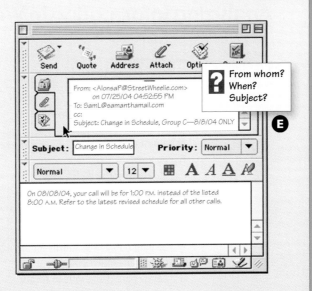

From: <AlonsaP@StreetWheelie.com> on 07/25/04 04:52:55 PM
To: SamL@samanthamail.com
cc:
Subject: Change in Schedule, Group C—8/8/04 ONLY

Subject: Change in Schedule   Priority: Normal

On 08/08/04, your call will be for 1:00 P.M. instead of the listed 8:00 A.M. Refer to the latest revised schedule for all other calls.

From whom? When? Subject?

Sam changes her calendar for August 8 but cannot find her latest revised schedule. She breathes a sigh of relief when she remembers that she can check her saved e-mail and print another copy. Look at Sam's **e-mail directory.**

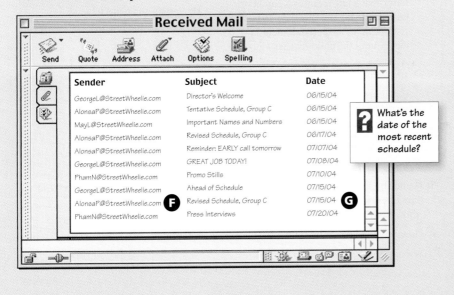

Received Mail

Sender	Subject	Date
GeorgeL@StreetWheelie.com	Director's Welcome	06/15/04
AlonsaP@StreetWheelie.com	Tentative Schedule, Group C	06/15/04
MayL@StreetWheelie.com	Important Names and Numbers	06/15/04
AlonsaP@StreetWheelie.com	Revised Schedule, Group C	06/17/04
AlonsaP@StreetWheelie.com	Reminder: EARLY call tomorrow	07/07/04
GeorgeL@StreetWheelie.com	GREAT JOB TODAY!	07/08/04
PhamN@StreetWheelie.com	Promo Stills	07/10/04
GeorgeL@StreetWheelie.com	Ahead of Schedule	07/15/04
AlonsaP@StreetWheelie.com	Revised Schedule, Group C	07/15/04
PhamN@StreetWheelie.com	Press Interviews	07/20/04

What's the date of the most recent schedule?

Test Practice

Answers and Model Rationales

1. **B** Students should realize that B is correct because the first paragraph of the letter says that the items on the contract are "as follows."

2. **H** Students should notice the phrase "with the bonus." H is correct because the bonus doubles Sam's earnings. F and G are incorrect because she will be paid the minimum hourly wage irrespective of her fulfillment of the contract. J is incorrect because "with the bonus" she will receive double the minimum wage.

3. **C** C is correct because the letter says "Because you are not yet age sixteen, a parent or guardian must be present whenever you are working." The ages in A, B, and D are not mentioned.

4. **J** F, G, and H are incorrect because waiting and the "no horseplay" rule would require people to be patient, responsible, and self-controlled.

5. **B** The memo states that the call is changed from one time to another. The memo does not change the date (A) and does not mention part or costume (C and D).

6. **G** The e-mail directory shows the e-mails Sam has received. Sam's favorite movies are not mentioned in the e-mail directory, so J is incorrect. It is impossible to know from the information given whether everyone Sam works with is in the directory, so F is incorrect. Students should realize that because there are a number of different senders in the e-mail directory, H is not the right choice.

Analyzing Information in Workplace Documents

Test Practice

1. The **business letter** discusses mainly Sam's —
   A audition
   B contract
   C ability to act
   D ability to ride a bike

2. The **business letter** points out that with the bonus, Sam will —
   F be paid only if she fulfills all conditions of her contract
   G not be paid if she fails to fulfill any conditions of her contract
   H be paid double if she fulfills all conditions of her contract
   J earn minimum wage for the project

3. Sam can **infer** from the **business letter** that a law requires a parent or guardian to be present when a child is working in the entertainment industry until the child reaches age —
   A ten
   B twelve
   C sixteen
   D eighteen

4. Sam's **workplace instructions** make it clear that while waiting, actors are expected to be all of the following *except* —
   F patient
   G responsible
   H self-controlled
   J loud

5. Sam's July 25 **e-mail memo** tells her about a change in —
   A date
   B time
   C part
   D costume

6. Sam's **e-mail directory** lists —
   F all the people she works with
   G e-mail she has received
   H e-mail she plans to send
   J her favorite movies

SKILLS FOCUS

Reading Skills
Analyze information in workplace documents.

Constructed Response

1. Name the **workplace documents** Sam has encountered. What is the purpose of each document?

2. How much will Sam be paid?

3. What equipment is Sam expected to provide?

4. What is the date of Sam's most recently revised schedule?

Test-Taking Tips

Remind students to look for qualifying words such as *mostly* and *except*.

For more information on how to answer multiple-choice questions, see **Test Smarts**, p. 920.

Constructed Response

1. Possible answers: a business letter that explains terms of employment; instructions that list rules of behavior at work; an e-mail memo about a schedule change.

2. the minimum hourly wage, plus a bonus equal to the sum of all paychecks if she fulfills the contract

3. a bike

4. July 15, 2004

Analyzing Information in Consumer Documents

Reading Focus
Consumer Documents

A consumer buys or uses what someone else sells. Have you ever treated a friend to an ice-cream cone or a movie? If so, both you and the person you treated were consumers. Even your pets can be considered consumers—of the food and the toys you buy for them. Consumers need information about the products and services they buy. **Consumer documents** provide that information. Let's look at some of the consumer documents Sam uses while she is working.

Locating Information: A Transit Map

Sam has to travel to work with her bike, and she doesn't look forward to a long bike ride from Walnut Creek to the movie location and back. Besides, her grandfather has to come with her, and he doesn't have a bike. Her grandfather could drive, but parking a car in San Francisco is expensive—even if you can find a parking space! So the two decide to take the Bay Area Rapid Transit System, known as BART. BART is a network of trains that can take you just about anywhere in the San Francisco Bay Area.

First, Sam and her grandpa log on to the Internet to look at the **BART system map.** They want to be sure they can get from their home in Walnut Creek to the Embarcadero Station, where the StreetWheelie production van will be waiting. They find the map that is shown on the next page.

SKILLS FOCUS

Reading Skills
Analyze information in consumer documents.

SKILLS FOCUS
pp. 899–904

Grade-Level Skills
■ Reading Skills
Analyze information in consumer documents.

Summary ◆ at grade level

To plan their commute to San Francisco, Sam and her grandfather use the Internet to look up a map of San Francisco's Bay Area Rapid Transit system, its information page on bicycle rules, its ticket-price guide, and its timetable.

PRETEACHING

Selection Starter

Build background. Ask how many students have ridden bus, subway, and train systems. Ask how they found out about routes, fares, transfers, and schedules in advance. Ask how train maps differ from street maps. What do train maps show? What do they omit? Why would you want to consult a schedule before traveling? Where is the best place to find out about fares? Tell students that this lesson will introduce them to some of the documents they might need to consult before planning a trip on public transportation.

Assign the Reading

Have students read p. 899 in class. Discuss the various documents Sam uses to plan her commute. Then, assign the reading and the Test Practice questions for homework.

HOMEWORK

RESOURCES: READING

Planning
■ *One-Stop Planner* CD-ROM with ExamView Test Generator

Differentiating Instruction
■ *Holt Reading Solutions*
■ *Supporting Instruction in Spanish*

Assessment
■ *Holt Assessment: Literature, Reading, and Vocabulary*

■ *One-Stop Planner* CD-ROM with ExamView Test Generator
■ *Holt Online Assessment*

Internet
■ go.hrw.com (Keyword: LE5 7-8)
■ *Elements of Literature Online*

A Reading Informational Text

? Locate information. What information does this map show? [Possible responses: The map shows all the stations in the BART system. It shows which line to take from any given station to another. It gives a basic indication of where the stations are in terms of a street map.]

[Answer to first call-out question: *Walnut Creek*—Pittsburg/Bay Point–Colma. *Embarcadero*—Richmond–Daly City/Colma, Pittsburg/Bay Point–Colma, Fremont–Daly City, and Dublin/Pleasanton–Daly City.]

B Reading Informational Text

? Locate information. Why does this map print each train line in a different color? [The colors make it much easier to see which line stops where and which line is the best choice for any given trip. If all the train lines were printed in the same color, riders would find the map hard to read.]

[Answer to second call-out question: Sam will have to take the Pittsburg/Bay Point–Colma line from Walnut Creek to Embarcadero station.]

BART System Map

Richmond–Daly City/Colma
Fremont–Daly City
Fremont–Richmond
Pittsburg/Bay Point–Colma
Dublin/Pleasanton–Daly City
P BART Parking

Which line should Sam take?

Which BART lines stop at Walnut Creek? at the Embarcadero?

Locating Information: Rules

Sam is glad to see that BART will take her directly from Walnut Creek to the Embarcadero station. She still needs more BART information: Is she allowed to bring a bike with her? She clicks on "Bikes on BART." Read the Web page on bicycle **rules** on the next page to see if Sam can take her bike on BART.

900 Collection 8 / Reading for Life

DIFFERENTIATING INSTRUCTION

Learners Having Difficulty
Have students look over the various documents before they begin reading the text. Point out the main headings, boldface type, bulleted lists, color printing, and other features that help guide readers to the important information they need. After students have spent a little time familiarizing themselves with the documents, they can read the text and answer the questions.

English-Language Learners
Although these consumer documents involve only place names, numerals for times, and basic vocabulary, many students may find the small print and unfamiliar formats daunting. Help students by showing them how to follow color-coded lines on the system map and how to look for the color-coded ticket information on the ticket guide.

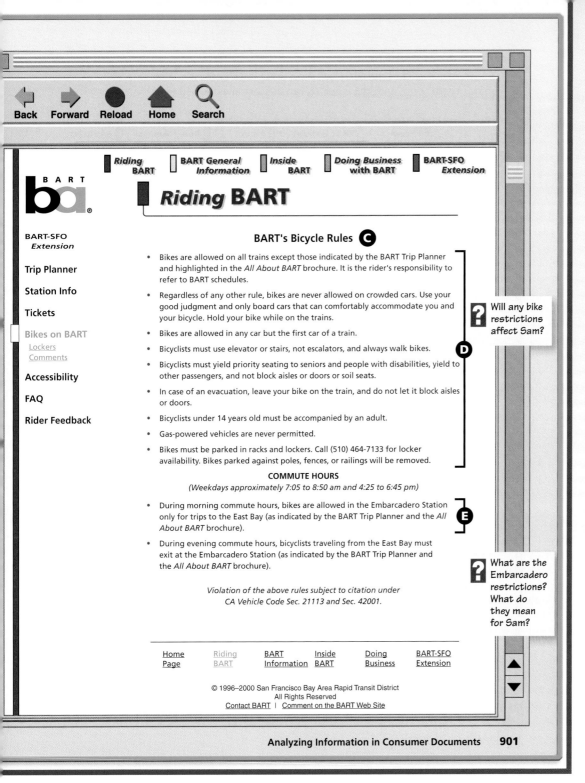

Riding BART

Riding BART | BART General Information | Inside BART | Doing Business with BART | BART-SFO Extension

BART-SFO Extension

Trip Planner

Station Info

Tickets

Bikes on BART
Lockers
Comments

Accessibility

FAQ

Rider Feedback

BART's Bicycle Rules **C**

- Bikes are allowed on all trains except those indicated by the BART Trip Planner and highlighted in the *All About BART* brochure. It is the rider's responsibility to refer to BART schedules.

- Regardless of any other rule, bikes are never allowed on crowded cars. Use your good judgment and only board cars that can comfortably accommodate you and your bicycle. Hold your bike while on the trains.

- Bikes are allowed in any car but the first car of a train.

- Bicyclists must use elevator or stairs, not escalators, and always walk bikes.

- Bicyclists must yield priority seating to seniors and people with disabilities, yield to other passengers, and not block aisles or doors or soil seats.

- In case of an evacuation, leave your bike on the train, and do not let it block aisles or doors.

- Bicyclists under 14 years old must be accompanied by an adult.

- Gas-powered vehicles are never permitted.

- Bikes must be parked in racks and lockers. Call (510) 464-7133 for locker availability. Bikes parked against poles, fences, or railings will be removed.

? Will any bike restrictions affect Sam?

D

COMMUTE HOURS
(Weekdays approximately 7:05 to 8:50 am and 4:25 to 6:45 pm)

- During morning commute hours, bikes are allowed in the Embarcadero Station only for trips to the East Bay (as indicated by the BART Trip Planner and the *All About BART* brochure).

- During evening commute hours, bicyclists traveling from the East Bay must exit at the Embarcadero Station (as indicated by the BART Trip Planner and the *All About BART* brochure).

E

Violation of the above rules subject to citation under CA Vehicle Code Sec. 21113 and Sec. 42001.

? What are the Embarcadero restrictions? What do they mean for Sam?

Home Page | Riding BART | BART Information | Inside BART | Doing Business | BART-SFO Extension

© 1996–2000 San Francisco Bay Area Rapid Transit District
All Rights Reserved
Contact BART | Comment on the BART Web Site

Analyzing Information in Consumer Documents 901

A Reading Informational Text

? Locate information. What information does this ticket guide not give the rider? [It doesn't tell how much a regular fare costs.]

[Answer to first call-out question: To find out the cost, Sam will have to use the Trip Planner.]

B Reading Informational Text

? Locate information. Who would be most likely to want a blue ticket? Why? [Someone who rides BART frequently but who isn't eligible for any of the discounts listed for students, children, senior citizens, or people with disabilities would purchase a blue ticket for the cheapest option.]

C Reading Informational Text

? Locate information. On which factors does BART determine these discount fares? [The fares are determined by the riders' ages and whether or not the riders have disabilities.] Which category of people travels for the least amount of money? [Children four years and under travel free.]

[Answers to second call-out question: Sam's best choice is the red ticket at a 75 percent discount since that ticket has the largest possible discount and no purchasing restrictions apply. The green ticket is Grandpa's best option because he can travel for 75 percent off the full fare.]

Locating Information: Ticket Guide

Now Sam checks the **ticket guide** to learn how much it will cost them. Since Grandpa is over sixty-five and Sam is twelve, can they get any discount fares?

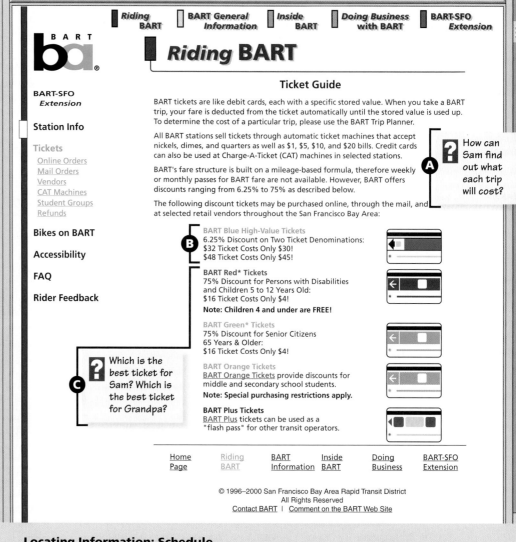

Locating Information: Schedule

To get the **BART schedule**, Sam goes to the trip-planning page and enters the name of the station they'll be leaving from and the name of the station they'll be arriving at. What she finds is on the next page.

History

The streets of San Francisco. During the mid-nineteenth century, horsecars—large passenger vehicles pulled by horses—were the only form of mass transit in cities. Horses had to work especially hard in San Francisco because it is built on a series of steep hills. This may be the reason that San Francisco was the first city in the world to build a cable-powered street railway. It ran along Clay Street and up Nob Hill.

San Francisco had no railway system until local voters agreed in 1961 to pay special taxes to fund its construction. BART includes seventy-one miles of track and connects residential neighborhoods with the thriving Market Street business district.

Like much of California, San Francisco is prone to earthquakes. Designers and builders worked hard to be sure that BART could withstand earthquakes. When a 1989 earthquake destroyed bridges and

expressways and halted the Oakland–San Francisco World Series just before the fourth game, BART was undamaged and continued to run on schedule.

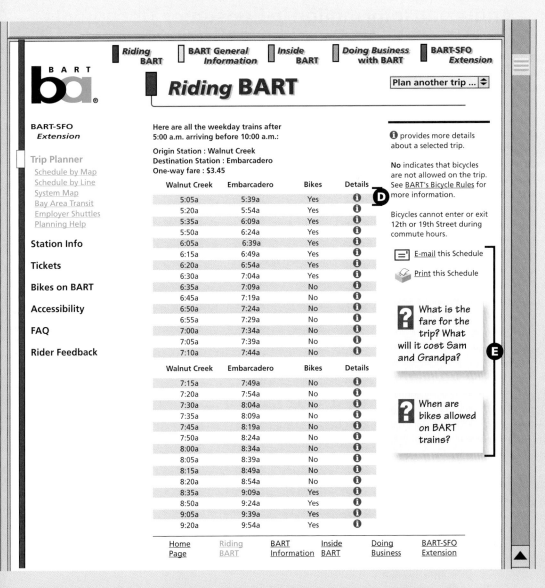

Here are all the weekday trains after
5:00 a.m. arriving before 10:00 a.m.:

Origin Station : Walnut Creek
Destination Station : Embarcadero
One-way fare : $3.45

Walnut Creek	Embarcadero	Bikes	Details
5:05a	5:39a	Yes	ⓘ
5:20a	5:54a	Yes	ⓘ
5:35a	6:09a	Yes	ⓘ
5:50a	6:24a	Yes	ⓘ
6:05a	6:39a	Yes	ⓘ
6:15a	6:49a	Yes	ⓘ
6:20a	6:54a	Yes	ⓘ
6:30a	7:04a	Yes	ⓘ
6:35a	7:09a	No	ⓘ
6:45a	7:19a	No	ⓘ
6:50a	7:24a	No	ⓘ
6:55a	7:29a	No	ⓘ
7:00a	7:34a	No	ⓘ
7:05a	7:39a	No	ⓘ
7:10a	7:44a	No	ⓘ

Walnut Creek	Embarcadero	Bikes	Details
7:15a	7:49a	No	ⓘ
7:20a	7:54a	No	ⓘ
7:30a	8:04a	No	ⓘ
7:35a	8:09a	No	ⓘ
7:45a	8:19a	No	ⓘ
7:50a	8:24a	No	ⓘ
8:00a	8:34a	No	ⓘ
8:05a	8:39a	No	ⓘ
8:15a	8:49a	No	ⓘ
8:20a	8:54a	No	ⓘ
8:35a	9:09a	Yes	ⓘ
8:50a	9:24a	Yes	ⓘ
9:05a	9:39a	Yes	ⓘ
9:20a	9:54a	Yes	ⓘ

Riding BART

BART General Information

Inside BART

Doing Business with BART

BART-SFO Extension

Plan another trip ...

BART-SFO *Extension*

Trip Planner
Schedule by Map
Schedule by Line
System Map
Bay Area Transit
Employer Shuttles
Planning Help

Station Info

Tickets

Bikes on BART

Accessibility

FAQ

Rider Feedback

ⓘ provides more details about a selected trip.

No indicates that bicycles are not allowed on the trip. See BART's Bicycle Rules for more information.

Bicycles cannot enter or exit 12th or 19th Street during commute hours.

E-mail this Schedule

Print this Schedule

? What is the fare for the trip? What will it cost Sam and Grandpa?

? When are bikes allowed on BART trains?

Home Page	Riding BART	BART Information	Inside BART	Doing Business	BART-SFO Extension

Thanks to her ability to use **consumer information materials**, Sam has found the correct BART line, discovered when bikes are allowed on the trains, learned about the cost of the tickets and discounts, and checked the schedules. She can do this from a library or the comfort of her home, thanks to the Internet and her ability to use consumer documents.

So look out, world. The name is Sam (Samantha Sallyann Lancaster, but call her Sam)— soon to be in a movie playing at a theater near *you*.

Analyzing Information in Consumer Documents **903**

INDEPENDENT PRACTICE

Analyzing Information in Consumer Documents

Test Practice

Answers and Model Rationales

1. **A** By referring back to page 900, students should realize this is the only possible response.

2. **G** The third bullet point of the bicycle rules clearly states that bikes are allowed in any car except the first.

3. **B** Sam is twelve, so her best choice is the red ticket. Grandpa is a senior citizen, so his best choice is the green ticket.

4. **J** By looking at the trip-planning Web page, students can find F, G, and H, but J appears only in the ticket guide.

5. **A** The 5:05 A.M. train from Walnut Creek is the only one that will reach Embarcadero and the van before 5:45 A.M.

Test-Taking Tips

Have students read each question, note which document it refers to, turn back to that document, and figure out which of the four answer choices is correct.

For more information on how to answer multiple-choice items, refer students to **Test Smarts**, p. 920.

Test Practice

1. Which type of **consumer document** would you consult to learn what BART line to take to get from one place to another?
   A   System map
   B   Bicycle rules
   C   Ticket guide
   D   Train schedule

2. According to the **bicycle rules,** in which cars of the train can you ride with a bike?
   F   Any car at all
   G   Any car but the first
   H   Any car but the last
   J   Only the first three cars

3. According to the **ticket guide,** Grandpa (age 75) and Sam (age 12) should buy —
   A   one blue and one red ticket
   B   one red and one green ticket
   C   one orange and one blue ticket
   D   two orange tickets

4. Reading the BART trip-planning Web page, you can learn all of the following *except* —
   F   the basic cost of the trip
   G   the schedule of departures and arrivals
   H   when bicycles are allowed
   J   available discounts

5. Sam must arrive two hours before her first call. If her first call is at 8:00 A.M., what is the latest she can leave the Walnut Creek station and still meet the van by 5:45 A.M.?
   A   5:05 A.M.
   B   5:20 A.M.
   C   5:35 A.M.
   D   5:50 A.M.

Constructed Response

1. Sam consults four **consumer documents** from the BART system. What is the purpose of each document?

2. Sam got all of her information about the BART system from the Internet. How might you get this same information if you did not have access to a computer?

SKILLS FOCUS

Reading Skills
Analyze information in consumer documents.

Constructed Response

1. The purpose of the BART system map is to provide information on the various stops along the train line. The purpose of the bicycle rules is to inform commuters about BART's bike policy. The purpose of the ticket guide is to provide ticket prices and information on discounts. The purpose of the trip-planning page is to provide a detailed train schedule.

2. Possible answer: I might call for information or pick up a flier from my nearest BART station.

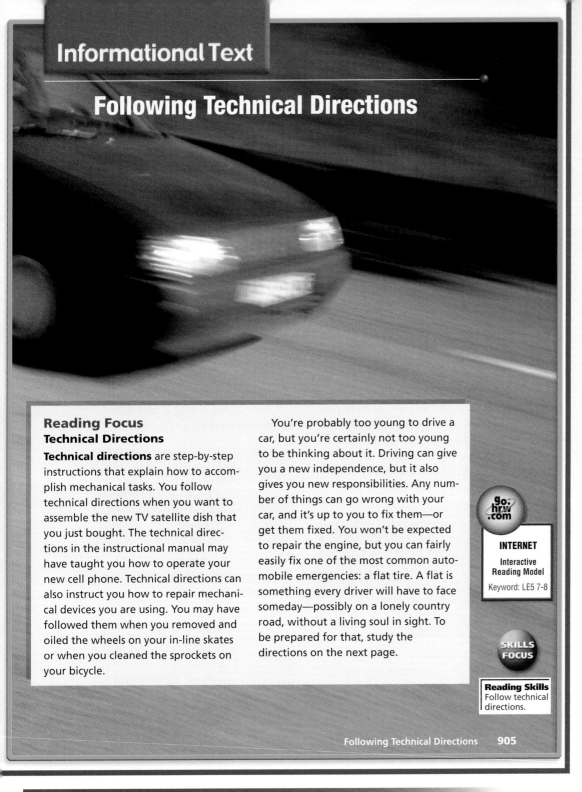

Following Technical Directions

Reading Focus
Technical Directions

Technical directions are step-by-step instructions that explain how to accomplish mechanical tasks. You follow technical directions when you want to assemble the new TV satellite dish that you just bought. The technical directions in the instructional manual may have taught you how to operate your new cell phone. Technical directions can also instruct you how to repair mechanical devices you are using. You may have followed them when you removed and oiled the wheels on your in-line skates or when you cleaned the sprockets on your bicycle.

You're probably too young to drive a car, but you're certainly not too young to be thinking about it. Driving can give you a new independence, but it also gives you new responsibilities. Any number of things can go wrong with your car, and it's up to you to fix them—or get them fixed. You won't be expected to repair the engine, but you can fairly easily fix one of the most common automobile emergencies: a flat tire. A flat is something every driver will have to face someday—possibly on a lonely country road, without a living soul in sight. To be prepared for that, study the directions on the next page.

go. hrw .com

INTERNET
Interactive
Reading Model
Keyword: LE5 7-8

SKILLS FOCUS

Reading Skills
Follow technical directions.

Selection Starter
Motivate. Ask how many students have had to take charge in emergencies such as a power failure or a sudden kitchen-sink flood. Did they know what to do? If they didn't know, what happened? Have students share stories of these minor disasters. Tell them that they are about to read directions that will explain what to do when an automobile tire goes flat.

Assign the Reading
Discuss the Informational Text page (p. 905) in class and assign the Test Practice for homework.

HOMEWORK

A Reading Informational Text
❓ **Follow directions.** Why can't you leave out the step of putting the brake on? [If the brake isn't on, the car can roll.]

B Reading Informational Text
❓ **Follow directions.** Point out the illustrations of each step in the directions. What is their purpose? [They clarify the verbal instructions. They show what the different tools look like, so the reader will recognize them.]

How to Change a Flat Tire

Before you can change a flat tire on your car, you first have to realize that the tire is flat. You might come out of your house in the morning and see the wheel rim resting on the road with the tire spread around it. You'll know right away the tire's flat. How can you tell, though, if it goes flat while you are driving? A first clue is that your car starts to pull to the right or the left even though you aren't turning the steering wheel. Another clue is that passing motorists honk and point as they drive by. Yet another clue is that the car starts bouncing up and down and making a loud *thumpity-thump-thump* sound.

When you suspect you have a flat tire, follow these procedures:

1 Park the car as far off the road as possible. Put the car in park (if you have an automatic transmission) or in gear (if you have a standard transmission), turn off the engine, and put on the emergency brake. Turn on your car's flashing lights. Now, get out and look at your tires. If you have a flat, put out emergency triangles or, at night, flares. (It's a good idea to carry warning triangles and flares in your trunk at all times in case of an emergency.)

2 Remove the spare tire from the trunk. Also take out the jack, the lug wrench, and related tools.

3 Remove the wheel cover from the flat tire, using a screwdriver or the end of the jack handle.

4 Loosen the lug nuts with the lug wrench, but do not remove them. Most lug nuts turn counterclockwise.

906 Collection 8 / Reading for Life

DIFFERENTIATING INSTRUCTION

Learners Having Difficulty
The illustrations in this article should help students follow the directions. Before they begin reading, point out the illustrations. Have students look again at each illustration after they read the step it depicts. Then, have them match up the tools and other objects in the illustrations with the copy in the text.

Advanced Learners
Acceleration. Have advanced learners explain how to operate a familiar technical device such as a CD player, video recorder, camera, microwave oven, or hand-held computer. Suggest that students write a list of instructions that would help someone operate the device. The instructions can include illustrations or diagrams. Students can then exchange their papers and rate

the directions. Are all necessary steps included? Are they clearly expressed? Are illustrations helpful? Is there any unnecessary information that can be deleted?

5 Position your jack. Different makes of cars come with different types of jacks, so check your owner's manual to learn how to use your jack. Make sure the jack is sitting on a solid, flat surface.

6 Lift the car with the jack until your flat tire is two or three inches off the ground. (*Never lie under the car when it is on the jack!*) **C**

7 Now, finish unscrewing the lug nuts. Put them inside the wheel **D** cover so you don't lose them.

8 Remove the flat tire, and replace it with the spare tire. Replace the lug nuts, and tighten them by hand.

9 Lower the jack until the spare tire is firmly on the ground. Remove the jack. Firmly tighten the lug nuts with the lug wrench. Work diagonally—tighten one on the top, then one on the bottom; one on the left, then one on the right; and so on.

10 Place the flat tire, the wheel cover, and all your tools in the trunk. As soon as you can, drive to a garage or a tire repair shop to get the tire fixed or replaced. You never want to be without a spare, because you never know when you'll get another flat!

C Reading Informational Text

❓ **Follow directions.** Why is this caution important? [If you got under the car and the jack slipped, you might be seriously injured or killed.]

D Reading Informational Text

❓ **Follow directions.** Why do you think you should loosen the lug nuts, then jack up the car, then take off the lug nuts, instead of jacking up the car first and removing the lug nuts in one step? [When the wheel is off the ground, it can turn around, making it difficult to loosen the tight lug nuts. Also, if you try to loosen the tight lug nuts while the car is on the jack, you might jolt the wheel and the car, which could cause the car to fall off the jack. The reason for not removing the lug nuts completely when you loosen them is so the wheel doesn't fall off while you are in the process of jacking the car up. If it did, it could roll away or land on you. Following the steps in the order given makes the job easier and can prevent accidents.]

GUIDED PRACTICE

Monitor students' progress. Have students explain to the class how to change a flat tire. Make sure they include all the necessary steps in the correct order.

MINI-LESSON Reading

Developing Word-Attack Skills
Remind students that the digraph *ch* most often stands for the sound /ch/ as in *change.* Then, point out that the digraph *ch* can also stand for the sound /k/. This letter-sound relationship commonly occurs in words that have Greek roots—for example, *technical* or *mechanical.*

Words from the same root often have similar letter-sound patterns. Display these words, which are related to *technical* and

mechanical. Have students identify the sound of *ch* in each word.

technique technology technician
mechanic mechanism mechanize

Activity. Display these sets of words. Have volunteers tell which word is related to the first one and has the same sound for *ch.* Answers are underlined.

1. *chronic*   chirp   chronicle
2. *technical*   trench   biotech
3. *archive*   archival   archery
4. *chorus*   chores   choreography
5. *chemist*   chemistry   cherish

Following Technical Directions

Following Technical Directions

Test Practice

Answers and Model Rationales

1. **C** When the tire is flat, you should not keep driving, so A and D are eliminated. Since you can change a tire yourself, there's no need to call your parents. "Park the car" (C) is the first direction in the article.

2. **G** Jacks and screwdrivers have nothing with which to grip the lug nuts. The lug nuts are too tight for you to loosen by hand. The directions tell you to use the lug wrench for this.

3. **C** The directions say not to get under the car when it's resting on the jack. You don't need to raise the car more than a couple of inches to change the tire, so B is incorrect. D is also incorrect because the jack can't remove the tire. Therefore, C is correct.

4. **G** You will need the lug nuts again, so putting them in a safe place like the inside of the wheel cover makes the most sense.

5. **B** You will probably want to do A and C, but first you should get the tire repaired (B) so you are not driving without a spare. You want to repair, not throw out, the flat tire, so D is incorrect.

Test Practice

1. When you think you have a flat tire, what should you do first?
   - **A** Drive the car to your family's garage.
   - **B** Call your parents, and ask them to pick you up.
   - **C** Park the car as far off the road as possible.
   - **D** Look out your window to see if the tire's flat.

2. The best tool for loosening the lug nuts is —
   - **F** a screwdriver
   - **G** a lug wrench
   - **H** a jack
   - **J** your hand

3. You should lift the car with the jack until —
   - **A** you can fit comfortably underneath the car
   - **B** the car is two to three feet in the air
   - **C** the flat tire is two to three inches off the ground
   - **D** the flat tire comes off the wheel

4. When you remove the lug nuts, you should —
   - **F** let them fall to the ground
   - **G** put them in the wheel cover
   - **H** throw them away
   - **J** feed them to a squirrel

5. After you have changed a flat tire, what should you do next?
   - **A** Call your parents to let them know what happened.
   - **B** Drive to a garage to get the flat tire fixed.
   - **C** Continue where you were going before you got the flat.
   - **D** Throw away the flat tire.

Constructed Response

1. How can you tell you have a flat tire? List three clues.
2. List the tools needed to fix a flat tire.
3. What should you do as soon as you can after you've changed your flat tire?

SKILLS FOCUS

Reading Skills
Follow technical directions.

Test-Taking Tips

When the text is a straightforward informational piece like this one, remind students that many of the multiple-choice questions will be answered in the text.

For more information on how to answer multiple-choice items, refer students to **Test Smarts**, p. 920.

Constructed Response

1. If the car is parked, you'll see the flat tire. If you're driving, clues that you have a flat include the car pulling left or right; other drivers trying to alert you; and the car bouncing and thumping.

2. Tools include a jack, a lug wrench, and a screwdriver.

3. You should replace the tire or have it repaired so you'll still have a spare.

Media Workshop

MULTIMEDIA PRESENTATION
Public-Service Announcement

In other workshops you have written expository papers, such as informative reports, where your chief purpose has been to present information. You have also written persuasive papers, where you have offered solutions to a problem or given your interpretation of a literary work.

In a public-service announcement, your object is both to share information and to advise or persuade your public about a specific course of action. If you search the World Wide Web, you will discover that public-service announcements are issued by governmental agencies, consumer advocates, and a variety of community groups. You will also discover that a number of young people who want to help their communities have written and produced public-service announcements.

A public-service announcement may appear in different forms. It may be produced as a newsletter, a poster, a radio or television presentation, or a Web site. It may even be animated and run for less than a minute.

Planning Your Announcement

1 Choosing a Focus

In a public-service announcement you wish to raise other people's awareness of a problem or situation and get them to take action. To get ideas for your own public-service message, you can explore local newspapers, newsletters, and bulletin boards; listen to radio and television announcements; and examine public-service announcements on the World Wide Web.

The subjects of public-service announcements range widely, including topics such as environmental concerns, safety tips, health issues, animal care, nutrition, and even

Assignment
Plan and deliver a public-service announcement.

Audience
Your classmates, teacher, friends, and other students.

RUBRIC
Evaluation Criteria

A successful public-service announcement

1. focuses on an issue of public concern

2. targets its audience

3. relies on facts, examples, and other evidence to support its points

4. may use print, visuals, and sound to deliver its message

Speaking and Listening Skills
Deliver a public-service announcement.

Media Workshop

Objectives
- Use appropriate planning skills to develop a public-service announcement.
- Revise the text to present the purpose of the message clearly, supply examples and evidence, incorporate various media, and conclude with a restatement of the message.
- Reflect on and assess one's writing process and public-service announcement.

PRETEACHING

Skills Starter

Motivate. Ask students to recall public-service announcements that they have heard on the radio or seen on television. Tell students to identify the main message of the announcement and to list any details that they remember. Explain to students that they will create a public-service announcement that catches their audience's attention and leaves a lasting impression.

DIRECT TEACHING

PLANNING YOUR ANNOUNCEMENT

Choosing a Focus

Encourage students to select as a focus a problem that they have experienced or have a deep interest in. If students select a topic that has been thoroughly explored already (for example, antidrug or antismoking announcements), remind them to strive to present familiar information in a fresh, creative way that will grab their audience's attention.

DIRECT TEACHING

Strategy Tip

Remind students that different audiences will respond differently to the way information is presented. Students may want to focus on a smaller, specific group, or they may want to address concerns of several groups or a larger, general audience. For example, adults may be more concerned with security issues for their children in regard to online etiquette, while teenagers may be more concerned with online shorthand. Students may want to address one or all of these groups in their presentations.

Researching Background Material

Remind students that they should always consult more than one source for their information. Some sources may have outdated statistics or biased views. Tell them to be on the lookout for sources that do not present alternative information in a fair manner. Tell students to find at least two sources, such as reputable newspapers, magazines, journals, and Web sites, to back up their facts.

Utilizing Different Media

Explain to students that they should feel free to experiment with how they present their public-service announcements. Students with interest in visual arts might want to create posters, actors might want to make video recordings, and musicians may want to incorporate songs into their presentations.

Research Strategies

- Most libraries are now equipped with online catalogs where you can locate sources. To access information, you can use **electronic databases.**

- To do research on the World Wide Web, you will need a **Web browser** to access information.

- For additional help, see Research Strategies in the Communication Handbook.

Suggested Topics

- how to behave at a school dance
- preparing for a test
- dealing with a bully
- a help line for new students
- rules for radio rookies
- conducting an interview
- tolerance for those who are different
- handling a library book
- dealing with teasing
- online etiquette

warnings about financial scams. Public-service announcements on the Web often can be accessed in more than one form. They might be available as both scripts and audios. Some use images and music to send their messages.

Consider your **purpose** and **audience.** A public-service announcement may have a large national audience or a local community audience, such as a school's student body. Choose a topic that will be of interest to your audience and that will hold their attention.

See the list on the left for suggestions for a public-service announcement that might be directed to other students in your school.

2 Researching Background Material

Learn as much as you can about the topic you have chosen for your public-service announcement. For example, if your topic is "online etiquette," you might begin by exploring a keyword like *netiquette* on a Web browser and by taking notes on the rules about online behavior. You might also take note of the special terms that are in current use, such as *flaming,* a word that means "belittling or putting down someone else's ideas." Gather the facts, examples, and reasons you will need to educate your audience.

3 Utilizing Different Media

A public-service announcement can be presented in print, or it can be presented in the form of a poster, an animated cartoon, or a recorded bulletin on radio or television. Your message can be accompanied by music, illustrations, or slides. Choose media that will express your ideas most effectively and dramatically.

RESOURCES: WRITING

Assessment

- *Holt Assessment: Writing, Listening, and Speaking*
- *One-Stop Planner* CD-ROM with ExamView Test Generator
- *Holt Online Assessment*
- *Holt Online Essay Scoring*

Internet

- go.hrw.com (Keyword: LE5 7-8)
- *Elements of Literature Online*

Developing a Script

1 Organizing Your Ideas

Even if your public-service announcement is brief, it should include an introduction, a body, and a conclusion. (If the message is to be aired on radio or television, it probably should not exceed one minute.)

Your **introduction** should be aimed at getting your audience's attention. If the technology is available, you can use music, a transparency, or a video clip to engage your listeners. Indicate the purpose of your announcement, and emphasize its importance.

In the **body** of your public-service announcement, present your information in a clear and logical manner. To support your points, use facts, statistics, examples, and reasons. You can introduce charts or other visual evidence to accompany your announcement.

In your **conclusion,** restate your main point. You may end with a slide, a photograph, or a dramatic quotation.

2 Formatting a Public-Service Announcement

Your public-service announcement can involve visuals and sound as well as texts. What will be the general makeup or arrangement of your announcement? Will it be delivered as a brochure or flier—that is, as a small pamphlet or handbill that can be distributed? Will it be recorded on tape to be aired on radio? Will it take the form of a colorful poster?

Decide on the best format for your public-service announcement. If you are using a visual format, you might use bullets to call out your main points. You can also vary the styles of type and the size of headings to create emphasis.

On the following page you'll find a script for a public-service announcement about netiquette. This announcement has been designed as a flier to be passed out by hand or posted on a bulletin board.

Media Elements

Visual Aids
Book and magazine
    illustrations
Posters
Photographs
Transparencies or slides

Audio Aids
Audiotapes of voices and
    sound effects
Web sites
Music recordings on CD or
    audiotape
Live instruments

Video Aids
Clips from movies or TV

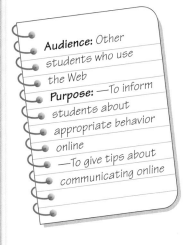

Audience: Other students who use the Web

Purpose: —To inform students about appropriate behavior online

—To give tips about communicating online

DEVELOPING A SCRIPT

Organizing Your Ideas

Tell students that if they choose to create a cartoon or a recorded bulletin for radio or television, their public-service announcement will be relatively brief. Students should spend extra time organizing and revising in order to find the most effective way to deliver their message in a short time span. Tell students to concentrate on using powerful visual images, presenting thought-provoking information, and concluding with a memorable slogan that will convey the point of their message in a condensed form.

Formatting a Public-Service Announcement

Tell students that they should treat their public-service announcements as advertisements for their ideas. A successful presentation uses eye-catching visuals and dramatic sound elements in a clear and organized format that best appeals to their audience's emotions, sense of humor, or sense of logic. Tell students that a well-chosen image, catchy phrase, or piece of music may persuade an audience to sympathize with their issue.

DIFFERENTIATING INSTRUCTION

Learners Having Difficulty

Students may feel overwhelmed with writing, organizing, and presenting a public-service announcement on their own. Encourage students having difficulty to work in groups. Tell students to delegate tasks and present their public-service announcement as a team. Remind students to update their partners frequently on any progress or problems they encounter.

English-Language Learners

Tell students that public-service announcements are often presented in several languages to reach a wide audience. Have English-language learners partner with fluent English-speaking students. Then, have them present a public-service announcement in English along with one that has been translated into the student's first language.

Public-Service Announcement Script

NETIQUETTE

When you "speak" to someone online, you need to observe certain rules of etiquette, just as you would in meeting someone face to face. Here are some do's and don'ts to help you maintain good relationships and have fun talking online.

Do's and Don'ts

DO pick an appropriate nickname, such as your first name or a short descriptive phrase.

DON'T use a nickname that will offend others or cause them to ignore you.

DO greet people politely. You can begin: "Hi" or "Hello everyone."

DON'T interrupt an ongoing conversation. Be sure you know the subject before you enter a conversation.

DO address individuals by using their nicknames: "LZJo, I like your idea."

DON'T type long, detailed messages. Give others a chance to speak.

DO type asterisks around a word or phrase you wish to emphasize.

DON'T type in capital letters or use boldface. This is like screaming at people.

DO use polite language. Discuss disagreements calmly. Always respect others' beliefs and opinions.

DON'T use or accept any verbal abuse. Ignore any person who uses offensive language or whose behavior is rude.

DO be careful when sharing personal information. Give out only details that you are comfortable sharing with strangers.

DON'T ask personal questions. Don't give out your last name, address, or phone number. Don't send photographs.

Chatting with your friends online can be great fun as long as you follow these simple rules and are considerate of one another.

Online Shorthand

AFK	Away from keyboard	FYI	For your information	OIC	Oh, I see	
B4	Before	K	OK	ROFL	Rolling on the floor laughing	
BRB	Be right back	L8R	Later			
BTW	By the way	LOL	Laugh out loud	THX	Thanks	
CUL	See you later	MSG	Message	WB	Welcome back	
EOM	End of message	NRN	No reply necessary	WTG	Way to go	

912   Collection 8 / Reading for Life

Evaluating and Revising

Use the following chart to evaluate and revise your public-service announcement.

Public-Service Announcement: Content and Organization Guidelines

Evaluation Questions	▶ Tips	▶ Revision Techniques
❶ Does your introduction state the purpose of your message?	▶ **Underline** the statement that shows the focus of your message.	▶ **Add** a statement that identifies your purpose and the importance of your message.
❷ Have you targeted your audience?	▶ **Bracket** words or phrases that identify your audience.	▶ If appropriate, **name** the individuals or groups who are affected.
❸ Have you supplied facts, examples, and other evidence to support your message?	▶ **Put a star** next to evidence that supports your message.	▶ **Add** facts, examples, and other details that support your main points.
❹ Did you use different forms of media in your presentation?	▶ **Put a check mark** next to each different form of media used in your presentation.	▶ When possible, **replace** print with another form of media, such as an illustration, a slide, or a video clip.
❺ Did you wrap up your message in your conclusion?	▶ **Underline** the statement that provides a conclusion to your message.	▶ **Add** a sentence that restates your position, or **add** a dramatic quotation.

On the next page is a public-service announcement that has been revised. Use the questions below the model to evaluate the writer's changes.

INTERNET

Media Tutorials

Keyword: LE5 7-8

Public-Service Announcement 913

EVALUATING AND REVISING

Content and Organization Guidelines

Have students meet in small groups to share their progress and discuss their ideas with each other. Students may want to form groups according to similar topics or by the types of media (print, audio, and video) they are using to produce their public-service announcements.

Publishing Tip

Students may want to submit their public-service announcements to government and nonprofit organizations that specialize in promoting awareness of the issues they have chosen to present.

TECHNOLOGY TIP

Tell students that they can make video recordings of public-service announcements that are aired on television and refer to them for ideas when they are producing their own. Students can also visit Web sites that are affiliated with advocacy groups or other organizations that produce public-service announcements.

EVALUATION GUIDELINES	**4**		**3**	**2**	**1**
Use these guidelines to quickly assess students' final drafts.	**Introduction states the purpose of the message.**	Introduction clearly states the purpose of the message in an attention-getting manner.	Introduction clearly states the purpose of the message.	Introduction vaguely states the purpose of the message.	Introduction is not included.
	Presentation targets audience and provides evidence to support the message.	Presentation persuasively targets audience and provides convincing evidence to support the message.	Presentation targets audience and provides clear evidence to support the message.	Presentation vaguely targets audience and provides minimal evidence to support the message.	Presentation does not target audience and provides insubstantial evidence to support the message.

(continued)

DIRECT TEACHING

Proofreading Tip

Tell students that as they proofread, they can alter the tone of their public-service announcements. Students may want to add slang or figures of speech to reach a younger audience. They may want to revise to a more formal tone to reach an older population.

GUIDED PRACTICE

Evaluating the Revision

Possible Answers

1. The writer added the sentence "A good rule is to be considerate of others." This detail provides a course of action that would aid in solving the problem and reinforces the message of this public-service announcement.

2. The writer deleted the sentence "What is the best way to handle this?" because the sentence was an unnecessary statement that offered no new information.

3. The writer moved the second sentence down to the end of the first paragraph. The change improves the flow of the text and leaves a strong impression on the reader.

PROOFREADING

TIP

- Ask a classmate to proofread your public-service announcement for errors in spelling, grammar, and mechanics.

Communications Handbook HELP

See Proofreaders' Marks.

PUBLISHING

TIPS

- Display your public-service announcement in an appropriate place, such as a bulletin board or the library.

- If your announcement has been taped, request permission to have it aired over the public-address system.

- Create a Web page for your class's public-service announcements.

Revision Model

When does teasing stop being a playful joke and turn into cruelty or meanness? Before you let your tongue slip, ask yourself, "How would I feel if someone said that about me?" You may think an insulting comment that embarrasses someone is quite innocent, but it is always ~~bad~~ rude to hurt a person's feelings. A good rule is to be considerate of others.

How should you ~~act~~ respond if someone teases you? ~~What is the best way to handle this?~~ Try to stay cool. Instead of showing anger, ignore the remark. Just laugh or walk away. If your response is good-natured, you will ~~keep~~ discourage the teaser from trying again.

Evaluating the Revision

1. Which details did the writer add? Do these details improve the message? Why or why not?

2. Which details did the writer delete? Why do you think these cuts were made?

3. How did the writer rearrange material? Do you think this change is an improvement? Explain.

(continued)

EVALUATION GUIDELINES		4	3	2	1
Use these guidelines to quickly assess students' final drafts.	**Different forms of media are used in the presentation.**	Different forms of media are creatively used in a thought-provoking presentation.	One form of media is creatively used in a thought-provoking presentation.	One form of media is used in a clear presentation.	One form of media is used in a vague presentation.
	Conclusion restates the main idea.	Conclusion restates the main idea in a thought-provoking and memorable way.	Conclusion clearly restates the main idea.	Conclusion vaguely restates the main idea.	There is no clear conclusion to the presentation.

Collection 8: Skills Review

Speaking and Listening Skills

Test Practice

DIRECTIONS: Read the following public-service announcement. Then, read the questions below it. Choose the best answer to each question, and mark your answers on your own piece of paper.

(1) Fellow middle schoolers, since our team placed first in the statewide debates, our school has become big news. (2) A reporter from the town newspaper wants to spend a day here, observing and asking questions. (3) The reporter has won several awards for her local coverage. (4) So here are some tips for what to do if you are interviewed. (5) Try to stay relaxed and keep your sense of humor. (6) Be as accurate as you can in your answers. (7) Listen to the questions carefully before you answer. (8) Take your time to respond. (9) If you don't understand a question, ask the interviewer to repeat or restate it. (10) We want the school to look good, so please do your best to make a good impression.

1. The best title for this announcement would be —
   A Conducting an Interview
   B How to Be Interviewed
   C Interviewer and Interviewee
   D Following Up an Interview

2. Which sentence is unnecessary and can be deleted?
   F sentence 3
   G sentence 5
   H sentence 7
   J sentence 9

3. The message of this public-service announcement would very likely be delivered —
   A over the school's public-address system
   B on a local radio station
   C in a town newspaper
   D on a billboard

4. Which of these additional tips would be appropriate?
   F Give the interviewer a list of questions.
   G Maintain eye contact throughout the interview.
   H Answer questions simply with a yes or no.
   J Review the interviewer's notes.

5. Which sentence reveals the underlying purpose of this public-service announcement?
   A sentence 1
   B sentence 2
   C sentence 4
   D sentence 10

SKILLS FOCUS

Speaking and Listening Skills
Analyze a public-service announcement.

Skills Review **915**

Test Practice

Answers and Model Rationales

1. **B** The public-service announcement offers information and advice for how to be interviewed by someone, so B is the best choice.

2. **F** G, H, and J all offer important details. F offers background information about a reporter, an unnecessary detail in this announcement.

3. **A** The target audience is the student body of a middle school. The best means to reach them would be over the school's public-address system, choice A.

4. **G** F, H, and J would not improve an interview. Only G, "Maintain eye contact throughout the interview," would be an appropriate tip.

5. **D** Sentence 10 reveals the underlying purpose of why these tips are given to the interviewees: to encourage the students to make the school look good.

APPLICATION

Have students create brief skits based on their public-service announcements to act out for the class or for the school. Encourage students to use visual and sound elements in their skits. Tell students to be prepared to give additional information and to answer questions about their topics.

EXTENSION

For homework, have students sketch ideas for a promotional item that would help raise awareness for the topic of their public-service announcements. Students can design items such as pencils, buttons, postcards, or toys with memorable slogans that might be distributed to their target audience.

READ ON

For Independent Reading

If students enjoyed the various types of informational texts in this collection, you might recommend the following magazines and Web sites for independent reading and investigation.

A Note on Web Sites

Web sites and online materials change continually and without notice. Holt, Rinehart and Winston cannot ensure the accuracy or appropriateness of these materials. Students, teachers, and guardians should assume responsibility for checking all online materials. The sites described on these Read On pages are well established and have been developed for—and in some cases, by—students.

Assessment Options

The following projects can help you evaluate and assess your students' outside work. Videotapes or audiotapes of completed projects may be included in students' portfolios.

■ **Write a news story.** Students who enjoy *Time for Kids* can try writing news stories of their own. Students should look at newspaper headlines to find current breaking stories that interest them, and then write their own feature stories on these topics. The articles in *Time for Kids* can serve as models for style, length, and so on. Students may want to write their stories on the computer so that they can scan in illustrations or graphics. You might have all students who pursue this project collaborate on a class newsmagazine.

Reading for Life: Magazines and Web Sites

Dig We Must

Do you dig ancient artifacts? If you do, unearth a copy of *Archaeology's dig*. This magazine covers the latest discoveries in the field of archaeology, from fossils to Vikings. It also features games and experiments and invites you to ask Dr. Dig all the questions you have about archaeology.

Up-to-Date

When a news story breaks, the magazine *Time for Kids* is there to report it. For the latest on history, sports, and culture, look on its Web site at www.timeforkids.com. You can contribute to *Time for Kids* by participating in its polls and writing letters in response to its stories and features.

Get Creative!

If you like writing, reading, and drawing, look for *Stone Soup: The Magazine by Young Writers and Artists.* Here you'll find short stories and poems written by kids from all around the world. Check out book reviews when you're looking for a new book to read. You may even decide to submit your own work for publication. Go to its Web site, www.stonesoup.com, for more links to sites for young writers, such as "ZuZu," "Young Girl Writers," and "Just Write."

Journey to the Past

Have you wondered how people lived during the Renaissance? Did you ever want to learn more about Mohammed, Charlemagne, and other leaders from world history? If you're curious about the past, read an issue of the magazine *Calliope*. You might not be able to put it down. In addition to its fantastic features, *Calliope* includes time lines, maps, and activities to enhance your understanding of history.

Using Academic Language

Informational Terms

As part of the review of consumer, public, and workplace documents, ask students to look back through the collection to find the meanings of the terms and phrases at right. Then, have students demonstrate their understanding of the terms by citing an informational selection from the collection (or an informational piece that they have read on their own) that illustrates the meanings of the following terms.

Consumer Documents (pp. 880, 899); **Advertisements** (p. 880); **Schedules** (p. 880); **Labels** (p. 880); **Warranties** (p. 880); **Contracts** (p. 880); **Instructional Manuals** (p. 880); **Workplace Documents** (pp. 880, 894); **Business Letter** (pp. 880, 894); **Application** (p. 880); **Employment Contract** (p. 880); **Social Security Number** (p. 881); **Work Permit** (p. 881); **Tax Form** (p. 881); **Insurance Forms** (p. 881); **Employee Manual** (p. 881); **Memorandums** (p. 881);

Nonfiction

The Ways of the World

Ever wondered where you can learn about the latest developments in computers and science? *Scientific American Explorations* magazine offers a comprehensive guide to technology and a whole lot more. Find out how to conduct science experiments in your home or classroom, and look into "Why and How," a feature that explains some of the mysteries of nature.

Endless Stories

The Web site storybookonline.net supplies compelling ways to practice your writing: Submit your own work of fiction, or collaborate with other writers on a story. Start your own stories, and let other writers contribute twists and turns to your plot. The site features links to book readings, fairy tales, and games.

Back Through Time

The Learning Curve's online "Millennium Exhibition" looks back on the last thousand years of England's history. Learn the importance of historic documents such as the Magna Carta. Read brief biographies of kings and queens, the story behind the invention of the printing press, and other interesting anecdotes. The "Millennium Exhibition" Web site is organized by century and can be found at learningcurve.pro.gov.uk/millennium /default.htm.

Friendly Advice

How do you decide what to buy and what to leave on the store shelf? *Consumer Reports* magazine offers guidance at its Web site designed for young people: zillions.org. Kids test such products as jeans and backpacks, evaluating their durability and safety. Their findings are then posted on the site.

Assessment Options

- **Submit a story or illustration.** Have students submit stories, poems, or illustrations to *Stone Soup* (see p. 916). Current issues of *Stone Soup,* either on library shelves or online, will give students a good idea of the quality and style of work that the magazine considers for publication. Students can look through their portfolios for examples of excellent work to submit, or they can write new stories and poems. Go over drafts with them, helping students to polish and refine their work. Encourage student illustrators to do the same with their art teacher.

- **Create an exhibition.** Students interested in history can create "Century Exhibition" modeled on the Learning Curve's "Millennium Exhibition." Working in a small group, students can choose an important document or artifact to represent each decade of the twentieth century in the United States. Possible choices for the 1920s include the Prohibition amendment to the Constitution or Louis Armstrong's trumpet, since this was the age of jazz. Encourage students to choose documents or objects that truly represent the entire decade. Then, using the "Millennium Exhibition" as a model, students can create their exhibit in a corner of the classroom.

E-mail Memos (p. 881); **Public Documents** (pp. 881, 888); **Newspaper Articles** (p. 881); **Announcement** (p. 888).

As part of the review of technical directions, ask students to look back through the collection to find the meanings of the terms listed below. Then, ask students to use these terms to explain how to use a mechanical device by following technical directions.
Instructional Manuals (p. 880); **Technical Directions** (pp. 880, 905).

Reteaching Lessons

Plot

Objective: To analyze elements of plot, including conflict, complications, climax, and resolution.

Direct Teaching: Introduce the lesson to the students with the following information:

> Every story or narrative is made up of a series of related events, called the plot. The plot answers the question "What happened?" When creating a plot, a writer involves characters in a conflict, challenges them with complications, pushes events to a climax, or peak of suspense, and finally wraps up the characters' story in a resolution. Together, this structure of related events makes up a narrative's plot.

Guided Practice: Have students re-read the first two and a half pages of "Rikki-tikki-tavi" (p. 14). Explain that in this section of the story, Rikki faces a minor obstacle, or conflict, that he quickly overcomes. Then, draw the following plot chain on the chalkboard:

Conflict	Complication 1	Complication 2	Resolution
Flood carries Rikki off.	Teddy thinks he's dead.		Family adopts Rikki.

Have volunteers complete this chain by describing the acts that revive Rikki and result in his adoption. Let students add more complication boxes and a climax box. Have them use time-order words, such as *first,*

next, then, and *after,* to make transitions between events. Make sure that all the events students record relate to the conflict at hand—Rikki's near drowning and his rescue by the family.

Independent Practice: Have students fill in a second chain based on the main conflict of the story—Rikki's fight with the cobras—using as many boxes as necessary. When students come to class with their completed plot chains, have them put the two chains together to reveal the entire plot of the story.
Possible chain:

Conflict	Complication 1	Complication 2	Complication 3
First Rikki meets Nag and is almost killed by Nagaina. He knows he must fight the cobras.	Then Teddy is threatened by another snake, Karait, but Rikki kills him and saves the boy.	Next Rikki learns through Chuchundra that the cobras have eggs and plan to kill the family and take over the house.	Knowing this, Rikki finds Nag in the bathroom and kills him, saving Teddy's father.

Complication 4	Complication 5	Climax	Resolution
In order to defeat Nagaina, Rikki gets Darzee's wife to distract the cobra while Rikki destroys her eggs.	Meanwhile, however, Nagaina threatens Teddy and his family on the veranda.	Finally, using her last egg, Rikki lures Nagaina away from Teddy and then pursues and kills her in her den.	Rikki has made the family and the garden safe, so Darzee sings a song of praise to the mongoose.

Forms of Prose

Objective: To analyze the purposes and characteristics of different forms of prose (for example, short story, novel, novella, essay).

Direct Teaching: Share the following ideas with the class:

Different forms of literature, such as short stories, novels, poems, articles, and essays, don't just have different forms and characteristics; they also have different purposes. A short story may be written to entertain, enlighten, inspire, or frighten its readers, while an article is more often written to inform or educate its readers or to capture a particular place, person, or event. An essay is often written to convince the reader of something or to explain a particular perspective. As you read, you should think about the author's purpose in writing the text. If you decide the author's purpose is to convince you of something, does he or she provide a logical argument to convince you, supported by credible evidence? If the author's purpose is to inspire or entertain you, does she or he challenge you with new ideas; striking imagery; eloquent, original language; and well-structured form? If the author's purpose is to frighten or create suspense, does the plot build tension and surprise you with unexpected twists and turns, or is the story predictable?

Guided Practice: Genre and purpose. Photocopy Selections by Genre (pp. T53–T58) in this teacher's edition, and distribute it to the class. Arrange students in pairs, and have them select three texts, one from the short stories, one from the novellas, and one from the essays. For each selection, partners should devise a statement of purpose. For instance, for the short story "Three Skeleton Key," students might write, "The purpose of the short story 'Three Skeleton Key' by George G. Toudouze is to frighten and entertain the reader using a suspenseful plot, foreshadowing, and precise details." Make sure students also express an opinion about how well the author fulfills his or her purpose.

Independent Practice: Genre and purpose. After partners have written their statements of purpose, they must decide whether or not the selection succeeds in accomplishing this purpose. For each selection, students should choose four passages or examples from the text (with page numbers) that help to fulfill or fail to fulfill the author's purpose. For instance, with "Three Skeleton Key," students might note that the story of the island's name on p. 40 works because it foreshadows the lighthouse keepers' fates and builds suspense. When partners have finished collecting support for their conclusions about how well the author achieved his or her purpose, have each pair share their findings with the rest of the class.

Interrelated Plot Events

Objective: To identify events that advance the plot, and determine how each event explains past or present action(s) or foreshadows future action(s).

Direct Teaching: Share the following information with students:

The plot of a narrative or story is more than just a list of what happens. It is a tightly structured web of related events. The plot usually begins with the introduction or exposition, which sets the scene. The exposition is followed by complications, which build to a climax. Good readers notice that some events move the plot forward, while other events may serve to clarify past or present actions in the story. Still other events may hint at, or foreshadow, future actions in the narrative. When you read, you should be thinking about how each event relates to what happens before and after it.

Guided Practice: Function of plot events. Divide the class into groups of four or five. First, have the groups review "Bargain" (p. 368) by A. B. Guthrie, using a reader's theater format. (Have one student assume the role of the narrator, another the role of Mr. Baumer, another Freighter Slade, and so on.) When students have finished re-reading the story, have each group select four events that are crucial to the advancement of the plot. Have the group summarize each event in writing, in a few sentences. Then, have students identify each event as part of the introduction or exposition, the complications or problems, the climax, or the resolution of the story. Students should then identify the function of each event in the plot. Does it clarify an earlier incident, hint, allusion, or description? Does it foreshadow what happens later in the plot? Does it contribute to the mounting tension before the story's climax?

Independent Practice: Interrelated time line. Have students take home a piece of poster paper and create an illustrated time line for "Bargain." For each event that students include, they should identify which part of the plot it belongs to and what function it serves in the story. Students should draw arrows that connect some events to the events they foreshadow and other arrows from later incidents to prior events they clarify.

[Possible time line:

1. Slade crumples the bill and twists Mr. Baumer's nose—*complication.* This event foreshadows future trouble between the two men.

↓

2. Mr. Baumer complains about Slade's stealing whisky—*exposition.* This event contributes background information about Slade and other freighters and foreshadows the means of Slade's death.

↓

3. Moore announces that Slade is dead—*climax.* This event heightens the mystery of Mr. Baumer's changed attitude toward Slade and marks the turning point in the conflict between the two men.

↓ ↑

4. The narrator notices the barrel from Slade's wagon containing poisonous wood alcohol—*resolution.* This event explains Mr. Baumer's different approach to Slade—he was simply waiting for Slade's evil temperament to cause his own inevitable downfall. It also resolves the conflict between the two men as a story of completed revenge.]

Characterization

> **Objective:** To analyze the methods writers use to reveal character.

Direct Teaching: Share the following thoughts with the class:

> We learn about the people around us in many different ways. We hear about them from their friends and family, we read their biographies or their own writings, we see their artwork, or we talk to them directly. Every detail we hear, see, or experience in relation to that person adds to our overall portrait of that person's character. In the same way, authors characterize the people in their stories through a wide range of techniques. While sometimes the narrator of a story will describe a character directly, like "good King Arthur," more often characterization is accomplished *indirectly*, through the character's thoughts, words, speech patterns, and actions or the thoughts, words, and actions of other characters. As you read, you should think about how even small details in a story contribute to characterization.

Guided Practice: Details of characterization. Have students re-read the short story "The Smallest Dragonboy" (p. 146), taking turns reading each paragraph aloud. Encourage students to interrupt the reading by raising their hands to note details that contribute to the characterization of Keevan, Beterli, Mende, K'last, Lessa, Keevan's dragon, and other characters on Pern. Write these details down on the chalkboard. Then, students should note the most important characteristics of each character and support their opinions with details from the chalkboard.

Independent Practice: Characterization web. Pair students up, and have each team construct a characterization web for a character in a story the class has read. In the center of each web, students should write the name of the selected character. Then students should choose three important characteristics of that character and arrange them around the center of the web. These characteristics should be described with a phrase or short sentence. For each characteristic, students should provide three details that communicate that characteristic to the reader. Remind students to choose a range of details from what the narrator, the character in question, and other characters say and do. For each detail, students should specify the source of the detail (narrator, character's words, actions, and so on) and the page number. Have the partners combine their webs to make a giant web for the story.

Characteristic 1:
Beterli's cruelty

a. taunting Keevan as a "babe" (quote from Beterli, p. 149)

b. his "contemptuous smile" (Beterli described by narrator, p. 149)

c. his attack on Keevan with the shovel (Beterli's action, p. 154)

Characteristic 2:
Beterli's arrogance

a. claiming the marked egg as his own (Beterli's action described, p. 150)

b. his disdain for the authority of the wingseconds (Keevan, thinking about Beterli, p. 149)

c. his guessing game with Keevan (quote from Beterli, p. 153)

Beterli

Characteristic 3:
Beterli's insecurity

a. recognizes Keevan as fast runner (quote from Beterli, p. 151)

b. not selected by dragons eight times (narrator's background, p. 150)

c. refusing to let others near "his" egg (Beterli described by narrator, p. 150)

Themes Across Genres

> **Objective:** To identify the theme of a work and analyze recurring themes across works.

Direct Teaching: Share the following information with the class:

> Part of what makes a literary theme or message powerful is that it doesn't apply just to the characters in a story or the speaker of a poem. Themes often have universal qualities that make them relevant to the lives of readers. Since a theme is often a general idea or statement about life, it may appear in a number of different contexts and genres. The importance of bravery, independence, and chivalry are emphasized in the medieval tales about King Arthur, but they are also emphasized in the *Star Wars* movie series. As good readers, you should be thinking not only about what general message or theme is being conveyed by a work but also about how it relates to similar themes in other works. By comparing and contrasting themes across works, you will have a better appreciation of what each writer is trying to say.

Guided Practice: Finding the theme. Have the class review the story "Amigo Brothers" (p. 484) and the article "Buddies Bare Their Affection for Ill Classmate" (p. 544), taking turns as each student reads aloud. When students are finished with the review, divide the class in half. One group will focus on the story, and the other group will focus on the article. Choose a student moderator for each group, and have the group discuss the overall theme of their work. Remind each moderator to focus on the big questions that each work raises about the nature of friendship, loyalty, and courage. How is friendship changed by competition or hardship? Does friendship make us stronger or weaker? How do people display loyalty to one another even when circumstances divide them or put them in different positions? When each group has finished brainstorming, have each student in each group write a statement about the theme or main idea of the work they focused on. Remind students that this statement should express the general observation or statement about life that the work communicates. Then, have students in each group exchange their statements with someone from the other group. These partners should compare and contrast their statements about the story and about the article, taking notes on the thematic overlap between the two works. Finally, partners should write a general thesis statement that applies to both the story and the article and present it to the class.

Independent Practice: Themes across genres. Have the class discuss the ideas about friendship that are expressed by "Amigo Brothers" and the news article. At home, have students select a poem, play, movie, or TV show that they think makes a strong statement about the nature of friendship. Students should present their selections in class, reading a passage (or describing a scene in detail) that they think illustrates the theme of the work. Between each presentation, have the class discuss how these themes relate to the themes in "Amigo Brothers" and the article and to the themes of the works presented earlier in class.

Point of View

Objective: To analyze point of view (e.g., first and third person, limited and omniscient, subjective and objective) in narrative text and explain how point of view affects the overall theme of the work.

Direct Teaching: Introduce the lesson to the students with the following information:

One of the most important things about any story is the point of view, or perspective, from which it is told. A story's point of view can affect not only the tone and style but also the message, or theme, that the author wants to communicate to the reader. Just as a detective story isn't as mysterious if it is told by the villain who committed the crime, so almost any story will say something different depending on who is telling it.

Guided Practice: Listening and speaking. Help students to recall the selection "Rikki-tikki-tavi" (p. 14) by Rudyard Kipling. Then, display on the chalkboard the following paragraph from the selection:

Darzee was a featherbrained little fellow who could never hold more than one idea at a time in his head, and just because he knew that Nagaina's children were born in eggs like his own, he didn't think at first that it was fair to kill them. But his wife was a sensible bird, and she knew that cobra's eggs meant young cobras later on; so she flew off from the nest and left Darzee to keep the babies warm and continue his song about the death of Nag. Darzee was very like a man in some ways.

Have a volunteer read the passage aloud. Have students listen carefully and then discuss whether the passage is told from a first- or third-person point of view. Ask students how they could tell that the passage is in the third person. [The narrator is not in the story but stands above it, describing all the events and people from a distance.] Remind students that an omniscient point of view reflects an all-knowing perspective, which allows us to hear the thoughts of different characters, while a limited point of view lets us hear only one character's

perspective on the world. Have another student read the passage aloud again, and ask students whether they think this passage is told from an omniscient or a limited point of view. Ask them to support their answers with evidence from the text. [We hear what different characters, Darzee and his wife, are thinking, and Darzee's behavior is compared with that of men in general. The perspective is all-knowing and omniscient.] Next, have students discuss the difference between an objective story and a subjective one. Ask students to decide whether the narrator's description of the birds is scientific, clinical, and detached (objective) or opinionated and full of feeling (subjective). [It is subjective.]

Independent Practice: Writing application. Have students take out a piece of paper. Read the passage aloud, and ask students to jot down a list of words and phrases from the passage that they think show the narrator's perspective on Darzee, his wife, and their behavior. [Possible responses: *featherbrained, could never hold more than one idea at a time, sensible, like a man in some ways.*] Have students share their lists with the class and discuss how the narrator seems to admire the sensible, brave actions of Darzee's wife and to criticize the foolish attitude of Darzee. Discuss how this passage might capture the overall theme of the story. Have students write down a statement using the form "Rudyard Kipling's 'Rikki-tikki-tavi' conveys the message that. . . . " [Responses will vary. Students might emphasize the idea that a sensible response to danger and evil requires taking precautions and having courage and that people often forget this because they are foolish or softhearted.]

Ask students to look at the passage on the chalkboard again, this time considering it from a different point of view. Have students use the other side of their paper to rewrite the passage from one of the following points of view:

1. **A subjective first-person point of view.** Remind students that this point of view might include the thoughts of Darzee and his unique "feather-brained" perspective on the cobras' eggs. Remind students to use first-person pronouns, like *I, me, mine, we, us,* and *ours*.

2. **An objective third-person point of view.** Point out that this point of view must describe the birds, the snakes, the eggs, and the forest from a completely *external* perspective. No thoughts or other subjective elements can be included in this point of view.

Whichever option students choose, remind them to try to capture the same message or theme of the original passage. When students have finished writing, have them share their rewrites with the class. Have them discuss how the different points of view affected the theme of the story.

Literary Criticism

Objective: To analyze a range of responses to a literary work, and to determine how the literary elements in the work shaped those responses.

Direct Teaching: Share the following thoughts with your students:

> In reading any story you shape your criticism in part by the literary elements of plot, character, setting, point of view, theme, and figurative language and in part by your life experiences. The author's artistry with words evokes certain images, associations, and ideas in your mind. These personal associations help to determine the way you respond to the work. For example, your response to Mildred D. Taylor's characters depends in part on your previous experience with people who talk in a black southern dialect and in part on what the characters say and do. If the characters you've met before were plain, honest folk, you'll probably assume these characters are too—until they prove otherwise. Because everyone's experiences are different, people respond to the same story in different ways.

Guided Practice: Rating three responses. Read the following three responses to *Song of the Trees* (p. 508). Consider to what extent each response is affected by the literary elements in the novella. Then, rate these responses from 1 (not affected much) to 3 (affected deeply).

> **Response 1.** This was a wonderful book about the way a family fights to defend what it owns. I cried when I read it because here in Russia my family has to fight to keep a tiny room in a cramped apartment. Please read this book. It is great. [2—affected by theme]

> **Response 2.** I didn't like this story because in the end the Logans actually lose most of the trees they are trying to protect. Although I was glad when Cassie's father forces Mr. Andersen to back off, the trees remaining at the close of the story stand like "lonely sentries" and are silent. This ending left me with a feeling of defeat. [3—affected by the resolution of the plot, simile, and personification]

> **Response 3.** I really liked this book. It was awesome. I recommend it to other students my age. It was easy to read and short. [1—not affected much by literary elements, only by length and readability of work]

Help students to see that response 3 does not discuss any literary elements. Response 1 focuses on theme and how the theme relates to the writer's own experience. Response 2 discusses the resolution of the plot and the author's use of simile and personification at the end of the novella. Therefore, this response is most strongly affected by the literary elements in the work.

Independent Practice: Literary Criticism. Challenge students to choose another work from this text and write a criticism to it that is shaped by various literary elements.

Cause and Effect

Objective: To analyze the cause-and-effect organizational pattern.

Direct Teaching: Introduce the lesson to the students with the following information:

> *Causes* **are reasons that things happen.** *Effects* **are results. When writers show why something happens, they're writing about causes; when they show what something leads to, they're writing about effects. Exploring causes and effects is one way to analyze an event or an issue. You can tell that a writer is exploring causes and effects when you notice signal words and phrases such as** *why,* *because, since, resulted in,* **and** *so.*

Guided Practice: Cause-and-effect chain. Have students re-read "A Mason-Dixon Memory" (p. 533). Point out the following sentences on pp. 537–538:

- "<u>Why</u> did she look and sound so nervous?"

- "'You mean I can't go to the park,' I stuttered, '<u>because</u> I'm a Negro?'"

- "'They don't allow Negroes in the park,' he said, '<u>so</u> I'm staying with Clifton.'"

Have volunteers identify the cause-and-effect signal words [underlined] in each excerpt. Next, put the following cause-and-effect chain on the chalkboard:

Independent Practice: Cause-and-effect chain. Assign students to make a second cause-and-effect chain for the experiences of Dondré Green. Tell them to write "Country club has racist admission policy" in the first box and to add as many boxes as they need to show how the policy affected Dondré, what actions his teammates took as a result, and what other effects the incident had. When students bring their completed cause-and-effect chains to class, have them use both chains to compare the causes and effects of both incidents.

> [Possible answers: Country club has racist admission policy. → Dondré is barred from playing. → Coach asks team to decide what to do. → Team walks out and forfeits tournament. → Louisiana citizens are outraged at the injustice. → Legislature proclaims Dondré Green Day. → Law is passed prohibiting racist policies for sports events at private clubs. → Dondré learns that love can conquer hatred and bigotry.]

Author's Argument

Objective: To analyze the development of an author's argument in informational texts.

Direct Teaching: Share the following explanation with students:

> In informational texts, perspective and point of view refer to the way the writer feels about a subject. On the subject of school vouchers, for example, there are many perspectives, or points of view. Some people think vouchers will help schools in poor-performing areas. Others think the threat of vouchers will make public schools try harder to improve their own instruction. Others think vouchers will spell the end of public education. Some like vouchers because they think vouchers will help their own private schools. These are all perspectives on the controversial topic of school vouchers.
>
> An argument is a kind of writing that uses evidence to try to persuade us to think or act in a certain way. We find many arguments in the editorial pages of newspapers. We could say that anyone who presents an argument has a point of view, or perspective, on a subject. If you present an argument in favor of school vouchers, it means your perspective on school vouchers is favorable.

Guided Practice: Analyzing an argument. In this exercise, students will trace the details of a writer's argument on a topic. Have students read the following brief letter about roads in wilderness areas. Tell them that as they read the letter, they are searching for the following three things:

1. the topic of the letter

2. evidence showing how the writer feels—and wants us to feel—about the topic

3. evidence "Concerned Hiker" uses to support position

Finally, they are evaluating the evidence; they are separating opinion from facts.

Roads Can Hurt Us

Just before the end of his presidency, President Clinton ordered that 60 million acres of our national forests be kept off limits to new roads. This ruling is very important and should not be overturned, for several reasons. First, roadless areas are sources of clean water. Second, they are vital to preserving endangered species. Opponents of roadless areas say that the ruling would have an adverse economic impact on the logging and mining industries; but this is not so, because more than half of the 192 million acres would be available for industry. Some people argue that new roads are needed for access to our national parks, but 360,000 miles of roads already exist in the national parks, and most of them are in great need of repair. Some argue that a ban on roads will put people nearby at greater risk of fire, but the rule permits the building of roads where there is a threat of fire. The public overwhelmingly supports a ban on roads in the national parks. It is heartbreaking to think of these wilderness areas defaced by ugly roads, the trees felled and hacked up. I believe that the president should save the rule to protect our wilderness.

—Signed,

Concerned Hiker

Independent Practice: Analyzing an argument. After students have read the letter, have them fill out a chart like this one:

Topic	
How the writer feels about the topic (the writer's perspective)	
Main point of the letter	
Key supporting details	

When the chart is filled out, have the students divide the supporting details into **facts** and **opinions.** (Facts carry much more weight than opinions in a serious argument.) Finally, have them **evaluate** the argument: Is it a convincing argument? Did Concerned Hiker fail to answer some objections to the ban on roads in wilderness areas?

[Possible answers for chart:

Topic—the ruling to prohibit road building in wilderness areas.

How the writer feels about the topic—The writer feels that it would be heartbreaking to build new roads in wilderness areas.

Main point of the letter—The arguments supporting new roads in wilderness areas are not supported by the facts; the writer feels that new road building should be banned.

Key supporting details—Roadless areas are sources of water; they support endangered species; half

the wilderness acres are still available for industry; many roads in national parks are in bad repair and should be fixed before new ones are built; provisions have been made for protection from fire; there is overwhelming public support.]

[Possible answers to questions:

Facts versus opinions—All of the above are facts except for the opinion that the building of roads would be heartbreaking. Ask students: Did the writer provide any factual support (statistics, for example) for the statement that the public over-whelmingly supports a ban on new roads in wilderness areas? (No)

Evaluation—In general this is a good argument, although the writer seems unable to resist the emotional appeal at the end. Ask students, however, how that appeal affected them. Did it influence them more or less than the factual evidence did?]

Resource Center

The Parisian Novels (The Yellow Books), Vincent van Gogh, 1888.

919

Test Smarts

by **Flo Ota De Lange and Sheri Henderson**

Strategies for Taking a Multiple-Choice Test

If you have ever watched a quiz show on TV, you know how multiple-choice tests work. You get a question and (usually) four choices. Your job is to pick the correct one. Easy! (Don't you wish?) Taking multiple-choice tests will get a whole lot easier when you apply these Test Smarts:

T rack your time.

E xpect success.

S tudy the directions.

T ake it all in.

S pot those numbers.

M aster the questions.

A nticipate the answers.

R ely on 50/50.

T ry. Try. Try.

S earch for skips and smudges.

Track Your Time

You race through a test for fear you won't finish, and then you sit watching your hair grow because you finished early, or you realize you have only five minutes left to complete eleven zillion questions. Sound familiar? You can avoid both problems if you take a few minutes before you start to estimate how much time you have for each question. Using all the time you are given can help you avoid making errors. Follow these tips to set **checkpoints:**

- How many questions should be completed when one quarter of the time is gone?

- What should the clock read when you are halfway through the questions?

- If you find yourself behind your check-points, you can speed up.

- If you are ahead, you can—and should— slow down.

Expect Success

Top athletes know that attitude affects performance. They learn to deal with their negative thoughts, to get on top of their mental game. So can you! But how? Do you compare yourself with others? Most top athletes will tell you that they compete against only one person: themselves. They know they cannot change another person's performance. Instead, they study their own performance and find ways to improve it. That makes sense for you too. You are older and more experienced than you were the day you took your last big test, right? So review your last scores. Figure out just what you need to do to top that "kid" you used to be. You can!

What if you get anxious? It's OK if you do. A little nervousness will help you focus. Of course, if you're so nervous that you think you might get sick or faint, take time to relax for a few minutes. Calm bodies breathe slowly. You can fool yours into feeling calmer and thinking more clearly by taking a few deep breaths—five slow counts in, five out. Take charge, take five, and then take the test.

Study the Directions

You're ready to go, go, go, but first it's wait, wait, wait. Pencils. Paper. Answer sheets. Lots of directions. Listen! In order to follow directions, you have to know them. Read all test directions as if they contain the key to lifetime happiness and several years' allowance. Then, read them again. Study the answer sheet. How is it laid out? Is it

1

2

3

4

or

1   2   3   4 ?

What about answer choices? Are they arranged

A   B   C   D

or

A   B

C   D ?

Directions count. Be very, very sure you know exactly what to do and how to do it before you make your first mark.

Take It All In

When you finally hear the words "You may begin," briefly **preview the test** to get a mental map of your tasks:

- Know how many questions you have to complete.
- Know where to stop.
- Set your time checkpoints.
- Do the easy sections first; easy questions are worth just as many points as hard ones.

Spot Those Numbers

"I got off by one and spent all my time trying to fix my answer sheet." Oops. Make it a habit to

- match the number of each question to the numbered space on the answer sheet every time
- leave the answer space on your answer sheet blank if you skip a question
- keep a list of your blank spaces on scratch paper or somewhere else—but *not* on your answer sheet. The less you have to erase on your answer sheet, the better.

Master the Questions

"I knew that answer, but I thought the question asked something else." Be sure—very sure—that you **know what a question is asking you.** Read the question at least twice before reading the answer choices. Approach it as you would a mystery story or a riddle. Look for clues. Watch especially for words like *not* and *except*—they tell you to look for the choice that is false or different from the other choices or opposite in some way. If you are taking a reading-comprehension test, read the selection, master all the questions, and then re-read the selection. The answers will be likely to pop out the second time around. Remember: A test isn't trying to trick you; it's trying to test your knowledge and your ability to think clearly.

Anticipate the Answers

All right, you now understand the question. Before you read the answer choices, **answer the question yourself. Then, read the choices.**

If the answer you gave is among the choices listed, it is probably correct.

Rely on 50/50

"I . . . have . . . no . . . clue." You understand the question. You gave an answer, but your answer is not listed, or perhaps you drew a complete blank. It happens. Time to **make an educated guess**—not a *wild* guess, but an *educated* guess. Think about quiz shows again, and you'll know the value of the 50/50 play. When two answers are eliminated, the contestant has a 50/50 chance of choosing the correct one. You can use elimination too.

Always read every choice carefully. **Watch out for distracters**—choices that may be true but are too broad, too narrow, or not relevant to the question. Eliminate the least likely choice. Then, eliminate the next, and so on until you find the best one. If two choices seem equally correct, look to see if "All of the above" is an option. If it is, that might be your choice. If no choice seems correct, look for "None of the above."

Try. Try. Try.

Keep at it. **Don't give up.** This sounds obvious, so why say it? You might be surprised by how many students do give up. Think of tests as a kind of marathon. Just as in any marathon, people get bored, tired, hungry, thirsty, hot, discouraged. They may begin to feel sick or develop aches and pains. They decide the test doesn't matter that much. They decide they don't care if it does—there'll always be next time; whose idea was this, anyway? They lose focus. Don't do it.

Remember: The last question is worth just as much as the first question, and the questions on a test don't get harder as you go. If the question you just finished was really hard, an easier one is probably coming up soon. Take a deep breath, and keep on slogging. Give it your all, all the way to the finish.

Search for Skips and Smudges

"Hey! I got that one right, and the machine marked it wrong!" If you have ever—ever—had this experience, pay attention! When this happens in class, your teacher can give you the extra point. On a machine-scored test, however, you would lose the point and never know why. So, listen up: All machine-scored answer sheets have a series of lines marching down the side. The machine stops at the first line and scans across it for your answer, stops at the second line, scans, stops at the third line, scans, and so on, all the way to the end. The machine is looking for a dark, heavy mark. If it finds one where it should be, you get the point. What if you left that question blank? A lost point. What if you changed an answer and didn't quite get the first mark erased? The machine sees two answers instead of one. A lost point. What if you made a mark to help yourself remember where you skipped an answer? You filled in the answer later but forgot to erase the mark. The machine again sees two marks. Another lost point. What if your marks are not very dark? The machine sees blank spaces. More lost points.

To avoid losing points, take time at the end of the test to make sure you

- did not skip any answers
- gave one answer for each question
- made the marks heavy and dark and within the lines

Correct:

Incorrect:

Get rid of smudges. Make sure there are no stray pencil marks on your answer sheet. Cleanly erase those places where you changed your mind. Check for little stray marks from pencil tapping. Check everything. You are the only person who can.

Reading Comprehension

Many tests have a section called **reading comprehension.** The good news is that you do not have to study for this part of the test. Taking a reading-comprehension test is a bit like playing ball. You don't know where the ball will land, so you have to stay alert to all possibilities. However, just as the ball can come at you in only a few ways, there are only a few kinds of questions on reading-comprehension tests. This discussion will help you identify the most common ones. Two kinds of texts are used here. The first one is an informational text. The second is an updated fairy tale.

DIRECTIONS: Read the following selection. Then, choose the best answer for each question. Mark each answer on your answer sheet in the square provided.

Night Lights on the High Seas

For centuries, lighthouses have been used to alert sailors that land is near, to point out dangerous rocks and reefs, and to cast a bright light into the night to guide ships on their way. Seafarers have relied on these structures since the days of ancient Egypt. The lighthouse built in 300 B.C. on Pharos, an island near Alexandria, was regarded as one of the Seven Wonders of the World.

Lighthouses help to guide ships at night by giving off an intense beam that flashes every few seconds. Until the eighteenth century, the source of light was an oak-log fire. Coal fire was used for many years after that, until electricity became common in the early twentieth century. Some modern lighthouses also send out radio signals to help ships find their way in foggy weather. Even in their modern form, lighthouses serve their ancient purpose as guiding lights, flashing specks of civilization in the dark, lonely waters of night.

ITEM 1 asks for vocabulary knowledge.

1. In the first paragraph, the word <u>seafarers</u> means —

   A oceans

   B sailors

   C fish

   D ships

Answer: Look at the surrounding sentences, or **context,** to see which definition fits.

A is incorrect. The word *ocean* is another word for "sea," but oceans do not rely on lighthouses.

B is the best answer. In the context of the passage, it makes sense that *sailors* have relied on lighthouses for centuries.

C is incorrect. Fish live and travel in the sea, but nothing in the passage indicates that they depend on lighthouses.

D is incorrect. The safety of ships on the ocean depends on lighthouses. However, it is the *sailors* on the ships who have "relied on these structures" for centuries.

ITEM 2 asks for close reading. Read carefully to see if the answer is stated directly in the text.

2. What was used to produce the light in lighthouses before the eighteenth century?

   F Wood

   G Coal

   H Gas

   J Electricity

Answer: Read the passage carefully to find the answer.

F is the correct answer. The second sentence of the second paragraph indicates that "until the eighteenth century, the source of light was an oak-log fire." The words *oak* and *log* clearly indicate that "wood" is the right choice.

ITEM 3 asks for an inference.

3. What is the main idea of this passage?

   A Working in a lighthouse is a dangerous job.

   B Modern lighthouses are very different from those of long ago.

   C The first lighthouse was built in 300 B.C. on the island of Pharos.

   D Lighthouses have helped guide ships for thousands of years.

Answer: Think about which statement covers the passage as a whole.

A is incorrect. The passage does not provide an explanation of working in a lighthouse.

B is incorrect. Lighthouses have not changed that much over the years.

C is incorrect. It is only one detail in the passage.

D is the best answer. It covers most of the details in the passage.

ITEM 4 asks for a prediction.

4. As more and more ships become equipped with navigational computers, what will probably happen?

   F More lighthouses will be built.

   G There will be more shipping accidents.

   H The number of lighthouses will be reduced.

   J Different energy sources will be used in lighthouses.

Answer: Find the information in the passage that supports a probable future outcome.

F is incorrect. Navigational computers will most likely reduce the need for lighthouses.

G is incorrect. The navigational computers will protect the ships from accidents.

H is the best answer. Navigational computers mean that ships will no longer need to rely on lighthouses for guidance.

J is incorrect. The passage does not say anything about new or different energy sources.

ITEM 5 asks you to recognize an opinion.

5. Which is an **opinion** expressed in the passage?

   A The beam from a lighthouse flashes every few seconds.

   B Modern lighthouses send out radio signals.

   C Pharos is an island near Alexandria.

   D The ocean waters are lonely at night.

Answer: A **fact** can be proved true or false. An **opinion,** a personal feeling or belief, cannot be proved true or false. **A, B,** and **C** are facts that can be proved true or false. **D is correct** because it is the only opinion.

ITEM 6 asks you to decide why the author wrote the passage.

6. What is the author's main **purpose** for writing this passage?

   F To entertain readers with an exciting story

   G To inform readers about the history of lighthouses

   H To persuade readers to visit a lighthouse

   J To describe what life in a lighthouse is like

Answer: Look at the information given in the passage, and decide what the writer's purpose was in writing.

F is incorrect. The writer does not tell a story.

G is the best answer. The writer presents information about the function of light-houses over time.

H is incorrect. The writer's purpose is not to persuade readers to visit a lighthouse.

J is incorrect. The writer never tells what it's like to live in a lighthouse.

DIRECTIONS: Read the following selection. Then, choose the best answer for each question. Mark each answer on your answer sheet in the space provided.

A Technologically Correct Fairy Tale:

Jack and the Beanstalk

There once was a poor widow who lived in a small cottage with her son, Jack. Jack was a good-hearted fellow who devoted all his time to a mega-computer game. Since Jack did not have a paying job, he and his widowed mother were very poor.

The day arrived when the widow had sold all her possessions via the Internet, except for an elderly cow. Jack was to sell the cow at the market since his mother was too frail to make the trip.

"Get a good price for her," the widow instructed.

"Yes, Mother," Jack answered.

Off he went with the cow in tow.

Out on the highway, Jack was stopped by a man who offered to trade him a handful of oddly shaped, brightly colored beans for the cow. "These are turbo-beans," the man whispered. While Jack didn't know exactly what that meant, he did know that the word *turbo* made the beans sound special, so he agreed to the trade. When he got home, he proudly handed the beans to his mother. She promptly tossed them out the window, declaring she didn't know what he could have been thinking. . . .

ITEM 1 is a vocabulary question. To answer it, consider the surrounding words, or **context,** to identify the best definition.

1. In the first paragraph the underlined word devoted means —
   A donated
   B avoided
   C captured
   D dedicated

A is incorrect. *Donated* means "gave someone something of value." It doesn't fit in this context.

B is incorrect. It doesn't fit the context, which shows what Jack did with his time, not what he didn't do.

C is incorrect. It doesn't fit in the context.

D is the best answer. In this context, *devoted* means "dedicated" or "gave one's time to a particular pursuit."

ITEM 2 is another vocabulary question.

2. In the second paragraph of the fairy tale, frail means —
   F proud
   G weak
   H stubborn
   J forceful

The best answer is G, since it offers the only reason why the widow would not be able to make the trip herself.

ITEM 3 is a factual question. Re-read the fairy tale, and you'll find the answer.

3. How did the widow sell all of her possessions, except for the old cow?
   A She sold them via the Internet.
   B She set up a shop on the highway.
   C She sold them to her neighbors.
   D She sold them to the man with the beans.

A is the best answer. The fairy tale clearly states that she sold her possessions on the Internet.

B is incorrect. Jack met the man with the beans on the main highway. The widow did not go there.

C is incorrect. Neighbors are not mentioned in the selection.

D is incorrect. Jack, not the widow, traded the cow for the beans.

ITEM 4 asks you to analyze a cause-and-effect relationship. Don't worry, though. The answer is in the text.

4. Because Jack didn't have a paying job, he and his mother were —

    F   supported by an uncle

    G   very poor

    H   reduced to stealing

    J   very angry

F is incorrect. An uncle is not mentioned in the story.

G is the best answer. The fairy tale says that they were poor.

H is incorrect. Stealing is not mentioned in the story.

J is incorrect. Anger is not mentioned in the story.

ITEM 5 requires that you make an **inference** based on the text.

5. Jack's mother didn't think beans for a cow was a good trade. How do you know this?

    A   She explains that a cow is worth more than a handful of beans.

    B   Jack was supposed to sell the cow.

    C   The man cheated Jack.

    D   She tossed the beans out the window.

A is incorrect. Jack's mother doesn't say this in the story.

B is incorrect. This is true, but it doesn't explain why his mother didn't think it was a good trade.

C is incorrect. This may be true, but it doesn't tell us how we know what Jack's mother thought of the trade.

D is the best answer. Her actions show what she thought of the trade.

ITEM 6 asks you to use your **prior knowledge** about fairy tales to predict the outcome of this tale.

6. If this story ended like a typical fairy tale, which of the following predictions would you make?

    F   The beans do, indeed, prove worthless.

    G   The beans become the key to lifelong happiness for Jack and his mother.

    H   The beans end up in a stew.

    J   The cow comes home.

F is incorrect. The fairy tale cannot have its "happily ever after" ending if the beans are worthless.

G is the best answer. In fairy tales, magical gifts from strangers often bring great rewards in the end.

H is incorrect. This is too ordinary an ending for a fairy tale.

J is incorrect. This ending is also too ordinary for a fairy tale.

Strategies for Taking Writing Tests

Writing a Story

Some tests may include writing prompts that ask you to write a narrative, or story. The following steps will help you write a **story.** The responses are based on this prompt.

> ### Prompt
>
> Write a short fictional narrative. The story should include major and minor characters, a thoroughly developed plot, and a definite setting.

STEP 1 **Read the prompt carefully.** Does the prompt ask you to write a **fictional story** (a made-up story) or an **autobiographical story** (a story of something that really happened to you)?

The word "fictional" tells me that the prompt is asking for a made-up story.

STEP 2 **Outline the plot of your narrative.** Explain the conflict, the climax, and the resolution.

Conflict—the main character, Sue, wants to win the fencing tournament. Climax—Sue fences against the champion. Resolution—Sue wins but feels bad when she sees her opponent crying.

STEP 3 **Identify the major and minor characters.** What do they look and act like? How do they sound when they speak?

Major character—Sue is tall and lanky; she is shy; she is very competitive. Minor character—Sue's competitor, Tory, is tall; she is confident and sometimes rude.

STEP 4 **Identify the setting of your narrative.** Where and when does your story take place?

The story takes place in January during the state fencing championships in a gymnasium.

STEP 5 **Draft your narrative, adding dialogue, suspense, and sensory details.**

I plan to create suspense by drawing out the moment when Sue must decide what to do when she sees Tory crying. I will use sensory details to describe how she feels. I will also include dialogue of her conversation with Tory.

STEP 6 **Revise and proofread your narrative.** Make sure that you have organized the events in your story in a logical order. Add transitions that show time, such as *earlier, afterward, at the same time,* and *later.*

Writing a Summary

Prompt

Read the article "The Body's Defenses," and then summarize it. In your summary, include the main idea and significant details of the article.

Some tests include writing prompts like the one to the right.

To write a **summary** of a passage, you rewrite in your own words the passage's main idea and significant details. The summary should both paraphrase and condense the original. A summary of a short passage should be about one-third as long. For a longer selection, a summary should include no more than one sentence for each paragraph.

The following steps will help you write an effective summary in response to a prompt.

▷ **STEP 1** **Read the passage carefully. Identify the main idea, and restate it in your own words.** What is the most important point the writer is making about the topic? How would *you* say it?

▷ **STEP 2** **Identify significant details to include in the summary.** Which details directly support the main idea? List at least one key idea or detail from each paragraph.

▷ **STEP 3** **Write the main idea and most significant details in a paragraph, using your own words.** Give details in the same order they are presented in the passage.

Writing a Response to Literature

On a writing test, you may be asked to write a **literary response**. Often on such tests, you will be given a literary selection to read and a prompt such as the one on the right.

Prompt

What sort of character is Andrew from the short story "Duffy's Jacket"? Analyze his thoughts, actions, and words.

The following steps and the partial student responses will help you respond to a prompt like the one above. The short story "Duffy's Jacket" can be found on pages 5–11.

STEP 1 **Read the prompt carefully, noting key words.** Key words might include a verb—such as *analyze, identify,* or *explain*—and a literary element—such as *plot, character, setting,* or *theme.*

The key words are "analyze" and "character."

STEP 2 **Read the selection at least twice.** Read first for the overall meaning of the work. Then, read the selection a second time, keeping the key words from the prompt in mind.

STEP 3 **Write a main idea statement.** Your main idea statement should give the title and author of the work and should directly address the prompt.

Andrew, the narrator of "Duffy's Jacket" by Bruce Coville, is similar to my friend Joss; both are easygoing and funny.

STEP 4 **Find specific examples and details from the selection to support your main idea.** If you include quotations from the literary work, remember to enclose them in quotation marks.

When Andrew's mom gets mad at Andrew for not reminding Duffy to get his jacket, Andrew thinks to himself, "What do I look like, a walking memo pad?"

STEP 5 **Draft, revise, and proofread your response.** To create coherence, use transitions between ideas, such as *for example, however,* and *finally.* When you have written your draft, re-read it to make sure you have presented your ideas clearly. Also, check to see that you have fully addressed all the key words in the prompt. Finally, proofread to correct mistakes in spelling, punctuation, and capitalization.

Using the T.H.E.M.E.S. Strategy on a Writing Test

Writing tests often ask you to write a **persuasive essay** in response to a prompt. Most of these prompts give you a topic, but you must identify your position and generate support for your position. Thinking of what to say in a limited amount of time is one of the most difficult parts of such a test.

Use the T.H.E.M.E.S. strategy, explained in the steps below, to generate support for a position quickly. The student responses are based on this prompt.

Prompt

The city council is considering building a parking garage or a park on an empty lot. Write an essay that takes a position on the issue and defends the position with relevant support.

Each letter in T.H.E.M.E.S. stands for a category you could use to trigger ideas for supporting your position in a persuasive essay.

T=Time   H=Health   E=Education   M=Money   E=Environment   S=Safety

▶ **STEP 1** **Identify your position on the topic given in the prompt.**

The city council should build a park.

▶ **STEP 2** **Use T.H.E.M.E.S to list benefits for your position.**

T = A park would take less time to build than a garage. H = People could use the park to exercise and remain healthy. E = People might become more aware, or educated, about the wildlife and plants that occupy the area. M = The city would save money because constructing playscapes and jogging trails is less expensive than clearing the land and building a garage. E = The environment would benefit because the trees and homes of animals are not destroyed. S = Without a garage, fewer cars may drive in the area, reducing the safety hazard of automobile accidents.

▶ **STEP 3** **Identify the three strongest reasons you developed using T.H.E.M.E.S.** Your strongest reasons will be those for which you have the most evidence and those that address readers' concerns about the topic.

My three strongest reasons for building a park are health benefits, reduced costs, and environmental benefits. These are the issues that I think concern my readers the most.

Handbook of Literary Terms

For more information about a topic, turn to the page(s) in this book indicated on a separate line at the end of the entries. To learn more about *Alliteration,* for example, turn to pages 577 and 601.

On another line are cross-references to entries in this handbook that provide closely related information. For instance, at the end of *Autobiography* is a cross-reference to *Biography.*

ALLITERATION The repetition of the same or very similar consonant sounds in words that are close together. Though alliteration usually occurs at the beginning of words, it can also occur within or at the end of words. Among other things, alliteration can help establish a mood, emphasize words, and serve as a memory aid. In the following example the *s* sound is repeated at the beginning of the words *silken* and *sad* and within the words *uncertain* and *rustling:*

> And the silken sad uncertain rustling of each
>   purple curtain
>
> —Edgar Allan Poe, from
> "The Raven"

See pages 577, 601.

ALLUSION A reference to a statement, a person, a place, or an event from literature, history, religion, mythology, politics, sports, or science. Allusions enrich the reading experience. Writers expect readers to recognize an allusion and to think, almost at the same time, about the literary work and the person, place, or event that it refers to. The following lines, describing a tunnel in the snow, contain an allusion to Aladdin, a character in *The Thousand and One Nights:*

> With mittened hands, and caps drawn low,
> To guard our necks and ears from snow,
> We cut the solid whiteness through.
> And, where the drift was deepest, made
> A tunnel walled and overlaid
> With dazzling crystal: we had read
> Of rare Aladdin's wondrous cave,
> And to our own his name we gave.
>
> —John Greenleaf Whittier,
> from "Snow-Bound"

The cave in the tale contains a magic lamp that helps Aladdin discover vast riches. By alluding to Aladdin's cave, Whittier makes us see the icy tunnel in the snow as a magical, fairy-tale place.

The cartoon below makes an allusion to a popular fairy tale.

*"Now, this policy will cover your home for fire, theft,
flood and huffing and puffing."*

See pages 174, 687.

ATMOSPHERE **The overall mood or emotion of a work of literature.** A work's atmosphere can often be described with one or two adjectives, such as *scary, dreamy, happy, sad,* or *nostalgic.* A writer creates atmosphere by using images, sounds, and descriptions that convey a particular feeling.

See also *Mood.*

AUTOBIOGRAPHY **The story of a person's life, written or told by that person.** Maijue Xiong wrote an autobiography called "An Unforgettable Journey" (page 403) about her escape from war-torn Laos as a child. Another well-known autobiographical work is Maya Angelou's *I Know Why the Caged Bird Sings.*

See pages 402, 499, 672, 846.
See also *Biography.*

BIOGRAPHY **The story of a real person's life, written or told by another person.** Milton Meltzer has written a number of biographies of historical figures, such as George Washington and Mark Twain. "Elizabeth I" (page 416) is his biography of the remarkable queen of England who reigned in the sixteenth century. Frequent subjects of biographies are movie stars, television personalities, politicians, sports figures, self-made millionaires, even underworld figures. Biographies are among the most popular forms of contemporary literature.

See pages 414, 479, 499, 853.
See also *Autobiography.*

CHARACTER **A person or animal who takes part in the action of a story, play, or other literary work.** In some works, such as Aesop's fables, a character is an animal. In myths and legends a character may be a god or a superhero. Most often a character is an ordinary human being, such as Kevin in "User Friendly" (page 272).

The process of revealing the personality of a character in a story is called **characterization.** A writer can reveal a character in the following ways:

1. by letting you hear the character speak

2. by describing how the character looks and dresses

3. by letting you listen to the character's inner thoughts and feelings

4. by revealing what other people in the story think or say about the character

5. by showing you what the character does—how he or she acts

6. by telling you directly what the character's personality is like (cruel, kind, sneaky, brave, and so on)

When a writer uses the first five ways to reveal a character, you must make an inference, based on the evidence the writer provides, to decide what the character is like. When a writer uses the sixth method, however, you don't make a decision but are told directly what kind of person the character is.

Characters can be classified as static or dynamic. A **static character** is one who does not change much in the course of a work. Mr. Andersen in "Song of the Trees" (page 509) is a static character. By contrast, a **dynamic character** changes as a result of the story's events. Keevan in "The Smallest Dragonboy" (page 147) is a dynamic character.

A character's **motivation** is any force that drives or moves the character to behave in a particular way. Many characters are motivated by the force of fear or love or ambition.

See pages 128–129, 130, 136, 146, 174, 190, 296.

CONFLICT **A struggle or clash between opposing characters or opposing forces.** In an **external conflict** a character struggles against some outside force. This outside force may be another character or society as a whole or a storm or a grizzly bear or even a machine. In "Three Skeleton Key" (page 39), the characters have an external conflict with a swarm of sea rats. An **internal conflict,** on the other hand, takes place within a character's mind. It is a struggle between opposing needs, desires, or emotions. In "After Twenty Years" (page 357), Officer Wells must resolve an internal conflict: Should he arrest an old friend or let him go?

See pages 2, 14.

CONNOTATION The feelings and associations that a word suggests. For example, *tiny*, *cramped*, and *compact* all have about the same dictionary definition, or **denotation,** but they have different connotations. A manufacturer of small cars would not describe its product as tiny or cramped. Instead, the company might say that its cars are compact. To grasp a writer's full meaning, you must pay attention not only to the literal definitions of words but also to their connotations. Connotations can be especially important in poetry.

See page 525.

DENOTATION The literal, dictionary definition of a word.

See page 525.
See also *Connotation.*

DESCRIPTION The kind of writing that creates a clear image of something, usually by using details that appeal to one or more of the senses: sight, hearing, smell, taste, and touch. Writers use description in all forms of fiction, nonfiction, and poetry. In "Fish Cheeks" (page 528), Amy Tan vividly describes the colors, sounds, and tastes of her family's Christmas celebration.

DIALECT A way of speaking that is characteristic of a particular region or group of people. A dialect may have a distinct vocabulary, pronunciation system, and grammar. In a sense, we all speak a dialect. One dialect usually becomes dominant in a country or culture and is accepted as the standard way of speaking. In the United States, for example, the formal written language is known as standard English. This is the dialect used in most newspapers and magazines.

Writers often reproduce regional dialects, or speech that reveals a character's economic or social class, in order to give a story local color. Mr. Baumer in "Bargain" (page 369) speaks in a dialect that reveals that his first language is German. The poem "Madam and the Rent Man" (page 561) is written in a dialect spoken in some urban African American communities in the northeastern United States.

See page 186.

DIALOGUE A conversation between two or more characters. Most stage dramas consist of dialogue together with stage directions. (Screenplays and teleplays sometimes include an unseen narrator.) The dialogue in a drama, such as *The Monsters Are Due on Maple Street* (page 59), must move the plot along and reveal its characters almost singlehandedly. Dialogue is also an important element in most stories and novels as well as in some poems and nonfiction. It is one of the most effective ways for a writer to show what a character is like. It can also add realism and humor.

In the written form of a play, dialogue appears without quotation marks. In prose or poetry, however, dialogue is usually enclosed in quotation marks.

A **monologue** is a part of a drama in which one character speaks alone.

See page 495.

DRAMA A story written to be acted for an audience. (A drama can also be appreciated and enjoyed in written form.) In a drama, such as *The Monsters Are Due on Maple Street* (page 59), the action is usually driven by characters who want something very much and take steps to get it. The related events that take place within a drama are often separated into **acts**. Each act is often made up of shorter sections, or **scenes**. Most plays have three acts, but there are many, many variations. The elements of a drama are often described as **introduction** or **exposition, complications, conflict, climax,** and **resolution**.

ESSAY A short piece of nonfiction prose that examines a single subject. Most essays can be categorized as either personal or formal.

The **personal essay** generally reveals a great deal about the writer's personality and tastes. Its tone is often conversational, sometimes even humorous. In a personal essay the focus is the writer's feelings and response to an experience.

The **formal essay** is usually serious, objective, and impersonal in tone. Its purpose is to inform readers about a topic or to persuade them to accept the writer's views.

See pages 479, 527, 533.

FABLE A brief story in prose or verse that teaches a moral or gives a practical lesson about how to get along in life. The characters of most fables are animals that behave and speak like human beings. Some of the most popular fables are attributed to Aesop, who is thought to have been a slave in ancient Greece.

See also *Folk Tale, Myth.*

FICTION A prose account that is made up rather than true. The term *fiction* usually refers to novels and short stories. Fiction may be based on a writer's experiences or on historical events, but characters, events, and other details are altered or added by the writer to create a desired effect. "A Rice Sandwich" (page 169) is a fictional account based on an episode in the writer's childhood.

See pages 478–479.
See also *Nonfiction.*

FIGURE OF SPEECH A word or phrase that describes one thing in terms of something else and is not literally true. Figures of speech always involve some sort of imaginative comparison between seemingly unlike things. The most common forms are **simile** ("The stars were like diamonds"), **metaphor** ("My soul is an enchanted boat"), and **personification** ("The sun smiled down on the emerald-green fields").

See pages 546, 548, 551, 555, 609.
See also *Metaphor, Personification, Simile.*

FLASHBACK An interruption in the action of a plot to tell what happened at an earlier time. A flashback breaks the usual movement of the narrative by going back in time. It usually gives background information that helps the reader understand the present situation. "A Mason-Dixon Memory" (page 534) contains a long flashback.

A break in the unfolding of a plot to an episode in the future is known as a **flash-forward.**

See page 533.

FOLK TALE A story with no known author that originally was passed on from one generation to another by word of mouth. Folk tales tend to travel, so similar plots and characters are found in several cultures. For example, "Yeh-Shen" (page 383) is a Chinese folk tale that is very similar to the European story of Cinderella. Folk tales often contain **fantastic** elements, or events that could not happen in the world as we know it.

See pages 696–697, 698, 707, 718, 724, 732, 747, 758.
See also *Fable, Myth.*

FORESHADOWING The use of clues to suggest events that will happen later in the plot. Foreshadowing is used to build suspense or create anxiety. In a drama a gun found in a bureau drawer in Act One is likely to foreshadow violence later in the play. In "Three Skeleton Key" (page 39), the story of three convicts who perished on the key foreshadows the danger the three lighthouse keepers will face.

> See pages 2, 38, 356.
> See also *Suspense.*

FREE VERSE Poetry without a regular meter or a rhyme scheme. Poets writing in free verse try to capture the natural rhythms of ordinary speech. To create their music, poets writing in free verse may use internal rhyme, repetition, alliteration, and onomatopoeia. Free verse also frequently makes use of vivid imagery. The following poem in free verse effectively uses images and the repetition of words to describe the effects of a family's eviction for not paying rent:

> **The 1st**
> What I remember about that day
> is boxes stacked across the walk
> and couch springs curling through the air
> and drawers and tables balanced on the curb
> and us, hollering,
> leaping up and around
> happy to have a playground;
>
> nothing about the emptied rooms
> nothing about the emptied family
>
> —Lucille Clifton

> See pages 576, 593.
> See also *Poetry, Rhyme, Rhythm.*

IMAGERY Language that appeals to the senses. Most images are visual—that is, they create pictures in your mind by appealing to the sense of sight. Images can also appeal to the sense of hearing, touch, taste, or smell or to several senses at once. The sensory images in "The Highwayman" (page 247) add greatly to the enjoyment of the poem. Though imagery is an element in all types of writing, it is especially important in poetry.

> See pages 546, 563.
> See also *Poetry.*

IRONY In general, a contrast between expectation and reality. Irony can create powerful effects, from humor to strong emotion. Here are three common types of irony:

1. **Verbal irony** involves a contrast between what is said or written and what is meant. If you were to call someone who failed a math test Einstein, you would be using verbal irony.

2. **Situational irony** occurs when what happens is very different from what is expected to happen. The surprise ending of "After Twenty Years" (page 357) involves situational irony.

3. **Dramatic irony** occurs when the audience or the reader knows something a character does not know. In Part 2 of "The Highwayman" (page 247), the reader feels an anxious sense of irony when King George's soldiers have Bess tied up. Although the highwayman doesn't yet know it, *we* know that a trap is set for him.

MAIN IDEA The most important idea expressed in a paragraph or in an entire essay. The main idea may be directly stated in a **topic sentence,** or you may have to look at all the details in the paragraph and make an **inference,** or educated guess, about its main idea.

> See page 393.

METAMORPHOSIS **A marvelous change from one shape or form to another one.** In myths the change is usually from human to animal, from animal to human, or from human to plant. Greek and Roman myths contain many examples of metamorphosis. The myth of Echo and Narcissus (page 290) tells how the vain youth Narcissus pines away for love of his own reflection until he is changed into a flower.

> See page 707.
> See also *Myth.*

METAPHOR **An imaginative comparison between two unlike things in which one thing is said to be another thing.** A metaphor is an important type of figurative language. Metaphors are used in all forms of writing and are common in ordinary speech. If you were to say someone has a heart of gold, you would not mean that the person's heart is actually made of metal. You would mean, instead, that the person is warm and caring. You would be speaking metaphorically.

Metaphors differ from similes, which use specific words (notably *like, as, than,* and *resembles*) to state comparisons. William Wordsworth's famous comparison "I wandered lonely as a cloud" is a simile because it uses *as.* If Wordsworth had written "I was a lonely, wandering cloud," he would have been using a metaphor.

PEANUTS reprinted by permission of United Feature Syndicate, Inc.

An **extended metaphor** is a metaphor that is developed, or extended, through several lines of writing or even throughout an entire poem. "I Like to See It Lap the Miles" (page 552) uses an extended metaphor to compare a train to a horse throughout the whole poem.

> See pages 255, 548, 551, 609.
> See also *Figure of Speech, Personification, Simile.*

MOOD **The overall emotion created by a work of literature.** A work of literature can often be described with one or more adjectives: *sad, scary, hopeful, exciting,* and so on. These are descriptions of the work's mood—its emotional atmosphere. For example, the mood of "Annabel Lee" (page 261) could be described as haunting or romantic. That mood has a lingering effect on its readers.

> See page 428.
> See also *Atmosphere.*

MOTIVATION See *Character.*

MYTH **A story that explains something about the world and typically involves gods or other superhuman beings.** Myths, which at one time were believed to be true, reflect the traditions of the culture that produced them. Almost every culture has **origin myths** (or **creation myths**), stories that explain how something in the world (perhaps the world itself) came to be. Myths may also explain many other aspects of nature. The ancient Greek myth of Echo and Narcissus (page 290), for example, explains the origins of a flower. Most myths are very old and were handed down orally long before being put in written form. In some of the world's greatest myths, a hero or even a god embarks on a **quest,** a perilous journey taken in pursuit of something of great value.

> See pages 646–647, 648–649, 654, 664, 675, 683.
> See also *Fable, Folk Tale.*

NONFICTION Prose writing that deals with real people, events, and places without changing any facts. Popular forms of nonfiction are the **autobiography,** the **biography,** and the **essay.** Other examples of nonfiction include newspaper stories, magazine articles, historical writing, scientific reports, and even personal diaries and letters.

Nonfiction writing can be subjective or objective. **Subjective writing** expresses the feelings and opinions of the writer. **Objective writing** conveys the facts without introducing any emotion or personal bias.

See pages 393, 402, 478–479.
See also *Autobiography, Biography, Fiction.*

NOVEL A fictional story that is usually more than one hundred book pages long. A novel uses all the elements of storytelling—**plot, character, setting, theme,** and **point of view.** A novel, because of its length, usually has more characters, settings, and themes and a more complex plot than a short story. Modern writers sometimes do not pay much attention to one or more of the novel's traditional elements. Some novels today are basically character studies that include only the barest story lines. Other novels don't look much beyond the surface of their characters and concentrate instead on plot and setting. A novel can deal with almost any topic. Many of the books recommended in the Read On sections of this text are novels. A **novella** is shorter than a novel and longer than a short story.

See pages 478–479, 508.

ONOMATOPOEIA The use of words whose sounds echo their sense. Onomatopoeia (än′ō·mat′ō·pē′ə) is so natural to us that we use it at a very early age. *Buzz, rustle, boom, ticktock, tweet,* and *bark* are all examples of onomatopoeia. Onomatopoeia is an important element in creating the music of poetry. In the following lines the poet creates a frenzied mood by choosing words that imitate the sounds of alarm bells:

> Oh, the bells, bells, bells!
> What a tale their terror tells
> Of Despair!
> How they clang, and clash, and roar!
> What a horror they outpour
> On the bosom of the palpitating air!
> Yet the ear, it fully knows
> By the twanging
> And the clanging
> How the danger ebbs and flows.
>
> —Edgar Allan Poe, from
> "The Bells"

See pages 577, 725.
See also *Alliteration.*

PERSONIFICATION A figure of speech in which a nonhuman or nonliving thing or quality is talked about as if it were human or alive. In "I Am of the Earth" (page 556), the poet personifies the earth as a mother.

See page 555.
See also *Figure of Speech, Metaphor, Simile.*

PLOT The series of related events that make up a story. Plot is what happens in a short story, novel, play, or narrative poem. Most plots are built on these bare bones: An **introduction,** or **exposition,** tells us who the characters are and what their **conflict** is. **Complications** arise as the characters take steps to resolve the conflict. The plot reaches a **climax,** the most emotional or suspenseful moment in the story, when the outcome is decided one way or another. The last part of a story is the **resolution,** when the characters' problems are solved and the story ends.

Not all works of fiction or drama have this traditional plot structure. Some modern writers experiment, often eliminating parts of a traditional plot in order to focus on elements such as character, point of view, or mood.

See pages 2–3, 4, 14, 57, 130, 820.
See also *Conflict.*

Handbook of Literary Terms   **937**

POETRY A kind of rhythmic, compressed language that uses figures of speech and imagery designed to appeal to emotion and imagination. We know poetry when we see it because it is usually arranged in a particular way on the page. Traditional poetry often has a regular pattern of rhythm (**meter**) and may have a regular **rhyme scheme.**

Free verse is poetry that has no regular rhythm or rhyme. "Names of Horses" (page 594) is a free-verse poem that is also an **elegy,** a poem that mourns the passing of something that is important to the writer. "Arithmetic" (page 607) is a free-verse poem that is also a **catalog poem,** a poem that lists the poet's thoughts or feelings about a subject. A major form of poetry is the **narrative poem,** which tells a story, such as "The High-wayman" (page 247). Two popular narrative forms are the **epic** and the **ballad.** Another major form of poetry is the **lyric poem,** which expresses a speaker's feelings. "I Ask My Mother to Sing" (page 569) is a lyric poem that is also a **sonnet**—a poem of fourteen lines that follows a strict form. The **ode** is a type of lyric poem that celebrates something. A lighthearted example is "Ode to Family Photographs" (page 573).

> See pages 246, 260, 546–547, 568, 572, 576–577, 578, 586, 589, 593, 606, 609.
> See also *Figure of Speech, Free Verse, Imagery, Refrain, Rhyme, Rhythm, Speaker, Stanza.*

POINT OF VIEW The vantage point from which a story is told. The most common points of view are the **omniscient,** the **third-person limited,** and the **first person.**

1. In the **omniscient** (äm·nish'ənt), or all-knowing, **point of view** the narrator knows everything about the characters and their problems. This all-knowing narrator can tell about the characters' past, present, and future. This kind of narrator can even tell what the characters are thinking or what is happening in other places. This narrator is not in

the story. Instead, he or she stands above the action, like a god. The omniscient is a very familiar point of view; we have heard it in fairy tales since we were very young. "Yeh-Shen" (page 383), a Chinese Cinderella story, is told from the omniscient point of view.

> Her loveliness made her seem a heavenly being, and the king suddenly knew in his heart that he had found his true love.

2. In the **third-person limited point of view,** the narrator focuses on the thoughts and feelings of only one character. From this point of view, you observe the action through the eyes and feelings of only one character in the story. "The Smallest Dragonboy" (page 147) is told from the third-person limited point of view.

> There was such a lot to know and understand about being a dragonrider that sometimes Keevan was overwhelmed. How would he ever be able to remember everything he ought to know at the right moment?

3. In the **first-person point of view,** one of the characters, using the personal pronoun *I,* is telling the story. You become very familiar with this narrator but can know only what he or she knows and can observe only what he or she observes. All information about the story must come from this character. In some cases the information is incorrect. "User Friendly" (page 272) is told from the first-person point of view of the boy whose computer starts acting funny.

> As I walked by the corner of my room, where my computer table was set up, I pressed the *on* button, slid a diskette into the floppy drive, then went to brush my

teeth. By the time I got back, the computer's screen was glowing greenly, displaying the message: *Good morning, Kevin.*

See pages 348–349, 356, 368, 382, 393.

REFRAIN A group of words repeated at intervals in a poem, song, or speech. Refrains are usually associated with songs and poems, but they are also used in speeches and other forms of literature. Refrains are most often used to create rhythm, but they may also provide emphasis or commentary, create suspense, or help hold a work together. Refrains may be repeated with small variations in a work in order to fit a particular context or to create a special effect.

See page 260.

RHYME The repetition of accented vowel sounds and all sounds following them in words close together in a poem. *Mean* and *screen* are rhymes, as are *crumble* and *tumble.* Rhyme has many purposes in poetry: It creates rhythm, lends a songlike quality, emphasizes ideas, organizes the poem (for instance, into stanzas or couplets), provides humor or delight, and makes the poem memorable.

Many poems—for example, "The Runaway" (page 587)—use **end rhymes,** rhymes at the end of a line. In the following stanza, *walls/calls/falls* form end rhymes, as do *hands/sands.* The pattern of end rhymes in a poem is called a **rhyme scheme.** To indicate the rhyme scheme of a poem, use a separate letter of the alphabet for each rhyme. For example, the rhyme scheme below is *aabba.*

> Darkness settles on roofs and walls,
> But the sea, the sea in the darkness calls;
> The little waves, with their soft,
>   white hands,
> Efface the footprints in the sands,
> And the tide rises, the tide falls.
>
> —Henry Wadsworth Longfellow,
>   from "The Tide Rises, the Tide Falls"

Internal rhymes are rhymes within lines. The following line has an internal rhyme (*turning/burning*):

> Back into the chamber turning, all my soul
>   within me burning
>
> —Edgar Allan Poe, from "The Raven"

Rhyming sounds need not be spelled the same way; for instance, *gear/here* forms a rhyme. Rhymes can involve more than one syllable or more than one word; *poet/know it* is an example. Rhymes involving sounds that are similar but not exactly the same are called **slant rhymes** (or **near rhymes** or **approximate rhymes**). *Leave/live* is an example of a slant rhyme. Poets writing in English often use slant rhymes because English is not a very rhymable language. It has many words that rhyme with no other word (*orange*) or with only one other word (*mountain/fountain*). Poets interested in how a poem looks on the printed page sometimes use **eye rhymes,** or **visual rhymes**—rhymes involving words that are spelled similarly but are pronounced differently. *Tough/cough* is an eye rhyme. (*Tough/rough* is a "real" rhyme.)

See pages 576–577, 586, 598.
See also *Free Verse, Poetry, Rhythm.*

RHYTHM A musical quality produced by the repetition of stressed and unstressed syllables or by the repetition of certain other sound patterns. Rhythm occurs in all language—written and spoken—but is particularly important in poetry.

The most obvious kind of rhythm is the regular pattern of stressed and unstressed syllables that is found in some poetry. This pattern is called **meter.** In the following lines describing a cavalry charge, the rhythm echoes the galloping of the attackers' horses:

Handbook of Literary Terms **939**

> ˘ ˘ ′ ˘ ′ ˘ ′ ˘
> The Assyrian came down like the wolf on the
> ′
> fold,
> ˘ ′ ˘ ′ ˘ ′ ˘
> And his cohorts were gleaming in purple and
> ′
> gold;
> ˘ ′ ˘ ′ ˘ ˘ ′ ˘ ′
> And the sheen of their spears was like stars on
> ˘ ′
> the sea,
> ˘ ˘ ′ ˘ ˘ ′ ˘ ˘ ′
> When the blue wave rolls nightly on deep
> ˘ ˘ ′
> Galilee.
>
> —George Gordon, Lord Byron,
> from "The Destruction of Sennacherib"

Marking the stressed (′) and unstressed (˘) syllables in a line is called **scanning** the line. Lord Byron's scanned lines show a rhythmic pattern in which two unstressed syllables are followed by a stressed syllable. Read the lines aloud and listen to this rhythmic pattern. Also, notice how the poem's end rhymes help create the rhythm.

Writers can also create rhythm by repeating words and phrases or even by repeating whole lines and sentences.

See pages 576–577, 578, 601.
See also *Free Verse, Poetry, Rhyme.*

SETTING **The time and place in which the events of a work of literature take place.** Most often the setting of a narrative is described early in the story. Setting often contributes to a story's emotional effect. In "Song of the Trees" (page 509), the forest setting helps create a soothing (yet mysterious) mood. Setting frequently plays an important role in a story's plot, especially one that centers on a conflict between a character and nature. In "Three Skeleton Key" (page 39), the characters must fight elements of a deadly setting to survive—they are threatened by a vast army of rats. Some stories are closely tied to particular settings, and it is difficult to imagine them taking place elsewhere. By contrast, other stories could easily take place in a variety of settings.

See page 296.

SHORT STORY **A fictional prose narrative that is usually ten to twenty book pages long.** Short stories were first written in the nineteenth century. Early short story writers include Sir Walter Scott and Edgar Allan Poe. Short stories are usually built on a plot that consists of at least these bare bones: the **introduction** or **exposition, conflict, complications, climax,** and **resolution.** Short stories are more limited than novels. They usually have only one or two major characters and one important setting.

See pages 478, 484, 508.
See also *Conflict, Fiction, Plot.*

SIMILE **A comparison between two unlike things, using a word such as *like, as, than,* or *resembles.*** The simile is an important type of figure of speech. In the following lines a simile creates a clear image of moths in the evening air:

> When the last bus leaves, moths stream
> toward lights like litter in wind.
>
> —Roberta Hill, from "Depot in Rapid City"

This example shows that similes can generate a strong emotional impact. By choosing to compare the moths to litter, the poet not only creates a picture in the reader's mind but also establishes a lonely, dreary mood.

See pages 255, 548, 609.
See also *Figure of Speech, Metaphor.*

SPEAKER **The voice talking in a poem.** Sometimes the speaker is identical to the poet, but often the speaker and the poet are not the same. The poet may be speaking as a child, a woman, a man, an animal, or even an object.

See also *Poetry.*

STANZA In a poem a group of consecutive lines that forms a single unit. A stanza in a poem is something like a paragraph in prose; it often expresses a unit of thought. A stanza may consist of any number of lines. "I'm Nobody!" (page 549) consists of two four-line stanzas, each expressing a separate idea. In some poems each stanza has the same rhyme scheme.

> See pages 546, 589.
> See also *Poetry, Rhyme.*

SUSPENSE The uncertainty or anxiety you feel about what will happen next in a story. In "Three Skeleton Key" (page 39), the narrator hooks your curiosity in the first sentences when he says he is about to describe his "most terrifying experience."

> See page 38.
> See also *Foreshadowing.*

SYMBOL A person, a place, a thing, or an event that has its own meaning *and* stands for something beyond itself as well. Examples of symbols are all around us—in music, on television, and in everyday conversation. The skull and crossbones, for example, is a symbol of danger; the dove is a symbol of peace; and the red rose stands for true love. In literature, symbols are often more personal. For example, in "Names/Nombres" (page 394), Julia Alvarez's name is a symbol of her cultural identity.

THEME The truth about life revealed in a work of literature. A theme is not the same as a subject. The subject of a work can usually be expressed in a word or two: *love, childhood, death.* The theme is the idea that the writer wishes to convey about a particular subject. The theme must be expressed in at least one sentence. For example, the subject of *The Monsters Are Due on Maple Street* (page 59) is alien invasion. The play's theme might be this: Prejudice is the fearful, unseen enemy within each of us.

A story can have several themes, but one will often stand out from the others. A work's themes are usually not stated directly. You have to think about all the elements of the work and use them to make an **inference,** or educated guess, about what the themes are.

It is not likely that two readers will ever state a theme in exactly the same way. Sometimes readers even differ greatly in their interpretations of theme. A work of literature can mean different things to different people.

> See pages 236–237, 238, 246, 260, 271, 289, 296, 428, 508.

TONE The attitude that a writer takes toward the audience, a subject, or a character. Tone is conveyed through the writer's choice of words and details. The poem "maggie and milly and molly and may" (page 599) is light and playful in tone. By contrast, the poem "Annabel Lee" (page 261) is serious in tone.

> See page 560.

Handbook of Literary Terms **941**

Handbook of Reading and Informational Terms

For more information about a topic, turn to the page(s) in this book indicated on a separate line at the end of the entry. To learn more about *Cause and Effect,* for example, turn to page 256.

On another line are cross-references to entries in this handbook that provide closely related information. For instance, the entry *Chronological Order* contains a cross-reference to *Text Structures.*

ANALOGY

1. An **analogy** is a point-by-point comparison made between two things to show how they are alike. An analogy shows how something unfamiliar is like something well-known.
2. Another kind of analogy is a **verbal analogy.** A verbal analogy is a word puzzle. It gives you two words and asks you to identify another pair of words with a similar relationship. In an analogy the symbol ":" means "is to." The symbol "::" means "as."

> Select the pair of words that best completes the analogy.
>
> Toe : foot :: _____
>
> | | |
> |---|---|
> | A | house : barn |
> | B | finger : hand |
> | C | road : path |
> | D | light : darkness |

> The correct answer is B: Toe : foot :: finger : hand, or "Toe is to foot as finger is to hand." The relationship is that of part to whole. A toe is part of the foot; a finger is part of the hand.

Another relationship often represented in verbal analogies is that of opposites:

> clear : cloudy :: bright : dark

Both sets of words are opposites. Clear is the opposite of cloudy, and bright is the opposite of dark.

Verbal analogies are often found in tests, where they are used to check vocabulary and thinking skills.

See pages 265, 288, 532.

ARGUMENT An **argument** is a position supported by evidence. Arguments are used to persuade us to accept or reject an opinion on a subject. Arguments are also used to persuade us to act in a certain way.

Supporting evidence can take the form of facts, statistics, anecdotes (brief stories that illustrate a point), and expert opinions. Not all arguments are logical. **Emotional appeals** find their way into most arguments, and you should learn to recognize them. Details that appeal to your feelings make an argument more interesting and memorable—but you should not accept an argument that is based only on an emotional appeal.

Athletes should not charge kids for autographs. The most popular players are the ones that fans ask for autographs. These players don't need extra money. They already earn millions of dollars. Kids are much poorer than star athletes. I had to spend six weeks of my allowance and borrow twenty dollars from my brother to attend a game. After the game I started waiting in line to get an autograph. The line broke up quickly when we heard that the player was charging fifty dollars for each autograph. We were all disgusted. After all, the athletes' fans make them famous. My soccer coach says players should see that an autograph is a way of saying "thank you" to a loyal fan. Signing a name isn't hard. It takes less than a minute. To be asked to pay for an autograph is an insult.	Position Opinion Fact Anecdote Emotional appeal Expert opinion Fact Emotional appeal

See pages 389, 672, 788.
See also *Evidence*.

BIAS (bī′əs) A leaning in favor of or against a person or issue is called a **bias.** Sometimes a writer's bias is obvious. For instance, Rudyard Kipling in "Rikki-tikki-tavi" (page 15) reveals his bias against snakes. In the conflict between the cobras and a mongoose, Kipling is clearly biased in favor of the mongoose. People are often not upfront about their biases. You should look for bias whenever writers or speakers make claims and assertions that they don't (or can't) support with logical reasons and facts. When people ignore, distort, or hide the facts that oppose their bias, they may be guilty of prejudice.

See page 816.

CAUSE AND EFFECT A **cause** is the event that makes something happen. An **effect** is what happens as a result of the cause. Storytellers use the cause-and-effect organizational pattern to develop their plots. Writers of historical texts use this organizational pattern to explain things like the causes and effects of war. Scientific writers use this organizational pattern to explain things like the causes and effects of an epidemic. Some of the words and phrases that point to causes and effects are *because, since, therefore, so that,* and *if . . . then.* Notice the cause-and-effect chain in the following summary of the Midas myth:

Because he did a favor for a god, Midas was granted the golden touch. Since everything he touched turned to gold, his daughter also turned to gold. Because of that, he asked to be released from the golden touch. Since gold had brought him such trouble, he then turned to nature and rejected riches.

See pages 256, 271, 284, 654, 726.
See also *Text Structures*.

CHRONOLOGICAL ORDER Most narrative texts, true or fictional, are written in **chronological order.** Writers use chronological order when they put events in the sequence, or order, in which they happened in time, one after the other. Recipes and technical directions are usually written in chronological order. When you read a narrative, look for words and phrases like *next, then,* and *finally.* Writers use such words as transitions to signal the order in which events or steps occur.

See also *Text Structures.*

COMPARE-AND-CONTRAST PATTERN

When you **compare,** you look for similarities, or likenesses. When you **contrast,** you look for differences. You've used comparison and contrast many times. For instance, you might compare and contrast the features of several dogs when you choose a puppy that is like the dog you used to have. When writers compare and contrast, they organize the text to help readers understand the **points of comparison,** the features that they're looking at.

A Venn diagram can help you tell similarities from differences. The one below compares and contrasts two stories: "Yeh-Shen" (page 383) and the Cinderella folk tale. Where the circles overlap, note how the stories are alike. Where there is no overlap, note differences.

Venn Diagram

"Cinderella" — "Yeh-Shen"

- helped by fairy godmother
- meets prince at ball

- has wicked stepmother
- wants to go to ball
- has wish granted
- has rags changed to beautiful clothes
- obeys one rule
- loses shoe
- is found by royalty

- helped by fish
- meets king when he is searching for owner of shoe

Differences   *Similarities*   *Differences*

An effective comparison-and-contrast text may be organized in the block pattern or the point-by-point pattern.

Block pattern. A writer using the block pattern first discusses all the points of subject 1, then goes on to discuss all the points of subject 2.

> **Subject 1—"Yeh-Shen":** In the Chinese folk tale "Yeh-Shen" a magic fish dies, but its spirit gives Yeh-Shen, a kind orphan, advice and help. It changes her rags into beautiful clothes. Her wicked stepmother treats Yeh-Shen badly. [*And so on*]
>
> **Subject 2—"Cinderella":** American children probably know best the Cinderella story in which a fairy godmother changes Cinderella's rags into beautiful clothes. Cinderella also has a wicked stepmother. [*And so on*]

Point-by-point pattern. A writer who uses the point-by-point pattern goes back and forth between the two things being compared and contrasted.

> In "Yeh-Shen" a magic fish helps the orphan girl. In "Cinderella," however, a fairy godmother helps the girl. In both stories, there is a wicked stepmother. [*And so on*]

Some of the words that signal comparison and contrast are *although, but, either . . . or, however,* and *yet.*

See pages 84, 164, 190, 296, 428, 484, 496, 746, 845.
See also *Text Structures.*

CONCLUSIONS A **conclusion** is a general summing up of the specific details in a text. The text below is from "Buddies Bare Their Affection for Ill Classmate" (page 544). One reader's conclusion based on these details follows the text.

> In Mr. Alter's fifth-grade class, it's difficult to tell which boy is undergoing chemotherapy. Nearly all the boys are bald. Thirteen of them shaved their heads so a sick classmate wouldn't feel out of place.
>
> **Conclusion:** These boys care a lot about their sick classmate.

See page 718.
See also *Evidence*.

CONNOTATION AND DENOTATION The **connotation** of a word is all the feelings and associations that have come to be attached to the word. The **denotation** of a word is its strict dictionary definition. Not all words have connotations. Words like *the, writer,* and *paper* do not have connotations. Words like *Democrat, Republican, conservative,* and *liberal* are loaded with associations and feelings.

The words *skinny, slender, gaunt,* and *lean* have approximately the same denotation. They all mean "thin; having little fat." There are important shades of meaning among those words, however. If a relative said you were skinny or gaunt, you'd probably feel hurt or angry. *Skinny* and *gaunt* have negative connotations. They suggest that the thin person may have been sick and is now unattractive. *Slender* and *lean,* on the other hand, have positive connotations. They suggest a healthy, athletic body.

See page 525.

CONTEXT CLUES When you don't know the meaning of a word, look for a clue to its meaning in the **context,** the words and sentences surrounding the unfamiliar word. Here are some common types of context clues. In each sentence, the unfamiliar word appears in boldface type; the clue is underlined.

Definition clue. Look for a familiar word that defines the meaning of the unfamiliar word.

> Keevan was rarely <u>bothered</u> by rivals, but he was **perturbed** to see Beterli wandering over to him.

The word *bothered* tells you that *perturbed* also means "something like bothered."

Example clue. Look for examples of the unfamiliar word. In the context of the sentence, the examples reveal the meaning of the unfamiliar word.

> **Tugs** and <u>other</u> <u>boats</u> were washed ashore by the tidal wave.

The words *other boats* tell you that a tug is a kind of boat.

Restatement clue. Look for words that restate the meaning of the unfamiliar word.

> We **delved** into the criminal's past—we <u>searched through</u> hundreds of pieces of evidence.

The restatement clue that helps you guess the meaning of *delved* is *searched through.* (*Delved* means "dug into; searched; investigated.")

Contrast clue. Look for words that contrast the unfamiliar word with a word or phrase in the sentence that you know.

> Although Helen wanted to **detain** the visitors, she had to <u>let</u> them <u>go.</u>

This sentence tells you that *detain* means the opposite of "let go."

See pages 289, 381, 427, 695.

EVIDENCE When you read informational and persuasive texts, you need to **assess,** or

946 Resource Center / Handbook of Reading and Informational Terms judge, the **evidence** that a writer uses to support a position. That means you need to read carefully, looking critically at the writer's claims and assertions. You need to evaluate the writer's sources. You also need to look at the writer's own background and expertise. One way to assess evidence is to give it the **3As test.** The *As* stand for *adequate, appropriate,* and *accurate.*

Adequate means "sufficient" or "enough." You have to see if the writer has provided enough evidence to support his or her position. For some positions, one or two supporting facts may be adequate. For others a writer may need to provide many facts, maybe even statistics. Sometimes a direct quotation from a well-respected expert, an authority on the subject, will be convincing.

You must make sure that the writer's evidence is **appropriate,** that it has direct bearing on the conclusion. Sometimes a writer presents a lot of flashy evidence, such as details loaded with emotional appeals. When you look at this kind of evidence closely, you realize that it doesn't have much, if anything, to do with the writer's conclusions.

To make sure that the evidence is **accurate,** or correct, check to see that it comes from a source you can trust. Don't assume that everything (or anything) you see online or even printed in a newspaper or book is accurate. If a fact, example, or quotation doesn't sound accurate, check it out. Look for the title of the magazine or book that the quotation comes from. Is it a reliable source? Look up the writer's background. Does the writer have the background and education to qualify him or her as an expert on the subject? Is the writer biased in some way?

See page 788.
See also *Argument.*

FACT AND OPINION A **fact** is a statement that can be proved true. Some facts are easy to prove by **observation.** For instance, *Cats make different vocal sounds* is a fact you can prove by listening to cats meow and purr. Other facts can be **verified,** or proved, if you look them up in a reliable source. You need to be sure that the source is **authoritative**—an official source that can be trusted, such as an encyclopedia. In fields where new discoveries are being made, you need to check facts in a *recently* published source.

An **opinion** expresses a personal belief or feeling. Sometimes strongly held opinions look and sound like facts. Dog lovers would never question the statement *Dogs are smarter than cats.* Cat lovers, however, would express the opposite opinion, *Cats are smarter than dogs,* and believe it just as strongly. Even if a statement sounds as if it's true, it's not a fact unless it can be proved. Here are some opinions:

> Travel to other planets will happen in my lifetime.
>
> We have the best football team in the United States.
>
> Every teenager should receive an allowance.

A **valid opinion** is a personal belief that is supported by facts. An **invalid opinion** is a belief that is either not supported by facts or is supported by illogical and wishful thinking.

Remember that what you see in print or on the Internet may or may not be true. If a statement looks like a fact but you suspect it's an opinion, check it out in a reliable source. Ask: Can this be proved true?

See pages 389, 402, 499, 672.

FALLACIOUS REASONING
Fallacious (fə·lā′shəs) means "false." **Fallacious reasoning** is false reasoning. Here are four major types of false reasoning:

1. **Hasty generalizations** are reached without considering enough facts. A

generalization is a conclusion drawn after considering as much of the evidence as possible. (See page 508.) If there is even one exception to the conclusion, your generalization is not true or valid.

Fact: "User Friendly" is a story with a surprise ending.

Fact: "After Twenty Years" is a story with a surprise ending.

Hasty generalization: All stories have surprise endings.

That conclusion is a hasty generalization. You could name many stories that do not have a surprise ending. Sometimes hasty generalizations can be corrected by using a qualifying word such as *most, usually, some, many,* or *often.* It is especially important to watch out for hasty generalizations when you're reading a persuasive text.

2. With **circular reasoning** a writer tries to fool you by restating the opinion in different words.

Hungry students can't study because they haven't had enough to eat.

Jean is the best candidate for student-council president because she's better than all the other candidates.

---

3. **Cause-and-effect fallacies.** One common **cause-and-effect fallacy** assumes that if something happens right before another event, the first event caused the next event.

I wasn't wearing my lucky shirt, so I failed my history test.

Another **cause-and-effect fallacy** names a single cause for a complicated situation that has many causes.

Popularity in middle school depends on wearing the right clothes.

---

4. The **either-or fallacy** suggests that there are only two sides to an issue.

Either you get a summer job, or you waste the whole summer.

See also *Argument, Evidence, Persuasion.*

5W-HOW? The first paragraph of a news story, called the **lead** (lēd) paragraph, usually answers the questions *who? what? when? where? why?* and *how?* Look for the answers to these **5W-How?** questions when you read a newspaper story or any eyewitness account.

See page 52.

GENERALIZATION A **generalization** is a broad statement that covers several particular situations. Scientists and detectives, for instance, begin their investigations by amassing many specific facts. Then they put the facts together and draw a conclusion about what all this evidence tells them, what it adds up to.

Fact: Cobras are poisonous.

Fact: Rattlesnakes are poisonous.

Fact: Garter snakes are not poisonous.

Generalization: Some snakes are poisonous.

The generalization *Most snakes are poisonous* would have been incorrect. Only three species out of a population of more than 2,500 species of snakes were considered. About four fifths of all snakes are not poisonous. To be valid, a generalization must be based on all the evidence (the facts) that can be gathered.

> See pages 508, 613, 675.
> See also *Stereotyping.*

GRAPHIC FEATURES **Graphic features** are design elements in a text. They include things like headings, maps, charts, graphs, and illustrations. Graphic features are visual ways of communicating information.

Some design elements you may find in a text are **boldface** and *italic* type; type in different styles (called fonts), sizes, and colors; bullets (dots that set off items in a list); and logos (like computer icons). For example, the Quickwrite heading in this book always appears with the pencil logo. Design elements make a text look more attractive. They also steer your eyes to different types of information and make the text easier to read.

A **heading** serves as a title for the information that follows it. Size and color set off from the rest of the text the type used for a heading. A repeated heading, like "Reading Skills" in this textbook, is always followed by the same type of material. Skimming the headings is one way to preview a text.

Graphic features such as **maps, charts,** and **graphs** display and sometimes explain complex information with lines, drawings, and symbols. Graphic features usually include these elements:

1. A **title** identifies the subject or main idea of the graphic.

2. **Labels** identify specific information.

3. A **caption** is text (usually under an illustration) that explains what you're looking at.

4. A **legend,** or **key,** helps you interpret symbols and colors, usually on a map.

Look for a **scale,** which relates the size or distance of something on a map to the real-life size and distance.

5. The **source** tells where the information in the graphic comes from. Knowing the source helps you evaluate the accuracy.

Different types of **maps** present special information. **Physical maps** show the natural landscape of an area. Shading may be used to show features like mountains and valleys. Different shades of color are often used to show different elevations (heights above sea level). **Political maps** show political units, such as states, nations, and capitals. The map of Canada, the United States, and Mexico shown here is a political map. **Special-purpose maps** present information such as the routes of explorers or the location of earthquake fault lines.

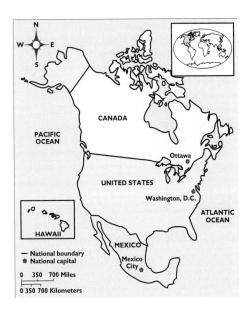

A **flowchart** shows a sequence of events or the steps in a process. Flowcharts are often used to show cause-and-effect relationships. See page 256 for an example of a flowchart. **Pie charts,** also called **circle graphs,** show how parts of a whole are related. A pie chart is a circle divided into different-sized sections, like slices of a pie. The emphasis in a pie chart is always on the proportions of the sections, not on the specific amounts of each section.

Pie Chart

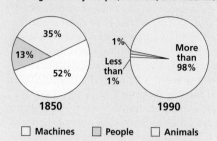

Distribution of Physical Labor in the United States: Percentage Done by People, Animals, and Machines

A **diagram** is a graphic that outlines the parts of something and shows how the parts relate to one another or how they work. You'll often find diagrams in technical directions, to show how a mechanical device works. Diagrams prove that a picture can be worth more than a thousand words. See page 906 for an example of a diagram.

A **time line** identifies events that take place over the course of time. In a time line, events are organized in chronological order, the order in which they happened. See pages 616–617 for a time line of an author's life.

Graphs usually show changes or trends over time. In line graphs, dots showing the quantity at different times are connected to

create a line. **Bar graphs** generally compare various quantities.

Bar Graph

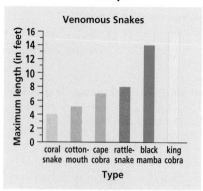

Line Graph

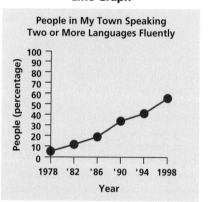

A **table** presents information arranged in rows and columns. There are many different types of tables. See page 903 for an example of a table showing a train schedule.

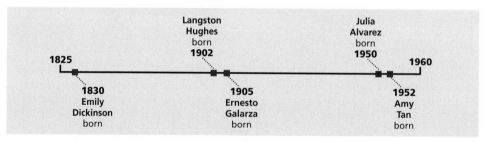

Tips for Understanding Graphic Features

1. Read the title, labels, and legend before you try to analyze the information.

2. Read numbers carefully. Note increases or decreases in sequences. Look for the direction or order of events and for trends and relationships.

3. Draw your own conclusions from the graphic. Then, compare your conclusions with the writer's conclusions.

See pages 32, 52.

IMAGES Descriptive writing appeals to the senses to create **mental images,** pictures in the reader's mind. Most description appeals to the sense of sight, but description can also appeal to one or more of the other senses. When you read a description, use the details to *visualize,* or form mental pictures of, the characters, settings, and events. Forming mental images is especially important when you read description in scientific texts.

See page 527.

INFERENCE An **inference** is an educated guess, a conclusion that makes sense because it's supported by evidence. The evidence may be a collection of **facts,** information that can be proved, or it may come from experiences in your own life. However, the evidence must provide some reason for believing that the conclusion is true if the inference is to be valid, or based on sound, logical thought. Nevertheless, people may draw different conclusions from the same evidence—especially if there isn't much evidence to go on.

> Bobby has recently transferred to your school. You ask Bobby to join you and a couple of other friends, Sam and Ali, at your house after school on Thursday. Bobby says, "Sorry. I have to go home right after school."

> **Inferences:** Sam infers that Bobby's parents are really strict. Ali infers that Bobby is stuck-up. You infer that Bobby doesn't like you.

As you read, you make inferences based on clues that the writer provides. For example, when you read a narrative, you **infer,** or guess, what will happen next based on what the writer has told you and on your own knowledge and experience. Sometimes a writer deliberately gives clues that lead you to different—and incorrect—inferences. That's part of the fun of reading. Until you get to the end of a suspenseful story, you can never be completely sure about what will happen next.

In O. Henry's short story "After Twenty Years" (page 357), a policeman speaks to a well-dressed man waiting in a doorway in New York City. The man is waiting for his boyhood friend, Jimmy. He hasn't seen Jimmy for more than twenty years. Read the following dialogue, and the inferences that follow it.

> "Did pretty well out West, didn't you?" asked the policeman.
>
> "You bet! I hope Jimmy has done half as well. He was a kind of plodder, though, good fellow as he was. I've had to compete with some of the sharpest wits going to get my pile. A man gets in a groove in New York. It takes the West to put a razor edge on him."
>
> **Inferences:** The policeman seems to be impressed by the man in the doorway. The well-dressed man thinks a lot of himself and looks down on his old friend Jimmy, who may have been too "good" to be successful.

See pages 57, 136, 146, 168.
See also *Evidence, Fact and Opinion.*

INSTRUCTIONAL MANUALS Instructional manuals tell you how to operate a specific device, such as a VCR or a car. Instructional manuals contain detailed directions, usually organized in chronological steps. Drawings and diagrams, such as flowcharts, might be included to help you understand the different parts of the device.

See page 81.

KWL CHART Using a **KWL chart** is a way to focus your reading and record what you learn. KWL means "What I **k**now, what I **w**ant to know, and what I **l**earned." When you use a KWL strategy, you first skim the text, looking at headings, subtitles, and illustrations. You decide what the topic of the text is. Then, on a blank sheet of paper, you draw a KWL chart. In the K column you note what you already know about the subject. In the W column you write down what you'd like to find out. After you finish reading the text, you write the answers under the L column to the questions you asked in the W column. Here is the beginning of a KWL chart based on "Sir Gawain and the Loathly Lady" (page 834).

K	W	L
What I **K**now	What I **W**ant to Know	What I **L**earned
Sir Gawain was a knight.	Why was the lady loathly?	

See also *Graphic Features.*

MAIN IDEA The most important point or focus of a passage is its **main idea.** Writers of essays, nonfiction narratives, and informational articles have one or more **main ideas** in mind as they write a text. The writer may state the main idea directly. More often the main idea is suggested, or implied. Then it's up to you, the reader, to **infer,** or guess at,

what it is. To infer the main idea, look at the key details in the text. See if you can create a statement that expresses a general idea that covers all these important details. When you are deciding on the main idea, look especially for a key passage at the beginning or end of the text. That's where a writer often refers to a key idea.

See pages 393, 480, 543.

NEWSPAPERS Newspapers are informational texts that present facts about current events. Newspapers may also contain feature articles that aim to entertain as well as inform. Newspapers often contain editorials that support a *position* for or against an issue. **Headlines** at the top of each story indicate the topic of the story. They are worded to catch your attention. The writer of a **news story** usually organizes the details in order of importance. If the article is running too long, the less important details can easily be cut from the end of the story.

See page 52.

OBJECTIVE WRITING Objective writing sticks to the facts. It does not reveal the writer's feelings, beliefs, or point of view about the subject. In a newspaper, news articles are usually written objectively. Readers of news articles want to get a true and accurate account of what happened. If they want to know a writer's point of view or perspective on the news, they turn to the **editorial page.** Editorials and letters to the editor are usually *not* written objectively. They are examples of **subjective writing.** See page 789 for an example of a letter to the editor.

See pages 393, 414.
See also *Subjective Writing.*

OUTLINING Outlining an informational text can help you identify main ideas and understand how they are related to one another. Outlining also shows you the important details that support each main idea. When you have an outline, you have a visual summary of the text.

Many readers start an outline by taking notes. Note taking is an especially good idea if you're reading a text with many facts, such as names and dates, that you want to remember.

Tips for Taking Notes

1. You can jot down notes in a notebook or on note cards. Put your notes in your own words, writing each main idea on its own note card or page.

2. As you continue to read, add details that relate to the important idea you have on each card.

3. Whenever you copy the writer's exact words, put quotation marks around them. Write down the page number for the source of each note.

After you have your notes on the text, you're ready to make an outline. Many outlines label the main ideas with Roman numerals. You need to have at least two headings at each level. This is how an outline might begin:

I. Main idea

A. Detail supporting main idea I

   1. Detail supporting A

      a. Detail supporting 1

      b. Detail supporting 1

   2. Detail supporting A

B. Detail supporting main idea I

II. Main idea

See page 266.

PERSUASION Persuasion is the use of language or pictures to convince us to think or act in a certain way. Recognizing **persuasive techniques** will help you evaluate the persuasion that you read, hear, and see all around you today. Here are some persuasive techniques to watch for:

1. **Logical appeals** are based on correct reasoning. Logic appeals to reason with opinions supported by strong factual evidence, such as facts, statistics, or statements by experts on the issue being considered.

2. **Emotional appeals** get your feelings involved in the argument. Some writers use vivid language and supporting evidence that arouse basic feelings, such as pity, anger, and fear. Persuasion tends to be most effective when it appeals to both your head and your heart. However, it's important to be able to recognize emotional appeals—and to be suspicious of how they can sway you.

3. **Logical fallacies** (fal′ə·sēz) are mistakes in reasoning. If you're reading a text quickly, fuzzy or dishonest reasoning may look as if it makes sense. See the entry for *Fallacious Reasoning* for examples of specific logical fallacies.

See pages 389, 788, 816.
See also *Argument.*

PREDICTIONS Guessing what will happen next in a narrative text is a reading skill called **making predictions.** To make predictions, you look for clues that **foreshadow,** or hint at, future actions. You try to connect those clues with past and present actions in the story. You quickly check your memory for other things you've read that are in any way like the story you're reading. You recall your real-life experiences. Then you make your predictions. As you read, you'll continuously revise your guesses, adjusting your predictions as new clues crop up.

See pages 38, 174, 246, 356, 368, 707.

PROPAGANDA **Propaganda** is an organized attempt to influence a large audience of readers, listeners, or TV watchers. Propaganda techniques are used in all kinds of persuasive texts. You see them especially in advertisements, speeches, and editorials. Some writers use propaganda to advance good causes—for instance, to persuade people to recycle, to exercise, or to join together to fight a terrible disease. However, many writers of propaganda use emotional appeals to confuse readers and to convince them that the writer's biased opinions are the only ones worth considering.

Common propaganda techniques include the following:

- The **bandwagon** appeal urges you to do or believe something because everyone else does.

> "Shop where the action is! Join the parade to Teen-Town Mall."

- The **testimonial** uses a famous person, such as an actor or an athlete, to testify that he or she supports the issue or uses the product.

> "I'm professional basketball player Hank Smith, and I drink Starade every day for quick and long-lasting energy."

- **Snob appeal** suggests that by using this product you can be superior to others—more powerful, wealthy, or beautiful.

> "You deserve this car. Don't settle for less than the best."

- **Stereotyping.** Writers who use stereotyping refer to members of a group as if they were all the same. (See also page 816.)

> Teenagers are bad drivers.
>
> Didn't I tell you that Martians can't be trusted?

- Writers using **name-calling** avoid giving reasons and logical evidence for or against an issue. Instead, they attack people who disagree with them by giving those people negative labels.

> That's just what I'd expect a nerd like you to say.
>
> I won't waste time listening to a puppet-politician whose strings are controlled by ill-informed special-interest groups.

PURPOSES OF TEXTS Texts are written for different **purposes:** to inform, to persuade, to express feelings, or to entertain. The purpose of a text, or the reason why a text is written, determines its **structure,** the way the writer organizes and presents the material.

READING RATE The speed at which you read a text is your **reading rate.** How quickly or slowly you should read depends on the type of text you are reading and your purpose for reading it.

Reading Rates According to Purpose

Reading Rate	Purpose	Example
Skimming	Reading for main points	Glancing at newspaper headlines; reviewing charts and headings in your science textbook before a test
Scanning	Looking for specific details	Looking for an author's name in a table of contents; looking in a geography book for the name of the highest mountain in North America
Reading for mastery	Reading to understand and remember	Taking notes on a chapter in your science textbook to study for a test; reading a story or poem for understanding

RETELLING The reading strategy called **retelling** helps you identify and remember events that advance the plot of a story. Retelling is also useful when you read informational texts, such as science or history texts. From time to time in your reading, stop for a moment. Review what's gone on before you go ahead. Focus on the important events or key details. Think about them, and retell them briefly in your own words. When you read history or science texts, you should stop after each section of the text and see if you can retell the key details to yourself.

See pages 4, 14, 732.

SQ3R The abbreviation **SQ3R** stands for a reading and study strategy that takes place in five steps: **s**urvey, **q**uestion, **r**ead, **r**etell, **r**eview. The SQ3R process takes time, but it helps you focus on the text—and it works.

- *S—Survey.* Glance through the text. Skim the headings, titles, charts, illustrations, and vocabulary words in boldface type. Read the first and last sentences of the major sections of the text, if they are indicated by headings.

- *Q—Question.* List the questions that you have. These may be questions that came out of your survey, or they may be general questions about the subject. Ask the questions that you hope to find answers to in the text.

- *R—Read.* Read the text carefully, keeping your questions in mind. As you read, look for answers. Take brief notes on the answers you find.

- *R—Retell.* Use your notes to write down the main ideas and important details in the text. Before you write, say your answers out loud. Listen to your answers to hear if they make sense.

- *R—Review.* Look back over the text. See if you can answer your questions without using the notes and answers you wrote down. Write a brief summary of the text so you'll be able to remember it later.

See page 415.

STEREOTYPING (ster′ē·ə·tīp′iŋ) Referring to all members of a group as if they were all the same is called **stereotyping.** Stereotyping ignores the facts about individuals. The most important fact about members of a group is that each individual person is *different* from all the others. Stereotyping does not allow for individual differences. Whenever you assess a writer's evidence, be on the lookout for stereotyping. When a writer makes a claim about an individual or a group and supports the assertion with a stereotype, you know that the writer is guilty of faulty reasoning. Here are some examples of stereotyping:

All teenagers are lazy.

Senior citizens have more money than they need.

All lawyers are dishonest.

All football players are dumb.

See page 816.
See also *Propaganda.*

SUBJECTIVE WRITING Writing that reveals and emphasizes the writer's personal feelings and opinions is called **subjective.** Subjective and objective writing are opposites. *Subjective* means "personal; resulting from feelings; existing only in the mind." *Objective* means "real; actual; factual; without bias." Writers may combine subjective and objective details in the same text. As a reader you must figure out which statements are based on subjective impressions and which are based on factual, objective evidence.

We expect subjectivity in some writing. We would expect an autobiography to reveal the writer's personal feelings. In a historical text, however, we expect objectivity—we want facts, not the writer's personal feelings.

See pages 393, 414.
See also *Objective Writing.*

SUMMARIZING Restating the main ideas or major events in a text is called **summarizing.** A summary of text is much shorter than the original. To summarize an informational text, you must include the main ideas and the important details that support those main ideas. To summarize a narrative, you must include the main events and be certain you have indicated cause and effect. In a summary, except for direct quotations from the text, you put the writer's ideas into your own words. (Every time you jot down a direct quotation, be sure to put quotation marks around it and write down the source.) Here is a summary of the selection from *Barrio Boy* by Ernesto Galarza (page 500):

> Ernesto's family had recently moved to Sacramento from Mazatlán, Mexico. This true account begins with Ernesto's mother taking him to school. The new school seems strange to Ernesto, who speaks no English. Ernesto finds out that many of his first-grade classmates are from other countries or have different ethnic backgrounds.

> Several of them, along with Ernesto, receive private English lessons from their teacher. The teachers at the school help Ernesto learn that he can be proud of being American while still feeling proud of his Mexican roots.

See pages 543, 664, 698.
See also *Main Idea.*

TEXT STRUCTURES There are some basic ways in which writers structure informational texts: **cause and effect, chronological order,** and **comparison-and-contrast.** Sometimes a writer will use one pattern throughout a text. Many writers will combine two or more patterns. These guidelines can help you analyze text structure:

1. Search the text for the main idea. Look for words that signal a specific pattern of organization.

2. Study the text for other important ideas. Think about how the ideas are connected to one another. Look for an obvious pattern.

3. Draw a graphic organizer that shows how the text seems to be structured. Your graphic organizer may look like one of the common text structures shown below.

The **cause-and-effect pattern** presents a series of causes and their effects. This example shows the effect of an earthquake, which led to another effect, which became the cause of another effect, and so on:

Causal Chain

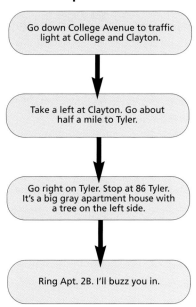

Chronological-order pattern shows events or ideas happening in time sequence. The example below gives directions for getting from school to a student's home:

Sequence Chain

Go down College Avenue to traffic light at College and Clayton.

↓

Take a left at Clayton. Go about half a mile to Tyler.

↓

Go right on Tyler. Stop at 86 Tyler. It's a big gray apartment house with a tree on the left side.

↓

Ring Apt. 2B. I'll buzz you in.

The comparison-and-contrast pattern points out similarities and differences. A Venn diagram can help you see how two subjects are alike and how they are different. Similarities are listed where the two circles overlap. Differences are shown where the circles don't overlap. This example compares a middle school with a high school.

Venn Diagram

Middle School
- smaller—500 students
- students from four K–5 schools
- everyone knows everyone else

Similarities
- classes same length
- many electives
- three foreign languages to choose from

High School
- Big school—2000 students
- Students from four middle schools
- More cliques; hard to get to know people

Differences   *Similarities*   *Differences*

Another kind of graphic organizer focuses on points of comparison (the features being compared).

Comparing and Contrasting

	Middle School	High School
Size of school		
Length of school day		
Sports program		

See pages 284, 496.
See also *Cause and Effect, Chronological Order, Compare-and-Contrast Pattern.*

TEXTBOOKS **Textbooks** are informational texts written to help students learn about a subject. This textbook is quite different in structure from a geography textbook. Nonetheless, both kinds of textbooks have certain elements in common. For example, they have the same general purpose. In addition, most textbooks present information followed by questions that help students determine whether they have learned the material. Finally, most textbooks contain a table of contents, an index, illustrations, charts, and other graphic features.

See page 32.

WRITER'S PERSPECTIVE **Perspective** is the way a person looks at a subject. Some people have a negative perspective, for instance, on violent computer games. They believe that such games may influence children to become violent. Other people have a positive perspective on violent computer games. They say that when children play such games, they may rid themselves of some of their aggressive feelings. Figuring out a writer's perspective can help you understand and evaluate what you are reading. The following paragraph is from Clifton Davis's "A Mason-Dixon Memory" (page 534). A statement describing Davis's perspective follows:

> In his words and in his life, Lincoln had made it clear that freedom is not free. Every time the color of a person's skin keeps him out of an amusement park or off a country-club fairway, the war for freedom begins again. Sometimes the battle is fought with fists and guns, but more often the most effective weapon is a simple act of love and courage.
>
> **Writer's perspective:** Prejudice still exists today, and it can be fought best with simple, nonviolent actions.

See pages 351, 364, 410.

Language Handbook

1 THE PARTS OF SPEECH

THE NOUN

1a. **A *noun* is a word used to name a person, a place, a thing, or an idea.**

PERSONS   giant, Miss Nettie Hopley, baby sitter, immigrant

PLACES   pasture, Italy, Sutter's Fort, Crocker Art Gallery

THINGS   quilt, key, frog, desk, Newbery Medal, *Voyager 2*

IDEAS   knowledge, friendliness, success, love, self-esteem

Compound Nouns

A *compound noun* is two or more words used together as a single noun. The parts of a compound noun may be written as one word, as separate words, or as a hyphenated word.

ONE WORD   butterfly, playground, Passover, classroom

SEPARATE WORDS   Golden Age, compact disc, post office

HYPHENATED WORD   self-control, bull's-eye, six-year-old

> **TIPS FOR SPELLING**
>
> Compound words may be written as one word, as separate words, or as a hyphenated word. To be sure you are spelling a compound word correctly, always use a current dictionary.

Collective Nouns

A *collective noun* is a word that names a group.

EXAMPLES   class   family   choir   herd   jury

Common Nouns and Proper Nouns

A *common noun* is a general name for a person, a place, a thing, or an idea. A *proper noun* names a particular person, place, thing, or idea. Proper nouns always begin with a capital letter. Common nouns begin with a capital letter in titles and when they begin sentences.

COMMON NOUNS   poem   nation   day

PROPER NOUNS   "The Runaway"   Japan   Friday

✓ QUICK CHECK 1

Identify the nouns in the following sentences. Classify each noun as *common* or *proper*. Also label any *compound* or *collective* nouns.

EXAMPLE   1. "Rikki-tikki-tavi" is a short story by Rudyard Kipling.

         1. *"Rikki-tikki-tavi"—compound, proper; short story—compound, common; Rudyard Kipling—compound, proper*

Quick Check 1: Answers

1. Rikki-tikki-tavi—compound, proper; pet—common; family—collective, common; India—proper

2. mongoose—common; Rikki-tikki—compound, proper; fear—common

3. teeth—common; person—common

4. cobra—common; bathroom—compound, common

5. lives—common; Teddy—proper; family—common

Try It Out: Possible Answers

1. As Cinderella wept under a willow tree, a fairy godmother suddenly appeared.

2. She waved a magic wand.

3. A pumpkin turned into a coach.

4. With another wave of the fairy godmother's wand, Cinderella's torn rags turned into a beautiful gown.

5. Overjoyed, Cinderella thanked the fairy godmother and rode to the ball at the castle.

Try It Out ✎

In the following paragraph, replace the vague nouns with exact, specific nouns.

[1] As a girl wept under a tree, a woman suddenly appeared. [2] She waved a magic stick. [3] A vegetable turned into a vehicle. [4] With another movement of the woman's stick, the girl's torn clothing turned into a beautiful dress. [5] Overjoyed, the girl thanked the woman and rode to the party at the building.

1. Rikki-tikki-tavi is the brave pet of a family in India.
2. A fierce little mongoose, Rikki-tikki knows no fear.
3. Although his teeth are sharp, he would never bite a person.
4. Instead, he kills a deadly cobra in the bathroom.
5. He saves the lives of Teddy and his family.

TIPS FOR WRITERS

Using Specific Nouns

Whenever possible, use specific, exact nouns. Using specific nouns will make your writing more accurate as well as more interesting.

NONSPECIFIC	Animals drank from the water.
SPECIFIC	Horses, cattle, and burros drank from the creek.

THE PRONOUN

1b. A *pronoun* is a word used in place of one or more nouns or pronouns.

EXAMPLES	Emily Dickinson took few trips; Dickinson spent most of Dickinson's time at Amherst.
	Emily Dickinson took few trips; **she** spent most of **her** time at Amherst.

The word that a pronoun stands for is called its ***antecedent.*** The antecedent is not always stated.

STATED	Dickinson wrote many **poems** and hid **them** in her room.
UNSTATED	**Who** edited *The Poems of Emily Dickinson*?

Personal Pronouns

A ***personal pronoun*** refers to the one speaking (*first person*), the one spoken to (*second person*), or the one spoken about (*third person*).

NOTE Some authorities prefer to call possessive forms of pronouns (such as *my, his,* and *their*) *possessive adjectives.* Follow your teacher's instructions regarding possessive forms.

PERSONAL PRONOUNS		
	SINGULAR	**PLURAL**
First Person	I, me, my, mine	we, us, our, ours
Second Person	you, your, yours	you, your, yours
Third Person	he, him, his, she, her, hers, it, its	they, them, their, theirs

Reflexive and Intensive Pronouns

A *reflexive pronoun* refers to the subject and directs the action of the verb back to the subject. An *intensive pronoun* emphasizes a noun or another pronoun. Reflexive and intensive pronouns have the same form.

FIRST PERSON	myself, ourselves
SECOND PERSON	yourself, yourselves
THIRD PERSON	himself, herself, itself, themselves

REFLEXIVE Emily Dickinson wrote **herself** notes on the backs of recipes.

INTENSIVE She did all the baking **herself.**

Demonstrative Pronouns

A *demonstrative pronoun* (*this, that, these, those*) points out a person, a place, a thing, or an idea.

EXAMPLE **This** is a collection of her poems.

Interrogative Pronouns

An *interrogative pronoun* (*what, which, who, whom, whose*) introduces a question.

EXAMPLE **What** were Dickinson's household duties?

Relative Pronouns

A *relative pronoun* (*that, what, which, who, whom, whose*) introduces a subordinate clause.

EXAMPLE Dickinson wrote of thoughts and feelings **that** she had.

Indefinite Pronouns

An *indefinite pronoun* refers to a person, a place, or a thing that is not specifically named. Many indefinite pronouns can also serve as adjectives.

Common Indefinite Pronouns

all	each	few	no one	several
any	either	many	nobody	some
both	everything	none	one	somebody

PRONOUN **Neither** of Emily's sisters was aware of the poems.

ADJECTIVE **Neither** sister was aware of the poems.

✓ QUICK CHECK 2

Identify each of the pronouns in the following sentences as *personal, reflexive, intensive, demonstrative, interrogative, relative,* or *indefinite*.

☞ *This, that, these,* and *those* can also be used as adjectives. See page 963.

☞ See pages 996–1000 for more on subordinate clauses.

Language Handbook

Quick Check 2: Answers

1. you—personal
2. herself—intensive; that—relative; she—personal
3. who—interrogative; her—personal
4. you—personal; this—demonstrative; your—personal; some—indefinite; her—personal
5. You—personal; yourself—reflexive; someone—indefinite; them—personal

NOTE An adjective may come before or after the word it modifies.

EXAMPLES **Each one** of the guests ate **steamed fish.** [The adjective *each* modifies *one.* The adjective *steamed* modifies *fish.*]

The **minister, proper** and **dignified,** was also **courteous.** [The adjectives *proper, dignified,* and *courteous* modify *minister.*]

EXAMPLE 1. I wonder about anyone who is famous.
1. *I—personal; anyone—indefinite; who—relative*

1. Are you famous or important?
2. Emily Dickinson herself declared that she wasn't.
3. Yet, who doesn't recognize her name today?
4. If you don't, this is your chance to read some of her poems.
5. You can decide for yourself if someone important wrote them.

THE ADJECTIVE

1c. An *adjective* is a word used to modify a noun or a pronoun.

To **modify** a word means to describe the word or to make its meaning more definite. An adjective modifies a word by telling *what kind, which one, how much,* or *how many.*

WHAT KIND?	WHICH ONE?	HOW MUCH? *or* HOW MANY?
noisy relatives	*those* days	*many* years
proper manners	*another* skirt	*more* guests
Mexican food	*next* lesson	*one* mistake

Articles

The most frequently used adjectives are *a, an,* and *the.* These adjectives are called **articles.** The adjectives *a* and *an* are **indefinite articles.** Each one indicates that the noun refers to someone or something in general. *A* is used before a word beginning with a consonant sound. *An* is used before a word beginning with a vowel sound.

EXAMPLES **An** early gift later caused Tan **an** embarrassing moment.
Her mother gave her **a** miniskirt.
It took him **an** hour to find **a** uniform that fit.

The adjective *the* is a **definite article.** It indicates that the noun refers to someone or something in particular.

EXAMPLE **The** minister's son attended **the** potluck dinner.

Proper Adjectives

A **proper adjective** is formed from a proper noun and begins with a capital letter.

PROPER NOUNS	PROPER ADJECTIVES
China	**Chinese** customs
America	**American** manners
Buddhist	**Buddhist** monk
Christmas	**Christmas** dinner

NOTE Some proper nouns, such as *Buddhist,* do not change spelling when they are used as adjectives.

Demonstrative Adjectives

This, that, these, and *those* can be used as adjectives and as pronouns. When these words modify a noun or a pronoun, they are called *demonstrative adjectives.* When used alone, these words are called *demonstrative pronouns.*

DEMONSTRATIVE ADJECTIVES	Is **this** story more interesting than **that** one?
	Those dishes are considered a delicacy.

DEMONSTRATIVE PRONOUNS	**That** is the way to hold chopsticks.
	Are **these** typical foods in China?

☞ For more about demonstrative pronouns, see page 961.

Nouns Used as Adjectives

When a noun modifies another noun or a pronoun, it is considered an adjective. Most compound nouns can be used as adjectives.

NOUNS	NOUNS USED AS ADJECTIVES
fish	**fish** scales
holiday	**holiday** menu
bicycle	**bicycle** tires
Christmas Eve	**Christmas Eve** celebration

✓ QUICK CHECK 3

Identify each adjective in the following sentences. Then, give the word the adjective modifies. Do not include the articles *a, an,* and *the.*

EXAMPLE   1. That name sounds strange to me.
           1. *That*—*name; strange*—*name*

1. Having an unusual name can be a problem for anyone.
2. That problem plagued Julia Alvarez all through school.
3. As a girl, she was known by many names—Judy, Jules, and even Alcatraz—but her family pronounced *Julia* "Hoo-lee-ah."
4. Those neighbors with a New York City accent said "Joo-lee-ah."
5. Family members told her to keep writing and her name would be famous.

Quick Check 3: Answers

1. unusual—name
2. That—problem
3. many—names; her—family
4. Those—neighbors; New York City—accent
5. Family—members; her—name; famous—name

☞ For more about subjects and verbs, see pages 970–973 and 1001–1003.

☞ For more information about objects, see pages 1005–1006.

 NOTE A verb may be transitive in one sentence and intransitive in another.

TRANSITIVE He **smelled** his grandfather's aftershave.

INTRANSITIVE Grandfather **smelled** good.

THE VERB

1d. A *verb* is a word used to express action or a state of being.

EXAMPLES Gary Soto **wrote** "The No-Guitar Blues."
Soto's stories **seem** realistic to me.

Every sentence must have a subject and a verb. The verb says something about the subject.

Action Verbs

1e. An *action verb* may express physical action or mental action.

PHYSICAL ACTION lean, watch, hop, say, push, toss, pull
MENTAL ACTION want, hope, regret, wonder, forget, dream

Transitive and Intransitive Verbs

(1) A *transitive verb* is an action verb that expresses an action directed toward a person or thing.

EXAMPLE He **held** a guitar. [The action of *held* is directed toward *guitar.*]

With transitive verbs, the action passes from the doer (the subject) to the receiver of the action. Words that receive the action of a transitive verb are called *objects*.

EXAMPLES She called **him.** [*Him* is the object of the verb *called.*]
The boy told the **villagers** a **lie.** [Both *villagers* and *lie* are objects of the verb *told.*]

(2) An *intransitive verb* expresses action (or tells something about the subject) without passing the action to a receiver.

EXAMPLE Fausto **waited** hopefully for a reward. [The action of *waited* is not directed toward a receiver. The verb *waited* does not have an object.]

Linking Verbs

1f. A *linking verb* links, or connects, the subject with a noun, a pronoun, or an adjective in the predicate.

EXAMPLES The dog's name **was** Roger. [name = Roger]
Los Lobos **became** Fausto's role models. [Los Lobos = role models]

Like intransitive verbs, linking verbs never take direct objects.

**Linking Verbs Formed
from the Verb _Be_**

am	were	should have been	was being
are	be	will have been	can be
being	been	has been	must be
is	may be	have been	might be
was	would be	will be	could be

Other Linking Verbs
appear, grow, seem, stay, become, look, smell, taste, feel, remain, sound, turn

Helping Verbs

1g. A _helping verb_ (_auxiliary verb_) helps the main verb to express an action or a state of being.

EXAMPLES **could** be   **may have** asked   **might have been** caught

COMMONLY USED HELPING VERBS	
Forms of _Be_	am, be, being, was, are, been, is, were
Forms of _Do_	do, does, did
Forms of _Have_	have, has, had
Other Helping Verbs	can, may, must, should, would, could, might, shall, will

A _verb phrase_ consists of a main verb and at least one helping verb.

EXAMPLE Fausto **could have kept** the money. [The main verb is _kept_.]

 **QUICK CHECK 4**

Identify the italicized verb in each of the following sentences as an _action verb_, a _linking verb_, or a _helping verb_. Then, for each action verb, tell whether the verb is _transitive_ or _intransitive_.

EXAMPLE **1.** Have you _read_ other poems by Shel Silverstein?
    1. _action verb, transitive_

1. Sarah Cynthia Sylvia Stout would not _take_ the trash out.
2. It _smelled_ bad.
3. She _did_n't care about that or about her family or friends.
4. Finally, she _was_ alone with her garbage.
5. That huge pile of garbage _reached_ to another state.

☞ See pages 1006–1007 for more information about linking verbs.

NOTE Some words may be either action verbs or linking verbs, depending on how they are used.

LINKING The dog **looked** hungry.
ACTION The dog **looked** for another orange peel.

NOTE Sometimes the verb phrase is interrupted by other words.

EXAMPLES **Will** you please **explain** the theme of this story? Fausto **did** not [_or_ didn't] **tell** the dog's owners the truth.

☞ For more information about verb phrases, see pages 970, 991, and 1002.

Language Handbook

Quick Check 4: Answers

1. action verb, transitive
2. linking verb
3. helping verb
4. linking verb
5. action verb, intransitive

Quick Check 5: Answers

1. sadly—cried
2. Too—soon; soon—sailed
3. not—would yield; most—desperate
4. harder—tried
5. Eventually—rescued

Try It Out: Possible Answers

1. wonderfully
2. refreshingly
3. completely
4. Rather
5. truly

> **NOTE** Adverbs may come before, after, or between the words they modify.
>
> **EXAMPLES** **Slowly,** the shark was circling.
> The shark was **slowly** circling.
> The shark was circling **slowly.**

☞ For more on modifiers in general, see Part 5: Using Modifiers.

Try It Out ✎

For each use of *very* below, substitute another adverb. You may wish to revise the sentence.

1. For entertainment, they imagined *very* delicious foods.
2. Douglas dreamed of a *very* cold honeydew melon.
3. At night on the sea, they felt *very* alone.
4. *Very* quickly, they pulled the sea turtle aboard.
5. After their rescue, a *very* fine cook helped them back to health.

THE ADVERB

1h. An *adverb* is a word used to modify a verb, an adjective, or another adverb.

MODIFYING A VERB They could **not** radio for help.

MODIFYING AN ADJECTIVE The sun was **extremely** hot.

MODIFYING ANOTHER ADVERB **Quite** bravely, they landed a shark.

An adverb tells *where, when, how,* or *to what extent* (*how much* or *how long*).

WHERE?	Killer whales are common **here.**
HOW?	The accident occurred **suddenly.**
WHEN?	**Then** the survivors depended on their wits.
TO WHAT EXTENT?	They were **exceptionally** careful with their supplies.

The word *not* is an adverb. When *not* is part of a contraction like *hadn't,* the *–n't* is an adverb.

✓ QUICK CHECK 5

Identify the adverb or adverbs in each of the following sentences. Then, give the word or phrase each adverb modifies.

EXAMPLE 1. Have you ever wondered about being shipwrecked?
1. *ever—Have wondered*

1. Neil cried sadly for their lost ship.
2. Too soon, a cargo vessel sailed into the distance.
3. Dougal Robertson would not yield to his most desperate fears.
4. He steeled himself and tried harder.
5. Eventually, a Japanese tuna fisher rescued them.

Using Descriptive Adverbs

The adverb *very* is overused. In your writing, try to replace *very* with more descriptive adverbs, or revise the sentence so that other words carry more of the descriptive meaning.

EXAMPLE Their ordeal at sea lasted a very long time.

REVISED Their ordeal at sea lasted an **extremely** long time.

or

Their ordeal at sea lasted **thirty-eight days.**

THE PREPOSITION

1i. **A *preposition* is a word used to show the relationship of a noun or a pronoun to another word in the sentence.**

Notice how a change in the preposition changes the relationship between *waves* and *rocks* in each of the following examples.

The waves crashed **under** the rocks.
The waves crashed **on** the rocks.
The waves crashed **against** the rocks.
The waves crashed **in front of** the rocks.

Commonly Used Prepositions

aboard	before	in	over
about	behind	in addition to	past
above	below	in front of	since
according to	beneath	inside	through
across	beside	in spite of	throughout
against	between	into	under
around	from	out of	without

The Prepositional Phrase

A preposition is usually followed by a noun or a pronoun. This noun or pronoun is called the **object of the preposition.** All together, the preposition, its object, and any modifiers of the object are called a **prepositional phrase.**

EXAMPLE   The family went **to beautiful Cocoa Beach.**

A preposition may have more than one object.

EXAMPLE   Tiffany sat **with David, Susan, and Amber.**

 QUICK CHECK 6

Identify the preposition or prepositions in each of the following sentences. Then, give the object of each preposition.

EXAMPLE   **1.** Do you know any stories about the sea?
  1. *about—sea*

1. Elizabeth told a sad story about her youth.
2. She had loved a man of the sea.
3. She never said the words to him.
4. One day, he didn't return from a fishing trip.
5. Still, according to Elizabeth, he is always with her.

NOTE Some words may be used as either prepositions or adverbs. To tell an adverb from a preposition, remember that a preposition is always followed by a noun or pronoun object.

NOTE Do not confuse a prepositional phrase that begins with *to* (*to town*) with a verb form that begins with *to* (*to run*).

☞ For more about prepositional phrases, see pages 985, 990, and 991–992.

Quick Check 6: Answers

1. about—youth
2. of—sea
3. to—him
4. from—trip
5. according to—Elizabeth; with—her

THE CONJUNCTION

1j. A *conjunction* is a word used to join words or groups of words.

(1) *Coordinating conjunctions* connect words or groups of words used in the same way.

Coordinating Conjunctions						
and	but	or	nor	for	so	yet

EXAMPLES Echo **or** Narcissus [two proper nouns]
down from Olympus **and** to the mountains [two prepositional phrases]
Echo angered Hera, **so** Hera punished her. [two independent clauses]

(2) *Correlative conjunctions* are pairs of conjunctions that connect words or groups of words used in the same way.

Correlative Conjunctions		
both . . . and	either . . . or	neither . . . nor
not only . . . but also	whether . . . or	

EXAMPLES **Both** the nymphs **and** Echo were loyal to Zeus. [two nouns]
She **not only** delayed Hera **but also** detained her. [two verbs with objects]
Either Echo would have love, **or** she would die. [two complete ideas]

THE INTERJECTION

1k. An *interjection* is a word used to express emotion. An interjection does not have a grammatical relation to other words in the sentence. Usually an interjection is followed by an exclamation point. Sometimes an interjection is set off by a comma.

EXAMPLES **Oh!** You surprised me.
Why, I've heard this story before.
Wow! What a story that was.
Well, Hera certainly isn't someone to cross!

NOTE When *for* is used as a conjunction, it connects groups of words that are sentences, and it is preceded by a comma. On all other occasions, *for* is used as a preposition.

CONJUNCTION The team forfeited the game, **for** they refused to play.

PREPOSITION Outraged, people shouted **for** fair play.

☞ Coordinating conjunctions that join independent clauses are preceded by a comma. See page 1019.

Common Interjections			
aha	hooray	ouch	wow
aw	oh	well	yikes
goodness	oops	whew	yippee

 QUICK CHECK 7

Identify the *conjunctions* and *interjections* in the following sentences.

EXAMPLE   1. Well, Echo was either unwise or unlucky.
   1. *Well—interjection; either . . . or—conjunction*

1. Echo not only answered Narcissus but also ran to and embraced him.
2. Oh! Why did Narcissus scoff and shove Echo away?
3. Goodness! Narcissus was a handsome but self-centered person.
4. Both Echo and Narcissus suffered because of his selfishness.
5. They were doomed, yet he lives on in the narcissus flower.

DETERMINING PARTS OF SPEECH

The part of speech of a word is determined by the way the word is used in a sentence. Many words can be used as more than one part of speech.

EXAMPLES   This **well** belongs to the golf course. [noun]
Well, Dondré was quite disappointed. [interjection]
He has always played **well.** [adverb]

Clifton Davis suddenly remembered an event from his **past.** [noun]
Didn't his team drive **past** the Lincoln Memorial? [preposition]
As they rode along, the lights of the city flew **past.** [adverb]

 QUICK CHECK 8

Identify the part of speech of the italicized word in each sentence.

EXAMPLE   1. *For* Dondré Green, it was a blessing in disguise.
   1. *preposition*

1. *Any* of the boys might have objected, but no one did.
2. They all would *back* him.
3. And they never looked *back.*
4. *Support* like that can make a man proud.
5. I wish everyone would *support* each other as those boys did!

Quick Check 7: Answers

1. not only . . . but also—conjunction; and—conjunction
2. Oh—interjection; and—conjunction
3. Goodness—interjection; but—conjunction
4. Both . . . and—conjunction
5. yet—conjunction

Quick Check 8: Answers

1. Any—pronoun
2. back—verb
3. back—adverb
4. Support—noun
5. support—verb

2 AGREEMENT

NUMBER

Number is the form of a word that indicates whether the word is singular or plural.

2a. **When a word refers to one person, place, thing, or idea, the word is *singular* in number. When a word refers to more than one, it is *plural* in number.**

SINGULAR	house	drum	wife	I	he	each
PLURAL	houses	drums	wives	we	they	all

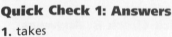 For more about plurals, see pages 1033–1034.

AGREEMENT OF SUBJECT AND VERB

2b. **A verb agrees with its subject in number.**

A subject and verb **agree** when they have the same number.

(1) Singular subjects take singular verbs.

EXAMPLE A **messenger gives** the king's orders.

(2) Plural subjects take plural verbs.

EXAMPLE Many **wives weep** after their husbands' departures during the war.

The first auxiliary (helping) verb in a verb phrase must agree with its subject.

EXAMPLES **He is** marching to war.
They are marching to war.

TIPS FOR SPELLING Generally, nouns ending in *s* are plural (*candles, ideas, neighbors, horses*), and verbs ending in *s* are singular (*sees, writes, speaks, carries*). However, verbs used with the singular pronouns *I* and *you* generally do not end in *s*.

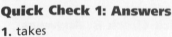 For more information about verb phrases, see pages 965, 991, and 993–994.

✓ QUICK CHECK I

For each of the following sentences, choose the correct form of the verb in parentheses.

EXAMPLE **1.** (*Do, Does*) you like folk tales like this one?
      1. *Do*

1. A tree spirit (*take, takes*) the shape of the absent husband.
2. Many days (*pass, passes*).
3. Then the husband (*return, returns*).
4. Dogs (*bark, barks*) at him.
5. The judge (*has, have*) suggested a solution.

Quick Check 1: Answers

1. takes
2. pass
3. returns
4. bark
5. has

Problems in Agreement

Prepositional Phrases Between Subjects and Verbs

2c. The number of a subject is not changed by a prepositional phrase following the subject.

NONSTANDARD One of the strongest heroes are Hercules.

STANDARD **One** of the strongest heroes **is** Hercules.

Indefinite Pronouns

Some pronouns do not refer to a definite person, place, thing, or idea and are therefore called *indefinite pronouns.*

2d. The following indefinite pronouns are singular: *anybody, anyone, each, either, everybody, everyone, neither, nobody, no one, one, somebody, someone.*

EXAMPLE **Neither** of these offers **relieves** him of his task.

2e. The following indefinite pronouns are plural: *both, few, many, several.*

EXAMPLE **Both** of the wild boar's tusks **frighten** Eurystheus.

2f. The following indefinite pronouns may be either singular or plural: *all, any, most, none, some.*

The number of these pronouns is often determined by the object in a prepositional phrase that follows the pronoun. If the pronoun refers to a singular object, the subject is singular. If the pronoun refers to a plural object, the subject is plural.

EXAMPLES **All** of the stable **needs** cleaning. [*All* refers to *stable.*]
All of the stalls **need** cleaning. [*All* refers to *stalls.*]

Compound Subjects

2g. Subjects joined by *and* usually take a plural verb.

EXAMPLE **Augeas** and **Eurystheus rule** kingdoms.

2h. When subjects are joined by *or* or *nor,* the verb agrees with the subject nearer the verb.

EXAMPLES Neither the **Hydra** nor Juno's huge **snakes defeat** Hercules.
Neither Juno's huge **snakes** nor the **Hydra defeats** Hercules.

COMPUTER NOTE You may want to create an indefinite-pronoun guide to help you use these pronouns correctly. First, summarize the information in rules 2d–2f and 2p–2r. Then, choose several examples to illustrate the rules. Using a computer, you can create a "Help" file in which to store this information. Call up your "Help" file whenever you run into difficulty with indefinite pronouns in your writing. If you don't use a computer, keep a writing notebook.

NOTE A compound subject that names only one person or thing takes a singular verb.

EXAMPLES The **friend** and **teacher** of Hercules **is** Chiron.
Law and **order suffers** when monsters roam the land.

Other Problems in Agreement

2i. **Collective nouns may be either singular or plural.**

A collective noun takes a singular verb when the noun refers to the group as a unit. A collective noun takes a plural verb when the noun refers to the individual parts or members of the group.

EXAMPLES   An oxen **herd goes** with Hercules. [The herd as a unit goes.]

The **herd call** to the stolen cattle. [The members of the herd individually call.]

2j. **When the subject follows the verb, find the subject, and make sure the verb agrees with it. The subject usually follows the verb in sentences beginning with** *here* **or** *there* **and in questions.**

EXAMPLES   There **is Centaurus,** and there **are** its **stars.**
Does the **fox** really not **want** the grapes?

The contractions *here's, there's,* and *where's* contain the verb *is* and should be used only with singular subjects.

NONSTANDARD   There's the constellations Hydra and Leo.
   STANDARD   There **are** the **constellations** Hydra and Leo.
   STANDARD   There's the **constellation** Hydra.

2k. **The contractions** *don't* **and** *doesn't* **must agree with their subjects.**

Use *don't* with plural subjects and with the pronouns *I* and *you*. Use *doesn't* with other singular subjects.

EXAMPLES   They **don't** like movies about Hercules, and **I don't** either.
This **film doesn't** seem realistic, but **that doesn't** matter to me.

2l. **Words stating amounts are usually singular.**

A word or phrase stating a weight, a measurement, or an amount of money or time is usually considered a single item. Such a word or phrase takes a singular verb.

EXAMPLE   Five **dollars is** too much for a movie ticket.

2m. **The title of a book or the name of an organization or country, even when plural in form, usually takes a singular verb.**

EXAMPLES   *Aesop's Fables* **is** on our reading list.
Has the **United States** signed the treaty?

NOTE When the subject of a sentence follows the verb, the word order is said to be *inverted*. To find the subject of a sentence with inverted order, restate the sentence in normal word order.

INVERTED   There **goes Hercules.**
NORMAL   Hercules **goes** there.

INVERTED   Into the clearing **stepped** the mighty **Hercules.**
NORMAL   The mighty **Hercules stepped** into the clearing.

2n. A few nouns, though plural in form, are singular and take singular verbs.

EXAMPLES   news, measles, mathematics, civics, mumps, physics

✓ QUICK CHECK 2

For the following sentences, correct each error in agreement.

EXAMPLE   **1.** There's many interesting stories about heroes.
   1. *There are many interesting stories about heroes.*

1. A flock of monstrous birds hover over the Stymphalian lake.
2. Doesn't the arrows of Hercules strike each bird in turn?
3. Neither Nereus nor his daughters foils Hercules.
4. The god of the oceans don't escape Hercules.
5. Some of the ancient myths seeks to explain actual geological or botanical facts.

AGREEMENT OF PRONOUN AND ANTECEDENT

2o. A pronoun agrees with its antecedent in number and gender.

An *antecedent* is the word the pronoun refers to. Some singular personal pronouns have forms that indicate gender. Masculine pronouns refer to males. Feminine pronouns refer to females. Neuter pronouns refer to things (neither male nor female) and sometimes to animals.

FEMININE	she	her	hers
MASCULINE	he	him	his
NEUTER	it	it	its

EXAMPLES   The **speaker** in "Annabel Lee" lost **his** bride.
Annabel Lee had given **her** heart to him.
Heaven sent **its** angels for Annabel Lee.

The antecedent of a personal pronoun can be another kind of pronoun, such as *each, neither,* or *one.* To determine the gender of a personal pronoun that refers to one of these other pronouns, look in the phrase that follows the antecedent.

EXAMPLES   **Each** of these **men** left **his** mark on the development of the American short story.
Neither of the **women** got what **she** wanted.

> **NOTE** When an antecedent may be either masculine or feminine, use both the masculine and the feminine forms.
>
> **EXAMPLES**   **No one** ever gave **his or her** approval of Poe's criticisms.
> **Everybody** wanted **his or her** writing in Poe's magazine.

Quick Check 2: Answers

1. hovers
2. Don't
3. foil
4. doesn't
5. seek

Problems in Agreement of Pronoun and Antecedent

Indefinite Pronouns

 For more about indefinite pronouns, see page 961.

2p. A singular pronoun is used to refer to *anybody, anyone, each, either, everybody, everyone, neither, nobody, no one, one, someone,* and *somebody.*

EXAMPLE   Each of these countries has **its** own Cinderella story.

2q. A plural pronoun is used to refer to *both, few, many,* and *several.*

EXAMPLES   **Both** of these stories take **their** characters from legend.
Many of these versions are similar, but **they** all differ.

2r. Either a singular or a plural pronoun may be used to refer to *all, any, most, none,* and *some.*

The number of the pronouns *all, any, most, none,* and *some* is determined by the object in the prepositional phrase following the pronoun.

EXAMPLES   **Some** of the story may come from the culture telling **it.**
[*Some* refers to the singular noun *story.*]
Some of the sisters are punished for **their** cruelty.
[*Some* refers to the plural noun *sisters.*]

Compound Subjects

2s. A plural pronoun is used to refer to two or more antecedents joined by *and.*

EXAMPLE   The **sisters and their mother** never share **their** fine clothing.

2t. A singular pronoun is used to refer to two or more singular antecedents joined by *or* or *nor.*

EXAMPLE   Neither **the mother nor a sister** shared **her** clothes.

Other Problems in Pronoun-Antecedent Agreement

 For more information about collective nouns, see page 959.

2u. Either a singular or a plural pronoun may be used with a collective noun.

EXAMPLES   The royal **family** was preparing **its** celebration.
The royal **family** are greeting **their** new princess.

2v. Words stating amounts usually take singular pronouns.

EXAMPLE   Admission costs five **dollars.** Maybe I can earn **it** in time.

2w. The title of a book or the name of an organization or a country, even when plural in form, usually takes a singular pronoun.

EXAMPLES I read *Folktales Around the World,* and **it** was great.
The **United Nations** can revise **its** charter.

2x. A few nouns, though plural in form, are singular and take singular pronouns.

EXAMPLE **Physics** is important, but **it** has nothing to do with folk tales.

✓ QUICK CHECK 3

For each blank in the following sentences, give a pronoun that will complete the meaning of the sentence. Then, identify the antecedent or antecedents of that pronoun.

EXAMPLE **1.** Kari or Leah will bring _____ copy of *The Glass Slipper.*
1. *her—Kari or Leah*

1. Aschenputtel and Cinderella got _____ names from ashes.
2. One of the stories features pigeons in _____ ending.
3. Many of the stories reward _____ heroes, but some don't.
4. The court cheered the prince and her and gave _____ a grand wedding.
5. Neither the prince nor the Pharaoh married the young woman _____ expected.

☞ See page 973 for a list of singular nouns that are plural in form.

Using Compound Antecedents

Sentences with singular antecedents joined by *or* or *nor* can sound awkward if the antecedents are of different genders. If the sentence sounds awkward, revise it to avoid the problem.

AWKWARD Ana or Ed will read her or his version of *Cinderella.*

REVISED **Ana** will read **her** version of *Cinderella,* or **Ed** will read **his.**

Similarly, a singular and a plural antecedent joined by *or* or *nor* can create an awkward or a confusing sentence. Revise such a sentence to avoid the problem.

AWKWARD Either my cousins or Mary will bring their video of *Cinderella.*

REVISED Either **my cousins** will bring **their** video of *Cinderella,* or **Mary** will bring **hers.**

Try It Out ✎

Revise each of the following sentences to eliminate awkward pronoun usage.

1. Neither her mother nor her sisters recognized that the girl was their own Aschenputtel.
2. Either birds or a fish help the heroine in their own way.
3. Did a fish or a falcon lend their help to Yeh-Shen?
4. Neither Yeh-Shen nor the king could have guessed her or his fate.
5. Joey or Linda will read his or her report on "Sealskin, Soulskin."

Quick Check 3: Answers

1. their—Aschenputtel and Cinderella
2. its—One
3. their—Many
4. them—prince and her
5. he—prince nor Pharaoh

Try It Out: Possible Answers

1. The mother and the sisters did not recognize that the girl was their own Aschenputtel.
2. Either birds help the heroine in their own way, or a fish does in its own way.
3. Did a fish or a falcon help Yeh-Shen?
4. Yeh-Shen and the king could not have guessed their fate.
5. Either Joey will read his report on "Sealskin, Soulskin," or Linda will read hers.

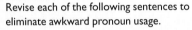

Language Handbook

NOTE Notice that the present participle and the past participle require helping verbs (forms of *be* and *have*).

☞ See page 990 for information about participles used as modifiers.

3 USING VERBS

THE PRINCIPAL PARTS OF A VERB

The four basic forms of a verb are called the **principal parts** of the verb.

3a. **The principal parts of a verb are the *base form*, the *present participle*, the *past*, and the *past participle*.**

BASE FORM	PRESENT PARTICIPLE	PAST	PAST PARTICIPLE
work	(is) working	worked	(have) worked
sing	(is) singing	sang	(have) sung

The principal parts of a verb are used to express the time that an action occurs.

PRESENT TIME   I **sing** rhythm and blues now.
We **are singing** along with the frog.

PAST TIME   The frog **sang** at the Big Time Weekly Concert.
We **have sung** there before.

FUTURE TIME   The audience **will sing** along with the frog.
By 8:00 P.M., we **will have sung** two numbers.

Regular Verbs

3b. **A *regular verb* forms its past and past participle by adding *–d* or *–ed* to the base form.**

BASE FORM	PRESENT PARTICIPLE	PAST	PAST PARTICIPLE
use	(is) using	used	(have) used
attack	(is) attacking	attacked	(have) attacked

Avoid the following common errors when forming the past or past participle of regular verbs:

1. leaving off the *–d* or *–ed* ending

NONSTANDARD   We use to think the frog couldn't sing.
STANDARD   We **used** to think the frog couldn't sing.

2. adding unnecessary letters

NONSTANDARD   The audience of animals attackted him.
STANDARD   The audience of animals **attacked** him.

✓ QUICK CHECK I

For each of the following sentences, supply the correct past or past participle form of the verb given in italics.

EXAMPLE 1. *discover*   Frog has _____ his singing talent.
          1. *discovered*

1. *cross*   He _____ over to the other side of the pond.
2. *visit*   He has _____ his friends to tell them of his wish to sing.
3. *join*   The birds already have _____ together to form a group.
4. *use*   Fox let Frog sing but also _____ a trick to fool Frog.
5. *leap*   When Frog was introduced, he _____ out on stage.

Irregular Verbs

3c. An *irregular verb* forms its past and past participle in some other way than by adding *–d* or *–ed* to the base form.

An irregular verb forms its past and past participle by

- changing vowels *or* consonants

	Base Form	Past	Past Participle
EXAMPLE	ring	rang	(have) rung

- changing vowels *and* consonants

	Base Form	Past	Past Participle
EXAMPLE	go	went	(have) gone

- making no changes

	Base Form	Past	Past Participle
EXAMPLE	spread	spread	(have) spread

> **TIPS FOR SPELLING**
>
> When you are not sure how to spell the principal parts of an irregular verb, look in a dictionary.

Avoid the following common errors when forming the past or past participle of irregular verbs:

1. using the past form with a helping verb

NONSTANDARD   Frog has went to the Big Time Weekly Concert.
STANDARD   Frog **went** to the Big Time Weekly Concert.
or
STANDARD   Frog **has gone** to the Big Time Weekly Concert.

2. using the past participle form without a helping verb

NONSTANDARD   I seen all of his shows.
STANDARD   I **have seen** all of his shows.

3. adding *–d* or *–ed* to the base form

NONSTANDARD   The elephant throwed a pineapple at the frog.
STANDARD   The elephant **threw** a pineapple at the frog.

Quick Check 1: Answers

1. crossed
2. visited
3. joined
4. used
5. leaped or leapt

Quick Check 2: Answers

1. brought
2. laid
3. led
4. built
5. caught

	COMMON IRREGULAR VERBS		

GROUP I: Each of these irregular verbs has the same form for its past and past participle.

BASE FORM	PRESENT PARTICIPLE	PAST	PAST PARTICIPLE
bring	(is) bringing	brought	(have) brought
build	(is) building	built	(have) built
catch	(is) catching	caught	(have) caught
hold	(is) holding	held	(have) held
lay	(is) laying	laid	(have) laid
lead	(is) leading	led	(have) led
say	(is) saying	said	(have) said
send	(is) sending	sent	(have) sent
spin	(is) spinning	spun	(have) spun
swing	(is) swinging	swung	(have) swung

 QUICK CHECK 2

For each of the following sentences, give the correct past or past participle form of the verb in parentheses.

EXAMPLE   **1.** Joey (*say*) he had the blues.
               1. *said*

1. Frog has (*bring*) rhythm and blues to the world.
2. Since then, many a guitarist has (*lay*) down a blues riff.
3. Many blues singers (*lead*) listeners to recall sad times.
4. Some musicians have (*build*) that sound using only a harmonica.
5. Others (*catch*) the beat with only their voice.

	COMMON IRREGULAR VERBS		

GROUP II: Each of these irregular verbs has a different form for its past and past participle.

BASE FORM	PRESENT PARTICIPLE	PAST	PAST PARTICIPLE
begin	(is) beginning	began	(have) begun
choose	(is) choosing	chose	(have) chosen
do	(is) doing	did	(have) done
draw	(is) drawing	drew	(have) drawn
go	(is) going	went	(have) gone
know	(is) knowing	knew	(have) known
run	(is) running	ran	(have) run
shake	(is) shaking	shook	(have) shaken
sing	(is) singing	sang	(have) sung
swim	(is) swimming	swam	(have) swum

978   Resource Center / Language Handbook

QUICK CHECK 3

For each of the following sentences, give the correct past or past participle form of the verb in parentheses.

EXAMPLE **I.** Louis Armstrong really (*know*) how to play jazz on his trumpet.
    I. *knew*

1. Some say rhythm and blues (*begin*) in the 1940s.
2. Like the frog, the legendary Muddy Waters (*draw*) crowds.
3. Who has (*sing*) with him?
4. Have you ever (*do*) the bump or the mashed potato?
5. In the story, the lion (*shake*) to the twist.

COMMON IRREGULAR VERBS			
GROUP III: Each of these irregular verbs has the same form for its base form, past, and past participle.			
BASE FORM	**PRESENT PARTICIPLE**	**PAST**	**PAST PARTICIPLE**
burst	(is) bursting	burst	(have) burst
cost	(is) costing	cost	(have) cost
cut	(is) cutting	cut	(have) cut
hit	(is) hitting	hit	(have) hit
hurt	(is) hurting	hurt	(have) hurt
let	(is) letting	let	(have) let
put	(is) putting	put	(have) put
read	(is) reading	read	(have) read
set	(is) setting	set	(have) set
spread	(is) spreading	spread	(have) spread

 QUICK CHECK 4

For each of the following sentences, give the correct past or past participle form of the verb in italics.

EXAMPLE **I.** How many people have been (*hurt*) by misunderstandings with others?
    I. *hurt*

1. *cost*   Slade and others like him have _____ Mr. Baumer a lot of money.
2. *hit*   Once, Slade _____ Mr. Baumer.
3. *let*   Yet, Mr. Baumer _____ Slade work for him.
4. *set*   Secretly, Mr. Baumer has _____ a trap for Slade.
5. *read*   Unlike Slade, Mr. Baumer _____ the warning.

Language Handbook

1. began
2. drew
3. sung
4. done
5. shook

Quick Check 4: Answers
1. cost
2. hit
3. let
4. set
5. read

Try It Out: Possible Answers

1. Butch retorted, "You lie!"
2. "Wow! That party was great!" beamed Tanya when the group met Monday morning at school.
3. "Way to go!" cried Jim's teammates, slapping him on the back after the game.
4. "Move it!" shouted the sergeant to the recruit.
5. "I can't believe you stabbed me in the back like that!" exclaimed Angela to her classmate.

Try It Out

Revise each of the following sentences to sound natural in a dialogue.

1. Butch replied, "I must say, old friend, that I cannot quite believe you."
2. "Gracious, what a marvelous party that was!" beamed Tanya when the group met Monday morning at school.
3. "Please accept our congratulations on a job well done," cried Jim's teammates, slapping him on the back after the game.
4. "I beg your pardon, but you are sitting in my seat," said the sergeant to the recruit.
5. "What an unfaithful friend you are to have spoken against me behind my back," exclaimed Angela to her classmate.

Using Nonstandard Verb Forms

TIPS FOR WRITERS

Using standard verb forms is important in almost all the writing that you do for school. Your readers expect standard usage in essays and reports. On the other hand, readers expect the dialogue in plays and short stories to sound natural. For dialogue to sound natural, it must reflect the speech patterns of real people, and real people speak in all sorts of nonstandard ways. Look at the following example from the short story "Bargain."

> "I think he hate me," Mr. Baumer went on. "That is the thing. He hate me for coming not from this country. I come here, sixteen years old, and learn to read and write, and I make a business, and so I think he hate me."

How might you translate this passage into standard English? How would that affect your impression of Mr. Baumer?

You may want to discuss the use of nonstandard verb forms with your teacher. Together you can decide how you can use such forms in your writing.

VERB TENSE

3d. The *tense* of a verb indicates the time of the action or state of being that is expressed by the verb.

Every verb has six tenses.

Present	Past	Future
Present Perfect	Past Perfect	Future Perfect

This time line shows how the six tenses are related to one another.

Past	*Present*	*Future*
existing or happening in the past	existing or happening now	existing or happening in the future

Past Perfect	*Present Perfect*	*Future Perfect*
existing or happening before a specific time in the past	existing or happening sometime before now or starting in the past and continuing now	existing or happening before a specific time in the future

Listing all forms of a verb in the six tenses is called **conjugating** a verb.

CONJUGATION OF THE VERB *WRITE*

PRESENT TENSE

SINGULAR	PLURAL
I write	we write
you write	you write
he, she, *or* it writes	they write

PAST TENSE

SINGULAR	PLURAL
I wrote	we wrote
you wrote	you wrote
he, she, *or* it wrote	they wrote

FUTURE TENSE

SINGULAR	PLURAL
I will write	we will write
you will write	you will write
he, she, *or* it will write	they will write

PRESENT PERFECT TENSE

SINGULAR	PLURAL
I have written	we have written
you have written	you have written
he, she, *or* it has written	they have written

PAST PERFECT TENSE

SINGULAR	PLURAL
I had written	we had written
you had written	you had written
he, she, *or* it had written	they had written

FUTURE PERFECT TENSE

SINGULAR	PLURAL
I will have written	we will have written
you will have written	you will have written
he, she, *or* it will have written	they will have written

NOTE In the future tense and in the future perfect tense, the helping verb *shall* is sometimes used in place of *will*.

Consistency of Tense

3e. Do not change needlessly from one tense to another.

When writing about events in the present, use verbs in the present tense. When writing about events in the past, use verbs in the past tense.

INCONSISTENT	When they were satisfied, they begin planting.
CONSISTENT	When they **are** satisfied, they **begin** planting.
CONSISTENT	When they **were** satisfied, they **began** planting.

Quick Check 5: Possible Answers

1. No one told them no, so they started to work.

2. It was hard, too; over and over, they carried dozens of sacks of dirt up the stairs.

3. None of the neighbors noticed them, or maybe they didn't mind.

4. At last, almost before they knew it, the rooftop was ready.

5. The rich, black earth waited for seeds.

COMPUTER NOTE

Most word processors can help you check your writing to be sure that you've used verbs correctly. Spelling checkers will highlight misspelled verb forms such as *drownded* or *costed*. Style-checking software can point out inconsistent verb tenses and may also highlight questionable uses of problem verb pairs such as *lie/lay* or *rise/raise*.

☑ QUICK CHECK 5

Read the following paragraph, and decide whether it should be rewritten in the present or past tense. Then, change the verb forms to make the verb tense consistent.

EXAMPLE   [1] These city boys enjoyed gardening when they get the chance.

1. These city boys enjoyed gardening when they got the chance.

or

1. These city boys enjoy gardening when they get the chance.

[1] No one tells them no, so they started to work. [2] It is hard, too; over and over, they carried dozens of sacks of dirt up the stairs. [3] None of the neighbors noticed them, or maybe they don't mind. [4] At last, almost before they know it, the rooftop is ready. [5] The rich, black earth waits for seeds.

SPECIAL PROBLEMS WITH VERBS

Sit and *Set*

(1) The verb *sit* means "rest in an upright, seated position." *Sit* seldom takes an object.

(2) The verb *set* means "put (something) in a place." *Set* usually takes an object.

BASE FORM	PRESENT PARTICIPLE	PAST	PAST PARTICIPLE
sit (rest)	(is) sitting	sat	(have) sat
set (put)	(is) setting	set	(have) set

EXAMPLES   Let's **sit** in the shade. [no object]

Let's **set** the buckets here. [Let's set what? *Buckets* is the object.]

Lie and *Lay*

(1) The verb *lie* means "rest," "recline," or "be in a place." *Lie* never takes an object.

(2) The verb *lay* means "put (something) in a place." *Lay* usually takes an object.

BASE FORM	PRESENT PARTICIPLE	PAST	PAST PARTICIPLE
lie (rest)	(is) lying	lay	(have) lain
lay (put)	(is) laying	laid	(have) laid

EXAMPLES   In the photograph, juicy, red watermelons **lay** on rich earth. [no object]

They **laid** dirt on the roof. [They laid what? *Dirt* is the object.]

Rise and *Raise*

(1) The verb *rise* means "go up" or "get up." *Rise* never takes an object.

(2) The verb *raise* means "lift up" or "cause (something) to rise." *Raise* usually takes an object.

BASE FORM	PRESENT PARTICIPLE	PAST	PAST PARTICIPLE
rise (go up)	(is) rising	rose	(have) risen
raise (lift up)	(is) raising	raised	(have) raised

EXAMPLES   My next-door neighbors **rise** very early in the morning. [no object]

They **raise** the blinds at dawn. [They raise what? *Blinds* is the object.]

 QUICK CHECK 6

For each of the following sentences, choose the correct verb form in parentheses.

EXAMPLE   **1.** Our garden (*lies, lays*) in the sunniest corner of our backyard.

    1. *lies*

1. Juan Guerrero (*raises, rises*) the bag containing the tomatillos he has grown.
2. Like Juan, other people also (*sat, set*) out their own plants each spring.
3. He will not just (*sit, set*) and remain idle.
4. Avoiding the heat of the day, Mr. Garcia also (*raises, rises*) early to tend his plot.
5. Once, only junk and trash (*lay, laid*) there, but now there is a beautiful garden.

Quick Check 6: Answers

1. raises
2. set
3. sit
4. rises
5. lay

Language Handbook

NOTE Possessive pronouns (such as *my, your,* and *our*) are also sometimes called ***possessive adjectives.***

☞ For more about possessive pronouns, see pages 960 and 1027.

NOTE To choose the correct pronoun in a compound subject, try each form of the pronoun separately.

EXAMPLE: Beterli and (*he, him*) quarreled. [*He* quarreled. *Him* quarreled.]

ANSWER: Beterli and **he** quarreled.

☞ For more about predicate nominatives, see page 1006.

4 USING PRONOUNS

CASE

Case is the form of a noun or a pronoun that shows how it is used. There are three cases: ***nominative, objective,*** and ***possessive.*** The form of a noun is the same for both the nominative and objective cases. A noun changes its form for the possessive case, usually by the addition of an apostrophe and an *s.*

Most personal pronouns have different forms for all three cases.

PERSONAL PRONOUNS		
SINGULAR		
NOMINATIVE CASE	**OBJECTIVE CASE**	**POSSESSIVE CASE**
I	me	my, mine
you	you	your, yours
he, she, it	him, her, it	his, her, hers, its
PLURAL		
NOMINATIVE CASE	**OBJECTIVE CASE**	**POSSESSIVE CASE**
we	us	our, ours
you	you	your, yours
they	them	their, theirs

The Nominative Case

4a. **A subject of a verb is in the nominative case.**

EXAMPLES **I** enjoy Anne McCaffrey's writing style. [*I* is the subject of *enjoy.*]

He and **she** were still at home. [*He* and *she* are the subjects of *were.*]

4b. **A *predicate nominative* is in the nominative case.**

A ***predicate nominative*** follows a linking verb and explains or identifies the subject of the verb. A personal pronoun used as a predicate nominative follows a form of the verb *be* (*am, is, are, was, were, be,* or *been*).

EXAMPLES The last one to arrive there was **he.** [*He* identifies the subject *one.*]

Could it be **she**? [*She* identifies the subject *it.*]

984 Resource Center / Language Handbook

The Objective Case

4c. A *direct object* is in the objective case.

A **direct object** follows an action verb and tells *who* or *what* receives the action of the verb.

EXAMPLES   The bronze dragon's choice amazed **us**. [*Us* tells *who* was amazed.]

Heth moved his wings and dried **them**. [*Them* tells *what* Heth dried.]

4d. An *indirect object* is in the objective case.

An **indirect object** comes between an action verb and a direct object and tells *to whom* or *to what* or *for whom* or *for what*.

EXAMPLES   Heth asked **him** a question. [*Him* tells *to whom* Heth asked a question.]

The dragon and his rider taught **them** a lesson. [*Them* tells *to whom* they taught a lesson.]

4e. An *object of a preposition* is in the objective case.

A **prepositional phrase** contains a preposition, a noun or pronoun called the **object of the preposition,** and any modifiers of that object.

EXAMPLES   like a **hero**   near **us**
            next to **Dr. Chang**   without **you** and **me**

A pronoun used as the object of a preposition should always be in the objective case.

EXAMPLES   A great honor had been bestowed on **him**.
            We went with **her** to the mall.

☑ QUICK CHECK I

For each of the following sentences, identify the correct personal pronoun in parentheses.

EXAMPLE   **1.** Rikki's gentleness surprised (*she, her*).
           1. *her*

1. Rikki had almost drowned, but an English boy named Teddy rescued (*he, him*).
2. Could a mongoose live with (*they, them*) happily?
3. Teddy's mother wasn't sure whether a mongoose would make a good pet, but Rikki gave (*she, her*) a surprise.
4. Didn't (*he, him*) save their lives?
5. "The winner of this battle will be (*I, me*)!" he vowed.

☞ For more about direct objects, see page 1005.

☞ For more about indirect objects, see page 1005.

☞ For a list of prepositions, see page 967. For more about prepositional phrases, see pages 967, 990, and 991–992.

Quick Check 1: Answers

1. him
2. them
3. her
4. he
5. I

Try It Out: Answers

1. The other candidates and we dashed to the Impression.
2. "Save a good place for my friends and me," someone called.
3. I wondered who would be first and thought, "Maybe it'll be I!"
4. When K'last asked me who Keevan was, I answered, "That's he."
5. Keevan was the smallest, yet it was he who impressed the bronze dragon.

Try It Out ✎

Revise each of the following sentences to show standard and polite usage of pronouns.

1. We and the other candidates dashed to the Impression.
2. "Save a good place for me and my friends," someone called.
3. I wondered who would be first and thought, "Maybe it'll be me!"
4. When K'last asked me who Keevan was, I answered, "That's him."
5. Keevan was the smallest, yet it was him who impressed the bronze dragon.

NOTE In spoken English, the use of *whom* is becoming less common. In fact, when you are speaking, you may correctly begin any question with *who* regardless of the grammar of the sentence. In written English, however, you should distinguish between *who* and *whom*.

TIPS FOR WRITERS

Improving Pronoun Usage

Expressions such as *It's me, That's her,* and *It was them* are accepted in everyday speaking. In writing, however, such expressions are generally considered nonstandard and should be avoided.

STANDARD   It is **I.**   That is **she.**   It was **they.**

Additionally, remember that it is considered polite to put first-person pronouns (*I, me, mine, we, us, ours*) last in compound constructions.

EXAMPLE   **The dragonriders and we** arrived at the Hatching Ground.

SPECIAL PRONOUN PROBLEMS

Who and Whom

The pronoun *who* has different forms in the nominative and objective cases. *Who* is the nominative form; *whom* is the objective form.

When deciding whether to use *who* or *whom* in a question, follow these steps:

STEP 1:	Rephrase the question as a statement.
STEP 2:	Decide how the pronoun is used in the statement—as subject, predicate nominative, object of the verb, or object of a preposition.
STEP 3:	Determine the case of the pronoun according to the rules of standard English.
STEP 4:	Select the correct form of the pronoun.

EXAMPLE: (*Who, Whom*) did Jerry see?

STEP 1:	The statement is *Jerry did see (who, whom).*
STEP 2:	The subject of the verb is *Jerry,* the verb is *did see,* and the pronoun is the direct object.
STEP 3:	A pronoun used as a direct object should be in the objective case.
STEP 4:	The objective form is *whom.*
ANSWER:	**Whom** did Jerry see?

Pronouns with Appositives

Sometimes a pronoun is followed directly by a noun that identifies the pronoun. Such a noun is called an **appositive.** To choose which pronoun to use before an appositive, omit the appositive, and try each form of the pronoun separately.

EXAMPLE: (*We, Us*) boys live in the Carolinas. [*Boys* is the appositive.] *We* live in the Carolinas. *Us* live in the Carolinas.

ANSWER: **We** boys live in the Carolinas.

Reflexive Pronouns

Reflexive pronouns (such as *myself, himself,* and *yourselves*) can be used as objects. Do not use the nonstandard forms *hisself* and *theirself* or *theirselves* in place of *himself* and *themselves*.

NONSTANDARD   Jerry prepared a fire for hisself.
STANDARD   Jerry prepared a fire for **himself.**

✓ QUICK CHECK 2

For each of the following sentences, choose the correct pronoun in parentheses.

EXAMPLE   **1.** May (*we, us*) students read aloud?
    1. *we*

1. For (*who, whom*) did the boy work?
2. Jerry did not often play with (*we, us*) in the neighborhood.
3. (*Who, Whom*) wrote *The Yearling*?
4. He promised (*hisself, himself*) that he would do a good job.
5. They seemed pleased with (*theirselves, themselves*).

5 USING MODIFIERS

COMPARISON OF MODIFIERS

A *modifier* is a word, a phrase, or a clause that describes or limits the meaning of another word. Two kinds of modifiers—*adjectives* and *adverbs*—may be used to compare things.

5a. The three degrees of comparison of modifiers are *positive, comparative,* and *superlative.*

POSITIVE	cold	loud	politely
COMPARATIVE	colder	louder	more politely
SUPERLATIVE	coldest	loudest	most politely

Regular Comparison

(1) Most one-syllable modifiers form their comparative and superlative degrees by adding *–er* and *–est.*

POSITIVE	sharp	calm	cold
COMPARATIVE	sharper	calmer	colder
SUPERLATIVE	sharpest	calmest	coldest

 For more about appositives, see page 995.

For more about reflexive pronouns, see page 961.

NOTE To show decreasing comparisons, all modifiers form their comparative and superlative degrees with *less* and *least.*

POSITIVE
 calm
 rapidly
COMPARATIVE
 less calm
 less rapidly
SUPERLATIVE
 least calm
 least rapidly

Quick Check 2: Answers

1. whom
2. us
3. Who
4. himself
5. themselves

Resources

Grammar and Language

■ *Language Handbook Worksheets,* pp. 47–56

(2) Some two-syllable modifiers form their comparative and superlative degrees by adding –er and –est. Others form their comparative and superlative degrees by using more and most.

POSITIVE	simple	sudden	quietly
COMPARATIVE	simpler	more sudden	more quietly
SUPERLATIVE	simplest	most sudden	most quietly

(3) Modifiers that have three or more syllables form their comparative and superlative degrees by using more and most.

POSITIVE	luxurious	fearfully	curious
COMPARATIVE	more luxurious	more fearfully	more curious
SUPERLATIVE	most luxurious	most fearfully	most curious

Irregular Comparison

Some modifiers do not form their comparative and superlative degrees by using the regular methods.

POSITIVE	bad	far	good	well	many	much
COMPARATIVE	worse	farther	better	better	more	more
SUPERLATIVE	worst	farthest	best	best	most	most

✓ QUICK CHECK I

TIPS FOR SPELLING

Drop the final silent e before a suffix beginning with a vowel.

EXAMPLES   safe + er = safer
ripe + est = ripest
gentle + er = gentler

Give the forms for the comparative and superlative degrees of the following modifiers.

EXAMPLE   **I.** colorful
             I. *more (less) colorful, most (least) colorful*

1. fine   5. daring   9. well
2. cautiously   6. comfortable   10. dainty
3. gladly   7. much
4. thankful   8. cozy

Uses of Comparative and Superlative Forms

5b.   **Use the comparative degree when comparing two things. Use the superlative degree when comparing more than two.**

COMPARATIVE	This mouse is **safer** than the Town Mouse. She sleeps **more soundly** than the Town Mouse.
SUPERLATIVE	This mouse is the **safest** one in the world. Of the three animals, the cat slept **most soundly.**

5c.   **Use *good* to modify a noun or a pronoun. Use *well* to modify a verb.**

EXAMPLE   The Town Mouse enjoyed **good food.** She **ate well.**

Quick Check 1: Answers

1. finer (less fine), finest (least fine)
2. more (less) cautiously, most (least) cautiously
3. more (less) gladly, most (least) gladly
4. more (less) thankful, most (least) thankful
5. more (less) daring, most (least) daring
6. more (less) comfortable, most (least) comfortable
7. more (less), most (least)
8. cozier (less cozy), coziest (least cozy)
9. better (less well), best (least well)
10. daintier (less dainty), daintiest (least dainty)

5d. Use adjectives, not adverbs, after linking verbs.

EXAMPLE   The Town Mouse's life seemed **wonderful.** [*not* wonderfully]

5e. Avoid using double comparisons.

A *double comparison* is the use of both *–er* and *more* (*less*) or both *–est* and *most* (*least*) to form a comparison. A comparison should be formed in only one of these two ways, not both.

EXAMPLE   The Country Mouse is **safer** [*not* more safer] than the Town Mouse.

5f. A *double negative* is the use of two negative words to express one negative idea.

Common Negative Words			
barely	never	none	nothing
hardly	no	no one	nowhere
neither	nobody	not (–n't)	scarcely

NONSTANDARD   She hasn't never liked cats.

STANDARD   She hasn't ever [*or* has never] liked cats.

✓ *QUICK CHECK 2*

The following sentences contain incorrect forms of comparison. Revise each sentence, using the correct form.

EXAMPLE   **1.** The acorns were the more delicious of all the foods.
           1. *The acorns were the most delicious of all the foods.*

1. Of course, the Town Mouse had the more finer foods.
2. However, the Country Mouse couldn't hardly enjoy those foods.
3. To the mice, was the cat most dangerous than the dog?
4. The Town Mouse ate worst on her visit to the country.
5. Of the two mice, which is the safest?

PLACEMENT OF MODIFIERS

5g. Place modifying words, phrases, and clauses as close as possible to the words they modify.

Notice how the meaning of the following sentence changes when the position of the phrase *from the country* changes.

Quick Check 2: Answers
1. Of course, the Town Mouse had the finer foods.
2. However, the Country Mouse could hardly enjoy those foods.
3. To the mice, was the cat more dangerous than the dog?
4. The Town Mouse did not eat well on her visit to the country.
5. Of the two mice, which is the safer?

The mouse **from the country** saw a cat. [The phrase modifies *mouse.*]

The mouse saw a cat **from the country.** [The phrase modifies *cat.*]

Prepositional Phrases

A *prepositional phrase* consists of a preposition, a noun or a pronoun called the *object of the preposition,* and any modifiers of that object. A prepositional phrase used as an adjective should be placed directly after the word it modifies.

MISPLACED   A cat would not be dangerous to the mice with a bell.

CLEAR   A cat **with a bell** would not be dangerous to the mice.

A prepositional phrase used as an adverb should be placed near the word it modifies.

MISPLACED   The mice had a meeting about the cat **in fear.**

CLEAR   **In fear,** the mice had a meeting about the cat.

Avoid placing a prepositional phrase in a position where it can modify either of two words. Place the phrase so that it clearly modifies the word you intend it to modify.

MISPLACED   The mouse said in the morning she would go. [Does the phrase modify *said* or *would go?*]

CLEAR   The mouse said she would go **in the morning.**

or

CLEAR   **In the morning,** the mouse said she would go.

Participial Phrases

A *participial phrase* consists of a verb form—either a present participle or a past participle—and its related words. A participial phrase modifies a noun or a pronoun. Like a prepositional phrase, a participial phrase should be placed as close as possible to the word it modifies.

MISPLACED   The mice hid from the cat scurrying fearfully.

CLEAR   **Scurrying fearfully,** the mice hid from the cat.

A participial phrase that does not clearly and sensibly modify any word in the sentence is a *dangling participial phrase.* To correct a dangling phrase, supply a word that the phrase can modify, or add a subject, a verb, or both to the dangling modifier.

DANGLING   Worried constantly, a plan was needed.

CLEAR   Worried constantly, **the mice** needed a plan.

or

CLEAR   The mice needed a plan **because they worried** constantly.

☞ For more about prepositions and prepositional phrases, see pages 967, 985, and 991–992.

☞ For more about participial phrases, see page 993.

Clauses

A *clause* is a group of words that contains a verb and its subject and that is used as a part of a sentence. An *adjective clause* modifies a noun or a pronoun. Most adjective clauses begin with a relative pronoun, such as *that, which, who, whom,* or *whose.* An *adverb clause* modifies a verb, an adjective, or another adverb. Most adverb clauses begin with a subordinating conjunction, such as *although, while, if,* or *because.*

Like phrases, clauses should be placed as close as possible to the words they modify.

MISPLACED   The fable was written by Aesop that we read today.
CLEAR   The fable **that we read today** was written by Aesop.

 QUICK CHECK 3

Each of the following sentences contains a misplaced or dangling modifier. Revise each sentence so that it is clear and correct.

EXAMPLE   **1.** A cat was frightening the mice with sharp claws and teeth.
   1. *A cat with sharp claws and teeth was frightening the mice.*

1. The mice complained about the cat at the meeting.
2. A bell could protect the mice on the cat.
3. Ringing loudly with each step, the mice could run away.
4. The plan had a flaw that he was suggesting.
5. An old mouse questioned the young mouse shaking his head sadly.

---

6   PHRASES

6a.   A *phrase* is a group of related words that is used as a single part of speech and does not contain a verb and its subject.

   VERB PHRASE   should have been stabled
PREPOSITIONAL PHRASE   with a shudder and whitened eyes

THE PREPOSITIONAL PHRASE

6b.   A *prepositional phrase* includes a preposition, a noun or pronoun called the *object of the preposition,* and any modifiers of that object.

EXAMPLES   The runaway was filled **with confusion and fear.**
   The colt **in front of them** climbed **up the wall.**

☞ For more about clauses, see Part 7: Clauses.

COMPUTER NOTE

A computer can help you find and correct nonstandard forms of modifiers such as *baddest, expensiver,* and *mostest.* However, the computer cannot help you make sure that a modifier is not misplaced or dangling. You will need to check the placement of your modifiers yourself.

☞ For more information about verb phrases, see pages 965, 970, and 1002.

☞ For a list of commonly used prepositions, see page 967.

Language Handbook

Quick Check 3: Possible Answers

1. At the meeting, the mice complained about the cat.
2. A bell on the cat could protect the mice.
3. Ringing loudly with each step, a bell would warn the mice to run away.
4. The plan that he was suggesting had a flaw.
5. Shaking his head sadly, an old mouse questioned the young mouse.

Resources

Grammar and Language

■ *Language Handbook Worksheets,* pp. 57–69

The Adjective Phrase

6c. An *adjective phrase* is a prepositional phrase that modifies a noun or a pronoun.

An adjective phrase tells *what kind* or *which one*.

EXAMPLES Robert Frost was a poet **of nature.** [What kind?]
"The Runaway" is the one **about a colt.** [Which one?]

More than one adjective phrase may modify the same word.

EXAMPLE A pasture **of snow on a mountain** upsets him. [The phrases *of snow* and *on a mountain* modify *pasture.*]

The Adverb Phrase

6d. An *adverb phrase* is a prepositional phrase that modifies a verb, an adjective, or an adverb.

An adverb phrase tells *how, when, where, why,* or *to what extent* (that is, *how long, how many,* or *how far*).

EXAMPLES The colt bolted **with a nervous snort.** [How?]
The colt seemed uneasy **because of the snow.** [Why?]
The poem takes place late **in the day.** [When?]
Frost had written poetry **for many years.** [How long?]

More than one adverb phrase may modify the same word or words.

EXAMPLE **At the Kennedy Inauguration,** Frost read **to the American people.**

An adverb phrase may be modified by an adjective phrase.

EXAMPLE **In his poem about the runaway,** Frost uses several verbals. [The adverb phrase modifies the verb *uses.* The adjective phrase modifies *poem.*]

 QUICK CHECK I

Identify the prepositional phrase or phrases in each numbered sentence in the following paragraph. Then, label each phrase as an *adjective phrase* or an *adverb phrase*. Give the word the phrase modifies.

EXAMPLE [1] They make judgments about the colt and its care.
1. *about the colt and its care—adjective phrase—judgments*

[1] Many of Robert Frost's poems contain imagery from nature. [2] These images say much about people and human nature. [3] "The Runaway" focuses on a colt's experiences during its first winter. [4] In the poem Frost shows observers' reactions to the colt. [5] The colt, the subject of conversation between the observers, is important to them.

Quick Check 1: Answers

1. of Robert Frost's poems—adjective phrase—many; from nature—adjective phrase—imagery

2. about people and human nature—adjective phrase—much

3. on a colt's experiences—adverb phrase—focuses; during its first winter—adjective phrase—experiences

4. In the poem—adverb phrase—shows; to the colt—adjective phrase—reactions

5. of conversation—adjective phrase—subject; between the observers—adjective phrase—conversation; to them—adverb phrase—important

VERBALS AND VERBAL PHRASES

A **verbal** is a form of a verb that is used as a noun, an adjective, or an adverb. There are three kinds of verbals: the *participle,* the *gerund,* and the *infinitive.*

Participles and Participial Phrases

6e. A *participle* is a verb form that can be used as an adjective.

There are two kinds of participles—*present participles* and *past participles.*

(1) *Present participles* end in *–ing.*

EXAMPLE The rats **swimming** ashore alarmed them. [*Swimming,* a form of the verb *swim,* modifies *rats.*]

(2) Most *past participles* end in *–d* or *–ed.* Others are irregularly formed.

EXAMPLES No one was on the **abandoned** ship. [*Abandoned,* a form of the verb *abandon,* modifies *ship.*]

The rats, **known** for their ferocity, swam toward the sailors. [*Known,* a form of the verb *know,* modifies *rats.*]

6f. A *participial phrase* consists of a participle and all the words related to the participle. The entire phrase is used as an adjective.

EXAMPLES **Seeing a ship nearby,** scores of rats dove into the sea. [The participial phrase modifies the noun *scores.* The noun *ship* is the direct object of the present participle *seeing.*]

We could see the sharks **feasting hungrily on the swarms of rats.** [The participial phrase modifies the noun *sharks.* The adverb *hungrily* and the adverb phrase *on the swarms of rats* modify the present participle *feasting.*]

☞ For information on placement of participial phrases, see page 990.

Gerunds and Gerund Phrases

6g. A *gerund* is a verb form ending in *–ing* that is used as a noun.

SUBJECT	**Singing** can be fun.
PREDICATE NOMINATIVE	My favorite pastime is **singing.**
OBJECT OF PREPOSITION	I warm up before **singing.**
DIRECT OBJECT	Do you enjoy **singing?**

6h. A *gerund phrase* consists of a gerund and all the words related to the gerund.

EXAMPLE **Counting the innumerable rats on the lighthouse** calmed the men. [The gerund phrase is the subject of the sentence. The noun *rats* is the direct object of the gerund *counting*.]

Infinitives and Infinitive Phrases

6i. An *infinitive* is a verb form that can be used as a noun, an adjective, or an adverb. Infinitives usually begin with *to*.

NOUNS **To escape** was their sole desire. [subject]
Was the sailors' fate **to become** dinner? [predicate nominative]
They had **to signal** but not **to let** the rats in. [direct objects]

ADJECTIVES The time **to signal** was now. [*To signal* modifies *time*.]
Who was the first man **to crack** under the pressure? [*To crack* modifies *man*.]

ADVERBS Rescuers were quick **to answer**. [*To answer* modifies *quick*.]
They came to the island **to tend** the light. [*To tend* modifies *came*.]

6j. An *infinitive phrase* consists of an infinitive and its modifiers and complements. The entire infinitive phrase may act as an adjective, an adverb, or a noun.

EXAMPLES Lighthouses are one way **to warn ships away from rocks.** [adjective]
The men were grateful **to see the ship.** [adverb]
To be rescued was their only hope. [noun]

☑ QUICK CHECK 2

Identify each italicized phrase in the following sentences as *participial*, *gerund*, or *infinitive*.

EXAMPLE 1. *Swimming in the sea* was easy for the rats.
    1. gerund

1. The rats, *lured by the scent,* approached the lighthouse.
2. *Seeing the laughing men* enraged the frenzied rats.
3. They tried *to get in through the windows and door.*
4. *Clawing and biting the metal, glass, and stone,* they succeeded.
5. What happened to the horrified men left *to fend for themselves*?

NOTE *To* plus a noun or a pronoun (*to class, to them, to the dance*) is a prepositional phrase, not an infinitive. Be careful not to confuse infinitives with prepositional phrases beginning with *to*.

INFINITIVE I want **to go.**
PREPOSITIONAL PHRASE I want to go **to sea.**

Quick Check 2: Answers

1. participial
2. gerund
3. infinitive
4. participial
5. infinitive

APPOSITIVES AND APPOSITIVE PHRASES

6k. An *appositive* is a noun or a pronoun placed beside another noun or pronoun to identify or explain it.

Appositives are often set off from the rest of the sentence by commas or dashes. However, when an appositive is necessary to the meaning of the sentence or when it is closely related to the word it refers to, no commas are necessary.

EXAMPLES The author **George G. Toudouze** wrote the story "Three Skeleton Key." [The noun *George G. Toudouze* identifies the noun *author*.]

The men saw a strange ship, **one** with Dutch lines and three masts. [The pronoun *one* refers to the noun *ship*.]

Their victims—the **captain** and **crew**—had vanished. [The nouns *captain* and *crew* explain who were the victims.]

6l. An *appositive phrase* consists of an appositive and its modifiers.

EXAMPLES Le Gleo, **one of the lighthouse keepers,** had horrible nightmares. [The adjective phrase *of the lighthouse keepers* modifies the appositive *one*.]

Rats, **the foul scourge of sailing ships,** pressed for entrance. [The article *the*, the adjective *foul*, and the adjective phrase *of sailing ships* modify the appositive *scourge*.]

☞ For information on the use of commas with appositives and appositive phrases, see page 1020.

✓ QUICK CHECK 3

Identify the appositives or appositive phrases in the following sentences. Give the word or words each appositive or appositive phrase identifies or explains.

EXAMPLE 1. The rats, a huge and hardy breed, swarmed the decks.
   1. *a huge and hardy breed—rats*

1. Three men—the narrator, Le Gleo, and Itchoua—stared in horror at the rats.
2. The entire crew would likely have perished but for the engineer, a brave man.
3. Terriers, dogs bred for hunting, were certainly no match for these vicious rats.
4. The supply boat, the last one of the month, would be no help because it would arrive too late.
5. His friend Le Gleo was never the same again.

Quick Check 3: Answers

1. the narrator, Le Gleo, and Itchoua—men
2. a brave man—engineer
3. dogs bred for hunting—Terriers
4. the last one of the month—supply boat
5. Le Gleo—friend

Try It Out: Possible Answers

1. Three Skeleton Key was a small rock about twenty miles offshore.

2. Three convicts, in hiding after escaping from prison, had died there.

3. People said that the dead men's skeletons danced at night.

4. To save money, he volunteered for the lighthouse job.

5. Having smooth, slick surfaces, the rocks were dangerous.

Resources

Grammar and Language

- *Language Handbook Worksheets,* pp. 70–77

Try It Out ✎

For each of the following items, use phrases to combine the short, choppy sentences into one smooth sentence.

1. Three Skeleton Key was a small rock. It was about twenty miles offshore.

2. Three convicts had died there. They were in hiding after escaping from prison.

3. People said that the dead men's skeletons danced. They danced at night.

4. He wanted to save money. He volunteered for the lighthouse job.

5. The rocks had smooth, slick surfaces. They were dangerous.

TIPS FOR WRITERS

Using Phrases to Combine Sentences

Knowing how to use different kinds of phrases can help you improve your writing. For example, to revise a series of choppy sentences, combine them by turning at least one sentence into a phrase.

CHOPPY	A beautiful ship approached. The ship was a Dutch three-master.
APPOSITIVE PHRASE	A beautiful ship, **a Dutch three-master,** approached.
PARTICIPIAL PHRASE	A beautiful Dutch ship **having three masts** approached.
INFINITIVE PHRASE	A beautiful Dutch three-master continued **to approach us.**

7 CLAUSES

7a. A *clause* is a group of words that contains a verb and its subject and that is used as a part of a sentence.

Every clause has a subject and a verb. However, not every clause expresses a complete thought.

COMPLETE THOUGHT   **Wagons delivered** milk daily.

INCOMPLETE THOUGHT   before **cars were invented**

The two kinds of clauses are the *independent clause* and the *subordinate clause.*

THE INDEPENDENT CLAUSE

7b. An *independent* (or *main*) *clause* expresses a complete thought and can stand by itself as a sentence.

                               S   V

INDEPENDENT CLAUSE   Joseph pulled the wagon.

THE SUBORDINATE CLAUSE

7c. A *subordinate* (or *dependent*) *clause* does not express a complete thought and cannot stand alone as a sentence.

                                   S   V

SUBORDINATE CLAUSE   that Pierre drove

The meaning of a subordinate clause is complete only when the clause is attached to an independent clause.

EXAMPLE   Joseph pulled the wagon **that Pierre drove.**

 QUICK CHECK I

Identify each of the following groups of words as an *independent clause* or a *subordinate clause*.

EXAMPLE   **1.** because Pierre was growing old
                1. *subordinate clause*

1. although Pierre did not read or write
2. everyone liked him
3. although he arrived early each day to get his wagon
4. when he spoke to his horse
5. Joseph knew every stop on the route

The Adjective Clause

7d.   An *adjective clause* is a subordinate clause that modifies a noun or a pronoun.

An adjective clause usually follows the word it modifies and tells *which one* or *what kind.*

EXAMPLES   Joseph knew every house **that they served.** [Which house?]

   Pierre was a man **who loved his job.** [What kind of man?]

An adjective clause is usually introduced by a *relative pronoun.*

Relative Pronouns				
that	which	who	whom	whose

A *relative pronoun* relates an adjective clause to the word that the clause modifies.

EXAMPLES   After work, Pierre, **who had seemed fit,** limped slowly. [The relative pronoun *who* relates the clause to the noun *Pierre.*]

   St. Joseph, **whose name the horse bore,** was also kind and faithful. [The relative pronoun *whose* relates the clause to the noun *St. Joseph.*]

Sometimes a relative pronoun is preceded by a preposition that is part of the adjective clause.

EXAMPLE   The character **to whom I am referring** is Jacques.

☞ For information on when to set off adjective clauses with commas, see rule 13i(1) on page 1020.

 NOTE   The relative pronouns *who* and *whom* are used to refer to people only. The relative pronoun *that* is used to refer both to people and to things. The relative pronoun *which* is used to refer to things only.

Quick Check 1: Answers

1. subordinate clause
2. independent clause
3. subordinate clause
4. subordinate clause
5. independent clause

QUICK CHECK 2

Identify the adjective clause in each of the following sentences. Give the relative pronoun and the word that the relative pronoun refers to.

EXAMPLE 1. Jacques, who was the foreman, seemed kind.
  1. *who was the foreman, who—Jacques*

1. Pierre Dupin worked for a milk company that was in Montreal.
2. The wagon that he drove carried milk to St. Catherine Street.
3. Pierre relied on his horse, whom he had named Joseph.
4. Joseph, whose coat was white, was large and reliable.
5. Pierre was offered a pension, which is a regular payment to a retired person.

The Adverb Clause

7e. An *adverb clause* is a subordinate clause that modifies a verb, an adjective, or an adverb.

An adverb clause tells *where, when, how, why, to what extent,* or *under what condition.*

EXAMPLES They live **where it never gets cold.** [Where?]

When he left, I cried. [When?]

Grover's room seems **as if it will never be the same.** [How?]

Because the weather was hot, the cool water felt good. [Why?]

My parents still miss him **as much as I do.** [To what extent?]

If I keep tickling him, he won't fall asleep. [Under what condition?]

An adverb clause is introduced by a *subordinating conjunction*—a word that shows the relationship between the adverb clause and the word or words that the clause modifies.

COMPUTER NOTE A computer can help you proofread your writing. Use the computer's "Search" function to locate any use of the words *after, as, before, since,* and *until.* Examine the use of such words at the beginnings of sentences. Determine whether the word begins a prepositional phrase or a subordinate clause. In most cases, an introductory prepositional phrase is not set off by a comma. An introductory adverb clause, however, should be followed by a comma.

NOTE Some subordinating conjunctions, such as *after, as, before, since,* and *until,* are also used as prepositions.

Common Subordinating Conjunctions			
after	as though	since	when
although	because	so that	whenever
as	before	than	where
as if	how	though	wherever
as long as	if	unless	whether
as soon as	in order that	until	while

An adverb clause does not always follow the word it modifies. When an adverb clause begins a sentence, the clause is followed by a comma.

EXAMPLE   Whenever King Midas touched something, it turned to gold.

Placement of Adverb Clauses

In most cases, the decision of where to place an adverb clause is a matter of style, not correctness. Both of the following sentences are correct.

> **Although she was almost unknown during her lifetime,** Emily Dickinson is now considered a major American poet.

> Emily Dickinson is now considered a major American poet **although she was almost unknown during her lifetime.**

Which sentence might you use in a paper on Emily Dickinson? The sentence to choose would be the one that looks and sounds better in the **context**—the rest of the paragraph to which the sentence belongs.

 QUICK CHECK 3

Identify the adverb clause in each of the following sentences. For each clause, circle the subordinating conjunction, and underline the subject once and the verb twice.

EXAMPLE   1. Many things change as you grow older.
              1. *as* you grow older

1. Grover worked on the computer whenever he could.
2. He packed all his things before he left.
3. Because he needed the computer, he took it too.
4. Although the room has been painted, it reminds me of him.
5. It won't be the same as long as he is gone.

The Noun Clause

7f.   A *noun clause* is a subordinate clause used as a noun.

A noun clause may be used as a subject, a complement (predicate nominative, indirect object, or direct object), or an object of a preposition.

SUBJECT	**What Mama promises** is tomorrow.
PREDICATE NOMINATIVE	She is **who makes us happy.**
INDIRECT OBJECT	She bids **whoever is sleeping** good morning.

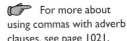 For more about using commas with adverb clauses, see page 1021.

Try It Out

Each of the following sentences contains an adverb clause. Decide whether you think each adverb clause is placed where it would read best in context. If the clause could be better placed, revise the sentence. If the clause reads best where it is, write *No change.*

[1] "The Highwayman" was an inevitable reading assignment when I was in school. [2] I now enjoy the poem although I laughed at it then. [3] Because it was remote in time and place, I did not relate to it. [4] The vocabulary and content seemed false because they were unfamiliar. [5] However, I discovered that this poem is filled with lively images when I read it carefully!

Try It Out: Possible Answers

1. When I was in school, "The Highwayman" was an inevitable reading assignment.
2. Although I laughed at it then, I now enjoy the poem.
3. I did not relate to it because it was remote in time and place.
4. No change.
5. However, when I read it carefully, I discovered that this poem is filled with lively images!

Quick Check 3: Answers

1. *whenever* he could
2. *before* he left
3. *Because* he needed the computer
4. *Although* the room has been painted
5. *as long as* he is gone

| DIRECT OBJECT | Choose **whichever you need most.** |
| OBJECT OF A PREPOSITION | A poem can be about **whatever you think is important.** |

Common Introductory Words for Noun Clauses

how	what	whatever	which
who	whoever	when	whichever
whom	whomever	where	that

☞ For guidelines on using *who* and *whom* correctly, see page 986. The same guidelines apply to *whoever* and *whomever.*

✓ QUICK CHECK 4

Identify the noun clause in each of the following sentences. Tell whether the noun clause is a *subject,* a *predicate nominative,* a *direct object,* an *indirect object,* or an *object of a preposition.*

EXAMPLE 1. Whatever we do affects our whole family.
1. *Whatever we do*—subject

1. What Evelyn Tooley Hunt is talking about is a mother's effect on her family.
2. This mother gives whoever is near warmth and brightness.
3. Similarly, she puts love into whatever she is cooking.
4. Notice that Hunt compares her warmth to grits and gravy.
5. A bright future is what her constant love promises.

8 SENTENCES

8a. A *sentence* is a group of words that has a subject and a verb and expresses a complete thought.

A sentence begins with a capital letter and ends with a period, a question mark, or an exclamation point.

EXAMPLES Sandra Cisneros wrote "Four Skinny Trees**.**"
Have you read any of her work**?**
What surprising rhythms she uses**!**

SENTENCE OR SENTENCE FRAGMENT?

A *sentence fragment* is a group of words that either does not have a subject and verb or does not express a complete thought.

| SENTENCE FRAGMENT | The rhythms in this story. [What about the rhythms in this story?] |
| SENTENCE | The rhythms in this story are based on repetition. |

Quick Check 4: Answers

1. What Evelyn Tooley Hunt is talking about—subject
2. whoever is near—indirect object
3. whatever she is cooking—object of a preposition
4. that Hunt compares her warmth to grits and gravy—direct object
5. what her constant love promises—predicate nominative

Resources

Grammar and Language

- *Language Handbook Worksheets,* pp. 78–87

SENTENCE FRAGMENT	After reading her story. [Who read her story? What happened then?]
SENTENCE	After reading her story, I looked at trees differently.

 QUICK CHECK 1

Tell whether each group of words is a *sentence* or a *sentence fragment*. If the word group is a sentence, correct it by adding a capital letter and end punctuation. If the word group is a sentence fragment, correct it by adding words to make a complete sentence, and also capitalize and punctuate it correctly.

EXAMPLE 1. one of my favorite writers
    1. *sentence fragment—One of my favorite writers is Sandra Cisneros.*

1. let me recommend this story
2. in front of her house grow four skinny trees
3. growing in the midst of concrete
4. where they don't belong
5. do you see a part of yourself in nature

THE SUBJECT AND THE PREDICATE

A sentence consists of two parts: a *subject* and a *predicate*.

8b. A *subject* tells whom or what the sentence is about. The *predicate* tells something about the subject.

   subj.   pred.
EXAMPLE Helen Callaghan played professional baseball.

Finding the Subject

Usually, the subject comes before the predicate. Sometimes, however, the subject may appear elsewhere in the sentence. To find the subject of a sentence, ask *Who?* or *What?* before the predicate. In sentences that begin with *here, there,* or *where,* ask *Here* (or *There* or *Where*) before the predicate, followed by *who?* or *what?* after the predicate.

EXAMPLES In the old photograph was a **woman at bat.** [Who was? A woman was.]
    By the way, **her son** plays for the Astros. [Who plays? Her son does.]
    Do **you** play baseball? [Who does play? You do play.]
    Where is **my notebook?** [Where is what? Where is my notebook.]

COMPUTER NOTE

If sentence fragments are a problem in your writing, a computer may be able to help you. Some style-checking programs can identify and highlight sentence fragments. Such programs are useful, but they aren't perfect. The best way to eliminate fragments from your writing is still to check each sentence yourself. Be sure that each expresses a complete thought and has a subject and a verb.

NOTE The subject of a sentence is *never* part of a prepositional phrase.

EXAMPLE **Many** of the women in the league attended the reunion. [Who attended? You might be tempted to say *women,* but *women* is part of the prepositional phrase *of the women. Many* attended.]

Quick Check 1: Answers

1. sentence—Let me recommend this story.
2. sentence—In front of her house grow four skinny trees.
3. sentence fragment—They are growing in the midst of concrete.
4. sentence fragment—They survive where they don't belong.
5. sentence—Do you see a part of yourself in nature?

Quick Check 2: Answers

1. The All-American Girls Professional Baseball League—complete subject; All-American Girls Professional Baseball League—simple subject; was started by Philip K. Wrigley—complete predicate; was started—simple predicate

2. It—complete subject and simple subject; enjoyed ten years of popularity—complete predicate; enjoyed—simple predicate

3. you—complete subject and simple subject; Have seen the movie about the Rockford Peaches—complete predicate; Have seen—simple predicate

4. The famous Rockford Peaches—complete subject; Rockford Peaches—simple subject; was only one of nine teams—complete predicate; was—simple predicate

5. a much older Callaghan—complete subject; Callaghan—simple subject; At the league's reunion many years later was—complete predicate; was—simple predicate

---

NOTE In this book, the term *subject* refers to the simple subject unless otherwise indicated.

NOTE In this book, the term *verb* refers to the simple predicate unless otherwise indicated.

☞ For more about verb phrases, see pages 965, 970, and 991.

The Simple Subject

8c. A *simple subject* is the main word or group of words in the complete subject.

EXAMPLES Her **mother** still had that old fire. [The complete subject is *her mother.*]

"The No-Guitar Blues" by Gary Soto is on the test. [The complete subject is *"The No-Guitar Blues" by Gary Soto.*]

The Simple Predicate, or Verb

8d. A *simple predicate,* or *verb,* is the main word or group of words in the complete predicate.

A **complete predicate** consists of a verb and all the words that describe the verb and complete its meaning. Usually, the complete predicate follows the subject in a sentence. Sometimes, however, the complete predicate appears at the beginning of a sentence. Other times, part of the predicate may appear on one side of the subject and the rest on the other side.

EXAMPLES In the darkness of a doorway **stood** a stranger.
On this night, he **had a meeting** with an old friend.
Would his friend **appear**?

A simple predicate may be a one-word verb, or it may be a verb phrase. A **verb phrase** consists of a main verb and its helping verbs.

EXAMPLES O. Henry's stories often **end** with a twist.
"After Twenty Years" **does** not **have** a happy ending.

✓ QUICK CHECK 2

Identify the *complete subject* and *simple subject* and the *complete predicate* and *simple predicate* in each of the following sentences.

EXAMPLE 1. On the mantel was an old baseball.
1. *an old baseball—complete subject; baseball—simple subject; on the mantel was—complete predicate; was—simple predicate*

1. The All-American Girls Professional Baseball League was started by Philip K. Wrigley.
2. It enjoyed ten years of popularity.
3. Have you seen the movie about the Rockford Peaches?
4. The famous Rockford Peaches was only one of nine teams.
5. At the league's reunion many years later was a much older Callaghan.

1002   Resource Center / Language Handbook

The Compound Subject

8e. A *compound subject* consists of two or more connected subjects that have the same verb. The usual connecting word is *and* or *or*.

EXAMPLES   Neither **Daedalus** nor **Icarus** escaped the king's anger.
Among Daedalus's gifts were **creativity, ingenuity,** and **skill.**

The Compound Verb

8f. A *compound verb* consists of two or more verbs that have the same subject.

A connecting word—usually *and, or,* or *but*—is used between the verbs.

EXAMPLE   He **flew** upward, **turned,** and **called** to his son.

Both the subject and the verb of a sentence may be compound.

                    S   S   V   V
EXAMPLE   **Icarus** and his **father put** on the wings and **took** off.
[Icarus put on the wings and took off. His father put on the wings and took off.]

 QUICK CHECK 3

Identify the *subjects* and the *verbs* in the following sentences.

EXAMPLE   **1.** Myths and fairy tales sometimes hide their meanings.
1. *Myths, fairy tales—subjects; hide—verb*

1. The myth of Icarus tells about creativity and warns of its dangers.
2. In this story, Daedalus and his son suffer a tragic fate.
3. Yet, did they not also create wings and fly?
4. You and I can read the story, learn, and avoid their mistakes.
5. "Echo and Narcissus" and this classic story can teach us much.

 Using Compound Subjects and Verbs

Using compound subjects and verbs, you can combine ideas and reduce wordiness in your writing. Compare the examples below.

WORDY   With his wings, Daedalus escaped. Icarus escaped also.

REVISED   With their wings, **Daedalus and Icarus escaped.**

Try It Out ✏

Using compound subjects and verbs, combine the following pairs of sentences.

1. Daedalus angered King Minos. Daedalus was imprisoned by King Minos.
2. Clouds sailed through the skies. Birds sailed through the skies.
3. Daedalus melted wax. Daedalus shaped a skeleton of a wing.
4. Daedalus flew close to his son, Icarus. Icarus flew close to his father.
5. Delos rushed by beneath them. Samos rushed by beneath them.

Quick Check 3: Answers

1. myth—subject; tells, warns—verbs
2. Daedalus, son—subjects; suffer—verb
3. they—subject; did create, fly—verbs
4. you, I—subjects; can read, learn, avoid—verbs
5. "Echo and Narcissus," story—subjects; can teach—verb

Try It Out: Possible Answers

1. Daedalus angered King Minos and was imprisoned by him.
2. Clouds and birds sailed through the skies.
3. Daedalus melted wax and shaped a skeleton of a wing.
4. Daedalus and his son, Icarus, flew close to each other.
5. Delos and Samos rushed by beneath them.

Language Handbook

9 COMPLEMENTS

9a. A *complement* is a word or a group of words that completes the meaning of a verb.

Every sentence has a subject and a verb. Often a verb also needs a complement to complete the meaning of the verb. A complement may be a noun, a pronoun, or an adjective. Each of the following subjects and verbs needs a complement to make a complete sentence.

INCOMPLETE	James Weldon Johnson became [what?]
COMPLETE	James Weldon Johnson became **a poet.**
INCOMPLETE	Johnson's poetry is [what?]
COMPLETE	Johnson's poetry is **wonderful.**
INCOMPLETE	Tamisha showed [what? to whom?]
COMPLETE	Tamisha showed **me** her **poem.**

As you can see, a complement may be a noun, a pronoun, or an adjective. An adverb is never a complement.

ADVERB	He writes **powerfully.** [*Powerfully* tells how he writes.]
COMPLEMENT	His writing is **powerful.** [The adjective *powerful* modifies the subject *writing.*]

A complement is never in a prepositional phrase.

OBJECT OF A PREPOSITION	The whole world was in **darkness.**
COMPLEMENT	The whole world was **darkness.**

☞ For more information about prepositional phrases, see pages 967, 985, 990, and 991–992.

✓ QUICK CHECK I

Identify the *subjects, verbs,* and *complements* in the sentences in the following paragraph. [Remember: A complement is never in a prepositional phrase.]

EXAMPLE [1] Will you read "The Creation" aloud?
   1. *you—subject; will read—verb; "The Creation"—complement*

[1] With his deep voice, James Earl Jones is a marvelous speaker. [2] Only his rich voice can do justice to a poem like "The Creation." [3] With lingering pauses and startling changes of volume, Jones's performance is awe-inspiring. [4] Can you find us a recording of his recitation? [5] No one will speak or move a muscle during the whole performance.

Quick Check 1: Answers

1. James Earl Jones—subject; is—verb; speaker—complement

2. voice—subject; can do—verb; justice—complement

3. performance—subject; is—verb; awe-inspiring—complement

4. you—subject; Can find—verb; us, recording—complements

5. No one—subject; will speak, move—verbs; muscle—complement

DIRECT OBJECTS

9b. A *direct object* is a noun or a pronoun that receives the action of the verb or that shows the result of the action. A direct object tells *what* or *whom* after a transitive verb.

EXAMPLE   In this poem, God creates **light, animals,** and all **things.** [The nouns *light, animals,* and *things* receive the action of the transitive verb *creates* and tell *what*.]

A direct object can never follow a linking verb because a linking verb does not express action.

LINKING VERB   People **became** living souls. [The verb *became* does not express action; therefore, it does not have a direct object.]

A direct object is never part of a prepositional phrase.

OBJECT OF A PREPOSITION   Humans gazed at the **moon.** [*Moon* is not the direct object of the verb *gazed; moon* is the object of the preposition *at*.]

INDIRECT OBJECTS

Like a direct object, an *indirect object* helps to complete the meaning of a transitive verb. If a sentence has an indirect object, it always has a direct object also.

9c. An *indirect object* is a noun or a pronoun that comes between the verb and the direct object and tells *to what* or *to whom* or *for what* or *for whom* the action of the verb is done.

EXAMPLE   In the last stanza, God gives **man** life. [The noun *man* tells *to whom* God has given life.]

Linking verbs do not have indirect objects. Also, an indirect object, like a direct object, is never in a prepositional phrase.

LINKING VERB   The cypress **is** a type of evergreen tree. [The linking verb *is* does not express action, so it cannot have an indirect object.]

INDIRECT OBJECT   Cypress trees give **swamps** deep shade. [The noun *swamps* shows *to what* cypress trees give shade.]

OBJECT OF A PREPOSITION   They give deep shade to the **swamps.** [The noun *swamps* is the object of the preposition *to*.]

> ☞ For more about transitive verbs, see page 964.

> ☞ For more about linking verbs, see pages 964–965 and 1006. For more about prepositional phrases, see pages 967, 985, 990, and 991–992.

> **NOTE** Like a direct object, an indirect object may be compound.
>
> **EXAMPLE**   Cypresses give **swamps** and **creeks** deep shade.

Quick Check 2: Answers

1. characterization—direct object
2. world—direct object
3. footsteps—direct object; us—indirect object
4. breath—direct object; humans—indirect object
5. humans—direct object

 QUICK CHECK 2

Identify the *direct objects* and the *indirect objects* in the following sentences. [Note: Not every sentence has an indirect object.]

EXAMPLE 1. Johnson's God has physical presence.
   1. *presence—direct object*

1. This poem delivers a strong characterization of God.
2. With the muscle of a worker, this God makes the world.
3. For Johnson, all the earth shows us His footsteps.
4. Not God's intellect but His body literally gives humans breath.
5. After all, God shaped humans in His own image.

👉 For information about linking verbs, see pages 964–965 and 1005.

NOTE Expressions such as "It is I" and "That was he" sound awkward even though they are correct. In conversation, you would likely say "It's me" and "That was him." Such nonstandard expressions may one day become acceptable in writing as well as in speech. For now, however, it is best to follow the rules of standard English in your writing.

NOTE A predicate nominative may be compound.

EXAMPLE Her helpers were **birds**, a **muskrat**, a **toad**, and a **turtle**.

SUBJECT COMPLEMENTS

A *subject complement* completes the meaning of a linking verb and identifies or describes the subject.

Common Linking Verbs

appear	become	grow	remain	smell	stay
be	feel	look	seem	sound	taste

EXAMPLES This unfortunate person became **Sky Woman.** [*Sky Woman* identifies the subject *person.*]
The story of Sky Woman is **sad.** [*Sad* describes the subject *story.*]

There are two kinds of subject complements—the *predicate nominative* and the *predicate adjective.*

Predicate Nominatives

9d. A *predicate nominative* is a noun or a pronoun that follows a linking verb and identifies the subject or refers to it.

EXAMPLE Sky Woman became the **Great Earth Mother.** [The compound noun *Great Earth Mother* is a predicate nominative that identifies the subject *Sky Woman.*]

Like subjects and objects, predicate nominatives never appear in prepositional phrases.

EXAMPLE The world was only a few **bits** of earth on a turtle. [The word *bits* is a predicate nominative that identifies the subject *world. Earth* is the object of the preposition *of,* and *turtle* is the object of the preposition *on.*]

Predicate Adjectives

9e. A *predicate adjective* is an adjective that follows a linking verb and describes the subject.

EXAMPLE   Sky Woman was **young** and **beautiful**. [The words *young* and *beautiful* are predicate adjectives that describe the subject *Sky Woman*.]

Some verbs, such as *look, grow,* and *feel,* may be used as either linking verbs or action verbs.

LINKING VERB   The Chief of Heaven **looked** angry. [*Looked* is a linking verb because it links the adjective *angry* to the subject *Chief of Heaven*.]

ACTION VERB   Sky Woman **looked** through the hole in the floor of Heaven. [*Looked* is an action verb because it expresses Sky Woman's action.]

 QUICK CHECK 3

Identify the subject complement in each of the following sentences. Then, label each as a *predicate nominative* or a *predicate adjective*.

EXAMPLE   1. Traditional stories are one way of understanding nature.
      1. *way—predicate nominative*

1. These stories may seem simple but may be quite complex.
2. After all, their theme is the whole world.
3. Sky Woman's misfortune was our good fortune.
4. With her fall, the world became possible.
5. Is anything, even luck, permanent?

 Using Action Verbs

Overusing the linking verb *be* can make writing dull and lifeless. As you evaluate your writing, you may get the feeling that nothing is *happening*, that nobody is *doing* anything. That feeling may be an indication that your writing contains too many *be* verbs. Wherever possible, replace a dull *be* verb with a verb that expresses action.

     BE VERB   "Sky Woman" **is** a traditional Seneca story.

ACTION VERB   Traditionally, the Seneca people **tell** the story of Sky Woman.

COMPUTER NOTE

The overuse of *be* verbs is a problem that a computer can help you eliminate. Use the computer's "Search" function to locate and highlight each occurrence of *am, are, is, was, were, be, been,* and *being.* In each case, determine whether the *be* verb is necessary or whether it could be replaced with an action verb for greater impact.

Try It Out ✎

Revise each of the following sentences by substituting an interesting action verb for the dull *be* verb.

1. The Chief of Heaven was angry at Sky Woman.
2. Paradise was the home of the Chief of Heaven, Sky Woman, and many animals and plants.
3. Animals of all kinds were her friends.
4. The shell of that turtle is now the earth.
5. Many things from the sky are now on earth.

Language Handbook   **1007**

Quick Check 3: Answers

1. simple, complex—predicate adjectives
2. world—predicate nominative
3. fortune—predicate nominative
4. possible—predicate adjective
5. permanent—predicate adjective

Try It Out: Possible Answers

1. The Chief of Heaven burned with anger at Sky Woman.
2. The Chief of Heaven, Sky Woman, and many animals and plants lived in paradise.
3. Animals of all kinds befriended her.
4. The shell of that turtle changed into the earth.
5. Many things from the sky now flourish on earth.

Language Handbook

10 KINDS OF SENTENCES

SENTENCES CLASSIFIED BY STRUCTURE

One way that sentences are classified is by **structure**—the kinds of clauses and the number of clauses the sentences contain.

The Simple Sentence

10a. A *simple sentence* has one independent clause and no subordinate clauses.

EXAMPLE Jean Fritz and her parents discussed her problem and found a clever solution to it.

Notice in the example above that a simple sentence may have a compound subject, a compound verb, or both.

☞ For more about compound subjects and compound verbs, see pages 971 and 1003.

The Compound Sentence

10b. A *compound sentence* has two or more independent clauses but no subordinate clauses.

The independent clauses are usually joined by a coordinating conjunction: *and, but, for, nor, or, so,* or *yet.* The independent clauses in a compound sentence may also be joined by a semicolon.

EXAMPLES Jared read *Old Yeller,* and then he saw the movie.

Anne McCaffrey has written many stories about dragons; in fact, she has contributed to their popularity.

☞ For more about using commas in compound sentences, see page 1019. For more about using semicolons, see pages 1021–1022.

The Complex Sentence

10c. A *complex sentence* has one independent clause and at least one subordinate clause.

EXAMPLE When I read one of Anne McCaffrey's stories, I want to ride a dragon.

Independent Clause   I want to ride a dragon

Subordinate Clause   When I read one of Anne McCaffrey's stories

QUICK CHECK I

Identify each of the following sentences as *simple, compound,* or *complex.*

EXAMPLE   I. *Homesick* was interesting to me because I
once lived abroad.

           I. *complex*

1. Boys and girls ran and played on the playground.
2. Jean Fritz did not feel like part of their world at the British school.
3. They sang "God Save the King," but she didn't.
4. Her problem disappeared after she spoke to her father.
5. She told her amah that *sewing machine* meant "hello."

 Using Varied Sentence Structure

Variety is the spice of life. It's also the spice of writing. By varying the length and the structure of your sentences, you can make your writing clearer and more interesting to read.

Simple sentences are best used to express single ideas. To describe more complicated ideas and to show relationships between them, use compound and complex sentences.

SENTENCES CLASSIFIED BY PURPOSE

In addition to being classified by structure, a sentence is also classified according to its purpose. The four kinds of sentences are *declarative, interrogative, imperative,* and *exclamatory.*

10d. A *declarative sentence* makes a statement. It is followed by a period.

EXAMPLE   I can guess what that is.

10e. An *interrogative sentence* asks a question. It is followed by a question mark.

EXAMPLE   What was the matter with Ted's bike?

10f. An *imperative sentence* gives a command or makes a request. It is followed by a period. A strong command is followed by an exclamation point.

EXAMPLES   Please open the door, Theo.
                 Look out!

 COMPUTER NOTE

A computer can help you analyze your writing for sentence length and structure. Programs are available that will tell you the average number of words in your sentences and the number of each kind of sentence you used. In this way, you can easily see which sentence structures you've mastered and which ones you'll need to work on.

Try It Out ✎

Read each of the following items containing short sentences. Decide what type of sentence structure would best express the ideas in each item. Then, rewrite the item.

1. Commas seemed complicated. Andrea Hull knew how to use them.
2. Andrea Hull knew more than young Jean. Andrea taught her many things.
3. Embroidery is beautiful. It can be tedious.
4. She stretched the cloth. She marked her pattern. She began stitching.
5. A design is finished. Everyone can enjoy it.

NOTE If an imperative sentence does not have a subject, the "understood" subject is always *you.*

EXAMPLE
(You) Do it now!

Quick Check 1: Answers

1. simple
2. simple
3. compound
4. complex
5. complex

Try It Out: Possible Answers

1. Though commas seemed complicated, Andrea Hull knew how to use them.
2. Andrea Hull, who knew more than young Jean, taught Jean many things.
3. Embroidery is beautiful, but it can be tedious.
4. After she stretched the cloth, she marked her pattern and began stitching.
5. After a design is finished, everyone can enjoy it.

Quick Check 2: Answers

1. interrogative
2. declarative
3. exclamatory
4. imperative
5. imperative

Resources

Grammar and Language

■ *Language Handbook Worksheets,* pp. 103–118

☞ For more on the different end marks of punctuation, see page 1018.

10g. An *exclamatory sentence* shows excitement or expresses strong feeling. An exclamatory sentence is followed by an exclamation point.

EXAMPLES   What a bargain this is!
We won regionals!

✓ QUICK CHECK 2

Classify each of the following sentences according to its purpose—*declarative, interrogative, imperative,* or *exclamatory.*

EXAMPLE   **1.** Explain the theme of this story, Andy.
1. *imperative*

1. Have you ever lived in a foreign country?
2. As a child, Jean Fritz attended a British school in China.
3. How wonderful the Yangtze River was!
4. Please take me there.
5. Read *Homesick,* and see for yourself.

11 WRITING EFFECTIVE SENTENCES

Combining Sentences

11a. Improve short, choppy sentences by combining them into longer, smoother sentences.

There are many ways to combine sentences. Here are a few examples.

(1) Insert words and phrases.

CHOPPY   The pan was hot. The pan was made of iron.
COMBINED   The **iron** pan was hot.

CHOPPY   Cook the steak. Cook it for five minutes.
COMBINED   Cook the steak **for five minutes.**

(2) Use coordinating conjunctions.

CHOPPY   Father likes steak. Mother does too.
COMBINED   Father **and** Mother like steak.

CHOPPY   The preparation was Chinese. The food was not.
COMBINED   The preparation was Chinese, **but** the food was not.

(3) Use subordinate clauses.

CHOPPY   Be careful. It is easy to be burned.
COMBINED   Be careful **because it is easy to be burned.**

CHOPPY I sliced the meat. It was already cooked.

COMBINED I sliced the meat **that was already cooked.**

 QUICK CHECK 1

Use the methods you've learned in this section to combine some of the choppy sentences in the following paragraph.

EXAMPLE [1] He is Chinese. [2] He is American.
  1. *He is Chinese and American.*

[1] "T-Bone Steak" is a poem about identity. [2] It was written by Wing Tek Lum. [3] The poet describes an ordinary moment. [4] This ordinary moment is filled with meaning. [5] The meaning is complex. [6] It includes self-assertion, rebellion, respect, and self-acceptance. [7] Preparing the meal is almost a ritual for the family. [8] It is a ritual that asserts their individuality. [9] The meal draws from Chinese and American customs. [10] Elements of both cultures contribute to the family's identity.

Revising Run-on Sentences

11b. **Avoid using run-on sentences.**

If you run together two complete sentences as if they were one sentence, you get a *run-on sentence.*

RUN-ON This poet values individuality, he also respects tradition.

Here are two of the ways you can revise run-on sentences.

1. You can make two sentences.

  REVISED This poet values individuality**.** **H**e also respects tradition.

2. You can use a comma and the coordinating conjunction *and, but,* or *or.*

  REVISED This poet values individuality**, but** he also respects tradition.

Revising Stringy Sentences and Wordy Sentences

11c. **Improve** *stringy* **and** *wordy sentences* **by making them shorter and more precise.**

Stringy sentences have too many independent clauses strung together with words like *and* or *but.*

STRINGY The Hummingbird King was betrayed, and an enemy betrayed him, and Kukul turned into a hummingbird, for the hummingbird symbolizes freedom for the Maya, and even today he watches everything.

> **NOTE** A *comma splice* is a kind of run-on sentence in which a comma is used without a coordinating conjunction to join independent clauses. The sample run-on sentence given under rule 11b is a comma splice.

Language Handbook

Language Handbook   1011

Quick Check 1: Possible Answers

Written by Wing Tek Lum, "T-Bone Steak" is a poem about identity. The poet describes an ordinary moment filled with complex meaning, which includes self-assertion, rebellion, respect, and self-acceptance. Preparing the meal is almost a ritual that asserts the family's individuality. The meal draws from Chinese and American customs, because elements of both cultures contribute to the family's identity.

Quick Check 2: Possible Answers

1. The world over, many legends tell of people being turned into animals.
2. Evidently, people feel a great kinship with animals.
3. Many of these legends feature an animal that was once a person with special powers.
4. Many animals do have powers that people do not have.
5. Perhaps these legends show that people sometimes envy animals.

Try It Out: Possible Answers

1. Many legends, myths, and fairy tales have survived for centuries because they address something important in people.
2. Their impossibility continually surprises and delights readers.
3. People have long told stories that explain both human behavior and natural forces.
4. Children and their parents read these stories or view them on film.
5. The needs of a culture, the details of a story, and its ending may change, but the readers remain.

To fix a stringy sentence, you can break the sentence into two or more sentences. You can also turn some of the independent clauses into phrases or subordinate clauses.

REVISED   When the Hummingbird King was betrayed by an enemy, Kukul turned into a hummingbird, the symbol of freedom for the Maya. Even today, he watches everything.

You can revise wordy sentences in three different ways.

1. Replace a group of words with one word.

WORDY   With great sorrow, they mourned their king.

REVISED   **Sorrowfully,** they mourned their king.

2. Replace a clause with a phrase.

WORDY   When Kukul's life ended, he turned into a hummingbird.

REVISED   **After his death,** Kukul turned into a hummingbird.

3. Take out a whole group of unnecessary words.

WORDY   What I mean to say is that Kukul is known as the *quetzal.*

REVISED   Kukul is known as the *quetzal.*

✓ QUICK CHECK 2

The following paragraph contains run-on, stringy, and wordy sentences. Revise them to improve the style of the paragraph.

EXAMPLE   [1] We know little about many ancient cultures due to the fact that records have been lost.

1. *We know little about many ancient cultures because records have been lost.*

[1] Many people all over the world have legends, these legends tell of people being turned into animals. [2] It seems evident that people must feel a great kinship with the animals. [3] Many of these legends feature an animal, and the animal was once a person, and that person had special powers. [4] The fact is that many animals have powers that people do not have. [5] Perhaps these legends are expressive of the idea that people sometimes have envy for animals.

Revising Wordy Sentences

TIPS FOR WRITERS

Extra words and phrases tend to make writing sound awkward and unnatural. As you revise your writing, read your sentences aloud to check for wordiness or a stringy style. If you run out of breath before the end of a sentence, it is likely stringy, wordy, or both.

Try It Out ✎

Revise each of the following sentences to eliminate wordiness and stringy style.

1. The reason that many legends, myths, and fairy tales have survived for centuries is that they address something important in people.
2. They continually surprise and delight readers due to the fact of their impossibility.
3. People have long told stories that explain human behavior and ones that explain natural forces in the world.
4. Children read these stories or view them on film, and so do their parents.
5. The needs of a culture change, and details of the story change, and the ending may change, but the readers remain.

12 CAPITAL LETTERS

12a. Capitalize the first word in every sentence.

EXAMPLE   **W**ho gets a place in the choir?

The first word of a sentence that is a direct quotation is capitalized even if the quotation begins within a sentence.

EXAMPLE   Francis Bacon states, "**K**nowledge is power."

Traditionally, the first word in a line of poetry is capitalized. However, some modern poets and writers do not follow this style. When you are quoting, follow the capitalization used in the source of the quotation.

EXAMPLE   **I**t was many and many a year ago,
          In a kingdom by the sea,
    That a maiden there lived whom you may know
          By the name of Annabel Lee;
    And this maiden she lived with no other thought
          Than to love and be loved by me.
              —Edgar Allan Poe, "Annabel Lee"

12b. Capitalize the pronoun *I*.

EXAMPLE   **I** enjoyed the book, but **I** didn't like the film.

12c. Capitalize the interjection *O*.

The interjection *O* is most often used on solemn or formal occasions. It is usually followed by a word in direct address.

EXAMPLE   Protect us in the battle, **O** great Athena!

☑ QUICK CHECK 1

Most of the following sentences contain errors in capitalization. If a sentence is correct, write *C*. If there are errors in the use of capitals, correct the word or words that should be changed.

EXAMPLE   **1.** William says that *i* am his best friend.
          1. *I*

1. If i need a ride, i will give you a call.
2. Loretta is in Maine, but Oh, how she would like to visit Paris.
3. oh no, I left my backpack on the bus!
4. Please accept these gifts, o Lord.
5. The poem ends with a question.

12d. Capitalize proper nouns.

A **common noun** is a general name for a person, a place, a thing, or an idea. A **proper noun** names a particular person, place, thing, or idea.

☞ For more about using capital letters in quotations, see page 1024.

NOTE The interjection *oh* requires a capital letter only at the beginning of a sentence. Otherwise, *oh* is not capitalized.

EXAMPLES   **O**h, look at the sunset!
We felt tired but, **oh**, so victorious.

---

* Grammar and Language

■ *Language Handbook Worksheets,* pp. 119–124

Quick Check 1: Answers

1. I, I
2. oh
3. Oh
4. O
5. C

Language Handbook   **1013**

Language Handbook   1013

You may be able to use your spelling checker to help you capitalize names correctly. Make a list of the names you write most often. Be sure that you have spelled and capitalized each name correctly. Then, add this list to your computer's dictionary or spelling checker.

NOTE In a hyphenated street number, the second part of the number is not capitalized.

EXAMPLE Seventy-eighth Street

NOTE Words such as *north, east,* and *southwest* are not capitalized when they indicate direction, but they are capitalized when they are part of a proper name.

EXAMPLES   go **s**outh for the winter
northeast of Atlanta
East **E**nd Cafe
Old **W**est Jamboree

NOTE The word *earth* is not capitalized unless it is used along with the names of other heavenly bodies that are capitalized. The words *sun* and *moon* are not capitalized.

A common noun is capitalized only when it begins a sentence or is part of a title. A proper noun is always capitalized. Some proper nouns consist of more than one word. In these names, short prepositions (those of fewer than five letters) and articles (*a, an, the*) are not capitalized.

| **COMMON NOUNS** | statue | man |
| **PROPER NOUNS** | Statue of Liberty | Eric the Red |

(1) Capitalize the names of persons and animals.

EXAMPLES   Franklin Chang-Díaz, Alice Walker, Lassie, Shamu

(2) Capitalize geographical names.

TYPE OF NAME	EXAMPLES
Towns, Cities	**S**an **D**iego, **J**amestown
Islands	Isle of **W**ight, **W**ake **I**sland
Counties, States	**C**ook **C**ounty, **N**ew **H**ampshire
Countries	**N**ew **Z**ealand, **G**ermany
Bodies of Water	**G**ulf of **M**exico, **I**ndian **O**cean
Forests, Parks	**S**herwood **F**orest, **Y**ellowstone **N**ational **P**ark
Streets, Highways	**R**oute 44, **W**est **F**ourth **S**treet
Mountains	**M**ount **W**ashington, **B**ig **H**orn **M**ountain
Continents	**S**outh **A**merica, **A**sia
Regions	the **W**est **C**oast, the **G**reat **P**lains

(3) Capitalize the names of planets, stars, and other heavenly bodies.

EXAMPLES   Jupiter   Sirius   Milky Way
Big Dipper   North Star

(4) Capitalize the names of teams, organizations, businesses, institutions, and government bodies.

TYPE OF NAME	EXAMPLES
Teams	**D**etroit **P**istons, **S**eattle **S**eahawks
Organizations	**G**irl **S**couts, **A**frican **S**tudies **A**ssociation
Businesses	**W**ilson's **V**acuum **W**orld, **S**easide **C**ycle **S**hop
Institutions	**C**ary **M**emorial **H**ospital, **H**illtop **H**igh **S**chool
Government Bodies	**A**ir **N**ational **G**uard, **D**epartment of **A**griculture

(5) Capitalize the names of historical events and periods, special events, and calendar items.

TYPE OF NAME	EXAMPLES
Historical Events	Battle of Bunker Hill, Yalta Conference
Historical Periods	Great Depression, Middle Ages
Special Events	Oklahoma State Fair, Cannes Film Festival
Calendar Items	Friday, Fourth of July

(6) Capitalize the names of nationalities, races, and peoples.

EXAMPLES   Greek, Asian, Caucasian, Hispanic, Shawnee

(7) Capitalize the names of religions and their followers, holy days, sacred writings, and specific deities.

TYPE OF NAME	EXAMPLES
Religions and Followers	Zen Buddhism, Christianity, Muslim
Holy Days	Passover, Lent, Ramadan
Sacred Writings	Tao Te Ching, Bible, Talmud, Koran
Specific Deities	Holy Spirit, Brahma, Allah, Jehovah

(8) Capitalize the names of buildings and other structures.

EXAMPLES   Ritz Theater, Golden Gate Bridge

(9) Capitalize the names of monuments and awards.

TYPE OF NAME	EXAMPLES
Monuments	Vietnam Veterans Memorial, Statue of Liberty
Awards	Newbery Medal, Purple Heart

(10) Capitalize the names of trains, ships, aircraft, and spacecraft.

TYPE OF NAME	EXAMPLES
Trains	*Silver Rocket, Orient Express*
Ships	*Nimitz, Santa Maria*
Aircraft	*Spirit of St. Louis, Air Force One*
Spacecraft	*Apollo 11, Columbia*

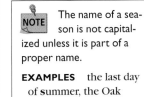

NOTE   The name of a season is not capitalized unless it is part of a proper name.

EXAMPLES   the last day of summer, the Oak Ridge Winter Carnival

NOTE   The word *god* is not capitalized when it refers to a mythological god. The names of specific gods, however, are capitalized.

EXAMPLE   The king of Greek gods was Zeus.

Quick Check 2: Answers

1. decisions of the United States Supreme Court
2. Three Skeleton Key, an island off Guiana
3. pictures of Saturn sent by Voyager 2
4. the Apaches of the Southwest
5. the Tomb of the Unknown Soldier

(11) Capitalize the brand names of business products.

EXAMPLES   Nike shoes, **B**uick station wagon, **W**rangler jeans

✓ *QUICK CHECK 2*

Correct each of the following expressions, using capital letters as needed.

EXAMPLE   1. the stone age
　　　　　　　1. *the Stone Age*

1. decisions of the united states supreme court
2. three skeleton key, an island off guiana
3. pictures of saturn sent by *voyager 2*
4. the apaches of the southwest
5. the tomb of the unknown soldier

👉 For more about proper nouns and proper adjectives, see pages 959 and 962–963.

12e. Capitalize proper adjectives.

A *proper adjective* is formed from a proper noun and is almost always capitalized.

PROPER NOUN   Rome, Islam, King Arthur
PROPER ADJECTIVE   **R**oman army, **I**slamic culture, **A**rthurian legend

12f. Do *not* capitalize the names of school subjects, except language classes and course names followed by a number.

EXAMPLES   I have tests in **E**nglish, **m**ath, and **A**rt II.

12g. Capitalize titles.

(1) Capitalize the title of a person when it comes before a name.

EXAMPLES   Does **Ms.** Tam know **Dr.** Politi or **Governor** Halsey?

Remember that correct capitalization of abbreviations is part of proper spelling. You may notice that certain abbreviations are capitalized.

EXAMPLES   Mr.   Ms.   U.S.   TV   Fla.
　　　　　　　NAACP

However, some abbreviations, especially those for measurements, are not capitalized.

EXAMPLES   in.   ft   lb   cc   ml

Consult a dictionary for the correct capitalization of an abbreviation.

---

(2) Capitalize a title used alone or following a person's name only when you want to emphasize the position of someone holding a high office.

EXAMPLES   We grew quiet as the **R**abbi rose to speak.
　　　　　　　Is he the **r**abbi at the new synagogue?

A title used alone in direct address is often capitalized.

EXAMPLES   Is the patient resting comfortably, **N**urse? What is your name, **S**ir [*or* sir]?

(3) Capitalize a word showing a family relationship when the word is used before or in place of a person's name.

EXAMPLES   Hey, **M**om, I received a letter from **Aunt** Christina and **Uncle** Garth.

Do not capitalize a word showing a family relationship when a possessive comes before the word.

EXAMPLES Angela's **m**other and my **g**randmother Daphne coach the softball team.

(4) Capitalize the first and last words and all important words in titles of books, magazines, newspapers, poems, short stories, historical documents, movies, television programs, works of art, and musical compositions.

Unimportant words in titles include

• prepositions of fewer than five letters (such as *at, of, for, from, with*)
• coordinating conjunctions (*and, but, for, nor, or, so, yet*)
• articles (*a, an, the*)

TYPE OF NAME	EXAMPLES
Books	*The Old Man and the Sea, Dust Tracks on a Road*
Magazines	*Sports Illustrated, Woman's Day*
Newspapers	*San Francisco Examiner, The Miami Herald*
Poems	"My Father Is a Simple Man," "Annabel Lee"
Short Stories	"The Naming of Names," "A Day's Wait"
Historical Documents	Bill of Rights, Emancipation Proclamation
Movies	*Stand and Deliver, Jurassic Park*
Television Programs	*FBI: The Untold Stories, A Different World*
Works of Art	*Birth of Venus, The Old Guitarist*
Musical Compositions	*The Marriage of Figaro,* "In the Pines"

 QUICK CHECK 3

Use capital or lowercase letters to correct each error in capitalization in the following sentences.

EXAMPLE 1. Did you know that dr. Santos subscribes to *field and stream?*

     1. Did you know that Dr. Santos subscribes to <u>Field and Stream</u>?

1. When my Aunt Rose and I went to Mexico, she introduced me to grandmother Villa.
2. Try looking up that word in *the american heritage dictionary.*
3. Did you hear commissioner of education boylan's speech?
4. Did the treasurer review the club's budget, senator?
5. When I get older, I hope I will be like the father in "My Father Is A Simple Man."

 NOTE The article *the* before a title is not capitalized unless it is the first word of the title.

EXAMPLES Is that the late edition of the *Chicago Sun-Times?* I read an interesting story in *The New Yorker.*

If you are not sure whether *the* is part of a magazine's title, look for the official title in the magazine's masthead or on the table-of-contents page. For a newspaper, look on the editorial page. For a book, look on the title page.

☞ For information on when to italicize (underline) a title, see page 1023. For information on using quotation marks for titles, see page 1026.

Quick Check 3: Answers

1. When my Aunt Rose and I went to Mexico, she introduced me to Grandmother Villa.
2. Try looking up that word in *The American Heritage Dictionary.*
3. Did you hear Commissioner of Education Boylan's speech?
4. Did the treasurer review the club's budget, Senator?
5. When I get older, I hope I will be like the father in "My Father Is a Simple Man."

Language Handbook

---

13 PUNCTUATION

END MARKS

An *end mark* is a mark of punctuation placed at the end of a sentence. The three kinds of end marks are the *period,* the *question mark,* and the *exclamation point.*

13a. Use a period at the end of a statement.

EXAMPLE   Kristi Yamaguchi is a world-champion figure skater**.**

13b. Use a question mark at the end of a question.

EXAMPLE   Did Gordon Parks write *The Learning Tree***?**

13c. Use an exclamation point at the end of an exclamation.

EXAMPLES   Wow**!** What a view**!**

13d. Use a period or an exclamation point at the end of a request or a command.

EXAMPLES   Please give me the scissors**.** [a request]
            Give me the scissors**!** [a command]

13e. Use a period after most abbreviations.

TYPES OF ABBREVIATIONS	EXAMPLES			
Personal Names	Pearl S. Buck		W.E.B. Du Bois	
Titles Used with Names	Mr.	Ms.	Jr.	Sr.	Dr.
States	Ky.	Fla.	Tenn.	Calif.
Addresses	St.	Blvd.	P.O. Box	
Organizations and Companies	Co.	Inc.	Corp.	Assn.
Times	A.M.	P.M.	B.C.	A.D.

Place A.D. before the number and B.C. after the number. For centuries expressed in words, place both A.D. and B.C. after the century.

EXAMPLES   A.D. 540   31 B.C.   sixth century B.C.   third century A.D.

When an abbreviation with a period ends a sentence, another period is not needed. However, a question mark or an exclamation point is used as needed.

EXAMPLES   This is my friend J. R**.**
            Have you met Nguyen, J. R**.?**

NOTE A two-letter state abbreviation without periods is used only when it is followed by a ZIP Code.

EXAMPLE
Austin, **TX** 78741

NOTE Some widely used abbreviations are written without periods.

EXAMPLES   UN, FBI, PTA, NAACP, PBS, CNN, YMCA, VHF

NOTE Abbreviations for most units of measure are written without periods.

EXAMPLES   cm, kg, ml, ft, lb, mi, oz, qt

The abbreviation for *inch* (*in.*) is written with a period to prevent confusion with the word *in.* If you're not sure whether to use periods with abbreviations, look in a dictionary.

QUICK CHECK I

Add end marks where they are needed in the following sentences.

EXAMPLE   I. Japanese haiku are very short poems
  I. *Japanese haiku are very short poems.*

1. Have you ever heard of Little Tokyo
2. It's a Japanese neighborhood in Los Angeles, Calif, bordered by First St, Third St, Alameda St, and Los Angeles St
3. Some friends of ours who live in Los Angeles, Mr and Mrs Cook, Sr, and their son, Al, Jr, introduced us to the area
4. They met our 11:30 AM flight from Atlanta, Ga, and took us to lunch at a restaurant in the Japanese Plaza Village
5. What a great afternoon we had with our friends

COMMAS

Items in a Series

13f. **Use commas to separate items in a series.**

Words, phrases, and clauses in a series are separated by commas to show the reader where one item in the series ends and the next item begins. Commas are always needed with three or more items in a series. Two items often do not need a comma.

WORDS IN A SERIES	*Hammock*, *canoe*, and *moccasin* are Native American words.
PHRASES IN A SERIES	Seaweed was in the water, on the beach, and in our shoes.
CLAUSES IN A SERIES	Tell us who was there, what happened, and why it happened.

If all items in a series are joined by *and* or *or*, commas are not needed.

EXAMPLE   I voted for Corey **and** Mona **and** Ethan.

13g. **Use a comma to separate two or more adjectives that come before a noun.**

EXAMPLE   An Arabian horse is a fast, beautiful animal.

Compound Sentences

13h. **Use a comma before *and, but, or, nor, for, so,* or *yet* when it joins independent clauses.**

EXAMPLE   I enjoyed *The King and I*, **but** *Oklahoma!* is still my favorite musical.

You may omit the comma before *and, but, or,* or *nor* if the clauses are very short and there is no chance of misunderstanding.

Quick Check 1: Answers

1. Have you ever heard of Little Tokyo**?**
2. It's a Japanese neighborhood in Los Angeles, Calif**.**, bordered by First St**.**, Third St**.**, Alameda St**.**, and Los Angeles St**.**
3. Some friends of ours who live in Los Angeles, Mr**.** and Mrs**.** Cook, Sr**.**, and their son Al, Jr**.**, introduced us to the area**.**
4. They met our 11:30 A**.** M**.** flight from Atlanta, Ga**.**, and took us to lunch at a restaurant in the Japanese Plaza Village**.**
5. What a great afternoon we had with our friends**!**

Interrupters

13i. Use commas to set off an expression that interrupts a sentence.

Two commas are needed if the expression comes in the middle of the sentence. One comma is needed if the expression comes at the beginning or the end of the sentence.

EXAMPLES   Yes, my favorite gospel singers, BeBe and CeCe Winans, were on TV, Ed.

(1) Use commas to set off a *nonessential* participial phrase or a *nonessential* subordinate clause.

A *nonessential* (or *nonrestrictive*) phrase or clause adds information to the sentence but can be omitted without changing the main idea of the sentence.

NONESSENTIAL PHRASE   Orpheus, **mourning his bride,** entered Hades.

NONESSENTIAL CLAUSE   Orpheus, **who was a musician,** met a cruel fate.

(2) Use commas to set off an appositive or an appositive phrase that is nonessential.

APPOSITIVE   The gray ferryman, **Charon,** did not charge him any fare.

APPOSITIVE PHRASE   Even Cerberus, **the dog at the gate,** listened.

(3) Use commas to set off words used in direct address.

EXAMPLE   Do you know, **Elena,** when the next bus is due?

(4) Use commas to set off a parenthetical expression.

A *parenthetical expression* is a side remark that either adds information or relates ideas in a sentence. Some of these expressions are not always used as interrupters. Use commas only when the expressions are parenthetical.

EXAMPLES   What, **in your opinion,** is the best solution to this problem? [parenthetical]
I have faith **in your opinion.** [not parenthetical]

Introductory Words, Phrases, and Clauses

13j. Use a comma after certain introductory elements.

(1) Use a comma after *yes, no,* or any mild exclamation such as *well* or *why* at the beginning of a sentence.

EXAMPLE   Yes, King Midas had been foolish.

NOTE   Do not set off an *essential* (or *restrictive*) phrase or clause. It cannot be omitted without changing the meaning of the sentence.

ESSENTIAL PHRASE   All the spirits **toiling in Hades** stopped and listened.

ESSENTIAL CLAUSE   The song **that Orpheus sang** charmed the king of Hades.

---

(2) Use a comma after an introductory prepositional phrase if the phrase is long or if two or more phrases appear together.

EXAMPLES **Long ago in a land called Lydia,** King Midas lived.
In the garden of his palace, he met Silenus.

(3) Use a comma after a participial phrase or an infinitive phrase that introduces a sentence.

PARTICIPIAL PHRASE **Threatened by Midas,** the satyr struck a bargain.

INFINITIVE PHRASE **To reward Midas,** Dionysus offered a gift.

(4) Use a comma after an introductory adverb clause.

EXAMPLE **When his daughter arrived,** he warned her to stay away.

Conventional Situations

13k. Use commas in certain conventional situations.

(1) Use commas to separate items in dates and addresses.

EXAMPLES They met on June 17, 1965, in Erie, Pennsylvania.
My address is 520 Cocoa Lane, Orlando, FL 32804.

(2) Use a comma after the salutation of a friendly letter and after the closing of any letter.

EXAMPLES Dear Aunt Margaret,   Sincerely yours,

✓ *QUICK CHECK 2*

Insert commas where they are needed in the following sentences.

EXAMPLE 1. This story the tale of King Midas warns us about greed.
1. *This story, the tale of King Midas, warns us about greed.*

1. Horrified by the sight of his daughter Midas wept.
2. Well Midas left the palace went to Dionysus and begged relief.
3. Dionysus sometimes a merciful god told him to go to Pactolus.
4. In the deep strong waters of the river Midas washed himself.
5. My friend do not make Midas's error or you may not find mercy.

Semicolons

13l. Use a semicolon instead of a comma between independent clauses when they are not joined by *and, but, or, nor, for, so,* or *yet.*

EXAMPLE Our parents settled our dispute; they gave us each half.

> **NOTE** Use a semicolon rather than a period between independent clauses only when the ideas in the clauses are closely related.
>
> **EXAMPLE** I called Leon; he will be here in ten minutes.

Quick Check 2: Answers

1. Horrified by the sight of his daughter, Midas wept.
2. Well, Midas left the palace, went to Dionysus, and begged relief.
3. Dionysus, sometimes a merciful god, told him to go to Pactolus.
4. In the deep, strong waters of the river, Midas washed himself.
5. My friend, do not make Midas's error, or you may not find mercy.

Try It Out: Possible Answers

1. The frogs wanted a king who could amuse them with royal customs. A strong ruler would be exciting, they thought.

2. Jupiter heard their request, and though he granted it, he felt they were foolish.

3. Jupiter threw down a large log, and it landed next to the frogs.

4. Was this strange, new king fearsome, or was he peaceful?

5. Strangely enough, these spoiled, bored frogs were not grateful. They petitioned Jupiter, who again granted their wish.

Quick Check 3: Answers

1. Some reptiles like a dry climate; others prefer a wet climate.

2. The first lunch period begins at 11:00 A.M.

3. Icarus flew too high; his wings melted.

4. In Ruth 1:16, Ruth pledges her loyalty to Naomi.

5. The frogs wanted a king; they got one.

Try It Out ✎

Decide whether each of the following sentences is better expressed as a single sentence or as two or more sentences. Then, write the sentence accordingly. Revise the sentence for style and clarity as well.

1. The frogs wanted a king, one who could amuse them with royal customs; they thought a strong ruler would be exciting.

2. Jupiter heard their request; he granted it; he felt they were foolish.

3. Jupiter threw down a large log; the log landed next to the frogs.

4. Was this strange, new king fearsome; was he peaceful?

5. Strangely enough, these spoiled, bored frogs were not grateful; they petitioned Jupiter, who again granted their wish.

NOTE Never use a colon directly after a verb or a preposition. Omit the colon, or reword the sentence.

INCORRECT My stepsister's favorite sports are: basketball, tennis, swimming, and bowling.

CORRECT My stepsister's favorite sports are basketball, tennis, swimming, and bowling.

NOTE Use a colon between chapter and verse in referring to passages from the Bible.

EXAMPLES John 3:16
Matthew 6:9–13

Using Semicolons

Semicolons are most effective when they are not overused. Sometimes it is better to separate a compound sentence or a heavily punctuated sentence into two sentences rather than to use a semicolon.

ACCEPTABLE In the jungles of South America, it rains every day, sometimes all day; the vegetation there, some of which is found nowhere else in the world, is lush, dense, and fast-growing.

BETTER In the jungles of South America, it rains practically every day, sometimes all day. The vegetation there, some of which is found nowhere else in the world, is lush, dense, and fast-growing.

Colons

13m. Use a colon before a list of items, especially after expressions like *as follows* or *the following*.

EXAMPLE Minimum equipment for camping includes the following: bedroll, utensils for eating, warm clothing, and rope.

13n. Use a colon in certain conventional situations.

(1) Use a colon between the hour and the minute.

EXAMPLES 11:30 P.M.   4:08 A.M.

(2) Use a colon after the salutation of a business letter.

EXAMPLES Dear Ms. Gonzalez: To Whom It May Concern:

☑ QUICK CHECK 3

Insert a colon or semicolon wherever one is needed in each sentence.

EXAMPLE 1. Daedalus made Minos the following furniture, weapons, and armor.

1. *Daedalus made Minos the following: furniture, weapons, and armor.*

1. Some reptiles like a dry climate others prefer a wet climate.

2. The first lunch period begins at 11 00 A.M.

3. Icarus flew too high his wings melted.

4. In Ruth 1 16, Ruth pledges her loyalty to Naomi.

5. The frogs wanted a king they got one.

14 PUNCTUATION

UNDERLINING (ITALICS)

Italics are printed letters that lean to the right, such as *the letters in these words.* In handwritten or typewritten work, indicate italics by underlining.

TYPED <u>Born Free</u> is the story of a lion that became a pet.

PUBLISHED *Born Free* is the story of a lion that became a pet.

COMPUTER NOTE If you use a computer, you may be able to set words in italics yourself. Most word-processing software and many printers are capable of producing italic type.

14a. Use underlining (italics) for titles of books, plays, periodicals, works of art, films, television programs, recordings, long musical compositions, trains, ships, aircraft, and spacecraft.

TYPE OF TITLE	EXAMPLES	
Books	*Barrio Boy*	*House Made of Dawn*
Plays	*Macbeth*	*Visit to a Small Planet*
Periodicals	*Hispanic*	*The New York Times*
Works of Art	*The Thinker*	*American Gothic*
Films	*Stand and Deliver*	*Jurassic Park*
Television Programs	*Home Improvement*	*Wall Street Week*
Recordings	*Unforgettable*	*Man of Steel*
Long Musical Compositions	*Don Giovanni*	*The Four Seasons*
Ships	*Calypso*	*USS Nimitz*
Trains	*Orient Express*	*City of New Orleans*
Aircraft	*Enola Gay*	*Spirit of St. Louis*
Spacecraft	*Apollo 12*	*USS Enterprise*

NOTE The article *the* before the title of a magazine or a newspaper is usually neither italicized nor capitalized when it is written within a sentence. Some periodicals do include *the* in their titles.

EXAMPLES My parents subscribe to **the** *San Francisco Chronicle.* On Sundays, we all share ***The*** *New York Times.*

☞ For examples of titles that are not italicized but enclosed in quotation marks, see page 1026.

14b. Use underlining (italics) for words, letters, and figures referred to as such.

EXAMPLES What is the difference between the words *affect* and *effect?*
Don't forget to drop the final *e* before you add *–ing* to that word.
Is the last number a *5* or an *8?*

Resources

Grammar and Language
■ *Language Handbook Worksheets,* pp. 135–139

Quick Check 1: Answers

1. Sometimes I forget the r in the word <u>friend</u> and write <u>fiend</u>.
2. Pablo Picasso's famous painting <u>Guernica</u> is named for a Spanish town that was bombed during the Spanish Civil War.
3. My father reads the <u>Washington Post</u> because he likes Carl Rowan's column.
4. The movie <u>My Left Foot</u> celebrates the accomplishments of a writer and artist who has serious disabilities.
5. Janice finally found her mistake; she had written the <u>4</u> in the wrong column.

> **NOTE** Do not use quotation marks for an *indirect quotation,* which is a rewording of a direct quotation.
>
> **DIRECT QUOTATION**
> Kaya asked, "What is your interpretation of the poem?"
>
> **INDIRECT QUOTATION**
> Kaya asked what my interpretation of the poem was.

✓ QUICK CHECK I

Underline the words that should be italicized in each of the following sentences.

EXAMPLE   1. Who will play the lead in Brian's Song?
   1. *Who will play the lead in <u>Brian's Song</u>?*

1. Sometimes I forget the r in the word friend and write fiend.
2. Pablo Picasso's famous painting Guernica is named for a Spanish town that was bombed during the Spanish Civil War.
3. My father reads the Washington Post because he likes Carl Rowan's column.
4. The movie My Left Foot celebrates the accomplishments of a writer and artist who has serious disabilities.
5. Janice finally found her mistake; she had written the 4 in the wrong column.

QUOTATION MARKS

14c. Use quotation marks to enclose a *direct quotation*— a person's exact words.

EXAMPLE   "Here is Eric's drawing of the runaway," said Ms. Rios.

14d. A direct quotation begins with a capital letter.

EXAMPLE   Brandon shouted, "**L**et's get busy!"

14e. When the expression identifying the speaker interrupts a quoted sentence, the second part of the quotation begins with a small letter.

EXAMPLE   "Gee," Angelo added, "**t**he boy in 'A Day's Wait' is a lot like my brother."

When the second part of a divided quotation is a separate sentence, it begins with a capital letter.

EXAMPLE   "Travel is exciting," said Mrs. Ash. "**S**pace travel is no exception."

14f. A direct quotation is set off from the rest of the sentence by a comma, a question mark, or an exclamation point, but not by a period.

Set off means "separated." If a quotation appears at the beginning of a sentence, place a comma after it. If a quotation falls at the end of a sentence, place a comma before it. If a quoted sentence is interrupted, place a comma after the first part and before the second part.

EXAMPLES   "I just read a story by Amy Tan**,**" Alyssa said.

Mark said**,** "I've read a couple of her stories, too."

"Alyssa**,**" asked Janet, "what story did you read?"

When a quotation ends with a question mark or an exclamation point, no comma is needed.

EXAMPLE   "Have you seen my brother**?**" Alicia asked.

14g. **A period or a comma is always placed inside the closing quotation marks.**

EXAMPLES   Ramón said, "My little brother loves Shel Silverstein's poems**."**

"My sister dóes too**,"** Paula responded.

14h. **A question mark or an exclamation point is placed inside the closing quotation marks when the quotation itself is a question or exclamation. Otherwise, it is placed outside.**

EXAMPLES   "Is the time difference between Los Angeles and Chicago two hours**?"** asked Ken. [The quotation is a question.]

Linda exclaimed, "I thought everyone knew that**!"** [The quotation is an exclamation.]

What did Sandra Cisneros mean in her story "Four Skinny Trees" when she wrote "Keep, keep, keep, trees say when I sleep**"?** [The sentence, not the quotation, is a question.]

I can't believe that Mom said, "I'm not planning to raise your allowance until next year**"!** [The sentence, not the quotation, is an exclamation.]

When both the sentence and the quotation at the end of the sentence are questions (or exclamations), only one question mark (or exclamation point) is used. It is placed inside the closing quotation marks.

EXAMPLE   Who wrote the poem that begins "How do I love thee**?"**

14i. **When you write dialogue (conversation), begin a new paragraph each time you change speakers.**

EXAMPLE   "Frog, how may we help you?"

"Uh, well, uh, you see," says Frog, "I would like to become a part of your group."

"That's wonderful," says the head bird.

"Yes, wonderful," echo the other birds.

"Frog, you may help us carry our worms," says the head bird.

"That's not what I had in mind," says Frog.

—Linda Goss, "The Frog Who Wanted to Be a Singer"

14j. When a quotation consists of several sentences, place quotation marks at the beginning and at the end of the whole quotation.

EXAMPLE "Take the garbage out. Clean your room. Have fun!" said Dad.

14k. Use single quotation marks to enclose a quotation within a quotation.

EXAMPLES "I said, 'The quiz will be this Friday,'" repeated Mr. Allyn.
"What poem begins with the words 'I'm Nobody'?" Carol asked.

14l. Use quotation marks to enclose titles of short works such as short stories, poems, articles, songs, episodes of television programs, and chapters and other parts of books.

TYPE OF TITLE	EXAMPLES	
Short Stories	"Papa's Parrot"	"Amigo Brothers"
Poems	"Early Song"	"The Runaway"
Articles	"Free Speech and Free Air" "How to Sharpen Your Wit"	
Songs	"La Bamba"	"Amazing Grace"
Episodes of Television Programs	"Heart of a Champion" "The Trouble with Tribbles"	
Chapters and Other Parts of Books	"Learning About Reptiles" "English: Origins and Uses"	

☞ For examples of titles that are italicized, see page 1023.

✓ **QUICK CHECK 2**

Revise the following sentences by adding commas, end marks, quotation marks, and paragraph breaks where necessary.

[1] Gordon, do you ever think about pencils Annie asked [2] I'm always wondering where I lost mine Gordon replied [3] Well said Annie let me tell you some of the things I learned about pencils [4] Sure Gordon said I love trivia [5] People have used some form of pencils for a long time Annie began [6] The ancient Greeks and Romans used lead pencils [7] However, pencils as we know them weren't developed until the 1500s, when people began using graphite [8] What's graphite asked Gordon [9] Graphite is a soft form of carbon Annie explained that leaves a mark when it's drawn over most surfaces [10] Thanks for the information, Annie Gordon said Now, do you have a pencil I can borrow?

Quick Check 2: Answers

[1] "Gordon, do you ever think about pencils?" Annie asked.
[2] "I'm always wondering where I lost mine," Gordon replied.
[3] "Well," said Annie, "let me tell you some of the things I learned about pencils."
[4] "Sure," Gordon said, "I love trivia."
[5] "People have used some form of pencils for a long time," Annie began. [6] "The ancient Greeks and Romans used lead pencils.
[7] However, pencils as we know them weren't developed until the 1500s, when people started using graphite."
[8] "What's graphite?" asked Gordon.
[9] "Graphite is a soft form of carbon," Annie explained, "that leaves a mark when it's drawn over most surfaces."
[10] "Thanks for the information, Annie," Gordon said. "Now, do you have a pencil I can borrow?"

15 PUNCTUATION

APOSTROPHES

15a. The *possessive case* of a noun or a pronoun shows owner-ship or relationship.

(1) To form the possessive case of a singular noun, add an apostrophe and an *s*.

EXAMPLES   a dog's collar   Cinderella's slipper

(2) To form the possessive case of a plural noun ending in *s*, add only the apostrophe.

EXAMPLES   doctors' opinions   hosts' invitations

(3) To form the possessive case of a plural noun that does not end in *s*, add an apostrophe and an *s*.

EXAMPLES   women's suits   geese's noise

(4) To form the possessive case of some indefinite pronouns, add an apostrophe and an *s*.

EXAMPLES   someone's opinion   no one's fault

15b. To form a contraction, use an apostrophe to show where letters have been left out.

A *contraction* is a shortened form of a word, figure, or group of words.

EXAMPLES	I am . . . . .I'm	they had . . . . .they'd
	1996 . . . .'96	where is . . . . . . .where's
	let us . . . . .let's	of the clock . . . .o'clock

The word *not* can be shortened to *–n't* and added to a verb, usually without changing the spelling of the verb.

EXAMPLES	is not . . . . .isn't	had not . . . . .hadn't
	do not . . . . .don't	should not . . .shouldn't
EXCEPTIONS	will not . . . .**won't**	cannot . . . .**can't**

Do not confuse contractions with possessive pronouns.

CONTRACTIONS	POSSESSIVE PRONOUNS
It's snowing. [*It is*]	**Its** front tire is flat.
Who's Clifton Davis? [*Who is*]	**Whose** idea was it?
There's only one answer. [*There is*]	This trophy is **theirs.**
They're not here. [*They are*]	**Their** dog is barking.

 NOTE A proper name ending in *s* may take only an apostrophe to form the possessive case if the addition of 's would make the name awkward to pronounce.
EXAMPLES
Ms. Masters' class
Hercules' feats

 NOTE Do not use an apostrophe with possessive personal pro-nouns.

EXAMPLES   **His** pan-tomime was good, but **hers** was better.

Language Handbook

Resources
Grammar and Language
■ *Language Handbook Worksheets,* pp. 140–146

Quick Check 1: Answers

1. My cousin Dorothy, everybody's favorite, usually gets all A's.
2. It isn't correct to use &'s in your compositions.
3. Many of my friends' scores were in the 80's and 90's
4. They'll meet us later, if it's not raining where we're going.
5. Who's signed up to try out for a part in *Antaeus*?

15c. Use an apostrophe and an *s* to form the plurals of letters, numerals, and signs, and of words referred to as words.

EXAMPLES   Your *2*'s look like *5*'s.
Don't use &'s in place of *and*'s.

✓ *QUICK CHECK 1*

Add an apostrophe wherever one is needed in the following sentences.

EXAMPLE   1. Who wrote "A Days Wait," class?
1. *Who wrote "A Day's Wait," class?*

1. My cousin Dorothy, everybodys favorite, usually gets all As.
2. It isnt correct to use &s in your compositions.
3. Many of my friends scores were in the 80s and 90s.
4. Theyll meet us later, if its not raining where were going.
5. Whos signed up to try out for a part in *Antaeus*?

HYPHENS

15d. Use a hyphen to divide a word at the end of a line.

(1) Divide a word only between syllables.

INCORRECT   Didn't Carrie write her science report on the tyrann-osaurs, the largest meat-eating dinosaurs?

CORRECT   Didn't Carrie write her science report on the tyran-nosaurs, the largest meat-eating dinosaurs?

(2) Divide an already hyphenated word at a hyphen.

INCORRECT   I went to the state fair with my sister and my broth-er-in-law.

CORRECT   I went to the state fair with my sister and my brother-in-law.

(3) Do not divide a word so that one letter stands alone.

INCORRECT   On our last class trip, all of us stayed o-vernight in a hotel.

CORRECT   On our last class trip, all of us stayed overnight in a hotel.

15e. Use a hyphen with compound numbers from *twenty-one* to *ninety-nine* and with fractions used as adjectives.

EXAMPLES   thirty-five   one-half   forty-eighth

Hyphens are used in some compound names. In such cases, the hyphen is part of the name's spelling.

PEOPLE   Daniel Day-Lewis
Orlando Hines-Smith

PLACES   Wilkes-Barre [city]
Stratford-on-Avon [borough]

If you are not sure whether a name is hyphenated, consult a reference source.

PARENTHESES

15f. Use parentheses to enclose material that is added to a sentence but is not considered of major importance.

EXAMPLES Mohandas K. Gandhi **(1869–1948)** led India's struggle for independence.

Ms. Matsuo served us the sushi **(sōō′shē)**.

Fill in the order form carefully. **(Do not use a pencil.)**

My great-uncle Chester **(he's Grandma's brother)** will stay with us.

DASHES

15g. Use a dash to indicate an abrupt break in thought or speech.

EXAMPLES Ms. Alonzo—she just left—will be one of the judges.

"You'll find it—oh, excuse me, Sir—over here," said the librarian.

✓ QUICK CHECK 2

For each of the following sentences, insert hyphens, parentheses, or dashes where they are needed.

EXAMPLE **1.** My grandfather, who is seventy five, can recite "The High wayman."

1. *My grandfather, who is seventy-five, can recite "The High-wayman."*

1. On Fifty third Street, there is a restaurant called The Highwayman.

2. The restaurant founded in 1925 draws half of its customers from tourists.

3. I painted its one hundred thirty one chairs a tedious job, to say the least.

4. Last night, the restaurant was oh, hi, Ed about one quarter full.

5. It's decorated like an inn my restaurant won't be.

Punctuating Parenthetical Information

Too many parenthetical expressions in a piece of writing can distract readers from the main idea. Keep your meaning clear by limiting the number of parenthetical expressions you use.

 NOTE Many words and phrases are used *parenthetically*; that is, they break into the main thought of a sentence. Most parenthetical elements are set off by commas or parentheses. Sometimes, parenthetical elements demand stronger emphasis. In such instances, a dash is used.

Try It Out ✎

Revise the following sentences to eliminate the parentheses. If you think the sentence is best written with parentheses, write *C*.

1. *Survive the Savage Sea* (true stories are my favorites) is about people on a raft.

2. Yellowstone National Park (established in 1872) covers territory in Wyoming, Idaho, and Montana.

3. The writer Langston Hughes (1902–1967) is best known for his poetry.

4. Alligators use their feet and tails to dig holes (called "gator holes") in marshy fields.

5. On the Sabbath we eat braided bread called challah (pronounced khä′ lə).

Language Handbook   1029

Quick Check 2: Possible Answers

1. On Fifty- third Street, there is a restaurant called The Highwayman.

2. The restaurant **(** founded in 1925 **)** draws half of its customers from tourists.

3. I painted its one hundred thirty-one chairs—a tedious job, to say the least.

4. Last night, the restaurant was —oh, hi, Ed—about one-quarter full.

5. It's decorated like an inn **(** my restaurant won't be **)**.

Try It Out: Possible Answers

1. *Survive the Savage Sea* is about people on a raft. True stories are my favorites.

2. Established in 1872, Yellowstone National Park covers territory in Wyoming, Idaho, and Montana.

3. C

4. Alligators use their feet and tails to dig holes, called "gator holes," in marshy fields.

5. C

Language Handbook

16 SPELLING

USING WORD PARTS

Many English words are made up of various word parts. Learning to spell the most frequently used parts can help you spell many words correctly.

Roots

16a. The *root* of a word is the part that carries the word's core meaning.

WORD ROOT	MEANING	EXAMPLES
–dict–	speak	dictation, dictionary
–duc–, –duct–	lead	educate, conductor
–ject–	throw	eject, reject
–ped–	foot	pedal, biped
–vid–, –vis–	see	videotape, invisible

Prefixes

16b. A *prefix* is one or more letters or syllables added to the beginning of a word or a word part to create a new word.

PREFIX	MEANING	EXAMPLES
anti–	against, opposing	antiwar, anticlimax
co–	with, together	coexist, codependent
in–	not	inaccurate, ineffective
re–	back, again	reclaim, rebuild
trans–	across, beyond	transport, translate

Suffixes

16c. A *suffix* is one or more letters or syllables added to the end of a word or a word part to create a new word.

SUFFIX	MEANING	EXAMPLES
–able	able, likely	readable, perishable
–ance, –ancy	act, quality	admittance, constancy
–ate	become, cause	captivate, activate
–ize	make, cause to be	socialize, motorize
–ness	quality, state	peacefulness, sadness

SPELLING RULES

ie and *ei*

16d. Except after *c*, write *ie* when the sound is long *e*.

EXAMPLES   achieve   believe   chief   field   piece
ceiling   conceit   deceit   deceive   receive

EXCEPTIONS   either   protein   neither   seize   weird

16e. Write *ei* when the sound is not long *e*, especially when the sound is long *a*.

EXAMPLES   foreign   forfeit   height   heir   their
freight   neighbor   reign   veil   weigh

EXCEPTIONS   ancient   conscience   patient   friend   efficient

✓ QUICK CHECK 1

Add the letters *ie* or *ei* to spell each of the following words correctly.

EXAMPLE   1. bel . . . ve
1. *believe*

1. gr . . . f
2. v . . . n
3. n . . . ce
4. sh . . . ld
5. . . . ght
6. perc . . . ve
7. pat . . . nce
8. th . . . f
9. r . . . ndeer
10. p . . . rce

–cede, –ceed, and *–sede*

16f. The only English word ending in *–sede* is *supersede*. The only words ending in *–ceed* are *exceed, proceed,* and *succeed*. Most other words with this sound end in *–cede*.

EXAMPLES   concede   intercede   precede   recede   secede

Adding Prefixes and Suffixes

16g. When adding a prefix to a word, do not change the spelling of the word itself.

EXAMPLES   mis + spell = **mis**spell   il + logical = **il**logical

16h. When adding the suffix *–ly* or *–ness* to a word, do not change the spelling of the word itself.

EXAMPLES   slow + ly = slow**ly**   dark + ness = dark**ness**

EXCEPTIONS   For words that end in *y* and have more than one syllable, change the *y* to *i* before adding *–ly* or *-ness*.
happy + ly = happ**ily**   lazy + ness = laz**iness**

NOTE This time-tested verse may help you remember the *ie* rule.

I before *e*
Except after *c*
Or when sounded like *a*,
As in *neighbor* and *weigh*.

The rhyme above and rules 16d and 16e apply only when the *i* and the *e* are in the same syllable.

Quick Check 1: Answers

1. grief
2. vein
3. niece
4. shield
5. eight
6. perceive
7. patience
8. thief
9. reindeer
10. pierce

NOTE When adding *—ing* to words that end in *ie*, drop the e and change the *i* to *y*.

EXAMPLES
lie + ing = **lying**
die + ing = **dying**

NOTE In some cases, the final consonant either may or may not be doubled.

EXAMPLE
cancel + ed = canceled
or cance**ll**ed

16i. **Drop the final silent e before a suffix beginning with a vowel.**

EXAMPLES line + ing = lin**ing**   desire + able = desir**able**

EXCEPTIONS Keep the final silent *e* in a word ending in *ce* or *ge* before a suffix beginning with *a* or *o*.
*notice + able = notic**e**able*
*courage + ous = courag**eous***

16j. **Keep the final silent e before a suffix beginning with a consonant.**

EXAMPLES hope + less = hope**less**   care + ful = care**ful**

EXCEPTIONS nine + th = nin**th**   argue + ment = argu**ment**

16k. **For words ending in y preceded by a consonant, change the y to i before any suffix that does not begin with i.**

EXAMPLES try + ed = tr**ied**   duty + ful = dut**iful**

16l. **For words ending in y preceded by a vowel, keep the y when adding a suffix.**

EXAMPLES pray + ing = pray**ing**   pay + ment = pay**ment**

EXCEPTIONS day—da**ily**   lay—la**id**   pay—pa**id**   say—sa**id**

16m. **Double the final consonant before a suffix beginning with a vowel if the word**

(1) **has only one syllable or has the accent on the last syllable**

and

(2) **ends in a single consonant preceded by a single vowel**

EXAMPLES sit + ing = sit**t**ing   begin + er = begin**n**er

EXCEPTIONS Do not double the final consonant in words ending in *w* or *x*.
mow + ing = mo**w**ing   wax + ed = wa**x**ed

Otherwise, the final consonant is usually not doubled before a suffix beginning with a vowel.

EXAMPLES sing + er = sing**er**   final + ist = final**ist**

 QUICK CHECK 2

Add the given prefix or suffix to each word listed at the top of the next page.

EXAMPLE **1.** display + ed
         1. *displayed*

1. im + migrate   5. semi + circle   9. carry + ed
2. re + settle   6. trace + able   10. advantage + ous
3. un + certain   7. jog + er
4. lucky + ly   8. dry + ness

Forming the Plurals of Nouns

16n. For most nouns, add –s.

EXAMPLES desks   ideas   shoes   friends   cameras   Wilsons

16o. For nouns ending in s, x, z, ch, or sh, add –es.

EXAMPLES gases   foxes   waltzes   inches   dishes   Suarezes

16p. For nouns ending in y preceded by a vowel, add –s.

EXAMPLES decoys   highways   alleys   Rileys

16q. For nouns ending in y preceded by a consonant, change the y to i and add –es.

EXAMPLES armies   countries   cities   ponies   allies   daisies

EXCEPTIONS For proper nouns ending in *y*, just add –s.
Brady—Bradys   Murphy—Murphys

16r. For some nouns ending in f or fe, add –s. For others, change the f or fe to v and add –es.

EXAMPLES beliefs   thieves   sheriffs   knives
giraffes   leaves   roofs   calves

16s. For nouns ending in o preceded by a vowel, add –s.

EXAMPLES radios   patios   stereos   igloos
Matteos

16t. For nouns ending in o preceded by a consonant, add –es.

EXAMPLES tomatoes   potatoes   echoes   heroes

EXCEPTIONS For musical terms and proper nouns, add -s.
alto—altos   soprano—sopranos
Blanco—Blancos   Nakamoto—Nakamotos

16u. The plural of a few nouns is formed in irregular ways.

EXAMPLES oxen   geese   feet   teeth   women   mice

16v. For most compound nouns, form the plural of the last word in the compound.

EXAMPLES bookshelves   push-ups   sea gulls   ten-year-olds

TIPS FOR SPELLING

In some names, marks that show pronunciation are just as important as the letters themselves.

PEOPLE Alemán   Böll   Ibáñez
Khayyám   Janáček   Eugène
PLACES Açores   Bogotá   Camagüey
Gîza   Köln   Sainte-Thérèse

If you're not sure about the spelling of a name, ask the person whose name it is, or check in a reference source.

Quick Check 2: Answers

1. immigrate
2. resettle
3. uncertain
4. luckily
5. semicircle
6. traceable
7. jogger
8. dryness
9. carried
10. advantageous

Quick Check 3: Answers

1. cargoes
2. diaries
3. Gómezes
4. sit-ups
5. children
6. videos
7. hooves
8. Japanese
9. *M*'s
10. *10*'s

Resources

Grammar and Language

■ *Language Handbook Worksheets,* pp. 154–157

When you use numbers in your writing, follow these guidelines:

• Spell out a number that begins a sentence.

EXAMPLE **Fifty** people received free tickets.

• Within a sentence, spell out numbers that can be written in one or two words.

EXAMPLE In all, **fifty-two** people worked on our play.

• If you use several numbers, some short and some long, write them all the same way. Usually, it is better to write them all as numerals.

EXAMPLE We sold **86** tickets today and **121** yesterday.

• Spell out numbers used to indicate order.

EXAMPLE Our team came in **third** [*not* 3rd] in the track meet.

16w. For compound nouns in which one of the words is modified by the other word or words, form the plural of the word modified.

EXAMPLES   brothers-in-law   maids of honor
eighth-graders   boy scouts

16x. For some nouns, the singular and the plural forms are the same.

SINGULAR AND PLURAL   Sioux   trout   sheep
deer   moose   series

16y. For numerals, letters, symbols, and words used as words, add an apostrophe and *–s.*

EXAMPLES   *4*'s   *s*'s $'s   *and*'s

✓ QUICK CHECK 3

Spell the plural form of each of the following items. [Note: An item may have more than one correct plural form. You only need to give one.]

EXAMPLE 1. &
1. &'s

1. cargo	**5.** child	**9.** *M*
2. diary	**6.** video	**10.** *10*
3. Gómez	**7.** hoof	
4. sit-up	**8.** Japanese	

17 GLOSSARY OF USAGE

This Glossary of Usage is an alphabetical list of words and expressions that are commonly misused in English. Throughout this section some examples are labeled *standard* or *nonstandard.* **Standard English** is the most widely accepted form of English. It is used in *formal* situations, such as in speeches and writing for school, and in *informal* situations, such as in conversation and everyday writing. **Nonstandard English** is language that does not follow the rules and guidelines of standard English.

---

all ready, already   *All ready* means "completely prepared." *Already* means "before a certain point in time."

EXAMPLES   Everyone was **all ready** for the show.
That bill has **already** been paid.

all right   Used as an adjective, *all right* means "unhurt" or "satisfactory." Used as an adverb, *all right* means "well enough." *All right* should always be written as two words.

EXAMPLES   Linda fell off the horse, but she is **all right.** [adjective]
Does this suit look **all right** on me? [adjective]
You did **all right** at the track meet. [adverb]

a lot   *A lot* should always be written as two words.

EXAMPLE   She knows **a lot** about computer software.

anywheres, everywheres, nowheres, somewheres   Use these words without the final *s*.

EXAMPLE   I didn't go **anywhere** [*not* anywheres] yesterday.

at   Do not use *at* after *where*.

EXAMPLE   Where is it? [*not* Where is it at?]

bad, badly   *Bad* is an adjective. *Badly* is an adverb.

EXAMPLES   The raw celery did not taste **bad.** [*Bad* modifies the noun *celery.*]
One little boy behaved **badly.** [*Badly* modifies the verb *behaved.*]

between, among   Use *between* when referring to two things at a time, even though they may be part of a group containing more than two.

EXAMPLES   In homeroom, Carlos sits **between** Bob and me.
Some players practice **between** innings. [Although a game has more than two innings, the practice occurs only *between* any two of them.]

Use *among* to refer to a group rather than separate individuals.

EXAMPLES   We saved ten dollars **among** the three of us. [As a group, the three saved ten dollars.]
There was disagreement **among** the fans about the coach's decision. [The fans are thought of as a group.]

bust, busted   Avoid using these words as verbs. Use a form of either *burst* or *break*.

EXAMPLES   The door **burst** [*not* busted] open and rats teemed in.
What would happen if the window **broke** [*not* busted]?

choose, chose   *Choose* is the present tense form of the verb *choose*. It rhymes with *whose* and means "select." *Chose* is the past tense form of *choose*. It rhymes with *grows* and means "selected."

EXAMPLES   Did you **choose** "Fish Cheeks" for your report?
Sara **chose** "Miss Awful."

NOTE   Many writers overuse *a lot*. Whenever you run across *a lot* as you revise your own writing, try to replace it with a more exact word or phrase.

☞ **among**   See **between, among.**
as   See **like, as.**
as if   See **like, as if, as though.**

☞ **because**   See **reason . . . because.**

👉 **doesn't, don't**
See page 972.

👉 **had of** See **could of.**

👉 **its, it's** See page 1027.

could of Do not write *of* with the helping verb *could*. Write *could have*. Also avoid *had of, ought to of, should of, would of, might of,* and *must of*.

EXAMPLE   All of Emily Dickinson's poems **could have** [*not* could of] been lost.

fewer, less *Fewer* is used with plural words. *Less* is used with singular words. *Fewer* tells "how many"; *less* tells "how much."

EXAMPLES   We sold **fewer** [*not* less] tickets than they did.
These plants require **less** water than those do.

good, well *Good* is always an adjective. Never use *good* as an adverb. Instead, use *well*.

EXAMPLE   Nancy sang **well** [*not* good] at the audition.

Well may also be used as an adjective to mean "healthy."

EXAMPLE   He didn't look **well** after eating the entire pizza.

had ought, hadn't ought *Had* should not be used with *ought*.

EXAMPLE   Eric **ought** [*not* had ought] to help us; he **oughtn't** [*not* hadn't ought] to have missed our meeting yesterday.

he, she, they Avoid using a pronoun along with its antecedent as the subject of a verb. This error is called the **double subject.**

NONSTANDARD   Linda Goss she is a famous writer.
   STANDARD   Linda Goss is a famous writer.

hisself *Hisself* is nonstandard English. Use *himself*.

EXAMPLE   Ira bought **himself** [*not* hisself] a polka-dot tie.

how come In informal situations, *how come* is often used instead of *why*. In formal situations, *why* should always be used.

INFORMAL   I don't know how come she didn't take the garbage out.
  FORMAL   I don't know **why** she didn't take the garbage out.

kind of, sort of In informal situations, *kind of* and *sort of* are often used to mean "somewhat" or "rather." In formal English, *somewhat* or *rather* is preferred.

INFORMAL   He seemed kind of embarrassed by our applause.
  FORMAL   He seemed **somewhat** embarrassed by our applause.

☑ **QUICK CHECK 1**

Revise each of the following sentences to correct any error in usage.

EXAMPLE   1. The author she had lived in China.
      1. *The author had lived in China.*

1. Alot of stars and planets have names from mythology.
2. Icarus had ought to have listened to his father.
3. If he had listened, he could of survived.
4. I wonder how come he didn't listen.
5. Surely, Daedalus's heart was busted by the death of his son.

learn, teach   *Learn* means "gain knowledge." *Teach* means "instruct" or "show how."

EXAMPLES   He is **learning** how to play the guitar.
His grandfather is **teaching** him how to play.

like, as   In informal situations, the preposition *like* is often used instead of the conjunction *as* to introduce a clause. In formal situations, *as* is preferred.

EXAMPLE   Look in the dictionary, **as** [*not* like] the teacher suggests.

like, as if, as though   In informal situations, the preposition *like* is often used for the compound conjunctions *as if* or *as though*. In formal situations, *as if* or *as though* is preferred.

EXAMPLES   They acted **as if** [*not* like] they hadn't heard him.
You looked **as though** [*not* like] you knew the answer.

of   Do not use *of* with other prepositions such as *inside, off,* and *outside.*

EXAMPLE   Did anyone fall **off** [*not* off of] the raft?

 **less**   See **fewer, less.**

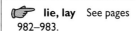 **lie, lay**   See pages 982–983.

☞ **might of, must of**
See **could of.**

☞ **ought to of**
See **could of.**

![Tips for Writers logo] **Revising Adverbs in Sentences**

In informal situations, the adjective *real* is often used as an adverb meaning "very" or "extremely." In formal situations, *extremely* or another adverb is preferred.

INFORMAL   I'm expecting a real important telephone call.

FORMAL   I'm expecting an **extremely** important telephone call.

reason . . . because   In informal situations, *reason . . . because* is often used instead of *reason . . . that.* In formal situations, use *reason . . . that,* or revise your sentence.

INFORMAL   The reason I did well on the test was because I had studied hard.

FORMAL   The **reason** I did well on the test was **that** I had studied hard.

some, somewhat   Do not use *some* for *somewhat* as an adverb.

EXAMPLE   My writing has improved **somewhat** [*not* some].

Try It Out ✎

Revise the following sentences by substituting another adverb for the word *real.* Use a variety of adverbs.

1. Hercules was real strong.
2. He accomplished many tasks that were real hard.
3. Stories of his labors are real interesting.
4. They have endured a real long time.
5. Even today, real young children know his story from television shows.

☞ **should of**
See **could of.**

☞ **somewheres**
See **anywheres,** etc.

Language Handbook   1037

Quick Check 1: Answers

1. A lot of stars and planets have names from mythology.
2. Icarus ought to have listened to his father.
3. If he had listened, he could have survived.
4. I wonder why he didn't listen.
5. Surely, Daedalus's heart was broken by the death of his son.

Try It Out: Possible Answers

1. Hercules was extremely strong.
2. He accomplished many tasks that were amazingly hard.
3. Stories of his labors are very interesting.
4. They have endured an exceptionally long time.
5. Even today, very young children know his story from television shows.

👉 **sort of** See **kind of, sort of.**

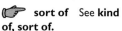
NOTE Here's an easy way to remember the difference between *stationary* and *stationery:*
You write a letter on station**ery**.

👉 **who's, whose** See page 1027.

👉 **would of** See **could of.**

stationary, stationery The adjective *stationary* means "in a fixed position." The noun *stationery* means "writing paper."

EXAMPLES Furnishings in a space capsule must be **stationary**.
I need a new box of **stationery**.

them *Them* should not be used as an adjective. Use *those.*

EXAMPLE The fox couldn't get **those** [*not* them] grapes.

way, ways Use *way*, not *ways*, in referring to a distance.

EXAMPLE They still had a long **way** [*not* ways] to go.

when, where Do not use *when* or *where* incorrectly in a definition.

NONSTANDARD In bowling, a "turkey" is when a person makes three strikes in a row.

STANDARD In bowling, a "turkey" is making three strikes in a row.

where Do not use *where* for *that.*

EXAMPLE I read **that** [*not* where] Pete Sampras won the match.

who, which, that The relative pronoun *who* refers to people only; *which* refers to things only; *that* refers to either people or things.

EXAMPLES Kim is the only one **who** got the right answer. [person]
My bike, **which** has ten speeds, is for sale. [thing]
He is the one person **that** can help you. [person]
This is the ring **that** I want to buy. [thing]

without, unless Do not use the preposition *without* in place of the conjunction *unless.*

EXAMPLE My mother said I can't go **unless** [*not* without] I finish my homework first.

✅ **QUICK CHECK 2**

Revise the following sentences to correct any error in usage.

EXAMPLE 1. The team forfeited the game like they had agreed to.
1. *The team forfeited the game as they had agreed to.*

1. The reason they forfeited was because Dondré couldn't play there.
2. What was going on inside of their heads?
3. They would not play without their teammate could play, too.
4. That story learned me something about loyalty.
5. True friendship is where people value each other as much as themselves.

Quick Check 2: Possible Answers

1. They forfeited because Dondré couldn't play there.
2. What was going on inside their heads?
3. They would not play unless their teammate could play, too.
4. That story taught me something about loyalty.
5. True friendship means that people value each other as much as themselves.

Spelling Handbook

COMMONLY MISSPELLED WORDS

No matter how many spelling rules you learn, you will find that it is helpful to learn to spell certain common words from memory. The fifty "demons" in the first list are words that you should be able to spell without any hesitation, even though they all contain spelling problems. Study them in groups of five until you are sure you know them.

The second, longer list contains words that you should learn if you do not already know them. They are grouped by tens so that you may study them ten at a time. In studying each list, pay particular attention to the underlined letters. These letters are generally the ones that pose problems for students.

For more on spelling, see spelling rules 16a–16y in the Language Handbook.

FIFTY SPELLING DEMONS

ache	cough	guess	once	though
again	could	half	ready	through
always	country	hour	said	tired
answer	doctor	instead	says	tonight
blue	does	knew	shoes	trouble
built	don't	know	since	wear
busy	early	laid	straight	where
buy	easy	meant	sugar	which
can't	every	minute	sure	whole
color	friend	often	tear	women

TWO HUNDRED SPELLING WORDS

abandon	commercial	February	nickel	separate
absolutely	committees	finally	nuisance	sergeant
acceptance	competition	flu	numerous	shepherd
accidentally	conceive	friendliness	obvious	similar
accommodate	condemn	generally	occasionally	solemn
accomplish	congratulations	governor	occurrence	sponsor
achieve	conscience	grammar	opportunity	straighten
acquaintance	conscious	gratitude	orchestra	subscription
acquire	convenience	guarantee	originally	succeed
actually	courteous	guardian	parallel	success
advertisement	criticism	gymnasium	parliament	sufficient
aisle	cylinder	height	patience	suppress
amount	dealt	hesitate	personal	surprise
analysis	deceit	humorous	persuade	surrounded
anticipate	definite	hypocrite	philosopher	suspense
anxiety	definition	ignorance	picnicking	tailor
apology	description	imagination	planned	temperament
apparent	desirable	immediately	possess	tendency
appearance	despair	incidentally	precede	theories
application	difficulties	individual	preferred	therefore
appreciation	disappointment	initial	prejudice	thorough
approach	discipline	inspiration	privilege	tobacco
assistance	discussion	intelligence	probably	tonsils
authority	diseased	interfere	procedure	tradition
beginning	distinction	interrupt	professor	tragedy
believe	distribution	judgment	pursuit	transferred
benefit	duplicate	knowledge	realize	truly
boundary	eligible	laboratory	receipt	unanimous
bouquet	embarrass	leisure	recommend	unnecessary
bulletin	engineering	lieutenant	referring	useful
business	equipped	luncheon	regularly	utilized
canceled	eventually	majority	relieve	vacuum
capacity	exactly	manufacture	repetition	various
carrier	exaggerate	marriage	research	vein
ceiling	excellent	mechanical	response	villain
challenge	existence	medieval	rhythm	violence
chorus	experience	mourn	satisfied	warrant
circuit	experiment	muscular	schedule	weird
colonel	fascinating	naturally	scissors	wholly
column	favorite	necessary	sense	writing

Communications Handbook

RESEARCH STRATEGIES

Using a Media Center or Library

To find a book, tape, film, or video in a library, start by looking in the **catalog.** Most libraries use an **online,** or computer, **catalog.**

Online catalogs vary from library to library. With some you begin searching for resources by **title, author,** or **subject.** With others you simply enter **keywords** for the subject you're researching. With either system, you enter information into the computer and a new screen will show you a list of materials or subject headings relating to your request. When you find an item you want, write down the title, author, and **call number,** the code of numbers and letters that shows you where to find the item on the library's shelves.

Some libraries still use card catalogs. A **card catalog** is a collection of index cards arranged in alphabetical order by title and author. Nonfiction is also cataloged by subject.

Electronic Databases. Electronic databases are collections of information you can access by computer. You can use these databases to find such resources as encyclopedias, almanacs, and museum art collections.

There are two kinds of electronic databases: **Online databases** are accessed at a computer terminal connected to a modem. The modem allows the computer to communicate with other computers over telephone lines. **Portable databases** are available on magnetic tape, diskette, or CD-ROM.

A **CD-ROM** (compact disc–read only memory) is played on a computer equipped with a CD-ROM player. If you were to look up *Amy Tan* on a CD-ROM guide to literature, for example, you could hear passages from her books and read critical analyses of her work.

Periodicals. Most libraries have a collection of magazines and newspapers. To find up-to-date magazine or newspaper articles on a topic, use a computerized index, such as *InfoTrac* or *EBSCO.* Some of these indices provide a summary of each article. Others provide the entire text, which you can read on-screen or print out. The *Readers' Guide to Periodical Literature* is a print index of articles that have appeared in hundreds of magazines.

Using the Internet

The **Internet** is a huge network of computers. Libraries, news services, government agencies, researchers, and organizations communicate and share information on the Net. The Net also lets you chat online with students around the world. For help in using the Internet to do research or to communicate with someone by computer, explore the options on the next page.

The Reference Section

Every library has materials you can use only in the library. Some examples are listed below. (Some reference works are available in both print and electronic form.)

Encyclopedias
Collier's Encyclopedia
The World Book Encyclopedia

General Biographical References
Current Biography Yearbook
The International Who's Who
Webster's New Biographical Dictionary

Special Biographical References
American Men & Women of Science
Biographical Dictionary of American Sports
Mexican American Biographies

Atlases
Atlas of World Cultures
National Geographic Atlas of the World

Almanacs
Information Please Almanac
The World Almanac and Book of Facts

Books of Quotations
Bartlett's *Familiar Quotations*

Books of Synonyms
Roget's International Thesaurus
Webster's New Dictionary of Synonyms

Communications Handbook **1041**

Communications Handbook **1041**

You've Got Mail!

E-mail is an electronic message sent over a computer network. On the Internet you can use e-mail to reach institutions, businesses, and individuals. When you e-mail places like museums, you may be able to ask **experts** about a topic you're researching. You can also use e-mail to chat with students around the country and around the world.

Internet forums, or newsgroups, let you discuss and debate lots of subjects with other computer users. You can write and send a question to a forum and get an answer from someone who may (or may not) know something about your topic.

Techno Tip

- If you get too few hits, use a more general word as your search term.

- If you get too many hits, use a more specific word as your search term.

The World Wide Web

The easiest way to do research on the Internet is on the World Wide Web. On the Web, information is stored in colorful, easy-to-access files called **Web pages.** Web pages usually have text, graphics, images, sound, and even video clips.

Using a Web Browser

You look at Web pages with a **Web browser,** a program for accessing information on the Web. Every page on the Web has its own address, called a **URL,** or Uniform Resource Locator. If you know the address of a Web page you want to go to, just enter it in the location field on your browser.

Hundreds of millions of Web pages are connected by **hyperlinks,** which let you jump from one page to another. These links are usually underlined or colored words or images, or both, on your computer screen. With hundreds of millions of linked Web pages, how can you find the information you want?

Using a Web Directory

If you're just beginning to look for a research topic, click on a **Web directory,** a list of topics and subtopics created by experts to help users find Web sites. Think of the directory as a giant index. Start by choosing a broad category, such as Literature. Then, work your way down through the subtopics, perhaps from Poetry to Poets. Under Poets, choose a Web page that looks interesting, perhaps one on Robert Frost.

Using a Search Engine

If you already have a topic and need information about it, try using a **search engine,** a software tool that finds information on the Web. To use a search engine, just go to an online search form and enter a **search term,** or keyword. The search engine will return a list of Web pages containing your search term. The list will also show you the first few lines of each page. A search term such as *Frost* may produce thousands of results, or **hits,** including weather data on frost. If you're doing a search on the poet Robert Frost, most of these thousands of hits will be of no use. To find useful material, you have to narrow your search.

"On the Internet, nobody knows you're a dog."

Refining a Keyword Search

To focus your research, use **search operators,** such as the words AND or NOT, to create a string of keywords. If you're looking for material on Robert Frost and his life in Vermont, for example, you might enter the following search term:

Frost AND Vermont NOT weather

The more focused search term yields pages that contain both *Frost* and *Vermont* and nothing about weather. The chart on the right explains how several search operators work.

Evaluating Web Sources

Since anyone can publish a Web page, it's important to evaluate your sources. Use these criteria to evaluate a source:

Authority

Who is the author? What is his or her knowledge or experience? Trust respected sources, such as the Smithsonian Institution, not a person's newsletter or Web page.

Accuracy

How trustworthy is the information? Does the author give his or her sources? Check information from one site against information from at least two other sites or print sources.

Objectivity

What is the author's **perspective,** or point of view? Find out whether the information provider has a bias or a hidden purpose.

Currency

Is the information up-to-date? For a print source, check the copyright date. For a Web source, look for the date on which the page was created or revised. (This date appears at the bottom of the site's home page.)

Coverage

How well does the source cover the topic? Could you find better information in a book? Compare the source with several others.

COMMON SEARCH OPERATORS AND WHAT THEY DO	
AND	Demands that both terms appear on the page; narrows search
+	Demands that both terms appear on the page; narrows search
OR	Yields pages that contain either term; widens search
NOT	Excludes a word from consideration; narrows search
–	Excludes a word from consideration; narrows search
NEAR	Demands that two words be close together; narrows search
ADJ	Demands that two words be close together; narrows search
" "	Demands an exact phrase; narrows search

Techno Tip
To evaluate a Web source, look at the top-level domain in the URL. Here is a sample URL with the top-level domain—a government agency—labeled.

top-level domain

http://www.loc.gov

Communications Handbook   **1043**

COMMON TOP-LEVEL DOMAINS AND WHAT THEY STAND FOR	
.edu	Educational institution. Site may publish scholarly work or the work of elementary or high school students.
.gov	Government body. Information is generally reliable.
.org	Usually a nonprofit organization. If the organization promotes culture (as a museum does), information is generally reliable; if it advocates a cause, information may be biased.
.com	Commercial enterprise. Information should be evaluated carefully.
.net	Organization offering Internet services. Information is generally reliable.

Listing Sources and Taking Notes

When you write a research paper, you must **document,** or identify, your sources so that readers will know where you found your material. You must avoid **plagiarism,** or presenting another writer's words or ideas as if they were your own.

Listing Sources

List each source, and give it a number. (You'll use these source numbers later, when you take notes.) Here's where to find the publication information (such as the name of the publisher and the copyright date) you'll need for different types of sources:

- **Print sources.** Look at the title and copyright pages of the book or periodical.

- **Online sources.** Look at the beginning or end of the document or in a separate electronic file. For a Web page, look for a link containing the word *About.*

- **Portable electronic databases.** Look at the start-up screen, the packaging, or the disc itself.

There are several ways to list sources. The chart on page 1045 shows the style created by the Modern Language Association.

Taking Notes

Here are some tips for taking notes:

- Put notes from different sources on separate index cards, sheets of paper, or computer files.

- At the top of each card, sheet of paper, or file, write a label telling what that note is about.

- At the bottom, write the numbers of the pages on which you found the information.

- Use short phrases, and make lists of details and ideas. You don't have to write full sentences.

- Use your own words unless you find material you want to quote. If you quote an author's exact words, put quotation marks around them.

The sample note card at the left shows how to take notes.

Preparing a List of Sources

Use your source cards to make a **works cited** list, which should appear at the end of your report. At the top of a sheet of paper, type and center the

Sample Note Card

Poe's Childhood and Youth	1
—Parents were actors—father deserted family, mother died before Poe's 3rd birthday	
—Raised by Frances and John Allan	
—Published first poems at age 18	p. 20

heading *Works Cited.* Below it, list your sources in alphabetical order. Follow the MLA guidelines for citing sources (see the chart below). The sample works cited list below shows you how to do this.

Sample Works Cited List

Anderson, M. K. Edgar Allan Poe: A Mystery. New York: Franklin Watts, 1993.

"The Life of a Poet." Edgar Allan Poe Historic Site Home Page. 2003. 19 Aug. 2003 <http://www.nps.gov/edal/brochure.htm>.

"Poe, Edgar Allan." The World Book Encyclopedia. 2003 ed.

The chart below shows citations of print, audiovisual, and electronic sources:

MLA GUIDELINES FOR CITING SOURCES	
Books	Give the author, title, city of publication, publisher, and copyright year. Anderson, M. K. Edgar Allan Poe: A Mystery. New York: Franklin Watts, 1993.
Magazine and newspaper articles	Give the author (if named), title of the article, name of the magazine or newspaper, date, and page numbers. "Did Rabies Fell Edgar Allan Poe?" Science News 2 Nov. 1996: 282.
Encyclopedia articles	Give the author (if named), title of the article, name of the encyclopedia, and edition (year). "Poe, Edgar Allan." The World Book Encyclopedia. 2003 ed.
Interviews	Give the expert's name, the words *Personal interview* or *Telephone interview,* and the date. M. K. Anderson. Telephone interview. 12 Jan. 2004.
Films, videotapes, and audiotapes	Give the title; producer, director, or developer; medium; distributor; and year of release. Edgar Allan Poe: Terror of the Soul. Prod. Film Odyssey. Videocassette. PBS Home Video, 1995.

Electronic materials, including CD-ROMs and online sources	Give the author (if named); title; title of project, database, periodical, or site; electronic posting date (online); type of source (CD-ROMs); city (CD-ROMs); distributor (CD-ROMs); publication date (CD-ROMs) or access date; and Internet address (if any).
	   "Poe, Edgar Allan." Grolier Multimedia Encyclopedia. CD-ROM. Danbury: Grolier Interactive, 2003.
	   "The Life of a Poet." Edgar Allan Poe Historic Home Site Page. 2003. 19 Aug. 2003 <http://www.nps.gov/edal/brochure.htm>.

PROOFREADERS' MARKS

Symbol	Example	Meaning
≡	New mexico	Capitalize lowercase letter.
/	next Spring	Lowercase capital letter.
∧	a book ∧quotations _of_	Insert.
ℛ	a good go℟d idea	Delete.
⌢ ⌣	a grape⌣fruit tree	Close up space.
√	does√it	Change order (of letters or words).
¶	¶"Who's there?" she asked.	Begin a new paragraph.
⊙	Please don't forget⊙	Add a period.
∧,	Maya∧did you call me?	Add a comma.
◇	Dear Mrs. Mills◇	Add a colon.
∧,	Columbus, Ohio∧, Dallas, Texas	Add a semicolon.
ˇ ˇ	ˇAre you OK?ˇ he asked.	Add quotation marks.

Giving and Listening to a Personal Narrative

Choosing a Story

To plan your oral narrative, you must find the right story to tell. (You might want to adapt the personal narrative you wrote for the Writing Workshop on pages 330–335.) Your story should have the following elements:

- **major and minor characters** that seem real
- **setting,** a definite time and place in which the story occurs
- **conflict,** a problem that the major characters must solve
- **plot,** made up of a **beginning** that sets the scene, **rising action** that leads to the story's **climax,** and a **resolution**

Make sure the story also has **dialogue** that brings the characters to life, **suspense** that makes listeners wonder what will happen next, and **action** that you can describe vividly or act out using movements, gestures, and facial expressions.

In addition, you need to consider the *purpose* and *audience* for your story. The **purpose** is to entertain, so you should choose a story that will appeal to the backgrounds and interests of your **audience,** namely, your teacher and classmates.

Planning Your Presentation

You can choose to tell the story as yourself, as a character involved in the story, or as an uninvolved narrator, but be sure to use a consistent **point of view** to keep your audience from becoming confused. Also, use the following strategies as you plan how to tell your story.

- **Describe the setting.** Use vivid language to describe each setting in the story. Focus on details that appeal to the senses. For example, if your story takes place in a garage, take time to describe the oil stains on the floor and the smell of gasoline in the air.

- **Describe the characters.** Bring your characters to life with specific details, such as the way they dress or talk.

- **Organize details in a logical way.** Organize your story in a way that will make sense and appeal to your listeners. Most listeners will expect a story to be told in **chronological order,** the order in which the events occur. As you organize your ideas, make sure they are **coherent**—all the events, actions, and dialogue should flow together smoothly.

Delivering Your Personal Narrative

Do not write out your narrative on a piece of paper, or you may be tempted just to read it aloud. Instead, jot down **notes** about key scenes, details, gestures, and so on, on an index card or sheet of paper. You can refer to your notes as you deliver your narrative without losing eye contact with your audience.

In your narrative, you must communicate the overall **mood,** or feeling, of the story, including your **attitude,** or what you think and feel about the situation and characters. You must also show the emotions of the individual characters in the story. Along with **movements, gestures,** and **facial expressions,** use these **speaking techniques** to make your narrative more effective:

- **Voice modulation.** Change the **tone** and **volume** of your voice to emphasize important moments, to build suspense, and to show emotion.

- **Inflection. Pitch** your voice to express shades of meaning or to share your attitude about the subject of the story.

- **Tempo.** Change the **speed** at which you talk to communicate emotion. A fast tempo often expresses excitement, while a slow one may reflect sadness or seriousness.

- **Enunciation.** Say each word clearly and precisely. Be sure not to slur words or drop word endings.

- **Eye contact.** Make eye contact with your audience members frequently. This will make them feel that you are speaking to each of them personally.

Rehearsing Your Presentation

To make your personal narrative the best it can be, you need to practice many times. Try following these steps:

REHEARSING A PERSONAL NARRATIVE	
Step 1	Rehearse your narrative several times. Practice your movements, gestures, and facial expressions in front of a mirror.
Step 2	Practice in front of a friend or relative, or tape your rehearsal with a video camera or tape recorder. Focus on making eye contact and speaking clearly and expressively. Ask your listener for feedback or play back the tape. Which parts of your narrative do you need to improve?
Step 3	Adjust your performance based on what your listener says or what you see or hear on the tape. Rehearse your narrative until you feel confident and do not need the notes much.

Responding to a Personal Narrative

In addition to giving your presentation, you will also listen carefully to your classmates' oral narratives and offer feedback on their performances. To **evaluate** a narrative's content, delivery, and overall impact, answer these questions.

- Are the story's content and organization **logical**? Have any important events or details been left out? What? Where?

- How does the speaker use movements, gestures, and facial expressions to portray characters in the story or to share his or her **attitude** about the subject of the story?

- How does the speaker's voice show his or her attitude? Do changes in **inflection** or **tempo** show amusement, or excitement?

- Does the presenter speak loudly and clearly and make **eye contact** with the audience?

Giving and Listening to a Persuasive Speech

Adapting a Persuasive Essay

When giving a persuasive speech, your purpose is to convince the people to whom you are speaking that your position on the issue is correct. Your speech needs to have strong content and appeal to your audience.

To find material for your speech, you may want to consider the persuasive essays you wrote for the assignments on pages 222–227 or 630–635. To adapt your essay into a speech, begin with a copy of your written essay. Identify your essay's **position** (your opinion statement), **reasons** and **evidence,** and **proposal** or **proposition.** Next, make notes on the copy using the following instructions.

- For a successful persuasive speech, you must consider your **audience.** Since your listening audience may be different from your essay's audience, you will need to reconsider what you include in your speech.

- As you choose **reasons** for your opinion and the **evidence** (anecdotes, facts, statistics, examples, and expert opinions) that supports your reasons, consider how they relate to your listeners. For example, if you give a speech in support of a better lunch menu in your school cafeteria to your classmates, you might describe better-tasting food. But if your audience is school administrators, you might give statistics that show how the new menu would improve attentiveness in class.

- Remember that your audience may not have the same **background information** as you do, particularly since you have researched your topic. Be sure that you explain in your speech any terms or ideas that may be unfamiliar to your listeners.

To organize your persuasive speech effectively, consider the following strategies for different **audiences** and **purposes**.

ORGANIZING IDEAS PERSUASIVELY		
If your audience . . .	**Your purpose is to . . .**	**Use this strategy:**
opposes your ideas	get them to consider your ideas	Acknowledge their point of view, and then list the reasons for your opinion.
agrees with your ideas	get them to take action	Strengthen their existing opinion by beginning with your opinion and then listing reasons. Close with your proposal, or call to action.
is unsure about your ideas	persuade them to agree with you	Open their minds to your position by beginning with reasons for your opinion.
does not care about your ideas	get them to consider your ideas	Start with information on how the issue affects them before giving your opinion and listing reasons.

As you organize your speech, remember that the **order** of your reasons and supporting evidence also has an impact on your audience. Do you want to start or end your speech with your strongest argument?

Delivering a Persuasive Speech

In persuasion, *how* you say something is often as important as *what* you say. A strong presenter can often make any argument more persuasive by using certain *speaking techniques*. How well can you pay attention to a speaker who quietly mumbles, who stumbles over words, who looks down while talking, or who races through a speech? To persuade your listeners, practice delivery techniques that will hold their attention, not distract them from your message.

To help audience members focus their attention on hearing your ideas, consider the speaking techniques below:

- **Enunciation.** Pronounce words carefully and clearly.
- **Vocal modulation.** Stress certain words and phrases through the volume of your voice.
- **Inflection.** Raise your voice at the end of a question, and lower it at the end of a statement.
- **Tempo.** Adjust the speed and rhythm of your speech.
- **Eye contact.** Keep the audience involved by looking at them.

Listening to a Speech

When you listen to **evaluate,** or judge, a speech, you should listen actively, giving the speaker your undivided attention. If you miss something that a speaker says, you may not get another chance to hear that information. While you listen to speeches, consider these tips to help you pay attention and get the message:

- Face the speaker, and listen quietly and attentively.
- Keep an open mind in weighing the reasons and evidence in the speech.
- Ask yourself if you understand the speaker's position.
- Take notes, writing down main ideas or details in your own words.

Remember that as a member of the audience, you can give the speaker **feedback.** For instance, after a speech you could ask for more information, politely counter a speaker's claim with your own ideas or experiences, or tell the speaker that you agree with his or her opinion.

Evaluating a Speech

One of the best ways for speakers to improve their speeches is to receive evaluations from their peers. When you are an audience member, the most useful thing you can do for your classmates is to give them honest, thorough, polite feedback about their speeches.

- When evaluating a speech's **content,** think about its message as well as the supporting reasons and evidence. The evidence the speaker provides should be **logical.** It should be relevant, or closely tied to the issue. To evaluate the **organization** of a speech, consider how easily you were able to follow the speaker's ideas.
- One of the most important elements of a persuasive speech is its **believability.** How knowledgeable and sincere does the speaker seem? Think about the strength of the speaker's reasons and evidence.
- By examining a speaker's **attitude**—his or her feelings toward the subject—you may find reasons to reject the speaker's position. You might discover a **bias,** or prejudice, the speaker holds. A biased speaker might present only one side of an issue, downplay information in favor of the other side, or keep his or her true purpose hidden from the listener.
- Criteria to consider when evaluating **delivery** are the speaker's use of presentation techniques, such as enunciation, voice modulation, inflection, tempo, and eye contact.

Giving and Listening to an Informative Speech

Delivering a speech can be a nerve-racking experience. If you prepare well, however, delivering a speech can also be fun. After all, when you give a speech, you are the center of attention. All eyes—and ears—are on *you*.

Planning an Informative Speech

To plan your speech, follow these steps:

- **Choose a focused topic.** You may want to base your speech on the informative report you wrote for the assignment on pages 864–869, or you might be ready to explore a different subject. Either way, make sure you **focus** your topic to keep your speech a manageable length. To focus your topic, ask yourself questions that are **relevant** (closely tied to the topic) and **concise** (brief and to the point).

- **Think about your purpose and audience.** For this speech, your general purpose is to share information with listeners. You should also decide on a specific purpose—what you hope to achieve through speaking. Ask yourself, "What do I want my audience to gain from my speech?" Then, write a sentence that answers your question. To make sure your listeners understand your purpose, plan to include a **thesis statement** at the beginning of your speech.

  As you plan your speech, think about what your audience may already know about your topic and what they might wonder about it. Thinking carefully about your listeners' backgrounds and interests will help you decide how to catch and hold their attention throughout your presentation.

■ **Gather support.** You can search the library for printed information on your topic by looking in the card catalog, the *Readers' Guide to Periodical Literature,* magazines, newspapers, and dictionaries. At many libraries you will also find videotapes, audiotapes, slides, microfiches, CD-ROMs, and Internet access. Some libraries offer access to **databases,** collections of specific types of information.

In order to give your audience a clear and accurate understanding of your topic, you will need to track down sources that offer a variety of **perspectives.**

Organizing Your Speech

Once you have collected ideas about your topic, you need to organize them in a way that will appeal to your **audience** and help you achieve your **purpose.**

Introduction   Your introduction is the audience's first impression of you *and* your topic, so plan it carefully. It should be just a few sentences and should

■ catch your listeners' interest

■ focus attention on your topic

■ make your listeners feel comfortable with you and your topic

■ end with a thesis statement that makes your purpose clear

As you plan your introduction, consider using one of the following openings. Notice that each example ends with a sentence that serves as the speaker's thesis statement.

OPENING TECHNIQUES	
Technique	**Student Example**
Begin with a question.	What do a dollar bill and a letter carrier's car have in common? Both display the bald eagle, the symbol of the United States. Bald eagles almost became extinct in the 1960s. You can see a real eagle today, however, because many people have worked hard to help eagles make an amazing comeback.
Begin with a personal anecdote.	On a recent vacation, I visited an area where eagles often nest. I spotted a bald eagle swooping down and grabbing a fish out of the water with its talons. Fortunately, that sight is one people can still hope to see in person. Bald eagles almost became extinct in the 1960s, but thanks to the hard work of many people, eagles have made an amazing comeback since then.
Begin with a startling fact.	The bald eagle has symbolized the United States since 1782—seven years longer than our Constitution has been in effect. Yet in the 1960s this majestic national symbol almost became extinct. Fortunately, thanks to the hard work of many people, bald eagles have made an amazing comeback since then.

Body To plan the body of your speech, you will need to choose an effective organizational structure and then create an outline. Thinking about your audience and your specific purpose will help you decide how to arrange the main ideas and support (details, descriptions, examples) in the body of your speech. If you are adapting a written report, revise the report outline to fit the audience and the time available.

Conclusion Like your introduction, your conclusion might be only a few sentences long, but those few sentences serve an important purpose—to reemphasize your main idea in a memorable way. Your audience should recognize immediately that you are ending your speech, not adding to it. Two effective ways to conclude an informative speech are in the following chart:

CONCLUDING TECHNIQUES	
Technique	**Student Example**
End with a summary of your findings.	Sadly, it was human factors—the need for lumber and land, the misunderstanding of the birds' role in nature, and the use of hazardous chemicals—that brought the bald eagle to the brink of extinction. Other human actions, such as enacting legislation and breeding programs, are now giving these great birds new hope.
End with an echo of your introduction.	The bald eagle is not completely out of danger yet, but its future looks brighter every day. If the eagles continue their comeback, future generations will see our national symbol as more than just a picture on a dollar bill or on a mail truck.

Sources Just as you listed your sources of information in your written research report, you will also need to give your sources credit in your speech. You should credit each source by mentioning its author, title, or both.

According to the National Foundation to Protect America's Eagles, there are now about 55,000 bald eagles in the United States.

In her book Bald Eagles, Karen Dudley explains that eagles that ate DDT laid thin-shelled eggs that broke easily.

Delivering Your Speech

Using **note** cards, practice your speech until you can get through it comfortably without stopping. Try rehearsing in front of a few friends or family members. Use natural gestures, and make **eye contact** with your listeners.

Consider including **audiovisual materials,** such as *charts, graphs, illustrations,* and *audio* or *video recordings,* in your speech. Audiovisual materials can make your ideas clearer and easier to remember for listeners or provide extra information in your speech.

Be sure that all materials can be heard and seen by all members of your audience. Always explain to your audience what the audiovisual material means, and continue to face the audience. Be sure to cue any audiotape or videotape before you speak to avoid wasting time rewinding or fast-forwarding during your speech.

Listening to an Informative Speech

To get the most out of the informative speeches you hear, follow these guidelines.

During the Speech

- Determine the speaker's **attitude** toward the topic. The speaker's word choice or tone of voice may reveal his or her feelings about the topic.

- Listen for **cues** that signal **main points,** such as changes in volume or tone of voice. Cues can also include transitional words and phrases such as *first, there are many reasons, most important,* and *in conclusion.*

- Ask yourself whether you **understand** what is being said well enough to explain the ideas to someone else. If not, try creating a rough outline or cluster diagram of the main idea and important points in the speech as you hear them.

- **Summarize** the main points of the speech in your own words.

After the Speech

- **Ask probing questions.** Ask the speaker to clarify any points in the speech that you did not understand. If any points you expected to be covered were left out, ask the speaker to address them. Ask for specific evidence to back any unsupported claims or conclusions the speaker may have made.

- **Provide constructive feedback.** Be specific in commenting on the speaker's content, organization, and delivery. Whenever possible, begin by complimenting specific things that you thought the speaker did well. When you ask questions or offer suggestions for improvement, be sure to phrase them politely.

Giving and Listening to a Poetry Reading

Many people experience poetry only by reading it in a book, but most poetry is meant to be read aloud. Long before writing and printing presses, people shared poems, stories, and even history through oral recitation. Today, the tradition of oral poetry continues at poetry readings, slams, and contests in places like schools, libraries, bookstores, and clubs.

Preparing for a Poetry Reading

To prepare to recite a poem at a poetry reading, start by selecting a poem that you like. Whether the poem is the work of a famous author or one of your own, choose one that you will enjoy reading aloud. Remember also to pick a poem that fits the time limits you are given. Once you have chosen a poem, work on preparing it for a reading by following these steps:

- **Study the poem for its meaning.** Learn all you can about the **speaker** of the poem. Learn about the speaker's attitude toward the poem's subject and toward the audience. Your study of the speaker will tell you what **tone** to take in your reading. Should it be happy or sad? serious or humorous? sincere or sarcastic?

- **Mark up a copy of the poem.** Mark the parts you want to emphasize, the places you need to pause, and the parts that should be read slowly or quickly. Remember not to stop at the end of lines of poetry unless a punctuation mark stops you.

Rehearsing for a Poetry Reading

Here are some ways you can make your presentation of a poem more enjoyable for yourself and your **audience**:

- **Get familiar with your poem.** You do not need to memorize your poem completely. You do, however, need to know it well enough that you can make **eye contact** with your audience while you are speaking. The better you understand your poem, the easier it will be to remember.

- **Practice reading your poem.** Practice several times by yourself. Then, read your poem into a **tape recorder.** Play each reading back and critique yourself. At least once before you present your poem, have a dress rehearsal. Read it to one or more family members or friends. Ask them for ways you might improve. You can stand still or move around, but you should not lose contact with your audience.

Presenting at a Poetry Reading

If you have followed all the preparation and practice steps described above, you'll have nothing to fear when you make your presentation. Just relax, speak loudly and clearly, look at your audience, and—most important of all—enjoy yourself!

Listening to a Poetry Reading

When you listen to a poetry reading, your **purpose** is to **enjoy** and to **appreciate,** just as when you listen to music or the dialogue in a movie. The first rule of good listening is, of course, to concentrate. As you listen, try to **visualize** what you are hearing. Close your eyes if it helps you picture what the words you are hearing describe.

Notice the **rhyme** and the **rhythm,** or beat, you feel when you hear the poem. For example, the rhythm of words in a poem about the ocean may be steady like waves lapping against the shore. Listen also for **sounds** in the poem. Do bees buzz? Does the snow sweep with repeated *s* sounds? The language of good poetry has both beauty and power. Listen for these qualities just as you do when you listen to music.

Every poem has a **speaker.** The reader should become the speaker of the poem. Is the reader's style right for the poem? For example, if the speaker of the poem is a mouse, the reader might use a high-pitched, hurried tone of voice.

Evaluating a Poetry Reading

Giving and receiving **feedback** for a poetry reading can help you sharpen your listening and presenting skills. Work with other students to evaluate poetry readings by filling out a chart like the one below. After all ratings have been given, add up the numbers and divide the total by six to find the average score.

Scale: 1—poor presentation

2—improvement needed

3—fair

4—good

5—excellent

Criteria	Rating
The reader uses the effects of rhyme, imagery, and language effectively to give the audience a clear impression of the poem.	
The reader's tone of voice is appropriate for the speaker's voice in the poem.	
The reader speaks at a speed that allows the audience to follow the words in the poem.	
The reader stresses appropriate words.	
The reader maintains eye contact with the audience.	
The reader is easy to hear and understand.	
TOTAL	
AVERAGE (Divide the TOTAL by six.)	

Interviewing

Interviews—coversations in which one person asks questions to obtain information—are more common than you might think. You've probably been interviewed—by a teacher, the school nurse, or a neighbor wanting you to baby-sit or mow the lawn. Sometime you may need to conduct an interview yourself. For example, you might interview a neighbor for an oral history project or a local official for an informative report. Here's how to get off to a good start.

Preparing for the Interview

A good interviewer is well prepared. Before you take out your pencil and note pad, follow these steps:

- **Research your topic.** If your interview focuses on a topic—kayaking, say—go to the library and find out all you can about it. The more you know, the better your questions will be.

- **Know your subject.** If your interview focuses on the ideas and life of the person you're interviewing (your subject), see if any newspaper or magazine articles have been written about him or her. If your subject is a writer, read her latest book; if he's an architect, go see—or find a picture of—a building he designed.

- **Make a list of questions.** Ask obvious questions rather than pretend you know the answer. Don't ask questions that can be answered with a simple yes or no. Avoid questions that might influence your subject, like "You hate losing, don't you?"

- **Set up a time and place for the interview.** Choose a place that's comfortable and familiar to your subject—interview a horse trainer at her ranch or a chemistry teacher in his lab. Be on time.

Conducting the Interview

You're seated across from your subject, pencil poised. How do you make the most of your opportunity? Follow these guidelines:

- **Set the ground rules.** If you want to tape-record or videotape the interview, ask your subject for permission before you begin. If you plan to quote your subject's exact words in a newspaper article or in an essay, you must ask for permission to do that, too.

- **Be courteous and patient.** Allow your subject plenty of time to answer your questions. Try not to interrupt. Respect the person's ideas and opinions, even if you disagree.
- **Listen carefully.** Don't rush on to your next question. If you're confused, ask for an explanation. If an answer reminds you of a related question, ask it—even if it isn't on your list.
- **Focus on your subject,** not on yourself. Avoid getting off on tangents, such as "Something like that happened to me. . . ."
- **Wrap things up.** A good interview is leisurely but doesn't go on forever. Know when to stop. You can always phone later to check a fact or ask a final question. Be sure to thank your subject.

Following Up the Interview

Your notebook is filled, and your mind is bursting with ideas. How do you get your thoughts in order? Follow these steps:

- **Review your notes.** As soon as possible, read through your notes and make sure your information is complete and clear.
- **Write a summary.** To make sure you understand what was said, write a summary of the main points of the interview.
- **Check your facts.** If you can, check the spelling of all names and technical facts against another source, such as an encyclopedia.

Being Interviewed

Sometime someone may want to interview you. Here are some tips:

- **Stay relaxed.** Listen carefully to each question before you begin your answer. If a question confuses you, ask the interviewer to reword it or repeat it. Take your time. Long, thoughtful answers are better than short, curt ones.
- **Be accurate.** Don't exaggerate. If you're not sure of something, say so.
- **Keep a sense of humor.**

Analyzing Electronic Journalism

Just as you can analyze the elements of fiction, you can analyze the elements of a TV news story. A TV news story is made up of words, images, and sounds. Television journalists use specific techniques for presenting these words, images, and sounds. Each of these techniques serves a specific purpose.

Analyzing Elements of TV News

Textual Elements   **Text** is the name given to the words you hear and sometimes see on the TV screen. When you hear text, it is presented by a *news anchor* or *news reporter*. The **news anchor** reads the text of the primary, or most important, news stories. The anchor also introduces other reporters and their news stories. **Reporters**—often reporting live from where a news event is happening—may provide additional information on the primary news stories or give information on secondary, or less important, news stories.

Because of time limitations on TV, news stories are short, usually no more than two to three minutes long. This means that news writers and reporters must carefully plan text to achieve their purposes—capturing and keeping your attention, engaging your mind and emotions, and informing you. In order to understand the effects of a news story, you must examine both the *structure* by which the text is arranged and *content* of the text. You must also think about how the structure helps determine the content.

To help viewers understand and remember the main points of a news story during the couple of minutes it is broadcast, the text usually follows a brief, simple, attention-getting **structure**, or order. The following graphic shows the typical news story structure.

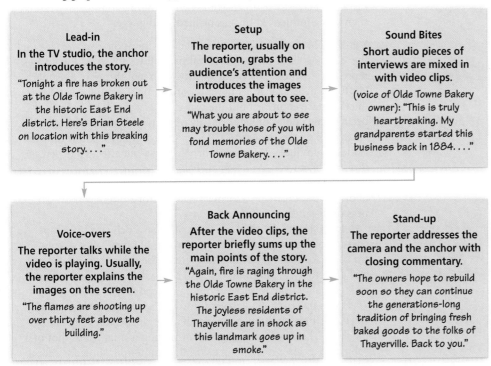

As you can see, the same information is repeated many times. Repeating the information gives viewers several chances to hear and understand the main point of a story.

Content The brief, repetitive structure of broadcast news stories limits the **content**, or information provided. Viewers may receive an oversimplified understanding of events, getting the basic facts without understanding the full meaning of the story. Because broadcast news stories are so short, they are often presented without much **context**—the whole situation or background information behind the story. As a result, viewers may not really be aware of the other issues related to the event.

Media Handbook   1063

Watch out for signs of **bias**—a slanted point of view, either in favor of or against an issue. Signs of bias include personal opinions and **loaded language**—words or phrases that carry strong positive or negative emotional impact, such as "a heartbreaking loss" or "an inspiring act." Try to form your own opinion about a story rather than being influenced by bias or loaded language.

Visual Elements   TV viewers tend to think of "live" images on the news as an accurate portrayal of reality. However, TV images represent just one piece of reality, as seen through a camera. **Photojournalists,** such as news reporters, photographers, and producers, make choices about the way each image will look. They also decide which **point of view,** or way of portraying the world, to show on the TV screen. As a critical TV viewer, you should know how the camera techniques TV photojournalists use can affect your perceptions of the news.

The **camera shot** is what the viewer sees on the television screen. Shots are put together to form a scene or story and may show closeness or distance.

A **long shot** is a shot made from far away, such as a landscape. A **cover shot**—a long shot at the beginning of a news story—can set the scene for the story. It may also create the impression of distance and objectivity. A long shot can also be used as **wallpaper,** an interesting visual image to show behind an anchor's narration.

A **close-up** is a shot taken very close to the subject. A close-up shot can show fine details, such as a detail of a craftsperson's hands weaving yarn. The camera may **zoom in** (moving from a wider shot of a subject to a closer one) to focus on the emotion in someone's face.

Long shot   Close-up

The **camera angle** is the viewpoint at which a camera is set when it is pointed toward a subject. Sometimes, conditions may limit the angles from which a cameraperson may shoot. For example, in filming a forest fire, a photojournalist may be able only to get shots taken from above, using a helicopter or airplane.

A **high angle** is a shot from above, with the camera looking down on the subject. A high camera angle can be used, for example, to provide an overview of a scene. A high camera angle can, however, make the subject look small, unimportant, and vulnerable.

High angle

A shot from below, with the camera looking up at the subject, is called a **low-angle** shot. A low camera angle can make the subject look tall and powerful. A low camera angle may distort reality, making subjects look much larger than they are.

Framing is the process by which the photojournalist decides which details to include or cut from the camera shot. Framing is used to focus on the subject, eliminate clutter, and engage the viewer's emotions. Unfortunately, framing can leave out important details, making a story seem less complex than it is. For example, the photojournalist who took the following pictures framed the right-hand shot so that just young women are shown in the frame. Viewers might wrongly conclude from the framed shot that the band is popular only with women, when in fact men are also fans.

Low angle

Full scene

Framed shot

Media Handbook **1065**

Props are all the objects that appear in a camera shot. Whether it is intentional or not, these props can add meaning to a shot. Possible problems arise if a prop distracts the viewer or demonstrates a bias for or against a particular opinion. For example, if the brand name of a computer is visible on camera, the reporter may unintentionally be advertising that computer company.

Audio Elements In addition to the text that you hear read by an anchor or reporter, there are other sounds that you may hear in a news report. Background noises captured on videotape, such as ambulance sirens, high winds, or hands clapping, add depth to a story. Sometimes you will hear the sounds of a busy newsroom behind a news anchor. Because music can affect viewers' emotions, network guidelines prohibit the use of music during a newscast. However, music is often used as a sound effect to open and close a program and to introduce commercial breaks.

Analyzing a TV News Story

Television newscasts blend textual, visual, and audio elements to create an effect greater than that which could be achieved through only one element. Still, before you can judge the effect of this blend, you need to analyze each of the individual elements. The following steps will help you identify the elements in a TV news broadcast and the techniques used to affect viewers:

▶ **STEP 1 Describe the news segment, identifying text, image, or sound techniques used in the segment.**

The story is a network news feature about the declining prairie dog population.

<u>Sound</u>: Prairie dogs bark and chatter through much of the story.

<u>Image</u>: The camera shows a long shot of a nearly deserted prairie dog town, medium shots of the remaining prairie dogs playing and eating, and a close-up of a rancher's face.

<u>Text</u>: The voice-over tells us that prairie dogs are in trouble because of disease and human activity and that they are a crucial part of the ecosystem. A rancher says he worries about them spreading disease. The story focuses on ways to handle the conflict between the environmental importance of prairie dogs and the needs of the ranchers and other people who consider them pests.

▶ **STEP 2** **Explain the purposes of each major technique.** (Hint: Think about why the producer might choose these techniques.)

<u>Sound</u>: The barking noises grab my attention.

<u>Image</u>: The long shot sets the scene. The medium shot shows prairie dog activities, and the close-up shot shows the rancher's weathered face.

<u>Text</u>: The words of the voice-over tell me why some people are concerned about prairie dogs, and the rancher's words tell me why other people consider them pests.

▶ **STEP 3** **Write an evaluation of the effects of the various techniques on you, the viewer.** (Hint: Think about how the techniques make you feel.)

The sounds the prairie dogs make in this story are kind of funny and cute. The long shot is a little sad because the prairie dog town is nearly empty. The medium shot is also really cute, and the prairie dogs act almost as if they have personalities. The close-up shows me the years of hard work the rancher has done. His expression is tired and tough at the same time— very different from the playful and vulnerable prairie dogs. The text gives specific reasons why prairie dogs are important to the ecosystem but only vague reasons why people exterminate them.

Overall, the techniques used in the story got my attention and the story was fairly informative. It may not have been totally balanced, though. The rancher's point of view seemed less important in the story than the case for saving the prairie dogs—probably because the prairie dogs were more appealing than the rancher and because the text went into more detail about the impact of their loss on the environment.

Analyzing a Documentary

Several decades ago, CBS aired Edward R. Murrow's *Harvest of Shame*. This documentary led to legislation that improved the lives of migrant farm workers, who travel from place to place to harvest crops.

Murrow followed the workers for a season, showing viewers what life was like for them. One **technique** that he used effectively was the **interview**—letting the workers speak for themselves. One woman he interviewed had been working in the fields since she was eight years old. She had worked ten hours that day and earned only one dollar. She had fourteen children to feed.

Media critics say that this documentary triggered changes in federal policy toward migrant workers. What made the documentary so effective in influencing and informing viewers?

- **A timely topic.** CBS aired the program on Thanksgiving Day, forcing viewers to connect the food they ate with the migrant workers who had harvested it.

- **Powerful images, words, and sounds.** Part of what gives images, words, and sounds power is their arrangement. For example, an image of cattle being shipped was placed next to an image of workers jammed into trucks. This technique, **juxtaposition** (side-by-side arrangement), showed viewers that the workers were treated like cattle. Filmmakers can also use sound techniques, such as **music** and **background noise,** to add to the messages they present.

- **A strong bias, or point of view.** The filmmaker's **attitude,** or **bias,** toward the subject can reflect the documentary's **purpose.** The creators of *Harvest of Shame* revealed their bias indirectly through the selection and arrangement of images and interviews. Clearly, they intended to influence, not just inform. Murrow also revealed his bias directly by urging viewers to help pass legislation to improve conditions for migrant workers.

Evaluating a Documentary

- As you watch a documentary, take notes on the topic; powerful images, words, and sounds; and the filmmaker's point of view and purpose.

- Also note techniques, such as interviews, juxtaposition, and music or background noise, used for effect.

- Use your notes to write an analysis of the documentary.

Glossary

The glossary that follows is an alphabetical list of words found in the selections in this book. Use this glossary just as you would use a dictionary—to find out the meanings of unfamiliar words. (Some technical, foreign, and more obscure words in this book are not listed here but instead are defined for you in the footnotes that accompany many of the selections.)

Many words in the English language have more than one meaning. This glossary gives the meanings that apply to the words as they are used in the selections in this book. Words closely related in form and meaning are usually listed together in one entry (for instance, *cower* and *cowered*), and the definition is given for the first form.

The following abbreviations are used:

adj.	adjective
adv.	adverb
n.	noun
v.	verb

Each word's pronunciation is given in parentheses. A guide to the pronunciation symbols appears at the bottom of this page. For more information about the words in this glossary or for information about words not listed here, consult a dictionary.

A

adaptation (ad′əp·tā′shən) *n.:* in biology, a change in structure, function, or form that improves an animal's or a plant's chances of survival. The protective coloration of some animals is a form of adaptation.

admonish (ad·män′ish) *v.:* warn or urge.

alleviate (ə·lē′vē·āt′) *v.:* relieve; reduce.

alliance (ə·lī′əns) *n.:* pact between nations, families, or individuals that shows a common cause.

amble (am′bəl) *v.:* walk without hurrying.

amplify (am′plə·fī′) *v.:* increase in strength.
—**amplified** *v.* used as *adj.*

antic (an′tik) *n.:* playful or silly act.

appalling (ə·pôl′iŋ) *adj.:* horrifying.

archaeologist (är′kē·äl′ə·jist) *n.:* scientist who studies the culture of the past, especially by excavating ancient sites.

arrogant (ar′ə·gənt) *adj.:* overly convinced of one's own importance.

artifact (ärt′ə·fakt′) *n.:* object made by people or adapted for human use.

ascend (ə·send′) *v.:* move up.

ashen (ash′ən) *adj.:* pale.

assent (ə·sent′) *n.:* agreement.

assure (ə·shoor′) *v.:* promise confidently.

avalanche (av′ə·lanch′) *n.:* mass of loosened snow, earth, rocks, and so on, suddenly and swiftly sliding down a mountain.

B

bedraggled (bē·drag′əld) *adj.:* hanging limp and wet; dirty.

bluff (bluf) *n.:* steep cliff.

bout (bout) *n.:* match; contest.

buckle (buk′əl) *v.:* collapse under pressure.

C

charade (shə·rād′) *n.:* obvious pretense or act.

chivalry (shiv′əl·rē) *n.:* code that governed knightly behavior, such as courage, honor, and readiness to help the weak.

---

at, āte, cär; ten, ēve; is, īce; gō, hôrn, look, tool; oil, out; up, fur; ə *for unstressed vowels, as a in* ago, u *in* focus; ′ *as in* Latin (lat′'n); chin; she; zh *as in* azure (azh′ər); thin; *the;* ŋ *as in* ring (riŋ)

---

churn (churn) *v.:* shake; stir.
—**churning** *v.* used as *adj.*
clamor (klam′ər) *n.:* loud, confused noise.
coexist (kō′ig·zist′) *v.:* live together peacefully.
commence (kə·mens′) *v.:* begin.
commotion (kə·mō′shən) *n.:* disturbance.
confrontation (kän′frən·tā′shən) *n.:* face-to-face meeting between opposing sides.
congregation (kän′grə·gā′shən) *n.:* gathering.
connoisseur (kän′ə·sur′) *n.:* person who is an expert on something.
consolation (kän′sə·lā′shən) *n.:* comfort.
contemplate (kän′təm·plāt′) *v.:* consider; look at or think about carefully.
contraption (kən·trap′shən) *n.:* strange machine or gadget.
converge (kən·vurj′) *v.:* close in.
—**converging** *v.* used as *adj.*
convoluted (kän′və·lōōt′id) *adj.:* complicated.
countenance (koun′tə·nəns) *n.:* face; appearance.
cower (kou′ər) *v.:* crouch and tremble in fear.
curt (kurt) *adj.:* rude, using few words.
—**curtly** *adv.*

D

decipher (dē·sī′fər) *v.:* interpret; find the meaning of.
defiant (dē·fī′ənt) *adj.:* boldly resisting authority.
delve (delv) *v.:* search.
deprivation (dep′rə·vā′shən) *n.:* loss; condition of having something taken away by force.
derisive (di·rī′siv) *adj.:* scornful and ridiculing.
descent (dē·sent′) *n.:* ancestry.
detain (dē·tān′) *v.:* hold back; delay.
dismal (diz′məl) *adj.:* miserable; gloomy.
—**dismally** *adv.*
dispel (di·spel′) *v.:* drive away.
dispute (di·spyōōt′) *n.:* argument.
domain (dō·mān′) *n.:* territory.

E

edible (ed′ə·bəl) *adj.:* fit to be eaten.
egotism (ē′gō·tiz′əm) *n.:* conceit; talking about oneself too much.
elude (ē·lōōd′) *v.:* escape cleverly.
elusive (ē·lōō′siv) *adj.:* hard to detect.
entreaty (en·trēt′ē) *n.:* earnest request.
erupt (ē·rupt′) *v.:* burst forth.
eternity (ē·tur′nə·tē) *n.:* very long time; forever.
ethnicity (eth·nis′ə·tē) *n.:* common culture or nationality.
excavate (eks′kə·vāt′) *v.:* uncover or expose by digging.
exotic (eg·zät′ik) *adj.:* foreign; not native.
explicit (eks·plis′it) *adj.:* definite; clearly stated.

F

fathom (fath′əm) *v.:* understand.
finicky (fin′ik·ē) *adj.:* fussy and extremely careful.
forfeit (fôr′fit) *v.:* lose the right to compete.
formidable (fôr′mə·də·bəl) *adj.:* awe-inspiring; impressive.
frenzied (fren′zēd) *adj.:* wild.
fumigate (fyōō′mə·gāt′) *v.:* clean out by spraying with chemical vapors.
—**fumigating** *v.* used as *n.*

G

ghastly (gast′lē) *adj.:* horrible; ghostlike.
goad (gōd) *v.:* push or drive.

H

habitual (hə·bich′ōō·əl) *adj.:* done or fixed by habit.
heritage (her′ə·tij) *n.:* traditions that are passed along.
horde (hôrd) *n.:* large, moving crowd.
hover (huv′ər) *v.:* hang in the air.
huddle (hud′′l) *v.:* nestle close together.

I

idiosyncrasy (id′ē·ō·sin′krə·sē) *n.:* peculiarity.

immense (i·mens′) *adj.:* enormous.
—**immensely** *adv.*

imminent (im′ə·nənt) *adj.:* about to happen.

implore (im·plôr′) *v.:* ask or beg.

imposter (im·päs′tər) *n.:* person who pretends to be someone or something that he or she is not.

impotent (im′pə·tənt) *adj.:* powerless.

inconsolable (in′kən·sōl′ə·bəl) *adj.:* unable to be comforted; brokenhearted.

incredulous (in·krej′oo·ləs) *adj.:* unbelieving.
—**incredulously** *adv.*

insolence (in′sə·ləns) *n.:* disrespect.

integrity (in·teg′rə·tē) *n.:* honesty; uprightness.

intelligible (in·tel′i·jə·bəl) *adj.:* understandable.

intent (in·tent′) *adj.:* concentrating deeply.
—**intently** *adv.*

interior (in·tir′ē·ər) *n.:* inner part of anything. The opposite of *interior* is *exterior.*

intimidate (in·tim′ə·dāt′) *v.:* frighten with threats.

intolerable (in·täl′ər·ə·bəl) *adj.:* unbearable.

intricate (in′tri·kit) *adj.:* complicated; full of detail.

invincible (in·vin′sə·bəl) *adj.:* unbeatable.

L

ligament (lig′ə·mənt) *n.:* in anatomy, band of tough tissue that connects bones and holds organs in place.

loathsome (lōth′səm) *adj.:* disgusting.

M

matinee (mat′'n·ā′) *n.:* afternoon performance of a play or a movie.

meager (mē′gər) *adj.:* slight; scanty.

menace (men′əs) *n.:* danger; threat.

minority (mī·nôr′ə·tē) *n.:* small group that differs from the larger, controlling group.

monarch (män′ərk) *n.:* sole and absolute leader.

monopoly (mə·näp′ə·lē) *n.:* exclusive control of a market.

muster (mus′tər) *v.:* call forth.

O

observatory (əb·zurv′ə·tôr′ē) *n.:* building equipped for scientific observation.

ominous (äm′ə·nəs) *adj.:* threatening.

P

parch (pärch) *v.:* make very hot and dry.
—**parched** *v.* used as *adj.*

particle (pärt′i·kəl) *n.:* tiny piece.

pensive (pen′siv) *adj.:* thoughtful.
—**pensively** *adv.*

persecution (pur′sə·kyoo′shən) *n.:* act of willfully injuring or attacking others because of their beliefs or ethnic backgrounds.

perturb (pər·turb′) *v.:* disturb; trouble.
—**perturbed** *v.* used as *adj.*

predominant (prē·däm′ə·nənt) *adj.:* main.
—**predominantly** *adv.*

presumptuous (prē·zump′choo·əs) *adj.:* too bold; arrogant.

prey (prā) *n.:* animal hunted or killed for food by another animal. Mice are prey to owls. Gazelles are prey to lions.

profane (prō·fān′) *adj.:* not religious.

R

ransack (ran′sak′) *v.:* search thoroughly for goods to steal; loot, rob.

reassure (rē′ə·shoor′) *v.:* comfort.
—**reassuring** *v.* used as *adj.*

recede (ri·sēd′) *v.:* move back.
—**receding** *v.* used as *adj.*

recognition (rek′əg·nish′ən) *n.:* knowing again.

refuge (ref′yooj) *n.:* shelter; protection.

refugee (ref′yo͞o·jē′) *n.:* person who flees home or country to escape war or persecution.

—**refugee** *n.* used as *adj.*

reluctance (ri·luk′təns) *n.:* unwillingness.

resolute (rez′ə·lo͞ot′) *adj.:* firm and purposeful; determined.

resolve (ri·zälv′) *v.:* decide.

rumple (rum′pəl) *v.:* wrinkle and make untidy.

—**rumpled** *v.* used as *adj.*

ruthless (ro͞oth′lis) *adj.:* without pity.

S

sabotage (sab′ə·täzh′) *v.:* obstruct or destroy.

sentinel (sent′n·əl) *n.:* watchful guard.

sentry (sen′trē) *n.:* guard.

shrewd (shro͞od) *adj.:* clever.

simultaneous (sī′məl·tā′nē·əs) *adj.:* occurring at the same time.

—**simultaneously** *adv.*

skirt (skʉrt) *v.:* avoid.

sophisticated (sə·fis′tə·kāt′id) *adj.:* worldly; elegant and refined.

sovereignty (säv′rən·tē) *n.:* control; authority.

species (spē′shēz) *n.:* in biology, a naturally existing population of similar organisms that usually breed only among themselves. The human species living today is called *Homo sapiens* ("wise man").

staid (stād) *adj.:* settled; quiet.

sterile (ster′əl) *adj.:* barren; lacking interest or vitality.

T

tirade (tī′rād′) *n.:* long, scolding speech.

torrent (tôr′ənt) *n.:* flood or rush.

tournament (to͝or′nə·mənt) *n.:* series of contests.

transfix (trans·fiks′) *v.:* cause to stand very still, as if nailed to the spot.

—**transfixed** *v.* used as *adj.*

transition (tran·zish′ən) *n.:* change; passage from one condition to another.

turbulent (tʉr′byə·lənt) *adj.:* wild; disorderly.

U

unrequited (un′ri·kwīt′id) *adj.:* not returned in kind.

unscrupulous (un·skro͞o′pyə·ləs) *adj.:* dishonest.

V

vain (vān) *adj.:* useless; having no result.

—**vainly** *adv.*

valiant (val′yənt) *adj.:* brave and determined.

variation (ver′ē·ā′shən) *n.:* difference.

W

wedge (wej) *n.:* pie-shaped slice.

Spanish Glossary

A

adaptation/adaptación *s.* en biología, un cambio de estructura, de función o de forma que mejora el potencial de supervivencia de una planta o de un animal. El color protectivo de ciertos animales es una forma de adaptación.

admonish/amonestar *v.* prevenir; advertir; reprender.

alleviate/aliviar *v.* mitigar; calmar; tranquilizar.

alliance/alianza *s.* coalición; liga; confederación; pacto entre naciones, familias o individuos con una causa común.

amble/deambular *v.* rondar; andar sin prisa; pasear.

amplify/amplificar *v.* ampliar; desarrollar; extender; incrementar en fuerza.

antic/travesura *s.* diablura; chiquillada.

artifact/artefacto *s.* conjunto de piezas que se adapta a un fin determinado.

appalling/espantoso *adj.* horrible; aterrador; grotesco.

archaeologist/arqueólogo *s.* científico que estudia los objetos y culturas antiguas especialmente mediante excavaciones de lugares antiguos.

arrogant/arrogante *adj.* soberbio; presuntuoso; orgulloso; convencido de su propia importancia.

ascend/ascender *v.* subir de un sitio a otro más alto.

ashen/pálido *adj.* exangüe; demacrado; sin color.

assent/asentimiento *n.* afirmación; consentimiento; confirmación; aceptación.

assure/asegurar *v.* afirmar; aseverar; prometer con seguridad.

avalanche/avalancha *s.* alud, masas grandes de nieve que se desprenden de las cumbres de las montañas, y al caer causan muchos daños.

avenge/vengar *v.* castigar; escarmentar; reivindicar.

B

bedraggled/destrozado *adj.* destrozado; manchado de barro.

bluff/acantilado *s.* talud; precipicio; barranco.

bout/combate *s.* pugilato; encuentro.

buckle/pandearse *v.* torcerse; caer bajo la presión.

C

charade/charada *s.* pasatiempo en que se trata de adivinar una palabra, haciendo una indicación sobre su significado, adivinanza.

chivalry/caballerosidad *s.* cortesía; urbanidad.

churn/batir *v.* remover; agitar.

clamor/clamor *s.* estruendo; ruido; fragor.

coexist/coexistir *v.* vivir juntos en armonía; convivir.

commence/comenzar *v.* empezar; dar comienzo a; iniciar.

commotion/conmoción *s.* tumulto; disturbio.

confrontation/confrontación *s.* careo; entrevista cara a cara entre oponentes.

congregation/congregación *s.* sociedad; agrupación; hermandad.

connoisseur/conocedor *s.* perito; entendido en alguna materia; inteligente.

consolation/consuelo *s.* alivio; desahogo; remedio.

contemplate/contemplar *v.* estudiar; considerar; poner atención en alguna cosa material o espiritual.

contraption/artefacto *s.* aparato; chisme; artilugio.

converge/converger *v.* confluir; reunirse; coincidir.

convoluted/retorcido *adj.* complicado; intrincado; sinuoso.

countenance/semblante *s.* cara; apariencia; fisonomía.

cower/acobardarse *v.* encogerse; amedrentarse; agacharse y temblar de miedo.

curt/brusco *adj.* parco; breve; lacónico.

D

decipher/decifrar *v.* interpretar, aclarar, describir lo oculto o dudoso.

defy/retador *adj.* desafiador; provocador; competidor; duelista.

delve/buscar *v.* explorar; hurgar; cavar.

deprivation/privación *s.* pérdida; falta; carencia.

derisive/burlón *adj.* socarrón; farsante.

descent/descendencia *s.* linaje; familia; estirpe.

detain/detener *v.* contener; suspender; arrestar.

dismal/deprimente *adj.* triste; patético; penoso.

dispel/disipar *v.* esfumar; eliminar; alejar; apartar.

dispute/disputa *s.* altercado; querella; contienda.

domain/dominio *s.* bienes; estados; posesión de tierras.

E

edible/comestible *adj.* que se puede comer; alimenticio.

egotism/egoísmo *s.* narcisismo; hablar demasiado de si mismo.

elude/eludir *v.* evitar; esquivar; rodear.

elusive/evasivo *adj.* escurridizo; esquivo; huidizo.

entreaty/peticion *s.* ruego; súplica.

erupt/arrojar *v.* entrar en erupción; dispersar.

eternity/eternidad *s.* perpetuidad; tiempo infinito; para siempre.

ethnicity/origen étnico *s.* cultura o nacionalidad en común.

excavate/excavar *v.* quitar de una cosa sólida parte de su masa haciendo un hoyo o cavidad en ella.

exude/exudar *v.* rezumar; sudar; transpirar.

exotic/exótico *adj.* extraño; raro; original.

explicit/explícito *adj.* claro; manifiesto; claramente explicado.

F

fathom/comprender *v.* entender; interpretar; concebir.

finicky/melindroso *adj.* quisquilloso; delicado; caprichoso; receloso.

forfeit/perder *v.* perder el derecho a competir.

formidable/formidable *adj.* tremendo; terrible; impresionante; que inspira la admiración.

frenzied/frenético *adj.* arrebatado; delirante; rabioso; extraviado.

fumigate/fumigar *v.* desinfectar; sanear; limpiar mediante vapores químicos.

G

ghastly/espantoso *adj.* horrible; lúgubre; parecido a la muerte.

goad/instigar *v.* aguijonear; incitar; alentar.

H

habitual/habitual *adj.* acostumbrado; inveterado; habituado.

heritage/herencia *s.* patrimonio; tradiciones que se heredan.

horde/horda *s.* multitud; tropa.

hover/colgar *v.* estar suspenso en el aire; revolotear; aletear.

huddle/amontonarse *v.* apiñarse; apretarse unos contra otros; acurrucarse.

I

idiosyncracy/idiosincrasia *s.* peculiaridad; especialidad.

immense/inmenso *adj.* enorme; desmesurado; colosal; gigantesco.

imminent/inminente *adj.* próximo; a punto de ocurrir.

implore/implorar *v.* suplicar; rogar; pedir con instancia.

imposter/impostor *adj.* se aplica al que engaña haciéndose pasar por lo que no es o por alguien que no es.

impotent/impotente *adj.* desautorizado; sin fuerza ni poder.

inconsolable/inconsolable *adj.* que no puede ser consolado o consolarse.

incredulous/incrédulo *adj.* suspicaz; prevenido.

insolence/insolencia *s.* desfachatez; descaro; frescura; falta de respeto.

integrity/integridad *s.* honradez; rectitud; probidad.

intelligible/inteligible *adj.* claro; evidente; legible; que se puede comprender.

intent/atento *adj.* considerado; muy concentrado en una tarea; dispuesto; vigilante.

interior/interior *adj.* interno; lo que está en la parte de dentro. El opuesto de *interior* es exterior.

intimidate/intimidar *v.* acobardar; amedrentar; atemorizar.

intolerable/intolerable *adj.* insoportable; insufrible; irritante.

intricate/intrincado *adj.* complicado; enredado; equívoco.

invincible/invencible *adj.* infranqueable; insuperable.

L

ligament/ligamento *s.* tendón; fibra; en anatomía, fibra segura que conecta huesos y mantiene órganos en su lugar.

loathsome/odioso *adj.* detestable; infame; horrible.

M

matinee/primera sesión *s.* función de la tarde.

meager/escaso *adj.* parco; pobre; exiguo.

menace/amenaza *s.* peligro; riesgo.

minority/minoría *s.* grupo pequeño que difiere del grupo mayor y en control.

monarch/monarca *s.* soberano; líder único y absoluto.

monopoly/monopolio *s.* consorcio; grupo; control exclusivo de un mercado.

muster/formar *v.* reunir; congregar.

O

observatory/observatorio *s.* mirador; edificio equipado para la observación científica.

ominous/siniestro *adj.* inquietante; adverso.

P

parch/secar *v.* tostar; abrasar; resecar; agostar.

particle/partícula *s.* átomo; fragmento minúsculo.

pensive/pensativo *adj.* meditabundo; ensimismado; absorto.

persecution/persecución *s.* acosamiento; perseguir o atacar a otros debido a sus creencias o procedencias.

perturb/perturbar *v.* inquietar; trastornar; alterar.

predominant/predominante *adj.* preponderante; superior; que prevalece.

presumptuous/presuntoso *adj.* presumido; arrogante; atrevido.

prey/presa *s.* captura; caza; víctima.

profane/profano *adj.* mundano; terrenal; que no es religioso.

R

ransack/rebuscar *v.* rebuscar; explorar; saquear; pillar; robar.

reassure/tranquilizar *v.* calmar; sosegar; aliviar.

recede/retroceder *v.* retirarse; volverse atrás.

recognition/reconocimiento *s.* evocación; recuerdo; volver a conocer.

refuge/refugio *s.* amparo; abrigo; protección.

refugee/refugiado *adj.* expatriado; persona que huye de su hogar o país para escapar de la guerra o persecución.

reluctance/desgana *s.* de mala gana, no dispuesto a ceder.

resolute/resuelto *adj.* determinado; firme; constante.

resolve/resolver *v.* decidir; arbitrar; despachar.

rumple/arrugar *v.* fruncir; marchitar.

ruthless/despiadado *adj.* cruel; feroz; sin compasión.

S

sabotage/sabotear *v.* estropear; arruinar; destrozar.

sentinel/centinela *s.* vigilante; guardián; celador.

sentry/guarda *s.* vigilante; celador; centinela.

shrewd/astuto *s.* perspicaz, de vivo ingenio, sutil.

simultaneous/simultáneo *adj.* sincrónico; paralelo; presente; que ocurre al mismo.

skirt/rodear *v.* circundar; contornear; bordear; evadir; prevenir; eludir.

sophisticated/sofisticado *adj.* mundano; carente de naturalidad.

sovereignty/soberanía *s.* control; autoridad; señorío; gobierno.

species/especie *s.* clase; en biología, una población natural de organismos similares que suelen procrearse únicamente entre ellos. La especie humana actual es *Homo sapiens* ("hombre sabio").

staid/serio *adj.* formal; quieto; moderado.

sterile/estéril *adj.* que no da fruto, o no produce nada.

T

tirade/diatriba *s.* perorata; sermón.

torrent/torrente *s.* arroyo; cascada; llover a cántaros; tumulto.

tournament/torneo *s.* liza; lucha; combate.

transfix/paralizar *v.* detener; suspender; inmovilizar.

transition/transición *s.* metamorfosis; evolución; etapa entre una condición a la otra.

turbulent/turbulento *adj.* perturbado; revuelto; agitado.

U

unrequited/no correspondido *adj.* un amor no correspondido; un servicio no recompensado.

unscrupulous/poco escrupuloso *adj.* inmoral; falto de principios morales; deshonesto.

V

vain/vano *adj.* sin éxito; infructuoso; inútil.

valiant/valiente *adj.* valeroso; bravo; indomable.

variation/variación *s.* muda; diferencia; diversificación.

W

wedge/trozo *s.* un pedazo en forma de pastel.

Acknowledgments

For permission to reprint copyrighted material, grateful acknowledgment is made to the following sources:

American Library Association: From Newbery Award Acceptance Speech by Mildred D. Taylor, 1977.

Américas, bimonthly magazine published by the General Secretariat of the Organization of American States in English and Spanish: From "Mongoose on the Loose" by Larry Luxner from *Américas*, July/August 1993, vol. 45, no. 4, p. 3. Copyright © 1993 by *Américas*.

Claudia Arnett: "Early Song" from *Collected Poems of Carroll Arnett/Gogisgi: Poems 1958–1995.* Copyright © 1979 by Gogisgi/Carroll Arnett. Published by Pavement Saw Press.

The Associated Press: "Buddies Bare Their Affection for Ill Classmate" by Associated Press from *Austin American-Statesman,* March 19, 1994. Copyright © 1994 by The Associated Press. From "Hatteras Lighthouse Completes Its Move" by Associated Press from *The New York Times,* July 10, 1999. Copyright © 1999 by The Associated Press.

Susan Bergholz Literary Services: "Names/Nombres" by Julia Alvarez. Copyright © 1985 by Julia Alvarez. First published in *Nuestro,* March 1985. "Chanclas" and "A Rice Sandwich" from *The House on Mango Street* by Sandra Cisneros. Copyright © 1984 by Sandra Cisneros. Published by Vintage Books, a division of Random House, Inc., and in hardcover by Alfred A. Knopf in 1994. All rights reserved. "Abuelito Who" from *My Wicked, Wicked Ways* by Sandra Cisneros. Copyright © 1987 by Sandra Cisneros. Published by Third Woman Press and in hardcover by Alfred A. Knopf. "The Place Where Dreams Come From" by Sandra Cisneros. Copyright © 1991 by Sandra Cisneros. "Salvador Late or Early" from *Woman Hollering Creek* by Sandra Cisneros. Copyright © 1991 by Sandra Cisneros. Published by Vintage Books, a division of Random House, Inc., and originally in hardcover by Random House, Inc. All rights reserved.

BOA Editions, Ltd.: "the 1st" *from good woman: poems and a memoir 1969–1980* by Lucille Clifton. Copyright © 1987 by Lucille Clifton. "I Ask My Mother to Sing" from *Rose* by Li-Young Lee. Copyright © 1986 by Li-Young Lee.

Brooks Permissions: "Home" from *Maud Martha* by Gwendolyn Brooks. Copyright © 1993 by Gwendolyn Brooks. Published by Third World Press, Chicago.

Arthur Cavanaugh: "Miss Awful" by Arthur Cavanaugh from *McCall's,* April 1969. Copyright © 1969 by Arthur Cavanaugh.

Laura Cecil, Literary Agent, on behalf of The James Reeves Estate: "The Sea" from *Complete Poems for Children* by James Reeves. Copyright © 1950 by James Reeves.

Judith Ortiz Cofer: "Aunty Misery," a Puerto Rican folktale translated by Judith Ortiz Cofer.

Don Congdon Associates, Inc.: "The Naming of Names" by Ray Bradbury from *Thrilling Wonder Stories.* Copyright © 1949 by Standard Magazines, Inc.; copyright renewed © 1976 by Ray Bradbury.

Bruce Coville c/o Ashley Grayson, Literary Agent: "Duffy's Jacket" from *Oddly Enough: Stories by Bruce Coville.* Copyright © 1989 by Bruce Coville.

Crown Publishers, Inc., an imprint of Random House Children's Books, a division of Random House, Inc.: "Overture" (retitled "The Power of Music") from *Nadja on My Way* by Nadja Salerno-Sonnenberg. Copyright © 1989 by Nadja Salerno-Sonnenberg.

Dell Publishing, a division of Random House, Inc.: "User Friendly" by T. Ernesto Bethancourt from *Connections: Short Stories,* edited by Donald R. Gallo. Copyright © 1989 by T. Ernesto Bethancourt.

Dial Books for Young Readers, a Member of Penguin Group (USA) Inc.: "The Flight of Icarus" from *Stories of the Gods and Heroes* by Sally Benson. Copyright 1940 and renewed © 1968 by Sally Benson. *Song of the Trees* by Mildred D. Taylor. Copyright © 1975 by Mildred Taylor.

Doubleday, a division of Random House, Inc.: Excerpt (retitled "The Only Girl in the World for Me") from *Love & Marriage* by Bill Cosby. Copyright © 1989 by Bill Cosby. "King Midas and the Golden Touch" from *Tales from Ancient Greece* by Pamela Oldfield. Copyright © 1988 by Grisewood and Dempsey, Ltd.

Dutton Children's Books, a Member of Penguin Group (USA) Inc.: *Merlin and the Dragons* by Jane Yolen. Copyright © 1995 by Jane Yolen; illustrations copyright © 1995 by Li Ming.

Esquire Magazine: "Three Skeleton Key" by George G. Toudouze from *Esquire,* January 1937. Copyright 1937 by Hearst Communications, Inc. All rights reserved. *Esquire* is a trademark of Hearst Magazines Property, Inc.

Farrar, Straus & Giroux, LLC: "Charles" from *The Lottery* by Shirley Jackson. Copyright © 1948, 1949 by Shirley Jackson; copyright renewed © 1976, 1977 by Laurence Hyman, Barry Hyman, Mrs. Sarah Webster, and Mrs. Joanne Schnurer. From "The Red Girl" from *Annie John* by Jamaica Kincaid. Copyright © 1985 by Jamaica Kincaid.

Edward Field: "Frankenstein" from *Counting Myself Lucky: Selected Poems 1963–1992* by Edward Field. Copyright © 1992 by Edward Field. Comment by Edward Field.

John Fleischman: "The Funeral Banquet of King Midas" by John Fleischman from *Muse,* vol. 4, no. 8, October 2000. Copyright © 2000 by John Fleischman.

Samuel French, Inc.: From *The Dream of Good Fortune: Arabian Nights* from *More from Story Theatre* by Paul Sills. Copyright © 1981 by Paul Sills. CAUTION: Professionals and amateurs are hereby warned that "The Dream of Good Fortune" being fully protected under the copyright laws of the United States of America, the British Commonwealth countries, including Canada, and the other countries of the Copyright Union, is subject to a royalty. All rights, including professional, amateur, motion picture, recitation, public reading, radio, television and cable broadcasting, and the rights of translation into foreign languages, are strictly reserved. Any inquiry regarding the availability of performance rights, or the purchase of individual copies of the authorized acting edition, must be directed to Samuel French, Inc., 45 West 25th Street, NY, NY 10010 with other locations in Hollywood and Toronto, Canada.

Abayomi Fuja: From "Oni and the Great Bird" from *Fourteen Hundred Cowries: Traditional Stories of the Yoruba,* collected by Abayomi Fuja. Copyright © 1962 by Oxford University Press.

The Gale Group: Quotes by Anne McCaffrey from "Anne McCaffrey" from *Something About the Author,* vol. 8, edited by Anne Commire. Copyright © 1976 by Gale Research Inc.

Greenwood Publishing Group, Inc., Westport, CT: "Sir Gawain and the Loathly Lady" from *The Oryx Multicultural Folktale Series: Beauties and Beasts* by Betsy Hearne. Copyright © 1993 by The Oryx Press.

Donald Hall: "Names of Horses" from *Kicking the Leaves* by Donald Hall. Copyright © 1975 by Donald Hall.

Harcourt, Inc.: "Arithmetic" from *The Complete Poems of Carl Sandburg.* Copyright © 1969, 1970 by Lilian Steichen Sandberg, Trustee. "Ode to Family Photographs" from *Neighborhood Odes* by Gary Soto. Copyright © 1992 by Gary Soto. "Mother and Daughter" from *Baseball in April and Other Stories* by Gary Soto. Copyright © 1990 by Gary Soto.

HarperCollins Publishers, Inc.: "Sarah Cynthia Sylvia Stout Would Not Take the Garbage Out" from *Where the Sidewalk Ends* by Shel Silverstein. Copyright © 1974 by Evil Eye Music, Inc. From *King Arthur: The Sword in the Stone* by Hudson Talbott. Copyright © 1991 by Hudson Talbott. Quotation by Hudson Talbott from jacket cover of *King Arthur: The Sword in the Stone,* written and illustrated by Hudson Talbott. Copyright © 1991 by Hudson Talbott. "Master Frog" from *The Brocaded Slipper and Other Vietnamese Tales* by Lynette Dyer Vuong. Text copyright © 1982 by Lynette Dyer Vuong. *The Crane Wife,* retold by Sumiko Yagawa, translated by Katherine Paterson. Text copyright © 1979 by Sumiko Yagama. Originally published in Japan by Fukuinkan-Shoten, Publishers, Inc., Tokyo.

Harvard University Press and the Trustees of Amherst College: "288: I'm Nobody! Who are you?" and "I Like to See It Lap the Miles" from *The Poems of Emily Dickinson,* edited by Thomas H. Johnson. Copyright © 1951, 1955, 1979 by the President and Fellows of Harvard College. Published by The Belknap Press of Harvard University Press, Cambridge, Mass.

Edward D. Hoch: "Zoo" by Edward D. Hoch. Copyright © 1958 by King-Size Publications, Inc.; copyright renewed © 1986 by Edward D. Hoch.

Henry Holt and Company, LLC: "The Runaway," "A Minor Bird," and "The Pasture" from *The Poetry of Robert Frost,* edited by Edward Connery Lathem. Copyright 1951 by Robert Frost; copyright 1923, © 1969 by Henry Holt and Company, Inc.

Houghton Mifflin Company: "The Great Musician" (retitled "Orpheus, the Great Musician") and "The Origin of the Seasons" from *Greek Myths* by Olivia Coolidge. Copyright © 1949 and renewed © 1977 by Olivia E. Coolidge. All rights reserved. "Bargain" from *The Big It and Other Stories* by A. B. Guthrie. Copyright © 1960 by A. B. Guthrie. All rights reserved.

Hyperion, an imprint of Disney's Children's Book Group, LLC: From *Dinorella: A Prehistoric Fairy Tale* by Pamela Duncan Edwards, illustrated by Henry Cole. Text copyright © 1997 by Pamela Duncan Edwards; illustrations copyright © 1997 by Henry Cole.

International Creative Management, Inc.: *The Monsters Are Due on Maple Street* by Rod Serling. Copyright © 1960 by Rod Serling.

Alfred A. Knopf, a division of Random House, Inc.: "Madam and the Rent Man," "Winter Moon," and "Harlem Night Song" from *The Collected Poems of Langston Hughes.* Copyright © 1994 by The Estate of Langston Hughes.

Lichtenstein Creative Media: Interview with Sandra Cisneros by Marit Haahr from *The Infinite Mind.* Copyright © 2002 by Lichtenstein Creative Media.

Little Brown and Company: From *Long Walk to Freedom* by Nelson Mandela. Copyright © 1994, 1995 by Nelson Rolihlahla Mandela.

Liveright Publishing Corporation: "All in green went my love riding" and "maggie and milly and molly and may" from *Complete Poems: 1904–1962* by E. E. Cummings, edited by George J. Firmage. Copyright © 1956, 1984, 1991 by the Trustees for the E. E. Cummings Trust.

Los Angeles Times: "Eeking out a Life" by Matt Surman from the *Los Angeles Times,* July 8, 2000. Copyright © 2000 by The Los Angeles Times.

Barry N. Malzberg for Arthur Porges: "The Ruum" by Arthur Porges. Copyright © 1953 by Mercury Press; copyright renewed © 1981 by Arthur Porges. Originally appeared in *The Magazine of Fantasy & Science Fiction,* October 1953.

Ashley Deal Matin: "Antaeus" by Borden Deal. Copyright © 1961 by Southern Methodist University Press. Quotation by Borden Deal.

Anne McCaffrey and agent, Virginia Kidd: "The Smallest Dragonboy" from *Get Off the Unicorn* by Anne McCaffrey. Copyright © 1973 and renewed © 2001 by Anne McCaffrey. First appeared in *Science Fiction Tales.*

Margaret K. McElderry Books, an imprint of Simon & Schuster Children's Publishing Division: From "The Search Goes On" from *The Mystery of the Ancient Maya* by Carolyn Meyer and Charles Gallenkamp. Copyright © 1985, 1995 by Carolyn Meyer and Charles Gallenkamp.

Pat Mora, www.patmora.com: "Gold" by Pat Mora. Copyright © 1998 by Pat Mora. Originally published by Harcourt Brace in *Home: A Journey Through America* by Thomas Locker and Candace Christiansen.

Motorola, Inc.: "Battery Removal/Replacement" from *Premier Cellular Telephone: Owner's Manual.* Copyright © 1994 by Motorola, Inc.

National Review: From "Canines to the Rescue" by Jonah Goldberg from the *National Review* web site accessed September 26, 2002, at http://www.nationalreview.com/goldberg/goldberg111201.shtml.

1080   Acknowledgments

NEA Today: From "Amy Tan: Joy, Luck, and Literature," an interview by Anita Merina from *NEA Today*, October 1991. Copyright © 1991 by the National Education Association of the United States.

Agate Nesaule: Comment by Agate Nesaule from *NPR Morning Edition*, October 24, 2000. Copyright © 2000 by Agate Nesaule.

New York Times Agency: From "In a Mix of Cultures, an Olio of Plantings" by Anne Raver from *The New York Times*, August 15, 1991. Copyright © 1991 by The New York Times Company.

W. W. Norton & Company, Inc.: "Rosa" from *On the Bus with Rosa Parks* by Rita Dove. Copyright © 1999 by Rita Dove.

Harold Ober Associates, Incorporated: "Stolen Day" by Sherwood Anderson from *This Week Magazine*, 1941. Copyright 1941 by United Newspapers Magazine Corporation; copyright renewed © 1968 by Eleanor Copenhaver Anderson.

Shaquille O'Neal: "A Good Reason to Look Up" by Shaquille O'Neal. Copyright © 1998 by Shaquille O'Neal.

Penguin Young Readers Group, a Member of Penguin Group (USA) Inc.: From "Elizabeth I" from *Ten Queens: Portraits of Women of Power* by Milton Meltzer. Copyright © 1998 by Milton Meltzer.

Persea Books, Inc. (New York): From "Who Is Your Reader?" from *The Effects of Knut Hamsun on a Fresno Boy* by Gary Soto. Copyright © 1983 and renewed © 1988 and © 2000 by Gary Soto.

Philomel Books, a division of Penguin Young Readers Group, a Member of Penguin Group (USA) Inc.: *Yeh-Shen: A Cinderella Story from China*, retold by Ai-Ling Louie. Text copyright © 1982 by Ai-Ling Louie.

G. P. Putnam's Sons, a Member of Penguin Group (USA) Inc.: From *Homesick* by Jean Fritz. Copyright © 1982 by Jean Fritz.

Random House, Inc.: "Girls, and the Circle of Death" (retitled "Girls") from *How Angel Peterson Got His Name* by Gary Paulsen. Copyright © 2003 by Gary Paulsen.

Random House UK Ltd: "Narcissus" (retitled "Echo and Narcissus") from *Tales the Muses Told* by Roger Lancelyn Green. Copyright © 1965 by Don Bolognese. Published by The Bodley Head.

The Saturday Review: "The Dinner Party" by Mona Gardner from *The Saturday Review of Literature*, vol. 25, no. 5, January 31, 1941. Copyright © 1979 by General Media Communications, Inc.

Scholastic Inc.: From *The Last Dinosaur* by Jim Murphy. Copyright © 1988 by Jim Murphy. "The Hummingbird King" from *The Hummingbird King: A Guatemalan Legend*, written and adapted by Argentina Palacios. Copyright © 1993 by Troll Communications LLC.

Andrew Scott Music: Lyrics from "The Impossible Dream" from *Man of La Mancha*. Lyrics by Joseph Darion. Copyright © 1965 by Joseph Darion.

Scribner, an imprint of Simon & Schuster Adult Publishing Group: "A Day's Wait" from *The Short Stories of Ernest Hemingway* by Ernest Hemingway. Copyright 1933 by Charles Scribner's Sons; copyright renewed © 1961 by Mary Hemingway.

Spoon River Poetry Press: "To A Golden-Haired Girl in a Louisiana Town" from *The Poetry of Vachel Lindsay*. Copyright © 1985 by Spoon River Poetry Press.

Suhrkamp Verlag: "The Burning of the Books" from *Selected Poems* by Bertolt Brecht, translated by H. R. Hays. Copyright 1947 by Bertolt Brecht and H. R. Hays; copyright © 1961 Suhrkamp Verlag Frankfurt am Main.

Amy Tan and Sandra Dijkstra Literary Agency: "Fish Cheeks" by Amy Tan. Copyright © 1987 by Amy Tan. Originally appeared in *Seventeen Magazine*, December 1987.

Temple University Press: From "The Xiong Family of Lompoc" from *Hmong Means Free: Life in Laos and America*, edited by Sucheng Chang. Copyright © 1994 by Temple University. All rights reserved.

Piri Thomas: "Amigo Brothers" from *Stories from El Barrio* by Piri Thomas. Copyright © 1978 by Piri Thomas.

Time Inc.: "Can We Rescue the Reefs?" by Ritu Upadhyay from *Time for Kids*, vol. 6, no. 9, November 10, 2000. Copyright © 2000 by Time Inc. From "From Page to Film" by Kathryn R. Hoffman from *Time for Kids*, November 8, 2002. Copyright © 2002 by Time Inc. From "The Torchbearer: Rosa Parks" by Rita Dove from *Time.com* web site, accessed September 25, 2002, at http://www.time.com/time/time100/heroes/profile/parks01.html. Copyright © 2002 by Time Inc.

The University of Arkansas Press: "Interview" by Sara Henderson Hay from *Story Hour*, University of Arkansas Press, 1982. Copyright © 1982 by Sara Henderson Hay.

University of Notre Dame Press: From *Barrio Boy* by Ernesto Galarza. Copyright © 1971 by University of Notre Dame Press. Quotation about *Barrio Boy* by Ernesto Galarza. Copyright © 1971 by University of Notre Dame Press.

University Press of Mississippi: Interview with Sandra Cisneros from *Interviews with Writers of the Post-Colonial World* by Reed Dasenbrock and Feroza Jussawalla.

John Updike: From "An Ode to Golf" by John Updike. Copyright © 2000 by John Updike. Originally published in *The New Yorker*. All rights reserved.

Anna Lee Walters: "I Am of the Earth" by Anna Walters from *Voices of the Rainbow: Contemporary Poetry by American Indians*, edited by Kenneth Rosen. Copyright © 1975 by Anna Lee Walters.

Mel White: "A Mason-Dixon Memory" by Clifton Davis, slightly adapted from *Reader's Digest*, March 1993. Copyright © 1993 by Mel White.

Roberta Hill Whiteman: From "Depot in Rapid City" by Roberta Hill from *A Book of Women Poets: From Antiquity to Now*, edited by Aliki Barnstone and Willis Barnstone.

The Wylie Agency, Inc.: "I Was Sleeping Where the Black Oaks Move" from *Jacklight* by Louise Erdrich. Copyright © 1984 by Louise Erdrich.

Al Young: "For Poets" by Al Young. Copyright © 1968 and © 1992 by Al Young.

Sources Cited
From "A Note from the Author" from *Oddly Enough: Stories* by Bruce Coville. Published by Harcourt, Inc., 1994, Orlando, FL.

Picture Credits

The illustrations and photographs on the Contents pages are picked up from pages in the textbook. Credits for those can be found either on the textbook page on which they appear or in the listing below.

A11, © Art Resource/NY; **A14,** Oeffentliche Kunstsammlung Basel, Kunstmuseum Assession no. 1569. © 2003 Artists Rights Society (ARS), New York/VG Bild-Kunst, Bonn; **A15,** Hunter Museum of American Art, Chattanooga, Tennessee. Museum purchase with funds provided by the Benwood Foundation and the 1982 Collectors' Group HMA 1982.10. © 2005 Gwendolyn Knight Lawrence/Artists Rights Society (ARS), New York; **A38-1,** Digital Image, © The Museum of Modern Art/Licensed by Scala/Art Resource, NY; **5,** © Getty Images, Inc.; **9,** © Craig Tuttle/CORBIS; **11,** Courtesy of Bruce Coville; **15,** © Joe McDonald/DRK Photo; (background) Michael Halbert; **16,** Dinodia/Omni–Photo Communications, Inc.; **19,** Renee Lynn/Photo Researchers, Inc.; **21,** Michael Fogden/Animals Animals; **25,** OSF/Senani/Animals Animals; **26,** Studio Carlo Dani/Animals Animals; **28,** Dr. E. R. Degginger/Color-Pic, Inc.; **29,** © Bettmann/CORBIS; **31,** (top and bottom) © PhotoDisc/Getty Images; **32,** Cover photo by John Fei Photography; **39,** Stephen Dalton/Photo Researchers, Inc.; **53,** © Joe McDonald/CORBIS; **56,** © Joe McDonald/CORBIS; **77,** © Bettmann/CORBIS; **81,** (top) Bob Daemmrich/PictureQuest, (bottom) Don Romero/PictureQuest; **84,** © David B. Mattingly; **86,** © David B. Mattingly; **93,** Drone © Erik C. Omtvedt; **96,** © Forrest J. Ackerman Collection/CORBIS; **101,** © Wood River Gallery/PictureQuest; **102,** © Getty Images, Inc.; **103,** © Pictures Now!; **109,** © Bettmann/CORBIS; **124,** (top left) Cover by Max Ginsberg, copyright © 1992 by Max Ginsberg, cover illustration from *Lyddie* by Katherine Paterson. Used by permission of Lodestar Books, an affiliate of Dutton Children's Books, a division of Penguin Young Readers Group, a member of Penguin Group (USA) Inc., 345 Hudson St., New York, NY 10014. All rights reserved, (top right) Cover © HRW, (bottom left) Cover art: David Gaadt, cover design: Joe Curcio. Used with permission, (bottom right) Cover from *Lupita Mañana by Patricia Beatty with Connections,* © HRW; Illustration by Diane Bennett/Daniele Collignon Represents; **125,** (top left) Cover from *Red Scarf Girl by Ji-Li Jiang with Connections,* © HRW (top right) Cover art: Queen Elizabeth I (1533–1603): The Pelican Portrait, c.1574 (oil on panel) by Nicholas Hilliard (1547–1619). © Walker Art Gallery, Liverpool, Merseyside, UK/Trustees of the National Museums & Galleries on Merseyside/Bridgeman Art Library, (bottom left) Cover from *The Snake Scientist* by Sy Montgomery. Jacket photograph copyright © 1999 by Nic Bishop. Reprinted by permission of Houghton Mifflin Company. All rights reserved, (bottom right) From *Behind the Headlines* by Thomas Fleming. Jacket by Michael Chesworth. Reprinted with permission from Walker and Company; **126,** © Manu Sassoonian/Art Resource, NY; **131,** © Tony Freeman/PhotoEdit/PictureQuest; **132,** © Image Bank/Getty Images; **134,** Courtesy of Gary Paulsen; **143,** Courtesy of Gary Soto; **161,** Courtesy of Anne McCaffrey; **169,** © PhotoDisc/Getty Images; **170,** © PhotoDisc/Getty Images; **171,** © Ruben Guzman; **175,** Orion Press; **184,** AP/Wide World Photos; **191,** © Omni–Photo Communications, Inc./Index Stock; **192,** © Andre Jenny/Focus Group/PictureQuest; **195,** © Bettmann/CORBIS; **198,** © Francis G. Mayer/CORBIS; **201,** © Pictures Now!; **203,** © Bettmann/CORBIS; **206,** © 1993 Tom Van Sant/The Geosphere Project/The Stock Market/CORBIS; **207,** © PhotoDisc/Getty Images; **208,** © Edward W. Bower/Getty Images, (inset) © PhotoDisc/Getty Images; **211,** © PhotoDisc/Getty Images; **212,** Keren Su/Stock Boston; **215,** Robert Knopes/Omni–Photo Communications, Inc.; **216,** © PhotoDisc/Getty Images; **219,** © PhotoDisc/Getty Images; **220,** © PhotoDisc/Getty Images; **221,** (top) Reprinted by permission of Penguin Putnam Books for Young Readers, (bottom) © 1993 Tom Van Sant/The Geosphere Project/The Stock Market/CORBIS; **232,** (top left) Jacket design by Eric Jon Nones from *Across the Grain* by Jean Ferris. Jacket illustration © 1990 by Eric Jon Nones. Reprinted by permission of Farrar, Straus and Giroux, LLC., (top right) Cover from *M. C. Higgins, the Great by Virginia Hamilton with Connections,* © HRW; Illustration by Sarajo Frieden, (bottom left) From *Harriet the Spy* (jacket cover) by Louise Fitzhugh, copyright. Used by permission of Random House Children's Books, a division of Random House, Inc., (bottom right) Cover art copyright © Ed Acuna. Used by permission of HarperCollins Publishers; **233,** (top left) The Royal Archives © 2003 Her Majesty Queen Elizabeth II, (top right) © 1995 by Bill Nye. Used with permission from Disney Enterprises, Inc., (bottom left) Used by permission of HarperCollins Publishers, (bottom right) Cover from *Castles* by Philip Steele. Cover art © John Jamieson. Used with permission from Kingfisher Publications; **235–236,** © Richard Cummins/CORBIS; **239,** © Hulton Archive/Getty Images; **241,** © Bettmann/CORBIS; **242,** © CORBIS; **243,** Private Collection/Ken Welsh/Bridgeman Art Library; **244,** © PhotoDisc/Getty Images; **250,** Amos Zezmer/Omni–Photo Communications, Inc.; **256,** British Museum, London/Bridgeman Art Library; **257,** North Wind Picture Archives; **258,** Christie's Images/© SuperStock; **260,** (top) © Lee Snider/CORBIS, (bottom) © Bettmann/CORBIS; **263,** (bottom left) © Bettmann/CORBIS, (bottom right) Courtesy of The Edgar Allan Poe Museum of The Poe Foundation, Inc.; **266,** Art Today; **267,** (top left) Photographs by Michael J. Deas, (top right) Art Today, (bottom) © PhotoDisc/Getty Images; **268,** Photographs by Michael J. Deas; **270,** (left) Art Today, (right) Photographs by Michael J. Deas; **281,** Tom Tondee; **286,** (top right) © PhotoDisc/Getty Images; **290,** Dr. E. R. Degginger; **291,** (border) Dr. E. R. Degginger; **299,** Paul Fusco/Magnum Photos, Inc.; **303,** Erich Hartmann/Magnum Photos, Inc.; **310,** © Zefa Visual Media-Germany/Index Stock Imagery; **315,** © Art Resource, NY; **317,** © Dave Ryan/Index Stock Imagery; **318,** © Bill Bachmann/Index Stock Imagery; **320,** Ann Aldrich; **322,** © Dave Ryan/Index Stock Imagery; **323,** © 2003 James Innes/Picture Perfect; **324,** © Paul Barton/The Stock Market/CORBIS; **325,** James Innes/Picture Perfect; **326,** James Innes/Picture Perfect; **327,** © Joe McNally; **328,** © SuperStock; **329,** Courtesy Vachel Lindsay Association; **344,** (top left) Cover art copyright © 1995 by Trevor Brown. Cover © 1995 by HarperCollins Publishers. Used by permission of HarperCollins Publishers, (top right) Cover from *Where the Red Fern Grows by Wilson Rawls with Connections,* © HRW; Illustration by Lori Lohstoeter/Lindgren & Smith Represents, (bottom left) Jacket art © 1997 Phil Boatwright. Used by permission of HarperCollins Publishers, (bottom right) Cover illustration © 1995 by Jody Hewgill. Used with permission from The Art Works, USA; **345,** (top left) Jacket used with permission from Harcourt, Inc. All Rights Reserved, (top right) Used with permission from Harcourt, Inc., (bottom left) Used with permission from Dorling Kindersley Publishing, Inc., (bottom right) Hodder Wayland Picture Library; **346,** © Art Resource/NY; **351,** © Robin Weiner/Mediapix/The Image Works; **352,** © Diane J. Ali; **357,**

Grace Davies/Omni–Photo Communications, Inc.; **361, 365,** ©
Bettmann/CORBIS; **366,** (top) AP Photo/Copyright Chuck Close,
High Museum of Art, Atlanta, (bottom) © Roger
Ressmeyer/CORBIS; **367,** © PhotoDisc/Getty Images, (inset) Bill
Bachmann/PictureQuest; **369,** Culver Pictures, Inc.; **379,** ©
Bettmann/CORBIS; **381,** Culver Pictures, Inc.; **387,** (bottom)
Reprinted by permission of McIntosh and Otis, Inc.; **389,** ©
PhotoDisc/Getty Images; **390,** © Jacqui Hurst/CORBIS, (inset) ©
PhotoDisc/Getty Images; **394,** Photo courtesy of Julia Alvarez.
Reprinted by permission of Susan Bergholz Literary Services, New
York. All rights reserved; **400,** © Francisco Villaflor/CORBIS; **403,**
(top) Courtesy of Maijue Xiong, (bottom) © Michael S. Yamashita/
CORBIS; **404, 405, 407,** Courtesy of Maijue Xiong; **410,** Courtesy
of Agate Nesaule; **411,** © Peter Turnley/CORBIS; **412,** (top) ©
Peter Turnley/CORBIS, (top middle) © David Turnley/CORBIS,
(bottom middle) © Peter Turnley/CORBIS, (bottom) © Lisa
Taylor/CORBIS; **417,** (top left) Copyright Scala/Art Resource, NY;
(top middle) Copyright National Trust/Art Resource, NY, (top right)
Copyright Giraudon/Art Resource, NY, (bottom left) Copyright
Scala/Art Resource, NY, (bottom right) Archivo Iconografico
SA/CORBIS; **419,** © CORBIS; **421,** (left) © Bettmann/CORBIS,
(middle) © Joel W. Rogers/CORBIS, (right) © Michael
Nicholson/CORBIS; **422,** © CORBIS; **423,** (left) © Archivo
Iconografico SA/CORBIS, (right) Copyright Erich Lessing/Art
Resource, NY; **424,** © CORBIS; **425,** Courtesy of Milton Meltzer;
427, (top) © Archivo Iconografico SA/CORBIS; **432,** © Philip
Gould/CORBIS; **435,** Karen Carr Studio; **436,** © Arthur Cohen
Photography/Scholastic Press; **438,** © Stephen Gassman/Index
Stock Imagery/PictureQuest; **441,** © The Image Bank/Getty Images;
442, (top) © Guy Gillette/Photo Researchers, Inc., (bottom) Photo
© Miriam Berkley; **443,** © Burstein Collection/CORBIS; **446,**
NASA/Omni–Photo Communications, Inc.; **461,** AP/Wide World
Photos; **474,** (top left) Cover art copyright © 1995 by Chris Miles.
Cover copyright © 1995 by HarperCollins Publishers. Used by
permission of HarperCollins Publishers, (top right) From *The Door
in the Wall* (jacket cover) by Marguerite De Angeli. Used by
permission of Random House Children's Books, a division of
Random House, Inc., (bottom left) Cover from *Treasure Island by
Robert Louis Stevenson with Connections,* © HRW; Illustration by
Brian Fox, (bottom right) Text and illustration copyright © 1992 by
Anni Axworthy. Used with permission by Charlesbridge Publishing,
Inc. All rights reserved; **475,** (top left) From *Knots in My Yo-yo String*
by Jerry Spinelli, copyright © 1998 by Jerry Spinelli. Cover
photograph copyright © 1998 by Penny Gentieu. Map copyright ©
1998 by Jennifer Pavlovitz. Used by permission of Alfred A. Knopf,
an imprint of Random House Children's Books, a division of
Random House, Inc., (top right) Used with permission from the
Salariya Book Co. Ltd., (bottom left) From *Postcards from France* by
Megan McNeill Libby, cover illustration © 1998 Rob Roth, (bottom
right) From *Made in China: Ideas and Inventions from Ancient China*
by Suzanne Williams, cover art by Andrea Fong. Used with
permission from Pacific View Press; **476–477,** © Digital
Vision/Getty Images; **481,** © The Image Bank/Getty Images; **482,**
(top) © Duomo/CORBIS, (bottom) © AFP/CORBIS; **491,** ©
PhotoDisc/Getty Images; **493,** Jim Pickerell/Stock Photo; **496,** ©
PhotoDisc/Getty Images; **497,** © Chris George/CORBIS; **500,** (top)
© Randy Duchaine/The Stock Market/CORBIS, (bottom) Gary
Conner/PhotoEdit; **504,** From *Barrio Boy* by Ernesto Galarza.
Copyright 1971 by The University of Notre Dame Press. Notre
Dame, Indiana 46556. Used by permission; **523,** Jack
Ackerman/Penguin USA; **529,** (inset) Grace Davies/Omni–Photo
Communications, Inc.; **530,** AP/Wide World Photos; **532,** ©
PhotoDisc/Getty Images; **534,** Saint Frederick High School
Yearbook; **539,** © Gerardo Somoza/CORBIS Outline; **541,** Saint

Frederick High School Yearbook; **544–545,** AP/Wide World
Photos; **552,** © SuperStock; **555,** Bridgeman Art Library; **556,**
Wunrow/Index Stock Imagery; **557,** Kevin Fall Collection; **558,**
Courtesy of Anna Lee Walters. Photograph by Ed McCombs; **560,**
Robert W. Kelley/TimePix; **563,** © Bettmann/CORBIS; **564,** © The
Brett Weston Archive/CORBIS; **566,** Peter Stein/Blackstar (Stock
Photo); **569,** © Jian Chen/Stock Connection/PictureQuest; **570,**
Arthur Furst; **572,** © Giantstep/Stone/Getty Images; **573,** © Ronnie
Kaufman/CORBIS; **574,** Courtesy of Gary Soto; **575,** © Ariel
Skelley/CORBIS; **581,** © Bettmann/CORBIS; **584,** AP/Wide World
Photos; **587,** (inset) Ralph Reinhold/Animals Animals; **590,** ©
Jeremy Woodhouse/PhotoDisc/Getty Images; **591,** ©
Bettmann/CORBIS; **594,** © Peter Finger/CORBIS; **596,** © Hugh
Chatfield, 2002; **598,** Ryuichi Nagasima/Photonica; **601, 603,**
Bridgeman Art Library; **604,** © Bettmann/CORBIS; **606,** © Art
Resource, NY; **610,** © Images.com/CORBIS; **611,** © Miriam
Berkley; **615,** © Bryce Harper; **616,** Vintage Books, a division of
Random House, Inc.; **617,** © AP/Wide World Photos; **618,** © Bryce
Harper; **620,** © Stone/Getty Images; **621,** © Grace Davies; **623,** ©
Jeff Greenberg/PhotoEdit, Inc.; **628,** © Don Farrall/PhotoDisc/Getty
Images; **629,** © Bettmann/CORBIS; **642,** (top left) From *Somewhere
in the Darkness* by Walter Dean Myers. Cover illustration copyright
© 1992 by Scholastic Inc. Reprinted by permission, (top right) Cover
from *Cut from the Same Cloth* by Robert D. San Souci, illustrated by
Brian Pinkney, copyright © 1993 by Brian Pinkney, illustrations. Used
by permission of Philomel Books, A division of Penguin Young
Readers Group, A Member of Penguin Group (USA) Inc., 345
Hudson St., New York, NY 10014. All rights reserved, (bottom left)
Cover, © HRW. Illustration by Higgins Bond/American Artist Rep.,
Inc., (bottom right) Cover from *Adam of the Road* by Elizabeth
Janet Gray, illustrated by Robert Lawson, copyright © 1942 by
Elizabeth Janet Gray and Robert Lawson, renewed © 1970 by
Elizabeth Janet Gray and John Boyd, Executor of the Estate of
Robert Lawson. Used with permission of Viking Penguin, a division
of Penguin Young Readers Group, a member of Penguin Group
(USA) Inc., 345 Hudson St., New York, NY 10014. All rights
reserved; **643,** (top left) Cover from *Amos Fortune: Free Man* by
Elizabeth Yates. Cover illustration © Lonnie Knabel, 1989. Used with
permission from Lonnie Knabel, (top right) From *Shrinking Forests*
by Jenny Tesar, used by permission of Blackbirch Press, (bottom left)
Used with permission from Dorling Kindersley Publishing, Inc.,
(bottom right) Used with permission from Grolier Publishing
Company; **644–645,** © CORBIS; **654,** Takashi Shima/Photonica;
655, Dr. E. R. Degginger/Color-Pic, Inc.; **666,** (bottom) © Getty
Images; **669,** © Michelle L. Smith; **673,** M. J. Quay/M. L. Falcone; **676,**
Lanny Provo/Photonica; **677,** © SuperStock; **679,** © UPI/CORBIS;
681, © Bettmann/CORBIS; **689,** © Rodica Prato; **690–692,**
University of Pennsylvania Museum, Philadelphia; **706,** © Photofest;
719, © SuperStock; **720,** © Bridgeman Art Library; **722,** ©
Christie's Images/CORBIS; **723,** © Samantha Loomis Paterson; **730,**
Arte Publico Press/University of Houston; **733,** Rollout Photograph
#4675 © Justin Kerr, 1990; **734–735,** © Robert Frerck/Getty
Images; **735,** The Granger Collection, New York; **739,** © Michael P.
Fogden/Bruce Coleman, Inc./PictureQuest; **741,** (top left) Laurie
Platt Winfrey, (top right) Chris Costello, (bottom left) © Erich
Lessing/Art Resource, NY, (bottom right) © Werner Forman/Art
Resource, NY; **743,** © Donne Bryant/Art Resource, NY; **764,** ©
Photofest; **765,** Courtesy: Special Collections, Carnegie Mellon
University Libraries; **782,** (top left) Reprinted by permission of
Carus Publishing Company, from *Patakin: World Tales of Drums and
Drummers* by Nina Jaffe, art by Christine Ronan, © 2001 by Carus
Publishing Company, (top right) Cover © Random House, text
copyright © 1996 by Gary Ferguson, Illustrations copyright © 1996
by Douglas Smith, (bottom left) Cover from *The Samurai's Tale* by

Illustrations

All art by Holt, Rinehart and Winston unless otherwise noted.

Index of Skills

Boldface page numbers indicate extensive treatment of a subject.

LITERARY SKILLS

Abbreviations key, 636
Academic language, 786
Accuracy, 787
Action, 129
Alliteration, 254, **577**, 585, 593, **601**, 608, 639, 758, 759, 763
Allusion, **174**, 185
Appearance, 128–129
Ars poetica, **609**
Attitude, 766
Author, 204, 437
Author study, 613
    message response chart, 619, 622, 626
Autobiography, **402, 499**, 505, 637
Basic situation, 2
Biographical narrative, **414**
Biography, **414**, 479, **499**, 637
Boldface, 786
Catalog poetry, **606**, 608
Causal chain, 271
Cause and effect, 271, 282, 294, 686, 842
    causal chain, 271
    chain of events, 686, 842
Chain of events, 686, 842
    flowchart, 271
Character, 50, 135, 136, 144, 162, 172, 185, **190**, 191, 193, 244, 294, **296**, 306, 316, 705, 711, 716, 746, 750, 765, **786**, 814
    action and, 129
    appearance of, 128–129
    character/setting/theme comparison chart, 304, 321
    cluster diagram for, 129
    discovery made by, 237
    dynamic, 296, 304
    imaginary, 84
    main, 204, 437, 484
    motivation, **146**, 162, **174**, 185, 244, 254, 786
    motive, 30, 254
    in narrative poetry, 246
    in nonfiction, 787
    reactions of other characters to, 129
    speech and, 129
    static, 296, 304
    theme and, 237
    thoughts and feelings of, 129
    traits, 132, **136**, 144, **190**, 194, 196, 229, 282, 724
    traits comparison chart, 196, 204, 205
Character/setting/theme comparison chart, 304, 321

Characterization, **128–129**, 135, 172, 229
    direct, **128**
    indirect, **128**
Character traits, 132, **136**, 144, **190**, 194, 196, 229, 282, 724
    comparison chart, 196, 204, 205
Chivalry, 842
Cinderella story, **746**
    comparison chart, 757, 763, 766
Climax, 3, 119, 437, 484, 622
Community, folk tales and, **697**
Comparing literature, 84, 190, 296, 428, 746, 845
    character traits comparison chart, 196, 204, 205
    Cinderella stories comparison chart, 757, 763, 766
    mood/theme comparison chart, 437, 443
    myth comparison chart, 670
    real hero comparison chart, 852, 860
    science fiction story comparison chart, 88, 106
Comparison, 84, 282, 484, 494, 814
Complications, 2, **57**, 78, 484
Conflict, 2, **14**, 30, 162, 204, 299, 437, 613, 621, 622, 763
    external, 2, **484**, 494
    internal, 2, **484**, 494
Contrast, 84, 484, 494, 814
Couplet, **589**, 592
Criticism, 871
Culture, folk tales and, **696–697**
Dialogue, 622
Differences, 626
Direct characterization, **128**
Discovery, character's theme and, 237
Dynamic character, 296, 304
Elegy, **593**, 597
End rhyme, **576**, **586**
Escape story, **697**
Essay, **479**, **527**, 531, **533**, 637
    humorous, **527**
    purpose of, 533
Events
    later, 119
    series of, 2
Everyday language, 613
Exact rhyme, **598**, 600
Exaggeration, **578**, 585
Experience comparison chart, 540
Extended metaphor, **551**, 554
External conflict, 2, **484**, 494
    internal- and external-conflict chart, 162
Fact, 499, 505

Fable, 778
Fantastic situations, 84
Fiction, **478**
    historical, **368**, 637
    novel, **478**, **508**, 637
    novella, **478**, **508**
    science, **84**, 85
    short story, **478**, **484**, **508**, 637
    See also Poetry.
Figurative language, 106, 621, 787
Figures of speech, **546**, **548**, **609**, 612
    extended metaphor, **551**, 554
    metaphor, 505, **548**, 550, **551**, 609, 613, 619, 626, 639
    personification, **555**, 559
    simile, **548**, 550, 608, 609, 621
First-person narrator, **168**, 172
First-person point of view, **349**, 362, **368**, 380, 469
Flashback, **533**, 536, 540
Folk tale, **696–697**
    community and, **697**
    culture and, **696–697**
    escape story, **697**
    motifs in, **696**
Foreshadowing, 2, **38**, 50, 68, 308, 362, 368
    suspense and, **38**, 50
Forms of poetry, **546**.
    See Poetry.
Forms of prose, **478–479**
    chart, 479.
    See Prose.
Frame story, 831
Freedom, 852
Free verse, **576**, **593**, 597, **606**, 608
    alliteration in, **593**, 597
    imagery in, **593**, 597
    onomatopoeia in, **593**, 597
    rhythm in, **593**, 608
Generalizations, 627, 680, 871
Giving/receiving chart, 555
Gods, **647**
    Greek/Roman gods and goddesses chart, 647
Goddesses, **647**
    Greek/Roman gods and goddesses chart, 647
Graphic organizers
    abbreviations key, 636
    chain of events, 686, 842
    chain of events flowchart, 271
    character cluster diagram, 129
    character/setting/theme comparison chart, 304, 321
    character traits comparison chart, 196, 204, 205
    Cinderella stories comparison chart, 757, 763, 766

rhyme in, 547, **576–577**, 585, **586,** 588, **598, 601,** 639
rhythm in, 547, **576, 578,** 593, 608
scanning, **576, 578,** 585
sonnet, **568,** 571
sound effects in, **546, 576–577, 601,** 605, 787
sounds of poetry chart, 605
stanzas in, 546, **589,** 592, 639
theme in, 592, 787
title and, 597
tone of, 608, 639
See also Figures of speech; Rhyme.
Point of view, 348–349, 408, 469
first-person, **349,** 362, **368,** 380, 469
objective, **393**
omniscient, **348,** 349, **356,** 362, **382,** 469
subjective, **393**
third-person-limited, **349,** 469
writer's, 78
Prediction, 505
Primary source, 787
Prior knowledge, 429
Problem, 484, 778
Prose, **478**
autobiography, **402, 499,** 505, 637
biography, **414,** 479, **499,** 637
chart, 479
essay, **479,** 527, 531, **533,** 637
fiction, **478**
forms of, **478–479**
historical fiction, **368,** 637
nonfiction, 478, **479, 787**
novel, **478, 508,** 637
novella, **478, 508**
short story, **478, 484, 508,** 637
Punctuation of poetry, **547**
Purpose, 531, 533
Quest, **820, 833,** 842
riddle and, **833**
Quotations, 814
Reading poetry, **547**
Real hero, **845**
comparison chart, 852, 860
Recurring themes, **289**
Repetition, **260,** 264, **601**
Resolution, 3, 119, 437, 484, 622, 763
Rhyme, 547, **576–577,** 585, **586,** 588, **598, 601,** 639
end, **576, 586**
exact, **598,** 600
internal, **576**
scheme, **577, 586,** 588, 639
slant, **598,** 600
See also Poetry.
Rhyming sounds, 264
Rhythm, 547, **576, 578,** 593, 608
free verse and, **593,** 608

meter and, **578**
scanning and, **578**
Riddle, **833**
Scanning, **576, 578,** 585
Science fiction, **84,** 85
elements of, 84
fantastic situations, 84
imaginary characters, 84
journey through time or space, 84
setting in the future, 84, 88
story comparison chart, 88, 106
story map, 88
surprise ending, 84, 304
technology, 84
Sensory images, 567
Sequence chart, 254, 860
Series of events, 2
Setting, 50, 88, 119, 264, **296**
character/setting/theme comparison chart, 304, 321
in narrative poems, 246, 254
in science fiction, 84, 88
Short short story, 484
Short story, **478, 484, 508,** 637
Similarities, 626
chart, 551
Simile, **548,** 550, 608, 609, 621
Slant rhyme, **598,** 600
Sonnet, **568,** 571
Sound effects in poetry, **546, 576–577, 601,** 605, 787
alliteration, 254, **577,** 585, 593, **601,** 608, 639
chart, 605
end rhyme, **576, 586**
free verse and, **576, 593,** 597, **606,** 608
internal rhyme, **576**
limerick and, **577**
meter, **576, 578,** 585
onomatopoeia, **577,** 593, 639, **718**
repetition, 260, 264, **601**
rhyme, 547, **576–577,** 585, **586,** 588, **598, 601,** 639
rhyme scheme and, **577, 586,** 588, 639
rhythm, 547, **576, 578,** 593, 608
scanning and, **576, 578,** 585
Spanish words, 613
Speaker, 469, 562
Speech, 129
Stanza, 546, **589,** 592, 639
Static character, 296, 304
Story, 38, **786–787**
character, **786**
details chart for wish, 731
graphic, 731
plot, **786–787**
short, **478, 484, 508,** 637
short short, 484
structure, 831
theme, **787**

Story map, 88, 144, 196, 321, 524, 716
Style, 598
Subjective point of view, **393**
Subjective writing, **393,** 399, 402, 408, **414,** 426
Summary, 204, 380, 670, 705, 763, 814
diagram, 670
Superhero, **698,** 705
Surprise ending, 84, 304
Suspense, **38,** 50
foreshadowing and, **38, 50**
Symbol, 78, 588
Taboo, **718,** 724
Technology, 84
Theme, **236–237,** 242, 244, 264, 282, 289, 294, **296,** 339, 362, 380, 388, **428,** 437, 443, 444, 524, 592, 746, 763, 786, **787**
character and, 237
character's discovery and, 237
character/setting/theme comparison chart, 304, 321
comparison chart, 237
as generalization, **508**
key passages and, 428
mood/theme comparison chart, 437, 443
in narrative poetry, 254
plot and, **236,** 238, 244
recurring, **289**
statement, 245
statement graphic, 245
title and, 237, 428
topic and, 238, 244, **246**
uncovering, 238
universal, **260**
Theme statement, 245
graphic, 245
Third-person-limited point of view, **349,** 469
Thoughts and feelings, 129
Three, motif of, 753, 757
Time line, 408, 616–617
Title, 204, 437, 439, 531, 588, 597
theme and, 237, 428
Tone, 343, 559, **560,** 562, 600, 608, 639, 746, 763, 764
Topic
plot and, 244
theme and, 238, 244, **246**
Trickster tale, 297
Underworld in myths, **664**
Universal theme, **260**
Venn diagram, 484
Wishes motif, **726**
wish story details chart, 731
Writer's point of view, 78
Writing
objective, **393,** 399, 408, **414,** 426, 469
subjective, **393,** 399, 402, 408, **414,** 426

INFORMATIONAL READING SKILLS

Multiple-meaning words, 122, 874
Mythology, making up words from, 687
Onomatopoeia, **725**
Personification, **671**
Place names, Greek and Roman, **681**
Precise verbs, 663
Prefixes, **163**, **663**, **815**, **832**
    Anglo-Saxon, **815**
    chart for Greek, 663
    Greek, **663**
    Latin, **815**
    word map for, 832
Pronoun references, unclear, **173**
    and antecedents, 173
Roman and Greek place names, **681**
Roots of words, 270
    chart of Greek, 819
    Greek, **819**
    Latin, **270**
Simile, **255**, 671
Specific words, using, **717**
Suffixes, **163**, **832**
    word map for, 832
Synonyms, 230, 472, **541**, 780
    word map for, 541
Vivid adjectives, 663
Word analogy, **532**
Word map, 541, 832
Word origins
    Anglo-Saxon, **809**
    etymology, **145**
    French, **843**
    Latin, **809**
Word roots, **163**
    word tree, 163
Word tree, 163, 653
Word web, 363

READING SKILLS

Accurate evidence, **788**, 791
Adequate evidence, **788**, 791
Affixes, Greek and Latin roots and.
    See Greek and Latin roots and
    affixes.
Appropriate evidence, **788**, 789, 791
Author's perspective, analyzing, **350**
    Perspective Wheel, 355
Boldface, 882, 883
Brainstorming map, 682
Causal chain, 271
Cause and effect, **271**, 282, **654**, 662
    causal chain, 271
    cause, **271**, 658, 660
    chain, **726**, 731
    chain chart, 726
    chain-of-events flowchart, 271
    effect, **271**, 655, 660, 661
    recognition of, **271**
Cause-and-effect chain, **726**, 731
    chart, 726

Character
    If—Then strategy, **130**, 135
    motivation of, 244
    plot and, **130**
    theme and, **244**
    tips for understanding, 130
Comparing and contrasting, **84**, **190**, **296**, **428**, **484**, **746**, **845**
    Venn diagram, 484
Conclusions, drawing, **718**, 724
Conflict, 613
Context clues, using, **289**
Details, **393**
Distinguishing fact from opinion, **402**, 408, **499**, 505
"Effects" phrases, 882
Expert testimony, 789
Evidence, evaluating, **788**, **791**
    accurate, **788**, 791
    adequate, **788**, 791
    appropriate, **788**, 789, 791
    expert testimony and, 789
    facts and, 788
    inaccurate, **788**, 791
    inadequate, **788**, 791
    inappropriate, **788**, 791
    opinions and, 788
    reliable sources and, 788
Facts, 788
    distinguished from opinions, **402**, 408, **499**, 505
Flashback, **533**, 536, 540
Foreshadowing, 38, 356, 368
Generalizations, making, **508**, **613**, **675**
    conflict and, 613
    message and, 613
    theme and, **508**
Graphic organizers
    brainstorming map, 682
    cause-and-effect chain chart, 726
    chain-of-events flowchart, 271
    informational text features chart, 887
    Perspective Wheel, 355
    prefixes chart, 652
    Retelling Summary Sheet, 4, **12**
    roots chart, 651
    SQ3R organizer, 415
    suffixes chart, 652
    summarizing diagram, 670
    text features chart, 887
    theme graphics, 245
    Venn diagram, 484
    vocabulary tree, 653
Graphics, 882
Greek and Latin roots and affixes, **650–653**
    prefixes, 650, **652**
    prefixes chart, 652
    roots chart, 651
    suffixes, 650, **652**
    suffixes chart, 652
    vocabulary tree, 653

Headings, 882, 883
If—Then strategy, **130**, 135
Illustrations, 886
Images, **527**, 531
Implications, 393
Inaccurate evidence, **788**, 791
Inadequate evidence, **788**, 791
Inappropriate evidence, **788**, 791
Inferences, 57, 68, 78, **136**, **146**, 162, **168**, 187, 229, 393, 571
Informational texts, reading. *See* Reading informational texts.
Italics, 882
Latin and Greek roots and affixes. *See* Greek and Latin roots and affixes.
Main idea, finding, **393**, 399, **480**, 483
    details and, **393**
    implications and, 393
    inferences and, 393
    reading informational texts and, 885
    topic and, 480
Message, 613
Motivation, 244
Numbered steps, 882
Opinions, 788
    distinguished from facts, **402**, 408, **499**, 505
"Opposite" phrases, 882
Paragraph, 883
    breaks, 885
Perspective, analyzing author's, **350**, 355
    Perspective Wheel, 355
Plot
    character and, **130**
    If—Then strategy, **130**, 135
    theme and, 238, **244**
    topic and, 244
Poetry, reading, **551**, **589**, **609**
    punctuation and, **589**
    thoughts and, **609**
Predicting, 38, 68, **174**, 185, **356**, **368**, 380, 505, **707**, 716
    foreshadowing and, 38, 356, 368
    suspense and, 38
Prefixes, 650, **652**
    chart, 652
Prior knowledge, using, **682**
    brainstorming map, 682
Punctuation in poetry, **589**
Reading informational texts, **882**
    boldface, 882, 883
    "effects" phrases, 882
    features chart, 887
    first paragraph, 883
    graphics, 882
    headings, 882
    illustrations, 886
    italics, 882
    main idea, 885
    numbered steps, 882

SPEAKING AND LISTENING SKILLS

Index of Skills   **1095**

RESEARCH AND STUDY SKILLS

INDEPENDENT READING

Index of Authors and Titles

Student Authors and Titles

For permission to reprint copyrighted material, grateful acknowledgment is made to the following sources:

Susan Bergholz Literary Services, New York: From "Notes to a Young(er) Writer" by Sandra Cisneros from *Americas Review,* vol.15, Spring 1987. Copyright © 1987 by Sandra Cisneros.

Arthur C. Clarke and the author's agents, Scovil Chichak Galen Literary Agency, Inc.: From "Space Flight: Imagination and Reality" by Sir Arthur C. Clarke from *The Planets,* edited by Byron Preiss. Copyright © 1985 by Arthur C. Clarke. Published by Bantam Books, a division of Random House, Inc.

St. James Press, a subsidiary of Gale Research Inc.: Quote by Gary Paulsen from *St. James Guide to Young Adult Writers,* 2nd ed. accessed March 11, 2003, at http://www.galenet.com/servlet/BioRC. Copyright © 2003 by The Gale Group.

Edward D. Hoch and Kurt Sercu: Quote from email interview with Edward D. Hoch by Kurt Sercu on April 25, 2002, accessed at http://neptune.spaceports.com/~queen/ The_Other_Side_Hoch.html. Copyright © 2002 by Edward D. Hoch and Kurt Sercu.

Sources Cited
From "A Lyrical Legacy: Part 1, An Interview with Poet, Essayist, Novelist & Memoirist Al Young" by Ray González from *The Bloomsbury Review,* Sept-Oct 2001. Published by The Bloomsbury Review, Denver, CO.

From interview with Judith Ortiz Cofer by Stephanie Gordon from *AWP Chronicle,* October/November 1997. Published by the Association of Writers & Writing Programs, Fairfax, VA.

Quote by Jim Murphy from "Jim Murphy" from *Something About the Author,* vol. 77. Published by Gale Research Inc., Farmington Hills, MI.